THE MEANING OF DIFFERENCE

American Constructions of Race, Sex and Gender, Social Class, Sexual Orientation, and Disability

A Text/Reader

Sixth Edition

Karen E. Rosenblum

George Mason University

Toni-Michelle C. Travis

George Mason University

THE MEANING OF DIFFERENCE: AMERICAN CONSTRUCTIONS OF RACE, SEX AND GENDER, SOCIAL CLASS, SEXUAL ORIENTATION, AND DISABILITY, SIXTH EDITION

Published by McGraw-Hill, a business unit of The McGraw-Hill Companies, Inc., 1221 Avenue of the Americas, New York, NY 10020. Copyright © 2012 by The McGraw-Hill Companies, Inc. All rights reserved. Previous editions © 2008, 2006, and 2003. No part of this publication may be reproduced or distributed in any form or by any means, or stored in a database or retrieval system, without the prior written consent of The McGraw-Hill Companies, Inc., including, but not limited to, in any network or other electronic storage or transmission, or broadcast for distance learning.

Some ancillaries, including electronic and print components, may not be available to customers outside the United States.

This book is printed on acid-free paper.

1 2 3 4 5 6 7 8 9 0 DOC/DOC 1 0 9 8 7 6 5 4 3 2 1

ISBN 978-0-07-811164-8
MHID 0-07-811164-1

Vice President & Editor-in-Chief: *Michael Ryan*
Vice President EDP/Central Publishing Services: *Kimberly Meriwether David*
Editorial Director: *William Glass*
Sponsoring Editor: *Gina Boedeker*
Editorial Coordinator: *Nikki Weissman*
Executive Marketing Manager: *Pamela S. Cooper*
Senior Project Manager: *Joyce Watters*
Buyer: *Susan K. Culbertson*
Design Coordinator: *Margarite Reynolds*
Cover Designer: *Mary-Presley Adams*
Cover Image Credit: *Royalty-Free/CORBIS*
Media Project Manager: *Sridevi Palani*
Compositor: *Glyph International*
Typeface: *10/12 Minion*
Printer: *R. R. Donnelley*

All credits appearing on page or at the end of the book are considered to be an extension of the copyright page.

Library of Congress Cataloging-in-Publication Data

The meaning of difference : American constructions of race, sex and gender,
social class, sexual orientation, and disability : a text/reader/Karen E.
Rosenblum, Toni-Michelle C. Travis [editors].—6th ed.
    p. cm.
  ISBN 978-0-07-811164-8 (alk. paper)
  1. United States—Social conditions—1980-   2. Cultural pluralism—United States.
  I. Rosenblum, Karen Elaine.   II. Travis, Toni-Michelle, 1947-
  HN59.2.M44 2011
  306.0973—dc22   2010049101

ABOUT THE AUTHORS

KAREN E. ROSENBLUM is associate professor of sociology at George Mason University in Fairfax, Virginia. She has served as the university's Vice President for University Life and was the founding director of the Women's Studies Program. In addition, she was a Fulbright Lecturer in Japan. Professor Rosenblum received her Ph.D. in sociology from the University of Colorado, Boulder. Her areas of research and teaching include sex and gender, language, and deviance.

TONI-MICHELLE C. TRAVIS is associate professor of government and politics at George Mason University in Fairfax, Virginia. Travis received her Ph.D. in political science from the University of Chicago. Her areas of research and teaching include race and gender dimensions of political participation, Virginia politics, and American government. She is a former chair of the African American Studies program and has served as the president of the National Capital Area Political Science Association and the Women's Caucus of the American Political Science Association. In addition, Professor Travis has been a fellow at the Rothermere American Institute, Oxford University. A political analyst, she is a frequent commentator on Virginia and national politics.

CONTENTS

Preface   *xi*

SECTION I—**CONSTRUCTING CATEGORIES OF DIFFERENCE**

FRAMEWORK ESSAY   2

WHAT IS RACE? WHAT IS ETHNICITY?

1. "Race" and the Construction of Human Identity
    Audrey Smedley   46

2. Who Is Black? One Nation's Definition
    F. James Davis   56

3. The Evolution of Identity
    The Washington Post   65

Personal Account: A Loaded Vacation
Niah Grimes   66

4. Real Indians: Identity and the Survival of Native America
    Eva Marie Garroutte   66

5. Asian American Panethnicity: Contemporary National and
    Transnational Possibilities
    Yen Le Espiritu   75

Personal Account: I Thought My Race Was Invisible
Sherri H. Pereira   88

6. Whiteness as an "Unmarked" Cultural Category
    Ruth Frankenberg   88

7. America's Changing Color Lines: Immigration, Race/Ethnicity, and Multiracial Identification
    Jennifer Lee and Frank D. Bean 94

Personal Account: The Price of Nonconformity
Julia Morgenstern 101

8. From Friendly Foreigner to Enemy Race
    John Tehranian 104

Personal Account: Master Status: Pride and Danger
Sumaya Al-Hajebi 111

WHAT IS SEX? WHAT IS GENDER?

9. The Gendered Society
    Michael S. Kimmel 113

Personal Account: Basketball
Andrea M. Busch 122

10. Where's the Rulebook for Sex Verification?
    Alice Dreger 123

11. All Together Now: Intersex Infants and IGM
    Riki Wilchins 124

WHAT IS SOCIAL CLASS?

12. What's Class Got to Do with It?
    Michael Zweig 130

13. More or Less Equal?
    The Economist 133

14. The Silver Spoon: Inheritance and the Staggered Start
    Stephen J. McNamee and Robert K. Miller Jr. 136

Personal Account: I Am a Pakistani Woman
Hoorie I. Siddique 145

WHAT IS SEXUAL ORIENTATION?

15. The Biology of the Homosexual
    Roger N. Lancaster 147

16. A New Paradigm for Understanding Women's Sexuality and Sexual Orientation
    Letitia Anne Peplau and Linda D. Garnets 157

17. The Heterosexual Questionnaire
    Martin Rochlin 166

WHAT IS DISABILITY?

18. Disability Definitions: The Politics of Meaning
    Michael Oliver 167

Personal Account: Invisibly Disabled
Heather L. Shaw   171

19.   A World of Their Own
      Liza Mundy   171

20.   Ethnicity, Ethics, and the Deaf-World
      Harlan Lane   177

SECTION II—**EXPERIENCING DIFFERENCE**

FRAMEWORK ESSAY   **194**

RACE AND ETHNICITY

21.   Formulating Identity in a Globalized World
      Carola Suárez-Orozco   221

Personal Account: Hair
Sarah Faragalla   235

22.   Latinos and the U.S. Race Structure
      Clara E. Rodríguez   235

23.   Everybody's Ethnic Enigma
      Jelita McLeod   242

Personal Account: My Strategies
Eric Jackson   243

SEX AND GENDER

24.   It's All in the Family: Intersections of Gender, Race, and Nation
      Patricia Hill Collins   245

25.   Proving Manhood
      Timothy Beneke   254

Personal Account: Just Something You Did as a Man
Francisco Hernandez   258

26.   Gendered Sexuality in Young Adulthood: Double Binds and Flawed Options
      Laura Hamilton and Elizabeth A. Armstrong   259

SEXUAL ORIENTATION

27.   Beyond the Closet: The Transformation of Gay and Lesbian Life
      Steven Seidman   269

Personal Account: Living Invisibly
Tara S. Ellison   276

28.   "Dude, You're a Fag": Adolescent Male Homophobia
      C. J. Pascoe   277

29.   Sexual Orientation and Sex in Women's Lives: Conceptual and
      Methodological Issues
      Esther D. Rothblum   286

SOCIAL CLASS

30. Class and the Transition to Adulthood
    Annette Lareau and Elliot B. Weininger   292
Personal Account: That Moment of Visibility
Rose B. Pascarell   300

31. Cause of Death: Inequality
    Alejandro Reuss   301

32. Why Are Droves of Unqualified, Unprepared Kids Getting into
    Our Top Colleges? Because Their Dads Are Alumni
    John Larew   305

DISABILITY

33. Public Transit
    John Hockenberry   310

34. "Can You See the Rainbow?" The Roots of Denial
    Sally French   317

35. Not Blind Enough: Living in the Borderland Called Legal Blindness
    Beth Omansky   323
Personal Account: A Time I Didn't Feel Normal
Heather Callender   330

SECTION III—**THE MEANING OF DIFFERENCE**

FRAMEWORK ESSAY   **332**

36. Blink in Black and White
    Malcolm Gladwell   351
Personal Account: Just Like My Mama Said
Anthony McNeill   356

37. See Baby Discriminate
    Po Bronson and Ashley Merryman   356

38. Between Barack and a Hard Place
    Tim Wise   363

39. The Model Minority: Asian American "Success" as a Race Relations Failure
    Frank Wu   370
Personal Account: Let Me Work for It!
Isabelle Nguyen   377

40. The Gender Revolution: Uneven and Stalled
    Paula England   378

LAW, PUBLIC POLICY, AND ECONOMY

41. Thirteen Key Supreme Court Cases and the Civil War Amendments   388

42. Segregation: The Rising Costs for America
    James H. Carr and Nandinee K. Kutty   418

Personal Account: Learning My Own Privilege
Mireille M. Cecil   427

43. Land Rich, Dirt Poor: Challenges to Asset Building in Native America
    Meizhu Lui, Bárbara J. Robles, Betsy Leondar-Wright,
    Rose M. Brewer, and Rebecca Adamson   428

44. Crossing the Color Line: A Historical Assessment and
    Personal Narrative of *Loving v. Virginia*
    Robert A. Pratt   442

POPULAR CULTURE

45. Framing Class: Media Representations of Wealth and Poverty in America
    Diana Kendall   448

46. Loot or Find: Fact or Frame?
    Cheryl I. Harris and Devon W. Carbado   453

Personal Account: He Hit Her
Tim Norton   462

47. The Protean N-Word
    Randall Kennedy   463

48. Disability and Representation
    Rosemarie Garland-Thomson   474

SECTION IV—**BRIDGING DIFFERENCES**

FRAMEWORK ESSAY   **480**

49. Lilly's Big Day
    Gail Collins   489

50. The Other Movement That Rosa Parks Inspired: By Sitting Down,
    She Made Room for the Disabled
    Charles Wilson   490

51. Influencing Public Policy
    Jeanine C. Cogan   492

52. What Can We Do? Becoming Part of the Solution
    Allan G. Johnson   502

Personal Account: Parents' Underestimated Love
Octavio N. Espinal   507

53. In Defense of Rich Kids
    William Upski Wimsatt   508

Personal Account: Where Are You From?
C.C.   511

54.   Uprooting Racism: How White People Can Work for Racial Justice
      Paul Kivel   512

55.   I/Me/Mine—Intersectional Identities as Negotiated Minefields
      Shuddhabrata Sengupta   517

      Credits   *C-1*
      Index   *I-1*

PREFACE

The Meaning of Difference is an effort to understand how difference is constructed in contemporary American culture: How do categories of people come to be seen as "different"? How does being "different" affect people's lives? What does difference mean at the level of the individual, social institution, or society? What difference does "difference" make? What is *shared* across the most significant categories of difference in America—race, sex/gender, sexual orientation, social class, and disability? What can be learned from their commonalities? That *The Meaning of Difference* is now in its sixth edition makes us hopeful that this comparative approach can be useful in understanding American conceptions and constructions of difference.

ORGANIZATION AND CONCEPTUAL FRAMEWORK

The Meaning of Difference is divided into four sections. Each section includes an opening Framework Essay and a set of readings, with the Framework Essay providing the conceptual structure by which to understand the readings. Thus, the Framework Essays are not simply introductions to the readings; they are the "text" portion of this **text/reader.**

The first section's Framework Essay and readings describe how categories of difference are *created;* the second considers the *experience* of difference; the third examines the *meanings* that are assigned to difference in ideology, law, public policy, the economy, and popular culture; and the fourth describes what people can do to *challenge and change these constructions* of difference.

Each of the readings included in the volume has been selected by virtue of its applicability to multiple categories of difference. For example, F. James Davis's conclusions about the construction of race (Reading 2) could be applied to a discussion of sexual identity or disability. How much of "x" does it take to locate someone as gay or straight, disabled or nondisabled, Middle-Eastern or American? Carola

Suarez-Orozco's discussion of identity formation in a globalized world (Reading 21) can be applied toward an understanding of racial identity formation and even to the formation of identities tied to sexuality. Similarly, Michael Oliver's rendering of an alternative Survey of Disabled Adults (Reading 18)—which parallels Martin Rochlin's classic Heterosexual Questionnaire (Reading 17)—serves as an example of the insights that can be gained by a change of perspective. In all, our aim has been to select readings that help identify both what is unique and what is shared across our experiences of difference.

DISTINGUISHING FEATURES

Five features make *The Meaning of Difference* distinctive:

- First, it offers a conceptual framework by which to understand the commonalities among these categories of difference. This encompassing conceptual approach makes *The Meaning of Difference* unique.
- Second, no other book provides an accessible and historically grounded discussion of the Supreme Court decisions critical to the creation of these differences.
- Third, *The Meaning of Difference* has been designed with an eye toward the pedagogic difficulties that often accompany this subject matter. Our experience has been that when the topics are *simultaneously* race, sex and gender, social class, sexual orientation, and disability no one group can be easily cast as victim or victimizer.
- Fourth, no other volume includes a detailed discussion and set of readings on how to challenge and change the constructions of difference.
- Finally, *The Meaning of Difference* is the first book of its kind to incorporate disability as a master status functioning in ways analogous to the operation of race and ethnicity, sex and gender, sexual orientation, and social class.

CHANGES IN THE SIXTH EDITION

This edition includes twenty-one new readings, six new personal accounts, and, in Reading 41, a discussion of the Supreme Court's 2009 *Ricci vs. DeStefano* decision on racial equity in hiring. In addition to increased attention to immigration and Middle Eastern Americans, the new readings—many from authors who have captured national attention—have been selected to speak to contemporary assumptions of a "post-racial" America. These new readings address topics such as

- the significance of the election of the country's first African American president (Tim Wise, Reading 38, "Between Barack and a Hard Place");
- the contemporary forms taken by prejudice and discrimination (Malcolm Gladwell, Reading 36, "Blink in Black and White"; Po Bronson and Ashley Merryman, Reading 37, "See Baby Discriminate"; C. J. Pascoe, Reading 28, "'Dude, You're a Fag'"; Paula England, Reading 40, "The Gender Revolution: Uneven and Stalled"; James Carr and Nandinee Kutty, Reading 42, "Segregation: The Rising Costs for America"; Riki Wilchins, Reading 11, "All Together Now: Intersex Infants and IGM");

- the historic and current experience of Middle Eastern and Muslim Americans (John Tehranian, Reading 8, "From Friendly Foreigner to Enemy Race");
- the widening American income gap and the ways it is perpetuated (*The Economist*, Reading 13, "More or Less Equal?"; Stephen McNamee and Robert Miller, Reading 14, "The Silver Spoon"); and
- the ways that people are shaped by and also use popular culture (Randall Kennedy, Reading 47, "The Protean N-Word"; Laura Hamilton and Elizabeth Armstrong, Reading 26, "Gendered Sexuality in Young Adulthood").

HIGHLIGHTS FROM THE SIXTH EDITION

This edition includes substantively revised and updated Framework Essays. For instance, Framework Essay II has been revised to provide a clearer overall structure, and Framework Essay III and that section's readings are now more closely aligned.

Several readings from the previous edition have been retained not only because of their wide popularity among students and faculty, but also because they are classics in the field. Included in this category are Patricia Hill Collins's "It's All in the Family: Intersections of Gender, Race, and Nation"; Yen Le Espiritu's "Asian American Panethnicity: Contemporary National and Transnational Possibilities"; F. James Davis's "Who Is Black? One Nation's Definition"; Ruth Frankenberg's "Whiteness as an 'Unmarked' Cultural Category"; Michael Oliver's "Disability Definitions"; Sally French's "Can you See the Rainbow?"; and Martin Rochlin's "The Heterosexual Questionnaire."

The volume also retains several readings that we believe will become classics, for example, John Hockenberry's "Public Transit"; Liza Mundy's "A World of Their Own"; Cheryl Harris and Devon Carbado's "Loot or Find: Fact or Frame?"; Shuddhabrata Sengupta's "I/Me/Mine—Intersectional Identities as Negotiated Minefields"; and Frank Wu's "The Model Minority: Asian American 'Success' as a Race Relations Failure."

SUPPLEMENTS

Instructor's Manual/Test Bank

An Instructor's Manual and Test Bank accompany this volume. Instructors can access this password-protected material on the Website that accompanies the sixth edition of *The Meaning of Difference* at www.mhhe.com/rosenblum6e.

ACKNOWLEDGMENTS

Many colleagues and friends have helped us clarify the ideas we present here. David Haines has been unfailing in his willingness to help Karen think through conceptual, technical, and ethical dilemmas. She could not imagine a colleague more supportive or wise. Theodore W. Travis provided insight on Supreme Court decisions, their relationship to social values, and their impact on American society. Since this project first emerged, Victoria Rader has been generous in sharing her knowledge as a teacher and writer. Her wisdom especially guided our development of the "Bridging Differences" section. We are also grateful to our colleague and friend Beth Omansky for helping us understand the critical relationship of disability to our work. Two other colleagues—Rose Pascarell and Jamey Piland—are owed special thanks both for their feedback and the good work they accomplish with students. As a friend and friendly editor, none could be better than Sheila Barrows. Cheryl Aston, Carol Henderson, and Addison Huber were generous with their time and skill in the final critical stages of manuscript production. Finally, we owe thanks to our students at George Mason University for sharing their experiences with us.

For this edition, we again convey our appreciation to Joan Lester and the Equity Institute of Emeryville, California, for their understanding of the progress that can be made through a holistic analysis.

Gina Boedeker, Jolynn Kilburg, and Nikki Weissman of McGraw-Hill shepherded this volume to completion. Fred Courtright's work on acquiring permissions was especially appreciated. As in previous editions, McGraw-Hill proved itself committed to a thorough review process by putting together a panel of accomplished scholars with broad expertise. All offered detailed and insightful critiques, and we are much in their debt:

Gary Bachman, Park University

Cynthia Bishop, Meredith College

Nicole Bromfield, Virginia Commonwealth University

Rosalind Fisher, University of West Florida

Anita Fleming-Rife, University of Northern Colorado

Nikitah Imani, James Madison University

Shepherd Jenks, Central New Mexico Community College

Danielle MacCartney, Webster University

Deanna McGaughey-Summers, University of Louisville

Aimee Moles, Louisiana State University-Baton Rouge

Kenneth Stewart, Angelo State University

Alison Thomas-Cottingham, Rider University

Becky Trigg, University of Alabama at Birmingham

Karen Rosenblum
Toni-Michelle Travis
George Mason University

CONSTRUCTING CATEGORIES OF DIFFERENCE

FRAMEWORK ESSAY

In this book we consider how *difference* is constructed in contemporary American society. We explore how categories of people are seen as significantly different from one another and how people's lives are affected by these conceptions of difference. The four sections of the book are organized around what we consider to be the key questions about difference: how it is constructed, how it is experienced by individuals, how meaning is attributed to difference, and how differences can be bridged.

We believe that race, sex, social class, sexual orientation, and disability are currently the primary axes of difference in American society—they are also what social scientists would call *master statuses.* In common usage, the term *status* means prestige or esteem. But for social scientists, the term describes positions in a social structure. In this sense, statuses are like empty slots (or positions) that individuals fill. The most obvious kinds of statuses are kinship and occupation, for example, uncle, mother-in-law, cousin, office manager, paramedic, disk jockey. At any time, an individual holds multiple statuses—kinship, occupational, religious—as well as race, sex, social class, sexual orientation, and disability statuses. (Age is another master status, although not one examined here.)

This latter set of statuses—the ones we focus on in this book—are significantly more powerful than most other social statuses. Social scientists refer to these as *master* statuses because they so profoundly affect a person's life: "in most or all social situations (master status) will overpower or dominate all other statuses. . . . Master status influences every other aspect of life, including personal identity" (Scott and Marshall, 2009:452–53). This does not mean, however, that people always understand the impact of the master statuses they occupy. Indeed, much of this book is about recognizing that impact.

This text will explore similarities in the operation of these master statuses. Although there are certainly differences of history, experience, and impact, we believe that similar processes are at work when people "see" differences of color, sex and gender, social class, sexual orientation, and disability, and we believe that there are similarities in the consequences of these master statuses for individuals' lives.

In preparing this volume, we noticed that talk about racism, sexism, and homophobia seemed to be everywhere—film, music, news reports, talk shows, sermons, and scholarly publications—and that the topics carried considerable intensity. These are controversial subjects; thus, readers may have strong reactions to these issues. Two perspectives—essentialism and constructionism—are core to this book; they should also help you understand your own reaction to the material.

The Essentialist and Constructionist Perspectives

The difference between the *constructionist* and *essentialist* perspectives is illustrated in the tale of the three umpires, first apparently told by social psychologist Hadley Cantril:

> Hadley Cantril relates the story of three baseball umpires discussing their profession. The first umpire said, "Some are balls and some are strikes, and I call them as they are." The second

replied, "Some's balls and some's strikes, and I call 'em as I sees 'em." The third thought about it and said, "Some's balls and some's strikes, but they ain't nothing 'till I calls 'em." (Henshel and Silverman, 1975:26)

The first umpire in the story can be described as an essentialist. When he says, "I call them as they are," he assumes that balls and strikes exist in the world regardless of his perception of them. For this umpire, balls and strikes are easily identified, and he is merely a neutral observer; he "regards knowledge as objective and independent of mind, and himself as the impartial reporter of things 'as they are'" (Pfuhl, 1986:5).

Thus, the essentialist perspective presumes that items in a category all share some "essential" quality, their "ball-ness" or "strike-ness." For essentialists, *race, sex, sexual orientation, disability,* and *social class* identify significant, empirically verifiable differences among people. From the essentialist perspective, each of these exists apart from any social processes; they are objective categories of real differences among people.

The second umpire is somewhat removed from pure essentialism. His statement, "I call 'em as I sees 'em," conveys the belief that while an independent, objective reality exists, it is subject to interpretation. For him, the world contains balls and strikes, but individuals may have different perceptions about which is which.

The third umpire, who says "they ain't nothing 'till I calls 'em," is a constructionist. He operates from the belief that "conceptions such as 'strikes' and 'balls' have no meaning except that given them by the observer" (Pfuhl, 1986:5). For this constructionist umpire, reality cannot be separated from the way a culture makes sense of it; strikes and balls do not exist until they are constructed through social processes. From this perspective, difference is created rather than intrinsic to a phenomenon. Social processes—such as those in political, legal, economic, scientific, and religious institutions—create differences, determine that some differences are more important than others, and assign particular meanings to those differences. From this perspective, the way a society defines difference among its members tells us more about that society than the people so classified. *The Meaning of Difference* operates from the constructionist perspective, since it examines how we have arrived at our race, sex, disability, sexual orientation, and social class categories.

Few of us have grown up as constructionists. More likely, we are essentialists who believe that master statuses such as race or sex entail clear-cut, unchanging, and in some way meaningful differences. Still, not everyone is an essentialist. Those from multiple racial or religious backgrounds are familiar with the ways in which identity is not clear-cut. They grow up understanding how definitions of self vary with the context; how others try to define one as belonging in a particular category; and how, in many ways, one's very presence calls prevailing classification systems into question. For example, the experience Jelita McLeod describes in Reading 24 of being asked "What are you?" is a common experience for multiracial people. Such experiences make evident the social constructedness of racial identity.

Most of us are unlikely to be exclusively essentialist or constructionist. As authors, we take the constructionist perspective, but we have still relied on essentialist terms we find problematic. The irony of questioning the idea of race but still talking about "blacks," "whites," and "Asians," or of rejecting a dualistic approach to sexual identity while still using the terms *gay* and *straight*, has not escaped us. Indeed, throughout our discussion we have used the currently favored essentialist phrase *sexual orientation* over the more constructionist *sexual preference*.[1]

Further, there is a serious risk that a text such as this falsely identifies people on the basis of *either* their sex, race, sexual orientation, disability, or social class, despite the fact that master statuses are not parts of a person that can be broken off from one another like the segments of a Tootsie Roll (Spelman, 1988). All of us are always *simultaneously* all of our master statuses, an idea encompassed by the concept of *intersectionality*. As Patricia Hill Collins describes it in Reading 24, "As opposed to examining gender, race, class, and nation, as separate systems of oppression, intersectionality explores how these systems mutually construct one another, . . . [how] certain ideas and practices surface repeatedly across multiple systems of oppression." Thus, while the readings in this section may make it seem as if these were separable statuses, they are not. Indeed, even the concept of master status could mislead us into thinking that there could be only one dominating status in one's life.

Both constructionism and essentialism can be found in the social sciences. Indeed, essentialism is the basis of probability theory and statistics, and it forms the bedrock for most social scientific research. Both perspectives also are evident in social movements, and those movements sometimes shift from one perspective to the other over time. For example, some feminists and most of those opposed to feminism have held the essentialist belief that women and men are inherently different. The constructionist view that sexual identity is chosen dominated the gay rights movement of the 1970s (Faderman, 1991; Armstrong, 2002), but today, most members of that movement take the essentialist approach that sexual identity is something one is born with. By contrast, some of those opposed to gay relationships now take the constructionist view that it is chosen. In this case, language often signals which perspective is being used. For example, sexual *preference* conveys active, human decision making with the possibility of change (constructionism), while sexual *orientation* implies something fixed and inherent to a person (essentialism).

Americans are now about equally split between those who hold essentialist and constructionist views on homosexuality—37 percent of those in a 2010 poll attributed being gay to upbringing and environment; 36 percent described it as a trait one is born with; 12 percent described it as both (Gallup, 2010). This is a significant reversal of the opinions held in the late 1970s, when only about 14 percent of respondents attributed homosexuality to an inborn trait. The shift toward an essentialist view occurred in the late 1990s, when, as Roger Lancaster describes in Reading 15, there was extensive media coverage of biological (i.e., essentialist) research on the origin of homosexuality.

---

[1]The term *sexual identity* seems now to be replacing *sexual orientation*. It could be used in either an essentialist or a constructionist way.

This example from journalist Darryl Rist shows the appeal that essentialist explanations might have for gay rights activists:

> [Chris Yates's parents were] Pentecostal ministers who had tortured his adolescence with Christian cures for sexual perversity. Shock and aversion therapies under born-again doctors and gruesome exorcisms of sexual demons by spirit-filled preachers had culminated in a plan to have him castrated by a Mexican surgeon who touted the procedure as a way to make the boy, if not straight, at least sexless. Only then had the terrified son rebelled.
>
> Then, in the summer of 1991, the journal *Science* reported anatomical differences between the brains of homosexual and heterosexual men. . . . The euphoric media—those great purveyors of cultural myths—drove the story wildly. Every major paper in the country headlined the discovery smack on the front page. . . . Like many others, I suspect, Chris Yates's family saw in this newly reported sexual science a way out of its wrenching impasse. After years of virtual silence between them and their son, Chris's parents drove several hundred miles to visit him and ask for reconciliation. Whatever faded guilt they might have felt for the family's faulty genes was nothing next to the reassurance that neither by a perverse upbringing nor by his own iniquity was Chris or the family culpable for his urges and actions. "We could never have condoned this if you could do something to change it. But when we finally understood that you were *born* that way, we knew we'd been wrong. We had to ask your forgiveness." (Rist, 1992:425–26)

Understandably, those who are discriminated against would find essentialist orientations appealing, just as the expansiveness of constructionist approaches would be appealing in more tolerant eras. Still, either perspective can be used to justify discrimination, since people can be persecuted for the choices they make as well as for their genetic inheritance.

Our inclusion of disability as a social construction may generate an intense reaction—many will want to argue that disability is about real physical, sensory, or cognitive differences, not social constructs. However, there are two factors at work here. One involves *impairment*, that is, "the physical, cognitive, emotional or sensory condition within the person as diagnosed by medical professionals" (Omansky, 2006:27). The second is "the loss or limitation of opportunities to take part in the normal life of the community on an equal level with others due to physical and social barriers" (Disabled People's International, 1982). This latter dimension, called *disability*, has been the emphasis of what is called the "social model" of disability, which contends that disability is created by social, political, and environmental obstacles—that is, that social processes turn impairments into disabilities (Barnes and Mercer, 2003; Oliver, 1990, 1996, 2009). This is a form of discrimination sometimes called *ableism.* In the historic words of Britain's Union of the Physically Impaired against Segregation (UPIAS), one of the first disability liberation groups in the world and the first run by disabled people themselves (Hunt, 2001),

> it is society which disables physically impaired people. Disability is something imposed on top of our impairment by the way we are unnecessarily isolated and excluded from full participation in society. Disabled people are therefore an oppressed group in society. (UPIAS, 1973:4)

That perspective is reflected in the 2007 United Nations Convention on the Rights of Persons with Disabilities.

> [D]isability should be seen as the result of the interaction between a person and his or her environment. Disability is not something that resides in the individual as the result of some impairment. . . . Disability resides in the society, not in the person. [For example,] in a society where corrective lenses are available for someone with extreme myopia (nearsightedness), this person would *not* be considered to have a disability, however someone *with the same condition* in a society where corrective lenses were not available would be considered to have a disability, especially if the level of vision prevented the person from performing tasks expected of this person. . . . (United Nations, 2007)

For example, John Hockenberry (Reading 33) and Charles Wilson (Reading 54) describe how mass transit systems that are inaccessible to wheelchair users "disable" them by making it difficult or impossible to work, attend school, or manage basic sociability. Beyond architectural, educational, and occupational barriers, disability is also constructed through cultural stereotypes and everyday interactions in which difference is defined as undesirable. We once heard a student with spina bifida tell a story addressing this point: In her first day at school, other students kept asking what was "wrong" with her. As she put it, she had always known she was different, but she hadn't thought she was "wrong."

Not only can disability be understood as the result of disabling environments and cultural stereotypes, but the categories of impairment and disability are also themselves socially constructed through medical and legal processes. "[I]llness, disease, and disability are not 'givens' in nature . . . but rather *socially constructed* categories that emerge from the interpretive activities of people acting together in social situations" (Schneider, 1988:65). Learning disabilities are an example of this process.

> Before the late 1800s when observers began to write about "word blindness," learning disability (whatever its name) did not exist, although the human variation to which it ambiguously refers did—sort of! People who today might be known as learning disabled may have formerly been known as "slow," "retarded," or "odd." But mostly they would not have been known as unusual at all. The learning difficulties experienced today by learning disabled youth have not been experienced by most youth throughout history. For example, most youth have not been asked to learn to read. Thus, they could not experience any reading difficulties, the most common learning disability. As we have expected youth to learn to read and have tried to teach them to do so, many youth have experienced difficulty. However, until the mid-1960s we typically did not understand those difficulties as the consequences of a learning disability. (Higgins, 1992:53)

The social model of disability first emerged out of the disabled people's movement in the 1970s in opposition to the "medical model," which approached disability as a matter of individual deficiencies or defects, rather than societal responses. From the perspective of the medical model, individuals have problems that need to be treated by medical specialists; from that of the social model, individual problems are the result of social structures that need to be changed. Thus, for adherents of the social model, the important questions are about civil rights such as equal access. The survey questions posed by Mike Oliver in Reading 18 show how the world is perceived differently from these two perspectives.

Why have we spent so much time describing the essentialist and constructionist perspectives? Discussions about race, sex, disability, sexual orientation, and social class generate great intensity, partly because they involve the clash of essentialist and constructionist assumptions. Essentialists are likely to view categories of people as "essentially" different in some important way; constructionists likely to see these differences as socially created and arbitrary. An essentialist asks what causes people to be different; a constructionist asks about the origin and consequence of the categorization system itself. While arguments about the nature and cause of racism, sexism, homophobia, and poverty are disputes about power and justice, from the perspectives of essentialism and constructionism they are also disputes about the meaning of differences in color, sexuality, and social class.

In all of this, the constructionist approach has one clear advantage. From that perspective, one understands that all this talk has a profound significance. Such talk is not simply *about* difference; it is itself the *creation* of difference. In the sections that follow, we examine how categories of people are named, dichotomized, and stigmatized—all toward the construction of difference.

Naming

Difference is constructed first by naming categories of people. Therefore, constructionists pay special attention to the names people use to refer to themselves and others—the times at which new names are asserted, the negotiations that surround the use of particular names, and those occasions when people are grouped together or separated out.

Asserting a Name   Both individuals and categories of people face similar issues in the assertion of a name. A change of name involves, to some extent, the claim of a new identity. For example, one of our colleagues wanted to be called by her full first name rather than by its shortened version because that had come to seem childish to her. It took a few times to remind people that this was her new name, and with most that was adequate. One colleague, however, argued that he could not adapt to the new name; she would just have to tolerate his continued use of the nickname. This was a small but public battle about who had the power to name whom. Did she have the power to enforce her own naming, or did he have the power to name her despite her wishes? Eventually, she prevailed.

A more disturbing example was a young woman who wanted to keep her maiden name after she married. Her fiancé agreed with her decision, recognizing that he would be reluctant to give up his name were the tables turned. When his mother heard of this possibility, however, she was outraged. In her mind, a rejection of her family's name was a rejection of her family. She urged her son to reconsider getting married.

Thus, asserting a name can create social conflict. On both a personal and societal level, naming can involve the claim of a particular identity and the rejection of others' power to impose a name. For example, is one Native American, American Indian, or Sioux; African American or black; girl or woman; Asian, Asian American, Korean, or Korean American; gay or homosexual; Chicano, Mexican American, Mexican, Latino/a, or Hispanic? For instance,

[j]ust who is Hispanic? The answer depends on whom you ask.

The label was actually coined in the mid-1970s by federal bureaucrats working under President Richard M. Nixon. They came up with it in response to concerns that the government was wrongly applying "Chicano" to people who were not of Mexican descent, and otherwise misidentifying and underserving segments of the population by generally classifying those with ancestral ties to the Spanish cultural diaspora as either Chicano, Cuban, or Puerto Rican.

Nearly three decades later, the debate continues to surround the term Hispanic and its definition. Although mainly applied to people from Latin American countries with linguistic and cultural ties to Spain, it also is used by the U.S. government to refer to Spaniards themselves, as well as people from Portuguese-speaking Brazil.

Especially on college campuses, a sizable and growing minority of people prefer "Latino," which does not have the same association with Spanish imperialism. That term is controversial as well, however, mainly because it stems from the term Latin America and wrongly implies ties to ancient Rome. (Schmidt, 2003)

Deciding what name to use for a category of people is not easy. It is unlikely that all members of the category use the same name; the name members use for one another may not be acceptable for outsiders to use; nor is it always advisable to ask what name a person prefers. We once saw an old friend become quite angry when asked whether he preferred the term *black* or *African American*. "Either one is fine with me," he replied, "*I* know what *I* am." To him, the question meant that he was being seen as a member of a category, not as an individual.

Because naming may involve a redefinition of self, an assertion of power, and a rejection of others' ability to impose an identity, social change movements often claim a new name, while opponents may express opposition by continuing to use the old name. For example, *black* emerged in opposition to *Negro* as the Black Power movement sought to distinguish itself from the Martin Luther King–led moderate wing of the civil rights movement. The term *Negro* had itself been put forward by influential leaders such as W. E. B. Du Bois and Booker T. Washington as a rejection of the term *colored* that had dominated the mid- to late 19th century—"[D]espite its association with racial epithets, 'Negro' was defined to stand for a new way of thinking about Blacks" (Smith, 1992:497–98). Similarly, in 1988, Ramona H. Edelin, president of the National Urban Coalition, proposed that *African American* be substituted for *black*. Now both terms are about equally in use.[2] Among blacks who have a preference, Gallup polls suggest a gradual trend toward the label "African American." Still, "a clear majority of blacks say they don't care which label is used" (Gallup, 2007), and some still prefer the term "Negro." "The immediate reason the word *Negro* is on the Census is simple enough: in the 2000 Census, more than 56,000 people wrote in *Negro* to describe their identity—even though it was already on the form. Some people, it seems, still strongly identify with the term, which used to be a perfectly polite designation," but is now considered by many an insult (Kiviat, 2010).

Each of these name changes—from *Negro* to *black* to *African American*—was first promoted by activists as a way to demonstrate their commitment to a new order. A similar theme is reflected in the history of the terms *Chicano* and *Chicanismo*. Although the origin of the terms is unclear, the principle was the same. As reporter

---

[2]Thus, one can find Black Studies, Afro-American Studies, and African American Studies programs in universities across the country.

Ruben Salazar wrote in the 1960s, "a Chicano is a Mexican-American with a non-Anglo image of himself" (Shorris, 1992:101). (*Anglo* is a colloquialism for *white* used in the southwestern and western United States.)

Similarly, the term *homosexual* was first coined in 1896 by a Hungarian physician hoping to decriminalize same-sex relations between men. It was incorporated into the medical and psychological literature of the time, which depicted nonprocreative sex as pathological. In the 1960s, activists rejected the pathological characterization along with the name associated with it, turning to the terms *gay*[3] and *lesbian* rather than *homosexual* (and using gay to refer to men, or both men and women). Later, the 1990s group Queer Nation transformed the epithet into a slogan—"We're here! We're queer! Get used to it!"

> Well, yes, "gay" is great. It has its place. . . . [But] using "queer" is a way of reminding us how we are perceived by the rest of the world. It's a way of telling ourselves we don't have to be witty and charming people who keep our lives discreet and marginalized in the straight world. . . . Queer, unlike gay, doesn't mean male. . . . Yeah, queer can be a rough word but it is also a sly and ironic weapon we can steal from the homophobe's hands and use against him. (Queer Nation Manifesto, 1990)

Now, all terms—homosexual, gay and lesbian, gay as including both women and men or just men, queer, and the acronyms GLBTQ (gay, lesbian, bisexual, transgender, and questioning) and LGBTQ—appear to be in common use. People who identify as asexual, that is, not experiencing sexual attraction, also appears to be a growing category, with the likelihood that the LGBTQ umbrella will expand to LGBTQA. While "queer" maintains some of its history as both pejorative and defiant, it is apparently acceptable enough to serve as the title of the popular reality cable show, *Queer Eye*, that aired from 2003–2007.

Just as each of these social movements has involved a public renaming that proclaims pride, the women's movement has asserted *woman* as a replacement for *girl*. A student who described a running feud with her roommate illustrates the significance of these terms. The student preferred the word *woman*, arguing that *girl*, when applied to females past adolescence, was insulting. Her female roommate just as strongly preferred the term *girl* and regularly applied it to the females she knew. Each of them had such strong feelings on the matter that it was apparent they would not last as roommates.

How could these two words destroy their relationship? It appears that English speakers use the terms *girl* and *woman* to refer to quite different qualities. *Woman*, like *man*, is understood to convey adulthood, power, and sexuality; *girl*, like *boy*, connotes youth, powerlessness, and irresponsibility. Thus, the two roommates were

---

[3]In the 17th century, *gay* became associated with an addiction to social pleasure, dissipation, and loose morality, and was used to refer to female prostitutes (e.g., *gay girl*). The term was apparently first used in reference to homosexuality in 1925 in Australia. "It may have been both the connotations of femininity and those of immorality that led American homosexuals to adopt the title 'gay' with some self-irony in the 1920s. The slogan 'Glad to Be Gay,' adopted by both female and male homosexuals, and the naming of the Gay Liberation Front, which was born from the Stonewall resistance riots following police raids on homosexual bars in New York in 1969, bear witness to a greater self-confidence" (Mills, 1989:102).

asserting quite different places for themselves in the world. One claimed adulthood; the other saw herself as not having achieved that yet. This explanation is offered by many females: It is not so much that they like being *girls*, as that they value youth and/or do not yet feel justified in calling themselves women. Yet this is precisely the identity the women's movement has asserted: "We cannot be girls anymore, we must be women."

As each of these cases shows, different categories of people may claim a wide range of names for themselves. A name may reflect the analysis and aspirations of a social movement, and it may be the battleground for competing conceptions of the world. The name invoked by movement activists may have no immediate bearing on the language used by people in the streets, or everyday language may come to be shaped by policymakers external to the social movement. Sometimes, a variety of names may be in use—each with a constituency that feels strongly that only some words are appropriate.

Of all the master statuses we are considering in this book, the naming of those with disabilities is perhaps the least settled. The term *handicapped*, which predominated in the period following World War II, shifted to *disabled* with the emergence of the disability rights movement in the 1970s. As we have seen, theorists from the British social model draw a distinction between *impairment*, referring to "the physical, cognitive, emotional or sensory condition within the person as diagnosed by medical professionals," and *disability*, which is reserved for the social processes that disable a person (Omansky, 2006:27)—but the U.S. disability rights movement uses *disability* to cover both of these features. The style guide for the American Psychological Association urges a "people first" approach, as in "people with disabilities" rather than "disabled people," and "people first" terminology has been formally authorized by some state and local governments. By contrast, one of the founders of the British disability rights movement—Mike Oliver—argued that *disabled people* is ultimately more appropriate:

> It is sometimes argued, often by [nondisabled] professionals and some disabled people, that 'people with disabilities' is the preferred term, for it asserts the value of the person first and the disability then becomes an appendage. This liberal and humanist view flies in the face of reality as it is experienced by disabled people themselves who argue that far from being an appendage, disability is an essential part of the self. In this view, it is nonsensical to talk about the person and the disability separately, and consequently, disabled people are demanding acceptance as they are, disabled people. (Oliver, 1990:xiii)

In all, the names that we call ourselves and others are rarely a matter of indifference; they are often carefully chosen to reflect worldview and aspirations, and they can materially shape our lives.

Creating Categories of People   While individuals and groups may assert names for themselves, governments also have the power to categorize. The history of the race and ethnicity questions asked in the U.S. Census illustrates this process.

Every census since the first one in 1790 has included a question about race. By 1970, the options for race were *white, Negro or black, American Indian* (with a request to print the name of the enrolled or principal tribe), *Japanese, Chinese, Filipino,*

Hawaiian, Korean, and *Other* with the option of specifying. The 1970 census began the practice of allowing the head of the household to identify the race of household members: before that, the census taker had made that decision based on the appearance of the family. Thus, the Census Bureau began treating race as primarily a matter of *self-*identification. Still, it was assumed that a person could only be a member of *one* racial group, so respondents were allowed only one option for each household member.

The 1970 census also posed the first ethnicity question, asking whether the individual was of Hispanic or non-Hispanic ancestry. (Ethnicity, which generally refers to national ancestry, is a subject we will return to shortly.) The Hispanic/non-Hispanic question was added at the recommendation of the Census Bureau's Hispanic Advisory Committee as a way to correct for the *differential undercount* of the Hispanic population. A differential undercount means that more people are undercounted in one category than in another; for example, the census yields a larger undercount of those who rent their homes than of those who own them. Undercounting primarily affects the data on low-income residents of inner cities. This is the case because the poor often move and are thus difficult to contact, are more likely to be illiterate or non-English speakers (there was no Spanish-language census form until 1990), and are more likely to be illegal immigrants afraid to respond to a government questionnaire. (The Constitution requires a count of *all* the people in the United States, not just those who are citizens or legal residents.) Because census data affect the distribution of billions of dollars of federal aid, as well as voting rights and civil rights enforcement, undercounting has a significant impact. Indeed, the Census Bureau estimates that, apart from the apportionment of seats in the U.S. House of Representatives, the census helps "determine how more than $400 billion dollars of federal funding each year [will be] spent on infrastructure and services like hospitals, job training centers, schools, senior centers, bridges, tunnels and other-public works projects, and emergency services" (U.S. Census 2010, http://2010.census.gov/2010census/why/ accessed on May 27, 2010).

To improve the collection of this data, in the 1970s the Commission on Civil Rights reviewed the race categorization practices of federal agencies and concluded that while "the designations do not refer strictly to race, color, national or ethnic origin," the categories were nonetheless what the general public understood to be *minority groups* (U.S. Commission on Civil Rights, 1973:39). The aim of this data collection was to pinpoint the extent of discrimination, not to identify all population categories.

This understanding of the meaning of "minority group" was part of a remarkable bipartisan consensus that characterized the decade following the 1964 Civil Rights Act.

It was a bipartisan project, including from both parties liberals and conservatives. . . . In the signature minority rights policy, affirmative action, the federal government went beyond African Americans and declared that certain groups were indeed "minorities"—an undefined term embraced by policymakers, advocates, and activists alike—and needed new rights and programs for equal opportunity and full citizenship. In the parlance of the period, minorities were groups seen as "disadvantaged" but not defined by income or education. African Americans were the paradigmatic minority, but there were three other ethnoracial minorities: Latinos, Asian Americans, and American Indians. Immigrants, women, and the disabled of all ethnic groups were also included and won new rights during this revolutionary period. (Skrentny, 2002:2)

It is in this context that, in 1977, the Office of Management and Budget (OMB) issued Statistical Directive No. 15, "Race and Ethnic Standards for Federal Statistics and Administrative Reporting," which established standard categories and definitions for all federal agencies, including the Bureau of the Census. Directive No. 15 defined four racial and one ethnic category: American Indian or Alaskan Native, Asian or Pacific Islander, Negro or Black, White, and Hispanic. "The questions [on the census] follow the categories required by the federal Office of Management and Budget for federal statistics" (U.S. Census, 2010). Thus, the question about Hispanic origin remains the only ethnicity question on the decennial census. A question asking respondents to identify their "ancestry or national origin" is, however, included in the Census Bureau's annual American Community Survey, which samples U.S. households. Reading 3, "The Evolution of Identity," shows how census questions on race and ethnicity changed between 1860 and 2000. Figure 1 shows the relevant questions in the 2010 census.

For our purposes, the most notable change has been recognition that a person may identify himself or herself as being a member of more than one racial group, although the census did not offer a category called *multiracial.* This change was one outcome of a comprehensive review and revision of OMB's Directive No. 15 that included public hearings, sample surveys of targeted populations, and collaboration among the more than 30 federal agencies that collect and use data on race and ethnicity. While this change was spurred by activists who identified themselves as multiracial, the bureau's pretesting also indicated that less than 2 percent of respondents would mark more than one race for themselves, and thus the historical continuity with previous censuses would not be compromised. The bureau's expectation was close to the mark—2.4 percent of the population, almost 7 million people, marked two or more races for themselves in the 2000 census. Since then, other Census Bureau surveys have found 1.7 percent of the population marking more than one race for themselves (U.S. Census Bureau, 2010b).

One change that was not made in the 2000 census, however, was inclusion of an ethnic category called *Arab* or *Middle Eastern* because public comment did not indicate agreement on a definition for this category. Thus, in the 2000 census Arab or Middle Eastern peoples continue to be categorized as *white.*

As in previous censuses, undercounting remains an important fiscal and political issue, given the disproportionate undercounting of people of color and the poor. Still, gay couples may well be the most undercounted population. Since the 1990 census, the form has provided *unmarried partner* as a possible answer to the question of how the people in the household are related to one another. The number of same-sex couples reporting themselves as "unmarried partners" increased more than 300 percent between the 1990 and 2000 censuses, to almost 600,000 couples, but that number is certainly less than a complete count because of respondents' reluctance to report (Cohn, 2001).

We end this phase of our discussion with two cautions. On a personal level, many of us find census categorizations objectionable. But as *citizens,* we still seek

➤ NOTE: Please answer BOTH Question 5 about Hispanic origin and Question 6 about race. For this census, Hispanic origins are not races.

5 Is this person of Hispanic, Latino, or Spanish origin?

☐ **No,** not of Hispanic, Latino, or Spanish origin

☐ Yes, Mexican, Mexican Am., Chicano

☐ Yes, Puerto Rican

☐ Yes, Cuban

☐ Yes, another Hispanic, Latino, or Spanish origin — *Print origin, for example, Argentinean, Colombian, Dominican, Nicaraguan, Salvadoran, Spaniard, and so on.* ↘

☐ _____

6 What is this person's race? *Mark* X *one or more boxes.*

☐ White

☐ Black, African Am., or Negro

☐ American Indian or Alaska Native — *Print name of enrolled or principal tribe.* ↘

☐ _____

☐ Asian Indian	☐ Japanese	☐ Native Hawaiian
☐ Chinese	☐ Korean	☐ Guamanian or Chamorro
☐ Filipino	☐ Vietnamese	☐ Samoan
☐ Other Asian — *Print race, for example, Hmong, Laotian, Thai, Pakistani, Cambodian, and so on.* ↘		☐ Other Pacific Islander — *Print race, for example, Fijian, Tongan, and so on.* ↘

☐ _____

☐ Some other race — *Print race.* ↘

☐ _____

FIGURE 1
Questions from the 2010 Census.
Source: U.S. Census Bureau, 2010 Census.

the benefits and protections of the laws and policies based on these data—and as citizens we share the goal of eliminating discriminatory practices.

[R]eliable racial data are crucial to enforcing our basic laws against intentional racial discrimination, which enjoy broad public support. For example, in order to demonstrate that an employer is engaging in a broad based "pattern or practice" of discrimination in violation of the Civil Rights Act of 1964, a plaintiff must rely on statistical proof that goes beyond the plight of an individual employee. Supreme Court precedent in such cases requires plaintiffs to show a statistically significant disparity between the proportion of qualified minorities in the local labor market and the proportion within the employer's work force. A disparity of more than two standard deviations creates a legal presumption that intentional discrimination is occurring, since a disparity of that magnitude almost never occurs by accident.

Demographic information, in other words, provides the "big picture" that places individual incidents in context. Voting rights cases require similar proof, as do many housing discrimination cases and suits challenging the discriminatory use of federal funds. Without reliable racial statistics, it would be virtually impossible for courts or agencies to detect institutional bias, and antidiscrimination laws would go unenforced. More fundamentally, we simply cannot know as a society how far we've come in conquering racial discrimination and inequality without accurate information about the health, progress and opportunities available to communities of different races. (Jenkins, 1999:15–16)

Still, when considering official counts of the population, we must be careful not to assume that what is counted is real. While census data contribute to the essentialist view that the world is populated by distinct, scientifically defined categories of people, this brief history demonstrates that not even those who collect the data make that assumption. As even the Census Bureau notes, "The concept of race as used by the Census Bureau reflects self-identification by people according to the race or races with which they most closely identify. These categories are socio-political constructs and should not be interpreted as being scientific or anthropological in nature. Furthermore, the race categories include both racial and national-origin groups" (U.S. Bureau of the Census, 2010a).

Aggregating and Disaggregating

The federal identification policies we have been describing collapsed nonwhite Americans into four categories: Hispanics, American Indians, Blacks, and Asian or Pacific Islanders. This process *aggregated* categories of people; that is, it combined, or "lumped together," different groups. For example, the category *Hispanic, Latino, or Spanish origin* includes 28 different census categories.[4] While census data can be used to separately research each of these, in public discussion the more common reference is to "Hispanics and Latinos," which both aggregates all those categories and masks which groups predominate (by proportion of the U.S. Hispanic/Latino population, Mexicans, Puerto Ricans, Cubans, and those from the Dominican Republic [U.S. Census Bureau, 2006–2008 American Community Survey]). On top of that, as the authors of *Multiple Origins, Uncertain Destinies* (Reading 45) remind us, the category "Hispanic and Latino" is used to encompass recent immigrants, Puerto Ricans (who are U.S. citizens), and those from "some of the earliest settlements in what is now the United States."

The difficulty with determining who counts as Hispanic is that Hispanics do not appear to share any properties in common. Linguistic, racial, religious, political, territorial, cultural, economic, educational, social class, and genetic criteria fail to identify Hispanics in all places and times. . . .

---

[4]The Census Bureau's Hispanic or Latino origin categories are Mexican, Puerto Rican, Cuban, Dominican Republic; Costa Rican, Guatemalan, Honduran, Nicaraguan, Panamanian, Salvadoran, Other Central American; Argentinian, Bolivian, Chilean, Colombian, Ecuadorian, Paraguayan, Peruvian, Uruguayan, Venezuelan, Other South American; Other Hispanic or Latino, including Spaniard, Spanish, Spanish American and All other Hispanic or Latino (U.S. Census Bureau, 2006–2008 American Community Survey).

[Nonetheless], we are treated as a homogeneous group by European Americans and African Americans; and even though Hispanics do not in fact constitute a homogeneous group, we are easily contrasted with European Americans and African Americans because we do not share many of the features commonly associated with these groups. (Gracia, 2000:204–5)

The groups that are lumped together in this aggregate have historically regarded one another as different, and thus in people's everyday lives the aggregate category is likely to *disaggregate*, or fragment, into its constituent national origin elements. For example, a 2009 Pew survey of *U.S.-born* Latino youth (ages 16–25) found that 41 percent refer to themselves first by the country their parents left, 33 percent called themselves American, and 21 percent referred to themselves as Hispanic or Latino/a. The proportions were similar among *immigrant* Latino/a youth, at 52 percent referring to themselves by the country of origin, 24 percent describing themselves as American, and 20 percent calling themselves Latino/a or Hispanic (Pew, 2009).

Still, survey responses about use of these self-identifications do not tell us much about the nature of interaction between groups under the umbrella term "Hispanic or Latino." On the one hand, one could conclude that "Mexicans, Puerto Ricans, and Cubans have little interaction with each other, most do not recognize that they have much in common culturally, and they do not profess strong affection for each other" (de la Garza et al., 1992:14). But on the other hand, "Identification with pan-ethnic labels varies across individuals and may be driven by the proximity of Latinos to other national-origin groups, levels of political awareness and interest, or even something as simple as familiarity with race and ethnic terminology in American society" (Fraga et al., 2010:11). In all, it is probably safe to say that the category *Latino/Hispanic* exists primarily, but not exclusively, from the perspective of non-Latinos.

Like all the differences masked by the terms *Latino* and *Hispanic*, among those in the category *Asian Pacific American* or *Asian American* are groups with different languages, cultures, and religions and sometimes centuries of mutual hostility. Like *Hispanic/Latino*, the category *Asian American* is based more on geography than on any cultural, racial, linguistic, or religious commonalities. "Asian Americans are those who come from a region of the world that *the rest of the world* has defined as Asia" (Hu-Dehart, 1994).[5]

---

[5]In census classification, the category *Asian* includes Asian Indian, Chinese, Filipino, Japanese, Korean, Vietnamese; *Other Asian* includes Bangladeshi, Bhutanese, Burmese, Cambodian, Hmong, Indo-Chinese, Indonesian, Iwo Jiman, Laotian, Malaysian, Maldivian, Mongolian, Nepalese, Okinawan, Pakistani, Singaporean, Sri Lankan, Thai, and Taiwanese. The category *Pacific Islander* includes Native Hawaiian, Guamanian or Chamorro, Samoan; *Other Pacific Islander* includes Carolinian, Chuukese, Fijian, Kiribati, Kosraean, Mariana Islander, Marshallese, Melanesian, Micronesian, New Hebridian, Palauan, Papua New Guinean, Pohnpeian, Polynesian, Saipanese, Solomon Islander, Tahitian, Tokelauan, Tongan, and Yapese (U.S. Census Bureau, 2001).

In 1980, Asian Indians successfully lobbied to change their census classification from *white* to *Asian American* by reminding Congress that historically, immigrants from India had been classed as *Asian*. With other Asians, those from India had been barred from immigration by the 1917 Immigration Act, prohibited from becoming naturalized citizens until 1946, and denied the right to own land by the 1920 Alien Land Law. Indeed, in 1923 the U.S. Supreme Court (in *Thind*) ruled that Asian Indians were nonwhite, and could therefore have their U.S. citizenship nullified (Espiritu, 1992:124–25). Thus, for most of their history in the United States, Asian Indians had been classed as *Asian*.

Much the same can be said for the terms *Middle East* and *Middle Eastern*. As John Tehranian writes in Reading 8, the term *Middle East* emerged at the beginning of the 20th century as part of geopolitical strategies. As a region that encompasses multiple continents, languages, ethnic groups, and religions, "the term is riddled in ambiguity, sometimes encompassing the entire North African coast, from Morocco to Egypt and other parts of Africa, including the Sudan and Somalia, the former Soviet Caucasus Republics of Georgia, Azerbaijan, and Armenia, and occasionally Afghanistan, Pakistan, and Turkistan. The Middle East is therefore a malleable geopolitical construct of relatively recent vintage."

Aggregate classifications have also been promoted by social movements. However, terms such as *Latino* or *Asian American* were not simply the result of federal classifications. Student activists inspired by the Black Power and civil rights movements first proposed the terms. As Yen Le Espiritu describes in Reading 5, college students coined the identifier *Asian American* in response to "the similarity of [their] experiences and treatment." *Asian American, Hispanic,* and *Latino* are examples of *panethnic* terms, that is, classifications that span national-origin identities. Panethnicity is "the development of bridging organizations and solidarities among subgroups of ethnic collectivities that are often seen as homogeneous by outsiders. . . . Those . . . groups that, from an outsider's point of view, are most racially homogeneous are also the groups with the greatest panethnic development" (Lopez and Espiritu, 1990:219–20).

The concept of panethnicity is useful but unstable in practice. "The elites representing such groups find it advantageous to make political demands by using the numbers and resources panethnic formations can mobilize. The state, in turn, can more easily manage claims by recognizing and responding to large blocs as opposed to dealing with the specific claims of a plethora of ethnically defined interest groups" (Omi, 1996:180). At the same time, competition and historic antagonisms make such alliances unstable. "At times it is advantageous to be in a panethnic bloc, and at times it is desirable to mobilize along particular ethnic lines" (Omi, 1996:181).

The disability movement is similar to panethnic movements in that it has brought together people with all types of impairments. This approach was a historic "first," running counter both to the tradition of organizing around specific impairments and to the fact that the needs of people with different impairments are sometimes in conflict. For example, some of the curb cuts that make wheelchair access possible can make walking more difficult for blind people who need to be able to feel the edges of a sidewalk with their canes. The aggregating of disabled people that began with the disability rights movement was reinforced in the 1990 Americans with Disabilities Act (ADA).

The terms *Native American* and *African American* are also aggregate classifications, but in this case they are the result of conquest and enslavement.

The "Indian," like the European, is an idea. The notion of "Indians" was invented to distinguish the indigenous peoples of the New World from Europeans. The "Indian" is the person on shore, outside of the boat. . . . There [were] hundreds of cultures, languages, ways of living in Native America. The place was a model of diversity at the time of Columbus's arrival.

> Yet Europeans did not see this diversity. They created the concept of the "Indian" to give what they did see some kind of unification, to make it a single entity they could deal with, because they could not cope with the reality of 400 different cultures. (Mohawk, 1992:440)[6]

Conquest made "American Indians" out of a multitude of tribes and nations that had been distinctive on linguistic, religious, and economic grounds. It was not only that Europeans had the unifying concept of *Indian* in mind—after all, they were sufficiently aware of cultural differences to generate an extensive body of specific treaties with individual tribes. It was also that conquest itself—encompassing as it did the appropriation of land, the forging and violation of treaties, and policies of forced relocation—structured the lives of Native Americans along common lines. Whereas contemporary Native Americans still identify themselves by tribal ancestry, rather than "Native American" or "American Indian," their shared experience of conquest also forged the common identity reflected in the collective name, *Native American.*

Similarly, the capture, purchase, and forced relocation of Africans, and their experience of forcibly being moved from place to place as personal property, created the category now called *African American.* This experience forged a single people out of a culturally diverse group; it produced an "oppositional racial consciousness," that is, a unity-in-opposition (Omi and Winant, 1994). "Just as the conquest created the 'native' where once there had been Pequot, Iroquois, or Tutelo, so too it created the 'black' where once there had been Asante or Ovimbundu, Yoruba or Bakongo" (Omi and Winant, 1994:66).

Even the categories of *gay and straight, male and female,* and *poor and middle class* are aggregations that presume a commonality by virtue of shared master status. For example, the category *gay and lesbian* assumes that sharing a sexual orientation binds people together despite all the issues that might divide them as men and women, people of color, or people of different social classes. And, just as in the cases we have previously discussed, alliances between gays and lesbians will depend on the circumstances and specific issues.

Still, our analysis has so far ignored one category of people. From whose perspective do the categories of *Native American, Asian American, African American, Middle Eastern American, Arab American,* and *Latino/Hispanic* exist? Since "difference" is always "difference *from,*" from whose perspective is "difference" determined? Who has the power to define "difference"? If "we" are in the boat looking at "them," who precisely are "we"?

Every perspective on the social world emerges from a particular vantage point, a particular social location. Ignoring who is in the boat treats that place as if it were just the view "anyone" would take. Historically, the people in the boat were

---

[6]The idea of *Europe* and the *European* is also a constructed, aggregate category. "Physically, Europe is not a continent. Where is the water separating Europe from Asia? It is culture that separates Europe from Asia. Western Europe roughly comprises the countries that in the Middle Ages were Latin Christendom, and Eastern Europe consists of those countries that in the Middle Ages were Eastern Orthodox Christendom. It was about A.D. 1257 when the Pope claimed hegemony over the secular emperors in Western Europe and formulated the idea that Europeans, Christians, were a unified ethnicity even though they spoke many different languages" (Mohawk, 1992:439–40).

European; at present, they are white Americans. As Ruth Frankenberg frames it in Reading 6, in America "whites are the nondefined definers of other people," "the unmarked marker of others' differentness." Failing to identify the "us" in the boat means that "white culture [becomes] the unspoken norm," a category that is powerful enough to define others while itself remaining invisible and unnamed. Indeed, Frankenberg argues that those with the most power in a society are best positioned to have their own identities left unnamed, thus masking their power.

The term *androcentrism* describes the world as seen from a male-centered perspective. For example, if we define a good employee as one who is willing to work extensive overtime, we are thinking from a male-centered perspective, since women's child-care responsibilities often preclude extra work commitments. We may also describe *Eurocentric* and *"physicalist"* (Russell, 1994) perspectives, that is, viewpoints that assume everyone is of European origin or physically agile. Similarly, the term *heteronormativity* turns our attention to the ways that heterosexuality is built into the assumptions and operation of all aspects of daily life, both sexual and nonsexual (Warner, 1993). Heteronormativity is one of a set of terms that has emerged to describe individual- and societal-level treatment of homosexuality. In 1972, in *Society and the Healthy Homosexual*, psychologist George Weinberg offered the term *homophobia* to describe the aversion to homosexuals that he found among people at the time. As he said later, "It was a fear of homosexuals which seemed to be associated with a fear of contagion, a fear of reducing the things one fought for—home and family. . . . [I]t led to great brutality as fear always does" (in Herek, 2004:7). The term was a watershed; it defined the problem as heterosexual intolerance, not homosexuality.

Weinberg was not thinking of homophobia in clinical terms (Herek, 2004); for example, phobias are usually experienced as "unpleasant and dysfunctional," which is not the case with "homophobia" (Herek, 2009). Nonetheless, the term is now pervasive and routinely identified as part of the triumvirate, "sexism, racism, and homophobia." One problem with that, however, is that homophobia focuses on individual prejudices rather than societal structures. Thus, in 1990, psychologist Gregory Herek offered the word *heterosexism* to describe "an ideological system that denies, denigrates, and stigmatizes any nonheterosexual form of behavior, identity, relationship or community" (Herek, 1990:316). A decade later, he suggested that the term *sexual prejudice* replace homophobia (Herek, 2000).

The concept of *heteronormativity* turns our attention to all the ways in which heterosexuality is presumed to be the natural, normal, and inevitable structure of society. It is the "view from the boat." First put forward by English professor Michael Warner, heteronormativity describes heterosexuality as akin to an "official national culture" (Berlant and Warner, 1998:547); a "sense of rightness—embedded in things and not just in sex—is what we call heteronormativity."

> People are constantly encouraged to believe that heterosexual desire, dating, marriage, reproduction, childrearing, and home life are not only valuable to themselves, but the bedrock on which every other value in the world rests. Heterosexual desire and romance are thought to be the very core of humanity. It is the threshold of maturity that separates the men from the boys (though it is also projected onto all boys and girls). It is both nature and culture. It is the

one thing celebrated in every film plot, every sitcom, every advertisement. It is the one thing to which every politician pays obeisance, couching every dispute over guns and butter as an effort to protect family, home, and children. What would a world look like in which all these links between sexuality and people's ideas were suddenly severed? Nonstandard sex has none of this normative richness, this built-in sense of connection to the meaningful life, the community of the human, the future of the world. (Warner, 1999:47).

[F]rom senior proms to conjugal rights in prison, from couples' discounts at hotels to the immediate immigration rights of foreign marital partners, from a nonchalant goodbye kiss at the airport to incessant male-female couples grinning down from billboards, to fairy tales with princes rescuing princesses. It is, indeed, difficult to find any aspect of modern life that does not include men desiring women and women desiring men as a premise, as necessary to being human as thinking and breathing. (Dennis, 2004:383)

In all, naming these perspectives helps us to see them as particular social locations, like the other master statuses we have considered. Indeed, it is possible to argue that, no matter what their master statuses, all Americans operate from these biases because they are built into the basic fabric of our culture.

Dichotomizing

Many forces promote the construction of aggregate categories of people. Frequently, these aggregates emerge as *dichotomies*. To dichotomize is not only to divide something into two parts; it is also to see those parts as mutually exclusive and in opposition. Dichotomization encourages the sense that there are only two categories, that everyone fits easily in one or the other, and that the categories stand in opposition to each other. In contemporary American culture, we appear to treat the master statuses of race, sex, class, sexual orientation, and disability as if each embodied "us" and "them"—as if for each master status, people could be easily sorted into two mutually exclusive, opposed groupings.[7]

Dichotomizing Race   Although three racial categories—*white, Negro,* and *Indian*—were identified throughout the 19th century, all were located within a white/nonwhite dichotomy. For example, in 1854, the California Supreme Court in *People v. Hall* held that blacks, mulattos, Native Americans, and Chinese were "not white" and therefore could not testify for or against a white man in court (Takaki, 1993:205–6). (Hall, a white man, had been convicted of killing a Chinese man on the testimony of one white and three Chinese witnesses; the Supreme Court overturned the conviction.) The same dichotomization can be seen in the Supreme Court's decision in *Plessy v. Ferguson* (1896) described in Reading 41.

Mexican residents of the southwest territories ceded to the United States in the 1848 Treaty of Guadalupe Hidalgo, however, "were defined as a white population and accorded the political-legal status of 'free white persons'" (Omi and Winant, 1994). European immigrants such as the Irish were initially treated as nonwhite,

---

[7]Springer and Deutsch (1981) coined the term *dichotomania* to describe the belief that there are male and female sides of the brain. We think that term also fits our discussion.

or at least not-yet-white. In turn, they lobbied for their own inclusion in American society on the basis of the white/nonwhite distinction.

> [Immigrants struggled to] equate whiteness with Americanism in order to turn arguments over immigration from the question of who was foreign to the question of who was white. . . . Immigrants could not win on the question of who was foreign. . . . But if the issue somehow became defending "white man's jobs" or "white man's government" . . . [they] could gain space by deflecting debate from nativity, a hopeless issue, to race, an ambiguous one. . . . After the Civil War, the new-coming Irish would help lead the movement to bar the relatively established Chinese from California, with their agitation for a "white man's government," serving to make race, and not nativity, the center of the debate and to prove the Irish white. (Roediger, 1994:189–90)

Historically, *American* has meant *white*, as many Americans of Asian ancestry learn when they are complimented on their English—a compliment that presumes that someone who is Asian could not be a native-born American.[8] A story from the 1998 Winter Olympics illustrates the same point. At the conclusion of the figure skating competition, MSNBC posted a headline that read "American Beats Out Kwan for Women's Figure Skating Title." The reference was to Michelle Kwan, who won the silver medal, losing the gold to Tara Lapinsky. But both Kwan and Lapinsky are Americans. While Kwan's parents immigrated from Hong Kong, she was born and raised in the United States, is a U.S. citizen, and was a member of the U.S. team. The network attributed the mistake to overworked staff and apologized. But for Asian American activists, this was an example of how people of Asian descent have remained perpetual foreigners in American society.

African American novelist Toni Morrison would describe this as a story about "how *American* means *white*":

> Deep within the word "American" is its association with race. To identify someone as South African is to say very little; we need the adjective "white" or "black" or "colored" to make our meaning clear. In this country it is quite the reverse. American means white, and Africanist people struggle to make the term applicable to themselves with . . . hyphen after hyphen after hyphen. (Morrison, 1992:47)

Because *American* means *white*, those who are not white are presumed to be recent arrivals and often told to go "back where they came from." Thus, we appear to operate within the dichotomized *racial* categories of *American/non-American*—these are racial categories, because they effectively mean *white/nonwhite*. The white/nonwhite binary itself contributes to making whiteness invisible:

> For most whites, most of the time, to think or speak about race is to think or speak about people of color, or perhaps, at times, to reflect on oneself (or other whites) in relation to people of color. But we tend not to think of ourselves or our racial cohort as racially distinctive. Whites' "consciousness" of whiteness is predominantly unconsciousness of whiteness. (Flagg, 1993:970)

---

[8]Since the historic American ban on Asian immigration remained in place until 1965, it is the case that a high proportion of Asian Americans are foreign-born. Nonetheless, about one-third of Asian Americans are U.S.-born—ranging from 58 percent of Japanese Americans to 24 percent of Korean Americans (U.S. Census Bureau, 2007).

Thus, "most Whites do not understand the need to assert a 'racial identity.' This is because Whites do not usually identify themselves by their race and so they do not readily see the significance of racial identity" (Okizaki, 2000:483).

Perhaps the clearest example of the contemporary dichotomiziation of race is provided by the "one-drop rule," which is described by F. James Davies in Reading 2. This "rule" began as law but now operates as an informal social practice, holding that people with any traceable African heritage should classify themselves as *black*. President Barack Obama's identification of himself as African American on the 2010 census is consistent with this practice. The rule, which grew out of the efforts of Southern whites to enforce segregation after the Civil War, came to be endorsed by *both* blacks and whites. Thus, as Jennifer Lee and Frank Bean note in Reading 7, only about 4 percent of black Americans identify themselves as having ancestry from more than one race, even though a much larger percentage have Native American and/or white ancestry.

In determining the future strength and significance of the one-drop rule, at least three important points bear consideration. First, there is a higher rate of multiracial identification among recent Asian and Latino immigrants to the United States than among those who are native-born, which might serve to weaken traditional American practices. Although, in other cultures, people of multiracial ancestry might have the option to define themselves as multiracial, U.S. culture has not historically supported that, especially for black Americans.

Second, an increase in intermarriage and the birth of children who grow up to describe themselves as multiracial might be an indicator that America is moving away from the dichotomization of race. This is precisely the topic that Lee and Bean, in Reading 7, investigate. Their analysis is that the racial boundaries between Latinos, Asian Americans, and whites are becoming more fluid, but that American blacks do not appear to be included in that racial blurring.

Third, a reduction in the strength of the one-drop rule may not mean that race has less of an impact on individuals. Rather, it may mean that America is moving to the tri-racial system—white, honorary white, and collective black—characteristic of Latin American countries (Bonilla-Silva, 2004).

Defining Race and Ethnicity

But what exactly *is* race? First, we need to distinguish *race* from *ethnicity*. Social scientists define *ethnic groups* as categories of people who are distinctive on the basis of national origin or heritage, language, or cultural practices. "Members of an ethnic group hold a set of common memories that make them feel that their customs, culture, and outlook are distinctive" (Blauner, 1992). Thus, racial categories encompass different ethnic groups—For example, in the early 1900s the American racial category *white* included ethnic groups such as Irish, Italian, Mexican, and Polish Americans. Now it includes Afghan, Kurd, Pakistani, Cuban, and Salvadoran Americans. Indeed, in Reading 20, Harlan Lane argues that there is a Deaf-World ethnic group distinct from those for whom deafness is a hearing impairment.

The concept of ethnicity attempts to capture people's actual practices, which do not always operate consistently or logically. For some, ethnic identity has waned over time; being an Italian American in the 1920s involved much more intensity of feeling, interaction, and political organization than it does now. For others, ethnic identity may retain its strength, but has been transformed over time. For example, Jews may be adherents of a religion and/or members of an ethnic group, since many who do not practice the religion still have a strong sense of being part of a people. Or, in recognizing that ethnic identity may involve some choice between national origin and religion, consider that a survey of Bosnian refugees in the United States found people identifying their ethnicity as either Bosnian, Bosnian Muslim, and Muslim, with many others refusing to answer the question at all as it raised the specter of the ethnic cleansing that had made them refugees (Haines, 2007).

Although, in many ways, ethnic group identification is more important to people than race, it is often obscured by race. For example, focusing only on race would hide the important differences between African Americans, Haitians, Somalis, Ethiopians, or Jamaicans—all black American ethnic groups. Similarly, many Americans with Middle Eastern heritage (who are classified as *white* in the census) are often misdescribed as *Arabs*, even though that term covers only those from Arabic-speaking countries. A scene in the movie *Crash* made this point: in vandalizing the store of an Iranian grocer, the looters left behind graffitti about "Arabs," but Iranians speak Farsi and do not consider themselves Arabic. Like the panethnic aggregations *Latino* or *Asian American*, beneath panethnic terms like *Middle Eastern* or *Arab American*, one will find strong ethnic attachments based on national origin or religion.

The term *race* first appeared in the Romance languages of Europe in the Middle Ages to refer to breeding stock (Smedley, 1993). A "race" of horses described common ancestry and a distinctive appearance or behavior. *Race* appears to have been first applied to New World peoples by the Spanish in the 16th century. Later it was adopted by the English, again in reference to people of the New World, and it generally came to mean *people, nation,* or *variety*. By the late 18th century, "when scholars became more actively engaged in investigations, classifications, and definitions of human populations, the term 'race' was elevated as the one major symbol and mode of human group differentiation employed extensively for non-European groups and even those in Europe who varied in some way from the subjective norm" (Smedley, 1993:39).

Though elevated to the level of science, the concept of race continued to reflect its origins in animal breeding. Farmers and herders had used the concept to describe stock bred for particular qualities; scholars used it to suggest that human behaviors could also be inherited. "Unlike other terms for classifying people . . . the term 'race' places emphasis on innateness, on the inbred nature of whatever is being judged" (Smedley, 1993:39). Like animal breeders, scholars also presumed that appearance revealed something about potential behavior. Just as the selective breeding of animals entailed the ranking of stock by some criteria, scholarly use of the concept of race involved the ranking of humans. Differences in skin color, hair texture, and the shape of head, eyes, nose, lips, and body were developed into an elaborate hierarchy of merit and potential for "civilization."

As described by Audrey Smedley in Reading 1, the idea of race emerged among all the European colonial powers, although their conceptions of it varied. However, only the British in colonizing North America and South Africa constructed a system of rigid, exclusive racial categories and a social order *based on race*, a "racialized social structure" (Omi and Winant, 1994). "[S]kin color variations in many regions of the world and in many societies have been imbued with some degree of social value or significance, but color prejudice or preferences do not of themselves amount to a fully evolved racial worldview" (Smedley, 1993:25).

This racialized social structure—which in America produced a race-based system of slavery and subsequently a race-based distribution of political, legal, and social rights—was a historical first. "Expansion, conquest, exploitation, and enslavement have characterized much of human history over the past five thousand years or so, but none of these events before the modern era resulted in the development of ideologies or social systems based on race" (Smedley, 1993:15, 25). Although differences of color had long been noted, societies had never before been built on those differences.

As scientists assumed that race differences involved more than simply skin color or hair texture, they sought the biological distinctiveness of racial categories—but with little success. In the early 20th century, anthropologists looked to physical features such as height, stature, and head shape to distinguish the races, only to learn that these are affected by environment and nutrition. More recently, the search has turned to genetics, only to find that those cannot be correlated with conventional racial classifications either. Even efforts to reach a consensus about how many races exist or what specific features distinguish one from another are problematic.

> If our eyes could perceive more than the superficial, we might find race in chromosome 11: there lies the gene for hemoglobin. If you divide humankind by which of two forms of the gene each person has, then equatorial Africans, Italians and Greeks fall into the "sickle-cell race"; Swedes and South Africa's Xhosas (Nelson Mandela's ethnic group) are in the healthy hemoglobin race. Or do you prefer to group people by whether they have epicanthic eye folds, which produce the "Asian" eye? Then the !Kung San (Bushmen) belong with the Japanese and Chinese. . . . [D]epending on which traits you pick, you can form very surprising races. Take the scooped-out shape of the back of the front teeth, a standard "Asian" trait. Native Americans and Swedes have these shovel-shaped incisors, too, and so would fall in the same race. Is biochemistry better? Norwegians, Arabians, north Indians and the Fulani of northern Nigeria . . . fall into the "lactase race" (the lactase enzyme digests milk sugar). Everyone else—other Africans, Japanese, Native Americans—form the "lactase-deprived race" (their ancestors did not drink milk from cows or goats and hence never evolved the lactase gene). How about blood types, the familiar A, B, and O groups? Then Germans and New Guineans, populations that have the same percentages of each type, are in one race; Estonians and Japanese comprise a separate one for the same reason. . . . The dark skin of Somalis and Ghanaians, for instance, indicates that they evolved under the same selective force (a sunny climate). But that's all it shows. It does *not* show that they are any more closely related in the sense of sharing more genes than either is to Greeks. Calling Somalis and Ghanaians "black" therefore sheds no further light on their evolutionary history and implies—wrongly—that they are more closely related to each other than either is to someone of a different "race." (Begley, 1995:67, 68)

As one anthropologist has put it, "Classifying people by color is very much like classifying cars by color. Those in the same classification look alike . . . but the classification tells you nothing about the hidden details of construction or about how the cars or people will perform" (Cohen, 1998:12). A "no-race" theory is now widely accepted in physical anthropology and human genetics. This perspective argues that "(1) Biological variability exists but this variability does not conform to the discrete packages labeled races. (2) So-called racial characteristics are not transmitted as complexes. (3) Races do not exist because isolation of groups has been infrequent; populations have always interbred" (Lieberman, 1968:128). Still, few scholars outside of anthropology seem to take this perspective into account.

> [I]t does not appear that this debate [about the existence of race] has had widespread impact on professionals in the fields of medicine, psychology, sociology, history, or political science.... [I]t will suffice to point out that virtually all scholars who write about "race and intelligence" assume that the "races" which they study are distinguished on the basis of biologically relevant criteria. So accepted is this fact that most scholars engaged in such research never consider it necessary to justify their assignment of individuals to this or that "race." ... [Thus], the layman who reads the literature on race and racial groupings is justified in assuming that the existent typologies have been derived through the application of theories and methods current in disciplines concerned with the biological study of human variation. Since the scientific racial classifications which a layman finds in the literature are not too different from popular ones, he can be expected to feel justified in the maintenance of his views on race. (Marshall, 1993:117, 121)

The complexities of incorporating a "no race" position into social science research is highlighted by how the professional associations in anthropology and sociology treat the concept. In 1998, the American Anthropological Association (AAA) adopted an unambiguous "Statement on Race": "Racial beliefs constitute myths about the diversity in the human species and about the abilities and behavior of people homogenized into 'racial' categories." For the American Sociological Association (ASA), however, that does not mean we should stop collecting data on race: its 2002 statement, "The Importance of Collecting Data and Doing Social Scientific Research on Race," urges the continued study of race as a *social* phenomenon because it affects major aspects of social life—including employment, housing, education, and health. The title of the ASA's 2002 press release about the statement reads, "Would 'Race' Disappear if the United States Officially Stopped Collecting Data on It?" Their answer to that is clearly "no"; anthropologists would certainly agree.

Thus, even though sociologists view race as social, not biological, their work could be interpreted to mean that race must refer to real biological differences. Reports on medical research also sometimes promote the same misconceptions. For example, in 2004 there was much fanfare about BiDil, the first American drug approved for use by a specific race or ethnic population. BiDil was found to be effective for black patients with advanced heart disease. If race were not "real," why would the drug have this effect? Actually, it is not clear that the drug *has* this effect.

> ... [A] small sub-sample of African Americans in the original clinical trial seemed to have fared better than did white people. Because the study was not designed to compare efficacy of BiDil in people of different races, a new clinical trial would have had to be approved to investigate such a hypothesis. However, rather than setting up a study designed to test this hypothesis, in March 2001, the FDA approved a full-scale clinical trial, undertaken only in black

men and women with heart disease. In June, 2005, after a hearing in which an FDA committee reviewed reports that BiDil was significantly more effective than a placebo, the drug's patent was approved for another 15 years as a race-specific drug. Indeed, the race-specific claim is what made the drug patentable. . . . Why the focus on race, and what is at stake? Part of the answer almost certainly lies in the role of prospective markets. . . . By making the drug race-specific, the patent extends another 13 years giving NitroMed exclusive rights to market the drug until 2020. (Duster, 2007:703)

Thus, the search for "race" based drugs continues: by one 2009 count, there are "nine clinical trials around the world studying diseases or treatments in groups defined by race or gender or both, including chronic hepatitis B in blacks and Hispanics and respiratory syncytial virus in Native American infants" (Adler, 16:2009). Most importantly, treating race as real and as based on "real" genetic markers gives us permission to ignore the *social* factors that affect the quality and length of people's lives.

By looking at what's in the blood, [geneticists] avoid the messy stuff that happens when humans interact with each other. It's easier to look inside the body because genes, proteins, and SNP patterns are far more measurable than the complex dynamics of society. . . .

When you're talking about genetic diseases, there's usually something in the environment that triggers their onset. Shouldn't we be talking about the trigger?

Take the case of black men and prostate cancer. African-American males have twice the prostate cancer rate that whites do. Right now, the National Cancer Institute is searching for cancer genes among black men. They're not asking, How come black men in the Caribbean and in sub-Saharan Africa have much lower prostate cancer rates than all American men?

A balanced approach might involve asking, Is there something in the American environment triggering these high rates? Is it diet, stress or what? (Dreifus, 2005, interview with Troy Duster, author of *Backdoor to Eugenics*, 2003)

Particularly on medical matters, some anthropologists contend that we would be better off thinking about "lineage" rather than race because then we would recognize the multiplicity of each of our individual inheritances and of the medically relevant genetic inheritances. Although "race implies dividing people into groups, lineage implies *connecting people through lines* (of descent)" (Thompson, 2006:3).

In all, "race is a biological fiction, but a social fact" (Rubio, 2001:xiv). Its primary significance is as a *social* concept. We "see" race; we expect it to tell us something significant about a person, and we organize social policy, law, and the distribution of wealth, power, and prestige around it. From the essentialist position, race is assumed to exist independently of our perception of it; it is assumed to significantly distinguish one group of people from another. From the constructionist perspective, race exists because we have created it as a meaningful category of difference among people.

Dichotomizing Sexual Orientation   Many similarities exist in the construction of race and sexual orientation categories. First, both are often dichotomized—into black/white, white/nonwhite, or gay/straight—and individuals are expected to fit easily into one category or the other. While the term *bisexual* has become increasingly common, the assumption that people are either gay or straight still appears to predominate.

For example, scientists continue to seek biological differences between gay and straight people just as they have looked for such differences between the "races." Usually the search is for what causes same-sex attraction, not for what causes heterosexuality—the point made by Martin Rochlin's Heterosexual Questionnaire (Reading 17). But, as with investigations of race difference, here as well the research is intrinsically suspect, because we are unlikely to find any biological structure or process that *all* gay people share but *no* straight people have (Sherman Heyl, 1989). Still, as Roger Lancaster describes in Reading 15, the conviction that such differences must exist propels the search and leads to the popularization of questionable findings.

> Dean Hamer first published his findings about the relationship of genes to sexuality in *Science* and, a little later, in a popular book called *The Science of Desire.* In both report and book, Hamer made clear that he did not figure he'd found a gay gene. He'd found a conspicuous concurrence of a specific genetic marker among self-declared homosexuals. The findings were statistically significant, but the relationship of the genetic marker to the behavior was as yet undetermined. None of which stopped the newspapers from using the euphonic "gay gene" in their headlines, nor other interested parties from citing this fantastic discovery as further proof of the firmly rooted, unchangeable nature of homosexuality. (Archer, 2002:135)

As with race, sexual orientation appears more straightforward than it really is. Because sexuality encompasses physical, social, and emotional attraction, as well as fantasies, self-identity, and actual sexual behavior over a lifetime, determining one's sexual orientation may involve emphasizing one of these features over the others. Just as the system of racial classification asks people to pick *one* race, the sexual orientation system requires that all the different aspects of sexuality be distilled into two possible choices.

For example, an acquaintance described the process by which he came to self-identify as gay. In high school and college he had dated and been sexually active with women, but his relations with men had always been more important to him. He looked to men for emotional and social gratification, as well as for relief from the "gender games" he felt required to play with women. He had been engaged to be married, but when that ended, he spent his time exclusively with other men. Eventually, he established a sexual relationship with another man and came to identify himself as gay. His experience reflects the varied dimensions of sexuality and shows the resolution of those differences by choosing a single sexual identity. Rather than say "I used to be straight but I am now gay," he described himself as always "really" having been gay.

Alfred Kinsey's landmark survey of American sexual practices showed that same-sex experience was more common than had been assumed, and that sexual practices could change over the lifespan. He suggested that instead of thinking about *homosexuals* and *heterosexuals* as if these were two discrete categories of people, we should recognize that sexual behavior exists along a continuum from those who are exclusively heterosexual to those who are exclusively gay. In Reading 16 Letitia Anne Peplau and Linda D. Garnets provide an interesting update to this approach by identifying the fluidity of women's sexuality across age and social contexts.

Further, there is no necessary correspondence between identity and sexual behavior (which Esther Rothblum explores for women in Reading 29). Someone who self-identifies as gay is still likely to have had some heterosexual experience; someone who self-identifies as straight may have had some same-sex experience; and even those who have had *no* sexual experience may lay claim to being gay or straight. Identity is not always directly tied to behavior. Indeed, a person who self-identifies as gay may have had *more* heterosexual experience than someone who self-identifies as straight. This distinction between identity and experience was underscored by the results of a 1994 national survey, still the most comprehensive American sex survey since Kinsey's. Only 2.8 percent of the men and 1.4 percent of the women identified themselves as gay, but an additional 7.3 percent and 7.2 percent, respectively, reported a same-sex experience or attraction (Michael, 1994).[9]

One last analogy between the construction of race and sexual orientation bears discussion. Most Americans would not question the logic of this sentence: "Tom has been married for 30 years and has a dozen children, but I think he's *really* gay." In a real-life illustration of the same logic, a young man and woman were often seen kissing on our campus. When this became the subject of a class discussion, a suggestive ripple of laughter went through the room: Everyone "knew" that the young man was really gay.

How could they "know" that? For such conclusions to make sense, we must believe that someone could be gay irrespective of his or her actual behavior. Just as it is possible in this culture for one to be "black" even if one looks "white," apparently one may be gay despite acting straight. Just as "black" can be established by any African heritage, "gay" is apparently established by displaying any behavior thought to be associated with gays, especially for men. Indeed, "gay" can be "established" by reputation alone, by a failure to demonstrate heterosexuality, or even by the demonstration of an overly aggressive heterosexuality. Therefore, "gay" can be assigned no matter what one actually does. In this sense, gay can function as an *essential identity* (Katz, 1975), that is, an identity assigned to an individual *irrespective of his or her actual behavior*, as in "I know she's a genius even though she's flunking all her courses." Because no behavior can ever conclusively prove one is *not* gay, this label is an extremely effective mechanism of social control.

In all, several parallels exist between race and sexual orientation classifications. With both, we assume there are a limited number of possibilities—usually two, but no more than three—and we assume individuals can easily fit into one or the other option. We treat both race and sexual orientation categories as encompassing populations that are internally homogeneous and profoundly dissimilar from each other. For both, this presumption of difference has prompted a wide-ranging search for the biological distinctiveness of the categories. Different races or sexual orientations are judged superior and inferior to one another, and members of each

---

[9]The 1992 National Health and Social Life Survey (NHSLS) was sponsored by the Robert Wood Johnson Foundation, The Henry J. Kaiser Family Foundation, the Rockefeller Foundation, The Andrew Mellon Foundation, the John D. and Catherine T. MacArthur Foundation, the New York Community Trust, and the American Foundation for AIDS Research under contract to the U.S. Department of Health and Human Services' National Institute for Child Health and Human Development. The NHSLS data set contains information on 1,604 variables gathered from interviews with a national probability sample of 3,432 American men and women between the ages of 18 and 59.

category historically have been granted unequal legal and social rights. Finally, we assume that sexual orientation, like skin color, tells us something meaningful about a person.

Dichotomizing Class   Any discussion of social class in the United States must begin with the understanding that Americans "almost never speak of themselves or their society in class terms. In other words, class is not a central category of cultural discourse in America" (Ortner, 1991:169). Indeed, considering the time and attention Americans devote to sexual orientation, sex/gender, or race, it is hard not to conclude that discussion of social class is "the last taboo" (Perrucci and Wysong, 2008). Because social class is so seldom discussed, the vocabulary for talking about it is not well developed.

> Class analyses . . . are not curricular themes covered in schools at the primary or secondary level and are seldom included in university-level courses. . . . Every major U.S. daily newspaper includes a separate business section, but none includes a separate "class" or even "labor" section. . . . Politicians typically avoid class-based rhetoric, especially the use of language and policy labels that might openly emphasize or reveal the conflicting economic and political interests of working-class versus privileged-class members. . . . [P]olitical candidates, especially presidential candidates, who violate what amounts to an unwritten rule against framing class inequalities as legitimate public policy issues, risk being accused of promoting divisive and disruptive "class warfare" by privileged-class-based mainstream media pundits. . . . Only two exceptions exist to the taboo on public discussions of class issues. First, it is acceptable to discuss the "middle class" and problems faced by this class. Because large numbers of Americans identify themselves as middle class, references to this group actually serve to disguise and mute class differences because the term is so inclusive . . . . The second exception to avoidance of class issues includes mass media glimpses into the lives of the privileged class, as well as tours of the excluded class. . . . The glamour of life at the top is routinely showcased on both conventional and tabloid style TV news magazines . . . . The grim realities of life-at-the-bottom experiences turn up most often on occasional PBS or cable TV documentaries. . . . (Perrucci and Wysong, 2008:48–50)

Yet despite its relative invisibility, as Michael Zweig notes in Reading 12, social class operates in ways quite similar to race and sex. That is, just as American culture offers interpretations of what differences in color or sex mean, it also provides interpretations about what differences in income, wealth, or occupation might mean. As sociologists Perrucci and Wysong noted in the quote above, social class is also often dichotomized, usually into those called *poor* and those called *middle class*. This social class dichotomization is particularly interesting in that it reflects an actual polarization of income and wealth among Americans, although not one accurately captured by "poor" and "middle class."

Since 1970, the distribution of wealth and income among Americans has become much more unequal, with an increasing gap between rich and poor and a declining number of families in the middle class (Wiefek, 2003). So the real social class division would appear to be between the rich and everyone else.

> The share of [all] income going to the top 10 percent of taxpayers rose from 32.9 percent in 1980 to 38.6 percent in 1988, then crept up to 39.6 percent in 1992 before rising rapidly

to 43.9 percent in the year 2000, roughly the percentage that prevailed in the late 1920s. . . . After 1973, the higher up in income distribution one looks, the greater the reconcentration of income. Whereas the share of income earned by the top 10 percent of taxpayers grew by 31 percent between 1973 and 2000, the share going to the top 5 percent rose by 45 percent, and that going to the top 1 percent nearly doubled, rising by 91 percent. In simple but stark terms, by the end of the twentieth century all of the declines in inequality achieved in the New and Fair Deals had been wiped out and the United States had unambiguously returned to levels of inequality not seen since the laissez-faire era of the 1920s. (Massey, 2007:35–6)

Reading 13 from *The Economist* describes it this way: "In the 1980s the poor fell further behind the middle classes, but since the 1990s those middle classes have been squeezed. Both groups have lost ground to the elite. Between 1947 and 1979, the top 0.1 percent of American earners were, on average, paid 20 times as much as the bottom 90 percent, . . . by 2006, the ratio had grown to 77." Nonetheless, Americans are more likely to assume the country is divided between the poor and the middle class, as if those in the highest brackets were "just like the rest of us."

Further, Americans often approach class standing as if it reflected an individual's merit as a person. More often than people of other nationalities, Americans explain success and failure in terms of *individual merit* rather than economic or social forces (Morris and Williamson, 1982)—even, as Stephen McNamee and Robert Miller describe in Reading 14, ignoring how much the intergenerational transfer of wealth—or the lack thereof—overwhelms individual merit.

But Americans have not always thought this way. In the early part of the 20th century, those who were poor were more likely to be considered hardworking, economically productive, constrained by artificial barriers, and probably in the majority. Today, however, "many of the least well off are not regarded as productive in any respect" (Arrow, Bowles, and Durlauf, 2000:x), and both popular opinion and social science research explain social class standing in terms of individual attributes and values rather than economic changes or discrimination (Kahlenberg, 1997; Mincey, 1994).

Americans now are prone to think that those who succeed financially do so on the basis of their own merit and that those who don't succeed have failed because they *lack* merit. Indeed, many talk about social class as if it were just the result of personal values or attitudes. Surveys indicate that over half of the American public believe "that lack of effort by the poor was the principal reason for poverty, or a reason at least equal to any that was beyond a person's control. . . . Popular majorities did not consider any other factor to be a very important cause of poverty—not low wages, or a scarcity of jobs, or discrimination, or even sickness" (Schwarz and Volgy, 1992:11).

This attribution of poverty and wealth to individual merit hides the complex reality of American social class. Although Americans are aware of a broad range of social class differences, the widespread conviction that one's station in life reflects one's ability and effort in many ways overshadows this awareness. In all, social class standing is taken to reveal one's core worth—a strikingly essentialist formulation.

Dichotomizing Sex   First, to clarify the terms *sex* and *gender,* most work in the social sciences has used *sex* to refer to females and males—that is, to chromosomal, hormonal, anatomical, and physiological differences—and *gender* to describe the socially constructed roles associated with each sex. Over the last 20 years or so, however, newspapers and magazines have increasingly used *gender* to cover both biological differences and social behavior. For example, it is now common to see descriptions of male and female voting patterns as *gender* differences, when they are actually *sex* differences. In popular culture generally, *sex* seems now to refer almost exclusively to sexual intercourse, whereas *gender* applies to the participants. Adding to the confusion, many scholars deliberately refer to biological sex as *gender* to underscore that it is socially constructed much as masculinity and femininity is. In these Framework Essays, we have maintained the traditional social science sex/gender distinction because we find it clearer.

Although the recognition can be unsettling, biological sex is as much a socially created dichotomy as race, sexual orientation, and gender. That is, like sexual orientation, sex refers to a complex set of attributes—anatomical, chromosomal, hormonal, physiological—that may sometimes be inconsistent with one another or with individuals' sense of their own identity. Rather than recognize that complexity, however, we commonly assume that there are two and only two sexes and that people can be easily classified as one or the other (Kessler and McKenna, 1978). The tenuous basis of these assumptions—and the fact that ultimately even *sex* is the product of a *decision*—is made clear in the case of South African runner Caster Semenya, described by Alice Dreger in Reading 10 and in Riki Wilchin's description of the ways we try to make bodies "at the margins" fit into our existing categories (in Reading 11).

Just as with race and sexual orientation, people are assigned to the categories of male or female irrespective of inconsistent or ambiguous evidence. Indeed, out of the imperative that there be consistency between the physical and psychological, some people undergo sex change surgery to produce a body consistent with their self-identities. Others will pursue psychotherapy to find an identity consistent with their bodies. In either case, it apparently makes more sense to use surgery and/or therapy to create consistency than to accept inconsistency: a man who feels like a woman must become a woman rather than just being a man who feels like a woman.

Throughout, one question is the most basic to the study of sex and gender: whether it is possible to escape the binaries of male/female and masculine/feminine. While transsexuals may change their sex to fit their gender and *transgendered* people may produce a gender that is different from their sex, neither moves beyond the world of two and only two sex/genders.

Dichotomization and Disability   Our discussion of race, sexual orientation, sex and gender, and social class has emphasized that each of these categories encompasses a continuum of behavior and characteristics rather than a finite set of discrete or easily separated groupings. It has also stressed that difference is a social creation—that differences of color or sex, for example, have no meaning other than what is attributed to them.

Can the same be said about disability? It is often assumed that people are easily classed as disabled or nondisabled, but that is no more true in this case than it is for the other master statuses. Sociologist Irving Zola provided the classic critique of how our use of statistics contributes to this misconception.

> The way we report statistics vis-à-vis disability and disease is generally misleading. If we speak of ratio figures for a particular disease as 1 in 8, 1 in 14, etc., we perpetuate what Rene Dubos (1961) once called "The Mirage of Health." For these numbers convey that if 1 person in 10 does get a particular disease, that 9 out of 10 do not. This means, however, only that those 9 people do not get that particular disease. It does not mean that they are disease-free, nor are they likely to be so. . . .
>
> Similarly deceptive is the now-popular figure of "43 million people with a disability" . . . for it implies that there are over 200 million Americans without a disability. . . . But the metaphor of being but a banana-peel slip away from disability is inappropriate. The issue of disability for individuals . . . is not *whether* but *when*, not so much *which one* but *how many* and *in what combination.* (Zola, 1993:18)

Apart even from how we count the disabled, how do we determine the disability of any particular person, on any particular day? Zola describes his experience of being able to work longer hours than others on an assembly line because his torso was in a brace (Zola, 1993); although he was "disabled," on the line he was also less disabled than others. This situation, where impairment is relative, is more the rule than the exception and thus undermines notions about fixed distinctions between disability and nondisability.

Constructing the "Other"

We have seen how the complexity of a population may be reduced to aggregates and then to a simplistic dichotomy. Aggregation assumes that those who share a master status are alike in "essential" ways. It ignores the multiple and conflicting statuses any individual inevitably occupies. Dichotomization especially promotes the image of a mythical "*other*" who is not at all like "us." Whether in race, sex, sexual orientation, social class, or disability, dichotomization yields a vision of "them" as profoundly different. Ultimately, dichotomization results in stigmatizing those who are less powerful. It provides the grounds for whole categories of people to become the objects of contempt.

Constructing "Others" as Profoundly Different   The expectation that "others" are profoundly different can be seen most clearly in the significance that has been attached to sex differences. In this case, biological differences between males and females have been the grounds from which to infer an extensive range of nonbiological differences. Women and men are assumed to differ from each other in behavior, perception, and personality, and such differences are used to argue for different legal, social, and economic roles and rights. The expectation that men and women are not at all alike is so widespread that we often talk about them as members of the "opposite" sex; indeed, it is not unusual to talk about the "war" between the sexes.

While this assumption of difference undergirds everyday life, few significant differences in behavior, personality, or even physical ability have been found between men and women of any age. Indeed, there are more differences *within* each sex than *between* the sexes. Susan Basow illustrates this point in the following:

> The all-or-none categorizing of gender traits is misleading. People just are not so simple that they either possess all of a trait or none of it. This is even more true when trait dispositions for groups of people are examined. Part [a] of Figure 2 illustrates what such an all-or-none distribution of the trait "strength" would look like: all males would be strong, all females weak. The fact is, most psychological and physical traits are distributed according to the pattern shown in Part [b] of Figure 2 with most people possessing an average amount of that trait and fewer people having either very much or very little of that trait.
>
> To the extent that females and males may differ in the average amount of the trait they possess (which needs to be determined empirically), the distribution can be characterized by *overlapping normal curves*, as shown in Part [c] of Figure 2. Thus, although most men are stronger than most women, the shaded area indicates that some men are weaker than some women and vice versa. The amount of overlap of the curves generally is considerable. Another attribute related to overlapping normal curves is that differences within one group are usually greater than the differences between the two groups. Thus, more variation in strength occurs within a group of men than between the average male and the average female. (Basow, 1992:8)

The lack of difference between women and men is especially striking given the degree to which we are all socialized to produce such differences. Thus, while boys and girls, and men and women, are often socialized to be different as well as being treated differently, this does not mean they inevitably *become* different. Yet, even though

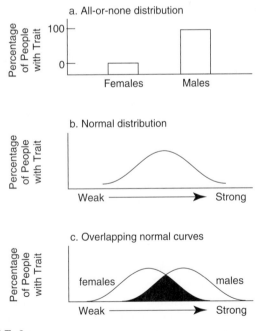

FIGURE 2
Three types of distribution for the trait "strength." (Basow, 1992:8; Figure 1)

decades of research have confirmed few sex differences, the search for difference continues and some suggest it may even have been intensified by the failure to find many differences.

The same expectation that the "other" differs in personality or behavior emerges in race, class, and sexual orientation classifications. Race differences are expected to involve more than just differences of color, those who are "gay" or "straight" are expected to differ in more ways than just their sexual orientation, and social classes are expected to differ in more than their income. In each case, scientific research is often directed toward finding such differences.

Sanctioning Those Who Associate with the "Other"   There are also similarities in the sanctions against those who cross race, sex, class, or sexual orientation boundaries. Parents sometimes disown children who marry outside of their racial or social class group, just as they often sever connections with children who are gay. Those who associate with the "other" are also in danger of being labeled a member of that category.

For example, during the Reconstruction period following the Civil War, the fear of invisible black ancestry was pervasive among southern whites, because that heritage would subject them to a restricted life based on *de jure* segregation. "Concern about people passing as white became so great that even behaving like blacks or willingly associating with them were often treated as more important than any proof of actual black ancestry" (Davis, 1991:56). Thus, Southern whites who associated with blacks ran the risk of being defined as black.

A contemporary parallel can be found in gay/straight relations. Those who associate with gays and lesbians or defend gay rights are often presumed—by gays and straights alike—to be gay. Many men report that when they object to homophobic remarks, they simply become the target of them. Indeed, the prestige of young men in fraternities and other all-male groups often rests on a willingness to disparage women and gays.

Similarly, few contemporary reactions are as strongly negative as that against men who appear feminine. Because acting like a woman is so disparaged, boys learn at an early age to control their behavior or suffer public humiliation. This ridicule has its greatest effect on young men; the power and prestige usually available to older men reduces their susceptibility to such accusations. Young men must avoid a long list of behavior for fear of being called feminine or gay: don't be too emotional, watch how you sit, don't move your hips when you walk, take long strides, don't put your hands on your hips, don't talk too much, don't let your voice show emotion, don't be too compliant or eager to please, etc.

Because boys and men who exhibit such traits are often assumed to be gay, they become targets for verbal and physical abuse. In Reading 28, for example, C.J. Pascoe describes the ubiquity and function of the "fag trope" in an American high school:

> Fag talk and fag imitations serve as a discourse with which boys discipline themselves and each other through joking relationships. Any boy can temporarily become a fag in a given social space or interaction. This does not mean that boys who identify as or are perceived to be homosexual aren't subject to intense harassment. Many are. But becoming a fag has as much to

do with failing at the masculine tasks of competence, heterosexual prowess, and strength or in any way revealing weakness or femininity, as it does with a sexual identity. This fluidity of the fag identity is what makes the specter of the fag such a powerful disciplinary mechanism. It is fluid enough that boys police their behaviors out of fear of having the fag identity permanently adhere. . . .

The popular linkage of effeminate behavior with a gay sexual orientation is so strong that it may be the primary criterion most Americans use to decide who is gay: A "masculine" man must be straight; a "feminine" man must be gay. But gender and sexual orientation are *separate* phenomena. Knowing that someone is a masculine man or a feminine woman does not tell us what that person's sexual orientation is—indeed, our guesses are most likely to be "false negatives"; that is, we are most likely to falsely identify someone as straight. Because we do not know who among us is gay, we cannot accurately judge how gay people behave.

In the world of mutual "othering," being labeled one of "them" is a remarkably effective social control mechanism. Boys and men control their behavior so that they are not called gay. Members of racial and ethnic groups maintain distance from one another to avoid the criticism that might be leveled by members of their own and other groups. These social controls are effective because all parties continue to enforce them.

Stigma

The term *stigma* comes from ancient Greece, where it meant a "bodily sign designed to expose something unusual and bad about the moral status of [an individual]." Such signs were "cut or burnt into the body to advertise that the bearer was a slave, a criminal, or a blemished person, ritually polluted, to be avoided, especially in public places" (Goffman, 1963:1). Stigmatized people are those "marked" as bad, unworthy, and polluted because of the category they belong to, for example, because of their disability, or their race, sex, sexual orientation, or social class category. The core assumption behind stigma is that internal merit is revealed through external features—for the Greeks, that a brand or a cut showed a person's lack of moral worth. This is not an unusual linkage. For example, physically attractive people are often assumed to possess a variety of positive attributes (Adams, 1982). We often assume that people who look good must *be* good.

Judgments of worth based on membership in certain categories have a self-fulfilling potential. Those who are judged superior by virtue of their membership in some category are given more opportunity to prove themselves; those who are judged less worthy by virtue of membership in a stigmatized category have difficulty establishing their merit no matter what they do. For example, social psychology data indicate that many whites perceive blacks as incompetent, regardless of evidence to the contrary: white subjects were "reluctant or unable to recognize that a black person is higher or equal in intelligence compared to themselves" (Gaertner and Dovidio, 1986:75). This would explain why many whites react negatively to affirmative action programs. If they cannot conceive of black applicants being *more* qualified than whites, they will see such programs as only mandates to hire the less qualified.

Stigma involves objectification and devaluation. *Objectification* means treating people as if they were objects, members of a category rather than possessors of individual characteristics. In objectification, the "living, breathing, complex individual" ceases to be seen or valued (Allport, 1958:175). In its extreme, those who are objectified are "viewed as having no other noteworthy status or identity. When that point is reached, a person becomes *nothing* but 'a delinquent,' 'a cripple,' 'a homosexual,' 'a black,' 'a woman.' The indefinite article 'a' underlines the depersonalized nature of such response" (Schur, 1984:30–1).

Examples of Stigmatized Master Statuses: Women, Poor People, and Disabled People   Sociologist Edwin Schur argues that because women are subject to both objectification and devaluation, they are discredited, that is, stigmatized. First, considering objectification, Schur argues that women are seen

> as all alike, and therefore substitutable for one another; as innately passive and objectlike; as easily ignored, dismissed, trivialized, treated as childlike, and even as a non-person; as having a social standing only through their attachments to men (or other non-stigmatized groups); and as a group which can be easily victimized through harassment, violence, and discrimination. (Schur, 1984:33)

Objectification occurs when women are thought of as generally indistinguishable from one another; for example, when someone says, "Let's get the woman's angle on this story." It also occurs when women are treated as nothing more than their body parts, for example, when young girls are assumed to be sexually promiscuous because they are big-breasted: they are nothing more than their cup size; they are objects.

African Americans, Latinos, Asian Americans, and gay/lesbian people are often similarly treated as indistinguishable from one another. Indeed, hate crimes have been defined by precisely this quality of interchangeability, such as an attack on *any* black family that moves into a neighborhood or the assault of *any* woman or man who looks gay. Hate crimes are also marked by excessive brutality and personal violence rather than property destruction—all of which indicate that the victims have been objectified (Levin and McDevitt, 2002).

Some members of stigmatized categories objectify themselves in the same ways that they are objectified by others. Thus, women may evaluate their own worth or the worth of other women in terms of physical appearance. In the process of self-objectification, a woman "joins the spectators of herself"; that is, she views herself as if from the outside, as if she were nothing more than what she looked like (Berger, 1963:50). Advertising routinely encourages one to make an object of oneself. For example, several years ago, in a cereal commercial, a bikini-clad woman posed before a mirror. She had lost weight for an upcoming vacation and was imagining herself as a stranger on the beach might see her. Thus, she made an object of herself. While physical appearance is also valued for men, it rarely takes precedence over all other qualities. Rather, men are more likely to be objectified in terms of wealth and power.

In addition to being objectified, there is a strong case that American women as a category remain devalued, a conclusion drawn from the characteristics most frequently attributed to men and women. Research conducted over the last 40 years has documented a remarkable consistency in those attributes. Both sexes are described as possessing valued qualities, but the characteristics attributed to men are more valued in the culture as a whole. For example, the female-valued characteristics include being talkative, gentle, religious, aware of the feelings of others, security oriented, and attentive to personal appearance. Male-valued traits include being aggressive, independent, unemotional, objective, dominant, active, competitive, logical, adventurous, and direct (Baron and Byrne, 2004; Sczesny et al., 2008).[10] (Remember that these attributes are only people's *beliefs* about sex differences.)

In many ways, the characteristics attributed to women are inconsistent with core American values. Although American culture values achievement, individualism, and action—all understood as male attributes—women are expected to subordinate their personal interests to the family and to be passive and patient. Therefore, "women are asked to become the kind of people that this culture does not value" (Richardson, 1977:11). Thus, it is more acceptable for women to display masculine traits, since these are culturally valued, than it is for men to display less-valued feminine characteristics. In contrast, women may be independent, unemotional, objective, dominant, active, competitive, logical, adventurous, and direct with few negative consequences. The characteristics we attribute to women are not valued for everyone, unlike the characteristics attributed to men.

Much of what we have described about the stigmatization of women applies to the poor as well. Indeed, being poor is a much more obviously shameful status than being female. The category *poor* is intrinsically devalued. At least in contemporary American culture, it is presumed that there is little commendable to be said about poor people; "they" are primarily constructed as a "problem." Poor people are also objectified; they are described as "*the* poor," as if they were all alike, substitutable for and interchangeable with one another.

> Most of the writing about poor people, even by sympathetic observers, tells us that they are different, truly strangers in our midst: Poor people think, feel, and act in ways unlike middle-class Americans. . . .
>
> We can think about poor people as "them" or as "us." For the most part, Americans have talked about "them." Even in the language of social science, as well as in ordinary conversation and political rhetoric, poor people usually remain outsiders, strangers to be pitied or despised, helped or punished, ignored or studied, but rarely full citizens, members of a larger community on the same terms as the rest of us. They are . . . "those people," objects of curiosity, analysis, prurience, or compassion, not subjects who construct their own lives and history. Poor people seem cardboard cutouts, figures in single dimension, members of inferior

---

[10]"Compared with White women, Black women are viewed as less passive, dependent, status conscious, emotional and concerned about their appearance. . . . Hispanic women tend to be viewed as more 'feminine' than White women in terms of submissiveness and dependence. . . . [A] similar stereotype holds for Asian women, but with the addition of exotic sexuality. . . . Native-American women typically are stereotyped as faceless . . . drudges without any personality. . . . Jewish women are stereotyped as either pushy, vain 'princesses' or overprotective, manipulative 'Jewish mothers' . . . working-class women are stereotyped as more hostile, confused, inconsiderate and irresponsible than middle-class women . . . and lesbians are stereotyped as possessing masculine traits" (Basow, 1992:4).

categories, rarely complex, multifaceted, even contradictory in the manner of other persons. (M. Katz, 1989:6, 126)

And, like women, poor people are not expected to display attributes valued in the culture as a whole.

Everything that we have described about stigma applies directly to the experience of disabled people. The concept of stigma was initially developed by sociologist Erving Goffman with disabled people in mind, and there are so many ways that the term applies that it is difficult to select a single focus. From assumptions that one is pitiable, sick, unhappy, incompetent, dependent, childlike, unattractive, and sexually undesirable, to notions that disability is a punishment for sin, disabled people are cast as essentially unworthy.

In addition to the stigma, those who are disabled—like many others in stigmatized categories—must also manage the paternalism of those who are not disabled. Taken from the position of a father toward his children, paternalism is the automatic assumption of superiority.

> Paternalism is often subtle in that it casts the oppressor as benign, as protector. . . . Paternalism often must transform its subjects into children or people with childlike qualities. . . . Paternalism is experienced as the bystander grabs the arm of a blind person and, without asking, 'helps' the person across the street. . . . It is most of all, however, the assumption that people with disabilities are intrinsically inferior and unable to take responsibility for their own lives. (Charlton, 2000:53)

For those of us outside the stigmatized group, a paternalistic attitude is dangerous because it keeps us from actually seeing the person in front of us: "A person who cannot see or is using a wheelchair for mobility may be a happy, prosperous, well-adjusted person, but most people encountering him or her immediately feel pity" (Charlton, 2000:55).

Stereotypes about People in Stigmatized Master Statuses   Finally, in an effort to capture the general features of what "we" say about "them," let us consider five common stereotypes about individuals in stigmatized master statuses.

First, they are presumed to lack the values the culture holds dear. Neither women nor those who are poor, disabled, gay, black, Asian American, or Latino are expected to be independent, unemotional, objective, dominant, active, competitive, logical, adventurous, or direct. Stigmatized people are presumed to lack precisely those values that nonstigmatized people are expected to possess.

Second, stigmatized people are likely to be seen as a problem. Certainly black, Latino, and Native American men and women, gay and lesbian people of all colors, white women, all disabled people, and people living in poverty are constructed as *having* problems and *being* problems. Often the implication is that they are also responsible for many of our national problems. While public celebrations often highlight the historic contributions of such groups to the culture, little in the public discourse lauds their current contributions. Indeed, those in stigmatized categories are often constructed as *nothing but a problem*, as if they did not exist apart from those problems. This was once illustrated by a black student who described her shock at hearing white students describe her middle-class neighborhood as a "ghetto."

Ironically, this depiction of stigmatized people as nothing but a problem is often accompanied by the trivialization of those problems. For example, Tim Wise (in Reading 38) describes the significant gap between black and white assessments of the persistence of race discrimination. In terms of sex discrimination, 61 percent of men compared to 45 percent of women, "believe that women have achieved equality of opportunity with men in the workplace" (Jones, 2005). Despite the participation of thousands of people in annual Gay Pride marches throughout the country, images from the parades typically trivialize participants by focusing on the small number in drag or leather. Indeed, much of what is disparaged as "gay lifestyle" has been forged by gay and lesbian people who have been excluded from mainstream, heterosexual society. Finally, despite dramatic federal reductions in the cash assistance programs to poor people begun in 1994 under President Bill Clinton's pledge to "end welfare as we know it,"[11] stereotypes about poor people getting government "handouts" persist. For example, polling from the early 2000s showed 49 percent of Americans agreeing that "poor people today do not have an incentive to work because they can get government benefits without doing anything in return" (Soss and Schram, 2007:116). Thus, the problems that stigmatized categories of people create for those in privileged statuses are highlighted, while the problems they experience are discounted, especially those problems created by "us."

Third, people in stigmatized master statuses are often stereotyped as lacking self-control; they are characterized as being lustful, immoral, and carriers of disease (Gilman, 1985, 1991). Currently, such accusations hold center stage in the depiction of gay men, but historically such charges have been leveled at African American, Latino, and Asian American men (e.g., Chinese immigrants in the late 19th century). Poor women and women of color have been and continue to be depicted as promiscuous, while poor men and women are presumed to be morally irresponsible.

Fourth, people in stigmatized categories are often marked as having too much or too little intelligence, and in either case as tending to deception or criminality. Many stigmatized categories of people have been assumed to use their "excessive" intelligence to unfair advantage. This was historically the charge against Jews, and now appears to be a characterization of Asian Americans.

> [T]he educational achievement of Asian American students was, and continues to be, followed by a wave of reaction. The image of Asian Americans as diligent super-students has often kindled resentment in other students. Sometimes called "damned curve raisers," a term applied first to Jewish students at elite East Coast colleges during the 1920s and 1930s, Asian American students have increasingly found themselves taking the brunt of campus racial jokes. (Takagi, 1992:60)

---

[11]"The number of recipients of Aid to Families with Dependent Children and Temporary Assistance to Needy Families [AFDC/TANF] fell by 68 percent between 1994 and 2006, and constant dollar spending on AFDC/TANF fell by 48 percent over the same period. A survey conducted by the *New York Times* in early 2009 suggested that even the recession of 2008 led to only miniscule increases in caseloads between 2007 and 2008." (Bane, 2009:75)

Fifth, people in stigmatized categories are depicted as both childlike and savagely brutal. Historically, characterizations of Native Americans, enslaved Africans, and Chinese immigrants reflected these conceptions. Currently, the same is true for the poor in their representation as both pervasively violent and irresponsible. A related depiction of women as both "virgins and whores" has been well documented in scholarship over time.

Perhaps because people in stigmatized master statuses are stereotyped as deviant, it appears that those who commit violence against them are less severely punished. For example, "most murders in the USA are intra-racial, that is, the alleged perpetrator and the victim are of the same race. . . . Yet of the 845 prisoners executed between 17 January 1977 and 10 April 2003, 53 percent were whites convicted of killing whites and 10 percent were blacks convicted of killing blacks" (Amnesty International, 2003). As one study of death row cases concluded, "minority death row inmates convicted of killing whites face higher execution probabilities than other capital offenders" (Jacobs et al, 2007:610). Although a number of factors are operating here, one conclusion is that stigmatized minority victims are valued less than white victims. The same conclusion could be reached in terms of the punishment meted out to those accused of sexual assault. "Major offenses *against* women, which we *profess* to consider deviant, in practice have been responded to with much ambivalence" (Schur, 1984:7). Indeed, some have argued that one way to recognize a stigmatized category of people is that the violence directed at them is not treated seriously (Schur, 1984).

Overall, individuals in stigmatized master statuses are represented not only as physically distinctive but also as the antithesis of the culture's desired behaviors and attributes. They are seen as not operating from cultural values. They are problems; they are immoral and disease ridden; their intelligence is questionable; they are childlike and savage. Such characterizations serve to dismiss claims of discrimination and unfair treatment, affirming that those in stigmatized categories deserve such treatment, that they are themselves responsible for their plight. Indeed, many of these stereotypes are also applied to teenagers, whom the media depict as violent, reckless, hypersexed, ignorant, out of control, and the cause of society's problems (Males, 1994).

A Final Comment

It is disheartening to think of oneself as a member of a stigmatized group, just as it is disheartening to think of oneself as thoughtlessly perpetuating stigma. Still, there are at least two important points to bear in mind. First, the characteristics attributed to stigmatized groups are similar across a great variety of master statuses. They are not tied to the actual characteristics of any particular group; in a way, they are quite impersonal. Second, people who are stigmatized have often formed alliances with those who are not stigmatized to successfully lobby against these attributions.

As we said at the outset of this essay, our hope is to provide you with a framework by which to make sense of what sex, disability, race, social class, and sexual orientation mean in contemporary American society. Clearly, these categorizations are complex; they are tied to emotionally intense issues that are uniquely American; and they have consequences that are both mundane and dramatic. From naming, to aggregating, to dichotomizing, and ultimately to stigmatizing, difference has a meaning for us. The readings in Section I explore the construction of these categorizations; the readings in Section II examine how we experience them; the readings in Section III address the meaning that is attributed to difference; and the readings in Section IV describe how we can bridge these differences.

KEY CONCEPTS

abelism/disablism Analogous to racism and sexism, a system of cultural, institutional, and individual discrimination against people with impairments. Disablism is the British term; disability oppression is synonymous. (page 5)

aggregate To combine or lump together (verb); something composed of different elements (noun). (pages 14–15)

-centrism or -centric Suffix meaning centered around, focused around, taking the perspective of. Thus, **androcentric** means focused around or taking the perspective of men; **heterocentric** means taking the perspective of heterosexuals; and **eurocentric** means having a European focus. (page 18)

constructionism The view that reality cannot be separated from the way a culture makes sense of it—that meaning is "constructed" through social, political, legal, scientific, and other practices. From this perspective, differences among people are created through social processes. (pages 2–7)

dichotomize To divide into two parts and to see those parts as mutually exclusive. (pages 19–31)

differential undercount In the census, undercounting more of one group than of another. (page 11)

disability The loss or limitation of opportunities to take part in the normal life of the community on an equal level with others because of physical and social barriers (page 10)

disaggregate To separate something into its constituent elements. (pages 14–15)

essential identity An identity that is treated as core to a person. Essential identities can be attributed to people even when they are inconsistent with actual behavior. (page 27)

essentialism The view that reality exists independently of our perception of it, that we perceive the meaning of the world rather than construct that meaning. From this perspective, there are real and important (essential) differences among categories of people. (pages 2–7)

ethnic group, ethnicity Those who share a sense of being a "people," usually based on national origin, language, or religion. (page 21)

gender Masculinity and femininity; the acting out of the behaviors thought to be appropriate for a particular sex. (page 30)

heteronormativity All the beliefs, norms, and social structures that contribute to the presumption that heterosexuality is the natural, normal, and inevitable structure of society (page 18)

impairment Physical, cognitive, emotional, or sensory conditions within the person as diagnosed by medical professionals (page 5)

intersectionality Consideration of the ways that master statuses interact and mutually construct one another. (page 4)

master status A status that has a profound effect on one's life, that dominates or overwhelms the other statuses one occupies. (page 2)

objectification Treating people as if they were objects, as if they were nothing more than the attributes they display. (page 35)

Other A usage designed to refer to those considered profoundly unlike oneself. (page 31)

panethnic A classification that spans ethnic identities. (page 16)

race The conception that people can be classified into groups based on skin color, hair texture, shape of head, eyes, nose, and lips. (pages 22–25)

sex The categories of male and female. (page 30)

status A position in society. Individuals occupy multiple statuses simultaneously, such as occupational, kinship, and educational statuses. (page 2)

stigma An attribute for which someone is considered bad, unworthy, or deeply discredited. (pages 34–39)

transgender People who systematically ignore or violate gender expectations; sometimes includes people who are transsexual. (page 9)

REFERENCES

Adams, Gerald R. 1982. Physical Attractiveness. *In the Eye of the Beholder: Contemporary Issues in Stereotyping,* edited by A. G. Miller, 253–304. New York: Praeger.

Adler, Jerry. 2009. What's Race Got to Do With It? *Newsweek,* January 12, 16.

Allport, Gordon. 1958. *The Nature of Prejudice.* Garden City, NY: Doubleday Anchor.

Amnesty International. 2003. Death by Discrimination: The Continuing Role of Race in Capital Cases. (http://web.amnesty.org/library/print/ENGAMR510462003.) Retrieved November 2, 2010.

Archer, Bert. 2002. *The End of Gay (and the Death of Heterosexuality).* New York: Thunder's Mouth Press.

Armstrong, Elizabeth A. 2002. *Forging Gay Identities: Organizing Sexuality in San Francisco, 1950–1994.* Chicago: University of Chicago Press.

Arrow, Kenneth, Samuel Bowles, and Steven Durlauf. 2000. Introduction. *Meritocracy and Economic Inequality,* edited by Kenneth Arrow, Samuel Bowles, and Steven Durlauf, ix–xv. Princeton, NJ: Princeton University Press.

Bane, Mary Jo. 2009. Poverty Politics and Policy. *Focus* 26(2):76–80. Retrieved June 6, 2010 (http://www.irp.wisc.edu/publications/focus/pdfs/foc262m.pdf).

Barnes, Colin, and Geof Mercer. 2003. *Disability.* Cambridge, UK: Polity Press.

Baron, Robert A., and Donn Byrne. 2004. *Social Psychology.* Boston: Pearson.

Basow, Susan A. 1992. *Gender: Stereotypes and Roles.* 3d ed. Pacific Grove, CA: Brooks/Cole Publishing.

Begley, Sharon. 1995. Three Is Not Enough. *Newsweek,* February 13, 67–69.

Berger, Peter L. 1963. *Invitation to Sociology: A Humanistic Perspective.* Garden City, NY: Doubleday Anchor.

Berlant, Lauren, and Michael Warner. 1998. Sex in Public. *Critical Inquiry* 24(2): 547–66.

Blauner, Robert. 1992. Talking Past Each Other: Black and White Languages of Race. *The American Prospect,* 10.

Bonilla-Silva, Eduardo. 2004. 'We Are All Americans': The Latin Americanization of Race Relations in the United States. *The Changing Terrain of Race and Ethnicity,* edited by Maria Krysan and Amanda E. Lewis, 149–83. New York: Russell Sage.

Charlton, James. 2000. *Nothing About Us Without Us: Disability Oppression and Empowerment.* Los Angeles, CA: University of California Press.

Choldin, Harvey M. 1986. Statistics and Politics: The "Hispanic Issue" in the 1980 Census. *Demography,* 23:403–18.

Cohen, G. 1995. *Self, Ownership, Freedom, and Equality.* Cambridge: Cambridge University Press.

Cohen, Mark Nathan. 1998. *Culture of Intolerance: Chauvinism, Class, and Racism in the United States.* New Haven, CT: Yale University Press.

Cohn, D'Vera. 2001. Counting of Gay Couples Up 300%. *Washington Post,* August 22, A.

Coles, Gerald. 1987. *The Learning Mystique: A Critical Look at "Learning Disabilities."* New York: Pantheon.

Conrad, Peter, and Joseph W. Schneider. 1980. *Deviance and Medicalization: From Badness to Sickness.* Philadelphia: Temple University Press.

Davis, F. James. 1991. *Who Is Black? One Nation's Rule.* University Park, PA: Pennsylvania State University Press.

de la Garza, Rudolfo O., Louis DeSipio, F. Chris Garcia, John Garcia, and Angelo Falcon. 1992. *Latino Voices: Mexican, Puerto Rican, and Cuban Perspectives on American Politics.* Boulder, CO: Westview Press.

Dennis, Jeffrey P. 2004. Heteronormativity. *Men and Masculinities: A Social, Cultural, and Historical Encyclopedia,* edited by Michael Kimmel and Amy Aronson, 382–83. Santa Barbara, CA: ABC-CLIO, Inc.

Disabled People's International. 1982. *Proceedings of the First World Congress.* Singapore: Disabled People's International.

Dreifus, Claudia. 2005. A Sociologist Confronts "The Messy Stuff": A Conversation with Troy Duster. *The New York Times,* October 18, Science Times.

Dubos, Rene. 1961. *Mirage of Health.* Garden City, NY: Anchor Books.

Duster, Troy. 2007. Medicalisation of Race. *Lancet* 369:702–04.

Espiritu, Yen Le. 1992. *Asian American Panethnicity: Bridging Institutions and Identities.* Philadelphia: Temple University Press.

Faderman, Lillian. 1991. *Odd Girls and Twilight Lovers: A History of Lesbian Life in Twentieth-Century America.* New York: Penguin Books.

Flagg, Barbara J. 1993. *"Was Blind, But Now I See": White Race Consciousness and the Requirement of Discriminatory Intent.* 91 Mich. L. Rev., 953–71.

Fraga, Luis Ricardo, John A. Garcia, Rodney E. Hero, Michael Jones-Correa, Valerie Martinez-Ebers, and Gary M. Segura. 2010. *Latino Lives in America: Making it Home.* Philadelphia: Temple University Press.

Gaertner, Samuel L., and John F. Dovidio. 1986. The Aversive Form of Racism. *Prejudice, Discrimination, and Racism,* edited by John F. Dovidio and Samuel L. Gaertner, 61–89. Orlando, FL: Academic Press.

Gallup, Inc. 2007. Black or African American? Retrieved May 26, 2010 (http://www.gallup.com/poll/28816/black-african-american.aspx).

Gallup, Inc. 2010. Americans' Acceptance of Gay Relations Crosses 50% Threshold. May 3–6. Retrieved June 23, 2010 (http://www.gallup.com/poll/135764/americans-acceptance-gay-relations-crosses-threshold.aspx).

Gallup Organization, Gallup Poll News Service. 2003. Q&A: Black-White Relations in the U.S.

Gilman, Sander. 1985. *Difference and Pathology: Stereotypes of Sexuality, Race, and Madness.* Ithaca, NY: Cornell University Press.

———. 1991. *The Jew's Body.* New York: Routledge.

Goffman, Erving. 1963. *Stigma: Notes on the Management of Spoiled Identity.* Englewood Cliffs, NJ: Prentice-Hall.

Gordon, Margaret T., and Stephanie Riger. 1989. *The Female Fear.* New York: The Free Press.

Gracia, Jorge J. E. 2000. Affirmative Action for Hispanics? Yes and No. *Hispanics/Latinos in the United States: Ethnicity, Race, and Rights,* edited by Jorge J. E. Gracia and Pablo De Greiff, 201–222. New York: Routledge.

Haines, David W. 2007. Ethnicity's Shadows: Race, Religion, and Nationality as Alternative Identities among Recent United States Arrivals. *Identities: Global Studies in Culture and Power,* 14:1–28.

Henshel, Richard L., and Robert A. Silverman. 1975. *Perceptions in Criminology.* New York: Columbia University Press.

Herek, Gregory M. 1990. The Context of Anti-gay Violence: Notes on Cultural and Psychological Heterosexism. *Journal of Interpersonal Violence, 5*(3), 316–33.

——— 2000. The Psychology of Sexual Prejudice. *Current Directions in Psychological Science, 9*(1): 19–22.

——— 2004. Beyond "Homophobia": Thinking about Sexual Stigma and Prejudice in the Twenty-first Century. *Sexuality Research and Social Policy, 1*(2): 6–24.

——— 2009. Sexual Stigma and Sexual Prejudice in the United States: A Conceptual Framework. In D. A. Hope (Ed.). *Contemporary Perspectives on Lesbian, Gay & Bisexual Identities: The 54th Nebraska Symposium on Motivation* (pp. 65–111). New York: Springer

Higgins, Paul C. 1992. *Making Disability: Exploring the Social Transformation of Human Variation.* Springfield, IL: Charles C. Thomas.

Hu-Dehart, Evelyn. 1994. Asian/Pacific American Issues in American Education. Presentation at the 7th Annual National Conference on Race and Ethnicity in American Higher Education, Atlanta, sponsored by The Southwest Center for Human Relations Studies, University of Oklahoma, College of Continuing Education.

Hunt, Judy. 2001. The Union of the Physically Impaired Against Segregation. Retrieved June 2, 2010 (http://www.labournet.net/other/0107/upias1.html).

Jacobs, David, Zhenchao Qian, Jason T. Carmichael, and Stephanie L. Kent. 2007. Who Survives on Death Row? An Individual and Contextual Analysis. *American Sociological Review,* 72(4):610–32.

Jenkins, Alan. 1999. See No Evil. *The Nation,* June 28: 15–19.

Jones, Jeffrey M. 2005. Gender Differences in Views of Job Opportunity. Gallup Poll, August 2. Retrieved June 27, 2010 (http://www.gallup.com/poll/17614/gender-differences-views-job-opportunity.aspx).

Kahlenberg, Richard D. 1997. *The Remedy: Class, Race, and Affirmative Action.* New York: Basic Books.

Katz, Jack. 1975. Essences as Moral Identities: Verifiability and Responsibility in Imputations of Deviance and Charisma. *American Journal of Sociology,* 80:1369–90.

Katz, Michael B. 1989. *The Undeserving Poor: From the War on Poverty to the War on Welfare.* New York: Pantheon Books.

Kessler, Suzanne J., and Wendy McKenna. 1978. *Gender: An Ethnomethodological Approach.* New York: John Wiley & Sons.

Kinsey, Alfred, Wardell Pomeroy, and Clyde Martin. 1948. *Sexual Behavior in the Human Male.* Philadelphia: W. B. Saunders.

Kiviat, Barbara. 2010. Should the Census Be Asking People if They Are Negro? *Time,* January 23. Retrieved May 28, 2010 (http://www.time.com/time/nation/article/0,8599,1955923,00.html).

Lemonick, Michael. 1992. Genetic Tests under Fire. *Time,* February 24, 65.

LeVay, Simon. 1991. A Difference in Hypothalmic Structure between Heterosexual and Homosexual Men. *Science,* 253:1034–37.

Levin, Jack, and Jack McDevitt. 2002. *Hate Crimes Revisited: America's War Against Those Who Are Different.* Boulder, CO: Westview Press.

Lieberman, Leonard. 1968. A Debate over Race: A Study in the Sociology of Knowledge. *Phylon,* 29:127–41.

Lopez, David, and Yen Espiritu. 1990. Panethnicity in the United States: A Theoretical Framework. *Ethnic and Racial Studies,* 13:198–224.

Males, Mike. 1994. Bashing Youth: Media Myths about Teenagers. *Extra!* March/April, 8–11.

Marshall, Gloria. 1993. Racial Classifications: Popular and Scientific. *The "Racial" Economy of Science: Toward a Democratic Future,* edited by Sandra Harding, 116–27. Bloomington, IN: Indiana University Press (Originally published 1968).

Massey, Douglas S. 2007. *Categorically Unequal: The American Stratification System.* New York: Russell Sage.

Michael, Robert T. 1994. *Sex in America: A Definitive Survey.* Boston: Little, Brown.

Mills, Jane. 1989. *Womanwords: A Dictionary of Words about Women.* New York: Henry Holt.

Mincey, Ronald B. 1994. *Confronting Poverty: Prescriptions for Change.* Cambridge: Harvard University Press.

Mohawk, John. 1992. Looking for Columbus: Thoughts on the Past, Present and Future of Humanity. *The State of Native America: Genocide, Colonization, and Resistance,* edited by M. Annette Jaimes, 439–44. Boston: South End Press.

Morris, Michael, and John B. Williamson. 1982. Stereotypes and Social Class: A Focus on Poverty. *In the Eye of the Beholder,* edited by Arthur G. Miller, 411–65. New York: Praeger.

Morrison, Toni. 1992. *Playing in the Dark.* New York: Vintage.

Office of Management and Budget. ———. October 1997. *Revisions to the Standards for the Classification of Federal Data on Race and Ethnicity.* Washington, DC: U.S. Government Printing Office.

Okizaki, Carrie Lynn H. 2000. "What are You?" Hapa-Girl and Multiracial Identity. 71 U. Colo. Law Review, 463–81.

Oliver, Michael. 1990. *The Politics of Disablement.* London: Macmillan.

———. 1996. *Understanding Disability.* New York: Palgrave.

———. 2009. *Understanding Disability: From Theory to Practice.* Second edition. London: Palgrave MacMillan.

Omansky, Beth. 2006. *Not Blind Enough: Living in the Borderland Called Legal Blindness.* Ph.D. Thesis, University of Queensland.

Omi, Michael. 1996. Racialization in the Post–Civil Rights Era. *Mapping Multiculturalism,* edited by A. Gordon and C. Newfield, 178–85. Minneapolis: University of Minnesota Press.

———and Howard Winant. 1994. *Racial Formation in the United States.* New York: Routledge.

Ortner, Sherry B. 1991. Reading America. Preliminary Notes on Class and Culture. *Recapturing Anthropology: Working in the Present,* edited by Richard G. Fox, 163–89. Santa Fe, NM: School of American Research Press.

Perrucci, Robert, and Earl Wyson. 2008. *The New Class Society: Goodbye American Dream?* Third edition. Lanham, MD.: Rowman & Littlefield.

Pew Research Center. 2009. Between Two Worlds: How Young Latinos Come of Age in America. December 11. Retrieved December 11, 2009 (http://pewresearch.org/pubs/1438/young-latinos-coming-of-age-in-america).

Pfuhl, Erdwin H. 1986. *The Deviance Process.* 2d ed. Belmont, CA: Wadsworth.

Queer Nation. Queer Nation Manifesto. 1990. Retrieved June 27, 2010 (http://www.digenia.se/andras%20texter/THE%20QUEER%20NATION%20MANIFESTO.htm).

Richardson, Laurel. 1977. *The Dynamics of Sex and Gender: A Sociological Perspective.* New York: Harper and Row.

———. 1988. *The Dynamics of Sex and Gender: A Sociological Perspective.* 3d ed. New York: Harper and Row.

Rist, Darrell Yates. 1992. Are Homosexuals Born That Way? *The Nation,* 255:424–29.

Roediger, David. 1994. *Towards the Abolition of Whiteness.* London: Verso.

Rubio, Philip F. 2001. *A History of Affirmative Action: 1619–2000.* Jackson: University of Mississippi Press.

Russell, Marta. 1994. Malcolm Teaches Us Too. *The Ragged Edge: The Disability Experience from the Pages of the First Fifteen Years of the Disability Rag,* edited by Barrett Shaw, 11–14. Louisville, KY: Avocado Press.

Schmidt, Peter. 2003. The Label "Hispanic" Irks Some, but Also Unites. *The Chronicle of Higher Education,* November 23, A9.

Schneider, Joseph W. 1988. Disability as Moral Experience: Epilepsy and Self in Routine Relationships. *Journal of Social Issues,* 44:63–78.

Schur, Edwin. 1984. *Labeling Women Deviant: Gender, Stigma, and Social Control.* New York: Random House.

Schwarz, John E., and Thomas J. Volgy. 1992. *The Forgotten Americans.* New York: W. W. Norton.

Scott, John, and Gordon Marshall. 2009. *Oxford Dictionary of Sociology.* Third edition revised. Oxford: Oxford University Press.

Sczesny, Sabine, Janine Bosak, Amanda B. Diekman, and Jean M. Twenge. 2008. Dynamics of Sex-Role Stereotypes. *Stereotype Dynamics: Language-based Approaches to the Formation, Maintenance, and Transformation of Stereotypes,* edited by Yoshihisa Kashima, Klaus Fiedler, and Peter Freytag, 135–61. New York: Taylor & Francis Group.

Shaffer, David R. 2005. *Social and Personal Development.* Sixth edition. Belmont, CA: Wadsworth.

Skrentny, John D. 2002. *The Minority Rights Revolution.* Cambridge, MA: Harvard University Press.

Soss, Joe, and Sanford Schram. 2007. A Public Transformed? Welfare Reform as Policy Feedback. *American Political Science Review,* 101(1):112–27.

Sherman Heyl, Barbara. 1989. Homosexuality: A Social Phenomenon. *Human Sexuality: The Societal and Interpersonal Context,* edited by Kathleen McKinney and Susan Sprecher, 321–49. Norwood, NJ: Ablex.

Shipman, Pat. 1994. *The Evolution of Racism: Human Differences and the Use and Abuse of Science.* New York: Simon and Schuster.

Shorris, Earl. 1992. *Latinos: A Biography of the People.* New York: W. W. Norton.

Smedley, Audrey. 1993. *Race in North America: Origin and Evolution of a Worldview.* Boulder, CO: Westview Press.

Smith, Tom W. 1992. Changing Racial Labels: From "Colored" to "Negro" to "Black" to "African American." *Public Opinion Quarterly,* 56:496–514.

Spelman, Elizabeth. 1988. *Inessential Woman.* Boston: Beacon Press.

Springer, S. P., and G. Deutsch. 1981. *Left Brain, Right Brain.* San Francisco: Freeman.

Steinberg, Stephen. 1989. *The Ethnic Myth: Race, Ethnicity, and Class in America.* Boston: Beacon Press.

Takagi, Dana Y. 1992. *The Retreat from Race: Asian-American Admission and Racial Politics.* New Brunswick, NJ: Rutgers University Press.

Takaki, Ronald. 1990. *Iron Cages: Race and Culture in 19th-Century America.* New York: Oxford University Press.

———. 1993. *A Different Mirror.* Boston: Little Brown.

Thompson, Eric C. 2006. The Problem of "Race" as a Social Construct. *Anthropology News* 47(2): 6–7.

Union of the Physically Impaired Against Segregation. 1976. Fundamental Principles of Disability. Retrieved June 2, 2010 (http://www.leeds.ac.uk/disability-studies/archiveuk/UPIAS/fundamental%20principles.pdf).

United Nations. 2007. Enable. Department of Economic and Social Affairs, Division for Social Policy and Development. Frequently Asked Questions: What is Disability and Who are Persons with Disabilities? Retrieved on June 3, 2010 (http://www.un.org/esa/socdev/enable/faqs.htm).

U.S. Census Bureau. 2001. *Census 2000 Summary File 2, Technical Documentation:* September 2001, SF2/01:G39–G41.

U.S. Census Bureau. 2007. The American Community—Asians: 2004. American Community Survey Results. Retrieved May 29, 2010 (http://www.census.gov/prod/2007pubs/acs-05.pdf).

U.S. Census Bureau. 2010a. State and Country QuickFacts. Retrieved June 3, 2010 (http://quickfacts.census.gov/qfd/states/00000.html).

U. S. Census Bureau. 2010b. The Whole Story: Real People, Real Questions, Real Answers. Retrieved May 29, 2010 (http://2010.census.gov/2010census/about/whole.php).

U.S. Census Bureau, American FactFinder. 2006–2008 data set. American Community Survey 3-Year Estimates, Hispanic or Latino Origin. Retrieved May 28, 2010 (http://factfinder.census.gov/servlet/DTTable?_bm=y&-geo_id=01000US&-ds_name=ACS_2008_3YR_G00_&-mt_name=ACS_2008_3YR_G2000_B03001).

U.S. Commission on Civil Rights. 1973. *To Know or Not to Know: Collection and Use of Racial and Ethnic Data in Federal Assistance Programs.* Washington, DC: U.S. Government Printing Office.

U.S. Department of Commerce. 2001. People Who Reported Two or More Races Are Young and Tend to Live in the West. *United States Department of Commerce News,* November 29.

U.S. Department of Education, 1990. *To Assure the Free Appropriate Public Education of All Handicapped Children: Twelfth Annual Report to Congress on the*

Implementation of the Education of the Handicapped Act. Washington, DC: U.S. Government Printing Office.

Warner, Michael. 1999. *The Trouble with Normal: Sex, Politics, and the Ethics of Queer Life.* Cambridge, MA: Harvard University Press.

Weinberg, George. 1973. *Society and the Healthy Homosexual.* Garden City, NY: Anchor.

Wiefek, Nancy. 2003. *The Impact of Economic Anxiety in Postindustrial America.* Westport, CT: Praeger.

Wilson, Clint, II, and Felix Gutierrez. 1985. *Minorities and the Media.* Beverly Hills, CA: Sage.

Zola, Irving K. 1993. Disability Statistics, What We Count and What It Tells Us: A Personal and Political Analysis. *Journal of Disability Policy Studies,* 4:10–37.

WHAT IS RACE? WHAT IS ETHNICITY?

READING 1

"Race" and the Construction of Human Identity

Audrey Smedley

HISTORICAL CONSTRUCTIONS OF IDENTITY

Historical records, including the Old and New Testaments of the Bible, evince scenarios of interethnic interaction that suggest some very different principles in operation throughout much of human history.[1] Ethnic groups have always existed in the sense that clusters of people living in demarcated areas develop lifestyles and language features that distinguish them from others and they perceive themselves as being separate societies with distinct social histories. Although some conflicts among different groups have been characteristic from the earliest recorded histories, hostilities were usually neither constant nor the basis on which long-term relationships were established.

One factor separates many in the contemporary world, at least some of our understandings of it, from earlier conceptions of human identity. That is that "ethnic" identity was not perceived as ineluctably set in stone. Individuals and groups of individuals often moved to new areas or changed their identities by acquiring membership in a different group. People of the ancient world seemed to have understood that cultural characteristics were external and acquired forms of behavior, and that "barbarians" could learn to speak the language of the Romans or the Greeks and become participants in those cultures, and even citizens of these states. Languages were indeed avenues to new social

identities, and ethnic identity itself was fluid and malleable.

Until the rise of market capitalism, wage labor, the Protestant Ethic, private property, and possessive individualism, kinship connections also operated as major indices that gave all peoples a sense of who they were. Even in the technologically and politically most advanced societies of the ancient world such as in Rome, kinship was the important diacritic of connectedness to the social system. In all of the mostly patrilineal societies of the Middle East. Africa, and the Mediterranean, the normal person was identified by who his or her father was. The long list of names of who begat whom in the Old Testament (Book of Genesis) attests to the importance, especially at the tribal and chiefdom levels, of genealogical identity.

Another important diagnostic of identity was occupation. Whether one was a farmer, carpenter, fisherman, tanner, brass worker, herdsman, philosopher, government official, senator, poet, healer, warrior, or harlot, was significantly salient in the eyes of the ancient world to require the label. Occupations determined to some extent how people were viewed and treated, as well as underscored their contribution to the society.

Throughout much of the period of the early imperial states, numerous groups were in contact with one another, and individuals often traveled from one region to another as traders, warriors, craftsmen, travelers, geographers, teachers, and so forth. From one end of the Mediterranean to another, in spite of the lack of modern forms of transportation, many men and women were interacting in an interethnic melange that included a wide range of cultures and peoples. From time to time, a conquest state would expand outward and incorporate some or most of this great variety. Populations did not necessarily lose any form of ethnic identity, but change was clearly understood as virtually inevitable as each society learned something new from the cultures of others. . . .

When Alexander conquered peoples and lands all the way to the Indus Valley in India, interacting

---

Audrey Smedley is professor emeritus of anthropology at Virginia Commonwealth University.

with "civilized" populations, nomadic pastoralists, settled villagers, and a variety of hunting and fishing peoples, he exhorted his warriors to intermarry with the peoples they conquered in order to learn their languages and cultures. Garrisons of military men were stationed all over the Roman world, from Brittany to the Danube and the Black Sea, from Gibraltar to the Tigris/Euphrates valley and the Indian Ocean, and soldiers often took local women as wives. When the armies of the Moroccan king brought down the Songhai empire in 1591, his soldiers stayed on the Western Sudan frontier area and intermarried with the local people. Most of northern Africa, including Egypt of the Delta, has been periodically invaded and ruled by outsiders for the last three thousand years or so. Hittites and Hyksos from the mountainous areas of Turkey, Assyrians, Persians, Syrians, Phoenicians, Greeks, Babylonians, Romans, and various more recent Turkish and Arabian groups have settled in the towns of the coasts and interacted with the indigenous Berbers and other peoples like the Libyan groups, the Garamantes, the Carthaginians, Syngambrians, and many others. Less well known is the fact that both the Greeks and the Romans used mercenaries from inner Africa (Nubians, Ethiopians, Kushites, among others) in conflicts such as the Persian and Peloponnesian wars (Herodotus, in Godolphin 1942).[2]

Peoples of different cultures coexisted for the most part without strife, with alien segments often functioning in distinct roles in the larger cities. One-third of the population of Athens were foreigners as early as the Classical period, five hundred years before the Christian era (Boardman et al. 1986:222). And the city of Alexandria was (and still is) a heterogeneous, sophisticated, and complex community under the Greeks, Romans, Christians, and Arabs. Carthage was founded in North Africa by Phoenicians, but peoples from all over the Mediterranean world and other parts of Africa made their residence, or served as slaves, in this great trading city. Moreover, men and women of different ethnic groups intermarried frequently, largely because marriage was often used

as a political or economic strategy. Men gave their daughters and sisters to other men, the historians tell us, because they desired political and/or economic alliances with powerful and wealthy men, without regard to ethnic origins. Timotheus was the son of a Jewish mother and a Greek father. Samson married a Philistine woman; Moses married an Ethiopian woman; and many leaders, and lesser men, of the Greeks and Romans married women not from their own societies.

Different societies and localized segments of larger societies were known either by their ethnic name for themselves or by the region, town, or village of their origins. That identities of this type were fluid is indicated by the depictions of individual lives. Paul of Tarsus traveled and preached extensively throughout much of the known Mediterranean world during the early Christian era and encountered individuals of different ethnic backgrounds. He even identified himself as a Roman on occasion when it was useful to do so. There are other examples of individuals in ancient writings who changed their ethnic identities for personal or private reasons.

Scholars who have studied African societies, especially African history, have also been aware of the malleability of ethnic identity on that continent. New ethnic groups have emerged out of the colonial period, and individuals have been known to transform themselves according to their ethnic or religious milieus. One may be a Christian in one context, and a Muslim in another, with no sense of ambivalence or deception. I have encountered this phenomenon myself. Most Africans spoke several different languages, and this facilitated the molding of multiple ethnicities by providing immediate access to cultural knowledge. In situations of potential or real conflict, allegiances could be firmly established without denial of the extrinsic nature of social/ethnic identities (Connah 1987; Davidson 1991).

In addition to identities that are predicated on place of birth, membership in kin groups, or descent in the male or female line from known ancestors, language spoken, and lifestyle to which individuals have been conditioned, another feature critical to individual identity in the state systems was social position. Aristocrats seemed to have been recognized even beyond the boundaries of their immediate societies. And certain men were widely famed for their specialized skills or crafts that set them above others. Every society had its large body of commoners and usually a great number of slaves captured in war or traded in when this enterprise became a common regional feature. Slaves were usually outsiders, but slavery was not considered by law and custom a permanent condition as slaves could be manumitted, redeemed by kinspeople, or could purchase their own freedom (Smedley [1993]1999: ch. 6). While enslavement was considered an unfortunate circumstance and most slaves did the menial and onerous tasks of society, the roles of slaves varied widely. There are numerous examples of slaves rising to political power in the ancient states of the Mediterranean and in the Muslim world. Often they held positions as generals who led armies of conquest and were frequently rewarded for their successes. Whole slave dynasties like the Mamluks in Egypt reigned in various areas of the Muslim world (Hitti 1953).

With the appearance of the proselytizing universal religions, Christianity and later Islam, that became competitors with one another for the souls of all human groups, a new focus of identity was gradually and increasingly placed on membership in a religious community. During the Middle Ages of Europe, Christians and Muslims were competing not only for land and souls, but for political power and influence. And various sects that developed within each large religious community complicated matters by fostering internal dissension and even warfare *inter alia*. Whether one was Sunni or Shiite, Protestant or Catholic, was a critical determinant of one's identity locally and in the wider world. As with other aspects of ethnicity and ethnic differences, individuals often changed their religious affiliation under circumstances prompted by self-interest, or self-preservation, as in the case of the 300,000 or more Jews who were forced to convert to Catholicism in Medieval Spain during the Inquisition (Castro 1971). Yet Christians, Jews, and

Muslims had lived together in relative amity, and even intermarried, for several hundred years after the Muslim conquests and before the rise of the Christian kingdoms to challenge Muslim power.

What was absent from these different forms of human identity is what we today would perceive as classifications into "racial" groups, that is, the organization of all peoples into a limited number of unequal or ranked categories theoretically based on differences in their biophysical traits. There are no "racial" designations in the literature of the ancients and few references even to such human features as skin color. Frank Snowden has demonstrated that ever since at least the second millennium B.C. the peoples of the Mediterranean world have interacted with other groups having a variety of physical traits that differed from the Italians and Greeks. Artistic depictions of Africans of clear "negroid" features have been found, and numerous statues and paintings throughout the classical era show that physical variations in different populations were recognized and accurately depicted (Snowden 1983).

Except for indigenous Americans, members of all three of the large geographic areas that came to be categorized as "races" in the nineteenth and twentieth centuries (Mongoloid, Negroid, and Caucasoid) interacted in the ancient world. Chinese porcelain vases have been found widely distributed in the East African coastal trading cities, indicating trade between these peoples at least two thousand years old. The peoples of the Malagasy Republic represent a mixture of African and Asian (Indonesian) ancestry dating back several thousand years. Greek sailors sailed down the Red Sea into the Indian Ocean and met East Africans long before the Christian era. The peoples of the Mediterranean regularly traded with dark-skinned peoples of the upper Nile valley (and all those in between) northwest Africa, and the contrasting lighter-skinned peoples of Northern Europe. Various states of the Mediterranean called upon and used Ethiopian warriors as mercenaries in their armies, as we have seen. Some of the more desired slaves were very fair-skinned Slavs (from whom the term *slave* was derived) who were traded down the Danube by

German tribesmen. Northern European slaves were shipped as far away as Egypt, Syria, Saudi Arabia, and the Muslim capital at Baghdad (Davis 1966).

What seems strange to us today is that the biological variations among human groups were not given significant social meaning. Only occasionally do ancient writers ever even remark on the physical characteristics of a given person or people. Herodotus, in discussing the habits, customs, and origins of different groups and noting variations in skin color, specifically tells us that this hardly matters. The Colchians are of Egyptian origin, he wrote, because they have black skins and wooly hair "which amounts to but little, since several other nations are so too."[3] Most writers explained such differences as due to natural environmental factors such as the hot sun causing people to be dark skinned. No structuring of inequality, whether social, moral, intellectual, cultural or otherwise, was associated with people *because of their skin color*, although all "barbarians" varied in some ways from the somatic norm of the Mediterranean world. But barbarians were not irredeemably so, and, as we have seen, nothing in the values of the public life denied the transformability of even the most backward of barbarians.

We in the contemporary Western world have often found it difficult to understand this phenomenon and assume that differences in skin color must have had some important meaning. Historians have tried to discover "racial" meanings in the literature of the ancients, assuming that these writers had the same attitudes and beliefs about human differences found in nineteenth- and twentieth-century North America. The reason for our myopia has to do with our deeply entrenched conditioning to the racial worldview (Smedley 1993, 1998). When "race" appeared in human history, it brought about a subtle but powerful transformation in the world's perceptions of human differences. It imposed social meanings on physical variations among human groups that served as the basis for the structuring of the total society. Since that time many people in the West have continued to link human identity to external physical features.

We have been socialized to an ideology about the meaning of these differences based on a notion of heredity and permanence that was unknown in the ancient world and in the Middle Ages.

RACE: THE MODERN CONCEPTION OF HUMAN DIFFERENCES AND HUMAN IDENTITY

In the eighteenth century this new mode of structuring inequality in human societies evolved in the American colonies and soon was present throughout the overseas territories of the colonizing countries of Western Europe. "Race" was a form of social identification and stratification that was seemingly grounded in the physical differences of populations interacting with one another in the New World, but whose real meaning rested in social and political realities. The term *race* had been used to refer to humans occasionally since the sixteenth century in the English language but was rarely used to refer to populations in the slave trade. It was a mere classificatory term like *kind, type,* or even *breed,* or *stock,* and it had no clear meaning until the eighteenth century. During this time, the English began to have wider experiences with varied populations and gradually developed attitudes and beliefs that had not appeared before in Western history and which reflected a new kind of understanding and interpretation of human differences. Understanding the foundations of race ideology is critical to our analysis.

English settlers in North America failed to assimilate the peoples whom they conquered; indeed they generally kept them at great length and social distance from themselves (Morgan 1975; Nash 1982). Indigenous Indians were different in both cultural and biological features, but this was not the necessary and sufficient reason for the English habits and policies of separateness. They had had a long history of enmity with earlier peoples, especially the Irish, on their very borders and had generated out of their hostility with the Irish an image of "savagery" that became institutionalized as a major part of public consciousness about "the other."

The policies and practices of the English in Ireland functioned to keep those Irish who refused to accept English domination segregated from themselves. Failing to even attempt an understanding of Irish customs and institutions, the English expressed an abiding contempt and hatred for both Irish culture and people that reached a crescendo during the sixteenth and seventeenth centuries when the English were also settling in the New World. It was an extreme form of ethnocentrism or ethnic chauvinism that some historians believe came close to being racial (Allen 1994; Canny 1973; Liggio 1976).

"Savagery" was an image about human differences that became deeply embedded in English life and thought and provided a foil against which they constructed their own identity as "civilized" Englishmen. They brought this image of what savagery was all about with them to the New World where it was soon imposed on the native populations when they, too, began to resist English encroachment. Savagery carried with it an enormous burden of negative and stereotypic characteristics grotesquely counterposed against the vision that the English had of themselves as a civilized people. Every new experience, along with a growing technological superiority, widened the differences and denigrated all other peoples who were not part of the civilized world. The concept of "civilized" polities in contrast to savagery and barbarism was beginning to take hold in much of Western Europe, and in this sense Englishmen were not much different from the rest of the Western world. But English notions of their own superiority were enhanced by their technological, material, and political successes, by their earlier successful split from the Catholic realm, by the early rise of merchant capitalism, the development of new forms of wealth, notions about individual freedom, property rights, and self-sufficiency, and by a growing sense of their own uniqueness even among other Europeans. This was summed up in the myth of Anglo-Saxonism (Horsman 1981).

"Race" emerged as a social classification that reflected this greatly expanded sense of human separateness and differences. Theodore Allen (1997) argues that the "invention" of the white race took place after an early, but unsuccessful, colonial revolt of servants and poor freedmen known as Bacon's Rebellion in 1676. Colonial leaders subsequently decided it would be useful to establish a division among the masses of poor to prevent their further collaboration against the governmental authorities. As African servants were vulnerable to policies that kept them in servitude indefinitely, and European servants had the protection of English law, colonial leaders developed a policy backed by new laws that separated African servants and freedmen from those of European background. Over the next half century, they passed numerous laws that provided resources and benefits to poor, white freedmen and other laws that restricted the rights of "Africans," "mulattoes," and "Indians."

Calling upon the model of the Chain of Being, and using natural differences in physical features, they created a new form of social identity. "Race" developed in the minds of some Europeans as a way to rationalize the conquest and brutal treatment of Native American populations, and especially the retention and perpetuation of slavery for imported Africans. As an ideology structuring social, economic, and political inequality, "race" contradicted developing trends in England and in Western European societies that promoted freedom, democracy, equality, and human rights. Europeans justified this attitude toward human differences by focusing on the physical features of the New World populations, magnifying and exaggerating their differences, and concluding that the Africans and Indians and their descendants were lesser forms of human beings, and that their inferiority was natural and/or God-given.

The creation of "race" and racial ideology imposed on the conquered and enslaved peoples an identity as the lowest status groups in society. Myths about their inferior moral, intellectual, and behavioral features had begun to develop and these facilitated proscription of any competition with Europeans. By the mid-eighteenth century, Negroes had been segregated from poor whites in the laws of most colonies and transformed into property as slaves in a state of permanent bondage.

Edmund Morgan (1975) also interpreted the actions of the early colonists in the process of establishing "racial" identities as stemming from the propertied colonists' fear of poor whites and possibly slaves engaging in rebellions together. Colonial leaders consciously formulated policies that would separate poor whites from Indians, blacks, and mulattoes and proceeded to provide the white poor, whom they had hitherto treated with contempt and hatred, with some privileges and special advantages.[4] In time, class divisions diminished in the minds of poor whites and they saw themselves as having something in common with the propertied class, symbolized by their light skins and common origins in Europe. With laws progressively continuing to reduce the rights of blacks and Indians, it was not long before the various European groups coalesced into a white "racial" category whose high-status identity gave them access to wealth, power, opportunity, and privilege.[5]

By the mid-nineteenth century virtually all Americans had been conditioned to this arbitrary ranking of the American peoples, and racial ideology had diffused around much of the world, including to the colonized peoples of the Third World and among Europeans themselves.

"RACE" AS IDENTITY

In the United States the biophysical features of different populations, which had become markers of social status, were internalized as sources of individual and group identities. After the Civil War, although slavery ended, race and racial ideology remained and were strengthened. African Americans particularly had to grapple with the reality of being defined as the lowest status group in American society and with the associated stereotyping that became increasingly part of the barriers to their integration into American society (Conrad 1969). And Native Americans had to try to reinvent their identities, whether in towns or isolated on remote reservations where traditional lifestyles were no longer possible. American society had made "race" (and the physical features connected to it)

equivalent to, and the dominant source of, human identity, superseding all other aspects of identity.

The problems that this has entailed, especially for the low-status "races," have been enormous, immensely complex, and almost intractable. Constant and unrelenting portrayals of their inferiority conditioned them to a self-imagery of being culturally backward, primitive, intellectually stunted, prone to violence, morally corrupt, undeserving of the benefits of civilization, insensitive to the finer arts, and (in the case of Africans) aesthetically ugly and animal-like. Because of the cultural imperative of race ideology, all Americans were compelled to the view that a racial status, symbolized by biophysical attributes, was the premier determinant of their identity. "Race" identity took priority over religion, ethnic origin, education and training, socioeconomic class, occupation, language, values, beliefs, morals, lifestyles, geographical location, and all other human attributes that hitherto provided all groups and individuals with a sense of who they were. The dilemma for the low-status races was, and still is, how to construct a positive identity for themselves in the light of the "racial" identity imposed on them by the dominant society.

In recent decades, one response to this dilemma on the part of some African Americans has been Afrocentrism (which is not the same as an older version of "Negritude" that black intellectuals had developed earlier in this century). And for some Indians a new form of "Nativism" has emerged, harkening back to a Native American lifestyle. Afrocentrism seeks to reidentify with the peoples and cultures of Africa and to elevate Africans to a position of esteem by emphasizing valuable aspects of African cultures. Some Afrocentrists also make assertions about the positive qualities of African people and seek to recognize and objectify Africanisms in the behavior of African-descended peoples who have been scattered all over the New World. Many assume or operate on the premise that all peoples who descended from Africans during the diaspora maintain certain behaviorisms that mark them off from other peoples. Their arguments seem similar to that of the biological determinists in the dominant society, but most would probably not go so far as to assert a genetic basis to certain "African"-originated behaviors. Those who take the position asserting a common African personality or behavior reflect the degree to which the ideology of "race" has been implanted in them. Like most Americans, they find it difficult to think beyond the racial worldview and draw upon the same strategies as white racists in claiming superior features for "African" people. At the same time, there are many Afrocentrists who are very conscious of the fact that theirs is a political position and that they are using the same biological arguments as racists, the people whom they theoretically oppose. They fail to realize that operating within the racial worldview, accepting its premises that biologically distinct races exist, each with unique cultural/behavioral features, and simply denying inferiority while asserting African superiority does nothing to change the racism in our society.

However, we also must understand that what Afrocentrism is really intended to do is to restore a sense of pride and dignity to ordinary African Americans, regardless of how whites and others regard their positions. By looking to the "real" Africa, studying her history, learning about and being involved in certain rituals and festivals that focus on African arts, dance, dress, music, and so on, some activists feel that they are engendering this pride and helping to remove the contempt and denigration that has accompanied our ideas about Africa in the past. They understand that for too long African Americans have been conditioned to the same negative beliefs about Africa and Africans as have whites and others and that there is a need to eliminate the self-deprecation and self-hatred that black Americans have experienced with regard to their African ancestry. . . .

THE NON-PROBLEM OF "MIXED-RACE" PEOPLE

One of the more tragic aspects of the racial worldview has been the seeming dilemma of people whose parents are identifiably of different "races."

Historically, "race" was grounded in the myth of biologically separate, exclusive, and distinct populations. No social ingredient in our race ideology allowed for an identity of "mixed-races." Indeed over the past century and a half, the American public was conditioned to the belief that "mixed-race" people (especially of black and white ancestry) were abnormal products of the unnatural mating of two species, besides being socially unacceptable in the normal scheme of things. The tragedy for "mixed" people is that powerful social lie, the assumption at the heart of "race," that a presumed biological essence is the basis of one's true identity. Identity is biology, racial ideology tells us, and it is permanent and immutable. The emphasis on and significance given to "race" precludes any possibility for establishing our premier identities on the basis of other characteristics. In this sense it may be argued that the myth of "race" has been a barrier to true human identities.

The unfortunate consequence of race ideology is that many of the people with this "mixed-race" background have also been conditioned to the belief in the biological salience of "race." Their efforts to establish a "Mixed-Race" category in the American census forms show a total misunderstanding of what "race" is all about, and this is, of course, a major part of the tragedy. Their arguments imply a feeling of having no identity at all because they do not exist formally (that is, socially) as a "biological" category.

The fact is that from the standpoint of biology, there have been "mixed" people in North America ever since Europeans first encountered indigenous Americans and the first Africans were brought to the English colonies in the 1620s. The average African American has about one-quarter of his or her genes from non-African (nonblack) ancestors, although most estimates are likely to be conservative (cf. Marks 1995; Reed 1969). There is a greater range of skin colors, hair textures, body sizes, nose shapes, and other physical features among black Americans than almost any other people identified as a distinct population. Virtually all of them could identify as of "mixed-race." But the physical markers of race status are always open to interpretation by others. "Race" as social status is in the eye of the beholder. "Mixed" people will still be treated as black if their phenotypes cause them to be so perceived by others. Insistence on being in a separate classification will not change that perception or the reaction of people to them.

What compounds and complicates matters is another lie that is one of the basic tenets, or constituent components, of the racial worldview: the myth that biology has some intrinsic connection to culture. Some advocates of a new "mixed-race" category have argued that they want to recognize the "culture" of their other parent. For example, in a black/white mixed marriage, a black parent presumably has "black" culture, and the white parent has "white" culture. These advocates fail to realize what anthropologists have long known, that there is no relationship between one's culture or lifestyle and one's genes or biological features. All native-born Americans share some basic cultural similarities, and the ancestors of modern African Americans have been "American" longer than the ancestors of most European Americans.[6] It is the ideological myths of the racial worldview that prevent us from seeing how very much alike culturally black and white Americans are. (This is not to suggest that there are not differences in the way blacks and whites experience our culture and lifestyle variations that reflect social-class differences and the isolation of inner-city populations.)

On the other hand, if one parent did come from a very different cultural background (e.g., recently emigrated from Asia), a child does not automatically have that culture because of the biology of the parent. Humans acquire culture; it is learned behavior. In order for Tiger Woods (a golfing star) to have Thai culture, he would have to *learn* the language and the elements of Thai culture. One can learn these without having a single gene from a Thai parent. Moreover, there is no reason why one should learn the cultures of ancestors merely because of some genetic or genealogical connections. None of us have the cultures of any of our ancestors two centuries ago because all cultures, including American culture, have changed, some of them drastically, during that time. Cultures constantly change without any corresponding changes in biological features.

Americans should understand clearly that humans learn cultural features from one another all the time because that has been one of the most profound experiences of human, and especially American, history. What prevents us from understanding this is that component in the ideology of "race," as we have seen, that holds that each race has separate, biologically determined patterns of cultural behavior. The racial worldview, with its emphasis on assumptions of innateness and immutability, makes it possible to interpret all forms of human behavior as hereditary. In fact, it almost mandates such a perspective because of powerful forces within our culture that preserve and promote hereditarian ideas. The belief in racially determined cultural behavior, despite all evidence to the contrary, is perpetuated in American society by the popular media and as a part of folk wisdom about human differences. Witness the inordinate attention to and sales of Herrnstein and Murray's *The Bell Curve* (1994). This belief has been a necessary component of the ideology of "race," because it helps to perpetuate the notion that major differences between "races" exist.

People who consider themselves of "mixed race" and experience some form of psychic stress because they feel they have no identity in American society, perhaps more than most, need to have understanding of this history. . . .

TRANSCENDING THE RESTRICTIONS OF "RACIAL" IDENTITY

Today scholars are beginning to realize that "race" is nothing more and nothing less than a social invention. It has nothing to do with the intrinsic, or potential, qualities of the physically differing populations, but much to do with the allocation of power, privilege, and wealth among them. *This conceptual separation of actual physical variations within the species from the socially invented characterizations of them represents a major paradigm shift in how many scholars now think about the human experience.* Anthropologists and biologists no longer see "races" as discrete populations defined by blood-group patterns or "types" defined by averages of statistical measurements. Biophysical variations are seen as continuous and gradual, overlapping population boundaries, fluid, and subject to evolutionary changes. In like manner, scholars honestly examining the history of American attitudes toward human differences have concluded that "race" was a social invention of the eighteenth century that took advantage of the superficial physical differences among the American population and the social roles that these peoples played, and transposed these into a new form of social stratification. The symbols of race identity became the substance.

Recognizing the reality of the racial worldview and how it developed as a sociocultural reality requires a whole new way of looking at human diversity in all of its many forms. It means that (1) we can better recognize and comprehend accurately and objectively the natural causes of human physical variations around the world without attempting to homogenize people into limited "racial" categories; (2) we can liberate ourselves from the need to utilize physical differences in apprehending human identities; (3) freed from the myths of racial determinism, we can now improve our understanding of the true nature of culture and cultural differences and begin to view the processes of cultural change in a more accurate light; and (4) we can begin to understand the real nature of "race" as a social construct and to deal with the problems that racial identities have imposed on people.

For example, using this new perspective, we would be able to avoid the problems encountered when scholars examine the African Diaspora and attempt to determine which peoples are legitimately black products of this massive process of displacement. Several years ago, two Asian students who had recently immigrated to the United States came to me confidentially after class with a puzzle. They wanted to know why were people like Hazel O'Leary (just appointed as U.S. Secretary of Energy) and Thurgood Marshall, Justice of the United States Supreme Court, identified as "black" in American society when it was obvious that they were not. I explained some of the history of the idea of "race" and the interactions among peoples in the New World. I also pointed out that there is a great deal more to the identification of African Americans than similarities in physical traits, that in fact, biological variations have little to do with the social categories of race. Indeed the people of the African Diaspora are a biogenetically diverse category of people who have an identity derived from common experiences of exploitation and racism. It is far more accurate and more fruitful to scholarship, and possibly to the future of humankind, to define African American people by their sense of *community, consciousness,* and *commitment* than by some mystical "racial" essence. It is the Community into which they were born and reared, a Consciousness of the historical realities and shared experiences of their ancestors, and a Commitment to the perspectives of their "blackness" and to the diminishing of racism that is critical to the identities of the Thurgood Marshalls and Hazel O'Learys of our society. The social categories of "race" have always encompassed more than mere physical similarities and differences. Theodore Allen tells us in the acknowledgements to his two-volume excoriation of white racism that he has learned to say, "I am not white" (1994).

Even without all of the intermixtures of peoples, some Americans have already experienced a high level of uncertainty about the "racial" status of individuals with whom they have had some interaction. Many peoples in the world, from Morocco to the Persian Gulf, to the islands in the South Pacific Ocean, have physical features that cause them to be "mistaken" for black Americans. In that broad band of the earth called the tropics we find indigenous peoples with tan to brown to dark brown skins, and hair that may be frizzly, kinky, curly, or straight. As more and more of these peoples either travel to the United States or are encountered by Americans on missions abroad, Americans must deal with their perceptions of these peoples. Some time ago, in the space of about eight months, I met a Samoan, a person from the New Guinea area, and a number of Arabs who in the course of conversations have indicated that they have been "mistaken" for blacks.[7] Many peoples from the southern regions of Saudi Arabia look very much like their neighboring Africans across the Red Sea, having evolved in the same climate and latitude (and having intermingled over eons of time). To try to maintain racial categories based on physical features in the face of the real world of human biological diversity, I suspect, will be increasingly difficult.

There is another option, one that we have not yet claimed in the establishing and referencing of our human identities. We cannot ignore the fact that since the fifteenth century, what has happened in the Americas, and to varying degrees in many parts of the Third World, has been the fusion of genetic materials from all of the great continents. So-called "racial" mixture has occurred extensively in Latin America, and to a lesser extent in North America, so that most people are descendants of ancestors from Europe, Africa, and the Americas, and in many places like the Caribbean, from Asia also (Graham 1990: Morner 1967). Throughout the colonial world, complex genetic mixtures among various peoples have taken place; and increasingly Europeans at home are participants in, and products of, new genetic combinations with individuals absorbed into their societies from distant lands.

In addition to the increasing genetic heterogeneity of individuals and groups, there is the obvious fact that cultural features have traveled all over the world independently of the spread of genetic material. In the midst of the Sahara desert, signs proclaim "Coca-Cola," everyone from the Siberian tundra to the Melanesian forests wears "jeans," African clothing and designs are found from Paris to Sydney, Australia, and Americans eat more pizzas and tacos (burritos, tortillas, etc.) than almost any other people outside of Italy and Mexico. White boys wear dreadlocks, and Chinese and other Asian, and increasingly African, ethnic restaurants are found around the world. Fast foods, music, dance, dress, Hollywood films, whole industrial complexes (including the world of computers), and a wide range of political, religious, and social beliefs have diffused around the world. Few cultures have not experienced the impact of such massive infusion of new traits.

The peoples who have resulted from all this continuous blending of genetic features and cultural traits are truly "universal" human beings, regardless of what languages they speak or cultures they participate in. The concept of "universal" human beings might very well in time obviate racial categories (but not ethnic identities) and may help to bring about the elimination of all such designations. Many persons will come to recognize themselves as "universal" human beings, and there should be perhaps an early census category that proclaims this reality. What anthropologists must do is to make sure that the ideas of "ethnicity" and "ethnic identity" do not become perceived as hereditary, permanent, and unalterable, but remain fluid forms of identity that will make us all "multicultural."

DISCUSSION QUESTIONS

1. Why was the social classification of race invented?
2. Is Afrocentrism a response to racism?

NOTES

1. Reference materials for this section were taken largely from the following: Boardman et al. (1986), Godolphin (1942), and Snowden (1983). But I have read widely in ancient history and am aware that such materials are not generally considered part of the anthropological repertoire. We need to realize that historical materials are widely available to all, and we should encourage students to avail themselves of them, especially since American students have been shown to be woefully ignorant of history and geography.
2. Herodotus lists more than two dozen different nations that fought on the different sides in the Persian wars: Arabians, Ethiopians, Armenians, Thracians, Libyans, and many others.
3. The Persian Wars, Book II, p. 130, in Godolphin (1942).

4. Morgan claims that the Virginia Assembly "deliberately did what it could to foster the contempt of whites for blacks and Indians" (1975:331).
5. For insightful analysis of this process, see also Allen (1994, 1997).
6. Bohannan and Curtin (1995:13) have observed that half the ancestors of African Americans were already here in the United States by 1780 while the median date for the arrival of European ancestors was "remarkably late, 1890s." We need more of this kind of honesty in recognizing historical realities on the part of scholars in all disciplines.
7. See Morsy (1994). When Arabs began to migrate to the Detroit area several generations ago, many were frequently mistaken for blacks. This became an acute problem in the area around Dearborn, Michigan, where many of them settled. There had long been a law in Dearborn that prohibited blacks from being in the city after sundown. The Dearborn police, among others, were often very confused.

REFERENCES

Allen, Theodore W. [1994]1997 *The Invention of the White Race*, vols. 1 and 2, London: Verso.

Boardman, John, J. Griffin, and O. Murray, eds. 1986 *The Oxford History of the Classical World*. Oxford: Oxford University Press.

Canny, Nicholas P. 1973 The Ideology of English Colonialization: From Ireland to America. *William and Mary Quarterly* (3rd ser.) 30:575–598.

Castro, Americo 1971 *The Spaniards*. Berkeley: University of California Press.

Connah, Graham 1987 *African Civilizations*. New York: Cambridge University Press.

Conrad, Earl 1969 *The Invention of the Negro*. New York: Paul S. Erikson.

Davidson, Basil 1991 *African Civilization Revisited*. Trenton, NJ: African World Press.

Davis, David Brion 1966 *The Problem of Slavery in Western Culture*. Middlesex, England: Penguin.

Godolphin, Francis R. B., ed. 1942 *The Greek Historians*, vols. 1 and 2. New York: Random House.

Graham, Richard, ed. 1990 *The Idea of Race in Latin America, 1870–1940*. Austin: University of Texas Press.

Hitti, Phillip 1953 *History of the Arabs*. London: Macmillan Publishing Co.

Horsman, Reginald 1981 *Race and Manifest Destiny*. Cambridge, MA: Harvard University Press.

Liggio, Leonard P. 1976 English Origins of Early American Racism. *Radical History Review* 3(1):1–26.

Marks, Jonathan 1995 *Human Biodiversity: Genes, Race, and History*. New York: Aldine de Gruyter.

Morgan, Edmund S. 1975 *American Slavery: American Freedom*. New York: W. W. Norton and Co.

Mörner, Magnus 1967 *Race Mixture in the History of Latin America*. Boston: Little, Brown.

Morsy, Soheir 1994 Beyond the Honorary "White" Classification of Egyptians: Societal Identity in Historical Context. In *Race*. S. Gregory and R. Sanjek, eds. Pp. 175–198. New Brunswick, NJ: Rutgers University Press.

Nash, Gary 1982 *Red, White, and Black: The Peoples of Early America*. Englewood Cliffs, NJ: Prentice Hall.

Reed, T.E. 1969 Caucasian Genes in American Negroes. *Science* 165 (3,895): 762–768.

Smedley, Audrey [1993]1999 *Race in North America: Origin and Evolution of a Worldview*. 2nd edition, revised and enlarged. Boulder, CO: Westview Press.

Snowden, Frank M., Jr. 1983 *Before Color Prejudice*. Revised edition. Cambridge, MA: Harvard University Press.

READING 2

Who Is Black? One Nation's Definition

F. James Davis

In a taped interview conducted by a blind, black anthropologist, a black man nearly ninety years old said: "Now you must understand that this is just a name we have. I am not black and you are not black either, if you go by the evidence of your eyes. . . . Anyway, black people are all colors. White people don't look all the same way, but there are more different kinds of us than there are of them. Then too, there is a certain stage [at] which you cannot tell who is white and who is black. Many of the people I see who are thought of as black could just as well be white in their appearance. Many of the white people I see are black as far as I can tell by the way they look. Now, that's it for looks. Looks don't mean much. The things that makes us different is how we think. What we believe is important, the ways we look at life" (Gwaltney, 1980:96).

How does a person get defined as a black, both socially and legally, in the United States?

F. James Davis is professor emeritus of sociology at Illinois State University.

What is the nation's rule for who is black, and how did it come to be? And so what? Don't we all know who is black, and isn't the most important issue what opportunities the group has? Let us start with some experiences of three well-known American blacks—actress and beauty pageant winner Vanessa Williams, U.S. Representative Adam Clayton Powell, Jr., and entertainer Lena Horne.

For three decades after the first Miss America Pageant in 1921, black women were barred from competing. The first black winner was Vanessa Williams of Millwood, New York, crowned Miss America in 1984. In the same year the first runner-up—Suzette Charles of Mays Landing, New Jersey—was also black. The viewing public was charmed by the television images and magazine pictures of the beautiful and musically talented Williams, but many people were also puzzled. Why was she being called black when she appeared to be white? Suzette Charles, whose ancestry appeared to be more European than African, at least looked like many of the "lighter blacks." Notoriety followed when Vanessa Williams resigned because of the impending publication of some nude photographs of her taken before the pageant, and Suzette Charles became Miss America for the balance of 1984. Beyond the troubling question of whether these young women could have won if they had looked "more black," the publicity dramatized the nation's definition of a black person.

Some blacks complained that the Rev. Adam Clayton Powell, Jr., was so light that he was a stranger in their midst. In the words of Roi Ottley, "He was white to all appearances, having blue eyes, an aquiline nose, and light, almost blond, hair" (1943:220), yet he became a bold, effective black leader—first as minister of the Abyssinian Baptist Church of Harlem, then as a New York city councilman, and finally as a U.S. congressman from the state of New York. Early in his activist career he led 6,000 blacks in a march on New York City Hall. He used his power in Congress to fight for civil rights legislation and other black causes. In 1966, in Washington, D.C., he convened the first black power conference.

In his autobiography, Powell recounts some experiences with racial classification in his youth that left a lasting impression on him. During Powell's freshman year at Colgate University, his roommate did not know that he was a black until his father, Adam Clayton Powell, Sr., was invited to give a chapel talk on Negro rights and problems, after which the roommate announced that because Adam was a Negro they could no longer be roommates or friends.

Another experience that affected Powell deeply occurred one summer during his Colgate years. He was working as a bellhop at a summer resort in Manchester, Vermont, when Abraham Lincoln's aging son Robert was a guest there. Robert Lincoln disliked blacks so much that he refused to let them wait on him or touch his luggage, car, or any of his possessions. Blacks who did got their knuckles whacked with his cane. To the great amusement of the other bellhops, Lincoln took young Powell for a white man and accepted his services (Powell, 1971:31–33).

Lena Horne's parents were both very light in color and came from black upper-middle-class families in Brooklyn (Horne and Schickel, 1965; Buckley, 1986). Lena lived with her father's parents until she was about seven years old. Her grandfather was very light and blue-eyed. Her fair-skinned grandmother was the daughter of a slave woman and her white owner, from the family of John C. Calhoun, well-known defender of slavery. One of her father's great-grandmothers was a Blackfoot Indian, to whom Lena Horne has attributed her somewhat coppery skin color. One of her mother's grandmothers was a French-speaking black woman from Senegal and never a slave. Her mother's father was a "Portuguese Negro," and two women in his family had passed as white and become entertainers.

Lena Horne's parents had separated, and when she was seven her entertainer mother began placing her in a succession of homes in different states. Her favorite place was in the home of her Uncle Frank, her father's brother, a red-haired, blue-eyed teacher in a black school in Georgia. The black children in that community asked her why she was so light and called her a "yellow bastard." She learned that when satisfactory evidence of respectable black parents is lacking, being light-skinned implies illegitimacy and having an underclass white parent and is thus a disgrace in the black community. When her mother married a white Cuban, Lena also learned that blacks can be very hostile to the white spouse, especially when the "black" mate is very light. At this time she began to blame the confused color line for her childhood troubles. She later endured much hostility from blacks and whites alike when her own second marriage, to white composer-arranger Lennie Hayton, was finally made public in 1950 after three years of keeping it secret.

Early in Lena Horne's career there were complaints that she did not fit the desired image of a black entertainer for white audiences, either physically or in her style. She sang white love songs, not the blues. Noting her brunette-white beauty, one white agent tried to get her to take a Spanish name, learn some Spanish songs, and pass as a Latin white, but she had learned to have a horror of passing and never considered it, although Hollywood blacks accused her of trying to pass after she played her first bit part in a film. After she failed her first screen test because she looked like a white girl trying to play black-face, the directors tried making her up with a shade called "Light Egyptian" to make her look darker. The whole procedure embarrassed and hurt her deeply. . . .

Other light mulatto entertainers have also had painful experiences because of their light skin and other caucasoid features. Starting an acting career is never easy, but actress Jane White's difficulties in the 1940s were compounded by her lightness. Her father was NAACP leader Walter White. Even with dark makeup on her ivory skin, she did not look like a black person on the stage, but she was not allowed to try out for white roles because blacks were barred from playing them. When she auditioned for the part of a young girl from India, the director was enthusiastic, although her skin color was too light, but higher management decreed that it was unthinkable for a Negro to play the part of an Asian Indian (White, 1948:338). Only after great

perseverance did Jane White make her debut as the educated mulatto maid Nonnie in the stage version of Lillian Smith's *Strange Fruit* (1944). . . .

THE ONE-DROP RULE DEFINED

As the above cases illustrate, to be considered black in the United States not even half of one's ancestry must be African black. But will one-fourth do, or one-eighth, or less? The nation's answer to the question "Who is black?" has long been that a black is any person with *any* known African black ancestry (Myrdal, 1944:113–18; Berry and Tischler, 1978:97–98; Williamson, 1980:1–2). This definition reflects the long experience with slavery and later with Jim Crow segregation. In the South it became known as the "one-drop rule," meaning that a single drop of "black blood" makes a person a black. It is also known as the "one black ancestor rule," some courts have called it the "traceable amount rule," and anthropologists call it the "hypo-descent rule," meaning that racially mixed persons are assigned the status of the subordinate group (Harris, 1964:56). This definition emerged from the American South to become the nation's definition, generally accepted by whites and blacks alike (Bahr, Chadwick, and Stauss, 1979:27–28). Blacks had no other choice. This American cultural definition of blacks is taken for granted as readily by judges, affirmative action officers, and black protesters as it is by Ku Klux Klansmen.

Let us not be confused by terminology. At present the usual statement of the one-drop rule is in terms of "black blood" or black ancestry, while not so long ago it referred to "Negro blood" or ancestry. The term "black" rapidly replaced "Negro" in general usage in the United States as the black power movement peaked at the end of the 1960s, but the black and Negro populations are the same. The term "black" is used [here] for persons with any black African lineage, not just for unmixed members of populations from sub-Saharan Africa. The term "Negro," which is used in certain historical contexts, means the same thing. Terms such as "African black," "unmixed Negro," and "all black" are used here to refer to unmixed blacks descended from African populations.

We must also pay attention to the terms "mulatto" and "colored." The term "mulatto" was originally used to mean the offspring of a "pure African Negro" and a "pure white." Although the root meaning of mulatto, in Spanish, is "hybrid," "mulatto" came to include the children of unions between whites and so-called "mixed Negroes." For example, Booker T. Washington and Frederick Douglass, with slave mothers and white fathers, were referred to as mulattoes (Bennett, 1962:255). To whatever extent their mothers were part white, these men were more than half white. Douglass was evidently part Indian as well, and he looked it (Preston, 1980:9–10). Washington had reddish hair and gray eyes. At the time of the American Revolution, many of the founding fathers had some very light slaves, including some who appeared to be white. The term "colored" seemed for a time to refer only to mulattoes, especially lighter ones, but later it became a euphemism for darker Negroes, even including unmixed blacks. With widespread racial mixture, "Negro" came to mean any slave or descendant of a slave, no matter how much mixed. Eventually in the United States, the terms mulatto, colored, Negro, black, and African American all came to mean people with any known black African ancestry. Mulattoes are racially mixed, to whatever degree, while the terms black, Negro, African American, and colored include both mulattoes and unmixed blacks. These terms have quite different meanings in other countries.

Whites in the United States need some help envisioning the American black experience with ancestral fractions. At the beginning of miscegenation between two populations presumed to be racially pure, quadroons appear in the second generation of continuing mixing with whites, and octoroons in the third. A quadroon is one-fourth African black and thus easily classed as black in the United States, yet three of this person's four grandparents are white. An octoroon has seven white great-grandparents out of eight and usually looks white or almost so. Most parents of black American children in recent decades have themselves been racially mixed, but often the fractions get complicated because the earlier details of the mixing were obscured generations ago. Like so many white Americans, black people are forced to speculate about some of the fractions—one-eighth this, three-sixteenths that, and so on. . . .

PLESSY, PHIPPS, AND OTHER CHALLENGES IN THE COURTS

Homer Plessy was the plaintiff in the 1896 precedent-setting "separate-but-equal" case of *Plessy v. Ferguson* (163 U.S. 537). This case challenged the Jim Crow statute that required racially segregated seating on trains in interstate commerce in the state of Louisiana. The U.S. Supreme Court quickly dispensed with Plessy's contention that because he was only one-eighth Negro and could pass as white he was entitled to ride in the seats reserved for whites. Without ruling directly on the definition of a Negro, the Supreme Court briefly took what is called "judicial notice" of what it assumed to be common knowledge: that a Negro or black is any person with any black ancestry. (Judges often take explicit "judicial notice" not only of scientific or scholarly conclusions, or of opinion surveys or other systematic investigations, but also of something they just assume to be so, including customary practices or common knowledge.) This has consistently been the ruling in the federal courts, and often when the black ancestry was even less than one-eighth. The federal courts have thus taken judicial notice of the customary boundary between two sociocultural groups that differ, on the average, in physical traits, not between two discrete genetic categories. In the absence of proof of a specific black ancestor, merely being known as a black in the community has usually been accepted by the courts as evidence of black ancestry. The separate-but-equal doctrine established in the Plessy case is no longer the law, as a result of the judicial and legislative successes of the civil rights movement, but the nation's legal definition of who is black remains unchanged.

State courts have generally upheld the one-drop rule. For instance, in a 1948 Mississippi case a young man, Davis Knight, was sentenced to five years in jail for violating the antimiscegenation statute. Less than one-sixteenth black, Knight said he was not aware that he had any black lineage, but the state proved his great-grandmother was a slave girl. In some states the operating definition of black has been limited by statute to particular fractions, yet the social definition—the one-drop rule—has generally prevailed in case of doubt. Mississippi, Missouri, and five other states have had the criterion of one-eighth. Virginia changed from one-fourth to one-eighth in 1910, then in 1930 forbade white intermarriage with a person with any black ancestry. Persons in Virginia who are one-fourth or more Indian and less than one-sixteenth African black are defined as Indians while on the reservation but as blacks when they leave (Berry, 1965:26). While some states have had general race classification statutes, at least for a time, others have legislated a definition of black only for particular purposes, such as marriage or education. In a few states there have even been varying definitions for different situations (Mangum, 1940:38–48). All states require a designation of race on birth certificates, but there are no clear guidelines to help physicians and midwives do the classifying.

Louisiana's latest race classification statute became highly controversial and was finally repealed in 1983 (Trillin, 1986:77). Until 1970, a Louisiana statute had embraced the one-drop rule, defining a Negro as anyone with a "trace of black ancestry." This law was challenged in court a number of times from the 1920s on, including an unsuccessful attempt in 1957 by boxer Ralph Dupas, who asked to be declared white so that a law banning "interracial sports" (since repealed) would not prevent him from boxing in the state. In 1970 a lawsuit was brought on behalf of a child whose ancestry was allegedly only one two-hundred-fifty-sixth black, and the legislature revised its law. The 1970 Louisiana statute defined a black as someone whose ancestry is more than one thirty-second black (La. Rev. Stat. 42:267). Adverse publicity about this law was

widely disseminated during the Phipps trial in 1983 (discussed below), filed as *Jane Doe v. State of Louisiana*. This case was decided in a district court in May 1983, and in June the legislature abolished its one thirty-second statute and gave parents the right to designate the race of newborns, and even to change classifications on birth certificates if they can prove the child is white by a "preponderance of the evidence." However, the new statute in 1983 did not abolish the "traceable amount rule" (the one-drop rule), as demonstrated by the outcomes when the Phipps decision was appealed to higher courts in 1985 and 1986.

The history in the Phipps (Jane Doe) case goes as far back as 1770, when a French planter named Jean Gregoire Guillory took his wife's slave, Margarita, as his mistress (Model, 1983:3–4). More than two centuries and two decades later, their great-great-great-great-granddaughter, Susie Guillory Phipps, asked the Louisiana courts to change the classification on her deceased parents' birth certificates to "white" so she and her brothers and sisters could be designated white. They all looked white, and some were blue-eyed blonds. Mrs. Susie Phipps had been denied a passport because she had checked "white" on her application although her birth certificate designated her race as "colored." This designation was based on information supplied by a midwife, who presumably relied on the parents or on the family's status in the community. Mrs. Phipps claimed that this classification came as a shock, since she had always thought she was white, had lived as white, and had twice married as white. Some of her relatives, however, gave depositions saying they considered themselves "colored," and the lawyers for the state claimed to have proof that Mrs. Phipps is three thirty-seconds black (Trillin, 1986:62–63, 71–74). That was more than enough "blackness" for the district court in 1983 to declare her parents, and thus Mrs. Phipps and her siblings, to be legally black.

In October and again in December 1985, the state's Fourth Circuit Court of Appeals upheld the district court's decision, saying that no one can change the racial designation of his or her parents or anyone else's (479 So. 2d 369). Said the majority of the court in its opinion: "That appellants might today describe themselves as white does not prove error in a document which designates their parents as colored" (479 So. 2d 371). Of course, if the parents' designation as "colored" cannot be disturbed, their descendants must be defined as black by the "traceable amount rule." The court also concluded that the preponderance of the evidence clearly showed that the Guillory parents were "colored." Although noting expert testimony to the effect that the race of an individual cannot be determined with scientific accuracy, the court said the law of racial designation is not based on science, that "individual race designations are purely social and cultural perceptions and the evidence conclusively proves those subjective perspectives were correctly recorded at the time the appellants' birth certificates were recorded" (479 So. 2d 372). At the rehearing in December 1985, the appellate court also affirmed the necessity of designating race on birth certificates for public health, affirmative action, and other important public programs and held that equal protection of the law has not been denied so long as the designation is treated as confidential.

When this case was appealed to the Louisiana Supreme Court in 1986, that court declined to review the decision, saying only that the court "concurs in the denial for the reasons assigned by the court of appeals on rehearing" (485 So. 2d 60). In December 1986 the U.S. Supreme Court was equally brief in stating its reason for refusing to review the decision: "The appeal is dismissed for want of a substantial federal question" (107 Sup. Ct. Reporter, interim ed. 638). Thus, both the final court of appeals in Louisiana and the highest court of the United States saw no reason to disturb the application of the one-drop rule in the lawsuit brought by Susie Guillory Phipps and her siblings.

CENSUS ENUMERATION OF BLACKS

When the U.S. Bureau of the Census enumerates blacks (always counted as Negroes until 1980), it does not use a scientific definition, but rather the one accepted by the general public and by the courts. The Census Bureau counts what the nation wants counted. Although various operational instructions have been tried, the definition of black used by the Census Bureau has been the nation's cultural and legal definition: all persons with any known black ancestry. Other nations define and count blacks differently, so international comparisons of census data on blacks can be extremely misleading. For example, Latin American countries generally count as black only unmixed African blacks, those only slightly mixed, and the very poorest mulattoes. If they used the U.S. definition, they would count far more blacks than they do, and if Americans used their definition, millions in the black community in the United States would be counted either as white or as "coloreds" of different descriptions, not as black.

Instructions to our census enumerators in 1840, 1850, and 1860 provided "mulatto" as a category but did not define the term. In 1870 and 1880, mulattoes were officially defined to include "quadroons, octoroons, and all persons having any perceptible trace of African blood." In 1890 enumerators were told to record the *exact* proportion of the "African blood," again relying on visibility. In 1900 the Census Bureau specified that "pure Negroes" be counted separately from mulattoes, the latter to mean "all persons with some trace of black blood." In 1920 the mulatto category was dropped, and black was defined to mean any person with any black ancestry, as it has been ever since.

In 1960 the practice of self-definition began, with the head of household indicating the race of its members. This did not seem to introduce any noticeable fluctuation in the number of blacks, thus indicating that black Americans generally apply the one-drop rule to themselves. One exception is that Spanish-speaking Americans who have black ancestry but were considered white, or some designation other than black, in their place of origin generally reject the one-drop rule if they can. American Indians with some black ancestry also generally try to avoid the rule, but those who leave the reservation are often treated as black.

At any rate, the 1980 census count showed that self-designated blacks made up about 12 percent of the population of the United States.

No other ethnic population in the nation, including those with visibly non-caucasoid features, is defined and counted according to a one-drop rule. For example, persons whose ancestry is one-fourth or less American Indian are not generally defined as Indian unless they want to be, and they are considered assimilating Americans who may even be proud of having some Indian ancestry. The same implicit rule appears to apply to Japanese Americans, Filipinos, or other peoples from East Asian nations and also to Mexican Americans who have Central American Indian ancestry, as a large majority do. For instance, a person whose ancestry is one-eighth Chinese is not defined as just Chinese, or East Asian, or a member of the mongoloid race. The United States certainly does not apply a one-drop rule to its white ethnic populations either, which include both national and religious groups. Ethnicity has often been confused with racial biology and not just in Nazi Germany. Americans do not insist that an American with a small fraction of Polish ancestry be classified as a Pole, or that someone with a single remote Greek ancestor be designated Greek, or that someone with any trace of Jewish lineage is a Jew and nothing else.

It is interesting that, in *The Passing of the Great Race* (1916), Madison Grant maintained that the one-drop rule should be applied not only to blacks but also to all the other ethnic groups he considered biologically inferior "races," such as Hindus, Asians in general, Jews, Italians, and other Southern and Eastern European peoples. Grant's book went through four editions, and he and others succeeded in getting Congress to pass the national origins quota laws of the early 1920s. This racist quota legislation sharply curtailed immigration from everywhere in the world except Northern and Western Europe and the Western Hemisphere, until it was repealed in 1965. Grant and other believers in the racial superiority of their own group have confused race with

ethnicity. They consider miscegenation with any "inferior" people to be the ultimate danger to the survival of their own group and have often seen the one-drop rule as a crucial component in their line of defense. Americans in general, however, while finding other ways to discriminate against immigrant groups, have rejected the application of the drastic one-drop rule to all groups but blacks.

UNIQUENESS OF THE ONE-DROP RULE

Not only does the one-drop rule apply to no other group than American blacks, but apparently the rule is unique in that it is found only in the United States and not in any other nation in the world. In fact, definitions of who is black vary quite sharply from country to country, and for this reason people in other countries often express consternation about our definition. James Baldwin relates a revealing incident that occurred in 1956 at the Conference of Negro-African Writers and Artists held in Paris. The head of the delegation of writers and artists from the United States was John Davis. The French chairperson introduced Davis and then asked him why he considered himself Negro, since he certainly did not look like one. Baldwin wrote, "He *is* a Negro, of course, from the remarkable legal point of view which obtains in the United States, but more importantly, as he tried to make clear to his interlocutor, he was a Negro by choice and by depth of involvement—by experience, in fact" (1962:19).

The phenomenon known as "passing as white" is difficult to explain in other countries or to foreign students. Typical questions are: "Shouldn't Americans say that a person who is passing as white is white, or nearly all white, and has previously been passing as black?" or "To be consistent, shouldn't you say that someone who is one-eighth white is passing as black?" or "Why is there so much concern, since the so-called blacks who pass take so little negroid ancestry with them?" Those who ask such questions need to realize that "passing" is so much more a social phenomenon than a biological one, reflecting the nation's unique definition of what makes a person black. The concept of "passing" rests on the one-drop rule and on folk beliefs about race and miscegenation, not on biological or historical fact.

The black experience with passing as white in the United States contrasts with the experience of other ethnic minorities that have features that are clearly non-caucasoid. The concept of passing applies only to blacks—consistent with the nation's unique definition of the group. A person who is one-fourth or less American Indian or Korean or Filipino is not regarded as passing if he or she intermarries and joins fully the life of the dominant community, so the minority ancestry need not be hidden. It is often suggested that the key reason for this is that the physical differences between these other groups and whites are less pronounced than the physical differences between African blacks and whites, and therefore are less threatening to whites. However, keep in mind that the one-drop rule and anxiety about passing originated during slavery and later received powerful reinforcement under the Jim Crow system.

For the physically visible groups other than blacks, miscegenation promotes assimilation, despite barriers of prejudice and discrimination during two or more generations of racial mixing. As noted above, when ancestry in one of these racial minority groups does not exceed one-fourth, a person is not defined solely as a member of that group. Masses of white European immigrants have climbed the class ladder not only through education but also with the help of close personal relationships in the dominant community, intermarriage, and ultimately full cultural and social assimilation. Young people tend to marry people they meet in the same informal social circles (Gordon, 1964:70–81). For visibly non-caucasoid minorities other than blacks in the United States, this entire route to full assimilation is slow but possible.

For all persons of any known black lineage, however, assimilation is blocked and is not promoted by miscegenation. Barriers to full opportunity and participation for blacks are still formidable, and a fractionally black person cannot escape these obstacles without passing as white and cutting off all ties to the black family and community. The pain of this separation, and condemnation by the black family and community, are major reasons why many or most of those who could pass as white choose not to. Loss of security within the minority community, and fear and distrust of the white world are also factors.

It should now be apparent that the definition of a black person as one with any trace at all of black African ancestry is inextricably woven into the history of the United States. It incorporates beliefs once used to justify slavery and later used to buttress the castelike Jim Crow system of segregation. Developed in the South, the definition of "Negro" (now black) spread and became the nation's social and legal definition. Because blacks are defined according to the one-drop rule, they are a socially constructed category in which there is wide variation in racial traits and therefore not a race group in the scientific sense. However, because that category has a definite status position in the society it has become a self-conscious social group with an ethnic identity.

The one-drop rule has long been taken for granted throughout the United States by whites and blacks alike, and the federal courts have taken "judicial notice" of it as being a matter of common knowledge. State courts have generally upheld the one-drop rule, but some have limited the definition to one thirty-second or one-sixteenth or one-eighth black ancestry, or made other limited exceptions for persons with both Indian and black ancestry. Most Americans seem unaware that this definition of blacks is extremely unusual in other countries, perhaps even unique to the United States, and that Americans define no other minority group in a similar way. . . .

DISCUSSION QUESTIONS

1. Is black a color category or a status?
2. Do you think passing still occurs?

REFERENCES

Bahr, Howard M., Bruce A. Chadwick, and Joseph H. Stauss. 1979. *American Ethnicity.* Lexington, MA: D.C. Heath & Co.

Baldwin, James. 1962. *Nobody Knows My Name.* New York: Dell Publishing Co.

Bennett, Lerone, Jr. 1962. *Before the Mayflower: A History of the Negro in America 1619–1962.* Chicago: Johnson Publishing Co.

Berry, Brewton. 1965. *Race and Ethnic Relations.* 3rd ed. Boston: Houghton Mifflin Co.

Berry, Brewton, and Henry L. Tischler. 1978. *Race and Ethnic Relations.* 4th ed. Boston: Houghton Mifflin Co.

Buckley, Gail Lumet. 1986. *The Hornes: An American Family.* New York: Alfred A. Knopf.

Gordon, Milton M. 1964. *Assimilation in American Life.* New York: Oxford University Press.

Grant, Madison. 1916. *The Passing of the Great Race.* New York: Scribner.

Gwaltney, John Langston. 1980. *Drylongso: A Self-Portrait of Black America.* New York: Vintage Books.

Harris, Melvin. 1964. *Patterns of Race in the Americas.* New York: W. W. Norton.

Horne, Lena, and Richard Schickel. 1965. *Lena.* Garden City, NY: Doubleday & Co.

Mangum, Charles Staples, Jr. 1940. *The Legal Status of the Negro in the United States.* Chapel Hill: University of North Carolina Press.

Model, F. Peter, ed. 1983. "Apartheid in the Bayou." *Perspectives: The Civil Rights Quarterly 15* (Winter–Spring), 3–4.

Myrdal, Gunnar, assisted by Richard Sterner and Arnold M. Rose. 1944. *An American Dilemma.* New York: Harper & Bros.

Ottley, Roi. 1943. *New World A-Coming.* Cleveland: World Publishing Co.

Powell, Adam Clayton, Jr. 1971. *Adam by Adam: The Autobiography of Adam Clayton Powell, Jr.* New York: Dial Press.

Preston, Dickson J. 1980. *Young Frederick Douglass: The Maryland Years.* Baltimore: Johns Hopkins University Press.

Trillin, Calvin. 1986. "American Chronicles: Black or White." *New Yorker,* April 14, 1986, pp. 62–78.

White, Walter. 1948. *A Man Called White: The Autobiography of Walter White.* New York: Viking Press.

Williamson, Joel. 1980. *New People: Miscegenation and Mulattoes in the United States.* New York: The Free Press.

The Evolution of Identity

The Washington Post

Decade to decade, the U.S. census has changed its classifications of race and ethnicity. Partially, this reflects the growing diversity of the country. It also reveals the nation's evolving politics and social mores. When the first census was taken in 1790, enumerators classified free residents as white or "other," while slaves were counted separately. By 1860, residents were classified as white, black or mulatto. Hispanic origin first became a category in 1970. Here are the categories used in the decennial counts from 1860 to 2000, as presented by AmeriStat (www.ameristat.org).

Race categories

1860	1870	1880	1890¹	1900²	1910	1920	1930	1940	1950	1960	1970	1980	1990	2000
White	White	White	White	White	White	White	White	White	White	White	White	White	White	White
Black	Black	Black	Black	Black (Negro descent)	Black	Black	Black	Black	Negro	Negro	Negro or Black	Black or Negro	Black or Negro	Black, African American or Negro
Mulatto	Mulatto	Mulatto	Mulatto		Mulatto	Mulatto								
			Quadroon											
			Octoroon											
	Chinese	Chinese	Chinese	Chinese	Chinese	Chinese	Chinese	Chinese	Chinese	Chinese	Chinese	Chinese	Chinese	Chinese
	Indian	Indian	Indian	Indian	Indian	Indian	Indian	Indian	Amer. Indian	Amer. Indian	Indian (Amer.)	Indian	Indian (Amer.)	Amer. Indian or Alaska Native
			Japanese	Japanese	Japanese	Japanese	Japanese	Japanese	Japanese	Japanese	Japanese	Japanese	Japanese	Japanese
						Filipino	Filipino	Filipino	Filipino	Filipino	Filipino	Filipino	Filipino	Filipino
						Hindu	Hindu	Hindu						
						Korean	Korean	Korean			Korean	Korean	Korean	Korean
							Mexican							
												Asian Indian	Asian Indian	Asian Indian
										Aleut		Aleut	Aleut	
										Eskimo		Eskimo	Eskimo	
										Hawaiian	Hawaiian	Hawaiian	Hawaiian	Native Hawaiian
										Part Hawaiian				
												Vietnamese	Vietnamese	Vietnamese
												Guamanian	Guamanian	Guamanian or Chamorro
												Samoan	Samoan	Samoan
													Other Asian Pacific Islander	**Other Asian** / **Other Pacific Islander**
					Other	Other	Other	Other	Other	Other	Other	Other	Other race	Some other race

ETHNICITY

1970	1980	1990	2000
Mexican	Mexican	Mexican	Mexican
	Mexican Amer.	Mexican Amer.	Mexican Amer.
	Chicano	Chicano	Chicano
Puerto Rican	Puerto Rican	Puerto Rican	Puerto Rican
Central/So. American			
Cuban	Cuban	Cuban	Cuban
Other Spanish	Other Spanish/Hispanic	Other Spanish/Hispanic	Other Spanish/Hispanic/Latino
(None of these)	Not Spanish/Hispanic	Not Spanish/Hispanic	Not Spanish/Hispanic/Latino

1 In 1890, mulatto was defined as a person who was three-eighths to five-eighths black. A quadroon was one-quarter black and an octoroon one-eighth black.

2 American Indians have been asked to specify their tribe since the 1900 Census.

Bold letters indicate first usage since 1860.

NOTE: Before the 1970 Census, enumerators wrote in the race of individuals using the designated categories. In subsequent censuses, respondents or enumerators filled in circles next to the categories with which the respondent identified. Also beginning with the 1970 Census, people choosing American Indian, other Asian, other race, or for the Hispanic question, other Hispanic categories, were asked to write in a specific tribe or group. Hispanic ethnicity was asked of a sample of Americans in 1970 and of all Americans beginning with the 1980 Census. The 2000 Census allowed Americans to select more than one race.

Sources: AmeriStat, "200 Years of U.S. Census Taking: Population and Housing Questions 1790–1990," U.S. Census Bureau. FROM: *The Washington Post*, Federal Page, August 13, 2001.

A Loaded Vacation

Every summer since I can remember, I go on vacation with my aunt and uncle. Last summer, my aunt took my cousin, brother, and me to Florida. My aunt grew up in Maryland along with my mother. She was college educated and until recently worked in corporate America. Now she owns her own daycare center.

I rarely thought about how my background was different from my aunt's until one night in Florida. We were all in the hotel suite when she asked me about my plans for the future and what I wanted to do with my degree, since I was entering college in the fall. I told her I wanted to be a lawyer. She told me that was going to be a hard goal to reach for a black female, but then again she said that I wasn't really black. I didn't understand. She went on to say that if I make it anywhere in life, it would be because I talk white. She said, "Just remember that, even though everything about you is white—your clothes, the way you talk, your friends—doesn't mean when they look at you they don't still see black."

I didn't know what to say. I sat there silently taking it all in. Was this the same aunt I'd known all my life? She told my brother that anything he accomplished would be due to his skin complexion, and that if he had been dark skinned "he wouldn't have a shot in hell, because white people determine how far we get in life." This went against everything I believed. I said, "What about my high GPA and the fact that I'm intelligent? That means nothing?" She said, "Exactly. Even with all of that, you'll only go as far as they let you."

After she finished ranting about how far we would go in life, she went on to say that we were foolish for having so many white friends, because white people were the devil. At that point I had to speak up. I told her that I've never had a problem with any of my white friends and that she shouldn't talk about people she's never met. She replied by saying, "All white people are the same. Some are just closet racists." I said that my best friend Monica is white. How could she be my best friend if she was racist? My aunt said, "She may be your friend now, but if the two of you got into any trouble she would throw you right under the bus." The conversation ended with her telling me how naive I was, and that one day I would learn the truth.

That day came, and soon. A few months after that dreadful vacation Monica and I got into trouble. Monica was only 17, whereas I was 18. Because of my age, I would not be let off with a phone call home. Monica took the blame and covered for me. Thanks to her, I don't have a criminal record. I thought about calling my aunt to tell her how wrong she had been, but I decided that there was no point in arguing. I knew the truth.

Niah Grimes

READING 4

Real Indians: Identity and the Survival of Native America

Eva Marie Garroutte

The most common tribal requirement for determining citizenship concerns "blood quantum," or degree of Indian ancestry. . . . About two-thirds of all federally recognized tribes of the coterminous

United States specify a minimum blood quantum in their legal citizenship criteria, with one-quarter blood degree being the most frequent minimum requirement.[1] (In the simplest instance, an individual has a one-quarter blood quantum if any one of her four grandparents is of exclusively Indian ancestry and the other three are non-Indian.) The remaining one-third of Indian tribes specify *no* minimum blood quantum. They often simply require that any new enrollee be a lineal (direct) descendant of another tribal member. . . .

Legal definitions of tribal membership regulate the rights to vote in tribal elections, to hold tribal office, and generally to participate in the political, and sometimes also the cultural, life of the tribe.

Eva Marie Garroutte is a professor of sociology at Boston College.

One's ability to satisfy legal definitions of identification may also determine one's right to share in certain tribal revenues (such as income generated by tribally controlled businesses). Perhaps most significantly, it may determine the right to live on a reservation or to inherit land interests there.

The tribes' power to determine citizenship allows them to delimit the distribution of certain important resources, such as reservation land, tribal monies, and political privileges. But this is hardly the end of the story of legal definitions of identity. The federal government has many purposes for which it, too, must distinguish Indians from non-Indians, and it uses its own, separate legal definition for doing so. More precisely, it uses a whole array of legal definitions. Since the U.S. Constitution uses the word "Indian" in two places but defines it nowhere, Congress has made its own definitions on an ad hoc basis.[2] A 1978 congressional survey discovered no less than *thirty-three* separate definitions of Indians in use in different pieces of federal legislation.[3] These may or may not correspond with those any given tribe uses to determine its citizenship.

Most federal legal definitions of Indian identity specify a minimum blood quantum—frequently one-quarter but sometimes one-half—but others do not. Some require or accept tribal citizenship as a criterion of federal identification, and others do not. Some require reservation residency, or ownership of land held in trust by the government, and others do not. Other laws affecting Indians specify *no* definition of identity, such that the courts must determine to whom the laws apply.[4] Because of these wide variations in legal identity definitions and their frequent departure from the various tribal ones, many individuals who are recognized by their tribes as citizens are nevertheless considered non-Indian for some or all federal purposes. The converse can be true as well.[5]

There are a variety of contexts in which one or more federal legal definitions of identity become important. The matter of economic resource distribution—access to various social services, monetary awards, and opportunities—probably comes immediately to the minds of many readers. The legal situation of Indian people, and its attendant opportunities and responsibilities, are the result of historic negotiations between tribes and the federal government. In these, the government agreed to compensate tribes in various ways for the large amounts of land and other resources that the tribes had surrendered, often by force.[6] Benefits available to those who can satisfy federal definitions of Indian identity are administered through a variety of agencies, including the Bureau of Indian Affairs, the Indian Health Service, the Department of Agriculture, the Office of Elementary and Secondary Education, and the Department of Labor, to name a few.[7]

Legal definitions also affect specific economic rights deriving from treaties or agreements that some (not all) tribes made with the federal government. These may include such rights as the use of particular geographic areas for hunting, harvesting, fishing, or trapping. Those legally defined as Indians are also sometimes exempted from certain requirements related to state licensure and state (but not federal) income and property taxation.[8] . . .

"IF HE GETS A NOSEBLEED, HE'LL TURN INTO A WHITE MAN"

North American Indians who successfully negotiate the rigors of legal definitions of identity at the federal level can achieve what some consider the dubious distinction of being a "card-carrying Indian." That is, their federal government can issue them a laminated document (in the United States, a CDIB; in Canada an Indian status card) that certifies them as possessing a certain "degree of Indian blood."

. . . Canadian-born country music singer Shania Twain has what it takes to be a card-carrying Indian: she is formally recognized as an Anishnabe (Ojibwe) Indian with band membership in the Temagami Bear Island First Nation (Ontario, Canada). More specifically, she is legally on record as possessing one-half degree Indian blood. Given this information, one might conclude that Twain's identity as an Indian person is more or less unassailable. It's not.

Controversy has engulfed this celebrity because of an anonymous phone call to a Canadian newspaper a few years ago that led to the disclosure of another name by which Shania was once known: Eileen Regina Edwards. Eileen/Shania was adopted by a stepfather in early childhood and took the surname of Twain at that time. So far well and good—except for one thing. Both sides of her *biological* family describe themselves not as Indian but as white. It is only Jerry Twain, her late stepfather, who was Indian.

As the adopted child of an Anishnabe man, Shania Twain occupies an unusual status. Though the U.S. government allows for the assignment of blood quantum only to biological descendants of Indian people, Canada allows for the naturalization of non-Native children through adoption.[9] Although Twain has stated that her white mother (now deceased) had told her, in childhood, that her biological father (also deceased) had some Indian heritage, his family denies the suggestion entirely. They say they are French and Irish. Ms. Twain explains: "I don't know how much Indian blood I actually have in me, but as the adopted daughter of my father Jerry, I became legally registered as 50-percent North American Indian. Being raised by a full-blooded Indian and being part of his family and their culture from such a young age is all I've ever known. That heritage is in my heart and my soul, and I'm proud of it."[10]

Twain has been sharply criticized, in both the United States and Canada, for not making the full details of her racial background clearer, especially to awards-granting agencies such as the First Americans in the Arts (FAITA), which honored her in February 1996 as a Native performer. FAITA itself has made no such complaint. The group states that it is satisfied that "Ms. Twain has not intentionally misrepresented herself." And more importantly, her adopted family defends her. An aunt observes: "She was raised by us. She was accepted by our band. If my brother were alive, he'd be very upset. He raised her as his own daughter. My parents, her grandparents, took her into the bush and taught her the [Native] traditions."[11]

Twain's case shows with uncommon clarity that legal and biological definitions are conceptually distinct. . . .

In their modern American construction, at least, biological definitions of identity assume the centrality of an individual's genetic relationship to other tribal members. Not just any degree of relationship will do, however. Typically, the degree of closeness is also important. And this is the starting point for much of the controversy that swirls around issues of biological Indianness. . . .

Sociologist Eugeen Roosens summarizes such common conceptions about the importance of blood quantum for determining Indian identity:

> There is . . . [a] principle about which the whites and the Indians are in agreement. . . . People with more Indian blood . . . also have more rights to inherit what their ancestors, the former Indians, have left behind. In addition, full blood Indians are more authentic than half-breeds. By *being* pure, they have more right to respect. They *are,* in all aspects of their being, more *integral.*[12]

Biological ancestry can take on such tremendous significance in tribal contexts that it overwhelms all other considerations of identity, especially when it is constructed as "pure." As Cherokee legal scholar G. William Rice points out, "Most [people] would recognize the full-blood Indian who was enrolled in a federally recognized tribe as an Indian, even if the individual was adopted at birth by a non-Indian family and had never set foot in Indian country nor met another Indian."[13] Mixed-race individuals, by contrast, find their identity claims considerably complicated. Even if such an individual can demonstrate conclusively that he has *some* Native ancestry, the question will still be raised: Is the *amount* of ancestry he possesses "enough"? Is his "Indian blood" sufficient to distinguish him from the mixed-blood individual spotlighted by an old quip: "If he got a nosebleed, he'd turn into a white man"?

Members of various tribes complain of factionalism between these two major groups—full bloods and mixed bloods—and they suggest that the division arose historically because of mixed bloods' greater access to the social resources of the dominant society and their enhanced ability to impose values and ideas upon others.[14] As Julie M., a citizen of the United Keetowah Band of Cherokee Indians, says: "For the Cherokee people, there's been this mixed blood/full blood kind of dynamic going from before the removal [in 1838, also known as the Trail of Tears]. . . . It's kind of like us-and-them. . . . It's almost been like a *war* in some cases. . . . It's a 'who's-really-going-to-be-in-control-of-the-tribe?' kind of thing." Many historians have similarly found it logical that political allegiances would tend to shift for those Indian people who formed alliances, through intermarriage, with members of the dominant society, and that this has made the division between full bloods and mixed bloods politically important.[15]

Modern biological definitions of identity, however, are much more complicated than this historical explanation can account for. This complexity did not originate in the ideas and experiences of Indian tribes. Instead, they closely reflect nineteenth- and early-twentieth-century theories of race introduced by Euro-Americans. These theories (of which there were a great many) viewed biology as definitive, but they did not distinguish it from culture. Thus, blood became quite literally the vehicle for the transmission of cultural characteristics. "'Half-breeds' by this logic could be expected to behave in 'half-civilized,' i.e., partially assimilated, ways while retaining one half of their traditional culture, accounting for their marginal status in both societies."[16]

These turn-of-the-century theories of race found a very precise way to talk about *amount* of ancestry in the idea of blood quantum, or degree of blood. The notion of blood quantum as a standard of Indianness emerged with force in the nineteenth century. Its most significant early usage as a standard of identification was in the General Allotment (Dawes) Act of 1887, which led to the creation of the Dawes Rolls [the "base roll" or written record of tribal membership in a specific year]. It has been part of the popular—and legal and academic—lore about Indians ever since.

Given this standard of identification, full bloods tend to be seen as the "really real," the quintessential Indians, while others are viewed as Indians in diminishing degrees. The original, stated intention of blood quantum distinctions was to determine the point at which the various responsibilities of the dominant society to Indian peoples ended. The ultimate and explicit federal intention was to use the blood quantum standard as a means to liquidate tribal lands and to eliminate government trust responsibility to tribes, along with entitlement programs, treaty rights, and reservations. Through intermarriage and application of a biological definition of identity Indians would eventually become citizens indistinguishable from all other citizens.[17]

Degree of blood is calculated, with reference to biological definitions, on the basis of the immediacy of one's genetic relationship to those whose bloodlines are (supposedly) unmixed. As in the case with legal definitions, the initial calculation for most tribes' biological definitions begins with a base roll, a listing of tribal membership and blood quanta in some particular year. These base rolls make possible very elaborate definitions of identity. For instance, they allow one to reckon that the offspring of, say, a full-blood Navajo mother and a white father is one-half Navajo. If that half-Navajo child, in turn, produces children with a Hopi person of one-quarter blood degree, those progeny will be judged one-quarter Navajo and one-eighth Hopi. Alternatively, they can be said to have three-eighths general Indian blood.

As even this rather simple example shows, over time such calculations can become infinitesimally precise, with people's ancestry being parsed into so many thirty-seconds, sixty-fourths, one-hundred-twenty-eighths, and so on. . . .

For those of us who have grown up and lived with the peculiar precision of calculating blood quantum, it sometimes requires a perspective less influenced by the vagaries of American history to remind us just how far from common sense the concepts underlying biological definitions of identity are. I recall responding to an inquiry from a Southeast Asian friend about what blood quantum was and how it was calculated. In mid-explanation, I noticed his expression of complete amazement. "That's the dumbest thing I ever heard," he burst out. "Who ever thought of *that*?"

The logic that underlies the biological definition of racial identity becomes even more curious and complicated when one considers the striking difference in the way that American definitions assign individuals to the racial category of "Indian," as opposed to the racial category "black." As a variety of researchers have observed, social attributions of black identity have focused (at least since the end of the Civil War) on the "one-drop rule," or rule of hypodescent.[18] . . .

Far from being held to a one-drop rule, Indians are generally required—both by law and by popular opinion—to establish rather *high* blood quanta in order for their claims to racial identity to be accepted as meaningful, the individual's own opinion notwithstanding. Although people must have only the slightest trace of "black blood" to be *forced* into the category "African American," modern American Indians must (1) formally produce (2) strong evidence of (3) often rather substantial amounts of "Indian blood" to be *allowed* entry into the corresponding racial category. The regnant biological definitions applied to Indians are simply quite different than those that have applied (and continue to apply) to blacks. Modern Americans, as Native American Studies professor Jack Forbes (Powhatan/Lenape/Saponi) puts the matter, "are *always finding 'blacks'* (even if they look rather un-African), and . . . *are always losing 'Indians.'*"[19]

BIOLOGICAL DEFINITIONS: CONTEXTS AND CONSEQUENCES

Biological definitions of Indian identity operate, in short, in some curious and inconsistent ways. They are nevertheless significant in a variety of contexts. And they have clear relationships, both direct and indirect, to legal definitions. The federal government has historically used a minimum blood quantum standard to determine who was eligible to receive treaty rights, or to sell property and manage

his or her own financial affairs.[20] Blood quantum is *one* of the criteria that determines eligibility for citizenship in many tribes; it therefore indirectly influences the claimant's relationship to the same kinds of rights, privileges, and responsibilities that legal definitions allow.[21]

But biological definitions of identity affect personal interactions as well as governmental decisions. Indian people with high blood quanta frequently have recognizable physical characteristics. As Cherokee Nation principal tribal chief Chad Smith observes, some people are easily recognizable as Indians because they pass "a brown paper bag test," meaning that their skin is "darker than a #10 paper sack." It is these individuals who are often most closely associated with negative racial stereotypes in the larger society. Native American Studies professor Devon Mihesuah makes a point about Indian women that is really applicable to either gender: "Appearance is the most visible aspect of one's race; it determines how Indian women define themselves and how others define and treat them. Their appearance, whether Caucasian, Indian, African, or mixed, either limits or broadens Indian women's choices of ethnic identity and ability to interact with non-Indians and other Indians."[22]

Every day, identifiably Indian people are turned away from restaurants, refused the use of public rest rooms, ranked as unintelligent by the education system, and categorized by the personnel of medical, social service, and other vital public agencies as "problems"—all strictly on the basis of their appearance. As Keetoowah Band Cherokee full-blood Donald G. notes, a recognizably Indian appearance can be a serious detriment to one's professional and personal aspirations: "It seems the darker you are, the less important you are, in some ways, to the employer. . . . To some, it would be discouraging. But I am four-fourths [i.e., full-blood] Cherokee, and it doesn't matter what someone says about me. . . . I feel for the person who doesn't like my skin color, you know?"

There are circumstances, however, in which it is difficult for the victims of negative racial stereotyping to maintain an attitude as philosophical as this. In one interview, a Mohawk friend, June L., illustrated the potential consequences of public judgments based on skin color. She reminded me of a terrifying episode that had once unfolded while I was visiting at her house. Our conversation was interrupted by a phone call informing this mother of five that her college-student son, who had spent the summer day working on a roof, had suddenly become ill while driving home. Feeling faint, he had pulled up to a local convenience store and made his way inside, asking for a drink of water. The clerk refused. Dangerously dehydrated, the young man collapsed on the floor from sunstroke. "The worst thing about it," June recalled, "was that I have to keep wondering: What was the reason for that? Did that clerk refuse to help my son because she was just a mean person? Or was it because she saw him stumble into the store and thought, 'Well, it's just some drunken Indian'?" Anxiety about social judgments of this kind are a fact of daily life for parents of children whose physical appearance makes their Indian ancestry clearly evident.

At the same time, June's remarks showed the opposite side to the coin of physical appearance. In some contexts, not conforming to the usual notions of "what Indians look like" can also be a liability:

> My aunt was assistant dean at a large Ivy League university. One day she called me on the phone. She had one scholarship to give out to an Indian student. One of the students being considered was blonde-haired and blue-eyed. The other one was black-haired and dark-skinned, and she looked Indian. The blonde girl's grades were a little better. My aunt didn't know what to do. She said to me, "Both these girls are tribal members. Both of them are qualified [for the scholarship]. They're sitting outside my office. What would *you* do?" I told her that, as an Indian person, there was only one thing I *could* say. Which was to give the money to the one with the dark skin. As Indian people, we *do* want to have Indian people that *look* like they're Indian to represent us.

Readers may be surprised by such a candid statement. But June's pragmatic reasoning takes account of certain historical realities. As she explained further, "We like people to *know* who's doing those accomplishments, like getting scholarships. We want them to know this is an Indian person doing this. Because I come from a background where if you looked Indian, you were put in special education because the schools said you couldn't learn. And it wasn't true. We need Indian people today who look Indian to show everyone the things we can do."

A physical appearance that is judged insufficiently "Indian" can also act as a barrier to participation in certain cultural activities. Bill T., a Wichita and Seneca minister in his mid-fifties, recalls that, in his youth, he witnessed light-skinned individuals who attempted to participate in powwow dances being evicted from the arena. "That kind of thing is still happening today," he added sadly, and other respondents readily confirmed this observation. A more unusual instance of the relevance of physical appearance to cultural participation was volunteered by Frank D., a Hopi respondent. His tribe's ceremonial dances feature the appearance of powerful spirit beings called kachinas, which are embodied by masked Hopi men. Ideally, the everyday, human identity of the dancers remains unknown to observers. Frank commented on the subject of tribal members whose skin tone is noticeably either lighter or darker than the norm:

Frank D.: Say, for instance, if a Hopi marries a black person . . . [and] you get a male child . . . it's gonna be darker skinned. It might even be black. A black kachina just wouldn't fit out here [at Hopi]. You see, everybody'd know who it is. He'd be very visible [in the ceremonial dances]. . . . It'd be very hard on that individual. Kids don't work the other way, too—if they're real light. . . . Kachinas gotta be *brown*.

Author: So there are certain ceremonial roles that people could not fill because of their appearance?

Frank D.: Well, they *could*, but it would be awful tough. A lot of these [ceremonial] things are done with secrecy. No one knows who the kachinas are. Or at least, the kids don't. And then, say you get somebody who really stands out, then everybody knows who that [dancer] is, and it's not good. For the ceremony—because everybody knows who that person is. And so the kids will start asking questions—"How come that kachina's so dark, so black?" or "How come that kachina's white?" They start asking questions and it's really hard. So I think, if you're thinking about kids, it's really better if kachinas are brown.

Finally, the physical appearance borne by mixed bloods may not only create barriers to tribal cultural participation; it may also offer an occasion for outrightly shaming them. Cornelia S. remembers her days at the Eufala Indian School:

> You *had* to be Indian to be [allowed admission] there. . . . But . . . if [certain students] . . . didn't look as Indian as we did, or if they looked like they were white, they were kind of looked down upon, like treated differently because [people would say] "oh, that's just a white person." . . . They just [would] tease 'em and stuff. Say "oh, whatcha doin' white boy" or "white girl"—just stuff like that.

Nor is the social disapproval of light-skinned mixed bloods strictly the stuff of schoolyard teasing. The same respondent added that even adults confront questions of blood quantum with dead seriousness:

> Us Indians, whenever we see someone else who is saying that they're Indian . . . or trying to be around us Indians, and act like us, and they don't look like they're Indian and we know that they're not as much Indian as *we* are, yeah, we look at them like they're not Indian and, ya know, don't really like why they're acting like that. . . . But you know, I'm not *that* far off . . . into judging other people and what color [they are].

The late author Michael Dorris, a member of the Modoc tribe (California), has written that humiliations related to his appearance were part of his daily experience. He describes (in his account of his family's struggle with his son's fetal alcohol syndrome, *The Broken Cord*) an encounter with a hospital admissions staff, to whom he had just identified himself and his son as Indians. "They surveyed my appearance with curiosity. It was an expression I recognized, a reaction, familiar to most people of mixed-blood ancestry, that said, 'You don't *look* like an Indian.' No matter how often it

happened, no matter how frequently I was blamed by strangers for not resembling their image of some Hollywood Sitting Bull, I was still defensive and vulnerable. 'I'm part Indian,' I explained."[23]

Even his tragic death has not safeguarded Dorris from insinuations about inadequate blood quantum. Shortly after his 1997 suicide, a story on his life and death in *New York* magazine reported that the author's fair complexion had always caused some observers to wonder about his racial identity and archly repeated a rumor: "It is said he . . . [eventually] discovered tanning booths."[24]

In short, many Indian people, both individually and collectively, continue to embrace the assumption that close biological connections to other Indian people—and the distinctive physical appearance that may accompany those connections—imply a stronger claim on identity than do more distant ones. As Potawatomi scholar of Native American Studies Terry Wilson summarizes, "Few, if any, Native Americans, regardless of upbringing in rural, reservation, or urban setting, ignore their own and other Indians' blood quantum in everyday life. Those whose physical appearances render their Indian identities suspect are subject to suspicious scrutiny until precise cultural explanations, especially blood quantum, are offered or discovered."[25]

DISCUSSION QUESTIONS

1. As Garroutte describes them, what are the various ways that one might be defined as a "real" Indian? When might these different definitions of "Indianness" conflict?
2. Thinking about June's description of her son being refused a drink of water and her advice about who should receive the Indian scholarship, do you see any consistencies or inconsistencies in her approach?

NOTES

1. Thornton surveyed 302 of the 317 tribes in the lower forty-eight states that enjoyed federal acknowledgment in 1997. He found that 204 tribes had some minimum blood quantum requirement, while the remaining

98 had none. Russell Thornton, "Tribal Membership Requirements and the Demography of 'Old' and 'New' Native Americans," *Population Research and Policy Review* 16 (1997): 37.

2. The two mentions of "Indians" in the Constitution appear in passages regarding the regulation of commerce and the taking of a federal census. The word "tribe" also appears once in the Constitution, in the Commerce Clause.

3. Sharon O'Brien, "Tribes and Indians: With Whom Does the United States Maintain a Relationship?" *Notre Dame Law Review* 66 (1991): 1481.

4. One particularly important law that provides no definition of "Indian" is the Major Crimes Act of 1885 (23 Stat. 385, U.S.C. Sec. 1153). It subjects reservation Indians to federal prosecution for certain offenses for which non-Indians would face only state prosecution.

5. For a detailed discussion of legal cases bearing on the definition of "Indian," see Felix S. Cohen, *Handbook of Federal Indian Law* (Charlottesville, Va.: Michie/Bobbs-Merrill, 1982).

6. Wilcomb E. Washburn, *Red Man's Land/White Man's Law: A Study of the Past and Present States of the American Indian* (New York: Charles Scribner's Sons, 1971).

7. These agencies administer resources and programs in areas such as education, health, social services, tribal governance and administration, law enforcement, nutrition, resource management, tribal economic development, employment, and the like. The most recently published source describing various programs and the requirements for participation is Roger Walk, *Federal Assistance to Native Americans: A Report Prepared for the Senate Select Committee on Indian Affairs of the US Senate* (Washington, D.C.: Government Printing Office, 1991). In fiscal year 2001, recognized tribes and their members had access to approximately four billion dollars of federal funding for various social programs. U.S. Government Accounting Office, *Indian Issues: Improvements Needed in Tribal Recognition Process,* Report to Congressional Requesters, Washington D.C.: Government Printing Office, November 2001.

8. Non-Indian students in my classes sometimes tell me that Indians also regularly receive such windfalls as free cars and monthly checks from the government strictly because of their race. It is my sad duty to puncture this fantasy; there is no truth in it. The common belief that Indians receive "free money" from the government probably stems from the fact that the government holds land in trust for certain tribes. As part of its trust responsibility, it may then lease that land, collect the revenue, and distribute it to the tribal members. Thus, some Indians do receive government checks, but these do not represent some kind of manna from heaven; they are simply the profits derived from lands which they own.

For details on the special, political-economic relationship of Indians to the federal government in relation to taxation and licensure, see Gary D. Sandefur, "Economic Development and Employment Opportunities for American Indians," in *American Indians: Social Justice and Public Policy,* ed. Donald E. Green and Thomas V. Tonneson, Ethnicity and Public Policy Series, vol. 9 (Milwaukee: University of Wisconsin System Institute on Race and Ethnicity, 1991), 208–22.

9. Aside from the issue of adopted children, the legal requirements for establishing legal status as Indian in Canada have been even more complicated and peculiar than the U.S. ones, and the tensions related to them even more severe. Until 1985, a Canadian Indian woman who married a legally non-Indian man lost her legal status as an Indian, and her children (who might have a blood quantum of one-half) could never be recognized as Indian under Canadian law. A non-Indian woman who married an Indian man, however, gained Indian status for herself and her children. Men could neither gain nor lose Indian status through marriage. When a 1985 bill amended the Indian Act, which governed such matters, the issue of "real Indianness" came to a head. Many Canadian Indian women and children sought and received Indian legal status, but when they attempted to return to the reservations, they often got a chilly welcome from Indian communities already overburdened with financial obligations to their existing population. Like their American counterparts, Canadian Indian bands continue to struggle with the issue of how to conceive the boundaries of their membership. For a good discussion of Canadian Indian identification policies, see Eugeen Roosens, *Creating Ethnicity: The Process of Ethnogenesis* (Newbury Park, Calif.: Sage, 1989).

10. Shania Twain quoted in Jackie Bissley, "Country Star Shania Twain's Candor Is Challenged," *Indian Country Today,* 9–16 April 1996.

11. Quoted in Jackie Bissley, "Country Singer Says Stories Robbing Her of Her Native Roots," *Indian Country Today,* 16–23 April 1996. Even Twain's unusual situation does not exhaust the intricate aspects of the Canadian legal system as it struggles with matters of Indian identity. Roosens describes other fine points of Indian identity in force north of the border over a period of several decades:

Since 1951, to be registered as an Indian one has to be the legitimate child of an Indian father. The ethnic origin of the mother is irrelevant. . . . Furthermore, if the grandmother on the Indian side of a mixed marriage (the father's mother) is a non-Indian by descent, then the grandchild loses his or her status at the age of 21. Thus, one can be officially born an Indian and lose this status at the age of maturity. (Roosens, *Creating Ethnicity,* 24)

12. Roosens, *Creating Ethnicity,* 41–42. Roosens is discussing the situation of Canadian Indians, but the same remarks apply to American Indians.

13. G. William Rice, "There and Back Again—An Indian Hobbit's Holiday: Indians Teaching Indian Law," *New Mexico Law Review* 26, no. 2 (1996): 176.

14. Melissa L. Meyer, "American Indian Blood Quantum Requirements: Blood Is Thicker than Family," in *Over the Edge: Remapping the American West,* ed. Valerie J. Matsumoto and Blake Allmendiger (Berkeley: University of California Press, 1999).

15. Historians such as Grace Steele Woodward and Marion Starkey have made this argument. But see also Julia Coates, "None of Us Is Supposed to Be Here" (Ph.D. diss., University of New Mexico, 2002) for a revisionist understanding of Cherokee history.

16. C. Matthew Snipp, "Who Are American Indians? Some Observations about the Perils and Pitfalls of Data for Race and Ethnicity," *Population Research and Policy Review* 5 (1986): 249. For excellent and intriguing discussions of the evolution of ideas about blood relationships among European and Euro-American peoples over several centuries, and transference of these ideas into American Indian tribal populations, see Meyer, "Blood Quantum Requirements," and Circe Sturm, *Blood Politics: Race, Culture, and Identity in the Cherokee Nation of Oklahoma* (Berkeley: University of California Press, 2002). See further Peggy Pascoe, "Miscegenation Law, Court Cases, and Ideologies of 'race' in Twentieth Century America," *Journal of American History* 83, no. 1 (June 1996): 44–69. For the processes by which some of these theories were rejected by scientists, see Elazar Barkan, *Retreat of Scientific Racism: Changing Concepts of Race in Britain and the United States between the World Wars* (Cambridge: Cambridge University Press, 1992).

17. Thomas Biolsi, "The Birth of the Reservation: Making the Modern Individual among the Lakota," *American Ethnologist* 22, no. 1 (February 1995): 28–49; Patrick Limerick, *The Legacy of Conquest: The Unbroken Past of the American West* (New York: W. W. Norton, 1988).

18. Naomi Zack, "Mixed Black and White Race and Public Policy," *Hypatia* 10, 1 (1995): 120–32; Ariela J. Gross, "Litigating Whiteness: Trials of Racial Determination in the Nineteenth-Century South," *Yale Law Journal* 108 (1998): 109–88.

19. Jack D. Forbes, "The Manipulation of Race, Caste, and Identity: Classifying AfroAmericans, Native Americans and Red-Black People," *Journal of Ethnic Studies* 17, no. 4 (1990): 24; original emphasis. Indians are "lost," in Forbes' sense, both to black *and* to white racial classifications, but at differing rates. Popular conventions of racial classification in America tend to prevent individuals with any discernible black ancestry from identifying themselves as Indians. As an interview respondent quoted by anthropologist Circe Sturm observes, "This is America, where being to any degree Black is the same thing as being to any degree pregnant." Sturm, *Blood Politics,* 188.

By contrast, individuals with discernible white ancestry are *sometimes* allowed by others to identify as Indian. In their case the legitimacy of their assertion is likely to be evaluated with reference to the *amount* of white ancestry, and with beliefs about whether that amount is enough to merely *dilute* or to entirely *compromise* Indian identity. Other factors, such as culture and upbringing, may also be taken into account. People of partial white ancestry, in other words, are typically somewhat more free (although not entirely free) to negotiate a legitimate identity as Indian than are people of partial black ancestry.

20. For further details on the historical impact of blood quantum on individuals' legal rights, see Felix S. Cohen, *Cohen's Handbook of Federal Indian Law* (Charlottesville, Va.: Michie/Bobbs-Merrill, 1982).

21. For a listing of the blood quantum requirements that different tribes require for tribal citizenship, see Edgar Lister, "Tribal Membership Rates and Requirements," unpublished table (Washington, D.C.: Indian Health Service, 1987). An edited version of the table appears in C. Matthew Snipp, *American Indians: The First of This Land* (New York: Russell Sage Foundation, 1989), appendix.

22. Devon A. Mihesuah, "Commonality of Difference: American Indian Women and History," in *Natives and Academics: Researching and Writing about American Indians,* ed. Devon A. Mihesuah (Lincoln: University of Nebraska Press, 1998), 42. For a fascinating and detailed discussion of the significance of appearance among contemporary Cherokees in Oklahoma, see Sturm, *Blood Politics,* 108–15.

23. Michael Dorris, *The Broken Cord* (New York: Harper Perennial, 1990), 22.

24. Eric Konigsberg, "Michael Dorris's Troubled Sleep," *New York Magazine,* 16 June 1997, 33. For a related article, see Jerry Reynolds, "Indian Writers: The Good, the Bad, and the Could Be, Part 2: Indian Writers: Real or Imagined," *Indian Country Today,* 15 September 1993.

25. Terry P. Wilson, "Blood Quantum: Native American Mixed Bloods," in *Racially Mixed People in America,* ed. Maria P. P. Root (Newbury Park, Calif.: Sage, 1992), 109.

READING 5

Asian American Panethnicity: Contemporary National and Transnational Possibilities

Yen Le Espiritu

In an article published in *Gidra*, an activist Asian American news magazine, Naomi Iwasaki (1999, under "Asian American or Not") writes, "You know, the hardest thing about pan-Asian solidarity is the 'pan' part. It forces us all to step outside of our comfort zones, whether they be constructed by ethnicity, class, home city, identity, whatever." Iwasaki's statement calls attention to the social constructedness of panethnicity—panethnic identities are self-conscious products of political choice and actions, not of inherited phenotypes, bloodlines, or cultural traditions. In my 1992 publication *Asian American Panethnicity: Bridging Institutions and Identities,* I identify the twin roots of Asian American panethnicity—in the racialization of Asian national groups by dominant groups and in Asian Americans' responses to those constructions. Employing a racial formation perspective (Omi and Winant 1986), I argue that the racialist constructions of Asians as homogeneous and interchangeable spawn important alliances and affiliations among ethnic and immigrant groups of Asian origin. Adopting the dominant group's categorization of them, Asian Americans have institutionalized pan-Asianism as their political instrument, thereby enlarging their own capacities to challenge and transform the existing structure of power. In other words, Asian Americans did not just adopt the pan-Asian concept but also transformed it to conform to their political, economic, and ideological needs.

Though powerful, pan-Asianism is not unproblematic: it can mask salient divisions, subsume nondominant groups, and create marginalities, all

Yen Le Espiritu is a professor of ethnic studies at the University of California, San Diego.

of which threatens the legitimacy and effectiveness of pan-Asianism and bolsters (however inadvertently) the racist discourses and practices that construct Asians as homogeneous. In the three decades since the emergence of the pan-Asian concept in the late 1960s, Asian American communities have changed in dramatic ways. No longer constrained by race-based exclusion laws, Asian immigrants began arriving in much larger numbers than before. Many of the post-1965 immigrants have little direct experience with the Asian American movement and little reason to think of themselves as Asian American rather than as immigrants, as low-wage workers, or as members of different national and ethnic groups (Espiritu et al. 2000, 131). Moreover, recent immigration has further diversified Asian Americans along cultural, generational, economic, and political lines—all of which have compounded the difficulties of forging pan-Asian identities and institutions.

This . . . review [of] the history of Asian American panethnicity in the United States *then to now* [pays] particular attention to the ways in which pan-Asian identities and institutions have been transformed by the post-1965 immigration and by changes in the global economy. The first section documents the social, political, and demographic factors that led to the emergence of pan-Asianism in the late 1960s and early 1970s. The second details how the post-1965 immigration has diversified the Asian American population and made it more difficult for groups to imagine shared origins and destinies. The third establishes that the construction of Asian American identities not only is a response to conditions in the United States but also is deeply bound to U.S. colonial and imperialist practices that propel the contemporary migration of Asians to the United States in the first place. The fourth discusses the political importance of cross-group affiliation, not only among Asians but also with other groups across class, ethnic, racial, and national lines. Of the four sections, the third conveys the central argument: pan-Asianism in the United States has been determined not exclusively by events and population changes in the United States but also by U.S.

colonialism and imperialism in Asia. Much of the published work in the field of U.S. immigration studies has remained "America-centric," focusing on the immigrants' "modes of incorporation" and the process of their "becoming American." In contrast, this [reading] takes a *critical transnational approach* to the study of Asian Americans, calling attention to the deep historical entanglements of immigration and imperialism.[1]

COMING TOGETHER: THE EMERGENCE OF PAN-ASIANISM

Arriving in the United States, nineteenth-century immigrants from Asian countries did not think of themselves as "Asians." Coming from specific districts and provinces in different nations, Asian immigrant groups did not even think of themselves as Chinese, Japanese, Korean, and so forth, but rather as people from Toishan, Hoiping, or some other district in Guandong Province in China or from Hiroshima, Yamaguchi, or some other prefecture in Japan. Members of each group considered themselves culturally and politically distinct. Historical enmities between their countries of origin further separated the groups even before their arrival in the United States. However, non-Asians had little understanding or appreciation of these distinctions. For the most part, outsiders accorded to people from Asia certain common characteristics and traits that were essentially supranational. Indeed, the exclusion acts and quotas limiting Asian immigration to the United States relied on racialist constructions of Asians as homogeneous (Lowe 1991, 28).

The development of panethnicity among Asian Americans has a short history. It was not until the late 1960s, with the advent of the Asian American movement, that a pan-Asian consciousness and constituency were first formed. Before the 1960s, Asians in the United States frequently practiced ethnic disidentification: distancing one's group from another group so as not to be mistaken for a member of that group and to avoid suffering the blame for its presumed misdeeds (Hayano 1981, 161, 162; Daniels 1988, 113). For example, in the

late nineteenth century, aware of Chinese exclusion, Japanese immigrant leaders did everything possible to distinguish themselves from the Chinese immigrants (Ichioka 1988, 250). In the end Japanese attempts at disidentification failed. With the passage of the 1924 Immigration Act, the Japanese joined the Chinese as a people deemed unworthy of becoming Americans. Less than two decades later, after the bombing of Pearl Harbor, it was the turn of the Chinese to disassociate themselves from the Japanese. Fearful that they would be targets of anti-Japanese activities, many Chinese immigrants took to wearing buttons that proclaimed positively, "I'm Chinese." Some Chinese immigrants—and also Korean and Filipino migrants—even joined the white persecution with buttons that added, "I hate Japs worse than you do" (Daniels 1988, 205; Takaki 1989, 370–71). These two examples are instructive not only as evidence of ethnic disidentification but also as documentation of the pervasiveness of racial lumping. Precisely because of racial lumping, persons of Asian ancestry found it necessary to disassociate themselves from other Asian groups.

The development of a pan-Asian consciousness and constituency reflected broader societal developments and demographic changes as well as the group's political agenda. Before World War II, pan-Asian unity was not feasible because the predominantly foreign-born Asian population did not share a common language. During the postwar years, owing to immigration restrictions and the growing dominance of the second and even third generations, U.S.-born Asians outnumbered immigrants. By 1960 approximately two-thirds of the Asian population in California had been born in the United States (Ong 1989, 5–8). With English as the common language, persons from different Asian backgrounds were able to communicate with one another (Ling 1984, 73) and in so doing to create a common identity associated with the United States. Also, the breakdown of economic and residential barriers during the postwar period provided the first opportunity for an unprecedented number of Asian Americans to come into intimate, sustained contact with the larger society—and with one another. Formerly homogeneous, the Asian ethnic enclaves started to house mixed-Asian communities, as well as non-Asian groups. Multigroup suburban centers also emerged. Paul Wong (1972, 34) reported that since the early 1960s Asian Americans of diverse national origins had moved into the suburbs outside the major Asian communities such as Berkeley and San Mateo, California. Although a small proportion of the local population, these Asian Americans tended to congregate in pockets; consequently, in some residential blocks a majority of the residents were Asian Americans.

Although broader social struggles and internal demographic changes provided the impetus for the Asian American movement, it was the Asian Americans' politics—explicitly radical, confrontational, and pan-Asian—that shaped the movement's content. Inspired by anticolonial revolutions in Asia and by black and Chicano revolutionary nationalism, college students of Asian ancestry sought to transcend inter-Asian ethnic divisions and to ally themselves with other "Third World" minorities (Blauner 1972, ch. 2; Omatsu 1994). Through pan-Asian organizations, publications, and Asian American studies programs, Asian American activists forged a pan-Asian consciousness by highlighting their shared resistance to Western imperialism and to U.S. racism. The pan-Asian concept enabled diverse Asian American groups to understand their "unequal circumstances and histories as being related" (Lowe 1991, 30). By the mid-1970s, "Asian American" had become a familiar term (Lott 1976, 30). Although first coined by college activists, the pan-Asian concept began to be used extensively by professional and community spokespersons to lobby for the health and welfare of Americans of Asian descent. Commenting on the "literally scores of pan-Asian organizations" in the mid-1970s, William Liu (1976, 6) asserted that "the idea of pan-Asian cooperation [was] viable and ripe for development."

The advent of state-sponsored affirmative action programs provided another material reason for Asian American subgroups to consolidate their efforts. Because the welfare state bureaucracy often treats all Asian Americans as a single administrative unit in distributing economic and political resources, it imposes a pan-Asian structure on persons and communities dependent on government support. As dealings with government bureaucracies increased, political organization along a pan-Asian line became necessary, not only because numbers confer power but also because the pan-Asian category is the institutionally relevant category in the political and legal system. Administratively treated as a homogeneous group, Asian Americans found it necessary—and even advantageous—to respond as a group. The pan-Asian strategy has led to some political victories. For example, Asian American legislators, community leaders, and organizations united to fight the Census Bureau's proposal to collapse all Asian racial codes into one summary category for the 1980 and 1990 censuses. Partly in response to the strength of their political lobbying, the Census Bureau finally conceded to the coalition's demand for a detailed enumeration of Asian subgroups.[2] Indeed, the emergence of the pan-Asian entity may be one of the most significant political developments in Asian American affairs. . . .

ETHNIC DIVERSIFICATION

Before the post-1965 immigration surge, the Asian American population was composed mainly of three ethnic groups: Japanese, Chinese, and Filipino. In 1970 Japanese Americans constituted the single largest group (41 percent of the Asian American population), followed by Chinese Americans (30 percent) and Filipino Americans (24 percent). Members of other national origins groups (mostly Koreans) represented less than 5 percent of the Asian American population total (Zhou and Gatewood 2000, 13). Coming of age in the 1960s, U.S.-born Japanese and Chinese Americans formed the core force of the Asian American movement on West Coast college campuses and in the Northeast (Espiritu 1992). In contrast, in 2000 the U.S. census recorded twenty-four national origins groups, and no single group accounted for more than one-quarter of the Asian American population. Although Japan has sent very few immigrants to the United States, the Philippines, China and Taiwan, Korea, India, and Vietnam have been on the list of the top ten sending countries since 1980 (USINS 1997). Reflecting these changing immigration patterns, in 2000 the Japanese American share of the Asian American population fell to only 8 percent, and the five largest Asian American groups were Chinese and Taiwanese (24 percent), Filipino (18 percent), Asian Indian (17 percent), Korean (11 percent), and Vietnamese (11 percent) (Barnes and Bennett 2002).[3] The new Asian American demographics have complicated the delicate pan-Asian alignments created in the 1960s and 1970s among the then-largest Asian American groups: Japanese, Chinese, and, to a lesser extent, Filipino Americans.

Generational Diversification

Between the 1940s and 1960s, when immigration from Asia was restricted, U.S.-born Asian Americans dominated the Asian American population. By the 1970s the foreign-born reemerged as a large majority. In 2000, 7.2 million Asian Pacific Americans—approximately 70 percent of the total Asian American population—were foreign-born (U.S. Department of Commerce 2002). The foreign-born component dominated all Asian American groups except for Japanese Americans; over 60 percent of Filipinos and nearly 80 percent of Vietnamese and other Asians were foreign-born (Zhou and Gatewood 2000, 14). Because of legal exclusion in the past, it is only among the two oldest immigrant groups—the Japanese and Chinese Americans—that a sizable third or fourth generation exists. Among Asian American children under eighteen years of age, more than 90 percent are either foreign-born or children of foreign-born parents (Zhou and Gatewood 2000, 23). Paul Ong and Suzanne Hee (1993) have predicted that the foreign-born segment will still be a majority in the year 2020.

Class Diversification

Post-1965 immigration has also increased the economic diversity of Asian Americans. In contrast to the largely unskilled immigrant population of the pre–World War II period, the new arrivals include not only low-wage service-sector workers but also significant numbers of white-collar professionals. According to the 1990 U.S. census, more than 60 percent of immigrants (age twenty-five or older) from India and Taiwan reported having attained a college degree (three times the proportion of average Americans), but fewer than 5 percent of those from Cambodia and Laos made such a report. Among the employed workers, about 45 percent of immigrants from India and Taiwan held managerial or professional occupations, more than twice the proportion of average American workers, but fewer than 5 percent of those from Laos and only about 10 percent of those from Cambodia had held such a position. Further, immigrants from India, the Philippines, and Taiwan reported a median household income of about $45,000, compared to $30,000 for average American households; those from Cambodia and highland Laos reported a median household income below $20,000. . . .

Implications for Panethnicity in Contemporary Asian America

By most accounts, the expanding diversity of Asian Americans has brought into question the very definition of Asian America—and along with it, the feasibility and appropriateness of pan-Asian identities and practices. In a major public policy report on the state of Asian America, editor Paul Ong (2000) suggests that the pan-Asian identity is "fragile," citing as evidence the group's ethnic and economic diversity as well as the growing population of bi- and multiracial Asian Americans who want to acknowledge their combined racial heritage.[4] Similarly, in the introduction to their substantial multidisciplinary reader on contemporary Asian America, editors Min Zhou and James Gatewood (2000, 27) caution that "differences in class background among the immigrant generation and divergent modes of incorporation of that generation can deter the formation of panethnicity." Comparing the experiences of affluent Chinese immigrants and Cambodian refugees, Aihwa Ong (1996, 751) concludes that the category "Asian American" "must confront the contradictions and instabilities within the imposed solidarity, brought about by the group's internal class, ethnic, and racial stratifications." In Asian American studies, many scholars have critically pointed to the field's privileging of East Asians (the "old" Asian Americans) over South and Southeast Asians (the "new" Asian Americans)—a clear indictment of the suppression of diverse histories, epistemologies, and voices within the pan-Asian framework. For example, in an edited volume on South Asians in Asian America aptly titled *A Part, Yet Apart*, Rajiv Shankar (1998, x) laments that South Asians "find themselves so unnoticed as an entity that they feel as if they are merely a crypto-group, often included but easily marginalized within the house of Asian America."

A CRITICAL TRANSNATIONAL APPROACH TO PAN-ASIAN ETHNICITY

Elsewhere (Espiritu and Ong 1994; Espiritu 1992, 1996), I have discussed at length one of the challenges facing the contemporary Asian American community: how do Asian Americans build pan-Asian solidarity amid increasing diversities? Like other Asian American scholars and activists, I have suggested that if Asian Americans are to build a self-consciously pan-Asian solidarity, they need to take seriously the heterogeneities among their ranks and overcome the narrow dominance of the professional class and that of the two oldest Asian American groups. I still subscribe to this view—that Asian Americans need to tend to the social, political, and economic inequalities that exist within their communities. At the same time, I am concerned that this view narrowly locates the "problems" of pan-Asian ethnicity *not* in the political and economic oppression or violence that produced massive displacements and migrations of Asians in the first place, but in the internal workings of the Asian American community itself. Thus

told, the internal diversities within Asian America become "interiorized," and the focus is shifted away from global politics and power and toward identity politics within Asian America. . . .

Certainly, ethnic, generational, and class diversity pose new obstacles for pan-Asian mobilization. But to begin and stop the analysis here would be to engage in an "America-centric" approach to the question of the relation between race, ethnicity, nation, and migration. From this perspective, the analysis of pan-Asian ethnicity begins when the immigrants arrive on U.S. soil. Thus told, intra-Asian differences—along ethnic, class, and generational lines—become naturalized, unmediated by global politics and power. Departing from this perspective, I resituate the discussion of pan-Asian relations within a critical transnational framework, one that is attentive to global relations, which set the context for immigration and immigrant life. That is, instead of just asking how the massive influx of immigrants from Asia—and the resultant diversification of the population along class, generational, and ethnic lines—has reshaped pan-Asian identities and practices, we also need to ask how the influx of immigrants from Asia—with its specific configurations—came into being in the first place. As I argue later, pan-Asian American "racial formation" has been determined not exclusively by events in the United States but also by U.S. geopolitical interests in Asia and needs for different types and sources of labor—all of which have produced the particular ethnic, generational, and class configurations that have rendered the term "Asian American" problematic for the post-1965 community.

In the United States public discussion on immigration is fundamentally about people who cross borders. The media, elected officials, and the general public often represent border crossers as desperate individuals migrating in search of the "land of opportunity." This representation makes invisible other important border crossers: U.S. colonizers, military, and corporations that invade and forcefully deplete the economic and cultural resources of less-powerful countries. Calling attention to global structures of inequality, recent social theorists have linked migration processes with the global penetration of Western economic systems, technological infrastructures, and popular cultures in non-Western countries (Burawoy 1976; Petras 1978; Portes 1978; Zolberg 1986). Although details vary, these works posit that the internalization of a capitalistic economic system in "Third World" countries has produced imbalances in their internal social and economic structures and subsequently spurred emigration. As Saskia Sassen (1992, 15) argues, "U.S. efforts to open its own and other countries to the flow of capital, goods, services, and information created the conditions that mobilized people for migration." Indeed, all of the nation-states from which the largest number of U.S. immigrants originate—Mexico, China (including Taiwan and Hong Kong), the Philippines, El Salvador, the Dominican Republic, South Korea, Guatemala, Vietnam, Laos, and Cambodia—have had sustained and sometimes intimate social, political, and economic relations with the United States.

A transnational approach that stresses the global structures of inequality is critical for understanding Asian immigration and Asian American lives in the United States. Linking global economic development with global histories of colonialism, Edna Bonacich and Lucie Cheng (1984) argue that the pre–World War II immigration of Asians to the United States has to be understood within the context of the development of capitalism in Europe and the United States and the emergence of imperialism, especially in relation to Asia. From World War II onward, as the world economy became much more globally integrated, Asia was the site for U.S. expansion. As a result, contemporary immigrants from the Philippines, South Vietnam, South Korea, Cambodia, and Laos come from countries that have been deeply disrupted by U.S. colonialism, war, and neocolonial capitalism (Lowe 1996). The "transnational porosity between the United States and Asia" (Kang 1997, 408) means that "there has been an important continuity between the considerable distortion of social relations in Asian countries affected by U.S. imperialist war

and occupation and the emigration of Asian labor to the United States" (Lowe 1996, 7).

The history of U.S. imperialism in Asia suggests that Asian American "racial formation" has never been exclusively shaped by events in the United States but has also been influenced by U.S. colonialism, neocolonialism, and militarism in Asia. However, the process of Asian American racial formation has been neither singular nor unified. Owing to the multiple contexts of colonialism and its various extensions within the development of global capitalism, Asians in the United States have experienced different processes of racialization specific to each group's historical and material conditions. It is these historical and material conditions—rather than intrinsic intra-Asian differences—that we need to investigate to understand the uneven formation of panethnicity among Asian Americans. . . . I confine my analysis to the experiences of Filipino immigrants and Vietnamese refugees—two groups with very different socioeconomic profiles—to illustrate the importance of a global conceptual framework in the theorizing of Asian American panethnicity.

Filipinos: Colonized Immigrant

In the twenty years following passage of the 1965 Immigration Act, about 40 percent of the documented immigration to the United States has come from Asia. The Philippines has been the largest source, with Filipinos comprising nearly one-quarter of the total Asian immigration. In the 1961 to 1965 period, fewer than 16,000 Filipinos immigrated to the United States, compared to more than 210,000 in the 1981 to 1985 period. Since 1979 over 40,000 Filipinos have been admitted annually, making the Philippines the second-largest source of all immigration, surpassed only by Mexico. Overall, the post-1965 Filipino immigrants constitute a relatively affluent group: in 1990 more than half joined the ranks of managers and professionals; their median household income exceeded that of all Americans and even that of whites; and the percentage of Filipino college graduates was twice that of all Americans. As Zhou and Gatewood (2000) report, many Filipino immigrants to the United States are college graduates with transferable job skills.

Unlike European or other Asian groups, Filipinos come from a homeland that was once a U.S. colony. Therefore, the Filipino American history of immigration and settlement can best be understood within the context of the colonial and postcolonial association between the Philippines and the United States. Since the 1960s the Philippines has sent the largest number of professional immigrants to the United States, the majority of whom are physicians, nurses, and other health-related practitioners (Rumbaut 1991). The overrepresentation of health professionals among contemporary Filipino immigrants is not accidental; it is the result of a U.S.-built economic infrastructure in the Philippines that proved to be ill suited to the needs of the local populace. During the 1960s, responding to the needs of the United States in its ongoing war effort in Vietnam, the Philippines (over)developed medical and nursing programs to provide personnel to care for the military and civilian casualties in Vietnam. This health professional educational infrastructure remained in place after the Vietnam War had ended and has continued to produce a surplus of physicians and nurses, many of whom migrate to the United States (Liu and Cheng 1994). The migration of Filipino health professionals was also a direct response to deliberate recruitment by U.S. hospitals, nursing homes, and health organizations seeking to address their perennial shortage of medical personnel.

In particular, the Philippines has become the major source of foreign-trained nurses in the United States, with at least 25,000 Filipino nurses arriving between 1969 and 1985. In fact, many women in the Philippines study nursing in the hope of securing employment abroad, and many of the nursing programs in the Philippines accordingly orient themselves toward supplying the U.S. market (Ong and Azores 1994). . . . By the 1960s Filipina nurses entered the United States through two major avenues: the Exchange Visitor Program and the new occupational preference categories of the Immigration Act of 1965.

Vietnamese: The Refugees

Unlike Filipino and most other contemporary immigrants, the Vietnamese were pushed out of their country and forced to leave without adequate preparation and with little control over their final destinations. Because refugees are less likely to be a self-selected labor force than economic migrants, their numbers include many unemployables: young children, the elderly, religious and political leaders, and people in poor mental and physical condition (Portes and Rumbaut 1990). They are also less likely to have acquired readily transferable skills and are more likely to have made investments (in training and education) specific to the country of origin. For example, significant numbers of Southeast Asian military personnel possess skills for which there is no longer a market in the United States. In a discussion of the economic diversity within Asian America, Evelyn Hu-DeHart (1999, 17) refers to Vietnamese and other Southeast Asian Americans as "the Other Asian America": "'traumatized' immigrants who do not arrive with families intact, and do not come armed with social skills and human capital that can be readily adapted to modern American society." Zhou and Gatewood (2000, 16) concur: "Southeast Asian refugees . . . were pushed out of their homelands by force and suffer tremendous postwar trauma and social displacement, compounded by a lack of education and professional skills, which negatively affects their resettlement."

The Vietnamese are the largest of the refugee groups to have settled in the United States since the mid-1970s. Their arrival is primarily the result of U.S. military intervention in Southeast Asia. I will not rehearse here the violent history of U.S. engagement in the Vietnam War, except to point out that the U.S. desire to contain the spread of communism in Southeast Asia rendered Vietnam completely dependent on U.S. financial and material assistance for its military, its administration, and its economy (Viviani 1984, 13). Soon after the withdrawal of U.S. troops from Vietnam in April 1975, the North Vietnamese took over South Vietnam, triggering an exodus of refugees who fled the country by sea, land, and air. Influenced by the pervasive American presence in their countries in the decade before 1975, some 135,000 Southeast Asian refugees—95 percent of whom were Vietnamese—fled to the United States that year. The number of refugees dropped to 15,000 in 1976 and 7,000 in 1977. Starting in 1978, a more heterogeneous second wave of refugees—the "boat people"—started streaming into the United States. Annual arrivals jumped from 20,574 in 1978 to 76,521 in 1979, to 163,799 in 1980. Their exodus was triggered by continued conflict, natural disasters, and deteriorating economic conditions in Vietnam and also by the legacy of thirty years of warfare, which "demolished cities, destroyed farmland, denuded forests, poisoned water sources, and left countless unexploded mines" (Chan 1991, 157). By 1990 Vietnamese Americans numbered over 615,000, constituting almost 10 percent of the nation's Asian American population.

The Vietnam War (as well as the Korean War) was a major direct and indirect contributor to the supply of working-class Asian immigrants. With the exception of the relatively small elite group who left at the fall of Saigon, most of the refugees lacked education, job skills, and measurable economic resources (Zhou 2001). In addition, the post-1978 refugees had suffered terrible tragedies under the new Communist regimes, survived brutal journeys to neighboring countries, and endured prolonged stays in refugee camps where they received little education and/or job training prior to their resettlement in the United States. Once in the United States, almost all of the refugees started out on public assistance (Zhou 2001, 188). Although their economic situation has improved over the years, the Vietnamese are still heavily concentrated in minimum-wage jobs and still disproportionately rely on public assistance to survive. By 1990 the poverty rate of the Vietnamese stood at 25 percent,

down from 28 percent in 1980 but still substantially higher than the national average (Zhou 2001).

Using the Filipino and Vietnamese cases as examples, I argue that different circumstances of exit—the product of different types of U.S. engagement in their respective countries—have shaped the size and timing of migration and the socio-economic composition of different Asian groups and thus have profoundly affected the process of group formation and differentiation in the United States. Given their divergent migration histories and disparate economic backgrounds, Asian groups from different ends of the class spectrum—such as Filipino Americans and Vietnamese Americans—have few material reasons to come together under the pan-Asian umbrella. Moreover, existing evidence indicates that pan-Asian organizations often reproduce these national and ethnic hierarchies as class and organizational hierarchies. . . .

PAN-ASIAN NATIONAL AND TRANSNATIONAL POSSIBILITIES

As we begin the twenty-first century, the Asian American community is at a crossroads: how is it to build pan-Asian solidarity amid increasing internal diversities and amid an increasingly racially polarized U.S. society? As I have argued here, Asian American panethnicity is a socially constructed identity that emerged in large part from the violence of racism and imperialism to contest and disrupt these structures of inequality and domination. But it is also a contested category, encompassing not only cultural differences but also social, political, and economic inequalities. In the past two decades underrepresented groups within the pan-Asian coalition have decried the dangers of an Asian American cultural and political agenda that erases differences or tokenizes and patronizes its less dominant members (Strobel 1996; Misir 1996; Nguyen 2002). But pan-Asian possibilities also abound. Since panethnic identities are self-conscious products of political choice and actions, I provide here examples of instances where Asian

Americans have made conscious choices to organize politically across difference.

The growing population of bi- and multiracial Asian Americans poses an immediate challenge to pan-Asianism. On the other hand, some existing evidence suggests that the growth in the population of multiracial Asians need not spell the end of pan-Asianism. For example, in their analyses of Asian American intermarriages from 1980 and 1990 census data, Larry Hajime Shinagawa and Gin Yong Pang (1996, 140–41) report a prominent countertrend toward pan-Asian interethnic marriages, regardless of gender, nativity, region, and generation: "For a span of ten years (1980 to 1990), nationally and for California, the number of Asian interethnic marriages approaches or now exceeds interracial marriages. Meanwhile, interethnic marriages for Asian Pacific men increased from 21.1 percent in 1980 to 64 percent in 1990, and for women from 10.8 percent to 45.5 percent." They attribute this rise to a combination of factors, including the large population increases and concentrations of Asian Americans, their growing similarities in socioeconomic attainment and middle-class orientation, and their growing racial consciousness in an increasingly racially stratified U.S. society.

But what of the multiracial children? According to the 2000 U.S. census, approximately 850,000 people reported that they were Asian and white, and 360,000 reported that they were two or more Asian groups (Barnes and Bennett 2002, table 4). While there exist no comprehensive data on the racial identification of multiracial Asians, the close contact with Asian American advocacy groups maintained by the Hapa Issues Forum (HIF)—a national multiracial Asian American organization—suggests that multiracial Asian and pan-Asian identities need not be mutually exclusive. From its inception, HIF has pursued a double political mission: pushing for recognition of multiracial Asians as well as for the civil rights agendas of existing Asian American groups. . . .

Asian American activists have also engaged in *proactive* efforts to draw together Asian Americans of different classes to organize against anti-Asian racism, defined not as random attacks against Asians but as a product of structural oppression and everyday encounters (Kurashige 2000, 15). The activities of the Asian Americans United, a panethnic community-based organization in Philadelphia, provide an example (Kurashige 2000). When large numbers of Southeast Asian immigrants began experiencing problems in Philadelphia with racist violence, educational inequality, and poor housing, a small group of educated East and South Asian American activists responded. Modeling themselves after the militant Yellow Seeds organization in the 1970s, group members insisted on anti-imperialist politics, a critique of racism as institutional and structural, and a focus on activist organizing and politics. They organized a successful rent strike and were part of a victorious legal campaign to institute bilingual education in the local schools. Most important, they sought to build relationships with working-class Southeast Asian communities by creating a youth leadership training program organized around a pan-Asian identity and radical politics. When a violent attack on Southeast Asian youths in that city by a group of white youths led to a fight that left one of the white attackers dead, city police and prosecutors portrayed the attackers as victims and laid the responsibility for the violence at the hands of the Southeast Asians. Although unable to secure full justice in the court cases that ensued, Asian Americans United seized on the incident as a means of educating its constituency about institutionalized racism. The group succeeded in mobilizing parts of the Asian American community around these efforts, and its success enabled it to move from panethnic to interethnic affiliation through an alliance with a Puerto Rican youth group also plagued by hate crimes, police brutality, and prosecutorial racism (Espiritu et al. 2000, 132). This example suggests that class need not be a source of cleavage among Asian Americans, and that the concerns of working-class Asian Americans *can* unite people at the grassroots level with class-conscious members of the intel-lectual and professional strata (Kurashige 2000).

Given our globalizing world and the resultant demographic changes, the construction of an Asian American identity is no longer situated—if indeed it ever was—only within Asian America but also through relations and struggles with other commu-nities of color. Today working-class immigrants of diverse backgrounds coexist with African American and U.S.-born Latinos in urban communities across the country. This "social geography of race" has produced new social subjects and new coalitions. For example, young Laotian women in northern California joined Chinese and Japanese Americans in panethnic struggles against anti-Asian racism and also against the "neighborhood race effects" of underfunded schools, polluted air and water, and low-wage jobs that they and their families share with their African American, Latino, Arab American, and poor white neighbors (Espiritu et al. 2000; Shah 2002). In the same way, recognizing their common histories of political fragmenta-tion and disfranchisement, Japanese, Chinese, and Mexicans in the San Gabriel Valley of Los Angeles County formed political alliances to work together on the redistricting and reapportionment process in the Valley (Saito 1998, 10).

Finally, given the internationalization and femi-nization of the labor force in recent decades, some Asian women in the United States *and* in Asia have begun to conceive of themselves as similarly situated racial, gendered, and classed subjects. The dominance of women in contemporary immigra-tion reflects the growth of female-intensive indus-tries in the United States, particularly in services, health care, microelectronics, and apparel manu-facturing. To escape the tightening labor market, employers in the United States have opted either to shift labor-intensive processes to less-developed countries or to import migrant labor, especially female, to fill low-wage, insecure assembly and service-sector jobs (Lim 1983; Hossfeld 1994). Women thus have become a rapidly growing seg-ment of the world's migratory and international workforce (Sacks and Scheper-Hughes 1987).

For post-1965 immigrant women from Asia, their politically insecure status as "alien" and their limited English proficiency have interacted with geographical segregation, racist and sexist hiring practices, and institutional barriers to recertifica-tion by U.S. professional boards to narrow greatly their occupational choices. Consequently, many Asian immigrant women, instead of gaining access to a better, more modern, and more liberated life in the United States, have been confined to low-paying service jobs and factory assembly-line work, especially in the garment and microelectronics in-dustries. The similarities in the labor conditions for Asian women here and in Asia, brought about by global capitalism, constitute the "situating grounds for a strategic transnational affiliation" (Kang 1997, 415). . . . The racialized feminization of labor gives rise to a "common context of struggle" among Asian women within, outside, and across the borders of the United States and has resulted in the establish-ment of numerous cross-border and transnational women's organizations, such as Gabriela, the sup-port committee for Maquiladora workers, and Asian Immigrant Women Advocates (Lowe 1996).

These cross-racial and cross-border alliances and the radical mobilization around gender issues underscore the centrality of "unlikely coalitions" in contemporary political organizing. As Angela Davis (1997, 322) points out, we can accomplish impor-tant things in the struggle for social justice if we focus on the creation of "unpredictable or unlikely coalitions grounded in political projects." A com-plex world requires a complex set of alliances. These unlikely coalitions, including pan-Asian coalitions, along with the antiglobal organizations that are seeking to impose workplace and environmental restraints on multinational corporations and capi-tal, could prove a potent force for social change at both the national and global levels.

CONCLUSION

Since the pan-Asian concept was forged in the late 1960s, the Asian American population has become much more variegated. The post-1965 immigration surge from Asia has fragmented Asian America more clearly than in the past along ethnic, generational, and class lines. This increasing diversity has brought into question the very feasibility and appropriateness of pan-Asian identities and practices, challenging Asian Americans to take seriously the social, political, and economic inequalities that exist within their communities. My main contention in this [reading] is that we cannot examine Asian American panethnicity solely in terms of racial politics within the framework of the U.S. nation-state. While important, this framework narrowly focuses on identity politics within Asian America, not on the global politics and power that produced massive displacements and migrations of Asians in the first place. Calling for a critical transnational perspective on the study of panethnicity, I argue instead that different circumstances of exit—the product of different types of U.S. engagement in different Asian countries—have shaped the size and timing of migration and the socioeconomic profile of different Asian groups and thus have profoundly affected their group formation and differentiation in the United States. This approach expands the discussion on pan-Asian ethnicity by viewing it as an integral part not only of Asian American studies or American studies but also of international and transnational studies. In all, the examples cited in this chapter confirm the plural and ambivalent nature of panethnicity: it is a highly contested terrain on which Asian Americans merge and clash over terms of inclusion but also an effective site from which to forge crucial alliances with other groups both within and across the borders of the United States in their ongoing efforts to effect larger social transformation.

Acknowledgments

I would like to thank Richard Delgado, Jean Stefancic, Nancy Foner, Josh DeWind, and the participants in the "Immigration, Race, and Ethnicity: Then and Now" workshops for their helpful comments on earlier versions of this chapter.

DISCUSSION QUESTIONS

1. What are the shortcomings of Asian American panethnicty?
2. How do ethnic, generational, and class diversity present obstacles for mobilization among Asian immigrants?

NOTES

1. For an extended discussion of the critical transnational approach to immigration, see Espiritu (2003). Certainly, I am not the first scholar to apply a critical transnational framework to the study of Asian Americans. Oscar Campomanes (1997), Sucheta Mazumdar (1990), Shirley Hune (1989), and others have written persuasively on the importance of conducting Asian American studies through an "international" frame.
2. For a detailed account of the disputes over the classification of Asian Americans in the 1980 and 1990 censuses, please see Espiritu (1992, ch. 5).
3. In 1990 the Japanese American share of the Asian American population was 12 percent, and the five largest Asian American groups were Chinese (23 percent), Filipino (19 percent), Asian Indian (11 percent), Korean (11 percent), and Vietnamese (8 percent).
4. According to the 2000 U.S. census, approximately 850,000 people reported that they were Asian and white, and 360,000 reported that they were two or more Asian groups (Barnes and Bennett 2002, table 4). The debate over the classification of multiracials in the 2000 census often posed the interests of multiracial Asian Americans—the right to claim their full heritage—in opposition to the civil rights needs of pan-Asian America—the possible loss of political clout that is tied to numbers (see Espiritu 2001, 31). Refusing this "splitting," Asian American multiracial organizations rejected the "stand-alone multiracial" category and endorsed the "check more than one" format because the latter would allow them to identify as multiracial *and* "still be counted with their Asian American brethren and sisters" (King 2000, 202). This stance suggests that multiracial Asian and pan-Asian identities need not be mutually exclusive.

REFERENCES

Barnes, Jessica, and Claudette E. Bennett. 2002. *The Asian Population 2000.* Washington: U.S. Department of Commerce.

Blauner, Robert. 1972. *Racial Oppression in America.* New York: Harper & Row.

Bonacich, Edna, and Lucie Cheng. 1984. "Introduction: A Theoretical Orientation to International Labor Migration." In *Labor Immigration Under Capitalism: Asian Workers in the United States Before World War II*, edited by Lucie Cheng and Edna Bonacich. Berkeley: University of California Press.

Burawoy, Michael. 1976. "The Functions and Reproduction of Migrant Labor: Comparative Material from Southern Africa and the United States." *American Journal of Sociology* 81(5, March): 1050–87.

Campomanes, Oscar. 1997. "New Formations of Asian American Studies and the Questions of U.S. Imperialism." *Positions* 5(2): 523–50.

Chan, Sucheng. 1991. *Asian Americans: An Interpretive History*. Boston: Twayne.

Daniels, Roger, 1988. *Asian America: Chinese and Japanese in the United States Since 1850*. Seattle: University of Washington Press.

Davis, Angela. 1997. "Interview with Lisa Lowe—Angela Davis: Reflections on Race, Class, and Gender in the USA." In *The Politics of Culture in the Shadow of Capital*, edited by Lisa Lowe and David Lloyd. Durham, N.C.: Duke University Press.

Espiritu, Yen Le. 1992. *Asian American Panethnicity: Bridging Institutions and Identities*. Philadelphia: Temple University Press.

———. 1995. *Filipino American Lives*. Philadelphia: Temple University Press.

———. 1996. "Crossroads and Possibilities: Asian Americans on the Eve of the Twenty-first Century." *Amerasia Journal* 22(2): vii–xii.

———. 2001. "Possibilities of a Multiracial Asian America." In *The Sum of Our Parts: Mixed Heritage Asian Americans*, edited by Teresa Williams-Leon and Cynthia L. Nakashima. Philadelphia. Temple University Press.

———. 2003. *Home Bound: Filipino American Lives Across Cultures, Communities, and Countries*. Berkeley: University of California Press.

Espiritu, Yen Le, and Paul Ong. 1994. "Class Constraints on Racial Solidarity Among Asian Americans." In *The New Asian Immigration in Los Angeles and Global Restructuring*, edited by Paul Ong, Edna Bonacich, and Lucie Cheng. Philadelphia: Temple University Press.

Espiritu, Yen Le, Dorothy Fujita Rony, Nazli Kibria, and George Lipsitz. 2000. "The Role of Race and Its Articulations for Asian Pacific Americans." *Journal of Asian American Studies* 3(2): 127–37.

Hayano, David. 1981. "Ethnic Identification and Disidentification: Japanese-American Views of Chinese Americans." *Ethnic Groups* 3(2): 157–71.

Hossfeld, Karen. 1994. "Hiring Immigrant Women: Silicon Valley's 'simple Formula.'" In *Women of Color in U.S. Society*, edited by Maxine Baca Zinn and Bonnie Thornton Dill. Philadelphia: Temple University Press.

Hu-DeHart, Evelyn. 1999. "Introduction: Asian American Formations in the Age of Globalization." In *Across the Pacific: Asian Americans and Globalization*, edited by Evelyn Hu-DeHart. Philadelphia: Temple University Press.

Hune, Shirley. 1989. "Expanding the International Dimension of Asian American Studies." *Amerasia Journal* 15(2): xix–xxiv.

Ichioka, Yuji. 1988. *The Issei: The World of the First Generation Japanese Americans, 1885–1924*. New York: Free Press.

Iwasaki, Naomi. 1999. "Pan-Asian What?" *Asian American Revolutionay Movement Ezine*, http://www.aamovement. net/narratives/panasian.html (accessed December 4, 2003).

Kang, Laura Hyun Yi. 1997. "Si(gh)ting Asian/American Women as Transnational Labor." *Positions* 5(2): 403–37.

King, Rebecca Chiyoko. 2000. "Racialization, Recognition, and Rights: Lumping and Splitting Multiracial Asian Americans in the 2000 Census." *Journal of Asian American Studies* 3(2): 191–217.

Kurashige, Scott. 2000. "Panethnicity and Community Organizing: Asian Americans United's Campaign Against Anti-Asian Violence." *Journal of Asian American Studies* 3(2): 163–90.

Ling, Susie Hsiuhan. 1984. "The Mountain Movers: Asian American Women's Movement in Los Angeles." M.A. thesis, University of California at Los Angeles.

Lim, Linda Y. C. 1983. "Capitalism, Imperialism, and Patriarchy: The Dilemma of Third-World Women Workers in Multinational Factories." In *Women, Men, and the International Division of Labor*, edited by June Nash and Maria Patricia Fernandez-Kelly. Albany: State University of New York Press.

Liu, John, and Lucie Cheng. 1994. "Pacific Rim Development and the Duality of Post-1965 Asian Immigration to the United States." In *The New Asian Immigration in Los Angeles and Global Restructuring*, edited by Paul Ong, Edna Bonacich, and Lucie Cheng. Philadelphia: Temple University Press.

Liu, William. 1976. "Asian American Research: Views of a Sociologist." *Asian Studies Occasional Report* 2: whole issue.

Lott, Juanita. 1976. "The Asian American Concept: In Quest of Identity." *Bridge* (November): 30–34.

Lowe, Lisa. 1991. "Heterogeneity, Hybridity, Multiplicity: Marking Asian American Differences." *Diaspora* 1 (1, Spring): 25–44.

———. 1996. *Immigrant Acts: On Asian American Cultural Politics*. Durham, N.C.: Duke University Press.

Mazumdar, Sucheta. 1990. "Asian American Studies and Asian Studies: Rethinking Roots." In *Asian Americans: Comparative and Global Perspectives*, edited by Shirley Hune et al. Pullman: Washington State University Press.

Misir, Deborah N. 1996. "The Murder of Navroze Mody: Race, Violence, and the Search for Order." *Amerasia Journal* 22(2): 55–76.

Nguyen, Viet Thanh. 2002. *Race and Resistance: Literature and Politics in Asian America.* New York: Oxford University Press.

Omatsu, Glenn. 1994. "'The Four Prisons and the Movements of Liberation: Asian American Activism from the 1960s to the 1990s." In *The State of Asian America: Activism and Resistance in the 1990s,* edited by Karin Aguilar-San Juan. Boston: South End.

Omi, Michael. 1993. "Out of the Melting Pot and into the Fire: Race Relations Policy." In *The State of Asian Pacific Americans: Policy Issues to the Year 2000.* Los Angeles: LEAP Asian Pacific American Public Policy Institute and UCLA Asian American Studies Center.

Omi, Michael, and Howard Winant. 1986. *Racial Formation in the United States: From the 1960s to the 1980s.* New York: Routledge & Kegan Paul.

Ong, Aihwa. 1996. "Citizenship as Subject Making: New Immigrants Negotiate Racial and Ethnic Boundaries." *Current Anthropology* 25(5): 737–62.

Ong, Paul, 1989. "California's Asian Population: Past Trends and Projections for the Year 2000." Los Angeles: Graduate School of Architecture and Urban Planning.

———. 2000. "The Asian Pacific American Challenge to Race Relations." In *The State of Asian Pacific Americans: Transforming Race Relations,* edited by Paul Ong. Los Angeles: LEAP Asian Pacific American Public Policy Institute and UCLA Asian American Studies Center.

Ong, Paul, and Tania Azores. 1994. "The Migration and Incorporation of Filipino Nurses." In *The New Asian Immigration in Los Angeles and Global Restructuring,* edited by Paul Ong, Edna Bonacich, and Lucie Cheng. Philadelphia: Temple University Press.

Ong, Paul, and Suzanne J. Hee. 1993. "The Growth of the Asian Pacific American Population. In *The State of Asian Pacific Americans: Policy Issues to the Year 2000.* Los Angeles: LEAP Asian Pacific American Public Policy Institute and UCLA Asian American Studies Center.

Petras, James. 1978. *Critical Perspectives of Imperialism and Social Class in the Third World.* New York: Monthly Review Press.

Portes, Alejandro. 1978. "Migration and Underdevelopment." *Politics and Society* 8: 1–48.

Portes, Alejandro, and Rubén Rumbaut. 1990. *Immigrant America: A Portrait.* Berkeley: University of California Press.

Rumbaut, Rubén. 1991. "Passages to America: Perspectives on the New Immigration." In *America at Century's End,* edited by Alan Wolfe. Berkeley and Los Angeles: University of California Press.

Sacks, Karen, and Nancy Scheper-Hughes. 1987. "Introduction." *Women's Studies* 13(3): 175–82.

Saito, Leland. 1998. *Race and Politics: Asian Americans, Latinos, and Whites in a Los Angeles Suburb.* Urbana and Chicago: University of Illinois Press.

Sassen, Saskia. 1992. "Why Migration." *Report on the Americas* 26(1, July): whole issue.

Shah, Bindi. 2002. "Making the 'American' Subject: Culture, Gender, Ethnicity, and the Politics of Citizenship in the Lives of Second-Generation Laotian Girls." Ph.D. diss., University of California at Davis.

Shankar, Rajiv. 1998. "Foreword: South Asian Identity in Asian America." In *A Part, Yet Apart: South Asians in Asian America,* edited by Lavina Dhingra Shankar and Rajini Srikanth. Philadelphia: Temple University Press.

Shinagawa, Larry Hajime, and Gin Yong Pang. 1996. "Asian American Panethnicity and Intermarriage." *Amerasia Journal* 22(2): 127–52.

Strobel, Leny Mendoza. 1996. "'Born-Again Filipino': Filipino American Identity and Asian American Panethnicity." *Amerasia Journal* 22(2): 31–54.

Takaki, Ronald. 1989. *Strangers from a Different Shore: A History of Asian Americans.* Boston: Little, Brown.

U.S. Department of Commerce. U.S. Census Bureau. 2002. "Coming to America: A Profile of the Nation's Foreign Born (2000 Update)." *Census Briefs: Current Population Survey, February 2002.* Washington: U.S. Census Bureau.

U.S. Immigration and Naturalization Service (USINS). 1997. *Statistical Yearbook of the Immigration and Naturalization Service, 1995.* Washington: U.S. Government Printing Office.

Viviani, Nancy. 1984. *The Long Journey: Vietnamese Migration and Settlement in Australia.* Carlton, Victoria: Melbourne University Press.

Wong, Paul. 1972. "The Emergence of the Asian-American Movement." *Bridge* 2(1): 33–39.

Zhou, Min. 2001. "Straddling Different Worlds: The Acculturation of Vietnamese Refugee Children." In *Ethnicities: Children of Immigrants in America,* edited by Rubén G. Rumbaut and Alejandro Portes. Berkeley: University of California Press.

Zhou, Min, and James V. Gatewood. 2000. "Introduction: Revisiting Contemporary Asian America." In *Contemporary Asian America: A Multidisciplinary Reader,* edited by Min Zhou and James V. Gatewood. New York: New York University Press.

Zolberg, Aristide. 1986. "International Factors in the Formation of Refugee Movement." *International Migration Review* 20(2, Summer): 151–69.

PERSONAL ACCOUNT

I Thought My Race Was Invisible

In a conversation with a close friend, I noticed that I am, to her, a representative of my entire racial category. To put things in perspective, my friend Janet and I have been friends for eight years. During this period, it has come up that I am a third-generation Japanese-American who has no ties to being Japanese other than a couple of sushi dishes I learned how to make from my grandmother. Nonetheless, whenever a question regarding "Asians" comes up, she comes to me as if I can provide the definitive answer to every Asian mystery.

Yesterday Janet asked me if there is a cultural reason why Asians "always drive so slow." Not having noticed that Asians drive slowly (in fact, I have noticed a number of Asians who actually exceed the speed limit), I commented that perhaps they are law-abiding citizens. She said that must explain it: "They are used to following the law." I thought, "Am I one of 'they'?" but didn't comment further. Before we switched subjects, she noted that she "knew there had to be a cultural reason" for their driving.

Janet then told me about a Vietnamese woman at the Hair Cuttery who cut her husband's hair. As is normal, her husband talked to the woman as she worked on his hair; he asked her what she did before working at the Hair Cuttery. She said that she used to work in the fields in California (i.e., she was a field hand). Janet told me of the healthy respect that she and her husband had for a woman who worked in the fields, put herself through cosmetology school, moved East, and became a professional hairstylist. She commented that "Blacks" should follow her example and work instead of complaining of their lot in life.

This conversation was interesting and a bit startling. Janet is a good friend who shares many interests with me. What I realized from this conversation, and in remembering others that were similar, is that she feels that I am a representative of the whole Asian race. Not only is this unrealistic, but it is surprising that she would imagine I could answer for my race given my lack of real cultural exposure. In relaying the story of the Vietnamese woman, I had a sense that she was complimenting me, and my race, for the industriousness "we" demonstrate. It seems to me that she approved of the "typically" Asian way of working (quietly, so as not to insult or offend), even though this woman was probably underpaid and overworked in her field hand job. While she approved of her reticence, Janet did not approve of "Black" complaints.

I realize that to Janet, I will always be Asian. I had not really thought about it before, but I never think of Janet as White; her race is invisible to me. I had thought that my race was invisible too; however, I realize now that I will always be the "marked" friend. This saddens me a bit, but I accept it with the knowledge that she is a close friend. Nonetheless, it is unfortunate to think that even between friends, race is an issue.

Sherri H. Pereira

READING 6

Whiteness as an "Unmarked" Cultural Category

Ruth Frankenberg

America's supposed to be the melting pot. I know that I've got a huge number of nationalities in my blood, but how do I—what do I call myself? And

Ruth Frankenberg (1957–2007) was a professor of American studies at the University of California, Davis. Her work helped define the field of whiteness studies.

hating this country as I do, I don't like to say I'm an American. Even though it is what I am. I hate identifying myself as only an American, because I have so much objections to Americans' place in the world. I don't know how I felt about that when I was growing up, but I never—I didn't like to pledge allegiance to the flag. . . . Still, at this point in my life, I wonder what it is that somebody with all this melting pot blood can call their own. . . .

Especially growing up in the sixties, when people *did* say "I'm proud to be Black," "I'm proud to be Hispanic," you know, and it became very popular to be proud of your ethnicity. And even feminists, you know, you could say, "I'm a woman," and be proud of it. But there's still a majority of the country that can't say they are proud of anything!

Suzie Roberts's words powerfully illustrate the key themes . . . that stirred the women I interviewed* as they examined their own identities: what had formed them, what they counted as (their own or others') cultural practice(s), and what constituted identities of which they could be proud. This [discussion] explores perceptions of whiteness as a location of culture and identity, focusing mainly on white feminist . . . women's views and contrasting their voices with those of more politically conservative women. . . .

[M]any of the women I interviewed, including even some of the conservative ones, appeared to be self-conscious about white power and racial inequality. In part because of their sense of the links and parallels between white racial dominance in the United States and U.S. domination on a global scale, there was a complex interweaving of questions about race and nation—whiteness and Americanness—in these women's thoughts about white culture. Similarly, conceptions of racial, national, and cultural belonging frequently leaked into one another.

On the one hand, then, these women's views of white culture seemed to be distinctively modern. But at the same time, their words drew on much earlier historical moments and participated in long-established modes of cultural description. In the broadest sense, Western colonial discourses on the white self, the nonwhite Other, and the white Other too, were very much in evidence. These discourses produced dualistic conceptualizations of whiteness versus other cultural forms. The women thus often spoke about culture in ways that reworked, and yet remained tied to, "older" forms of racism.

For a significant number of young white women, being white felt like being cultureless. Cathy Thomas, in the following description of whiteness, raised many of the themes alluded to by other feminist and race-cognizant women. She described what she saw as a lack of form and substance:

---

*Between 1984 and 1986 Ruth Frankenberg interviewed 30 white women, diverse in age, class, region of origin, sexuality, family situation and political orientation, all living in California at the time of the interviews.

. . . the formlessness of being white. Now if I was a middle western girl, or a New Yorker, if I had a fixed regional identity that was something palpable, then I'd be a white New Yorker, no doubt, but I'd still be a New Yorker. . . . Being a Californian, I'm sure it has its hallmarks, but to me they were invisible. . . . If I had an ethnic base to identify from, if I was even Irish American, that would have been something formed, if I was a working-class woman, that would have been something formed. But to be a Heinz 57 American, a white, class-confused American, land of the Kleenex type American, is so formless in and of itself. It only takes shape in relation to other people.

Whiteness as a cultural space is represented here as amorphous and indescribable, in contrast with a range of other identities marked by race, ethnicity, region, and class. Further, white culture is viewed here as "bad" culture. In fact, the extent to which identities can be named seems to show an inverse relationship to power in the U.S. social structure. The elisions, parallels, and differences between characterizations of white people, Americans, people of color, and so-called white ethnic groups will be explored [here].

Cathy's own cultural positioning seemed to her impossible to grasp, shapeless and unnameable. It was easier to know others and to know, with certainty, what one was *not*. Providing a clue to one of the mechanisms operating here is the fact that, while Cathy viewed New Yorkers and midwesterners as having a cultural shape or identity, women from the East Coast and the Midwest also described or mourned their own seeming lack of culture. The self, where it is part of a dominant cultural group, does not have to name itself. In this regard, Chris Patterson hit the nail on the head, linking the power of white culture with the privilege not to be named:

I'm probably at the stage where I'm beginning to see that you can come up with a definition of white. Before, I didn't know that you could turn it around and say, "Well what *does* white mean?" One thing is, it's taken for granted. . . . [To be white means to] have some sort of advantage or privilege, even if it's something as simple as not having a definition.

The notion of "turning it around" indicates Chris's realization that, most often, whites are the nondefined definers of other people. Or, to put it another way, whiteness comes to be an unmarked or neutral category, whereas other cultures are specifically marked "cultural."

Many of the women shared the habit of turning to elements of white culture as the unspoken norm. This assumption of a white norm was so prevalent that even Sandy Alvarez and Louise Glebocki, who were acutely aware of racial inequality as well as being members of racially mixed families, referred to "Mexican" music versus "regular" music, and regular meant "white."

Similarly, discussions of race difference and cultural diversity at times revealed a view in which people of color actually embodied difference and whites stood for sameness. Hence, Margaret Phillips said of her Jamaican daughter-in-law that: "She *really* comes with diversity." In spite of its brevity, and because of its curious structure, this short statement says a great deal. It implicitly designates whiteness as norm, and Jamaicans as having or bearing with them "differentness." At the risk of being crass, one might say that in this view, diversity is to the daughter-in-law as "the works" is to a hamburger—added on, adding color and flavor, but not exactly essential. Whiteness, seen by many of these women as boring, but nonetheless definitive, could also follow this analogy. This mode of thinking about "difference" expresses clearly the double-edged sword of a color- and power-evasive repertoire, apparently valorizing cultural difference but doing so in a way that leaves racial and cultural hierarchies intact.

For a seemingly formless entity, then, white culture had a great deal of power, difficult to dislodge from its place in white consciousness as a point of reference for the measuring of others. Whiteness served simultaneously to eclipse and marginalize others (two modes of making the other inessential). Helen Standish's description of her growing-up years in a small New England town captured these processes well. Since the community was all white, the differences at issue were differences between whites. (This also enables an assessment of the links between white and nonwhite "marked" cultures.) Asked about her own cultural identity, Helen

explained that "it didn't seem like a culture because everyone else was the same." She had, however, previously mentioned Italian Americans in the town, so I asked about their status. She responded as follows, adopting at first the voice of childhood:

> They are different, but I'm the same as everybody else. They speak Italian, but everybody else in the U.S. speaks English. They eat strange, different food, but I eat the same kind of food as everybody else in the U.S. . . . The way I was brought up was to think that everybody who was the same as me were "Americans," and the other people were of "such and such descent."

Viewing the Italian Americans as different and oneself as "same" serves, first, to marginalize, to push from the center, the former group. At the same time, claiming to be the same as everyone else makes other cultural groups invisible or eclipses them. Finally, there is a marginalizing of all those who are not like Helen's own family, leaving a residual, core or normative group who are the true Americans. The category of "American" represents simultaneously the normative and the residual, the dominant culture and a nonculture.

Although Helen talked here about whites, it is safe to guess that people of color would not have counted among the "same" group but among the communities of "such and such descent" (Mexican American, for example). Whites, within this discursive repertoire, became conceptually the real Americans, and only certain kinds of whites actually qualified. Whiteness and Americanness both stood as normative and exclusive categories in relation to which other cultures were identified and marginalized. And this clarifies that there are two kinds of whites, just as there are two kinds of Americans: those who are truly or only white, and those who are white but also something more—or is it something less?

In sum, whiteness often stood as an unmarked marker of others' differentness—whiteness not so much void or formlessness as norm. I associate this construction with colonialism and with the more recent assymetrical dualisms of liberal humanist views of culture, race, and identity. For the most part, this construction views nonwhite cultures as lesser, deviant, or pathological. However, another trajectory has been the inverse: conceptualizations of the cultures of peoples of color as somehow better than the dominant culture, perhaps more natural or more spiritual. These are positive evaluations of a sort, but they are equally dualistic. Many of the women I interviewed saw white culture as less appealing and found the cultures of the "different" people more interesting. As Helen Standish put it:

> [We had] Wonder bread, white bread. I'm more interested in, you know, "What's a bagel?" in other people's cultures rather than my own.

The claim that whiteness lacks form and content says more about the definitions of culture being used than it does about the content of whiteness. However, I would suggest that in describing themselves as cultureless these women are in fact identifying specific kinds of unwanted absences or presences in their own culture(s) as a generalized lack or nonexistence. It thus becomes important to look at what they *did* say about the cultural content of whiteness.

Descriptions of the content of white culture were thin, to say the least. But despite the paucity of signifiers, there was a great deal of consistency across the narratives. First, there was naming based on color, the linking of white culture with white objects—the clichéd white bread and mayonnaise, for example. Freida Kazen's identification of whiteness as "bland," together with Helen Standish's "blah," also signified paleness or neutrality. The images connote several things—color itself (although exaggerated, and besides, bagels are usually white inside, too), lack of vitality (Wonder bread is highly processed), and homogeneity. However, these images are perched on a slippery slope, at once suggesting "white" identified as a color (though an unappealing one) and as an absence of color, that is, white as the unmarked marker.

Whiteness was often signified in these narratives by commodities and brands: Wonder bread, Kleenex, Heinz 57. In this identification whiteness came to be seen as spoiled by capitalism, and as being linked with capitalism in a way that other cultures supposedly are not. Another set of signifiers that constructed whiteness as uniquely tainted by capitalism had to do with the "modern condition": Dot Humphrey described white neighborhoods as "more privatized," and Cathy Thomas used "alienated" to describe her cultural condition. Clare Traverso added to this theme, mourning her own feeling of lack of identity, in contrast with images of her husband's Italian American background (and here, Clare is again talking about perceived differences between whites):

> Food, old country, mama. Stories about a grandmother who can't speak English. . . . Candles, adobe houses, arts, music. [It] has emotion, feeling, belongingness that to me is unique.

In linking whiteness to capitalism and viewing nonwhite cultures as untainted by it, these women were again drawing on a colonial discourse in which progress and industrialization were seen as synonymous with Westernization, while the rest of the world is seen as caught up in tradition and "culture." In addition, one can identify, in white women's mourning over whiteness, elements of what Raymond Williams has called "pastoralism," or nostalgia for a golden era now gone by (but in fact, says Williams, one that never existed).[1]

The image of whiteness as corrupted and impoverished by capitalism is but one of a series of ways in which white culture was seen as impure or tainted. White culture was also seen as tainted by its relationship to power. For example, Clare Traverso clearly counterposed white culture and white power, finding it difficult to value the former because of the overwhelming weight of the latter:

> The good things about whites are to do with folk arts, music. Because other things have power associated with them.

For many race-cognizant white women, white culture was also made impure by its very efforts to maintain race purity. Dot Humphrey, for example, characterized white neighborhoods as places in which people were segregated by choice. For her, this was a good reason to avoid living in them.

The link between whiteness and domination, however, was frequently made in ways that both artificially isolated culture from other factors and obscured economics. For at times, the traits the women envied in Other cultures were in fact at least in part the product of poverty or other dimensions of oppression. Lack of money, for example, often means lack of privacy or space, and it can be valorized as "more street life, less alienation." Cathy Thomas's notion of Chicanas' relationship to the kitchen ("the hearth of the home") as a cultural "good" might be an idealized one that disregards the reality of intensive labor.

Another link between class and culture emerged in Louise Glebocki's reference to the working-class Chicanos she met as a child as less pretentious, "closer to the truth," more "down to earth." And Marjorie Hoffman spoke of the "earthy humor" of Black people, which she interpreted as, in the words of Langston Hughes, a means of "laughing to keep from crying." On the one hand, as has been pointed out especially by Black scholars and activists, the positions of people of color at the bottom of a social and economic hierarchy create the potential for a critique of the system as a whole and consciousness of the need to resist.[2] From the standpoint of race privilege, the system of racism is thus made structurally invisible. On the other hand, descriptions of this kind leave in place a troubling dichotomy that can be appropriated as easily by the right as by the left. For example, there is an inadvertent affinity between the image of Black people as "earthy" and the conservative racist view that African American culture leaves African American people ill equipped for advancement in the modern age. Here, echoing essentialist racism, both Chicanos and African Americans are placed on the borders of "nature" and "culture."

By the same token, often what was criticized as "white" was as much the product of middle-class status as of whiteness as such. Louise Glebocki's image of her fate had she married a white man was an image of a white-collar, nuclear family:

> Him saying, "I'm home, dear," and me with an apron on—ugh!

The intersections of class, race, and culture were obscured in other ways. Patricia Bowen was angry with some of her white feminist friends who, she felt, embraced as "cultural" certain aspects of African American, Chicano, and Native American cultures (including, for example, artwork or dance performances) but would reject as "tacky" (her term) those aspects of daily life that communities of color shared with working-class whites, such as the stores and supermarkets of poor neighborhoods. This, she felt, was tantamount to a selective expansion of middle-class aesthetic horizons, but not to true antiracism or to comprehension of the cultures of people of color. Having herself grown up in a white working-class family, Pat also felt that middle-class white feminists were able to use selective engagement to avoid addressing their class privilege.

I have already indicated some of the problems inherent in this kind of conceptualization, suggesting that it tends to keep in place dichotomous constructions of "white" versus Other cultures, to separate "culture" from other dimensions of daily life, and to reify or strip of history *all* cultural forms. There are, then, a range of issues that need to be disentangled if we are to understand the location of "whiteness" in the terrain of culture. It is, I believe, useful to approach this question by means of a reconceptualization of the concept of culture itself. A culture, in the sense of the set of rules and practices by means of which a group organizes itself and its values, manners, and worldview—in other words, culture as "a field articulating the life-world of subjects . . . and the structures created by human activity"[3]—is an indispensable precondition to any individual's existence in the world. It is nonsensical in terms of this kind of definition to suggest that anyone could actually have "no culture." But this is not, as I have suggested, the mode of thinking about culture that these women are employing.

Whiteness emerges here as inextricably tied to domination partly as an effect of a discursive "draining process" applied to both whiteness and Americanness. In this process, any cultural practice engaged in by a white person that is not identical to the dominant culture is automatically counted as either "not really white"—and, for that matter, not really American, either—(but rather of such and such descent), or as "not really cultural" (but rather "economic"). There is a slipperiness to whiteness here: it shifts from "no culture" to "normal culture" to "bad culture" and back again. Simultaneously, a range of marginal or, in Trinh T. Minh-ha's terminology, "bounded" cultures are generated. These are viewed as enviable spaces, separate and untainted by relations of dominance or by linkage to other structures or systems. By contrast, whiteness is conceived as axiomatically tied to dominance, to economics, to political structures. In this process, both whiteness and nonwhiteness are reified, made into objects rather than processes, and robbed of historical context and human agency. As long as the discussion remains couched in these terms, a critique of whiteness remains a double-edged sword: for one thing, whiteness remains normative because there is no way to name the cultural practices associated with it *as* cultural. Moreover, as I have suggested, whether whiteness is viewed as artificial and dominating (and therefore "bad") or civilized (and therefore "good"), whiteness and all varieties of nonwhiteness continue to be viewed as ontologically different from one another.

A genuine sadness and frustration about the meaning of whiteness at this moment in history motivated these women to decry white culture. It becomes important, then, to recognize the grains of truth in their views of white culture. It is important to acknowledge their anger and frustration about the meaning of whiteness as we reach toward a politicized analysis of culture that is freer of colonial and pastoral legacies.

The terms "white" and "American" as these women used them signified domination in international and domestic terms. This link is both accurate and inaccurate. While it is true that, by and large, those in power in the United States are white, it is also true that not all those who are white are in power. Nor is the axiomatic linkage between Americanness and power accurate, because not all Americans have the same access to power. At the same time, the link between whiteness, Americanness, and power *are* accurate because, as we have seen, the terms "white" and "American"

both function discursively to exclude people from normativity—including white people "of such and such descent." But here we need to distinguish between the fates of people of color and those of white people. Notwithstanding a complicated history, the boundaries of Americanness and whiteness have been much more fluid for "white ethnic" groups than for people of color.

There have been border skirmishes over the meaning of whiteness and Americanness since the inception of those terms. For white people, however, those skirmishes have been resolved through processes of assimilation, not exclusion. The late nineteenth and early twentieth centuries in the United States saw a systematic push toward the cultural homogenization of whites carried out through social reform movements and the schools. This push took place alongside the expansion of industrial capitalism, giving rise to the sense that whiteness signifies the production and consumption of commodities under capitalism.[4] But recognition of this history should not be translated into an assertion that whites were stripped of culture (for to do that would be to continue to adhere to a colonial view of "culture"). Instead one must argue that certain cultural practices replaced others. Were one to undertake a history of this "generic" white culture, it would fragment into a thousand tributary elements, culturally specific religious observances, and class survival mechanisms as well as mass-produced commodities and mass media.

There are a number of dangers inherent in continuing to view white culture as no culture. Whiteness appeared in the narratives to function as both norm or core, that against which everything else is measured, and as residue, that which is left after everything else has been named. A far-reaching danger of whiteness coded as "no culture" is that it leaves in place whiteness as defining a set of normative cultural practices against which all are measured and into which all are expected to fit. This normativity has underwritten oppression from the beginning of colonial expansion and has had impact in multiple ways: from the American pioneers' assumption of a norm of private property used to justify appropriation of land that within their worldview did not have an owner, and the ideological construction of nations like Britain as white,[5] to Western feminism's Eurocentric shaping of its movements and institutions. It is important for white feminists not to continue to participate in these processes.

And if whiteness has a history, so do the cultures of people of color, which are worked on, crafted, and created, rather than just "there." For peoples of color in the United States, this work has gone on as much in the context of relationships to imperialism and capitalism as has the production of whiteness, though it has been premised on exclusion and resistance to exclusion more than on assimilation. Although not always or only forged in resistance, the visibility and recognition of the cultures of U.S. peoples of color in recent times *is* the product of individual and collective struggle. Only a short time has elapsed since those struggles made possible the introduction into public discourse of celebration and valorization of their cultural forms. In short, it is important not to reify any culture by failing to acknowledge its createdness, and not to view it as always having been there in unchanging form.

Rather than feeling "cultureless," white women need to become conscious of the histories and specificities of our cultural positions, and of the political, economic, and creative fusions that form all cultures. The purpose of such an exercise is not, of course, to reinvert the dualisms and valorize whiteness so much as to develop a clearer sense of where and who we are.

DISCUSSION QUESTIONS

1. Why is whiteness considered to be lacking diversity?
2. How would you describe the cultural content of whiteness?

NOTES

1. Raymond Williams, *The Country and the City* (New York: Oxford University Press, 1978).
2. The classic statement of this position is W. E. B. Du Bois's concept of the "double consciousness" of Americans of African descent. Two recent feminist statements of similar positions are Patricia Hill Collins, *Black Feminist Thought: Knowledge, Consciousness, and the Politics of Empowerment* (Boston: Unwin Hyman, 1990); and Aida Hurtado, "Relating to Privilege: Seduction and Rejection in the Subordination of White Women and Women of Color," *Signs* 14, no. 4:833–55.
3. Paul Gilroy, *There Ain't No Black in the Union Jack.* London: Hutchinson, 1987.
4. See, for example, Winthrop Talbot, ed., *Americanization* (New York: H. W. Wilson, 1917), esp. Sophonisba P. Breckinridge, "The Immigrant Family," 251–52, Olivia Howard Dunbar, "Teaching the Immigrant Woman," 252–56, and North American Civic League for Immigrants, "Domestic Education among Immigrants," 256–58; and Kathie Friedman Kasaba, "'To Become a Person': The Experience of Gender, Ethnicity and Work in the Lives of Immigrant Women, New York City, 1870–1940," doctoral dissertation, Department of Sociology, State University of New York, Binghamton, 1991. I am indebted to Katie Friedman Kasaba for these references and for her discussions with me about working-class European immigrants to the United States at the turn of this century.
5. Gilroy, *There Ain't No Black in the Union Jack.*

READING 7

America's Changing Color Lines: Immigration, Race/Ethnicity, and Multiracial Identification

Jennifer Lee

Frank D. Bean

INTRODUCTION

. . . Unlike the immigrants who arrived at the turn of the twentieth century, today's immigrants are notable because they are mainly non-European. By the 1980s, only 12% of legal immigrants originated in Europe or Canada, whereas nearly 85% reported origins in Asia, Latin America, or the Caribbean (U.S. Immigration and Naturalization

Jennifer Lee is a professor of sociology at the University of California, Irvine. Frank D. Bean is a professor of sociology at the University of California, Irvine.

Service 2002, Waldinger & Lee 2001). According to National Research Council projections, by the year 2050, America's Latino and Asian populations are expected to triple, constituting about 25% and 8% of the U.S. population, respectively (Smith & Edmonston 1997). Once a largely biracial society with a large white majority and relatively small black minority—and a relatively impenetrable color line dividing these groups—the United States is now a society composed of multiple racial and ethnic groups. America's newcomers have undeniably altered the nation's racial and ethnic landscape.

At the same time that immigration has increased racial and ethic diversity in the United States, rises in rates of racial/ethnic intermarriage have also occurred. Over the past four decades—a time coinciding with the rise of the new immigration—intermarriage between whites and Asians and whites and Latinos have increased substantially, whether assessed on an individual or married-couple basis. For example, the percentages of Asian or Latino husbands or wives having spouses of another race or ethnicity exceeded 30% by the late 1990s, with the vast majority married to a white partner (Bean & Stevens 2003, p. 195). Similarly, the percentages of Asian or Latino marriages during the 1990s (defined as those with at least one spouse being a member of the race or ethnic group in question) that included a white spouse exceeded 50% in the third generation (Jacoby 2001, Waters 1999). Such rises in intermarriage have, in turn, led to a sizeable and growing multiracial population. Currently, 1 in 40 persons identifies himself or herself as multiracial, and this figure is twice as high for those under the age of 18 (Bean & Lee 2002, Grieco & Cassidy 2001). By the year 2050, as many as 1 in 5 Americans could claim a multiracial background (Farley 2001, Smith & Edmonston 1997).

It is not at all clear that today's immigrants see themselves, or for that matter that others see the immigrants, as either black or white. In short, most late-twentieth-century immigrants may be people of color, but the degree to which they view themselves and are viewed by others as closer to black or white is highly ambiguous. Today's

immigration thus may be moving the nation far beyond the traditional and relatively persistent black/white color line that has long divided the country, a demarcation reflecting the practice of slavery, its legacy of discrimination, and a history of black social and economic disadvantage (Bobo 1997; Clark 1965; Drake & Cayton 1993; Farley & Allen 1987; Massey & Denton 1993; Myrdal 1944; Patterson 1998a,b; Smelser et al. 2001; Wilson 1980, 1987). This fault line, of course, was famously forecast in 1903 by the prominent African American social theorist W.E.B. Du Bois when he prophesied that the "problem of the twentieth-century is the problem of the color line" (1997, p. 45). However, even in 1903, during a time of substantial immigration, it seems unlikely that Du Bois could have anticipated that America's racial and ethnic makeup would be so drastically changed by the late-twentieth-century immigration.

The arrival of unprecedented numbers of Asians and Latinos thus complicates the black/white portrait of America and calls into question where today's immigrants fit along its bipolar divide. If a black/white color line no longer characterizes the nature of racial/ethnic relations in the United States, and a new line is emerging, where will the line be redrawn? Although the birth of a new divide is certainly one possible scenario, another prospect is a shift toward unconditional boundary crossing and the fading of racial boundaries altogether. The rising rates of intermarriage combined with a growing multiracial population may indicate that boundaries are weakening overall, providing evidence of a declining significance of race for all groups.

Which of these scenarios more accurately depicts today's demographic scene and the changing nature of America's color lines is a question fraught with theoretical and social significance. Social scientists are beginning to wrestle with the question of whether today's immigrants are helping to blur racial boundaries generally or whether America's newcomers are simply crossing over the color line rather than helping to eradicate it (Alba 1999, Bean & Stevens 2003, Gans 1999, Gitlin 1995, Hollinger 1995, Lee & Bean 2003, Rodriguez 2000, Sanjek

1994, Skrentny 2001, Waters 1999). In this review, we attempt to address the question about the placement and strength of America's color lines by examining the extant theories and recent findings concerning immigrant incorporation, intermarriage, and multiracial identification in the United States, focusing specifically on intergroup differences among whites, blacks, Latinos, and Asians. After carefully reviewing the literature, we assess the implications of these findings for America's changing color lines. . . .

CHANGING RACIAL/ETHNIC BOUNDARIES

. . . Today, social scientists generally agree that race is a social rather than biological category and have documented the processes by which ethnic and racial boundaries have changed throughout our nation's history. For instance, previously "nonwhite" immigrant ethnic groups such as Irish, Italians, and eastern European Jews became "white," often by deliberately distinguishing themselves from blacks (Alba 1999, Brodkin 1998, Foner 2000, Gerstle 1999, Ignatiev 1995, Jacobson 1998, Perlmann & Waldinger 1997, Roediger 1991). Historians such as Ignatiev (1995) and Jacobson (1998) describe how white ethnics went to extreme measures to distance themselves from black Americans to achieve whiteness. Another critical factor that helped to change the status of Irish, Italians, and Jews from nonwhite to white was the end of large-scale European immigration in the 1920s. The cessation of massive immigration not only diminished fears about an overflow of allegedly racial inferiors, but also facilitated the economic incorporation of European immigrants, especially during the golden years following World War II (Foner 2000). In addition to the successful incorporation of white ethnics into the nation's economic and social structure, black migration patterns within the United States influenced the nation's color lines, redrawing the racial configuration along a stark binary black/white divide in which Irish, Italians, and Jews fell on the white side of the color line (Jacobson 1998).

However, many social scientists caution that the very fact that Irish, Italians, and Jews were not subject to the same type of systematic legal discrimination as African Americans illustrates that they were on a different plane from blacks to begin with, a standing that facilitated their eventual racial treatment as whites (Alba 1985, Foner 2000, Lieberson 1980). Moreover, the disappearance of national origin differences among European ethnics and the discontinuation of tendencies to view such differences not only in racial terms but in fact in rigid black/white terms contributed to the development of the idea that, for many European immigrants, race was an achieved rather than an ascribed status (Alba 1990, Gans 1979, Perlmann & Waldinger 1997, Waters 1990). But this in all likelihood was because such persons were viewed as nonwhite rather than black. In that time period's rigidly compartmentalized black/white world governed by the "one-drop" rule (which emphasized pure whiteness versus everything else), not being white did not necessarily involve actually being black, but it was like being black. Thus, it is not surprising that these national origin groups were treated as black. Perhaps because in fact they were not black, their status was eventually allowed to change, thus hastening the evolution and acceptance of the idea that at least some racial categories—maybe all except black—could in fact be changed.

White ethnics such as Italians, Irish, and eastern European Jews are not the only groups to have changed their status from nonwhite to white. Asian ethnic groups such as the Chinese in Mississippi and Japanese Americans also changed their racial status from almost black to almost white. Loewen (1971), for example, documents how Chinese Americans in the Mississippi Delta made conscious efforts to change their lowly racial status by achieving economic mobility, emulating the cultural practices of whites, intentionally distancing themselves from blacks, and rejecting fellow ethnics who married blacks, as well as their Chinese-black multiracial children. Spickard (1989) notes a similar process of change among Japanese Americans who were once at the bottom of the ethnic ladder along with blacks at the beginning of the twentieth century, but whose status improved dramatically just three-quarters of a century later.

The change in racial classification among ethnic groups from nonwhite to white or almost white vividly illustrates that race is a cultural rather than a biological category that has expanded over time to incorporate new immigrant groups. As Gerstle (1999, p. 289) explains, whiteness as a category "has survived by stretching its boundaries to include Americans—the Irish, eastern and southern Europeans—who had been deemed nonwhite. Contemporary evidence suggests that the boundaries are again being stretched as Latinos and Asians pursue whiteness much as the Irish, Italians, and Poles did before them." There are two points to underscore here: first, changes in ethnic and racial boundaries are a fundamental part of the immigrant incorporation experience; and second, racial and ethnic boundaries have stretched in the past and will undoubtedly continue to change. Although boundary changes may be a given, uncertainties remain about where the racial and ethnic divides will fade, where they will persist, and where today's newest immigrants will fall along these divides. It is impossible to predict exactly where the racial boundaries will be redrawn, but based on trends in immigrant incorporation, intermarriage, and multiracial identification, we can obtain a sense of the direction of these changes. . . .

INTERMARRIAGE IN THE UNITED STATES

At the beginning of the twentieth century, intermarriage between white ethnics was rare and nearly castelike, especially between "old" white ethnics and newer arrivals from eastern and southern Europe (Pagnini & Morgan 1990). Today, white ethnics intermarry at such high rates that only one-fifth of whites has a spouse with an identical ethnic background, reflecting the virtual disappearance of boundaries among white ethnic groups (Alba 1990; Lieberson & Waters 1988, 1993; Waters 1990). By contrast, marriage across racial groups,

while on the rise, is still relatively uncommon between some groups, and all groups continue to intermarry at rates lower than would be predicted at random (Moran 2001). For example, more than 93% of white and black marriages are endogamous, whereas only about 70% of Asian and Hispanic and 33% of American Indian marriages are (Harrison & Bennett 1995, Waters 2000b).

In one sense, that interracial marriage is not as common as white interethnic marriage should come as little surprise given that it was illegal in 16 states as recently as 1967, when the Supreme Court ruling Loving v. Commonwealth of Virginia overturned the last remaining antimiscegenation laws. The ruling had an enormous impact on the rise in interracial marriage, which increased tenfold within a 30-year period from 150,000 in 1960 to 1.6 million in 1990 (Jacoby 2001, Waters 2000b), far beyond what would be predicted by population growth alone. Trends in exogamy are significant because social scientists conceive of racial/ethnic intermarriage as a measure of decreasing social distance, declining racial/ethnic prejudice, and changing racial/ethnic group boundaries (Davis 1941, Fu 2001, Gilbertson et al. 1996, Gordon 1964, Kalmijn 1993, Lee & Fernandez 1998, Lieberson & Waters 1988, Merton 1941, Rosenfeld 2002, Tucker & Mitchell-Kernan 1990). Given its theoretical significance, we review recent findings on intermarriage between whites and nonwhites and explore their implications for America's color lines.

Today, about 13% of American marriages involve persons of different races, a considerable increase over the past three and a half decades (Bean & Stevens 2003, Lee & Bean 2003). Although the rise in interracial marriage might initially suggest that racial boundaries are eroding, recent findings indicate that not all racial/ethnic groups are equal partners in this growth. For instance, about 30% of married native-born Asians and Latinos have a spouse of a different racial background, mostly white. Among young (25- to 34-year-old) U.S.-born Asians and Latinos, the intermarriage figures are even higher; nearly two-thirds of married Asians and two-fifths of Latinos out-marry, again mostly with whites (Qian 1997). By contrast, only one-tenth of young blacks marry someone of a different racial background (Perlmann 2000).

Although the rate of intermarriage increased for all groups since 1970, on the whole the intermarriage rate for whites and blacks remains relatively low (Kalmijn 1993). In the late 1990s, among married whites and married blacks only 5.8% and 10.2% involved a member of another racial group, respectively (Bean & Stevens 2003). The intermarriage rates for Asians and Latinos are nearly three times as high as that of blacks and more than five times the rate of whites. Among married Asians and Latinos, 27.2% and 28.4% of marriages involve a member of another racial group, typically whites (Bean & Stevens 2003, Lee & Bean 2003). The comparatively higher rates of intermarriage among native-born Asians and Latinos indicate that as these groups incorporate into the United States, they not only become receptive to intermarriage but also are perceived by whites as suitable marriage partners (Moran 2001).

In sum, there appear to be three distinct trends in interracial marriage in the United States. First, intermarriage for all racial groups has increased dramatically over the past 35 years and will probably continue to rise. Second, intermarriage is not uncommon in the cases of newer immigrant groups such as Asians and Latinos (particularly among the young, native-born populations). Third, compared with Asians, Latinos, and American Indians, intermarriage is still relatively uncommon among blacks (Perlmann 2000).

The differential rates of intermarriage among nonwhite racial groups suggest that racial/ethnic boundaries are more prominent for some groups than for others. The significantly higher rates of intermarriage among Asians and Latinos indicate that racial/ethnic boundaries are more fluid and flexible, and racial/ethnic prejudice less salient for these groups. By contrast, the lower rates of intermarriage among blacks suggest that racial boundaries are more prominent, and the black/white divide more salient than the Asian/white or Latino/white divides. Hence, although boundaries are fading, boundary crossing among racial groups is not unconditional, and race is not declining in significance at the same pace for all groups.

THE MULTIRACIAL POPULATION IN THE UNITED STATES

The rise in interracial marriage has resulted in the growth of the multiracial population in the United States. This population became especially visible when, for the first time in the nation's history, the 2000 Census allowed Americans to select "one or more races" to indicate their racial identification. Brought about by a small but highly influential multiracial movement, this landmark change in the way the United States measures racial identification reflects the view that race is no longer conceived as a bounded category (DaCosta 2000; Farley 2001, 2002; Hirschman et al. 2000; Morning 2000; Waters 2000a; Williams 2001). In 2000, 6.8 million persons, or 2.4% of Americans, identified themselves as multiracial—about 1 in every 40 people. Although these figures may not appear large, a recent National Academy of Science study noted that the multiracial population could rise to 21% by the year 2050 when—because of rising patterns in intermarriage—as many as 35% of Asians and 45% of Hispanics might claim a multiracial background (Smith & Edmonston 1997). The growth of the multiracial population provides a new reflection on the nation's changing racial boundaries.

Although it has been apparent for some time that the multiracial population will continue to grow, the phenomenon has been relatively understudied in social science research. For example, only a handful of studies have examined the question of how interracial couples identify their multiracial children (Eschbach 1995, McKenney & Bennett 1994, Saenz et al. 1995, Xie & Goyette 1997, Waters 2000b), revealing that about 50% of American Indian/white and Asian/white intermarried couples report a white racial identity for their children. A somewhat larger but still not sizeable number of studies have examined the ways in which multiracial individuals self-identify, often based on small samples generating conflicting findings (Dalmage 2000; Harris & Sim 2002; Johnson et al. 1997; Korgen 1998; Root 1992, 1996; Salgado de Snyder et al. 1982; Spickard 1989; Stephan & Stephan 1989; Tizard & Phoenix 1993; Zack 1993). For example, Salgado de Snyder et al. (1982) find that 70% of multiracial children in California with one Mexican origin parent identify as Mexican, a rate much higher than Stephan & Stephan (1989) find for multiracial Hispanic college students in New Mexico, where only 44% adopt a Hispanic identity.

Previous research indicates that there are several important variables that affect the choice of racial identification among children of interracial unions, such as generational status, bilingualism, and proximity to a nonwhite community. For instance, in their studies of biracial children with one Asian parent, Saenz et al. (1995) and Xie & Goyette (1997) find that nativity and generational status matter. First-generation biracial Asian children are most likely to be identified as Asian compared with subsequent generations. However, the third-generation is more likely to be identified as Asian compared with their second-generation counterparts. Although this finding appears to contradict the classic assimilation model—which predicts fading ethnic identification with each successive generation—Xie & Goyette (1997) argue that choosing to identify one's child as Asian does not necessarily signify a stronger sense of racial identification. Rather, they posit that the racial identification of multiracial Asian children is largely optional, likening it to the ethnic options available for whites. Providing further support for this claim, Harris & Sim (2002) find in their study of multiracial youth that when asked to choose a single race, Asian/white youth are equally likely to identify as Asian or white, demonstrating that the racial identification of Asian/white multiracials is largely a matter of choice.

A second consistent finding is that speaking a language other than English at home significantly increases the likelihood that biracial children will adopt a nonwhite identity, supporting the thesis that language maintenance is critical in ethnic identity formation (Saenz et al. 1995; see also Portes & Rumbaut 2001, Zhou & Bankston 1998). A third finding is that neighborhood context matters, and exposure to the minority parent's culture increases the likelihood that biracial children will adopt a nonwhite identity (Harris & Sim 2002, Korgen 1998, Saenz et al. 1995, Stephan & Stephan 1989, Xie & Goyette 1997). For example, living among a large coethnic community or residing in a public use micro area (PUMA) that is greater than 20% Asian positively affects the degree to which interracially married Asians and whites identify their multiracial children as Asian (Saenz et al. 1995, Xie & Goyette 1997). Furthermore, Stephan & Stephan (1989) posit that the higher rates of multiracial identification of the Japanese in Hawaii (73%) compared with the Hispanics in New Mexico (44%) reflects the greater multicultural milieu in Hawaii, including a multiplicity of locally available labels for the multiracial/multiethnic population. Eschbach (1995) too discovers vast regional differences in the choice of an American Indian identity for American Indian/white multiracials—ranging from 33% to 73%.

Patterns of Multiracial Identification

. . . Mirroring trends in intermarriage, there appear to be three distinct patterns in multiracial identification. First, the multiracial population seems likely to continue to grow in the foreseeable future because of increasing intermarriage. Second, multiracial identification is not uncommon among the members of new immigrant groups such as Asians and Latinos (particularly for those under the age of 18). Third, at only 4.2%, multiracial identification remains relatively uncommon among blacks compared with Asians and Latinos. Why blacks are far less likely to report a multiracial background is particularly noteworthy considering that the U.S. Census Bureau estimates that at least three-quarters of the black population in the United States is ancestrally multiracial (Davis 1991, Spencer 1997). In other words, while at least 75% of black Americans have some alternative ancestry (mostly white) and thus could claim multiracial identities on that basis, just over 4% choose to do so, although recent studies reveal that younger black/white multiracials feel less constrained to adopt a black monoracial identity. For example, Korgen's (1998) study of 40 black/white adults reveals that only one-third of her sample under the age of 30 exclusively identifies as black. Moreover, Harris & Sim's (2002) study of multiracial youth shows that 17.1% of black/white adolescents choose white as the single race that best describes them.

Although younger blacks are less likely to report a black monoracial identity than older black cohorts, blacks overall are still far less likely to report multiracial backgrounds compared with Asians and Latinos. The tendency of black Americans to be less likely to report multiracial identifications undoubtedly is due to the legacy of slavery, including lasting discrimination and the formerly de jure and now de facto invocation of the "one-drop rule" of hypodescent (Davis 1991, Haney Lopez 1996, Nobles 2000). For no other racial or ethnic group in the United States and in no other country does the one-drop rule so tightly circumscribe a group's identity choices (Harris et al. 1993). Unlike the one-drop rule of hypodescent that has historically constrained racial identity options for multiracial blacks, the absence of such a traditional practice of labeling among multiracial Asians, Latinos, and American Indians leaves room for exercising discretion in the selection of racial/ethnic identities (Bean & Stevens 2003, Eschbach 1995, Harris & Sim 2002, Lee & Bean 2003, Stephan & Stephan 1989, Xie & Goyette 1997). The higher rates of multiracial reporting among Latinos and Asians, both as a proportion of the total Latino and Asian populations, and vis-à-vis blacks, indicate that racial boundaries are less constraining for these groups compared with blacks. Although boundary crossing may be more common for all groups, it appears that the legacy of institutional racism in the country, as exemplified in such practices as the informal rule of hypodescent, more forcefully constrains the identity options for blacks compared with other nonwhite groups.

In addition, because a significant proportion of Latinos and Asians in the United States are either immigrants or the children of immigrants, their understanding of race, racial boundaries, and the black/white color divide is shaped by a different set of circumstances than those of African Americans. Most importantly, what sets Latinos and Asians apart is that their experiences are not rooted in the same historical legacy of slavery with its systematic and persistent patterns of legal and institutional discrimination and inequality from which the tenacious black/white divide was born and cemented. Unlike African Americans who were forcefully brought to this country as slaves, today's Latino and Asian newcomers are voluntary migrants, and consequently their experiences are distinct from those of African Americans. The unique history and experience of black Americans in this country make the black/white racial gap qualitatively and quantitatively different from the Latino/white or Asian/white racial divides. For these reasons, racial/ethnic boundaries appear more fluid for the newest immigrants than for native-born blacks, consequently providing multiracial Asians and Latinos more racial options than their black counterparts.

In fact, some research even indicates that the racial boundaries among Latinos, Asians, and American Indians more generally are beginning to assume the fluidity and mutability of ethnicity. For instance, in their longitudinal study of high school students, Eschbach & Gomez (1998) note that only 68% of the more than 6500 students interviewed within a two-year period (1980 and 1982) consistently identified as Hispanic. They suggest that the change in racial/ethnic identification points to a process of transformation from ascribed to optional ethnicity. Similarly, Eschbach et al. (1998) note that the American Indian population grew from 827,000 in 1970 to 1.96 million in 1990—an increase far in excess of natural population growth. They posit that the change in racial identification from white to American Indian signifies the flexibility of racial boundaries for this group. Furthermore, as social scientists have documented, the racial identification for Asians has changed over time from "almost black" to "almost white," pointing to the mutability of boundaries for at least some

PERSONAL ACCOUNT

The Price of Nonconformity

I moved to the United States from Germany three years ago, and moved in with my American cousin and her family, which consists of her husband (who is Iranian) and two children, a boy and a girl. Things were going fine in the beginning, but then after three months I met my boyfriend and everything changed. Tony and I had been dating for about three weeks when I told my cousin I was seeing someone. She didn't seem to mind and just asked me to bring him over one night so she could meet him. A couple of days later, Tony stopped by the house to pick me up for dinner. We waited for my cousin to come home from her job, so they could be introduced. I will never forget the look on her face when she walked in the door and saw that Tony is black. Even though she contained herself quickly, it was obvious that she did not approve of this interracial relationship. For the next two months, she tried to keep me away from him by imposing curfews (I was 21 at the time), not allowing me to take the car, prohibiting him from coming into the house, ignoring him when he picked me up, and not talking to me when I was at home. All of this happened without her ever having to say that she didn't like him because he is black and I am white. But when all of her attempts to separate us failed, she had a talk with me that I will never forget.

She told me that I had no idea what I was getting myself into, and that a relationship between a black man and a white woman was unacceptable. Since we were from two different cultures—black vs. white—it would never work; our friends, family, and society would not accept it. Tony would never fit into my "white" life, and I would never fit into his "black" life. My friends would eventually turn away from me because I am with him, and also because the differences between my friends—who she assumed all to be white—and Tony would be insurmountable. Moreover, she was outraged that I would even consider having a black man's children. She said that my children would always be stigmatized as black children. They would suffer from prejudice and discrimination, and I was a terrible person for choosing that life for them.

So in the end, she gave me the choice of ending the relationship with Tony, or moving out. She said she could not allow such behavior in her house, since I was supposed to be a role model for her eleven-year-old daughter. She did not want her daughter to follow in my footsteps. Since I don't respond well to ultimatums, especially when they are as ridiculous and racist as this one, I packed my stuff and moved out shortly after this conversation.

Julia Morgenstern

Asian ethnic groups (Loewen 1971, Spickard 1989; see also Spickard & Fong 1995). Thus, recent findings suggest that at least for some Asians, Latinos, and American Indians, race is adopting the optional and symbolic character of white ethnicity. . . .

Acknowledgments

We thank the Russell Sage Foundation and the Center for Immigration, Population and Public Policy at the University of California, Irvine, for supporting the research on which this paper is based. This paper was partially completed while Jennifer Lee was a Fellow at the Center for Advanced Study in the Behavioral Sciences, with generous financial support provided by the William and Flora Hewlett Foundation, Grant #2000-5633, and while Frank D. Bean was a Visiting Scholar at the Russell Sage Foundation.

The Annual Review of Sociology is online at http://mutex.gmu.edu:3415.

DISCUSSION QUESTIONS

1. Where do new immigrants stand along the black/white color line?
2. How did race change from a biological to a cultural category?

REFERENCES

Alba RD. 1985. *Italian Americans: Into the Twilight of Ethnicity.* Engelwood. Cliffs, NJ: Prentice Hall.

Alba RD. 1990. *Ethnic Identity: The Transformation of White America.* New Haven, CT: Yale Univ. Press.

Alba RD. 1999. Immigration and the American realities of assimilation and multiculturalism. *Sociol. Forum* 14(1): 3–25.

Bean FD, Lee J. 2002. America's changing color lines: Immigration, racial/ethnic diversity, and multiracial identification. Presented at the Center for the Comparative Study of Race and Ethnicity, Stanford Univ.

Bean FD, Stevens G. 2003. *America's Newcomers and the Dynamics of Diversity.* New York: Russell Sage Found.

Bobo L. 1997. The color line, the dilemma, and the dream: Race relations in America at the close of the twentieth century. In *Civil Rights and Social Wrongs*, ed. J Higham, pp. 31–55. University Park: Penn. State Univ. Press.

Brodkin K. 1998. *How Jews Became White Folks and What That Says about Race in America.* New Brunswick, NJ: Rutgers Univ. Press.

Clark K. 1965. *Dark Ghetto: Dilemmas of Social Power.* New York: Harper and Row.

DaCosta K. 2000. Remaking the Color Line: Social Bases and Implications of the Multiracial Movement. Doc. Diss., Univ. Calif., Berkeley.

Dalmage HM. 2000. *Tripping on the Color Line: Black–White Multiracial Families in a Racially Divided World.* New Brunswick, NJ: Rutgers Univ. Press.

Davis FJ. 1991. *Who Is Black? One Nation's Definition.* University Park: Penn. State Univ. Press.

Davis K. 1941. Intermarriage in caste societies. *Am Anthropol.* 43:388–95.

Drake SC, Cayton HR. 1993 (1945). *Black Metropolis: A Study of Negro Life in a Northern City.* Chicago, IL: Univ. Chicago Press.

Du Bois WEB. 1997 (1903). *The Souls of Black Folk.* Boston, MA: Bedford Books.

Eschbach K. 1995. The enduring and vanishing American Indian: American Indian population growth and intermarriage in 1980. *Ethn. Racial. Stud.* 18(1): 89–108.

Eschbach K, Gomez C. 1998. Choosing Hispanic identity: Ethnic identity switching among respondents to high school and beyond. *Soc. Sci. Q.* 79(1): 74–90.

Eschbach K, Supple K, Snipp CM. 1998. Changes in racial identification and the educational attainment of American Indians, 1970–1990. *Demography* 35(1): 35–43.

Farley R. 2001. Identifying with multiple races. Rep. 01-491. Popul. Stud. Cent., Ann Arbor, MI: Univ. Mich.

Farley R. 2002. Racial identities in 2000: The response to the multiple-race response option. In *The New Race Question: How the Census Counts Multiracial Individuals*, ed. J Perlmann, MC Waters, pp. 33–61. New York: Russell Sage Found.

Farley R, Allen WR. 1987. *The Color Line and the Quality of Life in America.* New York: Russell Sage Found.

Foner N. 2000. *From Ellis Island to JFK: New York's Two Great Waves of Immigration.* New Haven, CT/New York: Yale Univ. Press/Russell Sage Found.

Fu V. 2001. Racial intermarriage pairing. *Demography* 38(2): 147–60.

Gans HJ. 1979. Symbolic ethnicity: The future of ethnic groups and cultures in America. *Ethn. Racial Stud.* 2: 1–20.

Gans HJ. 1999. The possibility of a new racial hierarchy in the twenty-first century United States. In *The Cultural Territories of Race*, ed. M Lamont, pp. 371–90. Chicago, IL/New York: Univ. Chicago Press/Russell Sage Found.

Gerstle G. 1999. Liberty, coercion, and the making of Americans. In *The Handbook of International Migration*, ed. C Hirschman, P Kasinitz, J DeWind, pp. 275–93. New York: Russell Sage Found.

Gilbertson G, Fitzpatrick JF, Yang L. 1996. Hispanic intermarriage in New York City: New evidence from 1991. *Int. Migr. Rev.* 30: 445–59.

Gitlin T. 1995. *The Twilight of Common Dreams.* New York: Metropolitan.

Gordon M. 1964. *Assimilation in American Life.* New York: Oxford Univ. Press.

Grieco EM, Cassidy RC. 2001. Overview of race and Hispanic origin. Census 2000 Brief. U.S. Dep. Commer., Econ. Stat. Admin. U.S. Census Bur.

Haney Lopez IF. 1996. *White by Law: The Legal Construction of Race.* New York: New York Univ. Press.

Harris DR, Sim JJ. 2002. Who is multiracial? Assessing the complexity of lived race. *Am. Sociol. Rev.* 67(4): 614–27.

Harris M, Consorte JG, Lang J, Byrne B. 1993. Who are the whites? Imposed census categories and the racial demography of Brazil. *Soc. Forces* 72(2): 451–62.

Harrison R, Bennett C. 1995. Racial and ethnic diversity. In *State of the Union: America in the 1990s*, Vol. 2: *Social Trends*, ed. R Farley. New York: Russell Sage Found.

Hirschman C, Alba R, Farley R. 2000. The meaning and measurement of race in the U.S. Census: Glimpses into the future. *Demography* 37: 381–93.

Hollinger DA. 1995. *Postethnic America: Beyond Multiculturalism.* New York: Basic Books.

Ignatiev N. 1995. *How the Irish Became White.* New York: Routledge.

Jacobson MF. 1998. *Whiteness of a Different Color: European Immigrants and the Alchemy of Race.* Cambridge, MA: Harvard Univ. Press.

Jacoby T. 2001. An end to counting race? *Commentary* 111(6): 37–40.

Johnson TP, Jobe JB, O'rourke D, Sudman S, Warnecke RB, et al. 1997. Dimensions of self-identification among multiracial and multiethnic respondents in survey interviews. *Eval. Rev.* 21(6):671–87.

Kalmijn M. 1993. Patterns in black/white intermarriage. *Soc. Forces* 72(1): 119–46.

Korgen KO. 1998. *From Black to Biracial: Transforming Racial Identity Among Americans.* Westport, CT: Praeger.

Lee J, Bean FD. 2003. Beyond black and white: Remaking race in America. *Contexts* 2(3): 26–33.

Lee SM, Fernandez M. 1998. Patterns in Asian American racial/ethnic intermarriage: A comparison of 1980 and 1990 census data. *Sociol. Perspect.* 41(2): 323–42.

Lieberson S. 1980. *A Piece of the Pie: Blacks and White Immigrants since 1880.* Berkeley: Univ. Calif. Press.

Lieberson S, Waters MC. 1988. *From Many Strands: Ethnic and Racial Groups in Contemporary America.* New York: Russell Sage Found.

Lieberson S, Waters MC. 1993. The ethnic responses of whites: What causes their instability, simplification, and inconsistency? *Soc. Forces* 72(2): 421–50.

Loewen J. 1971. *The Mississippi Chinese: Between Black and White.* Cambridge, MA: Harvard Univ. Press.

Massey DS, Denton NA. 1993. *American Apartheid: Segregation and the Making of the Underclass.* Cambridge, MA: Harvard Univ. Press.

McKenney NR, Bennett CE. 1994. Issues regarding data on race and ethnicity: The Census Bureau experience. *Public Health Rep.* 109(1): 16–25.

Merton RK. 1941. Intermarriage and the social structure: fact and theory. *Psychiatry* 4:361–74.

Moran RF. 2001. *Interracial Intimacy: The Regulation of Race and Romance.* Chicago IL: Univ. Chicago Press.

Morning A. 2000. Counting on the color line. Presented at the Annu. Meet. Popul. Assoc. Am., Los Angeles, CA, March.

Myrdal G. 1944. *An American Dilemma: The Negro Problem and Modern Democracy.* New York: Harper.

Nobles M. 2000. *Shades of Citizenship: Race and the Census in Modern Politics.* Stanford, CA: Stanford Univ. Press.

Pagnini DL, Morgan SP. 1990. Intermarriage and social distance among U.S. immigrants at the turn of the century. *Am. J. Sociol.* 96(2): 405–32.

Patterson O. 1998a. *The Ordeal of Integration.* Washington, DC: Civitas.

Patterson O. 1998b. *Rituals of Blood.* Washington, DC: Civitas.

Perlmann J. 2000. Reflecting the changing face of America: Multiracials, racial classification, and American intermarriage. In *Interracialism: Black-White Intermarriage in American History, Literature, and Law,* ed. W. Sollars, pp. 506–33. New York: Oxford Univ. Press.

Perlmann J, Waldinger R. 1997. Second generation decline? Children of immigrants, past and present—a reconsideration. *Int. Migr. Rev.* 31(4): 893–922.

Portes A, Rumbaut RG. 2001. *Legacies: The Story of the Immigrant Second Generation.* Berkeley: Univ. Calif. Press.

Qian Z. 1997. Breaking the racial barriers: Variations in interracial marriage between 1980 and 1990. *Demography* 34(2): 263–76.

Rodriguez CE. 2000. *Changing Race: Latinos, the Census, and the History of Ethnicity in the United States.* New York: NY Univ. Press.

Roediger DR. 1991. *The Wages of Whiteness.* New York: Verso.

Root MPP, ed. 1992. *Racially Mixed People in America.* Newbury Park, CA: Sage.

Root MPP, ed. 1996. *The Multiracial Experience: Racial Borders as the New Frontier.* Thousand Oaks, CA: Sage.

Rosenfeld MJ. 2002. Measures of assimilation in the marriage market: Mexican Americans 1970–1990. *J. Marriage Fam.* 64:152–62.

Saenz R, Hwang S, Aguirre BE, Anderson RN. 1995. Persistence and change in Asian identity among children of intermarried couples. *Sociol. Perspect.* 38(2): 175–94.

Salgado de Snyder N, Lopez CM, Padilla AM. 1982. Ethnic identity and cultural awareness among the offspring of Mexican interethnic marriages. *J. Early Adolesc.* 2:277–82.

Sanjek R. 1994. Intermarriage and the future of the races. In *Race,* ed. S Gregory, R Sanjek, pp. 103–30. New Brunswick, NJ: Rutgers Univ. Press.

Skrentny JD, ed. 2001. *Color Lines: Affirmative Action, Immigration, and Civil Rights Options for America.* Chicago, IL: Univ. Chicago Press.

Smelser NJ, Wilson WJ, Mitchell F, eds. 2001. *America Becoming: Racial Trends and their Consequences.* Washington, DC: Natl. Acad. Press.

Smith JP, Edmonston B. 1997. *The New Americans.* Washington, DC: Natl. Acad. Press.

Spencer JM. 1997. *The New Colored People: The Mixed-Race Movement in America.* New York: New York Univ. Press.

Spickard PR. 1989. *Mixed Blood.* Madison: Univ. Wis. Press.

Spickard PR, Fong R. 1995. Pacific Islander Americans and multiethnicity: A vision of America's future? *Soc. Forces* 73(4): 1365–83.

Stephan CW, Stephan WG. 1989. After intermarriage: Ethnic identity among mixed-heritage Japanese-Americans and Hispanics. *J. Marriage Fam.* 51: 507–19.

Tizard B, Phoenix A. 1993. *Black, White or Mixed Race? Race and Racism in the Lives of Young People of Mixed Parentage.* New York: Routledge.

Tucker MB, Mitchell-Kernan C. 1990. New patterns in Black American interracial marriage: The social structural context. *J. Marriage Fam.* 52: 209–18.

U.S. Bur. Census. 2002. Current Population Survey: Monthly Demographic File, March (Computer file). Washington, DC: U.S. Dep. Commer.

U.S. Immigr. Nat. Serv. 2002. *2000 INS Statistical Yearbook.* Washington, DC: USGPO.

Waldinger R, Lee J. 2001. New immigrants in urban America. In *Strangers at the Gates,* ed. R Waldinger, pp. 30–79. Berkeley: Univ. Calif. Press.

Waters MC. 1990. *Ethnic Options: Choosing Identities in America.* Berkeley: Univ. Calif. Press.

Waters MC. 1999. *Black Identities: West Indian Immigrant Dreams and American Realities.* Cambridge, MA: Harvard Univ. Press.

Waters MC. 2000a. Immigration, intermarriage, and the challenges of measuring racial/ethnic identities. *Am. J Public Health* 90:1735–37.

Waters MC. 2000b. Multiple ethnicities and identity in the United States. In *We Are a People*, ed. P Spikard, WJ Burroughs, pp. 23–40. Philadelphia, PA: Temple Univ. Press.

Williams K. 2001. Boxed In: The United States Multiracial Movement. Unpubl. Diss., Cornell Univ.

Wilson WJ. 1980. *The Declining Significance of Race.* Chicago, IL: Univ. Chicago Press. 2nd ed.

Wilson WJ. 1987. *The Truly Disadvantaged: The Inner City, the Underclass, and Public Policy.* Chicago, IL: Univ. Chicago Press.

Xie Y, Goyette K. 1997. The racial identification of biracial children with one Asian parent: Evidence from the 1990 Census. *Soc. Forces* 76:547–70.

Zack N. 1993. *Race and Mixed Race.* Philadelphia, PA: Temple Univ. Press.

Zhou M, Bankston CL III. 1998. *Growing Up American: How Vietnamese Children Adapt to Life in the United States.* New York: Russell Sage Found.

READING 8

From Friendly Foreigner to Enemy Race

Selective Racialization, Covering, and the Negotiation of Middle Eastern American Identity

John Tehranian

The term *Middle East* likely emerged in the 1850s from Britain's India Office.[1] It did not enjoy widespread usage in policy circles, however, until the early twentieth century, when it was used in the work of famed American naval strategist Admiral Alfred Thayer Mahan. In an article first published in September 1902, Mahan used the term *Middle East* to refer to a region of growing strategic importance in the emerging conflict pitting Britain and the United States against Germany and Russia.[2] Mahan appeared to define that region as ranging, on a north-south axis, from Turkey to the Arabian Peninsula and, on an east-west axis, from Iran to Egypt. Thus, the designation was borne of geopolitical considerations and its construction wrought with semiotic meaning. . . .

John Tehranian is a professor of law at Chapman University School of Law.

The term *Middle East* therefore appears to eschew the typical hallmarks of regional definitions, which are often based on continental, linguistic, or perceived ethnic boundaries. Observes Sedat Laciner,

> This so-called region neighbors two oceans (Indian and Atlantic) and six seas (Mediterranean, Red Sea, Persian Gulf, Black Sea, Aegean Sea and the Caspian Sea). It extends to three continents (Africa, Asia and Europe). It consists of ten sub-regions (Southern and Northern Caucasus, Northern Africa, Arabia, Greater Palestine and Syria, Mesopotamia, the Caspian Basin, Central Asia (Turkistan), and the Indian Peninsula). Three monotheistic religions (Islam, Christianity and Judaism), with their numerous sects and schools of thought, exist in this region. Thousands of religious and moral faiths, including atheism and paganism, are practiced in this wide geography and thus, it is one of the largest laboratories of the world. Although viewed by the West as all-Arab, the region consists of tens of different ethnic-linguistic communities, with Turks, Arabs and Persians as the main ones.[3]

At the same time, the term is riddled in ambiguity, sometimes encompassing the entire North African coast, from Morocco to Egypt, and other parts of Africa, including the Sudan and Somalia, the former Soviet, Caucasus Republics of Georgia, Azerbaijan, and Armenia, and occasionally Afghanistan, Pakistan, and Turkistan. The Middle East is therefore a malleable geopolitical construct of relatively recent vintage. . . .

A search of all reported federal and state court opinions reveals that there was not a single reference to the terms *Middle East* or *Middle Eastern* until 1946, when a New York court referred to a "European Middle Eastern Service Medal and Victory Medal" given to veterans.[4] Other than scattered references to similar medals, the next mention of the *Middle East* or *Middle Eastern* came in a 1955 IRS dispute involving the taxation of an oil worker who had taken employment in numerous countries, including Saudi Arabia, Lebanon, Syria, and Iraq. The court synoptically referred to the work as having resided in "Near or Middle Eastern countries."[5] The term was also used in a 1956 breach-of-contract suit in which the U.S. government failed to deliver certain airplane technology to "the Middle East" lest it be used in regional conflicts contrary to American foreign-policy interests.[6] Finally, several federal suits in 1957 linked the term to its most precious commodity, referring on numerous occasions to "Middle Eastern oil."[7] As these cases make clear, in the beginning, the Middle Eastern designation arose in a geopolitical and oil-related context.

In a time-honored process, the racialization of individuals from Turkey, Iran, and the Arab states as "Middle Eastern" came to serve broader economic and political needs. In their influential work on the formation of race, Michael Omi and Howard Winant highlight the "sociohistorical process by which racial categories are created, inhabited, transformed, and destroyed."[8] In prior eras, the racialization and stereotyping of various groups has taken on a distinctly utilitarian flavor.

Take the typecasting of African Americans through the course of history. . . . The demands of the plantation economy helped give rise to the Southern hierarchy and its black-white divide based on skin color (which supplanted the earlier hierarchy based on religious affiliation). As Richard Delgado reminds us, antiblack "prejudice sprang up with slavery. Previously, educated Europeans held generally positive attitudes toward Africans, recognizing the African civilization was highly advanced."[9] As slavery emerged, infantilization became commonplace in media portrayals, as blacks were stereotyped as buffoons unable to survive without the guidance of their masters. Blackface minstrelsy rose to popularity, in the guise of Sambo and other characters, conveying images of blacks as either "inept urban dandies or happy childlike slaves."[10] Following emancipation and the end of the Civil War, however, images became more ominous, with black men portrayed as rapists preying on white women and black women reduced to pliable domestic servants.[11] Stereotypes followed function, first legitimating slavery and later rationalizing lynching, segregation, imperialism, and Jim Crow.

Since "conquering nations generally demonize their subjects in order to rationalize exploiting them,"[12] Latino and Asian stereotypes have undergone a similar trajectory. As Delgado notes, "Anglo settlers in California and the Southwest began to circulate notions of Mexican inferiority only when the settlers came to covet Mexican lands and mining claims."[13] Similarly, early portraits of the Chinese and Japanese cast them as comical and hapless, though they were happily tolerated for their contribution to the American workforce. As economic and assimilatory fears related to these groups heightened, however, Charlie Chan–like stereotypes transformed and gave rise to the clichéd image of the wily, scheming, and menacing "Oriental" criminal mastermind.[14]

Quite simply, concludes Delgado, "Depictions vary depending on society's needs."[15] What then are we to make of the dramatic change in the status of Middle Easterners? It is hardly coincidence that it has occurred over the past generation—a time that has seen the Middle East rise to the forefront of global politics and economic importance due to its ample reserves of the great engine of industrialization: oil.

THE MIDDLE EASTERNER AS THE OTHER: THE SLIPPERY SLOPE FROM FRIENDLY FOREIGNER TO ENEMY ALIEN, ENEMY ALIEN TO ENEMY RACE

Inextricably intertwined with the rising tide of discrimination facing persons of Middle Eastern descent is the mythology surrounding racial construction and related religious and sociocultural perceptions. For prior generations, Middle Eastern Americans came closer to matching our constructed notions of whiteness. They were largely Christian; they came from an exotic but friendly, romantic, and halcyon foreign land imagined to contain magic lanterns, genies, flying carpets, and belly dancers; and they served as a chief vessel of the philosophical and cultural heritage of the West.[16] Thus, in previous generations, people of (what we now call) Middle Eastern descent were, more often than not, blended into the white category. . . .

[Now] in an era when we view the most immediate threat to our national security as emanating from the Middle East, it is not surprising that monolithic images of the Middle East and the Middle Easterner have leaped into existence. Middle Easterners have been irretrievably associated with Islam; they appear to hail from a decidedly unfriendly foreign land imagined to contain nothing but terrorists, obstreperous mobs chanting "Death to America," unabashed misogynistic polygamists, and religious fundamentalists; and they seem to represent a wholly different civilization from our own—one with which the inevitable and apocalyptic clash of civilizations is unfolding.[17] Thus, they are the quintessential Other, and the Middle Easterner category, imposed on them by society at large, has become their appellation.

In popular perception, in which the notion of assimilability constitutes the sine qua non of the majority's acceptance of an immigrant group, it is not surprising that Middle Easterners have fared poorly. As Karen Engle has noted, the past century has witnessed a radical transformation in majority perceptions of Middle Eastern individuals: they are, in short, no longer thought capable of assimilation.[18] The changing religious composition of Middle Eastern immigrants to the United States has played a key role in this transformation. As the naturalization cases make clear, perceptions of race are frequently conflated with perceptions of religion. In 1924, about two hundred thousand Arabs resided in the United States. Of these, 80 percent were from Syria and Lebanon, of which group a startling 90 percent were Christian.[19] Many of these immigrants had fled oppression and persecution under the Ottoman Empire.[20] Indeed, an early study of the emerging Syrian and Lebanese community at the turn of the century in New York City found that only 2 of 2,482 residents were Muslim.[21] As the author of the study noted, "The Moslems, Druses and Metâwely are not found in sufficient numbers to warrant more than passing mention."[22]

Given the tendency to conflate race with religious affiliation, and Christianity with assimilability, it is not surprising that, at the beginning of the twentieth century, courts declared Armenians and even some Arabs white by law, thereby entitling them to the privileges of whiteness, including naturalization. However, the composition of the Middle Eastern American population has undergone a dramatic change in recent years, especially in the public imagination. Contrary to popular perceptions, only 23 percent of present-day Arab Americans are Muslim.[23] However, about 60 percent of Arab immigrants arriving in the United States since 1965 identify themselves as Muslim.[24] As it has grown less Christian, the Middle Eastern population in the United States is thought of as less assimilable and, consequently, less white.

As faith in their assimilatory capacity has diminished, Middle Easterners have come to represent enemy aliens, and even an enemy race, in the popular imagination. In the past, the paradigmatic noncitizen was the "Mexican illegal alien, or the inscrutable, clannish Asian."[25] Today, it is the Arab terrorist, and this vision has firmly taken hold of our immigration policies. As Victor Romero argues, "post-9/11, the age-old stereotype of the foreign, Arab terrorist has been rekindled, and placing our immigration functions under the auspices of an executive department charged with 'homeland security' reinforces the idea that immigrants are terrorists."[26] The recent wave of registration and deportation policies aimed at individuals of Middle Eastern descent also highlights this trend. Take, for example, the National Security Entry-Exit Registration System (NSEERS), which was formally announced by the attorney general on June 6, 2002, and then supplemented with a special "call-in" registration in November 2002. The NSEERS singles out a limited class of noncitizens—male, nonimmigrant visa holders over the age of sixteen who are from one of twenty-five Muslim and Middle Eastern countries—for special registration requirements.[27] . . .

THE NEGOTIATION OF MIDDLE EASTERN IDENTITY: SELECTIVE RACIALIZATION AND COVERING

The negotiation of the Middle Eastern identity is mediated by a two-fold process that moves both from the top down and from the bottom up. From the top down, society at large engages in a practice that can best be described as *selective racialization*. From the bottom up, Middle Easterners, both privileged and damned by their proximity to the white dividing line, engage in persistent (and frequently effective) covering of their ethnic background. These two social forces combine to create a pernicious stereotyping feedback loop that enervates the political strength of the Middle Eastern community, heightens its invisibility, and leaves little effective resistance to the growing assaults against its civil rights.

A Theory of Selective Racialization

…Specifically, in society at large, Middle Easterners are consistently subjected to a process of *selective racialization*. This largely undocumented and predominantly subconscious mechanism has profound ramifications. Systematically, famous individuals of Middle Eastern descent are usually perceived as white. Meanwhile, *infamous* individuals of Middle Eastern descent are usually categorized as Middle Eastern. When Middle Eastern actors conform to social norms and advance positive values and conduct, their racial identity as the Other recedes to the background as they merge into the great white abyss. By contrast, when Middle Eastern actors engage in transgressive behavior, their racial identity as the Other immediately becomes a central, defining characteristic of who they are. The result is an endless feedback loop that calcifies popular prejudices. Wholesome and socially redeeming activities, which might otherwise subvert public misperceptions of the community, do not get associated with Middle Eastern identity. By contrast, the image of transgression is continually correlated with the Middle Eastern racial category, serving only to reinforce negative connotations with the community.

Our country is filled with individuals of Middle Eastern descent who have contributed constructively to American society. Yet surprisingly few of these Americans are actually perceived as Middle Easterners. Instead, their ethnicity is frequently whitewashed.[28] On one hand, this fact highlights the assimilability of Middle Eastern immigrants in the United States. On the other hand, it creates a problematic signposting of Middle Eastern identity when it becomes associated with transgressive activities.

The long list of Middle Eastern Americans includes individuals from virtually every aspect of American life, including athletes such as tennis player Andre Agassi (Persian/Armenian), Indy 500 champion Bobby Rahal (Lebanese), and NFL quarterbacks Doug Flutie and Jeff George (both Lebanese); entertainers such as actresses Cher (Armenian), Kathy Najimi (Lebanese), Catherine Bell (half Persian), and Gabrielle Anwar (half Persian), actors Danny Thomas (Lebanese) and Tony Shalhoub (Lebanese), radio deejay Casy Kasem (Palestinian/Lebanese), and singer Paul Anka (Lebanese); prominent entrepreneurs such as hoteliers the Maloof family (Lebanese) and Apple CEO Steve Jobs (half Syrian); and politicians and activists such as former New Hampshire governor and White House chief of staff John Sununu (Lebanese), former senator George Mitchell (half Lebanese), and prominent consumer advocate and presidential candidate Ralph Nader (Lebanese/Egyptian). Even "good" Middle Easterners who are perceived as nonwhite are not racialized as Middle Eastern. For example, although they are both half Lebanese, neither Salma Hayek, a famous actress, nor Shakira, an internationally renowned singer, is identified as Middle Eastern. Instead, they are almost universally considered Latina.

Some observers might point to the whitewashing of Americans of Middle Eastern descent as evidence of our evolving colorblindness. But such an argument is belied by the systematic racialization of transgressive individuals. When individuals lie at the cusp of the white/nonwhite divide, we unconsciously categorize them as the Other when they engage in wrongdoing but blend them into the white when they behave within social norms. Andre Agassi is a (white) tennis player, and Ralph Nader is a (white) politician. But Osama bin Laden is labeled an Arab terrorist and the Ayatollah Khomeini was a Middle Eastern Islamic fundamentalist. The act of selective racialization is by no means limited to geopolitical struggles. It occurs on a far more pedestrian, but nevertheless important, level. Take the case of Dodi Al-Fayed, the wealthy businessman who was dating Princess Diana following her divorce from Prince Charles. The escapades of the two, rumored to be engaged at the time of their deaths, were the subject of extensive media coverage. Throughout their relationship, Al-Fayed was repeatedly portrayed as an *Arab* businessman and *Middle Eastern* playboy—not merely an Englishman or a businessman without reference to his race. In other words, he was racialized. And the reason is clear: he was engaging in transgressive behavior, stealing away with the People's princess.

Other examples abound. Recently, Zenadine Zidane, a member of the French national soccer team, viciously headbutted Italian player Marco Materazzi in the finals of the 2006 World Cup. Zidane's violent outburst likely cost his team the championship and has gone down as one of the most infamous incidents in soccer history. While the incident sullied Zidane's previously untarnished reputation, it also did something else: it racialized Zidane in the United States. In the aftermath of the incident, Zidane went from simply being an otherwise ordinary native-born (white) Frenchman on the Gallican national soccer team to becoming an Arab. American media reports highlighted his Algerian roots. The racial subtext was all too clear—there was an implicit association of his apparent predilection for violence with his Arab background. He had brazenly violated social norms with his headbutt and, as such, had become a transgressor. Simultaneously, he went from being white to becoming the Other.

The process of selective racialization occurs with regularity in the mass media, serving to bolster and legitimize existing stereotypes. Although all the characters in the Middle Eastern-themed Disney film *Aladdin* share Arab descent, they are only selectively racialized. The chief wrongdoers—the greedy bazaar merchants, the thief Kazim, and the main antagonist, Jafar—all possess exaggerated stereotypical features. Both Kazim and Jafar

sport thick Arab accents, facial hair, and prominent hooked noses. By contrast, the movie's sympathetic protagonists—Aladdin, Princess Jasmine, and the Sultan—possess few of the features traditionally associated with Arabs. Instead, their physiognomy is quintessentially European, and they speak with no trace of a Middle Eastern accent.[29] In other words, the transgressive characters are Arabized and the wholesome characters are Anglicized, thereby heightening negative stereotypes linked to Middle Easterners while concurrently reinforcing positive associations with whiteness. . . .

Negotiating Middle Eastern Racial Status in the New America: Covering and Its Implications

Drawing from the work of Erving Goffman,[30] who once observed "that persons who are ready to admit possession of a stigma . . . may nonetheless make a great effort to keep the stigma from looming large,"[31] Kenji Yoshino calls attention to a rampant, yet relatively unappreciated, consequence of our national impulse toward assimilation—the covering of disfavored identities. Based on pressures to conform to social norms enforced by the dominant culture, a rational distaste for ostracism and social opprobrium can lead individuals to engage in the purposeful act of toning down traits that identify them with a stigmatized group. . . .

Applying Yoshino's model in the Middle Eastern context is both revealing and instructive: what, after all, could be more coercively assimilationist than forcibly designating an entire population white de jure while simultaneously treating that population as nonwhite de facto? Not surprisingly, Middle Easterners have sought refuge in covering as a strategic response to the discrimination they face. . . .

Largely due to the existence of distinctive phenotypic characteristics, many African Americans cannot pretend to be anything but African American and many Asian Americans cannot pretend to be anything but Asian American.[32] Many Middle Easterners, however, can realistically opt out of their racial categorization. Middle Easterners are more prone to racial ambiguity because successive waves of diverse populations have passed through the Middle East, making it a veritable racial melting pot since antiquity. Since the stereotypical image of the Middle Easterner is much darker in skin, hair, and eye color than the average Middle Easterner, those who naturally possess lighter skin, hair, and eyes are particularly nimble in their covering. Either way, with the simple change of a revealing first or last name, many Middle Easterners can become Italian, French, Greek, Romanian, Indian, Mexican, Puerto Rican, or Argentine.[33]

The gravitation toward covering is often irresistible, especially through its seductive illusion of simplifying the lives of its purveyors. In the wake of 9/11, Middle Easterners throughout the United States felt under attack and responded with a series of rational covering responses just to survive the wave of hate surging throughout the country.[34] Lebanese and Persian restaurants conspicuously displayed "Proud to be American" signs over their entrances. Cab drivers from the Middle East and South Asia decorated their vehicles with large American flags.[35] A series of hate crimes prompted many Muslim women and Sikh men to remove their head coverings out of fear of being perceived as Middle Eastern.[36]

Four axes of covering—association, appearance, affiliation, and activism[37]—are prevalent in the Middle Eastern community. Consider the phenomenon of association. As one associates more with recognized whites, one better performs whiteness and is therefore perceived as more white. When I first moved to Newport Beach, California, the former hometown of John Wayne and an oceanside hamlet renowned as a bastion of wealth and white conservatism, a friend of mine joked, "Don't worry—I'll be your white sponsor." His wry comment had historical antecedents. A decade after Congress passed the Chinese Exclusion Act of 1882 prohibiting any new immigration from China, Chinese immigrants already residing in the United States had to prove the legality of their presence by providing the testimony of "one credible *white* witness."[38] Mingling with the white is a powerful form of obtaining white bona fides.

In an illuminating passage from her essay *I Grew Up Thinking I Was White*, Iranian American writer Gelareh Asayesh describes the associational covering that she undertakes to assimilate:

> My National Public Radio accent takes me further than my parents' voices, laden with inflections from a faraway land. The options may be limited when it comes to skin color, but it is possible to improve one's status in other ways. I think of it as race laundering: the right clothes, the right car, the right neighborhood can help compensate for that fundamental imperfection: nonwhiteness.[39]

Asayesh's reflections help to explain why Iranian Americans—like many others trying to earn their white stripes—are so often concerned with projecting images of success and wealth. Iranian Americans in Los Angeles are well-known for making their homes in Beverly Hills, driving only a BMW or Mercedes, and dressing in the most high-priced designer fashions. For example, 1995's Alicia Silverstone vehicle *Clueless*, set in Beverly Hills, had an incisive and comical reference to the city's Persian residents. At one point, the lead character points away from the camera and comments, "that's the Persian mafia. You can't hang with them unless you own a BMW."[40] The camera then turns to reveal a throng of Iranian American teenagers outfitted stylishly in black, driving their German imports.

Throughout the Middle Eastern community, the manipulation of appearance also emerges as a quintessential form of covering. Middle Eastern women frequently dye their hair blond or wear colored contact lenses to downplay their more "ethnic" features. Middle Eastern men will go by the name "Mike" for Mansour, "Mory" for Morteza, "Al" for Ali, and "Moe" for Mohammed. Such tactics may appear petty and even futile, but they can be surprisingly effective. I was recently told a story about an Iranian American attorney who went by the name "Moe" instead of his birth-name, Mohammed. One day, he was selected for extra screening at the airport. After showing his identification to the TSA workers and undergoing the additional security measures, he calmly protested, wondering out loud if he had been targeted on the basis of his ethnicity. The TSA guard looked puzzled "It's not like your name is Mohammed or something," he guffawed. Absent the "Mohammed" stigma, Moe had become white. . . .

Many Iranians or Arabs of Jewish background cover by rationally exploiting mainstream (mis)-perceptions of "Jewishness" as both a religion and an ethnicity. For example, although the Jewish Iranian population is relatively large, especially in Los Angeles, the very existence of a Jewish Iranian population is a surprise to the many people who view Iran as an Islamic monolith. By identifying themselves to the world as Jewish, these Jewish Iranians tend to avoid any further questions about their ethnicity, as people assume their ethnicity is Jewish and that they therefore are white (i.e., Ashkenazi Jewish) and not Middle Eastern. A Jewish Iranian poet I once knew demonstrated her profound awareness of the way in which this popular misperception could be exploited for assimilatory purposes. Explaining the extent of her Persian pride, she pointed out that she had embraced her Iranian heritage despite the obvious covering tactics at her disposal "Since I'm Jewish, I don't have to be Iranian," she remarked. "Yet I choose to be."

Finally, with respect to activism, we have witnessed profound covering in the Middle Eastern community. As Kenji Yoshino argues, many minorities are reticent to become involved in the fight to protect their civil rights, lest they be associated with militant ethnics and become racialized. In the Middle Eastern American community, there is a profound wariness of political involvement, a fact revealed by the dearth of elected officials of Middle Eastern descent, even in areas with large concentrations. For example, it is believed that the highest ranking Iranian American public officeholder in the United States is Jimmy Delshad, the mayor of Beverly Hills.[41] Delshad was only elected to his post in 2007.[42] . . .

Beyond covering, Middle Eastern assimilation also crosses into the realm of passing and even conversion. As a matter of pride, many Middle Easterners (especially those from older generations, for which the importance of whiteness was perhaps more accentuated) insist on actually being considered white. In this regard, they are no different than prior immigrant groups. For example, in all but one of the many reported racial-prerequisite naturalization cases,[43] the petitioners claimed to be white, despite the fact that it was much harder to establish white, rather than black, status. At the time, many states had laws on the books declaring any individual with a single quantum of black blood to be black by law.[44]

In the continental United States, . . . white privilege still reigns supreme, and, naturally, immigrant groups still seek white recognition.[45] This is certainly true for the Iranian American population. The United States has seen a huge wave of immigration from Iran since the 1979 revolution. In 1996, it was estimated that almost 1.5 million Iranians resided in the United States, a figure that had grown from just a few thousand in the 1970s.[46] However, despite changes to the 2000 census, which allowed Middle Eastern individuals such as Iranian Americans to identify themselves as something other than just "white," it appears that very few Iranian Americans took the opportunity to do so. In fact, only 338,266 individuals in the United States identified themselves as Iranian.[47] The majority of Iranians, it seems, chose conversion. Any visitor to Los Angeles (often referred to as Tehrangeles or Irangeles) can attest that there are probably 338,266 individuals of Iranian descent living in Southern California, let alone the rest of the country.

The reason for this statistical discrepancy is not too difficult to ascertain: having fled a severely repressive government in their homeland, many Iranians have a profound mistrust of government. As a result, it is hardly surprising that they would balk at the chance to single themselves out conveniently to the government for identification and tracking purposes. Additionally, there is a strong desire within the Iranian community to assimilate. Ask typical Iranian Americans if they are white, and they will say, "Of course." Then, inevitably, they will tell you that the word *Iran* comes from the Sanskrit word meaning "Land of the Aryans" and that they, not the Germans, are the original Aryans. . . .

PERSONAL ACCOUNT

Master Status: Pride and Danger

I consider myself to be privileged in many things in life, but my one master status that is a bit controversial is being Muslim. By controversial, I mean that to some it might be a privilege to be Muslim, whereas to others, well . . . not so much. Aside from dealing with those who are racist, ignorant, and cruel, I think being Muslim is a privilege for me. For example, people will assume because I look like I am a practicing Muslim, that I won't be dishonest or conniving. People assume that I will be honest. Take, for example, the time I forgot my campus parking permit. The ticketing officer was writing me a ticket, but when I pled with him that I had just forgotten my parking pass, he said, "Well, you seem like you are a practicing young Muslim lady. I don't think you would be lying to me, so I'll take that ticket back."

I have actually tested this out. I once asked a non-Muslim woman friend to wear the hijab (head scarf) for one day, so it would be assumed she was Muslim. She went to the bookstore to buy a used textbook. When she got there, however, there were no used books, so she had to buy a new one, but she didn't have enough money. She explained to the clerk that she really needed the book for class right away, and asked if she could come back later to pay the rest. This is actually against the school policy. But the lady working at the register said to her, "Muslims usually don't cheat people. I am going to take your word for it," and let her buy the book at a used price (but put a hold on her account until the rest was paid). My friend was amazed.

Even with these positive experiences, being Muslim today can be very dangerous. I was in the 5th grade, sitting in the library fixing the TV monitor to play a video, when 9/11 happened. The flashing red news alert caught my eye. I stopped and sat there watching the crazy scene they were broadcasting. People were on fire and flying out of windows. Women were screaming, blood was all over the streets, and police and firefighters were everywhere. It was like a horror movie to me. Soon the library staff and administrators came to see what was going on. They quickly rushed me out and put the school on a complete shutdown. Parents were coming in to pick up their kids and teachers were crying. School was dismissed.

When we came back two days later, everyone was upset. We had classmates and teachers whose loved ones had been killed or injured. However, school had to continue, so everyone tried to have a normal day. During recess, a boy from another classroom came up to me and said, "I know I don't know you, but I want to warn you. My friend wants to kill you." I thought it was a joke. I ignored him and asked him to stay away. But he came back to me three times, until I finally became so annoyed by him that I complained to my teacher, asking if she could ask him to stay away.

The teacher called the boy, and soon his friend, and to her surprise and mine, the boy was right. His friend was carrying a gun and told the teacher and me straight up, "I am coming to kill her. She is Osama's daughter, and we have to kill these Muslims." The kid had a real gun, with a bullet. I was in shock. The teacher tried to take it from him, but he ran away. The police found him a few hours later, hiding somewhere in the forest right behind our school. I really wanted to believe it was just a joke, maybe just a nightmare, and I would wake up soon and things would be totally fine. It could not be reality, I thought . . . but it was reality.

It soon became the reality that I live every day. I get threatened at school, made fun of in public, discriminated against during work, and humiliated in the comfort of my home. I am reminded over and over again how my people are the cause of all these wars, are violent terrorists, and that I have to pay the price. People judge and discriminate against me on the basis of the acts of a few followers of my religion. They seem to forget that Muslims are humans just like they are. They forget that Islam is not made up of ten terrorists, but 1.4 billion people striving to live a better life just like they are. But even with all of this, as strong believers, we behold with patience, and we keep our heads up high, ignoring the comments. We are cautious about what we do and say, and every day we pray that we come back home to our families safely.

Although today's society portrays Muslims negatively, I think I am still privileged to be a Muslim. It is my number one identity. Before people even judge my gender/sex, my social status, my educational status, or anything else, they see "Muslim" written on my forehead. I am proud of that identity and always will be.

Sumaya Al-Hajebi

DISCUSSION QUESTIONS

1. As oil has become more important, why has there been a change in the image of the Middle East?
2. Describe the process of selective racialization and its consequences.

NOTES

1. Clayton R. Koppes, *Captain Mahan, General Gordon, and the Origins of the Term "Middle East,"* 12 MIDDLE EASTERN STUDIES 95, 95–96 (1976).
2. Alfred T. Mahan, *The Persian Gulf and International Relations,* in RETROSPECT AND PROSPECT 209, 237, 244–45 (1903).
3. Sedat Laciner, *Is There a Place Called "the Middle East"?* JOURNAL OF TURKISH WEEKLY OPINION, June 2, 2006, available online at http://www.turkishweekly.net/comments.php?id=2117#.
4. Fiore v. O'Connell, 66 N.Y.S.2d 173, 175 (N.Y. Sup. Ct. 1946).
5. Larsen v. Comm'r of Internal Revenue, 23 T.C. 599, 601 (Tax Court 1955).
6. Miller v. United States, 140 F. Supp. 789, 790, 792 (Ct. Cl. 1956).
7. Waldron v. British Petroleum Co., 149 F. Supp. 830, 836 (S.D.N.Y. 1957); United States v. Standard Oil Co. of California, 155 F. Supp. 121, 127 (S.D.N.Y. 1957).
8. Michael Omi and Howard Winant, RACIAL FORMATION IN THE UNITED STATES 55 (1994).
9. Richard Delgado, *Two Ways to Think about Race: Reflections on the Id, the Ego, an Other Reformist Theories of Equal Protection,* 89 GEO. L.J. 2279, 2283 (2001) (footnote omitted).
10. Richard Delgado & Jean Stefancic, *Images of the Outsider in American Law and Culture: Can Free Expression Remedy Systemic Social Ills?* 77 CORNELL L. REV. 1258, 1262–63 (1992).
11. *Id.*
12. Delgado, *supra*, at 2285.
13. *Id.* at 2283.
14. Delgado & Stefancic, *supra*, at 1271–72.
15. Delgado, *supra*, at 2285–86.
16. Of course, these romantic images have often served less than salutary ends, providing, as Edward Said has argued, implicit justification for colonial and imperial ambitions by the West toward the Middle East. *See* Edward Said, ORIENTALISM (1978).
17. *See, e.g.,* Samuel P. Huntington, THE CLASH OF CIVILIZATIONS AND THE REMAKING OF WORLD ORDER (1998).
18. *See* Karen Engle, *Constructing Good Aliens and Good Citizens; Legitimizing the War on Terror(ism),* 75 U COLO. L. REV. 59, 75 (2004) (discussing the stereotyping of

Middle Eastern individuals as religious extremists and terrorists incapable of assimilation in the United States).
19. Louise Cainkar, *The History of Arab Immigration to the U.S.: An Introduction for High School Students,* in ARAB AMERICAN ENCYCLOPEDIA (2000), available online at http://www.adc.org/education/AAImmigration.htm (accessed Sept. 12, 2006).
20. Lucius Hopkins Miller, A STUDY OF THE SYRIAN POPULATION OF GREATER NEW YORK 5 (1904).
21. *Id.* at 22.
22. *Id.* at 25.
23. Joyce Howard Price, *Census Counts 1.2 Million Arabs in U.S.: Most of Them Are Christian,* WASHINGTON TIMES, Dec. 4, 2003, at A1.
24. Engle, *supra*, at 74.
25. Victor Romero, *Race, Immigration and the Department of Homeland Security,* 19 ST. JOHN'S J. LEGAL COMMENT. 51, 55 (2004).
26. *Id.* at 52.
27. *See* Nancy Murray, *Profiled: Arabs, Muslims, and the Post-9/11 Hunt for the "Enemy Within,"* in CIVIL RIGHTS IN PERIL: THE TARGETING OF ARABS AND MUSLIMS 27, 44 (Elaine C. Hagopian ed., 2004).
28. Such a tack might be acceptable if we truly lived in a race-blind society in which racial perceptions were unimportant and all individuals were dissolved into a single catch-all "human" category. The "selective" aspect of the racialization process, however, belies the notion of race blindness.
29. Scott J. Simon, *Arabs in Hollywood: An Undeserved Image,* LATENT IMAGE (1996), available online at http://pages.emerson.edu/organizations/fas/latent_imageissues/1996-04/arabs.htm.
30. *See* Erving Goffman, STIGMA: NOTES ON THE MANAGEMENT OF SPOILED IDENTITY 12–13 (1963).
31. Kenji Yoshino, *Covering,* 111 YALE L. 169, 772–73.
32. There are certainly exceptions to this generalization, but I think it is fair to say that a determined individual of Middle Eastern descent would have a much easier time passing him- or herself off as a member of a different ethnic or racial group, or engaging in the act of covering, than an individual of African or East Asian descent. It should be noted that many Latinos, because of their inextricably mixed heritage, also "enjoy" the option of passing—for better or worse.
33. See, e.g., Lorraine Ali, *Laughter's New Profile,* NEWSWEEK, Apr. 22, 2002, at 61 (quoting a line from a routine performed by an Iranian American comedian: "Since September 11, when people ask me about my ethnicity I look them straight in the eye and say, 'I'm Italian' . . . We're all named Tony now.").
34. Sunita Patel, *Performative Aspects of Race: "Arab, Muslim, and South Asian" Racial Formation after September 11,* 10 ASIAN PAC. AM. L.J. 61, 83-84 (2005) (describing

many of the covering activities undertaken by individuals of Middle Eastern descent in the wake of 9/11.

35. *See, e.g.,* Muneer I. Ahmad, *A Rage Shared by Law: Post-September 11 Racial Violence as Crimes of Passion*, 92 CAL. L. REV. 1259, 1278–79 (2004); NEW YORKER, Nov. 5, 2001 (depicting on the cover a Sikh taxi driver whose cab is covered with American flags).

36. Patel, *supra*, at 84.

37. Kenji Yoshino, Covering: THE HIDDEN ASSAULT ON OUR CIVIL RIGHTS 125 (2006).

38. Geary Act of 1892, ch. 60, § 6, 27 Stat. 25 (1892) (repealed) (emphasis added).

39. Gelareh Asayesh, *I Grew Up Thinking I Was White*, in MY SISTER, GUARD YOUR VEIL; MY BROTHER, GUARD YOUR EYES: UNCENSORED IRANIAN VOICES 12, 17 (Lila Azam Zanganeh ed., 2006).

40. *Clueless* (Paramount Pictures 1995).

41. Prior to that, I would like to think that my uncle, Mansour Kia, was in the running for the title of highest ranking Iranian American elected official. He served as the mayor of the town of Stanton, Iowa (population: 714) at the turn of the century.

42. *In re* Cruz, 23 F. Supp. 774–75 (E.D.N.Y. 1938).

43. By the early 1900s, several Southern states had adopted this "one-drop" rule. *See* Luther Wright, Jr., *Who's Black, Who's White, and Who Cares? Reconceptualizing the United States's Definition of Race and Racial Classifications*, 48 VAND. L. REV. 513, 524 (1995) (documenting the progression of states toward the one-drop rule); Peter Wallenstein, TELL THE COURT I LOVE MY WIFE 142 (2002) (nothing that Georgia, Virginia, Alabama, and Oklahoma all had laws defining as black anyone with any drop of African ancestry); Plessy v. Ferguson, 163 U.S. 537 (1896) (assuming that the petitioner, who possessed only one-eighth African blood, was black for the purposes of segregation laws). *But see In re* Cruz, 23 F. Supp. at 775 (finding one-quarter African blood insufficient to gain someone recognition of African descent for naturalization purposes).

44. This trend is, of course, not limited to recent immigrant groups but has a long history. See, for example, the history of Irish, Greek, Italian, and Slavic assimilation in the United States. *See* NOEL IGNATIEV, HOW THE IRISH BECAME WHITE 2–3 (1995).

45. *See* Worldwide Persian Outreach, *The Persian Diaspora*, FARSINET, http://www.farsinet.com/pwo/diaspora.html (accessed Nov. 21, 2006). Another, more conservative, estimate suggests that the Iranian American population totaled approximately 540,000 by 2003. *See* Iranian Studies Group at MIT, *Factsheet on the Iranian-American Community* (2003), http://isg-mit.org/projects-storage/census/Factsheet.pdf.

46. Iranian Studies Group at MIT, *supra*.

WHAT IS SEX? WHAT IS GENDER?

READING 9

The Gendered Society

Michael S. Kimmel

In no country has such constant care been taken as in America to trace two clearly distinct lines of action for the two sexes, and to make them keep pace with the other, but in two pathways which are always different.

Alexis de Tocqueville
Democracy in America (1835)

Daily, we hear how men and women are different. They tell that we come from different planets. They

say we have different brain chemistries, different brain organization, different hormones. They say our different anatomies lead to different destinies. They say we have different ways of knowing, listen to different moral voices, have different ways of speaking and hearing each other.

You'd think we were different species, like, say lobsters and giraffes, or Martians and Venutians. In his best-selling book, pop psychologist John Gray informs us that not only do women and men communicate differently, but they also "think, feel, perceive, react, respond, love, need, and appreciate differently."[1] It's a miracle of cosmic proportions that we ever understand one another!

Yet, despite these alleged interplanetary differences, we're all together in the same workplaces, where we are evaluated by the same criteria for raises, promotions, bonuses, and tenure. We sit in the same classrooms, eat in the same dining halls,

---

Michael S. Kimmel is a professor of sociology at the State University of New York at Stony Brook.

read the same books, and are subject to the same criteria for grading. We live in the same houses, prepare and eat the same meals, read the same newspapers, and tune into the same television programs.

What I have come to call this "interplanetary" theory of complete and universal *gender difference* is also typically the way we explain another universal phenomenon: *gender inequality*. Gender is not simply a system of classification, by which biological males and biological females are sorted, separated, and socialized into equivalent sex roles. Gender also expresses the universal inequality between women and men. When we speak about gender we also speak about hierarchy, power, and inequality, not simply difference.

So the two tasks of any study of gender, it seems to me, are to explain both difference and inequality, or, to be alliterative, *difference* and *dominance*. Every general explanation of gender must address two central questions, and their ancillary derivative questions.

First: *Why is it that virtually every single society differentiates people on the basis of gender?* Why are women and men perceived as different in every known society? What are the differences that are perceived? Why is gender at least one—if not the central—basis for the division of labor?

Second: *Why is it that virtually every known society is also based on male dominance?* Why does virtually every society divide social, political, and economic resources unequally between the genders? And why is it that men always get more? Why is a gendered division of labor also an unequal division of labor? Why are women's tasks and men's tasks valued differently?

It is clear . . . that there are dramatic differences among societies regarding the type of gender differences, the levels of gender inequality, and the amount of violence (implied or real) that is necessary to maintain both systems of difference and domination. But the basic facts remain: *Virtually every society known to us is founded upon assumptions of gender difference and the politics of gender inequality.*

On these axiomatic questions, two basic schools of thought prevail: biological determinism and differential socialization. We know them as "nature" and "nurture," and the question of which is dominant has been debated for a century in classrooms, at dinner parties, by political adversaries, and among friends and families. Are men and women different because they are "hardwired" to be different, or are they different because they've been taught to be? Is biology destiny, or is it that human beings are more flexible, and thus subject to change?

Most of the arguments about gender difference begin . . . with biology. . . . Women and men *are* biologically different, after all. Our reproductive anatomies are different, and so are our reproductive destinies. Our brain structures differ, our brain chemistries differ. Our musculature is different. Different levels of different hormones circulate through our different bodies. Surely, these add up to fundamental, intractable, and universal differences, and these differences provide the foundation for male domination, don't they?

The answer is an unequivocal maybe. Or, perhaps more accurately, yes and no. There are very few people who would suggest that there are no differences between males and females. At least, I wouldn't suggest it. What social scientists call *sex differences* refer precisely to that catalog of anatomical, hormonal, chemical, and physical differences between women and men. But even here, as we shall see, there are enormous ranges of female-ness and male-ness. Though our musculature differs, plenty of women are physically stronger than plenty of men. Though on average our chemistries are different, it's not an all-or-nothing proposition—women do have varying levels of androgens, and men have varying levels of estrogen in their systems. And though our brain structure may be differently lateralized, males and females both do tend to use both sides of their brain. And it is far from clear that these biological differences automatically and inevitably lead men to dominate women. Could we not imagine, as some writers already have, a culture in which women's biological abilities to bear and nurse children might be seen as the expression of such ineffable power—the ability to create life—that strong men wilt in impotent envy?

In fact, in order to underscore this issue, most social and behavioral scientists now use the term *gender* in a different way than we use the word *sex*. Sex refers to the biological apparatus, the male and the female—our chromosomal, chemical, anatomical organization. Gender refers to the meanings that are attached to those differences within a culture. Sex is male and female; gender is masculinity and femininity—what it means to be a man or a woman. . . . And while biological sex varies very little, gender varies enormously. What it means to possess the anatomical configuration of male or female means very different things depending on where you are, who you are, and when you are living. . . .

The other reigning school of thought that explains both gender difference and gender domination is *differential socialization*—the "nurture" side of the equation. Men and women are different because we are taught to be different. From the moment of birth, males and females are treated differently. Gradually we acquire the traits, behaviors, and attitudes that our culture defines as "masculine" or "feminine." We are not necessarily born different; we become different through this process of socialization.

Nor are we born biologically predisposed toward gender inequality. Domination is not a trait carried on the Y chromosome; it is the outcome of the different cultural valuing of men's and women's experiences. Thus, the adoption of masculinity and femininity implies the adoption of "political" ideas that what women do is not as culturally important as what men do.

Developmental psychologists have also examined the ways in which the meanings of masculinity and femininity change over the course of a person's life. The issues confronting a man about proving himself and feeling successful will change, as will the social institutions in which he will attempt to enact those experiences. The meanings of femininity are subject to parallel changes, for example, among prepubescent women, women in

childbearing years, and postmenopausal women, as they are different for women entering the labor market and those retiring from it.

Although we typically cast the debate in terms of *either* biological determinism *or* differential socialization—nature versus nurture—it may be useful to pause for a moment to observe what characteristics they have in common. Both schools of thought share two fundamental assumptions. First, both "nature lovers" and "nurturers" see women and men as markedly different from each other—truly, deeply, and irreversibly different. (nurturers do allow for some possibility of change, but they still argue that the process of socialization is a process of making males and females different from each other—differences that are normative, culturally necessary, and "natural.") And both schools of thought assume that the differences *between* women and men are far greater and more decisive (and worthy of analysis) than the differences that might be observed *among* men or *among* women. Thus, both "nature lovers" and "nurturers" subscribe to some version of the interplanetary theory of gender.

Second, both schools of thought assume that gender domination is the inevitable outcome of gender difference, that difference causes domination. To the biologists, it may be because pregnancy and lactation make women more vulnerable and in need of protection, or because male musculature makes them more adept hunters, or that testosterone makes them more aggressive with other men and with women too. Or it may be that men have to dominate women in order to maximize their chances to pass on their genes. Psychologists of "gender roles" tell us that, among other things, men and women are taught to devalue women's experiences, perceptions, and abilities, and to overvalue men's.

I argue . . . that both of these propositions are false. First, . . . the differences between women and men are not . . . nearly as great as are the differences among women or among men. Many perceived differences turn out to be differences based less on gender than on the social positions people occupy. Second, I . . . argue that gender difference is the product of gender inequality, and not the other way around. In fact, gender difference is the chief outcome of gender inequality, because it is through the idea of difference that inequality is legitimated. As one sociologist recently put it, "The very creation of difference is the foundation on which inequality rests."[2]

Using what social scientists have come to call a "social constructionist" approach, . . . I make the case that neither gender difference nor gender inequality is inevitable in the nature of things, nor, more specifically, in the nature of our bodies. Neither are difference and domination explainable solely by reference to differential socialization of boys and girls into sex roles typical of men and women.

When proponents of both nature and nurture positions assert that gender inequality is the inevitable outcome of gender difference, they take, perhaps inadvertently, a political position that assumes that inequality may be lessened, or that its most negative effects may be ameliorated, but that it cannot be eliminated—precisely because it is based upon intractable differences. On the other hand, to assert, as I do, that the exaggerated gender differences that we see are not as great as they appear and that they are the result of inequality allows a far greater political latitude. By eliminating gender inequality, we will remove the foundation upon which the entire edifice of gender difference is built.

What will remain, I believe is not some non-gendered androgynous gruel, in which differences between women and men are blended and everyone acts and thinks in exactly the same way. Quite the contrary, I believe that as gender inequality decreases, the differences among people—differences grounded in race, class, ethnicity, age, sexuality *as well as* gender—will emerge in a context in which each of us can be appreciated for our individual uniqueness as well as our commonality.

MAKING GENDER VISIBLE FOR BOTH WOMEN AND MEN

. . . A dramatic transformation in thinking about gender . . . has occurred over the past thirty years. In particular, three decades of pioneering work by feminist scholars, both in traditional disciplines and in women's studies, has made us aware of the centrality of gender in shaping social life. We now know that gender is one of the central organizing principles around which social life revolves. Until the 1970s, social scientists would have listed only class and race as the master statuses that defined and proscribed social life. If you wanted to study gender in the 1960s in social science, for example, you would have found but one course designed to address your needs—"Marriage and the Family"—which was sort of the "Ladies Auxiliary" of the social sciences. There were no courses on gender. But today, gender has joined race and class in our understanding of the foundations of an individual's identity. Gender, we now know, is one of the axes around which social life is organized and through which we understand our own experiences.

In the past thirty years, feminist scholars properly focused most of their attention on women—on what Catharine Stimpson has called the "omissions, distortions, and trivializations" of women's experiences—and the spheres to which women have historically been consigned, such as private life and the family.[3] Women's history sought to rescue from obscurity the lives of significant women who had been ignored or whose work has been minimized by traditional androcentric scholarship, and to examine the everyday lives of women in the past—the efforts, for example, of laundresses, factory workers, pioneer homesteaders, or housewives to carve out lives of meaning and dignity in a world controlled by men. Whether the focus has been on the exemplary or the ordinary, though, feminist scholarship has made it clear that gender is a central axis in women's lives. . . .

But when we study men, we study them as political leaders, military heroes, scientists, writers, artists. Men, themselves, are invisible *as men*. Rarely, if ever, do we see a course that examines the lives of men as men. What is the impact of gender on the lives of these famous men? How does masculinity play a part in the lives of great artists, writers, presidents, etc. How does masculinity play out in the lives of "ordinary" men—in factories and on farms, in union halls and large corporations? On this score, the traditional curriculum suddenly draws a big blank. Everywhere one turns there are courses about men, but virtually no information on masculinity.

Several years ago, this yawning gap inspired me to undertake a cultural history of the idea of masculinity in America, to trace the development and shifts in what it has meant to be a man over the course of our history.[4] What I found is that American men have been very articulate in describing what it means to be a man, and in seeing whatever they have done as a way to prove their manhood, but that we haven't known how to hear them.

Integrating gender into our courses is a way to fulfill the promise of women's studies—by understanding men as gendered as well. In my university, for example, the course on nineteenth-century British literature includes a deeply "gendered" reading of the Brontës, that discusses their feelings about femininity, marriage, and relations between the sexes. Yet not a word is spoken about Dickens and masculinity, especially about his feelings about fatherhood and the family. Dickens is understood as a "social problem" novelist, and his issue was class relations—this despite the fact that so many of Dickens's most celebrated characters are young boys without fathers, and who are searching for authentic families. And there's not a word about Thomas Hardy's ambivalent ideas about masculinity and marriage in, say, *Jude the Obscure*. Hardy's grappling with premodernist conceptions of an apathetic universe is what we discuss. And my wife tells me that in her nineteenth-century American literature class at Princeton, gender was the main topic of conversation when the subject was Edith Wharton, but the word was never spoken when they discussed Henry James, in whose work gendered anxiety erupts variously as chivalric contempt, misogynist rage, and sexual ambivalence. James, we're told, is "about" the form of the novel, narrative technique, the stylistic powers of description and characterization. Certainly not about gender.

So we continue to act as if gender applied only to women. Surely the time has come to make

gender visible to men. As the Chinese proverb has it, the fish are the last to discover the ocean. . . .

THE CURRENT DEBATE

I believe that we are, at this moment, having a national debate about masculinity in this country—but that we don't know it. For example, what gender comes to mind when I invoke the following current American problems: "teen violence," "gang violence," "suburban violence," "drug violence," "violence in the schools?" And what gender comes to mind when I say the words "suicide bomber" or "terrorist hijacker"?

Of course, you've imagined men. And not just any men—but younger men, in their teens and twenties, and relatively poorer men, from the working class or lower middle class.

But how do our social commentators discuss these problems? Do they note that the problem of youth and violence is really a problem of young *men* and violence? Do they ever mention that everywhere ethnic nationalism sets up shop, it is young men who are the shopkeepers? Do they ever mention masculinity at all?

No. Listen, for example, to the voice of one expert, asked to comment on the brutal murder of Matthew Shepard, a gay twenty-one-year-old college student at the University of Wyoming. After being reminded that young men account for 80 percent to 90 percent of people arrested for "gay bashing" crimes, the reporter quoted a sociologist as saying that "[t]his youth variable tells us they are working out identity issues, making the transition away from home into adulthood."[5] This *"youth variable"*? What had been a variable about age and gender had been transformed into a variable about age. Gender had disappeared. That is the sound of silence, what invisibility looks like.

Now, imagine that these were all women—all the ethnic nationalists, the militias, the gay bashers. Would that not be *the* story, the *only* story? Would not a gender analysis be at the center of every single story? Would we not hear from experts on female socialization, frustration, anger, PMS, and everything else under the sun? But the fact that these are men earns nary a word.

Take one final example. What if it had been young girls who opened fire on their classmates in West Paducah, Kentucky, in Pearl, Mississippi, in Jonesboro, Arkansas, or in Springfield, Oregon? And what if nearly all the children who died were boys? Do you think that the social outcry would demand that we investigate the "inherent violence" of Southern culture, or simply express dismay that young "people" have too much access to guns? I doubt it. And yet no one seemed to mention that the young boys who actually committed those crimes were simply doing—albeit in dramatic form at a younger age—what American men have been taught to do for centuries when they are upset and angry. Men don't get mad; they get even. . . .

I believe that until we make gender visible for both women and for men we will not, as a culture, adequately know how to address these issues. That's not to say that all we have to do is address masculinity. These issues are complex, requiring analyses of the political economy of global economic integration, of the transformation of social classes, of urban poverty and hopelessness, of racism. But if we ignore masculinity—if we let it remain invisible—we will never completely understand them, let alone resolve them.

THE PLURAL AND THE POWERFUL

When I use the term *gender*, then, it is with the explicit intention of discussing both masculinity and femininity. But even these terms are inaccurate because they imply that there is one simple definition of masculinity and one definition of femininity. One of the important elements of a social constructionist approach—especially if we intend to dislodge the notion that gender differences alone are decisive—is to explore the differences *among* men and *among* women, since, as it turns out, these are often more decisive than the differences between women and men.

Within any one society at any one moment, several meanings of masculinity and femininity coexist. Simply put, not all American men and women are the same. Our experiences are also structured by class, race, ethnicity, age, sexuality, region. Each of these axes modifies the others. Just because we make gender visible doesn't mean that we make these other organizing principles of social life invisible. Imagine, for example, an older, black, gay man in Chicago and a young, white, heterosexual farm boy in Iowa. Wouldn't they have different definitions of masculinity? Or imagine a twenty-two-year-old wealthy Asian American heterosexual woman in San Francisco and a poor white Irish Catholic lesbian in Boston. Wouldn't their ideas about what it means to be a woman be somewhat different?

If gender varies across cultures, over historical time, among men and women within any one culture, and over the life course, can we really speak of masculinity or femininity as though they were constant, universal essences, common to all women and to all men? If not, gender must be seen as an ever-changing fluid assemblage of meanings and behaviors. In that sense, we must speak of *masculinities* and *femininities*, and thus recognize the different definitions of masculinity and femininity that we construct. By pluralizing the terms, we acknowledge that masculinity and femininity mean different things to different groups of people at different times.

At the same time, we can't forget that all masculinities and femininities are not created equal. American men and women must also contend with a particular definition that is held up as the model against which we are expected to measure ourselves. We thus come to know what it means to be a man or a woman in our culture by setting our definitions in opposition to a set of "others"—racial minorities, sexual minorities. For men, the classic "other" is, of course, women. It feels imperative to most men that they make it clear—eternally, compulsively, decidedly—that they are unlike women.

For most men, this is the "hegemonic" definition—the one that is held up as the model for all of us. It is as Virginia Woolf wrote in 1938, "the quintessence of virility, the perfect type of which all the others are imperfect adumbrations."[6] The hegemonic definition of masculinity is "constructed in relation to various subordinated masculinities as well as in relation to women," writes sociologist R. W. Connell. The sociologist Erving Goffman once described this hegemonic definition of masculinity like this:

> In an important sense there is only one complete unblushing male in America: a young, married, white, urban, northern, heterosexual, Protestant, father, of college education, fully employed, of good complexion, weight, and height, and a recent record in sports. . . . Any male who fails to qualify in any one of these ways is likely to view himself—during moments at least—as unworthy, incomplete, and inferior.[7]

Women contend with an equally exaggerated ideal of femininity, which Connell calls "emphasized femininity." Emphasized femininity is organized around compliance with gender inequality, and is "oriented to accommodating the interests and desires of men." One sees emphasized femininity in "the display of sociability rather than technical competence, fragility in mating scenes, compliance with men's desire for titillation and ego-stroking in office relationships, acceptance of marriage and childcare as a response to labor-market discrimination against women."[8] Emphasized femininity exaggerates gender difference as a strategy of "adaptation to men's power" stressing empathy and nurturance; "real" womanhood is described as "fascinating" and women are advised that they can wrap men around their fingers by knowing and playing by the "rules." In one research study, an eight-year-old boy captured this emphasized femininity eloquently in a poem he wrote:

If I were a girl, I'd have to attract a guy wear
  makeup; sometimes.

Wear the latest style of clothes and try to be
  likable.

I probably wouldn't play any physical sports like
  football or soccer.

I don't think I would enjoy myself around men
  in fear of rejection

or under the pressure of attracting them.[9]

GENDER DIFFERENCE AS "DECEPTIVE DISTINCTIONS"

The existence of multiple masculinities and femininities dramatically undercuts the idea that the gender differences we observe are due solely to differently gendered people occupying gender-neutral positions. Moreover, that these masculinities and femininities are arrayed along a hierarchy, and measured against one another, buttresses the argument that domination creates and exaggerates difference.

The interplanetary theory of gender assumes, whether through biology or socialization, that women act like women, no matter where they are, and that men act like men no matter where they are. Psychologist Carol Tavris argues that such binary thinking leads to what philosophers call the "law of the excluded middle," which, as she reminds us, "is where most men and women fall in terms of their psychological qualities, beliefs, abilities, traits and values."[10] It turns out that many of the differences between women and men that we observe in our everyday lives are actually not *gender* differences at all, but differences that are the result of being in different positions or in different arenas. It's not that gendered individuals occupy these ungendered positions, but that the positions themselves elicit the behaviors we see as gendered. The sociologist Cynthia Fuchs Epstein calls these "deceptive distinctions" because, while they appear to be based on gender, they are actually based on something else.[11]

Take, for example, the well-known differences in communication patterns observed by Deborah Tannen in her best-selling book *You Just Don't Understand.* Tannen argues that women and men communicate with the languages of their respective planets—men employ the competitive language of hierarchy and domination to get ahead; women create webs of inclusion with softer, more embracing language that ensures that everyone feels O.K. At home, men are the strong silent types, grunting monosyllabically to their wives, who want to use conversation to create intimacy.[12]

But it turns out that those very same monosyllabic men are very verbal at work, where they are in positions of dependency and powerlessness, and need to use conversation to maintain a relationship with their superiors at work; and their wives are just as capable of using language competitively to maximize their position in a corporate hierarchy. When he examined the recorded transcripts of women's and men's testimony in trials, anthropologist William O'Barr concluded that the witnesses' occupation was a more accurate predictor of their use of language than was gender. "So-called women's language is neither characteristic of all women, nor limited only to women," O'Barr writes. If women use "powerless" language, it may be due "to the greater tendency of women to occupy relatively powerless social positions" in society.[13] Communication differences turn out to be "deceptive distinctions" because rarely do we observe the communication patterns of dependent men and executive women. . . .

What about those enormous gender differences that some observers have found in the workplace? . . . Men, we hear, are competitive social climbers who seek advancement at every opportunity; women are cooperative team builders who shun competition and may even suffer from a "fear of success." But the pioneering study by Rosabeth Moss Kanter, reported in *Men and Women of the Corporation*, indicated that gender mattered far less than opportunity. When women had the same opportunities, networks, mentors, and possibilities for advancement, they behaved just as the men did. Women were not successful because they lacked opportunities, not because they feared success; when men lacked opportunities, they behaved in stereotypically "feminine" ways.[14]

Finally, take our experiences in the family. . . . Here, again, we assume that women are socialized to be nurturing and maternal, men to be strong and silent, relatively emotionally inexpressive arbiters of justice—that is, we assume that women do the work of "mothering" because they are socialized to do so. And again, sociological research suggests that our behavior in the family has somewhat less to do with gender socialization than with the family situations in which we find ourselves.

Research by sociologist Kathleen Gerson, for example, found that gender socialization was not very helpful in predicting women's family experiences. Only slightly more than half the women who were primarily interested in full-time motherhood were, in fact, full-time mothers; and only slightly more than half the women who were primarily interested in full-time careers had them. It turned out that marital stability, husbands' income, women's workplace experiences, and support networks were far more important than gender socialization in determining which women ended up full-time mothers and which did not.[15]

On the other side of the ledger, research by sociologist Barbara Risman found that despite a gender socialization that downplays emotional responsiveness and nurturing, most single fathers are perfectly capable of "mothering." Single fathers do not hire female workers to do the typically female tasks around the house; they do those tasks themselves. In fact, Risman found few differences between single fathers and mothers (single or married) when it came to what they did around the house, how they acted with their children, or even in their children's emotional and intellectual development. Men's parenting styles were virtually indistinguishable from women's, a finding that led Risman to argue that "men can mother and that children are not necessarily better nurtured by women than by men."[16] . . .

Based on all this research, you might conclude, as does Risman, that "if women and men were to experience identical structural conditions and role expectations, empirically observable gender differences would dissipate."[17] I am not fully convinced. There *are* some differences between women and men, after all. Perhaps, as this research suggests, those differences are not as great, decisive, or as impervious to social change as we once thought. . . .

THE MEANING OF MEAN DIFFERENCES

Few of the differences between women and men are hardwired into all males to the exclusion of all females, or vice versa. Although we can readily observe differences between women and men in rates of aggression, physical strength, math or verbal achievement, caring and nurturing, or emotional expressiveness, it is not true that all males and no females are aggressive, physically strong, and adept at math and science, and all females and no males are caring and nurturing, verbally adept, or emotionally expressive. What we mean when we speak of gender differences are mean differences, differences in the average scores obtained by women and men.

These mean scores tell us something about the differences between the two groups, but they tell us nothing about the distributions themselves, the differences *among* men or *among* women. Sometimes these distributions can be enormous: There are large numbers of caring or emotionally expressive men, and of aggressive and physically strong women. (See figure 1.) In fact, in virtually all the research that has been done on the attributes associated with masculinity or femininity, the differences among women and among men are far greater than the mean differences between women and men. We tend to focus on the mean differences, but they may tell us far less than we think they do.

What we think they tell us, of course, is that women and men are different, from different

planets. This is what I . . . call the interplanetary theory of gender difference—that the observed mean differences between women and men are decisive and that they come from the fact that women and men are biologically so physically different.

For example, even the idea that we are from different planets, that our differences are deep and intractable, has a political dimension: To call the "other" sex the "opposite" sex obscures the many ways we are alike. As the anthropologist Gayle Rubin points out:

> Men and women are, of course, different. But they are not as different as day and night, earth and sky, yin and yang, life and death. In fact from the standpoint of nature, men and women are closer to each other than either is to anything else—for instance mountains, kangaroos, or coconut palms. . . . Far from being an expression of natural differences, exclusive gender identity is the suppression of natural similarities.[18]

The interplanetary theory of gender difference is important not because it's right—in fact, it is wrong far more often than it is right—but because, as a culture, we seem desperately to *want* it to be true. That is, the real sociological question about gender is not the sociology of gender differences—explaining the physiological origins of gender difference—but the sociology of knowledge question that explores why gender difference is so important to us, why we cling to the idea of gender difference so tenaciously, why, I suppose, we shell out millions of dollars for books that "reveal" the deep differences between women and men, but will probably never buy a book that says, "Hey, we're all Earthlings!"

That, however, is [my] message. . . . Virtually all available research from the social and behavioral sciences suggests that women and men are not from Venus and Mars, but are both from planet Earth. We're not opposite sexes, but neighboring sexes—we have far more in common with each other than we have differences. We pretty much have the same abilities, and pretty much want the same things in our lives.

FIGURE 1

Schematic rendering of the overlapping distributions of traits, attitudes, and behaviors by gender. Although mean differences might obtain on many characteristics, these distributions suggest far greater similarity between women and men, and far greater variability among men and among women.

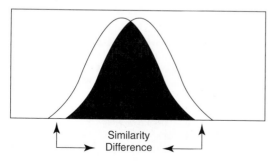

Similarity
Difference

PERSONAL ACCOUNT

Basketball

I frequently watch my boyfriend play basketball at an outdoor court with many other males in pick-up games. One time when I was there, there was a new face among the others waiting to play—a female face, and she was not sitting with the rest of the women who were watching. She was dressed and ready to play. I had never seen her in all the time I'd been there before, nor had I ever seen another woman there try to play.

For several games, she did not play. The guys formed teams and she was not asked to join. It was almost like there was a purposeful avoidance of her, with no one even acknowledging that she was there. Finally, she made a noticeable effort, and with some reluctance she was included in the next team waiting to play the winner of the current game. There were whispers and snickers among the guys, and I think it had a lot to do with the perception that she was challenging their masculinity. A "girl" was intruding into their area. My guess is that they were also somewhat nervous about the fact that she really might be good and embarrass some of them.

Anyway, the first couple of times up and down the court she was not given the ball despite the fact that she was wide open. The other guys on the team forced bad shots and tried super hard in what seemed like an effort to prove that she was not needed. The guy who was supposed to guard her on defense really didn't pay her much attention, and that same guy who she was guarding at the other end made sure he drove around her and scored on two occasions.

Finally, one time down the court she called for the ball and sank a shot from at least 16 feet. A huge feeling of relief and satisfaction came over me. Being a basketball player myself, I figured she was probably good or would not be there in the *first* place, but being a woman I was also happy to see her first shot go in. I found out later she had played basketball for a university and she had a great outside shot.

Even after she made one more shot off a rebound that ended up in her hands, she was not given the ball again. I suppose after some of the loud comments from some of the guys on the sidelines, that she was beating the male players out there, she wasn't going to get the ball again. I was kind of shocked that she wasn't *more* accepted even after she showed she was talented. I haven't seen her there since.

Andrea M. Busch

DISCUSSION QUESTIONS

1. What do you understand Kimmel to mean when he says that gender inequality produces gender difference? Can you give an example?

2. What is your reaction to Kimmel's position that we are engaged in a national debate about masculinity?

NOTES

1. John Gray, *Men Are from Mars, Women Are from Venus* (New York: HarperCollins, 1992), 5.

2. Barbara Risman, *Gender Vertigo* (New Haven: Yale University Press, 1998), 25. See also Judith Lorber, *Paradoxes of Gender* (New Haven: Yale University Press, 1994).

3. Catharine Stimpson, *Where the Meanings Are* (New York: Methuen, 1988).

4. See Michael Kimmel, *Manhood in America: A Cultural History* (New York: The Free Press, 1996).

5. Cited in James Brooke, "Men Held in Beatings Lived on the Fringes," *New York Times*, October 16, 1998, A16. Valerie Jenness, the sociologist who was quoted in the story, told me that she was *mis*quoted, and that of course she had mentioned gender as well as age—which suggests that the media's myopia matches that of the larger society.

6. Virginia Woolf, *Three Guineas* [1938] (New York: Harcourt, 1966), 142.

7. R. W. Connell, *Gender and Power* (Stanford: Stanford University Press, 1987), 183; Erving Goffman, *Stigma* (Englewood Cliffs, NJ: Prentice-Hall, 1963), 128.

8. Connell, *Gender and Power*, 183, 188, 187.

9. Cited in Risman, *Gender Vertigo*, 141.

10. Carol Tavris, "The Mismeasure of Woman," *Feminism and Psychology* (1993):153.

11. Cynthia Fuchs Epstein, *Deceptive Distinctions* (New Haven: Yale University Press, 1988).

12. Deborah Tannen, *You Just Don't Understand* (New York: William Morrow, 1991).

13. William O'Barr and Jean F. O'Barr, *Linguistic Evidence: Language, Power and Strategy—The Courtroom* (San Diego: Academic Press, 1995); see also Alfie Kohn, "Girl Talk, Guy Talk," *Psychology Today*, February 1988, 66.

14. Rosabeth M. Kanter, *Men and Women of the Corporation* (New York: Harper and Row, 1977).

15. Kathleen Gerson, *Hard Choices* (Berkeley: University of California Press, 1985); *No Man's Land* (New York: Basic Books, 1993).

16. Risman, *Gender Vertigo*, 70.

17. Risman, *Gender Vertigo*, 21.

18. Gayle Rubin, "The Traffic in Women," in *Toward an Anthropology of Women*, ed. R. R. Reiter, 179–80 (New York: Monthly Review Press, 1975).

READING 10

Where's the Rulebook for Sex Verification?

Alice Dreger

The only thing we know for sure about Caster Semenya, the world-champion runner from South Africa, is that she will live the rest of her life under a cloud of suspicion after track and field's governing body announced it was investigating her sex.

Why? Because the track organization, the I.A.A.F., has not sorted out the rules for sex typing and is relying on unstated, shifting standards.

To be fair, the biology of sex is a lot more complicated than the average fan believes. Many think you can simply look at a person's "sex chromosomes." If the person has XY chromosomes, you declare him a man. If XX, she's a woman. Right?

Wrong. A little biology: On the Y chromosome, a gene called SRY usually makes a fetus grow as a male. It turns out, though, that SRY can show up on an X, turning an XX fetus essentially male. And if the SRY gene does not work on the Y, the fetus develops essentially female.

Even an XY fetus with a functioning SRY can essentially develop female. In the case of Androgen Insensitivity Syndrome, the ability of cells to "hear" the masculinizing hormones known as androgens is lacking. That means the genitals and the rest of the external body look female-typical, except that these women lack body hair (which depends on androgen-sensitivity).

Women with complete Androgen Insensitivity Syndrome are less "masculinized" in their muscles and brains than the average woman, because the average woman makes and "hears" some androgens. Want to tell women with Androgen Insensitivity Syndrome they have to compete as men, just because they have a Y chromosome? That makes no sense.

So, some say, just look at genitals. Forget the genes—pull down the jeans! The I.A.A.F. asks drug testers to do this. But because male and female genitals start from the same stuff, a person can have something between a penis and a clitoris, and still legitimately be thought of as a man or a woman.

Moreover, a person can look male-typical on the outside but be female-typical on the inside, or vice versa. A few years ago, I got a call from Matthew, a 19-year-old who was born looking obviously male, was raised a boy, and had a girlfriend and a male-typical life. Then he found out, by way of some medical problems, that he had ovaries and a uterus.

Matthew had an extreme form of Congenital Adrenal Hyperplasia. His adrenal glands made so many androgens, even though he had XX chromosomes and ovaries, that his body developed to look male-typical. In fact, his body is mostly male-typical, including his muscle development and his self identity.

O.K., you say, if chromosomes and genitals do not work, how about hormones? We might assume that it is hormones that really matter in terms of whether someone has an athletic advantage.

Well, women and men make the same hormones, just in different quantities, on average. The average man has more androgens than the average woman. But to state the obvious, the average female athlete is not the average woman. In some

Alice Dreger is professor of clinical medical humanities and bioethics in the Feinberg School of Medicine at Northwestern University.

sports, she is likely to have naturally high levels of androgens. That is probably part of why she has succeeded athletically.

By the way, that is also why she is often flat-chested, boyish looking and may have a bigger-than-average clitoris. High levels of androgens can do all that.

Sure, in certain sports, a woman with naturally high levels of androgens has an advantage. But is it an unfair advantage? I don't think so. Some men naturally have higher levels of androgens than other men. Is that unfair?

Consider an analogy: Men on average are taller than women. But do we stop women from competing if a male-typical height gives them an advantage over shorter women? Can we imagine a Michele Phelps or a Patricia Ewing being told, "You're too tall to compete as a woman"? So why would we want to tell some women, "You naturally have too high a level of androgens to compete as a woman"? There seems to be nothing wrong with this kind of natural advantage.

So where do we draw the line between men and women in athletics? I don't know. The fact is, sex is messy. This is demonstrated in the I.A.A.F.'s process for determining whether Semenya is in fact a woman. The organization has called upon a geneticist, an endocrinologist, a gynecologist, a psychologist and so forth.

Sex is so messy that in the end, these doctors are not going to be able to run a test that will answer the question. Science can and will inform their decision, but they are going to have to decide which of the dozens of characteristics of sex matter to them.

Their decision will be like the consensus regarding how many points are awarded for a touchdown and a field goal—it will be a sporting decision, not a natural one, about how we choose to play the game of sex.

These officials should—finally—come up with a clear set of rules for sex typing, one open to scientific review, one that will allow athletes like Semenya, in the privacy of their doctors' offices, to find out, before publicly competing, whether they will be allowed to win in the crazy sport of sex. I bet

that's a sport no one ever told Semenya she would have to play.

DISCUSSION QUESTIONS

1. What criteria should guide scientists in deciding the sex of athletes?
2. In what ways does the application of scientific judgments affect decision making about the sex of athletes?

READING 11

All Together Now: Intersex Infants and IGM

Riki Wilchins

> "There is nothing abstract about the power that sciences and theories have to act materially and actually upon our bodies and our minds, even if the discourse that produces it is abstract. It is one of the forms of domination, its very expression."
>
> Monique Wittig, *The Straight Mind*

BODIES AT THE MARGINS

As Foucault once pointed out, the effects of discursive power are hard to see once a discourse is in place. Once we *see* gay, black, female, or transgender people, it's hard to imagine that they weren't always there. We imagine the cultural discourse about them just popped up in response; rather, it was the discourse that created such identities in the first place.

To clearly see discursive power at work, we need bodies at society's margins. Margins are margins because that's where the discourse begins to fray, where whatever paradigm we're in starts to lose its explanatory power and all those inconvenient exceptions begin to cause problems.

Riki Wilchins is the founding executive director of the Gender Public Advocacy Coalition.

We can see the marginalization of such bodies as evidence of their unimportance. Or we can see their marginalization as important evidence of the model's imperfection and begin to admit how the operations of language, knowledge, and truth have shaped our consciousness.

Once we might have turned to women, gays, transgender people, or even racial minorities for this kind of understanding. But as each of these groups has won greater or lesser degrees of social legitimacy, it has become necessary to look a little further out to find a really marginal, inconvenient body. We need a body that is still off the grid of cultural intelligibility, one that hasn't "set" yet into a socially recognized identity. What we need, of course, is a *herm*.

Cheryl Chase is a "true hermaphrodite." This is a very rare thing, since most intersex people are "only" pseudo-hermaphrodites.

When most people hear the word *hermaphrodite*, they're apt to think of a person born with "both sets of genitals," although this is actually impossible. *Hermaphrodite* is actually an archaic medical term, and the correct term is *intersex*.

According to Brown University medical researcher Dr. Anne Fausto-Sterling, one in every 2,000 births is intersex. As intersex activists say, these are children born with unexpected genitals, which is to say their genitals are perhaps worse, maybe better, or at least every bit as good as yours and mine (well, *yours* anyway).

Cheryl founded the Intersex Society of North America (ISNA), a national intersex advocacy group, and cofounded (with me) Hermaphrodites With Attitude—an intersex protest group, in itself a pretty rare thing. I just call her the Head Herm.

CONSTRUCTING CHERYL

"Cheryl" was born as "Charlie," a fairly happy, well-adjusted little boy. His doctor, however, was not as happy or well-adjusted.

For one thing, it must be admitted that Charlie had a pretty small penis. For another, Charlie had "ovaries" that contained both testicular and ovarian tissue.

Language is again a crucial issue here, especially at the margins, where labeling is the first discursive act that determines how a thing is seen and understood. For instance, if a boy has an ovary, is it still an ovary, especially if it also contains significant amounts of testicular tissue, as Cheryl's did? Medicine gives us no nonbinary options here, although the term *gonad* would do nicely enough.

Charlie was a year and a half old when—after tests, consultations, and diagnostic conferences—doctors decided that Charlie was actually a Cheryl. This meant his small penis was actually an abnormally large clitoris. So they cut it off.

Following the treatment protocols for a diagnosis of intersexuality, all evidence of Charlie's existence was hidden. Boy's clothes and toys were thrown out and replaced with girl's clothes and toys. Out blue, in pink.

Cheryl/Charlie's parents were warned to lie to her if he ever asked about her history, because the truth—intersexuality and surgery—would permanently traumatize the child. Doctors feared that acknowledging a history of intersexuality would undermine the sense of gender identity they had created in the child through secrecy and surgery.

Charlie had become Cheryl, but at an enormous price. The operation had removed a lot what the doctors thought was Charlie, but it also removed most of his erotic sensation, and along with it baby Cheryl's future ability to have an orgasm.

THE ABC'S OF IGM

"Intersexuality is a psychiatric emergency on the part of the doctors and parents, who treat it by cutting into the body of the infant, even though the adults—as the ones in distress—are the real patients."

Cheryl Chase

"The Academy is deeply concerned about the *emotional, cognitive, and body image* development of intersexuals, and believes that successful early genital surgery minimizes these issues."

Press Release on IGM from the American Academy of Pediatricians (emphasis added)

"Knowledge is not made for understanding; it is made for cutting."

Michel Foucault, *Language, Counter-Memory*

The surgical procedure Cheryl underwent is sometimes referred to as intersex genital mutilation. IGM refers to cosmetic genital cutting that is performed solely to make intersex infants resemble normal males and females. The definition of IGM does not include the small fraction of surgeries that are preformed to cure functional abnormalities, urinary obstructions, recurring infection, and so on.

It was not until the 1950s that IGM became a common pediatric practice. Prior to that, unless infants were born with genital deformities that caused ongoing pain or endangered their health, they were left alone. Today, according to Fausto-Sterling, about 1,000 infants are surgically altered for cosmetic reasons each year in U.S. hospitals, or about five every day.

Advocacy organizations like ISNA and GenderPAC do not advocate raising intersex children without a sex, which is a social impossibility anyway, at least right now. They do advocate forgoing permanent genital alteration of infants for strictly cosmetic reasons until they have grown old enough to participate in life-altering decisions about their own bodies and sexual health, and to offer informed consent.

LANGUAGE AS THE REAL

A pediatric nurse in one of my presentations complained, "But you don't mention all these tests we run to find out the infant's real sex." The discourse on intersex infants is concerned with discovering what binary sex they "really" are, so we can "fix" them properly. The possibility that intersex infants' sex might not be immediately available to us, that they might not have the sort of binary sex the doctors are so anxious to locate and assign, just doesn't register. Neither does the possibility that intersex bodies have nothing to tell us, or that these infants are whatever sex they are because that nonbinary outcome appears to the medical community (and indeed to most of society) as a logical impossibility.

As Cheryl notes, intersex is the sex that doesn't exist. First because it's always another sex "underneath" and, second, because as soon as it appears, we erase it. Whatever sex we "discover" in intersex infants' bodies is highly dependent upon what markers we choose—hormones, genitals, overall body structure, chromosomes, and gonads—and how we prioritize them.

Words are real; bodies are not.

There is no pretext of transparency here: We don't fit the words to the bodies; instead, it is the bodies that must fit the words. The only language we have for herm-bodies is directed toward pathologizing—and thereby delegitimating—them.

Nor can we raise the usual argument—"It's Nature's way"—when Sex is questioned. Clearly, Nature has other things in mind, even if we don't.

In this vein, I once tried to help a network producer who was searching for an intersex person to interview. He was interested only in one who had been surgically misassigned the "wrong sex." Our conversation went like this:

Producer: We're looking for someone whose sex was misassigned and who was then raised as the wrong sex, like John/Joan.

Me: How do we know if it was the wrong sex?

Producer: If they were really male but assigned female, or really female but assigned male.

Me: Okay. But what if they were really intersex?

Producer: Right. I get your point. But we're looking for someone who was misassigned.

Me: But if they're really intersex, then any assignment would be a misassignment.

Producer: Right. I get your point. Really.

Me: Why don't you interview Cheryl Chase? She/he's well known and very articulate.

Producer: Cheryl was misassigned?

Me: Yes. She/he was raised as a boy, then they decided she/he was a girl.

Producer: So she's really male?

Me: No, she/he's really Cheryl.

Producer: Right. I get it. I really do. But she's really a girl, right?

Me: Well, to me she/he looks like a woman, but do you mean hair, hormones, chromosomes, or genitals?

Producer: You know. Her *real* sex.

Me: Cheryl's real sex is intersex.

Producer: Uh-huh. I get it, honest. But can you give me an intersex person who was misassigned?

DISCOURSE: A PRACTICE WITH EFFECTS

Cheryl/Charlie had no say in what was done to him/her, nor had she/he complained that anything was wrong with him/her. The doctors and nurses involved were not spiteful or intolerant. On the contrary, they were dedicated healers, trained in pediatrics and deeply committed to Cheryl/Charlie's well-being. IGM is always considered compassionate surgery. Everything was done for his/her "own good."

Cheryl's mutilation did not result from the top-down power held by big institutions. Unlike that reliable villain, the State, the power involved was not that of repression and negation, so common when sex is involved. In fact, the discourse of Sex where Cheryl was involved did not *restrain* her Sex, but rather interpreted it, compelled it, and *demanded* it.

Her transformation from Charlie to Cheryl was carried out in a micro-politics of power: small, impersonal judgments and practices that involved myriad individuals, power that was held by no one in particular but exercised by practically everyone—except, of course, Charlie.

The power involved was productive, using language and meaning to interpret her genitals as defective, to produce her body as intersexed, and to require that she be understood through a lens of normal male and normal female. Through a series of silences and erasures, it socially produced a new person, one with a new name, history, wardrobe, bedroom decor, and toys.

This is not the familiar "big stick" approach to power that requires policemen, courts, and legislatures. That is something we are familiar with; at least it is something we know how to fight. The power that attached itself to Charlie's body is a different kind of power entirely, one we have little experience in dealing with, let alone have strategies to counter.

The Science involved in Charlie's surgery was also of a different order than we are accustomed to. That Science is logical, objective, and impartial. But the Science that has attached itself to herm-bodies is not disinterested at all, but rather interested in the most urgent way with preserving the universality of Sex and with defending society's interest in reproduction. In fact, one of IGM's basic rules is that any infant who might one day be able to become pregnant as an adult must be made into a female.

This kind of Science is characterized by a deliberate nonknowing, by its refusal to recognize the most obvious facts of the infant bodies before it. It is remarkable for its sturdy denial of any facts or interpretations that might contradict its own intentions.

THE SCIENCE OF SEX: PARTIAL, PASSIONATE, POLITICAL

Medical theories of Sex, like so much of theory, are concerned with the resolution and management of difference. Intersex infants represent one of society's most anxious fears—the multiplicity of Sex, the pinging under the binary hood, a noise in the engine of reproduction that must be located and silenced.

This kind of Science is not limited to bodies. Its psychiatric counterpart is called Gender Identity Disorder, or GID. GID does for insubordinate genders what IGM does for insubordinate genitals.

In GID, noncomplaining children as young as 3 and as old as 18 are made to undergo treatment that includes behavioral modification, confinement to psychiatric wards, and psychotropic medication, all because they transcend binary gender norms and/or cross-gender identify. These treatment measures are intended to help the child fit back into a defined gender role.

In many cases the psychiatrists who treat GID believe that norm-transcending "sissy boys" and "tomboy girls" are more likely to grow up to be gay, and GID treatment is designed to prevent homosexuality in adults. Yet gay activists largely ignore GID because they represent gay and lesbian Americans, and a 3-year-old doesn't have that kind of identity yet.

Of course the effort to regulate gender in children is not limited to those "at the margins." We have a host of social practices designed to masculinize boys and feminize girls that start at birth. For instance, infants who cry are more likely to be described as angry by adults who think they are boys, sad if they think they are girls. Caregivers are more likely to stroke and caress babies if they think they are girls and to bounce them if they think they are boys.

Up until a few years ago, the U.S. government was funding research into the best treatments for norm-transcending kids. Tax dollars were appropriated to pay for a new sort of knowledge manipulation: the prevention of "sissy boys." This has helped fuel a new counterscience devoted to providing biological basis for homosexuality. Our power *over* such bodies is enabled by the kinds of knowledge we create *about* them.

By asserting that the knowledge and language we create is transparent and objective, we confer enormous authority to it. We insulate it from criticism and deny its political origins; we justify excesses that might otherwise be unthinkable. At the margins, Science no longer asks but tells. Nature no longer speaks the truth, but is spoken to. Here, where our narrative of Sex breaks down, Knowledge finally bares its teeth.

IS IDENTITY POLITICS PERMANENTLY TROUBLED?

Cheryl can be understood as a genitally mutilated female, a genitally mutilated male, a transgender individual, an intersex individual, a man who sleeps with women, a woman who sleeps with women, or even a man with a vagina. This proved to be a real obstacle when Cheryl dealt with identity-based groups.

When we approached the board of a national women's organization for help, the organization's representatives responded that IGM was a terrible practice, and someone should stop it. But why, they wanted to know, was IGM a women's issue?

We pointed out that the overwhelming majority of infants diagnosed as "intersex" are otherwise unremarkable children whose clitorises happen to be larger than two standard deviations from the mean—an arbitrary measure equal to about three eighths of an inch. It turns out birth sex is like a menu. If your organ is less than three eighths of an inch long, it's a clitoris and you're a baby girl. If it's longer than an inch, it's a penis and you're a baby boy.

It is a startling example of the power of language, knowledge, and science to create bodies to realize that, if pediatricians agreed to increase this rule to, say, three standard deviations from the mean, thousands of intersex infants would be instantly "cured."

On the other hand, if they decided to decrease it to one-and-a half standard deviations, one third to half of the female readers of this book would suddenly find themselves intersexed, and therefore candidates for genital surgery.

But if it's in between, you're a baby herm: The organ is an enlarged clit, and it gets cut off. The pediatrician will apologetically explain to your parents that you were born genitally "deformed," but—through the miracle of modern Science—they can make you into a "normal little girl."

Of course, this never happens in reverse. No pediatrician will ever apologetically explain to your parents that, "I'm afraid your son's penis is going to be too big, maybe eight or nine inches long. No one will ever be attracted to him but homosexuals and oversexed women. If we operate quickly we can save him."

To help board members of the women's organization to understand, I showed them how to make a diagnosis. Holding up a thumb and forefinger about a quarter inch apart, I said, "female." Moving them about three-eighths of an inch apart, I said "intersex." I repeated this finger movement from "female" to "intersexed" over and over until heads began to nod.

Since many intersex infants were "really" women, this made IGM a women's issue. The board members even accepted Cheryl—a true hermaphrodite if ever there was one—as a woman.

Unfortunately, several board members insisted that since they were a women's group, I had to articulate everything in terms of "intersex" girls, a term with no meaning that contradicted everything I was trying to tell them.

Flushed with success, I asked a gathering of national gay organizations for their support on IGM, too. After what I thought was an impassioned presentation, they all agreed that IGM was a terrible practice and someone should stop it. But why, they wanted to know, was IGM a gay and lesbian issue? I pointed out that many intersex infants are heterosexualized as infants, surgically altered simply to ensure their bodies can accommodate a penis during intercourse.

Even worse, some doctors perform IGM out of the antique fear that girls with large clits (which no man likes) will repel potential husbands (which every woman needs), interfere with penetration (which every woman enjoys), and increase their chance of growing up to be masculinized lesbian women (which practically no woman wants to be). IGM was no longer an intersex issue or even a women's issue; it had become a gay issue.

I decided to cap my success by addressing a meeting of transgender organizations. Genderqueerness was their beat. This would be a walk in the park. And it was. They understood IGM right away. It was, they all agreed, a terrible practice, that someone should stop. But why, they wanted to know, was IGM a transgender issue?

Soft-pedaling Cheryl's identities as intersex, female, or lesbian, I focused like a laser on gender stereotypes. I pointed out that Cheryl had changed from one sex to another: She was transgender. Even more, IGM was a tell-tale example of enforcing exactly the kind of rigid, narrow, outdated gender stereotypes that hurt transgender people. In addition, a significant minority of transsexuals have some sort of organ development (such as hormonal imbalances and small or partial gonads) that could easily have gotten them diagnosed as intersex.

After extended discussion, IGM became a transgender issue.

Of course, none of these groups was ill intentioned or predisposed toward excluding intersex issues and IGM. They were all progressive, committed, and compassionate. Yet if national feminist groups even suspected that doctors performed clitoridectomies on thousands of baby girls each year, they would try to shut down hospitals across the country. If gay rights activists suspected that doctors were using hormones and surgery to erase thousands of potential lesbians each year, queer activists would be demonstrating in the halls of hospitals and lobbying in the halls of Congress.

But none of these scenarios have happened, all because an arbitrary definition means that these infants aren't female or possibly lesbian or even transgender. They're this other thing called intersex, which is not an issue for women or gays or transgender people; it's a medical issue. Presented with an enormously damaging and barbaric practice that harms thousands of kids, no group was able to embrace IGM as an issue. The rules of identity meant that intersex infants—the noise in the system—didn't fit....

DISCUSSIONS QUESTIONS

1. What are particular words, phrases, and concepts that especially contribute to the "need" for genital surgery?

2. Would you agree that the genital surgeries Wilchins describes are for cosmetic reasons?

WHAT IS SOCIAL CLASS?

READING 12

What's Class Got to Do with It?

Michael Zweig

Whether in regard to the economy or issues of war and peace, class is central to our everyday lives. Yet class has not been as visible as race or gender, not nearly as much a part of our conversations and sense of ourselves as these and other "identities." We are of course all individuals, but our individuality and personal life chances are shaped—limited or enhanced—by the economic and social class in which we have grown up and in which we exist as adults.

Even though "class" is an abstract category of social analysis, class is real. Since social abstractions can seem far removed from real life, it may help to consider two other abstractions that have important consequences for flesh-and-blood individuals: race and gender. Suppose you knew there were men and women because you could see the difference, but you didn't know about the socially constructed concept of "gender." You would be missing something vitally important about the people you see. You would have only a surface appreciation of their lives. If, based only on direct observation of skin color, you knew there were white people and black people, but you didn't know about "race" in modern society, you would be ignorant of one of the most important determinants of the experience of those white and black people. Gender and race are abstractions, yet they are powerful, concrete influences in everyone's lives. They carry significant meaning despite wide differences in experience within the populations of men, women, whites, blacks.

Similarly, suppose that based on your observation of work sites and labor markets you knew

there were workers and employers, but you didn't recognize the existence of class. You would be blind to a most important characteristic of the individual workers and employers you were observing, something that has tremendous influence in their lives. Despite the wide variety of experiences and identities among individual workers, capitalists, and middle class people, it still makes sense to acknowledge the existence and importance of class in modern society. In fact, without a class analysis we would have only the most superficial knowledge of our own lives and the experiences of others we observe in economic and political activity. . . .

When people in the United States talk about class, it is often in ways that hide its most important parts. We tend to think about class in terms of income, or the lifestyles that income can buy. . . . [But class can be better understood] as mainly a question of economic and political power. . . . Power doesn't exist alone within an individual or a group. Power exists as a relationship between and among different people or groups. This means that we cannot talk about one class of people alone, without looking at relationships between that class and others.

The working class is made up of people who, when they go to work or when they act as citizens, have comparatively little power or authority. They are the people who do their jobs under more or less close supervision, who have little control over the pace or the content of their work, who aren't the boss of anyone. They are blue-collar people like construction and factory workers, and white-collar workers like bank tellers and writers of routine computer code. They work to produce and distribute goods, or in service industries or government agencies. They are skilled and unskilled, engaged in over five hundred different occupations tracked by the U.S. Department of Labor: agricultural laborers, baggage handlers, cashiers, flight attendants, home health care aides, machinists, secretaries, short order cooks, sound technicians, truck drivers. In the United States, working class people are by far

Michael Zweig is a professor of economics at the State University of New York, Stony Brook.

the majority of the population. Over eighty-eight million people were in working class occupations in 2002, comprising 62 percent of the labor force.[1]

On the other side of the basic power relation in a capitalist society is the capitalist class, those most senior executives who direct and control the corporations that employ the private-sector working class. These are the "captains of industry" and finance, CEOs, chief financial officers, chief operating officers, members of boards of directors, those whose decisions dominate the workplace and the economy, and whose economic power often translates into dominant power in the realms of politics, culture, the media, and even religion. Capitalists comprise about 2 percent of the U.S. labor force.

There are big differences among capitalists in the degree of power they wield, particularly in the geographic extent of that power. The CEO of a business employing one hundred people in a city of fifty thousand might well be an important figure on the local scene, but not necessarily in state or regional affairs. On the national scale, power is principally in the hands of those who control the largest corporations, those employing over five hundred people. Of the over twenty-one million business enterprises in the United States, only sixteen thousand employ that many. They are controlled by around two hundred thousand people, fewer than two-tenths of 1 percent of the labor force.

Even among the powerful, power is concentrated at the top. It's one thing to control a single large corporation, another to sit on multiple corporate boards and be in a position to coordinate strategies across corporations. In fact, if we count only those people who sit on multiple boards, so-called interlocking directors, they could all fit into Yankee Stadium. They and the top political leaders in all branches of the federal government constitute a U.S. "ruling class" at the pinnacle of national power.

Capitalists are rich, of course. But when vice-president Dick Cheney invited a select few to help him formulate the country's energy policy shortly after the new Bush administration came into office in 2001, he didn't invite "rich people." He invited people who were leaders in the energy industry,

capitalists. The fact that they were also rich was incidental. Capitalists are rich people who control far more than their personal wealth. They control the wealth of the nation, concentrated as it is in the largest few thousand corporations. There is no lobby in Washington representing "rich people." Lobbyists represent various industries or associations of industries that sometimes coordinate their efforts on behalf of industry in general. They represent the interests that capitalists bring to legislative and regulatory matters.

Something similar operates for the working class. Over thirteen million people are in unions in the United States. Most of these unions—like the United Auto Workers (UAW); the American Federation of State, County, and Municipal Employees (AFSCME); the Carpenters; and the International Brotherhood of Teamsters (IBT)—maintain offices in Washington and in major and even smaller cities where their members work. In addition to engaging in collective bargaining at the workplace, these unions lobby for their members and occasionally coordinate their efforts to lobby for broader working class interests. Sixty-eight unions have joined under the umbrella of the American Federation of Labor, Congress of Industrial Organizations (AFL-CIO) to pool resources and try to advance the interests of working people in general. These organizations represent workers, not "the poor" or "middle-income people," even though some workers are poor and some have an income equal to that of some in the middle class.[2]

In between the capitalist and the working classes is the middle class. The "middle class" gets a lot of attention in the media and political commentary in the United States, but this term is almost always used to describe people in the middle of the income distribution. People sometimes talk about "middle class workers," referring to people who work for a wage but live comfortable if modest lives. Especially in goods-producing industries, unionized workers have been able to win wages that allow home ownership, paid vacations, nice cars, home entertainment centers, and other consumer amenities.

When class is understood in terms of income or lifestyle, these workers are sometimes called "middle class." Even leaders of the workers' unions use the term to emphasize the gains unions have been able to win for working people. "Middle class workers" are supposed to be "most people," those with stable jobs and solid values based in the work ethic, as opposed to poor people—those on welfare or the "underclass"—on one side, and "the rich" on the other. When people think about classes in terms of "rich, middle, and poor," almost everyone ends up in the middle.

Understanding class in terms of power throws a different light on the subject. In this view, middle class people are in the middle of the power grid that has workers and capitalists at its poles. The middle class includes professional people like doctors, lawyers, accountants, and university professors. Most people in the "professional middle class" are not self-employed. They work for private companies or public agencies, receive salaries, and answer to supervisors. In these ways they are like workers.

But if we compare professional middle class people with well-paid workers, we see important differences. A unionized auto assembly worker doing a lot of overtime makes enough money to live the lifestyle of a "middle class worker," even more money than some professors or lawyers. But a well-paid unionized machinist or electrician or autoworker is still part of the working class. Professors and lawyers have a degree of autonomy and control at work that autoworkers don't have. The difference is a question of class.

It is also misleading to equate the working class as a whole with its best-paid unionized members. Only 9 percent of private sector workers belong to unions, and millions of them are low-paid service employees. The relatively well-paid manufacturing industries are not typical of American business, and they are shrinking as a proportion of the total economy.

The middle class also includes supervisors in the business world, ranging from line foremen to senior managers below the top decision-making executives. As with the professional middle class, some people in the supervisory middle class are close to working people in income and lifestyle. We see this mostly at the lower levels of supervision, as with line foremen or other first-level supervisors. They often are promoted from the ranks of workers, continue to live in working class areas, and socialize with working class friends. But a foreman is not a worker when it comes to the power grid. The foreman is on the floor to represent the owner, to execute orders in the management chain of command. The foreman is in the middle—between the workers and the owners. When a worker becomes a supervisor, he or she enters the middle class. But just as the well-paid "middle class worker" is atypical, so "working class bosses" make up a small fraction of supervisory and managerial personnel in the U.S. economy.

We see something similar with small business owners, the third component of the middle class. Some come out of the working class and continue to have personal and cultural ties to their roots. But these connections do not change the fact that workers aspire to have their own business to escape the regimentation of working class jobs, seeking instead the freedom to "be my own boss." That freedom, regardless of how much it might be limited by competitive pressures in the marketplace and how many hours the owner must work to make a go of it, puts the small business owner in a different class from workers.

At the other end of the business scale, senior managers and high-level corporate attorneys and accountants share quite a bit with the capitalists they serve. They have considerable authority, make a lot of money, and revolve in the same social circles. But they are not the final decision makers. They are at a qualitatively different level in the power grid from those they serve, who pay them well for their service but retain ultimate authority. They, too, are in the middle class.

In all three sections of the middle class—professionals, supervisors, and small business owners—there are fuzzy borders with the working class and with the capitalists. Yet the differences in power, independence, and life circumstances among these classes support the idea of a separate middle class.

The middle class is about 36 percent of the labor force in the United States—sizable, but far from the majority, far from the "typical" American.

Like the working class and the capitalists, the middle class is represented in the political process by professional associations and small business groups. There is no "middle-income" lobby, but there are, for example, the Trial Lawyers Association, the American Medical Association, the American Association of University Professors, the National Association of Realtors.

Clearly, classes are not monolithic collections of socially identical people. We have seen that each class contains quite a bit of variation. Rather than sharp dividing lines, the borders between them are porous and ambiguous—important areas to study and better understand. Also, beyond the differences in occupations and relative power within classes, which lead to differences in incomes, wealth, and lifestyles, each class contains men and women of every race, nationality, and creed. Yet, despite these rich internal variations and ambiguous borders, a qualitative difference remains between the life experience of the working class compared with that of the professional and managerial middle class, to say nothing of differences both of these have with the capitalists.

DISCUSSION QUESTIONS

1. How is social class like and also different from race, sex, gender, and sexual orientation?
2. Would you agree with Zweig that "without a class analysis, we would have only the most superficial knowledge of our own lives and the experience of others"?

NOTES

1. For a detailed discussion of the class composition of the United States, on which these and the following findings are based, see Michael Zweig, *The Working Class Majority: America's Best Kept Secret* (Ithaca, NY: Cornell University Press, 2000), chap. 1.
2. Some middle class people are represented by unions, such as university professors in the American Federation of

Teachers (AFT) and legal aid attorneys in the UAW. Most union members are in the working class.

READING 13

More or Less Equal?

The Economist

The past 30 years have been a great time for the wealthy. Their businesses became more profitable; their equities and properties increased in value; for those who worked in investment banking or hedge funds, bonuses rose steeply. And the further up the income scale you went, the better the rich did. Just as the bottom 90% of the population have lagged far behind the top 10%, most of those in the top 10% have trailed the elite 1%. And that select 1% has looked in envy at the Croesus-like 0.1% at the very top of the tree.

Any explanation for this rise in inequality needs to account for several different trends. In the 1980s the poor fell further behind the middle classes, but since the 1990s those middle classes have been squeezed. Both groups have lost ground to the elite. Between 1947 and 1979 the top 0.1 % of American earners were, on average, paid 20 times as much as the bottom 90%, according to the Economic Policy Institute, a think-tank in Washington, DC; by 2006 the ratio had grown to 77. In 1979, 34.2% of all capital gains went to the top 1% of recipients; by 2005 the figure was 65.3%.

All this happened during a period when American workers' median real incomes stagnated (though the notional value [face value] of any health insurance would have risen steeply). In 2007, according to the Census Bureau, the median income of American male workers was $45,113, less than the $45,879 (in 2007 money) that they earned back in 1978. At no point over that 29-year period did median incomes pass the $46,000 mark. Families made ends meet because more women worked (and their real incomes did rise) and because they were able to borrow money to maintain their spending.

The classic tool for measuring inequality is the Gini coefficient. The higher it is, the less equal the society. In America the coefficient climbed steadily from 0.395 in 1974 to 0.47 in 2006 before dipping slightly to 0.463 in 2007. In Britain, according to the Institute for Fiscal Studies, the Gini has risen from 0.25 in 1979 to 0.35 in 2006 [1. The Gini coefficient, named after its originator Corrado Gini, measures the wealth or income inequality within a population. The coefficient can range from 0 to 1, with 0 indicating an equal distribution and 1 indicating complete inequality.] Figures from the United Nations suggest that America's Gini coefficient is lower than that of many developing countries but well above the levels recorded by egalitarian Denmark, Finland and Sweden, where it does not seem to have risen much.

The recent widening of inequalities marked a complete reversal of the previous trend. From the 1930s to the late 1970s wealth disparities in developed countries declined sharply. But which is the anomaly: the earlier period of high tax rates and rapidly growing state involvement in the economy, or the rising inequality of the past 30 years?

THE NORM AND THE EXCEPTION

Historically, it seems that the rich, like the poor, have always been with us. Even so, the change of course in the 1980s calls for an explanation, as does the fact that inequality has risen far more in some countries than in others. There is a clear gap between America's and Britain's "Anglo-Saxon" model and the rest.

That makes some explanations for the widening disparities look suspect. One is the widespread use of technology, which might be expected to favour those workers who are able to exploit it. But the Nordic economies are well up on technology; Finland, or instance, is home to Nokia, a huge mobile-telecoms group. Technological change may explain why unskilled workers have lost ground to graduates. But it does not explain why such a wide gap has emerged at the very top of the income scale,

with the top 0.1% outpacing other professional workers.

The disappearance of the ultra-high tax rates that were prevalent in the 1970s helped the rich hang on to their gains. But work by two academics, Thomas Piketty and Emmanuel Saez, shows that inequality has been just as marked in pre-tax as in post-tax incomes. And why did governments propose (and voters approve) such tax cuts in the first place? There was a feeling in the 1970s that the post-war economic model had been corroded by rising inflation and a series of oil shocks. That helped prepare the ground for the Reagan and Thatcher reforms.

As for inequality lower down the scale, a study of the literature by Robert Gordon and Ian Dew-Becker cites the decline in trade unionism as a big factor, at least for men. In 2005 only 14% of American workers were union members, compared with 27% in 1979. The decline in unionisation may also help to explain the political acceptance of the low-tax, low-regulation regime. Political parties are no longer as dependent as they were on union donations. Instead, they have had to cultivate the rich, who have gained greatly in lobbying power. A study in the late 1990s of congressional elections found that 81% of political donors earned more than $100,000 a year and only 5% earned less than $50,000.

The free-market consensus among parties in Western countries increased disillusionment among the poor, who felt they lacked any real choice between economic policies. That, in turn, made them less likely to cast their vote.

Domestic politics is clearly not the only factor. Many people would point to globalisation, in particular the opening up of the Indian and Chinese markets that vastly increased the global labour force, putting downward pressure on unskilled wages. But academic studies have not found this to be a big factor in explaining the level of wages for the unskilled in recent years.

Globalisation may, however, explain some of the changes at the very top of the scale. The emergence of a global market for talent in areas such as banking, the law and investment may explain why the top 0.1% have been so well rewarded.

In particular, the financial sector contributed an increasing proportion of stockmarket profits from the early 1980s to 2006. The greater acceptance of debt allowed private-equity firms and hedge funds to bet on rising asset prices with borrowed money, which is a quick route to riches when all goes well. There were plenty of incentives to take risk, in the expectation that someone else would pick up the tab when things went wrong. The willingness of central banks to use interest-rate cuts to bail out financial markets only added to the speculative enthusiasm.

Messrs Gordon and Dew-Becker point to the rise of "superstar" labour markets in which the best talent commands a huge premium. The clearest examples are found in entertainment and sport Name recognition gives an exponential kick to the incomes of celebrities like Madonna or David Beckham who can attract endorsements, souvenir sales and the rest. In financial markets, those who mastered the sophisticated instruments (such as derivatives) that emerged in the era of liberalisation were also able to cash in.

THE HALO EFFECT

Another group of beneficiaries, chief executives, may be in a different category. They benefited from the early use of share options in America. . . . Messrs Gordon and Dew-Becker are not sure whether the resulting wealth was due to their executive skill or to their ability to control boards and thus the amount they got paid. Some executives enjoy a "halo of reputation," the academics suggest, that causes directors to shower them with vast rewards when an equally capable but less famous alternative might have been willing to do the job at a small fraction of the price.

One thing holding back such executives was "outrage constraint," a fear that massive pay packages might attract unwelcome attention in the media. That may have led to an attempt to disguise executive pay, with the really big increases being awarded in the form of option grants and deferred compensation and benefits.

SPURS TO EFFORT

Leaving aside the moral issues, does inequality have any economic benefits? In the 1970s it was argued that high taxes had reduced incentives and thus economic growth. Entrepreneurs had to be motivated to build businesses and create jobs. But extensive study by economists has found little correlation, in either direction, between inequality and economic growth rates across countries.

One argument advanced in America is that wide income disparities might encourage more people to want to go to college, thus creating a better-educated workforce. But Lawrence Mishel of the Economic Policy Institute points out that several societies that are more egalitarian than America have higher college enrollment rates.

There might also be an argument in favour of wealth disparities if social mobility was high and the sons and daughters of office cleaners could fairly easily rise to become chief executives. But America and Britain, which follow the Anglo-Saxon model, have the highest intergenerational correlations between the social status of fathers and sons; the lowest are found in egalitarian Norway and Denmark. Things are even worse for ethnic minorities; a black American born in the bottom quintile of the population (by income) has a 42% chance of staying there as an adult, compared with 17% for a white person.

As a result talent is being neglected. Of American children with the highest test scores in eighth grade, only 29% of those from low-income families ended up going to college, compared with 74% of those from high-income families. Since the better-off can afford to keep their children in higher education and the poor cannot, breaking out of the cycle is hard.

Perhaps Americans put up with this system because they have unrealistic expectations of their chances of success. One study found that 2% of Americans described themselves as currently rich but 31% thought that they would become rich at some stage. In fact only 2–3% of those in the bottom half of the income distribution have a chance of becoming very well off (defined as having an annual income of more than $340,000). Just over half of those earning $75,000 a year think they will become very well off, but experience suggests that only 12–17% will make it.

Health outcomes too are decidedly unequal; the gap between the life expectancy of the top and bottom 10% respectively rose from 2.8 years to 4.5 between 1980 and 2000. That does not meet the definition of a fair society by John Rawls, a 20th-century philosopher, who described it as one in which a new entrant would be happy to be born even though he did not know his social position ahead of time.

However, these inequalities are likely to lessen now. For a start, this decade has so far seen a dismal performance by the stockmarket, which plays a crucial role in creating and maintaining wealth. Real annual returns from American stocks averaged –4.1% in the decade to the end of 2008.

THE PENDULUM SWINGS BACK

Property prices are already falling sharply. . . . Investment bankers are losing their jobs or at least seeing their bonuses cut, and hedge-fund managers are going out of business. As long as the credit crunch continues, it will be more difficult to use borrowed money to boost incomes. And corporate profits, which usually make a handsome contribution to the incomes of the rich, are declining steeply.

Much of this is what you would expect in a recession, and the poor will be suffering along with the rich. But although they may lose their jobs and default on their loans, they will not be troubled by collapsing asset prices because they do not own assets. Edward Wolff of New York University points out that the proportion of American households owning some stocks (including mutual funds and

401k pension plans) went up from 32% in 1983 to 51% in 2001. But only 32% of the population owned more than $10,000-worth of stock, and many middle-class people are only modestly affected by falling asset prices. The richest 10% of the American population owned 85% of all stocks. . . .

DISCUSSION QUESTIONS

1. Do you think Americans object to high degrees of income inequality? Why or why not?
2. Of the factors described as contributing to increasing inequality, which do you find most compelling?

READING 14

The Silver Spoon: Inheritance and the Staggered Start

Stephen J. McNamee and Robert K. Miller Jr.

> To heir is human.
>
> —Jeffrey P. Rosenfeld, *Legacy of Aging*

A common metaphor for the competition to get ahead in life is the foot race. The imagery is that the fastest runner—presumably the most meritorious—will be the one to break the tape at the finish line. But in terms of economic competition, the race is rigged. If we think of money as a measure of who gets how much of what there is to get, the race to get ahead does not start anew with each generation. Instead, it is more like a relay race in which we inherit a starting point from our parents. The baton is passed, and for a while, both parents and children run together. When the exchange is complete, the children are on their own as they position themselves for the next exchange to the next generation. Although each new runner may

Stephen J. McNamee is a professor of sociology at the University of North Carolina, Wilmington. Robert K. Miller, Jr. is a professor of sociology at the University of North Carolina, Wilmington.

gain or lose ground in the competition, each new runner inherits an initial starting point in the race.

In this intergenerational relay race, children born to wealthy parents start at or near the finish line, while children born into poverty start behind everyone else. Those who are born close to the finish line need no merit to get ahead. They already are ahead. The poorest of the poor, however, need to traverse the entire distance to get to the finish line on the basis of merit alone. In this sense, meritocracy applies strictly only to the poorest of the poor; everyone else has at least some advantage of inheritance that places him or her ahead at the start of the race.

In comparing the effects of inheritance and individual merit on life outcomes, the effects of inheritance come first, *followed by* the effects of individual merit—not the other way around. Figure 1 depicts the intergenerational relay race to get ahead. The solid lines represent the effects of inheritance on economic outcomes. The dotted lines represent the potential effects of merit. The "distance" each person needs to reach the finish line on the basis of merit depends on how far from the finish line each person starts the race in the first place.

It is important to point out that equivalent amounts of merit do not lead to equivalent end results. If each dash represents one "unit" of merit, a person born poor who advances one unit on the basis of individual merit over a lifetime ends up at the end of her life one unit ahead of where she started but still at or close to poverty. A person who begins life one unit short of the top can ascend to the top based on an equivalent one unit of merit. Each person is equally meritorious, but his or her end position in the race to get ahead is very different.

Heirs to large fortunes in the world start life at or near the finish line. Barring the unlikely possibility of parental disinheritance, there is virtually no realistic scenario in which they end up destitute—regardless of the extent of their innate talent or individual motivation. Their future is financially secure. They will grow up having the best of everything and having every opportunity money can buy.

Most parents want the best for their children. As a result, most parents try to do everything they can to secure their children's futures. Indeed, that parental desire to provide advantages for children may even have biological origins. Under the

FIGURE 1

The intergenerational race to get ahead. Note: solid lines are effects of inheritance; dashed lines are potential effects of merit.

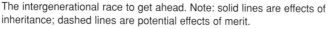

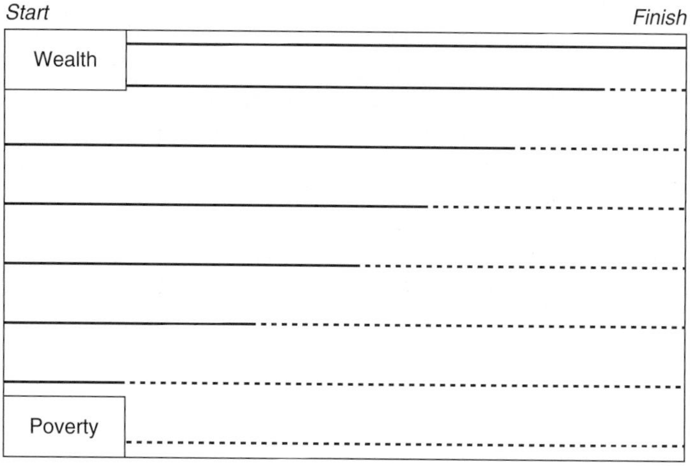

"inclusive fitness-maximizing" theory of selection, for instance, beneficiaries are favored in inheritance according to their biological relatedness and reproductive value. Unsurprisingly, research shows that benefactors are much more likely to bequeath estates to surviving spouses and children than to unrelated individuals or institutions (Schwartz 1996; Willenbacher 2003). In a form of what might be called "reverse inheritance," parents may invest in children to secure their own futures in the event that they become unable to take care of themselves. Parents may also invest in their children's future to realize vicarious prestige through the successes of their children, which may, in turn, be seen as a validation of their own genetic endowments or child-rearing skills.

Regardless of the source of parental motivation, most parents clearly wish to secure children's futures. To the extent that parents are successful in passing on advantages to children, meritocracy does not operate as the basis for who ends up with what. Despite the ideology of meritocracy, the reality in America, as elsewhere, is inheritance first and merit second.

INCOME AND WEALTH INEQUALITY

In considering how parents pass on advantages to children in the race to get ahead, researchers have usually looked at occupational mobility, that is, at how the occupations of parents affect the occupations of children. The results of this research show that parental occupation has strong effects on children's occupational prospects. Some of this effect is mediated through education; that is, the prestige of parental occupation increases the educational attainment of children, which in turn increases the prestige of the occupations they attain. Looking at occupational prestige alone, however, underestimates the full extent of inequality in society and overestimates the amount of movement within the system. A fuller appreciation of what is at stake requires examination of the kind and extent of economic inequality within the

system—who gets how much of what there is to get. Economic inequality includes inequalities of both income and wealth. Income is typically defined as the total flow of financial resources from all sources (e.g., wages and salaries, interest on savings and dividends, pensions, and government transfer payments such as social security, welfare payments, or other government payments) in a given period, usually annually. Wealth refers not to what people earn but to what they own. Wealth is usually measured as net worth that includes the total value of all assets owned (such as real estate, trusts, stocks, bonds, business equity, homes, automobiles, banking deposits, insurance policies, and the like) minus the total value of all liabilities (e.g., loans, mortgages, credit card and other forms of debt). For purposes of illustration, income and wealth inequalities are usually represented by dividing the population into quintiles and showing how much of what there is to get goes to each fifth, from the richest fifth of the population down to the poorest fifth. These proportions are illustrated in Table 1.

In terms of income, in 2005 the richest 20 percent of households received a 48.1 percent share of all income, compared to only 4 percent received by the bottom 20 percent. As income increases, so does its level of concentration. The top 15 percent alone accounts for 27 percent of the total, and the top 5 percent alone accounts for 21.1 percent of the total (Mishel, Bernstein, and Allegretto 2007, 59).

Moreover, income has great staying power over time. That is, the same households in the top income group now are very likely to have been in the top income group in previous years. Using longitudinal data and comparing income quintiles between 1969 and 1998, Mishel, Bernstein, and Allegretto (2007) note that most households in 1998 remained at or near where they were in 1969. Of those in the lowest income group in 1969, 53.3 percent remained in the lowest income fifth almost thirty years later, while 53.2 percent of those who were in the top income fifth remained there almost thirty years later. With regard to movement over the twenty-nine-year period, Mishel,

TABLE 1

SHARE OF TOTAL AVAILABLE HOUSEHOLD INCOME AND TOTAL NET WORTH

Income Group	Share of Income (%)	Share of Net Worth (%)
Top fifth	48.1	84.7
Fourth fifth	22.9	11.3
Third fifth	15.3	3.8
Second fifth	9.6	0.7
Bottom fifth	4.0	−0.5
Total	100.0	100.0

Source: Adapted from Lawrence Mishel, Jared Bernstein, and Sylvia Allegretto, *The State of Working America: 2006/2007*, Table 1.9, page 59 for share of income data, and Table 5.3, page 254 for share of net worth data. Copyright 2007 Cornell University. Used by permission of the publisher, Cornell University Press.

Bernstein, and Allegretto note that large intragenerational transitions are uncommon:

> Only 7.3% of those who began the period in the first fifth ended up in the top fifth, while only 9.2% fell from the top fifth to the lowest fifth. Those transitions that do occur are most likely to be a move up or down to the neighboring fifth. For example among the middle three-fifths, close to one half of the transitions were to the neighboring fifths. (2007, 105–6)

Another indication of income inequality is revealed by a comparison of pay for the chief executive officers of major corporations with that of rank-and-file employees. CEO pay as a ratio of average worker pay increased from 24 to 1 in 1965 to 262 to 1 in 2005, with much of the compensation package for CEOs coming in the form of stock options. Since CEO compensation is increasingly in the form of stock options, the ratio to worker pay in recent years is sensitive to changes in the market but always substantially higher than in previous decades; it is also substantially higher than the ratio of CEO to worker pay in other advanced industrial countries (Mishel, Bernstein, and Allegretto 2007, 202–7).

When wealth is considered, the disparities are much greater. In 2004, the richest 20 percent of American households accounted for 84.7 percent of total net household wealth. The bottom 40 percent combined, by contrast, held *less than one quarter of 1 percent* of all available net worth. At the bottom end of the wealth scale, 17 percent of households

had zero or negative net worth (Mishel, Bernstein, and Allegretto 2007, 257). In other words, a significant number of Americans either own nothing or owe more than they own.

As MIT economist Lester Thurow has observed, "Even among the wealthy, wealth is very unequally distributed" (1999, 200). In 2001, for instance, the top 1 percent of all wealth holders with an average household net worth of nearly $13 million and average annual income of over $1 million accounted for 34.3 percent of all net worth, 39.7 percent of financial wealth, and 20 percent of annual income (Wolff 2006). The top 1 percent of the wealthiest households (representing about three million Americans) is significant not only for the amount of wealth held that sets this group distinctly apart from the rest of American society but for the source of that wealth. Most of the wealth held by these top wealth holders comes not from wages and salary but from investments. In 2001 the top 1 percent of households held a staggering 57.3 percent of all business equity, 58 percent of all financial securities, 46.3 percent of all trusts, 44.1 percent of all stocks and mutual funds, and 34.9 percent of all nonhome real estate (Wolff 2006, 123). Because of the amount of ownership highly concentrated in this group, the top 1 percent of wealth holders are often referred to as "the ownership class" and are used as a proxy threshold for inclusion in the American "upper class."

In short, the degree of economic inequality in the United States is substantial by any measure. In fact, the United States now has greater income inequality and higher rates of poverty than other industrial countries (Mishel, Bernstein, and Allegretto 2007, 345; Kerbo 2006; Sieber 2005). Moreover, the extent of this inequality is increasing. One standard measurement of the extent of inequality is the Gini coefficient, which measures the extent of the discrepancy between the actual distribution of income and a hypothetical of the population receives the same percentage of income. Values of the Gini coefficient range between 0 and 1, where 0 indicates complete equality and 1 indicates complete inequality. Thus, the higher the number, the greater the degree of inequality. The U.S. Bureau of the Census (2007) reports that the Gini coefficient has steadily and incrementally increased from 0.406 in 1981 to 0.470 in 2006—representing a 16 percent increase over a twenty-five-year span.

Increases in wealth inequality are even more dramatic. The ratio of wealth of the top 1 percent of wealth holders to median wealth had increased from 125 times the median to 190 times by 2004 (Mishel, Bernstein, and Allegretto 2007, 253). In short, the gap between those who live off investments and the large majority of people who work for a living has widened considerably in recent decades.

Consideration of wealth as opposed to just income in assessing the total amount of economic inequality in society is critical for several reasons. First, the really big money in America comes not from wages and salaries but from owning property, particularly the kind that produces more wealth. If it "takes money to make money," those with capital to invest have a distinct advantage over those whose only source of income is wages. Apart from equity in owner-occupied housing, assets that most Americans hold are the kind that tend to *depreciate* in value over time: cars, furniture, appliances, clothes, and other personal belongings. Many of these items end up in used car lots, garage sales, and flea markets selling at prices much lower than their original cost. The rich, however, have a high proportion of their holdings in the kinds of wealth that *increase* in value overtime. Second, wealth is

especially critical with respect to inheritance. When people inherit an estate, they inherit accumulated assets—not incomes from wages and salaries. Inheritance of estates, in turn, is an important non-merit mechanism for the transmission of privilege across generations. In strictly merit terms, inheritance is a form of getting something for nothing.

INTERGENERATIONAL MOBILITY

Defenders of meritocracy sometimes argue that the *extent* of economic inequality is not a problem as long as there is ample *opportunity* for social mobility based on individual merit. Evidence, however, shows that a substantial amount of economic advantage is passed on across generations from parents to children. One way to measure the extent of intergenerational mobility is the correlation between parent and child incomes. Correlations can range from a low of 0 to a high of 1. If we had a pure merit system and assumed random transfer of genetic endowments across generations, we would expect a correlation of parent and adult child incomes approaching 0. On the other hand, in a strict caste system in which children inherit entirely the social position of parents and in which no mobility occurs, we would expect a correlation approaching 1. The correlation between parents' and adult children's incomes in the United States is actually about 0.50 (Mishel, Bernstein, and Allegretto 2007, 96), a correlation midway between these extremes. This figure is much larger than in almost all other industrial nations except the United Kingdom, which the United States closely follows (Mishel, Bernstein, and Allegretto 2007, 101; Isaacs 2008, 39).

Table 2 shows the extent of intergenerational wealth transfers from parents to children as calculated by economists Kerwin Charles and Erik Hurst (2003). This study compares wealth of children and parents in wealth quintiles. These data show a great deal of "stickiness" between generations, especially in the top and bottom quintiles. For instance, 36 percent of children born to parents in the lowest quintile remain in the lowest quintile as adults, while, correspondingly, 36 percent of those born

TABLE 2

INTERGENERATIONAL WEALTH TRANSMISSION FROM PARENTS TO CHILDREN

Child's Wealth Quintile	Parent's Wealth Quintile				
	Lowest (%)	Second (%)	Middle (%)	Fourth (%)	Top (%)
Lowest	36	26	16	15	11
Second	29	24	21	13	16
Middle	16	24	25	20	14
Fourth	12	15	24	26	24
Top	7	12	15	26	36
Total	100	100	100	100	100

Source: Charles and Hurst 2003.

to parents in the top wealth quintile remain there as adults. Most movement that does take place between generations occurs as "short-distance" mobility between adjacent quintiles, especially in the middle quintile ranges. In short, most people stay at, or very close to, where they started with most of the movement occurring as short-distance mobility in the middle ranges.

Another source of information on wealth transfers is the annual list of the four hundred wealthiest Americans published by *Forbes* magazine. An early study of the *Forbes* list, for instance, showed that at least 40 percent of the 1982 *Forbes* list inherited at least a portion of their wealth, and the higher on the list, the greater the likelihood that wealth was derived from inheritance (Canterbery and Nosari 1985). A more recent study of the 1997 *Forbes* list showed that the majority of individuals on the list (56 percent) inherited a fortune of at least $50 million (Collins 1997). Among the ten wealthiest Americans on the 2008 *Forbes* list, four (ranked three to six, respectively) are direct descendants of Sam Walton, founder of the Wal-Mart empire. The four Walton heirs have a combined estimated net worth of $93.1 billion (*Forbes* 2008).

Although there is some movement over time onto and off the *Forbes* list of the richest four hundred Americans, this does not mean that those who fall off the list have lost or squandered their wealth. Most likely, when wealthy individuals fall off the *Forbes* list, they have not lost wealth at all but rather have not gained it as quickly as others. Although those who fall off the four hundred list may have lost ground relative to others, they typically still have vast amounts of wealth and most likely remain within the upper 1 percent of the richest Americans.

The stability of wealth transfer across generations is particularly significant, given the amount of wealth available for transfer. Estimates are that $11.6 trillion will be available for transfer in the twenty-year period from 1998 to 2017 (7.1 trillion to heirs, 2.4 trillion to taxes, 1.7 trillion to charity and 0.5 trillion to estate fees) (Havens and Schervish 2003). Over a fifty-five-year period from 1998 through 2052, $41 trillion will be available for transfer ($25 trillion to heirs, $8 trillion to taxes, $6 trillion to charity, and $2 trillion to estate fees) (Havens and Schervish 2003). These vast amounts of wealth will not simply evaporate between generations, and, indeed, much of the intergenerational transfer will reach not only to the current generation of baby boomers but to their children as well, further solidifying continuity of wealth inequalities overtime.

Despite the evidence of wealth stability over time, much is made of the investment "risks" that capitalists must endure as a justification for returns on such investments. And to some extent, this is true. Most investments involve some measure of risk. The superwealthy, however, protect themselves as much as possible from the vicissitudes of "market forces"—most have professionally managed, diversified investment portfolios. As a result, established wealth has great staying power. In short, what is good for America is in general, good for the ownership class. The risk endured, therefore, is minimal. Instead of losing vast fortunes overnight, the more common scenario for the superrich is for the *amount* of their wealth to fluctuate with the ups and downs in the stock market as a whole. And, given the very high levels of aggregate and corporate wealth concentration in the economy, the only realistic scenario in which the ownership class goes under is one in which America as a whole goes under.

THE CUMULATIVE ADVANTAGES OF WEALTH INHERITANCE

Inheritance is more than bulk estates bequeathed to descendants; more broadly defined, it refers to the total impact of initial social-class placement at birth on future life outcomes. Therefore, it is not just the superwealthy who are in a position to pass advantages on to children. Advantages are passed on, in varying degrees, to all of those from relatively privileged backgrounds. Even minor initial advantages may accumulate during the life course. In this way, existing inequalities are reinforced and extended across generations. As Harvard economist John Kenneth Galbraith put it in the opening sentence of his well-known book *The Affluent Society*, "Wealth is not without its advantages and the case to the contrary, although it has often been made, has never proved widely persuasive" (1958, 13). Specifically, the cumulative advantages of wealth inheritance include the following.

Childhood Quality of Life

Children of the privileged enjoy a high standard of living and quality of life regardless of their individual merit or lack of it. For the privileged, this not only includes high-quality food, clothing, and shelter but also extends to luxuries such as entertainment, toys, travel, family vacations, enrichment camps, private lessons, and a host of other

indulgences that wealthy parents and even middle-class parents bestow on their children (Lareau 2003). Children do not earn a privileged lifestyle; they inherit and benefit from it long before their parents are deceased.

Knowing with Which Fork to Eat

Cultural capital refers to what one needs to know to function as a member of the various groups to which one belongs. All groups have norms, values, beliefs, ways of life, and codes of conduct that identify the group and define its boundaries. The culture of the group separates insiders from outsiders. Knowing and binding by these cultural codes of conduct is required to maintain one's status as a member in good standing within the group. By growing up in privilege, children of the elite are socialized into elite ways of life. This kind of cultural capital has commonly been referred to as "breeding," "refinement," "social grace," "savoir faire," or simply "class" (meaning upper class). Although less pronounced and rigid than in the past, these distinctions persist into the present. In addition to cultivated tastes in art and music ("highbrow" culture), cultural capital includes, but is not limited to, interpersonal styles and demeanor, manners and etiquette, and vocabulary. Those from more humble backgrounds who aspire to become elites must acquire the cultural cachet to be accepted in elite circle, and this is no easy task. Those born to it, however, have the advantage of acquiring it "naturally" through inheritance, a kind of social osmosis that takes place through childhood socialization (Lareau 2003).

Having Friends in High Places

Everybody knows somebody else. Social capital refers to the "value" of whom you know. For the most part, privileged people know other privileged people, and poor people know other poor people. Another nonmerit advantage inherited by children of the wealthy is a network of connections to people of power and influence. These are not connections that children of the rich shrewdly foster or cultivate on their own. The children of the wealthy travel in high-powered social circles. These connections provide access to power, information, and other resources. The difference between rich and poor is not in knowing people; it is in knowing people in positions of power and influence who can do things for you.

Early Withdrawals on the Family Estate

Children of the privileged do not have to wait until their parents die to inherit assets from them. Inter vivos transfers of funds and "gifts" from parents to children can be substantial, and there is strong evidence suggesting that such transfers account for a greater proportion of intergenerational transfers than lump-sum estates at death (Gale and Scholz 1994). Inter vivos gifts to children provide a means of legally avoiding or reducing estate taxes. In this way, parents can "spend down" their estates during their lives to avoid estate and inheritance taxes upon their deaths. Furthermore, in 2001 the federal government enacted legislation that is scheduled to ultimately phase out the federal estate tax. Many individual states have also reduced or eliminated inheritance taxes. The impact of these changes in tax law on intergenerational transfers is at this point unclear. If tax advantages were the only reasons for inter vivos transfers, we might expect parents to slow down the pace of inter vivos transfers. But it is unlikely that the flow of such transfers will be abruptly curtailed because they serve other functions. Besides tax avoidance, parents also provide inter vivos transfers to children to advance their children's current and future economic interests, especially at critical or milestone stages of the life cycle. These milestone events include going to college, getting married, buying a house, and having children. At each event, there may be a substantial infusion of parental capital—in essence an early withdrawal on the parental estate. One of the most common forms of inter vivos gifts is payment for children's education. A few generations ago, children may have inherited the family farm or the family business. With the rise of the modern corporation and the decline of family farms and businesses, inheritance increasingly takes on more fungible or liquid forms, including cash transfers. Indeed, for many middle-class Americans, education has replaced tangible assets as the primary form by which advantage is passed on between generations.

What Goes Up Doesn't Usually Come Down

If America were truly a meritocracy, we would expect fairly equal amounts of both upward and downward mobility. Mobility studies, however, consistently show much higher rates of upward than downward mobility. There are two key reasons for this. First, most mobility that people have experienced in American in the past century, particularly occupational mobility, was due to industrial expansion and the rise of the general standard of living in society as a whole. Sociologists refer to this type of mobility as "structural mobility," which has more to do with changes in the organization of society than with the merit of individuals. A second reason why upward mobility is more prevalent than downward mobility is that parents and extended family networks insulate children from downward mobility. That is, parents frequently "bail out," or "rescue," their adult children in the event of life crises such as sickness, unemployment, divorce, or other setbacks that might otherwise propel adult children into a downward spiral. In addition to these external circumstances, parents also rescue children from their own failures and weaknesses, including self-destructive behaviors. Parental rescue as a form of inter vivos transfer is not a generally acknowledged or well-studied benefit of inheritance. Indirect evidence of parental rescue may be found in the recent increase in the number of "boomerang" children, adult children who leave home only to return later to live with parents. Social scientists report that 34 percent of young adults are now moving back in with their parents during their twenties (*Contexts* 2008). The reasons for adult children returning to live at home are usually financial: adult children may be between jobs, between marriages, or without other viable means of self-support. Such living arrangements are likely to increase during periods of high unemployment, which in early 2009 topped 8 percent of the civilian labor force.

If America operated as a "true" merit system, people would advance solely on the basis of merit and fail when they lacked merit. In many cases however, family resources prevent, or at least reduce, "skidding" among adult children. One of the authors of this book recalls that when he left home as a adult, his parents took him aside and told him that no matter how bad things became for him out there in the world; if he could get to a phone, they would wire him money to come home. This was his insurance against destitution. Fortunately, he has not yet had to take his parents up on their offer, but neither has he forgotten it. Without always being articulated, the point is that this informal familial insurance against downward mobility is available in varying degrees, to all except the poorest of the poor, who simply have resources to provide.

Live Long and Prosper

From womb to tomb, the more affluent one is, the less the risk of injury, illness, and death (Budrys 2003; Cockerham 2000; National Center for Health Statistics 2007; Wermuth 2003). Among the many nonmerit advantages inherited by those from privileged backgrounds is higher life expectancy at birth and a greater chance of better health throughout life. There are several possible reasons for the strong and persistent relationship between socioeconomic status and health. Beginning with fetal development and extending through childhood, increasing evidence points to the effects of "the long reach of early childhood" on adult health (Smith 1999). Prenatal deprivations, more common among the poor, for instance, are associated with later life conditions such as retardation, coronary heart disease, stroke, diabetes and hypertension. Poverty in early childhood is also associated with increased risk of adult diseases. This may be due in part to higher stress levels among the poor. There is also evidence that cumulative wear and tear on the body over time occurs under conditions of repeated high stress. Another reason for

the health-wealth connection is that the rich have greater access to quality health care. In America, access to quality health care is still largely for sale to the highest bidder. Under these conditions, prevention and intervention are more widely available to the more affluent. Finally, not only does lack of income lead to poor health, but poor health leads to reduced earnings. That is, if someone is sick or injured, he or she may not be able to work or may have limited earning power.

Overall, the less affluent are at a health disadvantage due to higher exposure to a variety of unhealthy living conditions. As medical sociologist William Cockerham points out,

> Persons living in poverty and reduced socioeconomic circumstances have greater exposure to physical (crowding, poor sanitation, extreme temperatures), chemical and biochemical (diet, pollution, smoking, alcohol, and drug abuse), biological (bacteria, viruses) and psychological (stress) risk factors that produce ill health than more affluent individuals. (1998, 55).

Part of the exposure to health hazards is occupational. According to the Department of Labor, those in the following occupations (listed in order of risk) have the greatest likelihood of being killed on the job: fishers, timber cutters, airplane pilots, structural metal workers, taxicab drivers, construction laborers, roofers, electric power installers, truck drivers, and farm workers. With the exception of airline pilot, all the jobs listed are working-class jobs. Since a person's occupation is strongly affected by family background, the prospects for generally higher occupational health risks are in this sense at least indirectly inherited. Finally, although homicides constitute only a small proportion of all causes of death, it is worth noting that the less affluent are at higher risk for being victims of violent crime, including homicide.

Some additional risk factors are related to individual behaviors, especially smoking, drinking, and drug abuse—all of which are more common among the less affluent. Evidence suggests that these behaviors, while contributing to poorer health among the less affluent, are responsible for only one-third of the "wealth-health gradient" (Smith 1999, 157). These behaviors are also associated with higher

PERSONAL ACCOUNT

I Am a Pakistani Woman

I am a Pakistani woman, raised in the U.S. and Canada, and often at odds with the Western standard of beauty.

As a child in Nova Scotia and later growing up in New York and Indiana, I was proud of my uniqueness. On traditional Pakistani and Muslim holidays, I got to wear bright, fun clothes from my country and colorful jewelry. I had a whole rich tradition of my own to celebrate in addition to Christmas and Easter. However, as I started school, I somehow came to realize that being different wasn't so great—that in other people's viewpoint, I looked strange and acted funny. I learned the importance of fitting in and behaving like the other girls. This involved dressing well, giggling a lot, and having a superior, but flirtatious attitude toward boys. I was very outgoing and had very good grades, so outwardly I was able to "assimilate" with some success. But my sister, who was quiet and reticent, often took the brunt of other children's cruelty. I realize how proud and ashamed I was of my heritage when I look at my relationship with my family.

A lesson I learned early on in the U.S. was that being beautiful took a lot of money. It is painful, as an adult, for me to consider the inexorable, never-ending pressure that my father was under to embody the dominant, middle-class cultural expressions of masculinity, as in success at one's job, making a big salary, and owning status symbols. I resented him so much then for being a poor, untenured professor and freelance writer. I wanted designer clothes, dining out at nice restaurants, and a big allowance. Instead, I had a deeply spiritual thinker, writer, and theologian for a dad. I love(d) him and am so very grateful for what he's taught me, but as a child I didn't think of him as a success.

The prettiest girls in school all had a seemingly endless array of outfits, lots of makeup and perfume, and everything by the "right" designers. I hated my mom for making many of my clothes and buying things on sale (and my mom was a great seamstress). I felt a sense of hopelessness that I could never have the resources or opportunities necessary to compete, to be beautiful.

Instead I found safety in conformity. When I was in high school, the WASPy, preppy look was hot; it represented the epitome of success and privilege in America. I worked hard to purchase a wardrobe of clothes with a polo-horse insignia, by many hours at an after-school job. I tried to hide my exotic look behind Khakis, boat shoes, hair barrettes, and pearl studs. There was comfort in conformity. I saw the class "sex symbol" denigrated for wearing tight dresses and having a very well-developed body for a sixteen-year-old, and the more unique dressers dismissed as frivolous, trendy, and more than a little eccentric. You couldn't be too pretty, too ugly, too different—you had to just blend in.

Though I did it well, I perpetually felt like an imposter. This rigidly controlled, well-dressed preppy going through school with good grades in advanced placement classes in no way represented what I felt to be my true essence.

Hoorie I. Siddique

psychological as well as physical stress. Indeed, the less affluent are not just at greater risk for physical ailments; research has shown that the less affluent are at significantly higher risk for mental illness as well (Cockerham 2000; Feagin and McKinney 2003). Intriguing new evidence suggests that, apart from material deprivations, part of the link between wealth and health may be related to the psychological stress of relative deprivation, that is, the stress of being at the bottom end of an unequal social pecking order, especially when the dominant ideology attributes being at the bottom to individual deficiencies.

Despite the adage that "money can't buy happiness," social science research has consistently shown that happiness and subjective well-being tend to be related to the amount of income and wealth people possess (Frey and Stutzer 2002; Frank 2007a; Schnittker 2008). This research shows that people living in wealthier (and more democratic) countries tend to be happier and that rates of happiness are sensitive to overall rates of unemployment and inflation. In general, poor people are less happy than others, although increments that exceed average amounts of income only slightly increase levels of happiness. That is, beyond relatively low thresholds, additional increments of income and wealth are not likely to result in additional increments of happiness. Although money may not *guarantee* a long, happy, and healthy life, a fair assessment is that it aids and abets it. . . .

SUMMARY

The United States has high levels of both income and wealth inequality. In terms of the distribution of income and wealth, America is clearly not a middle-class society. Income and especially wealth are not evenly distributed, with a relatively small number of well-off families at one end and a small number of poor families much worse off at the other. Instead, the overall picture is one in which the bulk of the available wealth is concentrated in a narrow range at the very top of the system. In short, the distribution of economic resources in society is not symmetrical and certainly not bell-shaped: the poor who have the least greatly outnumber the rich who have the most. Moreover, in recent decades, by all measures, the rich are getting richer, and the gap between the very rich and everyone else has appreciably increased.

The greater the amount of economic inequality in society, the more difficult it is to move up within the system on the basis of individual merit alone. Indeed, the most important factor in terms of where people will end up in the economic pecking order of society is where they started in the first place. Economic inequality has tremendous inertial force across generations. Instead of a race to get ahead that begins anew with each generation, the race is in reality a relay race in which children inherit different starting points from parents. Inheritance, broadly defined as one's initial starting point in life based on parental position, includes a set of cumulative nonmerit advantages for all except the poorest of the poor. These include enhanced childhood standard of living, differential access to cultural capital, differential access to social networks of power and influence, infusion of parental capital while parents are still alive, greater health and life expectancy, and the inheritance of bulk estates when parents die. . . .

DISCUSSION QUESTIONS

1. On what grounds do McNamee and Miller conclude that America is not a middle class society? Is their conclusion supportable?
2. In what ways does America function as a meritocracy and in what ways does it not?

REFERENCES

Budrys, Grace. 2003. *Unequal Health: How Inequality Contributes to Health or Illness.* Lanham, MD: Rowman & Littlefield.

Canterbery, E. Ray, and Joe Nosari. 1985. "The Forbes Four Hundred: The Determinants of Super-Wealth." *Southern Economic Journal* 51: 1073–83.

Charles, Kerwin Kofi, and Erik Hurst. 2003. "The Correlation of Wealth across Generations." *Journal of Political Economy* 111, no. 6: 1155–82.

Cockerham, William. 1998. *Medical Sociology.* 7th ed. Upper Saddle River, NJ: Prentice Hall.

Collins, Chuck. 1997. *Born on Third Base: The Sources of Wealth of the 1997 Forbes 400.* Boston: United for a Fair Economy.

Contexts. 2008. "Turns Out You Can Go Home Again." *Contexts* 7, no. 3 (summer), P5.

Feagin, Joe. R., and Mary D. McKinney. 2003. *The Many Costs of Racism.* Lanham, MD: Rowman & Littlefield.

Frey, Bruno S., and Alois Stutzer. 2002. *Happiness and Economics: How the Economy and Institutions Affect Well-being.* Princeton, NJ: Princeton University Press.

Galbraith, John Kenneth. 1958. *The Affluent Society.* New York: Mentor Press.

Gale, William G., and John Karl Scholz. 1994. "Intergenerational Transfers and the Accumulation of Wealth." *Journal of Economic Perspectives* 8: 145–60.

Havens John J., and Paul G. Schervish. 2003. "Why the $41 Trillion Wealth Transfer Is Still Valid: A Review of Challenges and Comments." *Journal of Gift Planning,* no. 1: 11–15, 47–50

Isaacs Julia. 2008. "International Comparisons of Economic Mobility." Economic Mobility Project. Brookings Institution and Pew Charitable Trusts. www.economic mobility.org/reports_and_research/mobility_in_america?id=0003 (accessed April 7, 2009).

Kerbo Harold R. 2006. *World Poverty: Global Inequality and the Modern World System* Bosten: McGraw-Hill.

Lareau, Annette. 2003. *Unequal Childhood: Class, Race, and Family Life.* Berkeley: University of California Press.

Mishel, Lawrence, Jared Bernstein, and Sylvia Allegretto: 2007. *The State of Working America: 2006–2007.* Ithaca, NY: Cornell University Press.

National Center for Health Statistics. 2007. *Health, United States, 2007, with Chart-book on Trends in the Health of Americans*. Hyattsville, MD: National Center for Health Statistics, U.S. Department of Health and Human Services.

Rosenfeld, Jeffrey P. 1980. *Legacy of Aging: Inheritance and Disinheritance in Social Perspective*. Norwood, NJ: ABLEX.

Schwartz, T. P. 1996. "Durkheim's Prediction about the Declining Importance of the Family and Inheritance: Evidence from the Wills of Providence, 1775–1985. *Sociological Quarterly* 26: 503–19.

Sieber, Sam. D. 2005. *Second-Rate Nation: From the American Dream to the American Myth*. Boulder, CO: Paradigm.

Smith, James P. 1999. "Healthy Bodies and Thick Wallets: The Dual Relation between Health and Economic Status." *Journal of Economic Perspectives* 13: 145–66.

Thurow, Lester C. 1999. *Building Wealth: The New Rules for Individuals, Companies and Nations in a Knowledge-Based Economy*. New York: HarperCollins.

Wermuth, Laurie. 2003. *Global Inequality and Human Needs: Health and Illness in an Increasingly Unequal World*. Boston: Allyn Bacon.

Willenbacher, Barbara. 2003. "Individualism and Traditionalism in Inheritance Law in Germany, France, England, and the United States." *Journal of Family History* 28, no. 1: 208–25.

Wolff, Edward N. 2006. "Changes in Household Wealth in the 1980s and 1990s in the U.S." In *International Perspectives on Household Wealth*, ed. Edward N. Wolff, 107–50. Northhampton, MA: Elgar Publishing.

WHAT IS SEXUAL ORIENTATION?

READING 15

The Biology of the Homosexual

Roger N. Lancaster

Three studies, published close on each other's heels in the early 1990s, have been widely ballyhooed in the mass media as establishing the "organic seat," the "hormonal link," and the "genetic cause" of homosexual desire and gay identity: Simon LeVay's "gay brain" research, Michael J. Bailey and Richard Pillard's "gay twins" survey, and Dean Hamer's "gay gene" study. Major design flaws, problems with the definition and operationalization of terms, and alternative interpretations of the data were lost in the din of blaring headlines: "First Evidence of a Biological Cause for Homosexuality," "Genes Tied to Sexual Orientation; Study of Gay Men Bolsters Theory," "Study Shows Homosexuality Is Innate," "Genes Linked to Being Gay," "Report Suggests Homosexuality Is Linked to Genes," "Study Provides New Evidence of a 'Gay Gene'". . .[1]

Roger N. Lancaster is a professor of anthropology and cultural studies at George Mason University.

THE INTERSEXED HYPOTHALAMUS

Simon LeVay's much-cited "gay brain" study was published, with much fanfare, in 1991. The journal *Science* set the tone for press reportage, vigorously spinning LeVay's study to the media under its own press-release headline: "THE HOMOSEXUAL BRAIN: BIOLOGICAL BASIS FOR SEXUAL ORIENTATION?"[2]

LeVay found that the third interstitial nucleus of the hypothalamus (a neural structure at the base of the brain) is, on the average, smaller in gay men and straight women than in straight men.[3] (In theory, lesbians' hypothalami would resemble those of straight men—in other words, where gay men show a "feminized" pattern, lesbians would show a "masculinized" effect.). . . The hypothalamus affects certain endocrine functions and is thought to influence "basic urges" such as hunger, thirst, and sexual arousal. . . .

The results of LeVay's research were widely disseminated in mass-media outlets, but LeVay's data are less impressive than the public was led to believe, and his study is plagued with methodological problems. LeVay's study examined the hypothalami of forty-one cadavers. While living, nineteen of the subjects were described in hospital records as "homosexual" (a figure that includes one "bisexual"). We do not actually know for how long, or with what degree of consistency, or for that matter even *whether* the "homosexual" subjects described themselves as gay. We know only what someone saw fit to observe (speculate?) in their hospital records. We also do not know how the other subjects described themselves when they were alive, nor do we know *anything* about *anyone's* sexual fantasies or sexual histories, but for purposes of LeVay's study, the sixteen other male subjects are presumed to have been "heterosexual," and all six women subjects are presumed to have been "heterosexual." Many critics have commented on the vagueness—indeed, the capriciousness—of the labels and classifications employed by LeVay.

Needless to say, important aspects of LeVay's research were not always given due weight in science journalism. Note, for instance, that the much-reported difference between "gay" and "straight" men in LeVay's sample is a statistical average, not an absolute difference. Individual measurements overlap: Some of the men in the "gay" sample had larger hypothalami than most of the men in the "straight" sample. Since many individuals did not fit the "average" picture, one could not thus predict who was what simply by looking at his hypothalamus. Such results in such a small sample mean that the resulting numbers lie close to the statistical margin of error—and that the reclassification of a small number of brains in the study would render LeVay's findings statistically insignificant.[4]

To make matters more complicated, LeVay talks as though identifying, delineating, and measuring the third interstitial nucleus were a simple matter. This is not the case.[5] The nucleus LeVay measured is a tiny structure by no means clearly differentiated from the similar neural tissue surrounding it. The fact that LeVay, rather than a colleague, performed the measurements, coupled with the absence of a "blind rater" to confirm his measurements independently, departs from the usual standards in research of this sort and does nothing to lend credibility to the findings.[6]

Worse yet, *all* of the "homosexual" men in LeVay's sample died from AIDS-related illnesses. Both AIDS and HIV medical treatments are known to affect a variety of brain structures. LeVay's inclusion of six (again, presumably) "heterosexual" men who died

from AIDS scarcely addresses this problem.[7] Nor does the subsequent examination of the brain of one gay man who died from causes other than AIDS.[8]

In serious publications, LeVay rightly acknowledges that his results are open to a variety of interpretations. For instance, even if his results held—and to date his findings have not been replicated by a single subsequent study—it is by no means clear whether LeVay's average difference would measure biological "cause" or sociological "effect." As LeVay himself puts it, "It is not possible, purely on the basis of my observations, to say whether the structural differences were present at birth, and latter influenced the men to become gay or straight, or whether they arose in adult life, perhaps as a result of the men's sexual behavior."[9] It is also not possible to say whether the average structural differences have anything to do with sexual object choice per se or with other aspects of life associated with sexual object choice. Certainly, extended anxieties, social stress, the experience of inequality, sexual activity and inactivity, and various other cumulative life experiences affect organic processes, brain structures, and hormonal systems in human beings. . . .

LeVay has made far less cautious claims in public discussions of his study. LeVay's interpretation of his results, aggressively forwarded in a variety of media, is in no small part driven by his personal conviction that he was "born gay" and from his belief that the innatist scenario advances the social interests of gays and lesbians. LeVay thus favors a biologically reductive argument: The hypothalamus is the "seat" of sexual desire, and sexual object choice (or preference, or orientation) is physically *there*, in the third interstitial nucleus. As LeVay told *Newsweek*, "I felt if I didn't find any [differences between gay and straight men's hypothalami], I would give up a scientific career altogether."[10] . . .

BROTHERHOOD

Only months later the same year LeVay's study appeared, Michael Bailey and Richard Pillard published the results of a survey they conducted among gay men and their brothers.[11] The researchers recruited respondents by placing ads in gay newspapers across the Midwest and Southwest, ultimately gathering information on 56 pairs of identical (monozygotic) twins, 54 pairs of fraternal (dizygotic) twins, 142 non-twin brothers, and 57 pairs of adoptive brothers. They found that the "concordance rate" of homosexual self-identification—that is, the percentage of pairs in which both brothers called themselves gay—was highest for identical twins (52 percent), next highest for fraternal twins (22 percent), and lowest for non-twin and adoptive brothers (roughly 10 percent each).

Once again, methodological concerns and alternative interpretations were ignored or brushed aside. And once again, headlines trumpeted "mounting evidence" of a genetic basis for homosexuality.

How one interprets this data is largely a matter of the perspective one takes. As Ruth Hubbard and Elijah Wald dryly observe: "The fact that fraternal twins of gay men were roughly twice as likely to be gay as other biological brothers shows that environmental factors are involved, since fraternal twins are no more similar biologically than are other biological brothers."[12] Indeed, genetically unrelated adoptive brothers show the same concordance rate as blood brothers, which would further seem to falsify the genetic hypothesis. And by definition, the monozygotic twins are genetically identical—yet *only half* of the pairs were sexually concordant. Given the conditions and assumptions of Bailey and Pillard's study, this figure could be viewed as surprisingly high or as revealingly low. It could even indicate that sexual orientation has *no* genetic basis whatsoever.

This is because twin studies normally use pairs of identical twins who were separated at birth. Such studies thus attempt to view the development of genetically identical individuals in (supposedly) different environments.[13] Since the identical twins in Bailey and Pillard's study in fact *shared* a family environment, it is a non sequitur to claim that the comparatively high (although theoretically low?) degree of concordance is genetically caused. It might just as easily result from the fact that the two occupy the same environment. As Hubbard and Wald put it: "If being a fraternal twin exerts an environmental

influence, it does not seem surprising that this should be even truer for identical twins, who the world thinks of as 'the same' and treats accordingly, and who often share those feelings of sameness."[14] Gilbert Zicklin goes even further: "The intensely shared life of identical twins, including the phenomena of identification, mirroring, and imitation, might plausibly constitute fertile ground for the development of same-sex erotics."[15] Zicklin's suggestion is at least as plausible as the invocation of "genetic causation" to explain the 52 percent of identical-twin pairs who were concordant and "environmental factors" to account for the 48 percent who were discordant, an accounting that in no way follows from the data, but that dominated media presentations of the topic.

Consider the extraordinary anecdote related in *Newsweek*'s 1992 cover story, "Born or Bred: The Origins of Homosexuality."

> Until the age of twenty-eight, Doug Barnett (not his real name) was a practicing heterosexual. He was vaguely attracted to men, but with nurturing parents, a lively interest in sports and appropriate relations with women, he had little reason to question his proclivities. Then an astonishing thing happened: his identical twin brother "came out" to him, revealing he was gay. Barnett, who believed sexual orientation is genetic, was bewildered. He recalls thinking, "If this is inherited and we're identical twins—what's going on here?" To find out, he thought he should try sex with men. When he did, he says, "The bells went off, for the first time. Those homosexual encounters were more fulfilling." A year later both twins told their parents they were gay.[16]

The author of the *Newsweek* piece relates this tale as evidence of a fixed, clear-cut, and genetic basis for sexual orientation.[17] That is, no doubt, what the protagonist, "Doug Barnett," himself believes. But the tale could be read just as easily as a demonstration of the flux, ambiguity, and capriciousness—indeed, the *suggestibility*—of sexual desire. The subject's description of his life as a "practicing heterosexual" is in no sense unusual. In various surveys, beginning with the Kinsey study, large percentages of men whose sexual activity is predominately or exclusively heterosexual agree, in principle, that everyone experiences "vague feelings" of "occasional attraction" toward members of their own sex.[18] Such findings are conveniently forgotten in the current rush to geneticize and typologize desire. The *Newsweek* anecdote could be understood as a particularly sharp example of the "twinning" behavior Zicklin invokes. Indeed, if taken seriously, it could even be understood from a constructionist perspective—why not?—as a gauge of the social force of reductionist theories in shaping personal life and identity formation.

In the end, even if we take Bailey and Pillard's figures as reliable ones, we simply do not know which had more of an effect on the identical twins' sexuality, shared genes or a shared environment, and we cannot even be sure whether we are monitoring a genetic tendency through degrees of sibling relatedness, a social tendency for twins—especially identical twins—to be alike, to mimic mirror, and "twin" each other, or even a homoerotic tendency among identical twins.

So far, all of these interpretations lie within the realm of a generous reading of Bailey and Pillard's study—that is, within the assumption that their results are meaningful, that their numbers actually reflect real trends among siblings. But this is not necessarily the case.

The authors' sampling procedure almost guarantees a certain skewing. It is based on the self-selection of volunteers recruited through gay newspapers, rather than on a random sample of the general population. Given the stated aims of the study, which are clear enough in the ad, and given the cultural and political background of the question, which includes the active promotion of "innatist" scenarios in most gay newspapers, it is altogether possible that those who were most motivated to participate were those who already believed that sexual orientation is genetically determined. And it is altogether conceivable that those most likely to respond to the ad—to nominate themselves for study—would be concordant sets of identical twins.

These are not minor problems. They fatally undermine the study's reliability. As Zicklin elaborates:

The overrepresentation of concordant MZ [monozygotic, identical] twins is quite possible, since gay MZ twins are likely to be more interested in studies that highlight the special meaning of close biological connections, and they might also have less trepidation about participating since there is a greater likelihood that they would be "out" with one another than would any other pair of male siblings. Conversely, some twins who perceive themselves as discordant on sexual orientation may be motivated to avoid studies wherein this difference may be revealed. Thus Bailey and Pillard have a double problem: they attract the kind of twins who fit their hypothesis and deter the ones who might weaken it.[19]

Bailey and Pillard skirt the usual standards of twin studies, sampling procedures, and logical deduction. Again, only those already committed to the notion that homosexuals have biologically marked bodies would be swayed by this kind of evidence.

THE "GAY GENE"

The 1993 study by Dean Hamer and his associates is usually praised for being the most serious, sophisticated, and careful of the three major studies purporting to substantiate a link between genes and male homosexuality.

Hamer's research team recruited an original group of 76 gay men for a pedigree study. (A "pedigree study" is an attempt to determine how a trait is distributed among members of a kin group.) One or more relatives from 26 of these men's families were also interviewed, for a total of 122 participants. Hamer's team found elevated levels of homosexuality among gay men's maternal uncles and among their maternal cousins, linked by aunts, as compared to their paternally linked relatives. Hypothesizing transmission of a homosexual gene through the X chromosome, the researchers then recruited 38 pairs of gay brothers for a second pedigree study. These pairs of gay brothers were specifically culled from families without known lesbians or paternally linked homosexuals in order to eliminate subjects likely to display "nonmaternal" routes of "transmission." The second pedigree study found a somewhat more pronounced maternal pattern. Finally, the Hamer team performed

DNA linkage analysis on the 38 pairs of gay brothers from the second pedigree study, plus two pairs of gay brothers from the first study. Hamer et al. reported that 33 of 40 pairs (or 82 percent) shared a DNA marker, Xq28, located on the tip of the X chromosome. (The term "DNA marker" denotes a strip of DNA that is usually transmitted "whole" from parent to offspring; it thus allows geneticists to work with units of a few million base pairs of DNA, rather than trying to sort out individual genes from among several billion base pairs. Xq28, as the authors note, is large enough to contain several hundred genes.)[20] Hamer et al. conclude: "We have now produced evidence that one form of male homosexuality is preferentially transmitted through the maternal side and is genetically linked to chromosomal region Xq28." The authors suggest that a thorough mapping of the region will eventually yield a gene involved in homosexual expression, but they also suggest that more than one gene might contribute to sexual orientation, and that environmental factors also play a role.[21] ("Hey, Mom, Thanks for the Genes!" is the message that with minor variations appeared on gay T-shirts across the country—a line that proved even more popular than the camp come-on "How Big Is Your Hypothalamus?")

In his scientific (as opposed to journalistic or popularizing) publications, Hamer has been careful to avoid extreme variants of biological determinist arguments. Indeed, Hamer himself often points out that a "link" is not the same as a "cause." He distinguishes between "genetic influences" and "genetic destiny," and even while in search of a "gay gene," he often puts the term inside eyebrow-raising quotation marks.[22] Still, there is something less than fully congruous about searching for a "gay gene" while claiming that one does not exist, and the problems with Hamer's study are quite serious.

The pedigree studies invite certain preliminary observations. First, not all of the families in Hamer's samples exhibit the "maternal pattern" highlighted in the subsequent genetic study of gay brothers. The results suggest a "significant" but not dramatic elevation of homosexuality among the maternally linked relatives of gay men.

Next, some of the raw numbers supporting the idea of a maternal linkage are in fact quite low. In the first pedigree study, 7 of 96 gay men (7.3 percent) reported having a gay maternal uncle, as opposed to only 2 of 119 (1.7 percent) who reported a gay paternal uncle. But there is little difference between the 4 of 52 (7.7 percent) who reported a gay maternal cousin on their aunt's side and the 3 of 56 (5.4 percent) who reported a gay paternal cousin on their uncle's side.

In consequence, the difference between rates of homosexuality among maternal and paternal kin is statistically significant *only* if one assumes a (relatively low) 2 percent "base rate" of male homosexuality. As Edward Stein and others have pointed out, the difference becomes statistically insignificant if one assumes a (more plausible) base rate of 4 percent.[23]

Finally, given such small raw numbers, Hamer's pedigree analysis is open to charges that it fails to account for even the most obvious relevant effects of gender and family relations in American society. Women—mothers—play a much greater role than men in negotiating and cementing family ties, a tendency that is well established in the sociological and anthropological literature.[24] As a result, Americans tend to be closer to and to know more about their maternal relatives than their paternal ones. This sociological effect is likely to be even more pronounced in the case of gay men than in society at large. Given the role of fathers in perpetuating cultural expectations of masculinity, given the cultural anxieties that a gay son reflects upon his father, and given the nature of the idealized maternal role (nurturing caregiver), it is certainly conceivable that on the average, gay men tend to be closer to their mothers and to know more about their maternal, consanguineal kin than they are to their fathers, about whose blood relations they know correspondingly less.[25]

Hamer's team did attempt to apply a reasonable check on information provided by the gay men. They also interviewed at least one relative each for twenty-six participants (for a total of forty-six relatives interviewed). On this basis, Hamer concluded that the information provided by the seventy-six total participants was reliable. One might suggest, instead, that the claims were merely *consistent*: that one relative tended to think pretty much what another relative thought. Since extensive networks of the gay men's relatives were not systematically interviewed, either or both of the above sociological factors could fully account for the maternally skewed results of Hamer's pedigree study.[26]

At this point in a review of Hamer's study, it is usually conceded: "Yes, but Hamer's group nonetheless found *something*—a genetic marker—shared by gay brothers, and that is in itself significant." And after all, Hamer's group claims only to have established a genetic link for "one form" of male homosexuality—presumably the kind genetically transmitted along maternal lines. Still, there is considerably less significance here than one could glean from media reports, which took Hamer's study as the charmed third to seal the argument.

It is important to specify first what has *not* been shown by Hamer's group. First, no "gay gene" has been identified. Nor can we safely conclude that one is there, in Xq28, like a needle in the proverbial haystack, awaiting discovery. All kinds of traits "run in families" without having a genetic basis. And because human populations are quite variable, when a trait "runs in families,'" a "DNA sequence that is a marker for a particular trait in one family may not be associated with that trait in another."[27] The complexity of the relationships between genes, heredity, and even relatively simple phenotypic and behavioral characteristics has frustrated the search for genes "for" all manner of things that would appear far more straightforward than sexual desire.

There also is no genetic on/off switch for homosexuality. Even after a deliberate screening and selection process designed to produce a "maternal pattern" of "linkages," if not "transmission," not all the pairs of gay brothers whose X chromosomes were examined shared DNA markers for Xq28. A subsequent study by the Hamer group reported a somewhat lower percentage of Xq28 concordance among gay brothers.[28] Even a generous

interpretation of these results along the lines laid out by the authors clearly does not indicate a simple or direct genetic "cause" for homosexuality.

There is no conceivable genetic "test" for homosexuality. Specifically, it has been reported that a percentage of pairs of self-identified gay brothers, culled from certain highly selected samples, share a genetic marker. Note that this selectively culled group of gay brothers share that marker *with each other*, not with unrelated gay men. Thus, even if Hamer's results hold, no one can take a blood sample and look at this genetic marker to determine whether a person is gay or straight.

Finally, in larger terms, the search for an "organic seat" or "biological cause" of homosexuality remains an undemonstrated conceit—a mishmash of selective citation from the animal kingdom and speculative parallels to poorly understood human processes. Although various commentators have speculated that some gene in Xq28 *might* play a role in sexual orientation by way of neurohormonal links with the hypothalamus, no one has specified exactly how this might happen, much less tested a coherent hypothesis. In view of the aforementioned problems with LeVay's hypothalamus work, it is unlikely that they will. . . .

The questions raised about the reliability of Hamer's pedigree studies are crucial. Because the pedigree study is based on such poor design for sociological research, the likelihood is increased that the Xq28 concordance rates are the equivalent of "false positive" readings, results that appear to be significant but that are not replicated in subsequent research. (This kind of result happens all the time, even in unimpeachable, well-designed research.)

Notably, the Hamer group did not try to determine how many *nongay brothers* share this region of the chromosome with their gay brothers, much less whether pairs of straight brothers exhibit high rates of Xq28 concordance among themselves. This is not a trivial matter, because unless we know the Xq28 concordance rates for gay men with their heterosexual brothers, we have no way of interpreting the meaning of the 82 percent rate among gay brothers reported in the first study or the 67 percent rate reported in the Hamer group's follow-up study. Hamer's conclusions—that the gay men received a maternal chromosome for homosexuality and that Xq28 is *a* (or even *the*) genetic site involved in sexual orientation—depend on a viable control group that has never been established. The absence of such a control group renders Hamer's first study's results virtually meaningless.

The follow-up study, which found a lower rate of Xq28 consonance between gay brothers, did report a *very* small sample of eleven families in which two gay brothers shared the Xq28 marker and also had a nongay brother. It is reported that nine of the nongay brothers did not share the marker with their two gay brothers and that two did—but these numbers are very small indeed, scarcely adequate for a viable control group.

Perhaps most significantly, the Xq28 concordance rate for gay brothers fell from 83 percent in the first study to 67 percent in the second study. As Jonathan Marks makes clear in his discussion of inflated claims in the field of "behavioral genetics," the design of Hamer's study makes it extremely sensitive to a small number of families matching or not. The real question is not "Is there a gene for homosexuality?" but rather, "Is the 82 percent concordance result sufficiently different from the 50 percent rate that would occur by chance to be meaningful?" The concordance rate in the second study lies considerably closer to the 50 percent rate that would presumably occur in a DNA linkage analysis of pairs of brothers chosen entirely at random.[29]

More significant than any technical problems with Hamer's research design, however, are fundamental problems with the conception of the research and with the untested and untestable assumptions embedded therein. As is frequently the case with such research, the Hamer study implicitly understands phenotype (the aggregate physical and behavioral characteristics of an organism, usually understood as the product of a dynamic interaction between genes and environment) as the more or less direct expression of genotype (the state of the organism's genes, or the inherited genetic "givens" that are brought to the interaction), thus demoting "environmental" factors to an order of secondary importance. Whereas genes "for" this or that trait are conceived as playing a stable and "active" role in constructing the person, the environment serves as a backdrop and plays an essentially "passive" role, either speeding along the pre-given results or posing obstacles for the normal course of their expression.

This conception has the effect of obscuring the peculiar environment established by the study itself. Note the selection process that produced the sib-pair sample: There are always two gay brothers, maternally linked to other homosexual kin. We do not know how to compare this very specific sample with gay men who do *not* have gay brothers or other gay kin. This is no minor quibble, for the sampling procedure makes it impossible to distinguish environmental and social factors from genetic ones. There might well be major *social* differences between the development and experience of sexuality where a gay sibling is present, as opposed to sexual development and experience in other kinds of settings. Hamer has presumably accounted for this objection by claiming that he has identified "one form" of male homosexuality—presumably the kind genetically "transmitted" from mother to son. But this does not necessarily follow, and there are no compelling grounds for concluding it, unless one assumes that Xq28 in fact hides a "gay gene," which has not been demonstrated.

An alternative hypothesis, then: If older and successfully homosexual relatives serve as role models, fostering a sense of esteem for the homosexual feelings of younger relatives during crucial periods, then the "trait" in question might actually be "transmitted" *socially,* from uncle to nephew, from cousin to cousin, from brother to brother. . . . And the "form" of homosexuality identified here might mean only that there is an environmental difference—in that having a gay brother constitutes a different environment than not having a gay brother.

In this context, consider the most generous possible reading of Hamer's results, on their own terms—including the assumption that there must be some kind of "linkage" between genes and sexual object choice. Even assuming that Hamer's data, in toto, are reliable, there is no way of specifying exactly *what* is shared by gay brothers in Xq28: some gene *directly* related to sexuality and sexual orientation? Or some gene that has nothing to do with sexuality *directly*, but that can become linked, *indirectly* and under certain circumstances, to sexuality? In other words, the question of cause versus effect—indeed, of multiple causes and effects—has not been settled. Are consonant sibling pairs simply expressing a genetic predisposition toward homosexuality? Or are they being subtly socialized into homosexuality based on some other characteristic or set of traits? Or are they indirectly prodded toward the resolution of various conflicts through a homosexual outcome? Or even, yet again: Are they discovering and/or coming to emphasize a homosexual potential by way of some other characteristic, or by way of some other affinity with close kin?

Media reportage of genetic research like Hamer's invariably traffics in over-simplified, folkloric understandings of genetics and heritability. Headlines tell us that biologists have unearthed the "roots" of sexual orientation, or that geneticists have identified the gene "for" thrill seeking or a love of novelty. . . .[30] Such reportage, directed at the lay public, inevitably glosses complex technical questions. But it is not always clear that the research itself, considered apart from its splashy publicity, maintains a properly scientific approach to the question of heritability or the role of genetics in biological processes.

In the vernacular, heredity denotes what is "given," what is "in" the "blood": It is the part of human variation that is "caused" by genetic "nature," rather than by environmental "nurture." The folk conception of heredity also implies "immutability": The leopard cannot change his spots, and short of wearing colored contact lenses, human beings cannot change the color of their eyes.[31]

The biological conception of heritability is more precise and less deterministic. In biological terms, heritability is a measure of the likelihood that a trait present in one generation will recur in subsequent generations sharing a common gene pool in the same environment. Expressed as an equation, heredity includes both a numerator and a denominator. Richard Lewontin, Steven Rose, and Leon Kamin give that equation this way:

$$\text{Heritability} = H = \frac{\text{genetic variance}}{\text{genetic variance} + \text{environmental variance}}$$

where "genetic variance" refers to "the average performance of different genotypes" and "environmental variance" refers to the "variation among individuals of the same genotype."[32]

Two important qualifications follow from this formula. First, scientists attempting to determine the heritability of a trait assess average genetic variation. They do not measure genetic "causes." Second, environmental variation is part of the denominator—a basic point that is often forgotten in genetic research on complex human behaviors.

Note what limited arguments a properly biological conception of heritability and genetic factors actually permits. To say that a trait is "highly heritable"—that a high percentage of phenotypic variation is correlated to genetic variance—does not preclude saying that the trait also responds dramatically to environmental conditions. For example, if we say that height among a group of human beings has a heritability factor of about .9, or 90 percent, what this implies is that children in that group tend to be about the same height as their parents, all other things being equal.[33] But height also responds, impressively, to environmental factors, especially to childhood nutrition. Drought in the Sahel and famine in North Korea produce children whose height is substantially less than that of their parents, as is their body weight, among other things. In much of Asia, a shift away from traditional rice-and-fish staples to a cuisine more closely resembling the Western diet, with its emphasis on red meat, has dramatically raised the average height—along with body weight, average cholesterol levels, cardiovascular ailments, and the like. Heritability, then—even an extremely high measure of heritability—does not imply inevitability, immutability, or even genetic "causation." To say that a trait is "highly heritable" for a given population means only that the trait in question recurs at a certain rate among genetically related kin reproducing in a shared and relatively stable environment. It also implies a number of very substantial contingency clauses. If the environment changes, whether by accident, by migration, or as a result of changes introduced by the activity of the population itself, then the trait in question could also change dramatically.

To make matters yet more complicated, the heritability of a given trait can vary from group to group and place to place: "Some populations may have a lot of genetic variance for a character[istic], some only a little. Some environments are more variable than others."[34] For certain complex traits correlated to polygenic factors, environmental changes could signal the appearance of the trait in families where it was previously absent—or its elimination from lines where it had previously occurred. Finally, some simple, highly heritable traits in some species respond dramatically to changes in the environment—but not in any linear or straightforward way.[35] Famous experiments by Jens Clausen, David Keck, and William Heisey elegantly illustrate this principle.[36] The scientists took three clippings each from several different individual plants of the species *Achillea millefolium*. Such clippings will produce "clone" plants genetically identical to their parent plant and to each other. The scientists planted the clippings from each of the different plants in three different environments to observe how they grew under different conditions: one each at low, medium, and high elevations. The genetically identical plants grew to different heights at different elevations, but some were "tall" at low elevations, "short" at medium elevations, and "tall" again at high elevations. Others exhibited the opposite relationship: "short," "tall," and "short" from low to high elevation. Some showed a wide range of variation in different climates, others a narrow range. Although it was clear that the plants' heights were affected by elevation, it proved impossible to predict just how individuals would actually respond to different environments.[37]

Let us imagine, then, that homosexuality *has* a heritability factor, and that Hamer and his team are on to something. Even if one takes the Hamer results at face value—and I have tried to indicate some of what might be wrong with the research itself—and even if the findings withstand subsequent restudies, which is already very doubtful, the correlation of some form of sexual variation with some kind of genetic variation has many fewer implications than the lay public (or for that matter much of the science establishment) seems to think. Even a relatively high correlation—a high heritability factor (the worst-case scenario for partisans of a constructionist perspective)—could not preclude dramatic or unpredictable environmental effects on sexual orientation. Nor could it preclude the possibility that, under other circumstances, the "trait" in question could manifest itself differently or among altogether different kin groups.

Genetic research like Hamer's almost never announces itself with anything resembling the range of caveats appropriate for properly restrained biogenetic research. More often than not, it lapses into an essentially folkloric understanding of heritability; the search for "the" "gay" "gene," the confusion of "genetic correlation" with "genetic causation." That is because biologists, as a group, tend to be committed to an ideology of biological reductionism, with its reification of practices into things, even when such reduction runs contrary to their own best methods.[38] They also tend to reject the notion that science cannot answer every question.[39]

Readers will no doubt see where I stand. I do not believe that homosexuality is really susceptible to even "good" biological research. As a complex, meaningful, and motivated human activity, same-sex desire is simply not comparable to questions like eye color, hair color, or height. I am not even convinced that "desire" can be definitively identified, isolated from other human feelings, objectively classified, gauged, or compared. For how are we to measure the "occurrence" (or non-occurrence) of a "trait" that is itself relational, subtle, and subject to varied modalities and modulations? And how are we to measure environmental constancy across generations on a subject defined by contestation, volatility, and change?

DISCUSSION QUESTIONS

1. What are some of the flaws Lancaster identifies in this research on sexuality?
2. Should one study sexuality in the same way that one studies genetic traits such as eye or hair color?

NOTES

1. Thomas H. Maugh II and Nora Zamichow, *Los Angeles Times*, August 30, 1991. Malcolm Gladwell, *Washington Post*, December 17, 1991. Jamie Talan, *Newsday*, December 9, 1991. Kim Painter, *USA Today*, December 17, 1991. Natalie Angier, *New York Times*, July 16, 1993. Curt Suplee, *Washington Post*, October 31, 1995.
2. Anne Fausto-Sterling, *Myths of Gender: Biological Theories about Women and Men*, rev. ed. (1985; New York: Basic Books, 1992), 257.
3. Simon LeVay, "A Difference in Hypothalamic Structure between Heterosexual and Homosexual Men," *Science* 253 (1991): 1034–37.
4. See Edward Stein's calculations in *The Mismeasure of Desire: The Science, Theory, and Ethics of Sexual Orientation* (Oxford: Oxford University Press, 1999), 200–201.
5. Gail Vines, *Raging Hormones: Do They Rule Our Lives?* (Berkeley: University of California Press, 1994), 112. John Maddox, "Is Homosexuality Hardwired?" *Nature* 353 (1991): 13.
6. Gilbert Zicklin, "Media, Science, and Sexual Ideology: The Promotion of Sexual Stability," in *A Queer World: The Center for Lesbian and Gay Studies Reader*, ed. Martin Duberman (New York: New York University Press; 1997), 383.
7. See Simon LeVay, *The Sexual Brain* (Cambridge, Mass.: MIT Press, 1993), 121–22. William Byne, "LeVay's Thesis Reconsidered," in *A Queer World*, 325, and Stein, *The Mismeasure of Desire*, 201.
8. Stein, *The Mismeasure of Desire*, 210. Simon LeVay and Dean Hamer, "Evidence for a Biological Influence in Male Homosexuality," *Scientific American* 270 (May 1994): 44–49.
9. LeVay, *The Sexual Brain*, 122.
10. David Gelman with Donna Foote, Todd Barrett, and Mary Talbot, "Born or Bred?" *Newsweek*, February 24,

1992, 49. See also Ruth Hubbard and Elijah Wald, *Exploding the Gene Myth: How Genetic Information Is Produced and Manipulated by Scientists, Physicians, Employers, Insurance Companies, Educators, and Law Enforcers* (Boston: Beacon, 1993), 97–98.
11. Michael J. Bailey and Richard Pillard, "A Genetic Study of Male Sexual Orientation," *Archives of General Psychiatry* 48 (1991): 1089–96. See also Michael J. Bailey and Richard Pillard, "Are Some People Born Gay?" *New York Times*, December 17, 1991.
12. Hubbard and Wald, *Exploding the Gene Myth*, 97.
13. Actually, adoption procedures tend to select for relatively homogeneous, middle-class environments, even for twins separated at birth. And it turns out that many twins called "separated at birth" were not really so separated after all. Many such twins are actually reared by different sets of relatives in the same town.
14. Hubbard and Wald, *Exploding the Gene Myth*, 97.
15. Zicklin, "Media, Science, and Ideology," 385.
16. David Gelman et al., "Born or Bred: The Origins of Homosexuality," *Newsweek*, February 24, 1992, 46.
17. I leave aside here a discussion of all those terms that give away more than they need divulge of the author's presuppositions, for example, "nurturing" parents, a "lively interest" in sports, and "appropriate relations with women."
18. See the section entitled "Homosexual Outlet" in Alfred C. Kinsey et al., *Sexual Behavior in the Human Male* (Philadelphia: W. B. Saunders, 1948), 610–66.
19. Zicklin, "Media, Science, and Sexual Ideology," 384.
20. See Dean Hamer and Peter Copeland, *The Science of Desire: The Search for the Gay Gene and the Biology of Behavior* (New York: Simon and Schuster, 1994), 21.
21. Dean Hamer, Stella Hu, Victoria Magnuson, Nan Hu, and Angela Pattatucci, "A Linkage between DNA Markers on the X Chromosome and Male Sexual Orientation," *Science* 261 (1993): 321–27.
22. Hamer and Copeland, *The Science of Desire*, 203–4, 17–38.
23. Stein, *The Mismeasure of Desire*, 217. Neil Risch, E. Squires-Wheeler, and B. J. B. Keats, "Male Sexual Orientation and Genetic Evidence," *Science 262* (December 24, 1993): 2063–65.
24. On the matrilateral skewing of American and English kinship systems, especially but not exclusively patterns of kinship in the lower classes, see David M. Schneider and Raymond T. Smith, *Class Differences in American Kinship* (1973; Ann Arbor: University of Michigan Press, 1978), 9, 40–43, 53–55. On the significance of maternal kin work, see Micaela di Leonardo, "The Female World of Cards and Holidays: Women, Families, and the Work of Kinship," *Signs* 12, no. 3 (1987): 440–53.
25. See Zicklin, "Media, Science, and Sexual Ideology," 385.
26. In *The Science of Desire* and in response to Hamer's critics, Hamer and Copeland report that the Hamer team *did* attempt other checks: the first was to ponder the

distribution of *lesbian* relatives of the gay male subjects. Theoretically, if the maternal links simply reflected better knowledge of one's maternal kin, then there ought to also be elevated reportage of lesbianism along maternal lines. Hamer and Copeland report that the research team found no such pattern. The second check was to review lesbian informants' reportage of *gay male* relatives from a separate study. The authors report that there was no significant difference between maternal and paternal links for lesbian subjects (103–4). Of course, these "checks" assume that communication about relatives' sex lives occurs in a transparent environment unaffected by either sexual intolerance or gender inequalities—that talk about sex is uninflected by different maternal as opposed to paternal (and male as opposed to female, or mother-son, as opposed to mother-daughter, etc.) strategies of revelation and concealment. . . . It is by no means unthinkable that such factors could differentially distribute family knowledge about gays and lesbians. As Edward Stein demonstrates in *The Mismeasure of Desire* (218), it remains altogether plausible that the elevated maternal pattern of homosexuality reported by gay subjects is a *strictly* sociological effect, derived from partial knowledges, selectively revealed and asymetrically conveyed.

27. Hubbard and Wald, *Exploding the Gene Myth*, 75.
28. Stella Hu, Angela Pattatucci, C. Patterson, L. Li, D.W. Fulker, S. S. Cherny, L. Kruglak, and Dean Hamer, "Linkage between Sexual Orientation and Chromosome Xq28 in Males but Not in Females," *Nature Genetics* 11, no. 3 (1995): 248–56.
29. Jonathan Marks, "Behavioral Genetics," chapter 5 in *What It Means to Be 98 Percent Chimpanzee* (Berkeley: University of California Press, 2002).
30. Natalie Angier, "Variant Gene Tied to a Love of New Thrills," *New York Times*, January 2, 1996. See Angier's follow-up story later the same year, which reports a failure to replicate the original studies: "Maybe It's Not a Gene behind a Person's Thrill-Seeking Ways," *New York Times*, November 1, 1996.
31. Although the shorthand that refers to genetic "causes" is appealing when simple Mendelian traits such as eye color are under discussion, the idea of a genetic "cause" founders when polygenic traits are in question. Simple Mendelian traits account for only a small percentage of human traits. See Hubbard and Wald's discussion in *Exploding the Gene Myth*, 40–42.
32. R. C. Lewontin, Steven Rose, and Leon J. Kamin, *Not in Our Genes: Biology, Ideology, and Human Nature* (New York: Pantheon, 1984), 97.
33. To be more precise, it means that 90 percent of the variance in height for a population is accounted for by genetic variance. See Lewontin, Rose, and Kamin, *Not in Our Genes*, 97.
34. Ibid.
35. This important point is meticulously illustrated by Richard Lewontin, from whom I draw the following example, in *The Triple Helix: Gene, Organism, and Environment* (Cambridge, Mass.: Harvard University Press, 2000), 20–24.
36. Jens Clausen, David Keck, and William Heisey, *Experimental Studies on the Nature of Species, Vol. 3: Environmental Responses of Climatic Races of Achillea*, Carnegie Institution of Washington Publication 581 (1958), 1–129.
37. I leave aside certain well-known paradoxes of the scientific approach to heritability. Since heritability is a measure of *variance*, certain traits that are absolutely genetic show no variation—hence, zero heritability. (Imagine a population in which everyone has brown eyes.) Correlatively, if certain other traits "run in families" (because of where the families live) or are *socially* attached to a genetic trait (like skin color), they display high heritability, despite having plainly environmental origins. See Edward Stein's discussion in *The Mismeasure of Desire*, 142–44.
38. See Richard Lewontin's short masterpiece of science criticism, *Biology as Ideology: The Doctrine of DNA* (New York: HarperPerennial, 1992).
39. See John Horgan, *The End of Science: Facing the Limits of Knowledge in the Twilight of the Scientific Age* (Reading, Mass.: Addison-Wesley, 1996), and *The Undiscovered Mind—How the Human Mind Defies Replication, Medication, and Explanation* (New York: The Free Press, 1999).

READING 16

A New Paradigm for Understanding Women's Sexuality and Sexual Orientation

Letitia Anne Peplau

Linda D. Garnets

Scientific research on women's sexuality and sexual orientation is still a young endeavor. Nonetheless, several basic findings have been supported consistently by empirical research. Taken together, these findings highlight the need to reject old models of

Letitia Anne Peplau is a professor of social psychology at the University of California, Los Angeles. Linda D. Garnets is a professor of psychology and women studies at the University of California, Los Angeles.

women's sexual orientation and to develop a new paradigm that is grounded in scientific research and sensitive to the realities of women's lives. Too often, old theories have taken male experience as the norm for human experience. Yet there appear to be important differences in the sexualities of women and men that emerge when women's lives are the central focus of investigation. Consequently, we believe that a necessary research strategy will be to develop separate analyses of women's and men's sexualities, each based on a careful examination of the nature and antecedents of sexual orientation for that half of humankind. Whether or not generalizations and unified theories applicable to both sexes will eventually emerge remains to be seen.

We begin by summarizing well established empirical findings about women's sexualities. . . . As relevant, we note differences between women and men to underline the importance of research and theory that put women center stage. We then identify key ingredients in a new paradigm for understanding women's sexual orientation.

MENTAL HEALTH AND SEXUAL ORIENTATION: REJECTING THE ILLNESS MODEL

Implicit in many discussions of sexual orientation is the assumption that heterosexuals are normal and mentally healthy but homosexuals are abnormal and impaired in their psychological functioning (see review by Bullough & Bullough, 1997). This illness model has influenced theories about the causes of women's sexual orientation, as seen in the idea that lesbians have arrested psychosexual development. It has led to stereotypes of sexual-minority individuals as unhappy, maladjusted, and unable to form satisfying intimate relationships. A growing body of empirical work has refuted the illness model. Based on scientific evidence, the consensus among psychiatrists and psychologists is that homosexuality is not a form of pathology nor is it associated with mental illness or poor psychological functioning. On standardized measures of personal adjustment and psychological well-being,

gay and lesbian individuals (Gonsiorek, 1991), couples (Peplau & Spalding, 2000), and parents (Patterson & Redding, 1996) are comparable to their heterosexual counterparts. Although research about bisexuals is limited, Fox (1996) found no evidence of psychopathology in nonclinical samples of bisexual women and men.

In summary, the illness model of sexual orientation is no longer scientifically viable. One implication is that scientific researchers should avoid taking heterosexuality as the norm for mental health (see Herek, Kimmel, Amaro, & Melton, 1991, for research guidelines).

GENDER AND WOMEN'S SEXUAL ORIENTATION: REJECTING THE INVERSION MODEL

Early-20th-century sex experts such as Havelock Ellis (1928) and Krafft-Ebing (1908/1950) proposed an inversion model of homosexuality, suggesting that sexual orientation is closely tied to gender. Normal heterosexual women are feminine in their physiology, personality, and attractions to men. Lesbians are sexual inverts, women who are masculine in aspects of their physiology, personality, and attraction to women. The cumulative record of research on women's sexual orientation has repeatedly disconfirmed this model (see review by Peplau, Spalding, Conley, & Veniegas, 1999). There is no inherent link between heterosexuality and femininity in women or between homosexuality and masculinity in women. Biological models based on inversion premises, most notably the proposal that prenatal hormones "masculinize" the brains of females destined to be lesbians, have not been confirmed by scientific research.

Research . . . has demonstrated, instead, that there are consistent similarities among women, regardless of sexual orientation. Research on the centrality of intimacy and relationships to women's sexuality is illustrative. In addition, studies of bisexual women raise important questions about gender and sexual attractions (see Rust, 2000). Compared to other women, bisexual women appear to be less constrained by gender in their sexual and affectional attractions (Firestein, 1996). Bisexuals emphasize individual characteristics rather than gender in selecting a partner (Fox, 1996).

In summary, although the inversion model of sexual orientation remains popular, it lacks scientific support. There is no intrinsic association between gender conformity and women's sexual orientation; masculinity and femininity are linked to sexual orientation in some social contexts but not in others.

BIOLOGY AND WOMEN'S SEXUAL ORIENTATION: CHALLENGING BIOLOGICAL MODELS

Empirical research has failed to demonstrate that biological factors are a major influence in the development of women's sexual orientation. (In addition to the review by Veniegas and Conley, 2000, see also Bailey, 1995; Peplau et al., 1999.) Lesbian and heterosexual women are indistinguishable in their body build (A. Ellis, 1963). Researchers generally agree that there is no causal relationship between adult sex hormone levels and sexual orientation (Byne, 1995). Studies of the impact of prenatal sex hormones on human development show that the great majority of women exposed to atypical levels of sex hormones before birth are heterosexual in their attractions and behavior. According to one leading expert, "the main bone of contention is whether variations in the prenatal hormonal milieu have any effect at all and, if they do, are [they] of any practical significance" (Zucker, Bradley, & Lowry Sullivan, 1992, p. 93). Investigations of sexual orientation and brain structure in women have never been conducted.

Currently, the most promising biological research on women's sexual orientation focuses on genetics (Bailey & Pillard, 1995). Research has found that lesbians are more likely than heterosexual women to report having homosexual relatives. Studies of twins reared together find greater concordance (similarity) between the sexual orientation of monozygotic ("identical") twins than between

dizygotic twins or adoptive sisters. Proponents of genetic perspectives see these findings as encouraging. In contrast, skeptics emphasize possible limitations of the studies (e.g., McGuire, 1995) and the need for studies of twins reared apart. The one study that attempted to identify a genetic marker for homosexuality in women was unsuccessful (Hu et al., 1995). A definitive understanding of possible genetic influences on women's sexual orientation must await future research.

In summary, there is little evidence that biological factors are a major determinant of women's sexual orientation. In a recent review, Baumeister (2000, p. 356) acknowledged gaps in the available evidence, but nonetheless concluded, "the currently available data offer the best guess that male homosexuality is more strongly linked to innate or genetic determinants while female homosexuality remains more subject to personal choice and social influence." Although additional research will fill in gaps in our knowledge, there is no reason to expect that biological factors play anything other than a minor and probably indirect role in women's sexual orientation.

THE FLUIDITY OF WOMEN'S SEXUALITY

Scholars from many disciplines have noted that women's sexuality tends to be fluid, malleable, and capable of change over time. This point is often made in comparison to men, whose sexuality and sexual orientation are viewed as less flexible and more automatic. Recently social psychologist Roy Baumeister (2000) systematically reviewed empirical research on gender differences in erotic plasticity. Baumeister defined *plasticity* as the degree to which a person's sex drive can be shaped and altered by cultural, social, and situational pressures. By contrast, a lack of plasticity would indicate that a person's sexuality is more rigidly patterned early in life, as a result of biological and/or childhood influences.

The concept of sexual fluidity is the cornerstone of a new paradigm for understanding women's sexuality and sexual orientation. If women's sexuality is not primarily determined by biological programming but is instead responsive to social contexts, then theories about women's experiences must be social psychological in focus. To make the case for this core idea, we next review evidence from Baumeister and others that supports three specific predictions concerning the fluidity of female sexuality.

Influence of the Social Environment

A first prediction is that to the extent that sexuality is plastic and malleable, it can be shaped by a range of social and situational influences. Baumeister (2000) marshaled considerable evidence showing that such factors as education, religion, and acculturation have greater impact on aspects of women's sexuality than on men's. Consider the link between education and sexual orientation. The National Health and Social Life Survey (Laumann, Gagnon, Michael, & Michaels, 1994, p. 305) found that completing college doubled the likelihood that a man identified as gay or bisexual but was associated with a 900% increase in the percentage of women identifying as lesbian/bisexual (from 0.4% of women high school graduates to 3.6% of college graduates). Similarly, the association between religious conservatism and a heterosexual identity was stronger among women than men. Also consistent with the plasticity hypothesis is evidence that active involvement in the 1970s feminist movement led some women to turn away from sexual relations with men and to establish relationships with women (e.g., Kitzinger, 1987; Rosenbluth, 1997; Whisman, 1996). Pearlman (1987) explained that "many of the new, previously heterosexual, radical lesbians had based their choice as much on politics as on sexual interest in other women" (p. 318).

Within-Person Variation or Change Over Time

A second prediction by Baumeister (2000) is that some degree of erotic plasticity would make it possible for an individual to have nonexclusive attractions toward both women and men. In addition, plasticity would permit a woman to change aspects of her sexuality or sexual orientation across the lifespan. There is considerable evidence that both nonexclusive attractions and change over time do characterize the experiences of some women (see Rust, 2000). American women who are not exclusively heterosexual are more likely to be bisexual rather than exclusively homosexual in their attractions and relationships (e.g., Laumann et al., 1994; Weinberg, Williams, & Pyror, 1994). For example, a recent study of 6,935 self-identified lesbians from all 50 states found that 77% of lesbians had had one or more male sexual partners during their lifetime (Diamant, Schuster, McGuigan, & Lever, 1999). The study's authors cautioned health care providers and others not to "assume that a woman who identifies herself as a lesbian has not had any sexual contact with men, or that such contact was only in the distant past" (p. 2734). Baumeister documented that this pattern of bisexual attraction and behavior is significantly more common among women than men.

Further, both women's identification as lesbian, bisexual, or heterosexual and women's actual behavior can vary over time. In an early study of bisexuality in women, Blumstein and Schwartz (1976) interviewed women who had a long-term heterosexual relationship followed by a long-term lesbian relationship. Some of these women subsequently returned to relationships with men. Other researchers have also documented the experiences of married women who switch course and start a new life with a female partner (e.g., Kitzinger & Wilkinson, 1995). The reverse pattern also occurs: Women who identified as lesbians may begin sexual relationships with men (e.g., Bart, 1993; Rust, 1992).

Claims about the potential erotic plasticity of women do *not* mean that most women will actually exhibit change over time. At a young age, many women adopt patterns of heterosexuality that are stable across their lifetime. Some women adopt enduring patterns of same-sex attractions and relationships. To the extent that the social influences acting on a woman remain constant, there is little reason to expect change based on the sexual plasticity hypothesis. The key point is that at least some women are capable of variation and change, and that such plasticity appears to be more characteristic of women than men (cf. Diamond, 2000). . . .

Attitude-Behavior Consistency

A third issue relevant to sexual fluidity concerns the consistency among an individual's sexual attitudes, desires, and behavior. Baumeister (2000) argued that "if women's behavior is more malleable by situational forces than men's, then women will be more likely than men to do things contrary to their general attitudes" (p. 359). In the area of sexual orientation, the plasticity hypothesis would challenge the popular belief that sexual desires, behavior, and identity are invariably interconnected. To be sure, many individuals do report complete consistency: A woman might identify as lesbian, be attracted exclusively to women, and have sex with women partners only. But exceptions to this pattern of consistency are common. For example, a woman who identifies as lesbian might develop a strong attraction to a man. A woman may have strong attractions to both men and women but not identify as bisexual. A heterosexual woman may employ homoerotic fantasies when having sex with her male partner. . . .

CHILDHOOD INFLUENCES ON WOMEN'S SEXUAL ORIENTATION

It is often believed that childhood experiences in the family and with peers are formative in shaping many aspects of adult personality, attitudes, and behavior. From this perspective, one would expect that sexual orientation is strongly influenced by childhood experiences. Yet empirical research has so far failed to identify events or activities that predictably point a girl in our culture on the path toward lesbian or bisexual attractions (Bohan, 1996).

Efforts to test psychoanalytic theories about the family history antecedents of sexual orientation have failed (e.g., Bell, Weinberg, & Hammersmith,

1981; Downey & Friedman, 1998). Furthermore, the sexual orientation of parents appears to have limited impact on the sexual orientation of their children: most lesbians were raised by heterosexual parents and most children raised by gay or lesbian parents become heterosexual adults (e.g., Bailey & Dawood, 1998; Patterson, 1997). There is some suggestive evidence that gender nonconformity in childhood may be correlated with adult sexual orientation (e.g., Bailey & Zucker, 1995). Based on retrospective reports, lesbians are more likely than heterosexual women to remember having been a tomboy as a child. Such studies are inconclusive, however, because memories of childhood may be colored by adult experiences. Equally important, most tomboys grow up to be heterosexuals.

Two issues concerning childhood influences on women's sexual orientation are noteworthy. First, according to the sexual plasticity hypothesis, we might expect women's sexuality to be more strongly influenced by childhood events than men's sexuality. Baumeister (2000) considered and rejected this possibility on empirical grounds. His review of research on childhood gender nonconformity, sexual dysfunction, and paraphilias suggested the opposite: that childhood experiences have stronger and more lasting effects on male than female sexuality. So, for example, the correlation between adult sexual orientation and retrospective reports of childhood gender nonconformity is significantly higher among men than among women (Bailey & Zucker, 1995). To explain this apparent contradiction, Baumeister (p. 368) proposed that "male sexuality may undergo a childhood phase (akin to imprinting in animals) during which social and environmental influences can have a major influence." In contrast, females may have no such critical period and so exhibit greater sexual fluidity across the lifecycle. This speculation needs empirical investigation (cf. Weinrich, 1987).

Second, it is possible that important early antecedents of women's sexual orientation have simply been overlooked by researchers and could be identified with further effort. For instance, in a society that is hostile to homosexuality, lesbians may be women who are willing to challenge convention and take social risks. Researchers have not investigated whether the development of personality characteristics such as risk taking or independence affects adult sexual orientation in women. Longitudinal studies charting the development of sexual orientation in women over time would be valuable.

SOCIOCULTURAL INFLUENCES ON WOMEN'S SEXUAL ORIENTATION

Identity

Sexual identity can be defined as "an individual's enduring sense of self as a sexual being that fits a culturally created category and accounts for one's sexual fantasies, attractions, and behavior" (Savin-Williams, 1995, p. 166). Historical changes in cultural interpretations of women's romantic relationships illustrate how cultural categories shape identity. The romantic friendships between women that flourished in the 18th and 19th centuries were socially acceptable and had no implications for a woman's identity (Faderman, 1981). As the 20th century unfolded, however, the identity of "lesbian" emerged, and social attitudes about these relationships changed. Faderman (1991, p. 303) explained that

> love between women, especially those of the middle class, was dramatically metamorphosed from romantic friendships [into] "lesbianism" once the sexologists formulated the concept, economic factors made it possible for large numbers of women to live independently of men, and mobility allowed many women to travel to places where they might meet others who accepted the lesbian label.

Historians contend that the creation of "homosexual" and "heterosexual" as defining identities is a relatively recent development (e.g., Katz, 1995). As Rust (2000) has discussed, these sexual identities then set the stage for the emergence of a new social identity, that of the bisexual person.

Institutions

Another way in which cultures influence sexual orientation is through the creation of social institutions that provide both opportunities for and constraints on women's sexuality and relationships. As Blumstein and Schwartz (1990, p. 310) observed, these social arrangements can "be as concrete as a woman being unable to have heterosexual experience because her interactions with men are always chaperoned, or as subtle as her being unable to have sexual relations outside of her marriage because she is a suburban housewife who . . . never finds herself in the company of men."

As another example, living in same-sex institutions also tends to increase the likelihood of romantic and erotic relationships between women. In the 1920s, Katharine Davis (1929) surveyed more than 2,000 graduates of women's colleges. Fully 42% of the sample reported that they had had an intense emotional relationship with another woman in college; 1 woman in 5 reported having a sexual relationship with a best friend in college. Same-sex relationships are also common among prison populations and appear to be more prevalent among women than men in prison (see review in Baumeister, 2000; Rust, 2000): In both cases, institutions created for nonsexual purposes—education and incarceration—provide settings that foster same-sex bonds between women.

An important implication of cross-cultural and historical findings is that researchers cannot assume that the experiences of contemporary American women are universal or even typical of the full range of women's erotic attractions and relationships. More broadly, the phenomena of sexual orientation are not fixed and universal, but rather highly variable across time and place. Researchers interested in understanding the general nature of female sexuality must look beyond their immediate cultural and historical context.

Sexual Prejudice

The experiences of contemporary lesbian and bisexual women must be understood in the context of widespread prejudice against sexual minorities in our society (see Herek, 2000). Indeed, bisexual women may encounter negative attitudes not only from heterosexuals but from lesbians as well (Rust, 1993). Similarly, individuals who are both ethnic and sexual minorities may encounter sexual prejudice from both mainstream society and from their own racial/ethnic communities (Rust, 1996; Savin-Williams, 1996).

Sexual prejudice is closely linked to attitudes about gender and women's sexuality. Lesbians and gay men are disliked in part because they are perceived to violate traditional gender roles (Storms, 1978). Gender nonconformity is a central theme in antigay stereotypes, which depict lesbians as masculine or unfeminine and gay men as effeminate or unmasculine (Herek, 1984; Kite & Deaux, 1987). Furthermore, antigay prejudice is stronger among heterosexuals who endorse traditional, restrictive attitudes about gender and family roles and who reject equality between the sexes (Herek, 1984).

All people are affected by sexual prejudice and discrimination. Women who identify as lesbian or bisexual must navigate through hostile social environments and may experience difficult dilemmas about when to conceal versus reveal their sexual orientation and intimate relationships. Women who are uncertain about their sexual orientation may be discouraged from considering sexual-minority options. Sexual prejudice also touches the lives of heterosexuals. Fear of being labeled gay is a powerful socialization influence (see Hyde & Jaffee, 2000). Regardless of their sexual orientation, girls and women who appear to be masculine in their appearance or interests, who dress in nontraditional clothes or resist a man's sexual advances, who work in nontraditional occupations or appear assertive risk being called lesbians (Kite, 1994). As a result, heterosexuals may experience social pressure to conform to traditional gender roles in order to avoid the stigmatizing label of homosexuality. For example, varsity women athletes often wear dresses, makeup, jewelry or long hair to avoid being considered lesbian (Blinde & Taub, 1992).

In summary, cultural and historical research documents the varied patterns of women's sexuality and erotic relationships. These findings add support to characterization of women's sexuality as potentially fluid and influenced by social forces.

THE IMPORTANCE OF RELATIONSHIPS FOR WOMEN'S SEXUALITY AND SEXUAL ORIENTATION

For many theorists, especially those taking male experiences as their model, sexuality and sexual orientation are first and foremost about sexual behavior. Increasingly, however, researchers with diverse theoretical orientations have suggested that love and intimacy are more important for understanding women's sexuality than for understanding men's sexuality (e.g., Golden, 1996; Weinrich, 1987). For example, Regan and Berscheid (1996, p. 116) asked young heterosexual adults, "What is sexual desire?" These comments are illustrative:

> *Man:* Sexual desire is wanting someone . . . in a physical manner. No strings attached. Just for uninhibited *sexual intercourse.* (italics in original)
> *Woman:* Sexual desire is the longing to be emotionally intimate and to express love for another person.

Regan and Berscheid concluded that men were more likely to "sexualize" and women to "romanticize" the experience of sexual desire. Similarly, based on their study of bisexuals, Weinberg and colleagues (1994, p. 7) concluded: "For men it was easier to have sex with other men than to fall in love with them. For women it was easier to fall in love with other women than to have sex with them." We are not suggesting that eroticism is unimportant in women's lives or irrelevant to their sexual orientation. Rather, we think it is crucial to acknowledge and analyze the central role emotional intimacy often has for women's sexual experiences. Similarly, we do not propose that emotional intimacy is unimportant to men's lives or their sexual orientation.

Gender differences in sexuality have been widely discussed (e.g., Sprecher & McKinney, 1993). In general, women have been characterized as having a relational or partner-centered orientation to sexuality and men as having a recreational or body-centered orientation (e.g., Baldwin & Baldwin, 1997; DeLamater, 1987). Both biological and social explanations have been proposed for these differences. Oliver and Hyde (1993) reviewed five theoretical perspectives—sociobiology, neoanalytic, social learning, social roles, and script theory—all of which predict sex differences in sexuality—for instance, that compared to males, females will have a smaller number of sex partners and hold more negative attitudes toward premarital sex. Several lines of research provide empirical support for these generalizations and suggest that they may apply regardless of sexual orientation. . . .

Multiple Pathways

The emerging view of scholars is that sexual orientation is multiply determined by many influences. No single factor reliably predicts whether a woman embarks on a path toward heterosexuality, homosexuality, bisexuality, or some other pattern. Further, there are multiple developmental pathways leading to common outcomes (see Diamond & Savin-Williams, 2000). In contemporary society, a woman's assertion that she is heterosexual or lesbian may be based on quite diverse and non-linear developmental trajectories. Women may be drawn to a particular lifestyle for differing reasons. Knowing that a woman labels herself as heterosexual, lesbian, or bisexual does not necessarily inform us about the pattern of her life experiences or the nature of her current erotic thoughts and feelings. Indeed, Pattatucci (1998) criticized research on sexual orientation for concentrating on "end states" (i.e., self-identification as lesbian) and ignoring how individuals reach that point. Demo and Allen (1996, p. 426) urged researchers to focus on the "multiple trajectories and social contexts . . . shaping individual lives; . . . the transitions and turning-points lesbians and gay men experience form their families of origin through the families they form and maintain as adults." . . .

DISCUSSION QUESTIONS

1. How is the fluidity of women's sexuality manifested?
2. What common assumptions and prejudices about sexuality are being undermined by the research summarized in this article?

REFERENCES

Bailey, J. M. (1995). Biological perspectives on sexual orientation. In A. R. D'Augelli & C. J. Patterson (Eds.), *Lesbian, gay and bisexual identities over the lifespan* (pp. 104–135). New York: Oxford University Press.

Bailey, J. M., & Dawood, K. (1998). Behavioral genetics, sexual orientation, and the family. In C. J. Patterson & A. R. D'Augelli (Eds.), *Lesbian, gay, and bisexual identities in families* (pp. 3–18). New York: Oxford University Press.

Bailey, J. M., & Pillard, R. C. (1995). Genetics of human sexual orientation. In R. C. Rosen (Ed.), *Annual Review of Sex Research* (Vol. 6, pp. 136–150). Mason City, IA: Society for the Scientific Study of Sexuality.

Bailey, J. M., & Zucker, K. J. (1995). Childhood sex-typed behavior and sexual orientation: A conceptual analysis and quantitative review. *Developmental Psychology, 31*, 43–55.

Baldwin, J. D., & Baldwin, J. I. (1997). Gender differences in sexual interest. *Archives of Sexual Behavior, 26*(2), 181–210.

Bart, P. (1993). Protean women: The liquidity of female sexuality and the tenaciousness of lesbian identity. In S. Wilkinson & C. Kitzinger (Eds.), *Heterosexuality: Feminism and psychology reader* (pp. 246–252). London: Sage.

Baumeister, R. F. (2000). Gender differences in erotic plasticity: The female sex drive as socially flexible and responsive. *Psychological Bulletin, 126*, 347–374.

Bell, A. P., Weinberg, M. S., & Hammersmith, S. K. (1981). *Sexual preference.* Bloomington: Indiana University Press.

Blinde, E. M., & Taub, D. E. (1992). Women athletes as falsely accused deviants: Managing the lesbian stigma. *Sociological Quarterly, 33*, 521–533.

Blumstein, P. W., & Schwartz, P. (1976). Bisexuality in women. *Archives of Sexual Behavior, 5*(2), 171–181.

Blumstein, P. W., & Schwartz, P. (1990). Intimate relationships and the creation of sexuality. In D. M. McWhirter, S. A. Sanders, & J. M. Reinisch (Eds.). *Homosexuality/heterosexuality* (pp. 307–320). New York: Oxford.

Bohan, J. S. (1996). *Psychology and sexual orientation.* New York: Routledge.

Bullough, V. L., & Bullough, B. (1997). The history of the science of sexual orientation 1880–1980. *Journal of Psychology and Human Sexuality, 9*(2), 1–16.

Byne, W. (1995). Science and belief: Psychobiological research on sexual orientation. *Journal of Homosexuality, 28*(3/4), 303–344.

Davis, K. B. (1929). *Factors in the sex life of twenty-two hundred women.* New York: Harper

DeLamater, J. (1987). Gender differences in sexual scenarios. In K. Kelley (Ed.), *Females, males and sexuality: Theories and research* (pp. 127–129). Albany: State University of New York Press.

Demo, D. H., & Allen, K. R. (1996). Diversity within lesbian and gay families: Challenges and implications for family theory and research. *Journal of Social and Personal Relationships, 13*(3), 415–434.

Diamant, A. L., Schuster, M. A., McGuigan, K., & Lever, J. (1999). Lesbians' sexual history with men. *Archives of Internal Medicine, 159,* 2730–2736.

Diamond, L. M. (2000). Sexual identity, attractions and behavior among young sexual-minority women over a two-year period. *Developmental Psychology, 36,* 241–250.

Diamond, L. M. & Savin-Williams, R. C. (2000). Explaining diversity in the development of same-sex sexuality among young women. *Journal of Social Issues, 56*(2), 297–313.

Downey, J. I., & Friedman, R. C. (1998). Female homosexuality: Classical psychoanalytic theory reconsidered. *Journal of the American Psychoanalytic Association, 46*(2), 471–506.

Ellis, A. (1963). Constitutional factors in homosexuality. In H. G. Beigel (Ed.), *Advances in sex research* (pp. 161–186). New York: Harper and Row.

Ellis, H. (1928). *Studies in the psychology of sex. Vol. II: Sexual inversion.* Philadelphia: F. A. Davis.

Faderman, L. (1981). *Surpassing the love of men.* New York: Morrow.

Faderman, L. (1991). *Odd girls and twilight lovers.* New York: Columbia University Press.

Firestein, B. A. (1996). Bisexuality as a paradigm shift: Transforming our disciplines. In B. Firestein (Ed.), *Bisexuality: The psychology and politics of an invisible minority* (pp. 263–291). Thousand Oaks, CA: Sage.

Fox, R. (1996). Bisexuality in perspective: A review of theory and research. In B. Firestein (Ed.), *Bisexuality: The psychology and politics of an invisible minority* (pp. 3–50). Thousand Oaks, CA: Sage.

Golden, C. (1996). What's in a name? Sexual self-identification among women. In R. C. Savin-Williams & K. M. Cohen (Eds.), *The lives of lesbians, gays and bisexuals* (pp. 229–247). New York: Harcourt Brace.

Gonsiorek, J. (1991). The empirical basis for the demise of the illness model of homosexuality. In J. Gonsiorek &

J. Weinrich (Eds.), *Homosexuality: Research implications for public policy* (pp. 115–136). Newbury Park, CA: Sage.

Herek, G. M. (1984). Beyond homophobia: A social psychological perspective on attitudes toward lesbians and gay men. *Journal of Homosexuality, 10*(1/2), 1–21.

Herek, G. M. (2000). The psychology of sexual prejudice. *Current Directions in Psychological Science, 9,* 19–22.

Herek, G. M., Kimmel, D. C., Amaro, H., & Melton, G. B. (1991). Avoiding heterosexual bias in psychological research. *American Psychologist 46,* 957–963.

Hu, S., Pattatucci, A. M., Patterson, C., Li, L., Fulker, D. W., Cherny, S. S., Kruglyak, L., & Hamer, D. (1995). Linkage between sexual orientation and chromosome Xq28 in males but not in females. *Nature Genetics, 11,* 248–256.

Hyde, J. S. & Jaffee, S. R. (2000). Becoming a heterosexual adult: The experiences of young women. *Journal of Social Issues, 56*(2), 283–296.

Katz, J. N. (1995). *The invention of heterosexuality.* New York: Dutton.

Kite, M. E. (1994). When perceptions meet reality: Individual differences in reactions to gay men and lesbians. In B. Greene & G. Herek (Eds.), *Lesbian and gay psychology: Theory, research, and clinical applications* (pp. 25–53). Thousand Oaks, CA: Sage.

Kite, M. E. & Deaux, K. (1987). Gender belief systems: Homosexuality and the implicit inversion theory. *Psychology of Women Quarterly, 11,* 83–96.

Kitzinger, C. (1987). *The social construction of lesbianism.* London: Sage.

Kitzinger, C., & Wilkinson, S. (1995). Transitions from heterosexuality to lesbianism. *Developmental Psychology, 31,* 95–104.

Krafft-Ebing, R. (1950). *Psychopathia sexualis* (F. J. Rebman, Trans.). Brooklyn, NY: Physicians and Surgeons Book Co. (Original work published 1908)

Laumann, E. O., Gagnon, J. H., Michael, R. T., & Michaels, S. (1994). *The social organization of sexuality: Sexual practices in the United States.* Chicago, IL: University of Chicago Press.

McGuire, T. R. (1995). Is homosexuality genetic? A critical review and some suggestions. *Journal of Homosexuality, 28*(1/2), 115–145.

Oliver, M. B., & Hyde, J. S. (1993). Gender differences in sexuality: A meta-analysis. *Psychological Bulletin, 114*(1), 29–51.

Pattatucci, A. M. L. (1998). Biopsychosocial interactions and the development of sexual orientation. In C. J. Patterson & A. R. D'Augelli (Eds.), *Lesbian, gay and bisexual identities in families* (pp. 19–39). New York: Oxford University Press.

Patterson, C. J. (1997). Children of lesbian and gay parents. In T. H. Ollendick & R. J. Prinz (Eds.), *Advances in clinical child psychology* (Vol. 19, pp. 235–282). New York: Plenum Press.

Patterson, C. J., & Redding, R. E. (1996). Lesbian and gay parents and their children: Legal and public policy implications of social science research. *Journal of Social Issues*, 52, 29–50.

Pearlman, S. F. (1987). The saga of continuing clash in lesbian community, or will an army of ex-lovers fail? In Boston Lesbian Psychologies Collective (Ed.), *Lesbian psychologies* (pp. 313–326). Urbana, IL: University of Illinois Press.

Peplau, L. A., & Spalding, L. R. (2000). The close relationships of lesbians, gay men, and bisexuals. In C. Hendrick & S. S. Hendrick (Eds.), *Close relationships: A sourcebook* (pp. 111–124). Thousand Oaks, CA: Sage.

Peplau, L. A., Spalding, L. R., Conley, T. D., & Veniegas, R. C. (1999). The development of sexual orientation in women. *Annual Review of Sex Research*, 10, 70–99.

Regan, P. C., & Berscheid, E. (1996). Beliefs about the state, goals, and objects of sexual desire. *Journal of Sex and Marital Therapy*, 22, 110–120.

Rosenbluth, S. (1997). Is sexual orientation a matter of choice? *Psychology of Women Quarterly*, 21, 595–610.

Rust, P. C. (1992). The politics of sexual identity: Sexual attraction and behavior among lesbian and bisexual women. *Social Problems*, 39(4), 366–386.

Rust, P. C. (1993). Neutralizing the political threat of the marginal woman: Lesbians' beliefs about bisexual women. *Journal of Sex Research*, 30(3), 214–228.

Rust, P. C. (1996). Managing multiple identities: Diversity among bisexual men and women. In B. Firestein (Ed.), *Bisexuality: The psychology and politics of an invisible minority* (pp. 53–83). Thousand Oaks, CA: Sage.

Rust, P. C. (2000). Bisexuality: A contemporary paradox for women. *Journal of Social Issues*, 56(2), 205–221.

Savin-Williams, R. C. (1995). Lesbian, gay male, and bisexual adolescents. In A. R. D'Augelli & C. J. Patterson (Eds.), *Lesbian, gay and bisexual identities over the lifespan* (pp. 165–189). New York: Oxford University Press.

Savin-Williams, R. C. (1996). Ethnic-minority and sexual-minority youths. In R. C. Savin-Williams & K. M. Cohen (Eds.), *The lives of lesbians, gays and bisexuals* (pp. 152–165). New York: Harcourt Brace.

Sprecher, S., & McKinney, K. (1993). *Sexuality*. Newbury Park, CA: Sage.

Storms, M. D. (1978). Attitudes toward homosexuality and femininity in men. *Journal of Homosexuality*. 3(3), 257–263.

Veniegas, R. C. & Conley, T. D. (2000). Biological research on women's sexual orientations: Evaluating the scientific evidence. *Journal of Social Issues*, 56(2), 267–282.

Weinberg, M. S., Williams, C. J., & Pryor, D. W. (1994). *Dual attraction: Understanding bisexuality*. New York: Oxford.

Weinrich, J. D. (1987). *Sexual landscapes*. New York: Scribner.

Whisman, V. (1996). *Queer by choice*. New York: Routledge.

Zucker, K. J., Bradley, S. U., & Lowry Sullivan, C. B. (1992). Gender identity disorder in children. *Annual Review of Sex Research*, 3, 73–120.

READING 17

The Heterosexual Questionnaire

Martin Rochlin

This Heterosexual Questionnaire reverses the questions that are very often asked of gays and lesbians by straight people. By having to answer this type of question, the heterosexual person will get some intellectual and emotional insight into how oppressive and discriminatory a "straight" frame of reference can be to lesbians and gays.

1. What do you think caused your heterosexuality?
2. When and how did you first decide you were a heterosexual?
3. Is it possible that your heterosexuality is just a phase you may grow out of?
4. Is it possible that your heterosexuality stems from a neurotic fear of others of the same sex?
5. If you've never slept with a person of the same sex, is it possible that all you need is a good gay lover?
6. To whom have you disclosed your heterosexual tendencies?
7. Why do you heterosexuals feel compelled to seduce others into your lifestyle?
8. Why do you insist on flaunting your heterosexuality? Can't you just be what you are and keep it quiet?
9. Would you want your children to be heterosexual, knowing the problem they'd face?
10. A disproportionate majority of child molesters are heterosexuals. Do you consider it safe to expose your children to heterosexual teachers?
11. Even with all the societal support marriage receives, the divorce rate is spiraling. Why are there so few stable relationships among heterosexuals?

Martin Rochlin (1928–2003) was one of the founders of the Association of Gay Psychologists and a leader in the campaign that led to removing homosexuality from the list of mental disorders in the *Diagnostic and Statistical Manual of Mental Disorders*.

12. Why do heterosexuals place so much emphasis on sex?

13. Considering the menace of overpopulation, how could the human race survive if everyone were heterosexual like you?

14. Could you trust a heterosexual therapist to be objective? Don't you fear that the therapist might be inclined to influence you in the direction of his or her own leanings?

15. How can you become a whole person if you limit yourself to compulsive, exclusive heterosexuality and fail to develop your natural, healthy homosexual potential?

16. There seem to be very few happy heterosexuals. Techniques have been developed that might enable you to change if you really want to. Have you considered trying aversion therapy?

DISCUSSION QUESTIONS

1. What is your reaction to the Heterosexual Questionnaire?

2. What are the assumptions behind these questions?

WHAT IS DISABILITY?

READING 18

Disability Definitions: The Politics of Meaning

Michael Oliver

THE IMPORTANCE OF DEFINITIONS

The social world differs from the natural world in (at least) one fundamental respect; that is, human beings give meanings to objects in the social world and subsequently orient their behavior towards these objects in terms of the meanings given to them. W. I. Thomas (1966) succinctly puts it thus: "if men define situations as real, they are real in their consequences." As far as disability is concerned, if it is seen as a tragedy, then disabled people will be treated as if they are the victims of some tragic happening or circumstance. This treatment will occur not just in everyday interactions but will also be translated into social policies which

Michael Oliver is professor emeritus of disability studies at the University of Greenwich in the United Kingdom.

will attempt to compensate these victims for the tragedies that have befallen them.

Alternatively, it logically follows that if disability is defined as social oppression, then disabled people will be seen as the collective victims of an uncaring or unknowing society rather than as individual victims of circumstance. Such a view will be translated into social policies geared towards alleviating oppression rather than compensating individuals. It almost goes without saying that at present, the individual and tragic view of disability dominates both social interactions and social policies.

A second reason why definitions are important historically centres on the need to identify and classify the growing numbers of the urban poor in modern industrial societies. In this process of identification and classification, disability has always been an important category, in that it offers a legitimate social status to those who can be defined as unable to work as opposed to those who may be classified as unwilling to do so (Stone, 1985). Throughout the twentieth century this process has become ever more sophisticated, requiring access to expert knowledge, usually residing in the ever-burgeoning medical and paramedical professions. Hence the simple dichotomy of the nineteenth century has given way to a whole new range of definitions based upon clinical criteria or functional limitation.

A third reason why definitions are important stems from what might be called "the politics of minority groups." From the 1950s onwards, though earlier in the case of alcoholics, there was a growing realisation that if particular social problems were to be resolved, or at least ameliorated, then nothing more or less than a fundamental redefinition of the problem was necessary. Thus a number of groups including women, black people and homosexuals, set about challenging the prevailing definitions of what constituted these problems by attacking the sexist and racist biases in the language used to underpin these dominant definitions. They did this by creating, substituting or taking over terminology to provide more positive imagery (e.g., gay is good, black is beautiful, etc.). Disabled people too have realised that dominant definitions of disability pose problems for individual and group identity and have begun to challenge the use of disablist language. Whether it be offensive (cripple, spastic, mongol, etc.) or merely depersonalising (the handicapped, the blind, the deaf, and so on), such terminology has been attacked, and organisations of disabled people have fostered a growing group consciousness and identity.

There is one final reason why this issue of definitions is important. From the late fifties onwards there was an upswing in the economy and an increasing concern to provide more services for disabled people out of an ever-growing national cake. But clearly, no government (of whatever persuasion) was going to commit itself to a whole range of services without some idea of what the financial consequences of such a commitment might be. Thus, after some pilot work, the Office of Population Censuses and Surveys (OPCS) was commissioned in the late sixties to carry out a national survey in Britain which was published in 1971 (Harris, 1971). Subsequent work in the international context (Wood, 1981) and more recently a further survey in this country, which has recently been published (Martin, Meltzer and Elliot, 1988), built on and extended this work. However, this work has proceeded isolated from the direct experience of disability as experienced by disabled people themselves, and this has led to a number of wide-ranging and fundamental criticisms of it. . . .

THE POLITICS OF MEANING

It could be argued that in polarising the tragic and oppressive views of disability, a conflict is being created where none necessarily exists. Disability has both individual and social dimensions and that is what official definitions from Harris (1971) through to WHO [World Health Organization] (Wood, 1981) have sought to recognize and to operationalize. The problem with this, is that these schemes, while acknowledging that there are social dimensions to disability, do not see disability as arising from social causes. . . .

This view of disability can and does have oppressive consequences for disabled people and can be quite clearly shown in the methodology adopted by the OPCS survey in Britain (Martin et al., 1988). [Table 1 presents] a list of questions drawn from the face-to-face interview schedule of this survey.

TABLE 1
SURVEY OF DISABLED ADULTS—OPCS, 1986

Can you tell me what is wrong with you?

What complaint causes your difficulty in holding, gripping or turning things?

Are your difficulties in understanding people mainly due to a hearing problem?

Do you have a scar, blemish or deformity which limits your daily activities?

Have you attended a special school because of a long-term health problem or disability?

Does your health problem/disability mean that you need to live with relatives or someone else who can help look after you?

Did you move here because of your health problem/disability?

How difficult is it for you to get about your immediate neighborhood on your own?

Does your health problem/disability prevent you from going out as often or as far as you would like?

Does your health problem/disability make it difficult for you to travel by bus?

Does your health problem/disability affect your work in any way at present?

These questions clearly ultimately reduce the problems that disabled people face to their own personal inadequacies or functional limitations. It would have been perfectly possible to reformulate these questions to locate the ultimate causes of disability as within the physical and social environments [as they are in Table 2].

This reformulation is not only about methodology or semantics, it is also about oppression. In order to understand this, it is necessary to understand that, according to OPCS's own figures, 2231 disabled people were given face-to-face interviews (Martin et al., 1988, Table 5.2). In these interviews, the interviewer visits the disabled person at home and asks many structured questions in a structured way. It is in the nature of the interview process that the interviewer presents as expert and the disabled person as an isolated individual inexperienced in research, and thus unable to reformulate the

TABLE 2

ALTERNATIVE QUESTIONS

Can you tell me what is wrong with society?

What defects in the design of everyday equipment like jars, bottles and tins causes you difficulty in holding, gripping or turning them?

Are your difficulties in understanding people mainly due to their inabilities to communicate with you?

Do other people's reactions to any scar, blemish or deformity you may have, limit your daily activities?

Have you attended a special school because of your education authority's policy of sending people with your health problem or disability to such places?

Are community services so poor that you need to rely on relatives or someone else to provide you with the right level of personal assistance?

What inadequacies in your housing caused you to move here?

What are the environmental constraints which make it difficult for you to get about in your immediate neighborhood?

Are there any transport or financial problems which prevent you from going out as often or as far as you would like?

Do poorly designed buses make it difficult for someone with your health problem/disability to use them?

Do you have problems at work because of the physical environment or the attitudes of others?

questions in a more appropriate way. It is hardly surprising that, given the nature of the questions and their direction that, by the end of the interview, the disabled person has come to believe that his or her problems are caused by their own health/disability problems rather than by the organization of society. It is in this sense that the process of the interview is oppressive, reinforcing onto isolated, individual disabled people the idea that the problems they experience in everyday living are a direct result of their own personal inadequacies or functional limitations. . . .

IMPAIRMENT: A STRUCTURED ACCOUNT

Recently it has been estimated that there are some 500 million severely impaired people in the world today, approximately one in ten of the population (Shirley, 1983). These impairments are not randomly distributed throughout the world but are culturally produced.

> The societies men live in determine their chances of health, sickness and death. To the extent that they have the means to master their economic and social environments, they have the means to determine their life chances. (Susser and Watson, 1971, p. 45)

Hence in some countries impairments are likely to stem from infectious diseases, poverty, ignorance and the failure to ensure that existing medical treatments reach the population at risk (Shirley, 1983). In others, impairments resulting from infectious diseases are declining, only to be replaced by those stemming from the aging of the population, accidents at work, on the road or in the home, the very success of some medical technologies in ensuring the survival of some severely impaired children and adults and so on (Taylor, 1977). To put the matter simply, impairments such as blindness and deafness are likely to be more common in the Third World, whereas heart conditions, spina bifida, spinal injuries and so on, are likely to be more common in industrial societies.

Again, the distribution of these impairments is not a matter of chance, either across different societies or within a single society, for

> Social and economic forces cause disorder directly; they redistribute the proportion of people at high or low risk of being affected; and they create new pathways for the transmission of disorders of all kinds through travel, migration and the rapid diffusion of information and behaviour by the mass communication media. Finally, social forces affect the conceptualisation, recognition and visibility of disorders. A disorder in one place and at one time is not seen as such in another; these social perceptions and definitions influence both the provision of care, the demands of those being cared for, and the size of any count of health needs. (Susser and Watson, 1971, p. 35)

Social class is an important factor here both in terms of the causes of impairments or what Doyal (1979) calls degenerative diseases, and in terms of outcomes, what Le Grand (1978) refers to as long-standing illnesses.

Just as we know that poverty is not randomly distributed internationally or nationally (Cole and Miles, 1984; Townsend, 1979), neither is impairment, for in the Third World at least

> Not only does disability usually guarantee the poverty of the victim but, most importantly, poverty is itself a major cause of disability. (Doyal, 1983, p. 7)

There is a similar relation in the industrial countries. . . . Hence, if poverty is not randomly distributed and there is an intrinsic link between poverty and impairment, then neither is impairment randomly distributed.

Even a structured account of impairment cannot, however, be reduced to counting the numbers of impaired people in any one country, locality, class or social group, for

> Beliefs about sickness, the behaviours exhibited by sick persons, and the ways in which sick persons are responded to by family and practitioners are all aspects of social reality. They, like the health care system itself, are cultural constructions, shaped distinctly in different societies and in different social structural settings within those societies. (Kleinman, 1980, p. 38)

The discovery of an isolated tribe in West Africa where many of the population were born with only two toes illustrates this point, for this made no difference to those with only two toes or indeed the rest of the population (Barrett and McCann, 1979). Such differences would be regarded as pathological in our society, and the people so afflicted subjected to medical intervention.

In discussing impairment, it was not intended to provide a comprehensive discussion of the nature of impairment but to show that it occurs in a structured way. However

> such a view does not deny the significance of germs, genes and trauma, but rather points out that their effects are only ever apparent in a real social and historical context, whose nature is determined by a complex interaction of material and nonmaterial factors. (Abberley, 1987, p. 12)

This account of impairment challenges the notion underpinning personal tragedy theory, that impairments are events happening to unfortunate individuals. . . .

DISCUSSION QUESTIONS

1. Can you list some words that have changed meaning over time?
2. Why must minority groups continue to challenge definitions?

REFERENCES

Abberley, P. (1987). "The Concept of Oppression and the Development of a Social Theory of Disability," *Disability, Handicap and Society*, Vol. 2, no. 1, 5–19.

Barrett, D., and McCann, E. (1979). "Discovered: Two Toed Man," *Sunday Times Colour Supplement*, n.d.

Cole, S., and Miles, I. (1984). *Worlds Apart* (Brighton: Wheatsheaf).

Doyal, L. (1979). *The Political Economy of Health* (London: Pluto Press).

Doyal L. (1983). "The Crippling Effects of Underdevelopment" in Shirley, O. (ed.).

Harris, A. (1971). *Handicapped and Impaired in Great Britain* (London: HMSO).

Le Grand, J. (1978). "The Distribution of Public Expenditure: the Case of Health Care," *Economica*, Vol. 45.

PERSONAL ACCOUNT

Invisibly Disabled

I am a disabled individual. I am an invisibly disabled person, which makes me not disabled enough. My earliest memories are of being in pain. Unfortunately, when those around me could not see my pain and, when doctors could not diagnose my pain, it was decided for me that my pain did not exist. If someone grabbed my arm and it was not "that hard," I learned I was not supposed to say it hurt, because it didn't *really* hurt—at least not them. This is when I began to put my disabilities in the closet.

I was 17 years old when I went to a rheumatologist about my medical problems. I heard the words, "Well, I am sorry to tell you this, but your daughter has fibromyalgia." I smiled with relief to finally find out what it was that was causing my problems. "Great, so . . . how do we fix it?" I asked. The look on his face was serious and almost sad as he told me, "Well, there is no cure. What I mean is we can treat some of the symptoms." That is when it hit me; I would be in pain for the rest of my life. The medications I have had to take since I was 17 have caused their own medical conditions. When I was 19, my rheumatologist realized I had rheumatoid arthritis as well, and when I was 22, I began showing the signs of what I would later find out is myoclonic epilepsy. At the age of 27, I experienced a full seizure; my body was flipping around like a fish out of water on the floor. The only time I ever remember being so scared was waking up as a child not being able to feel my legs.

With all that I am because of, in spite of, and thanks to my disabilities, I continue to try to keep them to myself and people close to me. Making my disabilities visible to someone is a choice I do not make lightly, or very often. From experience, I know they will make certain judgments about me and/or view me differently. Most of all, I fear people not believing me. It takes most people a long time to believe I am in pain at all, and explaining that I have had a lifetime of masking my pain is always a pointless endeavor.

I find myself using phrases like "I'm all right" and "Don't worry about me" because worrying about me will do no good, and I am all right—I am not completely helpless on the ground and unable to move, not yet anyway. As long as others are seeing me as able, I feel and act more able. It makes it more of a reality to some extent. Every time I see someone who is physically disabled treated poorly because of their disability, I take it personally. I see my own future and become angry, because I know they would not treat me that way since they view me as able . . . for now.

Heather L. Shaw

Martin, J., Meltzer, H., and Elliot, D. (1988). *The Prevalence of Disability Amongst Adults* (London: HMSO).

Shirley, O. (ed.) (1983). *A Cry for Health: Poverty and Disability in the Third World* (Frome: Third World Group and ARHTAG).

Stone, D. (1985). *The Disabled State* (London: Macmillan).

Susser, M., and Watson, W. (2nd ed.) (1971). *Sociology in Medicine* (London: Oxford University Press).

Taylor, D. (1977). *Physical Impairment—Social Handicap* (London: Office of Health Economics).

Thomas, W. I. (1966). In Janowitz, M. (ed.), *Organization and Social Personality: Selected Papers* (Chicago: University of Chicago Press).

Townsend, P. (1979). *Poverty in the United Kingdom* (Harmondsworth: Penguin).

Wood, P. (1981). *International Classification of Impairments, Disabilities and Handicaps* (Geneva: World Health Organization).

READING 19

A World of Their Own

Liza Mundy

As her baby begins to emerge after a day of labor, Sharon Duchesneau has a question for the midwife who is attending the birth. Asking it is not the easiest thing, just now. Sharon is deaf, and communicates using American Sign Language, and the combination of intense pain and the position she

---

Liza Mundy is a feature writer for the *Washington Post*.

has sought to ease it—kneeling, resting her weight on her hands—makes signing somewhat hard. Even so, Sharon manages to sign something to Risa Shaw, a hearing friend who is present to interpret for the birth, which is taking place in a softly lit bedroom of Sharon's North Bethesda home.

"Sharon wants to know what color hair you see," Risa says to the midwife.

The midwife cannot tell because the baby is not—quite—visible. He bulges outward during contractions, then recedes when the contraction fades. But now comes another contraction and a scream from Sharon, and the midwife and her assistant call for Sharon to keep pushing but to keep it steady and controlled. They are accustomed to using their voices as a way of guiding women through this last excruciating phase; since Sharon can't hear them, all they can hope is that she doesn't close her eyes.

"Push through the pain!" shouts the midwife.

"Little bit!" shouts her assistant, as Risa frantically signs.

And suddenly the baby is out. One minute the baby wasn't here and now the baby is, hair brown, eyes blue, face gray with waxy vernix, body pulsing with life and vigor. A boy. "Is he okay?" signs Sharon, and the answer, to all appearances, is a resounding yes. There are the toes, the toenails, the fingers, the hands, the eyes, the eyelashes, the exquisite little-old-man's face, contorted in classic newborn outrage. The midwife lays the baby on Sharon and he bleats and hiccups and nuzzles her skin, the instinct to breast-feed strong.

"Did he cry?" signs Sharon, and the women say no, he cried remarkably little.

"His face looks smushed," Sharon signs, regarding him tenderly.

"It'll straighten out," says the midwife.

Presently the midwife takes the baby and performs the Apgar, the standard test of a newborn's condition, from which he emerges with an impressive score of nine out of a possible 10. "He's very calm," she notes as she weighs him (6 pounds 5 ounces), then lays him out to measure head and chest and length. She bicycles his legs to check the flexibility of his hips; examines his testicles to make sure they are descended; feels his vertebrae for gaps.

All in all, she pronounces the baby splendid. "Look how strong he is!" she says, pulling him gently up from the bed by his arms. Which means that it is, finally, possible to relax and savor his arrival. Everyone takes turns holding him: Sharon; her longtime partner, Candace McCullough, who is also deaf, and will be the boy's adoptive mother; their good friend Jan DeLap, also deaf; Risa Shaw and another hearing friend, Juniper Sussman. Candy and Sharon's five-year-old daughter, Jehanne, is brought in to admire him, but she is fast asleep and comically refuses to awaken, even when laid on the bed and prodded. Amid the oohing and aahing someone puts a cap on the baby; somebody else swaddles him in a blanket; somebody else brings a plate of turkey and stuffing for Sharon, who hasn't eaten on a day that's dedicated to feasting. Conceived by artificial insemination 38 weeks ago, this boy, Gauvin Hughes McCullough, has arrived two weeks ahead of schedule, on Thanksgiving Day.

"A turkey baby," signs Sharon, who is lying back against a bank of pillows, her dark thick hair spread against the light gray pillowcases.

"A turkey baster baby," jokes Candy, lying next to her.

"A perfect baby," says the midwife.

"A perfect baby," says the midwife's assistant.

But there is perfect and there is perfect. There is no way to know, yet, whether Gauvin Hughes McCullough is perfect in the specific way that Sharon and Candy would like him to be. Until he is old enough, two or three months from now, for a sophisticated audiology test, the women cannot be sure whether Gauvin is—as they hope—deaf.

Several months before his birth, Sharon and Candy—both stylish and independent women in their mid-thirties, both college graduates, both holders of graduate degrees from Gallaudet University, both professionals in the mental health field—sat in their kitchen trying to envision life if their son turned out not to be deaf. It was something they had a hard time getting their minds around. When they were looking for a donor to inseminate Sharon, one thing they knew was that they wanted a deaf donor. So they contacted a local sperm bank and asked whether the bank would provide one. The sperm bank said no; congenital deafness is precisely the sort of condition that, in the world of commercial reproductive technology, gets a would-be donor eliminated.

So Sharon and Candy asked a deaf friend to be the donor, and he agreed.

Though they have gone to all this trouble, Candy and Sharon take issue with the suggestion that they are "trying" to have a deaf baby. To put it this way, they worry, implies that they will not love their son if he can hear. And, they insist, they will. As Sharon puts it: "A hearing baby would be a blessing. A deaf baby would be a special blessing."

As Candy puts it: "I would say that we wanted to increase our chances of having a baby who is deaf."

It may seem a shocking undertaking: two parents trying to screen in a quality, deafness, at a time when many parents are using genetic testing to screen out as many disorders as science will permit. Down's syndrome, cystic fibrosis, early-onset Alzheimer's—every day, it seems, there's news of yet another disorder that can be detected before birth and eliminated by abortion, manipulation of the embryo or, in the case of in vitro fertilization, destruction of an embryo. Though most deafness cannot be identified or treated in this way, it seems safe to say that when or if it can, many parents would seek to eliminate a disability that affects one out of 1,000 Americans.

As for actively trying to build a deaf baby. "I think all of us recognize that deaf children can have perfectly wonderful lives," says R. Alta Charo, a professor of law and bioethics at the University of Wisconsin. "The question is whether the parents have violated the sacred duty of parenthood, which is to maximize to some reasonable degree the advantages available to their children. I'm loath to say it, but I think it's a shame to set limits on a child's potential."

In the deaf community, however, the arrival of a deaf baby has never evoked the feelings that it does among the hearing. To be sure, there are many deaf parents who feel their children will have an easier life if they are born hearing. "I know that my parents were disappointed that I was deaf, along with my brother, and I know I felt, just for a fleeting second, bad that my children were deaf," says Nancy Rarus, a staff member at the National Association of the Deaf. Emphasizing that she is speaking personally and not on behalf of the association, she adds, "I'm a social animal, and it's very difficult for me to talk to my neighbors. I wish I could walk up to somebody and ask for information. I've had a lot of arguments in the deaf community about that. People talk about 'The sky's the limit,' but being deaf prevents you from getting there. You don't have as many choices."

"I can't understand," she says, "why anybody would want to bring a disabled child into the world."

Then again, Rarus points out, "there are many, many deaf people who specifically want deaf kids." This is true particularly now, particularly in Washington, home to Gallaudet, the world's only liberal arts university for the deaf, and the lively deaf intelligentsia it has nurtured. Since the 1980s, many members of the deaf community have been galvanized by the idea that deafness is not a medical disability, but a cultural identity. They call themselves Deaf, with a capital D, a community whose defining and unifying quality is American Sign Language (ASL), a fluent, sophisticated language that enables deaf people to communicate fully, essentially liberating them—when they are among signers—from one of the most disabling aspects of being deaf. Sharon and Candy share the fundamental view of this Deaf camp; they see deafness as an identity, not a medical affliction that needs to be fixed. Their effort—to have a baby who belongs to what they see as their minority group—is a natural outcome of the pride and self-acceptance the Deaf movement has brought to so many. It also would seem to put them at odds with the direction of reproductive technology in general, striving as it does for a more perfect normalcy.

But the interesting thing is—if one accepts their worldview, that a deaf baby could be desirable to some parents—Sharon and Candy are squarely part of a broader trend in artificial reproduction. Because, at the same time that many would-be parents are screening out qualities they don't want, many are also selecting for qualities they do want. And in many cases, the aim is to produce not so much a superior baby as a specific baby. A white baby. A black baby. A boy. A girl. Or a baby that's been even more minutely imagined. Would-be parents can go on many fertility clinic Web sites and type in preferences for a sperm donor's weight, height, eye color, race, ancestry, complexion, hair color, even hair texture.

"In most cases," says Sean Tipton, spokesman for the American Society of Reproductive Medicine, "what the couples are interested in is someone who physically looks like them." In this sense Candy and Sharon are like many parents, hoping for a child who will be in their own image.

And yet, while deafness may be a culture, in this country it is also an official disability, recognized under the Americans with Disabilities Act. What about the obligation of parents to see that their child has a better life than they did?

Then again, what does a better life mean? Does it mean choosing a hearing donor so your baby, unlike you, might grow up hearing?

Does it mean giving birth to a deaf child, and raising it in a better environment than the one you experienced?

What if you believe you can be a better parent to a deaf child than to a hearing one?

"It would be nice to have a deaf child who is the same as us. I think that would be a wonderful experience. You know, if we can have that chance, why not take it?"

This is Sharon, seven months pregnant, dressed in black pants and a stretchy black shirt, sitting at their kitchen table on a sunny fall afternoon, Candy beside her. Jehanne, their daughter, who is also deaf, and was conceived with the same donor they've used this time, is at school. The family has been doing a lot of nesting in anticipation of the baby's arrival. The kitchen has been renovated, the backyard landscaped. Soon the women plan to rig a system in which the lights in the house will blink one rhythm if the TTY—the telephonic device that deaf people type into—is ringing; another rhythm when the front doorbell rings; another for the side door. They already have a light in the bedroom that will go on when the baby cries.

In one way, it's hard for Sharon and Candy to articulate why they want to increase their chances of having a deaf child. Because they don't view deafness as a disability, they don't see themselves as bringing a disabled child into the world. Rather, they see themselves as bringing a different sort of normal child into the world. Why not bring a deaf child into the world? What, exactly, is the problem? In their minds, they are no different from parents who try to have a girl. After all, girls can be discriminated against. Same with deaf people. Sharon and Candy have faced obstacles, but they've survived. More than that, they've prevailed to become productive, self-supporting professionals. "Some people look at it like, 'Oh my gosh, you shouldn't have a child who has a disability,'" signs Candy. "But, you know, black people have harder lives. Why shouldn't parents be able to go ahead and pick a black donor if that's what they want? They should have that option. They can feel related to that culture, bonded with that culture."

The words "bond" and "culture" say a lot; in effect, Sharon and Candy are a little like immigrant parents who, with a huge and dominant and somewhat alien culture just outside their door, want to ensure that their children will share their heritage, their culture, their life experience. If they are deaf and have a hearing child, that child will move in a world where the women cannot fully follow. For this reason they believe they can be better parents to a deaf child, if being a better parent means being better able to talk to your child, understand your child's emotions, guide your child's development, pay attention to your child's friendships. "If we have a hearing child and he visits a hearing friend, we'll be like, 'Who is the family?'" says Candy. "In the deaf community, if you don't know a family, you ask around. You get references. But with hearing families, we would have no idea."

They understand that hearing people may find this hard to accept. It would be odd, they agree, if a hearing parent preferred to have a deaf child. And if they themselves—valuing sight—were to have a blind child, well then, Candy acknowledges, they would probably try to have it fixed, if they could, like hearing parents who attempt to restore their child's hearing with cochlear implants. "I want to be the same as my child," says Candy. "I want the baby to enjoy what we enjoy."

Which is not to say that they aren't open to a hearing child. A hearing child would make life rich and interesting. It's just hard, before the fact, to know what it would be like. "He'd be the only hearing member of the family," Sharon points out, laughing. "Other than the cats." . . .

Candy usually signs with both hands, using facial expressions as well as signs. This is all part of ASL, a physical language that encompasses the whole body, from fingers to arms to eyebrows, and is noisy, too: There is lots of clapping and slapping in ASL, and in a really great conversation, it's always possible to knock your own eyeglasses off.

When she drives, though, Candy also signs one-handed, keeping the other hand on the wheel. Chatting with Sharon, she maneuvers her Volvo through Bethesda traffic and onto I-270, making her way north toward Frederick, home to the Maryland School for the Deaf. State residential schools have played a huge role in the development of America's deaf community. Historically, deaf children often left their homes as young as five and grew up in dorms with other deaf kids. This sometimes isolated them from their families but helped to create an intense sense of fellowship among the deaf population, a group that, though geographically spread out, is essentially a tribe, a small town, a family itself.

Now that people are more mobile, families with deaf children often relocate near a residential school for the deaf, where the young children are more likely to be day students. Jehanne is one; today she's waiting for them in a low corridor inside the elementary school building at MSD, petite, elfin, dimpled, with tousled brown hair and light brown, almost amber eyes. Essentially, the baby Sharon is carrying represents a second effort that they're making because the first was so successful. (Candy tried to have their second child, but a year of efforts didn't take.) At her own infant audiology test, Jehanne was diagnosed as profoundly deaf. In their baby book, under the section marked "first hearing test," Candy wrote, happily, "Oct. 11, 1996—no response at 95 decibels—DEAF!"

This afternoon, Jehanne greets her mothers and begins immediately to sign. She has been signed to since birth and, unlike her mothers, has been educated from the start in sign. At five she is beginning to read English quite well; when they're riding in the car, she'll notice funny shop names, like Food Lion and For Eyes. But she is also fluent in ASL, more fluent even than Sharon.

The women have arrived to visit Jehanne's kindergarten classroom, which in most ways is similar to that of any other Maryland public school; the kids are using flashcards to learn about opposites, conducting experiments to explore concepts like wet and dry, light and heavy. The classes are small, and teachers are mostly deaf, which is something new; years ago, even at MSD, deaf people weren't permitted to teach the young kids, because it was believed that sign would interfere with their learning to read. Now that's all changed. Sign is used to teach them reading. They learn science in sign; they sign while doing puzzles, or gluing and pasting, or coloring, or working in the computer lab.

There is a speech therapy class, but it's optional, and a far cry from the ones that Sharon and Candy remember, where laborious hours were spent blowing on feathers to see the difference between a "b" and a "p." In general, Sharon and Candy have tried not to make what they see as the mistakes their own parents did. Sharon, for example, resents having been made to wear hearing aids and denied the opportunity to learn sign, while Candy—who really wanted to try a hearing aid when she was little—was told by her father that she couldn't because it would be expensive and pointless, anyway. Trying to chart a middle course, they let Jehanne decide for herself whether she wanted to try a hearing aid; she did, one summer when attending camp at Gallaudet. It was hot pink. She wore it about a week. . . .

"Do you think this baby's hearing?" Candy asks Sharon afterward, when they are having lunch in downtown Frederick.

"I don't know," says Sharon. "I can say that I hope the baby's deaf, but to say I feel it's deaf, no."

They are talking about an old saying in the deaf community: If the mother walks into a place with loud music, and the baby moves, the baby is hearing. "If you base it on that, I do think it's deaf," says Sharon.

"I just say to myself that the baby's deaf," Candy says. "I talk as if the baby's deaf. If the baby's hearing, I'll be shocked."

"You better be prepared," Sharon tells her. "With Jehanne, I prepared myself. It could happen." Thinking about it, she speculates: "A hearing child would force us to get out and find out what's out there for hearing children. Maybe that would be nice."

Candy looks at her, amazed.

"It's not that it's my preference," says Sharon. "But I'm trying to think of something positive." . . .

In trying to know how to think about Sharon and Candy's endeavor, there are any number of opinions a person might have. Any number of abstract ideas a person might work through in, say, an ethics course. Are the women being selfish? Are they inflicting too much hardship on the child? How does one think of them compared with, say, a mother who has multiple embryos implanted in the course of fertility treatments, knowing that this raises the likelihood of multiple births and, with it, birth defects in some or all of the babies? Morally, how much difficulty can a parent impose on a child in order to satisfy the desire to have a child, or to have a certain kind of child?

A person can think about this, and think about it, but eventually will run up against the living, breathing fact of the child herself. How much difficulty have Sharon and Candy imposed on Jehanne? They haven't deafened her. They've given life to her. They've enabled her to exist. If they had used

a hearing donor, they would have had a different child. That child would exist, but this one wouldn't. Jehanne can only exist as what she is: Jehanne, bright, funny, loving, loved, deaf.

And now what about Gauvin, who, at three months, already resembles his sister? He has the same elfin face shape, the same deep dimples when he smiles. On his head is a light fuzz of hair; bulkier now, alert and cheery, he's wearing gray overalls and groovy red leather sneakers. The question that will be answered this February afternoon, at Children's National Medical Center, is whether Gauvin, like Jehanne, is deaf. Whether the coin has landed on the same side twice. By now, Gauvin has had an initial hearing screening, which he failed. They considered this good news, but not conclusive. From there he was referred to this one, which is more sophisticated. The preliminaries take awhile. Sharon lays Gauvin in a crib and a technician applies conductive paste at points around his head, then attaches electrodes to the paste. He needs to be asleep for the test, in which microphones will be placed in his ears and a clicking noise sent through the wires. Through the electrodes, a machine will monitor the brain response. If the waves are flat, there is no hearing. He stirs and cries, so Sharon breast-feeds him, wires dangling from his head, until he falls asleep. The technician slips the microphone in his ear, turns on the clicking noise—up and up, louder and louder—and the two women look at the computer screen. Even at 95 decibels, a sound so loud that for hearing people it's literally painful, the line for the left ear is flat. But there is a marked difference in the right. For softer sounds the line is flat, but at 75 decibels there is a distinct wave. The technician goes to fetch the doctor, and the mothers contemplate their sleeping son, who, it appears, might be neither deaf nor hearing but somewhere in between.

The doctor, Ira Weiss, bustles in; he is a white-haired, stocky man, jovial and accustomed to all sorts of parents, hearing and deaf, happy and sobbing.

The technician points to the wave and suggests that perhaps it represents some noise that Gauvin himself was making. "No," says the doctor, "I think it's not just noise." Sharon looks up at Candy and lets out a little breath. The doctor disappears to get a printout of the results, then returns, reading it. Gauvin, he says, "has a profound hearing loss in his left ear and at least a severe hearing loss in his right ear.

"It does appear," he adds, "that his right ear has some residual hearing. There might be some usable hearing at this time. Given the mother's history, it will probably get worse over time. If you want to take advantage of it, you should take advantage of it now. Right now it's an ear that could be aided, to give him a head start on spoken English. Obviously, he's going to be a fluent signer."

At this stage, Weiss says later, a hearing parent would probably try a hearing aid, in the hope that with it, that right ear could hear something. Anything. A word, here and there. A loud vowel. Maybe just enough residual sound to help him lip-read. Maybe just enough to tell him when to turn his head to watch someone's lips. Hearing parents would do anything—anything—to nudge a child into the hearing world. Anything—anything—to make that child like them. For a similar reason, Sharon and Candy make the opposite choice. If he wants a hearing aid later, they'll let him have a hearing aid later. They won't put one on him now. After all, they point out, Sharon's hearing loss as a child occurred at below 40 decibels, which meant that under certain conditions she could make out voices, unaided. Gauvin's, already, is far more severe than hers. Bundling Gauvin up against the cold, they make their way down the corridor, and into the car, and home, where they will tell Jehanne, and Jan, and friends, and family, a sizable group, really, that wants to know. He is not as profoundly deaf as Jehanne, but he is quite deaf. Deaf enough.

DISCUSSION QUESTIONS

1. What reactions do you have to Sharon and Candy's wish for a deaf child?
2. Would you have wanted them to wish for a child who was not hearing impaired?

READING 20

Ethnicity, Ethics, and the Deaf-World

Harlan Lane

It has become widely known that there is a Deaf-World in the United States, as in other nations, citizens whose primary language is American Sign Language (ASL) and who identify as members of that minority culture. The size of the population is not known, but estimates generally range from half a million to a million members (Schein, 1989). The English terms *deaf* and *hearing impaired* are commonly used to designate a much larger and more heterogeneous group than the members of the Deaf-World. Most of the 20 million Americans (Binnie, 1994) who are in this larger group had conventional schooling and became deaf after acculturation to hearing society; they communicate primarily in English or one of the spoken minority languages; they generally do not have Deaf spouses; they do not identify themselves as members of the Deaf-World or use its language, participate in its organizations, profess its values, or behave in accord with its mores; rather, they consider themselves hearing people with a disability. Something similar is true of most nations: There is a Deaf-World, a relatively small group of visual people (Bahan, 2004; Padden & Humphries, 1988) who use a natural visual-gestural language and who are often confused with the larger group who view themselves as hearing impaired and use a spoken language in its spoken or written form. To acknowledge this contrast, often signaled in the scholarly literature by capital-D *Deaf* versus small-d *deaf*, is not to deny that there is a gray area between the two; for example, some hard-of-hearing people are active in the American Deaf-World; others are not. Oral deaf adults and late-deafened adults

Harlan Lane is a professor of psychology at Northeastern University.

usually consider that they have a hearing impairment and do not self-identify as members of the Deaf-World.

This article is concerned exclusively with the smaller group, the Deaf-World. It aims to show that the Deaf-World qualifies as an ethnic group, and that an unsuitable construction of the Deaf-World as a disability group has led to programs of the majority that aim to discourage Deaf children from participating in the Deaf-World (programs such as oral education and cochlear implant surgery) and that aim to reduce the number of Deaf births, programs that are unethical from an ethnic group perspective. In other words, this article makes the case that our ethical standards for the majority's treatment of Deaf people depend, not surprisingly, on whether our representation of the Deaf-World is that of a disability group on the one hand or an ethnic group on the other.

THE DEAF-WORLD IS AN ETHNIC GROUP

Internal Properties

Table 1 shows the criteria that have been advanced by social scientists for characterizing a social group as an ethnic group.

Collective Name

The members of this group have a collective name in their manual-visual language by which they refer to themselves. We refer to them by that name in adopting the English gloss of their compound sign: the *Deaf-World.*

TABLE 1

PROPERTIES OF ETHNIC GROUPS: DISTINCT

Collective name	Customs
Feeling of community	Social structure
Norms for behavior	Language
Values	Art forms
Knowledge	History
Kinship	

Feeling of Community

Self-recognition, and recognition by others, is a central feature of ethnicity (Barth, 1969; A. D. Smith, 1986). Americans in the Deaf-World do indeed feel a strong identification with that world and show great loyalty to it. This is not surprising: The Deaf-World offers many Deaf Americans what they could not find at home: easy communication, a positive identity a surrogate family. The Deaf-World has the highest rate of endogamous marriages of any ethnic group—an estimated 90% (Schein, 1989).

Norms for Behavior

In Deaf culture, there are norms for relating to the Deaf-World: for decision making, consensus is the rule, not individual initiative; for managing information; for constructing discourse; for gaining status; for managing indebtedness; and many more such rules. Cultural rules are not honored all the time by everyone any more than are linguistic rules. Such rules tell what you must know as a member of a particular linguistic and cultural group; what one actually does or says depends on a host of intervening factors, including other rules that have priority.

Distinct Values

The underlying values of an ethnic group can often be inferred from cultural norms. A value that appears to be fundamental in the Deaf-World is allegiance to the culture, which is expressed in prizing one's relation to the Deaf-World, in endogamous marriage, in gaining status by enhancing the group and acknowledging its contributions, in the giving of culturally related names, in consensual decision making, in defining oneself in relation to the culture, in distributed indebtedness, in the priority given to evidence that arises from experience as a member of the culture, in treasuring the language of the Deaf-World, and in promoting among Deaf people dissemination of culturally salient information (cf., Lane, 2004a; Mindess, 1999; T. Smith, 1997).

Knowledge

Deaf people have culture-specific knowledge, such as who their leaders are (and their characteristics); the concerns of rank-and-file members of the Deaf-World; important events in Deaf history; how to manage trying situations with hearing people. Knowing when and with whom to use ASL and when to use English- marked varieties of sign language is an important part of being recognized as Deaf (Johnson & Erting, 1989).

Customs

The Deaf-World has its own ways of doing introductions and departures, of taking turns in a conversation, of speaking frankly and of speaking politely; it has its own taboos.

Social Structure

There are numerous organizations in the American Deaf-World: athletic, social, political, literary, religious, fraternal, and many more (Lane, Hoffmeister, & Bahan, 1996). As with many ethnic minorities, there are charismatic leaders who are felt to embody the unique characteristics of the whole ethnic group (A. D. Smith, 1986).

Language

"The mother tongue is an aspect of the soul of a people. It is their achievement par excellence. Language is the surest way for individuals to safeguard or recover the authenticity they inherited from their ancestors as well as to hand it on to generations yet unborn" (Fishman, 1989, p. 276). Competence in ASL is a hallmark of Deaf ethnicity in the United States and some other parts of North America. A language not based on sound is the primary element that sharply demarcates the Deaf-World from the engulfing hearing society.

The Arts

First, the language arts: ASL narratives, storytelling, oratory, humor, tall tales, word play, pantomime, and poetry. Theatre arts and the visual arts also address Deaf culture and experience.

History

Ethnic groups construct rootedness, with forms of expression that include history, territory and genealogy. The Deaf-World has a rich history recounted in stories, books, films, and the like. Members of the Deaf-World have a particular interest in their history for "[T]he past is a resource in the collective quest for meaning [and ethnic identity]" (Nagel, 1994, p. 163). A sense of common history unites successive generations (Fishman, 1982, 1989; A. D. Smith, 1986).

Kinship

Many ethnic groups have a belief in the land of their ancestors. However, "territory is relevant not because it is actually possessed but because of an alleged and felt connection. The land of dreams is far more significant than any actual terrain" (A. D. Smith, 1986, p. 34). Land that the Deaf-World in the United States has traditionally felt an attachment to includes the residential schools; Deaf travel is often planned around visits to some of those schools. There is a Deaf utopian vision of "a land of our own" expressed in folk tales, novels, journalism, theater, and political discussions (Bullard, 1986; Lane, 1984; Levesque, 1994; Van Cleve & Crouch, 1989; Winzer, 1986). Deaf-Worlds are to be found around the globe, and when Deaf members from two different cultures meet, they feel a strong bond although they share no common territory and are limited in their ability to communicate with one another. In this, they are like Diaspora groups, such as the Jews. And, like the Diaspora ethnic minorities worldwide, prejudice and discrimination in the host society encourage them to cultivate their ethnicity to maintain their dignity despite social marginalization.

Some scholars maintain that the core of ethnicity lies in the cultural properties we have examined, so kinship is not necessary for the Deaf-World or any other group to qualify as an ethnic group

(Barth, 1969; Petersen, 1980; Schneider, 1972; Sollors, 2001). Others say kinship should be taken in its social meaning as "those to whom we owe primary solidarity" (Schneider, 1969). "*Ethnie* embody the sense of being a large unique family; the members feel knit to one another and so committed to the cultural heritage, which is the family's inheritance" (A. D. Smith, 1986, p. 49). What is involved is a sense of tribal belonging, not necessarily genetic and blood ties. Certainly, there is a strong sense of solidarity in the Deaf-World; the metaphor of family goes far in characterizing many Deaf-World norms and practices.

What kinship is really about, other scholars contend, is a link to the past; it is about "intergenerational continuity" (Fishman, 1989). The Deaf-World does pass its norms, knowledge, language, and values from one generation to the next: first through socialization of the child by Deaf adults (parent or other) and second through peer socialization. Here, however, there is a significant difference from other ethnic groups: For many Deaf children, socialization into Deaf culture starts late, usually when the Deaf child meets other Deaf children in school (Johnson & Erting, 1989). Members of the Deaf-World have a great handicap and a great advantage when it comes to intergenerational continuity. The handicap is that their hearing parents usually have a different ethnocultural identity that, lacking a shared language, they cannot pass on to their children. Moreover, they commonly do not advocate in the schools, community, courts, and so on for their Deaf child's primary language. Minority languages without parental and community support are normally endangered. The great advantage of the Deaf-World lies in the fact that there will always be intergenerational continuity for sign language because there will always be visual people who take possession of that language in preference to any other and with it the wisdom and values of generations of Deaf people before them. (Although one can imagine an intervention in the future that would provide high-fidelity hearing to Deaf children and thus threaten intergenerational continuity, it seems likely that most countries will not be able to afford it, and that most Deaf parents will continue to refuse such interventions with their Deaf children.)

When we think of kinship, yet other scholars maintain, what is at stake is common ancestors, what Joshua Fishman (1977) termed paternity—real or putative biological connections across generations. Johnson and Erting (1989) suggested that what is primary in this biological criterion for kinship is not genealogy but biological resemblance across generations. In that case, members of the Deaf-World are kin because Deaf people resemble one another biologically in their reliance on vision for language and for much else (Johnson & Erting, 1989). To some extent, like the members of many other ethnic groups, Deaf people come by their biological resemblance through heredity more often than not. The estimate commonly cited is 50% of all people born deaf with little or no usable hearing are so for hereditary reasons (Reardon et al., 1992). However, another 20% are Deaf for reasons unknown; many of those may be hereditarily Deaf people not aware of the role of their ancestry (S. Smith, 1995).

To summarize in the words of social scientist Arthur Smith

> By involving a collective name, by the use of symbolic images of community, by the generation of stereotypes of the community and its foes, by the ritual performance and rehearsal of ceremonies, by the communal recitation of past deeds and ancient hero's exploits, men and women partake of a collectivity and its historic fate which transcend their individual existences. (A. D. Smith, 1986, p. 46)

Many scholars in the field of ethnicity believe that these "internal" properties of the ethnic group just reviewed must also be accompanied by an "external" property a boundary separating the minority from other ethnicities, in particular, the majority ethnicity (Barth, 1969). Does the Deaf-World in the United States occupy its own ecological niche? Does it look to itself for the satisfaction of certain needs, while looking to the larger society for the satisfaction of other needs—and conversely?

Ethnic Boundaries

Table 2 shows, at the left, activities that are primarily conducted by Deaf people for Deaf people in the Deaf-World in the United States; at the right, activities in the hearing world that impact Deaf people; and in the middle, areas of overlap. The more Deaf people celebrate their language and culture, the more they affirm their distinct identity, the more they reinforce the boundary delineating them from the hearing world. Language comes first for it always plays a powerful role in maintaining ethnic boundaries, but especially so in the case of Deaf people because bearing people are rarely fluent in visual language and members of the Deaf-World are rarely fluent in spoken language. Next, Deaf-World social activities are organized and conducted by Deaf people with little or no hearing involvement. On the other hand, law enforcement is a hearing world activity. Religious services overlap the Deaf and hearing worlds; there are missions to the Deaf, Deaf pastors, and signed services, but the operation of the house of worship is generally in hearing hands. All in all, the Deaf-World keeps to itself for many of its activities; it collaborates in a few with the hearing world; and it leaves the really broad responsibilities such as law enforcement to the larger society; in this, it is like other ethnic groups, such as Hispanic Americans.

This brief survey is intended to show that the Deaf-World in the United States today meets the

TABLE 2

DEAF-WORLD—HEARING WORLD BOUNDARIES

Deaf-World	Overlap	Hearing world
Sign language	Interpreter services	Spoken language
Social activities	Religious services	Law enforcement
Sign language teaching	Consumer goods and services	Employment (not Deaf related)
Political activities	Deaf history	Military services
Athletics	Deaf education	Garbage collection
Arts and leisure	Deaf service agencies	Medical care
Finding employment		Banking
Publishing		Transportation

criteria put forth for ethnic groups (also see Erting, 1978, 1982; Johnson & Erting, 1979, 1982, 1984, 1989; Markowicz & Woodward, 1978; Padden & Markowicz, 1976). Classifying the Deaf-World as an *ethnic group* should encourage those who are concerned with Deaf people to do appropriate things: learn their language, defend their heritage against more powerful groups, study their ethnic history; and so on. In this light, the Deaf-World should enjoy the rights and protections accorded other ethnic groups under international law and treaties, such as the United Nations Declaration of the Rights of Persons Belonging to National or Ethnic, Religious and Linguistic Minorities (United Nations, 2003a).

REASONS ADVANCED TO VIEW THE DEAF-WORLD AS A DISABILITY GROUP

Is it also appropriate to label the Deaf-World a disability group? We do not ask whether Deaf people in fact have a disability because it is not a matter of fact: Disability, like ethnicity, is a social construct, not a fact of life, although it is a property of such constructs that they appear misleadingly to be a fact of life. For example, the social problem of alcoholism evidently consists of this: Many Americans suffer from alcoholism; there are specially trained people to help them (alcoholism counselors, psychologists, psychiatrists, and others) and special facilities to care for them, such as detox centers. However, this understanding of alcoholism dates from the latter half of the 20th century. In the first half, the temperance movement branded excessive drinking as voluntary, and the movement promoted not treatment but prohibition. With the shift in the construction of alcoholism from illegal (and immoral) behavior to illness, the need was for medical research and treatment, halfway houses, hospital wards, outpatient clinics, and specialized hospitals (Gusfield, 1982).

Homosexuality went from moral flaw, to crime, to treatable disability, to a minority group seeking civil rights (Conrad & Schneider, 1980). Shortness came to be seen as a disability of childhood, not a normal variation, when growth enzyme was discovered, not before (Downie et al., 1996; Werth, 1991). Mild mental retardation came to be seen as a disability, not merely normal human variation in intellect, with the arrival of the IQ test (Gelb, 1987). In societies in which sign language use is mostly restricted to Deaf people, hearing people commonly see being Deaf as a serious problem requiring professional intervention; but in societies in which sign language use is widespread because of a substantial Deaf population—on Martha's Vineyard and Bali, for example—being Deaf is simply seen as a trait, not a disability (Lane, Pillard, & French, 2000).

The case of the forest dwellers of Central Africa is instructive. Their short stature, some 4.5 feet on average, allows them modest caloric requirements, easy and rapid passage through dense jungle cover in search of game, and construction of small huts rapidly disassembled and reassembled for self-defense and hunting. The Bantu villagers, formerly herdsmen, now farmers, have contempt for the pygmies because of their puny size, and they in turn have contempt for the villagers who are "clumsy as elephants" in the forest, much too tall to move swiftly and silently; they "do not know how to walk" (Turnbull, 1962, p. 79). Each group considers the other handicapped by their physical size. Each fails to appreciate how physical makeup, culture, and environment are intertwined.

Despite all this evidence that disability is constructed in a given society at a given time, many writers addressing ethics and Deaf people, apparently unaware of disability studies and medical anthropology, simply adopt the naïve materialist view when it comes to disability: "Almost by definition deaf persons . . . have a disability" (Gonsoulin, 2001, p. 554). "I maintain that the inability to hear is a deficit, a disability, a lack of perfect health" (D. S. Davis, 1997, p. 254). And, their ethical conclusions turn on this postulate. We understand, however, that disability is a label that can be applied with more or with less aptness to a particular group. That application is not a matter of chance, even less is it foreordained; it is powerfully influenced by the "technologies of normalization" (Foucault, 1980, p. 21) that exist to mitigate what is seen as a disability for they have a great stake in retaining that conception of the group. In the next section, arguments that have been made for including members of the Deaf-World among disability groups are examined critically.

Oppression from Deaf Bodies

Advocates of classifying Deaf people with disability groups claim that Deaf people have this in common with people who avowedly have disabilities: They are discriminated against because general social customs do not accommodate their bodies. Deaf people are indeed discriminated against in school, on the job, and in gaining access, but it is much more their language that is the target of discrimination than their bodies: "The major impact of deafness is on communication" (Baynton, 2000, p. 391). Thus, the Deaf are more like oppressed language minorities than oppressed disability groups. Like many Hispanic Americans, for example, many Deaf people have difficulty learning in school because the teacher cannot communicate with them fluently; they have difficulty getting a job when the job requires good English; they miss out on important information because it has not been provided in their language.

Still, say the Deaf-are-disabled advocates, why not acknowledge the many things that physically different people share by using a common label (Baynton, 2002). After all, some disability activists make a claim for disability culture, just as there is a Deaf culture; many oppose mainstreaming, as do many Deaf activists. Both groups pay the price of social stigma, and stigmatized groups—among them disabled people, blacks, women, gays, and the Deaf—are often claimed to be biologically inferior. Moreover, both the Deaf-World and disability groups struggle with the troubled-persons industries for control of their destiny (Gusfield, 1984). Both endeavor to promote their construction of their identity in competition with the efforts of professionals to promote *their* constructions

(Finkelstein, 1981). Finally, because there are great differences among disability groups, accommodating one more with its unique issues need not be a problem.

At one level, oppressed minorities do indeed share important traits and a common struggle for the defense and valuing of their diversity. At that level, disabled people, blacks, women, gays, the Deaf, and other language minorities can inform and reinforce one another's efforts. They can promote an understanding of the value of diversity, learn successful strategies from one another, and use their combined numbers to urge government in the right directions. At another level, however, many practical truths apply only to individual minorities, with their own makeup, demographics, histories, and cultures. To minimize that diversity with the same global representation would undermine the most cherished goal of each group: to be respected and valued for its difference. After all, beyond being stigmatized because of their physical difference, what, practically speaking, do the Deaf have in common with gays, women, blacks, Little People, and people with mobility impairment, for example? Deaf people have been subject to the globalizing disability label, and it has widely led to the wrong questions and the wrong answers, which are considered later in this article under reasons to reject it. This is the pragmatic answer to disability scholar Lennard Davis's proposal that Deaf people abandon the category of ethnicity in favor of a coalition with gays, hearing children with Deaf parents, and people with disabilities (L. Davis, 2002): Their agendas are utterly different.

The Shared Struggle for Rights

Another argument advanced for Deaf people to embrace the disability label is that it might assist them in gaining more of their rights (Baynton, 2002). For example, interpreters are not normally provided in the classroom for members of ethnic groups; Deaf people have them in many places under a disability umbrella. However, much that is important to Deaf people has come through

an understanding of the Deaf-World as an ethnic group. Let us cite the burgeoning of ASL in high schools and colleges in the United States and the increasing acceptance of ASL classes in fulfillment of the foreign language and culture requirement; the mushrooming of scholarship in the last 40 years concerning Deaf ethnicity—history, arts, social structure, culture, and language; the flourishing of the interpreting profession; the development of the discipline of Deaf studies; bilingual bicultural Deaf education; the growing community of nations that formally recognize their national sign language. All these gains reflect an understanding of the Deaf as an ethnic group.

Although the disability label seems inappropriate for the Deaf-World, its members have not aggressively promoted governmental understanding of its ethnicity and of the poor fit of the disability label. As a result, the majority's accommodation of the Deaf has come under a disability label, and Deaf people must in effect subscribe to that label to gain their rights in access to information, in education, and in other areas. This is the Deaf dilemma: retain some important rights as members of their society at the expense of being mischaracterized by that society and government or surrender some of those rights in the hope of gradually undermining that misconstruction. This dilemma is reminiscent of similarly oppressive choices offered to other minority groups: for gays to embrace the disability label and be spared classification as a criminal and entry into the army; for women to conform to the masculine idea of the feminine ideal and gain men's support and approval.

In principle, it should be possible for members of the Deaf-World in the United States to base their demand for language access on existing legislation and court rulings protecting language minorities. For example, in the field of education, the U.S. Congress has passed two types of statutes to remedy the disadvantage experienced by language-minority students who cannot communicate freely in the classroom by using their primary language: the Bilingual Education Act (P.L. 89–10, Title VII, 1965), which provides funding for a variety of programs promoting the use of minority languages in the schools, and civil rights statutes (P.L. 88–352, Title VI, 1964; P.L. 93–380, 1974), which impose an affirmative duty on the schools to give children who speak a minority language an equal educational opportunity by lowering the English language barriers. The provision of language rights in Deaf education should bring with it appropriate school curricula and materials, teachers who are ethnic models, interpreters, real television access through sign language, and video-telephone communication. But, in practice that would require that the public come to understand the Deaf-World as the Deaf-World understands itself. Until this happens, the Deaf-World can expect scant support from other ethnic groups.

Among the obstacles to a change from the disability to the ethnic construction of Deaf people are the numerous professional organizations predicated on the disability construction and who wish to own the problem of Deaf children. "To 'own' a social problem is to possess the authority to name that social condition a problem and to suggest what might be done about it" (Gusfield, 1989, p. 433). Consider just two of the many organizations that have Deaf children as clients. The American Academy of Otolaryngology, with over 10,000 members, has registered two paid lobbyists in Washington; the American Speech-Language-Hearing Association, with 115,925 members, has three (http://sopr.senate.gov). Members of these organizations collaborate with government officials in approving treatments, in drawing up legislation, and in evaluating proposed research and training activities. The Deaf-World has none of these advantages in seeking to promote an ethnic understanding of being Deaf.

FOUR REASONS TO REJECT THE DISABILITY LABEL

It "Doesn't Compute"

The overwhelming reason to reject the view of culturally Deaf people as members of a disability group concerns how Deaf people see themselves.

People who have grown up Deaf and have become integrated into Deaf culture are naturally aware of their biological difference, but they do not, as a rule, see in that difference a reason to consider them members of a disability group. This is a very strong argument for rejecting the disability label because there is no higher authority on how a group should be regarded than the members of the group themselves. Some writers, convinced that the Deaf have a disability and baffled by their refusal to acknowledge it, conclude that Deaf people are simply denying the truth of their disability to avoid stigma (Baynton, 2002; Finkelstein, 1991; Gonsoulin, 2001). But, many people have, like the Deaf, physical differences that are not accommodated (Zola, 1993)—relatively short and tall people, for example—and they also deny they have a disability. Surely, in doing so they are not simply trying to avoid stigma. The gender preferences of gay men and women were at one time viewed as an expression of mental illness. In rejecting that disability categorization, the gay rights movement was not simply trying to avoid a stigma; it was trying instead to promote a new representation of gay men and women that would be better for them, their families, and the wider society (Conrad & Schneider, 1980).

When Gallaudet University's president, I. King Jordan, was asked on the television program *Sixty Minutes* if he would like to be hearing, he replied: "That's almost like asking a black person if he would rather be white . . . I don't think of myself as missing something or as incomplete. . . . It's a common fallacy if you don't know Deaf people or Deaf issues. You think it's a limitation" (Fine & Fine, 1990). Deaf scholars like I. King Jordan, Tom Humphries, and MJ Bienvenu in the United States and Paddy Ladd in England are not rejecting the disability label because they want to avoid stigma associated with disability (Ladd, 2003). That would be to give them little credit. Rather, they are rejecting it because, as Tom Humphries has said so well, "It doesn't compute" (1993, pp. 6, 14). In ASL, the sign with a semantic field that most overlaps that of the English "disability" can be glossed in English

LIMP-BLIND-ETC. I have asked numerous Deaf informants to give me examples from that category: They have responded by citing people in wheelchairs, blind people, mentally retarded people, and people with cerebral palsy, among others, but no informant has ever listed Deaf, and all reject it as an example of a disability group when asked.

Further examples of how the disability label does not compute come from Deaf preferences in marriage and childbearing. Like the members of many ethnic groups, culturally Deaf people prefer to socialize with and to marry other members of their cultural group; as noted, the Deaf have one of the highest endogamous marriage rates of any ethnic group (Schein, 1989). When it comes to Deaf preferences in childbearing, there are no hard statistics, but in interviews with the press and with me, Deaf parents have expressed a wish for children like themselves—much as all parents do who do not see themselves as disabled. "I want my daughter to be like me, to be Deaf," one expectant Deaf mother declared in an interview with the *Boston Globe*. She explained that she came from a large Deaf family, all of whom had hoped that her baby would be born Deaf (Saltus, 1989; also see Mills, 2002). Other expectant Deaf parents reportedly say it will be fine either way, Deaf or hearing. These views contrast sharply with the tendency of disability groups. A study of blind people, for example, reported that they tend to shun the company of other blind people, associate with each other only when there are specific reasons for doing so, seek sighted mates, and do not wish to transmit their blindness to their children (Deshen, 1992). Leaders of the disability rights movement call for ambivalence: They want their physical difference valued, as a part of who they are; at the same time, they do not wish to see more children and adults with disabilities in the world (Abberley, 1987; Lane, 1995).

We should not be surprised that Deaf people want Deaf spouses, welcome Deaf children, and prefer to be together with other culturally Deaf people—in clubs, in school, at work if possible, in leisure activities, in political action, in sports, and so on—in short, they see being Deaf as an inherent good. Do not ethnic groups characteristically value their physical difference, from the pygmies of the Iturbi forest in Central Africa to the tall pale inhabitants of, say, Finland? Of course they do, so it is perfectly expected that culturally Deaf people positively value the Deaf difference and that hearing folks find in their own cultures a preference for hearing bodies, despite their poorer performance on some visual processing tasks compared to the Deaf (Lane, 2004a).

Thus, embracing the disability label in hopes it might assist Deaf people in gaining more of their rights is fundamentally flawed because Deaf people do not believe it. For Deaf people to surrender anyway to how others define them is to misrepresent themselves, and that is the first reason to reject the disability label.

Greater Risk for the Deaf Child

There are many penalties for misrepresenting, for allowing the disability label. An important penalty concerns the risk to the Deaf child. It appears that children are at greater medical and surgical risk when their bodies differ from their parents in important ways that age alone does not explain. Parents want children like themselves, and if they are significantly unlike, they will listen to the doctors who say they can reduce or eliminate the difference, sometimes harming the child in the process. It is very tempting to locate the source of the social stigma with the child rather than the society; after all, the child is right there and much more manageable than an entire society. Moreover, the technologies of normalization are knocking at the door. However, the medicalization of difference deflects us from the real issue, which is the stigmatizing of difference in our society. When children who have undergone surgical normalizing become adults, many decry what was done to them as children.

For example, it has been the practice in the United States to operate on children with ambiguous genitalia, most often carving a vagina in male children because the surgical methods are not available to create a suitable penis. Once grown to adulthood, these and other intersexuals have been campaigning to dissuade urologists from continuing to perform this maiming surgery on children (Dreger, 1998). Little People, when their parents are not dwarfs, are frequently subjected as children to bone-breaking surgery for limb lengthening. It is painful, it is risky, and it is incapacitating. At best, it places the child in a no-man's land, neither short as a dwarf nor average size, and most adult dwarfs are utterly opposed to the surgery (Kennedy, 2003). There are many more victims of the medical-surgical imperative. One thinks of the horrors visited on the mentally ill, like frontal lobotomy (Valenstein, 1986), and those visited on homosexuals, such as deconditioning (Conrad & Schneider, 1980). Not all medical intervention in social issues is bad, of course; sometimes, it serves us well, and it derives great prestige from doing so. That is just why it overreaches at times and why we have to be wary of its abuse.

Cochlear Implant Surgery.   Now to label the Deaf child as having a disability places that child at risk for interventions like cochlear implant surgery. Cochlear implant surgery lasts about 3.5 hours under general anesthesia and requires hospitalization from 2 to 4 days. A broad, crescent-shaped incision is made behind the operated ear, and the skin flap is elevated. A piece of temporalis muscle is removed. A depression is drilled in the skull and reamed to make a seat for the internal electrical coil of the cochlear implant. A section of the mastoid bone is removed to expose the middle ear cavity. Further drilling exposes the membrane of the round window on the inner ear. Observing the procedure under a microscope, the surgeon pierces the membrane. A wire about 18mm long is pushed through the opening. The wire seeks its own path as it moves around and up the coiled inner ear. The microstructure of the inner ear is destroyed; if there was any residual hearing in the ear, it is likely destroyed as well. The auditory nerve itself is unlikely to be damaged, however, and the implant stimulates the auditory nerve directly. The internal

coil is then sutured into place. Finally, the skin is sewn back over the coil.

Clear Risks.   The surgery and general anesthesia entail medical and surgical risks. The incidence of bacterial meningitis in implanted children is 30 times higher than in age-matched unimplanted children (Daneshi et al., 2000; Reefhuis et al., 2003). Other risks include anesthesia risk (Svirsky, Teoh, & Neuburger, 2004); loss of vestibular function (Huygen et al., 1995); cerebrospinal fluid leak (Reefhuis et al., 2003); facial nerve stimulation and injury (Kelsall et al., 1997); and damage to the carotid artery (Gastman et al., 2002). The surgery can have fatal consequences (Jalbert, 2003). Nine of ten candidates for pediatric implant surgery, those with no or little usable hearing, were born Deaf (Allen, Rawlings & Remington, 1994; Center for Assessment, 1992). Such children rarely receive the main benefit sought: fluency in a spoken language (Lane & Bahan, 1998). Compounding the harm, special educators who work with the surgical team commonly urge oral educational programs on the parents and discourage sign language use (Tye-Murray, 1992). If implanted children are unable to learn spoken English and are prevented from mastering ASL, they will remain language-less for many years. Developmental milestones for signed languages are similar to those for spoken languages, and the later the acquisition of ASL, the poorer its mastery on the average (Mayberry & Eichen, 1991; Newport, 1990; Petitto, 1993). It is inexcusable to leave a child without fluent language for years on end. Medicine is coming to realize that it is the overall quality of life of the person and not just the concerned organ that must be considered (Reisenberg & Glass, 1989).

Dubious Benefits.   Advocates for childhood implantation acknowledge that "implants do not restore normal hearing," and that, after the operation, "long-term habilitation continues to be essential" (Balkany et al., 2002, p. 356). According to a recent report, 59% of implanted children are judged by their parents to be behind their hearing peers in reading, and 37% are behind in math (Christiansen & Leigh, 2004). It seems unlikely these children will be full-fledged members of the hearing world (Lane, 1999; Lane & Bahan, 1998).

We know that early acquisition of ASL facilitates later mastery of English (Padden & Ramsey, 2000; Strong & Prinz, 1997). This linguistic intervention might deliver greater English mastery than implant surgery; the comparison study has not been done. On the contrary, every study that has compared the performance of children with cochlear implants to an unimplanted control group employed controls that apparently had not mastered any language (see, for example, the literature review in Geers, Nicholas, & Sedey, 2003). . . .

If medical and surgical procedures used with children who are Deaf, or intersexuals, or dwarfs required informed consent from adults *like* the child, they would almost never take place. And, when the parents are like the child, in fact they rarely take place. . . .

Survival Risk for the Deaf-World

A third argument against the disability label for the Deaf-World concerns the risk to the Deaf-World as a whole if that representation prevails. A majority of people in the Deaf-World have inherited their ethnicity. Deaf inheritance and a failure to understand the ethnic status of culturally Deaf people have historically and at present placed the Deaf-World in jeopardy of ethnocide and even genocide. Despite surgical and medical experiments on large numbers of Deaf children in the 19th century, medicine made no inroads against the Deaf-World as a whole. However, developments in biology in the late 19th century gave rise to the eugenics movement, which sought to improve the race and eliminate the Deaf-World, among other groups considered undesirable, by selective breeding. From the point of view of the variety of humankind favored by selective breeding, the practice is eugenic; from the point of view of the varieties disfavored, it is genocidal.

The most famous advocate of regulating Deaf marriage to reduce Deaf childbirth was one of the founders of oral education in America, Alexander Graham Bell, who devoted his great wealth and prestige to these eugenic measures (Lane, 1984). When the American Breeders Association created a section on eugenics "to emphasize the value of superior blood and the menace to society of inferior blood," Bell agreed to serve. He engaged the issue of eugenics and the Deaf population beginning in the 1880s. Sign language and residential schools were creating a Deaf community, he warned, in which Deaf people intermarried and reproduced, a situation fraught with danger to the rest of society. He sounded the alarm in his *Memoir Upon the Formation of a Deaf Variety of the Human Race*, presented to the National Academy of Sciences in 1883. Because there are familial patterns of deafness, Bell wrote, "It is to be feared that the intermarriage of such persons would be attended by calamitous results to their off-spring" (Bell, 1883, p. 11).

Bell argued, with breathtaking hubris, that to avoid this calamity, we must "commence our efforts on behalf of the deaf-mute by changing his social environment" (1883, p. 46). Residential schools, where most Deaf children acquired language, identity, and a life partner, should be closed and Deaf people educated in small day schools. Sign language should be banished; Deaf teachers fired. Bell's *Memoir* received wide newspaper coverage. Bell's actions led many to believe that there would be, or already were, laws prohibiting Deaf marriage. There was much consternation among Deaf people contemplating marriage. Some hearing parents of Deaf children chose to have their children sterilized (Mitchell, 1971).

A 1912 report from Bell's eugenics section of the Breeders' Association cites his census of blind and Deaf persons and lists "socially unfit" classes to "be eliminated from the human stock" (American Genetic Association, 1912, p. 3). The model eugenic law called for the sterilization of feebleminded, insane, criminalistic ("including the delinquent and the wayward"), epileptic, inebriate, diseased, blind, Deaf, deformed, and dependent people ("including orphans, ne'er-do-wells, the homeless, tramps, and paupers"). By the time of World War I, 16 states in the United States had sterilization laws in force. By 1940, 30 states had such laws (Haller, 1963). Physicians were actively involved in this eugenics movement (May & Hughes, 1987). . . .

Deaf Eugenics Today

Audiometric testing, labeling, special needs schooling, genetic research and counseling, surgery, and reproductive control all are means of currently or potentially exercising power over the Deaf body. In 1992, researchers at Boston University announced that they had identified the so-called genetic error responsible for a common type of inherited deafness. The director of the National Institute on Deafness and Other Communication Disorders [sic] called the finding a "major breakthrough that will improve diagnosis and genetic counseling and ultimately lead to substitution therapy or gene transfer therapy" ("BU Team," 1992, p. 6; "Deafness gene," 1992, p. 141). The goal of such efforts as gene transfer therapy is, of course, to reduce Deaf births, ultimately altogether. Thus, a new form of medical eugenics applied to Deaf people is envisioned, in this case by an agency of the U.S. government The primary characteristics of Deaf people with this particular genetic background to be eliminated are numerous Deaf relatives, sign language fluency, facial features such as widely spaced eyebrows, and coloring features such as white forelock and freckling (Fraser, 1976).

Imagine the uproar if medical scientists trumpeted a similar breakthrough for any other ethnic minority, promising a reduction in that ethnic group's children—promising fewer Navajos, fewer Jews, whatever the ethnic group. The Australian government indeed undertook a decades-long eugenic program to eliminate its aboriginal peoples by placing their children in white boarding houses in the city, where it was hoped they would marry white and have white children. In 1997, a government commission of inquiry classified these and other measures as genocide (National Inquiry, 1997). Under international law, an activity that has the foreseeable effect of diminishing or eradicating

a minority group, even if it is undertaken for other reasons and is not highly effective, is guilty of genocide (National Inquiry, 1997; United Nations, 2003b). Why do governments fail to apply this moral principle and law to the Deaf? Americans fail to see the danger of pursuing a genocidal program in this instance because most Americans see Deaf people as having a disability arising from an impairment. And, the goal of eradicating a disability, although it may be in some circumstances unwise and unethical, is not seen as genocide.

If culturally Deaf people were understood to be an ethnic group, they would have the protections offered to such groups. It is widely held as an ethical principle that the preservation of minority cultures is a good. The variety of humankind and cultures enriches all cultures and contributes to the biological, social, and psychological well-being of humankind. Laws and covenants, such as the United Nations Declaration of the Rights of Persons Belonging to National or Ethnic, Religious and Linguistic Minorities (United Nations, 2003a), are founded on a belief in the value of protecting minority cultures. The declaration calls on states to foster their linguistic minorities and ensure that children and adults have adequate opportunities to learn the minority language. It further affirms the right of such minorities to enjoy their culture and language and participate in decisions on the national level that affect them. Programs that substantially diminish minority cultures are engaged in ethnocide and may constitute crimes against humanity. . . .

Wrong Solutions

Because they are an ethnic group whose language and mores were long disparaged, Deaf people commonly feel solidarity with other oppressed groups, the more so as the Deaf-World includes such groups as people with disabilities, seniors, women, blacks, and so on. Deaf people have special reasons for solidarity with hard-of-hearing and late-deafened people; their combined numbers have created services, commissions, and laws that the Deaf-World alone probably could not have achieved. Solidarity, yes, but when culturally Deaf people allow their ethnic identity to be subsumed under the construct of disability, they set themselves up for wrong solutions and bitter disappointments. After all, members of the Deaf-World differ from disabled people in their language and cultural experience, in their body of knowledge, in their system of rules and values, and in their models for selfhood.

If the Deaf-World were to embrace a disability identity, it would urge on Americans an understanding from which grow solutions that Deaf people oppose. Priorities of the disabilities rights movement include better medical care, rehabilitation services, and personal assistance services (Shapiro, 1993). Deaf people do not attach particular importance to any of these services and instead campaign for acceptance of their language and better and more interpreters. Whereas the disability rights movement seeks independence for people with disabilities, Deaf people cherish interdependence with other Deaf people. These differences in values and priorities far outweigh the areas, such as fighting job discrimination, in which Deaf goals are potentially advanced by joining ranks with disability groups. . . .

This article has presented a case that the sign language–using minority in the United States, the Deaf-World, is best viewed as an ethnic group, and it has cited reasons why it is inappropriate to view the Deaf-World as a disability group: Deaf people themselves do not believe they have a disability; the disability construction brings with it needless medical and surgical risks for the Deaf child; it also endangers the future of the Deaf-World. Finally, the disability construction brings bad solutions to real problems because it is predicated on a misunderstanding.

All of these objections to the disability construction of culturally Deaf people apply to the proposal that Deaf people be understood as both an ethnic group and a disability group at the same time. Taking up such a position would weaken the Deaf-World claim on ethnicity (is there any other ethnic group that is a disability group?) while inviting

the risks and wrong solutions described here. The ethically troubling practices in which surgeons, scientists, and educators are engaged—operating on healthy Deaf children, seeking the means to diminish and ultimately eradicate the Deaf-World, opposing the Deaf child's right to full and fluent language—exist because this ethnic group is misunderstood as a disability group. They will not be avoided by affirming, contrary to the group's own judgment, that it is a disability group but also an ethnic group.

How we ultimately resolve these ethical issues goes well beyond Deaf people; it will say a great deal about what kind of society we are and the kind of society in which we wish to live. Difference and diversity not only have evolutionary significance but, I would argue, are a major part of what gives life its richness and meaning; ethnic diversity is a basic human good, and to choose to be with one's own kind is a fundamental right. There is reason for hope: Society *can* adopt a different understanding of a people. Native Americans were once seen as savages; black Americans as property; women as utterly dependent. The case for Deaf ethnicity built by the social sciences is powerful. Increasingly, linguists take account of ASL, sociologists of the social structure of the Deaf-World, historians of its history, educators of its culture, and so on. It remains to reform those other professions that have an outdated understanding or a representation that suits their agenda but not that of Deaf people. The challenge to the professions that seek to be of service to Deaf children and adults is to replace the normativness of medicine with the curiosity of ethnography.

DISCUSSION QUESTIONS

1. Is the ethnic group model of Deaf-World preferable to the disability model as Lane contends? What grounds should be used in making that calculation?
2. Why hasn't the ethnic group approach that Lane recommends so far taken hold in pubic policy or popular opinion?

REFERENCES

Abberley, P. (1987). The concept of oppression and the development of a social theory of disability. *Disability, Handicap and Society, 2,* 5-19.

Allen, T. E., Rawlings, B. W., & Remington, F. (1994). Demographic and audiologic profiles of deaf children in Texas with cochlear implants. *American Annals of the Deaf, 138,* 260–266.

American Genetic Association, Eugenics Section. (1912). *American sterilization laws. Preliminary report of the Committee of the Eugenics Section of the American Breeders Association to study and to report on she best practical means for cutting off the defective germ plasm in the human population.* London: Eugenics Educational Society.

Bahan, B. (2004, April). *The visual people.* Paper presented at the conference Deaf Studies Today, Utah Valley State College, Orem.

Balkany, T. J., Hodges, A. V., Eshraghi, A. A., Butts, S., Bricker, K., Lingvai, J., et al. (2002). Cochlear implants in children—a review. *Acta Oto-laryngologica (Stockholm), 122,* 356–362.

Balkany, T., Hodges, A., & Goodman, K. (1999). Authors' reply [to Lane and Bahan]. *Otolaryngology—Head and Neck Surgery, 121,* 673–675.

Barth, F. (1969). *Ethnic groups and boundaries.* Boston: Little-Brown.

Baynton, D. (2000). Bodies and environments. In P. Blanet (Ed.), *Employment, disability and the Americans with Disabilities Act* (pp. 387–411). Evanston, IL: Northwestern University Press.

Baynton, D. (2002, July). *Deafness and disability.* Paper presented at the Deaf Studies Think Tank, Gallaudet University, Washington, DC.

Bell, A. G. (1883). *Memoir upon the formation of a deaf variety of the human race.* Washington, DC: Volta Bureau.

Binnie, C. (1994). The future of audiologic rehabilitation: Overview and forecast. In J. P. Gagné & N. Tye-Murray (Eds.), *Research in audiological rehabilitation* (pp. 13–24). Cedar Falls, IA: American Academy of Rehabilitative Audiology.

BU team finds genetic cause of Waardenburg syndrome. (1992, March). *Deaf Community News,* p. 6.

Bullard, D. (1986) *Islay.* Silver Spring, MD: TJ Publishers.

Center for Assessment and Demographic Studies, Gallaudet University. (1992). *Annual survey of hearing-impaired children and youth 1991–1992. Age at onset of deafness for students with profound hearing losses.* Washington, DC: Gallaudet University.

Christiansen, J. D., & Leigh, L. W. (2004). Children with cochlear implants: Changing parent and Deaf community perspectives. *Archives of Otolaryngology Head and Neck Surgery, 130,* 673–677.

Conrad, P., & Schneider, J. (1980). *Deviance and medicalization.* Columbus, OH: Merrill.

Daneshi, A., Farhadi, M., Emamjomeh, H., & Hasanzadeh, S. (2000). Management and the control of gusher during cochlear implant surgery. *Advances in Oto-Rino-Laryngology, 57,* 120–122.

Davis, L. (2002). *Postdeafness.* Paper presented at the Deaf Studies Think Thank, Gallaudet University, Washington, DC.

Deafness gene. (1992, February 18). *New York Times,* p. 141, B7, C 2.

Deshen, S. (1992). *Blind people.* Albany: State University of New York Press.

Downie, A. B., Mulligan, J., McCaughey, E. S., Stratford, R. J., Betts, P. R., & Voss, L. D. (1996). Psychological response to treatment in short normal children. *Archives of Disorders of Childhood, 76,* 92-95.

Dreger, A. (l998). *Hermaphrodites and the medical invention of sex.* Cambridge, MA: Harvard University Press.

Erting, C. (1978). Language policy and Deaf ethnicity in the United States. *Sign Language Studies, 19,* 139–152.

Erting, C. (1982). *Deafness, communication and social identity: An anthropological analysis of interaction among parents, teachers and deaf children in a preschool.* Unpublished doctoral dissertation, American University, Washington, DC.

Fine, H., & Fine, P. (Executive Producers). (1990, March). *Sixty Minutes.* New York, NY: Columbia Broadcasting System.

Finkelstein, V. (1981). Disability and the helper-helped relationship. In A. Brechin, P. Liddiard, & J. Swain (Eds.), *Handicap in, a social world,* (pp. 58–64). Sevenoaks, UK: Beckenham, Hodder, & Stoughton.

Finkelstein, V. (1991) "We" are not disabled, "you" are. In S. Gregory & G. M. Hartley (Eds.), *Constructing Deafness,* (pp. 265–271). London: Pinter.

Fishman, J. (1977). Language and ethnicity. In H. Giles (Ed.), *Language ethnicity, and intergroup relations* (pp. 15–57). New York: Academic Press.

Fishman, J. (1982). A critique of six papers on the socialization of the deaf child. In J. B. Christiansen (Ed.), *Conference highlights: National research conference on the social aspects of deafness* (pp. 6–20). Washington, DC: Gallaudet College.

Fishman, J. (1989). *Language and ethnicity in minority sociolinguistic perspective.* Philadelphia: Multilingual Matters.

Foucault, M. (1980). *Power/knowledge: Selected interviews and other writings, 1972–1977.* Brighton, UK: Harvester Press.

Fraser, G. R. (1976). *The causes of profound deafness in childhood.* Baltimore, MD: Johns Hopkins Press.

Gastman, B. R., Hirsch, B. E., Sando, I., Fukui, M. B., & Wargo M. L. (2002). The potential risk of carotid injury in cochlear implant surgery. *Laryngoscope, 112,* 262–266.

Geers, A. E., Nicholas, J. G., & Sedey, A. L. (2003). Language skills of children with early cochlear implantation. *Ear and Hearing, 24*(Suppl.), 46S–58S.

Gelb, S. A. (1987). Social deviance and the "discovery" of the moron. *Disability, Handicap and Society, 2,* 247–258.

Gonsoulin, T. P. (2001). Cochlear implant/Deaf-World dispute: Different bottom elephants. *Otolaryngology—Head and neck surgery, 125,* 552–556.

Gusfield, J. (1982). Deviance in the welfare state: The alcoholism profession and the entitlements of stigma. In M. Lewis (Ed.), *Research in social problems and public policy* (Vol. 2., pp. 1–20). Greenwich, CT: JAI Press.

Gusfield, J. (1984). On the side: Practical action and social constructivism in social problems theory. In J. Schneider & J. Kitsuse (Eds.), *Studies in the sociology of social problems* (pp. 31–51). Rutgers, NJ: Ablex.

Gusfield, J. (1989). Constructing the ownership of social problems: Fun and profit in the welfare state. *Social Problems, 36,* 431–441.

Haller, M. (1963). *Eugenics: Hereditarian attitudes in American thought.* New Brunswick, NJ: Rutgers University Press.

Humphries, T. (1993). Deaf culture and cultures. In K. M. Christensen & G. L. Delgado (Eds.), *Multicultural issues in deafness,* (pp. 3–15). White Plains, NY: Longman.

Huygen, P. L., Hinderink, J. B., van den Broek, P., van den Borne, S., Brokx, J. P., Mens, L. H., et al. (1995). The risk of vestibular function loss after intracochlear implantation. *Acta Otolaryngologica, Pt. 2*(Suppl. 520), 270–272.

Jalbert, Y. (2003). Décès suite à un, implant cochléaire: Pas un type b. *Canadian Medical Association Journal, 168,* 256.

Johnson, R. E., & Erting, C. (1979, November). *Sign, solidarity, and socialization.* Paper presented at the meeting of the American Anthropological Association, Cincinnati, OH.

Johnson, R. E., & Erting, C. (1982). Linguistic socialization in the context of emergent deaf ethnicity. In C. Erting & R. Meisegeier (Eds.), *Working papers no. 1: Deaf children and the socialization process.* Washington, DC: Gallaudet College. (Unpaginated document).

Johnson, R. E., & Erting, C. (1984). Linguistic socialization in the context of emergent Deaf ethnicity. In K. Kernan (Ed.), *Wenner-Gren Foundation working papers in anthropology.* New York: Wenner-Gren.

Johnson, R. E., & Erting, C. (1989). Ethnicity and socialization in a classroom for Deaf children. In C. Lucas (Ed.), *The sociolinguistics of the Deaf community* (pp. 41–84). New York, NY: Academic Press.

Kelsall, D. C., Shallop, J. K., Brammeier, T. G., & Prenger, E. C. (1997). Facial nerve stimulation after Nucleus 22-channel cochlear implantation. *American Journal of Otology, 18,* 336–341.

Kennedy, D. (2003). *Little people.* New York: St. Martin's Press

Ladd, P. (2003). *Understanding deaf culture: In search of Deafhood.* London: Multilingual Matters.

Lane, H. (1984). *When the mind hears: A history of the Deaf.* New York: Random House.

Lane, H. (1995). Constructions of deafness. *Disability and Society, 10,* 171–89.

Lane, H. (2004a). *A Deaf artist in early America: The worlds of John Brewster Jr.* Boston: Beacon Press.

Lane, H., & Bahan, B. (1998). Effects of cochlear implantation in young children: A review and a reply from a Deaf-World perspective. *Otolaryngology: Head and Neck Surgery 119,* 297–308.

Lane, H., Pillard, R., & French, M. (2000). Origins of the American Deaf-World: Assimilating and differentiating societies and their relation to genetic patterning. *Sign Language Studies, 1,* new series, 17–44.

Levesque, J. (1994). It's a Deaf Deaf Deaf-World. *DCARA News, 15,* 2.

Markowicz, H., & Woodward, J. (1978). Language and the maintenance of ethnic boundaries in the Deaf community. *Communication and Cognition, 11,* 29–37.

May, D., & Hughes, D. (1987). Organizing services for people with mental handicap: The Californian experience. *Disability, Handicap and Society, 2,* 213–230.

Mayberry, R., & Eichen, E. (1991). The long-lasting advantage of learning sign language in childhood: Another look at the critical period for language acquisition. *Journal of Memory and Language, 30,* 486–512.

Mills, M. (2002, April 9). Women: I am happy my child is Deaf. *The Guardian,* 8.

Mindess, A. (1999). *Reading between the signs: Intercultural communication for sign language interpreters.* Yarmouth, ME: Intercultural Press.

Mitchell, S. H. (1971). The haunting influence of Alexander Graham Bell. *American Annals of the Deaf. 116,* 349–356.

Nagel, J. (1994). Constructing ethnicity: Creating and recreating ethnic identity and culture. *Social problems, 41,* 152–176.

National Inquiry Into the Separation of Aboriginal and Torres Strait Islander Children From Their Families. (1997). *Bringing them home.* New South Wales, Australia: Sterling Press.

Newport, E. Maturational constraints on language learning. *Cognitive Science, 14,* 11–28.

Padden C., & Humphries, T. (1998). *Deaf in America: Voices from a culture.* Cambridge MA: Harvard University Press.

Padden, C., & Markowicz, H. (1976). Cultural conflicts between hearing and deaf communities. In F. B. Crammatte & A. B. Crammatte (Eds.), *Seventh World Congress of the World Federation of the Deaf* (pp. 407–411). Silver Spring, MD: National Association of the Deaf.

Padden, C., & Ramsey, C. (2000). American Sign Language and reading ability in Deaf children. In C. Chamberlain, J. Morford, & R. Mayberry (Eds.), *Language acquisition by eye* (pp. 165–189). Maway, NJ: LEA.

Petersen, W. (1980). Concepts of ethnicity. In S. Thernstrom (Ed.), *Harvard encyclopedia of American ethnic groups* (pp. 234–242). Cambridge, MA: Harvard University Press.

Petitto, L. (1993). On the ontogenetic requirements for early language acquisition. In E. de Boysson-Bardies, S. de Schonen, P. Jusczyk, & J. Morton (Eds.), *Developmental neurocognition: Speech and face processing in the first year of life* (pp. 365–383). New York: Kluwer Academic Press.

Ramsey, P. (1970). *The patient as person.* New Haven, CT: Yale University Press.

Reardon, W., Middleton-Price, H., Malcolm, S., Phelps, P., Bellman, S., Luxon, L., et al. (1992). Clinical and genetic heterogeneity in X-linked deafness. *British Journal of Audiology, 26,* 109–114.

Reefhuis, J., Honein, M. A., Whitney, C. G., Chamany, S., Mann, E. A., Biernath, K. R., et al. (2003). Risk of bacterial meningitis in children with cochlear implants. *New England Journal of Medicine, 349,* 435–445.

Reisenberg, D., & Glass, R. M. (1989). The medical outcomes study. *Journal of the American Medical Association, 262,* 943.

Saltus, R. (1989, July 10). Returning to the world of sound. *Boston Globe,* pp. 27, 29.

Schein J. D. (1989). *At home among strangers.* Washington, DC: Gallaudet University Press.

Schneider, D. M. (1969). Kinship, nationality and religion in American culture: Toward a definition of kinship. In R. F. Spencer (Ed.), *Forms of symbolic action* (pp. 116–125) Seattle, WA: University of Washington Press.

Schneider, D. M. (1972). What is kinship all about? In P. Reining (Ed.), *Kinship studies in the Morgan centennial year* (pp. 32–64). Washington, DC: Anthropological Society of Washington.

Shapiro, J. P. (1993). *No pity: People with disabilities forging a new civil rights movement.* New York: Times Books.

Smith, A. D. (1986). *The ethnic origin of nations.* Cambridge, UK: Blackwell.

Smith, S. (1995). Overview of genetic auditory syndromes. *Journal of the American Academy of Audiology, 6,* 1–14.

Smith, T. (1997). *Deaf people in context.* Unpublished doctoral dissertation, University of Washington, Seattle.

Sollors, W. (2001). Ethnic groups/ethnicity: Historical aspects. In N. J. Smelser & P. B. Baltes (Eds.), *International encyclopedia of the social sciences* (pp. 4813–4817). New York: Elsevier.

Strong, M., & Prinz, P. (1997). A study of the relationship between American Sign Language and English literacy. *Journal of Deaf Studies and Deaf Education, 2,* 37–46.

Svirsky, M., Teoh, S.-W., & Neuburger, H. (2004). Development of language and speech perception in congenitally, profoundly deaf children as a function of age at cochlear implantation. *Audiology, Neuro-Otology, 9,* 224–233.

Turnbull, C. M. (1962). *The forest people.* New York: Simon & Schuster.

Tye-Murray, N. (1992). *Cochlear implants and children: A handbook for parents, teachers and speech and hearing professionals.* Washington, DC: Alexander Graham Bell Association for the Deaf.

United Nations. (1948). *Convention on the Prevention and Punishment of the Crime of Genocide.* Resolution 96/I.

United Nations. (1992). *Declaration on the Rights of Persons Belonging to National or Ethnic, Religious and Linguistic Minorities.* Resolution 47/135.

United Nations (2003a). Declaration on the rights of persons belonging to national or ethnic, religious and linguistic minorities Resolution 47/135. In E. Osmanczyk & A. Mango (Eds.), *Encyclopedia of the United Nations and international agreements.* New York: Routledge.

United Nations (2003b). Genocide Convention, 1948 Resolution 96/1. In E. Osmanczyk & A. Mango (Eds.), *Encyclopedia of the United Nations and international agreements* (pp. 293–294). New York: Routledge.

Valenstein, E. (1986). *Great and desperate cures.* New York: Basic Books.

Van Cleve, J., & Crouch, B. (1989). *A place of their own: Creating the deaf community in America.* Washington, DC: Gallaudet University Press.

Werth, B. (1991, June 16). How short is too short? *New York Times Magazine,* Section 6, pp. 14–17, 28–29, 47.

Winzer, M. A. (1986). Deaf-Mutia: Responses to alienation by the deaf in the mid-19th century. *American Annals of the Deaf, 131,* 29–32.

Zola, I. K. (1993). Disability statistics, what we count and what it tells us. *Journal of Disability Policy Studies, 4,* 9–39.

EXPERIENCING DIFFERENCE

FRAMEWORK ESSAY

In the first framework essay, we considered the social construction of difference as master statuses were named, aggregated, dichotomized, and stigmatized. Now we turn to *experiencing* these statuses. A story from a friend provides an illustration of what we mean by this. In 1997, she and her husband had wanted to see *Men in Black* when it opened in the theaters, but they had not been able to find a babysitter for their eight-year-old daughter. They had watched many movies as a family and thought their daughter had a good understanding of the difference between real and pretend, so they decided it would be all right to take her with them to the show. They were wrong.

> Our perception of the movie was that while there was plenty of action, it was definitely a comedy. The "alien monsters" were ridiculous to us, inspiring laughter or mild disgust like that of a yucky bug you find in your bathroom and flush down the toilet. Jenny, however, found the movie to be scary and gross. It was beyond her ability to laugh away as something that was "pretend." She hid her eyes through 90 percent of the movie and did not agree with us that it was funny. She talked for months about how scary it was and chastised us for letting her see it.

This story holds a small lesson about *experiencing* your social status. What we notice in the world depends in large part on the statuses we occupy; in this way we may be said to *experience* our social status. Jenny thought the movie was scary both because of the unique person she is and because of her age, a master status. Her parents did not see the movie that way for the same reasons. All experienced the movie through their unique personalities and as people of certain ages.

Although we do not specifically address age in this book, it operates in ways that are analogous to race, sex, class, sexual orientation, and disability. For example, being young affects the way a person is treated in innumerable ways: at a minimum, restrictions on driving, employment, military enlistment, marriage, abortion, admission to movies, and alcohol and cigarette consumption; higher insurance rates; mandatory school attendance; and "status offenses" (acts that are illegal only for minors). In addition, minors are excluded from voting and exercising other legal rights.

In these ways, those defined as "young" are treated differently than those who are not so defined. Because of that treatment, those who are younger see the world differently from those who are older and no longer operating within these constraints. The young notice things that older people need not notice, because they are not subject to the same rules. Our experiences are tied to the statuses we occupy.

A different example of experiencing one's status comes from the autobiography of one of the first black students in an exclusive white prep school. She recalls what it was like to hear white students say, "It doesn't matter to me if somebody's white or black or green or purple. I mean people are just people." While she appreciated the students' intentions, she also heard her own *real* experience being trivialized by comparison to the Muppets. Her status helps to explain what she noticed in these conversations (Cary, 1991:83–84).

In all, you experience your social statuses; you live through them. They are the filters through which you see and make sense of the world, and in large measure they account for how you are treated and what you notice. In the sections that follow, we will focus on the experiences of both privilege and stigma associated with master statuses.

THE EXPERIENCE OF PRIVILEGE

Just as status helps to explain what we notice, it also explains what we *don't* notice. In the following classroom discussion between a black and a white student, the white student argues that because she and the black student are both female, they should be allies. The black woman responds,

> "When you wake up in the morning and look in the mirror, what do you see?"
>
> "I see a woman," replied the white woman.
>
> "That's precisely the issue," replied the black woman. "I see a black woman. For me, race is visible every day, because it is how I am *not* privileged in this culture. Race is invisible to you [because it is how you are privileged]." (Kimmel and Messner, 1989:3; emphasis added)

Thus, we are likely to be unaware of the statuses that *privilege* us, that is, provide us with advantage, and acutely aware of those that are the source of trouble—those that yield negative judgments and unfair treatment. Indeed, the mirror metaphor used by the black woman in this conversation emerges frequently among those who are stigmatized: "I looked in the mirror and saw a gay man." These moments of suddenly realizing your social position with all of its life-shaping ramifications are usually about recognizing how some statuses leave you stigmatized and under-privileged, but they are rarely about how you might be privileged or advantaged by other statuses.

Examples of Privilege

This use of the term *privilege* was first developed by Peggy McIntosh (1989) from her experience of teaching women's studies courses. Over time, McIntosh noticed that while many men were willing to grant that women were disadvantaged (or "un-derprivileged") because of sexism, it was far more difficult for them to acknowledge that they were themselves advantaged (or "overprivileged") because of it. Extending the analysis to race, McIntosh generated a list of the ways in which she, as a white woman, was overprivileged by virtue of racism. Her list of over forty white privi-leges included the following:

> I do not have to educate my children to be aware of systemic racism for their daily protection.
>
> I can arrange my activities so that I will never have to experience feelings of rejection owing to my race.
>
> I can be sure [that] if I need legal or medical help, my race will not work against me.
>
> I can take a job with an affirmative action employer without having my co-workers on the job suspect that I got it because of my race.
>
> I can worry about racism without being seen as self-interested or self-seeking.

As she talked to people about her list, McIntosh learned about other white privileges: "A black woman said she was glad to hear me 'working on my own people,' because if she said these things about white privilege, she would be seen as a militant." Someone else noted that one privilege of being white was being able to be oblivious of those privileges. "Those in privileged groups are educated [to be oblivious] about what it is like for others, especially for others who have to be in their presence" (McIntosh, 1989).

Privilege makes life easier: it is easier to get around, to get what one wants, and to be treated in an acceptable manner. For example, perhaps the privilege least noticed by nondisabled people is the simple ease of getting around—accessing buildings, restaurants, and movie theaters; accessing print information such as store names, bus stops, and street signs; riding public transportation; using public bathrooms; in short, having fairly uncomplicated access to the world. By contrast, notice the rage and exhaustion that reporter John Hockenberry describes as he tries to hail a cab or use the Brooklyn subway (Reading 33). Or ponder the indignity detailed in *Tennessee v. Lane*, the 2004 Supreme Court case about county court houses that lacked elevators, which meant that paraplegic people had to crawl or be carried up the steps (Reading 41). Thus, one usually unnoticed privilege of not being disabled is the ability to get around. Life is just easier, because everything is designed for your use.

While privilege makes people's lives easier, it also makes their lives safer. For example, many black and Hispanic students describe being closely monitored by security guards for shoplifting when they are in department stores. Indeed, in one class discussion of this, an African American student mentioned that she had the habit of walking through stores with her hands held out, palms open in front of her, to prove that she was not stealing. In effect, it is "safer" for white people to shoplift, since attention is focused on black and Latino customers.

This point was conveyed in a 2009 episode of ABC's *Primetime: What Would You Do?*, which was set in a public park in a predominately white New Jersey suburb. Called "Teen Vandals," a hidden camera recorded the reaction of passersby to a group of white teenagers (who were actors) destroying a car. Almost no one called the police or attempted to stop them. As one of the white actors commented later, "I was actually shocked to see how many people would actually take a good look at what we were doing and just walk on by without even interfering at all" (*Primetime*, 2009). By contrast, people did call the police about the black teenagers who were sleeping in a nearby car waiting for their turn to act as vandals. Not surprisingly, when it was time for those actors to destroy the car, there were numerous calls to the police and attempts to stop them. Thus, one privilege of being white is the presumption that you are not really criminal, violent, or dangerous to others.

While whites do not generally assume that other whites are a threat to them, they often assume that of blacks.[1] The percentage appears to be declining, but surveys indicate that about half of whites think blacks are aggressive or violent (Smith, 2001). This is especially important because if one assumes that a person or group is dangerous, taking preemptive action against them to ward off violence is more likely to

---

[1] Despite whites' fear of violence at the hands of African Americans, crime is predominately *intra*racial.

be seen as legitimate. An example of the consequence of this belief is provided by law professor and author Patricia J. Williams:

> My best friend from law school is a woman named C. For months now I have been sending her drafts of this book, filled with many shared experiences, and she sends me back comments and her own associations. Occasionally we speak by telephone. One day, after reading the beginning of this chapter, she calls me up and tells me her abiding recollection of law school. "Actually, it has nothing to do with law school," she says.
>
> "I'll be the judge of that," I respond.
>
> "Well," she continues, "It's about the time I was held at gunpoint by a SWAT team."
>
> It turns out that during one Christmas vacation C. drove to Florida with two friends. Just outside Miami they stopped at a roadside diner. C. ordered a hamburger and a glass of milk. The milk was sour, and C. asked for another. The waitress ignored her. C. asked twice more and was ignored each time. When the waitress finally brought the bill, C. had been charged for the milk and refused to pay for it. The waitress started to shout at her, and a highway patrolman walked over from where he had been sitting and asked what was going on. C. explained that the milk was sour and that she didn't want to pay for it. The highway patrolman ordered her to pay and get out. When C. said he was out of his jurisdiction, the patrolman pulled out his gun and pointed it at her.
>
> ("Don't you think," asks C. when I show her this much of my telling of her story, "that it would help your readers to know that the restaurant was all white and that I'm black?" "Oh, yeah," I say. "And six feet tall.")
>
> Now C. is not easily intimidated and, just to prove it, she put her hand on her hip and invited the police officer to go ahead and shoot her, but before he did so *he* should try to drink the damn glass of milk, and so forth and so on for a few more descriptive rounds. What cut her off was the realization that, suddenly and silently, she and her two friends had been surrounded by eight SWAT team officers, in full guerrilla gear, automatic weapons drawn. Into the pall of her ringed speechlessness, they sent a local black policeman, who offered her twenty dollars and begged her to pay and be gone. C. describes how desperately he was perspiring as he begged and, when she didn't move, how angry he got—how he accused her of being an outside agitator, that she could come from the North and go back to the North, but that there were those of "us" who had to live here and would pay for her activism.
>
> C. says she doesn't remember how she got out of there alive or why they finally let her go; but she supposes that the black man paid for her. But she does remember returning to the car with her two companions and the three of them crying, sobbing, all the way to Miami. "The damnedest thing about it," C. said, "was that no one was interested in whether or not I was telling the truth. The glass was sitting there in the middle of all this, with the curdle hanging on the side, but nobody would taste it because a black woman's lips had touched it." (Williams, 1991:56–57)

The privilege of not being considered criminal was highlighted in a nationwide review of the cases in which an undercover, plainclothes, or off-duty police officer was fatally shot by fellow police officers (New York State Task Force on Police-on-Police Shootings, 2010). The review did not find any racial pattern in the shootings of undercover and plainclothes officers because training and prevention measures have long been in place,

> . . . but the reality is strikingly different for off-duty officers. As far as we can determine, 1982 was the last year in which an off-duty, white police officer was killed in a mistaken-identity, police-on-police shooting anywhere in the United States. Since then, nine off-duty officers of color have been killed in such shootings. . . . (New York State Task Force on Police-on-Police Shootings, 2010:iii)

Thus, white off-duty officers who have to display their guns in a police action are safer than their black or Hispanic colleagues because other officers are less likely to assume they are criminal.

This assumption of white *non*-criminality is reinforced on a daily basis by television news reporting. In comparison with actual arrest rates, local news shows appear to underrepresent whites as perpetrators and overrepresent African Americans (Dixon and Linz, 2000; Entman and Rojeck, 2000; Entman, 1990, 1994). Because television is the primary news source for most Americans, the underrepresentation of whites as criminals yields a distorted view of the connection between race and crime.

> Even when suspects were clearly white, studies demonstrated that when white viewers were asked to identify the suspect later, they consistently misidentified the suspect as African American, a disturbing finding that suggests that white viewers have been primed through years of viewing African Americans almost exclusively as criminals to see *all* criminals as African American [Oliver, 1999; Oliver et al. 2004]. (Stabile, 2006:178)

As English and journalism professor Carol Stabile (2006) concluded from her review of U.S. crime news since the 1830s, African Americans have been criminalized with a persistence unlike that experienced by any other group. While the threats presumably posed by Irish, Eastern European, and Chinese immigrants were framed in the same terms as those for African Americans, for those groups the stereotypes have faded over time. Not so for African Americans. Even methamphetamine users, who are predominately white, fare better in the media:

> Where crack addicts were cast as people disposed to escape reality and responsibility . . . white [methamphetamine] users were [cast as] rural, hardworking members of the working class. Driven by circumstances to drug use, they found themselves hopeless captives to a powerful substance. The message was clear: white drug users were victims of their circumstances and therefore deserving of sympathy and rehabilitation; black drug addicts were social parasites, beyond redemption and worthy of nothing more than punishment. (Stabile, 2006:172–3)

Indeed, the privilege of *not* being assumed to be a "real" criminal has consequences even in terms of the degree to which behaviors are criminalized. For example,

> In the late 1970s, crack first came on the scene in the form of cocaine freebasing. Many of its users were stockbrokers and investment bankers, rock stars, Hollywood types, and a few pro athletes. Some of them began to get into trouble with this form of cocaine use, showing up in hospital emergency rooms and police stations. Congress passed new laws to extend health insurance coverage to include drug treatment. The treatment industry expanded the number of beds available.
>
> In the mid-1980s, crack use spread into America's inner cities among impoverished African Americans and Latinos. Some of them began to get into trouble with this form of cocaine use, showing up in hospital emergency rooms and police stations. Congress passed new laws to extend the length of criminal sentences for crack offenses. The prison industry expanded the number of cells available. (Reinarman and Levine, 2004:182)

This comparison of crack cocaine and cocaine powder users is not frivolous. In the late 1980s, federal sentencing laws established a *mandatory* five-year sentence for *first-time* possession of five grams of crack cocaine. By contrast, it takes 500 grams (1.1 pounds) of cocaine powder to trigger the five-year sentence—an intentional 100:1 differential that was established based on the hyperbole that crack was somehow 100 times more powerful than cocaine. (Crack is cocaine powder "cooked" with baking soda and water.) The same ratio was applied to the 10-year mandatory sentence trigged by 50 grams of crack cocaine but 5 kilograms (11 pounds) of cocaine powder. Revisions since 2007 have raised the trigger amount and reduced, but not eliminated, the sentencing differential. Nonetheless, the stage had been set for the differential imprisonment of black men.

> In the early 1970s, blacks were about twice as likely as whites to be arrested for a drug offense. The great growth in drug arrest rates through the 1980s had a large effect on African Americans. At the height of the drug war in 1989, arrest rates for blacks had climbed to 1,460 per hundred thousand compared to 365 for whites. Throughout the 1990s, drug arrest rates remained at these historically high levels. (Western, 2006:46)

These differential arrest rates are in contrast to what we know about drug usage. National surveys of high school drug use have long shown that white students self-report more drug use than black students (Johnson et al., 2004), and self-report surveys of black and white adults show similar levels of drug use (Western, 2006).

By the end of the 1990s, "60 percent of all federal prisoners were drug offenders and the share of drug offenders in state prison had more than doubled" (Western, 2006:58). The United States now has an incarcerated population (prisons and jails combined) of almost 2.2 million, exceeding its historic average by a factor of nearly five (Western, 2006:13) and far exceeding that of any other developed nation (Walmsley, n.d.). Within this incarcerated population, blacks outnumber whites by an eight-to-one ratio (Western, 2006).

Thus, as a category, whites experience the privileges of not being presumed criminal, not being depicted as criminal, not being at risk of preemptive violence, and able to pursue their "vices" with less chance of punishment. If they do not appear to be Middle Eastern, both whites and blacks are at little risk of being considered terrorists; if they do not look like immigrants, especially Hispanic immigrants, they are at little risk of being detained and deported. These privileges are the outcome of *racial profiling.*

Racial profiling—singling out members of a race or ethnic group for heightened police surveillance—is a way to act on the assumption that whole categories of people are dangerous. It became the subject of public debate following a 1996 Supreme Court decision that allowed the police to use routine traffic stops to investigate drug possession and other crimes. African Americans and Latinos argued that they were disproportionately pulled over—guilty of nothing more than "driving while black," or "driving while brown." Research by several social scientists confirmed the allegations, and national attention was focused by a 1998 shooting in which two New Jersey state troopers fired eleven shots into a van carrying black and Latino men from the Bronx to a basketball camp, wounding three of the passengers. At their sentencing, the troopers "said their supervisors had trained them to focus on black- and brown-skinned drivers because, they were told, they were more likely to be drug traffickers" (Kocieniewski, 2002). Thus, a national consensus against racial profiling—supported by public opinion, state legislation, and new federal policies barring racial profiling at the borders—began to emerge.

That consensus fractured with the September 11, 2001, terrorist attacks. Public opinion swung dramatically toward support of profiling Middle Eastern Americans as well as immigrants and visitors from the Middle East.[2] Special national security measures were implemented—most notably the National Security Entry-Exit Registration System that requires male nonimmigrant visa holders (that is, those who are temporary visitors) from twenty-five Middle Eastern countries to attend in-person interviews at an immigration office; to provide notification of a change of address, employment, or school; and to use designated ports for exiting the country (U.S. Immigration and Customs Enforcement, 2010).

Unlike the experience of most other American minorities and white women who, over time, have come to enjoy greater protection of their civil rights, Middle Eastern Americans have experienced the erosion of those protections, not only since the 2001 attacks, but also following the attack on Israeli athletes in the 1972 Olympic games in Munich, during the 1979 Iranian hostage crisis, and in the first Gulf War of 1990-1991—which were variously followed by limitations on Arab immigration and access to permanent resident status, increased FBI surveillance, restrictions on student visas, and increasing suspicion of Middle Eastern Americans (Tehranian, 2009). Even in 1991, polls found that 59 percent of Americans associated Arabs with terrorism; 58 percent, with violence; and 56 percent, with religious fanaticism (Tehranian, 2009:122).

As federal immigration laws have changed, not being subject to racial profiling has provided those who appear to be native-born, non-immigrants with the privilege of not being detained or deported. By contrast, two laws passed in 1996 (the Antiterrorism and Effective Death Penalty Act and the Illegal Immigration Reform and Immigrant Responsibility Act) made *lawful permanent residents* deportable for virtually any crime, from major offenses to shoplifting or drunk driving, depending on the wording of local statutes. (A *lawful permanent resident* is a visa status that allows the person to live and work in the U.S., travel outside the country and return, and apply for U.S. citizenship after 5 years.)

The laws are retroactive, in that permanent residents can be deported for crimes that did not warrant deportation at the time they were committed or that they committed as minors, and they are applied even to those who entered the country as children and have never actually resided in the country to which they are remanded (Atencia, 1999; Richards 2003). If the home country refuses to accepted the detainee once the U.S. prison time has been served, the detainee probably faces lifetime imprisonment in the United States. Nor can the outcome be changed by an immigration judge: "The legislation Congress passed in 1996 precluded immigration judges from considering

---

[2]Indeed, some have argued that the endorsement of racial profiling became a way to prove one's "Americanness": "Other people of color have become 'American' through the process of endorsing racial profiling. Whites, African Americans, East Asian Americans and Latinas/os are now deemed safe and not required to prove their allegiance" (Volpp, 2002:1584).

whether deportation would be excessively harsh in light of the immigrants' family relationships, community ties, U.S. military service records, or the possibility of persecution if returned to their country of origin" (Human Rights Watch, 2007).

While it is illegal to deport a U.S. citizen, there are increasing reports of that happening (Stevens, 2008; Amnesty International, 2009), as citizens are also sometimes swept up in immigration raids and imprisoned until they are able to convince authorities of their legal status. A 2008 survey of Latinos reported that "one-in-ten Hispanic adults—native-born U.S. citizens (8 percent) and immigrants (10 percent) alike—report that in the past year the police or other authorities have stopped them and asked them about their immigration status" (Pew Hispanic Center, 2008). Since detainees may be sent to any one of 300 detention centers and are likely to be poor, claims of citizenship are not easily resolved.

Whether the population profiled is Latino, African American, Middle Eastern, or immigrant, and whether the enforcing agency involves federal immigration, local police, or airport security, the efficacy of such profiling has long been questioned, specifically because *behavior*-based evaluations are more productive than race-based ones. For example, in terms of using traffic stops to uncover drugs, guns, or criminals, "when stops and searches are not racialized, they are more productive" (Harris, 2003:77). "Profiling is a crude substitute for behavior-based enforcement and . . . invites screeners to take a less vigilant approach to individuals who don't fit the profile, even if they engage in conduct that should cause concern" (Carter, 2002:12). In all, those of us who do not look Middle Eastern, black, Hispanic, or foreign born have the privilege of not being treated like criminals, illegal immigrants, or terrorists.

A different privilege, likely to be invisible to those in single-race families, is the privilege of being recognized as a family. The following account by a mother illustrates how the failure to perceive a family is linked to the expectation of black criminality.

> When my son was home visiting from college, we met in town one day for lunch. . . . On the way to the car, one of us thought of a game we'd often played when he was younger.
>
> "Race you to the car!"
>
> I passed my large handbag to him, thinking to more equalize the race since he was a twenty-year-old athlete. We raced the few blocks, my heart singing with delight to be talking and playing with my beloved son. As we neared the car, two young white men yelled something at us. I couldn't make it out and paid it no mind. When we arrived at the car, both of us laughing, they walked by and mumbled "Sorry" as they quickly passed, heads down.
>
> I suddenly understood. They hadn't seen a family. They had seen a young Black man with a pocketbook, fleeing a pursuing middle-aged white woman. My heart trembled as I thought of what could have happened if we'd been running by someone with a gun.
>
> Later I mentioned the incident in a three-day diversity seminar I was conducting at a Boston corporation. A participant related it that evening to his son, a police officer, and asked the son what he would have done if he'd observed the scene.
>
> The answer: "Shot out his kneecaps." (Lester, 1994:56–7)

Turning now from privileges of race to *privileges of sexual orientation,* the most obvious privilege enjoyed by heterosexuals is that they are allowed to be open about their relationships—which is, after all, what heteronormativity is all about. From idle conversation and public displays of affection, to the legal and religious approval embodied in marriage, heterosexuals are able to declare that they love and are loved. That privilege is not just *denied* to people in same-sex relationship; they are actively punished for such expressions by ostracism, physical assault, unemployment, and even loss of child custody and visitation—not so surprising given the still uncertain legal recognition of gay families.

Even the ability to display a picture of one's partner on a desk at work stands as an invisible privilege of heterosexuality.

> Consider, for example, an employee who keeps a photograph on her desk in which she and her husband smile for the camera and embrace affectionately. . . . [T]he photo implicitly conveys information about her private sexual behavior. [But] most onlookers (if they even notice the photo) do not think of her partner primarily in sexual terms. . . .
>
> [But] if the photograph instead shows the woman in the same pose with a same-sex partner, everyone is likely to notice. As with the first example, the photograph conveys the information that she is in a relationship. But the fact that the partner is a woman overwhelms all other information about her. The *sexual* component of the relationship is not mundane and implicit as with the heterosexual spouse. (Herek, 1992:95–6; emphasis added)

Because heterosexual public affection is so commonplace, it rarely conjures up images of sexual activity. But that is exactly what we may think of when we see a same-sex couple embrace or even hold hands. This is why gay and lesbian people are often accused of "flaunting" their sexuality: *any* display of affection between them is understood by many heterosexuals as virtually a display of the sex act.

These attitudes do, however, appear to be changing. For example, "Americans' support for the moral acceptability of gay and lesbian relations crossed the symbolic 50 percent threshold in 2010. At the same time, the percentage calling these relations 'morally wrong' dropped to 43 percent, the lowest in Gallup's decade-long trend" (Gallup, 2010). That change is almost entirely attributable to the increasing acceptance of same-sex relationships among men, especially those younger than 50; indeed, the 2010 poll was the first in which men were more accepting of these relationships than women. Still, appreciating abstractly supportive poll data is not the same as feeling safe enough to express affection in public settings. For gay and lesbian people, it is likely the latter will remain difficult for some time.

In the realm of *class privilege*, several readings in this book address the considerable differences in health, life span, educational access, and quality of life that accompany American class differences. But these are perhaps the more visible privileges of being middle and upper class. Less apparent is the privilege of being treated as a deserving and competent member of the community. Higher education institutions provide a number of examples of this. One of the boons of the legacy admission system, described by John Larew in Reading 32, is its invisibility. The students admitted to universities this way—who are predominately middle- and upper-class whites—don't have their qualifications questioned by faculty or other students, nor are they likely to agonize about whether they deserved to be admitted.

> Like many children of University of Virginia graduates, Mary Stuart Young of Atlanta, Georgia, wore Cavalier orange and blue long before she took an SAT or mailed an application.

"Coming here just felt right," said Young, 21, who expects to graduate with a religious studies degree. . . . "This was where I should be."

After all, with two generations of faithful alumni backing her, Young doubled her chances of getting into Thomas Jefferson's university. (Associated Press, 2003)

One of the privileges of being a legacy admission rather than an affirmative action admission is that you are treated as a deserving and competent member of the community, rather than someone who is not qualified to be there.

The assumption that students are middle or upper class is pervasive within higher education, so working-class students often find schools oblivious or even antagonistic to their needs. Students are presumed to understand how college works, because it is assumed that their parents are college graduates and can advise them: "In an article on working class students in higher education, one student was paraphrased as saying that college is a very unforgiving place. It is unforgiving not of those who don't know the rules, but rather of those who did not know the rules before arriving on campus" (Tokarczyk, 2004:163). Thus, one of the privileges of being a college student from the middle or upper classes is that you come to the university with a good deal of information about how it works.

"Working class students often have difficulty in their studies partially because colleges and universities—elite and nonelite—refuse to recognize that many students must work" (Tokarczyk, 2004:163). For example, schools that require unpaid internships, off-campus experiences, or study abroad trips may forget not only the costs associated with these requirements but also the fact that working-class students may have to quit their jobs to fulfill the requirement. The same is true of faculty office hours—set as if students could easily arrange their schedules to fit the professor's. If working-class students were seen as deserving and competent members of the community, their needs would be factored in automatically, not as a "special favor."

In all, one of the privileges of being middle or upper class is that higher education—which is absolutely critical to upward mobility—is in sync with one's experience. As Annette Lareau and Elliot Weininger describe in Reading 30, this cultural "fit" has been fostered by middle-class child rearing practices, as well as parental interventions in high school and the transition to college. But beyond that, those who go to college can expect to have their life experiences and perspectives treated as the norm. The institution will be organized around those experiences in ways large and small, from assuming that everyone should live on campus (and bear the expense of room and board) to assuming they will be able to cover the cost of texts or forgo employment. In these ways, students from the middle or upper classes have the privilege of feeling like they belong.

Overall, two privileges shape the experience of those in nonstigmatized statuses: *entitlement* and the privilege of being *unmarked*. Entitlement is the belief that one has the right to be respected, acknowledged, protected, and rewarded. This is so much taken for granted by those in nonstigmatized statuses that they are often shocked and angered when it is denied them.

[After the lecture, whites in the audience] shot their hands up to express how excluded they felt because [the] lecture, while broad in scope, clearly was addressed first and foremost to the women of color in the room. . . . What a remarkable sense of entitlement must drive their willingness to assert their experience of exclusion! If I wanted to raise my hand every time I felt excluded, I would have to glue my wrist to the top of my head. (Ettinger, 1994:51)

Like entitlement, the privilege of occupying an unmarked status is shared by most of those in nonstigmatized categories. *Dentist* is an *unmarked* status; *woman dentist* is *marked*. Unmarked categories convey the usual and expected distribution of individuals in social statuses—the distribution that does not require any special comment. Thus, the unmarked category tells us what a society takes for granted.

Theoretically, the unmarked category might include anyone, but in truth it refers to white males. How do we know that? Because other occupants of that status are usually marked: woman dentist, black dentist, and so on. While the marking of a status signals infrequency—there are few female astronauts or male nurses—it may also imply inferiority. A "woman dentist" or a "black dentist" may be considered less qualified.

Thus, a final privilege of those who are not stigmatized is that their master statuses are not used to discount their accomplishments or imply that they serve only special interests. Someone described as "a politician" is presumed to operate from a universality that someone described as "a white male politician" is not. Because white male politicians are rarely described as such, their anchoring in the reality of their own master statuses is hidden. In this way, those in marked statuses appear to be operating from an "agenda," or "special interest" while those in unmarked statuses can appear to be agenda-free. Being white and male thus becomes invisible, because it is not regularly identified as important. For this reason, some recommend identifying *everyone's* race and sex as a way to recognize that we are all grounded in our master statuses.

In all, privilege is usually invisible to those who possess it; they may assume that everyone is treated as they are. When they learn about instances of discrimination, they may think that the incident was exceptional rather than routine, that the victim was overreacting or misinterpreting, or that the victim must have provoked the encounter. Such responses do not necessarily deny that the incident took place; rather, they deny that the event carries any negative or special meaning.

Through such dismissals, those operating from positions of privilege can deny the experience of those without privilege. For example, college-age students often describe university administrators as unresponsive until they have their parents call to complain. If the parents later said, "I don't know why *you* had such a problem with those people; they were very nice to *me*. Did you do something to antagonize them?" that would indicate they were oblivious to their privileged status in the university setting as well as unaware of their student's underprivileged status in it.

Dismissals like these treat the stigmatized person like a child inadequate to judge the world. Often such dismissals are framed in terms of the very stigma about which people are complaining. In this way, what stigmatized people say about their status is discounted precisely because they are stigmatized. The implication is that those who occupy a stigmatized status are somehow the ones *least* able to assess its consequence. The effect is to dismiss precisely those who have had the most experience with the problem.

This process, called *looping* or *rereading,* is described by many who have studied the lives of patients in psychiatric hospitals (Rosenhan, 1973; Schur, 1984; Goffman, 1961, 1963). If a patient says, "The staff here are being unfair to me," and the staff respond, "Of course he would think that—he's crazy," they have reread, or looped, his words through his status. His words have been heard in view of his stigma and dismissed for exactly that reason.

These dismissals serve a function. Dismissing another's experience of status-based mistreatment masks the possibility that one has escaped such treatment precisely because of one's privilege. If we do not acknowledge that *their* status affects *their* treatment, we need not acknowledge that *our* status affects *our* treatment. Thus, we avoid the larger truth that those who are treated well, those who are treated poorly, and all the rest in between are always evaluated both as individuals and as occupants of particular esteemed and disesteemed categories.

THE EXPERIENCE OF STIGMA

We have so far considered the privileges conferred by some master statuses; now we examine the stigma conferred by other master statuses.

In his classic analysis of stigma, sociologist Erving Goffman (1963) distinguished between the *discredited,* whose stigma is immediately apparent to an observer (for example, race, sex, some disabilities), and the *discreditable,* whose stigma can be hidden (for example, sexual orientation, cognitive disabilities, or social class). Since stigma plays out differently in the lives of the discredited and the discreditable, each will be examined separately.

The Discreditable: "Passing"

The discreditable are those who are *passing,* that is, not publicly acknowledging the stigmatized statuses they occupy. (Were they to acknowledge that status, they would become discredited.) The term *passing* comes from "passing as white," which emerged as a phenomenon after 1875 when southern states reestablished racial segregation through hundreds of "Jim Crow"[3] laws. At that point, some African Americans passed as white as a way to get better-paying jobs.

> [S]ome who passed as white on the job lived as black at home. Some lived in the North as white part of the year and as black in the South the rest of the time. More men passed than women . . . the vast majority who could have passed permanently did not do so, owing to the pain of family separation, condemnation by most blacks, their fear of whites, and the loss of the security of the black community. . . . Passing as white probably reached an all-time peak between 1880 and 1925. (Davis, 1991:56–57)

"Passing as white" is now quite rare and strongly condemned by African Americans. We will use the term *passing* here to refer to those who have not made

---

[3]"Jim Crow" was "a blackface, singing-dancing-comedy characterization portraying black males as child-like, irresponsible, inefficient, lazy, ridiculous in speech, pleasure-seeking, and happy, [and was] a wide-spread stereotype of blacks during the last decades before emancipation . . . " (Davis, 1991:51). Whites created segregation in the South after the Civil War by imposing what were called "Jim Crow" laws.

their stigmatized status evident. For example, in Reading 8, John Tehranian describes the ways Muslim Americans may sometimes mask their identity. "Passing" is similar to the phrase "being in the closet," which is usually applied to gays. Steven Seidman, in Reading 27, argues that passing was at its peak for lesbian and gay Americans between 1950 and 1980 and plays somewhat less of a role in people's lives now. Still, it remains a significant concern and topic of discussion for both gays and straights.

One may engage in passing by chance as well as by choice. For example, the presumption that everyone is heterosexual can have the effect of putting gay people in the closet even when they had not intended to be. During a series of lectures on the family, one of our faculty colleagues realized that he had been making assignments, lecturing, and encouraging discussion under the assumption that all of the students in the class had, or wanted to have, heterosexual relationships. His actions forced gay and lesbian students to choose between announcing or remaining silent about their status. Had he assumed that students would be involved only with others of the same race, he would have created a similar situation for those in interracial relationships. Thus, assumptions about others' private lives—for example, by asking whether someone is married—may have the effect of making them choose between a lie lying or an announcement of something they may consider private.

Since most heterosexuals assume that everyone is heterosexual, many social encounters either put gay people in the closet or require that they announce their status. For example, in the first session of one class, a student opened his remarks by saying, "Well, you all know I am a gay man, and as a gay man I think. . . ." The buzz of conversation stopped, other students stared at him, and one asked, "How would we know you were gay?" The student pointed to a pink triangle he had pinned to his book bag and explained that he thought they knew that someone wearing it would be gay. (Pink triangles were assigned to gay men during the Nazi era. Still, his logic was questionable: Anyone supportive of gay rights might wear the triangle.) This announcement—which moved the student from a discreditable to a discredited status—may have been intended to keep his classmates from making overtly antigay comments in his presence. His strategy was designed to counter the negative consequences of passing.

> Every encounter with a new classful of students, to say nothing of a new boss, social worker, loan officer, landlord, doctor, erects new closets [that] . . . exact from at least gay people new surveys, new calculations, new draughts and requisitions of secrecy or disclosure. Even an *out* gay person deals daily with interlocutors about whom she doesn't know whether they know or not [or whether they would care]. . . . The gay closet is not a feature only of the lives of gay people. But for many gay people it is still the fundamental feature of social life; there can be few gay people . . . in whose lives the closet is not a shaping presence. (Sedgwick, 1990:68)

Inadvertent passing is also experienced by those whose racial status is not immediately apparent. An African American acquaintance of ours who looks white is often in settings in which others do not know that she is African American—or in which she does not know if they know. Thus, she must regularly decide how and when to convey that information. This is important to her as a way to discourage racist remarks, since whites sometimes assume it is acceptable to make racist remarks to one another (as men may assume it is acceptable to make sexist remarks to other men, or as straights presume it acceptable to make antigay remarks to those they think are also straight). It is also important to her that others know she is black so that they understand the meaning of her words—so that they will hear her words through her status as an African American woman. Those whose stigma is not apparent must go to some lengths to avoid being in the closet by virtue of others' assumptions.

Those with relatively invisible disabilities also face the tension of inadvertent passing. Beth Omansky, in Reading 35, describes the experiences of those who are legally, rather than totally, blind. Observers who assume the person is fully sighted can react with disbelief or even anger when they learn otherwise; others may insist that the person behave as if they were totally blind, to avoid confusing observers. Either way, the person suffers the consequence of inadvertent passing.

Still, passing may be an intentional choice. For example, one of our students, who was in the process of deciding that he was gay, had worked for many years at a local library, where he became friends with several of his coworkers. Much of the banter at work, however, involved disparaging gay, or presumably gay, library patrons. As he grappled with a decision about his own sexual identity, his social environment reminded him that being gay is a stigmatized status in American society. This student did not so much face prejudice personally (since he was not "out" to his work friends) as he faced an "unwilling acceptance of himself by individuals who are prejudiced against persons of the kind he can be revealed to be" (Goffman, 1963:42). Thus, he was not the person his friends took him to be. While survey data indicate that those who personally know a gay man hold more positive feelings about gays in general (Herek and Glunt, 1993), the decision to publicly reveal a stigma that others have gone on record as opposing is not made lightly.

Revealing stigma changes one's interactions, even with those who are not particularly prejudiced. Such revelations are likely to alter important relationships. Parents sometimes disown gay children, just as they do children involved in interracial relationships. Thus, the decision to pass or be "out" is not easily made. For the discreditable, what Goffman euphemistically described as "information management" is at the core of one's life. "To tell or not to tell; to let on or not to let on; to lie or not to lie; and in each case, to whom, how, when, and where" (Goffman, 1963:42). Such choices are faced daily by those who are discreditable—not just by those who are gay and lesbian, but also by those who are poor, have been imprisoned, attempted suicide, terminated a pregnancy through abortion, are HIV-positive, are drug or alcohol dependent, or who have been the victims of incest or rape. By contrast, those who do not occupy stigmatized statuses don't have to invest emotional energy in monitoring information about themselves; they can choose to talk openly about their personal history.

Passing has both positive and negative aspects. On the positive side, passing lets the stigmatized person exert some power over the situation; the person controls the information, the flow of events, and their privacy. By withholding his or her true identity until choosing to reveal it, the person may create a situation in which others' prejudices are challenged. Passing also limits one's exposure to verbal and physical abuse, allows for the development of otherwise forbidden relationships, and improves employment security by minimizing one's exposure to discrimination.

On the negative side, passing consumes a good deal of time, energy, and emotion. It introduces deception and secrecy even into close relationships. Passing also denies others the opportunity to prove themselves unprejudiced, and it makes one vulnerable to blackmail by those who do know about one's stigma.

The Discredited: The Problems of Visibility

While the discreditable face problems of invisibility, *visibility* is the problem for those who are discredited. Those who are discredited suffer from undue attention and are subject to being stereotyped.

Being discredited means that one's stigma is immediately apparent to others. As essayist bell hooks describes, those who are discredited often have little patience for those who at least have the option of passing.

> Many of us have been in discussions where a non-white person—a black person—struggles to explain to white folks that while we can acknowledge that gay people of all colors are harassed and suffer exploitation and domination, we also recognize that there is a significant difference that arises because of the visibility of dark skin. . . . While it in no way lessens the severity of such suffering for gay people, or the fear that it causes, it does mean that in a given situation the apparatus of protection and survival may be simply not identifying as gay. In contrast, most people of color have no choice. No one can hide, change, or mask dark skin color. White people, gay and straight, could show greater understanding of the impact of racial oppression on people of color by not attempting to make these oppressions synonymous, but rather by showing the ways they are linked and yet differ. (hooks, 1989:125)

For the discredited, stigma is likely to always shape interaction even though its effect may not play out in ways one can easily determine. Florynce Kennedy, a black activist in the civil rights and women's movements, once commented that the problem with being black in America was that you never knew whether what happened to you, good or bad, was because of your talents or because you were black (Kennedy, 1976). This situation was described in 1903 by sociologist W. E. B. Du Bois as the "*double consciousness*" of being black in America. The concept was key to Du Bois's classic, *The Souls of Black Folk,* for which he was rightfully judged "the father of serious black thought as we know it today" (Hare, 1982:xiii). Du Bois described double consciousness this way:

> the Negro . . . [is] gifted with a second-sight in this American world—a world which yields him no true self-consciousness, but only lets him see himself through the revelation of the other world. It is a peculiar sensation, this double consciousness, this sense of always looking at one's self through the eyes of others, of measuring one's soul by the tape of a world that looks on in amused contempt and pity. One ever feels his twoness. . . . (1982:45)

This is the sense of seeing oneself through the eyes of a harshly critical other, and it relates to our discussion of objectification in the first Framework Essay. When those who are stigmatized view themselves from the perspective of the nonstigmatized, they have reduced themselves to objects. This theme of double or "fractured" consciousness can also be found in contemporary analyses of women's experience.

The greatest effect of being visibly stigmatized is on one's life chances—literally, one's chances for living. Thus, the readings in this book detail differences in income, employment, health, lifespan, education, targeting for violence, and the likelihood of arrest and imprisonment. In this essay, however, we will consider the more mundane difficulties created by stigmatization, particularly the sense of being "on stage."

The discredited often have the feeling of being watched or on display when they are in settings dominated by nonstigmatized people. For example, when women walk through male-dominated settings, they often feel they are on display in terms of their physical appearance. Asian, black, and Latino students in majority white universities often describe a sense of being on display in campus dining facilities. In such cases, the discredited are likely to feel that others are judging them in terms of their stigma.

As sociologist Rosabeth Moss Kanter (1980, 1993) has shown, this impression is probably true. When Kanter studied corporate settings in which one person was visibly different from the others, that person was likely to get a disproportionate share of attention. In fact, people in the setting were likely to closely monitor what the minority person did, which meant his or her mistakes were more likely to be noticed—and the mistakes of those in the rest of the group were more likely to be overlooked because everyone was busy watching the minority person. Even in after-work socializing, the minority person was still subject to disproportionate attention.

Kanter also found that the minority person's behavior was likely to be interpreted in terms of the prevailing stereotypes about the members of that category. For example, when there were only a few men in a setting dominated by women, the men were subject to intense observation, and their behavior was filtered through the stereotypes about men. Perceptions were distorted to fit the preexisting beliefs.

Without the presence of a visibly different person, members of a setting are likely to see themselves as different from one another in various ways. Through contrast with the visibly different person, however, they notice their own similarities. In this way, majority group members may construct dichotomies—"us" and "them"—out of settings in which there are a few who are different. It is not surprising that those who are visibly different sometimes isolate themselves in response.

Still, none of this is inevitable. Kanter argues that once minority membership in a setting reaches 15 percent, these processes abate. Until that point, however, those who are in the minority (or visibly stigmatized) are the subject of a good deal of attention. As a consequence, they are often accused of flaunting their difference, of being "so" black, Latino, gay, and so on—of making a show of their status.

This is a charge that the nonstigmatized often level at those who are stigmatized. Although there are certainly occasions in which the discredited may deliberately make a show of their status, Kanter's work indicates that when their numbers are low in a setting, they are likely to be charged with being too visible no matter what they do. When they are subjected to a disproportionate amount of attention and viewed through the lenses of stereotypes, almost anything the discredited do is likely to be noticed and attributed to the category to which they belong.

Those who are visibly stigmatized react to this excess of attention in various ways. Some are careful to behave in ways contrary to expectations. At other times, however, people may deliberately make reference to their stigmatized status. For example, in adolescence, light-skinned black men are often derided by their black and white peers as not "really" black, and so they may go to great lengths to counter that charge.

Overt displays of one's stigmatized status may also have an entertaining side. For example, many bilingual Latino students talk about how much they enjoy a loud display of Spanish when Anglos are present; some Asian American students have described their pleasure in pursuing extended no-English-used card games in public spaces on campus. Black and gay adolescents sometimes entertain themselves by loudly affecting stereotypical behavior and then watching the disapproving looks from observers. Those who do not occupy stigmatized statuses may better appreciate these displays by remembering their experience of deliberately acting like "obnoxious teenagers" in public settings. Thus, for some, flaunting their difference may also be fun.

In all, those who are visibly stigmatized—who cannot or will not hide their identity—generate a variety of mechanisms to try to neutralize that stigma and the undue attention that follows.

The Expectations of Those Who Share One's Stigma

The shame associated with stigma may keep people from affiliating with one another, as has sometimes been the case among disabled people; or stigma may be the grounds for coming together in collective pride, as has often been the case for American race and ethnic groups. For those stigmatized by color, sex, or social class, family members often provide the lessons about what to expect from those in and outside the category, as well as the "lessons" about how "people like us" are supposed to behave.[4] For those who are gay and lesbian, the lessons are usually provided later in life by members of the gay community.

Particularly for those with visible stigma, there are also frequent reminders that one will be seen as representative of *all* members of the category. Thus, many in stigmatized categories must factor in virtually everyone's opinion: What will others in my category think? What will those who are not stigmatized think? Indeed, they may even be criticized for failing to deal with themselves as stigmatized— "After all, who do you think you are?" In a sense, members of stigmatized categories may monitor one another much as they are policed by those outside the category, with the difference that those within their category can at least claim to be defending them.

This point is illustrated in a story by the late tennis champion Arthur Ashe (1993). (Ashe was the first, and still only, African American to win tennis's Grand Slam singles title.) Ashe described watching his daughter play with a gift she had just received—a white doll—as they sat in the audience of a televised match in his honor. When the cameras panned his section of seats, he realized that he needed

---

[4]*People Like Us* (2001) is a well-known PBS documentary about social class in America. One message it describes is "don't get above your raising."

to get the doll away from his daughter or risk the anger of some black viewers who would argue that by letting his child play with a white doll, he appeared to be a bad role model for the black community.

A different example is provided by a Mexican American acquaintance who worked in an office with only a few other Hispanics, most of whom felt that the routes to upward mobility were closed to them. Together they drafted a letter to the firm's president detailing their concerns and seeking some corrective action. Although he had qualms about signing the letter, our acquaintance felt there was no alternative. Because he worked for management, he was then called in to explain his behavior, which his supervisor saw as disloyal. Thus, he was put in the position of having to explain that, as a Chicano, he could not have refused to sign the letter.

Codes of conduct for those in stigmatized categories often require loyalty to the group, a fact of life, of which, in this case, the supervisor was unaware of. Indeed, the operating rule for many in stigmatized categories is to avoid public disagreement with one another or public airing of the group's "dirty laundry." Such codes are not trivial, because when the codes are violated, members of stigmatized categories risk ostracism from a critical support network. The reality of discrimination makes it foolhardy to reject those who share one's stigma. What would it have meant to Arthur Ashe to lose the support of other African Americans? To whom would our acquaintance have turned in that organization had he refused to sign the letter? When they are unaware of these pressures, those in privileged categories may make impossible demands of those who are stigmatized; when they are aware of these pressures, however, such requests are clear tests of loyalty.

Complexities in the Experience of Privilege and Stigma

Separating out the discussion of privileged and stigmatized statuses, as we have done here, has the benefit of allowing us to focus on these processes, but it carries multiple risks, especially that of making people's experience appear less complicated than it is. There are several of these complexities to consider.

First, stigma doesn't always produce disadvantage; it can sometimes yield a benefit, but not as frequently as the benefits that follow from privilege. For example, discrimination is sometimes measured through what are called "audit studies." In this case, researchers select, match, and train people (called testers) to play the part of an applicant for a job or apartment. "By presenting equally qualified individuals who differ only by race or ethnicity, researchers can assess the degree to which racial considerations affect access to opportunities" (Pager and Shepherd, 2008:185). While audit studies have found evidence of racial discrimination in a variety of arenas (for example, in housing rental and purchase and call-backs on job resumes [Pager and Shepherd, 2008]), minority testers will still sometimes advance further than their white counterparts in a process. Thus, minority testers will sometimes experience preferential treatment, but they will not experience *as much* preferential treatment as their white counterparts.

Thus, concerns about "reverse discrimination" can often miss the mark. While blacks, Latinos, Asian Americans, or white women are sometimes favored—for example, in employment—they are not favored as *frequently* as white males. In her study of black and white graduates of a Baltimore technical school, Diedre Royster

(2003) offers an example of how this complexity can be ignored. One of her white informants described being turned down for a job with the state police. He was standing with a group of other white applicants, when one trooper approached them to say, "I'm sorry, fellas. Unfortunately, if you were black you would have had the job."

> For the whites involved in these sorts of interchanges, this is a win/win situation. The white applicant wins; he (or sometimes she) is reinforced in his (or her) belief that on merits he or she would have succeeded. . . . The white trooper (or other employing agency official dispensing bad advice) wins because he has found a way to deliver the news such that he and his agency will not encounter any hostility, despite the fact that they are rejecting applicants. [The trooper didn't say], "I'm sorry, fellas. We only had twenty-five places; two of them went to the sons of troopers, three went to cousins and neighbors, one went to a political connection, four were reserved for minority or female applicants (and frankly, those applicants had really strong records), and we had tons of great applicants for the remaining fifteen positions. In fact, we had three hundred applicants with scores higher than any of you." (Royster, 2003:170–71)

Thus, advantages may follow from stigma as well as privilege, though in different proportions and with different levels of visibility. This point is made by the dissenting justices in the Supreme Court's 2009 decision in *Ricci v. DeStefano* (Reading 41).

Second, analyzing stigma and privilege separately risks ignoring that those with privilege are nonetheless affected by stigma, even though they are not themselves stigmatized. For example, homophobia and sexism shape interaction between straight men—as Tim Beneke and C. J. Pascoe make clear in Readings 24 and 28—just as racism affects how white men and women interact; for example, in the expectation that white men need to be the protectors of white women. Likewise, the stigma of disability affects the friends and relatives of those who are disabled, interactions between those who are not disabled about injury and illness, and even people's response to their own bodies. In all, privilege exists in interaction with stigma.

Third, as we mentioned in the first Framework Essay, while it may appear that people can be easily separated into two categories—stigmatized and privileged—every individual occupies several master statuses. The privilege or stigma that might be associated with one status emerges in the context of *all* of one's other statuses. For example, a middle-class, heterosexual, Mexican American male may be privileged in terms of class, sex, and sexual orientation, but stigmatized by virtue of being Chicano. Given the invisibility of privilege, he is more likely to notice the ways in which his ethnic status stigmatizes him than to notice all the privileges that follow from his other statuses. Nevertheless, he is *simultaneously* all of his statuses; the privileges and disadvantages of each emerge in the context of all the others. Whereas an Anglo male and a Latino male may both be said to experience the privilege of sex, they do not experience the *same* privilege.

This is what sociologist Pat Hill Collins, in her classic article, "It's All in the Family: Intersections of Gender, Race, and Nation" (Reading 24), described as *intersectionality:* "As opposed to examining gender, race, class, and nation, as separate systems of oppression, intersectionality explores how these systems mutually construct one another." Intersectionality helps us focus on how people live at the intersection, or convergence, of multiple dichotomies. For example, getting assistance in the form of welfare as a single mother is much different than getting assistance in the form of unemployment as a man (Fraser; 1997). In the former, recipients must prove they are deserving, show how the money is spent, and are generally stigmatized. By contrast, the latter is not stigmatized, payments are in cash, and reporting requirements are relatively limited. Thus, individuals live at the *intersection* of multiple statuses. Shuddhabrata Sengupta describes this on a global dimension in Reading 55.

Fourth, while individuals may experience both privilege and stigma, some stigmas are so strong that they can cancel out the privileges other statuses might provide. This is often the case for people who are disabled. For example, the student quoted below describes how using a wheelchair "canceled out" expectations that she was intelligent.

> I find that people automatically assume your intelligence level is lower. They sort of talk maybe slower to you or in a patronizing way. . . . They don't speak right at you or act like you know anything. And they're always surprised to find out that I'm a college student. . . . They think "How could you go to U of M?" Sometimes they'll even say that. (McCune, 2001:7)

There is much evidence that the stigma of being black in America cancels privileges that might be expected to follow from being middle class. For example,

> A large body of published research reveals that racial and ethnic minorities experience a lower quality of health services and are less likely to receive even routine medical procedures than are white Americans. Relative to whites, African Americans—and in some cases, Hispanics—are less likely to receive hemodialysis and kidney transplantation, and are likely to receive a lower quality of basic clinical services such as intensive care, even when variations in such factors as insurance status, income, age, co-morbid conditions, and symptom expression are taken into account. . . . The majority of studies . . . find that racial and ethnic disparities remain even after adjustment for socioeconomic differences and other healthcare access-related factors. (Institute of Medicine, 2003:1,2)

Fifth, separating out discussions of privilege and stigma can mistakenly connote that they are equivalent. For example, when Latino students in one class talked about their pleasure in speaking Spanish, their Anglo friend immediately described how excluded she felt on those occasions. While they understood her reaction, the Latino students made it clear that they were not willing to forgo the opportunity to speak Spanish: their friend would just have to understand it wasn't anything personal. The question that emerged for the students listening to this exchange was about equivalent "rights." Isn't the Latino exclusion of Anglos the same as the Anglo exclusion of Latinos?

As a way to approach this, consider the following two statements about gays and straights. In what ways are the statements similar, and in what ways different?

> A heterosexual says, "I can't stand gays. I don't want to be anywhere around them."
> A gay says, "I can't stand straights. I don't want to be anywhere around them."

While the statements are almost identical, the speakers come from very different positions of power. A heterosexual could probably structure his or her life so as to rarely interact with anyone gay, or at least anyone self-identified as gay. Most important, however, the heterosexual's attitude is consistent with major social, political, legal, and religious practices. Thus, the heterosexual in this example speaks from a position of some power, if only that derived from alignment with dominant cultural practices.

This is not the case for the gay person in this example, who is unlikely to be able to avoid contact with straights—and who would probably pay a considerable economic cost for self-segregation if that were attempted. There are no powerful institutional supports for hatred of heterosexuals. Similarly, whatever pleasure there might be in exclusiveness, it would exist against a backdrop of relative powerlessness, discrimination, and stigmatization. The same might be said of men's disparagement of women compared with women's disparagement of men. As a student once wrote,

> As a male I have at times been on the receiving end of comments like, "Oh, you're just like all men," or "Why can't men show more emotion?" but these comments or the sentiments behind them do not carry any power to affect my status. Even in the instance of a black who sees me as a representative of all whites, his vision of me does not change my privileged status.

Thus, the exclusiveness of those in privileged statuses exists in a context of relative powerfulness, a sense of entitlement, infrequent discrimination based on master status, and a general ability to avoid those who might be prejudiced against people like themselves. The forms of exclusion available to stigmatized people are unlikely to tangibly affect the lives of those in privileged statuses. Being able to exclude someone from a dance or a club is not as significant as being able to exclude that person from a job or residence. This is what is meant when it is said that members of stigmatized categories may be prejudiced but not discriminatory; they do not have access to the institutional power by which to significantly affect the lives of those in nonstigmatized groups.

Similarly, the term *racist* carries different connotations for blacks and whites. As Bronson and Merryman describe in Reading 37, among whites, being color conscious is often considered to be a sign of being racist. If, as the civil rights movement taught, color should not make a difference in the way people are treated, whites who make a point of *not* noticing race argue that they are being polite and not racist (Frankenberg, 1993).

But given America's historical focus on race, it seems unrealistic for any of us to claim that we are oblivious to it. Although many consider it impolite to mention race, differential treatment does not disappear as a consequence. Further, a refusal to notice race conveys that being black, Asian, or Latino is a "defect" and that is indelicate (for whites) to mention. Thus, it can be argued that colorblindness is not really a strategy of politeness; rather, it is a strategy of power evasion. Because race, sex, sexual orientation, or disability clearly make a difference in people's lives, pretending not to see those statuses is a way to avoid noticing their effect. The alternative would be a strategy of awareness, that is, of paying systematic attention to the impact of these statuses on oneself and others (Frankenberg, 1993).

Finally, the understanding of what it means to be stigmatized or privileged changes in the course of a person's identity development. A composite overview of the changes in race and ethnic identity development (Cross, 1971, 1978; Hazen, 1992, 1994;

Helms, 1990; Morton and Atkinson, 1983; Thomas, 1970; Thomas and Thomas, 1971) helps make this point. These stages might also be applied to sex, class, and sexual orientation identities. One important caution is necessary, however: Not everyone necessarily goes through each of these stages. For example, it is argued that African Americans are rarely found in the first of the stages we detail below (Hazen, 1992).

For those in stigmatized statuses, the first stage of identity development involves an internalization of the culture's negative imagery. This stage may include the disparagement of others in one's group and a strong desire to be accepted by dominant group members. For women, this might mean being highly critical of other women. For people who are low income or gay, this stage might entail feelings of shame. For people of color, it might involve efforts to lighten one's skin, straighten one's hair, or have an eye tuck.

In the next stage, anger at the dominant culture emerges, usually as the result of specific encounters with discrimination. Philosopher Sandra Bartky (1990), focusing on women's discovery of the extent of sexism, describes this as a period in which sexism seems to be everywhere. Events and objects that previously had been neutral are discovered to be sexist; it becomes impossible to get through the day without becoming enraged—and the injustices one discovers are communicated to everyone within earshot. One's own behavior is also subject to increased scrutiny: "Am I being sexist to buy a doll for my niece?" Situations that used to be straightforward become moral tests.

This may be followed by what is sometimes called an immersion stage, because it involves involvement in one's own culture. In the previous stage, the individual is focused on evaluating and reacting to the dominant culture. In this stage, however, the focus shifts to one's own group. Dominant group members and the dominant group culture become less relevant to one's pursuits. This is often a period of participation in segregated activities and organizations as one seeks distance from dominant group members. Although anger is somewhat lessened here, the process of reevaluating one's old identity continues.

The final stage is described as a period of integration, as one's stigmatized status becomes integrated with the other aspects of one's life rather than taking precedence over them. Still, an opposition to prejudice and discrimination continues. At this point, one can distinguish between supportive and unsupportive dominant group members, and thus one is more likely to establish satisfying relations with them.

For those who do *not* occupy stigmatized statuses, the first stage of race or ethnic identity development is described as an unquestioning acceptance of dominant group values. This acceptance might take shape as being oblivious to discrimination or as espousing supremacist ideologies.

In the next stage, one becomes aware of others' stigmatization, often through an eye-opening encounter with discrimination. Such an experience may produce a commitment to social change or a sense of powerlessness. As is the case for those in stigmatized statuses, in this stage those in privileged statuses also find themselves overwhelmed by all the forms of discrimination they see, often accompanied by a sense of personal guilt. In an attempt to affiliate and offer assistance, they may seek alliances with those in stigmatized statuses. On college campuses, this timing may not be promising, since many of those in stigmatized statuses are at a high level of anger at those in privileged groups.

We have sometimes had white students of European ancestry describe a kind of envy that emerges at this point. As one said, black and Latino/a ethnic identity made him feel like "I just don't have anything." Even though his own ancestry was a mix of Russian Jew, Italian Catholic, and Scotch Irish Protestant, none of these seemed as compelling as the black, Asian, and Hispanic identities he saw around him.

This student's reaction reflects the transformed ethnic identity of the grandchildren and great-grandchildren of people who arrived in the peak immigration period of 1880 to 1920. At that time, Hungarians, Bohemians, Slovaks, Czechs, Poles, Russians, and Italians differed culturally and linguistically from one another and from the Irish, German, Scandinavian, and English immigrants who preceded them. Over the generations—and through intermarriage—this ethnic distinctiveness has been replaced by a socioeconomic "convergence" (Alba, 1990). Among non-Hispanic whites, ethnic ancestry no longer shapes occupation, residence, or political interest, nor is it the basis of the creation of communities of interest.[5] While many enjoy ethnic food and celebrations or have strong feelings attached to stories of immigration, the attachment is likely to be symbolic rather than meaningful. Ethnic identifications are also more likely to be situational and self-selected—for example, highlighting the Russian but ignoring the Irish and German sides of the family.

Eventually, however, those in privileged statuses focus less on trying to win the approval of those in stigmatized groups and instead explore the history of privileged and stigmatized statuses. Learning how privilege has affected one's own life is often a central question in this period.

The final stage involves integrating one's privileged statuses with all the other aspects of one's life, recognizing those in stigmatized categorizations as distinctive individuals rather than romanticizing them as a category ("just because oppressors are bad, doesn't mean that the oppressed are good" [Spivak, 1994]), and understanding that many with privilege have worked effectively against discrimination.

Passage through the stages of ethnic or racial identity is positively related to self-esteem for all American race and ethnic groups, but the relationship is stronger for those who are Asian American, African American, and Latino than for those who are white (Hazen, 1994:55). Indeed, on various measures of self-esteem, African

---

[5]An exception to the process of convergence among European-originated groups may be white, urban, Catholic ethnics. Throughout the 19th century, American Catholic churches were established as specifically ethnic churches (called "nationality churches"). These mostly urban churches were tailored to serve a particular ethnic group, which often included sending a priest from the home country who spoke the immigrants' native language. Thus, within a single urban area one might find separate Irish, Italian, and Polish Catholic churches, as well as effectively separate Catholic schools. The formation of ethnic churches meant that parishes also became ethnically segregated. On occasion, those parishes came to constitute stable, distinctive, working-class ethnic enclaves, for example, such as those found in Chicago. In these cases, ethnic identity continues as an active, viable reality.

Americans score significantly higher than those in other race or ethnic groups (Hazen, 1992).

CONCLUSION

In all, focusing on stigma and privilege uncovers social processes that might otherwise be invisible, but also risks understating the complexity of people's experiences. Indeed, building an analysis around stigma highlights victim status, as if the entire experience of a group could be characterized by stigma rather than coping and resistance. This point is illustrated in a classroom conversation we once observed, in which an African American student explained to his white classmates that he and his sister both self-identified as black, even though their mother was white. At that point a white student asked why he didn't call himself white since he looked white and that status would yield him more privilege. In response, he detailed all the qualities he prized in the black community and said he would never give up that status to be white. Much of what he said was new to the white students; many had never thought there was anything positive about being black in America.

The student's question reflected the common assumption that those who are stigmatized wish they belonged to the privileged group. Yet the woman who had asked the question was clear that she never wanted to be a male, which was equally surprising to the men in the class. Thus, many men presume there is nothing positive about being female, many straights assume there is nothing positive about being gay, many nondisabled people assume that disability ensures misery and loneliness, and many in the middle and upper classes assume there is nothing positive in life for those who are poor. But most people value and appreciate the statuses they occupy. We may wish those statuses weren't stigmatized or overprivileged, but that does not mean we would want to be other than who we are.

Our goal in this essay was to provide you with a framework by which to make sense of people's experience of privilege and stigma. Because there is a great deal of material that illustrates privilege and stigma, for this section we have tried to select readings with broad applicability.

KEY CONCEPTS

discredited and discreditable The discredited are those whose stigma is known or apparent to others. The discreditable are those whose stigma is unknown or invisible to others; they are not yet discredited. (pages 205–210)

double consciousness A concept first offered by W. E. B. Du Bois to describe seeing oneself (or members of one's group) through the eyes of a critical, dominant group member. (page 208)

entitlement The belief that one has the right to respect, protection, reward, and other privileges. (page 203)

looping or rereading Interpreting (and usually dismissing) someone's words or actions because of the status that the person occupies. (page 205)

marked and unmarked statuses A marked status is one identified as "special" in some way, for example, a *blind* musician or a *woman* doctor. Unmarked statuses, such as musician or doctor, do not have such qualifiers. (page 204)

passing Not revealing a stigmatized identity. (pages 205–208)

privilege The advantages provided by some statuses. (pages 195–204)

REFERENCES

Alba, Richard D. 1990. *Ethnic Identity: The Transformation of White America.* New Haven, CT: Yale University Press.

Amnesty International. 2009. Immigrants Languish in Detention in U.S. March 26. Retrieved on June 25, 2010 (http://www.amnesty.org/en/news-and-updates/news/migrants-languish-detention-us-20090326).

Ashe, Arthur. 1993. *Days of Grace.* New York: Ballantine.

Associated Press. 2003. Are Legacy College Admissions Racist? March 5.

Atencia, Diana P. 1999. Deportation Defense Under 1996 Laws. Retrieved June 22, 2010 (http://library.findlaw.com/1999/Nov/1/129798.html).

Bartky, Sandra. 1990. *Femininity and Domination: Studies in the Phenomenology of Oppression.* New York: Routledge.

Carter, Tom. 2002. Profiling Is "Flawed" Tool to Beat Terror. *The Washington Times,* January 14, 12.

Cary, Lorene. 1991. *Black Ice.* New York: Knopf.

Cross, W. E., Jr. 1971. The Negro-to-Black Conversion Experience: Toward a Psychology of Black Liberation. *Black World,* 20 (9):13–17.

———. 1978. The Thomas and Cross Models of Psychological Nigrescence: A Review. *The Journal of Black Psychology,* 5(1):13–31.

Davis, F. James. 1991. *Who Is Black? One Nation's Definition.* University Park, PA: Pennsylvania University Press.

Dixon, Travis L. and Daniel Linz. 2000. Overrepresentation and Underrepresentation of African Americans and Latinos as Lawbreakers on Television News. *Journal of Communication* 50:131–154.

Du Bois, W. E. B. 1982. *The Souls of Black Folk.* New York: Penguin. (Originally published in 1903.)

Entman, Robert. 1990. Modern Racism and the Image of Blacks in Local Television News. *Critical Studies in Mass Communication* 7:332–345.

Entman, Robert. 1994. Representation and Reality in the Portrayal of Blacks on Network Television News. *Journalism Quarterly* 71:509–520.

Entman, Robert M. and Andrew Rojecki. 2000. *The Black Image in the White Mind: Media and Race in America.* Chicago: University of Chicago Press.

Ettinger, Maia. 1994. The Pocahontas Paradigm, or Will the Subaltern Please Shut Up? *Tilting the Tower,* edited by Linda Garber, 51–55. New York: Routledge.

Frankenberg, Ruth. 1993. *White Women, Race Matters: The Social Construction of Whiteness.* Minneapolis: University of Minnesota Press.

Fraser, Nancy. 1997. *Justice Interruptus: Critical Reflections on the "Postsocialist" Condition.* New York: Rutledge.

French, Sally. 1996. Simulation Exercises in Disability Awareness Training: A Critique. *Beyond Disability: Towards an Enabling Society,* edited by Gerald Hales, 114–23. London: Sage Publications.

Gallup, Inc. 2007. Tolerance for Gay Rights at High-Water Mark. Retrieved June 24, 2010 (http://www.gallup.com/poll/27694/tolerance-gay-rights-highwater-mark.aspx).

Gallup, Inc. 2010. Americans' Acceptance of Gay Relations Crosses 50% Threshold. May 3–6. Retrieved June 23, 2010 (http://www.gallup.com/poll/135764/americans-acceptance-gay-relations-crosses-threshold.aspx).

Goffman, Erving. 1961. *Asylums.* New York: Doubleday Anchor.

———. 1963. *Stigma: Notes on the Management of Spoiled Identity.* Englewood Cliffs, NJ: Prentice-Hall.

Hare, Nathan. 1982. W. E. Burghart Du Bois: An Appreciation, pp. xiii–xxvii in *The Souls of Black Folk.* New York: Penguin. (Originally published in 1969.)

Harris, David. 2002. Flying While Arab: Lessons from the Racial Profiling Controversy. *Civil Rights Journal,* 6(1):8–14.

———. 2003. The Reality of Racial Disparity in Criminal Justice: The Significance of Data Collection. *Law and Contemporary Problems,* 66(3):71–95.

Hazen, Sharlie Hogue. 1992. *The Relationship between Ethnic/Racial Identity Development and Ego Identity Development.* Ph.D. proposal, Department of Psychology, George Mason University.

———. 1994. *The Relationship between Ethnic/Racial Identity Development and Ego Identity Development.* Ph.D. dissertation, Department of Psychology, George Mason University.

Helms, J. E. 1990. An Overview of Black Racial Identity Theory. *Black and White Racial Identity: Theory, Research, and Practice,* edited by J. E. Helms, 9–33. New York: Greenwood Press.

Herek, Gregory M. 1992. The Social Context of Hate Crimes. *Hate Crimes: Confronting Violence against Lesbians and Gay Men,* edited by Gregory Herek and Kevin Berrill, 89–104. Newbury Park, CA: Sage.

———, and Eric K. Glunt. 1993. Heterosexuals Who Know Gays Personally Have More Favorable Attitudes. *The Journal of Sex Research,* 30:239–44.

Hocker, Cliff. 2004. Worst Labor Market for Black Professionals in 25 Years. *Black Enterprise,* May, 26.

hooks, bell. 1989. *Talking Back: Thinking Feminist, Thinking Black.* Boston: South End Press.

Human Rights Watch. 2007. U.S.: Mandatory Deportation Law Harms American Families. July 17. Retrieved on June 22, 2010 (http://www.hrw.org/en/news/2007/07/17/us-mandatory-deportation-laws-harm-american-families).

Institute on Race and Justice. Racial Profiling Data Collection Resource Center. Northeastern University. Retrieved on June 21, 2010 (http://www.racialprofilinganalysis.neu.edu/index.php)

Institute of Medicine, Board on Health Sciences. 2003. *Unequal Treatment: Confronting Racial and Ethnic Disparities in Health Care.* Washington, DC: National Academy of Sciences.

Johnson, Lloyd D., Patrick M. O'Malley, Jerald G. Bachman, and John E. Schulenberg. 2004. *Monitoring the Future Survey Results on Drug Use, 1975–2003.* Bethesda, Md.: National Institute on Drug Abuse.

Kanter, Rosabeth Moss. 1993. *Men and Women of the Corporation.* New York: Basic Books. (Originally published in 1976.)

———, with Barry A. Stein. 1980. *A Tale of 'O': On Being Different in an Organization.* New York: Harper and Row.

Kennedy, Florynce. 1976. *Color Me Flo: My Hard Life and Good Times.* Englewood Cliffs, NJ: Prentice-Hall.

Kimmel, Michael S., and Michael A. Messner, eds. 1989. *Men's Lives.* New York: Macmillan.

Kocieniewski, David. 2002. New Jersey Troopers Avoid Jail in Case That Highlighted Profiling. *The New York Times,* January 15, A1.

Lester, Joan. 1994. *The Future of White Men and Other Diversity Dilemmas.* Berkeley, CA: Conari Press.

McCune, Pat. 2001. What Do Disabilities Have to Do with Diversity? *About Campus* May-June, pp. 5–12.

McIntosh, Peggy. 1989. White Privilege: Unpacking the Invisible Knapsack. *Peace and Freedom* July/August 1989. (No page numbers.) Wellesley Centers for Women, Wellesley, MA.

Morton, G., and D. R. Atkinson. 1983. Minority Identity Development and Preference for Counselor Race. *Journal of Negro Education,* 52(2):156–61.

New York State Task Force on Police-on-Police Shootings. 2010. *Reducing Inherent Danger: Report of the Task Force on Police-on-Police Shootings.* Retrieved on June 20, 2010 (http://www.ny.gov/governor/reports/pdf/Police_on_Police.pdf).

Oliver, Mary Beth. 1999. Caucasian Viewers' Memory of Black and White Criminal Suspects in the News. *Journal of Communication* 49(3):46–60.

Oliver, Mary Beth, Ronald J. Jackson II, Niddi N. Moses, and Celnisha L. Dangerfield. 2004. The Face of Crime: Viewers' Memory of Race-Related Facial Features of Individuals Pictures in the News. *Journal of Communication* 54(1):88–104.

Pager, Devah and Hana Shepherd. 2008. The Sociology of Discrimination: Racial Discrimination in Employment, Housing, Credit, and Consumer Markets. *Annual Review of Sociology* 34:181–209.

Pew Hispanic Center. 2008. 2008 National Survey of Latinos. September 18. Retrieved on June 25, 2010. http://pewhispanic.org/files/reports/93.pdf

Preston, Julia. 2008. Perfectly Legal Immigrants until They Applied for Citizenship. *New York Times.* April 12. Retrieved June 22, 2010 (http://www.nytimes.com/2008/04/12/us/12naturalize.html#).

Primetime: What Would You Do? Teen Vandals. February 25, 2009 http://abcnews.go.com/video/playerIndex?id=6953414

Richards, Randall. 2003. Associated Press. *The Seattle Times.* Retrieved July 5, 2010 (http://www.thefreelibrary.com/The+deportation+of+crime+U.S.+policy+causing+problems+elsewhere.(ROP...-a0110245579).

Reinarman, Craig and Harry G. Levine. 2004. Crack in the Rearview Mirror: Deconstructing Drug War Mythology. *Social Justice* 31(1-2):182–197

Rosenhan, D. L. 1973. On Being Sane in Insane Places. *Science,* 179:250–58.

Ross, Stephen, and John Yinger. 2002. *The Color of Credit: Mortgage Discrimination, Research Methodology, and Fair-Lending Enforcement.* Cambridge, MA: MIT Press.

Royster, Diedre A. 2003. *Race and the Invisible Hand: How White Networks Exclude Black Men from Blue Collar Jobs.* Berkeley: University of California Press.

Schur, Edwin. 1984. *Labeling Women Deviant: Gender, Stigma, and Social Control.* New York: Random House.

Sedgwick, Eve Kosofsky. 1990. *The Epistemology of the Closet.* Berkeley: University of California Press.

Smith, Tom W. 2001. *Intergroup Relations in a Diverse America: Data from the 2000 General Social Survey.* The American Jewish Committee. www.ajc.org.

Spivak, Gayatre. 1994. George Mason University Cultural Studies presentation.

Stabile, Carol. 2006. *White Victims, Black Villains: Gender, Race, and Crime News in U.S. Culture.* New York: Routledge.

Stevens, Jacqueline. 2008. Amid Anti-Immigrant Fervor, ICE Deporting More American Citizens. *Nation.* June 10. Retrieved June 22, 2010 (http://www.alternet .org/immigration/87467/?page=entire).

Tehranian, John. 2009. *Whitewashed: America's Invisible Middle Eastern Minority.* New York: New York University Press.

Thomas, C. 1970. Different Strokes for Different Folks. *Psychology Today* 4(4):48–53, 78–80.

———, and S. Thomas. 1971. Something Borrowed, Something Black. In *Boys No More: A Black Psychologist's View of Community,* edited by C. Thomas. Beverly Hills, CA: Glencoe Press.

Tokarczyk, Michelle M. 2004. Promises to Keep: Working Class Students and Higher Education. *What's Class Got to Do with It? American Society in the Twenty-First Century,* edited by Michael Zweig, 161–167. Ithaca, NY: ILR Press.

U.S. Bureau of the Census. 2008. Median Income of People with Income in Constant (2007) Dollars by Sex, Race, and Hispanic Origin: 1990 to 2007. U.S. Census Bureau, *Current Population Reports,* P60–235.

U.S. Immigration and Customs Enforcement. 2010. Retrieved June 22, 2010 (http://www.ice.gov/pi/ specialregistration/archive.htm#what).

Volpp, Leti. 2002. The Citizen and the Terrorist. *UCLA Law Review* 49(5):1575–1600.

Walmsley, Roy. n.d. World Prison Population List. Seventh edition. International Centre for Prison Studies, King College London. Retrieved June 21, 2010 (http://www.kcl.ac.uk/depsta/law/research/icps/ downloads/world-prison-pop-seventh.pdf0)

Western, Bruce. 2006. *Punishment and Inequality in America.* New York: Russell Sage.

Williams, Richard, Reynold Nesiba, and Eileen Diza McConnell. 2005. The Changing Face of Inequality in Home Mortgage Lending. *Social Problem* 52(2):181–208.

Williams, Patricia J. 1991. Teleology on the Rocks. *The Alchemy of Race and Rights.* Cambridge, MA: Harvard University Press.

RACE AND ETHNICITY

Formulating Identity in a Globalized World

Carola Suárez-Orozco

Increasing globalization has stimulated an unprecedented flow of immigrants worldwide. These newcomers—from many national origins and a wide range of cultural, religious, linguistic, racial, and ethnic backgrounds—challenge a nation's sense of unity. Globalization threatens both the identities of the original residents of the areas in which newcomers settle and those of the immigrants and their children. Integrating immigrants and the subsequent generations into the receiving society is a primary challenge of globalization; failing to do so, however, will have long-term social implications. The ability to formulate an identity that allows comfortable movement between worlds will be at the very heart of achieving a truly "global soul" (Iyer 2000).

At the beginning of the new millennium, there are over 175 million immigrants and refugees worldwide. In the United States alone, 32.5 million, or approximately 11.5 percent of the population, are immigrants (U.S. Bureau of the Census 2000). This is not simply a U.S. phenomenon, however. In 2000, 4.2 percent of the population in the United Kingdom and 5.6 percent of the population in France, was foreign-born. In other nations the percentage of foreign-born is greater than in the United States: 11.8 percent in Sweden, 17.4 percent in Canada, and 23.6 percent in Australia (Migration Information 2003). In almost all these countries, this trend has been steadily increasing. It is important to note that these figures reflect only the first generation. If one considers the children of these immigrants—the second generation—clearly,

many more individuals are involved in the task of negotiating a new identity that synthesizes elements of the culture of origin with those of the receiving culture.

The ever increasing flows of individuals from myriad backgrounds provide a number of aesthetic, cognitive, social, and marketplace opportunities. The ability to code-switch—to move fluidly between languages and cultures—has obvious social advantages. Bicultural and bilingual competence enables individuals to fluidly adapt themselves to evolving situations (Titone 1989). This skill has advantages for entering many professions in the business, diplomatic, and social service sectors. Sommer argues that bilingualism is essential for democracy as it "depends on constructing those miraculous and precarious points of contact from mismatches among codes and people" (Sommer 2004). Indeed, shortly after the last large wave of migration at the turn of the twentieth century, Stonequist argued that the marginality afforded to those individuals in between cultures could lead to individuals who play the essential role of cultural ambassadors adept at interpreting and bridging difference (Stonequist 1937). The cognitive flexibility that this multiple perspective taking requires is becoming an ever more essential trait for the global citizen (Gardner, this volume; Suárez-Orozco and Qin-Hilliard, this volume).

IMMIGRANT STRESS

Multiple pathways structure immigrants' journeys into their new homes. Immigrants and refugees are motivated by a variety of factors—relief from political, religious, or ethnic persecution (in the case of refugees); economic incentives; as well as the opportunity to be reunited with family members. Although for many immigrant families, migration results in substantial gains, it provides many challenges to the individuals involved. It removes individuals from many of their relationships and predictable contexts—extended families and

Carola Suárez-Orozco is co-director of the Howard Immigration Projects and a scholar-in-residence at the Ross Institute.

friends, community ties, jobs, living situations, customs, and often languages. Immigrants are stripped of many of their sustaining social relationships as well as the social roles that provide them with culturally scripted notions of how they fit into the world, resulting in acculturative stress (Berry 1997; C. Suárez-Orozco and M. Suárez-Orozco 2001).

Immigrant youth face particular challenges. They often immigrate not just to new homes but also to new family structures (C. Suárez-Orozco, Todorova, and Louie 2002). In our study of four hundred immigrant youth who came to the United States from a variety of origins, including Central America, China, the Dominican Republic, Mexico, and Haiti, we found that fully 85 percent of the youth in this project had been separated from one or both parents for periods of several months to several years (C. Suárez-Orozco et al. 2002). To compound this form of parental unavailability, many immigrant parents work long hours, rendering them relatively physically absent in the lives of their children. Further, depression and anger that may be associated with the migratory experience may make many immigrant parents psychologically unavailable to their children (Athey and Ahearn 1991). These forms of absence all too frequently leave immigrant children to their own devices long before it is developmentally ideal. Although in some cases it can lead to hyperresponsible children, in other cases it leads to depressed youth who are drawn to the lure of alternative family structures such as gangs—a particular risk for boys (Vigil 1988).

THE SECOND GENERATION

The challenges of the first generation are considerably different from those of the second generation. The first generation is largely concerned with surviving and adjusting to the new context. These immigrants may go through a variety of normative adverse reactions following the multiple losses of migration, including anxiety and depression. However, the first generation is protected from these psychological sequelae by several factors. The dual frame of reference by which immigrants can compare their current situation with that left behind often allows them to feel relatively advantaged in the new context (C. Suárez-Orozco and M. Suárez-Orozco 1995). Optimism is at the very heart of the immigrant experience: the possibility of a better tomorrow acts as both a tremendous motivator as well as a form of inoculation against encountered frustrations and barriers. Further, first-generation immigrants are often energized by the desire to support loved ones—by sending remittances home to those left behind, as well as by building the best possible life for their children. While not an easy road, it is one with a clear identity. Immigrants who arrive as adults maintain a sense of identity rooted deeply in their birthplaces. Many expatriates are, of course, quite comfortable in their new homeland. Nevertheless they tend to retain an outsider status as the cultural and linguistic hurdles are simply too high to be surmounted within one generation (C. Suárez-Orozco and M. Suárez-Orozco 2001).

The path for their children, the second generation, is less straightforward, offering a variety of pathways. For these youth, forging a sense of identity may be their single greatest challenge. Do they feel comfortable in their homeland? Do they feel accepted by the "native-born" of the host country? What relationship do they have with their parents' country of origin? Is their sense of identity rooted "here," "there," everywhere, or nowhere?

THE ARCHITECTURE OF CULTURAL IDENTITY

Stage versus Context

Erik Erikson (1968) argued that in the developmental stage of adolescence, identity is the critical maturational task. In forming an identity, youth attempt to create a self-identity that is consistent with how others view them. Identity is less challenging when there is continuity among the various social milieus youth encounter—home, school, neighborhood, and country. In the era of globalization, however, social spaces are more discontinuous and fractured than ever before.

A number of psychologists have claimed that identity goes through a variety of permutations during adolescence as the individual experiments with different identity strategies. Some argue that all youth move steadily from a stage of ethnic or "racial unawareness," to one of "exploration," to a final stage of an "achieved" sense of racial or ethnic identity (Marcia 1966). Others point out that the process of identity formation is, rather than being linear, more accurately described as "spiraling" back to revisit previous stages, each time from a different vantage point (Parham 1989).

Achieved and Ascribed Identities

Identity formation, I would argue, is not simply a process by which one passes through a variety of stages on the way to achieving a stable identity. Rather it is a process that is fluid and contextually driven. If raised in Beijing and immigrating as an adult, one may "discover" that one is "Asian" for the first time at age thirty. Prior to immigrating, that same individual in Beijing may never have considered her racial or ethnic identity (or if she did, it would be a neighborhood identity). In the Chinatown of the host society, the identity will be one of northern mainland Chinese origin (in contrast to Cantonese speakers from Hong Kong or Canton); but in the heartland of the host country the identity may become a more complex, "pan-Asian" construct. The social context is essential in predicting which identity is constructed (Suárez-Orozco 2000).

The tension between the dominant culture and minority newcomers lies at the heart of the ethnic and cultural identity formation drama of immigrants and their children (DeVos 1980). Youth are challenged to navigate between achieved identities and ascribed or imposed identities (C. Suárez-Orozco and M. Suárez-Orozco 2001). Achieved identity is the extent to which an individual achieves a sense of belonging—"I am a member of *this* group." An ascribed identity is imposed either by coethnics—"You are a member of *our* group"—or by members of the dominant culture—"You are a member of *that* group."

For some groups the imposed or ascribed identity is considerably stronger than for others. In the United States, for example, African identity is firmly ascribed, whereas Italian identity can be assumed at will. The degree to which ascribed origins are imposed may also evolve over time. At the turn of the twentieth century in Boston, having Irish origins had significant negative implications, whereas at the turn of the twenty-first century, being from Ireland merits little notice and can be articulated at will (for St. Patrick's Day events but not necessarily in a job interview).

Phenotypic racial features have considerable implications for the ease of assimilation. Historically, immigrants coming from Europe to the United States could more easily assimilate once they lost their accents and changed their names. The ability to join the mainstream unnoticed is more challenging when one is racially marked. Questions as to where one is "really from" or compliments made to Asian Americans who have been in the United States many generations on their English fluency lead to what law professor Frank H. Wu (2002) refers to as "perpetual foreigner syndrome." In this era of globalization, the fact that many immigrants of color originate in the developing world (Africa, Asia, the Caribbean, and Latin America) and enter postindustrial regions traditionally populated by Europeans (Europe, North America, Australia) makes "passing," or fully assimilating unnoticed, no longer possible for most new arrivals.

Contact with Cultures

Culture provides one with generally shared understandings and models for making meaning of one's experiences. Cultural beliefs present standards of behavior that are internalized over time, and cultural traditions offer a soothing sense of social safety. At the heart of these shared understandings are the interpersonal networks of relations in which one is embedded.

In order to maintain a sense of affinity with one's culture of origin, sustained contact is required. Regular visits back to the homeland—in what is described as a transnational existence—facilitates maintenance of the parent culture (Levitt 1996). Living in an ethnic enclave limits the opportunity for regular interaction with members of the mainstream culture. Ethnic communities, such as Chinatown in San Francisco, Mexican barrios in Los Angeles, the Dominican neighborhood in Washington Heights (in Manhattan), the Cuban enclave in Miami, and the like, nurture a sense of culture of origin without requiring return visits to the homeland. The strength of the effect of these ethnic neighborhoods and enclaves is determined by the density of the local ethnic population, the strength of the collective coethnic identity, the community's cohesiveness, and the availability of cultural role models.

If there is little contact with the culture of origin, however, then all of the "cultural lessons" fall upon the shoulders of the parents to teach. Parents are, no doubt, a critical source of information in the quest to form an identity. Immigration, however, undermines parents' ability to act as guides, by removing the "map of experience" necessary to successfully escort children in the new culture (Hoffman 1989). Without effortless proficiency in the new cultural expectations and practices, immigrant parents are less able to provide guidance in the ways of negotiating the currents of a complex society; in addition, they must rely on their children for cultural interpretations. As a seasoned immigrant comments to a prospective migrant in the novel *Accordion Crimes*, "the natural order of the world is reversed. The old learn from the children" (Proulx 1996).

The ease with which elements of the parent culture can be incorporated into the new culture will to some extent be affected by the "cultural distance" between the parent and new culture (Berry 1997). Youth growing up within dual contexts characterized by great degrees of dissimilarity between cultural beliefs and social practices are likely to suffer from greater identity confusion than those coming from more convergent cultural backgrounds (Arnett 2002). This would suggest that in the United States the children of rural Hmong in northern California (Fadiman 1998; Portes and Rumbaut 2001) or Yemeni immigrants in the Midwest would face more challenges than the children of Canadian immigrants in New England.

The fact that many immigrants enter highly segregated neighborhoods with large coethnic or minority populations complicates the potential for identification with mainstream culture. If there is little contact with the mainstream middle class in any form other than media representations encountered on television or in movies, identifying with the host culture becomes something of an abstraction.

Performing Identity

How does an individual demonstrate his ethnic affiliation? At the most basic level, the ethnic label an individual chooses signifies his identity (Maestes 2000; Waters 1996). Sociological research has used the self-selected label as a way of examining identity. Whether a second-generation person of Mexican origin calls herself Mexican or Mexican American, or Latina, or Chicana seems to be linked to quite different patterns of incorporation and engagement in schooling (Matute-Bianchi 1991; Portes and Rumbaut 2001; Waters 1996). Individuals who adopt a self-referential label that includes their parents' country of origin seem to do better in school than their counterparts who select a panethnicity (such as Hispanic or Latino) or who refer only to their country of residence (such as American). The same is true with self-selected labels adhered to by persons of Caribbean origin: Waters (1997) has demonstrated that Caribbean-origin youth who call themselves Jamaican American, for example, appear to have different perceptions of discrimination and opportunities than those who call themselves African American.

Feelings of belonging to rather than alienation from the various cultural groups an individual may be part of also has important implications (DeVos and Suárez-Orozco 1990). Whether or not one feels affiliation with and acceptance in the groups under consideration may be related to one's ability to incorporate elements of the culture into one's sense of self. Does the individual value his culture of origin? Does he feel accepted by other members of that culture? Is he drawn to the new culture (or cultures)? Does he feel welcome and incorporated into the new culture (or cultures)? Does he *wish* to be incorporated into the new culture, or does he find it alienating? These attitudes will have much to do with the fusion of culture that the individual internalizes (Maestes 2000).

Participation in a series of *ethnic activities,* as well as the *dominant culture's* activities and social practices, is one of the clearest ways in which cultural identity is performed (Maestes 2000). What language does the individual report feeling most comfortable using (Maestes 2000)? In what circumstances does she use the language of origin—spontaneously or under duress? What is the culture of the friends to whom she is drawn? Are these friends mostly persons of the individual's culture of origin, of the dominant culture, or of a range of origins? What religious practices are important, and to what degree? Do these practices occur on a daily basis, or are they more occasional, with a primarily social function? What foods does the individual most enjoy, particularly in social settings? What holidays does she celebrate? Are they largely those of the culture of origin, of the host society, or some combination? What entertainment choices does she make? Selections made in sports participation (baseball versus basketball versus soccer, for example), music (salsa versus rap versus pop), radio or television (ethnic versus mainstream), movies and videos (country of origin versus Hollywood versus an eclectic selection) can provide insight into relative comfort and affiliation with the points of cultural contact (Louie 2003).

The Ethos of Reception

The general social climate, or ethos of reception, plays a critical role in the adaptation of immigrants and their children (C. Suárez-Orozco and M. Suárez-Orozco 2001). Unfortunately, intolerance for newcomers is an all-too-common response all over the world. Discrimination against immigrants of color is particularly widespread and intense in many areas receiving large numbers of

new immigrants, including Europe (Suárez-Orozco 1996), the United States (Espenshade and Belanger 1998), and Japan (Tsuda 2003). As today's immigrants are more diverse than ever before in ethnicity, skin color, and religion, they are particularly subject to the pervasive social trauma of prejudice and social exclusion (Tatum 1997).

The exclusion can take a structural form (when individuals are excluded from the opportunity structure) as well as an attitudinal form (in the form of disparagement and public hostility). These structural barriers and the social ethos of intolerance and racism encountered by many immigrants of color intensify the stresses of immigration. Although the structural exclusion suffered by immigrants and their children is tangibly detrimental to their ability to participate in the opportunity structure, prejudicial attitudes and psychological violence also play a toxic role. Philosopher Charles Taylor argues that "our identity is partly shaped by recognition or its absence, often by the misrecognition of others, and so a person or group of people can suffer real damage, real distortion, if the people or society around them mirrors back to them a confining or demeaning or contemptible picture of themselves" (Taylor 1994). How can youth of immigrant origin incorporate the notion that they are unwanted "aliens" who do not warrant the most basic rights of education and health care?

The Social Mirror

Child psychoanalyst D. W. Winicott suggests that a child's sense of self is profoundly shaped by the reflections mirrored back to him by significant others (Winicott 1971). Indeed, all human beings are dependent upon the reflection of themselves mirrored by others. "Others" include not just the mother (which was Winicott's principal concern) but also relatives, adult caretakers, siblings, teachers, peers, employers, people on the street, and even the media (C. Suárez-Orozco 2000). When the reflected image is generally positive, the individual (adult or child) is able to feel that she is worthwhile and competent. When the reflection is generally negative, it is extremely difficult to maintain an unblemished sense of self-worth.

These reflections can be accurate or inaccurate. When the reflection is a positive distortion, the response to the individual may be out of proportion to his actual contribution or achievement. In the most benign case, positive expectations can be an asset. In the classic "Pygmalion in the Classroom" study, teachers who believed that certain children were brighter than others (based on the experimenter randomly assigning some children that designation, unsubstantiated in fact) treated the children more positively and assigned them higher grades (Rosenthal and Feldman 1991). It is possible that some immigrant students, such as Asians, benefit somewhat from positive expectations of their competence as a result of being members of a "model minority"—though no doubt at a cost (Takaki 1993).

It is the negative distortions, however, that are most worrisome. What is the effect for children who receive mirroring from society that is predominantly negative and hostile? Such is the case with many immigrant and minority children (see Maira, 2004). Commenting on the negative social mirroring toward Muslim students after September 11, Iraqi American Nuar Alsadir eloquently stated: "The world shouldn't be a funhouse in which we're forced to stand before the distorting mirror, begging for our lives" (Alsadir 2002). W. E. B. Du Bois famously articulated the challenge of what he termed "double-consciousness"—a "sense of always looking at one's self through the eyes of others, of measuring one's soul by the tape of a world that looks on in amused contempt and pity" (Du Bois 1903/1989). When the expectations are of sloth, irresponsibility, low intelligence, and even danger, the outcome can be toxic. When these reflections are received in a number of mirrors, including the media, classroom, and street, the outcome is devastating (Adams 1990).

Research from the Harvard Immigration Project, a study of youth immigrating to the United States from China, Central America, the Dominican Republic, Haiti, and Mexico, suggests that immigrant children are keenly aware of the prevailing ethos of hostility in the dominant culture (C. Suárez-Orozco 2000). A sample of four hundred children were asked to complete the sentence "Most Americans think that [Chinese, Dominicans, Central Americans, Haitians, Mexicans—depending on the child's country of origin] are _____." Disturbingly, fully 65 percent of the respondents provided a negative response to the sentence-completion task. The modal response was "bad"; others—even more disconcerting—included "stupid," "useless," "garbage," "gang members," "lazy," and "we don't exist" (C. Suárez-Orozco 2000).

What meanings do youth construct from and how do they respond to this negative social mirror? One possible pathway is for youth to become resigned to the negative reflections, leading to hopelessness and self-depreciation that may in turn result in low aspirations and self-defeating behaviors. The general affect associated with this pathway is depression and passivity. In this scenario, the child is likely to respond with self-doubt and shame, setting low aspirations in a kind of self-fulfilling prophecy: "They are probably right. I'll never be able to do anything." Other youth may mobilize to resist the mirrors and injustices they encounter. I differentiate between two types of resistance. The first is a project infused with hope, a sense of justice, and faith in a better tomorrow. The other form of resistance is eventually overcome by alienation leading to anomie, hopelessness, and a nihilistic view of the future. In this latter case, youth may actively resist the reflections they encounter but are unable to maintain hope for change or a better future. Without hope, the resulting anger and compensatory self-aggrandizement may lead to acting-out behaviors including the kinds of dystopic cultural practices typically associated with gang membership. For these youth, the response is "If you think I'm bad, let me show you just how bad I can be" (C. Suárez-Orozco and M. Suárez-Orozco 2001).

The social trajectories of youth are more promising for those who are able to actively maintain and cultivate a sense of hope for the future. Whether they are resigned, oblivious, or resistant to the reflections in the social mirror, those who are able to maintain hope are in fundamental ways partially inoculated to the toxicity they may encounter. These youth are better able to maintain pride and preserve their self-esteem. In these circumstances, their energies are mobilized in the service of day-to-day coping. Some may not only focus on their own advancement but also harness their energies in the service of their communities by volunteering to help others, acting as role models, or advocating and mobilizing for social change. In this scenario, youth respond to the negative social mirror as a goad toward "I'll show you I can make it in spite of what you think of me" (C. Suárez-Orozco and M. Suárez-Orozco 2001).

Social Disparagement and Academic Outcomes

Children of color are particularly subject to negative expectations that have profound implications for their academic performance (Weinstein 2002). Cross-cultural data from research focused on a variety of disparaged minorities in a number of contexts all over the world suggest that exposure to a negative social mirror adversely affects academic engagement. This research provides insight into a number of critical questions: In ethnically diverse and increasingly transnational societies, how does schooling relate to hierarchies of inequality (Freire 1995)? Does the educational system reproduce inequalities by replicating the existing social order? Or does schooling help to overcome social inequalities by emerging as an avenue for status mobility?

What is the experience of self in cultures where patterned inequality shapes social interactions? Anthropological cross-cultural evidence from a variety of regions suggests that the social context and ethos of reception plays an important role in immigrant adaptation. Ogbu (1978) has argued that minorities who were originally incorporated against their will through conquest and enslavement are more likely to give up on educational avenues as a route to social mobility than are those of immigrant origin who enter a new society voluntarily. DeVos

and M. Suárez-Orozco (1990) have demonstrated that a cultural and symbolic ethos of reception saturated with psychological disparagement and racist stereotypes has profound implications for the identity formation of minority and immigrant children, as well as for their schooling experiences.

In cases in which racial and ethnic inequalities are highly structured, such as for Algerians in France, Koreans in Japan, or Mexicans in California, "psychological disparagement" and "symbolic violence" may permeate the experience of many minority youth. Members of these groups not only are effectively locked out of the opportunity structure (through segregated and inferior schools and work opportunities in the least desirable sectors of the economy) but also commonly become the objects of cultural violence. The stereotypes of inferiority, sloth, and violence justify the sense that they are less deserving of full participation in the dominant society's opportunity structure. Facing such charged attitudes, which assault and undermine their sense of self, minority children may come to experience the institutions of the dominant society—especially its schools—as alien terrain reproducing an order of inequality (DeVos and M. Suárez-Orozco 1990). While all groups face structural obstacles, not all groups elicit and experience the same attitudes from the dominant culture. Some immigrant groups elicit more negative attitudes, encountering a more negative social mirror than others do. In U.S. public opinion polls, for example, Asians are seen more favorably than Latinos (Espenshade and Belanger 1998).

In past generations, assimilationist trajectories demonstrated a correlation between length of residence in the United States and better schooling, health, and income outcomes (Gordon 1964; M. Suárez-Orozco and Paez 2002). While assimilation was a goal and a possibility for immigrants of European origin, resulting in a generally upwardly mobile journey (Child 1943; Higham 1975), this alternative is more challenging for immigrants of color today. Further, increasing "segmentation" in the American economy and society is shaping new patterns of immigrant adaptation (Gans 1992;

Portes and Rumbaut 2001; Rumbaut 1997; Waters 1999; Zhou 1997).

Certainly, a preponderance of evidence suggests that structural factors such as neighborhood segregation and poverty (see Massey and Denton 1993; Orfield and Yun 1999), as well as family-level factors (including parents' education and socioeconomic status), are significant predictors of long-term educational outcomes for children (Coleman et al. 1966). In a society powerfully structured by "the color line" (Du Bois 1903/1989), however, race and color are significant vectors for understanding the adaptations of immigrant youth of color.

Stanford University social psychologist Claude Steele has led new theoretical and empirical work on how "identity threats," based on group membership, can profoundly shape academic achievement. In a series of ingenious experimental studies, Steele and his colleagues have demonstrated that under the stress of a stereotype threat, performance goes down on a variety of academic tasks. For example, when high-achieving African American university students are told before taking an exam that the test has proven to differentiate between blacks and whites, in favor of whites, their performance was significantly worse than when they were not told that the test differentiated between groups (Steele 1997). Steele maintains that when negative stereotypes about one's group prevail, "members of these groups can fear being reduced to the stereotype" (Steele 1997, p. 614). He notes that in these situations, self-handicapping goes up. This "threat in the air" has not only an immediate effect on the specific situation that evokes the stereotype threat but also a cumulative erosive effect when events that evoke the threat continually occur. He argues that stereotype threat shapes both intellectual performance and intellectual identity.

How are identity and agency implicated in educational processes and outcomes? John Ogbu and his colleagues have done seminal work in the area of immigration, minority status, and schooling in plural societies (Matute-Bianchi 1991; Ogbu 1978, 1987). Inspired by George DeVos's comparative studies of social stratification and status inequality (DeVos 1973; DeVos and M. Suárez-Orozco 1990),

Ogbu argued that parental and other socioeconomic factors explain only part of the variance; when these factors are controlled for, differences become evident. On one hand, immigrants tend to develop cultural models and social practices that serve them well in terms of educational adaptations and outcomes. On the other hand, "involuntary minorities," after generations of living with structural inequities and symbolic violence, tend to develop social practices and cultural models that remove them from investing in schooling as the dominant strategy for status mobility.

A number of theorists of the new immigration have begun to examine how race and color complicate the process of immigrant adaptation. Waters (1999) claims that in this "race conscious society a person becomes defined racially and identity is imposed upon [him or her] by outsiders" (p. 6). She reports that her black West Indian immigrant informants are shocked by the level of racism against blacks in the United States. Though they arrive expecting structural obstacles (such as discrimination in housing and promotions), what they find most distressing is the level of both overt and covert prejudice and discrimination. Black immigrants tend to bring with them a number of characteristics that contribute to their relative success in the new setting. For their children, however, "over the course of one generation the structural realities of American race relations and the American economy undermine the cultures of the West Indian immigrants and create responses among the immigrants, and especially their children, that resemble the cultural responses of African Americans to long histories of exclusion and discrimination" (Waters 1999, p. 6). While cross-sectional data have been used to identify this transgenerational pattern, preliminary data from the Harvard Longitudinal Immigrant Student Adaptation study suggest that among many immigrant youth of color, this process unfolds at a rapid pace within a few years of migration.

In response to marginalization they encounter in their ethnic homeland, for example, Japanese Brazilians resist assimilationist cultural pressures by strengthening their Brazilian national identity. Similar trends found among Haitians in Miami

(Stepick 1997), Dominicans in Providence, Rhode Island (Bailey 2001), and Caribbean American youth in New York (López 2002,) suggest that for many of today's new arrivals, the journey is a process of racial and ethnic self-discovery and self-authoring. New identities are crafted in the process of immigrant uprooting and resettlement through continuous feedback between the subjective sense of self and what is mirrored by the social milieu (Erikson 1968; C. Suárez-Orozco and M. Suárez-Orozco 2001).

Given that today nearly 80 percent of the new immigrants are of color, emigrating from the "developing world"—Latin America, the Caribbean, and Asia (Edmonston and Passel 1994; Fix and Passel 1994)—a pattern of racialization and adversarial identity formation within the school context is deeply concerning. In our increasingly globalized world, education becomes ever more crucial for functioning (Bloom, 2004; Suárez-Orozco and Qin-Hilliard, 2004). Formulating identities that allow individuals to move fluidly from context to context becomes critical to future functioning as global citizens.

IDENTITY PATHWAYS

Identities and styles of adaptation are highly context dependent and fluid. An immigrant youth might first gravitate toward one style of adaptation. Over time, as she matures and as her context changes, she may be drawn into new attitudes and social behaviors.

In some cases the identity that is forged is highly focused upon the culture of origin, with coethnics as the primary point of reference. In some of these cases, an identity that is adversarial to the dominant culture may emerge. In other cases youth of immigrant origin may embrace total assimilation and complete identification with mainstream American culture. In still other cases a new ethnic identity that incorporates selected aspects of *both* the culture of origin and mainstream American culture is forged. All of these identity styles have clear implications for adaptation to the new society, including the schooling experiences of immigrant youth. Within the same family, each child may adopt his or her own style, resulting in various siblings occupying very different sectors of the identity spectrum.

Coethnic Identities

Some immigrant-origin youth maintain a largely coethnic focus. Some may do so because they have limited opportunity to make meaningful contact with other groups in the host culture. Others may be responding to an understanding that a group with which they may have extensive contact is even more disparaged than they are as immigrants. Hence, Caribbean-origin individuals may distinguish themselves from African Americans in an attempt to ward off further disparagement (Waters 1999; Zéphir 2001).

Other youth of immigrant origin may develop an adversarial stance, constructing identities around rejecting—after having been rejected by—the institutions of the dominant culture. Princeton sociologist Alejandro Portes observes, "As second-generation youth find their aspirations for wealth and social status blocked, they may join native minorities in the inner city, adopting an adversarial stance toward middle-class white society, and adding to the present urban pathologies" (Portes 1993).

Immigrant children who find themselves structurally marginalized and culturally disparaged are more likely to respond to the challenges to their identities by developing an adversarial style of adaptation (Vigil 2002). These children of immigrants are responding in ways similar to those of other marginalized youth in the United States—such as many inner-city poor African Americans and Puerto Ricans (and elsewhere, such as Koreans in Japan or Algerians in France). Likewise, many of the disparaged and disenfranchised second-generation Italian American, Irish American, and Polish American adolescents of previous waves of immigration demonstrated a similar profile.

Today, some youth of immigrant origin respond to marginalization and the poisoned mirror by developing adversarial identities. Among children of immigrants who gravitate toward adversarial styles, embracing aspects of the culture of the dominant group is equated with giving up one's own ethnic identity (Fordham and Ogbu 1986). Like other disenfranchised youth, children of immigrants who develop adversarial identities tend to encounter problems in school and drop out, and consequently face unemployment in the formal economy. . . .

Ethnic Flight

The children of immigrants who shed their cultures structure their identities most strongly around the dominant mainstream culture (Berry 1997). Taking ethnic flight, these youth may feel most comfortable spending time with peers from the mainstream culture rather than with their less acculturated peers. For these youth, learning to speak standard English not only serves an instrumental function of communicating but also becomes an important symbolic act of identifying with the dominant culture. Among these youth, success in school may be seen not only as a route for individualistic self-advancement but also as a way to symbolically and psychologically move away from the world of the family and the ethnic group.

Often this identification with the mainstream culture results in a weakening of ties to members of one's own ethnic group. These young people all too frequently are alienated from their less acculturated peers, having little in common with them or even feeling superior to them. While they may gain access to privileged positions within mainstream culture, they must still deal with issues of marginalization and exclusion.

Even when immigrant-origin youth do not feel haughty toward their ethnic peers, they may find the peer group unforgiving of any behaviors that could be interpreted as "ethnic betrayal." It is not necessary for the child of an immigrant to consciously decide to distance himself from his culture. Among some ethnic groups, merely being a good student will result in peer sanctions. Accusations of "acting white" or being a "coconut," "banana," or "Oreo" (brown, yellow, or black on the outside and white on the inside) are frequent (Fordham and Ogbu 1986).

In an earlier era of scholarship, this style of adaptation was termed "passing" (DeVos 1992). While

there were gains for the children of immigrants who "disappeared" into the mainstream culture, there were also hidden costs—primarily in terms of unresolved shame, doubt, and self-hatred. While passing may have been a common style of adaptation among those who phenotypically looked like the mainstream, it is not easily available to today's immigrants of color, who visibly look like the "other." Further, while ethnic flight is a form of adaptation that can be adaptive in terms of "making it" by the mainstream society's standards, it frequently comes at a significant social and emotional cost.

Transcultural Identities

Between the coethnic and ethnic flight gravitational fields, we find the large majority of children of immigrants. The task of immigration for these children is crafting a transcultural identity. These youth must creatively fuse aspects of two or more cultures—the parental tradition and the new culture or cultures. In so doing, they synthesize an identity that does not require them to choose between cultures but rather allows them to incorporate traits of both cultures while fusing additive elements (Falicov 2002).

For Latinos, this state is what Ed Morales refers to as "living in Spanglish." He defines "the root of Spanglish [as] a very universal state of being. It is displacement from one place, home, to another place, home, in which one feels at home in both places, yet at home in neither place. . . . Spanglish is the state of belonging to at least two identities at the same time, and not being confused or hurt by it" (Morales 2002, pp. 7–8). Such is the identity challenge of youth of immigrant origin—their developmental task requires crafting new cultural formations out of two systems that are at once their own and foreign. These children achieve bicultural and bilingual competencies that become an integral part of their sense of self.

Among youth engaged in bicultural styles, the culturally constructed social strictures and patterns of social control of their immigrant parents and elders maintain a degree of legitimacy. Learning standard English and doing well in school are viewed as competencies that do not compromise their sense of who they are. These youth network, with similar ease, among members of their own ethnic group as well as with students, teachers, employers, colleagues, and friends of other backgrounds. A number of studies in the past two decades have demonstrated a link between racial and ethnic identity pathways and academic outcomes (Gibson 1988; Ogbu and Herbert 1998). These studies suggest that those who forge transcultural identities are more successful academically.

Many who successfully "make it" clearly perceive and appreciate the sacrifices loved ones have made to enable them to thrive in a new country. Rather than wishing to distance themselves from parents, these youth come to experience success as a way to "pay back" their parents for their sacrifices. At times, they experience a form of "survivor guilt" as a result of the deprivation their parents and other family members have suffered in order to move to the new land. Among many such adolescents, success in school serves not only the instrumental function of achieving self-advancement and independence but also, perhaps even more important, the expressive function of making the parental sacrifices worthwhile through the son or daughter's "becoming a somebody." For such youth, "making it" may involve restitution by "giving back" to parents, siblings, peers, and other less fortunate members of the community.

A transcultural identity is the most adaptive of the three styles. It blends the preservation of the affective ties of the home culture with the acquisition of instrumental competencies required to cope successfully in the mainstream culture. This identity style not only serves the individual well but also benefits the society at large. It is precisely such transcultural individuals whom Stonequist identified as being best suited to become the "creative agents" who might "contribute to the solution of the conflict of races and cultures" (Stonequist 1937, p. 15).

Transcultural identities are particularly adaptive in this era of globalism and multiculturalism. By acquiring competencies that enable them to operate within more than one cultural code, immigrant youth are at an advantage. The unilinear assimilationist model, which results in styles of adaptation I term ethnic flight, is no longer feasible. Today's immigrants are not unambivalently invited to join the mainstream society. The rapid abandonment of the home culture implied in ethnic flight almost always results in the collapse of the parental voice of authority. Furthermore, lack of group connectedness results in anomie and alienation. The key to a successful adaptation involves acquiring competencies that are relevant to the global economy while maintaining the social networks and connectedness essential to the human condition. Those who are at ease in multiple social and cultural contexts will be most successful and will be able to achieve higher levels of maturity and happiness.

Gendered Differences

An emerging body of literature reveals that boys from disparaged minority backgrounds seem to be particularly at risk of being marginalized, beginning in the educational system (Brandon 1991; Gibson 1988; J. Lee 2002; Portes and Rumbaut 2001; Qin-Hilliard 2003; Waters 1996). Consistent with this literature, data from the Harvard Immigration Project suggest that immigrant boys tend to demonstrate lower academic achievement (as measured by report card outcomes) and encounter more challenges in school than immigrant girls. Boys report feeling less support from teachers and staff and are more likely to perceive school as a negative, hostile, and racist environment (Qin-Hilliard 2003; Suárez-Orozco and Qin-Hilliard 2004). . . .

Several factors may contribute to this pattern. The negative social mirror that boys of color encounter appears to be significantly more distorting than that encountered by girls (López 2002). Boys of color are consistently viewed by members of the mainstream society they encounter as more threatening than are girls. Another factor that may help to explain boys' poorer school performance is peer pressure. Many researchers have noted that peer pressure to reject school is quite strong among boys (Gibson 1993; C. Suárez-Orozco and M. Suárez-Orozco 2001; Waters 1996). Furthermore, behaviors that gain boys respect with their peers often bring them into conflict with their teachers. Some researchers point out that immigrant boys are more pressured by their peers to reject school than immigrant girls from the same ethnic background (Gibson 1993; C. Suárez-Orozco and M. Suárez-Orozco 2001; Waters 1996). Gender differences in family responsibilities at home may also play a role in explaining differences in academic outcomes between girls and boys. Research findings consistently suggest that, compared with their brothers, immigrant girls have many more responsibilities at home (S. Lee 2001; Olsen 1997; Sarroub 2001; Smith 2002, Valenzuela 1999; Waters 1996). While these factors may account for this gendered pattern of academic engagement, more research is required to unpack the source of this trend.

EDUCATING THE GLOBAL CITIZEN

. . . Is there such a thing as a global identity? In recent decades, American youth culture has come to dominate the cultural scene among adolescents living in urban centers in Europe, Latin America, and Asia (C. Suárez-Orozco and M. Suárez-Orozco 2001). This pattern seems to be driven in large part by global media, including movies, television, music videos and recordings, and the Internet, as well as global marketing of such brands as Coca-Cola, McDonald's, and Nike (Arnett 2002). Whether this attraction to global brands translates into internalized cultural practices remains to be seen. . . .

Psychologist Jeffrey Jensen Arnett, however, argues that globalization has clear implications for identity development among youth. He maintains that "most people in the world now develop a bicultural identity," which incorporates elements of the local culture with an awareness of a relation to the global culture (Arnett 2002, p. 777). As a result, he and others maintain that identity confusion may be increasing among youth (Nsamenang 2002). For many, however, the identity is less *bicultural* than a "complex *hybrid*" (Arnett 2000, p. 778) or *trans-cultural* (C. Suárez-Orozco and M. Suárez-Orozco 2001). Indeed, ethnic identity options may involve more than simply two cultures. For those who remain in the land of birth with a legacy of colonization, the challenge is to reconcile local traditions with the imported practices *and* globalized culture (Nsamenang 2002). In the words of Henry Louis Gates Jr.: "Today the ideal of wholeness has largely been retired. And cultural multiplicity is no longer seen as the problem but as a solution—a solution to the confines of identity itself. Double consciousness, once a disorder, is now a cure. Indeed, the only complaint we moderns have is that Du Bois was too cautious in his accounting. He'd conjured 'two souls, two thoughts, two unreconciled strivings.' Just two, Dr. Du Bois? Keep counting" (Gates 2003, p. 31). . . .

DISCUSSION QUESTIONS

1. In what ways are the experiences of first and second-generation immigrants likely to differ?
2. What factors shape the identities of immigrant youth? To improve the outcome for immigrant youth, what would you recommend?

REFERENCES

Adams, P. L. (1990). Prejudice and exclusion as social trauma. In *Stressors and adjustment disorders.* J. D. Noshpitz and R. D. Coddington, eds. New York: John Wiley and Sons.

Alsadir, N. (2002). Invisible woman. *New York Times Magazine,* November 17, p. 98.

Arnett, J. J. (2002). The psychology of globalization. *American Psychologist* 57(10): 774–783.

Athey, J. L., and F. L. Ahearn (1991). *Refugee children: Theory, research, and services.* Baltimore, MD: John Hopkins University Press.

Bailey, B. H. (2001). Dominican-American ethnic/racial identities and United States social categories. *International Migration Review* 35(3): 677–708.

Bloom, David E. (2004) Globalization and Education: An Economic Perspective. In *Globalization: Culture and education in the new millennium.* M. M. Suárez-Orozco and Desireé Baolian Qin-Hilliard, eds. Berkeley: University of California Press.

Brandon, P. (1991). Gender differences in young Asian Americans' educational attainment. *Sex Roles* 25(1–2): 45–61.

Child, I. L. (1943). *Italian or American? The second generation in conflict.* New Haven, CT: Yale University Press.

Coleman, J., et al. (1966). *Equality and educational opportunity.* Washington, DC: U.S. Government Printing Office.

DeVos, G. (1973). *Socialization for achievement: Essays on the cultural psychology of the Japanese.* Berkeley: University of California Press.

DeVos, G. (1980). Ethnic adaptation and minority status. *Journal of Cross-Cultural Psychology* 11(1): 101–125.

_____ (1992). The passing of passing. In *Social cohesion and alienation: Minorities in the United States and Japan.* G. DeVos, ed. Boulder, CO: West-view Press.

DeVos, G., and M. Suárez-Orozco (1990). *Status inequality: The self in culture.* Newbury Park, CA: Sage Publications.

Du Bois, W. E. B. (1989). *The souls of black folks.* New York: Bantam. (Original work published 1903).

Edmonston, B., and J. Passel, eds. (1994). *Immigration and ethnicity: The integration of America's newest arrivals.* Washington, DC: Urban Institute.

Erikson, E. (1968). *Identity: Youth and crisis.* New York: W. W. Norton.

Espenshade, T., and M. Belanger (1998). Immigration and public opinion. In *Crossings: Mexican immigration in interdisciplinary perspective.* M. M. Suárez-Orozco, ed. Cambridge, MA: David Rockefeller Center for Latin American Studies.

Fadiman, A. (1998). *The spirit catches you and you fall down: A Hmong child, her American doctors, and the collision of two cultures.* New York: Farrar, Straus & Giroux.

Falicov, C. J. (2002). The family migration experience: Loss and resilience. In *Latinos: Remaking America.* M. M. Suarez-Orozco and M. M. Paez, eds. Berkeley: University of California Press.

Fix, M., and J. Passel (1994). *Immigration and immigrants: Setting the record straight.* Washington, DC: Urban Institute.

Fordham, S., and J. U. Ogbu (1986). Black students' school success: Coping with the burden of "acting white." *Urban Review* 18(3): 176–206.

Freire, P. (1995). *Pedagogy of the oppressed.* New York: Continuum.

Gans, H. (1992). Second-generation decline: Scenarios for the economic and ethnic futures of the post-1965 American immigrants. *Ethnic and Racial Studies* 15(April): 173–192.

Gardner, Howard. (2004). How education changes: Considerations of history, science, and values.

Gates, H. L., Jr. (2003) Both sides now. *New York Times Book Review,* April 4, p. 31.

Gibson, M. A. (1988). *Accommodation without assimilation: Sikh immigrants in an American high school.* Ithaca, NY: Cornell University Press.

_____ (1993). Variability in immigrant students' school performance: The U.S. case. Unpublished manuscript. Washington, DC.

Gordon, M. M. (1964). *Assimilation in American life: The role of race, religion, and national origins.* Oxford, UK: Oxford University Press.

Higham, J. (1975). *Send these to me: Jews and other immigrants in urban America.* New York: Atheneum.

Hoffman, E. (1989). *Lost in translation: A life in a new language.* New York: Penguin Books.

Iyer, P. (2000). *The global soul.* New York: Vintage Press.

Lee, J. (2002). Racial and ethnic achievement gap trends: Reversing the progress toward equity? *Educational Researcher* 31(1):3–12.

Lee, S. (2001). More than "model minorities" or "delinquents": A look at Hmong American high school students. *Harvard Educational Review,* 71(3): 505–528.

Levitt, P. (2001). *The transnational villagers.* Berkeley: University of California Press.

López, N. (2002). *Hopeful girls, troubled boys: Race and gender disparity in urban education.* New York: Routledge.

Louie, J. (2003). Media in the lives of immigrant youth. In *The Social worlds of immigrant youth: New directions for youth development.* C. Suárez-Orozco and I. Todorova, eds. New York: Jossey-Bass.

Maestes, M. (2000). *Acculturation and ethnic identity measures for Latinos and Asian Americans: Analyses of methodology and psychometrics.* Lincoln: University of Nebraska.

Maira, Sunaina. (2004). Imperial feelings: Youth culture, citizenship, and globalization.

Marcia, J. (1966). Development and validation of ego-identity status. *Journal of Personality and Social Psychology* 3: 551–558.

Massey, D., and N. Denton (1993). *American apartheid.* Cambridge, MA: Harvard University Press.

Matute-Bianchi, M. E. (1991). Situational ethnicity and patterns of school performance among immigrant and non-immigrant Mexican descent students. In *Minority status and schooling: A comparative study of immigrant and involuntary minorities.* M. A. Gibson and J. Ogbu, eds. New York: Garland Publishing.

Migration Information (2003). *Global Data.* Retrieved January 3, 2003, from http://www.migrationinformation.org/GlobalData/countrydata/data.cfm.

Morales, E. (2002). *Living in Spanglish: The search for Latino identity in America.* New York: LA Weekly Books.

Nsamenang, B. (2002). Adolescence in sub-Saharan Africa: An image constructed from Africa's triple inheritance. In *The world's youth: Adolescence in eight regions of the globe.* B. B. Brown, R. Larson, and T. S. Saraswathi, eds. New York: Cambridge University Press.

Ogbu, J. U. (1978). *Minority education and caste: The American system in cross-cultural perspective.* New York: Academic Press.

_____ (1987). Variability in minority school performance: A problem in search of an explanation. *Anthropology and Education Quarterly* 18(4): 312–334.

Ogbu, J. U., and S. Herbert (1998). Voluntary and involuntary minorities: A cultural-ecological theory of school performance with some implications for education. *Anthropology and Education Quarterly* 29: 155–188.

Olsen, L. (1997). *Made in America: Immigrant students in our public schools.* New York: The New Press.

Orfield, G. (2002). Commentary. In *Latinos: Remaking America.* M. Suárez-Orozco and M. M. Paez, eds. Berkeley: University of California Press; Cambridge, MA: David Rockefeller Center for Latin American Studies.

Orfield, G., and J. T. Yun (1999). *Resegregation in American schools.* Cambridge, MA: The Civil Rights Project, Harvard University.

Parham, T. (1989). Cycles of psychological nigrescence. *Counseling Psychologist* 17(2): 187–226.

Portes, A. (1993). The "New Immigration." Press release, School of International Relations, Johns Hopkins University.

Portes, A., and R. G. Rumbaut (2001). *Legacies: The story of the second generation.* Berkeley: University of California Press.

Proulx, E. A. (1996). *Accordion crimes.* New York: Scribners.

Qin-Hilliard, D. B. (2003). Gendered expectations and gendered experiences: Immigrant students' adaptation in U.S. schools. In *The social worlds of immigrant youth: New directions for youth development.* C. Suárez-Orozco and I. Todorova, eds. New York: Jossey-Bass.

Rosenthal, D. A., and S. S. Feldman (1991). The influence of perceived family and personal factors on self-reported school performance of Chinese and Western high school students. *Journal of Research on Adolescents* 1: 135–154.

Rumbaut, R. (1997). *Passages to adulthood: The adaptation of children of immigrants in Southern California.* New York: Russell Sage Foundation.

Sarroub, L. K. (2001). The sojourner experience of Yemeni American high school students: An ethnographic portrait. *Harvard Educational Review* 71(3): 390–415.

Smith, R. (2002). Gender, ethnicity, and race in school and work outcomes of second-generation Mexican Americans. In *Latinos: Remaking America.* M. M. Suarez-Orozco and M. M. Paez, eds. Berkeley: University of California Press.

Sommer, D. (2004). *Bilingual aesthetics: A new sentimental education.* Raleigh, NC: Duke University Press.

Steele, C. (1997). A threat in the air: How stereotypes shape intellectual identity and performance. *American Psychologist* 52(6): 613–629.

Stepick, A. (1997). *Pride against prejudice: Haitians in the United States.* Boston: Allyn & Bacon.

Stonequist, E. V. (1937). *The marginal man.* New York: Scribner and Sons.

Suárez-Orozco, C. (2000). Identities under siege: Immigration stress and social mirroring among the children of immigrants. In *Cultures under siege: Social violence and trauma.* A. Robben and M. Suárez-Orozco, eds. Cambridge, UK: Cambridge University Press.

Suárez-Orozco, C., and D. B. Qin-Hilliard (2004). The cultural psychology of academic engagement: Immigrant boys' experiences in U.S. schools. In *Adolescent boys in context.* N. Way and J. Chu, eds. New York: New York University Press.

Suárez-Orozco, C., and M. Suárez-Orozco (1995). *Transformations: Immigration, family life, and achievement motivation among Latino adolescents.* Stanford, CA: Stanford University Press.

Suárez-Orozco, C., and M. Suárez-Orozco (2001). *Children of immigration* (1st ed.). Cambridge, MA: Harvard University Press.

Suárez-Orozco, C., I. Todorova, and J. Louie (2002). Making up for lost time: The experience of separations and reunifications among immigrant families. *Family Process* 41(4): 625–643.

Suarez-Orozco, M., and Desirée Baolian Qin-Hilliard. (2004) Globalization: Culture and education in the new millennium.

Suárez-Orozco, M. M. (1996). Unwelcome mats. *Harvard Magazine* 98: 32–35.

Suárez-Orozco, M. M., and Paez, M. M. (2002). *Latinos: Remaking America.* Berkeley: University of California Press.

Takaki, R. (1993). *A different mirror: A history of multicultural America.* New York: Little, Brown.

Tatum, B. (1997). *"Why are all the black kids sitting together in the cafeteria?" and other conversations about race.* New York: Basic Books.

Taylor, C. (1994). *Multiculturalisim: Examining the politics of recognition.* Princeton: Princeton University Press.

Titone, R. (1989). The bilingual personality as a metasystem: The case of code switching. *Canadian Society for Italian Studies* 3: 55–64.

Tsuda, T. (2003). *Strangers in the ethnic homeland: Japanese Brazilian return migration in transnational perspective.* New York: Columbia University Press.

U.S. Bureau of the Census (2000). *Current population reports.* Washington, DC.

Valenzuela, A. (1999). Gender roles and settlement activities among children and their immigrant families. *American Behavioral Scientist* 42(4): 720–742.

Vigil, J. D. (1988). *Barrio gangs: Street life and identity in Southern California.* Austin: University of Texas Press.

Waters, M. (1996). The intersection of gender, race, and ethnicity in identity development of Caribbean American teens. In *Urban girls: Resisting stereotypes, creating identities.* B. J. R. Leadbeater and N. Way, eds. New York: New York University Press.

Waters, M. (1997). Ethnic and racial identities of second-generation black immigrants in New York City. *International Migration Review* 28(4): 795–820.

PERSONAL ACCOUNT

Hair

I never hated my hair until I moved to America. My parents always told me that I was beautiful and that my full head of hair and thick curls were unique. I used to think so too, until we moved. In Egypt, other girls had curly hair, and it was commonplace for curly hair to be left wild and untamed. But in the States, words like "frizzy," "nappy," "poufy," and "interesting" were used to describe my hair. I have been approached many times by people wanting to touch my hair, and often it has been compared to dogs or carpet. This was hurtful, because I wanted so badly to be accepted as a beautiful person. I wanted to be acknowledged for characteristics like being intelligent and committed to my education, not my carpet-dog hair. School pictures were a nightmare; I am still taunted by boys from my elementary school about how my hair used to look, with threats that they will show my pictures to other people.

I began to think that beautiful hair was straight and shiny, like all the white girls had. That is when I began to straighten my hair. Enormous time and effort went into finding the latest "best way to make hair flat." Money was spent on hair products, hair irons, and blow dryers, all for the satisfaction of going to school the next day and finally being told that my hair looked pretty. When I went to the hair salon, I was charged extra for having curly hair and had to listen to unbearable comments from the stylists, not to mention their body language. Since my hair was curly, stylists knew no other way to straighten it than by blow-drying it into a "fro" and then using the hair iron afterwards. I was subject to many stares, grunts, and groans as the stylists expressed that my hair was not just a burden for me, but for them as well. All the while, I deceived myself into thinking that straight hair was more manageable and less of a burden than outrageously curly hair.

It has taken me more than ten years to realize that all this is wrong, and that I should go back to loving my hair for what it is and not wishing I had someone else's. Now, I am going through the slow process of growing it out and letting myself go back to my natural hair—wild, free, and untamed curliness.

My hair has played a huge part in establishing my feelings as a minority in the United States. Although the United States Census defines Egyptians as white, I certainly don't feel white. The words used to describe my hair are often used to describe black hair. I believe that my hair has caused much confusion for other people in terms of racial categorization. While my features and skin color might categorize me as white, my hair is black. Likewise, I'm not sure what race most people perceive me to be. I have been told I look Hispanic, Dominican, and half-black. This used to confuse me when I was younger. Am I one of the black, white, or Hispanic kids? Today, I don't describe myself as Arab or Middle Eastern. Rather, I'm Sarah, from Egypt, plain and simple.

Sarah Faragalla

Waters, M. (1999). *Black identities: West Indian dreams and American realities. Cambridge,* MA: Harvard University Press.

Weinstein, R. (2002). *Reaching higher: The power of expectations in schooling.* Cambridge, MA: Harvard University Press.

Winicott, D. W. (1971). *Playing and reality.* Middlesex, UK: Penguin.

Wu, F. H. (2002). *Yellow: Race in America beyond black and white.* New York: Basic Books.

Zéphir, F. (2001). *Trends in ethnic identification among second-generation Haitian immigrants in New York City.* Westport, CT: Bergin & Garvey.

Zhou, M. (1997). Growing up American: The challenge confronting immigrant children and children of immigrants. *Annual Review* 23: 63–95.

READING 22

Latinos and the U.S. Race Structure

Clara E. Rodríguez

According to definitions common in the United States, I am a light-skinned Latina, with European features and hair texture. I was born and raised in

Clara E. Rodríguez is a professor of sociology at Fordham University's College at Lincoln Center.

New York City; my first language was Spanish, and I am today bilingual. I cannot remember when I first realized how the color of one's skin, the texture of one's hair, or the cast of one's features determined how one was treated in both my Spanish-language and English-language worlds. I do know that it was before I understood that accents, surnames, residence, class, and clothing also determined how one was treated.

Looking back on my childhood, I recall many instances when the lighter skin color and European features of some persons were admired and terms such as "pelo malo" (bad hair) were commonly used to refer to "tightly curled" hair. It was much later that I came to see that this Eurocentric bias, which favors European characteristics above all others, was part of our history and cultures. In both Americas and the Caribbean, we have inherited and continue to favor this Eurocentrism, which grew out of our history of indigenous conquest and slavery (Shohat and Stam 1994).

I also remember a richer, more complex sense of color than this simple color dichotomy of black and white would suggest, a genuine esthetic appreciation of people with some color and an equally genuine valuation of people as people, regardless of color. Also, people sometimes disagreed about an individual's color and "racial" classification, especially if the person in question was in the middle range, not just with regard to color, but also with regard to class or political position.[1]

As I grew older, I came to see that many of these cues or clues to status—skin color, physical features, accents, surnames, residence, and other class characteristics—changed according to place or situation. For example, a natural "tan" in my South Bronx neighborhood was attractive, whereas downtown, in the business area, it was "otherizing." I also recall that the same color was perceived differently in different areas. Even in Latino contexts, I saw some people as lighter or darker, depending on certain factors, such as their clothes, occupations, and families.[2] I suspect that others saw me similarly, so that in some contexts, I was very light, in others darker, and in still others about the same

as everyone else. Even though my color stayed the same, the perception and sometimes its valuation changed.

I also realize now that some Latinos' experiences were different from mine and that our experiences affect the way we view the world. I know that not all Latinos have multiple or fluctuating identities. For a few, social context is irrelevant. Regardless of the context, they see themselves, and/or are seen, in only one way. They are what the Census Bureau refers to as *consistent*; that is, they consistently answer in the same way when asked about their "race." Often, but not always, they are at one or the other end of the color spectrum.

My everyday experiences as a Latina, supplemented by years of scholarly work, have taught me that certain dimensions of race are fundamental to Latino life in the United States and raise questions about the nature of "race" in this country. This does not mean that all Latinos have the same experiences, but that for most, these experiences are not surprising. For example, although some Latinos are consistently seen as having the same color or "race," many Latinos are assigned a multiplicity of "racial" classifications, sometimes in one day! I am reminded of the student who told me after class one day, "When people first meet me, they think I'm Italian, then when they find out my last name is Mendez, they think I'm Spanish, then when I tell them my mother is Puerto Rican, they think I'm nonwhite or Black." Although he had not changed his identity, the perception of it changed with each additional bit of information.

Latino students have also told me that non-Latinos sometimes assume they are African American. When they assert they are not "Black" but Latino, they are either reproved for denying their "race" or told they are out of touch with reality. Other Latinos, who see Whites as Other-than-me are told by non-Latinos, "But you're white." Although not all Latinos have such dramatic experiences, almost all know (and are often related to) others who have.

In addition to being reclassified by others (without their consent), some Latinos shift their own self-classifications during their lifetime. I have known Latinos, who became "black," then "white," then "human beings," and finally "Latino"—all in a relatively short time. I have also known Latinos for whom the sequence was quite different and the time period longer. Some Latinos who altered their identities came to be viewed by others as legitimate members of their new identity group. I also saw the simultaneously tricultural, sometimes trilingual, abilities of many Latinos who manifested or projected a different self as they acclimated themselves to a Latino, African American, or White context (Rodríguez 1989:77).

I have come to understand that this shifting, context-dependent experience is at the core of many Latinos' life in the United States. Even in the nuclear family, parents, children, and siblings often have a wide range of physical types. For many Latinos race is primarily cultural; multiple identities are a normal state of affairs; and "racial mixture" is subject to many different, sometimes fluctuating, definitions.

Some regard *racial mixture* as an unfortunate or embarrassing term, but others consider the affirmation of mixture to be empowering. Lugones (1994) subscribes to this latter view and affirms "mixture," *mestizaje,* as a way of resisting a world in which purity and separation are emphasized, and one's identities are controlled: "Mestizaje defies control through simultaneously asserting the impure, curdled multiple state and rejecting fragmentation into pure parts . . . [T]he mestiza . . . . has no pure parts to be 'had,' controlled." (p. 460) Also prevalent in the upper classes is the hegemonic view that rejects or denies "mixture" and claims a "pure" European ancestry. This view also is common among middle- and upper-class Latinos, regardless of their skin color or place of origin. In some areas, people rarely claim a European ancestry, such as in indigenous sectors of Latin America, in parts of Brazil and in some coastal areas in Colombia, Venezuela, Honduras, and Panama (see, e.g., Arocha 1998; De la Fuente 1998). Recently, some Latinos have encouraged another view in which those historical components that were previously denied and denigrated, such as indigenous and African ancestry, were privileged (see, e.g., Moro; *La Revista de Nuestra Vida* [Bogota, Colombia, September 1998]; *La Voz del Pueblo Taino* [The Voice of the Taino People], official newsletter of the United Confederation of Taino People, U.S. regional chapter, New York, January 1998).

Many people, however—mostly non-Latinos—are not acquainted with these basic elements of Latino life. They do not think much about them; and when they do, they tend to see race as a "given," an ascribed characteristic that does not change for anyone, at any time. One is either white or not white. They also believe that "race" is based on genetic inheritance, a perspective that is just another construct of race.

Whereas many Latinos regard their "race" as primarily cultural, others, when asked about their race, offer standard U.S. race terms, saying that they are White, Black, or Indian. Still others see themselves as Latinos, Hispanics, or members of a particular national-origin group *and* as belonging to a particular race group.[3] For example, they may identify themselves as Afro-Latinos or white Hispanics. In some cases, these identities vary according to context, but in others they do not.

I have therefore come to see that the concept of "race" can be constructed in several ways and that the Latino experience in the United States provides many illustrations of this. My personal experiences have suggested to me that for many Latinos, "racial" classification is immediate, provisional, contextually dependent, and sometimes contested. But because these experiences apply to many non-Latinos as well, it is evident to me that the Latino construction of race and the racial reading of Latinos are not isolated phenomena. Rather, the government's recent deliberations on racial and ethnic classification standards reflect the experiences and complexities of many groups and individuals who are similarly involved in issues pertaining to how they see themselves and one another (U.S. Dept. of Commerce 1995; U.S. Office of Management and Budget 1995, 1997a, 1997b, 1999).

Throughout my life, I have considered racism to be evil and I oppose it with every fiber of my being. I study race to understand its influence on the lives of individuals and nations because I hope that honest, open, and well-meaning discussions of race and ethnicity and their social dynamics can help us appreciate diversity and value all people, not for their appearance, but for their character.

It was because of my personal experiences that I first began to write in this area and that I was particularly sensitive to Latinos' responses to the census' question about race. The U.S. Census Bureau's official position has been that race and ethnicity are two separate concepts. Thus, in 1980 and in 1990, the U.S. census asked people to indicate their "race"—white, black, Asian or Pacific Islander, American Indian or "other race"—and also whether or not they were Hispanic. Latinos responded to the 1990 census' question about race quite differently than did non-Latinos. Whereas less than 1% of the non-Hispanic population reported they were "other race," more than 40% of Hispanics chose this category. Latinos responded similarly in the previous decennial census (Denton and Massey 1989; Martin, DeMaio, and Campanelli 1990; Rodríguez 1989, 1990, 1991; Tienda and Ortiz 1986). Although the percentages of different Hispanic groups choosing this category varied, all chose it more than did non-Hispanics.

In addition, the many Hispanics who chose this category wrote—in the box explicitly asking for race—the name of their "home" Latino country or group, to "explain" their race—or "otherness."[4] The fact that these Latino referents were usually cultural or national-origin terms, such as Dominican, Honduran, or Boricua (i.e., Puerto Rican) underscores the fact that many Latinos viewed the question of race as a question of culture, national origin, and socialization rather than simply biological or genetic ancestry or color. Indeed, recent studies have found that many Latinos understand "race" to mean national origin, nationality, ethnicity, culture (Kissam, Herrera, and Nakamoto 1993), or a combination of these and skin color (Bates et al. 1994:109; Rodríguez 1991, 1992, 1994; Rodríguez

and Cordero-Guzmán 1992). For many Latinos, the term *race* or *raza* is a reflection of these understandings and not of those often associated with "race" in the United States, e.g., defined by hypodescent.[5] Studies have found that Latinos also tend to see race along a continuum and not as a dichotomous variable in which individuals are either white or black (Bracken and de Bango 1992; Rodríguez and Hagan 1991; Romero 1992).

This does not mean that there is one Latino view of race. Rather, there are different views of race within different countries, classes, and even families. Latinos' views of race are dependent on a complex array of factors, one of which is the racial formation process in their country of origin. Other variables also influence their views of race, for example, generational differences, phenotype, class, age, and education. But even though there is not just one paradigm of Latin American race, there are some basic differences between the way that Latinos view race and the way that race is viewed overall in the United States.

In the United States, rules of hypodescent and categories based on presumed genealogical-biological criteria have generally dominated thinking about race. Racial categories have been few, discrete, and mutually exclusive, with skin color a prominent element. Categories for mixtures—for example, mulatto—have been transitory. In contrast, in Latin America, racial constructions have tended to be more fluid and based on many variables, like social class and phenotype. There also have been many, often overlapping, categories, and mixtures have been consistently acknowledged and have had their own terminology. These general differences are what Latinos bring with them to the United States, and they influence how they view their own and others' "identity."

Although Latinos may use or approach "race" differently, this does not mean that "race" as understood by Latinos does not have overtones of racism or implications of power and privilege—in either Latin America or the United States. The depreciation and denial of African and Amerindian characteristics are widespread.[6] Everywhere in Latin

America can be found ". . . a pyramidal class structure, cut variously by ethnic lines, but with a local, regional and nation-state elite characterized as 'white.' And white rules over color within the same class; those who are lighter have differential access to some dimensions of the market" (Torres and Whitten 1998:23).

Suffice it to say at this point that in my many years of research in this area, I have noticed in my and others' work that "race" is a recurring, sometimes amusing and benign, and sometimes conflictual issue.[7] For Latinos' responses to questions of race are seldom as simple and straightforward as they tend to be for most non-Hispanic Whites (Rodríguez et al. 1991).

In the past, new immigrants immediately underwent a racialization process, which conveyed an implicit hierarchy of color and power. The two elements of this racialization process were (1) the acceptance of and participation in discrimination against people of color (Bell 1992; Du Bois 1962:700 ff; Morrison 1993) and (2) negotiations regarding the group's placement in the U.S. racial-ethnic queue (Jacobson 1998; Rodríguez 1974; Smith 1997; Takaki 1994). Immigrants undergoing this racialization process discriminated implicitly or explicitly against others because of their color and status. Indeed, some immigrants realized that one way to become "White," or more acceptable to Whites, was to discriminate against others seen as "nonwhite" (Ignatiev 1995; Kim 1999; Loewen 1971). Kim (1999) reviewed the historical experience of Asian Americans being triangulated with Blacks and Whites through a simultaneous process of valorization and ostracism. This racial triangulation continued to reinforce White racial power and insulate it from minority encroachment or challenge.

Some immigrants discriminated against Blacks and/or other depreciated minorities, by not living with "them," not hiring "them" in enclave economies, or articulating prejudices against "them." Institutionalized discrimination and normative behavior aided racialization so that, for example, it became difficult to rent or sell to members of certain groups because of exclusionary practices. Nearly all immigrant groups experienced this seldom-mentioned, but indisputable dimension of the Americanization process. Critical to the racialization process was the belief that there is always some "other" group to which one is superior. Indeed, this process has been an effective means of protecting the status quo because it made it difficult to understand and pursue areas of common interest and resulted in divide-and-conquer outcomes.

Latinos—and many other groups—come to the United States with different views on race and with their own racial hierarchies. The relation of these people's racialization to their hierarchies in the United States has not been widely studied. But it is clear that when they arrive, they too become part of a racialization process in which they are differentiated according to the official perception of their race, which may or may not be the same as their own perception. This racial reclassification immerses immigrants in a social education process in which they first learn—and then may ignore, resist, or accept—the state-defined categories and the popular conventions about race (particularly one's own) (Rodríguez 1994).

The racialization process also includes contradictory views of the way that Hispanics are generally regarded. At one extreme, Hispanics are a Spanish-speaking white ethnic group, who are simply the most recent in the continuum of immigrant groups and are expected to follow the traditional path of assimilation. Another view holds that the term *Hispanic*—which has generally not been unknown to new immigrants from Latin America—is subtly "colored" by negative and racial associations. For example, the stereotyped image (for both Hispanics and non-Hispanics) of a Hispanic is "tan." Within this perspective, Hispanics are often referred to as "light skinned," not as white. Yet, many Hispanics would be seen as White, Black, or Asian if it were not known that they were Hispanic. But seeing Hispanics/Latinos as "light" clearly restricts their "Whiteness" and thus makes them nonwhite by default, but not a member of other race groups. Thus, many Hispanics entering this country become generically "nonwhite" to themselves, or to others, regardless of their actual phenotype or ancestry.

The United States' racialization process affects all groups' sense of who they are, and how they are seen, in regard to color and race. There are few studies of this concerning Latinos, but some auto-biographies suggest that the racialization process has had a significant impact (see, e.g., Rivera 1983; Rodríguez 1992; Santiago 1995; Thomas 1967). Whether this has been a dissonant impact and has affected Latinos' mobility and the quality of life has not yet been determined.

Some Latinos, influenced by movements such as the Black Power movement, Afrocentrism, pan-Africanism and African diaspora philosophies, and the celebration of negritude, have come to see themselves, and sometimes their group, as Black. Terms like *Afro-Latino, black Cuban,* and *black Panamanian* are now common, and some Latinos celebrate their African roots. Others focus on their Amerindian or indigenous component, while still others see themselves only as white or mixed or identify themselves only ethnically.

A Dominican student of mine told me that each of her and her husband's children claimed a different identity. So they had one Black child, one White child, and one Dominican child. Each of the children had different friends and tastes. Many variables contribute to and interact with the racialization process to determine how individuals decide on their group affiliation. Generation, phenotype, previous and current class position, and the size and accessibility of one's cultural or national-origin group, as well as the relative size of other groups, all affect how individual Latinos identify themselves.

My own life experiences have demonstrated the social constructedness of race, and subsequent research has shown that "race" is not fixed, is imperfectly measured, is at variance with scientific principles, is often conflated with the concept of "ethnicity," and is under increasing scientific criticism and popular interrogation. Nonetheless, race is still real; it still exists.[8] We may question its necessity, the right of anyone to establish such markers, and its validity as a scientific concept. We may see

it as unjust and want to change it. But we must acknowledge its significance in our lives. It can be deconstructed, but it cannot be dismissed.

DISCUSSION QUESTIONS

1. What do you think Rodríguez means when she says that for Latinos, race is "cultural"?
2. What do you think is the impact of American racial constructions on immigrant Latino Americans?

NOTES

1. In her study of Spanish speaking Caribbeans, Dominguez states that "An individual may be identified as *indio, trigueno, blanco, prieto,* or whatever in different contexts by different people or even by the same person" (1986:275).
2. Except when specifically referring to women, I use the word *Latino* to refer to both women and men. At the descriptive level, my analyses of how Latinas and Latinos classify themselves racially have not revealed significant differences. But under more controlled conditions, some labor market differences by race and gender have been noted (Gómez n.d.; Rodríguez 1991).
3. I use both *Hispanic* and *Latino,* in part because both terms are used in the literature and I've tried to use those of the authors I cite when discussing their work. Works based on census material, for example, tend to use the term *Hispanic,* mainly because this is the category under which the data were collected. Other works refer to surveys employing the term *Latino.* See the following for different arguments concerning the preferred term: Gimenez 1989; Hayes-Bautista and Chapa 1987; Oboler 1995; Treviño 1987.
4. According to Jorge del Pinal, 42.7% of the Hispanics who chose the "other race" category in the 1990 census gave a Latino referent. However, 94.3% of "other race" persons who provided a write-in gave a Latino referent. (Personal communication, July 30, 1999.) In addition, two-thirds of all those who did not specify their race wrote in their Hispanic ethnicity (U.S. Office of Management and Budget 1995:44689).
5. *Hypodescent* is also referred to as the "one-drop rule," in which "one drop" of "nonwhite or Black blood" determines a person's "race."
6. The degree to which racism is perceived and experienced within the Latino framework may be related to phenotype. Consequently, those farthest from either the local mean or the ideal European model may be those most subject to, and therefore most aware of, racism and

discrimination. In the dominant United States framework, those farthest from the stereotype "Latin look" may be those who are most acutely aware of, or in the best position to observe, discrimination.

7. See Davis et al. (1998a:III-22-23) for light and humorous discussions of skin color in cognitive interviews.

8. Marks (1994) maintains that folk concepts of race— flawed and scientifically deficient as they may be—are passed down from generation to generation, just as genetic material is inherited. This is part of what keeps the concept of "race" real.

REFERENCES

Arocha, Jaime. 1998. "Inclusion of Afro-Colombians: Unreachable National Goal?" *Latin American Perspectives* 25 (3) (May):70–89.

Bates, Nancy A., Manuel de la Puente, Theresa J. DeMaio, and Elizabeth A. Martin. 1994. "Research on Race and Ethnicity: Results from Questionnaire Design Tests." Paper presented at the U.S. Census Bureau's annual research conference, March 20–23, Rosslyn, VA.

Bell, Derrick. 1992. *Faces at the Bottom of the Well: The Permanence of Racism.* New York: Basic Books.

Bracken, Karen, and Guillermo de Bango. 1992. "Hispanics in a Racially and Ethnically Mixed Neighborhood in the Greater Metropolitan New Orleans Area." *Ethnographic Evaluation of the 1990 Decennial Census Report* 16. Prepared under Joint Statistical Agreement 89–45 with Hispanidad '87, Inc. Washington, DC: U.S. Bureau of the Census.

Davis, Diana K., Johnny Blair, Howard Fleischman, and Margaret S. Boone. 1998a. *Cognitive Interviews on the Race and Hispanic Origin Questions on the Census 2000 Dress Rehearsal Form.* Report prepared by Development Associates, Inc., Arlington, VA, under contract from the U.S. Census Bureau, Population Division, May 29.

De La Fuente, Alejandro. 1998. "Race, National Discourse, and Politics in Cuba: An Overview." *Latin American Perspectives* 25 (3) (May): 43–69. Issue 100 entitled "Race and National Identity in the Americas" and edited by Helen Safa.

Denton, N. A., and D. S. Massey. 1989. "Racial Identity among Caribbean Hispanics: The Effect of Double Minority Status on Residential Segregation." *American Sociological Review* 54:790–808.

Domínguez, Virginia R. 1986. *White by Definition: Social Classification in Creole Louisiana.* New Brunswick, NJ: Rutgers University Press.

Du Bois, W. E. B. 1962. *Black Reconstruction in America, 1860–1880.* Cleveland: World Publishing.

Gimenez, Martha. 1989. "Latino/'Hispanic'—Who Needs a Name? The Case against a Standardized Terminology." *International Journal of Health Services* 19 (3): 557–571.

Gómez, Christina. n.d. "The Continual Significance of Skin Color: An Exploratory Study of Latinos in the Northeast." *Hispanic Journal of Behavioral Sciences,* currently under review.

Hayes-Bautista, D. E., and J. Chapa. 1987. "Latino Terminology: Conceptual Basis for Standardized Terminology." *American Journal of Public Health* 77: 61–68.

Ignatiev, Noel. 1995. *How the Irish Became White.* New York: Routledge & Kegan Paul.

Jacobson, Mathew. 1998. *Becoming Caucasian: Whiteness and the Alchemy of the American Melting Pot.* Cambridge, MA: Harvard University Press.

Kim, Claire Jean. 1999. "The Racial Triangulation of Asian Americans." *Politics and Society* 27(1)(March): 105–138.

Kissam, Edward, Enrique Herrera, and Jorge M. Nakamoto. 1993. "Hispanic Response to Census Enumeration Forms and Procedures." Task order no. 46-YABC-2-0001, contract no. 50-YABC-2-66027, submitted by Aguirre International, 411 Borel Ave., Suite 402, San Mateo, CA 94402, to U.S. Bureau of the Census, Center for Survey Methods Research, March.

Lugones, María. 1994. "Purity, Impurity, and Separation." *Signs* 19 (2) (Winter): 459–479.

Marks, Jonathan. 1994. "Black, White, Other: Racial Categories Are Cultural Constructs Masquerading as Biology." *Natural History,* December, pp. 32–35.

Martin, E., T. J. DeMaio, and P. C. Campanelli. 1990. "Context Effects for Census Measures of Race and Hispanic Origin." *Public Opinion Quarterly* 54 (4): 551–566.

Morrison, Toni. 1993. "On the Backs of Blacks." *Time,* special issue (Fall), p. 57.

Oboler, Suzanne. 1995. *Ethnic Labels/Latino Lives: Identity and the Politics of (Re) Presentation in the United States.* Minneapolis: University of Minnesota Press.

Rivera, Edward. 1983. *Family Installments: Memories of Growing up Hispanic.* New York: Penguin Books.

Rodríguez, Clara. 1974. "Puerto Ricans: Between Black and White." *Journal of New York Affairs* 1 (4): 92–101.

———. 1989. *Puerto Ricans: Born in the USA.* Boston: Unwin Hyman.

———. 1990. "Racial Identification among Puerto Ricans in New York." *Hispanic Journal of Behavioral Sciences* 12 (4) (November): 366–79.

———. 1991. "The Effect of Race on Puerto Rican Wages." In *Hispanics in the Labor Force: Issues and Policies,* ed. Edwin Melíndez, Clara Rodríguez, and Janice Barry Figueroa. New York: Plenum Press.

———. 1992. "Race, Culture and Latino 'Otherness' in the 1980 Census." *Social Science Quarterly* 73 (4) (December): 930–937.

———. 1994. "Challenging Racial Hegemony. Puerto Ricans in the United States." In *Race,* ed. R. Sanjek and S. Gregory. New Brunswick, NJ: Rutgers University Press.

Rodríguez, Clara, Aida Castro, Oscar García, and Analisa Torres. 1991. "Latino Racial Identity: In the Eye of the Beholder?" *Latino Studies Journal* 2 (3) (December): 33–48.

Rodríguez, Clara, and Hector Cordero-Guzmán. 1992. "Placing Race in Context." *Ethnic and Racial Studies* 15 (4): 523–542.

Rodríguez, Nestor, and Jacqueline Hagan. 1991. *Investigating Census Coverage and Content among the Undocumented: An Ethnographic Study of Latino Immigrant Tenants in Houston. Ethnographic Evaluation of the 1990 Decennial Census Report* 3. Prepared under Joint Statistical Agreement 89-34 with the University of Houston, U.S. Bureau of the Census, Washington, DC.

Romero, Mary. 1992. *Ethnographic Evaluation of Behavioral Causes of Census Undercount of Undocumented Immigrants and Salvadorans in the Mission District of San Francisco, California. Ethnographic Evaluation of the 1990 Decennial Census Report* 18. Prepared under Joint Statistical Agreement 89-41 with the San Francisco State University Foundation, U.S. Bureau of the Census, Washington, DC.

Santiago, Roberto. 1995. "Black and Latino." *In Boricuas: Influential Puerto Rican Writings, an Anthology,* ed. Roberto Santiago. New York: Ballantine Books.

Shohat, Ella, and Robert Stam. 1994. *Unthinking Eurocentrism: Multiculturalism and the Media.* New York: Routledge & Kegan Paul.

Smith, Rogers M. 1997. *Civic Ideals: Conflicting Visions in U.S. History.* New Haven, CT: Yale University Press.

Takaki, Ronald. 1994. *From Different Shores: Perspectives on Race and Ethnicity in America.* 2d ed. New York: Oxford University Press.

Thomas, Piri. 1967. *Down These Mean Streets.* New York: Knopf.

Tienda, M., and V. Ortiz. 1986. "'Hispanicity' and the 1980 Census." *Social Science Quarterly* 67 (March): 3–20.

Torres, Arlene, and Norman E. Whitten Jr., eds. 1998. *Blackness in Latin America and the Caribbean.* Vol. 2. Bloomington: Indiana University Press.

Treviño, F. M. 1987. "Standardized Terminology for Standardized Populations." *American Journal of Public Health* 77: 69–72.

U.S. Department of Commerce. 1995. "1996 Race and Ethnic Targeted Test; Notice." *Federal Register,* 60:231:62010-62014. December 1. Washington, DC: U.S. Government Printing Office.

U.S. Office of Management and Budget (OMB). 1995. "Standards for the Classification of Federal Data on Race and Ethnicity; Notice." *Federal Register,* part 6, vol. 60, no. 166, pp. 44674–44693, August 28.

———. 1997a. "Recommendations from the Interagency Committee for the Review of the Racial and Ethnic Standards to the Office of Management and Budget Concerning Changes to the Standards for the Classification of Federal Data on Race and Ethnicity; Notice." *Federal Register,* 62:131:36874–36946, July 9.

———. 1997b. "Revisions to the Standards for the Classification of Federal Data on Race and Ethnicity; Notices." *Federal Register,* 62:210:58782-58790, October 30.

———. 1999. "Provisional Guidance on the Implementation of the 1997 Standards for the Collection of Federal Data on Race and Ethnicity." Prepared by Tabulation Working Group, Interagency Committee for the Review of Standards for Data on Race and Ethnicity, Washington, DC, February 17.

READING 23

Everybody's Ethnic Enigma

Jelita McLeod

The forty-something black man I was sharing an elevator with looked at me for a while before he asked the question I had been expecting. He wanted to know my ethnicity.

"I'm mixed," I told him. "Half-Caucasian, half-Asian."

"Oh," he said, disappointed. "I thought you were one of us."

I knew what the question would be because people have been asking me the same thing as long as I can remember. I've found that curiosity easily overrides courtesy. I am asked in stores, on the bus, on the street, in line at McDonald's, even in public bathrooms. Almost always the inquirers are total strangers, as if not knowing me allows them to abandon social graces they might otherwise feel the need to display. Sometimes they will ask me straight out, but very often they use coded language, as in "What's your background?" Then there's "Where are you from?" which is really a two-part question, to be followed by "Where are you *really* from?"

Why is it that people feel they can approach me for this personal information? Would they ask total strangers their age or marital status? What do they need the information for? Are they census takers?

Jelita McLeod is an award-winning writer who works in education and public relations.

PERSONAL ACCOUNT

My Strategies

I speak differently around different people. When I am with white people I use my vocabulary, sharp wit, and smooth, concise statements. I try to keep my grammar in line and use acceptable slang and swearing. When I am in a formal setting, court, school, work, etc., I do the above, but I also change my inflection. I also use no slang or swearing. My white voice has gotten me loans, jobs, and makes my life easier. On the flip side when I am around black people, my speech is totally different. Black people, mostly, talk in a manner that is all inclusive. They don't want to talk down to anyone, or over anyone's head. Using a large vocabulary for no reason is considered rude and frowned upon. You are considered a snob. Black people worry about everyone understanding, seeing if you are on the level, and creating a relaxed environment. We are probably tired of talking in a fake manner all day, so the manner we choose has to be more relaxed.

White people size you up by the way you talk plus other things. If I were to use slang or talk in the manner I do around black people, I would be considered stupid and faking it. Yet when I talk with a high vocabulary and diction that is taken as the way I talk and assumed to be natural. Since it is the most comfortable for whites, and matches their own manner of speaking, they don't contest its authenticity. So when speaking I have to remember who I am talking to; context is, again, everything. I slip around my close friends often though, and they stare at me. "What it do Liz?" This will get no response beyond, ". . . what?" This isn't to say anything about all white people; these are general statements from my life. I know plenty of white people who have learned or always knew how to talk in the manner that black people do, but they are the exceptions. The same goes for black people. It stands to reason that if we can talk in a different manner, that white people can also learn.

There are other things I have to remember when moving between groups. Eye contact is a big one, because most black people don't like it, yet white people think you are distracted if you don't use it. I also don't like eye contact, but have learned to use it as needed. Hand shakes are another issue, which factors in age, sex, race, etc. I won't go into the differences because it would be another paper. Needless to say, a lot of effort goes in to small tasks. I have to keep my ghetto pass and still not be thought silly and stupid.

Usually when someone figures out I am biracial, I'll have to pass some stupid test. It is usually a series of questions displaying their limited understanding. Here is a transcript:

Person A: I don't mean to be racist, but. . . . (This means that they are going to say something very racist, always.)

Eric: Sigh, I am biracial. (To try and stop them before they offend me.)

Person A: No you're not, really?

Eric: Father is a large black man.

Person A: NO WAY, laughter. You look so white.

Eric: Yep.

Person A: Is he like all the way black, or like really light?

Eric: Nope, *as black as you think black is.*

Person A: (Now apologizes for their racist comment that started this.) Yeah, but aren't you like still white, you look white? Do you have siblings? Which parent did you live with?

Eric: Happy to meet such a race expert. Yes, my older brother, Gene, and I have the same parents and he looks black. I lived with my mother, but saw my father whenever I wished.

Person A: But you look white, phhhh, look at you, you're white.

Eric: Thank you I needed someone to tell me my race, thus saving all that time I would have spent already knowing.

Person A: Don't get mad or anything. I'm just saying, you look white, you act white.

Eric: *How is it that black people act?*

This could continue, but by now I usually end it by going to do something, or they start to get uncomfortable and change the subject. Things in italics are usually omitted if I have to work with the person at a job or in a class. No reason to be hostile if I am going to see them often. When I was very young I had to get used to people openly laughing at me. I still don't know why they laugh, but they always do. As if I said my father was a polar bear, thus making me half polar bear. That example is the only way I can try to make sense of it. I am so used to

(Continued)

PERSONAL ACCOUNT *(Continued)*

the tests that I can usually answer their questions before they ask.

Often the test is to prove you are black. My name is easy because Eric Michael Jackson is easy to pass as a black name. Most people will buy this right away. Then everything they knew about me gets converted to stigma mode, unless they are black, then it gets un-stigmatized. I also have to use stereotypes to prove who I am at times. I feel this is wrong, but it is better than punching someone in the face. Thus, all my actions for a limited time become black. I like chicken. This wasn't an issue when I was white, now it is. I can't say I know anyone, other than people who don't eat meat, who don't love chicken.

I enjoy seeing the looping and re-reading upon my newly discovered blackness. Before when I had an opinion on matters regarding race I was thought a tad extreme, but they could see my point. Now they either don't want to talk about it because any discussion of race outside ones own group is no longer "pc", or

because they feel I'll get all black on them. As if I'll stand up and shout, "Free Mumia and H. Rap Brown!" then curse them for years of oppression. In reality they just disregard what I say because I am "biased." They are not biased because being white apparently gives you this supreme understanding of how things work. I remind them I am also white, something they like to remind me of as well, and then I get a "not really." So I am only white when it suits them, and then I am black the rest of the time. Where I am from, I was white enough to go in your home, but I won't be dating your daughter. I have often had people boast I was the first black man in their home. This usually makes me want to leave right away. Looking back on it, my entire life has been a sociological study and I just never knew it. I knew what ethnocentrism was when I was ten.

P. S. teachers hate it when you call them that, like twenty times a day.

Eric Jackson

Once, in a truly surreal episode, a casino dealer stopped in the middle of a hand of poker to ask me, as if he couldn't stand to wait a second longer. After I offered my usual answer, he shook his finger in my face and said he wasn't convinced, that I didn't look white enough. He was Asian.

I wonder why, after having been subjected to this treatment for years, I still respond. I can't remember a time when doing so has resulted in a pleasant encounter or a meaningful conversation. Yet I've never quite found the strength to meet such inquiries with "It's none of your business" or, better yet, silence. What's quite strange is that people often feel the need to comment, as if what I've told them is an opinion they can't quite agree with. Comedian Margaret Cho tells a story about a TV producer who asked her to act "a little more Chinese," to which she replied, "But I'm Korean." "Whatever," the producer said. I had a similar experience with a man in a bookstore, who crept out from behind a shelf of cookbooks to ask me where I was from. Before I had a chance to say anything, he guessed: "Japan?" I could have said Oregon, where my father

is from, but I knew he wouldn't go for that, so I said, "Indonesia." "Ah," he said. "Close." It's not close. Not really. Not unless you consider London close to Djibouti. The distances are similar.

In the game of "Name that Ethnicity," I am the trick question. I have been mistaken for almost every Asian nationality, but also as Hispanic, Native American, Arab and, of course, African American. There's something in being a chameleon. It's human nature to look for unifying bonds. When people think that they have something in common with you, particularly something so personal as identity, they feel they know you and they imagine that you have an innate understanding of them, too. They will speak to you in a certain unguarded way. The idea that any person can be truly "color-blind" is a fallacy. As long as the human eye can detect differences in skin tone, eye shape, hair texture, these differences will play a role in how we interact with one another. Because of my ambiguous appearance, I have experienced from people the kind of familiarity they would normally reserve for one of their "own."

The unfortunate consequence of this ambiguity is the misunderstanding I frequently encounter from those who haven't gotten the full story. The Mexican immigration official who looks disgusted when I can't understand Spanish, as I surely should. The kindly Vietnamese waiter who helps me "remember" how to pronounce the names of dishes. This puts me in the slightly ridiculous position of being apologetic for not being what people expect me to be, however unreasonable.

When I think back to the man in the elevator, I feel disappointed, too. The way he said "I thought you were one of us" made me feel as if we might have bonded but now couldn't, as if I'd been refused entry into a club because I didn't have the right password. My immediate reaction was that I was missing out on something. But I see the artificiality of this classification mentality. If the opportunity for bonding existed before he knew my ethnic makeup, wasn't it still there after he found out? After all, I was still the same person.

When my parents were married, my grandfather was against the union. His objection was that the children of mixed marriages had no foothold in any one community but instead were doomed to a lifetime of identity crises and disorientation.

If my grandfather were still alive, I'd tell him that the crisis comes not from within, but from without.

I know who I am. It's everyone else that's having trouble.

DISCUSSION QUESTIONS

1. Does an ambiguous appearance lead to stereotypic assumptions?
2. If you don't identify with the questioner, what are the likely consequences?

SEX AND GENDER

READING 24

It's All in the Family: Intersections of Gender, Race, and Nation

Patricia Hill Collins

When former vice president Dan Quayle used the term *family values* near the end of a speech at a political fundraiser in 1992, he apparently touched a national nerve. Following Quayle's speech, close to three hundred articles using the term *family values* in their titles appeared in the popular press. Despite the range of political perspectives expressed on "family values," one thing remained clear—"family values," however defined, seemed central to national well-being. The term *family*

values constituted a touchstone, a phrase that apparently tapped much deeper feelings about the significance of ideas of family, if not actual families themselves, in the United States.

Situated in the center of "family values" debates is an imagined traditional family ideal. Formed through a combination of marital and blood ties, ideal families consist of heterosexual couples that produce their own biological children. Such families have a specific authority structure; namely, a father-head earning an adequate family wage, a stay-at-home wife, and children. Those who idealize the traditional family as a private haven from a public world see family as held together by primary emotional bonds of love and caring. Assuming a relatively fixed sexual division of labor, wherein women's roles are defined as primarily in the home and men's in the public world of work, the traditional family ideal also assumes the separation of work and family. Defined as a natural or biological arrangement based on heterosexual attraction, this

Patricia Hill Collins is a professor of sociology at the University of Maryland.

monolithic family type articulates with governmental structures. It is organized not around a biological core, but a state-sanctioned, heterosexual marriage that confers legitimacy not only on the family structure itself but on children born into it (Andersen 1991).[1]

The power of this traditional family ideal lies in its dual function as an ideological construction and as a fundamental principle of social organization. As ideology, rhetoric associated with the traditional family ideal provides an interpretive framework that accommodates a range of meanings. Just as reworking the rhetoric of family for their own political agendas is a common strategy for conservative movements of all types, the alleged unity and solidarity attributed to family is often invoked to symbolize the aspirations of oppressed groups. For example, the conservative right and Black nationalists alike both rely on family language to advance their political agendas.

Moreover, because family constitutes a fundamental principle of social organization, the significance of the traditional family ideal transcends ideology. In the United States, understandings of social institutions and social policies are often constructed through family rhetoric. Families constitute primary sites of belonging to various groups: to the family as an assumed biological entity; to geographically identifiable, racially segregated neighborhoods conceptualized as imagined families; to so-called racial families codified in science and law; and to the U.S. nation-state conceptualized as a national family.

The importance of family also overlaps with the emerging paradigm of intersectionality. Building on a tradition from Black Women's Studies, intersectionality has attracted substantial scholarly attention in the 1990s.[2] As opposed to examining gender, race, class, and nation, as separate systems of oppression, intersectionality explores how these systems mutually construct one another, or, in the words of Black British sociologist Stuart Hall, how they "articulate" with one another (Slack 1996). Current scholarship deploying intersectional analyses suggests that certain ideas and practices surface repeatedly across multiple systems of oppression and serve as focal points or privileged social locations for these intersecting systems.[3]

The use of the traditional family ideal in the United States may function as one such privileged exemplar of intersectionality.[4] In this [essay], I explore how six dimensions of the traditional family ideal construct intersections of gender, race, and nation. Each dimension demonstrates specific connections between family as a gendered system of social organization, race as ideology and practice in the United States, and constructions of U.S. national identity. Collectively, these six dimensions illuminate specific ways that ideological constructions of family, as well as the significance of family in shaping social practices, constitute an especially rich site for intersectional analysis. . . .

MANUFACTURING NATURALIZED HIERARCHY

One dimension of family as a privileged exemplar of intersectionality lies in how it reconciles the contradictory relationship between equality and hierarchy. The traditional family ideal projects a model of equality. A well-functioning family protects and balances the interests of all its members—the strong care for the weak, and everyone contributes to and benefits from family membership in proportion to his or her capacities. In contrast to this idealized version, actual families remain organized around varying patterns of hierarchy. As Ann McClintock observes, "the family image came to figure *hierarchy within unity* [emphasis in original] as an organic element of historical progress, and thus became indispensable for legitimating exclusion and hierarchy within nonfamilial social forms such as nationalism, liberal individualism and imperialism" (McClintock 1995, 45). Families are expected to socialize their members into an appropriate set of "family values" that simultaneously reinforce the hierarchy within the assumed unity of interests symbolized by the family and lay the foundation for many social hierarchies. In particular, hierarchies of gender, wealth, age, and sexuality within actual family units correlate with comparable hierarchies in U.S. society. Individuals typically learn their assigned place in hierarchies of race, gender, ethnicity, sexuality, nation, and social class in their families of origin. At the same time, they learn to view such hierarchies as natural social arrangements, as compared to socially constructed ones. Hierarchy in this sense becomes "naturalized" because it is associated with seemingly "natural" processes of the family.

The "family values" that underlie the traditional family ideal work to naturalize U.S. hierarchies of gender, age, and sexuality. For example, the traditional family ideal assumes a male headship that privileges and naturalizes masculinity as a source of authority. Similarly, parental control over dependent children reproduces age and seniority as fundamental principles of social organization. Moreover, gender and age mutually construct one another; mothers comply with fathers, sisters defer to brothers, all with the understanding that boys submit to maternal authority until they become men. Working in tandem with these mutually constructing age and gender hierarchies are comparable ideas concerning sexuality. Predicated on assumptions of heterosexism, the invisibility of gay, lesbian, and bisexual sexualities in the traditional family ideal obscures these sexualities and keeps them hidden. Regardless of how individual families grapple with these hierarchical notions, they remain the received wisdom to be confronted.

In the United States, naturalized hierarchies of gender and age are interwoven with corresponding racial hierarchies, regardless of whether racial hierarchies are justified with reference to biological, genetic differences or to immutable cultural differences (Goldberg 1993). The logic of the traditional family ideal can be used to explain race relations. One way that this occurs is when racial inequality becomes explained using family roles. For example, racial ideologies that portray people of color as intellectually underdeveloped, uncivilized children require parallel ideas that construct Whites as intellectually mature, civilized adults. When applied to race, family rhetoric that deems adults more

developed than children, and thus entitled to greater power, uses naturalized ideas about age and authority to legitimate racial hierarchy. Combining age and gender hierarchies adds additional complexity. Whereas White men and White women enjoy shared racial privileges provided by Whiteness, within the racial boundary of Whiteness, women are expected to defer to men. People of color have not been immune from this same logic. Within the frame of race as family, women of subordinated racial groups defer to men of their groups, often to support men's struggles in dealing with racism. . . .

This notion of naturalized hierarchy learned in family units frames issues of U.S. national identity in particular ways. If the nation-state is conceptualized as a national family with the traditional family ideal providing ideas about family, then the standards used to assess the contributions of family members in heterosexual, married-couple households with children become foundational for assessing group contributions to overall national well-being. Naturalized hierarchies of the traditional family ideal influence understandings of constructions of first- and second-class citizenship. For example, using a logic of birth order elevates the importance of time of arrival in the country for citizenship entitlements. Claims that early-migrating, White Anglo-Saxon Protestants are entitled to more benefits than more recent arrivals resemble beliefs that "last hired, first fired" rules fairly discriminate among workers. Similarly, notions of naturalized gender hierarchies promulgated by the traditional family ideal—the differential treatment of girls and boys regarding economic autonomy and free access to public space—parallel practices such as the sex-typing of occupations in the paid labor market and male domination in government, professional sports, the streets, and other public spaces.

As is the case with all situations of hierarchy, actual or implicit use of force, sanctions and violence may be needed to maintain unequal power relations. However, the very pervasiveness of violence can lead to its invisibility. For example, feminist efforts to have violence against women in the home taken seriously as a bona fide form of violence and not just a private family matter have long met with resistance. In a similar fashion, the extent of the violence against Native American, Puerto Rican, Mexican-American, African-American, and other groups who were incorporated into the United States not through voluntary migration but via conquest and slavery remains routinely overlooked. Even current violence against such groups remains underreported unless captured in a dramatic fashion, such as the videotaped beating of motorist Rodney King by Los Angeles police officers. Despite their severity and recent increase, hate crimes against gays, lesbians, and bisexuals also remain largely invisible. Through these silences, these forms of violence not only are neglected, they become legitimated. . . .

Subordinated groups often face difficult contradictions in responding to such violence (Crenshaw 1991). One response consists of analyzing one or more hierarchies as being socially constructed while continuing to see others as naturalized. In African-American civil society, for example, the question of maintaining racial solidarity comes face-to-face with the question of how naturalized hierarchies construct one another. Maintaining racial solidarity at all costs often requires replicating hierarchies of gender, social class, sexuality, and nation in Black civil society.

LOOKING FOR A HOME: PLACE, SPACE, AND TERRITORY

The multiple meanings attached to the concept of "home"—home as family household, home as neighborhood, home as native country—speak to its significance within family as a privileged exemplar of intersectionality. In the United States, the traditional family ideal's about place, space, and territory suggest that families, racial groups, and nation-states require their own unique places or "homes." Because "homes" provide spaces of privacy and security for families, races, and nation-states, they serve as sanctuaries for group members. Surrounded by individuals who seemingly share similar objectives, these homes represent idealized, privatized spaces where members can feel at ease.

This view of home requires certain gendered ideas about private and public space. Because women are so often associated with family, home space becomes seen as a private, feminized space that is distinct from the public, masculinized space that lies outside its borders. Family space is for members only—outsiders can be invited in only by family members or else they are intruders. Within these gendered spheres of private and public space, women and men again assume distinctive roles. Women are expected to remain in their home "place." Avoiding the dangerous space of public streets allows women to care for children, the sick, and the elderly, and other dependent family members. Men are expected to support and defend the private, feminized space that houses their families. Actual U.S. families rarely meet this ideal. . . .

ON "BLOOD TIES": FAMILY, RACE, AND NATION

Presumptions of "blood ties" that permeate the traditional family ideal reflect another dimension of how family operates as a privileged exemplar of intersectionality. In the United States, concepts of family and kinship draw strength from the flow of blood as a substance that regulates the spread of rights (Williams 1995). While the legal system continues to privilege heterosexual married couples as the preferred family organization, the importance given to bonds between mothers and children, brothers and sisters, grandmothers and grandchildren, illustrates the significance of biology in definitions of family. Representing the genetic links among related individuals, the belief in blood ties naturalizes the bonds among members of kinship networks. Blood, family, and kin are so closely connected that the absence of such ties can be cause for concern. As the search of adoptees for their "real" families or blood relatives suggests, blood ties remain highly significant for definitions of family.

Given the significance attached to biology, women of different racial groups have varying responsibilities in maintaining blood ties. For example, White women play a special role in keeping family bloodlines pure. Historically, creating White families required controlling White women's sexuality, largely through social norms that advocated pre-marital virginity. By marrying White men and engaging in sexual relations only with their husbands, White women ensured the racial purity of White families. Thus, through social taboos that eschewed pre-marital sexuality and interracial marriage for White women, White families could thereby avoid racial degeneration (Young 1995). When reinserted into naturalized hierarchies of gender, race, class, and nation, and institutionally enforced via mechanisms such as segregated space and state-sanctioned violence, efforts to regulate sexuality and marriage reinforced beliefs in the sanctity of "blood ties."

. . . Definitions of race as family in the United States traditionally rested on biological classifications legitimated by science and legally sanctioned by law. By grouping people through notions of physical similarity, such as skin color, facial features, or hair texture, and supported by law and custom, scientific racism defined Whites and Blacks as distinctive social groups (Gould 1981). Just as members of "real" families linked by blood were expected to resemble one another, so were members of racial groups descended from a common bloodline seen as sharing similar physical, intellectual, and moral attributes. Within this logic, those lacking biological similarities became defined as family outsiders, while racially different groups became strangers to one another.

. . . U.S. national identity may be grounded more in ethnic nationalism than is typically realized. Notions of U.S. national identity that take both family and race into account result in a view of the United States as a large national family with racial families hierarchically arranged within it. Representing the epitome of racial purity that is also associated with U.S. national interests, Whites constitute the most valuable citizens. In this racialized nation-state, Native Americans, African-Americans, Mexican Americans, and Puerto Ricans become second-class citizens, whereas people of color from the Caribbean, Asia, Latin America, and Africa encounter more difficulty becoming naturalized citizens than immigrants

from European nations. Because all of these groups are not White and thereby lack appropriate blood ties, they are deemed to be less-worthy actual and potential U.S. citizens. . . .

MEMBERSHIP HAS ITS PRIVILEGES: RIGHTS, OBLIGATIONS AND RULES

By suggesting an ideal relationship between the rights and responsibilities of family membership, the traditional family ideal operates as a privileged exemplar of intersectionality in yet another way. In a situation in which notions of belonging to a family remain important to issues of responsibility and accountability, individuals feel that they "owe" something to, and are responsible for, members of their families. For example, people within family units routinely help their family members by babysitting, lending money, helping relatives find employment and housing, or caring for the elderly. Family members linked by blood are entitled to these benefits merely by belonging. Even when family members lack merit, they are entitled to benefits simply because they belong. Beyond this issue of access to entitlements, individuals incur differential responsibilities that depend on their placement in family hierarchies. For example, women are expected to perform much of the domestic labor that keeps the family going, whereas men's duties lie in providing financial support.

In a similar fashion, U.S. citizens by birth or naturalization acquire certain rights and responsibilities that accrue from membership. Citizens are promised entitlements such as equal protection under the law, access to unemployment insurance, old age pensions, free public education, and other social welfare benefits. Citizens are also expected to fulfill certain obligations to one another. U.S. citizens are expected to pay taxes, observe the law, and engage in military service when required. In contrast to the rights and responsibilities provided insiders, outsiders lack both the entitlements provided group members and the obligations attached to belonging. Similar to non-family members, non-U.S. citizens are neither entitled to citizenship benefits nor responsible for national duties. . . .

In a situation of naturalized hierarchy, conceptualizing U.S. national identity as composed of racial groups that collectively comprise a U.S. national family fosters differential patterns of enforcement of the rights and obligations of citizenship. Members of some racial families receive full benefits of membership while others encounter inferior treatment. Gender hierarchies add additional complexity. African-American women's experiences with entitlement criteria for 1930s Social Security programs, for example, illustrate how institutionalized racism and gender-specific ideology public policies shaped national public policy. Race was a factor in deciding which occupations would be covered by Social Security. Two occupational categories were expressly excluded from coverage: agricultural and domestic workers, the two categories that included most African-American women. Also, by providing differential benefits to men and women through worker's compensation (for which Black women did not qualify) and mother's aid, from its inception, Social Security encompassed ideas about gender. Eligibility rules rewarded women who remained in marriages and were supported by their husbands but penalized women who became separated or divorced or who remained single and earned their own way. Black women who were not in stable marriages lacked access to spousal and widows benefits that routinely subsidized White women. In this case, the combination of race-targeted polices concerning occupational category and gender-targeted policies concerning applicants' marital status worked to exclude Black women from benefits (Gordon 1994). On paper, Black women may have been first-class U.S. citizens, but their experiences reveal their second-class treatment.

FAMILY GENEALOGY: INHERITANCE AND THE FAMILY WAGE

. . . Focusing on wealth not only references contemporary economic inequality but also incorporates the historical origins and reproduction of class differences over time. Despite ideas that social mobility is widespread, U.S. children routinely enjoy or suffer the economic status of their parents. Families constitute important sites for inheritance, not solely of cultural values, but of property. Families use wealth to create opportunities, secure a desired standard of living, and pass their social class status to their children. In this process, the family home becomes more than a private respite from the demands of the public sphere. When "family values" and "property values" become intertwined, homes in racially segregated neighborhoods become important investments. The traditional family ideal shows the family not only occupying a home, but owning it. Ensconced in tax policies that provide lucrative benefits for homeowners, for many Americans, the single-family home as a tangible symbol of wealth remains central to the American dream (Coontz 1992). Wealth matters because, if one adheres to rules of marriage and childbearing, it is directly transferable from generation to generation.

. . . Despite the historical concentration of wealth among a small percentage of families, the intergenerational transmission of wealth through family also operates among working-class families. Traditional analyses view working-class families in purely wage-earning terms. Such families are thought to have no property to pass on to their children, and are seen as mere employees of other more wealthy families. However, the notion of working-class men being entitled to a "family wage" emerges at the intersection of expectations of family inheritance and a naturalized gender hierarchy. In this situation, working-class men inherit opportunities to earn a wage and are expected to use that wage to support their families. According to this logic, women's and children's social class status derives from that of men.

When these relationships regulating intergenerational property transmission are racialized, as they are in the United States, another level of complexity emerges. In her analysis of how racism undermined the War on Poverty program, Jill Quadagno describes the resistance that craft unions put forth when pressured to change entrenched patterns of racial discrimination. As Quadagno points out, the right of unions to select their own members was seen as a "property right of the working class. This was a most compelling argument for nepotism—the tradition of passing on the craft from fathers to sons" (Quadagno 1994, 65). Among Philadelphia plumbers, 40 percent of the apprentices were sons of members. Fathers wanted their sons to be trained as plumbers and to continue in the business. Practices such as these virtually ensured that African-Americans and other groups were excluded from lucrative positions. Quadagno quotes one construction worker who explains the concept of property rights and property transmission in White working-class families:

> Some men leave their sons money, some large investments, some business connections and some a profession. I have none of these to bequeath to my sons. I have only one worthwhile thing to give: my trade. . . . For this simple father's wish it is said that I discriminate against Negroes. Don't all of us discriminate? Which of us when it comes to choice will not choose a son over all others? (quoted in Quadagno 1994, 65)

In effect, racial discrimination in education, employment, and housing historically reflected White working-class understandings of these social locations as "private property" to be disposed of as inherited wealth. . . .

FAMILY PLANNING

The significance of the family as an exemplar of intersectionality can also be seen in one final dimension of family rhetoric. Family planning comprises a constellation of options, ranging from coercion to choice, from permanence to reversibility regarding reproduction of actual populations. In the case of individual families, decision-making lies with family members; they decide whether to have children, how many children to have, and how those children will be spaced. Feminist scholars in particular have identified how male control over women's sexual and reproductive capacities has been central to women's oppression (see, for example, Raymond 1993). . . .

Social policies designed to foster the health of the United States conceptualized as a national family follow a family planning logic, as demonstrated via eugenic thinking. Early twentieth century "racial hygiene" or eugenic movements compellingly illustrate the thinking that underlies population policies designed to control the motherhood of different groups of women for reasons of nationality and race (Haller 1984; Proctor 1988). Eugenic philosophies and the population policies they supported emerged in political economies with distinctive needs, and in societies with particular social class relations. Common to eugenic movements throughout the world was the view that biology was central to solving social problems. Societies that embraced eugenic philosophies typically aimed to transform social problems into technical problems amenable to biological solutions effected via social engineering. Eugenic approaches thus combined a "philosophy of biological determinism with a belief that science might provide a technical fix for social problems" (Proctor 1988, 286).

Three elements of eugenic thinking seem remarkably similar to themes in American public policy. Those embracing eugenic thinking saw "race and heredity—the birth rates of the fit and the unfit—as the forces that shape[d] . . . political and social developments" (Haller 1984, 78). First, eugenic thinking racializes segments of a given population by classifying people into mutually exclusive racial groups. Because the United States has operated as a racialized state since its inception, race remains a fundamental principle of U.S. social organization. While racial meanings change in response to political and economic conditions, the fundamental belief in race as a guiding principle of U.S. society remains remarkably hardy. Associating diverse racial groups with perceived national interests, a second element of eugenic thinking, also has a long history in the United States. The third feature of eugenic thinking, the direct control of different racial groups through various measures also is present in U.S. politics. So-called positive eugenic—efforts to increase reproduction among the better groups who allegedly carried the outstanding qualities of their group in their genes—and negative eugenic—efforts to prevent the propagation by less desirable groups—also have affected U.S. public policy. . . .

With the civil rights, women's, anti-war, and other social movements of the 1950s and 1960s, as well as the growing nonwhite immigrant population of the 1970s and 1980s, the United States experienced profound change. Omi and Winant (1994) interpret the expanding conservative social projects that emerged during this period as a direct response to the perceived gains of Blacks and women. One core feature characterizing the rhetoric of social projects of the Right was a return to the family values of the traditional U.S. family. By associating the ideal family with U.S. national interests, these movements linked those interests to their own political agendas concerning race and gender. Returning to "family values" not only invoked racial and gendered meanings, it set the stage for reviving a logic of eugenic that could be applied to adolescent pregnancy, women's poverty, street crime, and other social issues.

In this context, contemporary American social policies from the 1960s through the "family values" debate of the 1990s become more comprehensible. When attached to state policy in a racialized nation-state, questions of controlling the sexuality and fertility of women from diverse race, social class, and citizenship groups become highly politicized. For example, White women, especially those of the middle class, are encouraged to reproduce. In contrast, women of color, especially those lacking economic resources or not in state sanctioned marriages, are routinely discouraged from having children (Raymond 1993). Population policies such as providing lavish services to combat infertility for White, middle class women, while offering a limited range of Norplant, Depo Provera, and sterilization to poor African-American women constitute contemporary reflections of the logic of eugenic thinking (Davis 1981; Nsiah-Jefferson 1989). . . .

RECLAIMING FAMILY

Family occupies such a prominent place in the language of public discourse in the United States that rejecting it outright might be counterproductive for groups aiming to challenge hierarchies. Because the family functions as a privileged exemplar of intersectionality in structuring hierarchy, it potentially can serve a similar function in challenging that hierarchy. . . .

Given the power of family as ideological construction and principle of social organization, Black nationalist, feminist, and other political movements in the United States dedicated to challenging social inequality might consider recasting intersectional understandings of family in ways that do not reproduce inequality. Instead of engaging in endless criticism, reclaiming the language of family for democratic ends and transforming the very conception of family itself might provide a more useful approach.

DISCUSSION QUESTIONS

1. What is an example of a subordinated group other than African Americans that faces contradictions such as those described by Collins?
2. What is the role of family and race in U.S. national identity?

NOTES

1. By dislodging beliefs in the naturalness or normality of any one family form, feminist scholarship analyzes the significance of specific notions of family to gender oppression (Thorne 1992). As Stephanie Coontz (1992) reports, this traditional family ideal never existed, even during the 1950s, a decade that is often assumed to be the era of its realization. Feminist anthropologists also challenge the traditional family ideal by demonstrating that the heterosexual, married couple form in the United States is neither "natural," universal, nor cross-culturally normative (Collier et al. 1992). Recent family scholarship suggests that large numbers of U.S. families never experienced the traditional family ideal, and those who may have once achieved this form are now abandoning it (Coontz 1992; Stacey 1992).
2. In the early 1980s, several African-American women scholar-activists called for a new approach to analyzing Black women's lives. They claimed that African-American women's experiences were shaped not just by race but also by gender, social class, and sexuality. In this tradition, works such as *Women, Race, and Class* by Angela Davis (1981), "A Black Feminist Statement" drafted by the Combahee River Collective (1982), and Audre Lorde's

(1984) classic volume *Sister Outsider* stand as groundbreaking works that explore interconnections among systems of oppression. Subsequent work aimed to name this interconnected relationship with terms such as *matrix of domination* (Collins 1990), and *intersectionality* (Crenshaw 1991). Because Black lesbians were at the forefront in raising the issue of intersectionality, sexuality was one of the emphases in early work by African-American women. However, pervasive homophobia in African-American communities, as evidenced by the reaction to the works of Alice Walker, Ntosake Shange, Michele Wallace and other early modern Black feminists, diverted attention from intersectional analyses that emphasized sexuality. The absence of a developed tradition of queer theory in the academy also worked against more comprehensive intersectional analyses. For early intersectional analyses that included sexuality, see the essays in Barbara Smith's (1983) edited volume *Home Girls: A Black Feminist Anthology*.

3. A wide range of topics, such as the significance of primatology in framing gendered, raced views of nature in modern science (Haraway 1989); the social construction of Whiteness among White women in the United States (Frankenberg 1993); race, gender, and sexuality in the colonial conquest (McClintock 1995); and the interplay of race, class, and gender in welfare state policies in the United States (Brewer 1994: Quadagno 1994) have all received an intersectional treatment. Moreover, the initial emphasis on race, social class, and gender has expanded to include intersections involving sexuality, ethnicity, and nationalism (Anthias and Yuval-Davis 1992; Parker et al. 1992; Daniels 1997).

4. Theoretical and empirical work on women of color's location in work and family not only challenges the traditional family ideal, but paves the way for the more general question of family as a privileged site of intersectionality. For work in this tradition, see Dill 1988, Zinn 1989, and Glenn 1992.

REFERENCES

Andersen, Margater L. 1991. Feminism and the American family ideal. *Journal of Comparative Family Studies* 22(2) (Summer): 235–46.

Anthias, Floya, and Nira Yuval-Davis. 1992. *Racialized boundaries: Race, nation, gender, colour and class in the anti-racist struggle*. New York: Routledge.

Brewer, Rose, 1994. Race, gender and US state welfare policy: The nexus of inequality for African American families. In *Color, class and country: Experiences of gender*, ed. Gay Young and Bette Dickerson. London: Zed Books.

Collier, Jane, Michelle Z. Rosaldo, and Sylvia Yanagisako. 1992. Is there a family?: New anthropological views. In *Rethinking the family*. See Thorne and Yalom 1992.

Collins, Patricia Hill. 1990. *Black feminist thought: Knowledge, consciousness, and the politics of empowerment*. New York: Routledge, Chapman and Hall.

Combahee River Collective. 1982. A Black feminist statement. In *But some of us are brave*, ed. Gloria T. Hull, Patricia Bell Scott, and Barbara Smith. Old Westbury, NY: Feminist Press.

Coontz, Stephanie. 1992. *The way we never were: American families and the nostalgia trap*. New York: Basic Books.

Crenshaw, Kimberle. 1991. Mapping the margins: Intersectionality, identity politics, and violence against women of color. *Stanford Law Review* 43(6): 1241–99.

Daniels, Jessie. 1997. *White lies*. New York: Routledge.

Davis, Angela Y. 1981. *Women, race, and class*. New York: Random House.

Dill, Bonnie Thornton. 1988. Our mothers' grief: Racial ethnic women and the maintenance of families. *Journal of Family History* 13(4): 415–31.

Frankenberg, Ruth. 1993. *The social construction of whiteness: White women, race matters*. Minneapolis: University of Minnesota Press.

Glenn, Evelyn Nakano. 1992. From servitude to service work: Historical continuities in the racial division of paid reproductive labor. *Signs* 18(1): 1–43.

Goldberg, David Theo. 1993. *Racist culture: Philosophy and the politics of meaning*. Cambridge, MA: Blackwell.

Gordon, Linda. 1994. *Pitied but not entitled: Single mothers and the history of welfare*. Cambridge: Harvard University Press.

Gould, Stephen Jay. 1981. *The mismeasure of man*. New York: W. W. Norton.

Haller, Mark H. 1984 [1963]. *Eugenics: Hereditarian attitudes in American thought*. New Brunswick: Rutgers University Press.

Haraway, Donna. 1989. *Primate visions: Gender, race, and nature in the world of modern science*. New York: Routledge, Chapman and Hall.

Lorde, Audre. 1984. *Sister outsider*. Trumansberg, NY: Crossing Press.

McClintock, Anne. 1995. *Imperial leather*. New York: Routledge.

Nsiah-Jefferson, Lautie. 1989. Reproductive laws, women of color, and low-income women. In *Reproductive laws for the 1990s*, ed. Sherrill Cohen and Nadine Taub. Clifton, NJ: Humana Press.

Omi, Michael, and Howard Winant. 1994. *Racial formation in the United States: From the 1960s to the 1990s*. New York: Routledge.

Parker, Andrew, Mary Russo, Doris Sommer, and Patricia Yaeger, eds. 1992. *Nationalisms and sexualities*. New York: Routledge.

Proctor, Robert N. 1988. *Racial hygiene: Medicine under the Nazis*. Cambridge: Harvard University Press.

Quadagno, Jill. 1994. *The color of welfare: How racism undermined the war on poverty*. New York: Oxford University Press.

Raymond, Janice. 1993. *Women as wombs: Reproductive technologies and the battle over women's freedom.* San Francisco: Harper San Francisco.

Slack, Jennifer Daryl. 1996. The theory and method of articulation in cultural studies. In *Stuart Hall: Critical dialogues in cultural studies,* ed. David Morley and Kuan-Hsing Chen. New York: Routledge.

Smith, Barbara, ed. 1983. *Home girls: A Black feminist anthology.* New York: Kitchen Table Press.

Stacey, Judith. 1992. Backward toward the postmodern family: Reflections on gender, kinship, and class in the Silicon Valley. In *Rethinking the family.* See Thorne and Yalom 1992.

Thorne, Barrie. 1992. Feminism and the family: Two decades of thought. In *Rethinking the family: Some feminist questions.* See Thorne and Yalom 1992.

Thorne, Barrie, and Marilyn Yalom, eds. 1992. *Rethinking the family: Some feminist questions,* Boston: Northeastern University Press.

Williams, Brackette F. 1995. Classification systems revisited: Kinship, caste, race, and nationality as the flow of blood and the spread of rights. In *Naturalizing power: Essays in feminist cultural analysis,* ed. Sylvia Yanagisako and Carol Delaney. New York: Routledge.

Young, Robert J. C. 1995. *Colonial desire: Hybridity in theory, culture and race.* New York: Routledge.

Zinn, Maxine Baca. 1989. Family, race, and poverty in the eighties. *Signs* 14(4): 875–84.

READING 25

Proving Manhood

Timothy Beneke

Instead of coming to ourselves . . . we grow all manner of deformities and enormities.

Saul Bellow

. . . Why is it that successfully enduring distress is so central to proving manhood and proving superiority to women, not only in the United States, but in most of the cultures of the world? And why is it that manhood is something to be *proved*? And how do we confer manhood on men without also conferring upon them superiority to women? Or is the

very business of conferring manhood inherently problematic? . . .

COMPULSIVE MASCULINITY

By compulsive masculinity I mean the compulsion or need to relate to, and at times create, stress or distress as a means of both proving manhood and conferring on boys and men superiority over women and other men. Failure to do so results in the social or private perception that one is less than a man. One must take distress "like a man" or run the risk of being perceived as feminine—a "sissy" or "mama's boy."

The content of the stress and distress can be usefully divided into three general categories:

1. That which would hurt anyone, e.g., physical pain, physical danger, large quantities of alcohol.
2. That which poses a psychological danger owing to the meaning it is given in relation to manhood, e.g., failing to win a sporting contest, losing physical strength and skill as one ages, and crying in public.
3. That which poses the greatest threat of all to manhood (a special case of category 2)—women. . . .

I will further divide compulsive masculinity into what I witness (and manifest) as an American man and what can be gleaned from other cultures through anthropological and other data. It is useful to keep in mind the distinction between activities performed as masculinity-proving in themselves (like many rites of passage), and activities like work where proving masculinity is not the primary goal, but rather a secondary gratification that influences how work is done.

COMPULSIVE MASCULINITY IN THE UNITED STATES

American culture is replete with examples of compulsive masculinity. Witness Norman Mailer writing about Muhammad Ali, who had recently lost an agonizing championship fight to Joe Frazier, in *Life* magazine in March of 1971: "For Ali had shown

---

Timothy Beneke is a freelance writer and anti-rape activist.

America what we all had hoped was secretly true. He was a man. He could endure moral and physical torture and he could stand."[1]

It wasn't enough that Ali had shown himself to be a great fighter; winning had been too easy for him. Ali had taken Frazier's punishment "like a man" and remained competent and whole: "he could stand." He did not give up or burst into tears or go soft. According to Mailer "we *all*" could only be sure he was a man if he suffered and endured. Otherwise he was too much of a woman and not a real man, or he was a boy and, implicitly, too soft and attached to his mother—too feminine. Mailer assumes that admirers of Ali tacitly subscribed to this manhood ideology and that readers of *Life* magazine already understood it. No explanation was required.

That one of America's most famous writers could write this about America's (then) most famous athlete in one of America's most popular magazines suggests the pervasiveness of this ideology. It was, and largely still is, central to American culture.

Tom Wolfe wrote about the "right stuff" that was required of men to be test pilots and astronauts. What was this right stuff? It was the ability to repeatedly endure severe physical and psychological distress—high g's; intense, physically induced anxiety; and rapid heartbeats—while remaining cool, competent, and able to make snap, life-or-death decisions. And this right stuff—possessed only by the few—Wolfe says, is nothing other than masculinity itself.[2]

Sociologist Michael Kimmel offers many examples in his essay on the cult of masculinity in the United States.[3] The National Commission on the Causes and Prevention of Violence stated that "proving masculinity may require frequent rehearsals of toughness, the exploitation of women, and quick aggressive responses" (237). To "rehearse toughness" is to repeatedly prove one's ability to withstand stress as a preparation for greater stress. Kimmel quotes General Homer Lea, writing in 1898: "the greatest danger that a long period of profound peace offers to a nation is that

of creating effeminate tendencies in young men" (241). Without war to "masculinize" men, they are in danger of becoming like women. And the Boy Scout Manual of 1914 states:

> The wilderness is gone, the Buckskin Man is gone, the painted Indian has hit the trail over the Great Divide, the hardships and privations of pioneer life which did so much to develop sterling manhood are now but a legend of history, and we must depend upon the Boy Scout movement to produce the MEN of the future. (243)

Again, without stress or distress through which men could test their manhood, they risk becoming women or remaining boys.

It seems that virtually anything men experience as stressful can serve as an occasion to prove manhood, so long as it is also something experienced as stressful by women. It would appear unlikely that American men could prove masculinity doing something women find easy to do. Although, with the advent of a "mythopoetic men's movement," where men take pride and may even compete in displaying their feelings, it is possible that the ability to cry in public, something women do more easily than men, may become a means of proving manhood.

American men take pride in handling alcohol like a man—getting sick or drunk, becoming incompetent, too easily can threaten one's manhood. Boys and even men feel superior to women and other men through their greater capacity to handle "grossness": unpleasant sounds and smells, insects and rodents, dirt, and so on.

The whole domain of male sports constitutes an occasion for proving manhood. The ability to withstand physical pain and intense psychological pressure, as Ali had done, and remain competent, is a central part of this. Moments of physical danger, like facing a fast-moving baseball when at bat or on the field, or evading tacklers while carrying a football, are similar occasions. The sheer psychological pressure exerted by the importance of winning or performing well enables one to prove manhood.

Hypermasculine G. Gordon Liddy, of radio talk and Watergate fame, as a child toughened himself by placing his hand on a burning flame without flinching and eating a cooked rat.[4] And part of what makes some popular aftershave lotions like Old Spice manly is the stinging pain they cause when rubbed on the face.

What defines a sissy on the playground is regression in the face of stress: bursting into tears when hurt, growing soft and "choking" at a crucial moment in a sporting event, giving in to fear and refusing to accept dares or take risks.

Work is another realm where the ethos of the playground is often transferred and where competence has often been equated with masculinity. It is an open question to what extent the training one receives to become a doctor, lawyer, or other professional is motivated by compulsive masculinity—and to what extent the entrance of large numbers of women into the higher levels of these professions will change them.[5] Nor is it clear the degree to which proving manhood constitutes a source of creativity in work.

Clearly, the army claims to make a man out of its entrants.[6] A popular television commercial for the army presents a solider about to parachute from a plane. We hear a voice-over of him writing to his father, telling him that he would have been proud of him today. The solider remembers what his father told him: "Being a man means putting your fear aside and doing your job."

The degree to which work is motivated by ulterior, manhood-proving needs is an issue that demands exploration. And, as technology increasingly renders men's superior physical strength of less value, mastering technology itself increasingly becomes an important realm for proving manhood, as the popularity of the television sitcom, *Home Improvement*, ironically attests.

Another means of proving manhood requires resisting the impulse to "go soft" and empathize with or nurture those who are suffering or weaker—a skill strongly needed to remain cold-blooded when confronting suffering or horror. It would appear that at least some of the evils of the world, e.g., sexism, fascism, homophobia, and racism, are, in varying degrees, then, ways that men prove their

manhood. Men engaging in a gang bang, committing political torture, bashing a gay man; white men deriding blacks and boys torturing a bug, are all in danger of being regarded as less manly by other men if they empathize with or try to help the rape or torture victim, the gay or black man, even the bug. They resist the impulse to empathize with victims in order to prove manhood. Though men aren't likely to explicitly regard these experiences as suffering "taken like a man," it is what's expected of them.

And, similarly, men mock and feel superior to women or men whose need to nurture is easily aroused at the sight of babies or cuddly animals. The capacity to experience other beings as "cute" is the capacity to have one's desire to nurture aroused. Many men find this threatening to their manhood. Men rather often, and women seldom, refer sarcastically to the actions of others as "cute." Typically, it is a way of saying that, in trying to be clever, another man has been incompetent; "cute" is, in this sense, a denigration of manhood. If a baseball pitcher throws an odd pitch or a basketball player shoots a wild and spectacular shot, they may be accused of "trying to be cute," that is, of not being a real man. "Getting cute" is perceived as the equivalent of seeking nurturance, being feminine, and is thus unacceptable.

Learning to swear is an interesting domain for proving manhood; saying what (supposedly) no "good" woman would say is a way of advertising one's toughness and separation from women; one learns to endure the implicit fear of one's parents, and maybe, God. A good swear is the opposite of a good cry; it hardens one in a self-image of toughness and attempts to inspire fear in one's real or imagined cohorts and adversaries.

Symbols of masculinity often contain and express a history of suffering successfully endured. Think of tattoos, sculpted muscles, and scars. Such symbols convey a willingness and capacity to suffer for a masculine identity, an achieved and visible toughness.

Threats to manhood need not be explicit, conscious, or labeled; they can be deeply internalized and can manifest themselves as shadowy anxiety, guilt, or defensiveness, among other things. Proving manhood need not be dramatic or overt, rather, typically, it becomes internalized and characterological. What makes the need to prove manhood compulsive is that it can never be satisfied; one is momentarily a man and then the doubts reassert themselves—you're only as masculine as your last demonstration of masculinity. Men internalize a draconian model of masculinity that is inherently masochistic.

Relating to stress together is a common way that men bond—the greater the stress the stronger the bond. The extraordinary connection men feel at war has often been observed.[7] Compulsive masculinity is inherently social, no matter how isolated the man or boy engaging in it.[8]

Women constitute the third major category of stress that threatens manhood. . . .

First, the presence of women when a man is encountering masculinity-threatening stress compounds the stress. Part of proving manhood includes being perceived by women as a "real man."

Second, in the realm of sex, manhood is proved through one's capacity to find sexual partners and to remain potent with them. Sex is often dominative for men, and sexual problems are typically seen more as problems of failed manhood than as sexual problems.[9] In American culture we seldom explicitly regard sex as an occasion to take distress "like a man." But we do regard it as a proving ground for masculinity, either in terms of success at finding sexual partners or performance in sex.

Third, men's competition with women in the workplace is increasingly a threat to masculinity; competence at work has been a defining feature of male identity and men's superiority to women. . . .

COMPULSIVE MASCULINITY AND SEXISM

Compulsive masculinity is inexorably tied to sexism—in proving manhood a man is proving his superiority to women by enduring distress that women supposedly cannot endure. The domination and degradation of women are a basic defense used to bolster men's vulnerable masculinity. Where men are compulsively masculine, they are also sexist. What follows are some assumptions of sexist men, stated at their most extreme and stereotypical:[10]

> Men and women are inherently different.
> Real men are superior to women and superior to men who do not live up to models of masculinity.
> Activities normally associated with women are demeaning for men to engage in.
> Men should not feel or express vulnerable or sensitive emotions: the manly emotions are lust and anger.
> Toughness and the domination of others are central to men's identity.
> Sex is less about pleasure or relating and more about proving manhood and asserting power.
> Gay men are failed men.

Relatively few men may actively express such beliefs; far more men feel them than express them. But it is safe to say that all men in American society must—to some degree—negotiate their identities by way of such ideas. I am struck by the powerful psychic resonance such ideas have for me, even though I do not intellectually subscribe to them. They are far more alive in my emotions than I would like them to be. For instance, I react with anxiety to the thought of engaging in certain "women's activities" like sewing; I still have trouble acknowledging, much less expressing, vulnerable emotions; the element of performance as an end in itself is still more alive in my sex life than I want it to be. And it has been a struggle to acknowledge the liberatory potential that gay men offer straight men.

I find it impossible to imagine compulsive masculinity without sexism. The inability to empathize with women, to experience "vulnerable" emotions, to engage in egalitarian sex, or to empathize with gays is tied to the need to prove manhood by never regressing under stress.

DISCUSSION QUESTIONS

1. Is proving masculinity primarily about demonstrating superiority to women?
2. Do you think the need to prove manhood is as strong now as it was for your parents' generation?

PERSONAL ACCOUNT

Just Something You Did as a Man

In a class we had discussed the ways men stratify themselves in terms of masculinity. I decided I would put that discussion to the test at work.

As I sat at a table, one of my coworkers approached me with a copy of a popular men's magazine, which portrays nude women. He said, "Frank, there is this bitch in here with the most beautiful big tits I have ever seen in my life." I told him that I wasn't interested in looking at the magazine because I had decided I did not agree with the objectification of women. His reply was, "What's the matter, are you getting soft on us?" I joked that it was not a matter of getting soft, it was simply a decision I had made due to a "new and improved consciousness."

At my job, talk about homosexuals, the women who walk by, and graphic (verbal) depictions of sexual aggression toward women abound, but on this occasion I either rejected the conversation or said nothing at all. By the end of the day I was being called, sometimes jokingly and sometimes not, every derogatory homosexual slur in the English language. I was no longer "one of the boys." I did not engage in the "manly" discourse of the day so therefore I was labeled (at best) a "sissy."

My coworkers assumed that I had had or was about to have a change of sexual orientation simply because I did not engage in their conversations about women and homosexuals. Since men decide how masculine another man is by how much he is willing to put down women and gays, I was no longer considered masculine.

This experience affected me as much as it did because it opened my eyes to a system of stratification in which I have been immersed but still had no idea existed. Demeaning women and homosexuals, to me, was just something you did as a man. But to tell you the truth, I don't think I could go back to talking like that. I am sure that my coworkers will get used to my new thinking, but even if they don't I believe that it is worth being rejected for a cause such as this. I had not thought about it, but I would not want men talking about my sisters and mother in such a demeaning way.

Francisco Hernandez

NOTES

1. Norman Mailer, *Existential Errands* (New York: Signet, 1974), 43.
2. Tom Wolfe, *The Right Stuff* (New York: Bantam, 1980), 22.
3. Michael Kimmel, "The Cult of Masculinity: American Social Character and the Legacy of the Cowboy," in *Beyond Patriarchy*, ed. Michael Kaufman (Oxford: Oxford University Press, 1983). Also see Kimmel's lucid and rich *Manhood in America* (New York: The Free Press, 1995), which promises to establish manhood-proving as an independent force in American history.
4. Gordon Liddy, *Will* (New York: St. Martin's Press, 1980), 24.
5. The issue of how work, indeed the Weberian rationalization of modern society, is informed and motivated by manhood-proving motivations is one that awaits demystification. For instance, will the massive entry of women into medical school alter the masochistic structure of medical training? The degree to which training for the professions is modeled on military training no doubt relates to the general militarization of society. The moral logic of the warrior still can be found throughout the world of work. Christine L. Williams has produced two thoughtful empirical studies about work and gender: *Still a Man's World: Men Who Do "Women's" Work* (Berkeley: University of California Press, 1995), and *Gender Differences at Work: Women and Men in Nontraditional Occupations* (Berkeley: University of California Press, 1989).
6. The likelihood that one will have to go to war some day is no doubt a major, underdiscussed factor among the objective social forces constructing masculinity and sexism. If a sense that someday they will have to fight and kill is drilled into men, if they have to be willing to risk death, to die as part of their gendered identity, then childhood becomes war preparedness and women become objects of protection and thus inferior.
7. See Glenn Gray, *The Warriors* (New York: Harper and Row, 1967).
8. This is as good a place as any to suggest a possible relation between compulsive masculinity and creativity. To wit, I am intrigued by a parallel between creating and conquering stress as a means of proving manhood, and creating and conquering stress as a part of the creative process in art. Sometimes in the creative process, an internalized dare is produced as one writes the first line of a poem (or puts the first daub of paint on canvas), and prepares for the second. Does compulsive masculinity

make such creative processes more psychically congenial to boys and men? There is considerable evidence that boys are more risk-taking in their cognitive styles than girls. And if creating and conquering distress separates men from mothers, does the same process in art gratify a need in men to emulate mothers by giving birth to something new? I owe this last observation to Jim Stockinger.

9. See Jeffrey Fracher and Michael Kimmel, "Hard Issues and Soft Spots: Counseling Men About Sexuality," in *Men's Lives*, eds. Michael Kimmel and Mike Messner (New York: Macmillan Publishing, 1989).

10. This summary is adopted from Harry Christian's useful *The Making of Anti-sexist Men* (London: Routledge and Kegan Paul, 1994), 10–11.

READING 26

Gendered Sexuality in Young Adulthood: Double Binds and Flawed Options

Laura Hamilton
Indiana University, Bloomington

Elizabeth A. Armstrong
University of Michigan

Paul, McManus, and Hayes (2000) and Glenn and Marquardt (2001) were the first to draw attention to the hookup as a distinct social form. As Glenn and Marquardt (2001, 13) explain, most students agree that "a hook up is anything 'ranging from kissing to having sex,' and that it takes place outside the context of commitment." Others have similarly found that *hooking up* refers to a broad range of sexual activity and that this ambiguity is part of the appeal of the term (Bogle 2008). Hookups differ from dates in that individuals typically do not plan to do something together prior to sexual activity. Rather, two people hanging out at a party, bar, or place of residence will begin talking, flirting, and/or dancing. Typically, they have been drinking. At

some point, they move to a more private location, where sexual activity occurs (England, Shafer, and Fogarty 2007). While strangers sometimes hook up, more often hookups occur among those who know each other at least slightly (Manning, Giordano, and Longmore 2006).

England has surveyed more than 14,000 students from 19 universities and colleges about their hookup, dating, and relationship experiences. Her Online College Social Life Survey (OCSLS) asks students to report on their recent hookups using "whatever definition of a hookup you and your friends use."[1] Seventy-two percent of both men and women participating in the OCSLS reported at least one hookup by their senior year in college.[2] Of these, roughly 40 percent engaged in three or fewer hookups, 40 percent between four and nine hookups, and 20 percent 10 or more hookups. Only about one-third engaged in intercourse in their most recent hookups, although—among the 80 percent of students who had intercourse by the end of college—67 percent had done so outside of a relationship.

Ongoing sexual relationships without commitment were common and were labeled "repeat," "regular," or "continuing" hookups and sometimes "friends with benefits" (Armstrong, England, and Fogarty 2009; Bogle 2008; Glenn and Marquardt 2001). Ongoing hookups sometimes became committed relationships and vice versa; generally, the distinction revolved around the level of exclusivity and a willingness to refer to each other as "girlfriend/boyfriend" (Armstrong, England, and Fogarty 2009). Thus, hooking up does not imply interest in a relationship, but it does not preclude such interest. Relationships are also common among students. By their senior year, 69 percent of heterosexual students had been in a college relationship of at least six months.

To date, however, scholars have paid more attention to women's experiences with hooking up than relationships and focused primarily on ways that hookups may be less enjoyable for women than for men. Glenn and Marquardt (2001, 20) indicate that "hooking up is an activity that women sometimes

Laura Hamilton is completing her Ph.D. in sociology at Indiana University, Bloomington. Elizabeth A. Armstrong is a professor of sociology at the University of Michigan.

find rewarding but more often find confusing, hurtful, and awkward." Others similarly suggest that more women than men find hooking up to be a negative experience (Bogle 2008, 173; Owen et al. 2008) and focus on ways that hookups may be harmful to women (Eshbaugh and Gute 2008; Grello, Welsh, and Harper 2006).

This work assumes distinct and durable gender differences at the individual level. Authors draw, if implicitly, from evolutionary psychology, socialization, and psychoanalytic approaches to gender—depicting women as more relationally oriented and men as more sexually adventurous (see Wharton 2005 for a review). For example, despite only asking about hookup experiences, Bogle (2008, 173) describes a "battle of the sexes" in which women want hookups to "evolve into some semblance of a relationship," while men prefer to "hook up with no strings attached" (also see Glenn and Marquardt 2001; Stepp 2007).

The battle of the sexes view implies that if women could simply extract commitment from men rather than participating in hookups, gender inequalities in college sexuality would be alleviated. Yet this research—which often fails to examine relationships—ignores the possibility that women might be the losers in both hookups and relationships. Research suggests that young heterosexual women often suffer the most damage from those with whom they are most intimate: Physical battery, emotional abuse, sexual assault, and stalking occur at high rates in youthful heterosexual relationships (Campbell et al. 2007; Dunn 1999). This suggests that gender inequality in college sexuality is systemic, existing across social forms.

Current research also tends to see hooking up as solely about gender, without fully considering the significance of other dimensions of inequality. Some scholars highlight the importance of the college environment and traditional college students' position in the life course (Bogle 2008; Glenn and Marquardt 2001). However, college is treated primarily as a context for individual sexual behavior rather than as a key location for class reproduction. Analyzing the role of social class in sex and

relationships may help to illuminate the appeal of hookups for both college women and men.

METHOD

The strength of our research strategy lies in its depth: We conducted a longitudinal ethnographic and interview study of a group of women who started college in 2004 at a university in the Midwest, collecting data about their entire sexual and romantic careers. . . .

A research team of nine, including the authors, occupied a room on an all-female floor in a mixed-gender dormitory. When data collection commenced, Laura was a graduate student in her early twenties and Elizabeth an assistant professor in her late thirties. The team also included a male graduate student, an undergraduate sorority member, and an undergraduate with working-class roots. Variation in age, approach, and self presentation among team members allowed for different relationships with participants and brought multiple perspectives to data analysis—strengths of team ethnography (Erickson and Stull 1998).

Fifty-three 18- to 20-year-old unmarried women (51 freshmen, two sophomores) lived on the floor for at least part of the year. No one opted out of the ethnographic study. All but two identified as heterosexual.[3] All participants were white, a result of low racial diversity on campus overall and racial segregation in campus housing. Sixty-eight percent came from middle-, upper-middle-, or upper-class backgrounds; 32 percent came from working- or lower-middle-class backgrounds. Forty-five percent were from out of state; all of these women were from upper-middle-class or upper-class families. Thirty-six percent, mostly wealthier women, joined sororities in their first year.

Assessment of class background was based on parental education and occupation, student employment during the school year, and receipt of student loans. We refer to those from middle-, upper- middle-, or upper-class backgrounds as "more privileged" and those from working- or lower-middle-class backgrounds as "less privileged." There were distinct differences between women in these groups. Less privileged women did not have parents with college degrees and struggled to afford college. In contrast, more privileged women had at least one, and more often two, parents with degrees. They received a great deal of parental support, keeping their loans to a minimum and allowing most to avoid working during the year.

The residence hall in which they lived was identified by students and staff as one of several "party dorms." The term refers to the presumed social orientation of the modal resident, not to partying within the dorm itself. Students reported that they requested these dormitories if they were interested in drinking, hooking up, and joining the Greek system. This orientation places them in the thick of American youth culture. Few identified as feminist, and all presented a traditionally feminine appearance (e.g., not one woman had hair shorter than chin length). Most planned to marry and have children.

We observed throughout the academic year, interacting with participants as they did with each other—watching television, eating meals, helping them dress for parties, sitting in as they studied, and attending floor meetings. We let the women guide our conversations, which often turned to "boys," relationships, and hooking up. We also refrained from revealing our own predispositions, to the extent that women openly engaged in homophobic and racist behaviors in front of us. Our approach made it difficult for women to determine what we were studying, which behaviors might be interesting to us, and in which ways we might be judgmental. Consequently, we believe they were less likely to either underreport or exaggerate sexual behavior, minimizing the effects of social desirability. . . .

THE POWER OF GENDER BELIEFS

A battle of the sexes approach suggests that women have internalized a relational orientation but are unable to establish relationships because hooking up—which men prefer—has come to dominate college sexual culture. Rather that accepting stated individual-level preferences at face value we focus on the interactional contexts in which preferences are formed and expressed. We show that gender beliefs about what women should and should not do posed problems for our participants in both hookups and relationships.

The "Slut" Stigma

Women did not find hookups to be unproblematic. They complained about a pervasive sexual double standard. As one explained, "Guys can have sex with all the girls and *it makes them more of a man*, but if a girl does then all of a sudden she's a ho, and she's not as quality of a person" (10-1* emphasis added). Another complained, "Guys, they can go around and have sex with a number of girls and they're not called anything" (6-1). Women noted that it was "easy to get a reputation" (11-1) from "hooking up with a bunch of different guys" (8-1) or "being wild and drinking too much" (14-3). Their experiences of being judged were often painful; one woman told us about being called a "slut" two years after the incident because it was so humiliating (42-3).

Fear of stigma constrained women's sexual behavior and perhaps even shape their preferences. For example, several indicated that they probably would "make out with more guys" but did not because "I don't want to be a slut" (27-2). Others wanted to have intercourse on hookups but instead waited until they had boyfriends. A couple hid their sexual activity until the liaison was "official." One said, "I would not spend the night there [at the fraternity] because that does not look good, but now everyone knows we're boyfriend/girlfriend, so it's like my home now" (15-1). Another woman, who initially seemed to have a deep aversion to hooking up, explained, "I would rather be a virgin for as much as I can than go out and do God knows who." She later revealed a fear of social stigma, noting that when women engage in nonromantic sex, they "get a bad reputation. I know that I wouldn't want that reputation" (11-1). Her comments highlight the

---

*Number indicates participant and wave of the interview.

feedback between social judgment and internalized preference.

Gender beliefs were also at the root of women's other chief complaint about hookups—the disrespect of women in the hookup scene. The notion that hooking up is okay for men but not for women was embedded in the organization of the Greek system, where most parties occurred: Sorority rules prohibited hosting parties or overnight male visitors, reflecting notions about proper feminine behavior. In contrast, fraternities collected social fees to pay for alcohol and viewed hosting parties as a central activity. This disparity gave fraternity men almost complete control over the most desirable parties on campus—particularly for the under-age crowd (Boswell and Spade 1996; Martin and Hummer 1989).

Women reported that fraternity men dictated party transportation, the admittance of guests, party themes such as "CEO and secretary ho," the flow of alcohol, and the movement of guests within the party (Armstrong, Hamilton, and Sweeney 2006). Women often indicated that they engaged in strategies such as "travel[ing] in hordes" (21-1) and not "tak[ing] a drink if I don't know where it came from" (15-1) to feel safer at fraternity parties. Even when open to hooking up, women were not comfortable doing so if they sensed that men were trying to undermine their control of sexual activity (e.g., by pushing them to drink too heavily, barring their exit from private rooms, or refusing them rides home). Women typically opted not to return to party venues they perceived as unsafe. As one noted, "I wouldn't go to [that house] because I heard they do bad things to girls" (14-1). Even those interested in the erotic competition of party scenes tired of it as they realized that the game was rigged. . . .

The Relationship Imperative

Women also encountered problematic gender beliefs about men's and women's different levels of interest in relationships. As one noted, women fight the "dumb girl idea"—the notion "that every girl wants a boy to sweep her off her feet and fall in love" (42-2). The expectation that women should want to be in relationships was so pervasive that many found it necessary to justify their single status to us. For example, when asked if she had a boyfriend, one woman with no shortage of admirers apologetically explained, "I know this sounds really pathetic and you probably think I am lying, but there are so many other things going on right now that it's really not something high up on my list. . . . I know that's such a lame-ass excuse, but it's true" (9-3). Another noted that already having a boyfriend was the only "actual, legitimate excuse" to reject men who expressed interest in a relationship (34-3).

Certainly, many women wanted relationships and sought them out. However, women's interest in relationships varied, and almost all experienced periods during which they wanted to be single. Nonetheless, women reported pressure to be in relationships all the time. We found that women, rather than struggling to get into relationships, had to work to avoid them.

The relational imperative was supported by the belief that women's relational opportunities were scarce and should not be wasted. Women described themselves as "lucky" to find a man willing to commit, as "there's not many guys like that, in college" (15-1). This belief persisted despite the fact that most women were in relationships most of the time. As one woman noted, "I don't think anyone really wants to be in a serious relationship, but most, well actually all of us, have boyfriends" (13-1). Belief in the myth of scarcity also led women to stay in relationships when they were no longer happy. A woman who was "sick of" her conflict-ridden relationship explained why she could not end it: "I feel like I have to meet somebody else. . . . I go out and they're all these asshole frat guys. . . . That's what stops me. . . . Boys are not datable right now because . . . all they're looking for is freshman girls to hook up with. . . . [So] I'm just stuck. I need to do something about it, but I don't know what" (30-3). It took her another year to extract herself from this relationship. Despite her fears, when she decided she was ready for another relationship, she quickly found a boyfriend.

Women also confronted the belief that all women are relationally insatiable. They often told stories of men who acted entitled to relationships, expected their relational overtures to be accepted, and became angry when rebuffed—sometimes stalking the rejecting woman. As one explained about a friend, "Abby was having issues with this guy who likes her. He was like, 'You have to like me. . . . I'm not gonna take no for an answer. I'm gonna do whatever it takes to date you'" (24-3). Another noted that "last semester, this guy really wanted to date me, and I did not want to date him at all. He flipped out and was like, 'This is ridiculous, I don't deserve this'" (12-3). A third eventually gave in when a man continually rejected her refusals: "I was like, if I go [out with him]. . . . maybe he'll stop. Because he wouldn't stop." She planned to act "extremely conservative" as a way to convince him that he did not want to be with her (39-4).

Gender beliefs may also limit women's control over the terms of interaction within relationships. If women are made to feel lucky to have boyfriends, men are placed in a position of power, as presumably women should be grateful when they commit. Women's reports suggest that men attempted to use this power to regulate their participation in college life. One noted, "When I got here my first semester freshman year, I wanted to go out to the parties . . . and he got pissed off about it. . . . He's like, 'Why do you need to do that? Why can't you just stay with me?'" (4-2). Boyfriends sometimes tried to limit the time women spent with their friends and the activities in which they participated. As a woman explained, "There are times when I feel like Steve can get . . . possessive. He'll be like . . . 'I feel like you're always with your friends over me.' He wanted to go out to lunch after our class, and I was like, 'No, I have to come have this interview.' And he got so upset about it" (42-3). Men's control even extended to women's attire. Another told us about her boyfriend, "He is a very controlling person. . . . He's like, 'What are you wearing tonight?' . . . It's like a joke but serious at the same time" (32-4).

Women also became jealous; however, rather than trying to control their boyfriends, they often tried to change themselves. One noted that she would "do anything to make this relationship work." She elaborated, "I was so nervous being with Dan because I knew he had cheated on his [prior] girlfriend . . . [but] I'm getting over it. When I go [to visit him] now . . . I let him go to the bar, whatever. I stayed in his apartment because there was nothing else to do" (39-3). Other women changed the way they dressed, their friends, and where they went in the attempt to keep boyfriends.

When women attempted to end relationships, they often reported that men's efforts to control them escalated. We heard 10 accounts of men using abuse to keep women in relationships. One woman spent months dealing with a boyfriend who accused her of cheating on him. When she tried to break up, he cut his wrist in her apartment (9-2). Another tried to end a relationship but was forced to flee the state when her car windows were broken and her safety was threatened (6-4). Men often drew on romantic repertoires to coerce interaction after relationships had ended. One woman told us that her ex-boyfriend stalked her for months—even showing up at her workplace, showering her with flowers and gifts, and blocking her entry into work until the police arrived (25-2).

INTERSECTIONALITY: CONTRADICTIONS BETWEEN CLASS AND GENDER

Existing research about college sexuality focuses almost exclusively on its gendered nature. We contend that sexuality is shaped simultaneously by multiple intersecting structures. In this section, we examine the sexual and romantic implications of class beliefs about how ambitious young people should conduct themselves during college. Although all of our participants contended with class beliefs that contradicted those of gender, experiences of this structural intersection varied by class location. More privileged women struggled to meet gender and class guidelines for sexual behavior, introducing a difficult set of double binds. Because these class beliefs reflected a privileged path to adulthood, less privileged women found them foreign to their own sexual and romantic logics.

More Privileged Women and the Experience of Double Binds

The Self-development Imperative and the Relational Double Bind

The four-year university is a classed structural location. One of the primary reasons to attend college is to preserve or enhance economic position. The university culture is thus characterized by the self-development imperative, or the notion that individual achievement and personal growth are paramount. There are also accompanying rules for sex and relationships: Students are expected to postpone marriage and parenthood until after completing an education and establishing a career.

For more privileged women, personal expectations and those of the university culture meshed. Even those who enjoyed relationships experienced phases in college where they preferred to remain single. Almost all privileged women (94 percent) told us at one point that they did not want a boyfriend. One noted, "All my friends here . . . they're like, 'I don't want to deal with [a boyfriend] right now. I want to be on my own'" (37-1). Another eloquently remarked, "I've always looked at college as the only time in your life when you should be a hundred percent selfish. . . . I have the rest of my life to devote to a husband or kids or my job . . . but right now, it's my time" (21-2).

The notion that independence is critical during college reflected class beliefs about the appropriate role for romance that opposed those of gender. During college, relational commitments were supposed to take a backseat to self-development. As an upper-middle-class woman noted, "College is the only time that you don't have obligations to anyone but yourself. . . . I want to get settled down and figure out what I'm doing with my life before

[I] dedicate myself to something or someone else" (14-4). Another emphasized the value of investment in human capital: "I've always been someone who wants to have my own money, have my own career so that, you know, 50 percent of marriages fail. . . . If I want to maintain the lifestyle that I've grown up with . . . I have to work. I just don't see myself being someone who marries young and lives off of some boy's money" (42-4). To become self-supporting, many privileged women indicated they needed to postpone marriage. One told us, "I don't want to think about that [marriage]. I want to get secure in a city and in a job. . . . I'm not in any hurry at all. As long as I'm married by 30, I'm good" (13-4). Even those who wanted to be supported by husbands did not expect to find them in college, instead setting their sights on the more accomplished men they expected to meet in urban centers after college.

More privileged women often found committed relationships to be greedy—demanding of time and energy. As one stated, "When it comes to a serious relationship, it's a lot for me to give into that. [What do you feel like you are giving up?] Like my everything. . . . There's just a lot involved in it" (35-3). These women feared that they would be devoured by relationships and sometimes struggled to keep their self-development projects going when they did get involved. As an upper-class woman told us, "It's hard to have a boyfriend and be really excited about it and still not let it consume you" (42-2). This situation was exacerbated by the gender beliefs discussed earlier, as women experienced pressure to fully devote themselves to relationships.

Privileged women reported that committed relationships detracted from what they saw as the main tasks of college. They complained, for example, that relationships made it difficult to meet people. As an upper-middle-class woman who had just ended a relationship described, "I'm happy that I'm able to go out and meet new people. . . . I feel like I'm doing what a college student should be doing. I don't need to be tied down to my high school boyfriend for two years when this is the time to be meeting people" (14-3). A middle-class woman similarly noted that her relationship with her boyfriend made it impossible to make friends on the floor her first year. She explained, "We were together every day. . . . It was the critical time of making friends and meeting people, [and] I wasn't there" (21-2).

Many also complained that committed relationships competed with schoolwork (also see Holland and Eisenhart 1990). An upper-middle-class woman remarked, "[My boyfriend] doesn't understand why I can't pick up and go see him all the time. But I have school. . . . I just want to be a college kid" (18-3). Another told us that her major was not compatible with the demands of a boyfriend. She said, "I wouldn't mind having a boyfriend again, but it's a lot of work. Right now with [my major] and everything . . . I wouldn't have time even to see him" (30-4). She did not plan to consider a relationship until her workload lessened.

With marriage far in the future, more privileged women often worried about college relationships getting too serious too fast. All planned to marry—ideally to men with greater earnings—but were clear about the importance of temporary independence. . . .

The Appeal of Hookups and the Sexual Double Bind   In contrast, hookups fit well with the self-development imperative of college. They allowed women to be sexual without the demands of relationships. For example, one upper-class woman described hooking up as "fun and non-threatening." She noted, "So many of us girls, we complain that these guys just want to hook up all the time. I'm going, these guys that I'm attracted to . . . get kind of serious." She saw her last hookup as ideal because "we were physical, and that was it. I never wanted it to go anywhere" (34-2). Many privileged women understood, if implicitly, that hooking up was a delay tactic, allowing sex without participation in serious relationships.

As a sexual solution for the demands of college, hooking up became incorporated into notions of what the college experience should be. When asked which kinds of people hook up the most,

one woman noted, "All. . . . The people who came to college to have a good time and party" (14-1). With the help of media, alcohol, and spring break industries, hooking up was so institutionalized that many took it for granted. One upper-middle-class woman said, "It just happens. It's natural" (15-1). They told us that learning about sexuality was something they were supposed to be doing in college. Another described, "I'm glad that I've had my one-night stands and my being in love and having sex. . . . Now I know what it's supposed to feel like when I'm with someone that I want to be with. I feel bad for some of my friends. . . . They're still virgins" (29-1).

High rates of hooking up suggest genuine interest in the activity rather than simply accommodation to men's interests. Particularly early in college, privileged women actively sought hookups. One noted, "You see a lot of people who are like, 'I just want to hook up with someone tonight.' . . . It's always the girls that try to get the guys" (41-1). Data from the OCSLS also suggest that college women like hooking up almost as much as men and are not always searching for something more. Nearly as many women as men (85 percent and 89 percent, respectively) report enjoying the sexual activity of their last hookup "very much" or "somewhat," and less than half of women report interest in a relationship with their most recent hookup.

In private, several privileged women even used the classed logic of hooking up to challenge stereotyped portrayals of gender differences in sexuality. As one noted, "There are girls that want things as much as guys do. There are girls that want things more, and they're like, 'Oh it's been a while [since I had sex].' The girls are no more innocent than the guys. . . . People think girls are jealous of relationships, but they're like, 'What? I want to be single'" (34-1). When asked about the notion that guys want sex and girls want relationships another responded, "I think that is the absolute epitome of bullshit. I know so many girls who honestly go out on a Friday night and they're like, 'I hope I get some ass tonight.' They don't wanna have a boyfriend! They just wanna hook up with someone.

And I know boys who want relationships. I think it goes both ways" (42-2). These women drew on gender-neutral understandings of sexuality characteristic of university culture to contradict the notion of women's sexuality as inevitably and naturally relational.

For more privileged women, enjoyment of hookups was tightly linked to the atmosphere in which they occurred. Most were initiated at college parties where alcohol, music, attractive people, sexy outfits, and flirting combined to generate a collective erotic energy. As one woman enthusiastically noted, "Everyone was so excited. It was a big fun party" (15-1). Privileged women often "loved" it when they had an "excuse to just let loose" and "grind" on the dance floor. They reported turning on their "make-out radar" (18-1), explaining that "it's fun to know that a guy's attracted to you and is willing to kiss you" (16-1). The party scene gave them a chance to play with adult sexualities and interact for purely sexual purposes—an experience that one middle-class woman claimed "empowered" her (17-1).

Hookups enabled more privileged women to conduct themselves in accordance with class expectations, but as we demonstrated earlier, the enforcement of gender beliefs placed them at risk of sanction. This conflict gets to the heart of a *sexual double bind*: While hookups protected privileged women from relationships that could derail their ambitions, the double standard gave men greater control over the terms of hooking up, justified the disrespectful treatment of women, supported sexual stigma, and produced feelings of shame.

Less Privileged Women and the Experience of Foreign Sexual Culture

Women's comfort with delaying commitment and participating in the hookup culture was shaped by class location. College culture reflects the beliefs of the more privileged classes. Less privileged women arrived at college with their own orientation to sex and romance, characterized by a faster transition into adulthood. They often attempted to build both relationships and career at the same time. As a result, the third of the participants from less privileged backgrounds often experienced the hookup culture as foreign in ways that made it difficult to persist at the university.

Less privileged women had less exposure to the notion that the college years should be set aside solely for educational and career development. Many did not see serious relationships as incompatible with college life. Four were married or engaged before graduating—a step that others would not take until later. One reminisced, "I thought I'd get married in college. . . . When I was still in high school, I figured by my senior year, I'd be engaged or married or something. . . . I wanted to have kids before I was 25" (25-4). Another spoke of her plans to marry her high school sweetheart: "I'll be 21 and I know he's the one I want to spend the rest of my life with. . . . Really, I don't want to date anybody else" (6-1).

Plans to move into adult roles relatively quickly made less privileged women outsiders among their more privileged peers. One working-class woman saw her friendships dissolve as she revealed her desire to marry and have children in the near future. As one of her former friends described,

> She would always talk about how she couldn't wait to get married and have babies. . . . It was just like, Whoa. I'm 18. . . . Slow down, you know? Then she just crazy dropped out of school and wouldn't contact any of us. . . . The way I see it is that she's from a really small town, and that's what everyone in her town does . . . get married and have babies. That's all she ever wanted to do maybe? . . . I don't know if she was homesick or didn't fit in. (24-4)

This account glosses over the extent to which the working-class woman was pushed out of the university—ostracized by her peers for not acclimating to the self-development imperative and, as noted below, to the campus sexual climate. In fact, 40 percent of less privileged women left the university, compared to 5 percent of more privileged women. In all cases, mismatch between the sexual culture of women's hometowns and that of college was a factor in the decision to leave.

Most of the less privileged women found the hookup culture to be not only foreign but hostile. As the working-class woman described above told us,

> I tried so hard to fit in with what everybody else was doing here. . . . I think one morning I just woke up and realized that this isn't me at all; I don't like the way I am right now. . . . I didn't feel like I was growing up. I felt like I was actually getting younger the way I was trying to act. Growing up to me isn't going out and getting smashed and sleeping around. . . . That to me is immature. (28-1)

She emphasized the value of "growing up" in college. Without the desire to postpone adulthood, less privileged women often could not understand the appeal of hooking up. As a lower-middle-class woman noted, "Who would be interested in just meeting somebody and then doing something that night? And then never talking to them again? . . . I'm supposed to do this; I'm supposed to get drunk every weekend. I'm supposed to go to parties every weekend . . . and I'm supposed to enjoy it like everyone else. But it just doesn't appeal to me" (5-1). She reveals the extent to which hooking up was a normalized part of college life: For those who were not interested in this, college life could be experienced as mystifying, uncomfortable, and alienating.

The self-development imperative was a resource women could use in resisting the gendered pull of relationships. Less privileged women did not have as much access to this resource and were invested in settling down. Thus, they found it hard to resist the pull back home of local boyfriends, who—unlike the college men they had met—seemed interested in marrying and having children soon. One woman noted after transferring to a branch campus, "I think if I hadn't been connected with [my fiancé], I think I would have been more strongly connected to [the college town], and I think I probably would have stayed" (2-4). Another described her hometown boyfriend: "He'll be like, 'I want to see you. Come home.' . . . The stress he was putting me under and me being here my first

year. I could not take it" (7-2). The following year, she moved back home. A third explained about her husband, "He wants me at home. . . . He wants to have control over me and . . . to feel like he's the dominant one in the relationship. . . . The fact that I'm going to school and he knows I'm smart and he knows that I'm capable of doing anything that I want . . . it scares him" (6-4). While she eventually ended this relationship, it cost her an additional semester of school.

Women were also pulled back home by the slut stigma, as people there—perhaps out of frustration or jealousy—judged college women for any association with campus sexual culture. For instance, one woman became distraught when a virulent sexual rumor about her circulated around her hometown, especially when it reached her parents. Going home was a way of putting sexual rumors to rest and reaffirming ties that were strained by leaving.

Thus, less privileged women were often caught between two sexual cultures. Staying at the university meant abandoning a familiar logic and adopting a privileged one—investing in human capital while delaying the transition to adulthood. As one explained, attending college led her to revise her "whole plan": "Now I'm like, I don't even need to be getting married yet [or] have kids. . . . All of [my brother's] friends, 17- to 20-year-old girls, have their . . . babies, and I'm like, Oh my God. . . . Now I'll be able to do something else for a couple years before I settle down . . . before I worry about kids" (25-3). These changes in agendas required them to end relationships with men whose life plans diverged from theirs. For some, this also meant cutting ties with hometown friends. One resolute woman, whose friends back home had turned on her, noted, "I'm just sick of it. There's nothing there for me anymore. There's absolutely nothing there" (22-4).

DISCUSSION

Public gender beliefs are a key source of gender inequality in college heterosexual interaction. They undergird a sexual double standard and a relational imperative that justify the disrespect of women who hook up and the disempowerment of women in relationships—reinforcing male dominance across social forms. Most of the women we studied cycled back and forth between hookups and relationships, in part because they found both to be problematic. These findings indicate that an individualist, battle of the sexes explanation not only is inadequate but may contribute to gender inequality by naturalizing problematic notions of gender difference.

We are not, however, claiming that gender differences in stated preferences do not exist. Analysis of the OCSLS finds a small but significant difference between men and women in preferences for relationships as compared to hookups: After the most recent hookup, 47 percent of women compared to 37 percent of men expressed some interest in a relationship. These differences in preferences are consistent with a multilevel perspective that views the internalization of gender as an aspect of gender structure (Risman 2004). As we have shown, the pressure to internalize gender-appropriate preferences is considerable, and the line between personal preferences and the desire to avoid social stigma is fuzzy. However, we believe that widely shared beliefs about gender difference contribute more to gender inequality in college heterosexuality than the substantively small differences in actual preferences. . . .

DISCUSSION QUESTIONS

1. What are the ways that social class shapes sexuality for college men as well as for college women?
2. What problems and advantages follow from the self-development and relationship imperatives?

NOTES

1. Online College Social Life Survey data collection is ongoing. Thus, numbers vary slightly according to the version of the data set. This article references data prepared and distributed by Reuben J. Thomas on February 26, 2009.
2. This number is consistent with that reported by Paul, McManus, and Hayes (2000). Glenn and Marquardt (2001) found lower rates, perhaps because they include students attending religious and commuter colleges. Recently, Owen et al. (2008) found that white students, those who drink, and students with higher parental income are more likely to hook up.
3. The two women who identified as lesbian or bisexual are included as they also had sex with men. How the women on this floor responded to lesbianism is explored elsewhere (Hamilton 2007).

REFERENCES

Armstrong, Elizabeth A., Paula England, and Alison C. K. Fogarty. 2009. Orgasm in college hookups and relationships. In *Families as they really are,* edited by B. Risman. New York: Norton.

Bogle, Kathleen A. 2008. *Hooking up: Sex, dating, and relationships on campus.* New York: New York University Press.

Campbell, Jacquelyn C. Nancy Glass, Phyllis W. Sharps, Kathryn Laughon, and Tina Bloom. 2007. Intimate partner homicide. *Trauma, Violence, & Abuse* 8:246–69.

Dunn, Jennifer L. 1999. What love has to do with it: The cultural construction of emotion and sorority women's responses to forcible interaction. *Social Problems* 46:440–59.

England, Paula, Emily Fitzgibbons Shafer, and Alison C.K. Fogarty. 2007. Hooking up and forming romantic relationships on today's college campuses. In *The gendered society reader,* edited by M. Kimmel. New York: Oxford University Press.

Glenn, Norval, and Elizabeth Marquardt. 2001. *Hooking up, hanging out, and hoping for Mr. Right: College women on mating and dating today.* New York: Institute for American Values.

Manning, Wendy D., Peggy C. Giordano, and Monica A. Longmore. 2006. Hooking up: The relationship contexts of "nonrelationship" sex. *Journal of Adolescent Research* 21:459–83.

Paul, Elizabeth L., Brian McManus, and Allison Hayes. 2000. "Hookups": Characteristics and correlates of college students' spontaneous and anonymous sexual experiences. *Journal of Sex Research* 37:76–88.

Risman, Barbara J. 2004. Gender as a social structure: Theory wrestling with activism. *Gender & Society* 18: 429–50.

SEXUAL ORIENTATION

READING 27

Beyond the Closet: The Transformation of Gay and Lesbian Life

Steven Seidman

SEXUAL IDENTITY

Identities refer to the way we think of ourselves and the self image we publicly project.[1] No doubt our identities are related to how we feel about ourselves and to our character or personality; as such, the image we publicly fashion might feel like a spontaneous expression of who we really are. Yet we can project an identity only through acting purposefully. The decisions we make about the way we dress, walk, and talk, the language we use and how we use it, who we associate with, and where and with whom we live make a statement about who we are. These practices announce to the world something about our gender, sexuality, parental status, social class, ethnic identity, and countless other markers of identity. In other words, we fashion identities by drawing on a culture that already associates identities with certain behaviors, places, and things.

Identities are complex. We don't have just one and in the course of our lives we can alter—add or subtract—identities. We make choices about which identity or identities to make into a core part of our self-definition and which will be treated as "threads" or secondary.

If an identity such as being a wife is considered "core," it will shape an individual's decisions about friends, residence, social activities, and employment. A core identity will be a key part of one's

Steven Seidman is a professor of sociology at SUNY Albany.

public presentation; it will carry over to diverse situations and remain part of varied social roles. It will be a chief way you want friends, coworkers, acquaintances, and kin to see and respond to you. For example, if being Jewish is a core identity, an individual will fashion a public self that consistently signals this identity by means of clothes, language, social activities, and friends. Decisions about partners or lovers, work, residence, and donations of time and money will likely be shaped by a core identity. By contrast, approaching identity as a thread suggests that an identity is important or self-defining in only some situations. While we may have only one or two core identities, we have many identity threads. For example, when I'm at home my identity as a parent may be paramount but at work it's my identity as a professor that matters; while as an active member of the gay community it is being gay that is crucial.

Not all identities are chosen or easily managed. There may be social pressure to approach certain identities as core ones; other individuals may disregard your wish to make this or that identity into a core or a thread. For example, for many people, race and gender function as a core identity. If you're black, others will likely assume and react as if this racial identity is primary regardless of your wishes.

During what we might call the heyday of the closet era, between roughly 1950 and 1980, some closeted individuals downplayed their homosexuality as an identity. They managed what was publicly considered a deviant identity by defining homosexuality as a secondary part of themselves, something akin to a peculiar appetite or an unusual sexual impulse. Yet for some individuals the sheer magnitude of energy and focus spent managing this stigmatized identity, and the fact that avoiding suspicion and exposure sometimes shaped a whole way of life, meant that homosexuality functioned as a sort of hidden core identity.

For individuals who decided to come out during this period of heightened public homophobia, the intensity of the struggle for acceptance of the self, and the anticipation that disclosure would likely bring a major lifestyle change, pressured some individuals to make homosexuality a focus of their lives. The pervasiveness of public fear and loathing of homosexuals that sustained the closet made coming out a deliberate, intense life drama. It is hardly surprising that many of these individuals would come to define their homosexuality as a core identity. Also, during these years many individuals migrated to urban centers and built protective subcultures. Becoming a part of these enclaves often meant fashioning a life around a core gay identity, as one became integrated into the dense social networks of an exclusive outsider world.

To the extent that the closet has less of a role in shaping gay life, the dynamics of identity change somewhat. As the lives of at least some gays look more like those of straights, as gays no longer feel compelled to migrate to urban enclaves to feel secure and respected, gay identity is often approached in ways similar to heterosexual identity—as a thread. However, it is a thread of a minority rather than a dominant majority—more like being a Muslim-American than like being a Protestant American. Given gays' historically embattled status, individuals will often be deliberate in publicly asserting a gay identity in order to make a personal statement of pride or a political statement. Many people continue to claim a core gay identity, despite the lessening of public acts of homophobia and social repression. Today, individuals may choose to adopt a core gay identity as a lifestyle or for political reasons. For example, individuals may migrate to urban subcultures and fashion lives around being gay, but less to escape a claustrophobic, hostile social milieu than to find kindred spirits who share particular lifestyle choices.

It occurred to me, as my research progressed, that as some of us are living more openly and freely, heterosexuals are now routinely exposed to positive images of being gay and to actual gay individuals. I wondered whether straight Americans might alter the way they approach sexual identity. I decided to interview mostly younger folk, roughly age seventeen to early twenties. I figured that any change in the culture of heterosexual identity would be easier to detect in younger people.

I found contradictory patterns. On the one hand, as straight individuals viewed gays as normal, some reported being less attached to or less assertive of a heterosexual identity. These individuals told me that they do not act to avoid gays or any suspicion of being gay by deliberately flagging a heterosexual identity. They have deemphasized heterosexuality as an identity and some have said they no longer consider sexuality an important marker of identity. They prefer to identify themselves and others in nonsexual ways; for example, in terms of gender, social values, occupation, or as just "people." On the other hand, some individuals respond to the new gay visibility by becoming more purposeful about being seen as heterosexual. I was particularly interested in those individuals who said they view gays as ordinary people. Many of these individuals told me that they want to be recognized as straight. Some said that it's because that's who they are. Perhaps that's true, but it's also the case that claiming a heterosexual identity confers real social and cultural privileges.

The heightened sense of identity among heterosexuals and their deliberateness about asserting a heterosexual identity is, I think, something new. In the era of the closet, everyone was simply assumed to be straight; to be sure, individuals also projected a straight identity by being homophobic or gender conventional. Today, as it becomes less acceptable to be publicly homophobic, and as many gays and straights look and act alike, some individuals are deliberate in presenting a public heterosexual identity.

HETEROSEXUAL DOMINANCE

I work in one of the most liberal institutions in America, a research university, in one of the most liberal states in the nation, New York. Among colleagues and administrators, I feel respected as an individual and as a scholar who studies and writes about gay life. I have never experienced anything remotely close to discrimination or disrespect—at least not for reasons of sexual orientation. Still, my institution does not offer domestic partnership benefits for same-sex partners; gays are not included in the university policy of promoting respect for social diversity; there has never been any effort to hire openly gay professors; and except for myself and a handful of faculty who teach women's studies and English, I know of no faculty that includes lesbian and gay scholarship as part of his or her regular course offerings. In short, the personal aspects of my work life are "virtually normal," but my public status is that of a second-class citizen.

If gay life is freer and more open for many of us today, it is not because heterosexual dominance has ended. Discriminatory social policies and laws continue to organize American institutional life. Still, there has been something of a shift, at least in emphasis, in the way that heterosexual privilege is enforced. In many social settings, homophobic and blatantly repressive institutional practices are losing legitimacy as gays are seen as ordinary, "normal" human beings deserving rights and respect. We have cautiously been invited to join the community of Americans, but so far the invitation has not extended beyond tolerance of a minority; heterosexual dominance has not been seriously challenged. How is it that gays can be viewed as normal but are still unequal?[2]

To understand changes in patterns of heterosexual dominance, I decided to look at commercial films. Since the early 1960s, homosexuals have regularly appeared on the screen. However, the dramatic rise in their visibility since the 1990s makes film useful for charting shifts in how homosexuality is understood and regulated.

After analyzing almost fifty films that appeared between 1960 and 2000, I've concluded that for most of these years heterosexual dominance worked by polluting homosexuality. The homosexual was viewed as such a despicable and disgusting figure that no one would want to openly declare herself a homosexual. Conversely, the heterosexual was defined as a pure and ideal status. Moreover, to the extent that homosexuals were imagined as predators, child molesters, disease spreaders, or cultural subversives, the state and other social institutions

were given a broad social mandate to protect respectable citizens by purging America of any visible signs of homosexuality. This culture of homosexual pollution contributed significantly to creating the conditions that we have come to call "the closet."

Until the mid-1990s, the image of the polluted homosexual dominated the screen. Then there was a striking change: the rise of the "normal gay." In films such as *Philadelphia, In and Out, The Object of My Affection, As Good as It Gets,* and *My Best Friend's Wedding,* gays step forward as "normal" human beings. Normality carries ambiguous political meaning. The status of normality means that gays are just like any other citizens. We have the same needs, feelings, commitments, loyalties, and aspirations as straight Americans. Accordingly, we deserve the same rights and respect. But normal also carries another normative sense: the normal gay is expected to exhibit specific kinds of traits and behaviors. He is supposed to be gender conventional, well adjusted, and integrated into mainstream society; she is committed to home, family, career, and nation.

This claim to normality justifies social integration but only for normal-looking and acting gays and lesbians. Moreover, to the extent that the normal gay aspires only to be a full-fledged citizen or to be accepted into America as is, her integration does not challenge heterosexual dominance. The politics of the normal gay involves minority rights, not the end of heterosexual privilege.

THE POLITICS OF SEXUAL CITIZENSHIP

The closet was not only a response to a culture that polluted and scandalized homosexuality. Stigma and the shame it induced would surely create ambivalence around being seen as homosexual, but they would not necessarily keep homosexuals silent and secretive. If many gay individuals chose to organize public heterosexual lives, it was in no small part because of a government that waged a war against homosexuals. From the 1950s onward, the state enacted laws and policies that persecuted and prosecuted homosexuals. If exposure risked public disgrace and the loss of job and family, is it any wonder that many individuals opted for a closeted life?

Throughout most of American history homosexuals were not the targets of state control. From the beginning of the republic through much of the nineteenth century, homosexuality was not viewed as the basis for a distinct self-identity, and homosexual behavior was not the focus of specific laws. Homosexual behavior was outlawed as an act of "sodomy," which referred to a wide range of nonmarital, nonprocreative acts. This changed in the late nineteenth and early twentieth centuries as a variety of powerful social groups enlisted the state to battle what they saw as the spread of vice, divorce, and sexual and gender deviance. The state became heavily involved in regulating the intimate affairs of its citizens. Still, it wasn't until the 1950s and 1960s that the government mobilized its considerable resources and authority to crack down on homosexuals. At this point, the closet became the defining reality of gay life in America.

Homosexual repression and pollution was met with political resistance. From the beginning, the modern gay movement has been divided between a rights-oriented assimilationist and a liberationist agenda. Both wings of the movement made dismantling the closet a chief political aim. Except for a short period in the early 1970s and a brief flourish in the late 1980s and early 1990s (ACT UP and Queer Nation), a rights agenda has dominated the chief organizations of the gay movement. Its aim, roughly speaking, is to bring gays into the circle of citizenship and social respectability.

The rights-oriented movement has had many successes. Repressive laws have been repealed or now go unenforced; and positive rights have been established in many municipalities, workplaces, and institutions of all sorts. These social gains have made it possible for many of us to organize fairly routine personal and public lives. And, as many of us have come to feel a strong sense of self-integrity and social entitlement, mainstream gay politics has responded by shifting its agenda from gaining tolerance (decriminalization) to achieving civil and political equality. In this regard, it is not accidental that battles around gay marriage and gays in the military have gained prominence. There cannot be real equality without equal marital and military rights.

As the rights wing of the gay movement moved forward confidently, as there developed multimillion-dollar national organizations battling for our rights, the voices of some critics have also grown sharper and louder. Liberationism didn't, after all, expire in the mid-1970s or the mid-1990s. It survived on the margins, in the culture of academics, artists, writers, and some activists. And, as the rights movement has helped gays gain a footing in the social mainstream, liberationists have expressed concerns. While some critics wrongly interpret the struggle for rights as a desire to mimic straight life, liberationists have also understood, in a way that rights advocates have not, that heterosexual dominance is deeply rooted in the institutions and culture of American society. Gaining equal rights, including the right to marry and serve in the military, will not bring about full social equality. Without challenging a culture of advertising, television, film, music, literature, and news that makes heterosexuality the norm and the ideal, there cannot be social equality. Until our public schools hire openly gay teachers and administrators, and incorporate the teaching of gay lives, families, culture, and politics into the curriculum, there may be tolerance but not social equality. Until our workplaces celebrate events such as Coming Out Day and the anniversary of Stonewall, until companies advertise to attract gay consumers, promote openly gay employees to managerial and supervisory positions, encourage gay employees to bring their partners and dates to work-related social events, and offer the full range of health and other social benefits to gay employees, civic equality will remain an unrealized promise. We need a movement that broadens rights activism to include an agenda of across-the-board institutional equality and cultural justice.[3]

The struggle for gay equality should not be isolated from other social and sexual conflicts. From lesbian feminists and gay liberationists to queer activists, a liberationist tradition has sought to broaden our thinking about the politics of sexuality. They invite us to view the politics of sexual identity as part of a larger network of sexual and social conflicts.

From a liberationist perspective, bringing gays into the circle of good sexual citizens would still leave in place a sexual order that unnecessarily restricts the range of desires, behaviors, and relationships that are considered acceptable and worthy of value and social support. In other words, the idea of a good sexual citizen is associated with specific sexual-gender norms—what we might call a notion of "normal sexuality." Only sexual desires and acts that are viewed as normal are acceptable. Behaviors between consenting adults that fall outside the boundaries of normal sexuality may be labeled "abnormal," "diseased," or "unhealthy"; individuals who engage in these behaviors may be perceived as sick, immoral, and socially dangerous.

My sense is that, despite some dissent and conflict, there is a dominant culture that associates normal sexuality with sex that is exclusively between adults, that conforms to dichotomous gender norms that is private, tender, caring, genitally centered, and linked to love, marriage, and monogamy. There is then a wide range of consensual adult practices that are potentially vulnerable to stigma and social punishment; for example, rough or S/M (sadomasochistic) sex, "casual" sex, multiple-partner sex, group and fetishistic sex, and commercial and public sex. Individuals who engage in some of these acts will be scandalized as "bad citizens"; demands will be heard to use repressive or therapeutic interventions to protect good citizens from contamination—that is, being seduced, molested, or infected by disease-carrying sexual deviants.

The gay movement should not ignore this broader sexual political context. Like it or not, a movement seeking gay equality inevitably supports or challenges a wide network of sexual control. Obviously, it challenges the outsider status of gays. But, to the extent that this movement appeals to a narrow set of sexual norms associated with the good citizen to justify its claim for rights and respect, it reinforces the outsider status of many sexual agents who engage in consensual, victimless practices. In fact, as the "normal gay" is integrated as a good citizen, other sexual outsiders may stand in for the homosexual as representing the "bad" or dangerous sexual citizen. Polluting specific sexual citizens as "bad" and dangerous (for example, sex workers, libertines, sexually aggressive women, sexually active youth, pregnant young women) establishes certain sexual acts or lifestyles (commercial sex, multiple-partner sex, youthful sexuality) as unacceptable; those who engage in these acts risk public disgrace or worse. Bringing gays into the fold of the good citizen may not then bring about expanded choice for all citizens. It may evoke fears of disorder, and this may bring about the tightening of sexual control for all citizens.

Liberationists remind gays that there are many types of outsiders. There are outsiders among insiders (for example, straights whose desires run to the nonconventional) and insiders among outsiders (gays who are thoroughly straight-looking-and-acting). So, yes, gays need and deserve equal rights and full, across-the-board social equality. But there are battles around sexual regulation that need to be waged beyond gay rights and equality. Liberationist voices need to be heard.

A MULTICULTURAL AMERICA

Gays' changing social status is connected to the making of America as a multicultural nation. The United States is becoming a society that is more socially diverse than it has been at any other time in its history. And, for many of its citizens, respecting and valuing group differences is a key part of this nation's identity.

Today, many Americans see themselves as national citizens but also as members of particular cultural communities. We are proud to be American but also to be women, African American, Chinese, Irish, Catholic, Muslim, Latino/a, gay, or part of a disabled community. And we don't confine our differences to private life; we assert our group identities in social and political life. We bring our differences into the cultural and institutional arena and expect them to be respected.

Outsider groups, including gays, have benefited from this multicultural remaking of America. For example, Americans are today expected to initially withhold judgment when encountering individuals who are culturally different. We are encouraged to consider varied points of view on sexuality, family, politics, education, and faith. For individuals and groups who are marginal or who have been outside of what is considered "the mainstream," a multicultural national ideal makes it possible for them to at least get a public hearing. In a multicultural society, public space, however cramped and marginal, is created for outsider groups to make their case to be respected as part of the spectrum of legitimate social difference.

At a deeper level, as a national culture takes shape that values group differences, there is occurring something of a shift from "absolutist" to "pragmatic" types of moral reasoning. The former makes judgments on the basis of transcendent worldviews. For example, divorce might be criticized because it violates a fixed, absolute norm of permanent marriage established by religion, tradition, or natural-law thinking. By contrast, a pragmatic approach offers loose guidelines in making judgments; it acknowledges that there can be varied legitimate moral points of view and that these should be reckoned with. This approach encourages a more situation-specific style of moral decision making; individual needs, purposes, and possible social consequences should be considered. Judgments about the ethics of divorce should weigh issues of individual well-being and public welfare and perhaps involve some sort of calculus of advantage and disadvantage. Absolute thinking is not so much declining as making room for pragmatic moral styles.

A pragmatic moral culture encourages gay integration. If an identity or way of life can be deemed worthy of social respect because it promotes personal and social well-being, and cannot be shown to have clear social harm, gays need only make the case that homosexuality is both victimless and, like heterosexuality, essential to personal happiness. To

the extent that a pragmatic moral style gains a social footing, those who aim to deny gays' rights and respect by relying on absolutist arguments (for example, that homosexuality is a sin or disease) may be put on the defensive, as they are accused of intolerance, authoritarianism, or cultural backwardness.

Changes in America's moral culture pressure institutions to accommodate group differences. In the past few decades, we've seen institutions make real efforts to incorporate people of color, women, ethnic minorities, the disabled, and gays. In each case, though, social accommodation has meant tolerance, not full social equality.

Group differences are recognized but understood as products of prejudice and discrimination. Inequalities are to be remedied by education and the establishment of equal rights and opportunity. In effect, complex cultural communities such as those of blacks, the deaf, or gays, are viewed as temporary social adaptations to intolerance. Individual members of these groups are assumed to share core national values, beliefs, and social goals. As outsiders are tolerated and integrated into the social mainstream, their participation in these particular cultural communities is expected to weaken. These ethnic-like identities will become merely personal or symbolic, if they do not entirely disappear. At least that's the expectation and hope. In this view of a multicultural America, group differences are recognized, but integration through legal rights and identity normalization leaves the dominant social norms and hierarchies in place.

For example, confronted with the women's movement the state and other social institutions responded by narrowing its agenda to one of granting women's formal equality. As men and women become equal national citizens or bearers of equal rights as workers, family members, and political citizens, gender differences other than those that relate to rights, equal opportunity, and respect are understood as personal. However, many in the women's movement claim that there are important differences in social values and outlook between men and women; these differences have mostly been ignored by our institutions.

The way multiculturalism currently works in the United States leaves in place the dominant social groups and social norms. A social order that is disproportionately shaped by the interests of, say, men, whites, the abled, or straights is not seriously threatened by enfranchising gays, women or blacks. Still, integrating outsider groups such as these improves the quality of their lives and may have important unintended consequences. For example, the state, pressured by various groups, has passed a great deal of legislation that expands individual control over bodily, sexual, and intimate expression. Thus, the legalization of abortion in *Roe v. Wade* and a wave of legislation aimed at protecting women from sexual harassment and violence has expanded women's capacity to make sexual-intimate choices. Appealing to an ideal of sexual autonomy that is implicit in this legislation, women may claim a right to remain single, to be single parents, or to choose other women as their partners.

Although this liberal state practice promotes tolerance, it has considerable limits and can be stalled or reversed. In general, as the agenda of social movements has shifted from abstract civil rights to actual institutional equality, the state has retreated from an agenda of promoting diversity. Thus, as gay marriage became a national issue after the Hawaii Court of Appeals case, the U.S. Congress passed, with the overwhelming support of the Democrats and the president, the Defense of Marriage Act, which restricted marriage to heterosexuals. Nevertheless, to the extent that the state endorses the right of individuals to control their own bodies and sexual expression, gays can appeal to this principle to make demands for tolerance and equality. . . .

DISCUSSION QUESTIONS

1. Under what circumstances would sexual identity be a thread identity, and when would it be a core identity?

2. How does the film and popular culture image of the "normal gay" both help and hinder the gay rights movement?

NOTES

1. My ideas about identity have benefited from the sociological views of Erving Goffman, in particular *The Presentation of the Self in Everyday Life* (Garden City, N.Y.: Doubleday, 1959) and *Stigma: Notes on the Management of Sexual Identity* (Englewood Cliffs, N.J.: Prentice-Hall, 1963). I have also drawn considerably from poststructural approaches that emphasize the relational and performative character of identity. In this regard, see Judith Butler, *Gender Trouble: Gender and the Subversion of Identity* (New York: Routledge, 1990), and Diana Fuss, *Essentially Speaking: Feminism, Nature, and Difference* (New York: Routledge, 1990), and "Inside/Out," in *Inside/Out. Lesbian Theories, Gay Theories*, ed. Diana Fuss (New York: Routledge, 1991). The work of historians and social scientists has been crucial in recent discussion of sexual identity. For a sampling of this work, see Jeffrey Weeks, *Coming Out: Homosexual Politics in Britain from the Nineteenth Century to the Present* (London: Quarter, 1977), and *Sexuality and Its Discontents* (London: Routledge, 1985); John D'Emilio, *Sexual Politics, Sexual Communities: The Making of a Homosexual Minority in the United States, 1940–1970* (Chicago: University of Chicago Press, 1983); Lillian Faderman, *Odd Girls and Twilight Lovers: A History of Lesbian Life in Twentieth-Century America* (New York: Columbia University Press, 1991); George Chauncey, *Gay New York: Gender, Urban Culture, and the Making of the Gay Male World, 1890–1940* (New York: Basic Books, 1994); Kenneth Plummer, *Sexual Stigma: An Interactionist Account* (London: Routledge, 1975); Kristin Esterberg, *Lesbian and Bisexual Identities: Constructing Communities, Constructing Selves* (Philadelphia: Temple University Press, 1997); Arlene Stein, *Sex and Sensibility: Stories of a Lesbian Generation* (Berkeley: University of California Press, 1997); Joshua Gamson, *Freaks Talk Back: Tabloid Talk Shows and Sexual Nonconformity* (Chicago: University of Chicago Press, 1998); and Viviane Namaste, *Invisible Lives: The Erasure of Transsexual and Transgendered People* (Chicago: University of Chicago Press, 2000).

2. In thinking about heterosexual dominance, I've drawn considerably from gay liberationism and lesbian feminism. Key texts include Dennis Altman, *Homosexual Oppression and Liberation* (New York: Avon Books, 1971); Nancy Myron and Charlotte Bunch, eds. *Lesbianism and the Women's Movement* (Baltimore: Diana Press, 1975); Karla Jay and Allen Young, eds., *Out of the Closets: Voices of Gay Liberationism* (New York: New York University Press, 1992 [1972]); and Mark Blasius and Shane Phelan, eds., *We Are Everywhere: A Historical Sourcebook of Gay and Lesbian Politics* (New York: Routledge, 1997). Among the key works inspired by these traditions are Adrienne Rich,

PERSONAL ACCOUNT

Living Invisibly

For me, coming out is a Sisyphean task. Because of my invisible differences, I constantly have to reveal different parts of my identity. It's not an easy task, either. When I come out as a lesbian/queer woman, people are often surprised because I don't "look" queer. I can count on one hand the number of times I have been recognized by a stranger as part of the LGBT "family." Some people are also surprised to learn that I'm half Taiwanese. I am also half-white, and often assumed to be white, making my race another invisible identity. Because of this, there have been times when people have made racist jokes—either about Asians or other groups—because they thought I was white, and thus thought that these were "acceptable" jokes to tell in my presence.

Invisible identities work differently from other differences. I am lucky not to be harassed on the street because of my race, and since I don't appear queer to your average passerby, I don't usually get harassed for that. I benefit from the privilege of passing as a straight and white, but most days I wish that I could give up that privilege. It is extremely difficult to live your life where some of the most important things about you are hidden. For example, I never know when it is appropriate to come out as queer in class, and almost feel guilty if I never do, even though it may not always be necessary or appropriate. Because I am invisible, I bear the burden of disclosure. When someone assumes that I'm heterosexual, I have to correct her or him (my mother still doesn't believe that I'm queer). When someone assumes that I'm white, I do the same. Regardless, I come out all the time to new people in my life, and each time I do, I hope that they will be able to handle the information with care and respect.

Most people respond well when I come out to them, and I can breathe another sigh of relief when my peers accept me. College, especially, has been a (mostly) safe space for me to be out and proud about my race and sexuality. Living with my multiple invisible identities has taught me to be more assertive in all areas of my life, and I have learned to take risks. I know quite well how privilege works, and how that privilege can be taken away in an instant. I am also proud of all of my identities. The difficulty of coming out is well worth the satisfaction and pride I have of living my life the way that I have always wanted to.

Tara S. Ellison

"Compulsory Heterosexuality and Lesbian Existence," *Signs* 5 (Summer 1980): 631–60; Michael Warner, "Fear of a Queer Planet," *Social Text* 9 (1991): 3–17; Eve Sedgwick, *Epistemology of the Closet* (Berkeley: University of California Press, 1990); and, in the British context, Stevie Jackson, *Heterosexuality in Question* (London: Sage, 1999). In the past few years there has emerged an empirical literature that speaks to the ways compulsory heterosexuality operates in different institutions and societies. See Mary Louise Adams, *The Trouble with Normal: Postwar Youth and the Making of Heterosexuality* (Toronto: University of Toronto Press, 1997); Karen Dubinsky, *Improper Advances: Rape and Heterosexual Conflict in Ontario, 1880–1929* (Chicago: University of Chicago Press, 1993); Debbie Epstein and Richard Johnson, *Schooling Sexualities* (Buckingham: Open University Press, 1998); Chrys Ingraham, *White Weddings: Romancing Heterosexuality in Popular Culture* (New York: Routledge, 1999); Mairtin Mac An Ghaill, *The Making of Men: Masculinities, Sexualities, and Schooling*

(Buckingham: Open University Press, 1994); Anna Marie Smith, "The Good Homosexual and the Dangerous Queer: Resisting the 'New Homophobia,'" in *New Sexual Agendas*, ed. Lynn Segal (New York: New York University Press, 1997); D. Steinberg, D. Epstein, and R. Johnson, eds., *Border Patrols: Policing the Boundaries of Heterosexuality* (London: Cassell, 1997); and Lisa Duggan, "The Social Enforcement of Heterosexuality and Lesbian Resistance," in *Class, Race, and Sex: The Dynamics of Control*, eds. Amy Swerdlow and Hannah Lessinger (Boston: G. K. Hall, 1983), 75–92.

3. In thinking about lesbian and gay politics beyond questions of rights and equality, my ideas have been sharpened by the work of Michel Foucault, *The History of Sexuality, Vol. 1: An Introduction* (New York: Vintage, 1980); Gayle Rubin, "Thinking Sex: Notes for a Radical Theory of the Politics of Sexuality," in *Pleasure and Danger: Exploring Female Sexuality*, ed. Carole Vance (Boston: Routledge, 1984); Pat Califia, *Public Sex: The Culture of Radical Sex* (Pittsburgh: Cleis, 1994); Sedgwick, *Epistemology of the*

Closet; Vaid, *Virtual Equality;* Combahee River Collective, "A Black Feminist Statement," in *All the Women Are White, All the Blacks Are Men, But Some of Us Are Brave: Black Women's Studies,* eds. Gloria Hull, Patricia Bell Scott, and Barbara Smith (Old Westbury, N.Y.: Feminist Press, 1982); Shane Phelan, *Getting Specific: Postmodern Lesbian Politics* (Minneapolis: University of Minnesota Press, 1994); Diane Richardson, "Constructing Sexual Citizenship: Theorizing Sexual Rights," *Critical Social Policy 20* (2000): 100–35; Jeffrey Weeks, "The Sexual Citizen," in *Love and Eroticism,* ed. Mike Featherstone (London: Sage, 1999), pp. 35–52.

READING 28

Dude, You're a Fag: Adolescent Male Homophobia

C. J. Pascoe

The sun shone bright and clear over River High's annual Creative and Performing Arts Happening, or CAPA. During CAPA the school's various art programs displayed students' work in a fairlike atmosphere. The front quad sported student-generated computer programs. Colorful and ornate chalk art covered the cement sidewalks. Tables lined with student-crafted pottery were set up on the grass. Tall displays of students' paintings divided the rear quad. To the left of the paintings a television blared student-directed music videos. At the rear of the back quad, a square, roped-off area of cement served as a makeshift stage for drama, choir, and dance performances. Teachers released students from class to wander around the quads, watch performances, and look at the art. This freedom from class time lent the day an air of excitement because students were rarely allowed to roam the campus without a hall pass, an office summons, or a parent/faculty escort. In honor of CAPA, the school district bussed in elementary school students from the surrounding grammar schools to participate in the day's festivities.

C. J. Pascoe is a professor of sociology at Colorado College.

Running through the rear quad, Brian, a senior, yelled to a group of boys visiting from the elementary schools, "There's a faggot over there! There's a faggot over there! Come look!" Following Brian, the ten-year-olds dashed down a hallway. At the end of the hallway Brian's friend Dan pursed his lips and began sashaying toward the little boys. As he minced, he swung his hips exaggeratedly and wildly waved his arms. To the boys Brian yelled, "Look at the faggot! Watch out! He'll get you!" In response, the ten-year-olds raced back down the hallway screaming in terror. Brian and Dan repeated this drama throughout the following half hour, each time with a new group of young boys.

Making jokes like these about faggots was central to social life at River High. Indeed, boys learned long before adolescence that faggots were simultaneously predatory and passive and that they were, at all costs, to be avoided. Older boys repeatedly impressed upon younger ones through these types of homophobic rituals that whatever they did, whatever they became, however they talked, they had to avoid becoming a faggot.

Feminist scholars of masculinity have documented the centrality of homophobic insults and attitudes to masculinity (Kimmel 2001; Lehne 1998), especially in school settings (Burn 2000; Kimmel 2003; Messner 2005; Plummer 2001; G. Smith 1998; Wood 1984). They argue that homophobic teasing often characterizes masculinity in adolescence and early adulthood and that antigay slurs tend to be directed primarily at gay boys. This [discussion] both expands on and challenges these accounts of relationships between homophobia and masculinity. Homophobia is indeed a central mechanism in the making of contemporary American adolescent masculinity. A close analysis of the way boys at River High invoke the faggot as a disciplinary mechanism makes clear that something more than simple homophobia is at play in adolescent masculinity. The use of the word *fag* by boys at River High points to the limits of an argument that focuses centrally on homophobia. Fag is not only an identity linked to homosexual boys but an identity that can temporarily adhere to heterosexual boys as well. The fag trope is also a racialized disciplinary mechanism.

Homophobia is too facile a term with which to describe the deployment of *fag* as an epithet. By calling the use of the word *fag* homophobia—and letting the argument stop there—previous research has obscured the gendered nature of sexualized insults (Plummer 2001). Invoking homophobia to describe the ways boys aggressively tease each other overlooks the powerful relationship between masculinity and this sort of insult. Instead, it seems incidental, in this conventional line of argument, that girls do not harass each other and are not harassed in this same manner. This framing naturalizes the relationship between masculinity and homophobia, thus obscuring that such harassment is central to the formation of a gendered identity for boys in a way that it is not for girls.

Fag is not necessarily a static identity attached to a particular (homosexual) boy. Fag talk and fag imitations serve as a discourse with which boys discipline themselves and each other through joking relationships. Any boy can temporarily become a fag in a given social space or interaction. This does not mean that boys who identify as or are perceived to be homosexual aren't subject to intense harassment. Many are. But becoming a fag has as much to do with failing at the masculine tasks of competence, heterosexual prowess, and strength or in any way revealing weakness or femininity as it does with a sexual identity. This fluidity of the fag identity is what makes the specter of the fag such a powerful disciplinary mechanism. It is fluid enough that boys police their behaviors out of fear of having the fag identity permanently adhere and definitive enough so that boys recognize a fag behavior and strive to avoid it.

An analysis of the fag discourse also indicates ways in which gendered power works through racialized selves. The fag discourse is invoked differently by and in relation to white boys' bodies than it is by and in relation to African American boys' bodies. While certain behaviors put all boys at risk for becoming temporarily a fag, some behaviors can be enacted by African American boys without putting them at risk of receiving the label. The racialized meanings of the fag discourse suggest that something more than simple homophobia is involved in these sorts of interactions. It is not that gendered homophobia does not exist in African American communities. Indeed, making fun of "negro faggotry seems to be a rite of passage among contemporary black male rappers and filmmakers" (Riggs 1991, 253). However, the fact that "white women and men, gay and straight, have more or less colonized cultural debates about sexual representation" (Julien and Mercer 1991, 167) obscures varied systems of sexualized meanings among different racialized ethnic groups (Almaguer 1991). Thus far male homophobia has primarily been written about as a racially neutral phenomenon. However, as D. L. King's (2004) recent work on African American men and same-sex desire pointed out, homophobia is characterized by racial identities as well as sexual and gendered ones.

WHAT IS A FAG? GENDERED MEANINGS

"Since you were little boys you've been told, 'Hey, don't be a little faggot,'" explained Darnell, a football player of mixed African American and white heritage, as we sat on a bench next to the athletic field. Indeed, both the boys and girls I interviewed told me that *fag* was the worst epithet one guy could direct at another. Jeff, a slight white sophomore, explained to me that boys call each other fag because "gay people aren't really liked over here and stuff." Jeremy, a Latino junior, told me that this insult literally reduced a boy to nothing, "To call someone *gay* or *fag* is like the lowest thing you can call someone. Because that's like saying that you're nothing."

Most guys explained their or others' dislike of fags by claiming that homophobia was synonymous with being a guy. For instance, Keith, a white soccer-playing senior, explained, "I think guys are just homophobic." However, boys were not equal-opportunity homophobes. Several students told me that these homophobic insults applied only to boys and not to girls. For example, while Jake, a handsome white senior, told me that he didn't like gay people, he quickly added, "Lesbians, okay, that's *good*." Similarly Cathy, a popular white cheerleader, told me, "Being a lesbian is accepted because guys think, 'Oh that's cool.'" Darnell, after telling me that boys were warned about becoming faggots, said, "They [guys] are fine with girls. I think it's the guy part that they're like ewwww." In this sense it was not strictly homophobia but a gendered homophobia that constituted adolescent masculinity in the culture of River High. It is clear, according to these comments, that lesbians were "good" because of their place in heterosexual male fantasy, not necessarily because of some enlightened approach to same-sex relationships. A popular trope in heterosexual pornography depicts two women engaging in sexual acts for the purpose of male titillation. The boys at River High are not unique in making this distinction; adolescent boys in general dislike gay men more than they dislike lesbians (Baker and Fishbein 1998). The fetishizing of sex acts between women indicates that using only the term *homophobia* to describe boys' repeated use of the word *fag* might be a bit simplistic and misleading.

Girls at River High rarely deployed the word *fag* and were never called fags. I recorded girls uttering *fag* only three times during my research. In one instance, Angela, a Latina cheerleader, teased Jeremy, a well-liked white senior involved in student government, for not ditching school with her: "You wouldn't 'cause you're a faggot." However, girls did not use this word as part of their regular lexicon. The sort of gendered homophobia that constituted adolescent masculinity did not constitute adolescent femininity. Girls were not called dykes or lesbians in any sort of regular or systematic way. Students did tell me that *slut* was the worst thing a girl could be called. However, my field notes indicate that the word *slut* (or its synonym *ho*) appeared one time for every eight times the word *fag* appeared.

Highlighting the difference between the deployment of *gay* and *fag* as insults brings the gendered nature of this homophobia into focus. For boys and girls at River High *gay* was a fairly common synonym for "stupid." While this word shared the sexual origins of *fag*, it didn't *consistently* have the skew of gender-loaded meaning. Girls and boys often used *gay* as an adjective referring to inanimate objects and male or female people, whereas they used *fag* as a noun that denoted only unmasculine males. Students used *gay* to describe anything from someone's clothes to a new school rule that they didn't like. For instance, one day in auto shop, Arnie pulled out a large older version of a black laptop computer and placed it on his desk. Behind him Nick cried, "That's a gay laptop! It's five inches thick!" The rest of the boys in the class laughed at Arnie's outdated laptop. A laptop can be gay, a movie can be gay, or a group of people can be gay. Boys used *gay* and *fag* interchangeably when they referred to other boys, but *fag* didn't have the gender-neutral attributes that *gay* frequently invoked.

Surprisingly, some boys took pains to say that the term *fag* did not imply sexuality. Darnell told me, "It doesn't even have anything to do with being gay." Similarly, J. L., a white sophomore at Hillside High (River High's cross-town rival), asserted, "*Fag*, seriously, it has nothing to do with sexual preference at all. You could just be calling somebody an idiot, you know?" I asked Ben, a quiet, white sophomore who wore heavy-metal T-shirts to auto shop each day, "What kind of things do guys get called a fag for?" Ben answered, "Anything . . . literally, anything. Like you were trying to turn a wrench the wrong way, 'Dude, you're a fag.' Even if a piece of meat drops out of your sandwich, 'You fag!'" Each time Ben said, "You fag," his voice deepened as if he were imitating a more masculine boy. While Ben might rightly *feel* that a guy could be called a fag for "anything . . . literally, anything," there were actually specific behaviors that, when enacted by most boys, could render them more vulnerable to a *fag* epithet. In this instance Ben's comment highlights the use of *fag* as a generic insult for incompetence, which in the world of River High, was central to a masculine identity. A boy could get called a fag for exhibiting any sort of behavior defined as unmasculine (although not necessarily behaviors aligned with femininity): being stupid or incompetent, dancing, caring too much about clothing, being too emotional, or expressing interest (sexual or platonic) in other guys. However, given the extent of its deployment and the laundry list of behaviors that could get a boy in trouble, it is no wonder that Ben felt a boy could be called fag for "anything." These nonsexual meanings didn't replace sexual meanings but rather existed alongside them.

One-third (thirteen) of the boys I interviewed told me that, while they might liberally insult each other with the term, they would not direct it at a homosexual peer. Jabes, a Filipino senior, told me, "I actually say it *[fag]* quite a lot, except for when I'm in the company of an actual homosexual person. Then I try not to say it at all. But when I'm just hanging out with my friends I'll be like, 'shut up, I don't want to hear you any more, you stupid fag.'" Similarly J. L. compared homosexuality to a disability, saying there was "no way" he'd call an actually gay guy a fag because "there's people who are the retarded people who nobody wants to associate with. I'll be so nice to those guys, and I hate it when people make fun of them. It's like, 'Bro do you realize that they can't help that?' And then there's gay people. They were born that way." According to this group of boys, gay was a legitimate, or at least biological, identity.

There was a possibility, however slight, that a boy could be gay and masculine (Connell 1995). David, a handsome white senior dressed smartly in khaki pants and a white button-down shirt, told me, "Being gay is just a lifestyle. It's someone you choose to sleep with. You can still throw around a football and be gay." It was as if David was justifying the use of the word *fag* by arguing that gay men could be men if they tried but that if they failed at it (i.e., if they couldn't throw a football) then they deserved to be called a fag. In other words, to be a fag was, by definition, the opposite of masculine, whether the word was deployed with sexualized or nonsexualized meanings. In explaining this to me, Jamaal, an African American junior, cited the explanation of the popular rap artist Eminem: "Although

I don't like Eminem, he had a good definition of it. It's like taking away your title. In an interview they were like, 'You're always capping on gays, but then you sing with Elton John.' He was like 'I don't mean gay as in gay.'" This is what Riki Wilchins (2003) calls the "Eminem Exception. Eminem explains that he doesn't call people 'faggot' because of their sexual orientation but because they're weak and unmanly" (72). This is precisely the way boys at River High used the term *faggot*. While it was not necessarily acceptable to be gay, at least a man who was gay could do other things that would render him acceptably masculine. A fag, by the very definition of the word, could not be masculine.

This distinction between fag as an unmasculine and problematic identity and gay as a possibly masculine, although marginalized, sexual identity is not limited to a teenage lexicon; it is reflected in both psychological discourses and gay and lesbian activism. Eve Sedgwick (1995) argues that in contemporary psychological literature homosexuality is no longer a problem for men so long as the homosexual man is of the right age and gender orientation. In this literature a homosexual male must be an adult and must be masculine. Male homosexuality is not pathologized, but gay male *effeminacy* is. The lack of masculinity is the problem, not the sexual practice or orientation. Indeed, the edition of the *Diagnostic and Statistical Manual of Mental Disorders* (a key document in the mental health field) that erased homosexuality as a diagnosis in the 1970s added a new diagnosis in its wake: Gender Identity Disorder. According to Sedgwick, the criteria for diagnosis are different for girls and boys. A girl has to actually assert that she is a boy, indicating a psychotic disconnection with reality, whereas a boy need only display a preoccupation with female activities. The policing of boys' gender orientation and of a strict masculine identity for gay men is also reflected in gay culture itself. The war against fags as the specter of unmasculine manhood appears in gay male personal ads in which men look for "straight-appearing, straight-acting men." This concern with both straight and gay men's masculinity not only reflects teenage boys' obsession with hypermasculinity but also points to the conflict at the heart of the contemporary "crisis of masculinity" being played out in popular, scientific, and educational arenas.

BECOMING A FAG: FAG FLUIDITY

"The ubiquity of the word *faggot* speaks to the reach of its discrediting capacity" (Corbett 2001, 4). It's almost as if boys cannot help shouting it out on a regular basis—in the hallway, in class, or across campus as a greeting. In my fieldwork I was amazed by the way the word seemed to pop uncontrollably out of boys' mouths in all kinds of situations.[1] To quote just one of many instances from my field notes: two boys walked out of the PE locker room, and one yelled, "Fucking faggot!" at no one in particular. None of the other students paid them any mind, since this sort of thing happened so frequently. Similar spontaneous yelling of some variation of the word *fag*, seemingly apropos of nothing, happened repeatedly among boys throughout the school. This and repeated imitations of fags constitute what I refer to as a "fag discourse."

Fag discourse is central to boys' joking relationships. Joking cements relationships among boys (Kehily and Nayak 1997; Lyman 1998) and helps to manage anxiety and discomfort (Freud 1905). Boys both connect with one another and manage the anxiety around this sort of relationship through joking about fags. Boys invoked the specter of the fag in two ways: through humorous imitation and through lobbing the epithet at one another. Boys at River High imitated the fag by acting out an exaggerated "femininity" and/or by pretending to sexually desire other boys. As indicated by the introductory vignette in which an older boy imitated a predatory fag to threaten little boys, male students at River High linked these performative scenarios with a fag identity. They also lobbed the *fag* epithet at each other in a verbal game of hot potato, each careful to deflect the insult quickly by hurling it toward someone else. These games and imitations made up a fag discourse that highlighted the fag not as a static but rather as a fluid identity that boys constantly struggled to avoid.

In imitative performances the fag discourse functioned as a constant reiteration of the fag's existence, affirming that the fag was out there; boys reminded themselves and each other that at any moment they could become fags if they were not sufficiently masculine. At the same time these performances demonstrated that the boy who was invoking the fag was *not* a fag. Emir, a tall, thin African American boy, frequently imitated fags to draw laughs from other students in his introductory drama class. One day Mr. McNally, the drama teacher, disturbed by the noise outside the classroom, turned to the open door, saying, "We'll shut this unless anyone really wants to watch sweaty boys playing basketball." Emir lisped, "I wanna watch the boys play!" The rest of the class cracked up at his imitation. No one in the class actually thought Emir was gay, as he purposefully mocked both same-sex sexual desire (through pretending to admire the boys playing basketball) and an effeminate gender identity (through speaking with a lisp and in a high-pitched voice). Had he said this in all seriousness, the class most likely would have responded in stunned silence. Instead, Emir reminded them he was masculine by immediately dropping the fag act. After imitating a fag, boys assure others that they are not a fag by instantly becoming masculine again after the performance. They mock their own performed femininity and/or same-sex desire, assuring themselves and others that such an identity deserves derisive laughter. . . .

The constant threat of the fag regulated boys' attitudes toward their bodies in terms of clothing, dancing, and touching. Boys constantly engaged in repudiatory rituals to avoid permanently inhabiting the fag position. Boys' interactions were composed of competitive joking through which they interactionally created the constitutive outside and affirmed their positions as subjects.

EMBODYING THE FAG: RICKY'S STORY

Through verbal jockeying, most boys at River continually moved in and out of the fag position. For the one boy who permanently inhabited the fag position, life at River High was not easy. I heard about Ricky long before I met him. As soon as I talked to any student involved with drama, the choir, or the Gay/Straight Alliance, they told me I had to meet Ricky. Ricky, a lithe, white junior with a shy smile and downcast eyes, frequently sported multi-colored hair extensions, mascara, and sometimes a skirt. An extremely talented dancer, he often starred in the school's dance shows and choreographed assemblies. In fact, he was the male lead in "I've Had the Time of My Life," the final number in the dance show. Given how important other students thought it was that I speak to him, I was surprised that I had to wait for nearly a year before he granted me an interview. His friends had warned me that he was "heterophobic" and as a result was reluctant to talk to authority figures he perceived were heterosexual. After I heard his stories of past and present abuse at the hands of negligent adults, cruel teenagers, and indifferent school administrators, I understood why he would be leery of folks asking questions about his feelings, experiences, and opinions. While other boys at River High engaged in continual repudiatory rituals around the fag identity, Ricky embodied the fag because of his homosexuality and his less normative gender identification and self-presentation.

Ricky assumed (rightly so in this context) that other people immediately identified him with his sexuality. He told me that when he first met people, "they'll be like, 'Can I ask you a personal question?' And I'm like, 'sure.' And they say, 'Are you gay?' And I'm like, 'Yeeeaahh.' 'Okay, can I ask you another question?' And I'm like, 'Sure.' And they'll go, 'Does it hurt?' It always goes . . ." He rolled his eyes dismissively, telling me, "They go straight up to the most personal question! They skip everything else. They go straight to that. Sometimes I'll get the occasional 'Well, how did you know that you were [gay]?'" He answered with "For me it's just always been there. I knew from the time I could think for myself on. It was pretty obvious," he concluded gesturing to his thin frame and tight fitting tank top with a flourish. . . .

. . . Figuring out the social map of the school was central to Ricky's survival. Homophobic harassment at the hands of teachers and students characterized his educational experience. When he was beat up in a middle school PE class, the teacher didn't help but rather fostered this sort of treatment:

> They gave them a two-day suspension and they kind of kept an eye on me. That's all they could do. The PE coach was very racist and very homophobic. He was just like "faggot this" and "faggot that." I did not feel comfortable in the locker room and I asked him if I could go somewhere else to change, and he said, "No, you can change here."

Sadly, by the time Ricky had reached River High he had become accustomed to the violence.

> In a weird sense, in a weird way, I'm comfortable with it because it's just what I've known for as long as I can remember. I mean, in elementary school, I'm talking like sixth grade, I started being called a fag. Fifth grade I was called a fag. Third grade I was called a fag. I have the paperwork, 'cause my mom kept everything, I still have them, of kids harassing me, saying "Gaylord," at that time it was "Gaylord."

Contrary to the protestations of boys . . . that they would never call someone who was gay a fag, Ricky experienced this harassment on a regular basis, probably because he couldn't draw on identifiably masculine markers such as athletic ability or other forms of dominance to bolster some sort of claim on masculinity.

Hypermasculine environments such as sporting events continued to be venues of intense harassment at River High. "I've had water balloons thrown at me at a football game. Like, we [his friends Genevieve and Lacy] couldn't have stayed at the homecoming game. We had to go." The persecution began immediately at the biggest football game of the year. When he entered with his friend Lacy, "Two guys that started walking up to get tickets said, 'There's the fucking fag.'" When Ricky responded with "Excuse me?" the boy shot back, "Don't talk to me like you know me." The boy and his friends started to threaten Ricky. Ricky said, "He started getting into my face, and his friends started saying, 'Come on, man, come on, man'" as if they were about to hit Ricky. Ricky felt frustrated that "the ticket people are sitting there not doing a damn thing. This is right in front of them!" He found Ms. Chesney, the vice principal, after the boys finally left. While Ms. Chesney told him, "We'll take care of it," Ricky said he never heard about the incident again. Later at the game he and Lacy had water bottles thrown at them by young boys yelling, "Oh look, it's a fag!" He said that this sentiment echoed as they tried to sit in the bleachers to watch the half-time show, which he had choreographed: "Left and right, 'What the fuck is that fag doing here?' 'That fag has no right to be here.' Blah blah blah. That's all I heard. I tried to ignore it. And after a while I couldn't take it and then we just went home." While many of the boys I interviewed said they would not actually harass a gay boy, that was not Ricky's experience. He was driven out of the event he had choreographed because of the intense homophobic harassment. . . .

Ricky developed different strategies to deal with the fag discourse, given that he was not just *a* fag but *the* fag. While other boys lobbed the epithet at one another with implied threats of violence (you are not a man and I am, so watch out), for Ricky that violence was more a reality than a threat. As a result, learning the unwritten rules of a particular school and mapping out its social and physical landscape was literally a matter of survival. He found River High to be one of the most homophobic schools he had attended: "It's the most violent school I think that I've seen so far. With all the schools the verbal part about, you know the slang, 'the fag,' the 'fuckin' freak,' 'fucking fag,' all that stuff is all the same. But this is the only school that throws water bottles, throws rocks, and throws food, ketchup, sandwiches, anything of that nature."[2]

While there is a law in California protecting students from discrimination based on sexual identity, when Ricky requested help from school authorities he was ignored, much as in his interaction with the vice principal at the homecoming game. Ricky responded to this sort of treatment with several evasion strategies. He walked with his eyes downcast to avoid meeting other guys' eyes, fearing that they would regard eye contact as a challenge or an invitation to a fight. Similarly he varied his route to and from school:

> I had to change paths about three different times walking to school. The same people who drive the same route know, 'cause I guess they leave at the same time, *so* they're always checking something out. But I'm always prepared with a rock just in case. I have a rock in my hand so if anything happens I just chuck one back. I always walk with something like that.

Indeed, when I was driving him home from the interview that day, boys on the sidewalk glared at him and made comments I couldn't hear. He also, with the exception of the homecoming football game, avoided highly sexualized or masculinized school events where he might be subject to violence.[3]

RACIALIZING THE FAG

While all groups of boys, with the exception of the Mormon boys, used the word *fag* or fag imagery in their interactions, the fag discourse was not deployed consistently or identically across social groups at River High. Differences between white boys' and African American boys' meaning making, particularly around appearance and dancing, reveal ways the specter of the fag was racialized. The specter of the fag, these invocations reveal, was consistently white. Additionally, African American boys simply did not deploy it with the same frequency as white boys. For both groups of boys, the *fag* insult entailed meanings of emasculation, as evidenced by Darnell's earlier comment. However, African American boys were much more likely to tease one another for being white than for being a fag. Precisely because African American men are so hypersexualized in the United States, white men are, by default, feminized, so *white* was a stand-in for *fag* among many of the African American boys at River High. Two of the behaviors that put a white boy at risk for being labeled a fag didn't function in the same way for African American boys.

Perhaps because they are, by necessity, more invested in symbolic forms of power related to appearance (much like adolescent girls), a given African American boy's status is not lowered but enhanced by paying attention to clothing or dancing. Clean, oversized, carefully put-together clothing is central to a hip-hop identity for African American boys who identify with hip-hop culture. Richard Majors (2001) calls this presentation of self a "cool pose" consisting of "unique, expressive and conspicuous styles of demeanor, speech, gesture, clothing, hairstyle, walk, stance and handshake," developed by African American men as a symbolic response to institutionalized racism (211). Pants are usually several sizes too big, hanging low on the hips, often revealing a pair of boxers beneath. Shirts and sweaters are similarly oversized, sometimes hanging down to a boy's knees. Tags are frequently left on baseball hats worn slightly askew and perched high on the head. Meticulously clean, unlaced athletic shoes with rolled-up socks under the tongue complete a typical hip-hop outfit. In fact, African American men can, without risking a fag identity, sport styles of self and interaction frequently associated with femininity for whites, such as wearing curlers (Kelley 2004). These symbols, at River High, constituted a "cool pose." . . .

Dancing was another arena that carried distinctly fag-associated meanings for white boys but masculine meanings for African American boys who participated in hip-hop culture. White boys often associated dancing with fags. However, dancing did not carry this sort of sexualized gender meaning for all boys at River High. For African American boys dancing demonstrates membership in a cultural community (Best 2000). At River, African American boys frequently danced together in single-sex groups, teaching each other the latest dance moves, showing off a particularly difficult move, or making each other laugh with humorous dance moves. In fact, while in drama class Liam and Jacob [who are white] hit each other and joked through the entire dancing exercise, Darnell and Maro [who are African American] seemed very comfortable touching one another. They stood close to one another, heel to toe, as they were supposed to. Their bodies touched, and they gently and gracefully moved the other's arms and head in a way that was tender, not at all like the flailing of the two white boys. . . .

None of this is to say that the sexuality of boys of color wasn't policed. In fact, because African American boys were regarded as so hypersexual, in the few instances I documented in which boys were punished for engaging in the fag discourse, African American boys were policed more stringently than white boys. It was as if when they engaged in the fag discourse the gendered insult took on actual combative overtones, unlike the harmless sparring associated with white boys' deployments. The intentionality attributed to African American boys in their sexual interactions with girls seemed to occur as well in their deployment of the fag discourse. One morning as I waited with the boys on the asphalt outside the weight room for Coach Ramirez to arrive, I chatted with Kevin and Darrell. The all-male, all-white wrestling team walked by, wearing gold and black singlets. Kevin, an African American sophomore, yelled out, "Why are you wearing those faggot outfits? Do you wear those tights with your balls hanging out?" The weight-lifting students stopped their fidgeting and turned to watch the scene unfold. The eight or so members of the wrestling team stopped at their SUV and turned to Kevin. A small redhead whipped around and yelled aggressively, "Who said that?!" Fingers from wrestling team members quickly pointed toward Kevin. Kevin, angrily jumping around, yelled back as he thrust his chest out, "Talk about jumping me, nigger?" He strutted over, advancing toward the small redhead. A large wrestler sporting a cowboy hat tried to block Kevin's approach. The redhead meanwhile began to jump up and down, as if warming up for a fight. Finally the boy in the cowboy hat pushed Kevin away from the team and they climbed in the truck, while Kevin strutted back to his classmates, muttering, "All they know how to do is pick somebody up. Talk about jumping me . . . weak-ass wrestling team. My little bro could wrestle better than any of those motherfuckers."

It would seem, based on the fag discourse scenarios I've described thus far, that this was, in a sense, a fairly routine deployment of the sexualized and gendered epithet. However, at no other time did I see this insult almost cause a fight. Members of the white wrestling team presumably took it so seriously that they reported the incident to school authorities. This in itself is stunning. Boys called each other fag so frequently in everyday discussion that if it were always reported most boys in the school would be suspended or at least in detention on a regular basis. This was the only time I saw school authorities take action based on what they saw as a sexualized insult. As a result Mr. J. explained that somebody from the wrestling team told him that Kevin was "harassing" them. Mr. J. pulled Kevin out of weight-lifting class to discuss the incident. According to him, Kevin "kept mouthing off" and it wasn't the first time he had been in trouble, so they decided to expel him and send him to Hillside.

While Kevin apparently had multiple disciplinary problems and this interaction was part of a larger picture, it is important that this was the only time that I heard any boy (apart from Ricky) tattle on another boy for calling him gay or fag. Similarly it was the only time I saw punishment meted out by the administration. So it seems that . . . intentionality was more frequently attributed to African American boys. They weren't just engaging in the homophobic bantering to which teachers like Mr. Kellogg turned a blind eye or in which Mr. McNally participated. Rather, they were seen as engaging in actual struggles for dominance by attacking others. Because they were in a precarious economic and social position, the ramifications for African American boys for engaging in the fag discourse were more serious. Precisely because some of them were supposed to be attending, not River High, but the "bad" school, Chicago, in the neighboring school district, when they did encounter trouble their punishment was more severe.

REFRAMING HOMOPHOBIA

Homophobia is central to contemporary definitions of adolescent masculinity. Unpacking multilayered meanings that boys deploy through their uses of homophobic language and joking rituals makes clear that it is not just homophobia but a gendered and racialized homophobia. By attending to these meanings, I reframe the discussion as a fag discourse rather than simply labeling it as homophobia. The fag is an "abject" (Butler 1993) position, a position outside masculinity that actually constitutes masculinity. Thus masculinity, in part, becomes the daily interactional work of repudiating the threatening specter of the fag. . . .

DISCUSSION QUESTIONS

1. What are the social uses and consequences of "fag discourse"?
2. Is that discourse racialized?

NOTES

1. In fact, two of my colleagues, both psychotherapists, suggested that the boys exhibited what we could think of as a sort of "Fag Tourette's Syndrome."
2. Though River was not a particularly violent school, it may have seemed like that to Ricky because sexuality-based harassment increases with grade level as gender differentiation becomes more intense. As youth move from childhood into adolescence there is less flexibility in terms of gender identity and self-presentation (Shakib 2003).
3. There were two other gay boys at the school. One, Corey, I learned about after a year of fieldwork. While he wasn't "closeted," he was not well known at the school and kept a low profile. The other out gay boy at the school was Brady. While he didn't engage in the masculinity rituals of the other boys at River High, he didn't cross-dress or engage in feminine-coded activities as did Ricky. As such, when boys talked about fags, they referenced Ricky, not Brady or Corey.

REFERENCES

Almaguer, Tomas. 1991. "Chicano Men: A Cartography of Homosexual Identity and Behavior." *Differences* 3, no. 2: 75–100.

Baker, Janet G., and Harold D. Fishbein. 1998. "The Development of Prejudice towards Gays and Lesbians by Adolescents," Journal of Homosexuality 36, no. 1:89–100.

Burn, Shawn Meghan. 2000. "Heterosexuals' Use of 'Fag' and 'Queer' to Deride One Another: A Contributor to Heterosexism and Stigma." *Journal of Homosexuality* 40, no. 2:1–11.

Butler, Judith. 1993. *Bodies That Matter: On the Discursive Limits of "Sex."* New York: Routledge.

Connell, R. W. 1995. *Masculinities.* Berkeley: University of California Press.

Corbett, Ken. 2001. "Faggot = Loser." *Studies in Gender and Sexuality* 2, no. 1:3–28.

Freud, Sigmund. 1905. *The Basic Writings of Sigmund Freud.* Translated by A. A Brill. New York: Modern Library.

Julien, Isaac, and Kobena Mercer. 1991. "True Confessions: A Discourse on Images of Black Male Sexuality." In *Brother to Brother: New Writings by Black Gay Men,* edited by Essex Hemphill, 167–73. Boston: Alyson Publications.

Kehily, Mary Jane, and Anoop Nayak. 1997. "'Lads and Laughter': Humour and the Production of Heterosexual Masculinities." *Gender and Education* 9, no.1:69–87.

Kelley, Robin D. G. 2004. "Confessions of a Nice Negro, or Why I Shaved My Head." In *Men's Lives,* edited by Michael Kimmel and Michael Messner, 335–41. Boston: Allyn and Bacon.

Kimmel, Michael S. 2001. "Masculinity as Homophobia: Fear, Shame, and Silence in the Construction of Gender Identity." In *The Masculinities Reader,* edited by Stephen Whitehead and Frank Barrett, 266–87. Cambridge: Polity Press.

———. 2003. "Adolescent Masculinity, Homophobia, and Violence Random School Shootings, 1982–2001." *American Behavioral Scientist* 46, no. 10:1439–58.

King, J. L. 2004. *On the Down Low: A Journey into the Lives of Straight Black Men Who Sleep with Men.* New York: Broadway Books.

Lehne, Gregory. 1998. "Homophobia among Men: Supporting and Defining the Male Role." In *Men's Lives,* edited by Michael Kimmel and Michael Messner 237–49 Boston: Allyn and Bacon.

Lyman, Peter. 1998. "The Fraternal Bond as a Joking Relationship: A Case Study of the Role of Sexist Jokes in Male Group Bonding." In *Men's Lives,* edited by Michael Kimmel and Michael Messner, 171–93. Boston: Allyn and Bacon.

Majors, Richard. 2001. "Cool Pose: Black Masculinity and Sports." In *The Masculinities Reader,* edited by Stephen Whitehead and Frank Barrett, 208–17. Cambridge-Polity Press.

Messner, Michael 2005. "Becoming 100% Straight." In *Gender through the Prism of Difference,* edited by Maxine Baca Zinn, Pierrette Hondagneu-Sotelo, and Michael Messner, 227–32. New York: Oxford University Press.

Plummer, David C. 2001, "The Quest for Modern Manhood: Masculine Stereotypes, Peer Culture and the Social Significance of Homophobia." *Journal of Adolescence* 24, no. 1:15–23.

Riggs, Marlon. 1991. "Black Macho Revisited: Reflections of a Snap! Queen." In *Brother to Brother: New Writings by Black Gay Men,* edited by Essex Hemphill 253–60. Boston: Alyson Publications.

Sedgwick, Eve Kosofsky. 1995. "'Gosh, Boy George, You Must Be Awfully Secure in Your Masculinity!'" In *Constructing Masculinity,* edited by Maurice Berger, Brian Wallis, and Simon Watson, 11–20. New York: Routledge.

Shakib, Sohaila. 2003. "Female Basketball Participation: Negotiating the Conflation of Peer Status and Gender Status from Childhood through Puberty." *American Behavioral Scientist* 46, no. 4:1405–22.

Smith, George W. 1998. "The Ideology of 'Fag': The School Experience of Gay Students." *Sociological Quarterly* 39, no. 2:309–35.

Wilchins, Riki. 2003. "Do You Believe in Fairies?" *Advocate,* February 4, 72.

Wood, Julian. 1984. "Groping Towards Sexism: Boy's Sex Talk." In *Gender and Generation,* edited by Angela McRobbie and Mica Nava, 54–84. London: Macmillan.

READING 29

Sexual Orientation and Sex in Women's Lives: Conceptual and Methodological Issues

Esther D. Rothblum

In the novel *Never Say Never* (Hill, 1996), two co-workers, Leslie, who is a lesbian, and Sara, who is heterosexual, become close friends. Though it is obvious to the reader and to both women that they are sexually attracted to each other, the suspense builds as to whether or not Leslie and Sara will "consummate" their relationship—that is, become genitally sexual. Whether or not the women do "it" will affect the reader's perception as to whether the book had a happy ending (they became lovers) or an unhappy one (they remained "just friends"). It will also determine whether Sara "becomes" a lesbian.

What is sexual orientation? What does it mean to be a heterosexual, bisexual, or lesbian woman? Are these terms on a continuum or separate categories? Can all women categorize themselves in one of these three ways? This article will discuss conceptual issues of sexual orientation in women.

Esther D. Rothblum is a professor of women's studies at San Diego State University.

Closely related to sexual orientation is the concept of sexual behavior. Sexual orientation is usually defined in terms of the gender of one's sexual partner. This article will ask the question, what is "sex" for women? Finally, there has been so little research addressing these concepts that some methodological issues for future research will be presented.

CONCEPTUAL ISSUES IN SEXUAL ORIENTATION

Dichotomous Definitions

Fehr (1988) views categorical definitions as "classical" in the sense that they are defined by specific inclusion and exclusion criteria. She states:

> Category membership is therefore an all-or-none phenomenon; any instance that meets the criterion is a member; all others are non-members. Boundaries between concepts are thus clearly defined. Because each member must possess the particular set of attributes that is the criterion for category inclusion, all members have a full and equal degree of membership and therefore are equally representative of the category. (p. 558)

Similarly, Rosch (1978) has argued that categories in language can be structured into a model of best fits, followed by examples that resemble these best fits to some extent.

In a categorical definition of sexual orientation, all aspects of sexual orientation—desire, behavior, and identity—are presumed to be congruent. The terms "heterosexual" and "lesbian" are often used in ways that presume these are unidimensional. When a woman says that she is a "lesbian," we may take for granted that this identity includes homogeneity of sexual behavior, sexual fantasies, and participation in a lesbian community, for example. Consider the following quotation:

> I have been heterosexual as some homosexuals say they have been homosexual: forever. Already, at the age of 5, I was attracted (in some diffuse sense of "attract") to male movie stars in ways that were different from my fascination with female stars. Demands by lesbian separatists earlier in the Second Wave

that heterosexual feminists vacate their relationships with men seemed to me then and seem to me still both cruel and impossible. . . . The impossibility, for women like me, is akin to the impossibility I would feel if, in obedience to political fiat, I were asked to change my fingerprints. (Bartky, 1992, p. 426)

This quotation is noteworthy for highlighting several issues usually assumed about sexual orientation: that it forms at an early age, that it involves sexual attraction, and that it can't be changed. The quote is unusual in that heterosexual women are rarely asked to describe their own sexuality, since heterosexuality is the "default" sexual orientation in Western societies.

Let us assume that sexual orientation is categorical. This would imply that there is a distinct boundary between being a lesbian on the one hand and a heterosexual woman on the other. At one extreme, we could picture a woman who has felt sexual/affectional desire only toward females since she was a girl. Similarly, this woman has had sexual relations only with other females. She considers herself a lesbian and has integrated into the lesbian community.

In reality, few women fit this image. Young girls who are attracted to other girls and women quickly learn to hide these feelings from others and even from themselves. They may date boys and even get married in order to fit the dominant heterosexual lifestyles. Women who do have the courage to express sexual desire and relations with other women may avoid using the term "lesbian" to describe themselves because of its negative connotations.

At the other extreme, a woman may always have been attracted to males and had sexual relations only with men. Yet we know little about heterosexuality among women. Media images of women depict them as very sexual, but in passive, objectified roles (see Umiker-Sebeok, 1981, for a review of this literature). At the same time, there may be pressure by parents and schools for young women to remain celibate, and there are few approved roles for women to be heterosexually active outside of marriage (see Hyde and Jaffee, 2000). Consequently, even heterosexual women may know little about their own sexual desire and attraction.

Some of the earliest writings about sexual orientation focused on "stages" that gay men and lesbians go through in the process of coming out. Generally these stages described an initial sense of difference and identity confusion that eventually was replaced by identity acceptance and synthesis (see Cass, 1979; Coleman, 1981). In this way, lesbians were presumed to move from lack of congruence to congruence between identity and behavior.

How would a categorical definition of sexual orientation include bisexuality? Bisexuality may be viewed as a separate category for women who are attracted to and have sexual relationships with women and men. In the past, categorical definitions of sexual orientation would have excluded bisexuality, viewing bisexuals as women in transition to be lesbians, or as lesbians who wanted a less stigmatizing self-description (Rust, 2000b). Development of a strong bisexual movement and bisexual communities has demonstrated that bisexuality is not transient and in fact may be an even more stigmatized term than lesbianism.

In sum, a dichotomous definition of sexual orientation is bipolar, with heterosexual women and lesbians as opposite constructs. Bisexuality is seen as either nonexistent or as a transitional phase between being heterosexual and lesbian (this point is discussed in detail by Rust, 2000a). There is congruence between sexual identity, behavior, and desire. Thus, if a woman experiences any same-gender behavior or attraction, she is presumed to be a lesbian with a same-gender identity as well.

Continuous Definitions

On the other hand, sexual orientation can be conceptualized as multifaceted. Consider this quotation:

> How does my heterosexuality contribute to my feminist politics? That is an impossible question for me to answer because, although I have lived monogamously with a man I love for over 26 years, I am not and never have been a "heterosexual." But neither have I ever been either a "lesbian" or a "bisexual." What I am—and have been for as long as I can remember—is someone whose gender and sexuality have just never seemed to mesh very well with the available cultural categories, and *that*—rather than my presumed heterosexuality—is what has most profoundly informed my feminist politics (Bem, 1992. p. 436)

This statement describes the experience of many women who have unsuccessfully tried to "fit" into categorical definitions. Even as new terminology has entered counterculture vocabularies (e.g., "queer" to describe people who do not have a mainstream sexual orientation), these individuals continue to feel marginalized and disenfranchised. . . .

In sum, from a continuous perspective, sexual orientation is a multidimensional concept that varies in degree and intensity. Sexual orientation is viewed as diverse, with each individual having a unique template of erotic and affectional identity, behavior, fantasies, relationships (including relationship status), and emotional attachments, all of which can change over time (Garnets & Kimmel, 1993). These components can be (and often are) incongruous, so there is no simple relationship among behavior, identity, and desire. For example, many more people engage in same-gender sexual behavior than those who identify as lesbian, gay, or bisexual.

RESEARCH ON SEXUAL ORIENTATION

Most research in this area has used categorical definitions of sexual orientation, such as asking participants to check off whether they are lesbian, bisexual, or heterosexual. Furthermore, a survey entitled "Lesbian Mental Health Survey" (Oetjen & Rothblum, 2000) is unlikely to obtain many respondents who identify as bisexual or heterosexual. Nor will it interest women who are sexually involved with women but who do not identify as lesbian. Such categorical methods introduce a level of artificiality that may not in fact correspond with the identity or experiences of women respondents. . . .

In a recent study, Jessica Morris and I (1999) examined the interrelationships among various dimensions of sexual orientation. The study examined the way in which over 2,000 women who answered a "Lesbian Wellness Survey" were distributed on five aspects of lesbian sexuality and the coming out process. The five aspects were sexual orientation on the "Kinsey Scale" (Kinsey, Pomeroy, & Martin, 1948; Kinsey, Pomeroy, Martin, & Gebhard, 1953); years out (length of time of self-identity as lesbian/gay/bisexual); outness/disclosure (amount of disclosure of sexual orientation to others); sexual experience (proportion of sexual relationships with women compared to men); and lesbian activities (extent of participation in lesbian community events). The intercorrelations among these dimensions were quite low, indicating that being lesbian is not a homogeneous experience.

Closer examination by the demographic characteristics of race/ethnicity and age revealed a diversity of experience. African American, Native American, and Latina respondents had moderate correlations among the aspects of the lesbian experience, whereas the intercorrelations of White and Asian American respondents tended to be mild or nonsignificant. The results indicate that researchers who are studying one aspect of the lesbian experience (e.g., outness to others) need to ensure that they are not assuming such behavior based on other dimensions (such as frequent participation in lesbian community activities or years of being out), especially among White and Asian American lesbians. Most studies of sexual orientation have focused on members of the visible gay and lesbian communities (there is still relatively little research on people who are bisexual). By recruiting participants at lesbian community events or using mailing lists of lesbian news letters, for example, researchers are stratifying by lesbian *self-identity*. . . .

The limited research on dimensions of women's sexual orientation, whether conducted directly in lesbian/bisexual women's communities or via national surveys, indicates that identity as lesbian or bisexual, sexual activity with women, and sexual desire are separate and (somewhat) overlapping dimensions. This raises the question whether sexual orientation for women should be defined on the basis of sexual activity/attraction and, if so, what *does* sex mean for women?

CONCEPTUAL ISSUES IN FEMALE SEXUAL ACTIVITY

In the United States, the concept of "sex" is so closely linked with genital intercourse that most heterosexual women will not "count" experiences that didn't include this aspect of sexual activity. When asked when they first had "sex," women who have sex with men will often "count" the first time they had sexual intercourse with a man, even if this experience was not particularly sexual for them and even if they had prior sexual experiences that were quite arousing and even led to orgasm (see Rothblum, 1994, for a review). Loulan (1993) has described how female adolescents who have engaged in a variety of sexual activities but have not had intercourse will say that they have not "gone all the way." Thus, women's definition of what constitutes sexual activity with a male partner is often separate from their own sexual arousal and desire.

"Sex" when both partners are female is even more complex. On the one hand, lesbians and bisexual women will say that sex between women allows for a greater variety of sexual expression, exactly because it is not focused on intercourse (see Rothblum, 1999, for a review). On the other hand, sexual activity between women is socially constructed in the lesbian/bisexual communities to mean certain activities and not others. Two women who are "just" kissing and cuddling, for example, have not "gone all the way" (Rothblum, 1999). Interestingly, the current Vermont Youth Behavior Risk Survey (Vermont Department of Health, 1999) asks respondents whether they have had "intercourse" with males only, females only, both males and females, or neither. It is difficult to say how female adolescents will conceptualize "intercourse" between two females, but the wording of this item reflects the salience of the word "intercourse" to mean sexual activity in research.

Research on female sexuality has found lesbians to engage in sexual activity with relatively low frequency. A major survey of sexual activity among 12,000 people (Blumstein & Schwartz, 1983) indicated that lesbians are less likely to have genital sex than are married heterosexual, cohabiting heterosexual, or gay male couples. Loulan (1988) surveyed over 1,500 lesbians and found the majority (78%) to have been celibate for some period of time. Most had been celibate for less than 1 year, 35% had been celibate from 1 to 5 years, and 8% for 6 years or more. The national survey by Laumann et al. (1994) similarly found women to be lower than men on rates of sexual behavior.

The results of these surveys were interpreted as reflecting women's lack of socialization to initiate sexual encounters. Survey authors also indicated that lesbians, being women, placed more focus on love, affection, and romance than on genital sexual activity (e.g., Klinkenberg & Rose, 1994). Thus, heterosexual and bisexual women may have sex more often because men are more likely to want and initiate sexual activity.

It is difficult to obtain accurate data on sexual behavior. Sexual activity is private, and women in particular are not socialized to discuss details of sexual activity. This issue is confounded for lesbians and bisexual women, who may live in areas where same-gender sexual activity is against the law and who may lose their jobs or custody of their children if such knowledge became public. Most sex surveys have been criticized for being of questionable accuracy, as people may not respond honestly for a variety of reasons (see Laumann et al., 1994, for a discussion).

Certainly the low rates of sexual "activity" found in these surveys may in part be due to how sexual behavior is traditionally defined. What are the implications of lesbians engaging in genital sex less than heterosexual women or than men, yet at the same time using a genital-based definition to define "sex"? Is there a way that women of all sexual orientations should discuss the relative devaluation of alternatives to genital sex? Can we reclaim erotic, nongenital experiences as "real" sex?

CONCEPTUAL ISSUES IN FEMALE SEXUAL DESIRE

The lack of congruence between female sexual behavior and desire implies that sexual behavior per se may not be what is most important to

women and may not define their sexual identity. On the one hand, women in Western societies live in a culture of sex (Rothblum, 1994) in which images of women being sexual are everywhere in the media and are used to promote a wide range of products in the economy. On the other hand, the overemphasis on sex ignores the reality that women have related passionately and emotionally to other women all their lives.

Some years ago, Kathy Brehony and I (Rothblum & Brehony, 1993) interviewed self-identified lesbians who considered themselves to be in a couple but who were not currently sexual with their partners (and may never have had sex with these partners). Here are some examples of the ways of relating that we found (all names are pseudonyms):

Laura became attracted to her heterosexual roommate, Violet. Violet seemed to encourage the relationship in multiple ways, such as having heart-shaped tattoos made with each other's names and telling Laura it was okay that people mistook them for lovers. When Laura suggested they become lovers, Violet said she couldn't do it. Laura was devastated.

Elizabeth and Marianne were briefly genitally sexual, then Marianne broke that off, saying that the age difference of 20 years was too great for her. Marianne, the younger of the two, became involved sexually with another woman, Eve, and Elizabeth decided to move out of state to get away. Elizabeth and Marianne continued their relationship over the telephone, and both agree that they are the most important people in each other's lives. Elizabeth says about Eve, Marianne's sexual partner, "she will never have access to the total person that I have."

Sarah and Hannah have a primary relationship, but without sex. They have an agreement that they can have other lovers, but only men. Sarah is confused because she is a lesbian, and now her friends only see her with male lovers. It has shaken her whole identity as a lesbian. Hannah is primarily heterosexual. They are both afraid that sex would make them even more intense, given their closeness already.

These examples bring up a number of themes related to sexual desire. When two members of a couple disagree on what constitutes sex and thus whether or not they are having sex, they may also differ on whether or not they are in a real relationship. Even when both members of the couple agree that their genitally asexual relationship makes them a real couple, society in general may not agree with this definition. The couple may hide their asexuality from their community in much the same way that women in past centuries hid their sexuality from the community at large. Societal validation is especially important for women who are not heterosexual, in light of the fact that many of these women felt invisible to society at large when growing up or while coming out. Furthermore, the examples above came from self-identified lesbians; others may exist among women who are passionate about women yet who are married to men, in celibate religious orders, or extremely closeted even to themselves.

METHODOLOGICAL ISSUES FOR FUTURE RESEARCH

. . . In conclusion, what can we say about female sexuality at the end of the millennium? Sexual behavior is still defined in genital ways that may not accurately reflect the totality of women's sexual experiences. Sexual behavior is only one dimension of women's sexuality, and not highly interrelated with sexual desire, attraction, sexual orientation, and so on. There is increasing knowledge that even the concept of gender itself is flexible, complex, and multidimensional, so that knowing who is a "woman" is not as clear-cut as once believed. Far fewer women may be heterosexual in the traditional sense, indicating that more research on women's sexuality is necessary to learn about women's ways of being in sexual relationships. Even for women who *are* heterosexual, little is known about this "mainstream" group, such as how they came to be heterosexual, the ways that they might question their heterosexuality, and how their sexual desire and attraction differs from those of women who are bisexual or lesbian. Women's sexuality is an area in which we don't

even know what most of the questions are, let alone the answers.

DISCUSSION QUESTIONS

1. What assumptions about women's sexuality does this article encourage us to question?
2. Should "sex" be defined as only genital intercourse?

REFERENCES

Bartky, S. L. (1992). Hypatia unbound: A confession. *Feminism & Psychology, 2,* 426–428.

Bem, S. L. (1992). On the inadequacy of our sexual categories: A personal perspective. *Feminism & Psychology, 3,* 436–437.

Blumstein, P., & Schwartz, P. (1983). *American couples.* New York: William Morrow.

Cass, V. C. (1979). Homosexual identity formation: A theoretical model. *Journal of Homosexuality, 4,* 219–235.

Coleman, E. (1981). Developmental stages of the coming out process. *Journal of Homosexuality, 4,* 31–43.

Fehr, B. (1988). Prototype analysis of the concepts of love and commitment. *Journal of Personality and Social Psychology, 55*(4), 557–579.

Garnets, L. D., & Kimmel, D. C. (1993). Introduction: Lesbian and gay male dimensions in the psychological study of human diversity. In L. D. Garnets & D. C. Kimmel (Eds.), *Psychological perspectives on lesbian and gay male experiences* (pp. 1–51). New York: Columbia University Press.

Hill, L. (1996). *Never say never.* Tallahassee, FL: Naiad Press.

Hyde, J. S., & Jaffee, S. R. (2000). Becoming a heterosexual adult: The experiences of young women. *Journal of Social Issues, 56*(2), 283–296.

Kinsey, A. C., Pomeroy, W., & Martin, C. (1948). *Sexual behavior in the human male.* Philadelphia: W. B. Saunders.

Kinsey, A. C., Pomeroy, W. B., Martin, C. F., & Gebhard, P. H. (1953). *Sexual behavior in the human female.* Philadelphia: Saunders.

Klinkenberg, D., & Rose, S. (1994). Dating scripts of lesbians and gay men. *Journal of Homosexuality, 26,* 23–35.

Laumann, E. O., Gagnon, J. H., Michael, R. T., & Michaels, S. (1994). *The social organization of sexuality: Sexual practices in the Untied States.* Chicago: University of Chicago Press.

Loulan, J. (1988). Research on the sex practices of 1566 lesbians and the clinical applications. *Women and Therapy, 7,* 221–234.

Loulan, J. (1993). Celibacy. In E. D. Rothblum & K. A. Brehony (Eds.), *Boston marriages: Romantic but asexual* relationships among contemporary lesbians. Amherst, MA: University of Massachusetts Press.

Morris, J. F., & Rothblum, E. D. (1999). Who fills out a "lesbian" questionnaire? The interrelationship of sexual orientation, years out, disclosure of sexual orientation, sexual experience with women, and participation in the lesbian community. *Psychology of Women Quarterly, 23*(3), 537–557.

Oetjen, H., & Rothblum, E. D. (2000). When lesbians aren't gay: Factors affecting depression among lesbians. *Journal of Homosexuality, 39*(1), 49–73.

Rosch, E. (1978). Principles of categorization. In E. Rosch & B. B. Lloyd (Eds.), *Cognition and categorization* (pp. 27–48). Hillsdale, NJ: Erlbaum.

Rothblum, E. D. (1994). I only read about myself on bathroom walls: The need for research on the mental health of lesbians and gay men. *Journal of Consulting and Clinical Psychology, 62*, 213–220.

Rothblum, E. D. (1999). Poly-friendships. *Journal of Lesbian Studies, 3*, 71–83.

Rothblum, E. D., & Brehony, K. A. (Eds.). (1993). *Boston marriages: Romantic but asexual relationships among contemporary lesbians.* Amherst, MA: University of Massachusetts.

Rust, P. C. (2000a). Bisexuality: A contemporary paradox for woman. *Journal of Social Issues, 56*(2), 205–221.

Rust, P. C. (2000b). *Bisexuality in the United States: A reader and guide to the literature.* New York: Columbia University Press.

Umiker-Sebeok, J. (1981). The seven ages of woman: A view from American magazine advertisements. In C. Mayo & N. M. Henley (Eds.), *Gender and nonverbal behavior* (pp. 209–252). New York: Springer-Verlag.

Vermont Department of Health. (1999). Vermont Youth Behavior Risk Survey. Unpublished survey currently in progress.

SOCIAL CLASS

READING 30

Class and the Transition to Adulthood

Annette Lareau and Elliot B. Weininger

On the basis of the original observational and interview data, [Annette Lareau's] *Unequal Childhoods* argues that a great deal of parental behavior is driven by cultural repertoires that vary sharply across social classes but not across racial groups. Middle class child rearing, the book asserts, generally conforms to the logic of *concerted cultivation,* according to which parents view it as their duty to actively foster the development of their children's potential skills and talents. By contrast, the book notes, working class and poor child rearing conforms to a logic of the *accomplishment of natural growth,* according to which parents assume that

if they provide their children with love, feed and clothe them, and keep them safe, the children will grow and thrive spontaneously.

Lareau examined how these contrasting cultural orientations operate in three domains of everyday life. In the area of time use, she found that middle class children are enrolled in numerous age-specific leisure activities that are believed to transmit important life skills, while their working class and poor counterparts are generally granted autonomy in the use of leisure time. In the area of language use, middle class parents generally emphasize the development of verbal reasoning, frequently drawing their children into conversation and offering them chances to negotiate, whereas working class and poor parents are more likely to use directives when conversing with their children, to engage in brief exchanges of information, and to rely more on physical discipline than on negotiation. Lastly, in the area of institutional contacts, middle class parents generally consider it appropriate to closely monitor the behavior of institutional agents (such as teachers and other school officials) and to intervene on behalf of their children if they deem that their children's best interests are not being

Annette Lareau is a professor of sociology at Temple University. Elliot Weininger is a professor of sociology at the State University of New York, Brockport.

served, whereas working class parents consider these agents' authority and responsibility to be broad and not open to challenge.

In this [discussion], we narrow the focus to one domain of everyday life—contacts between families and key institutions—and draw on the follow-up data to assess the extent to which the two cultural orientations to child rearing at the center of *Unequal Childhoods* have persisted through time. Our goal is to determine whether notions of concerted cultivation and the accomplishment of natural growth aptly characterized parental behavior as the children were making the transition out of high school. . . .

CLASS AND THE TRANSITION TO ADULTHOOD

. . . In this section, we compare two young African American women who each aspired to a medical career. Tara Carroll grew up in a poor family and dreamed of becoming a nurse. Stacey Marshall grew up in a middle class family and hoped to become a pediatrician. Tara was raised by her grandmother when she was younger and later moved in with her mother (her father was in prison). Stacey's biological parents had raised her since birth. Both young women had a sibling who was approximately two years older. The careers they aspired to required a science background. During middle school, both had struggled with math; neither young woman was naturally gifted in the subject.

Comparing Tara's and Stacey's transitions from high school shows that the differences in parental interventions in education observed when the children were younger have persisted. For example, in keeping with the cultural logic of the accomplishment of natural growth, Tara's mother placed the responsibility for applying to college on her daughter.

> Well, I let Tara make her choices. She told me what she wanted to do, and I let her do it. I should have participated more, yes, but because of my [work] schedule, I couldn't. . . . I should have participated more and pushed a little more. You know, get on the

Internet and find scholarships, utilize that. Get her to write and sell herself more. You have to do essays to participate for scholarships. I should have been a little bit more pushy that way.

Although she had a car, and all of the schools Tara was interested in were within a one-hour drive of their home, Tara's mother did not visit any. The visits that Tara experienced were arranged at the "health academy" in her public high school. Tara's mother also did not recall ever having seen an application. Tara filled out the forms at school, with assistance from teachers: "Every college that she applied to, all I saw was the letters, yea or nay, and that was hurtful for her—everybody kept turning her down." Her Mother also lacked basic information about crucial aspects of Tara's education: "I wish I could find that letter. All I remember is that [her GPA] was above average. I don't know exactly what it was. I think it was around a B."

Tara's knowledge was limited too. As a senior, she had to ask her counselor what a "3.4" meant:

> I had went to my counselor, his name was Mr. Bradley, and he did my GPA, like combined my averages, like, add[ed] up all my grades. . . . I remember, it was close to a 3.5 or it was like a 3.4. [I said] something like, "Well, what's that?" He was like, "That's a B." So I knew I did good overall [in] high school.

Tara's combined SAT scores totaled 690. She applied to six or seven colleges, including a number of schools whose representatives had made visits to her high school. In addition to assistance from teachers, Tara received advice from an aunt who had graduated from college. Still, she was unable to overcome some of the challenges the applications posed:

> I only got one recommendation. I didn't know a lot of teachers in there, um, but I had one teacher I really liked. Her name was Ms. Thomas. She gave me a letter of recommendation. . . . I had to get one more, but I couldn't. I tried to get one from my counselors, my counselor, but he came up with an excuse, like, um [*she changes her voice*], "You know, I got a lot of people to do, and I got to take time," some ol' excuse, and he had to see if he had time. And I was supposed

to get one more, and that was from my English teacher . . . his name was Mr. Rogers. He was the head coordinator of my [school within a school] health academy. But he never got around to writin' it. He just kept saying, "Remind me, remind me, remind me." And I never got a chance to get that letter of recommendation from him, so I only had one.

Tara applied to colleges where the median SAT scores were 100 to 300 points above her own scores. She was rejected everywhere. She went to community college "as a last resort" to pursue her hope of becoming a nurse. She enrolled in an anatomy and physiology course but soon found that she did not like the instructor. Although she went to the instructor's office hours, she still did not understand the material, did not feel comfortable asking questions, and did not know that she could have sought help from an adviser. She simply stopped going to class. Since she did not formally drop the course, she failed it and will have to take it again. She says she is "taking a break from school" but hopes to go back in the future. Put differently, although Tara had relatively high grades and a fervent desire to attend college and had energetically visited colleges and filled out numerous applications, her college search failed to yield admission to a four-year college because of her lack of informal knowledge about the higher education system and the fact that she applied to schools that were quite selective (reflecting her high aspirations). Both she and her mother found the process to be "hurtful."

Middle class parents, especially mothers, generally have active roles in the college application process. Often parents guide their children every step of the way. For example, Stacey Marshall's experience with college applications was quite different from Tara's. From the beginning, Stacey received considerable adult support. Middle class parents, having gone to college themselves and having sought out detailed information from their social networks, generally feel comfortable providing their children with informal advice on academic matters. Stacey's mother worked in the computer industry and had a master's degree. In addition, she had long been committed to an especially active

form of concerted cultivation. She reported that she had "kept tabs with the teacher" all through her daughter's primary and secondary education: "I was then and remained through high school kind of a visible parent in the school district, letting them know that I was watching what was going on."

Stacey's mother was concerned about her daughter's desire to be a premed student because she was aware that math was not Stacey's strong suit:

> She had the traumatic experience near the end of the [fifth-grade] year where she had gotten what I believe was her very first C. . . . Math has haunted her ever since. [*Pauses.*] Even now, there is this insecurity, this feeling that "I can't do it," which in my mind puts a damper on that desire to go into medicine, because she's got to deal with that math.

Nor, in her mother's opinion, had Stacey chosen to enroll in sufficiently challenging classes in high school: "Stacey was always a B-plus student with the ability to be A-minus, [who] never wanted to accept a challenge to go for a more challenging class. She did stick with the sciences. The counselor and I forced her into that."[1]

Indeed, Stacey's mother actively sought ways to further the development of her daughter's natural sciences skills. She mentioned, for example, that the summer before Stacey's senior year she and her husband had spent "a lot of money" (at least $1,500) to have Stacey attend a ten-day "young people in science" program suggested by a high school microbiology teacher.

After Stacey grew three inches in a single summer and was no longer competitive in gymnastics, she was persuaded to play basketball for her middle school. She became a basketball star in high school. During her senior year, she was recruited by Ivy League schools. Her combined SAT scores were 1060, and her grades were a B average. Although Stacey desperately wanted to go to Columbia and the basketball program there would have helped her gain admission, her parents told her the financial aid gap (over $15,000 per year) was too large and that therefore she could not go. (Privately, she reported still feeling "bitter" about her parents' unilateral decision.) Her mother worked hard to collect extensive information about the acceptance policies of various colleges; she guided her daughter to colleges that she thought would be a good fit for Stacey and that also reflected her daughter's desire not to be too far from home. Ultimately, Stacey was admitted to a selective state university three hours from home; as a member of the women's basketball team, she was given a full scholarship.[2]

During Stacey's freshman year, her parents continued to play the same sort of active role they had taken throughout the college application process. Her mother helped her select courses strategically: "I said, 'Look, you have got to get out of calculus. Because first semester you don't want your GPA to get too low, because then you can never dig yourself out of it.' And so she was calling me about 'what should I take?'"

Her mother's advice concerned both the immediate decision and, more importantly, the resources Stacey needed to use to make effective decisions in general:

> She emailed me first, and then she called me one night at eleven o'clock. And it was like, "Well, I can take the cinema course." I said, "*Stacey.*" [*Laughs.*] I said, "Do you know anything about this? Do they even give you a description?" [She said,] "Wellllll, no, not really." But she . . . was on the computer; she could see that there were seats in this class; the time was right. I said, "Sometimes you can be jumping out of the frying pan into the fire. This course may have an interesting name, but, one, it sounds like, yeah, you'd be watching movies, but two, you'll probably be writing about [them]. You have these other courses where you will be writing. You are telling me that you don't like to write." She said, "Well, I don't know. I guess I see your point."

Stacey's mother continued:

> "In the meantime, you have an academic adviser. . . ." I really stressed with her that *she* needed to establish communication with those people. I said, "You need to call Alesha. Call Alesha, set up an appointment, and *go to talk to her*. Talk to her about your major. And see what advice she can give to you. That is what she is getting paid for."

Indeed, in some ways, her mother appeared to be trying to teach Stacey to be less dependent:

> I think that she was used to, throughout school, to me making a call or talking to a teacher as part of my parental responsibility. A couple of times I got emails from her while she was at college with questions like, "What should I do?" or, "What do you think?" And as the year wore on, there were some things that I would say, "Look, Stacey, this is *your* responsibility. I can't go and talk to this professor. This is college. [Stacey's university] doesn't even send me your grades. [*Laughs.*] They won't tell me anything. . . ."

Stacey Marshall clearly benefited from her mother's informal guidance. Although it is uncertain whether she will be able to successfully pursue her university's premed curriculum, it is much more likely that Stacey will graduate from college than it is that Tara will, although both are attached to the idea.

To summarize, comparing Tara Carroll's experiences with Stacey Marshall's suggests that middle class children have more informational resources at their disposal as they negotiate college than do working class and poor youth. Also, the comparison reveals a striking similarity in the overall cultural logic of child rearing that parents followed when their children were in fourth grade and when their children were in high school, even though the problems and concerns shifted considerably.

NATURAL GROWTH CONTINUES

Many students, particularly those of working class and poor origins, do not attend college. A significant number, particularly in urban communities, drop out of high school. Since Lareau's study drew on this population, it is not surprising that a number of the youth in her study struggled in high school. A number dropped out. Some graduated from high school and attempted to start, but quickly stopped, attending community college. Their mothers and fathers were extremely concerned about their educational progress. But since parents generally defined education as the school's responsibility, parents played much less of a role in critically overseeing or intervening in their children's high school experiences than did middle class parents. When mothers did try to intervene, they reported that they were unable to alter the course of events. Put differently, in *Unequal Childhoods* Lareau reported that working class and poor families spent scarce resources taking care of children and keeping them safe. Unlike the middle class parents, the working class and poor parents did not see it as their duty to continuously develop their children's talents and skills. . . .

Overall, parents continued to try to keep their children safe and to protect them. Parents (many of whom were high school dropouts) continued to cede responsibility for education to the school and, in addition, to the children themselves. Unlike middle class parents, the less-privileged parents did not micro-manage core aspects of the school experience. Nor did they seem to possess potentially important informal knowledge, such as the academic status hierarchy of their local public high schools. In the case of Katie Brindle, a white girl from a poor background, this apparent lack of information had long-term consequences. When Katie was about to enter high school, her mother's primary concern was her daughter's safety. Her mother did not want Katie to go across town to attend a school in a different neighborhood. This more distant school was much more highly ranked academically than the one that her mother directed her daughter to attend, although it is unclear whether either she or Katie knew this. Katie recalled that she had "wanted to go to Lincoln High. But my mom said I could only take the Washington or Franklin [choices] because they were in the neighborhood."

Saying that she was "wild" and that there was nothing her mother could have done to change that, Katie reported that she "never really went to high school." Her teenage years were punctuated by truancy, fighting, alcohol, and drugs. At age seventeen, she became pregnant, dropped out of school, and gave birth to a daughter, who is now being raised mainly by Katie's sister. As with many working class and poor youth in the study, she has received substantial assistance from her family. Her mother found her a job and got up with the baby at night when Katie was recovering from the cesarean section surgery. Her sister often took care of the baby and, when Katie was "running the streets," offered to raise the child. Her mother and sister also gave her gifts of cash and food. Katie hopes to get a GED one day; in the meantime, she works with her mother cleaning houses.

An orientation to schooling similar to the Brindles' was evident in other poor and working class families. Parents showed love and concern for their children in many different ways, but since they did not define their proper role as including the management of school careers, they had limited information about the options available to their children. For example, the Greeleys, another poverty-level white family, relied on school personnel for guidance when Mark, their eldest son, was ready for high school. As one of the few whites in an inner-city middle school, Mark had had a difficult time, frequently getting into fights. His mother explained that in selecting a high school for Mark, she "went by the word of his [middle school] school counselor, who said that this would be a great school for him. It's smaller, no one has issues, no one has problems." The school, however, did not prove to be a good choice. Mark was again one of the few white students, and he again had problems. Although he later transferred to a different high school, he became increasingly disengaged and eventually dropped out.

As Mark's problems were escalating, his mother attempted to intercede. She called "the school" to find out what she could do. This effort proved futile:

> I called the school. And I asked them, what, what—you know, "My son doesn't wanna come to school—what legal—what can I do legally?" There's nothing I can do when he's seventeen—if he don't wanna go, he don't have to go. It's just that simple. They can quit when they're sixteen, but you have to have the parents' permission, and he has to have a job. But, you know, he just didn't go to school the last month, and then he was seventeen. So . . . there's nothin' that I could've made him do.

Mark dropped out of high school when he was sixteen. He got a job stocking grocery shelves at night for $10 an hour. At the time of the follow-up interview, he lived at home, and his mother frequently drove him to work.

All three of Ms. Greeley's children have scored high enough on standard IQ tests to qualify for school-based gifted programs. (A teacher recommended that Mark be tested, and Ms. Greeley then had his siblings tested as well.) Nevertheless, none of the Greeley children have done well academically, although Mark's sister is likely to graduate from high school. Their mother noted ruefully that

> Pammy was one hundred forty-something [IQ score], and Rick was one hundred forty-something. But none of them did nothing with it. I think if situations . . . I don't know—I just believe that it's because of circumstances and situations and environment. They didn't flourish, you know, they didn't flourish. I mean, it might be the same anywhere. [But] I think if schools were different and they had different opportunities to go to better schools—they didn't. Unfortunately, when you're poor, you have to go to the neighborhood school, you know. They didn't have—there was no choices of going anywhere else—you have to go to the neighborhood school.

Ms. Greeley's reliance on school officials when making key decisions concerning her children's schooling, coupled with her sense of powerlessness in the face of negative events, was typical of working class and poor parents in the study, and it closely echoed the sensibility that was apparent among them some ten years earlier—namely, the supposition that responsibility for their children's education was properly relegated to educators. . . .

CONCERTED CULTIVATION CONTINUES

Not all of the middle class adolescents went to college. But in every case, their parents took an extremely active role in their transition out of high school; such parental actions are rarely accounted for in the current models of educational transitions.

Mothers in particular did not hesitate to intervene. For example, the mother of Garrett Tallinger, a white middle class young man, reported:

> MS. TALLINGER: In talking to the guidance people, I said, "I think he's capable of honors [enrolling in the honors courses]. But obviously you-all need to decide that. . . ." One of the things I did know was that the more competitive colleges look at what is available in a high school, and if you're not taking the most rigorous of what's available, that's a strike against you in terms of their evaluating your transcript. And so I wanted Garrett, as is true with all my kids, I want them to take the most rigorous [courses] that they're possibly capable of taking.
> LAREAU: And how did you know that?
> MS. TALLINGER: Well, from friends who work in admissions offices. I mean, a very good friend used to work in admissions. And she said, "It's very important." And actually then talking to some other parents that had taken their daughter on a tour of Yale and Duke. He told a funny story of visiting at Duke, and the question to the person guiding the admissions discussions . . . the question from the student was, "Well, is it better to take honors calculus and get a B or take regular calculus and get an A?" He says, "It's better to take honors calculus and get an A." [*Laughs.*]

For many middle class parents in the study, friends' experiences with the college admission process proved to be an important source of information.

Garrett did enroll in rigorous high school courses, including AP economics, AP calculus, AP English literature, and two years of both physics and history. His weighted grade point average was 4.26 (which he believes is equivalent to an unweighted average of 3.78). In guiding their son's school career, the Tallingers tapped multiple resources, including the expertise school personnel. For example, it was Garrett's ninth grade math teacher who facilitated his entrance into the highest levels of math, including, AP calculus. Nevertheless, Garrett's mother took steps promptly anytime she felt that her son's best interests were not being fully served by the school. Thus, when a scheduling problem threatened to prevent Garrett from taking college preparatory courses in both math and English, she quickly intervened:

I did have to go fight about his schedule, because they went into this new scheduling system, and if he wanted to take the AP English and AP calculus, they were given at the same time. I was like, "C'mon, this is not—you gotta figure something out. I mean, I can't believe Garrett's the only person this is impacting. You have to figure a way for these kids to maximize their opportunities, and they have to switch things around." So that I did fight for.

Ms. Tallinger's efforts to directly manage Garrett's education closely resembled her behavior, and that of other middle class parents, some ten years earlier, when the children were in elementary school. . . .

For Alexander Williams, an African American middle class young man, college visits began during sophomore year of high school. By the time he made his final choice, he had visited Duke, Columbia, Dartmouth, Brandeis, Georgetown, Haverford, Northwestern, and a few others. During the follow-up interview, he recalled being annoyed that he had had to spend his spring break in junior year visiting campuses: "I didn't want to go to visit colleges on my spring break," he said, but then quickly added, "No, it was fun." He applied early-decision to Columbia, which meant that he was committed to going if he got admitted. With an A average and SAT scores of 1350, he was reasonably confident. He explained: "I didn't apply anywhere else, and if I hadn't gotten in, I would have had about a week and a half to apply everywhere else." His father had not been enthusiastic about this strategy: "I think that my mom was pretty sure I would get in; my dad was wondering why I hadn't applied anywhere else." Put differently, compared to Tara Carroll's mother, Alexander's mother had considerable informal knowledge about the higher education system, was aware of his skills, and guided him through the process ("my mom was pretty sure I would get in"). In other cases, the middle class students visited and toured many schools but, after narrowing their preferences, applied to a small number of potential colleges.

Even after their children have begun their college careers, middle class parents often remain deeply involved. The Tallingers reported that they speak with Garrett frequently and give him advice. During the follow-up interview, his father offered this example:

> He called us the end of last semester when it was time to register for this fall's semester, and he said he was going to get up and get out of business school—he wanted to be a teacher. And it surprised me a little bit. I didn't have anything against it; I was supportive. I told him, "Do what you want, whatever makes you happy." . . . I said, "Garrett, you just need to realize that . . ."—his high school coach, who he idolizes, who's been a high school teacher now for twenty years or something . . . I mean, you know he makes probably high fifty thousands or sixty thousand dollars a year and will probably never make a whole lot more than that. He has a great life, loves his life. So I said, "You just need to be aware of that." He kind of went, "Oh, really?" [*Chuckles.*] I said, "Yeah." 'Cause he's just unaware of these kinds of things. . . . It was on a Thursday, so on Friday afternoon he called and said, "Well, I'm in the business school." So he stayed in the business school.

By providing their son with regular input during his college career, Mr. and Ms. Tallinger helped Garrett align his short-term educational choices with his long-term goals. Other middle class parents in the study saw themselves as being so central to their children's postsecondary school career that they often used the term "we" during the follow-up interviews. Ms. Handlon, for instance, in reporting with embarrassment that her daughter Melanie (a white middle class young woman) had dropped out of community college, said, "We only made it one semester."[3] This pattern of parental involvement is not unique to the young people in this study. As one college administrator notes, "The 'helicopter parent,' or hovering parent who repeatedly tries to intervene and manage his or her child's life, seems to be a growing phenomenon on many campuses" (White 2005).[4]

CONCLUSIONS

In this [discussion] we have taken up the question of how families from different class locations negotiate children's transition out of high school. In much current research, this transition is construed in terms of choices made by the isolated individuals of statistical decision theory (or, at most, by generic "students and their parents"). The key decision-making parameters of these models include the potential returns to additional schooling, students' academic abilities, and their available resources. We suggested that these models might usefully be juxtaposed with empirical data on the decisionmaking process as it actually occurs.

Our central finding is that substantial class differences exist in the role played by the family, and in particular by parents. In our ethnographic data, parental involvement is an overwhelmingly middle class phenomenon. Moreover, it takes numerous forms. Middle class parents may help their children formulate effective strategies while they are still in high school (for example, by overseeing the choice of appropriate courses), help them evaluate their individual academic strengths and weaknesses, and help them realistically assess the costs and benefits of specific courses of action (including not just whether to attend college but also, for example, what to major in once there). Thus, if, as Stephen Morgan (2005) has asserted, high school decisionmakers are confronted with considerable uncertainty with respect to these crucial factors, then our data suggest that parental involvement may help them reduce this ambiguity. However, it is important to recognize that middle class parental involvement often goes beyond providing advice to include, at times, directly interceding to ensure that their children's interests (as perceived) are well served. These interventions can take the form of speaking with high school counselors about course selection, complaining to school officials when AF course schedules conflict, working closely with their children—sentence by sentence—on college essays, planning (and funding) a large number of visits to potential colleges, and other actions. Indeed, the heavy involvement of middle class parents in the complex and long-term process of preparing for and applying to college is one of our most notable findings. To varying degrees, middle class parents and their children form a collective in which concerted action on the part of each family member is carefully directed toward a shared goal over the course of a child's high school career.

Among working class and poor children, by contrast, parental involvement appears to be substantially rarer. Parents do not typically see it as part of their job to monitor the minutiae of their children's educational careers or to play a central role in making or helping their children make key decisions about their post–high school path. Thus, these parents usually do not try to help their children evaluate the potential long-term implications of their high school course selection or assess their career interests in light of their academic strengths and weaknesses. Nor did we document any conversations in working class or poor families that were comparable to the one between Garrett Tallinger and his father concerning the long-term financial payoff to a particular college program, or even to college attendance in general. Additionally most did not have experience with the college application process themselves, and neither could they draw on the cumulative experience of a network of college-educated friends; therefore, they could not serve their children as a significant source of information. Consequently, working class and poor children are more likely to rely exclusively on teachers, counselors, and school officials for assistance when making key decisions. Moreover, direct interventions in schooling by working class or poor parents are rare; when they do occur, as with Mark Greeley's mother, they are less likely to be successful.

Working class and poor parents are no less deeply committed, however, to the well being of their children than are middle class parents. The less-privileged parents in the study helped their children frequently and in many ways. They babysat, paid car insurance, supplied transportation to and from work sites, set up job interviews, and provided other crucial emotional and financial support. Some of the working class and poor parents championed college, and some were deeply disappointed that their children did not, in the end, attend. Nevertheless, compared with middle class parents, their enthusiastic "pushing" typically

PERSONAL ACCOUNT

That Moment of Visibility

I never realized how much my working-class background and beliefs played a role in my education. My family, friends, and neighbors never placed much importance on college. Instead, we were strongly encouraged to find work immediately after high school so we could support ourselves financially. My sisters and I were encouraged to do secretarial work until we married. There was no particular positive status attached to obtaining a degree except maybe the chance of making a lot of money. In fact, friends who went to college were looked at somewhat suspiciously. Among my reference group, college was often seen as a way to get out of having to work.

No one in my family had ever gone to college. It was not financially feasible and a college environment was equal to the unknown. It really was scary terrain. When I decided to go to a local community college after having worked for five years in a secretarial position, family and friends could not understand my decision. Why would I choose college when I already had a job? I could pay bills, buy what I needed, and I had a savings account. So I started by taking a course a semester—and I barely got through the first course. Although I received a good grade, I felt incredibly isolated, like I was an impostor who did not belong in a classroom. I had no idea how someone in college was supposed to act. I stayed silent, scared, and consciously invisible most of the time. I was not even close to making a commitment to a college education when I signed up for a second course—but because my job paid for it (one of the benefits), I felt I had nothing to lose. I signed up for Introduction to Juvenile Delinquency and midway through, our class received an assignment to do a fifteen-page self-analysis applying some of the theories we were learning. The

thought of consciously revealing myself when I was trying so hard not to look, act, or be different was not something I was willing (or, I think, able at the time) to do. When I discussed the assignment with the people close to me, they agreed that the assignment was too personal and revealing. I decided not to do it and I also decided that college was probably not for me.

I went to see my professor (who was the only woman in her department) to let her know that I was refusing to do the assignment and would not complete the course. We had spoken two or three times outside of class and she knew a little about me. I knew that she was also from a working-class background and had returned to school after working some years. I felt the least I could do was tell her I was quitting the class. When I said that I was unwilling to do the assignment, she stared at me for some time, and then asked me what I would prefer to write about. I was stunned that I was noticed and was being asked what I would like to do. When I had no reply, she asked if I would write a paper on the importance of dissent. All I could think to say was yes. I completed the course successfully and found an ally in my department. I can't overstate the importance of that moment of acknowledgment. It was the first time I felt listened to. It was the moment when you feel safe enough to reveal who you are, the deep breath you can finally take when you figure out that the person you're talking to understands, appreciates, and may even share your identity.

I think of this experience as a turning point for me—when I realized that despite all my conscious efforts to be invisible and to "pass," it was that moment of visibility and acknowledgment that kept me in school.

Rose B. Pascarell

was less informed and less useful in enabling their children to navigate the complexities involved in pursuing higher education.

The portrait that emerges from these data is strikingly consistent with the one presented in *Unequal Childhoods.* In particular, class-specific cultural orientations to child rearing retain their purchase on family behavior—at least in the area of

relations to institutions—approximately ten years after the original data collection took place. Thus, the behavior of middle class parents in managing their children's high school career and transition into college can be viewed straightforwardly as an extension of the same "concerted cultivation" child rearing strategy they practiced earlier. Similarly, the propensity of working class and poor parents to assume that their children's education is the responsibility of professional educators constitutes an extension of the "accomplishment of natural growth" approach. This indicates that the cultural dispositions identified in *Unequal Childhoods*, are highly durable.

We conclude by pointing out that these dispositions have profound consequences when they come into contact with the standards gatekeeping institutions such as colleges. The ability to negotiate the (absurdly) complex process of applying to college is enhanced dramatically by the presence of parents whose informal knowledge covers the myriad factors involved (the costs, the entry requirements, the strengths and weaknesses and status of potential schools) and who are inclined to involve themselves deeply in their children's institutional lives. As such, we maintain that this knowledge, and the associated dispositions, may be viewed as a form of "cultural capital"—one that is clearly implicated in the long-term persistence of class inequality. . . .

DISCUSSION QUESTIONS

1. What is a cultural repertoire?
2. Is education the responsibility of the school or the parent?

NOTES

1. Stacey's mother regretted that she did not force her daughter to take more AP and honors classes: "I kick myself for that. I think that she would have gotten in more writing and more reading. She was a kid who hated to read. She's at a college that is very challenging. . . . I think that she is challenged."
2. Children do not, of course, always conform to their parents' wishes. Stacey's older sister Fern, who also played basketball, chose a selective public university with an excellent basketball team that was located in a relatively rural location. Her mother was vociferously opposed to the choice because she thought, given her daughter's temperament, she would be better off in an urban setting. Fern found the basketball coach to be very difficult. (Her mother wrote a letter to school officials complaining about the treatment the coach was giving her team.) Fern transferred at the end of her freshman year to a school close to home. Not wanting to sit out a year, per NCAA rules, she transferred from a Division 1 school to a lower division. She liked that school much better; with a major in business, she was planning to get an MBA.

3. Melanie Handlon worked for a while in a coffee shop and then went to cosmetology school. Her case highlights the important variability within class. . . .
4. According to *The Chronicle of Higher Education*, the University of Vermont has hired "parent bouncers" to help keep parents away from their children at college orientations and to allow them to make their course selections without parental input (Will 2005).

REFERENCES

Morgan, Stephen. 2005. *On the Edge of Commitment: Educational Attainment and Race in the United States.* Stanford, Calif.: Stanford University Press.

White, Wendy S. 2005. "Students, Parents, Colleges: Drawing the Lines." *Chronicle of Higher Education* 52(17): B16.

Will, Eric. 2005. "Parent Trap." *Chronicle of Higher Education* 51(46): A4.

READING 31

Cause of Death: Inequality

Alejandro Reuss

INEQUALITY KILLS

You won't see inequality on a medical chart or a coroner's report under "cause of death." You won't see it listed among the top killers in the United States each year. All too often, however, it is social inequality that lurks behind a more immediate cause of death, be it heart disease or diabetes, accidental injury or homicide. Few of the top causes of death are "equal opportunity killers." Instead, they tend to strike poor people more than rich people, the less educated more than the highly educated, people lower on the occupational ladder more than those higher up, or people of color more than white people.

Alejandro Reuss is an economist, historian, and frequent contributor to *Dollars and Sense* magazine.

Statistics on mortality and life expectancy do not provide a perfect map of social inequality. For example, the life expectancy for women in the United States is about six years longer than the life expectancy for men, despite the many ways in which women are subordinated to men. Take most indicators of socioeconomic status, however, and most causes of death, and it's a strong bet that you'll find illness and injury (or "morbidity") and mortality increasing as status decreases.

Men with less than 12 years of education are more than twice as likely to die of chronic diseases (e.g., heart disease), more than three times as likely to die as a result of injury, and nearly twice as likely to die of communicable diseases, compared to those with 13 or more years of education. Women with family incomes below $10,000 are more than three times as likely to die of heart disease and nearly three times as likely to die of diabetes, compared to those with family incomes above $25,000. African Americans are more likely than whites to die of heart disease; stroke; lung, colon, prostate, and breast cancer, as well as all cancers combined; liver disease; diabetes; AIDS; accidental injury; and homicide. In all, the lower you are in a social hierarchy, the worse your health and the shorter your life are likely to be.

THE WORSE OFF IN THE UNITED STATES ARE NOT WELL OFF BY WORLD STANDARDS

You often hear it said that even poor people in rich countries like the United States are rich compared to ordinary people in poor countries. While that may be true when it comes to consumer goods like televisions or telephones, which are widely available even to poor people in the United States, it's completely wrong when it comes to health.

In a 1996 study published in *The New England Journal of Medicine*, University of Michigan researchers found that African-American females living to age 15 in Harlem had a 65% chance of surviving to age 65, about the same as women in India.

Meanwhile, Harlem's African-American males had only a 37% chance of surviving to age 65, about the same as men in Angola or the Democratic Republic of Congo. Among both African-American men and women, infectious diseases and diseases of the circulatory system were the prime causes of high mortality.

It takes more income to achieve a given life expectancy in a rich country like the United States than it does to achieve the same life expectancy in a less affluent country. So the higher money income of a low-income person in the United States, compared to a middle-income person in a poor country, does not necessarily translate into a longer life span. The average income per person in African-American families, for example, is more than five times the per capita income of El Salvador. The life expectancy for African-American men in the United States, however, is only about 67 years, the same as the average life expectancy for men in El Salvador.

HEALTH INEQUALITIES IN THE UNITED STATES ARE NOT JUST ABOUT ACCESS TO HEALTH CARE

Nearly one-sixth of the U.S. population lacks health insurance, including about 44% of poor people. A poor adult with a health problem is only half as likely to see a doctor as a high-income adult. Adults living in low-income areas are more than twice as likely to be hospitalized for a health problem that could have been effectively treated with timely outpatient care, compared with adults living in high-income areas. Obviously, lack of access to health care is a major health problem.

But so are environmental and occupational hazards; communicable diseases; homicide and firearm-related injuries; and smoking, alcohol consumption, lack of exercise, and other risk factors. These dangers all tend to affect lower-income people more than higher-income, less educated people more than more-educated, and people of color more than whites. African-American children are more than twice as likely as white children to be hospitalized for asthma, which is linked to air pollution. Poor men are nearly six times as likely as high-income men to have elevated blood-lead levels, which reflect both residential and workplace environmental hazards. African-American men are more than seven times as likely to fall victim to homicide as white men; African-American women, more than four times as likely as white women. The less education someone has, the more likely they are to smoke or to drink heavily. The lower someone's income, the less likely they are to get regular exercise.

Michael Marmot, a pioneer in the study of social inequality and health, notes that so-called diseases of affluence—disorders, like heart disease, associated with high calorie and high-fat diets, lack of physical activity, etc.—are most prevalent among the least affluent people in rich societies. While recognizing the role of such "behavioral" risk factors as smoking in producing poor health, he argues, "It is not sufficient . . . to ask what contribution smoking makes to generating the social gradient in ill health, but we must ask, why is there a social gradient in smoking?" What appear to be individual "lifestyle" decisions often reflect a broader social epidemiology.

GREATER INCOME INEQUALITY GOES HAND IN HAND WITH POORER HEALTH

Numerous studies suggest that the more unequal the income distribution in a country, state, or city, the lower the life expectancies for people at all income levels. One study published in the *American Journal of Public Health,* for example, shows that U.S. metropolitan areas with low per capita incomes and low levels of income inequality have lower mortality rates than areas with high median incomes and high levels of income inequality. Meanwhile, for a given per capita income range, mortality rates always decline as inequality declines.

R. G. Wilkinson, perhaps the researcher most responsible for relating health outcomes to overall levels of inequality (rather than individual income levels), argues that greater income inequality causes worse health outcomes independent of its effects on poverty. Wilkinson and his associates suggest several explanations for this relationship. First, the bigger the income gap between rich and poor, the less inclined the well off are to pay taxes for public services they either do not use or use in low proportion to the taxes they pay. Lower spending on public hospitals, schools, and other basic services does not affect wealthy people's life expectancies very much, but it affects poor people's life expectancies a great deal. Second, the bigger the income gap, the lower the overall level of social cohesion. High levels of social cohesion are associated with good health outcomes for several reasons. For example, people in highly cohesive societies are more likely to be active in their communities, reducing social isolation, a known health risk factor. (See Thad Williamson, "Social Movements Are Good for Your Health")

Numerous researchers have criticized Wilkinson's conclusions, arguing that the real reason income inequality tends to be associated with worse health outcomes is that it is associated with higher rates of poverty. But even if they are right and income inequality causes worse health simply by bringing about greater poverty, that hardly makes for a defense of inequality. Poverty and inequality are like partners in crime. "[W]hether public policy focuses primarily on the elimination of poverty or on reduction in income disparity," argue Wilkinson critics Kevin Fiscella and Peter Franks, "neither goal is likely to be achieved in the absence of the other."

DIFFERENCES IN STATUS MAY BE JUST AS IMPORTANT AS INCOME LEVELS

Even after accounting for differences in income, education, and other factors, the life expectancy for African Americans is less than that for whites. U.S. researchers are beginning to explore the relationship between high blood pressure among African

Americans and the racism of the surrounding society. African Americans tend to suffer from high blood pressure, a risk factor for circulatory disease, more often than whites. Moreover, studies have found that, when confronted with racism, African Americans suffer larger and longer-lasting increases in blood pressure than when faced with other stressful situations. Broader surveys relating blood pressure in African Americans to perceived instances of racial discrimination have yielded complex results, depending on social class, gender, and other factors.

Stresses cascade down social hierarchies and accumulate among the least empowered. Even researchers focusing on social inequality and health, however, have been surprised by the large effects on mortality. Over 30 years ago, Michael Marmot and his associates undertook a landmark study, known as Whitehall I, of health among British civil servants. Since the civil servants shared many characteristics regardless of job classification—an office work environment, a high degree of job security, etc.—the researchers expected to find only modest health differences among them. To their surprise, the study revealed a sharp increase in mortality with each step down the job hierarchy—even from the highest grade to the second highest. Over ten years, employees in the lowest grade were three times as likely to die as those in the highest grade. One factor was that people in lower grades showed a higher incidence of many "lifestyle" risk factors, like smoking, poor diet, and lack of exercise. Even when the researchers controlled for such factors, however, more than half the mortality gap remained.

Marmot noted that people in the lower job grades were less likely to describe themselves as having "control over their working lives" or being "satisfied with their work situation," compared to those higher up. While people in higher job grades were more likely to report "having to work at a fast pace," lower-level civil servants were more likely to report feelings of hostility, the main stress-related risk factor for heart disease. Marmot concluded that "psycho-social" factors—the psychological

costs of being lower in the hierarchy—played an important role in the unexplained mortality gap. Many of us have probably said to ourselves, after a trying day on the job, "They're killing me." Turns out it's not just a figure of speech. Inequality kills—and it starts at the bottom.

DISCUSSION QUESTIONS

1. What explanation can you offer for why the rich are less likely to support public services in communities with a wide income gap between the rich and poor?

2. Why do you think there might be social class differences in smoking, drinking, or exercise?

REFERENCES

Lisa Berkman, "Social Inequalities and Health: Five Key Points for Policy-Makers to Know," February 5, 2001, Kennedy School of Government, Harvard University.

Kevin Fiscella and Peter Franks, "Poverty or income inequality as predictors of mortality: longitudinal cohort study," *British Medical Journal* 314: 1724–8, 1997.

Arline T. Geronimus, et al., "Excess Mortality among Blacks and Whites in the United States," *The New England Journal of Medicine* 335 (21), November 21, 1996.

Health, United States, 1998, with Socioeconomic Status and Health Chartbook, National Center for Health Statistics, www.cdc.gov/nchs.

Human Development Report 2000, UN Development Programme.

Ichiro Kawachi, Bruce P. Kennedy, and Richard G. Wilkinson, eds., *The Society and Population Health Reader, Volume I: Income Inequality and Health*, 1999.

Nancy Krieger, Ph.D., and Stephen Sidney, M.D., "Racial Discrimination and Blood Pressure: The CARDIA Study of Young Black and White Adults," *American Journal of Public Health* 86 (10), October 1996.

Michael Marmot, "Social Differences in Mortality: The Whitehall Studies," *Adult Mortality in Developed Countries: From Description to Explanation*, Alan D. Lopez, Graziella Caselli, and Tapani Valkonen, eds., 1995.

Michael Marmot, "The Social Pattern of Health and Disease," *Health and Social Organization: Towards a Health Policy for the Twenty First Century*, David Blane, Eric Brunner, and Richard Wilkinson, eds., 1996.

Thad Williamson, "Social Movements Are Good for Your Health," *Dollars and Sense,* May/June, 2001.

World Development Indicators 2000, World Bank.

READING 32

Why Are Droves of Unqualified, Unprepared Kids Getting into Our Top Colleges? Because Their Dads Are Alumni

John Larew

Growing up, she heard a hundred Harvard stories. In high school, she put the college squarely in her sights. But when judgment day came, the Harvard admissions guys were frankly unimpressed. Her academic record was solid—not special. Extracurriculars, interview, recommendations? Above average, but not by much. "Nothing really stands out" one admissions officer scribbled on her application folder. Wrote another, "Harvard not really the right place."

At the hyperselective Harvard, where high school valedictorians, National Merit Scholar finalists, musical prodigies—11,000 ambitious kids in all—are rejected annually, this young woman didn't seem to have much of a chance. Thanks to Harvard's largest affirmative action program, she got in anyway. No, she wasn't poor, black, disabled, Hispanic, native American, or even Aleutian. She got in because her mom went to Harvard.

Folk wisdom at Harvard holds that "Mother Harvard does not coddle her young." She sure treats her grandkids right, though. For more than 40 years, an astounding one-fifth of Harvard's students have received admissions preference because parents attended the school. Today, these overwhemingly affluent, white children of alumni—"legacies"—are three times more likely to be accepted to Harvard than high school kids who lack that handsome lineage.

Yalies, don't feel smug: Offspring of the Old Blue are two-and-a-half times more likely to be accepted than their unconnected peers. Dartmouth this year admitted 57 percent of its legacy applicants, compared to 27 percent of nonlegacies. At the University of Pennsylvania, 66 percent of legacies were admitted last year—thanks in part to an autonomous "office of alumni admissions" that actively lobbies for alumni children before the admissions committee. "One can argue that it's an accident, but it sure doesn't look like an accident," admits Yale Dean of Admissions Worth David.

If the legacies' big edge seems unfair to the tens of thousands who get turned away every year, Ivy League administrators have long defended the innocence of the legacy stat. Children of alumni are just smarter; they come from privileged backgrounds and tend to grow up in homes where parents encourage learning. That's what Harvard Dean of Admissions William Fitzsimmons told the campus newspaper, the *Harvard Crimson,* when it first reported on the legacy preference last year. Departing Harvard President Derek Bok patiently explained that the legacy preference worked only as a "tie-breaking factor" between otherwise equally qualified candidates.

Since Ivy League admissions data is a notoriously classified commodity, when Harvard officials said in previous years that alumni kids were just better, you had to take them at their word. But then federal investigators came along and pried open those top-secret files. The Harvard guys were lying.

This past fall, after two years of study, the U.S. Department of Education's Office for Civil Rights (OCR) found that, far from being more qualified or even equally qualified, the average admitted legacy at Harvard between 1981 and 1988 was significantly *less* qualified than the average admitted nonlegacy. Examining admissions office ratings on academics, extracurriculars, personal qualities, recommendations, and other categories, the OCR concluded that "with the exception of the athletic rating, [admitted] nonlegacies scored better than legacies in *all* areas of comparison."

Exceptionally high admission rates, lowered admission standards, preferential treatment . . . hmmm. These sound like the cries heard in the

---

John Larew wrote this article when he was editor of Harvard's student newspaper, *The Harvard Crimson.*

growing fury over affirmative action for racial minorities in America's elite universities. Only no one is outraged about legacies.

- In his recent book, *Preferential Policies,* Thomas Sowell argues that doling out special treatment encourages lackluster performance by the favored and resentment from the spurned. His far-ranging study flits from Malaysia to South Africa to American college campuses. Legacies don't merit a word.
- Dinesh D'Souza, in his celebrated jeremiad *Illiberal Education,* blames affirmative action in college admissions for declining academic standards and increasing racial tensions. Lowered standards for minority applicants, he hints, may soon destroy the university as we know it. Lowered standards for legacies? The subject doesn't come up.
- For all his polysyllabic complaints against preferential admissions, William F. Buckley Jr. (Yale '50) has never bothered to note that son Chris (Yale '75) got the benefit of a policy that more than doubled his chance of admission.

With so much silence on the subject, you'd be excused for thinking that in these enlightened times hereditary preferences are few and far between. But you'd be wrong. At most elite universities during the eighties, the legacy was by far the biggest piece of the preferential pie. At Harvard, a legacy is about twice as likely to be admitted as a black or Hispanic student. As sociologists Jerome Karabel and David Karen point out, if alumni children were admitted to Harvard at the same rate as other applicants, their numbers in the class of 1992 would have been reduced by about 200. Instead, those 200 marginally qualified legacies outnumbered all black, Mexican-American, native American, and Puerto Rican enrollees put together. If a few marginally qualified minorities are undermining Harvard's academic standards as much as conservatives charge, think about the damage all those legacies must be doing.

Mind you, colleges have the right to give the occasional preference—to bend the rules for the brilliant oboist or the world-class curler or the guy whose remarkable decency can't be measured by the SAT. (I happened to benefit from a geographical edge: It's easier to get into Harvard from West Virginia than from New England.) And until standardized tests and grade point average perfectly reflect the character, judgment, and drive of a student, tips like these aren't just nice, they're fair. Unfortunately, the extent of the legacy privilege in elite American colleges suggests something more than the occasional tie-breaking tip. Forget meritocracy. When 20 percent of Harvard's student body gets a legacy preference, aristocracy is the word that comes to mind.

A CASTE OF THOUSANDS

If complaining about minority preferences is fashionable in the world of competitive colleges, bitching about legacies is just plain gauche, suggesting an unhealthy resentment of the privileged. But the effects of the legacy trickle down. For every legacy that wins, someone—usually someone less privileged—loses. And higher education is a high-stakes game.

High school graduates earn 59 percent of the income of four-year college graduates. Between high school graduates and alumni of prestigious colleges, the disparity is far greater. A *Fortune* study of American CEOs shows the usual suspects—graduates of Yale, Princeton, and Harvard—leading the list. A recent survey of the Harvard Class of 1940 found that 43 percent were worth more than $1 million. With some understatement, the report concludes, "A picture of highly advantageous circumstances emerges here, does it not, compared with American society as a whole?"

An Ivy League diploma doesn't necessarily mean a fine education. Nor does it guarantee future success. What it *does* represent is a big head start in the rat race—a fact Harvard will be the first to tell you. When I was a freshman, a counselor at the Office of Career Services instructed a group of us to make the Harvard name stand out on our résumés: "Underline it, boldface it, put it in capital letters."

Of course, the existence of the legacy preference in this fierce career competition isn't exactly news. According to historians, it was a direct result of the influx of Jews into the Ivy League during the twenties. Until then, Harvard, Princeton, and Yale had admitted anyone who could pass their entrance exams, but suddenly Jewish kids were outscoring the WASPs. So the schools began to use nonacademic criteria—"character," "solidity," and, eventually, lineage—to justify accepting low-scoring blue bloods over their peers. Yale implemented its legacy preference first, in 1925—spelling it out in a memo four years later: The school would admit "Yale sons of good character and reasonably good record . . . regardless of the number of applicants and the superiority of outside competitors." Harvard and Princeton followed shortly thereafter.

Despite its ignoble origins, the legacy preference has only sporadically come under fire, most notably in 1978's affirmative action decision, *University of California Board of Regents v. Bakke.* In his concurrence, Justice Harris Blackmun observed, "It is somewhat ironic to have us so deeply disturbed over a program where race is an element of consciousness, and yet to be aware of the fact, as we are, that institutions of higher learning . . . have given conceded preferences to the children of alumni."

If people are, in fact, aware of the legacy preference, why has it been spared the scrutiny given other preferential policies? One reason is public ignorance of the scope and scale of those preferences—an ignorance carefully cultivated by America's elite institutions. It's easy to maintain the fiction that your legacies get in strictly on merit as long as your admissions bureaucracy controls all access to student data. Information on Harvard's legacies became publicly available not because of any fit of disclosure by the university, but because a few civil rights types noted that the school had a suspiciously low rate of admission for Asian-Americans, who are statistically stronger than other racial groups in academics.

While the ensuing OCR inquiry found no evidence of illegal racial discrimination by Harvard, it did turn up some embarrassing information about how much weight the "legacy" label gives an otherwise flimsy file. Take these comments scrawled by admissions officers on applicant folders:

- "Double lineage who chose the right parents."
- "Dad's [deleted] connections signify lineage of more than usual weight. That counted into the equation makes this a case which (assuming positive TRs [teacher recommendations] and Alum IV [alumnus interview]) is well worth doing."
- "Lineage is main thing."
- "Not quite strong enough to get the clean tip."
- "Classical case that would be hard to explain to dad."
- "Double lineage but lots of problems."
- "Not a great profile, but just strong enough #'s and grades to get the tip from lineage."
- "Without lineage, there would be little case. With it, we'll keep looking."

In every one of these cases, the applicant was admitted.

Of course, Harvard's not doing anything other schools aren't. The practice of playing favorites with alumni children is nearly universal among private colleges and isn't unheard of at public institutions, either. The rate of admission for Stanford's alumni children is "almost twice the general population," according to a spokesman for the admissions office. Notre Dame reserves 25 percent of each freshman class for legacies. At the University of Virginia, where native Virginians make up two-thirds of each class, alumni children are automatically treated as Virginians even if they live out of state—giving them a whopping competitive edge. The same is true of the University of California at Berkeley. At many schools, Harvard included, all legacy applications are guaranteed a read by the dean of admissions himself—a privilege nonlegacies don't get.

LITTLE WHITE ELIS

Like the Harvard deans, officials at other universities dismiss the statistical disparities by pointing to the superior environmental influences found in the homes of their alums. "I bet that, statistically, [legacy qualifications are] a little above average, but not by much," says Paul Killebrew, associate director of admissions at Dartmouth. "The admitted group [of legacies] would look exactly like the profile of the class."

James Wickenden, a former dean of admissions at Princeton who now runs a college consulting firm, suspects otherwise. Wickenden wrote of "one Ivy League university" where the average combined SAT score of the freshman class was 1,350 out of a possible 1,600, compared to 1,280 for legacies. "At most selective schools, [legacy status] doubles, even trebles the chances of admission," he says. Many colleges even place admitted legacies in a special "Not in Profile" file (along with recruited athletes and some minority students), so that when the school's SAT scores are published, alumni kids won't pull down the average.

How do those kids fare once they're enrolled? No one's telling. Harvard, for one, refuses to keep any records of how alumni children stack up academically against their nonlegacy classmates—perhaps because the last such study, in 1956, showed Harvard sons hogging the bottom of the grade curve.

If the test scores of admitted legacies are a mystery, the reason colleges accept so many is not. They're afraid the alumni parents of rejected children will stop giving to the colleges' unending fundraising campaigns. "Our survival as an institution depends on having support from alumni," says Richard Steele, director of undergraduate admissions at Duke University, "so according advantages to alumni kids is just a given."

In fact, the OCR exonerated Harvard's legacy preference precisely because legacies bring in money. (OCR cited a federal district court ruling that a state university could favor the children of out-of-state alumni because "defendants showed that the alumni provide monetary support for the university.") And there's no question that alumni provide significant support to Harvard: Last year, they raised $20 million for the scholarship fund alone.

In a letter to OCR defending his legacies, Harvard's Fitzsimmons painted a grim picture of a school where the preference did not exist—a place peeved alumni turned their backs on when their kids failed to make the cut. "Without the fundraising activities of alumni," Fitzsimmons warned darkly, "Harvard could not maintain many of its programs, including needs-blind admissions."

Ignoring, for the moment, the question of how "needs-blind" a system is that admits one-fifth of each class on the assumption that, hey, their parents might give us money, Fitzsimmons's defense doesn't quite ring true. The "Save the Scholarship Fund" line is a variation on the principle of "Firemen First," whereby bureaucrats threatened with a budget cut insist that essential programs rather than executive perks and junkets will be the first to be slashed. Truth be told, there is just about nothing that Harvard, the richest university in the world, could do to jeopardize needs-blind admissions, provided that it placed a high enough priority on them.

But even more unclear is how closely alumni giving is related to the acceptance of alumni kids. "People whose children are denied admission are initially upset," says Wickenden, "and maybe for a year or two their interest in the university wanes. But typically they come back around when they see that what happened was best for the kids." Wickenden has put his money where his mouth is: He rejected two sons of a Princeton trustee involved in a $420 million fundraising project, not to mention the child of a board member who managed the school's $2 billion endowment, all with no apparent ill effect.

Most university administrators would be loath to take such a chance, despite a surprising lack of evidence of the legacy/largess connection. Fitzsimmons admits Harvard knows of no empirical research to support the claim that diminishing legacies would decrease alumni contributions, relying instead on "hundreds, perhaps thousands of conversations with alumni whose sons and daughters applied."

No doubt some of Fitzsimmons's anxiety is founded: It's only natural for alumni to want their kids to have the same privileges they did. But the historical record suggests that alumni are far more tolerant than administrators realize. Admit women and blacks? *Well, we would,* said administrators earlier this century—*but the alumni just won't have it.* Fortunately for American universities, the bulk of those alumni turned out to be less craven than administrators thought they'd be. As more blacks and women enrolled over the past two decades, the funds kept pouring in, reaching an all-time high in the eighties.

Another significant historical lesson can be drawn from the late fifties, when Harvard's selectiveness increased dramatically. As the number of applications soared, the rate of admission for legacies began declining from about 90 percent to its current 43 percent. Administration anxiety rose inversely, but Harvard's fundraising machine has somehow survived. That doesn't mean there's *no* correlation between alumni giving and the legacy preference, obviously; rather, it means that the people who would withhold their money at the loss of the legacy privilege were far outnumbered by other givers. "It takes time to get the message out," explains Fitzsimmons, "but eventually people start responding. We've had to make the case [for democratization] to alumni, and I think that they generally feel good about that."

HEIR CUT

When justice dictates that ordinary kids should have as fair a shot as the children of America's elite, couldn't Harvard and its sister institutions trouble themselves to "get the message out" again? Of course they could. But virtually no one—liberal or conservative—is pushing them to do so.

"There must be no goals or quotas for any special group or category of applicants," reads an advertisement in the right-wing *Dartmouth Review.* "Equal opportunity must be the guiding policy. Males, females, blacks, whites, Native Americans, Hispanics . . . can all be given equal chance to matriculate, survive, and prosper based solely on individual performance."

Noble sentiments from the Ernest Martin Hopkins Institute, an organization of conservative

Dartmouth alumni. Reading on, though, we find these "concerned alumni" aren't sacrificing *their* young to the cause. "Alumni sons and daughters," notes the ad further down, "should receive some special consideration."

Similarly, Harvard's conservative *Salient* has twice in recent years decried the treatment of Asian-Americans in admissions, but it attributes their misfortune to favoritism for blacks and Hispanics. What about legacy university favoritism—a much bigger factor? *Salient* writers have twice endorsed it.

What's most surprising is the indifference of minority activists. With the notable exception of a few vocal Asian-Americans, most have made peace with the preference for well-off whites.

Mecca Nelson, the president of Harvard's Black Students Association, leads rallies for the hiring of more minority faculty. She participated in an illegal sit-in at an administration building in support of Afro-American studies. But when it comes to the policy that Asian-American activist Arthur Hu calls "a 20-percent-white quota," Nelson says, "I don't have any really strong opinions about it. I'm not very clear on the whole legacy issue at all."

Joshua Li, former co-chair of Harvard's Asian-American Association, explains his complacency differently: "We understand that in the future Asian-American students will receive these tips as well."

At America's elite universities, you'd expect a somewhat higher standard of fairness than that—especially when money is the driving force behind the concept. And many Ivy League types *do* advocate for more just and lofty ideals. One of them, as it happens, is Derek Bok. In one of Harvard's annual reports, he warned that the modern university is slowly turning from a truth-seeking enterprise into a money-grubbing corporation—at the expense of the loyalty of its alums. "Such an institution may still evoke pride and respect because of its intellectual achievements," he said rightly. "But the feelings it engenders will not be quite the same as those produced by an institution that is prepared to forgo income, if need be, to preserve values of a nobler kind."

Forgo income to preserve values of a nobler kind—it's an excellent idea. Embrace the preferences for the poor and disadvantaged. Wean alumni from the idea of the legacy edge. And above all, stop the hypocrisy that begrudges the great unwashed a place at Harvard while happily making room for the less qualified sons and daughters of alums.

After 70 years, it won't be easy to wrest the legacy preference away from the alums. But the long-term payoff is as much a matter of message as money. When the sons and daughters of today's college kids fill out *their* applications, the legacy preference should seem not a birthright, but a long-gone relic from the Ivy League's inequitable past.

DISCUSSION QUESTIONS

1. Do you think legacy preferences are unfair? Why or why not? How do you think they compare to minority preferences?
2. John Larew, then editor of the *Harvard Crimson*, was the first to bring the subject of legacy preference to national attention. Since then, these preferences have received a good deal of media attention. Do you think that legacy admissions are now stigmatized admissions like affirmative action admissions?

DISABILITY

READING 33

Public Transit

John Hockenberry

New York was not like Iran.

It was a shock to return to the United States in 1990, where it routinely took an act of God to hail a taxi. There was nothing religious about New York City, even on Christmas Eve. I had taken a cab from midtown to Riverside Church on the west side of Manhattan only to find that my information about a Christmas Eve service there was mistaken. The church was padlocked, which I only discovered after getting out of the cab into the forty-mile-an-hour wind and the twenty-degree weather. I tried all of the doors of the church and found myself alone at close to midnight, without a taxi, on December 24 at 122d Street and Riverside Drive.

I was wearing a wool sports jacket and a heavy scarf, but no outer jacket. There were no cars on

the street. Being wrong about the service and having come all the way uptown was more than a little frustrating. I suspected that I was not in the best psychological condition to watch the usual half-dozen or so New York cabs pass me by and pretend not to see me hailing them. I knew the most important thing was to try and not look like a panhandler. This was always hard. Many times in New York I had hailed a cab only to have the driver hand me a dollar. Once I was so shocked that I looked at the cabbie and said, as though I were correcting his spelling, "No, I give you the money."

"You want a ride?" he said. "Really?"

The worst were the taxis that stopped but had some idea that the wheelchair was going to put itself into the trunk. After you hopped into the backseat, these drivers would look at you as though you were trying to pull a fast one, tricking them into having to get out of their cabs and load something in the trunk that you had been cleverly hiding. Some cabbies would say that I should have brought someone with me to put the chair in, or that it was too heavy for them to lift. My favorite excuse was also the most frequent, "Look, buddy, I can't lift that chair. I have a bad back."

"I never heard of anyone who became paralyzed from lifting wheelchairs," I'd say. My favorite reply never helped. If the drivers would actually load the

---

John Hockenberry is the host of *The Takeaway*, a live national news program. He has been a broadcast journalist for National Public Radio and *ABC News*, and is the author of *Moving Violations: War Zones, Wheelchairs, and Declarations of Independence*.

chair, you could hear them grumbling, throwing it around to get it to fit, and smashing the trunk lid down on it. When we would arrive at our destination, the driver would throw the chair at me like it was a chunk of nuclear waste and hop back behind the wheel. The only thing to do in these situations was to smile, try not to get into a fight, and hope the anger would subside quickly so you could make it wherever you were going without having a meltdown.

There were some drivers who wouldn't load the chair at all. For these people, at one time, I carried a Swiss army knife. The rule was, if I had to get back out of a cab because a driver wouldn't load my chair, then I would give the driver a reason to get out of his cab shortly after I was gone. I would use the small blade of the knife to puncture a rear tire before the cab drove away, then hail another one. A few blocks ahead, when the first driver had discovered his difficulties, he was generally looking in his trunk for the tire jack when I passed by, waving.

The trouble with this idea was that other people often did not have the same righteous attitude that I did about tire puncturing in Manhattan traffic, and using knives to get freelance revenge in New York City under any circumstances. Most of my friends put me in the same league with subway vigilante Bernard Goetz, and concluded that I needed serious help. So I had stopped using the Swiss army knife and was without it that Christmas Eve on 122nd and Riverside Drive.

The first cab drove toward me and slowed down; the driver stared, then quickly drove by. A second cab approached. I motioned emphatically. I smiled and tried to look as credible as I could. Out in this December wind, I was just another invisible particle of New York misery. The driver of the second cab shook his head as he passed with the lame, catch-all apologetic look New York cabbies use to say, "No way, Mac. Sorry, no way I can take you."

I had one advantage. At least I was white. Black males in New York City have to watch at least as many cabs go by as someone in a wheelchair does before getting a ride. Black male friends of mine say they consciously have to rely on their ritzy trench coats or conservative "Real Job" suits to counter skin color in catching a cab. If I could look more white than crippled, I might not freeze to death on Christmas Eve. I was a psychotic, twentieth-century hit man named Tiny Tim, imagining all sorts of gory ways to knock off a cabbie named Scrooge. The wind was blowing furiously off the Hudson, right up over Riverside Drive.

A third cab drove by. I wondered if I could force a cab to stop by blocking the road. I wished I had a baseball bat. For a period of a few minutes, there was no traffic. I turned and began to roll down Riverside. After a block, I turned around, and there was one more empty cab in the right lane coming toward me. I raised my hand. I was sitting directly under a streetlight. The cabbie clearly saw me, abruptly veered left into the turn lane, and sat there, signaling at the red light.

I rolled over to his cab and knocked on the window. "Can you take a fare?" The driver was pretending I had just landed there from space, but I was freezing and needed a ride, so I tried not to look disgusted. He nodded with all of the enthusiasm of someone with an abscessed tooth. I opened the door and hopped onto the backseat. I folded the chair and asked him to open the trunk of his cab.

"Why you want me to do that?" he said.

"Put the chair in the trunk, please." I was half-sitting in the cab, my legs still outside. The door was open and the wheelchair was folded next to the cab. "No way, man," he said. "I'm not going to do that. It's too damn cold." I was supposed to understand that I would now simply thank him for his trouble, get back in my wheelchair, and wait for another cab. "Just put the chair in the trunk right now. It's Christmas Eve, pal. Why don't you just pretend to be Santa for five fucking minutes?" His smile vanished. I had crossed a line by being angry. But he also looked relieved, as though now he could refuse me in good conscience. It was all written clearly on his face. "You're crazy, man. I don't have to do nothing for you." I looked at him once more and said, "If you make me get back into this chair, you are going to be very sorry." It was a moment of visceral anger. There was no turning back now. "Go away, man. It's too cold."

I got back into the chair. I placed my backpack with my wallet in it on the back of my chair for safekeeping. I grabbed his door and, with all of my strength, pushed it back on its hinges until I heard a loud snap. It was now jammed open. I rolled over to his passenger window, and two insane jabs of my right fist shattered it. I rolled around to the front of the cab, and with my fist in my white handball glove took out first one, then the other headlight. The light I was bathed in from the front of the cab vanished. The face of the driver could now be seen clearly, illuminated by the dashboard's glow.

I could hear myself screaming at him in a voice that sounded far away. I knew the voice, but the person it belonged to was an intruder in this place. He had nothing to do with this particular cabbie and his stupid, callous insensitivity; rather, he was the overlord to all such incidents that had come before. Whenever the gauntlet was dropped, it was this interior soul, with that screaming voice and those hands, who felt no pain and who surfed down a wave of hatred to settle the score. This soul had done the arithmetic and chosen the weapons. I would have to live with the consequences.

I rolled over to the driver's seat and grabbed the window next to his face. I could see that he was absolutely terrified. It made me want to torture him. I hungered for his fear; I wanted to feel his presumptions of power and physical superiority in my hands as he sank up to his neck in my rage, my fists closed around his throat. I attacked his half-open window. It cracked, and as I hauled my arm back to finish it, I saw large drops of blood on the driver's face. I looked at him closely. He was paralyzed with fear and spattered with blood. There was blood on his window, as well. A voice inside me screamed, "I didn't touch you, motherfucker. You're not bleeding. Don't say that I made you bleed. You fucking bastard. Don't you dare bleed!"

I rolled back from the cab. It was my own blood shooting from my thumb. It gushed over the white leather of my glove: I had busted an artery at the base of my thumb, but I couldn't see it because it was inside the glove. Whatever had sliced my thumb had gone neatly through the leather first,

and as I rolled down the street I could hear the cabbie saying behind me, "You're crazy, man, you're fucking crazy." I rolled underneath a street lamp to get a closer look. It was my left hand, and it had several lacerations in addition to the one at the base of my thumb. It must have been the headlight glass. The blood continued to gush. Wind blew it off my fingers in festive red droplets, which landed stiffly on the frozen pavement under the street lamp. Merry Christmas.

Up the street, a police squad car had stopped next to the cab, which still had its right rear door jammed open. I coasted farther down the street to see if I could roll the rest of the way home. With each push of my hand on the wheel rim of my chair, blood squirted out of my glove. I could feel it filled with blood inside. The cops pulled up behind me. "Would you like us to arrest that cabbie? Did he attack you?" All I could think of was the indignity of being attacked by him. I thought about screaming, "That piece of human garbage attacked me? No way. Maybe it was me who attacked him as a public service. Did you donut eaters ever think of that? I could have killed the bastard. I *was* trying to kill him, in fact. I insist that you arrest me for attempted murder right now, or I will sue the NYPD under the Americans with Disabilities Act." I thought better of this speech. Intense pain had returned my mind to practical matters. Spending the night in jail for assaulting a cabbie after bragging about it while bleeding to death seemed like a poor way to cap off an already less than stellar Christmas Eve.

"Everything's fine, officer. I'll just get another taxi." I continued to roll one-handed and dripping down Riverside Drive. The cops went back to talk to the cabbie, who was screaming now. I began to worry that he was going to have me arrested, but the cops drove back again. Once more, the officer asked if I wanted to file a complaint against the cabbie. As more blood dripped off my formerly white glove, the officers suggested that I go to the hospital. They had figured out what had happened. As I started to explain, they told me to get in the squad car. "Let's just say it was an unfortunate accident," one officer said. "I don't think he'll ever stop for someone in a wheelchair again. If we can get you to the emergency room in time, maybe you won't lose your thumb."

I got in the backseat while the cops put the chair in the trunk. Seven blocks away was the emergency room of St. Luke's Hospital. Christmas Eve services at St. Luke's included treatment of a young woman's mild overdose. An elderly man and his worried-looking wife were in a corner of the treatment room. His scared face looked out from beneath a green plastic oxygen mask. A number of men stood around watching CNN on the waiting-room television. A woman had been brought in with fairly suspicious-looking bruises on her face and arms. One arm was broken and being set in a cast. She sat quietly while two men talked about football in loud voices. The forlorn Christmas decorations added to the hopelessness of this little band of unfortunates in the emergency room.

When I arrived, everything stopped. Police officers are always an object of curiosity, signaling the arrival of a shooting victim or something more spectacular. For a Christmas Eve, the gushing artery at the base of my thumb was spectacular enough. The men sitting around the emergency room shook their heads. The overdose patient with the sunken cocaine eyes staggered over to inspect the evening's best carnage. "Where did you get that wheelchair?" She looked around as though she was familiar with all of the wheelchairs in this emergency room from previous visits. "It's my own," I replied. "That's a good idea," she said. "Why didn't I think of that?"

I got nine stitches from a doctor who suggested politely that whatever my complaint with the taxi driver, I was one person on the planet who could ill afford to lose a thumb. The deep laceration was just a few millimeters from the nerve and was just as close to the tendon. Severing either one would have added my thumb to an already ample chorus of numbness and paralysis. The thought of losing the use of my thumb was one thing, but what was really disturbing was the thought of its isolation on my hand, numb in the wrong zone. Trapped on a functional hand, a numb and paralyzed thumb would have no way of communicating with my numb and paralyzed feet. It would be not only paralyzed, it

would be in exile: an invader behind enemy lines, stuck across the checkpoint on my chest.

Today, there is a one-inch scar that traces a half circle just to the left of my knuckle. The gloves were a total loss, but they no doubt saved my thumb. Nothing could save my pride, but pride is not always salvageable in New York City. I have taken thousands of cabs, and in each case the business of loading and unloading delivers some small verdict on human nature. Often it is a verdict I am in no mood to hear, as was the case on that Christmas Eve. At other times, the experience is eerie and sublime. At the very least, there is the possibility that I will make a connection with a person, not just stare at the back of an anonymous head.

In my life, cabbies distinguish themselves by being either very rude and unhelpful or sympathetic and righteous. Mahmoud Abu Holima was one of the latter. It was his freckles I remembered, along with his schoolboy nose and reddish-blond hair, which made his Islamic tirades more memorable. He was not swarthy like other Middle Eastern cabbies. He had a squeaky, raspy voice. He drove like a power tool carving Styrofoam. He used his horn a lot. He made constant references to the idiots he said were all around him.

He was like a lot of other New York cabbies. But out of a sea of midtown yellow, Mahmoud Abu Holima was the one who stopped one afternoon in 1990, and by stopping for me he wanted to make it clear to everyone that he was not stopping for anyone else, especially the people in expensive-looking suits waiting on the same street corner I was. His decision to pick me up was part of some protest Mahmoud delivered to America every day he drove the streets of Manhattan.

His cab seemed to have little to do with transporting people from place to place. It was more like an Islamic institute on wheels. A voice in Arabic blared from his cassette player. His front seat was piled with books in Arabic and more cassettes. Some of the books were dog-eared Korans. There were many uniformly bound blue and green books open, marked, and stacked in cross-referenced chaos, the arcane and passionate academic studies of a Muslim cabbie studying hard to get ahead and lose his day job, interrupting his studies in midsentence to pick up a man in a wheelchair.

I took two rides with him. The first time I was going somewhere uptown on Third Avenue. Four cabs had passed me by. He stopped. He put the chair in the trunk and, to make more space there, brought stacks of Arabic books from the trunk into the front seat. He wore a large, knit, dirty-white skullcap and was in constant motion. He seemed lost in the ideas he had been reading about before I got in. At traffic lights, he would read. As he drove, he continually turned away from the windshield to make eye contact with me. His voice careened from conversation to lecture, like his driving. He ignored what was going on around him on the street. He told me he thought my wheelchair was unusually light. He said he knew many boys with no legs who could use such a chair. There were no good wheelchairs in Afghanistan.

"Afghanistan, you know about the war in Afghanistan?" he asked.

I said I knew about it. He said he wasn't talking about the Soviet invasion of Afghanistan and the American efforts to see that the Soviets were defeated. He said that the war was really a religious war. "It is the war for Islam." On a lark, in my broken, rudimentary Arabic, I asked him where he was from. He turned around abruptly and asked, "Where did you learn Arabic?" I told him that I had learned it from living in the Middle East. I apologized for speaking so poorly. He laughed and said that my accent was good, but that non-Muslims in America don't speak Arabic unless they are spies. "Only the Zionists really know how to speak," he said, his voice spitting with hatred.

I thanked him for picking me up. He removed my chair from his trunk, and as I hopped back into it I explained to him that it was difficult sometimes to get a cab in New York. He said that being in America was like being in a war where there are only weapons, no people. "In Islam," he said, "the people are the weapons."

"Why are you here?" I asked him.

"I have kids, family." He smiled once, and the freckles wrinkled on his nose and face, making him look like Tom Sawyer in a Muslim prayer cap. The scowl returned as he drove away. He turned up the cassette. The Arabic voice was still audible a block away.

The second time I saw him, I remembered him and he remembered me. He had no cassettes this time. There were no books in the car, and there was plenty of room in the trunk for my chair this time. Where were all of the books? He said he had finished studying. I asked him about peace in Afghanistan and the fact that Iran and Iraq were no longer at war. He said something about Saddam Hussein I didn't catch, and then he laughed. He seemed less nervous but still had the good-natured intensity I remembered from before. "Are you from Iran?" I asked him, and this time he answered. He told me he was from Egypt. He asked me if I knew about the war in Egypt, and I told him I didn't.

Before he dropped me off, he said that he wanted me to know when we would lose the war against Islam. He said that we won't know when we have lost. "Americans never say anything that's important." He looked out the window. His face did not express hatred as much as disappointment. He shook his head. "It is quiet now."

He ran a red light and parked squarely in the middle of an intersection, stopping traffic to let me out. Cars honked and people yelled as I got into the wheelchair. He scowled at them and laughed. I laughed too. I think I said to him, "*Salaam*," the Arabic word for peace and good-bye. He said something that sounded like "*Mish Salaam fi Amerika*," no peace in America. Then he said, "*Sa'at.*" In Arabic, it means difficult. He got into his cab, smiled, and drove away. On February 26, 1993, cabbie, student of Islam, and family man Mahmoud Abu Holima, along with several others, planted a bomb that blew up in the World Trade Center. Today, he is serving a life sentence in a New York prison. . . .

When I returned to New York City from the Middle East in 1990, I lived in Brooklyn, just two blocks from the Carroll Street subway stop on the F train. It was not accessible, and as there appeared to be no plans to make it so, I didn't think much about the station. When I wanted to go into Manhattan,

I would take a taxi, or I would roll up Court Street to the walkway entrance to the Brooklyn Bridge and fly into the city on a ribbon of oak planks suspended from the bridge's webs of cable that appeared from my wheelchair to be woven into the sky itself. Looking down, I could see the East River through my wheelchair's spokes. Looking up, I saw the clouds through the spokes of the bridge. It was always an uncommon moment of physical integrity with the city, which ended when I came to rest at the traffic light on Chambers Street, next to city hall.

It was while rolling across the bridge one day that I remembered my promise to Donna, my physical therapist, about how I would one day ride the rapid transit trains in Chicago. Pumping my arms up the incline of the bridge toward Manhattan and then coasting down the other side in 1990, I imagined that I would be able physically to accomplish everything I had theorized about the subway in Chicago in those first days of being a paraplegic back in 1976. In the Middle East, I had climbed many stairways and hauled myself and the chair across many filthy floors on my way to interviews, apartments, and news conferences. I had also lost my fear of humiliation from living and working there. I was even intrigued with the idea of taking the train during the peak of rush hour when the greatest number of people of all kinds would be underground with me.

I would do it just the way I had told Donna back in the rehab hospital. But this time, I would wire myself with a microphone and a miniature cassette machine to record everything that happened along the way. Testing my own theory might make a good commentary for an upcoming National Public Radio program about inaccessibility. Between the Carroll Street station and city hall, there were stairs leading in and out of the stations as well as to transfer from one line to another inside the larger stations. To get to Brooklyn Bridge/City Hall, I had to make two transfers, from the F to the A, then from the A to the 5, a total of nearly 150 stairs.

I rolled up to the Brooklyn Carroll Street stop on the F train carrying a rope and a backpack and

wired for sound. Like most of the other people on the train that morning I was on my way to work. Taking the subway was how most people crossed the East River, but it would have been hard to come up with a less practical way, short of swimming, for a paraplegic to cover the same distance. Fortunately, I had the entire morning to kill. I was confident that I had the strength for it, and unless I ended up on the tracks, I felt sure that I could get out of any predicament I found myself in, but I was prepared for things to be more complicated. As usual, trouble would make the story more interesting.

The Carroll Street subway station has two staircases. One leads to the token booth, where the fare is paid by the turnstiles at the track entrance, the other one goes directly down to the tracks. Near the entrance is a newsstand. As I rolled to the top of the stairs, the man behind the counter watched me closely and the people standing around the newsstand stopped talking. I quickly climbed out of my chair and down onto the top step.

I folded my chair and tied the length of rope around it, attaching the end to my wrist. I moved down to the second step and began to lower the folded chair down the steps to the bottom. It took just a moment. Then, one at a time, I descended the first flight of stairs with my backpack and seat cushion in my lap until I reached a foul-smelling landing below street level. I was on my way. I looked up. The people at the newsstand who had been peering sheepishly down at me looked away. All around me, crowds of commuters with briefcases and headphones walked by, stepping around me without breaking stride. If I had worried about anything associated with this venture, it was that I would just be in the way. I was invisible.

I slid across the floor to the next flight of stairs, and the commuters arriving at the station now came upon me suddenly from around a corner. Still, they expressed no surprise and neatly moved over to form an orderly lane on the side of the landing opposite me as I lowered my chair once again to the bottom of the stairs where the token booth was.

With an elastic cord around my legs to keep them together and more easily moved (an innovation

I hadn't thought of back in rehab), I continued down the stairs, two steps at a time, and finally reached the chair at the bottom of the steps. I stood it up, unfolded it, and did a two-armed, from-the-floor lift back onto the seat. My head rose out of the sea of commuter legs, and I took my place in the subway token line.

"You know, you get half price," the tinny voice through the bulletproof glass told me, as though this were compensation for the slight inconvenience of having no ramp or elevator. There, next to his piles of tokens, the operator had a stack of official half-price certificates for disabled users. He seemed thrilled to have a chance to use them. "No, thanks, the tokens are fine." I bought two and rolled through the rickety gate next to the turnstiles and to the head of the next set of stairs. I could hear the trains rumbling below.

I got down on the floor again, and began lowering the chair. I realized that getting the chair back up again was not going to be as simple as this lowering maneuver. Most of my old theory about riding the trains in Chicago had pertained to getting up to the tracks, because the Chicago trains are elevated. Down was going well, as I expected, but up might be more difficult.

Around me walked the stream of oblivious commuters. Underneath their feet, the paper cups and straws and various other bits of refuse they dropped were too soiled by black subway filth to be recognizable as having any connection at all to their world above. Down on the subway floor, they seemed evil, straws that could only have hung from diseased lips, plastic spoons that could never have carried anything edible. Horrid puddles of liquid were swirled with chemical colors, sinister black mirrors in which the bottoms of briefcases sailed safely overhead like rectangular airships. I was freshly showered, with clean white gloves and black jeans, but in the reflection of one of these puddles, I too looked as foul and discarded as the soda straws and crack vials. I looked up at the people walking by, stepping around me, or watching me with their peripheral vision. By virtue of the fact that my body and clothes were in contact with places they feared to touch, they saw and feared me much as they might fear sudden assault by a mugger. I was just like the refuse, irretrievable, present only as a creature dwelling on the rusty edge of a dark drain. By stepping around me as I slid, two steps at a time, down toward the tracks, they created a quarantined space, just for me, where even the air seemed depraved.

I rolled to the platform to wait for the train with the other commuters. I could make eye contact again. Some of the faces betrayed that they had seen me on the stairs by showing relief that I had not been stuck there, or worse, living there. The details they were too afraid to glean back there by pausing to investigate, they were happy to take as a happy ending which got them off the hook. They were curious as long as they didn't have to act on what they had learned. As long as they didn't have to act, they could stare.

I had a speech all prepared for the moment anyone asked if I needed help. I felt a twinge of satisfaction over having made it to the tracks without having to give it. My old theory, concocted while on painkillers in an intensive care unit in Pennsylvania, had predicted that I would make it. I was happy to do it all by myself. Yet I hadn't counted on being completely ignored. New York is such a far cry from the streets of Jerusalem, where Israelis would come right up to ask how much you wanted for your wheelchair, and Arabs would insist on carrying you up a flight of stairs whether you wanted to go or not. . . .

I rolled to the stairs and descended into a corridor crowded with people coming and going. "Are you all right?" A black woman stopped next to my chair. She was pushing a stroller with two seats, one occupied by a little girl, the other empty, presumably for the little boy with her, who was standing next to a larger boy. They all beamed at me, waiting for further orders from Mom.

"I'm going down to the A train," I said. "I think I'll be all right, if I don't get lost."

"You sure you want to go down there?" She sounded as if she was warning me about something. "I know all the elevators from having these kids," she said. "They ain't no elevator on the A train, young man." Her kids looked down at me as if to say, *What can you say to that?* I told her that I knew there was no elevator and that I was just seeing how many stairs there were between Carroll Street and city hall. "I can tell you, they's lots of stairs." As she said good-bye, her oldest boy looked down at me as if he understood exactly what I was doing, and why. "Elevators smell nasty," he said.

Once on the A train, I discovered at the next stop that I had chosen the wrong side of the platform and was going away from Manhattan. If my physical therapist, Donna, could look in on me at this point in my trip, she might be more doubtful about my theory than I was. By taking the wrong train, I had probably doubled the number of stairs I would have to climb.

I wondered if I could find a station not too far out where the platform was between the tracks, so that all I had to do was roll to the other side and catch the inbound train. The subway maps gave no indication of this, and the commuters I attempted to query on the subject simply ignored me or seemed not to understand what I was asking. Another black woman with a large shopping bag and a brown polka-dotted dress was sitting in a seat across the car and volunteered that Franklin Avenue was the station I wanted. "No stairs there," she said.

At this point, every white person I had encountered had ignored me or pretended that I didn't exist, while every black person who had come upon me had offered to help without being asked. I looked at the tape recorder in my jacket to see if it was running. It was awfully noisy in the subway, but if any voices at all were recorded, this radio program was going to be more about race than it was going to be about wheelchair accessibility. It was the first moment that I suspected the two were deeply related in ways I have had many occasions to think about since.

At Franklin Avenue I crossed the tracks and changed direction, feeling for the first time that I was a part of the vast wave of migration in and out of the Manhattan that produced the subway, all the famous bridges, and a major broadcast industry in traffic reporting complete with network rivals and local personalities, who have added words like *rubbernecking* to the language. I rolled across the platform like any other citizen and onto the train with ease. As we pulled away from the station, I thought how much it would truly change my life if there were a way around the stairs, if I could actually board the subway anywhere without having to be Sir Edmund Hillary.

DISCUSSION QUESTIONS

1. As Hockenberry notes, black men and disabled people share the inability to get cabs to pick them up. Why does that experience make them so angry?

2. Why do people shun interaction with the disabled?

READING 34

"Can You See the Rainbow?" The Roots of Denial

Sally French

CHILDHOOD

Some of my earliest memories are of anxious relatives trying to get me to see things. I did not understand why it was so important that I should do so, but was acutely aware of their intense anxiety if I could not. It was aesthetic things like rainbows that bothered them most. They would position me with great precision, tilting my head to precisely the right angle, and then point to the sky saying "Look, there it is; look, there, there . . . THERE!" As far as I was concerned there was nothing there, but if I said as much their anxiety grew even more intense; they would rearrange my position and the whole scenario would be repeated.

Sally French is a senior lecturer at The Open University in the United Kingdom.

In the end, despite a near total lack of color vision and a complete indifference to the rainbow's whereabouts, I would say I could see it. In that way I was able to release the mounting tension and escape to pursue more interesting tasks. It did not take long to learn that in order to avert episodes such as these and to protect the feelings of the people around me, I had to deny my disability.

The adults would also get very perturbed if ever I looked "abnormal." Being told to open my eyes and straighten my face, when all I was doing was trying to see, made me feel ugly and separate. Having adults pretend that I could see more than I could, and having to acquiesce in the pretence, was a theme throughout my childhood.

Adults who were not emotionally involved with the issue of whether or not I could see also led me along the path of denial. This was achieved by their tendency to disbelieve me and interpret my behavior as "playing up" when I told them I could not see. Basically they were confused and unable to cope with the ambiguities of partial sight and were not prepared to take instruction on the matter from a mere child. One example of this occurred in the tiny country primary school that I attended. On warm, sunny days we had our lessons outdoors where, because of the strong sunlight, I could not see to read, write or draw. It was only when the two teachers realized I was having similar difficulties eating my dinner that they began to doubt their interpretation that I was a malingerer. On several occasions I was told off by opticians when I failed to discriminate between the different lenses they placed before my eyes. I am not sure whether they really disbelieved me or whether their professional pride was hurt when nothing they could offer seemed to help; whatever it was I rapidly learned to say "better" or "worse," even though all the lenses looked the same.

It was also very difficult to tell the adults, when they had scraped together the money and found the time to take me to the pantomime or wherever, that it was a frustrating and boring experience. I had a strong sense of spoiling other people's fun, just as a sober person among a group of drunken friends may have. As a child, explaining my situation without appearing disagreeable, sullen and rude was so problematic that I usually denied my disability and suffered in silence. All of this taught me from a very early age that, while the adults were working themselves up about whether or not I could see rainbows, my own anxieties must never be shared.

These anxieties were numerous and centered on getting lost, being slow, not managing and, above all, looking stupid and displaying fear. I tried very hard to be "normal," to be anonymous and to merge with the crowd. Beaches were a nightmare; finding my way back from the sea to specific people in the absence of landmarks was almost impossible, yet giving in to panic was too shameful to contemplate. Anticipation of difficulties could cause even greater anguish than the difficulties themselves and was sufficient to ruin whole days. The prospect of outings with lots of sighted children to unfamiliar places was enough to make me physically ill, and with a bewildering mix of remorse and relief, I would stay at home.

Brownie meetings were worrying if any degree of independent movement was allowed; in the summer when we left the confines and safety of our hut to play on the nearby common, the other children would immediately disperse, leaving me alone among the trees, feeling stupid and frightened and wondering what to do next. The adults were always adamant that I should join in, that I should not miss out on the fun, but how much they or the other children noticed my difficulties I do not know; I was never teased or blamed for them, they were simply never discussed, at least not with me. This lack of communication gave me a powerful unspoken message that my disability must be denied.

By denying the reality of my disability I protected myself from the anxiety, disapproval, frustration and disappointment of the adults in my life. Like most children I wanted their acceptance, approval and warmth, and quickly learned that this could best be gained by colluding with their perceptions of my situation. I denied my disability in response to their denial, which was often motivated by a benign attempt to integrate me in a world which they perceived as fixed. My denial of disability was thus not a psychopathological reaction, but a sensible and rational response to the peculiar situation I was in.

Special School

Attending special school at the age of nine was, in many ways, a great relief. Despite the crocodile walks,[1] the bells, the long separations from home, the regimentation and the physical punishment, it was an enormous joy to be with other partially sighted children and to be in an environment where limited sight was simply not an issue. I discovered that many other children shared my world and, despite the harshness of institutional life, I felt relaxed, made lots of friends, became more confident and thrived socially. For the first time in my life I was a standard product and it felt very good. The sighted adults who looked after us were few in number with purely custodial roles, and although they seemed to be in a permanent state of anger, provided we stayed out of trouble we were basically ignored. We lived peer-orientated, confined and unchallenging lives where lack of sight rarely as much as entered our heads.

Although the reality of our disabilities was not openly denied in this situation, the only thing guaranteed to really enthuse the staff was the slightest glimmer of hope that our sight could be improved. Contact lenses were an innovation at this time, and children who had previously been virtually ignored were nurtured, encouraged and congratulated, as they learned to cope with them, and were told how good they looked without their glasses on. After I had been at the school for about a year, I was selected as one of the guinea pigs for the experimental "telescopic lenses" which were designed, at least in part, to preserve our postures (with which there was obsessive concern) by enabling us to read and write from a greater distance. For most of us they did not work.

I remember being photographed wearing the lenses by an American man whom I perceived to be very important. First of all he made me knit while wearing them, with the knitting held right down on my lap. This was easy as I could in any case knit without looking. He was unduly excited and enthusiastic and told me how much the lenses were helping. I knew he was wrong. Then he asked me to read, but this changed his mood completely; he became tense, and before taking the photograph he pushed the book, which was a couple of inches from my face, quite roughly to my knees. Although I knew he had cheated and that what he had done was wrong, I still felt culpable for his displeasure and aware that I had failed an important test.

We were forced to use equipment like the telescopic lenses even though it did not help, and sometimes actually made things worse; the behavior of the adults clearly conveyed the message, "You are not acceptable as you are." If we dared to reject the equipment we were reminded of the cost, and asked to reflect on the clever and dedicated people who were tirelessly working for the benefit of ungrateful creatures like ourselves. No heed was ever taken of our own suggestions; my requests to try tinted lenses were always ignored and it was not until I left school that I discovered how helpful they would be.

The only other times that lack of sight became an issue for us at the school were during the rare and clumsy attempts to integrate us with able-bodied children. The worst possible activity, netball,[2] was usually chosen for this. These occasions were invariably embarrassing and humiliating for all concerned and could lead to desperate maneuvers on the part of the adults to deny the reality of our situation—namely that we had insufficient sight to compete. I am reminded of one netball match, with the score around 20/nil, during which we overheard the games mistress[3] of the opposing team anxiously insisting that they let us get some goals. It was a mortifying experience to see the ball fall through the net while they stood idly by. Very occasionally local Brownies would join us for activities in our extensive grounds. We would be paired off with them for a treasure hunt through the woods, searching for milk-bottle tops—the speed at which they found them was really quite amazing. They seemed to know about us, though, and would be very kind and point the "treasure" out, and even let us pick it up ourselves sometimes, but relying on their bounty spoiled the fun and we wished we could just talk to them or play a different game.

Whether the choice of these highly visual activities was a deliberate denial of our disabilities or simply a lack of imagination on the part of the adults, I do not know. Certainly we played such games successfully among ourselves, and as we were never seen in any other context, perhaps it was the latter. It was only on rare occasions such as these that our lack of sight (which had all but been forgotten) and the artificiality of our world became apparent.

As well as denying the reality of their disabilities, disabled children are frequently forced to deny painful feelings associated with their experiences because their parents and other adults simply cannot cope with them. I am reminded of a friend who, at the age of six or seven, was repeatedly promised expensive toys and new dresses provided she did not cry when taken back to school; we knew exactly how we must behave. Protecting the feelings of the adults we cared about became an arduous responsibility which we exercised with care.

Bravery and stoicism were demanded by the institution too; any outward expression of sadness was not merely ridiculed and scorned, it was simply not allowed. Any hint of dejection led to stern reminders that, unlike most children, we were highly privileged to be living in such a splendid house with such fantastic grounds—an honor which was clearly not our due. There was no one to turn to for comfort or support, and any tears which were shed were, of necessity, silent and private. In contrast to this, the institution, normally so indifferent to life outside its gates, was peculiarly concerned about our parents' states of mind. Our letters were meticulously censored to remove any trace of despondency and the initial letter of each term had a compulsory first sentence: "I have settled down at school and am well and happy." Not only were we compelled to deny our disabilities, but also the painful feelings associated with the lifestyles forced upon us because we were disabled.

Such was our isolation at this school that issues of how to behave in the "normal" world were rarely addressed, but at the next special school I attended, which offered a grammar school education and had an entirely different ethos, much attention was paid to this. The headmaster, a strong, resolute pioneer in the education of partially sighted children, appeared to have a genuine belief not only that we were as good as everyone else, but that we were almost certainly better, and he spent his life tirelessly battling with people who did not share his view.

He liked us to regard ourselves as sighted and steered us away from any connection with blindness; for example, although we were free to go out by ourselves to the nearby town and beyond, the use of white canes was never suggested although many of us use them now. He delighted in people who broke new, visually challenging ground, like acceptance at art school or reading degrees in mathematics, and "blind" occupations, like physiotherapy, were rarely encouraged. In many ways his attitudes and behavior were refreshing, yet he placed the onus to achieve and succeed entirely on ourselves; there was never any suggestion that the world could adapt, or that our needs could or should be accommodated. The underlying message was always the same: "Be superhuman and deny your disability."

ADULTHOOD

In adulthood, most of these pressures to deny disability persist, though they become more subtle and harder to perceive. If disabled adults manage to gain control of their lives, which for many is very difficult, these pressures may be easier to resist. This is because situations which pose difficulties, create anxieties or cause boredom can be avoided, or alternatively adequate assistance can be sought; many of the situations I was placed in as a child I now avoid. As adults we are less vulnerable and less dependent on other people, we can more easily comprehend our situation, and our adult status makes the open expression of other people's disapproval, frustration and disbelief less likely. In addition, disabled adults arouse less emotion and misplaced optimism than disabled children, which serves to dilute the insatiable drive of many professionals to cure or "improve" us. Having said this, many of the problems experienced by disabled adults are similar to those experienced by disabled children.

Disabled adults frequently provoke anxiety and embarrassment in others simply by their presence. Although they become very skillful at dealing with this, it is often achieved at great cost to themselves by denying their disabilities and needs. It is not unusual for disabled people to endure boredom or distress to safeguard the feelings of others. They may, for example, sit through lectures without hearing or seeing rather than embarrass the lecturer, or endure being carried rather than demanding an accessible venue. In situations such as these reassuring phrases such as "I'm all right" or "Don't worry about me" become almost automatic.

One of the reasons we react in this way, rather than being assertive about our disabilities, is to avoid the disapproval, rejection and adverse labeling of others, just as we did when we were children. Our reactions are viewed as resulting from our impairments rather than from the ways we have been treated. Thus being "up front" about disability and the needs which emanate from it can easily lead us to be labeled "awkward," "selfish" or "warped." Such labeling is very difficult to endure without becoming guilty, anxious and depressed; it eats away at our confidence, undermining our courage and leading us to deny our disabilities.

Disbelief remains a common response of able-bodied people when we attempt to convey the reality of our disabilities. If, for example, I try to explain my difficulty in coping with new environments, the usual response is, "Don't worry we all get lost" or "It looks as if you're doing fine to me." Or when I try to convey the feelings of isolation associated with not recognizing people or not knowing what is going on around me, the usual response is "You will in time" or "It took me ages too." This type of response renders disabled people "just like everyone else." For those of us disabled from birth or early childhood, where there is no experience of "normality" with which to compare our situation, knowing how different we really are is problematic and it is easy to become confused and to have our confidence undermined when others insist we are just the same.

An example of denial through disbelief occurred when I was studying a statistics component as part of a course in psychology. I could see absolutely nothing of what was going on in the lectures and yet my frequent and articulate requests for help were met with the response that all students panic about statistics and that everything would work out fine in the end. As it happens it did, but only after spending many hours with a private tutor. As people are generally not too concerned about how we "got there," our successes serve to reinforce the erroneous assumption that we really are "just like everyone else." When I finally passed the examination, the lecturer concerned informed me, in a jocular and patronizing way, that my worries had clearly been unfounded! When people deny our disabilities they deny who we really are.

This tendency to disbelieve is exacerbated by the ambiguous nature of impairments such as partial sight. It is very hard for people to grasp that although I appear to manage "normally" in many situations, I need considerable help in others. The knowledge of other people's perceptions of me is sufficiently powerful to alter my behavior in ways which are detrimental to myself; for example, the knowledge that fellow passengers have seen me use a white cane to cross the road, can be enough to deter me from reading a book on the train. A more common strategy among people with limited sight is to manage roads unaided, thereby risking life and limb to avoid being labeled as frauds.

A further reaction, often associated with the belief that we are really no different, is that because our problems are no greater than anyone else's we do not deserve any special treatment or consideration. People who react in this way view us as whining and ungrateful complainers whenever we assert ourselves, explain our disabilities, ask that our needs be met or demand our rights. My most recent and overt experience of this reaction occurred during a visit to Whitehall to discuss the lack of transport for disabled people. Every time I mentioned a problem which disabled people encounter, such as not being able to use the underground system or the buses, I was told in no uncertain terms that many other people have transport problems too; what about old people, poor people, people who live in remote areas? What was so special about disabled people, and was not a lot being done for them anyway? I was the only disabled person present in this meeting and my confidence was undermined sufficiently to affect the quality of my argument. Reactions such as this can easily give rise to feelings of insecurity and doubt; it is, of course, the case that many people do have problems, but disabled people are among them and cannot afford to remain passive or to be passed by.

College

At the age of 19, after working for two years, I started my physiotherapy training at a special segregated college for blind and partially sighted students. For the first time in my life my disability was, at least in part, defined as blindness. Although about half the students were partially sighted, one of the criteria for entry to the college was the ability to read and write braille (which I had never used before) and to type proficiently, as, regardless of the clarity of their handwriting, the partially sighted students were not permitted to write their essays or examinations by hand, and the blind students were not permitted to write theirs in braille. No visual teaching methods were used in the college and, for those of us with sight, it was no easy matter learning subjects like anatomy, physiology and biomechanics without the use of diagrams.

The institution seemed unable to accept or respond to the fact that our impairments varied in severity and gave rise to different types of disability. We were taught to use special equipment which we did not need and were encouraged to "feel" rather than "peer" because feeling, it was thought, was aesthetically more pleasing, especially when dealing with the poor, unsuspecting public. There was great concern about the way we looked in our professional roles; white canes were not allowed inside the hospitals where we practiced clinically, even by totally blind students, and guide dogs were completely banned. It appeared that the blind students were expected to be superhuman whereas the partially sighted students were expected to be blind. Any attempt to defy or challenge these rules was very firmly quashed so, in the interests of "getting through," we outwardly denied the reality of our disabilities and complied.

Employment

Deciding whether or not to deny disability probably comes most clearly to the fore in adult life when we attempt to gain employment. Until very recently it was not uncommon to be told very bluntly that, in order to be accepted, the job must be done in exactly the same way as everyone else. In many ways this was easier to deal with than the situation now, where "equal opportunity" policies have simultaneously raised expectations and pushed negative attitudes underground, and where, in reality, little has changed. Although I have no way of proving it, I am convinced that the denial of my disability has been absolutely fundamental to my success in gaining the type of employment I have had. I have never completely denied it (it is not hidden enough for that) but rather, in response to the interviewers' skeptical and probing questions, I have minimized the difficulties I face and portrayed myself in a way which would swell my headmaster's pride.

Curiously, once in the job, people have sometimes decided that certain tasks, which I can perform quite adequately, are beyond me, while at the same time refusing to relieve me of those I cannot do. At one college where I worked it was considered impossible for me to cope with taking the minutes of meetings, but my request to be relieved of invigilating large numbers of students, on the grounds that I could not see them, was not acceded to; once again the nature of my disability was being defined by other people. On the rare occasions I have been given "special" equipment or consideration at work it has been regarded as a charitable act or donation for which I should be grateful and beholden. This behavior signals two distinct messages: first that I have failed to be "normal" (and have therefore failed), and second that I must ask for nothing more.

In these more enlightened days of "equal opportunities," we are frequently asked and expected to educate others at work about our disabilities. "We know nothing about it, you must teach us" is the frequent cry. In some ways this is a positive development but, on the other hand, it puts great pressure on us because few formal structures have been developed in which this educative process can take place. In the absence of proactive equal opportunity policies, we are rarely taken seriously and what we say is usually forgotten or ignored. Educating others in this way can also mean that we talk of little else but disability, which, as well as becoming boring to ourselves, can lead us to be labeled adversely or viewed solely in terms of problems. Challenging disabling attitudes and structures, especially as a lone disabled person, can become frustrating and exhausting, and in reality it is often easier and (dare I say) more functional, in the short term at least, to cope with inadequate conditions rather than fight to improve them. We must beware of tokenistic gestures which do little but put pressure on us.

CONCLUSION

The reasons I have denied the reality of my disability can be summarized as follows:

1. To avoid other people's anxiety and distress.
2. To avoid other people's disappointment and frustration.
3. To avoid other people's disbelief.
4. To avoid other people's disapproval.
5. To live up to other people's ideas of "normality."
6. To avoid spoiling other people's fun.
7. To collude with other people's pretenses.

I believe that from earliest childhood denial of disability is totally rational given the situations we find ourselves in, and that to regard it as a psychopathological reaction is a serious mistake. We deny our disabilities for social, economic and emotional survival and we do so at considerable cost to our sense of self and our identities; it is not something we do because of flaws in our individual psyches. For those of us disabled from birth or early childhood, denial of disability has deeply penetrating and entangled roots; we need support and encouragement to make our needs

known, but this will only be achieved within the context of genuine structural and attitudinal change.

In this paper I have drawn upon my life experiences and personal reactions to elucidate the pressures placed upon disabled people to deny the reality of their experience of disability. This approach is limited inasmuch as personal experiences and responses can never be divorced from the personality and biography of the person they concern. In addition these pressures will vary according to the individual's impairment. But with these limitations in mind, I am confident that most disabled people will identify with what I have described and that only the examples are, strictly speaking, mine.

DISCUSSION QUESTIONS

1. What are all the ways that French and those around her conspire to deny that she is disabled?
2. Would those in other stigmatized statuses have experiences similar to French's?

NOTES

1. Walking two-by-two in a long file.
2. Girls' basketball.
3. Physical education teacher.

READING 35

Not Blind Enough: Living in the Borderland Called Legal Blindness

Beth Omansky

. . . Human beings are uncomfortable with uncertainty. For instance, when waiting for medical test results or news about a missing loved one, how often we hear people say, "It's the not knowing

Beth Omansky is a researcher and writer involved in the international disability studies community and is engaged in disability advocacy in Portland, Oregon. She researched the social construction of blindness as part of her Ph.D. in social work from the University of Queensland, Australia.

that's so hard." The human mind, including sight and vision, seeks to make order out of chaos—to organise and categorise, and to find comfort in closure, which relieves the anxieties of uncertainty. Moreover, in an ocularcentric world, the predominant method of making sense of the surrounding environment is sight (Elkins 1996). After all, social culture informs us that "seeing is believing." Because legal blindness is abundantly ambiguous, the sighted might fail to apprehend how borderland blind people make sense of the physical world; what is more, they feel tentative about how to treat borderland blind people or even to trust that those who claim the identity of legal blindness are, in fact, blind.

Unlike totally blind people, borderland blind people are often accused of fraud because they act too sighted. John Hull (1990, pp. 67–69) describes this social phenomenon in a journal entry titled, "You Bastard! You're Not Blind." Hull tells of a passerby repeatedly yelling at him, insisting that he was not *really* blind; Hull's orientation and mobility skills failed to replicate societal stereotypes of how blindness presents itself in everyday life.

Borderland blind people are subjected to pressures that totally blind people do not endure; they are pushed and pulled back and forth across the border between sightedness and blindness, resulting in disallowance of citizenship in both lands, which leaves them in a state of what Black American pacifist civil rights leader, Bayard Rustin, aptly called "social dislocation" (D'Emilio 2004).

Totally blind people fall into a discrete stereo-typed classification of blindness as darkness (Monbeck 1973), which in many ways is comforting to sighted people because they do not have to guess what the blind person can or cannot see. In an effort to relieve their own dubiety, sighted people might try to force borderland blind people to choose one side or the other—usually pushing them into the socially preferred land of the sighted—a land in which they experience egregious inequality. Borderland blind people are vulnerable to attempted regulation by disquieted but well-meaning acquaintances, friends and family, who yearn for their loved one to be "normal"; in reaction, borderland blind people might internally regulate their own behaviour or else succumb to external pressures as they try to "pass" even during times when they clearly reside on the blind side of the pale. The dynamics of such interactions press everyone concerned into denial (French 1993). Participants in this study reported experiences which echo these phenomena.

PATROLLING THE BORDER

. . . This subtheme is consistent with Sally French's personal account, "Can You See the Rainbow?" [Reading 34], which receives the most reprint permission requests of her entire body of work (personal communication, September 2003). . . .

Two of [one of my informant's] anecdotes are consistent with French's reminiscences. Uncomfortable with the contradictions of "border" behaviour, a companion requested that Larry refrain from reading the newspaper in restaurants while his guide dog lay at his side because it would "confuse" sighted restaurant-goers and give them false impressions of what blindness is. Perhaps she was afraid observers would disbelieve Larry's claim of blindness, and by association, might just reflect on her own character. She also urged him to call colours by the names most commonly used by sighted people despite the fact that he saw them as another colour. For example, if he sees a building as brown even though he knows it's red, he calls it brown, but she thinks he should call it red because that's what it is to sighted people and also, to how he used to see it. She is more comfortable with him pretending to see as sighted people do, and as he used to even though she did not know him before he went blind. Colours are important to Larry's profession as an artist and photographer; so now he encounters a conundrum common to legal blindness. Which is more valid? An accurate description of what the borderland blind person sees, or is the sighted population's naming and interpretation of things *more* valid because it is the majority opinion? And if the latter is accepted as "truth," does this place borderland blind people in the position of having to lie about their own experience to satisfy sighted people's perception of "reality"—of truth? . . .

I, too, have often experienced people placing me on the sighted ("normal") side of the border despite my own choice to stake my claim on the blindness side. On two separate occasions, sighted people grabbed my white cane away from me when my picture was about to be taken. As I posed in front of a statue of George Mason on the campus where we had just attended my master's degree graduation ceremony, one of my relatives walked up and took my cane from my hand. I understood and appreciated his good intentions, but I didn't like it. I didn't say anything because I didn't want to cause tension between us or hurt his feelings. Another time I was getting my picture taken at the Molly Malone statue in Dublin, Ireland. The man in charge of the statue looked through his camera to set the pose, and then reached up in an attempt to remove my cane from my hand. I was not as surprised as I was at graduation, so this time I refused to hand it over and got my picture taken as I am. I guess they both thought the cane was unsightly, which, come to think of it, is a pretty telling word.

Stephen Kuusisto's (1998, p. 13) family left him with a mixed message that placed him on the fence of the border, ill-equipped to fit in on either side; first, that he was blind, and next, that he "was taught to disavow it." He explains the emotional consequences thus, "I grew bent over like the dry tinder grass. I couldn't stand up proudly, nor could I retreat" (Kuusisto 1998, p. 13).

Sighted people do not always attempt to place blind people on the sighted side: a critical factor is acceptance of their loved one's blindness. For example, Larry's daughter accepted his blindness from the outset, and she understands the limitations of an ocularcentric built environment. Every year, she sends him a new bright yellow parka because she wants him to be easily seen by motorists. Soon after Larry told his family that he had become blind, one of his sons offered to act as driver on a trip across the country—a role Larry traditionally assumed. His son told him that he would drive, and Larry still could take photographs of the Southwest desertscape, just as he had always done on previous trips.

RESISTANCE AND CHALLENGE IN EVERYDAY LIFE

Larry, Catherine, J. R. and I have been subjected to social treatment based on common myths about blind people, and we each found various ways to challenge these stereotypes. We all used humour as a strategy to resist and challenge societal misperceptions about blindness. J. R. believes that those who use humour are the ones who "survive" blindness.

For instance, when Larry shook hands with someone to whom he was introduced, he made a "lucky guess" that the person was a piano player. The person making the introduction cried out in amazement, "Oh, my God! How did you get that?" Larry then spun a yarn about how his blindness gave him special hypersensitivity to touch. Larry laughed as he told me, "So you know I am definitely just perpetrating a hoax."

One of J. R.'s anecdotes speaks directly to the stereotype that blindness means darkness (Monbeck, 1973), and it also highlights what it is like to be both observer and observed. When J. R. goes to the optician's office he observes that people notice that he wears tinted (not dark) glasses, yet he carries a white cane. He jokes, "They think, 'Oh you have glasses you're not blind.'" But then, there is the presence of the white cane. J. R. suspects the observers wonder about the optician's abilities, thinking, "This is the best they can do?" His anecdote illustrates the cognitive dissonance sighted people experience when they witness the alterity of legal blindness. But J. R.'s social commentary was not as funny to me once I connected the dots back to when I was fired from my much-needed receptionist job at the optician's office because, "It looked bad" for the optical company.

J. R. told about when he was using his white cane during an outing, and a child asked her mother, "Why is that man using that white stick?" The mother explained that he used the cane because he is blind. As J. R. passed them, he said to the mother, "Don't tell her about the 25 bonus points," which refers to the old joke about drivers earning "bonus points" for running over a blind person. He made his point that he is well aware of "blind" jokes.

None of the participants reported engaging in self-demeaning humour; instead, they turned the joke onto society in the form of social observation, and they all used humour to resist internalised oppression—a strategy used by many authors (e.g., Hull 1990; Knipfel 1999; Kudlick 2005; Kuusisto 1998; Michalko 1998, 1999).

Blind People as Public Property

Frequently, acting blind (i.e., using low vision aids and other blindness skills) elicits invasive, infantilising questions from strangers such as, "Oh my, what happened to you?" or, "How do you cross the street by yourself?" or, "Aren't you afraid?" Sometimes this line of questioning is followed with something along the lines of, "Oh, you're just so brave," or, "You're such an inspiration." Strangers seem to have no compunction about prying into private medical and even financial matters as if they have a right to know; and if the blind person refuses to answer, the strangers either redouble their efforts or turn away as if they were the ones insulted. Larry manages blindness questions in different ways depending upon whether they come from strangers, acquaintances or family. He said:

> It's like they wonder what it is that you see . . . if it's like my niece . . . I'll take more care in analogies and stuff like that whereas if it's my brother or my sister-in-law or one of the guys I'm with, um, I would just give them a couple of different things.

Larry reports, however, that as for the general public, he doesn't "give a shit what they think." Be that as it may, he remains aware of how people might perceive him.

Borderland blind people report that they make decisions about whether they should disclose their visual impairment from moment to moment and situation to situation. Act sighted or flaunt blindness? Or should they just do what they need to do to get around without feeling the need to explain themselves to anyone? Self-disclosure decisions are aroused by the needs of embodied consequences of blindness; by awareness of societal attitudes and predictable consequences of presenting oneself as blind; and by issues around identity. All these factors influence how blind (and other disabled) people negotiate a world "from the vantage point of the atypical" (Linton 1998, p. 6).

As illustration, fast-food restaurants almost always hang their menus high up on walls several feet behind the service counter. Blind people cannot read the sign for two reasons; first, their impairment limits their sensory ability to read print from a distance; and second, the location, position and font size of the menu is rendered inaccessible because the restaurant designers falsely assumed their customers are all sighted. Faced with the barrier of an inaccessible menu, borderland blind customers must decide whether to "ask for help" (request access), knowing through past experience their request might evoke pity, disdain, or that they will be outright shunned. One alternative I adopted in the past is to memorize what I wish to order and just order the same thing every time I go to that restaurant. Blind people often choose this option to avoid making themselves vulnerable to stigmatization, rudeness, public embarrassment or pity, but the downside is that they surrender gastronomic variety (Gordon 1996; Linton 1998).

Restaurants can be particularly troublesome for borderland blind people because the ocularcentric environment and the embodied experience bump up against the pressure of social graces. The fancier the restaurant, the dimmer the lighting most likely is. People sit across from each other, so the table width breaches any possibility of eye contact; add flickering candles, an undercurrent of simultaneously humming conversations punctuated with loud laughter, and now the setting becomes a recipe for social *faux pas* and other mishaps. Catherine said:

> [t]hey just think you're absolutely stupid. And it's just like you can't get away from that. That's your embarrassment . . . And then it's all over. It's all over. [Laughs] And then you go to the bathroom and cry . . . breathe . . . panic attack. It's like, Christ! Why can't anything go right? Why couldn't the mashed potatoes be over here? Why couldn't the butter be . . . ?

Finding the bathroom in a dark restaurant is like running an obstacle course—wending one's way through tables, booths, wait staff carrying head-level trays, feet and handbags in aisles, coats on chair backs, swinging kitchen doors with wait staff moving quickly in all directions, and the dark hallway that inevitably houses the rest rooms, which are more than likely not clearly marked because the signs are hung high above eye level, written in fancy script, or marked with artistically gender-specific designs with no print as clues:

> I cannot count on both hands how many times I've walked into the men's room in restaurants because no one was around to whom I could ask direction. When I see a urinal on the wall, I turn around and head off into the restroom next door, hoping no one saw me enter or leave.

ASKING FOR HELP

When borderland blind people ask for impairment-related assistance, they must identify themselves as blind. It is very difficult to pass as sighted and ask for help reading a street sign six feet above where you are standing. Identity is a two-way social process; people identify themselves and people are identified by others (Rosenblum & Travis 1996). Since borderland blind people may not use typical blindness artifacts (e.g., white cane, dark glasses) the sighted public may respond to requests for assistance in demeaning, curt or other unhelpful ways. Sighted people might be more ready to offer help to someone who is obviously blind; yet they may feel intruded upon by an unidentifiable borderland blind person. Catherine said:

> Yeh, you have to ask everyone, and it's like people, they can be really—brush you off mean. You have to be really cordial and demure as a blind person.

Larry's reluctance to ask for help is bound up in his desire for self-sufficiency. He said:

> . . . to find out that yeah you know damn it I need help reading this label because I don't know if it's apple juice or apple vinegar . . . So um, there was a

time when I wouldn't have bought it. That's, that's the thing that can eat at you. You know?

POLICING ONE'S SELF

The traditional medical establishment, indeed, all of society, teaches disabled people to act like everyone else if they hope to lead successful lives—they have to act "normal," which requires them to "overcome" their impairments. But as Linton (1998), Michalko (2002), and others note, people do not "overcome" as that is impossible; people live with their impairments. As Linton (1998) observes:

> "overcoming" disability [sic] assumes that there is something inferior about their group membership, and the responsibility is left on the individual to work harder to be successful and to triumph over what otherwise would be a tragic life (p. 17).

Another message in the concept of "overcoming" is that the person has gone beyond societal expectations of what people with impairments can achieve; the person has overcome the "social stigma of having a disability" (Linton 1998, p. 17).

I Can See Clearly Now: Passing as Sighted

"Passing" is an interactional social tool employed by all people, in one way or another, as they produce personal identities within (and influenced by) the cultural contexts in which they live. Some blind people employ premeditated strategies as they attempt to pass as sighted and/or to engage in social interaction in ways that are understood and unquestioned by sighted people. Michalko (1999) and Hull (1990) describe intricate ways they negotiate meeting and greeting oncoming people beyond their field of vision. Michalko (1998) uses eye contact with sighted people. He stays aware not only of his seeing, but of how and where he directs his eyes so that sighted people assume he is making direct eye contact. If he gazes where he needs to in order to see them, he appears as though he is not looking at the other person at all. I have central vision loss, so when I look at a person's face, they often think

I am looking behind them or looking at their hair instead of into their eyes:

> Depending on where I am and who I'm with, I might try to appear as if I'm making eye contact. Sometimes I will tell people that even though it appears I'm not looking at them, I really am, but I have to feel emotionally ready for an onslaught of nosy questions before I do that.

Catherine said she has problems with relationships just because of her vision. She can't pick up signals such as body language or a "certain look" to know, for example, if someone is "getting pissed off." In concert with Michalko (1999) and Hull (1990), Catherine can't identify people approaching her. She has to learn the sound of their walk. She said, "I have to know them because you can feel people's energy in a way." But, when borderland blind people use familiar clues to identify people or things, sighted people disbelieve their blindness, and then they have to re-assert that, yes, they really are blind, which is another social pitfall distinctive to the borderland. The struggle to be believed can be emotionally draining because such disbelief assaults their integrity and essential as well as social identity. Catherine said:

> . . . it's like you're always having to confirm "I'm blind but I'm not too blind." It's like back and forth, and you're just like constantly pulling at them and you don't realize that; and they don't realize that you feel like you're manipulating the crap out of them and that they're invalidating you. And they're invalidating your blindness. You're just like, either way I go they hate me. [Laughs] It's like you just feel like you're hated even though you know yes, no it's not about you.

Borderland blind people might attempt to pass or, at the very least, to remain unnoticed, which keeps things simpler in social situations. Explaining one's blindness several times a day to several different strangers gets tiresome, distracting and boring. Catherine believes sighted people act like "little anthropologists" trying to figure out blindness culture, and ". . . in the process they're destroying the living hell out of it and objectifying your blindness, and objectifying you, and, oh. This is *huge*."

Sometimes borderland blind people deny themselves use of access equipment such as white canes or low vision glasses; or they might take unnecessary risks such as not asking a passerby what colour the traffic light is at an idle intersection—all to avoid the attention that a "spoiled identity" attracts (Goffman 1986). *Passing* is *acting*, that is, to practice in a creative, methodical way, how to perform as something they are not—sighted. Larry said that his need for perfectionism drives how he presents himself in public:

> Yeah, the challenge is greater; therefore the perfection has to be greater . . . See, if people come up to you and say, "Gee I didn't know you were blind." I say I hit a home run.

Catherine hesitates to use her blindness as an excuse even when it is a quite legitimate reason for a particular behaviour, explaining, "You don't want to blame it on you being blind though, that's the problem." She describes her reticence to be judged by sighted people:

> . . . when a lot of things are caused by not seeing you don't want to keep saying it over and over again because people get kind of like, okay, you're going to blame everything on that, you know . . . You have to be really self sufficient sounding, even if you're kind of leaving out bits of the reason. . . .

I understand Catherine's reasoning. I think long and hard before invoking blindness as a reason for something I did or did not do because I am concerned that people will think I'm using my blindness—as Sally French (1993) writes, "playing up"; they might think I'm a complainer or not "adjusted." Multiple identities further confound the dilemma. For example:

> I think people might misconstrue my holding money close up to my face to read the denominations on bills, or feel the edges of coins to tell quarters with their ridged edges apart from smooth-edged pennies and nickels. I'm concerned that people will think I'm

doing all this because I am Jewish; that is, inviting them to invoke stereotypes about Jews having an extreme attachment to money. I guess I'd rather be thought of as a pitiful blind person than a money-hungry Jew. So, I try to be inconspicuous.

Personal Costs of Passing or Coming Out

A lot of thought, creativity, time and energy gets spent carrying out strategies for passing as sighted, and the personal costs can be high. Catherine said that when she self-discloses her blindness, she feels vulnerable, and she does her best to resist falling prey to the negative societal stereotypes that blind people are "fools" (Monbeck 1973). She said:

> [Y]ou don't see it. And so you're constantly dealing with these things that come at you and you don't know what it is . . . Um, ah, and you know it's like having to explain to people. It's like yeah I might not see but . . . you *cannot* pull one over on me.

Sometimes people choose not to disclose their blindness, which results in exclusion from activities not because of sighted people leaving them out, but because they have left themselves out. On the other hand, they might disclose their impairments and ask for what they need despite feeling awkward and running the risk of being treated as different. Either way, there is a trade-off. . . .

Just because someone asks for what he or she needs does not guarantee they will get it. J. R. talked about people who think they know what blind people are going through, and say something like, "Oh gee, my brother knew a friend who was, had a friend who was blind, or something like that," and then proceed to give unwanted or the wrong kind of assistance. Blind people tell stories about sighted people grabbing them by the arm at street corners, and then tugging them across the street even though they had not asked for assistance or even wanted to go across the street in the first place. One evening, a woman grabbed me as I made my way through a theatre aisle and literally pulled me to where she thought I wanted to go without ever asking if I needed assistance (Omansky Gordon 2003, p. 224). Apparently, my white cane drafted her into do-gooder duty. Rod Michalko (1998) relates a story about someone pressing a dollar in his hand as he and his dog guide stood at a traffic light together. He told the man he did not need it, and asked him to take it back. The man insisted Rod take it. So, he did, and then gave it to a panhandler. . . .

DISCUSSION QUESTIONS

1. Why would people who are legally blind be reluctant to ask for help?
2. What are the costs and benefits of passing as sighted?

REFERENCES

D'Emilio, John, 2004. *Lost Prophet: The Life and Times of Bayard Rustin.* Chicago: University of Chicago Press.

Elkins, James, 1996. *The Object Stares Back.* New York: Simon & Schuster.

French, Sally, 1993. Can You See the Rainbow? The Roots of Denial. In John Swain, Vic Finkelstein, Sally French & Michael Oliver (eds.), *Disabling Barriers, Enabling Environments.* London: Open University Press.

Goffman, Erving, 1986. *Stigma: Notes on the Management of a Spoiled Identity.* Englewood Cliffs, NJ: Prentice-Hall.

Gordon, Beth. 1996. I am Legally Blind. In Rosenblum, Karen E. & Toni-Michele C. Travis (eds.) *The Meaning of Difference: American Constructions of Race, Sex and Gender, Social Class, and Sexual Orientation.* New York: McGraw-Hill.

Hull, John, 1990. *Touching the Rock: An Experience of Blindness.* New York: Pantheon Books.

Knipfel, Jim, 1999. *Slack Jaw.* New York: Penguin Putnam.

Kudlick, Catherine J., 2005. The Blind Man's Harley: White Canes and Gender Identity in America. In *Signs: Journal of Women and Culture in Society,* vol. 30, no. 2, pp. 1589–1606.

Kuusisto, Stephen, 1998. *Planet of the Blind: A Memoir.* New York: G. K. Hall.

Linton, Simi, 1998. *Claiming Disability: Knowledge and Identity.* New York: New York University Press.

Michalko, Rod, 1998. *Mystery of the Eye and the Shadow of Blindness.* Toronto: University of Toronto Press.

———, 1999. *The Two in One: Walking with Smokie, Walking with Blindness.* Philadelphia: Temple University Press.

———, 2002. *The Difference That Disability Makes.* Philadelphia: Temple University Press.

PERSONAL ACCOUNT

A Time I Didn't Feel Normal

I was tested for Learning Disabilities (LD) when I was in third grade and diagnosed with being ADD and LD because of short-term memory loss and mild dyslexia. I thought nothing of it because I didn't really understand what it meant. All I knew was it got me out of class to go work with a woman on my schoolwork. However, the next year I moved from Ohio to Virginia and discovered that I was different from most of my peers. It got worse when I got to fifth grade because I still had to leave class twice a week to go work with the disabilities counselor with two other kids in my class. I soon realized that people would actually talk down to me in my class because I wasn't really "one of them," that I wasn't as smart. The stereotype, even at such a young age, about being LD was not a good one. The other two kids that were in my LD class were not exactly popular and a little weird. So because I was with them, I became one of them. I would get made fun of and stopped really trying in class because if I messed up people would look at me as though it was expected that I would do things wrong. It got so bad that I told my mom I didn't want to go back to school. I asked her to home school me so that I wouldn't have to deal with the other kids in my class judging me and making me feel like I was stupid. My mom refused to do it, so I did the only other thing I could think of: I forced my way out of the LD program at my school. I don't know how I got them to let me out but I felt that it was the only way for me to be "normal." I continued to struggle throughout my school career but I wasn't treated as differently, I was more socially accepted.

Today, I don't have a problem with telling people about my "disabilities," but back then I would never have admitted it. I have grown to the point where my "disabilities" don't really affect me all that much. I've learned to cope with them and still do well in school. So, I don't feel like an idiot, or stupid, or a lesser student because of my LD anymore. However, back then I would cry because I thought I wasn't as smart as everyone else and that there was something wrong with me that made me different from everyone else. I felt isolated at times and envied my friends who were "normal." My parents did what they could to help me with my homework and in overcoming my difficulties, but no one really stuck up for me at school or seemed to care how I felt, or even notice how upset I was. I am a better person today because of this though; I realize how hard it is for people to be treated as though there is something wrong with them even though there really isn't. Judging people for their "disabilities" is wrong and cruel and people really need to step back and think about how their actions affect others.

Heather Callender

Monbeck, Michael, 1973. *The Meaning of Blindness: Attitudes Toward Blindness and Blind People.* Bloomington: Indiana University Press.

Omansky Gordon, Beth, 2003. I am Legally Blind. In Rosenblum, Karen E. & Toni-Michelle C. Travis (eds.), *The Meaning of Difference: American Constructions of Race, Sex and Gender, Social Class, and Sexual Orientation.* New York: McGraw-Hill.

Rosenblum, Karen E. & Toni-Michelle C. Travis, 1996, (eds.). *The Meaning of Difference: American Constructions of Race, Sex and Gender, Social Class, and Sexual Orientation.* New York: McGraw-Hill.

THE MEANING OF DIFFERENCE

FRAMEWORK ESSAY

In the first framework essay we considered how contemporary American master statuses are named, dichotomized, and stigmatized. In the second essay, we focused on the experience of privilege and stigma that accompanies those master statuses. In this third section, we will look at the meaning that is conferred on difference. In effect, what difference does difference make?

The readings in this section highlight social institutions that have some of the strongest effects on what difference ultimately means—the economy, public policy, law, popular culture. The concept of ideology gets special attention here because it both shapes and is shaped by the operation of these social institutions.

In looking at ideology and social institutions, our approach parallels the metaphor of the "birdcage" developed by philosopher Marilyn Frye in her now classic discussion of the concept of oppression (1983). Frye suggests that if we are to understand how categories of people are "pressed" by social forces, we must attend to the *systematic* and *systemic* nature of this "press." Using the metaphor of a birdcage, she argues that oppression cannot be understood by looking at only one obstacle or "wire"; one must consider the *set of wires* that together form the cage. Ideology, economy, policy, law, and popular culture *together and in interaction* form the "cage" that people confront. Above and beyond the construction and experience of difference, these social forces give difference tangible meaning; they make difference matter.

Ideology

The concept of *ideology* was first elaborated by Marx and Engels, particularly in *The German Ideology* (1846). It is now a concept used throughout the social sciences and humanities. In general, an ideology can be defined as a widely shared belief or idea that has been constructed and disseminated by the powerful that primarily reflects their experiences and that functions for their benefit.

Ideologies are anchored in the experiences of their creators; thus, they offer only a partial view of the world. "Ideologies are not simply false, they can be 'partly true,' and yet also incomplete [or] distorted. . . . [They are not] consciously crafted by the ruling class and then injected into the minds of the majority; [they are] instead *produced* by specifiable, complex, social conditions" (Brantlinger, 1990:80). Because those who control the means of disseminating ideas have a better chance of having their ideas prevail, Marx and Engels concluded that "the ideas of the ruling class are in every epoch the ruling ideas." Ideologies have the power to supplant, distort, or silence the experiences of those outside their production.

The idea that people are rewarded on the basis of their merit is an example of an ideology. It is an idea promoted by those with power—for example, teachers and supervisors—and many opportunities are created for the expression of the belief. Report cards, award banquets, and merit raises are all occasions for the expression of the belief that people are rewarded on the basis of their merit.

But certainly, most know this idea is not really true: as Stephen McNamee and Robert Miller illustrate in Reading 14, people are not rewarded only, or even primarily, on the basis of their merit. The idea that merit is rewarded is only partly true and reflects only *some* people's experiences. The frequent repetition of the idea, however, has the potential to overwhelm contrary experience. Even those who have not generally experienced people being rewarded on merit are likely to subscribe to this philosophy, because they hear it so often. In any event, there are few safe opportunities to describe beliefs to the contrary or have those beliefs widely disseminated.

Thus, the idea that people are rewarded on the basis of merit is an ideology. It is a belief that reflects primarily the experiences of those with power, but it is presented as universally valid. The idea overwhelms and silences the voices of those who are outside its production. In effect, ideologies ask us to discount our own experience.

This conflict between one's own experience and the ideas conveyed by an ideology is implied in W. E. B. Du Bois's description of the "double consciousness" experienced by African Americans that is discussed in Framework Essay II. It is also what many feminists refer to as the double or fractured consciousness experienced by women. In both cases, the dominant ideas fail to reflect the real-life experiences of people in these categories. For example, the *actual* experience of poverty, discrimination, teen motherhood, disability, sexual assault, or life in a black neighborhood or in a gay relationship rarely coincide with the public discussion on these topics. Because those in stigmatized categories do not control the production or distribution of the prevailing ideas, *their* experience is not likely to be reflected in them. The ideology not only silences their experience; it may invalidate it even in their own minds: "I must be the one who's crazy!" In this way, the dominant discourse can invade and overwhelm our own experience (D. Smith, 1978, 1990).

An ideology that so dominates a culture that it becomes the prevailing and unquestioned belief was described in the 1920s by Italian political theorist Antonio Gramsci as the *hegemonic*, or ruling, ideology. Gramsci argued that social control was primarily accomplished by the control of ideas and that whatever was considered to be "common sense" was especially effective as a mechanism of social control (Omi and Winant, 1994:67). Commonsense beliefs are likely to embody widely shared ideas that primarily reflect the interests and experience of those who are powerful. We are all encouraged to adhere to common sense even when that requires discounting our own experience. The discussion of natural-law language that follows highlights that process.

Conveying Ideologies: Natural-Law Language and Stereotypes

Hegemonic, or ruling, ideologies often take the form of commonsense beliefs that are especially embodied in *natural-law language* and *stereotypes.*

Natural-Law Language   When people use the word *natural,* they usually mean that something is inevitable, predetermined, or outside human control (Pierce, 1971). *Human nature* and *instinct* are often used in the same way. For example, "It's only natural to care about what others think," "It's human nature to want to get ahead," or "It's just instinctive to be afraid of someone different" all convey the sense that something is inevitable, automatic, and independent of one's will.

Thus, it is not surprising when, in discussions about discrimination, someone says, "It's only natural for people to be prejudiced," or "It's human nature to want to be with your own kind." Each of these commonsense ideas conveys a belief in the inevitability of discrimination and prejudice, as if such processes emerged independently of anyone's will.

Even when describing something we oppose, the word *natural* can convey a sense of inevitability. For example, "I am against racism, but it's only natural," puts nature on the side of prejudice. Arguing that something is natural because it happens frequently has the same consequence. "All societies have discriminated against women," implies that something that happens frequently is therefore inevitable. But in truth, something that happens frequently more likely means that there is an extensive set of social controls ensuring the outcome.

At least three consequences follow from using natural-law language. First, it ends discussion, as if having described something as natural makes any further exploration of the topic unnecessary. This makes sense, given that the word *natural* is equated with inevitability: If something is inevitable, there is little sense in questioning it.

Second, because natural-law language treats behavior as predetermined, it overlooks the actual cultural and historical variation of human societies. If something is natural, it should always happen. Yet virtually no human behavior emerges everywhere and always; all social life is susceptible to change. Thus, natural-law language ignores the variability of social life.

Third, natural-law language treats individuals as passive, lacking an interest in or control over social life. If it is "natural" to dislike those who are different, then there is really nothing we can do about that feeling. It is no one's responsibility; it is just natural. If there is nothing I can do about my own behavior, I can expect to do little about the behavior of others. Human nature thus is depicted as a limitation beyond which people cannot expect to move (Gould, 1981). Describing certain behavior as "only natural" implies that personal and social change are impossible.

In all these ways—by closing off discussion, masking variation and change, and treating humans as passive—natural-law language tells us not to question the world that surrounds us. Natural-law language has this effect whatever its specific content: "It's only natural to discriminate." "It's only natural to want to have children." "It's only natural to marry and settle down." "Inequality is only natural; the poor will always be with us." "Aggression and war are just human nature." "Greed is instinctive." Indeed, in several of the early Supreme Court decisions described in Reading 41—for example, *Dred Scott v. Sanford, Minor v. Happersett, Plessy v. Ferguson, Elk v. Wilkins*—being a slave, black, Native American, and/or female is treated as a "natural class," a limited and fixed "condition" that cannot be ameliorated by racial ancestry, wealth, talent, transportation to a new state, and so on.

Overall, natural-law language not only discourages questions, it carries a covert recommendation about what you *ought* to do. If something is "just natural," you cannot prevent others from doing it, and you are well advised to do it yourself. Thus, natural-law language serves as a forceful mechanism of social control (Pierce, 1971).

Natural-law language is used to reinforce hegemonic ideologies. It reduces the complexity and historic variability of the social world to a claim for universal processes, offering a partial and distorted truth that silences those with contrary experience. Natural-law language can make discrimination appear to be natural, normal, and inevitable. It tells us simply to accept the world around us and not seek to improve it. Thus, natural-law language itself creates and maintains ideas about difference.

"People just want to be with their own kind": Natural-law language that both reproduces and repudiates social hierarchies   As we have said, describing something as "natural" helps us to ignore how *social* forces—for example, those of economy, policy, and law—have created the conditions that we attribute to "nature."

For example, the idea that blacks and whites naturally live in separate neighborhoods because they "like living with their own kind" makes it seem as if these groups have *always* been segregated and indeed choose that segregation. But as James Carr and Nandinee Kutty describe in Reading 42, the "hypersegregation and isolation" experienced by African Americans is not only of fairly recent origin; it is the product of specific discriminatory actions enshrined in law and public policy, as well as the failure of federal policies to correct that damage. The policies that have diminished discrimination in employment and segregation in education—and have also generated a broad social consensus that these are valuable outcomes—have not materialized regarding residential segregation (Bonastia, 2006). In turn, the persistence of this segregation deeply limits groups' access to the resources for an improved life: education, jobs, transportation, safety, recreation, nutrition, and health care.

A variety of factors contribute to residential segregation—from the local "tipping point" at which the nonwhite population in a neighborhood becomes large enough to prompt white flight; to an individual's willingness to live in a neighborhood in which there are few others from their race or ethnic group; to deliberate discrimination on the part of landlords, real estate agents, and mortgage lenders. The latter, overt discrimination, continues to be found in housing audits.

> For example, between 2000 and 2002 the Department of Housing and Urban Development conducted an extensive series of audits measuring housing discrimination against blacks, Latinos, Asians, and Native Americans, including nearly 5500 paired tests in nearly 30 metropolitan areas. . . . The study results reveal bias across multiple dimensions, with blacks experiencing consistent adverse treatment in roughly one in five housing searches and Hispanics experiencing consistent adverse treatment in roughly one out of four housing searches (both rental and sales). Measured discrimination took the form of less information offered about units, fewer opportunities to view units, and in the case of home buyers, less assistance with financing, and steering into less wealthy communities and neighborhoods with a higher proportion of minority residents. . . . Asian . . . homebuyers experienced similar levels of consistent adverse treatment. The highest levels of discrimination among the groups was experienced by Native American renters. . . . (Pager and Shepherd, 2008:188)

In all, the residential segregation that appears "just natural" is constituted not simply by individual acts of discrimination, but by the social structural forces of economy, policy, law, and ideology. Though its levels have "modestly declined" since 1980 (Pager and Shepherd, 2008:188), residential segregation continues even though "surveys consistently show that whites and blacks alike prefer integrated neighborhoods by wide margins" (Ford, 2008:287–8).

Similarly, Robert Pratt's discussion of the Supreme Court's 1967 rejection of state laws banning interracial marriage (*Loving v. Virginia*) details the historic prohibitions on interracial marriage that have contributed to our current ideas that people "just naturally" love and marry others of the same race (Reading 44). In this case, however, while law no longer bars such marriages, the persistence of these beliefs about what is "natural" may help explain the relatively low rate of black-white intermarriage described by Jennifer Lee and Frank Bean in Reading 7 and the preferences that emerge in on-line dating sites. As the authors of a 2009 study of Yahoo! Personals found, "Race is one of the main selection criteria for white internet daters—whites express racial preferences even more commonly than religious or educational preferences" (Feliciano, et al., 2009:49–50).

This is the case despite surveys now showing historically high acceptance of interracial marriage among whites: "While a majority of black adults have consistently approved of marriage between whites and nonwhites since Gallup began asking this question of blacks in 1968, only 17 percent of whites approved in 1968. It wasn't until 1997 that a majority of whites expressed approval toward black-white marriages. [In 2004], 70 percent of whites and 80 percent of blacks approve of marriage between whites and blacks" (Ludwig, 2004). Like the contrast between actual residential segregation and survey results that affirm the desire to live in an integrated neighborhood, here the contrast is between a low rate of actual interracial dating and marriage, and surveys that show historically high levels of their acceptance.

Why is residential segregation reproduced even when people say they do not want to live in segregated environments? Why do interracial marriage and dating remain infrequent despite attitudes that are increasingly tolerant? Although there are many factors at work, the gap between attitudes and behavior highlights one of the paradoxes of our time, that "*it is possible to reproduce racial categories [and hierarchies] even while ostensibly repudiating them*" (Winant, 2004:47). Unfortunately, all of this real complexity is masked by a claim that "it's only natural for people to want to stay with their own kind."

Stereotypes   A *stereotype* is a prediction that "members of a group will behave in certain ways" (Andre, 1988:259)—for example, that black men will have athletic ability or that Asian American students will excel in the sciences. As Frank Wu wrote in Reading 39, "Before I can talk about Asian American experiences at all, I have to kill off the model minority myth because the stereotype obscures many realities."

Stereotypes assume that all the individuals in a category possess the same characteristics. Stereotypes persist despite evidence to the contrary because they are not formulated in a way that is testable or falsifiable (Andre, 1988). In this way, stereotypes differ from descriptions. Description offers no prediction; it can be tested for accuracy and rejected when wrong. Description also encourages explanation and a consideration of historical variability.

For example, "Most great American athletes are African American." is a description. First, there is no prediction that a particular African American can be expected to be a good athlete, or that someone who is white will be a poor one. Second, the claim is verifiable; that is, it can be tested for accuracy and proven wrong (e.g., by asking what proportion of the last two decades' American Olympic medal winners were African American). Third, the statement turns our attention to explanation and historical variation: Why might this be the case? Has this always been the case?

In contrast, "African Americans are good athletes." is a stereotype. It attempts to characterize a whole population, thus denying the inevitable differences among the people in the category. It predicts that members of a group will behave in a particular way. It cannot be verified since there is no direct way to test the claim. Further, the stereotype denies the reality of historical and cultural variation by suggesting that this has always been the case. Thus, stereotypes essentialize: they assume that if you know something about the physical package someone comes in, you can predict that person's behavior.

Both stereotypes and natural-law language offer broad-based predictions about behavior. Stereotypes predict that members of a particular category will possess particular attributes; natural-law language predicts that certain behavior is inevitable. Neither stereotypes nor natural-law language is anchored in any social or historical context, and for that reason, both are frequently wrong. Basketball great Bill Russell's reaction when asked if he thought African Americans were "natural" athletes makes clear the similarity of natural-law language and stereotyping. As Russell said, this was a stereotypic image of African American athletes that deprecated the skill and effort he brought to his craft—as if he was great because he was black rather than because of the talent he cultivated in hours of practice.

Model-minority stereotypes and immigration   As we have said, stereotypes explain life outcomes by attributing some essential, shared quality to all those in a particular category. The current depiction of Asian Americans as a "model minority" is a good example of this. This stereotype masks the considerable economic, educational, and occupational heterogeneity among Asian Americans. For example, the proportion of those holding college degrees varies considerably among Asian American groups, at rates of 64 percent for Asian Indians, 46 percent for Chinese, 42 percent for Filipinos, 40 percent for Japanese, 44 percent for Koreans, and 14 percent for Vietnamese (Le, 2007). The model-minority stereotype is itself a fairly recent invention. Among those now called "model minority" are groups who were previously categorized as undesirable immigrants, denied citizenship through naturalization, and placed in internment camps as potential traitors.

Further, model-minority stereotypes conflate legal immigrants and refugees, groups that have had very different paths to the United States. About 5 percent of all those legally admitted to the country since 2000 have been refugees.

> There are many reasons for that small size, but one reason is that refugees are, by and large, different from Americans and often more different from Americans than are other immigrants. . . . The reasons why refugees are different are multiple. One reason is that refugees are often already different in their home countries: whether because of religion, race or ethnicity, social background, or political opinions. Refugees are rarely typical representatives of the countries from which they come. That is why they have to leave. Consider some recent

examples. The most recent set of refugees from Somalia are hardly Somali in an ethnic sense; rather they are Bantu people trafficked north into Somalia as labor. The refugees coming from Myanmar (Burma) are not ethnic Burmese; rather, they are hill tribes who have fled from a government dominated by ethnic Burmese who differ from them in culture, language, politics, and often religion. . . . Many other differences come from the disrupted nature of refugee lives, much less the frequent horrors of which they have been victims and witnesses. One consequence is that, unlike other immigrants, most refugees have limited opportunity for planning their migration. They must seize opportunities to flee on quick notice, must navigate complex geographical and political mazes, and must usually make such a sharp break with their home country that they cannot return. They thus tend to lack the social resources of kin and community on which most immigrants can rely. . . .

[Also] refugees . . . often lack the three factors that a vast body of research indicates are crucial for finding work in America: English competence (and refugees sometimes lack literacy in any language); education (often limited and almost certainly interrupted for most refugees); and occupational skills (particularly a problem for refugees coming from agricultural backgrounds). (Haines, 2010)

Nonetheless, many refugees are likely to be faced with these "model minority" stereotypes.

In American culture, stereotypes are often driven by the necessity to explain why some categories of people succeed more than others (Steinberg, 1989). Thus, the model-minority stereotype is often used to claim that if racism has not been an impediment to Asian Americans' success, it could not have hurt African Americans' likelihood of success.

The myth of the Asian-American "model minority" has been challenged, yet it continues to be widely believed. One reason for this is its instructional value. For whom are Asian Americans supposed to be a "model"? Shortly after the Civil War, southern planters recruited Chinese immigrants in order to pit them against the newly freed blacks as "examples" of laborers willing to work hard for low wages. Today, Asian Americans are again being used to discipline blacks. . . . Our society needs an Asian-American "model minority" in an era anxious about a growing black underclass. (Takaki, 1993:416)

A brief review of U.S. immigration policy explains the misguided nature of the comparison between African and Asian Americans. Until 1965, U.S. immigration was restricted by quotas that set limits on the number of immigrants from each nation based on the percentage of people from that country residing in the United States at the time of the 1920 census. This had the obvious and intended effect of severely restricting immigration from Asia, as well as that from Southern and Eastern Europe and Africa. The civil rights movement of the 1960s raised national embarrassment about this quota system (Skrentny, 2002), such that in 1965 Congress replaced national-origin quotas with an annual 20,000-person limit for every nation regardless of its size. Within that quota, preference went first to those who were relatives of U.S. citizens and then to those with occupational skills needed in America.

The result was a total increase in immigration and a change in its composition. Because few individuals from non-European countries could immigrate on the grounds of having family in America—previous restrictions would have made that almost impossible—the quotas were filled with people meeting designated *occupational* needs. Thus, those immigrating to the United States since 1965 have had high educational and occupational profiles. The middle- and upper-class professionals and entrepreneurs who have immigrated to the United States did not suddenly become successful here; rather, they continued their home-country success here. These high occupational and educational profiles have characterized immigrants from African as well as Asian countries.

Interestingly, the contemporary comparison—if Asian Americans can make it, why can't African Americans?—echoes an earlier question: If European immigrants can make it, why can't African Americans? The answer to that question is summarized as follows:

> Conditions within the cities to which they had migrated [beginning in the 1920s], not slavery, strained blacks' ability to retain two-parent families. Within those cities, blacks faced circumstances that differed fundamentally from those found earlier by European immigrants. They entered cities in large numbers as unskilled and semiskilled manufacturing jobs were leaving, not growing. The discrimination they encountered kept them out of the manufacturing jobs into which earlier immigrants had been recruited. One important goal of public schools had been the assimilation and "Americanization" of immigrant children; by contrast, they excluded and segregated blacks. Racism enforced housing segregation, and residential concentration among blacks increased at the same time it lessened among immigrants and their children. Political machines had embraced earlier immigrants and incorporated them into the system of "city trenches" by which American cities were governed; they excluded blacks from effective political power until cities had been so abandoned by industry and deserted by whites that resistance to black political participation no longer mattered. All the processes that had opened opportunities for immigrants and their children broke down for blacks. (Katz, 1989:51)

Whites' racial stereotypes: The persistence and disavowal of bias   The relationship between stereotypes, prejudice, and discrimination has long been the subject of research in the field of social psychology. Like the paradox we noted earlier between the simultaneous reproduction and repudiation of racial hierarchies, here we see the simultaneous persistence and disavowal of bias.

> Since the inception of research on stereotyping and prejudice, social psychologists have documented two seemingly contradictory observations: the pervasiveness of these phenomena and the presence of culturally valued norms that repudiate them. A plethora of research demonstrates that stereotyping and prejudice abound, so much so that they seem to be part of the cultural fabric. Despite initial assertions that these stereotypes were becoming less consensual (Gilbert, 1951; Karlins, Coffman, and Walters, 1969), closer examination indicates wide agreement on the content of ethnic stereotypes even now (Devine and Elliott, 1995; Maden, Guyll, and Aboufadel, 2001). Recent research paints a similar picture, with a Web-based measure that captures individuals' less conscious (i.e., implicit) ethnic attitudes. Data gathered from several thousand people show that 68% of respondents had more generally negative associations toward black than toward white people. (Sinclair and Lun, 2010:214–215).

Thus, in terms of a willingness to endorse principles of integration and job equality, surveys show a dramatic and sustained improvement in whites' attitudes (Sinclair and Lun, 2010:215). Yet, alongside support for these principles, the research points to pervasive and persistent negative stereotypes hold by whites about blacks (Bobo, 2003).

Grappling with this inconsistency, some theorists have argued that the old-fashioned, explicit forms of racism have been replaced by new, more subtle manifestations. Because these new forms are so unlike the old ways that prejudice was displayed, dominant group members may not recognize their own bias. For example, in the readings included here, Malcolm Gladwell takes the Implicit Association Test and describes his shock at the levels of unconscious stereotyping the test reveals (Reading 36); Po Bronson and Ashley Merryman consider the messages that are conveyed by white parents' belief that it is better not to discuss race with their children (Reading 37); and Tim Wise describes "Racism 2.0," which leads whites to conclude that racism must no longer exist because an African American has been elected President (Reading 38).

The obliviousness to prejudice—especially one's own—is an aspect of what social psychologists Samuel Gaertner and John Dovidio have described as *aversive racism*. Unlike those who are overtly prejudiced, aversive racists are unaware of their negative attitudes, instead considering themselves unprejudiced and even supportive of racial equality. Despite endorsing the principles of fair treatment, they feel personally so uneasy with blacks that they tend to avoid interracial interaction.

> When interracial interaction is unavoidable, aversive racists experience anxiety and discomfort, and consequently they try to disengage from the interaction as quickly as possible. In addition, because part of the discomfort that aversive racists experience is due to a concern about acting inappropriately and appearing prejudiced, aversive racists are motivated primarily by avoiding wrongdoing in interracial interactions. (Gaertner and Dovidio, 2005:619)

Out of their discomfort and desire to minimize interaction—especially in the absence of situational norms that compel engagement—aversive racists are likely to discriminate against blacks but in ways they are unaware of: for example, by failing to help blacks in emergencies to the same extent that they would help whites. As Gaertner and Dovidio summarize the research literature, "Taken together, the results from a substantial number of studies drawing on a range of different paradigms demonstrate the systematic operation of aversive racism producing in Whites a failure to help, to hire or admit, and to treat Blacks fairly under the law" (Gaertner and Dovidio, 2005:623).

In the context of an overall change from "old-fashioned" to "modern" racism, whites are more likely to attribute discrimination to isolated events or individuals, or to the failings of minorities themselves. For example,

> ... [T]o Whites, the [New York City police] officers who tortured Abner Louima constitute a few bad apples. To Blacks, these officers represent only the tip of the iceberg. [Hatian immigrant Abner Louima was beaten and sexually assaulted by police after he was arrested outside a Brooklyn nightclub in 1997.]
>
> To Whites, the Texaco tapes are shocking. To Blacks, the tapes merely reflect that in this one instance the guilty were caught. [In 1996, a Texaco executive turned over audiotapes of Texaco executives making racist remarks and plotting to purge the documents in a discrimination

case. Ultimately, Texaco paid more than $115 million for having failed to hire, promote, and treat its black staff with general decency.]

But differences in perception cut deeper than this. . . . Although many Whites recognize that discrimination plays some part in higher rates of unemployment, poverty, and a range of hardships in life that minorities often face, the central cause is usually understood to be the level of effort and cultural patterns of the minority group members themselves (Schuman, 1971; Apostle et al., 1983; Kluegel and Smith, 1986; Schuman, et al., 1997). For minorities, es-pecially Blacks, it is understood that the persistence of race problems has something to do with how our institutions operate. For many Whites, larger patterns of inequality are understood as mainly something about minorities themselves. . . . [T]he most popular view holds that blacks should "try harder," should get ahead "without special favors," and fall behind because they "lack motivation." (Bobo, 2001:281–282)

Social Institutions and the Support of Ideologies

The specific messages carried by natural-law language and stereotypes are often echoed by social institutions. The term *social institution* refers to the established mechanisms by which societies meet their predictable needs. For example, the need to socialize new members of the society is met by the institutions of the family and education. In addition to these, social institutions include science, law, religion, poli-tics, the economy, military, medicine, mass media, and popular culture. Ideologies—in our case ideologies about the meaning of difference—naturally play a significant role in the operation of social institutions. In the discussion that follows, we will consider how late-19th- and early-20th-century science and popular culture con-structed the meaning of race, class, sex, disability, and sexual orientation differences. Just as Roger Lancaster (Reading 15), Riki Wilchins (Reading 11), Michael Kimmel (Reading 9), and Marilyn French (Reading 34) describe for the contemporary pe-riod, in this historic material there is also a troubling congruence among scientific pronouncements, popular culture messages, and the prejudices of the day.

Science   The need to explain the meaning of human difference forcefully emerged when 15th-century Europeans encountered previously unknown regions and peoples. "Three centuries of exploration brought home as never before the tremen-dous diversity of human behavior and life patterns within environments and under circumstances dramatically different from those of Europe. . . . Out of that large laboratory of human experience was born the [idea of the] conflict between nature and nurture" (Degler, 1991:4–5).

The "nature-nurture" conflict offered two ways to explain human variation. Explanations from the nature side stressed that the diversity of human societies, and the ability of some to conquer and dominate others, argued for significant bio-logical differences among populations. Explanations from the nurture side argued that human diversity resulted from historical, environmental, and cultural differ-ence. From the nature side, humans were understood to act out biologically driven behaviors. From the nurture side, humans were something of a *tabula rasa*, a blank slate, on which particular cultural expectations were inscribed.

Whether nature or nurture was understood to dominate, however, the discussion of the meaning of human difference always assumed that people could be ranked as to their worth (Gould, 1981). Thus, the real question was whether the rankings reflected in social hierarchies were the result of nature, and thus inevitable and fixed, or whether they could be affected by human action and were thus subject to change.

The question was not merely theoretical. The 1800s in America witnessed appropriation of Native American territories and the forced relocation of vast numbers of people under the Indian Removal Act of 1830; and the 1848 signing of the Treaty of Guadalupe Hidalgo ended the Mexican-American War and ceded what is now Texas, New Mexico, California, Utah, Nevada, Colorado, and Arizona to the United States with 75,000 Mexican nationals residing in those territories becoming U.S. citizens. The 19th century also included passage of the 1892 Chinese Exclusion Act; a prolonged national debate about slavery and women's suffrage; and the arrival of an unprecedented number of poor and working-class immigrants from Southern and Eastern Europe. The century closed with the internationally publicized trial of Irish playwright Oscar Wilde, who was sentenced to two years' hard labor for "gross indecency," which in that case meant homosexuality.

Thus, a profound question was whether social hierarchy reflected natural, permanent, and inherent differences in capability (the nature side) or was the product of specific social and historical circumstances and therefore susceptible to change. Because Africans were held by whites in slavery, did that mean Africans were by their nature inferior to whites? Were Native Americans literally "savages" occupying some middle ground between animals and civilized humans, and did they therefore benefit from domination by those who supposedly were more advanced? Did the dissimilarity of Chinese immigrants from American whites mean they were not "human" in the way whites were? If homosexuality was congenital as was the thinking in the 1800s, did that mean homosexuals were profoundly different from heterosexuals? Were women closer to plants and animals than to civilized men? Were the deaf also "dumb"? Were the poor and working classes composed of those who not only lacked the talents by which to rise in society but also passed their defects on to their children? In all, were individuals and categories of people located in the statuses for which they were best suited? This was the question driving public debate. If one believed that the social order simply reflected immutable biological differences, the answer to that question would probably be "Yes." That would not have been the case, however, for those who believed these differences were the outcome of specific social and historical processes overlaying a shared humanity. In all, the question behind the nature-nurture debate was about the *meaning* of what appeared to be *natural* difference. The answer to that question was shaped by the hegemonic ideologies of the time—especially those informed by science.

Charles Darwin's publication of *The Origin of the Species* (1859) and *The Descent of Man* (1871) shifted the weight of popular and scholarly opinion. In particular, his conclusions challenged the two central beliefs of the time. First, his idea of evolutionary change challenged "traditional, Christian belief in a single episode of creation of a static, perfect, and unchanging world." The significance of evolutionary change was clear: "If the world were not created perfect, then there was no implicit justification for the way things were . . ." (Shipman, 1994:18).

Second, Darwin's work implied that all humans share a common ancestry. If differences among birds were the result of their adaptation to distinctive environments, then *their differences existed within an overall framework of similarity and common ancestry*. By analogy, the differences within human populations might also be understood as "variability within overall similarity" (Shipman, 1994:22)—a shocking possibility at the time even for Darwin. "It was the age of imperialism and most non-Europeans were regarded, even by Darwin, as 'barbarians'; he was astonished and taken aback by their wildness and animality. The differences among humans seemed so extreme that the humanity . . . of some living groups was scarcely credible" (Shipman, 1994:19).

Darwin's idea that change in the physical environment resulted in the perpetuation of some species and demise of others (the idea of natural selection), however, bolstered a pre-existent concept of "survival of the fittest." This phrase had been coined by English sociologist Herbert Spencer, who had been considering the evolutionary principles of human societies several years before Darwin published *The Origin of the Species*.

Spencer's position, eventually called *social Darwinism,* was extremely popular in the United States. Spencer strongly believed that modern societies are inevitably improvements over earlier forms of social organization and that progress would necessarily follow from unimpeded competition for social resources. In all, social Darwinism argued that those who are more advanced will naturally rise to the top of any stratification ladder.

Through social Darwinism, the prevailing hierarchies—slave owner over people held in slavery, white over Mexican and Native American, native born over immigrant, upper class over poor, male over female—could be attributed to natural processes and justified as a reflection of inherent differences among categories of people. As one sociologist at the turn of the century framed it, "under the tutelage of Darwinism the world returns again to the idea that *might* as evidence of fitness has something to do with *right*" (Degler, 1991:13). Thus, the ideology of social Darwinism was used to justify slavery, colonialism, immigration restrictions, the criminalization of homosexuality, the forced relocation of Native Americans, and the legal subordination of women. Because social Darwinism affirmed that difference meant defect, it was also compatible with the historical oppression of disabled people.

The social Darwinist position was used by those opposed to providing equal education for women. Just when American institutions of higher education were opening to women—Vassar College was founded in 1865, Smith and Wellesley colleges ten years later, and by 1870 many state universities had become coeducational—biologist Edward Clarke published *Sex in Education* (1873), which argued that the physical energy education required would endanger women's reproductive abilities (an idea first put forward by Spencer). Clarke's case was based on meager and questionable empirical evidence: seven clinical cases, only one of which actually supported his position (Sayers, 1982:14). His work was a response to *social* rather than scientific developments, since it was prompted by no new discoveries in biology. Nonetheless, the book was an immediate and enduring success. For the next thirty years, it was used in the argument against equal education despite the accumulation of evidence refuting its claims. While Clarke's research should have been suspect, it instead became influential in policymaking. In part, "the reason why Clarke's argument seemed so serviceable to those opposed to women's higher education was that it was couched in biological terms and thus appeared to offer a legitimate scientific basis for conservative opposition to equal education" (Sayers, 1982:11).

In a similar fashion, science shaped ideas about the meaning of same-sex relationships. In Europe, by the turn of the century, a gay rights movement had arisen in Germany and gay themes had emerged in French literature. At the same time, however, an international move to criminalize sexual relations between men gathered momentum. A revision of the German criminal code increased the penalties for male homosexuality; the British imprisoned Oscar Wilde; and Europe and the United States experienced a social reform movement directed against prostitution and male homosexuality. The possibility of sexual relations between women was not considered until later.

The move to criminalize homosexuality was countered by physicians arguing, from a social Darwinist position, that homosexuality is the product of "hereditary weakness" and is thus beyond individual control. Though their hope was for increased tolerance, those who took this position offered the idea of "homosexuality as a medical entity and the homosexual as a distinctive kind of person" (Conrad and Schneider, 1980:184). Thus, they contributed to the idea that heterosexual and homosexual people were biologically different from each other.

Science also supported the argument that people of different skin colors were different in significant, immutable ways. Certainly Spencer's idea of the survival of the fittest was understood to support the ideology that whites were superior to all people of color: thus, "the most prevalent form of social Darwinism at the turn of the century was actually racism, that is, the idea that one people might be superior to another because of differences in their biological nature" (Degler, 1991:15).

The scientific defense of American slavery first emerged with the work of two eminent scientists, Swiss naturalist Louis Agassiz and Philadelphia physician Samuel Morton. Agassiz immigrated to America in 1840 and became a professor at Harvard. There he garnered immense popularity by countering the biblically based theory of the unity of all people (which attributed racial differences to "degeneration" from a shared origin) with a "scientific" theory that different races had descended from different moments of creation—"different Adams" as it was called (Gould, 1981:39). Morton tested Agassiz's theories by measuring the skull capacity of people of different races. His idea was that the size of the skull would correlate with the intelligence of the race, and his results "matched every good Yankee's prejudices—whites on top, Indians in the middle, and blacks on the bottom; and among whites, Teutons and Anglo-Saxons on top, Jews in the middle, and Hindus on the bottom" (Gould, 1981:53).

As we now know, Morton's findings were simply wrong. Others who replicated his measurements did not arrive at the same conclusions about skull capacity: There were "*no* significant differences among races for Morton's own data" (Gould, 1981:67). There is no evidence that Morton intended to deceive. Rather, his assumptions of white superiority were so firm that he was oblivious to his own errors and illogic, errors that yielded the conclusion of white superiority only because of his miscalculations.

The use of questionable research to support prevailing beliefs was also evident in the development of intelligence testing. In 1904, Alfred Binet, director of the psychology lab at the Sorbonne, was commissioned by the French minister of public education to develop a test to identify children whose poor performance in school might indicate a need for special education. Binet developed a test with a series of tasks that children of "normal" intelligence were expected to have mastered. Binet's own claims for the test were fairly limited. He did not equate intelligence with the score produced by his test, arguing that intelligence was too complex a factor to be reduced to a simple number. Nor did he construe his test as measuring inborn, permanent, or inherited limitations (Gould, 1981).

Binet's hesitations regarding the significance of the test, however, were ignored by the emerging field of American psychology, which used intelligence as a way to explain social hierarchies. "The people who are doing the drudgery are, as a rule, in their proper places," wrote H. H. Goddard, who introduced the Binet test to America. Stanford psychologist Lewis M. Terman (author of the Stanford-Binet IQ test) argued that "the children of successful and cultured parents test higher than children from wretched and ignorant homes for the simple reason that their heredity is better" (Degler, 1991:50). Indeed, "Terman believed that class boundaries had been set by innate intelligence" (Gould, 1981:183).

Such conclusions were used to shape decisions about the distribution of social resources. For example, intelligence was described as a capacity like the capacity of a jug to hold a certain amount of milk. A pint jug could not be expected to hold a quart of milk; similarly, it was pointless to waste "too much" education on someone whose capacity was supposedly limited. Intelligence Quotient (IQ) tests were used to assess mental deficiency, including the newly developed categories of idiots, imbeciles, and morons. Morons were judged the highest of the "mental defectives," with the potential to be trained to function in society. Nonetheless, Goddard recommended that they be "institutionalized, carefully regulated, made happy by catering to their limits, . . . prevented from breeding" (Gould, 1981:160), and not allowed into the country as immigrants. Toward that end, intelligence tests were used to identify the "mental defectives" as they landed at Ellis Island:

> [C]onsider a group of frightened men and women who speak no English and who have just endured an oceanic voyage in steerage. Most are poor and have never gone to school; many have never held a pencil or pen in their hand. They march off the boat; one of Goddard's . . . [inspectors] takes them aside shortly thereafter, sits them down, hands them a pencil, and asks them to reproduce on paper a figure shown to them a moment ago, but now withdrawn from their sight. Could their failure be a result of testing conditions, of weakness, fear, or confusion, rather than of innate stupidity? Goddard considered the possibility, but rejected it. (Gould, 1981:166)

In the early decades of the 20th century, the eugenics movement, a form of social Darwinism, spearheaded the use of forced sterilization to limit the growth of "defective" populations. Eugenicists lobbied for state laws endorsing the sterilization of the "feebleminded, insane, criminalistic, epileptic, inebriate, diseased, blind, deaf, deformed, and dependent" (Lombardo, n.d.). The practice was approved by the

Supreme Court in *Buck v. Bell* in 1927, with Justice Oliver Wendell Holmes, Jr., writing the majority opinion:

> It is better for all the world, if instead of waiting to execute degenerate offspring for crime or to let them starve for the imbecility, society can prevent those who are manifestly unfit from continuing their kind. . . . Three generations of imbeciles are enough.

Only in 1942, in *Skinner v. Oklahoma*, did the Supreme Court back away from its position, but by that point thirteen states had laws allowing the sterilization of criminals. Thus,

> sterilization of people in institutions for the mentally ill and mentally retarded continued through the mid-1970's. At one time or another, 33 states had statutes under which more than 60,000 Americans endured involuntary sterilization. The *Buck v. Bell* precedent allowing sterilization of the so-called "feebleminded" has never been overturned. (Lombardo, n.d.)

The findings of intelligence testers were also used to advocate particular social policies such as restrictions on immigration. While it is not clear that the work of intelligence testers directly affected the Immigration Restriction Act of 1924 (Degler, 1991), the ultimate shape of the legislation limited immigration from Southern and Eastern Europe, which was consistent with intelligence testers' claims about the relative intelligence of the "races" in Europe. These quotas barred the admission of European Jews fleeing the impending holocaust.

Still, by 1930, a considerable body of research showed that social environment more than biology accounted for differing IQ scores and that the tests themselves measured not innate intelligence but familiarity with the culture of those who wrote the tests. In the end, the psychologists who had promoted intelligence testing were forced to repudiate the idea that intelligence is inherited or that it can be separated from cultural knowledge.[1]

Whether measuring cranial capacity, developing paper-and-pencil intelligence tests, worrying about the effect of education on women, or arguing for hereditary weakness as an explanation of homosexuality, the work of these scientists supported the prevailing ideologies about the merit and appropriate social position of people of different sexes, races, ethnic groups, sexual orientations, and social classes. Most of these scientists were not overtly motivated by ideology; indeed they were sometimes troubled by their own findings. Still, their research was riddled with technical errors and questionable findings. Their research proved "the surprising malleability of 'objective,' quantitative data in the interest of a preconceived idea" (Gould, 1981:147). Precisely because their research confirmed prevailing beliefs, it was more likely to be celebrated than scrutinized.

Why were these findings eventually repudiated? Since they offered a defense of the status quo and confirmed the prevailing ideology, who would have criticized them?

---

[1] ". . . There is also a lot of evidence for the whole American population, for American ethnic groups, and for populations wherever tests are given that IQ is changing in ways that can't possibly be genetic because they happen too fast. It is widely recognized that average IQs are increasing fairly rapidly. These changes in IQ clearly must have more to say about relationships between testing and real performance, or about social patterns of learning, than about biologically rooted 'intelligence.' The genes of a large population don't change that fast unless there is a very dramatic episode of natural selection such as an epidemic" (Cohen, 1998:210).

First, the scientific defense of immutable hierarchy was eroded by the steady accumulation of evidence about the "intellectual equality and therefore the equal cultural capacity of all peoples" (Degler, 1991:61). A good deal of the research that made that point was produced by the many "prominent or soon to be prominent" scholars of African American, Chinese, and European immigrant ancestry who, after finally being admitted to institutions of higher education, were pursuing scientific research. African American scholars such as W. E. B. Du Bois and E. Franklin Frazier, and scholars of recent European immigrant ancestry such as anthropologists Franz Boas, Alfred Kroeber, and Edward Sapir, trenchantly criticized the social science of the day and by their very presence challenged the prevailing expectations about the "inherent inferiority" of people like themselves (Degler, 1991).

The presumptions about the meaning of race were also challenged by increased interracial contact. The 1920s began the Great Migration, in which hundreds of thousands of African Americans from the rural South moved to northern cities. This movement continued through two world wars as black, Latino, Asian, and Native American men joined the armed forces and women followed wartime employment opportunities. The 1920s also brought the Harlem Renaissance, an outpouring of creativity from black writers, scholars, and artists in celebration of African and African American culture. Overall, white social scientists "gained an unprecedented opportunity to observe blacks in a fresh and often transforming way" (Degler, 1991:197). Their attitudes and expectations changed as a result of this increased contact.

In sum, the scientific argument for the inherent inferiority of some groups of people was advanced by upper-class, native-born, white male faculty members of prestigious universities. Few others would have had the means with which to disseminate their ideas or the prestige to make those ideas influential. These theories of essential difference were not written by Native Americans, Mexicans, women, gays, African Americans, or immigrants from Asia or Southern and Eastern Europe. Most of these people lacked access to the public forums to present their experiences until the rise of the antislavery, suffrage, labor, and gay rights movements. Insofar as the people in these categories could be silenced, it was easier to depict them as essentially and profoundly different.

Popular Culture   Like the sciences, popular culture (the forms of entertainment available for mass consumption such as popular music, theater, film, literature, and television) may convey ideologies about difference and social stratification. At virtually the same time that social Darwinism gained popularity in America—indeed within two years of Louis Agassiz's arrival in the United States in 1840—America's first minstrel show was organized. Like social Darwinism, minstrel shows offered a defense of slavery.

Minstrel shows, which became an enormously popular form of entertainment, were musical variety shows in which white males in "blackface" ridiculed blacks, abolitionism, and women's suffrage. Their impact can be seen in the movies and cartoons of the 1930s and 1940s and in current American stereotypes. As the shows traveled the country, their images were impressed on whites who often had no direct contact with blacks and thus no information to contradict the minstrel images.

The three primary characters of the minstrel show were the happy slave, Zip Coon, and the mammy (Riggs, 1987). The image of the happy slave—singing and dancing, naive and childlike, taken care of through old age by the white master as a virtual member of the family—asserted that blacks held in slavery were both content and cared for. Zip Coon was a northern, free black man characterized by an improper use of language and laughable attempts to emulate whites; the caricature was used to show that blacks lacked the intelligence to handle freedom. The mammy was depicted as a large and presumably unattractive black woman fully devoted to the white family she served. Like the happy slave, the mammy was unthreatening and content—no sexual competition to the white mistress of the house, no children of her own needing attention, committed to and fulfilled by her work with her white family. Thus, the characters of the minstrel show hid the reality of slavery. The happy slave and mammy denied the brutality of the slave system. Zip Coon denied the reality of blacks' organization of the underground railroad, their production of slave narratives in books and lectures, and their undertaking of slave rebellions and escapes.

In all, minstrel shows offered an ideology about slavery constructed by and in the interests of those with power. They ridiculed antislavery activists and legitimatized the status quo. Minstrel shows asserted that blacks did not mind being held as slaves and that they did not suffer loss and pain in the same way whites did. The minstrel show was not the only source of this ideology, but as a form of popular entertainment, it was a very effective means of disseminating such beliefs. The shows traveled to all parts of the country, with a hostile racial message masked as mere entertainment.

But within popular culture, an effective counter to the ideology of the minstrel show emerged through the speakers of the antislavery lecture circuit and the publication of numerous slave narratives. Appearing as early as 1760, these narratives achieved an enormous and enduring popularity among northern white readers. Frederick Douglass, former slave and the renowned antislavery activist, was the most famous public lecturer on the circuit and wrote a best-selling slave narrative. Whether as book or lecture, slave narratives provided an image of blacks as human beings. Access to these life histories provided the first opportunity for most whites to see a shared humanity between themselves and those held in slavery (Bodziock, 1990). Thus, slave narratives directly countered the images of the minstrel show. Although popular culture may offer a variety of messages, all parties do not meet equally on its terrain. Those with power have better access and more legitimacy, but popular culture cannot be so tightly controlled as to entirely exclude the voice of the less powerful.

Conclusion

As we have seen, ideologies confer meaning on difference; they both shape and are shaped by social institutions. Their content is not fixed, nor need it be internally consistent. Most important in terms of the subject matter of this text, ideologies can simultaneously reproduce and repudiate, maintain and disavow social hierarchies.

KEY CONCEPTS

aversive racism Unrecognized prejudices that affect behavior. (page 350)

hegemonic Dominating or ruling. A *hegemonic ideology* is a belief that is pervasive in a culture. (page 343)

ideology A widely shared belief that primarily reflects the experiences of those with power, but is presented as universally valid. (pages 342–343)

natural-law language Language that treats human behavior as bound by natural law. (pages 343–345)

social Darwinism The belief that those who dominate a society are necessarily the fittest. (page 353)

social institution Established system for meeting societal needs; for example, the family. (page 351)

stereotype A characterization of a category of people as all alike, as possessing the same set of characteristics and likely to behave in the same ways. (pages 346–351)

REFERENCES

Adam, Barry D. 1987. *The Rise of a Gay and Lesbian Movement.* Boston: G. K. Hall & Co.

Adelman, Robert M. 2005. The Roles of Race, Class, and Residential Preferences in the Neighborhood Racial Composition of Middle Class Blacks and Whites. *Social Science Quarterly,* 86(1):209–28.

Andre, Judith. 1988. Stereotypes: Conceptual and Normative Considerations. *Racism and Sexism: An Integrated Study,* edited by Paula S. Rothenberg, 257–62. New York: St. Martin's Press.

Apostle, Richard, Charles Glock, Thom Piazza, and Marijean Suelzle. 1983. *The Anatomy of Racial Attitudes.* Berkeley, CA: University of California Press.

Bobo, Lawrence D. 2001. Racial Attitudes and Relations at the Close of the Twentieth Century. *America Becoming: Racial Trends and Their Consequences,* edited by Neil J. Smelser, William Julius Wilson, and Faith Mitchell, 264–301. Washington, DC: National Academy Press.

———, and James Kluegel. 1997. Status, Ideology, and Dimensions of Whites' Racial Beliefs and Attitudes: Progress and Stagnation. *Racial Attitudes in the 1990s: Continuity and Change,* edited by S. Tuch and J. Martin, 93–120. Westport, CT: Praeger.

Bodziock, Joseph. 1990. The Weight of Sambo's Woes. *Perspectives on Black Popular Culture,* edited by Harry B. Shaw, 166–79. Bowling Green, OH: Bowling Green State University Popular Press.

Bonastia, Christopher. 2006. *Knocking at the Door: The Federal Government's Attempt to Desegregate the Suburbs.* Princeton, NJ: Princeton University Press.

Brantlinger, Patrick. 1990. *Crusoe's Footprints: Cultural Studies in Britain and America.* New York: Routledge.

Cohen, Mark Nathan. 1998. *Culture of Intolerance: Chauvinism, Class, and Race in the United States.* New Haven, CT: Yale University Press.

Conrad, Peter, and Joseph W. Schneider. 1980. *Deviance and Medicalization.* Philadelphia: Temple University Press.

Degler, Carl N. 1991. *In Search of Human Nature: The Decline and Revival of Darwinism in American Social Thought.* New York: Oxford University Press.

Devine, Patricia G., and Andrew J. Elliott. 1995. Are Racial Stereotypes Really Fading?: The Princeton Trilogy Revisited. *Personality and Social Psychology Bulletin,* 21:1139–50

Feliciano, Cynthia, Belinda Robnett and Golnaz Komaie. 2009. "Gendered Racial Exclusion among White Internet Daters" *Social Science Research,* 38(1): 39–54.

Ford, Richmond Thompson. 2008. *The Race Card: How Bluffing about Bias Makes Race Relations Worse.* New York: Farrer, Straus and Giroux.

Frye, Marilyn. 1983. *The Politics of Reality: Essays in Feminist Theory.* Freedom, CA: The Crossing Press.

Gaertner, Samuel L., and John F. Dovidio. 2005. Understanding and Addressing Contemporary Racism: From Aversive Racism to the Common Ingroup Identity Model. *Journal of Social Issues,* 61:615–639.

Gilbert, G M. (1951) Stereotype Persistence and Change among College Students. *Journal of Abnormal and Social Psychology,* 46:245–54.

Gould, Stephen Jay. 1981. *The Mismeasure of Man.* New York: W. W. Norton.

Haines, David W. 2010. Safe Haven in America? Thirty Years after the Refugee Act of 1980. *Global Studies Review.* George Mason University, Spring 2010. Retrieved June 13, 2010 (http://www.globality-gmu.net/archives/2063).

Katz, Michael B. 1989. *The Undeserving Poor.* New York: Pantheon Books.

Karlins, Marvin., Coffman, Thomas L., and Walters, Gary. 1969. On the Fading of Social Stereotypes:

Studies in Three Generations of College Students. *Journal of Personality and Social Psychology,* 13:1–16.

Kluegel, James, and Eliot Smith. 1986. *Beliefs about Inequality: Americans' Views of What Is and What Ought to Be.* New York: Aldine de Gruyter.

Le, C. N. 2007. Socioeconomic Statistics & Demographics," *Asian-Nation: The Landscape of Asian America.* http://www.asian-nation.org/model-minority .shtml (accessed May 2007).

Lombardo, P. n.d. "Eugenic Sterilization Laws," *The Eugenics Archive,* Dolan DNA Learning Center, Cold Spring Harbor Laboratory. http://www.eugenicsarchive .org/eugenics/list3.pl (accessed June 2005).

Ludwig, Jack. 2004. Acceptance of Interracial Marriage at Record High: Religion and Social Trends. Gallup, Inc. Retrieved June 13, 2010 (http://www.gallup.com/ poll/11836/Acceptance-Interracial-Marriage-Record- High.aspx).

Madon, Stephanie, Max Guyll, Kathy Abuoufadel, Eulices Montiel, Alison Smith, Polly Palumbo, and Lee Jussim. 2001. Ethnic and National Stereotypes: The Princeton Trilogy Revisited and Revised. *Personality and Social Psychology Bulletin,* 27:966–1010.

Marshall, Gordon. 1994. *The Concise Oxford Dictionary of Sociology.* Oxford, UK: Oxford University Press.

Massey, Douglas S. 2001. Residential Segregation and Neighborhood Conditions in U.S. Metropolitan Areas. *America Becoming: Racial Trends and Their Consequences,* edited by Neil J. Smelser, William Julius Wilson, and Faith Mitchell, 391–424. Washington, DC.: National Academy Press.

Omi, Michael, and Howard Winant. 1994. *Racial Formation in the United States.* New York: Routledge.

Pager, Devah, and Hana Shepherd. 2008. The Sociology of Discrimination: Racial Discrimination in Employment, Housing, Credit, and Consumer Markets. *Annual Review of Sociology,* 34:181–209.

Pew Research Center for the People and the Press. 2003. Race: Most Americans Do Not Object to Interracial Dating or Marriage. Retrieved June 13, 2010 (http:// www.publicagenda.org/charts/most-americans-do- not-object-interracial-dating-or-marriage).

Pierce, Christine. 1971. Natural Law Language and Women. *Woman in Sexist Society,* edited by Vivian Gornick and Barbara K. Moran, 242–58. New York: New American Library.

Riggs, Marlon. 1987. *Ethnic Notions.* California Newsreel (video).

St. John, C., and T. Heald-Moore. 1995. Fear of Black Strangers. *Social Science Research* 24:262–80.

Sayers, Janet. 1982. *Biological Politics: Feminist and Antifeminist Perspectives.* London: Tavistock Publications.

Schuman, Howard. 1971. Free Will and Determinism in Beliefs about Race. *Majority and Minority: The Dynamics of Racial and Ethnic Relations,* edited by N. Yetman and C. Steeh, 375–80. Boston: Allyn & Bacon.

———, Charlotte Steeh, Lawrence Bobo, and Maria Krysan. 1997. *Racial Attitudes in America: Trends and Interpretations.* Rev. ed. Cambridge: Harvard University Press.

Shipman, Pat. 1994. *The Evolution of Racism: Human Differences and the Use and Abuse of Science.* New York: Simon and Schuster.

Sinclair, Stacey, and Janetta Lun. 2010. Social Tuning of Ethnic Attitudes. *The Mind in Context,* edited by Batja Mesquita, Lisa Feldman Barrett, and Elliot R. Smith, 214–32. New York: Guilford Press.

Skrentny, John D. 2002. *The Minority Rights Revolution.* Cambridge, MA: Harvard University Press.

Smith, Dorothy. 1978. A Peculiar Eclipsing: Women's Exclusion from Men's Culture. *Women's Studies International Quarterly* 1:281–95.

———. 1990. *The Conceptual Practices of Power: A Feminist Sociology of Knowledge.* Boston: Northeastern University Press.

Smith, Tom. 1990. Ethnic Images. General Social Survey Technical Report, No. 19, National Opinion Research Center. University of Chicago.

Steinberg, Steven. 1989. *The Ethnic Myth: Race, Ethnicity, and Class in America.* Boston: Beacon Press.

Takaki, Ronald. 1993. *A Different Mirror: A History of Multicultural America.* Boston: Little, Brown.

Winant, Howard. 2004. *The New Politics of Race: Globalism, Difference, Justice.* Minneapolis, MN: University of Minnesota Press.

READING 36

Blink in Black and White

Malcolm Gladwell

Over the past few years, a number of psychologists have begun to look more closely at the role unconscious—or, as they like to call them, implicit—associations play in our beliefs and behavior, and much of their work has focused on a very fascinating tool called the Implicit Association Test (IAT). The IAT was devised by Anthony G. Greenwald, Mahzarin Banaji, and Brian Nosek, and it is based on a seemingly obvious—but nonetheless quite profound—observation. We make connections much more quickly between pairs of ideas that are already related in our minds than we do between pairs of ideas that are unfamiliar to us. What does that mean? Let me give you an example. Below is a list of words. Take a pencil or pen and assign each name to the category to which it belongs by putting a check mark either to the left or to the right of the word. You can also do it by tapping your finger in the appropriate column. Do it as quickly as you can. Don't skip over words. And don't worry if you make any mistakes.

Male	Female
John	
Bob	
Amy	
Holly	
Joan	
Derek	
Peggy	
Jason	
Lisa	
Matt	
Sarah	

Malcolm Gladwell is a staff writer for *The New Yorker*.

That was easy, right? And the reason that was easy is that when we read or hear the name "John" or "Bob" or "Holly," we don't even have to think about whether it's a masculine or a feminine name. We all have a strong prior association between a first name like John and the male gender, or a name like Lisa and things female.

That was a warm-up. Now let's complete an actual IAT. It works like the warm-up, except that now I'm going to mix two entirely separate categories together. Once again, put a check mark to either the right or the left of each word, in the category to which it belongs.

Male or Career	Female or Family
Lisa	
Matt	
Laundry	
Entrepreneur	
John	
Merchant	
Bob	
Capitalist	
Holly	
Joan	
Home	
Corporation	
Siblings	
Peggy	
Jason	
Kitchen	
Housework	
Parents	
Sarah	
Derek	

My guess is that most of you found that a little harder, but that you were still pretty fast at putting the words into the right categories. Now try this:

Male or Family	Female or Career
....	Babies ....
....	Sarah..............................
....	Derek.............................
....	Merchant..........................
....	Employment ....
....	John.............................
....	Bob ....
....	Holly.............................
....	Domestic ....
....	Entrepreneur.....................
....	Office.............................
....	Joan ....
....	Peggy ....
....	Cousins ....
....	Grandparents....................
....	Jason.............................
....	Home.............................
....	Lisa ....
....	Corporation.....................
....	Matt.............................

Did you notice the difference? This test was quite a bit harder than the one before it, wasn't it? If you are like most people, it took you a little longer to put the word "Entrepreneur" into the "Career" category when "Career" was paired with "Female" than when "Career" was paired with "Male." That's because most of us have much stronger mental associations between maleness and career-oriented concepts than we do between femaleness and ideas related to careers. "Male" and "Capitalist" go together in our minds a lot like "John" and "Male" did. But when the category is "Male or Family," we have to stop and think—even if it's only for a few hundred milliseconds—before we decide what to do with a word like "Merchant."

When psychologists administer the IAT, they usually don't use paper and pencil tests like the ones I've just given you. Most of the time, they do it on a computer. The words are flashed on the screen one at a time, and if a given word belongs in the left-hand column, you hit the letter *e,* and if the word belongs in the right-hand column, you hit the letter *i.* The advantage of doing the IAT on a computer is that the responses are measurable down to the millisecond, and those measurements are used in assigning the test taker's score. So, for example, if it took you a little bit longer to complete part two of the Work/Family IAT than it did part one, we would say that you have a moderate association between men and the workforce. If it took you a lot longer to complete part two, we'd say that when it comes to the workforce, you have a strong automatic male association.

One of the reasons that the IAT has become so popular in recent years as a research tool is that the effects it is measuring are not subtle; as those of you who felt yourself slowing down on the second half of the Work/Family IAT above can attest, the IAT is the kind of tool that hits you over the head with its conclusions. "When there's a strong prior association, people answer in between four hundred and six hundred milliseconds," says Greenwald. "When there isn't, they might take two hundred to three hundred milliseconds longer than that—which in the realm of these kinds of effects is huge. One of my cognitive psychologist colleagues described this as an effect you can measure with a sundial."

If you'd like to try a computerized IAT, you can go to www.implicit.harvard.edu. There you'll find several tests, including the most famous of all the IATs, the Race IAT. I've taken the Race IAT on many occasions, and the result always leaves me feeling a bit creepy. At the beginning of the test, you are asked what your attitudes toward blacks and whites are. I answered, as I am sure most of you would, that I think of the races as equal. Then comes the test. You're encouraged to complete it quickly. First comes the warm-up. A series of pictures of faces flash on the screen. When you see a black face, you press *e* and put it in the left-hand category. When you see a white face, you press *i* and put it in the right-hand category. It's *blink, blink, blink:* I didn't have to think at all. Then comes part one.

European American or Bad	African American or Good
..............................Hurt................................	
..............................Evil.................................	
..............................Glorious...........................	

.... Wonderful ....

And so on. Immediately, something strange happened to me. The task of putting the words and faces in the right categories suddenly became more difficult. I found myself slowing down. I had to think. Sometimes I assigned something to one category when I really meant to assign it to the other category. I was trying as hard as I could, and in the back of my mind was a growing sense of mortification. Why was I having such trouble when I had to put a word like "Glorious" or "Wonderful" into the "Good" category when "Good" was paired with "African American" or when I had to put the word "Evil" into the "Bad" category when "Bad" was

paired with "European American"? Then came part two. This time the categories were reversed.

European American or Good	African American or Bad
..............................Hurt................................	
..............................Evil.................................	
..............................Glorious...........................	

.... Wonderful ....

And so on. Now my mortification grew still further. Now I was having no trouble at all.

Evil? *African American or Bad.*
Hurt? *African American or Bad.*
Wonderful? *European American or Good.*

I took the test a second time, and then a third time, and then a fourth time, hoping that the awful feeling of bias would go away. It made no difference. It turns out that more than 80 percent of all those who have ever taken the test end up having pro-white associations, meaning that it takes them measurably longer to complete answers when they are required to put good words into the "Black" category than when they are required to link bad things with black people. I didn't do quite so badly. On the Race IAT, I was rated as having a "moderate automatic preference for whites." But then again, I'm half black. (My mother is Jamaican.)

So what does this mean? Does this mean I'm a racist, a self-hating black person? Not exactly. What it means is that our attitudes toward things like race or gender operate on two levels. First of all, we have our conscious attitudes. This is what we choose to believe. These are our stated values, which we use to direct our behavior deliberately. The apartheid policies of South Africa or the laws in the American South that made it difficult for African Americans to vote are manifestations of conscious discrimination, and when we talk about racism or the fight for civil rights, this is the kind of discrimination that we usually refer to. But the IAT measures something else. It measures our second level of attitude, our racial attitude on an *unconscious* level—the immediate, automatic associations that tumble out before we've even had time to think. We don't deliberately choose our unconscious attitudes. And . . . we may not even be aware of them. The giant computer that is our unconscious silently crunches all the data it can from the experiences we've had, the people we've met, the lessons we've learned, the books we've read, the movies we've seen, and so on, and it forms an opinion. That's what is coming out in the IAT.

The disturbing thing about the test is that it shows that our unconscious attitudes may be utterly incompatible with our stated conscious values. As it turns out, for example, of the fifty thousand African Americans who have taken the Race IAT so far, about half of them, like me, have stronger associations with whites than with blacks. How could we not? We live in North America, where we are surrounded every day by cultural messages linking white with good. "You don't choose to make positive associations with the dominant group,"

says Mahzarin Banaji, who teaches psychology at Harvard University and is one of the leaders in IAT research. "But you are required to. All around you, that group is being paired with good things. You open the newspaper and you turn on the television, and you can't escape it."

The IAT is more than just an abstract measure of attitudes. It's also a powerful predictor of how we act in certain kinds of spontaneous situations. If you have a strongly pro-white pattern of associations, for example, there is evidence that that will affect the way you behave in the presence of a black person. It's not going to affect what you'll choose to say or feel or do. In all likelihood, you won't be aware that you're behaving any differently than you would around a white person. But chances are you'll lean forward a little less, turn away slightly from him or her, close your body a bit, be a bit less expressive, maintain less eye contact, stand a little farther away, smile a lot less, hesitate and stumble over your words a bit more, laugh at jokes a bit less. Does that matter? Of course it does. Suppose the conversation is a job interview. And suppose the applicant is a black man. He's going to pick up on that uncertainty and distance, and that may well make him a little less certain of himself, a little less confident, and a little less friendly. And what will you think then? You may well get a gut feeling that the applicant doesn't really have what it takes, or maybe that he is a bit standoffish, or maybe that he doesn't really want the job. What this unconscious first impression will do, in other words, is throw the interview hopelessly off course.

Or what if the person you are interviewing is tall? I'm sure that on a conscious level we don't think that we treat tall people any differently from how we treat short people. But there's plenty of evidence to suggest that height—particularly in men—does trigger a certain set of very positive unconscious associations. I polled about half of the companies on the Fortune 500 list—the list of the largest corporations in the United States—asking each company questions about its CEO. Overwhelmingly, the heads of big companies are, as I'm sure comes as no surprise to anyone, white men, which undoubtedly reflects some kind of implicit bias. But they are also almost all tall: in my sample, I found that on average, male CEOs were just a shade under six feet tall. Given that the average American male is five foot nine, that means that CEOs as a group have about three inches on the rest of their sex. But this statistic actually understates the matter. In the U.S. population, about 14.5 percent of all men are six feet or taller. Among CEOs of Fortune 500 companies, that number is 58 percent. Even more striking, in the general American population, 3.9 percent of adult men are six foot two or taller. Among my CEO sample, almost a third were six foot two or taller.

The lack of women or minorities among the top executive ranks at least has a plausible explanation. For years, for a number of reasons having to do with discrimination and cultural patterns, there simply weren't a lot of women and minorities entering the management ranks of American corporations. So, today, when boards of directors look for people with the necessary experience to be candidates for top positions, they can argue somewhat plausibly that there aren't a lot of women and minorities in the executive pipeline. But this is not true of short people. It is possible to staff a large company entirely with white males, but it is not possible to staff a large company without short people. There simply aren't enough tall people to go around. Yet few of those short people ever make it into the executive suite. Of the tens of millions of American men below five foot six, a grand total of ten in my sample have reached the level of CEO, which says that being short is probably as much of a handicap to corporate success as being a woman or an African American. (The grand exception to all of these trends is American Express CEO Kenneth Chenault, who is both on the short side—five foot nine—and black . . .).

Is this a deliberate prejudice? Of course not. No one ever says dismissively of a potential CEO candidate that he's too short. This is quite clearly the kind of unconscious bias that the IAT picks up on. Most of us, in ways that we are not entirely aware of, automatically associate leadership ability with imposing physical stature. We have a sense of what a leader is supposed to look like, and that stereotype is so powerful that when someone fits it, we simply become blind to other considerations. And this isn't confined to the executive suite. Not long ago, researchers who analyzed the data from four large research studies that had followed thousands of people from birth to adulthood calculated that when corrected for such variables as age and gender and weight, an inch of height is worth $789 a year in salary. That means that a person who is six feet tall but otherwise identical to someone who is five foot five will make on average $5,525 more per year. As Timothy Judge, one of the authors of the height-salary study, points out: "If you take this over the course of a 30-year career and compound it, we're talking about a tall person enjoying literally hundreds of thousands of dollars of earnings advantage." Have you ever wondered why so many mediocre people find their way into positions of authority in companies and organizations? It's because when it comes to even the most important positions, our selection decisions are a good deal less rational than we think. We see a tall person and we swoon. . . .

DISCUSSION QUESTIONS

1. Do you think some of your unconscious attitudes may be different from your stated conscious values? Why?
2. What are some examples of two words that are not usually thought of together?

NOTES

For more on the IAT, see Anthony G. Greenwald, Debbie E. McGhee, and Jordan L. K. Schwartz, "Measuring Individual Differences in Implicit Cognition: The Implicit Association Test," *Journal of Personality and Social Psychology* 74, no. 6 (1998): 1464–1480.

For an excellent treatment of the height issue, see Nancy Etcoff, *Survival of the Prettiest: The Science of Beauty* (New York: Random House, 1999), 172.

The height-salary study can be found in Timothy A. Judge and Daniel M. Cable, "The Effect of Physical Height on Workplace Success and Income: Preliminary Test of a Theoretical Model," *Journal of Applied Psychology* 89, no. 3 (June 2004): 428–441.

Just Like My Mama Said

I remember when I was just a little boy, my mother used to tell me, "Anthony you have to work twice as hard in life as everyone else, because being black means that you already have one strike against you." When I was growing up in a predominately black area, I did not know what she meant by this. Then we moved to an area that was filled with white people. I found myself constantly lagging behind, and I couldn't figure out why.

When I was 19 years old, I hit rock bottom and had nothing. I then remembered what my mama had said, and I began to work twice as hard as everyone else. I managed to afford my own apartment and eventually get married.

My wife is white, but her parents dislike me because of my color. They told her all the stereotypes about "the black male" and swore to her that I would follow suit. Soon after we moved in together, I was laid off from my job. I began to worry that she would think her parents were correct, so I tried to teach her about the black experience. I began to worry that her parents would negatively influence her and I would lose her. I was ready to give in and let her parents win, when I remembered something that my mama had said: "Sometimes you can't teach people; they have to learn on their own." Little did I know an appropriate lesson would soon follow.

As I was going through the want ads, I saw an advertisement for a job delivering pianos. The job paid more money than I had ever earned. I set up an interview for that evening. When my then-fiancée arrived home, I put on a shirt and a tie, grabbed my résumé, and headed for the interview. When I asked her if she thought I would get the job, she said, "I don't see why not. You work hard, you have good references, and you are enrolled in school." Needless to say I felt pretty good about my chances. I interviewed with a middle-aged white lady. The interview went very well. She nearly assured me that I had the job, but said that she just needed to run it by the storeowner. She left and returned with the owner minutes later. He was a middle-aged man of apparently white and Asian descent. He looked at me for a few seconds, and our eyes met. Then he shook his head and said, "No this is not who I want for the job" and walked out. The lady and I dejectedly looked at each other. She attempted to make an excuse for him, but I told her, "Don't worry, it's not your fault." I walked out and told my fiancée what had happened. We rode home in silence. She had just gotten her first taste of what it is like to be black in America.

Anthony McNeill

READING 37

See Baby Discriminate

Po Bronson

Ashley Merryman

At the children's research lab at the University of Texas, a database is kept on thousands of families in the Austin area who have volunteered to be available for scholarly research. In 2006 Birgitte Vittrup

recruited from the database about a hundred families, all of whom were Caucasian with a child 5 to 7 years old.

The goal of Vittrup's study was to learn if typical children's videos with multicultural storylines have any beneficial effect on children's racial attitudes. Her first step was to give the children a Racial Attitude Measure, which asked such questions as:

How many White people are nice?
(Almost all) (A lot) (Some) (Not many)
(None)

How many Black people are nice?
(Almost all) (A lot) (Some) (Not many)
(None)

Po Bronson is a writer of nonfiction. Ashley Merryman is a writer and attorney.

During the test, the descriptive adjective "nice" was replaced with more than 20 other adjectives, like "dishonest," "pretty," "curious," and "snobby."

Vittrup sent a third of the families home with multiculturally themed videos for a week, such as an episode of *Sesame Street* in which characters visit an African-American family's home, and an episode of *Little Bill,* where the entire neighborhood comes together to clean the local park.

In truth, Vittrup didn't expect that children's racial attitudes would change very much just from watching these videos. Prior research had shown that multicultural curricula in schools have far less impact than we intend them to—largely because the implicit message "We're all friends" is too vague for young children to understand that it refers to skin color.

Yet Vittrup figured explicit conversations with parents could change that. So a second group of families got the videos, and Vittrup told these parents to use them as the jumping-off point for a discussion about interracial friendship. She provided a checklist of points to make, echoing the shows' themes. "I really believed it was going to work," Vittrup recalls.

The last third were also given the checklist of topics, but no videos. These parents were to discuss racial equality on their own, every night for five nights.

At this point, something interesting happened. Five families in the last group abruptly quit the study. Two directly told Vittrup, "We don't want to have these conversations with our child. We don't want to point out skin color."

Vittrup was taken aback—these families volunteered knowing full well it was a study of children's racial attitudes. Yet once they were aware that the study required talking openly about race, they started dropping out.

It was no surprise that in a liberal city like Austin, every parent was a welcoming multiculturalist, embracing diversity. But according to Vittrup's entry surveys, hardly any of these white parents had ever talked to their children directly about race. They might have asserted vague principles—like "Everybody's equal" or "God made all of us" or

"Under the skin, we're all the same"—but they'd almost never called attention to racial differences.

They wanted their children to grow up colorblind. But Vittrup's first test of the kids revealed they weren't colorblind at all. Asked how many white people are mean, these children commonly answered, "Almost none." Asked how many blacks are mean, many answered, "Some," or "A lot." Even kids who attended diverse schools answered the questions this way.

More disturbing, Vittrup also asked all the kids a very blunt question: "Do your parents like black people?" Fourteen percent said outright, "No, my parents don't like black people"; 38 percent of the kids answered, "I don't know." In this supposed race-free vacuum being created by parents, kids were left to improvise their own conclusions—many of which would be abhorrent to their parents.

Vittrup hoped the families she'd instructed to talk about race would follow through. After watching the videos, the families returned to the Children's Research Lab for retesting. To Vittrup's complete surprise, the three groups of children were statistically the same—none, as a group, had budged very much in their racial attitudes. At first glance, the study was a failure.

Combing through the parents' study diaries, Vittrup realized why. Diary after diary revealed that the parents barely mentioned the checklist items. Many just couldn't talk about race, and they quickly reverted to the vague "Everybody's equal" phrasing.

Of all those Vittrup told to talk openly about interracial friendship, only six families managed to actually do so. And, for all six, their children dramatically improved their racial attitudes in a single week. Talking about race was clearly key. Reflecting later about the study, Vittrup said, "A lot of parents came to me afterwards and admitted they just didn't know what to say to their kids, and they didn't want the wrong thing coming out of the mouth of their kids."

We all want our children to be unintimidated by differences and have the social skills necessary for a diverse world. The question is, do we make it worse, or do we make it better, by calling attention to race?

The election of President Barack Obama marked the beginning of a new era in race relations in the United States—but it didn't resolve the question as to what we should tell children about race. Many parents have explicitly pointed out Obama's brown skin to their young children, to reinforce the message that anyone can rise to become a leader, and anyone—regardless of skin color—can be a friend, be loved, and be admired.

Others think it's better to say nothing at all about the president's race or ethnicity—because saying something about it unavoidably teaches a child a racial construct. They worry that even a positive statement ("It's wonderful that a black person can be president") still encourages a child to see divisions within society. For the early formative years, at least, they believe we should let children know a time when skin color does not matter.

What parents say depends heavily on their own race: a 2007 study in the *Journal of Marriage and Family* found that out of 17,000 families with kindergartners, nonwhite parents are about three times more likely to discuss race than white parents; 75 percent of the latter never, or almost never, talk about race.

In our new book, *NurtureShock,* we argue that many modern strategies for nurturing children are backfiring—because key twists in the science have been overlooked. Small corrections in our thinking today could alter the character of society long term, one future citizen at a time. The way white families introduce the concept of race to their children is a prime example.

For decades, it was assumed that children see race only when society points it out to them. However, child-development researchers have increasingly begun to question that presumption. They argue that children see racial differences as much as they see the difference between pink and blue—but we tell kids that "pink" means for girls and "blue" is for boys. "White" and "black" are mysteries we leave them to figure out on their own.

It takes remarkably little for children to develop in-group preferences. Vittrup's mentor at the University of Texas, Rebecca Bigler, ran an experiment in three pre-school classrooms, where 4- and 5-year-olds were lined up and given T shirts. Half the kids were randomly given blue T shirts, half red. The children wore the shirts for three weeks. During that time, the teachers never mentioned their colors and never grouped the kids by shirt color.

The kids didn't segregate in their behavior. They played with each other freely at recess. But when asked which color team was better to belong to, or which team might win a race, they chose their own color. They believed they were smarter than the other color. "The Reds never showed hatred for Blues," Bigler observed. "It was more like, 'Blues are fine, but not as good as us.'" When Reds were asked how many Reds were nice, they'd answer, "All of us." Asked how many Blues were nice, they'd answer, "Some." Some of the Blues were mean, and some were dumb—but not the Reds.

Bigler's experiment seems to show how children will use whatever you give them to create divisions—seeming to confirm that race becomes an issue only if we make it an issue. So why does Bigler think it's important to talk to children about race as early as the age of 3?

Her reasoning is that kids are developmentally prone to in-group favoritism; they're going to form these preferences on their own. Children naturally try to categorize everything, and the attribute they rely on is that which is the most clearly visible.

We might imagine we're creating color-blind environments for children, but differences in skin color or hair or weight are like differences in gender—they're plainly visible. Even if no teacher or parent mentions race, kids will use skin color on their own, the same way they use T-shirt colors. Bigler contends that children extend their shared appearances much further—believing that those who look similar to them enjoy the same things they do. Anything a child doesn't like thus belongs to those who look the least similar to him. The spontaneous tendency to assume your group shares characteristics—such as niceness, or smarts—is called essentialism.

Within the past decade or so, developmental psychologists have begun a handful of longitudinal studies to determine exactly when children develop bias. Phyllis Katz, then a professor at the University of Colorado, led one such study—following 100 black children and 100 white children for their first six years. She tested these children and their parents nine times during those six years, with the first test at 6 months old.

How do researchers test a 6-month-old? They show babies photographs of faces. Katz found that babies will stare significantly longer at photographs of faces that are a different race from their parents, indicating they find the face out of the ordinary. Race itself has no ethnic meaning per se—but children's brains are noticing skin-color differences and trying to understand their meaning.

When the kids turned 3, Katz showed them photographs of other children and asked them to choose whom they'd like to have as friends. Of the white children, 86 percent picked children of their own race. When the kids were 5 and 6, Katz gave these children a small deck of cards, with drawings of people on them. Katz told the children to sort the cards into two piles any way they wanted. Only 16 percent of the kids used gender to split the piles. But 68 percent of the kids used race to split the cards, without any prompting. In reporting her findings, Katz concluded: "I think it is fair to say that at no point in the study did the children exhibit the Rousseau type of color-blindness that many adults expect."

The point Katz emphasizes is that this period of our children's lives, when we imagine it's most important to not talk about race, is the very developmental period when children's minds are forming their first conclusions about race.

Several studies point to the possibility of developmental windows—stages when children's attitudes might be most amenable to change. In one experiment, children were put in cross-race study groups, and then were observed on the playground to see if the interracial classroom time led to interracial play at recess. The researchers found mixed study groups worked wonders with the first-grade children, but it made no difference with third graders. It's possible that by third grade, when parents usually recognize it's safe to start talking a little about race, the developmental window has already closed.

The other deeply held assumption modern parents have is what Ashley and I have come to call the Diverse Environment Theory. If you raise a child with a fair amount of exposure to people of other races and cultures, the environment becomes the message. Because both of us attended integrated schools in the 1970s—Ashley in San Diego and, in my case, Seattle—we had always accepted this theory's tenets: diversity breeds tolerance, and talking about race was, in and of itself, a diffuse kind of racism.

But my wife and I saw this differently in the years after our son, Luke, was born. When he was 4 months old, Luke began attending a preschool located in San Francisco's Fillmore/Western Addition neighborhood. One of the many benefits of the school was its great racial diversity. For years our son never once mentioned the color of anyone's skin. We never once mentioned skin color, either. We thought it was working perfectly.

Then came Martin Luther King Jr. Day at school, two months before his fifth birthday. Luke walked out of pre-school that Friday before the weekend and started pointing at everyone, proudly announcing, "That guy comes from Africa. And she comes from Africa, too!" It was embarrassing how loudly he did this. "People with brown skin are from Africa," he'd repeat. He had not been taught the names for races—he had not heard the term "black" and he called us "people with pinkish-whitish skin." He named every kid in his schoolroom with brown skin, which was about half his class.

My son's eagerness was revealing. It was obvious this was something he'd been wondering about for a while. He was relieved to have been finally given the key. Skin color was a sign of ancestral roots.

Over the next year, we started to overhear one of his white friends talking about the color of their skin. They still didn't know what to call their skin, so they used the phrase "skin like ours." And this notion of ours versus theirs started to take on a meaning of its own. As these kids searched for their identities, skin color had become salient.

Soon, I overheard this particular white boy telling my son, "Parents don't like us to talk about our skin, so don't let them hear you."

As a parent, I dealt with these moments explicitly, telling my son it was wrong to choose anyone as his friend, or his "favorite," on the basis of skin color. We pointed out how certain friends wouldn't be in our lives if we picked friends for their color. Over time he not only accepted but embraced this lesson. Now he talks openly about equality and the wrongfulness of discrimination.

Not knowing then what I do now, I had a hard time understanding my son's initial impulses. Katz's work helped me to realize that Luke was never actually colorblind. He didn't talk about race in his first five years because our silence had unwittingly communicated that race was something he could not ask about.

The Diverse Environment Theory is the core principle behind school desegregation today. Like most people, I assumed that after 30 years of desegregation, it would have a long track record of scientific research proving that the Diverse Environment Theory works. Then Ashley and I began talking to the scholars who've compiled that very research.

In the summer of 2007, led by the Civil Rights Project, a dozen scholars wrote an amicus brief to the U.S. Supreme Court supporting school desegregation in Louisville, Ky., and Seattle. By the time the brief reached the court, 553 scientists had signed on in support. However, as much as the scientists all supported active desegregation, the brief is surprisingly circumspect in its advocacy: the benefits of desegregation are qualified with words like "may lead" and "can improve." "Mere school integration is not a panacea," the brief warns.

UT's Bigler was one of the scholars heavily involved in the process of its creation. Bigler is an adamant proponent of desegregation in schools on moral grounds. "It's an enormous step backward to increase social segregation," she says. However, she also admitted that "in the end, I was disappointed with the amount of evidence social psychology could muster [to support it]. Going to integrated schools gives you just as many chances to learn stereotypes as to unlearn them."

The unfortunate twist of diverse schools is that they don't necessarily lead to more cross-race relationships. Often it's the opposite. Duke University's James Moody—an expert on how adolescents form and maintain social networks—analyzed data on more than 90,000 teenagers at 112 different schools from every region of the country. The students had been asked to name their five best male friends and their five best female friends. Moody matched the ethnicity of the student with the race of each named friend, then compared the number of each student's cross-racial friendships with the school's overall diversity.

Moody found that the more diverse the school, the more the kids self-segregate by race and ethnicity within the school, and thus the likelihood that any two kids of different races have a friendship goes down.

Moody included statistical controls for activities, sports, academic tracking, and other school-structural conditions that tend to desegregate (or segregate) students within the school. The rule still holds true: more diversity translates into more division among students. Those increased opportunities to interact are also, effectively, increased opportunities to reject each other. And that is what's happening.

As a result, junior-high and high-school children in diverse schools experience two completely contrasting social cues on a daily basis. The first cue is inspiring—that many students have a friend of another race. The second cue is tragic—that far more kids just like to hang with their own. It's this second dynamic that becomes more and more visible as overall school diversity goes up. As a child circulates through school, she sees more groups that her race disqualifies her from, more lunchroom tables she can't sit at, and more implicit lines that are taboo to cross. This is unmissable even if she, personally, has friends of other races. "Even in multiracial schools, once young people leave the classroom, very little interracial discussion takes place because a desire to associate with one's own ethnic group often discourages interaction between groups," wrote Brendesha Tynes of the University of Illinois at Urbana-Champaign.

All told, the odds of a white high-schooler in America having a best friend of another race is only 8 percent. Those odds barely improve for the second-best friend, or the third-best, or the fifth. For blacks, the odds aren't much better: 85 percent of black kids' best friends are also black. Cross-race friends also tend to share a single activity, rather than multiple activities; as a result, these friendships are more likely to be lost over time, as children transition from middle school to high school.

I can't help but wonder—would the track record of desegregation be so mixed if parents reinforced it, rather than remaining silent? It is tempting to believe that because their generation is so diverse, today's children grow up knowing how to get along with people of every race. But numerous studies suggest that this is more of a fantasy than a fact.

Is it really so difficult to talk with children about race when they're very young? What jumped out at Phyllis Katz, in her study of 200 black and white children, was that parents are very comfortable talking to their children about gender, and they work very hard to counter-program against boy-girl stereotypes. That ought to be our model for talking about race. The same way we remind our daughters, "Mommies can be doctors just like daddies," we ought to be telling all children that doctors can be any skin color. It's not complicated what to say. It's only a matter of how often we reinforce it.

Shushing children when they make an improper remark is an instinctive reflex, but often the wrong move. Prone to categorization, children's brains can't help but attempt to generalize rules from the examples they see. It's embarrassing when a child blurts out, "Only brown people can have breakfast at school," or "You can't play basketball; you're white, so you have to play baseball." But shushing them only sends the message that this topic is unspeakable, which makes race more loaded, and more intimidating.

To be effective, researchers have found, conversations about race have to be explicit, in unmistakable terms that children understand. A friend of mine repeatedly told her 5-year-old son, "Remember, everybody's equal." She thought she was getting the message across. Finally, after seven months of this, her boy asked, "Mommy, what's 'equal' mean?"

Bigler ran a study in which children read brief biographies of famous African-Americans. For instance, in a biography of Jackie Robinson, they read that he was the first African-American in the major leagues. But only half read about how he'd previously been relegated to the Negro Leagues, and how he suffered taunts from white fans. Those facts—in five brief sentences were omitted in the version given to the other children.

After the two-week history class, the children were surveyed on their racial attitudes. White children who got the full story about historical discrimination had significantly better attitudes toward blacks than those who got the neutered version. Explicitness works. "It also made them feel some guilt," Bigler adds. "It knocked down their glorified view of white people." They couldn't justify in-group superiority.

Minority parents are more likely to help their children develop a racial identity from a young age. April Harris-Britt, a clinical psychologist and professor at the University of North Carolina at Chapel Hill, found that all minority parents at some point tell their children that discrimination is out there, but they shouldn't let it stop them. Is this good for them? Harris-Britt found that some preparation for bias was beneficial, and it was necessary—94 percent of African-American eighth graders reported to Harris-Britt that they'd felt discriminated against in the prior three months.

But if children heard these preparation-for-bias warnings often (rather than just occasionally), they were significantly less likely to connect their successes to effort, and much more likely to blame their failures on their teachers—whom they saw as biased against them.

Harris-Britt warns that frequent predictions of future discrimination ironically become as destructive as experiences of actual discrimination:

"If you overfocus on those types of events, you give the children the message that the world is going to be hostile—you're just not valued and that's just the way the world is."

Preparation for bias is not, however, the only way minorities talk to their children about race. The other broad category of conversation, in Harris-Britt's analysis, is ethnic pride. From a very young age, minority children are coached to be proud of their ethnic history. She found that this was exceedingly good for children's self-confidence; in one study, black children who'd heard messages of ethnic pride were more engaged in school and more likely to attribute their success to their effort and ability.

That leads to the question that everyone wonders but rarely dares to ask. If "black pride" is good for African-American children, where does that leave white children? It's horrifying to imagine kids being "proud to be white." Yet many scholars argue that's exactly what children's brains are already computing. Just as minority children are aware that they belong to an ethnic group with less status and wealth, most white children naturally decipher that they belong to the race that has more power, wealth, and control in society; this provides security, if not confidence. So a pride message would not just be abhorrent—it'd be redundant.

Over the course of our research, we heard many stories of how people—from parents to teachers—were struggling to talk about race with their children. For some, the conversations came up after a child had made an embarrassing comment in public. A number had the issue thrust on them, because of an interracial marriage or an international adoption. Still others were just introducing children into a diverse environment, wondering when and if the timing was right.

But the story that most affected us came from a small town in rural Ohio. Two first-grade teachers, Joy Bowman and Angela Johnson, had agreed to let a professor from Ohio State University, Jeane Copenhaver-Johnson, observe their classrooms for the year. Of the 33 children, about two thirds were white, while the others were black or of mixed-race descent.

It being December, the teachers had decided to read to their classes *'Twas the Night B'fore Christmas,* Melodye Rosales's retelling of the Clement C. Moore classic. As the teachers began reading, the kids were excited by the book's depiction of a family waiting for Santa to come. A few children, however, quietly fidgeted. They seemed puzzled that this storybook was different: in this one, it was a black family all snug in their beds.

Then there was the famed clatter on the roof. The children leaned in to get their first view of Santa and the sleigh as Johnson turned the page—

And they saw that Santa was black.

"He's black!" gasped a white little girl.

A white boy exclaimed, "I thought he was white!"

Immediately, the children began to chatter about the stunning development. At the ripe old ages of 6 and 7, the children had no doubt that there was a Real Santa. Of that they were absolutely sure. But suddenly there was this huge question mark. Could Santa be black? And if so, what did that mean?

While some of the black children were delighted with the idea that Santa could be black, others were unsure. A couple of the white children rejected this idea out of hand: a black Santa couldn't be real.

But even the little girl the most adamant that the Real Santa must be white came around to accept the possibility that a black Santa could fill in for White Santa if he was hurt. And she still gleefully yelled along with the Black Santa's final "Merry Christmas to All! Y'all Sleep Tight."

Other children offered the idea that perhaps Santa was "mixed with black and white"—something in the middle, like an Indian. One boy went with a two-Santa hypothesis: White Santa and Black Santa must be friends who take turns visiting children. When a teacher made the apparently huge mistake of saying that she'd never seen Santa, the children all quickly corrected her: everyone had seen Santa at the mall. Not that that clarified the situation any.

The debate raged for a week, in anticipation of a school party. The kids all knew Real Santa was the guest of honor.

Then Santa arrived at the party—and he was black. Just like in the picture book.

Some white children said that this black Santa was too thin: that meant that the Real Santa was the fat white one at Kmart. But one of the white girls retorted that she had met the man and was convinced. Santa was brown.

Most of the black children were exultant, since this proved that Santa was black. But one of them, Brent, still doubted—even though he really wanted a black Santa to be true. So he bravely confronted Santa.

"There ain't no black Santas!" Brent insisted.

"Lookit here." Santa pulled up a pant leg.

A thrilled Brent was sold. "This is a black Santa!" he yelled. "He's got black skin and his black boots are like the white Santa's boots."

A black-Santa storybook wasn't enough to crush every stereotype. When Johnson later asked the kids to draw Santa, even the black kids who were excited about a black Santa still depicted him with skin as snowy white as his beard.

But the shock of the Santa storybook was the catalyst for the first graders to have a yearlong dialogue about race issues. The teachers began regularly incorporating books that dealt directly with issues of racism into their reading.

And when the children were reading a book on Martin Luther King Jr. and the civil-rights movement, both a black and a white child noticed that white people were nowhere to be found in the story. Troubled, they decided to find out just where in history both peoples were.

DISCUSSION QUESTIONS

1. Assess the likelihood that these research conclusions would be implemented. What factors would support and oppose its implementation?
2. What are the implications of this research for child rearing, education, and public policy?

READING 38

Between Barack and a Hard Place

Tim Wise

Once Barack Obama became the Democratic Party's nominee for president of the United States, two questions emerged most prominently in media and personal discussions of his candidacy. The first of these, most often put forward by those who were seeking to draw rather sweeping and positive conclusions from their query, was typically posed as, "What does it say about race in America that a black man now stands on the precipice of becoming, arguably, the most powerful person in the world?" The second, presented somewhat more skeptically than the first, and more likely offered up by those whose hopefulness was a bit more tempered by an appreciation of history, most often sounded like this: "Is white America really ready for a black president?"

While we can hardly be surprised at how quickly these became the principal questions asked in the run-up to the November 2008 election, both nonetheless stemmed from premises that were largely false, or at least glaringly problematic. And as with any question that emanates from a false or incomplete starting point, such interrogations as these ultimately led down mundane analytic corridors, to destinations that, although interesting, were never truly the places to which we needed to travel.

For while the political ascent of Barack Obama, culminating with his victory in November over challenger John McCain, certainly says something about race, what it says is far from that which most—including those typically asking the question in the first place—seem to believe. Yes, it suggests that blind and irrational bigotry of the kind that animated so much white opinion for so

Tim Wise is an American anti-racist activist who has for over 20 years taught methods to address and dismantle racism.

long in the United States may well have receded (though not as much as we'd like to think). But given the evidence regarding entrenched racial inequities in employment, education, health care, criminal justice, housing and elsewhere—and the studies indicating these are due in large measure to discrimination, either past, present, or a combination of the two—it most definitely does not suggest that racism has been truncated as an ongoing social problem for persons of color generally.

Though Obama's victory falls well short of proving that racism has been vanquished in America, for reasons I will explore shortly, it is still worth noting some of the positive aspects of the Obama victory when it comes to race. For although I will insist that his rise says far less than many would suggest, we would do well to at least note a few of the beneficial outcomes, so we know what we have to build on in the future.

First, Obama's election to the presidency demonstrates that old-fashioned racism (or what I call Racism 1.0), though still far too prevalent in the nation, is capable of being defeated, especially when an effective coalition is put together, and when those who otherwise might fall back into patterns of bias and discrimination can be convinced that their interests (economic, for instance) should outweigh their tendency to act on the basis of skin color. Given the harrowing state of the American economy as voters went to the polls in November, and given the Obama campaign's message that his opponent would only provide tax relief to the wealthiest Americans while largely continuing the economic policies of the Bush administration, many voters (including white working-class voters who had been turning against Democrats for a generation) turned to Obama. Even if they harbored ongoing prejudices toward African Americans generally (and evidence suggests that many still did), they were prepared to vote their pocketbooks and break with a long tradition, stretching back decades, whereby so many of them had ignored economic interests for the sake of apparent "racial bonding," against communities of color.

Especially heartening was the fact that part of the strategy for gaining the support of white working-class voters was to directly confront them on their racism when it was expressed, rather than finessing it. Labor leader Richard Trumka, for instance, as well as other labor organizers and Obama's own campaign in Ohio developed strategies for taking on white racism directly, rather than trying to sidestep it, in the hopes that voters would simply do the right thing for economic reasons alone. By calling out white racism and forcing white working folks to think about the irrationality of racial bonding—especially in the face of an economic free fall—these organizers planted the seeds of potential cross-racial alliance, which, if tended carefully, could bear fruit in the future.[1]

Secondly, and on a related note, the level of cross-racial collaboration (especially among youth) that made Obama's victory possible was something rarely seen in American politics, or history. Although many, including myself, would rather see such mobilizing take place in arenas other than mainstream electoral politics, the fact is, efforts of this nature have to start somewhere. For young people who forged real and meaningful movement relationships in the Obama campaign, the possibility that they may continue to engage in grassroots organizing in years to come—and much of it around issues of racial justice—cannot be ignored. Long-term sustained activism is always more likely for those who have formed those genuine relationships and worked together for a common purpose, as so many young blacks, whites, Latinos and Asian Americans did in this election cycle. Likewise, that so many of the Obama campaigners witnessed racism up close and personal—while either canvassing or making phone calls for the campaign—can only have served to heighten these folks' sensitivity to the problem of racism in America. So although the average white person may view Obama's win as evidence of the death of racism (more on this below), those who worked on his behalf will have a hard time coming to that conclusion, having seen and heard so much raw and unexpurgated bigotry on the campaign trail.[2]

Finally, Obama's win indicates that when a person of color has the opportunity to make his case day after day, for at least a year and a half (and really more, since Obama had been introduced to the public four years earlier during the 2004 Democratic National Convention), he is fully capable of demonstrating to the satisfaction of millions of whites (if still not most), his intelligence, wisdom, and leadership capabilities, sufficiently to win the job for which he is in effect, interviewing. So far so good.

But the bad news, and let us not forget it, is that most job interviews don't last for eighteen months, and don't involve millions of decision-makers, where at least in theory the biases of some can be canceled out by the open-mindedness of others. Rather, most job-seekers are facing a mere handful of evaluators, often only one, and if there is any significant bias in the heart or mind of that person (or if that person adheres, even subconsciously, to negative stereotypes about folks of color), the job applicant who is black or brown faces an uphill climb that Obama's success cannot erase or transform. Likewise, most persons of color don't have the luxury of whipping out their memoir when applying for a mortgage loan, while searching for an apartment, or when they are stopped by a police officer on suspicion of illegal activity and saying, "Here, read this; it'll show you what a great guy I am." Most folks of color face far less deliberative snap judgments on the part of employers, landlords, teachers, and cops, and in those instances, the ability of racial bias to taint the process of evaluation is of no small concern.

So, rather than ask what Obama's success means in terms of race and racism in the United States in the twenty-first century, the better question may be what doesn't his success mean for those things? What does it *not* tell us about how far we've come, and how far we still have to go?

As for the second of the two most often asked questions, while many whites may well not have been prepared to vote for a black—or as some may prefer, biracial—man for the presidency, there is another issue almost completely overlooked by the press: the possibility that Obama might well have won the nation's highest office in spite of ongoing traditional white racism, and yet because of a newer, slicker

Racism 2.0, in which whites hold the larger black community in low regard and adhere, for instance, to any number of racist stereotypes about African Americans—and yet carve out acceptable space for individuals such as Obama who strike them as different, as exceptions who are not like the rest. That this "enlightened exceptionalism" manages to accommodate individual people of color, even as it continues to look down upon the larger mass of black and brown America with suspicion, fear, and contempt, suggests the fluid and shape-shifting nature of racism. It indicates that far from vanishing, racism has become more sophisticated and that Obama's rise could, at least in part, stem from the triumph of racism, albeit of a more seemingly ecumenical type than that to which we have grown accustomed.

If some whites are willing to vote for a person of color, but only to the extent they are able to view that person as racially unthreatening, as different from "regular" black people, as somehow less than truly black, or as having "transcended race" (a term used with regularity to describe Obama over the past few years), then white racism remains quite real, quite powerful, and quite operative in the life of the nation. More than that, even in the case of the electoral success of a man of color, it might well have remained central to the outcome. The only question, really, was which kind of racism was likely to show up most prominently on election day? Would it be the traditional old-fashioned kind, rooted in conscious bigotry and hate, the Racism 1.0, which historically has caused many whites to act toward black folks with suspicion, violence, distrust, fear, and anxiety, and which—if it is prevalent enough—could have resulted in Obama's defeat? Or would it be the newer, slicker, enlightened exceptionalism, or Racism 2.0, which still holds the larger black and brown communities of our nation in low regard but is willing to carve out exceptions for those who make some whites sufficiently comfortable? We now have our answer to that question, if we're willing to examine it. But one thing about which we should be clear as we conduct that examination is this: the election of Barack Obama was not the result of a national evolution to a truly antiracist consciousness or institutional praxis. And this we know for reasons we shall now explore.

SAME AS IT EVER WAS: BARACK OBAMA AND THE PROBLEM OF WHITE DENIAL

That white folks would find it tempting, in light of Obama's mass appeal and his ascent to the presidency, to declare the struggle against racism over should surprise no one. As we'll see below, even when the system of racism and white supremacy was more firmly entrenched, white folks by and large failed to see what all the fuss was about. So needless to say, with Barack Obama now in the nation's top political position, it is to be expected that once again white America would point to such a thing as firm confirmation that all was right with the world. Indeed, the day after Obama's victory, the *Wall Street Journal* editorial page intoned: "One promise of his victory is that perhaps we can put to rest the myth of racism as a barrier to achievement in this splendid country."[3]

Even before Obama had been declared the winner of the election, proclamations of racism's early death were becoming ubiquitous. And so, ten days before the vote, columnist Frank Rich, writing in the *New York Times*, declared that concerns about white racism possibly sinking Obama's ship were so obviously absurd as to indicate evidence of "prevailing antiwhite bias" on the part of the media types who continually raised the subject. He went on to explain that white America's distrust of blacks "crumbles when they actually get to know specific black people."[4] Though Rich's point about the willingness of whites to open up to individual blacks once they become familiar with them may be true for many, he, like most commentators, ignores the fact that most black folks will not get the chance to be known in this way by the average white person. As such, to proclaim a phenomenon observable in the presidential race (whites, getting to know Obama and choosing him in the voting booth) as common or likely to obtain in everyday situations and encounters seems a bit far-fetched.

Then there was columnist Richard Cohen, who said in the *Washington Post* on the morning of the election, "It is not just that he (Obama) is post-racial; so is the nation he is generationally primed to lead," and then closed his piece by suggesting, in a bizarre appropriation of civil rights movement language, "we have overcome."[5]

On a personal note, about a week before the election I received an e-mail from a young white man who proclaimed his desire for Obama to win so that the nation would finally be able to "stop talking about racism, and move on to more important subjects," and so that "blacks would have to stop whining about discrimination, and focus on pulling themselves up by their bootstraps instead."

On election eve, before Obama had accumulated enough electoral votes to be proclaimed the winner, former New York City mayor (and Republican presidential candidate) Rudy Giuliani had made clear what an Obama victory would mean for the nation. Speaking of what appeared at that moment to be a sure Obama win, Giuliani noted that if the trend at that point in the evening held up, "we've achieved history tonight and we've moved beyond . . . the whole idea of race and racial separation and unfairness."[6] Interestingly, not only did none of the other commentators challenge Giuliani's formulation, but they also failed to note the obvious irony of his comment. Namely, if an Obama win by necessity would indicate the veritable death of racism in the United States, then would an Obama loss have suggested deeply entrenched bigotry in the eyes of Giuliani and others making the same argument? Had McCain won, could we have expected these prophets of achieved color blindness to condemn their fellow voters for being so obviously racist as to vote against a black man? After all, if voting for Obama means people have put away racism, by definition, voting against him would have to mean they had not, right? Actually no, of course, but such a conclusion is where arguments like that of Giuliani necessarily lead.

In truth, such a proposition (that the victory of one person of color signifies a victory over racism aimed at nearly 90 million) is very nearly the definition of lunacy. And note, it is the kind of proposition one would never make regarding sexism in a place like Pakistan, just because Benazir Bhutto was twice elected prime minister of the place; or in India, Israel, or Great Britain, by virtue of all three having elected women as the heads of their respective states. Surely, had Hillary Clinton captured the nomination of her party and gone on to win in November, no one with even a scintilla of common sense would have argued that a result such as this signaled the obvious demise of sexism in the United States. But that is essentially what so many would have us believe to be true of racism, thanks to the national effort that elected Barack Obama.

What white America has apparently missed, in spite of all the Black History Month celebrations to which we have lately been exposed, is that there have always been individually successful persons of color. Their pictures adorn the walls of our elementary school classrooms; their stories get told, albeit in an abbreviated and sanitized way, every February, when corporations and the Ad Council take to the airwaves to tell us about so-and-so great black inventor, or so-and-so great black artist, or so-and-so great black literary giant. What remains unsaid, but which forms the background noise of all this annual praise for the triumphs of black Americans (or, at other times, Latinos and Latinas, Asian-Pacific Americans, or the continent's indigenous persons), is the systematic oppression that marked the society at the time when most of their achievements transpired. In other words, even in the midst of crushing oppression these hearty souls managed to find a way out of no way, as the saying goes. But that hardly suggests that their singular achievements, even multiplied hundreds of times over, actually rendered the system any less oppressive for all the rest. Thus, Madame C.J. Walker managed to become a millionaire developing and selling beauty products to black women in 1911. This achievement, though of importance in the history of American entrepreneurship, and to the narrative of black success, nonetheless fails to alter the fact that, on balance, 1911 was not a good year to be black in the United States, Madame Walker

notwithstanding. Though I am hardly so naïve as to suggest that nothing has changed since 1911, the point still holds: the triumph of individuals of color cannot, in itself, serve as proof of widespread systemic change.

Although it is possible that the political success of Barack Obama could serve to open the minds of whites as to the potentiality of effective black leadership, it is also possible that it might deepen the denial in which so much of the white public has been embedded for generations. And although Obama's success has had a measurable effect on young men and women of color, who appear empowered by his example—and this could lead to greater levels of accomplishment for still more persons of color, thereby producing a ripple effect when it comes to collective racial uplift—it is also possible that this sense of pride may be stalled if Obama is unable to deliver on his promise of "Change We Can Believe In," thanks to the exigencies of Washington politics. Long story short, what the rise of Obama comes to mean, regarding race or any other subject, remains to be seen.

But what we can say, without fear of contradiction, is that it does not signify, as some would have it, a fundamental diminution of institutional racism in the United States at present. Contrary to the proclamations of conservatives, both white and of color—such as Abigail Thernstrom and Ward Connerly, who have been among the chief critics and organized opponents of affirmative action programs since the mid-1990s—Obama's ability to attract white votes (and even then, let us remember, a minority of those) hardly suggests that we can put away various civil rights remedies and proclaim opportunities to be truly open and equitable. That white America may desperately want Obama's success to serve as the final nail in the political coffin of civil rights activism—and even the media seems to have evinced this hope, as with the August 2008 *New York Times* article that asked whether Obama marks the "end of black politics" altogether—hardly speaks to whether it should be used as that nail, or whether there is evidence to support the notion that his individual victories are proxies for institutional transformation.[7]

Though the evidence about our nation's progress says something else altogether, it turns out that white folks have never paid much attention to the evidence, and so denial has long carried the day. This, of course, is no shock in 2009. After all, it is not only the age of Obama, but the age of Oprah Winfrey, Denzel Washington, Colin Powell, Tiger Woods, the Williams sisters, J-Lo, Jackie Chan, Lucy Liu, Russell Simmons, P. Diddy, and any number of dizzyingly successful folks of color in the worlds of entertainment, sports, and politics. Hip-hop is, for most youth of whatever race, at least part of the sound track of their lives. With such apparent signs of progress, who can blame white folks for thinking the work has been done, and that it is now time to move on to other subjects, leaving the stale topic of racism in the dustbin of history?

Given such a transformation of popular culture as we have seen in the past few decades, it should hardly surprise us to read that according to a summer 2008 Gallup/*USA Today* poll, more than three in four whites say that blacks have "just as good a chance as whites to get any job for which they are qualified" (a proposition with which fewer than half of African Americans agree). Likewise, it can't be much of a shock to learn that 80 percent of whites polled say blacks have "just as good a chance as whites to get a good education," while fewer than half of blacks agree. Or that 85 percent of whites claim blacks have "just as good a chance to get any housing they can afford," while only 52 percent of blacks agree. Or that only about a third of whites accept the proposition that discrimination has played a major role in producing income disparities between whites and blacks.[8] Or that, according to a survey for CNN and *Essence* magazine, only one in nine whites believe racial discrimination against blacks is still a very serious problem, while nearly four times that many say it's not a serious problem at all.[9] And all this, despite a July 2008 *New York Times*/CBS poll, in which seven in ten blacks said they had suffered a specific discriminatory incident (up from 62 percent who said this in 2000).[10] No, there is nothing particularly surprising about any of this. The outward trappings of major transformative change appear to be everywhere, causing whites and blacks both, in the wake of Obama's victory, to announce their hope and expectations that race relations will improve in coming years.[11] So white denial (and perhaps even a bit from persons of color themselves) makes sense. It fits the visuals beamed into our living rooms, incomplete as they are.

But as predictable as this denial may be today—and however maddening it must be to the persons of color whose very sanity and judgment, indeed life experiences are being called into question by such denial—it is far more enraging to realize that the inability or unwillingness of white America to see racial discrimination as a problem is a pathology with a lengthy and disturbing pedigree. Putting aside the fact that, as with the examples above, we seem to be able to name all the really powerful black and brown folks on a couple of hands—and this, one might suggest, indicates that they are, by definition, exceptions to a much different-looking rule—the bigger problem with white denial is that it isn't a modern malady.

Though whites may now be seeking to use Obama as evidence of racism's eradication, let us remember that long before he burst onto the national scene—indeed, even at a time when he was an infant, well before anyone could have foreseen what he would become, and even before the passage of modern civil rights legislation—white Americans were fairly nonchalant about the problems facing persons of color, choosing in most cases to deny what all their senses (and surely their eyes, fixed on the television as most already were by the early 1960s) had to be telling them: that they were living in an apartheid nation; that theirs was no land of freedom and democracy, no oasis of liberty, but rather a formal white supremacy, a racially fascistic state for millions of people.

And so, in 1963, roughly two-thirds of whites told Gallup pollsters that blacks were treated equally in white communities. Even more along the lines of delusion, in 1962, nearly 90 percent of whites said black children were treated equally in terms of educational opportunity.[12] All of which is to say that in August 1963, as 200,000 people marched on Washington, and as they stood there in the sweltering heat, listening to Dr. Martin Luther King Jr.'s famous "I Have a Dream" speech, most whites seeing the news that evening were, in effect, thinking to themselves, what's the problem, exactly? Dream? Why dream? Everything is just fine now. Isn't it?

Or consider the 1950s, and the way in which white denial manifested so prominently among the very persons who had been most implicated in the maintenance of white domination. So, for instance, when racist forces in Congress issued their "Southern Manifesto" in response to Supreme Court rulings invalidating racially separate schools, they noted with no apparent misgiving that the push for desegregation was "destroying the amicable relations between the white and Negro races that have been created through 90 years of patient effort by the good people of both races. It has planted hatred and suspicion where there has been heretofore friendship and understanding."[13]

Although modern polling techniques weren't in place in the 1930s one can imagine few whites at that time seeing racism and the oppression of black people as a major concern. Likewise, even at the height of overt white supremacist rule in the United States—during the 1890s, as Black Codes and massive violence against post-emancipation blacks were reaching their zenith[14]—one can read editorials in newspapers all around the South in which it was proclaimed how well whites and blacks got along, and how everything would be just fine if those "yankees" would just stop messing with Dixie. And of course it was in the mid-nineteenth century that a well-respected physician of his day, Dr. Samuel Cartwright, opined that enslaved blacks occasionally ran away due to a mental illness, drapetomania, which apparently rendered them incapable of fully appreciating just how good they had it. In short, at no point in American history have whites, by and large, believed that folks of color were getting a raw deal. That we were wrong in every generation prior to the current one in holding such a rosy and optimistic view apparently gives most whites little pause. And so we continue

to reject claims of racism as so much whining, as "playing the race card" or some such thing, never wondering, even for a second, how a bunch who have proven so utterly inept at discerning the truth for hundreds of years can at long last be trusted to accurately intuit other people's reality. . . .

DISCUSSION QUESTIONS

1. What can we reasonably infer about white Americans' racial attitudes from Barack Obama's presidential victory?
2. Is Wise's evidence for the nature and persistence of white denial compelling?

NOTES

1. Jessie Daniels, "Ground Game in PA: Anti-Racist Organizing," *RacismReview.com,* November 5, 2008. Also, this author consulted with the Obama campaign in Ohio a few months before the election, specifically on how to address racism encountered by canvassers and phone bankers calling on behalf of Obama in working class communities. That the campaign was open to the suggestion that they couldn't merely "pivot" back to economics when racism was evident, but instead needed to confront it directly (albeit respectfully), suggests that the ability to turn the Obama experience for many volunteers into antiracist training may be stronger than many suspect.
2. I personally received several dozen e-mails during the 2008 campaign from Obama volunteers to the effect that they were often shocked by the extent of the racism they experienced during the campaign, and additionally heard stories to that extent from others across the nation who had worked for Obama, either as canvassers or phone solicitors.
3. "President Elect Obama," *Wall Street Journal,* November 5, 2008, http://online.wsj.com
4. Frank Rich, "In Defense of White Americans," *New York Times,* October 25, 2008.
5. Richard Cohen, "The Election That LBJ Won," *Washington Post,* November 4, 2008: A17.
6. *NBC News* transcript, "Decision 2008," November 4, 2008, 9:00 P.M., LexisNexis News, www6.lexisnexis.com.
7. Matt Bai, "Is Obama the End of Black Politics," *New York Times,* August 6, 2008.
8. Susan Page and William Risser, "Poll: Racial divide narrowing but persists" *USA Today,* July 23, 2008.
9. CNN/Essence Poll, July 23, 2008, CNN *Politics.com.*
10. New York Times/CBS Poll, *NYTimes.com,* July 15, 2008.

11. Paul Steinhauser, "In poll, African Americans say election a 'dream come true,'" *CNN Politics.com*, November 11, 2008.

12. The Gallup Organization, Gallup Poll Social Audit, Black-White Relations in the United States, 2001 Update (July 10, 2001), 7–9.

13. Joe R. Feagin, *Systemic Racism: A Theory of Oppression* (NY: Routledge, 2006), 166–167.

14. In the post-emancipation South, Black Codes restricted where African Americans could live and work, in such a way as to virtually re-establish enslavement. In combination with vagrancy laws that essentially defined blacks without jobs or money as criminals and then leased them out to plantation owners and other commercial interests to "work off" their "crimes," these codes formed the backbone of late-nineteenth-century white supremacy. Additionally, massive violence against blacks swept the nation in the wake of emancipation. According to testimony in Congress, read into the equivalent of the Congressional Record at the time, literally tens of thousands of blacks were murdered in the first few years after emancipation: this on top of the several thousand whose deaths are recorded in official lynching records from the 1890s onward. For detailed analyses of post-emancipation oppression and violence see, Douglas A. Blackmon, **Slavery by Another Name: The Re-Enslavement of Black Americans from the Civil War to World War Two** (NY: Doubleday, 2008), and James Clarke, **The Lineaments of Wrath: Race, Violent Crime, and American Culture** (Transaction Publishers, 2001).

READING 39

The Model Minority: Asian American "Success" as a Race Relations Failure

Frank Wu

Student: "Asians are threatening our economic future. . . . We can see it right here in our own school. Who are getting into the best colleges, in disproportionate numbers? Asian kids! It's not fair."

Teacher: "Uh . . . That certainly was an unusual essay. . . . Unfortunately, it's racist."

Frank Wu is chancellor, dean, and law professor at Hastings College of Law in San Francisco, California.

Student: "Um . . . are you sure? My parents helped me."

Garry Trudeau
Recycled Doonesbury: Second
Thoughts on a Gilded Age

REVENGE OF THE NERDS

I am not the model minority. Before I can talk about Asian American experiences at all, I have to kill off the model minority myth because the stereotype obscures many realities. I am an Asian American, but I am not good with computers. I cannot balance my checkbook, much less perform calculus in my head. I would like to fail in school, for no reason other than to cast off my freakish alter ego of geek and nerd. I am tempted to be very rude, just to demonstrate once and for all that I will not be excessively polite, bowing, smiling, and deferring. I am lazy and a loner, who would rather reform the law than obey it and who has no business skills. I yearn to be an artist, an athlete, a rebel, and, above all, an ordinary person.

I am fascinated by the imperviousness of the model minority myth against all efforts at debunking it. I am often told by nice people who are bewildered by the fuss, "You Asians are all doing well. What could you have to complain about anyway? Why would you object to a positive image?" To my frustration, many people who say with the utmost conviction that they would like to be color blind revert to being color conscious as soon as they look at Asian Americans, but then shrug off the contradiction. They are nonchalant about the racial generalization, "You Asians are all doing well," dismissive in asking "What could you have to complain about anyway?" and indifferent to the negative consequences of "a positive image."

Even people who are sympathetic to civil rights in general, including other people of color, sometimes resist mentioning civil rights and Asian Americans together in the same sentence. It is as if Asian American civil rights concerns can be ruled out categorically without the need for serious consideration of the facts, because everyone knows that Asian Americans are prospering.

Consider the term "overachiever." I am reluctant to accept the title for myself, and not out of Asian modesty. To be called an "overachiever" begs the question: What, exactly, is it that individuals have achieved over—what others expected of them or what they deserve?

In either case, overachievers have surprised observers by surpassing the benchmark, and their exploits are not quite right. They will get their comeuppance sooner or later. Applied to an entire racial group, as "overachiever" is to Asian Americans, the implications are troubling. Asian Americans, often thought of as intellectuals, will be consigned to the same fate as intellectuals. As Columbia University historian Richard Hofstadter stated in the opening pages of his *Anti-intellectualism in American Life,* "The resentment from which the intellectual has suffered in our time is a manifestation not of a decline in his position but of his increasing prominence."[1]

And so it is with Asian Americans. "You Asians are all doing well anyway" summarizes the model minority myth. This is the dominant image of Asians in the United States. Ever since immigration reforms in 1965 led to a great influx of Asian peoples, we have enjoyed an excellent reputation. As a group, we are said to be intelligent, gifted in math and science, polite, hard working, family oriented, law abiding, and successfully entrepreneurial. We revere our elders and show fidelity to tradition. The nation has become familiar with the turn-of-the-century Horatio Alger tales of "pulling yourself up by your own bootstraps" updated for the new millennium with an "Oriental" face and imbued with Asian values.

This miracle is the standard depiction of Asian Americans in fact and fiction, from the news media to scholarly books to Hollywood movies. From the 1960s to the 1990s, profiles of whiz kid Asian Americans became so common as to be cliches. In 1971, *Newsweek* magazine observed that we were "outwhiting the whites."[2] *People* magazine one year made celebrities of the five Asian American teenagers who swept the highest prizes in the annual Westinghouse science talent search in an article headlined "Brain Drain Boon for the U.S.," and it

followed up the next year by profiling an entire family of Asian American winners.[3] Brown University history professor Stephen Graubard wrote an op-ed for *The New York Times* asking "Why Do Asian Pupils Win Those Prizes?"[4] The Asian refugee who was a finalist in a spelling bee, but who lost on the word "enchilada," has become legendary.[5] *Time, Newsweek, Sixty Minutes,* and other media outlets have awarded Asian Americans the title "model minority."[6] *Fortune* magazine dubbed us the "superminority."[7] *The New Republic* heralded, "the triumph of Asian Americans" as "America's greatest success story" and *Commentary* magazine referred to Asian Americans as "a trophy population."[8] The *New York Times* announced that we are "going to the head of the class."[9] The *Washington Post* said in a headline, "Asian Americans Outperform Others at School and Work."[10] Smith College sociologist Peter Rose has described Asian Americans as making a transition "from pariahs to paragons."[11] Memoirist Richard Rodriguez and Washington Post columnist William Raspberry have wondered whether Hispanics and blacks, respectively, might be able to emulate Asian immigrants.[12] A minority group could become the equivalent of a white real estate developer: *Advertising Age* quoted a consultant who opined that Asian Americans were "the Donald Trumps of the 1990s."[13]

Conservative politicians especially like to celebrate Asian Americans. President Ronald Reagan called Asian Americans "our exemplars of hope."[14] President George [H.] Bush, California Governor Pete Wilson, House Speaker Newt Gingrich—all have been unduly awed by the model minority myth. In a brief for the *Heritage Foundation Policy Review,* California politician Ron Unz said that Asian Americans come from an "anti-liberal Confucian tradition" that "leaves them a natural constituency for conservatives."[15] In the *National Review,* author William McGurn made the model minority myth a partisan parable: "Precisely because Asian Americans are making it in their adoptive land, they hold the potential not only to add to Republican rolls but to define a bona-fide American language of civil rights."[16]

According to the model minority myth, Asian immigrants have followed the beacon of economic opportunity from their homes in China, Japan, Korea, the Philippines, India, Vietnam, and all the other countries on the Asian continent and within the Pacific Rim. They might be fleeing despotism or Communism, backwardness or the deprivations of war and famine, but whatever the conditions of their past they know that the legend of Golden Mountain, to use the Cantonese phrase, guides their future.

They arrive in America virtually penniless. They bring barely more than the clothes on their backs. Their meager physical possessions are less important than their mental capacity and work ethic. Thanks to their selfless dedication to a small business or an advanced degree in electrical engineering—or both—they are soon achieving the American Dream.

They run a corner grocery in Manhattan, offering the freshest fruits and vegetables and serving up a take-out luncheon buffet priced by the pound. They buy a dry cleaning establishment in Los Angeles, featuring one-hour turnaround times and giving discounts to police officers. They start a motel franchise, which spreads throughout the Midwest, boasting such low rates with amenities like free cable television that other proprietors have no choice but to post signs identifying their accommodations inaccurately as "Native American Owned." They begin a computer chip manufacturing plant in the Silicon Valley, inventing the hottest miniaturized gadgets before selling their shareholdings and retiring at thirty-five. Or they open a boutique in Washington, D.C., with a display case of real-hair wigs on the wall above a bevy of manicurists chatting among themselves in another language while painting their customers' nails. . . .

They come to dominate their trades after less than a decade, reducing their competition to the verge of bankruptcy and then buying up their warehouse stocks. Their associations become monopolies, lending money cooperatively among their own members to preserve their collective advantage. In some cities, they hold more than half the commercial licenses and operate a majority of the downtown "mom and pop"

retail outlets. Hospitals and universities have departments wholly staffed by Asian immigrants. Private industries ranging from automobile manufacturers to software developers to government agencies, such as the Defense Department, depend on them for research and development.

In turn, their American-born progeny continue the tradition with their staggering academic prowess. They start off speaking pidgin, some of them even being held back a grade to adjust. They are willing to do as they are told, changing their given names to Anglicized Christian names chosen with the help of their teachers and their friends and told matter of factly to their parents. Above all, they study, study, study.

They are brought up under the strict tutelage of parents who have sacrificed everything in the hopes that their children will garner more than what they themselves have lost. The parents defer everything for themselves and invest it in their young, giving them the mission of redeeming the family. They maintain that anything less than a straight-A report card will shame the ancestors, and they beat their children for receiving a single B-plus. The elders have faith in the school system. They instill respect for educators. They take their children to weekend language lessons instead of allowing them to watch Saturday morning cartoons on television.

The no-nonsense regimen works wonders. A parade of prodigies named Chang, Nguyen, and Patel takes the prizes at piano recitals and proceeds to graduate from high school with honors as valedictorian, salutatorian, and the rest of the top ten of the class, receiving full scholarships to the Ivy League colleges en route to graduate school and advanced professional training. . . .

In the view of other Americans, Asian Americans vindicate the American Dream. A publicity campaign designed to secure the acceptance of Asian Americans could hardly improve perceptions. They have done better here than they ever could have dreamed of doing in their homelands. They are living proof of the power of the free market and the absence of racial discrimination. Their good fortune flows from individual self-reliance and community self-sufficiency, not civil rights activism or government welfare benefits. They believe that merit and effort pay off handsomely and justly, and so they do. Asian Americans do not whine about racial discrimination; they only try harder. If they are told that they have a weakness that prevents their social acceptance, they quickly agree and earnestly attempt to cure it. If they are subjected to mistreatment by their employer, they quit and found their own company rather than protesting or suing.

This caricature is the portrait of the model minority. It is a parody of itself. . . .

Regrettably, the model minority myth embraced by the pundits and the public alike is neither true nor truly flattering. Instead, it is a stock character that plays multiple roles in our racial drama. Like any other myth forming our collective narrative of race, it is ultimately more revealing than reassuring. Complimentary on its face, the model minority myth is disingenuous at its heart.

As well-meaning as it may be, the model minority myth ought to be rejected for three reasons. First, the myth is a gross simplification that is not accurate enough to be seriously used for understanding 10 million people. Second, it conceals within it an invidious statement about African Americans along the lines of the inflammatory taunt: "They made it; why can't you?" Third, the myth is abused both to deny that Asian Americans experience racial discrimination and to turn Asian Americans into a racial threat.

GERMS OF TRUTH WITHIN THE MYTH

Like many racial stereotypes, the model minority myth has a germ of truth. The problem, however, is that the germ becomes exaggerated and distorted. On its own terms, the myth is not even persuasive as a description of the status of Asian Americans. In earning power, for example, the evidence points toward a disparity between what individual white Americans and what individual Asian Americans are paid—and not for lack of trying on the part of Asian Americans.

To figure out the facts, University of Hawaii sociology professor Herbert Barringer led a team that conducted the most comprehensive review of the research literature ever done. Barringer concludes that with respect to income, "in almost every category . . . whites showed advantages over most Asian Americans."[17]

Barringer proceeds cautiously because he is contesting the model minority myth. Even controlling for nativity—that is, native-born versus foreign-born—Barringer finds that Asian Americans who are native-born earn less money than white Americans who are native-born and possibly even than white Americans who are foreign-born. That means that Asians without cultural and language difficulties may earn less than white Americans who may have such difficulties. Barringer observes that "there seems to be no compelling reason to argue for parity" between Asian Americans and white Americans, but he does agree that Asian Americans "have certainly done much better with incomes than have blacks and Hispanics." He states that Asian Americans, including such ethnic groups as Vietnamese immigrants, might show "decided improvements" over time. He prefers "the most favorable interpretation," that "most Asian Americans are overeducated compared to whites for the incomes they earn."[18]

That interpretation, however, is most favorable to white Americans and not Asian Americans. Translated into practical terms, it means that white Americans are paid more than Asian Americans who are equally qualified. Either Asian Americans are not hired for the higher-paying jobs, or they are hired but are still paid less. . . .

The fact that Asian Americans are better educated than white Americans on average undermines rather than supports the model minority myth. The gap between Asian Americans and white Americans that appears with income reverses itself with education. It was consistent throughout the 1980s and 1990s. In 1980, approximately 36 percent of foreign-born Asian Americans had finished college compared with 16 percent of native-born citizens. In 1990, about 42 percent of Asian Americans had finished college compared with 25 percent of the general population. Every Asian American ethnic group, except Filipinos, attends college at higher rates than do white Americans. Chinese Americans, Indian Americans, and Korean Americans attend college at about twice the rate of white Americans. The entering classes of Ivy League schools are now as high as 20 percent Asian American, California schools such as University of California–Berkeley and UCLA as much as twice that percentage as Asian Americans become a plurality on campuses with no majority. Considering all educational institutions, Asian American overrepresentation is much lower but still significant: As of 1993, Asian Americans made up 5.3 percent of the college student body but approximately 2.9 percent of the general population. Their desire for education is increasing even as that of other groups is decreasing. Between 1979 and 1989, Asian Americans increased their numbers of Ph.D. recipients by 46 percent while whites and blacks decreased their numbers by 6 and 23 percent, respectively. By 1997, Asian Americans were receiving 12 percent of the doctorates conferred by U.S. universities, and they received more than one-quarter of the doctorates in engineering disciplines.

Although the average educational levels of Asian Americans might be taken as substantiating the model minority myth, the more plausible reading is that Asian Americans have had to overcompensate. Asian Americans receive a lower return on investment in education. They gain less money than white Americans on average for each additional degree. . . .

Moreover, Asian immigrants start off relatively privileged. This admission must be made gingerly, so that it will not be taken as corroboration of the model minority myth. In actuality, it undercuts the myth. Most Asian Americans are not rich. But some Asian immigrants are relatively fortunate compared to the many Asians who reside in Asia, and some of them are relatively fortunate compared to native-born Americans (including, incidentally, native-born Asian Americans), even though they have not had an easy time of it in coming to the United

States and even though they experience prejudice. A major study of diversity in the power elite found that almost none of the Chinese Americans who served on the boards of directors for Fortune 1000 companies were "authentic bootstrappers."[19] Almost all of them had come from well-to-do families in China, Taiwan, and Hong Kong.

University of California at Santa Cruz sociologist Deborah Woo examined more closely the media coverage of "a Korean-born immigrant who once worked the night shift at 7-Eleven to put himself through school" and who sold his company for $1 billion, as well as another Korean-born immigrant, a Silicon Valley entrepreneur who lived on ramen noodles and had to pawn his belongings to pay his phone bill, but gave $15 million to the San Francisco Asian Art Museum, "mak[ing] Horatio Alger look like a slacker."[20] Woo delved into the backgrounds of these examples of the model minority myth. In the former instance, the individual was able to start his company because he had received a government contract through a minority set-aside program. In the latter, the man was descended from the royal family that ruled Korea until the Japanese takeover of 1905, and he had been a university professor and an executive in the family business in Korea before emigrating. They are still impressive people, but they have not come from the ghetto. The sheen comes off the model minority myth once the real stories are revealed.

Asian immigrants personify "brain drain": the selective nature of immigration. More than half of the professional immigrants to the United States are Asian; Asian men are well over a majority of the professional immigrants in technical occupations. Indian doctors are the single largest ethnic group in the medical profession in this country, at about 4 percent of the total number of physicians; 11 percent of Indian men in the United States and 7 percent of Indian women hold medical degrees. Filipina women are over half the total number of registered nurses who were trained abroad; thousands more come every year. In 1990, 20 percent of all Filipino Americans listed their area of employment as health care. For many

Asian ethnicities in the United States, such as Indians, the earliest cohort of immigrants following immigration policy reforms are the most qualified, and the continuing stream is less elite. Among some Asian ethnicities, such as Filipinos, the foreign-born generally make more money than the native-born. Under restrictive immigration policies, individuals who have skills that are in high demand in the United States have greater opportunities to acquire a green card. . . .

The model minority myth also masks great disparities among Asian ethnic groups. Japanese Americans and Chinese Americans are closest to equality with whites, but Vietnamese Americans and other Southeast Asian refugees languish at the bottom of the economic pyramid, along with blacks. . . .

Finally, the figures for Asian Americans are rendered unreliable by the careless inclusion of Asians who reside in the United States but who are not Asian Americans at all.[21] Hundreds of business executives with Japanese-based multinational companies spend stints of up to a few years here. Their upper-management salaries add to the average Asian American income, but they are no more representative of either Asians overseas or Asian immigrants than a white American vice president of a Fortune 500 company who was an expatriate manager in Europe would be either average of Americans or of Europeans themselves. They are part of a transnational overclass. . . .

Upon anything more than cursory reflection, the model minority myth becomes mystifying. The model minority myth is misleading not only because it takes for granted that racial groups rather than individual persons are the best basis for thinking about human lives, but also because it equates status and conduct. These most pernicious qualities of the myth are hidden in the open. Whatever else might be said about the myth, it cannot be disputed that it is a racial generalization. As such, it contains the premise that people can be arranged by racial group, and, furthermore, that the differences between racial groups are more significant than either the similarities between racial groups

or the differences within them. It makes race the main feature of an individual as well as the leading division among people. . . .

The model minority myth persists, despite violating our societal norms against racial stereotyping and even though it is not accurate. Dozens of amply documented and heavily annotated government studies and scholarly papers, along with a handful of better magazine and newspaper articles supplemented by television segments and public speeches, all intended to destroy the myth, have had negligible effect on popular culture. . . .

The myth has not succumbed to individualism or facts because it serves a purpose in reinforcing racial hierarchies. Asian Americans are as much a "middleman minority" as we are a model minority. We are placed in the awkward position of buffer or intermediary, elevated as the preferred racial minority at the expense of denigrating African Americans. Asian American writers and scholars have not hesitated to call the phenomenon what it is. Novelist Frank Chin has described it as "racist love," contrasting it with "racist hate" of other people of color. DePaul University law professor Sumi Cho has explained that Asian Americans are turned into "racial mascots," giving right-wing causes a novel messenger, camouflaging arguments that would look unconscionably self-interested if made by whites about themselves. University of California at Irvine political scientist Claire Kim has argued that Asian Americans are positioned through "racial triangulation," much as a Machiavellian would engage in political triangulation for maximum advantage. Law professor Mari Matsuda famously declared, "we will not be used" in repudiating the model minority myth.[22]

Whatever the effects are called, Asian Americans become pawns. We are not recognized in our own right but advanced for ulterior motives. Michael S. Greve, a leading advocate against racial remedies, said that the controversy over anti-Asian discrimination could be used to attack affirmative action: It presented "an opportunity to call, on behalf of a racial minority (i.e., the Asian applicants), for an end to discrimination. It was an appeal that, when made on behalf of whites, is politically hopeless and, perhaps, no longer entirely respectable."[23] . . .

BACKLASH FROM THE MYTH

The model minority myth hurts Asian Americans themselves. It is two-faced. Every attractive trait matches up neatly to its repulsive complement, and the aspects are conducive to reversal. If we acquiesced to the myth in its favorable guise, we would be precluded from rejecting its unfavorable interpretations. We would already have accepted the characteristics at issue as inherent.

The turnaround is inevitable during a military crisis or economic downturn. To be intelligent is to be calculating and too clever; to be gifted in math and science is to be mechanical and not creative, lacking interpersonal skills and leadership potential. To be polite is to be inscrutable and submissive. To be hard working is to be an unfair competitor for regular human beings and not a well-rounded, likable individual. To be family oriented is to be clannish and too ethnic. To be law abiding is to be self-righteous and rigidly rule-bound. To be successfully entrepreneurial is to be deviously aggressive and economically intimidating. To revere elders is to be an ancestor-worshipping pagan, and fidelity to tradition is reactionary ignorance.

Asian Americans cannot win by winning. . . .

The model minority myth does more than cover up racial discrimination; it instigates racial discrimination as retribution. The hyperbole about Asian American affluence can lead to jealousy on the part of non-Asian Americans, who may suspect that Asian Americans are too comfortable or who are convinced [that] Asian American gains are their losses. Through the justification of the myth, the humiliation of Asian Americans or even physical attacks directed against Asian Americans become compensation or retaliation. . . .

It would be bad enough if the model minority myth were true. Everyone else would resent Asian Americans for what Asian Americans possess. It is worse that the model minority myth is false. Everyone else resents Asian Americans for

what they believe Asian Americans possess. Other Americans say that their resentment is about riches and not race, but they assume that Asian Americans are rich on the basis of race; there is no escaping that the resentment is racial. Above all, the model minority myth is a case study in the risks of racial stereotypes of any kind. It is the stereotyping itself, not the positive or negative valence it assumes temporarily, that is dangerous. A stereotype confines its subjects. The myth was neither created by nor is it controlled by Asian Americans. It is applied to but not by Asian Americans.

DISCUSSION QUESTIONS

1. Is being a model minority a burden?
2. How would you feel about "positive stereotypes" being applied to a group that you were a member of?

NOTES

1. Richard Hofstadter, 1963. *Anti-intellectualism in American Life*. New York: Knopf, 6.
2. "Success Story: Outwhiting the Whites," *Newsweek*, June 21, 1971, 24.
3. David Grogan, "Brain Drain Boon for the U.S.: Students of Asian-American Families with Rare Genetic Gifts and a Reverence for Learning Sweep a Science Contest for the Nation's High-Schoolers," *People*, April 21, 1986, 30; Mary Shaughnessy, "When the Westinghouse Talent Scout Dealt Out Their Awards, They Gave the Kuos a Full House," *People*, June 8, 1987, 149.
4. Stephen G. Graubard, "Why Do Asian Pupils Win Those Prizes?" *New York Times*, January 29, 1988, A35.
5. "Minestrone, Ratatouille and Strudel," *Washington Post*, June 14, 1983, A18.
6. David Brand, "The New Whiz Kids: Why Asian Americans Are Doing So Well, and What It Costs Them," *Time*, August 31, 1987, 42; Martin Kasindorf, "Asian Americans: A Model Minority," *Newsweek*, December 6, 1982, 39.
7. Anthony Ramirez, "America's Super Minority," *Fortune*, November 24, 1986, 148.
8. Daniel A. Bell, "The Triumph of Asian Americans: America's Greatest Success Story," *New Republic*, July 15, 1985, 24; Louis Winnick, "America's 'Model Minority,'" *Commentary* (August 1990): 23.
9. Fox Butterfield, "Why Asians Are Going to the Head of the Class: Some Fear Colleges Use Quotas to

PERSONAL ACCOUNT

Let Me Work for It!

I remember once in a sociology of education class that I was asked to describe my educational experience. At first, I was quick to say that it was very positive. Although racial remarks and jokes were passed around school, teachers and administrators paid little or no attention to them. I always felt uneasy with such remarks, but because the teachers and administrators would play ignorant to what was being said, I felt that maybe I was being too sensitive. Therefore, I learned to suck it up and was taught to view such comments as harmless.

Still, at a very young age I was very aware of racism and sexism. Both of my Vietnamese parents came to the United States when they were 20 years old. They arrived right before the Vietnam War ended, which explains the stigmatization they experienced. "VC" was a common epithet addressed to my dad along with "Gook" and "Charlie." My mom, on the other hand, struggled with gender/racial stereotypes such as being labeled mindless, dependent, and subservient. I can recall many times watching people mentally battering my parents. Numerous looks of disgust and intolerance of my parents' accent or confusion with the English language were some unpleasant cases that I experienced. Yet the snide remarks and mistreatment thrown at my parents remain the most hurtful. Many times my parents were told that their lack of proficiency in English would doom them from success and from any self-worth. They were also ostracized for holding on to their Vietnamese culture and were persuaded to assimilate to the American culture. The accumulation of these events reinforced the idea that being different, in this case Vietnamese, was negative. As far as I was concerned, my family was my only community. It was only within my family that I felt the sense of security, love, support, and, most importantly, connection. After all, I was just a "Gook" like my parents.

Yet I experienced support and love at school. I can trace this feeling all the way back to third grade. I remember how I was constantly praised for being so bright, even before turning in my first assignment. This did not send alarms to my brain. As a student, I felt great. I felt validated. But looking back on it now, there are alarms going off for me. Why? Because now I wonder if I was being labeled as a model student, a positive stereotype. Many Americans have held positive stereotypes about Asians and their work/study ethic, and making these stereotypes prior to a person's performance can create the possibility of drowning in the pressure of high expectations. Teachers have always had unreasonably high expectations for me. Although I did not experience this as pressure, I do feel that I have been robbed of the equal chance to prove myself, to see my mistakes and grow. I feel that I have so much to give, but my audience is content with what they "know" of me (which is usually built upon assumptions). I was never given the chance to work for the standing ovation; nor was I given the privilege of criticism.

At the personal level, the model minority stereotype has denied me human dignity, individuality, and the acknowledgment of my own strengths and weaknesses. I feel that I have been prejudged in this fictitious view of Asian Americans. These positive portrayals depict Asians as so flawless that they are robbed of any humanity. Some may feel indifferent to my story or ask if I really reject the positive stereotype. My only reply is this: positive and negative stereotyping are different sides of the same coin. Both invalidate individuals as human beings and lead to negative consequences.

Isabelle Nguyen

Limit Admissions," *New York Times*, August 3, 1986, Educational Supplement, 18.
10. Spencer Rich, "Asian Americans Outperform Others in School and at Work: Census Data Outlines 'Model Minority,'" *Washington Post*, October 10, 1985, A1.
11. Peter I. Rose, *Tempest-Tost: Race, Immigration, and the Dilemmas of Diversity* (New York: Oxford University Press, 1997).
12. Richard Rodriguez, "Asians: A Class by Themselves; A Formal Model for Minority Education," *Los Angeles Times*, October 11, 1987, E1. Among William Raspberry's several articles on Asian Americans are "Asian Americans—Too Successful?" *Washington Post*, February 10, 1990, A23; "The Curse of Low Expectations," *Washington Post*, March 4, 1988, A25; and "When White Guilt Won't Matter," *Washington Post*, November 4, 1987, A23.

13. Alice Z. Cuneo, "Asian Americans: Companies Disoriented about Asians: Fast-Growing but Diverse Market Holds Key to Buying Power," *Advertising Age,* July 9, 1990, S2.

14. Rose, *Tempest-Tost,* 4.

15. Ron K. Unz, "Immigration or the Welfare State: Which Is Our Real Enemy?" *Heritage Foundation Policy Review* (Fall 1994): 33.

16. William McGurn, "The Silent Majority: Asian Americans' Affinity with Republican Party Principles," *National Review,* June 24, 1991, 19. Stuart Rothenberg and William McGurn, "The Invisible Success Story: Asian Americans and Politics," *National Review,* Sept. 15, 1989, 17. After the 2000 Presidential elections, in which Asian Americans supported Gore over Bush, the editor of *National Review* changed his mind about the prospects of Asian Americans belonging to the conservative "investor class" rather than representing the liberal "impact of immigration." John O'Sullivan, "Following the Returns: Investor Class or Immigrant Tide?" *National Review,* Dec. 18, 2000, 30.

17. Herbert R. Barringer, *Asians and Pacific Islanders in the United States* (New York: Russell Sage Foundation, 1993), 265.

18. Ibid., 266–67. *See* U.S. Department of Labor, Federal Glass Ceiling Commission, *A Solid Investment: Making Full Use of the Nation's Human Capital* (Washington, D.C.: Government Printing Office, 1995) and Federal Glass Ceiling Commission, *Good for Business: Making Full Use of the Nation's Human Capital* (Washington, D.C.: Government Printing Office, 1995).

19. Richard L. Zweigenhaft and G. William Domhoff, *Diversity in the Power Elite: Have Women and Minorities Reached the Top?* (New Haven, Conn.: Yale University Press, 1998), 140–57.

20. Deborah Woo, *Glass Ceilings and Asian Americans: The New Fear of Workplace Barriers* (Walnut Creek, Calif.: Alta Mira Press, 2000), 26–30.

21. U.S. Civil Rights Commission, *The Economic Status of Asian Americans* (Washington, D.C.: Government Printing Office, 1988), 86.

22. Frank Chin and Jeffrey Paul Chan, "Racist Love," in Richard Kostelanetz, ed., *Seeing Through the Shuck* (New York: Ballantine, 1972), 65; Sumi Cho, "Redeeming Whiteness in the Shadow of Internment: Earl Warren, Brown, and a Theory of Racial Redemption," *Boston College Law Review* 40 (1988): 120; Clair Jean Kim, "The Racial Triangulation of Asian Americans," in Gordon H. Chang, ed., *Asian Americans and Politics: Perspectives, Experiences, Prospects* (Washington, D.C.: Woodrow Wilson Center/Stanford University Press 2001), 39–78; Mari Matsuda, "We Will Not Be Used: Are Asian Americans the Racial Bourgeoisie?" in *Where Is Your Body* (Boston: Beacon Press, 1996), 149–159. Matsuda delivered the talk at the 1990 dinner of the Asian Law Caucus in San Francisco, California, where she first used the phrase.

23. Michael S. Greve, "The Newest Move in Law Schools' Quota Game," *Wall Street Journal,* October 5, 1992, A12. Recognizing the divisive role Asian Americans being inserted into, the Japanese American Citizens League withdrew its support for proposed legislation attacking affirmative action in 1989. One of the sponsors of the bill had said of the effort: "So, in a way, we want to help Asian Americans, but at the same time we're using it as a vehicle to correct what we consider to be a societal mistake on the part of the United States." Robert W. Stewart, "'Merit Only' College Entry Proposal Failing: Opposition by Japanese Americans to Admissions Policy Change Frustrates GOP Sponsor," *Los Angeles Times,* December 9, 1989, B12.

READING 40

The Gender Revolution: Uneven and Stalled

Paula England

We sometimes call the sweeping changes in the gender system since the 1960s a "revolution." Women's employment increased dramatically (Cotter, Hermsen, and England 2008); birth control became widely available (Bailey 2006); women caught up with and surpassed men in rates of college graduation (Cotter, Hermsen, and Vanneman 2004, 23); undergraduate college majors desegregated substantially (England and Li 2006); more women than ever got doctorates as well as professional degrees in law, medicine, and business (Cotter, Hermsen, and Vanneman 2004, 22–23; England et al. 2007); many kinds of gender discrimination in employment and education became illegal (Burstein 1989; Hirsh 2009); women entered many previously male-dominated occupations (Cotter, Hermsen, and Vanneman 2004, 10–14); and more women were elected to political office (Cotter,

Paula England is a professor of sociology at Stanford University and an affiliate of the Clayman Institute for Gender Research.

Hermsen, and Vanneman 2004, 25). As sweeping as these changes have been, change in the gender system has been uneven—affecting some groups more than others and some arenas of life more than others, and change has recently stalled. My goal in this article is not to argue over whether we should view the proverbial cup as half empty or half full (arguments I have always found uninteresting) but, rather, to stretch toward an understanding of why some things change so much more than others. To show the uneven nature of gender change, I will review trends on a number of indicators. While the shape of most of the trends is not in dispute among scholars, the explanations I offer for the uneven and halting nature of change have the status of hypotheses rather than well-documented conclusions.

I will argue that there has been little cultural or institutional change in the devaluation of traditionally female activities and jobs, and as a result, women have had more incentive than men to move into gender-nontraditional activities and positions. This led to asymmetric change; women's lives have changed much more than men's. Yet in some subgroups and arenas, there is less clear incentive for change even among women; examples are the relatively low employment rates of less educated women and the persistence of traditionally gendered patterns in heterosexual romantic, sexual, and marital relationships.

I also argue, drawing on work by Charles and Bradley, that the type of gender egalitarianism that did take hold was the type most compatible with American individualism and its cultural and institutional logics, which include rights of access to jobs and education and the desideratum of upward mobility and of expressing one's "true self" (Charles 2011; Charles and Bradley 2002, 2009). One form this gender egalitarianism has taken has been the reduction of discrimination in hiring. This has made much of the gender revolution that has occurred possible; women can now enter formerly "male" spheres. But co-occurring with this gender egalitarianism, and discouraging such integration is a strong (if often tacit) belief in gender essentialism—the notion that men and

women are innately and fundamentally different in interests and skills (Charles forthcoming; Charles and Bradley 2002, 2009; Ridgeway 2009). A result of these co-occurring logics is that women are most likely to challenge gender boundaries when there is no path of upward mobility without doing so, but otherwise gender blinders guide the paths of both men and women.

DEVALUATION OF "FEMALE" ACTIVITIES AND ASYMMETRIC INCENTIVES FOR WOMEN AND MEN TO CHANGE

Most of the changes in the gender system heralded as "revolutionary" involve women moving into positions and activities previously limited to men, with few changes in the opposite direction. The source of this asymmetry is an aspect of society's valuation and reward system that has not changed much—the tendency to devalue and badly reward activities and jobs traditionally done by women.

Women's Increased Employment

One form the devaluation of traditionally female activities takes is the failure to treat child rearing as a public good and support those who do it with state payments. In the United States, welfare reform took away much of what little such support had been present. Without this, women doing child rearing are reliant on the employment of male partners (if present) or their own employment. Thus, women have had a strong incentive to seek paid employment, and more so as wage levels rose across the decades (Bergmann 2005). As Figure 1 shows, women's employment has increased dramatically. But change has not been continuous, as the trend line flattened after 1990 and turned down slightly after 2000 before turning up again. This turndown was hardly an "opt-out revolution," to use the popular-press term, as the decline was tiny relative to the dramatic increase across 40 years (Kuperberg and Stone 2008; Percheski 2008). But the stall after 1990 is clear, if unexplained.

FIGURE 1

Percentage of U.S. men and women employed, 1962–2007

Source: Cotter, Hermsen, and Vanneman (2009).

Note: Persons are considered employed if they worked for pay anytime during the year. Refers to adults aged 25 to 54.

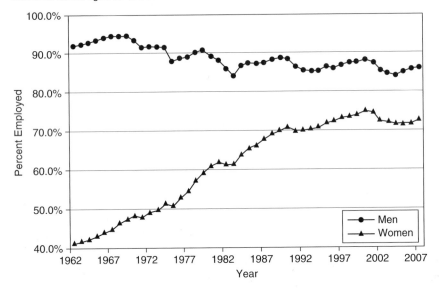

Figure 1 also shows the asymmetry in change between men's and women's employment; women's employment has increased much more than men's has declined. There was nowhere near one man leaving the labor force to become a full-time homemaker for every woman who entered, nor did men pick up household work to the extent women added hours of employment (Bianchi, Robinson, and Milkie 2006). Men had little incentive to leave employment.

Among women, incentives for employment vary. Class-based[1] resources, such as education, affect these incentives. At first glance, we might expect less educated women to have higher employment rates than their better-educated peers because they are less likely to be married to a high-earning man. Most marriages are between two people at a similar education level (Mare 1991), so the less educated woman, if she is married, typically has a husband earning less than the husband of the college graduate. Her family would seem to need the money from her employment more than the family headed by two college graduates. Let us call this the "need for income" effect. But the countervailing "opportunity cost" factor is that well-educated women have more economic incentive for employment because they can earn more (England, Garcia-Beaulieu, and Ross 2004). Put another way, the opportunity cost of staying at home is greater for the woman who can earn more. Indeed, the woman who did not graduate from high school may have potential earnings so low that she could not even cover child care costs with what she could earn. Thus, in typical cases, for the married college graduate, her own education encourages her employment, while her husband's high earnings discourage it. The less educated woman typically has a poor husband (if any), which encourages her employment, while her own low earning power discourages her employment.[2] It is an empirical question whether the "need for income" or "opportunity cost" effect predominates.

Recent research shows that the opportunity-cost effect predominates in the United States and other affluent nations. England, Gornick, and Shafer (2008) use data from 16 affluent countries circa 2000 and show that, in all of them, among women partnered with men (married or cohabiting), those with more education are more likely to be employed. Moreover, there is no monotonic relationship between partner's earnings and a woman's employment; at top levels of his income, her employment is deterred. But women whose male partners are at middle income levels are more likely to be employed than women whose partners have very low or no earnings, the opposite of what the "need for income" principle suggests. . . .

Women Moving into "Male" Jobs and Fields of Study

The devaluation of and underpayment of predominantly female occupations is an important institutional reality that provides incentives for both men and women to choose "male" over "female" occupations and the fields of study that lead to them. Research has shown that predominantly female occupations pay less, on average, than jobs with a higher proportion of men. At least some of the gap is attributable to sex composition because it persists in statistical models controlling for occupations' educational requirements, amount of skill required, unionization, and so forth. I have argued that this is a form of gender discrimination—employers see the worth of predominantly female jobs through biased lenses and, as a result, set pay levels for both men and women in predominantly female jobs lower than they would be if the jobs had a more heavily male sex composition (England 1992; Kilbourne et al. 1994; England and Folbre 2005). While the overall sex gap in pay has diminished because more women have moved into "male" fields (England and Folbre 2005), there is no evidence that the devaluation of occupations because they are filled with women has diminished (Levanon, England, and Allison 2009). Indeed, as U.S. courts have interpreted the law, this type

of between-job discrimination is not even illegal (England 1992, 225–51; Steinberg 2001), whereas it is illegal to pay women less than men in the same job, unless based on factors such as seniority, qualifications, or performance. Given this, both men and women continue to have a pecuniary incentive to choose male-dominated occupations. Thus, we should not be surprised that desegregation of occupations has largely taken the form of women moving into male-dominated fields, rather than men moving into female-dominated fields.

Consistent with the incentives embedded in the ongoing devaluation of female fields, desegregation of fields of college study came from more women going into fields that were predominantly male, not from more men entering "female" fields. Since 1970, women increasingly majored in previously male-dominated, business-related fields, such as business, marketing, and accounting; while fewer chose traditionally female majors like English, education, and sociology; and there was little increase of men's choice of these latter majors (England and Li 2006, 667–69). . . .

Women have also recently increased their representation in formerly male-dominated professional degrees, getting MDs, MBAs, and law degrees in large numbers. Women were 6 percent of those getting MDs in 1960, 23 percent in 1980, 43 percent in 2000, and 49 percent in 2007; the analogous numbers for law degrees (JDs) were 3, 30, 46, and 47 percent, and for MBAs (and other management first-professional degrees), 4, 22, 39, and 44 percent (National Center for Education Statistics 2004–2008). There was no marked increase in the proportion of men in female-dominated graduate professional programs such as library science, social work, or nursing (National Center for Education Statistics 2009).

As women have increasingly trained for previously male-dominated fields, they have also integrated previously male-dominated occupations in management and the professions in large numbers (Cotter, Hermsen, and Vanneman 2004, 10–13). Women may face discrimination and coworker resistance when they attempt to integrate these fields, but they have a strong pecuniary incentive to do so. Men lose money and suffer cultural disapproval when they choose traditionally female-dominated fields; they have little incentive to transgress gender boundaries. While some men have entered female-intensive retail service jobs after losing manufacturing jobs, there is little incentive for voluntary movement in this direction, making desegregation a largely one-way street.

What about employers' incentives? There is some debate about whether, absent equal employment legislation, employers have an incentive to engage in hiring and placement discrimination or are better off simply hiring gender-blind (for debate, see Jackson 1998; England 1992, 54–68). Whichever is true, legal enforcement of antidiscrimination laws has imposed some costs for hiring discrimination (Hirsh 2009), and this has probably reduced discrimination in hiring, contributing to desegregation of jobs.

The "Personal" Realm

"The personal is political" was a rallying cry of 1960s feminists, urging women to demand equality in private as well as public life. Yet conventions embodying male dominance have changed much less in "the personal" than in the job world. Where they have changed, the asymmetry described above for the job world prevails. For example, parents are more likely to give girls "boy" toys such as Legos than they are to give dolls to their sons. Girls have increased their participation in sports more than boys have taken up cheerleading or ballet. Women now commonly wear pants, while men wearing skirts remains rare. A few women started keeping their birth-given surname upon marriage (Goldin and Shim 2004), with little adoption by men of women's last names. Here, as with jobs, the asymmetry follows incentives, albeit nonmaterial ones. These social incentives themselves flow from a largely unchanged devaluation of things culturally defined as feminine. When boys and men take on "female" activities, they often suffer disrespect, but under some circumstances, girls and women gain respect for taking on "male" activities.

What is more striking than the asymmetry of gender change in the personal realm is how little gendering has changed at all in this realm, especially in dyadic heterosexual relationships. It is still men who usually ask women on dates, and sexual behavior is generally initiated by men (England, Shafer, and Fogarty 2008). Sexual permissiveness has increased, making it more acceptable for both heterosexual men and women to have sex outside committed relationships. But the gendered part of this—the double standard—persists stubbornly; women are judged much more harshly than men for casual sex (Hamilton and Armstrong 2009; England, Shafer, and Fogarty 2008). The ubiquity of asking about height in Internet dating Web sites suggests that the convention that men should be taller than their female partner has not budged. The double standard of aging prevails, making women's chances of marriage decrease with age much more than men's (England and McClintock 2009). Men are still expected to propose marriage (Sassler and Miller 2007). Upon marriage, the vast majority of women take their husband's surname. The number of women keeping their own name increased in the 1970s and 1980s but little thereafter, never exceeding about 25 percent even for college graduates (who have higher rates than other women) (Goldin and Shim 2004). Children are usually given their father's surname; a recent survey found that even in cases where the mother is not married to the father, 92 percent of babies are given the father's last name (McLanahan forthcoming). While we do not have trend data on all these personal matters, my sense is that they have changed much less than gendered features of the world of paid work.

The limited change seen in the heterosexual personal realm may be because women's incentive to change these things is less clear than their incentive to move into paid work and into higher-paying "male" jobs. The incentives that do exist are largely noneconomic. For example, women may find it meaningful to keep their birth-given surnames and give them to their children, and they probably enjoy sexual freedom and initiation, especially if they are not judged adversely for it. But these noneconomic benefits may be neutralized by the noneconomic penalties from transgressing gender norms and by the fact that some have internalized the norms. When women transgress gender barriers to enter "male" jobs, they too may be socially penalized for violating norms, but for many this is offset by the economic gain.

CO-OCCURRING LOGICS OF WOMEN'S RIGHTS TO UPWARD MOBILITY AND GENDER ESSENTIALISM

I have stressed that important change in the gender system has taken the form of women integrating traditionally male occupations and fields of study. But even here change is uneven. The main generalization is shown by Figure 2, which divides all occupations by a crude measure of class, calling professional, management, and nonretail sales occupations "middle class," and all others "working class" (including retail sales, assembly work in manufacturing, blue-collar trades, and other non-professional service work). Using the index of dissimilarity to measure segregation, Figure 2 shows that desegregation has proceeded much farther in middle-class than working-class jobs. Middle-class jobs showed dramatic desegregation, although the trend lessened its pace after 1990. By contrast, working-class jobs are almost as segregated as they were in 1950! Women have integrated the previously male strongholds of management, law, medicine, and academia in large numbers. But women have hardly gained a foothold in blue-collar, male-dominated jobs such as plumbing, construction, truck driving, welding, and assembly in durable manufacturing industries such as auto and steel (Cotter, Hermsen, and Vanneman 2004, 12–14). This is roughly the situation in other affluent nations as well (Charles and Grusky 2004). This same class difference in trend can be seen if we compare the degree of segregation among those who have various levels of education; in the United States, sex segregation declined much more dramatically

FIGURE 2

Sex segregation of middle-class and working-class occupations in the United States, 1950–2000

Source: Cotter, Hermsen, and Vanneman (2004, 14).

Note: Middle-class occupations include professional, management, and nonretail sales. All others are classified as working-class occupations.

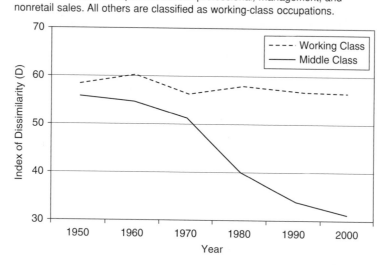

since 1970 for college graduates than any other group (Cotter, Hermsen, and Vanneman 2009, 2004, 13–14).

Why has desegregation been limited to high-level jobs? The question has two parts: why women did not integrate blue-collar male jobs in significant numbers, and why women did integrate professional and managerial jobs in droves. Why one and not the other? Many factors were undoubtedly at work,[3] but I will focus on one account, which borrows from Charles and Bradley (Charles forthcoming; Charles and Bradley 2002, 2009). In the United States and many Western societies today, a certain kind of gender egalitarianism has taken hold ideologically and institutionally. The logic is that individuals should have equal rights to education and jobs of their choice. Moreover, achievement and upward mobility are generally valued. There is also a "postmaterialist" aspect to the culture which orients one to find her or his "true self." The common ethos is a combination of "the American dream" and liberal individualism. Many women, like men, want to "move up" in earnings and/or status, or at least avoid moving down. But up or down relative to what reference group? I suggest that the implicit reference group is typically those in the previous generation (or previous birth cohorts) of one's own social class background and one's own sex. For example, women might see their mothers or aunts as a reference, or women who graduated with their level of education 10 years ago. Persons of the same-sex category are the implicit reference group because of strong beliefs in gender essentialism, that notion that men and women are innately and fundamentally different (Charles forthcoming; Ridgeway 2009). While liberal individualism encourages a commitment to "free choice" gender egalitarianism (such as legal equality of opportunity), ironically, orienting toward gender-typical paths has probably been encouraged by the emerging form of individualism that stresses finding and expressing one's "true self." Notions of self will in fact be largely socially constructed, pulling from socially salient identities. Because of the omnipresent nature of gender in the culture (Ridgeway 2009;

West and Zimmerman 1987), gender often becomes the most available material from which to construct aspirations and may be used even more when a job choice is seen as a deep statement about self (Charles and Bradley 2009).

Given all this, I hypothesize that if women can move "up" in status or income relative to their reference group while still staying in a job typically filled by women, then because of gender beliefs and gendered identities, they are likely to do so. If they cannot move up without integrating a male field, and demand is present and discrimination not too strong, they are more likely to cross the gender boundary. Applying this hypothesis, why would women not enter male blue-collar fields? To be sure, many women without college degrees would earn much more in the skilled blue-collar crafts or unionized manufacturing jobs than in the service jobs typically filled by women at their education levels—jobs such as maid, child care worker, retail sales clerk, or assembler in the textile industry. So they have an economic incentive to enter these jobs. But such women could also move "up" to clerical work or teaching, higher status and better paying but still traditionally female jobs. Many take this path, often getting more education.

In contrast, consider women who assumed they would go to college and whose mothers were in female-dominated jobs requiring a college degree like teacher, nurse, librarian, or social worker. For these women, to move up in status or earnings from their reference group options requires them to enter traditionally male jobs; there are virtually no heavily female jobs with higher status than these female professions. These are just the women, usually of middle-class origins, who have been integrating management, law, medicine, and academia in recent decades. For them, upward mobility was not possible within traditional boundaries, so they were more likely to integrate male fields.

In sum, my argument is that one reason that women integrated male professions and management much more than blue-collar jobs is that the women for whom the blue-collar male jobs would have constituted "progress" also had the option to move up by entering higher-ranking female jobs via more education. They thus had options for upward mobility without transgressing gender boundaries not present for their middle-class sisters. . . .

CONCLUSION

Change in the gender system has been uneven, changing the lives of some groups of people more than others and changing lives in some arenas more than others. Although many factors are at play, I have offered two broad explanations for the uneven nature of change.

First, I argued that, because of the cultural and institutional devaluation of characteristics and activities associated with women, men had little incentive to move into badly rewarded, traditionally female activities such as homemaking or female-dominated occupations. By contrast, women had powerful economic incentives to move into the traditionally male domains of paid employment and male-typical occupations; and when hiring discrimination declined, many did. These incentives varied by class, however; the incentive to go to work for pay is much stronger for women who can earn more; thus employment levels have been higher for well-educated women. I also noted a lack of change in the gendering of the personal realm, especially of heterosexual romantic and sexual relationships.

Second, I explored the consequences of the co-occurrence of two Western cultural and institutional logics. Individualism, encompassing a belief in rights to equal opportunity in access to jobs and education in order to express one's "true self," promotes a certain kind of gender egalitarianism. It does not challenge the devaluation of traditionally female spheres, but it encourages the rights of women to upward mobility through equal access to education and jobs. To be sure, this ideal has been imperfectly realized, but this type of gender egalitarianism has taken hold strongly. But co-occurring with it, somewhat paradoxically, are strong (if tacit) beliefs in gender essentialism—that men and women are innately and fundamentally different in interests and skills (Charles 2011

Charles and Bradley 2002, 2009; Ridgeway 2009). Almost no men and precious few women, even those who believe in "equal opportunity," have an explicit commitment to undoing gender differentiation for its own sake. Gender essentialism encourages traditional choices and leads women to see previous cohorts of women of their social class as the reference point from which they seek upward mobility. I concluded that the co-occurrence of these two logics—equal opportunity individualism and gender essentialism—make it most likely for women to move into nontraditional fields of study or work when there is no possible female field that constitutes upward mobility from the socially constructed reference point. This helps explain why women integrated male-dominated professional and managerial jobs more than blue-collar jobs. Women from working-class backgrounds, whose mothers were maids or assemblers in nondurable manufacturing, could move up financially by entering blue-collar "male" trades but often decide instead to get more education and move up into a female job such as secretary or teacher. It is women with middle-class backgrounds, whose mothers were teachers or nurses, who cannot move up without entering a male-dominated career, and it is just such women who have integrated management, law, medicine, and academia. Yet even while integrating large fields such as academia, women often gravitate toward the more female-typical fields of study.

As sociologists, we emphasize links between parts of a social system. For example, we trace how gender inequality in jobs affects gender inequality in the family, and vice versa (England and Farkas 1986). Moreover, links between parts of the system are recognized in today's prevailing view in which gender is itself a multilevel system, with causal arrows going both ways from macro to micro (Risman 2004). All these links undoubtedly exist, but the unevenness of gender-related change highlights how loosely coupled parts of the social system are and how much stronger some causal forces for change are than others. For example, because it resonated with liberal individualism well, the part of the feminist message that urged giving women equal access to jobs and education made considerable headway and led to much of what we call the gender revolution. But even as women integrated employment and "male" professional and managerial jobs, the part of feminism challenging the devaluation of traditionally female activities and jobs made little headway. The result is persistently low rewards for women who remain focused on mothering or in traditionally female jobs and little incentive for men to make the gender revolution a two-way street.

While discussing the uneven character of gender change, I also noted that the type of gender change with the most momentum—middle-class women entering traditionally male spheres—has recently stalled (Cotter, Hermsen, and Vanneman 2004, 2009). Women's employment rates stabilized, desegregation of occupations slowed down, and desegregation of fields of college study stopped. Erosion of the sex gap in pay slowed as well (Cotter, Hermsen, and Vanneman 2009). While the reason for the stalling is unclear, like the unevenness of change, the stalling of change reminds us how contingent and path-dependent gender egalitarian change is, with no inexorable equal endpoint. Change has been as much unintended consequence of larger institutional and cultural forces as realization of the efforts of feminist organizing, although the latter has surely helped.[4] Indeed, given the recent stalling of change, future feminist organizing may be necessary to revitalize change.

DISCUSSION QUESTIONS

1. What is gender egalitarianism?
2. What stereotypes and double standards still remain for women?

NOTES

1. In this article, I use the term *class* to cover both categoric notions of class and gradational notions of socioeconomic position. Often I use education or occupation as imperfect but readily available indicators of class.
2. A complementary hypothesis about why employment rates are lower for less educated women is that,

compared to women with more education, they place a higher value on motherhood and find less intrinsic meaning in the jobs they can get. In this vein, Edin and Kefalas (2005) argue that low-income women place a higher value on motherhood because they have so few alternative sources of meaning. However, Ferree (1976) found that working-class women were happier if employed; they worked for the money but also gained a sense of competence, connectedness, and self-determination from their jobs. McQuillan et al. (2008) find that neither education nor careerism is associated with the value placed on motherhood. Overall, there is no clear conclusion on class differences in how women value motherhood and jobs.

3. One important additional factor is that blue-collar male jobs have been contracting (Morris and Western 1999), so integrating them would have been more difficult even if women had wanted to do so. Moreover, male coworkers may fight harder to harass and keep women out of blue-collar than professional and managerial jobs; lacking class privilege, blue-collar men may feel a stronger need than more privileged men to defend their gender privilege. Finally, it is possible that the Equal Employment Opportunity Commission had an institutional bias toward bringing cases challenging discrimination in high-level managerial and professional positions, particularly when they became concerned with the "glass ceiling." This could explain why Burstein (1989) found more discrimination cases in high-level jobs.

4. Risman (2009) reminds us that our own teaching has probably had an effect on keeping feminism alive, as today's young feminists often say that the college classroom is where they began to identify as feminists.

REFERENCES

Bailey, Martha J. 2006. More power to the pill: The impact of contraceptive freedom on women's life cycle labor supply. *Quarterly Journal of Economics* 121:289–320.

Bergmann, Barbara. 2005. *The economic emergence of women*. 2nd ed. New York: Basic Books.

Bianchi, Suzanne, John P. Robinson, and Melissa A. Milkie. 2006. *Changing rhythms of American family life*. New York: Russell Sage Foundation.

Burstein, Paul. 1989. Attacking sex discrimination in the labor market: A study in law and politics. *Social Forces* 67:641–65.

Charles, Maria. 2011. A world of difference: International trends in women's economic status. *Annual Review of Sociology*.

Charles, Maria, and Karen Bradley. 2002. Equal but separate: A cross-national study of sex segregation in higher education. *American Sociological Review* 67:573–99.

Charles, Maria, and Karen Bradley. 2009. Indulging our gendered selves: Sex segregation by field of study in 44 countries. *American Journal of Sociology* 114:924–76.

Charles, Maria, and David B. Grusky. 2004. *Occupational ghettos: The worldwide segregation of women and men.* Stanford, CA: Stanford University Press.

Cotter, David A., Joan M. Hermsen, and Paula England. 2008. Moms and jobs: Trends in mothers' employment and which mothers stay home. In *American families: A multicultural reader*, 2nd ed., edited by Stephanie Coontz, with Maya Parson and Gabrielle Raley, 379–86. New York: Routledge.

Cotter, David A., Joan M. Hermsen, and Reeve Vanneman. 2004. *Gender inequality at work.* New York: Russell Sage Foundation.

Cotter, David A., Joan M. Hermsen, and Reeve Vanneman. 2009. End of the gender revolution website, http://www.bsos.umd.edu/socy/vanneman/endofgr/default.html (accessed December 14, 2009).

Edin, Kathryn, and Maria Kefalas. 2005. *Promises I can keep: Why poor women put motherhood before marriage.* Berkeley: University of California Press.

England, Paula 1992. *Comparable worth: Theories and evidence.* New York; Aldine.

England, Paula, Paul Allison, Su Li, Noah Mark, Jennifer Thompson, Michelle Budig, and Han Sun. 2007. Why are some academic fields tipping toward female? The sex composition of U.S. fields of doctoral degree receipt, 1971–2002. *Sociology of Education* 80:23–42.

England, Paula, and George Farkas. 1986. *Households, employment, and gender: A social, economic, and demographic view.* New York: Aldine.

England, Paula, and Nancy Folbre. 2005. Gender and economic sociology. In *The handbook of economic sociology*, edited by N. J. Smelser and R. Swedberg, 627–49. New York: Russell Sage Foundation.

England. Paula, Carmen Garcia-Beaulieu, and Mary Ross. 2004. Women's employment among Blacks, whites, and three groups of Latinas: Do more privileged women have higher employment? *Gender & Society* 18 (4): 494–509.

England, Paula, Janet C. Gornick, and Emily Fitzgibbons Shafer. 2008. Is it better at the top? How women's employment and the gender earnings gap vary by education in sixteen countries. Paper presented at the 2008 annual meeting of the American Sociological Association.

England, Paula, and Su Li. 2006. Desegregation stalled: The changing gender composition of college majors, 1971–2002. *Gender & Society* 20:657–77.

England, Paula, and Elizabeth Aura McClintock. 2009. The gendered double standard of aging in U.S. marriage markets. *Population and Development Review* 35:797–816.

England, Paula, Emily Fitzgibbons Shafer, and Alison C. K. Fogarty. 2008. Hooking up and forming romantic relationships on today's college campuses. In *The gendered society reader*, 3rd ed., edited by Michael Kimmel and Amy Aronson, 531–46. New York: Oxford University Press.

Ferree, Myra Marx. 1976. Working-class jobs: Paid work and housework as sources of satisfaction. *Social Problems* 23 (4):431–41.

Goldin, Claudia, and Maria Shim. 2004. Making a name: Women's surnames at marriage and beyond. *Journal of Economic Perspectives* 18:143–60.

Hamilton, Laura, and Elizabeth A. Armstrong. 2009. Gendered sexuality in young adulthood: Double binds and flawed options. *Gender & Society* 23:589–616.

Hirsh, C. Elizabeth. 2009. The strength of weak enforcement: The impact of discrimination charges on sex and race segregation in the workplace. *American Sociological Review* 74 (2):245–71.

Jackson, Robert Max. 1998. *Destined for equality: The inevitable rise of women's status.* Cambridge, MA: Harvard University Press.

Kilbourne, Barbara Stanek, Paula England, George Farkas, Kurt Beron, and Dorothea Weir. 1994. Returns to skills, compensating differentials, and gender bias: Effects of occupational characteristics on the wages of white women and men. *American Journal of Sociology* 100:689–719.

Kuperberg, Arielle, and Pamela Stone. 2008. The media depiction of women who opt out. *Gender & Society* 2:497–517.

Levanon, Asaf, Paula England, and Paul Allison. 2009. Occupational feminization and pay: Assessing causal dynamics using 1950-2000 census data. *Social Forces* 88:865–92.

Mare, Robert D. 1991. Five decades of educational assortative mating. *American Sociological Review* 56:15–32.

McLanahan, Sara. Forthcoming. Children in fragile families. In *Families in an unequal society*, edited by Marcia Carlson and Paula England. Stanford, CA: Stanford University Press.

McQuillan, Julia, Arthur L. Greil, Karina M. Shreffler, and Veronica Tichenor. 2008. The importance of motherhood among women in the contemporary United States. *Gender & Society* 22:477–96.

Morris, Martina, and Bruce Western. 1999. Inequality in earnings at the close of the twentieth century. *Annual Review of Sociology* 25:623–57.

National Center for Education Statistics. 1971–2003. *Digest of education statistics.* Washington, DC: Government Printing Office.

National Center for Education Statistics. 2004–2007. Table numbers by year: 2004: 253, 2005: 252, 2006: 58, 2007: 264, 2008: 279. http://nces.ed.gov/programs/digest (accessed December 14, 2009).

Percheski, Christine. 2008. Opting out? Cohort differences in professional women's employment rates from 1960 to 2000. *American Sociological Review* 73:497–517.

Ridgeway, Cecilia L. 2009. Framed before we know it: How gender shapes social relations. *Gender & Society* 23:145–60.

Risman, Barbara J. 2004. Gender as a social structure: Theory wrestling with activism. *Gender & Society* 18:429–50.

Risman, Barbara J. 2009. From doing to undoing: Gender as we know it. *Gender & Society* 23:81–84.

Sassler, Sharon, and Amanda Miller. 2007. Waiting to be asked: Gender, power and relationship progression among cohabiting couples. Presented at the annual meeting of the American Sociological Association, New York, August.

Steinberg, Ronnie J. 2001. Comparable worth in gender studies. In *International encyclopedia of the social and behavioral sciences*, vol. 4, edited by Neil J. Smelser and Paul B, Baltes. Cambridge: Cambridge University Press.

West, Candace, and Donald H. Zimmerman. 1987. Doing gender. *Gender & Society* 1:125–51.

LAW, PUBLIC POLICY, AND ECONOMY

READING 41

Thirteen Key Supreme Court Cases and the Civil War Amendments

Individuals' lives are affected not only by social practices but also by law as interpreted in the courts. Under U.S. federalism, Congress makes laws, the president swears to uphold the law, and the Supreme Court interprets the law. When state laws appear to be in conflict with the United States Constitution or when the terminology of the Constitution is vague, the Supreme Court interprets such laws. We will focus here on Supreme Court rulings that have defined the roles individuals are allowed to assume in American society.

As the supreme law above laws enacted by Congress, the U.S. Constitution determines individual and group status. A brief document, the Constitution describes the division of power between the federal and state governments, as well as the rights of individuals. Only 16 amendments to the Constitution have been added since the ratification of the Bill of Rights (the first 10 amendments). Although the Constitution appears to be sweeping in scope—relying on the principle that all men are created equal—in reality it is an exclusionary document. It omitted women, Native Americans, and African Americans except for the purpose of determining a population count. In instances where the Constitution was vague on the rights of

each of these groups, clarification was later sought through court cases.

Federalism provides four primary methods by which citizens may influence the political process. First, the Constitution grants citizens the right to petition the government, that is, the right to lobby. Second, as a civic duty, citizens are expected to vote and seek office. Once in office, citizens can change conditions by writing new legislation, known as *statutory law*. Third, changes can be achieved through the lengthy procedure of passing constitutional amendments, which affect all citizens. Controversial amendments have often become law after social movement activists advocated passage for several years or after a major national upheaval, such as the Civil War.

Last, the Constitution provides that citizens can sue to settle disputes. Through this method, sweeping social changes can take place when Supreme Court decisions affect all the individuals in a class. Thus, the assertion of individual rights has become a key tool of those who were not privileged by the Constitution to clarify their status in American society.

An examination of landmark cases reveals the continuous difficulties some groups have had in securing their rights through legal remedy. The Court has often taken a narrow perspective on which classes of people were to receive equal protection of the law or were covered under the privileges and immunities clause.[1] Each group had to bring suit in every area where barriers existed. For example, white women who were citizens had to sue to establish that they had the right to inherit property, to serve on juries, to enter various professions, and in general to be treated as a class apart from their husband and family. Blacks sued to attend southern state universities and law schools, to participate in the all-white Democratic Party primary election,[2] to attend public schools that had been ordered to desegregate by the Supreme Court, and to vote without having to pay a poll tax. When these landmark cases were decided, they were perceived to herald sweeping changes in policy. Yet they proved to be only a guide to determining the rights of individuals.

I. *DRED SCOTT V. SANFORD* (1857)

Before the Civil War, the Constitution was not precise on whether one was simultaneously a citizen of a given state and of the entire United States. Slavery further complicated the matter because the status of slaves and free persons of color was not specified in the Constitution, nor were members of either group considered citizens. Each state had the option of determining the status and rights of these nonwhites.

A federal form of government permitted flexibility by allowing states to differ on matters such as rights for its citizens. Yet as it was a newly invented form of government, a number of issues that were clear under British law were not settled until the Thirteenth, Fourteenth, and Fifteenth Amendments were added to the United States Constitution. Federalism raised questions about rights and privileges because a citizen was simultaneously living under the laws of a state and of the United States. Who had rights and privileges guaranteed by the Constitution? Did all citizens have all rights and privileges?

For example, what was the status of women? The Constitution provided for citizenship, but it did not specify which rights and privileges were granted to female citizens. State laws considered white men and white women citizens, yet white women were often not allowed to own property, sue in court, or vote. Under federalism, each state

enacted laws determining the rights and status of free blacks, slaves, white men, and white women so long as the laws did not conflict with the United States Constitution.

The *Dred Scott* case of 1846 considered the issues of slavery, property, citizenship, and the supremacy of the United States over individual states when a slave was taken to a free territory. The Court's holding primarily affected blacks, now called African Americans,[3] who sought the benefits of citizenship. Broadly, the case addressed American citizenship, a matter not clearly defined until passage of the Fourteenth Amendment in 1868.

Dred Scott was an enslaved man owned by Dr. John Emerson, a U.S. Army surgeon stationed in Missouri. When Emerson was transferred to Rock Island, Illinois, where slavery was forbidden, he took Dred Scott with him. Emerson was subsequently transferred to Fort Snelling, a territory (now Minnesota) where slavery was forbidden by the Missouri Compromise of 1820. In 1838, he returned to Missouri with Dred Scott.

In 1846, Scott brought suit in a Missouri circuit court to obtain his freedom on the grounds he had resided in free territory for periods of time. Scott won the case and his freedom. However, the judgment was reversed by the Missouri Supreme Court. Later, when Emerson's brother-in-law, John Sanford—who was a citizen of New York—arranged for the sale of Scott, the grounds were established for Scott to take his case to the federal circuit court in Missouri. The federal court ruled that Scott and his family were slaves and therefore the "lawful property" of Sanford. With the financial assistance of abolitionists, Scott appealed his case to the Supreme Court.

The Court's decision addressed these key questions:

1. Are blacks citizens?
2. Are blacks entitled to sue in court?
3. Can one have all the privileges and immunities of citizenship in a state, but not the United States?
4. Can one be a citizen of the United States and not be qualified to vote or hold office?

Excerpts from the Supreme Court Decision in *Dred Scott v. Sanford*[4]

Mr. Chief Justice Taney delivered the opinion of the Court:

... The question is simply this: Can a Negro, whose ancestors were imported into this country and sold as slaves, become a member of the political community formed and brought into existence by the Constitution of the United States, and as such become entitled to all the rights, and privileges and immunities, guaranteed by that instrument to the citizen? One of which rights is the privilege of suing in a court of the United States. ...

The question before us is whether the class of persons described are constituent members of this sovereignty? We think they are not, and that they are not included, and were not intended to be included, under the word "citizens" in the Constitution, and can therefore claim none of the rights and privileges which that instrument provides for and secures to citizens of the United States.

In discussing this question, we must not confound the rights of citizenship which a State may confer within its own limits and the rights of citizenship as a member of the Union. It does not by any means follow, because he has all the rights and privileges of a citizen of a State, that he must be a citizen of the United States. He may have all of the rights and privileges of a citizen of a State, and yet not be entitled to the rights and privileges of a citizen in any other State. ...

Undoubtedly a person may be a citizen . . . although he exercises no share of the political power, and is incapacitated from holding particular office. Those who have not the necessary qualifications cannot vote or hold the office, yet they are citizens.

The court is of the opinion, that . . . Dred Scott was not a citizen of Missouri within the meaning of the Constitution of the United States, and not entitled as such to sue in its courts: and, consequently, that the Circuit Court had no jurisdiction. ...

II. THE CIVIL WAR AMENDMENTS

The Civil War (1861–1865) was fought over slavery, as well as the issue of supremacy of the national government over the individual states.

After the Civil War, members of Congress known as the Radical Republicans sought to protect the freedom of the former slaves by passing the Thirteenth, Fourteenth, and Fifteenth Amendments. These amendments, especially the Fourteenth, have provided the foundation for African Americans— as well as women, gays, Native Americans, immigrants, and those who are disabled—to bring suit for equal treatment under the law.

Amendment XIII, 1865

(Slavery)

This amendment prohibited slavery and involuntary servitude in the United States. The entire amendment follows:

Section 1. Neither slavery nor involuntary servitude, except as a punishment whereof the party shall have been duly convicted, shall exist within the United States, or any place subject to their jurisdiction.

Section 2. Congress shall have power to enforce this article by appropriate legislation.

Amendment XIV, 1868

(Citizenship, Due Process, and Equal Protection of the Laws)

This amendment defined citizenship; prohibited the states from making or enforcing laws that abridged the privileges or immunities of citizenship; forbade states to deprive persons of life, liberty, or property without due process of law; and forbade states to deny equal protection of the law to any person. Over time, the Fourteenth Amendment became the most important of the Reconstruction amendments. Key phrases such as "privileges and immunities," "deprive any person of life, liberty, or the pursuit of justice," and "deny to any person within its jurisdiction equal protection of the law" have caused this amendment to be the subject of more Supreme Court cases than any other provision of the Constitution. The entire amendment follows:

Section 1. All persons born or naturalized in the United States, and subject to the jurisdiction thereof, are citizens of the United States and of the State wherein they reside. No State shall make or enforce any law which shall abridge the privileges or immunities of citizens of the United States; nor shall any State deprive any person of life, liberty, or property, without due process of law; nor deny to any person within its jurisdiction the equal protection of the laws.

Section 2. Representatives shall be apportioned among the several States according to their respective numbers, counting the whole number of persons in each State, excluding Indians not taxed. But when the right to vote at any election for the choice of electors for President and Vice President of the United States, Representatives in Congress, the Executive and Judicial officers of a State, or the members of the Legislature thereof, is denied to any of the male inhabitants of such State, being twenty-one years of age, and citizens of the United States, or in any way abridged, except for participation in rebellion, or other crime, the basis of representation therein shall be reduced in proportion which the number of such male citizens shall bear to the whole number of male citizens twenty-one years of age in such State.

Section 3. No person shall be a Senator or Representative in Congress, or elector or President and Vice President, or hold any office, civil or military, under the United States, or under any State, who, having previously taken an oath, as a member of Congress, or as an officer of the United States, or as a member of any State legislature, or as an executive or judicial officer of any State, to support the Constitution of the United States, shall have engaged in insurrection or rebellion against the same, or given aid or comfort to the enemies thereof. But Congress may by a vote of two-thirds of each House, remove such disability.

Section 4. The validity of the public debt of the United States, authorized by law, including debts incurred for payments of pensions and bounties for services in suppressing insurrection or rebellion, shall not be questioned. But neither the United States nor any State shall assume or pay any debt or obligation incurred in aid of insurrection or rebellion against the United States, or any claim for the loss or emancipation of any slave, but all such debts, obligations and claims shall be held illegal and void.

Section 5. The Congress shall have power to enforce, by appropriate legislation, the provisions of this article.

Amendment XV, 1870
(The Right to Vote)

The entire amendment follows:

Section 1. The right of citizens of the United States to vote shall not be denied or abridged by the United States or by any State on account of race, color, or previous condition of servitude.

Section 2. The Congress shall have power to enforce this article by appropriate legislation.

As we have seen, the Thirteenth, Fourteenth, and Fifteenth Amendments were added to the Constitution expressly with former slaves in mind. In Section 1 of the Fourteenth Amendment, the definition of *citizenship* was clarified and granted to blacks. In the Fifteenth Amendment, black males, former slaves, were granted the right to vote. For women, however, the situation was different.

During the 19th century, there was no doubt that white females were U.S. citizens, but their rights as citizens were unclear. For example, although they were citizens, women were not automatically enfranchised. Depending on state laws, they were barred from owning property, holding office, or voting. The 1872 case of *Bradwell v. The State of Illinois* specifically tested whether women as United States citizens had the right to become members of the bar. More generally, it addressed whether the rights of female citizens included the right to pursue any employment.

III. *MINOR V. HAPPERSETT* (1875)

The Fifteenth Amendment was not viewed as a triumph for women because it specifically denied them the vote. Section 2 of the Fourteenth Amendment for the first time made reference to males as citizens. Since black men were included but women of all races were omitted, women were left to continue to seek changes through the courts. This was a difficult route, because in subsequent cases, judges often held a narrow view that the legislators wrote the amendment only with black males in mind. Thus, a pattern was soon established in which white women followed black men and women in asserting their rights as citizens, as seen in the 1875 case of *Minor v. Happersett.* In *Dred Scott*, the question was whether Scott was a citizen; in *Minor*, the question was whether *Minor* as a citizen had the right to vote. In both cases, the Supreme Court said no.

Virginia Minor, a native-born, free, white citizen of the United States and the state of Missouri, and over the age of 21 wished to vote for president, vice president, and members of Congress in the election of November 1872. She applied to the registrar of voters but was not allowed to vote because she was not a "male citizen of the United States." As a citizen of the United States, Minor sued under the privileges and immunities clause of the Fourteenth Amendment.

The Court's decision addressed these key questions:

1. Who is covered under the term *citizen?*
2. Is suffrage one of the privileges and immunities of citizenship?
3. Did the Constitution, as originally written, make all citizens voters?
4. Did the Fifteenth Amendment make all citizens voters?
5. Can a state confine voting to only male citizens without violating the Constitution?

Although women were citizens of the United States and of the state where they resided, they did not automatically possess all the privileges granted to male citizens, such as suffrage. This landmark case was not overturned until the passage of the Nineteenth Amendment, which enfranchised women, in 1920.[5]

Excerpts from the Supreme Court Decision in *Minor v. Happersett*[6]

Mr. Chief Justice Waite delivered the opinion of the Court:

. . . It is contended [by Minor's counsel] that the provisions of the Constitution and laws of the State of Missouri which confine the right of suffrage and registration therefore to men, are in violation of the Constitution of the United States, and therefore void. The argument is, that as a woman, born or naturalized in the United States and subject to the jurisdiction thereof as a citizen of the United States and of the State in which she resides, she has the right of suffrage as one of the privileges and immunities of her citizenship, which the State cannot by its laws or Constitution abridge.

There is no doubt that women may be citizens. . . .

. . . From this it is apparent that from the commencement of the legislation upon this subject alien women and alien minors could be made citizens by naturalization, and we think it will not be contended that . . . native women and native minors were already citizens by birth.

. . . More cannot be necessary to establish the fact that sex has never been made one of the elements of citizenship in the United States. In this respect men have never had an advantage over women. The same laws precisely apply to both. The Fourteenth amendment did not affect the citizenship of women any more than it did of men . . . therefore, the rights of Mrs. Minor do not depend upon the amendment. She has always been a citizen from her birth, and entitled to all the privileges and immunities of citizenship. The amendment prohibited the State, of which she is a citizen, from abridging any of her privileges and immunities as a citizen of the United States. . . .

. . . The direct question is, therefore, presented whether all citizens are necessarily voters.

The Constitution does not define the privileges and immunities of citizens. For that definition we must look elsewhere.

. . . The [Fourteenth] amendment did not add to the privileges and immunities of a citizen. It simply furnished an additional guaranty for the protection of such as he already had. No new voters were necessarily made by it.

. . . No new State has ever been admitted to the Union which has conferred the right of suffrage upon women, and this has never been considered a valid objection to her admission. . . .

. . . Certainly, if the courts can consider any question settled, this is one. For nearly ninety years the people have acted upon the idea that the Constitution, when it conferred citizenship, did not necessarily confer the right of suffrage. . . . Our province is to decide what the law is, not to declare what it should be.

The *Dred Scott*, *Bradwell*, and *Minor* cases point to the similarity in the status of black men and women of all races in 19th-century America. As one judicial scholar noted, race and sex were comparable classes, distinct from all others. Historically, these "natural classes" were considered permanent and unchangeable.[7] Thus, both slavery and the subjugation of women have been described as a caste system where one's status is fixed from birth and not alterable based on wealth or talent.[8]

Indeed, the connection between the enslavement of black people and the legal and social standing of women was often traced to the Old Testament. Historically, slavery was justified on the grounds that one should look to Abraham; the Bible refers to Abraham's wives, children, men servants, maid servants, camels, and cattle as his property. A man's wife and children were considered his slaves. By the logic of the 19th century, if women were slaves, why shouldn't blacks be also?

Thus, the concepts of race and sex have been historically linked. Since "the doctrines were developed by the same people for the same purpose it is not surprising to find anti-feminism to be an echo of racism, and vice versa."[9]

Additional constitutional amendments were necessary if women and African Americans were to exercise the privileges of citizenship that were automatically granted to white males. Nonetheless, even after amendments were enacted, African Americans still had to fight for enforcement of the law.

IV. *PLESSY V. FERGUSON* (1896)

After the Civil War, the northern victors imposed military rule on the South.[10] White landowners and former slaveholders often found themselves with unproductive farmland and no free laborers. Aside from the economic loss of power, white males were in a totally new political environment: Black men had been elevated to citizens; former slaves were now eligible to vote, run for office, and hold seats in the state or national legislature. To ensure the rights of former slaves, the U.S. Congress passed the Civil War Amendments and provided federal troops to oversee federal elections.

However, when federal troops were withdrawn from the southern states in 1877, enfranchised black men became vulnerable to former masters who immediately seized political control of the state legislatures. In order to solidify political power, whites rewrote state constitutions to disenfranchise black men. To ensure that all blacks were restricted to a subordinate status, southern states systematically enacted "Jim Crow" laws, rigidly segregating society into black and white communities. These laws barred blacks from using the same public facilities as whites, including schools, hospitals, restaurants, hotels, and recreation areas. With the cooperation of southern elected officials, the Ku Klux Klan, a white supremacist, terrorist organization, grew in membership. The return of political power to whites without any federal presence to protect the black community set the stage for "separate but equal" legislation to become a constitutionally valid racial doctrine.

Under slavery, interracial sexual contact was forbidden, but white masters nonetheless had the power to sexually exploit the black women who worked for them. The children of these relationships, especially if they looked white, posed potential inheritance problems because whites feared that such children might seek to exercise the privileges accorded to their white fathers. In order to keep all children of such relationships subordinate in the two-tiered racial system, descent was based on the race of the mother. Consequently, regardless of color, all the children of black women were defined as black.

This resulted in a rigid biracial structure where all persons with "one drop" of black blood were labeled black. Consequently, the "black" community consisted of a wide range of skin color based on this one-drop rule. Therefore, at times individuals with known black ancestry might look phenotypically white. This situation created a group of African Americans who had one-eighth or less African ancestry.

Louisiana was one of the few states to modify the one-drop rule of racial categorization because it considered mulattoes a valid racial category. A term derived from Spanish, *mulatto* refers to the offspring of a "pure African Negro" and a "pure white." Over time, *mulatto* came to encompass children of whites and "mixed Negroes."

These were the social conditions in 1896, when Homer Adolph Plessy, a mulatto, sought to test Louisiana laws that imposed racial segregation. Plessy and other mulattoes decided to test the applicability of the law requiring racial separation on railroad cars traveling in interstate transportation.

In 1890, Louisiana had followed other southern states in enacting Jim Crow laws that were written in compliance with the Equal Protection Clause of Section 1 of the Fourteenth Amendment. These laws required separate accommodations for white and black railroad passengers. In this case, Plessy, a U.S. citizen and a resident of Louisiana who was one-eighth black, paid for a first-class ticket on the East Louisiana Railway traveling from New Orleans to Covington, Louisiana. When he entered the passenger train, Plessy took a vacant seat in a coach designated for white passengers. He claimed that he was entitled to every "recognition, right, privilege, and immunity" granted to white citizens of the United States by the Constitution. Under Louisiana law, the conductor, who knew Plessy, was required to ask him to sit in a coach specifically assigned to nonwhite persons. By law, passengers who sat in the inappropriate coach were fined or imprisoned. When Plessy refused to comply with the order, he was removed from the train and imprisoned.

The decision in *Plessey v. Ferguson* established that separation of the races was legal under the U.S. constitution, it solidified the power of whites over blacks in southern states. Through state laws, and with the additional federal weight in the *Plessy* decision, whites began to enforce rigid separation of the races in every aspect of life.

In *Plessy*, Justice John Marshall Harlan wrote the only dissenting opinion. Usually in Supreme Court cases, attention is focused on the majority, rather than the dissenting opinion. However, in this case Justice Harlan's dissent is noteworthy because his views on race and citizenship pointed out a line of reasoning that eventually broke down segregation and second-class citizenship for blacks.

Justice Harlan's background as a Kentucky slaveholder who later joined the Union side during the Civil War is cited as an explanation of his views. Some scholars speculate that his shift from slaveholder to a defender of the rights of blacks was caused by his observation of beatings, lynchings, and the use of intimidation tactics against blacks in Kentucky after the Civil War. In a quirk of history, when *Plessy v. Ferguson* was overturned in 1954 by a unanimous opinion in *Brown v. Board of Education*, Justice Harlan's grandson was a member of the Supreme Court.

The Court's decision addressed these key questions:

1. How is a black person defined?
2. Who determines when an individual is black or white?
3. Does providing separate but equal facilities violate the Thirteenth Amendment?
4. Does providing separate but equal facilities violate the Fourteenth Amendment?
5. Does a separate but equal doctrine imply inferiority of either race?
6. Can state laws require the separation of the two races in schools, theaters, and railway cars?
7. Does the separation of the races when applied to commerce within the state of Louisiana abridge the privileges and immunities of the "colored man,"[11] deprive him of equal protection of the law, or deprive him of his property without due process of law under the Fourteenth Amendment?

Excerpts from the Supreme Court Decision in *Plessy v. Ferguson*[12]

Mr. Justice Brown delivered the opinion of the Court:

> . . . An [1890] act of the General Assembly of the State of Louisiana, provid[ed] for separate railway carriages for the white and colored races.

. . . No person or persons, shall be admitted to occupy seats in coaches, other than the ones assigned to them on account of the race they belong to.

. . . The constitutionality of this act is attacked upon the ground that it conflicts both with the Thirteenth Amendment of the Constitution, abolishing slavery, and the Fourteenth Amendment, which prohibits certain restrictive legislation.

. . . A statute which implied merely a legal distinction between the white and colored races . . . has no tendency to destroy the legal equality of the two races, or reestablish a state of servitude.

. . . The object of the amendment [the Fourteenth Amendment] was undoubtedly to enforce the absolute equality of the two races before the law, but in the nature of things it could not have been intended to abolish distinctions based upon color, or a commingling of the two races upon terms unsatisfactory to either.

Laws permitting and even requiring their separation in places where they are liable to be brought into contact do not necessarily imply the inferiority of either race to the other, and have been generally, if not universally recognized as within the competency of the state legislatures in the exercise of their police power. The most common instance of this is connected with the establishment of separate schools for white and colored children, which has been held to be a valid exercise of the legislative power even by courts of States where the political rights of the colored race have been longest and most earnestly enforced. One of the earliest of these cases is that of *Roberts v. City of Boston*, 5 Cush. 198, in which the Supreme Judicial Court of Massachusetts held that the general school committee of Boston had power to make provision for the instruction of colored children in separate schools established exclusively for them, and to prohibit their attendance upon the other schools.

. . . We are not prepared to say that the conductor, in assigning passengers to the coaches according to their race, does not act at his peril. . . . The power to assign to a particular coach obviously implies the power to determine to which race the passenger belongs, as well as the power to determine who, under the laws of the particular State, is to be deemed a white, and who is a colored person.

. . . We consider the underlying fallacy of the plaintiff's argument to consist in the assumption that the enforced separation of the two races stamps the colored race with a badge of inferiority. If this be so, it is not by reason of anything found in the act, but solely because the colored race chooses to put that construction upon it. . . . The argument also assumes that social prejudices may be overcome by legislation, and that equal rights cannot be secured to the negro except by an enforced commingling of the two races. We cannot accept this proposition. If the two races are to meet upon terms of social equality, it must be the result of natural affinities, a mutual appreciation of each other's merits and a voluntary consent of individuals.

. . . If the civil and political rights of both races be equal one cannot be inferior to the other civilly or politically. If one race be inferior to the other socially, the Constitution of the United States cannot put them upon the same plane.

It is true that the question for the proportion of colored blood necessary to constitute a colored person, as distinguished from a white person, is one upon which there is a difference of opinion in the different States, some holding that any visible admixture of black blood stamps the persons as belonging to the colored races, others that it depends upon the preponderance of blood . . . still others that the predominance of white blood must only be in the proportion of three fourths. . . . But these are questions to be determined under the laws of each State. . . .

Mr. Justice Harlan in the dissenting opinion:

. . . It was said in argument that the statute of Louisiana does not discriminate against either race, but prescribes a rule applicable alike to white and colored citizens. . . . [But] everyone knows that the statute in question had its origin in the purpose, not so much to exclude white persons from railroad cars occupied by blacks, as to exclude colored people from coaches occupied by or assigned to white persons.

. . . It is one thing for railroad carriers to furnish, or to be required by law to furnish, equal accommodations for all whom they are under a legal duty to carry. It is quite another thing for government to forbid citizens of the white and black races from traveling in the same public conveyance, and to punish officers of railroad companies for permitting persons of the two races to occupy the same passenger coach. If a State can prescribe, as a rule of civil conduct, that whites and blacks shall not travel as passengers in the same railroad coach, why may it not so regulate the use of the streets of its cities and towns as to compel white citizens to keep on one side of a street and black citizens to keep on the other? Why may it not, upon like grounds, punish whites and blacks who ride together in street cars or in open vehicles on a public road or street? Why may it not require sheriffs to assign whites to one side of a court-room and blacks to the other? And why may it not also prohibit the commingling of the two races in the galleries of legislative halls or in public assemblages convened for the consideration of the political questions of the day? Further, if this statute of Louisiana is consistent with the personal liberty of citizens, why may not the State require the separation in railroad coaches of native and naturalized citizens of the United States, or of Protestants and Roman Catholics?

. . . In my opinion, the judgment this day rendered will, in time, prove to be quite pernicious as the decision made by this tribunal in the Dred Scott case.

. . . The thin disguise of "equal" accommodations for passengers in railroad coaches will not mislead anyone, nor atone for the wrong this day done.

Thus, the *Plessy v. Ferguson* decision firmly established the separate but equal doctrine in the South until the National Association for the Advancement of Colored Persons (NAACP) began to systematically attack Jim Crow laws. It is ironic that in *Plessy* the systematic social, political, and economic suppression of blacks in the South through Jim Crow laws was justified in terms of a case decided in the northern city of Boston, where the segregation of schools occurred in practice (*de facto*), but not by force of law (*de jure*). In that 1849 case (*Roberts v. City of Boston*, 5 Cush. 198), a parent had unsuccessfully sued on behalf of his daughter to attend a public school. Thus, educational access became both the first and last chapter—in the 1954 case of *Brown v. Board of Education*—of the doctrine of separate but equal.

V. *YICK WO V. HOPKINS* (1886)

In the 1880s, the questions of citizenship and the rights of citizens were raised again by Native Americans and Asian immigrants. While the status of citizenship for African Americans was settled by the Thirteenth and Fourteenth Amendments, the extent of the privileges and immunities clause still needed clarification. Yick Wo, a Chinese immigrant living in San Francisco, brought suit under the Fourteenth Amendment to see if it covered all persons in the territorial United States regardless of race, color, or nationality.

The Chinese were different from European immigrants because they came to the United States under contract to work as laborers building the transcontinental railroad. When Chinese workers remained, primarily in California, after the completion of the railroad in 1869, Congress became anxious about this "foreign element" that was non-Christian and non-European. Chinese immigrants were seen as an economic threat because they would work for less than white males. To address the issue of economic competition, the Chinese Exclusion Act was passed in 1882 to prohibit further immigration to the United States. This gave the Chinese the unique status among immigrants of being the only group barred from entry into the United States and barred from becoming naturalized U.S. citizens.

Yick Wo, a subject of the Emperor of China, went to San Francisco in 1861, where he operated a laundry at the same premise for 22 years with consent from the Board of Fire Wardens. When the consent decree expired on October 1, 1885, Yick Wo routinely reapplied to continue to operate a laundry. He was, however, denied a license. Of the over 300 laundries in the city and county of San Francisco, about 240 were owned by Chinese immigrants. Most of these laundries were wooden, the most common construction material used at that time, although it posed a fire hazard. Yick Wo and more than 150 of his countrymen were arrested and charged with carrying on business without having special consent, while those who were not subjects of China and were operating some 80 laundries under similar conditions, were allowed to conduct business.

Yick Wo stated that he and 200 of his countrymen with similar situations petitioned the Board of Supervisors for permission to continue to conduct business in the same buildings they had occupied for more than 20 years. The petitions of all the

Chinese were denied, while all petitions of those who were not Chinese were granted (with one exception).

Did this prohibition of the occupation and destruction of the business and property of the Chinese laundrymen in San Francisco constitute the proper regulation of business, or was it discrimination and a violation of important rights secured by the Fourteenth Amendment?

The Court's decision addressed these key questions:

1. Does this municipal ordinance regulating public laundries within the municipality of San Francisco violate the United States Constitution?
2. Does carrying out this municipal ordinance violate the Fourteenth Amendment?
3. Does the guarantee of protection of the Fourteenth Amendment extend to all persons within the territorial jurisdiction of the United States regardless of race, color, or nationality?
4. Are the subjects of the Emperor of China who, temporarily or permanently, reside in the United States entitled to enjoy the protection guaranteed by the Fourteenth Amendment?

Excerpts from the Supreme Court Decision in *Yick Wo v. Hopkins*[13]

Mr. Justice Matthews delivered the opinion of the Court:

> . . . In both of these cases [*Yick Wo v. Hopkins* and *Wo Lee v. Hopkins*] the ordinance involved was simply a prohibition to carry on the washing and ironing of clothes in public laundries and washhouses, within the city and county of San Francisco, from ten o'clock p.m. until six o'clock a.m. of the following day. This provision was held to be purely a police regulation, within the competency of any municipality.
>
> . . . The rights of the petitioners are not less because they are aliens and subjects of the Emperor of China.
>
> The Fourteenth amendment to the Constitution is not confined to the protection of citizens. It says: "Nor shall any State deprive any person of life, liberty, or property without due process of law; nor deny to any person within its jurisdiction the equal protection of the laws." These provisions are universal in their application, to all persons within the territorial jurisdiction, without regard to any differences of race, or color, or of nationality; and the equal protection from the laws is a pledge of the protection of equal laws. . . .
>
> Though the law itself be fair on its face and impartial in appearance, yet, it is applied and administered by public authority with an evil eye and unequal hand, so as practically to make unjust and illegal discriminations between persons in similar circumstances. . . .
>
> . . . No reason whatever, except the will of the supervisors, is assigned why they should not be permitted to carry on, in the accustomed manner, their harmless and useful occupation, on which they depend for a livelihood. And while this consent of the supervisors is withheld from them and from two hundred others who have also petitioned, all of whom happened to be Chinese subjects, eighty others, not Chinese subjects, are permitted to carry on similar business under similar conditions. The fact of this discrimination is admitted. No reason for it is shown, . . . no reason for it exists except hostility to the race and nationality to which the petitioners belong, and which in the eye of the law is not justified. The discrimination is, therefore, illegal, and the public administration which enforces it is a denial of the equal protection of the laws and a violation of the Fourteenth amendment of the Constitution. The imprisonment of the petitioners is, therefore illegal, and they must be discharged.

The decision in *Yick Wo* demonstrated the Court's perspective that the Fourteenth Amendment applied to all persons, citizens and noncitizens.

VI. *ELK V. WILKINS* (1884)

In the late 19th century, Native Americans constituted a problematic class when the Supreme Court considered citizenship. Although Native Americans were the original inhabitants of the territory that became the United States, they were considered outside the concept of citizenship. They were viewed as a separate nation, and described as uncivilized, alien people who were not worthy of citizenship in the political community. As Native Americans were driven from their homeland and pushed farther west, the United States government developed a policy of containment by establishing reservations. Native Americans who lived with their tribes on such reservations were presumed to be members of "not strictly speaking, foreign states, but alien nations." The Constitution made no provisions for naturalizing Native Americans or defining the status of those who chose to live in the territorial United States rather than be assigned to reservations. It was presumed that Native Americans would remain on the reservations. The framers of the Constitution had not given any thought as to when or how a Native American might become a U.S. citizen. When the Naturalization Law of 1790 was written, only Europeans were anticipated as future citizens. The citizenship of Native Americans was not settled until 1924, when a statutory law, not a constitutional amendment, granted citizenship.

Elk v. Wilkins raised the question of citizenship and voting behavior as a privilege of citizenship. In 1857, the Court had easily dismissed Dred Scott's suit on the grounds that he was not a citizen. Since he did not hold citizenship, he could not sue. *Minor v. Happersett* in 1872 considered the citizenship and voting issue with a female plaintiff. In that case, citizenship was not in doubt but the court stated that citizenship did not automatically confer the right to suffrage. In *Elk,* a Native American claimed citizenship and the right to vote. Before considering the right to vote, the Court first examined whether Elk was a citizen and the process by which one becomes a citizen.

As midwestern cities emerged from westward expansion in the 1880s, a few Native Americans left their reservations to live and work in those cities. John Elk left his tribe and moved to Omaha, Nebraska, under the jurisdiction of the United States. In April 1880, he attempted to vote for members of the city council. Elk met the residency requirements in Nebraska and Douglas County for voting. Claiming that he complied with all of the statutory provisions, Elk asserted that under the Fourteenth and Fifteenth Amendments, he was a citizen of the United States who was entitled to exercise the franchise, regardless of race or color. He further claimed that Wilkins, the voter registrar, "designedly, corruptly, willfully, and maliciously" refused to register him for the sole reason that he was a Native American.

The Court's decision addressed these key questions:

1. Is a Native American still a member of an Indian tribe when he voluntarily separates himself from his tribe and seeks residence among the white citizens of the state?
2. What was the intent of the Fourteenth Amendment regarding who could become a citizen?
3. Can Native Americans become naturalized citizens?
4. Can Native Americans become citizens of the United States without the consent of the U.S. government?
5. Must Native Americans adopt the habits of a "civilized" life before they become U.S. citizens?
6. Is a Native American who is taxed a citizen?

Excerpts from the Supreme Court Decision in *Elk v. Wilkins*[14]

Mr. Justice Gray delivered the opinion of the Court.

. . . The plaintiff . . . relies on the first clause of the first section of the Fourteenth amendment of the Constitution of the United States, by which "all persons born or naturalized in the United States, and subject to the jurisdiction thereof, are citizens of the United States and of the State wherein they reside"; and on the Fifteenth amendment, which provides that "the right of citizens of the United States to vote shall not be denied or abridged by the United States or by any State on account of race, color, or previous condition of servitude."

. . . The question then is, whether an Indian, born a member of the Indian tribes within the United States, is, merely by reason of his birth within the United States, and of his afterwards voluntarily separating himself from his tribe and taking up his residence among white citizens, a citizen of the United

States, within the meaning of the first section of the Fourteenth amendment of the Constitution.

. . . The Indian tribes, being within the territorial limits of the United States, were not, strictly speaking, foreign States; but they were alien nations, distinct political communities, with whom the United States might and habitually did deal, as they thought fit, either through treaties made by the President and Senate, or through acts of Congress in the ordinary forms of legislation. The members of those tribes owed immediate allegiance to their several tribes, and were not a part of the United States. They were in a dependent condition, a state of pupilage, resembling that of a ward to his guardian.

. . . They were never deemed citizens of the United States, except under explicit provisions of treaty or statute to that effect, either declaring a certain tribe, or such members of it as chose to remain behind on the removal of the tribe westward, to be citizens, or authorizing individuals of particular tribes to become citizens. . . .

This [opening] section of the Fourteenth amendment contemplates two sources of citizenship, and two sources only: birth and naturalization.

. . . Slavery having been abolished, and the persons formerly held as slaves made citizens. . . . But Indians not taxed are still excluded from the count [U.S. Census count for apportioning seats in the U.S. House of Representatives],[15] for the reason that they are not citizens. Their absolute exclusion from the basis of representation, in which all other persons are now included, is wholly inconsistent with their being considered citizens.

. . . Such Indians, then, not being citizens by birth, can only become so in the second way mentioned in the Fourteenth amendment, by being "naturalized in the United States," by or under some treaty or statute.

. . . The treaty of 1867 with the Kansas Indians strikingly illustrates the principle that no one can become a citizen of a nation without its consent, and directly contradicts the supposition that a member of an Indian tribe can at will be alternately a citizen of the United States and a member of the tribe.

. . . But the question whether any Indian tribes, or any members thereof, have become so far advanced in civilization, that they should be let out of the state of pupilage, and admitted to the privileges and responsibilities of citizenship, is a question to be decided by the nation whose wards they are and whose citizens they seek to become, and not by each Indian for himself.

. . . And in a later case [Judge Deady in the District Court of the United States for the District of Oregon] said: "But an Indian cannot make himself a citizen of the United States without the consent and co-operation of the government. The fact that he has abandoned his nomadic life or tribal relations, and adopted the habits and manners of civilized people, may be a good reason why he should be made a citizen of the United States, but does not of itself make him one. To be a citizen of the United States is a political privilege which no one, not born to, can assume without its consent in some form.

Mr. Justice Harlan in the dissenting opinion:

. . . We submit that the petition does sufficiently show that the plaintiff is taxed, that is, belongs to the class which, by the laws of Nebraska, are subject to taxation.

. . . The plaintiff is a citizen and *bona fide* resident of Nebraska. . . . He is subject to taxation, and is taxed, in that State. Further: The plaintiff has become so far incorporated with the mass of the people of Nebraska that . . . he constitutes a part of her militia.

By the act of April 9, 1866, entitled "An Act to protect all persons in the United States in their civil rights, and furnish means for their vindication" (14 Stat. 27), it is provided that "all persons born in the United States and not subject to any foreign power, excluding Indians not taxed, are hereby declared to be citizens of the United States." . . . Beyond question, by that act, national citizenship was conferred directly upon all persons in this country, of whatever race (excluding only "Indians not taxed"), who were born within the territorial limits of the United States, and were not subject to any foreign power. Surely every one must admit that an Indian, residing in one of the States, and subject to taxation, there, became by force alone of the act of 1866, a citizen of the United States, although he may have been, when born, a member of a tribe.

. . . If he did not acquire national citizenship on abandoning his tribe [moving from the reservation] and . . . by residence in one of the States, subject to the complete jurisdiction of the United States, then the Fourteenth amendment has wholly failed to accomplish, in respect of the Indian race, what, we think, was intended by it, and there is still in this country a despised and rejected class of persons, with no nationality; who born in our territory, owing no allegiance to foreign power, and subject, as residents of the States, to all the burdens of government, are yet not members of any political community nor entitled to any of the rights, privileges, or immunities of citizens of the United States.

In all, the Court never addressed Elk's right to vote because the primary question involved Elk's citizenship. By excluding him from citizenship because he had not been naturalized and because there was no provision for naturalization, John Elk was left outside of the political community as was Dred Scott.

VII. *BROWN V. BOARD OF EDUCATION* (1954)

Unlike many of the earlier cases brought by individual women, blacks, or Native Americans, *Brown v. Board of Education* was the result of a concerted campaign against racial segregation led by Howard University School of Law graduates and the NAACP. In the 1930s, the NAACP Legal Defense Fund began to systematically fight for fair employment, fair housing, and desegregation of public education. Key lawyers in the campaign against segregation were Charles Houston, Thurgood Marshall, James Nabrit, and William Hastie. Marshall later became a Supreme Court justice, Nabrit became president of Howard University, and Hastie became a federal judge.

By using the Fourteenth Amendment, *Brown* became the key case in an attempt to topple the 1896 separate but equal doctrine. Legal strategists knew that educational opportunity and better housing conditions were essential if black Americans were to achieve upward mobility. While one group of lawyers focused on restrictive covenant cases,[16] which prevented blacks from buying housing in white neighborhoods, another spearheaded the drive for blacks to enter state-run professional schools.

In 1954, suits were brought in Kansas, South Carolina, Virginia, and Delaware on behalf of black Americans seeking to attend nonsegregated public schools. However, the case is commonly referred to as *Brown v. Board of Education*. The plaintiffs in the suit contended that segregation in the public schools denied them equal protection of the laws under the Fourteenth Amendment. The contention was that since segregated public schools were not and could not be made equal, black American children were deprived of equal protection of the laws.

The Court's unanimous decision addressed these key questions:

1. Are public schools segregated by race detrimental to black children?
2. Does segregation result in an inferior education for black children?
3. Does the maintenance of segregated public schools violate the Equal Protection Clause of the Fourteenth Amendment?
4. Is the maintenance of segregated public school facilities *inherently* unequal?
5. What was the intent of the framers of the Fourteenth Amendment regarding distinctions between whites and blacks?
6. Is the holding in *Plessy v. Ferguson* applicable to public education?
7. Does segregation of children in public schools *solely on the basis of race*, even though the physical facilities and other "tangible" factors may be equal, deprive the children of the minority group of equal educational opportunities?

Excerpts from the Supreme Court Decision in *Brown v. Board of Education*[17]

Mr. Chief Justice Warren delivered the opinion of the Court:

> . . . In each of these cases [NAACP suits in Kansas, South Carolina, Virginia, and Delaware] minors of the Negro race, through their legal representatives, seek the aid of the courts in obtaining admission to the public schools of their community on a nonsegregated basis. . . . This segregation was alleged to deprive the plaintiffs of the equal protection of the

laws under the Fourteenth Amendment. In each of the cases other than the Delaware case, a three-judge federal district court denied relief to the plaintiffs on the so-called "separate but equal" doctrine announced by this Court in *Plessy v. Ferguson,* 163 U.S. 537. Under that doctrine, equality of treatment is accorded when the races are provided substantially equal facilities, even though these facilities be separated. . . .

The plaintiffs contend that segregated schools are not "equal" and cannot be made "equal," and that hence they are deprived of the equal protection of the laws.

. . . The most avid proponents of the post–[Civil] War amendments undoubtedly intended them to remove all legal distinctions among "all persons born or naturalized in the United States."

In the first cases in this Court construing the Fourteenth Amendment, decided shortly after its adoption, the Court interpreted it as proscribing all state imposed discriminations against the Negro race. The doctrine of "separate but equal" did not make its appearance in this Court until 1896 in the *Plessy v. Ferguson, supra,* involving not education but transportation.

In these days, it is doubtful that any child may reasonably be expected to succeed in life if he is denied the opportunity of an education. Such an opportunity where the state has undertaken to provide it, is a right which must be made available to all on equal terms.

We come then to the question presented: Does segregation of children in public schools solely on the basis of race, even though the physical facilities and other "tangible" factors may be equal, deprive the children of the minority group of equal educational opportunities? We believe that it does.

To separate them [the children] from others of similar age and qualifications solely because of their race generates a feeling of inferiority as to their status in the community that may affect their hearts and minds in a way unlikely ever to be undone.

We conclude that in the field of public education the doctrine of "separate but equal" has no place. Separate educational facilities are inherently unequal. Therefore, we hold that the plaintiffs and others similarly situated for whom the actions have been brought are, by reason of the segregation complained of, deprived of the equal protection of the laws guaranteed by the Fourteenth Amendment.

. . . We have now announced that such segregation is a denial of the equal protection of the laws.

VIII. *LAU V. NICHOLS* (1974)

In the 19th century, Native Americans and Asian immigrants sought to exercise rights under the Fourteenth Amendment although it had been designed explicitly to protect blacks. In the 20th century, issues first raised by African Americans, such as equality in public education, again presented other minority groups with an opportunity to test their rights under the Constitution.

Brown v. Board of Education forced the Court to consider the narrow question of the distribution of resources between black and white school systems. The *Brown* decision addressed only education. It did not extend to the other areas of segregation in American society, such as the segregation of public transportation (e.g., buses) or public accommodations (e.g., restaurants and hotels). Indeed, *Brown* had not even specified how the integration of the school system was to take place. All of these questions were taken up by the Civil Rights movement that followed the *Brown* decision.

Once the separate but equal doctrine was nullified in education, immigrants raised other issues of equality. In the 1970s, suits were brought on behalf of the children of illegal immigrants, non-English-speaking children of Chinese ancestry, and children of low-income parents.

In *Lau v. Nichols,* a non-English-speaking minority group questioned equality in public education. The case was similar to *Brown* because it concerned public education, the Equal Protection Clause of the Fourteenth Amendment, and the suit was brought on behalf of minors; but the two cases also differed in many respects. The 1954 decision in *Brown* was part of a series of court cases attacking segregated facilities primarily in southern states. It addressed only the issues of black-white interaction.

In *Lau v. Nichols,* a suit was brought on behalf of children of Chinese ancestry who attended public schools in San Francisco. Although the children did not speak English, their classes in school were taught entirely in that language. (Some of the children received special instruction in the English language; others did not.) The suit did not specifically ask for bilingual education, nor did the Court require it, but *Lau* led to the development of such programs. In bilingual education, the curriculum is taught in children's native language, but they are also given separate instruction in the English language, and over time they are moved into English throughout their courses.

The *Lau* decision hinged in part on Department of Health, Education, and Welfare guidelines that prohibited discrimination in federally assisted programs. The decision was narrow because it instructed only the lower court to provide appropriate relief. The Court's ruling did not guarantee minority language rights, nor did it require bilingual education.

The Court's decision addressed these key questions:

1. Does a public school system that provides for instruction only in English violate the equal protection clause of the Fourteenth Amendment?
2. Does a public school system that provides for instruction only in English violate section 601 of the Civil Rights Act of 1964?
3. Do Chinese-speaking students who are in the minority receive fewer benefits from the school system than the English-speaking majority?
4. Must a school system that has a minority of students who do not speak English provide bilingual instruction?

Excerpts from the Supreme Court Decision in *Lau v. Nichols*[18]

Mr. Justice Douglas delivered the opinion of the Court:

The San Francisco, California, school system was integrated in 1971 as a result of a federal court decree. The District Court found that there are 2,856 students of Chinese ancestry in the school system who do not speak English. Of those who have that language deficiency, about 1,000 are given supplemental courses in the English language. About 1,800 however, do not receive that instruction.

This class suit brought by non-English-speaking Chinese students against officials responsible for the operation of the San Francisco Unified School District seeks relief against the unequal educational opportunities, which are alleged to violate, *inter alia,* the Fourteenth Amendment. No specific remedy is urged upon us. . . .

The Court of Appeals [holding that there was no violation of the Equal Protection Clause of the Fourteenth Amendment or of section 601 of the Civil Rights Act of 1964] reasoned that "[e]very student brings to the starting line of his educational career different advantages and disadvantages caused in part by social, economic and cultural background, created and continued completely apart from any contribution by the school system." . . . Section 71 of the California Education Code states that "English shall be the basic language of instruction in all schools." That section permits a school district to determine "when and under what circumstances instruction may be given bilingually." . . .

Under these state-imposed standards there is no equality of treatment merely by providing students with the same facilities, textbooks, teachers, and curriculum; for students who do not understand English are effectively foreclosed from any meaningful education.

. . . We know that those who do not understand English are certain to find their classroom experiences wholly incomprehensible and in no way meaningful.

We do not reach the Equal Protection Clause argument which has been advanced but rely solely on section 601 of the Civil Rights Act of 1964, 42 U.S.C. section 2000d. to reverse the Court of Appeals.

That section bans discrimination based "on the ground of race, color, or national origin, in any program or activity receiving Federal financial assistance." The school district involved in this litigation receives large amounts of federal financial assistance. The Department of Health, Education, and Welfare (HEW), which has authority to promulgate regulations prohibiting discrimination in federally assisted school systems, in 1968 issued one guideline that "[s]chool systems are responsible for assuring that students of a particular race, color, or national origin are not denied the opportunity to obtain the education generally obtained by other students in the system." In 1970 HEW made the guidelines more specific, requiring school districts that were federally funded "to rectify the language deficiency in order to open" the instruction to students who had "linguistic deficiencies." . . .

It seems obvious that the Chinese-speaking minority receive fewer benefits than the English-speaking majority from respondents' school system which denies them a meaningful opportunity to participate in the educational program—all earmarks of the discrimination banned by the regulations. . . .

Lau differed from *Brown* because it was decided not on the basis of the Fourteenth Amendment but on the Civil Rights Act of 1964. In reference to *Brown*, the justices noted that equality of treatment was not achieved by providing students with the same facilities, textbooks, teachers, or curriculum. *Lau* underscores the idea that equality may not be achieved by treating different categories of people in the same way.

IX. *SAN ANTONIO SCHOOL DISTRICT V. RODRIGUEZ* (1973)

The 1973 case of *San Antonio School District v. Rodriguez* raised the question of equality in public education from another perspective. As was the case in *Brown* and *Lau*, the Fourteenth Amendment required interpretation. However, unlike the earlier cases, the issue was the financing of local public schools.

Education is not a right specified in the Constitution. Under a federal system, education is a local matter in each state. This allows for the possibility of vast differences among states and even within states on the quality of instruction, methods of financing, and treatment of nonwhite students. Whereas the *Brown* decision examined inequality between races, *San Antonio* considered inequality based on financial resources through local property taxes. *San Antonio* raised the question of the consequence of the unequal distribution of wealth among Texas school districts. As with *Brown* and *Lau*, minors were involved; however, the issue was not race or language instruction but social class. Did the Texas school system discriminate against the poor?

Traditionally, the states have financed schools based on property tax assessments. Since wealth is not evenly distributed, some communities are able to spend more on education and provide greater resources to children. This is the basis of the *San Antonio* case, where the charge was that children in less affluent communities necessarily received an inferior education because those communities had fewer resources to draw on. The Rodriguez family contended that the Texas school system of financing public schools through local property taxes denied them equal protection of the laws in violation of the Fourteenth Amendment.

Financing public schools in Texas entailed state and local contributions. About half of the revenues were derived from a state-funded program that provided a minimal educational base; each district then supplemented state aid with a property tax. The Rodriguez family brought a class action suit on behalf of school children who claimed to be members of poor families who resided in school districts with a low property tax base. The contention was that the Texas system's reliance on local property taxation favored the more affluent and violated equal protection requirements because of disparities between districts in per-pupil expenditures.

The Court's decision addressed these key questions:

1. Does Texas's system of financing public school education by use of a property tax violate the Equal Protection Clause (Section 1) of the Fourteenth Amendment?
2. Does the Equal Protection Clause apply to wealth?
3. Is education a fundamental right?
4. Does this state law impinge on a fundamental right?
5. Is a state system for financing public education by a property tax that results in interdistrict disparities in per-pupil expenditures unconstitutionally arbitrary under the Equal Protection Clause?

Excerpts from the Supreme Court Decision in *San Antonio School District v. Rodriguez*[19]

Mr. Justice Powell delivered the opinion of the Court:

. . . The District Court held that the Texas system [of financing public education] discriminates on the basis of wealth in the manner in which education is provided for its people. Finding that wealth is a "suspect" classification and that education is a "fundamental" interest, the District Court held that the Texas system could be sustained only if the State could show that it was premised upon some compelling state interest.

. . . We must decide, first, whether the Texas system of financing public education operates to the disadvantage of some suspect class or impinges upon a fundamental right explicitly or implicitly protected by the Constitution, thereby requiring strict judicial scrutiny. If so, the Texas scheme must still be examined to determine whether it rationally furthers some legitimate, articulated state purpose and therefore does not constitute an invidious discrimination in violation of the Equal Protection Clause of the Fourteenth Amendment.

. . . In concluding that strict judicial scrutiny was required, the [District] court relied on decisions dealing with the rights of indigents to equal treatment in the criminal trial and appellate processes, and on cases disapproving wealth restrictions on the right to vote. Those cases, the District Court concluded, established wealth as a suspect classification. Finding that a local property tax system discriminated on the basis of wealth, it regarded those precedents as controlling. It then reasoned, based on decisions of this Court affirming the undeniable importance of education, that there is a fundamental right to education and that, absent some compelling state justification, the Texas system could not stand.

We are unable to agree that this case, which in significant aspects is *sui generis,* may be so neatly fitted under the Equal Protection Clause. Indeed, we find neither the suspect-classification nor the fundamental-interest analysis persuasive.

The wealth discrimination discovered by the District Court in this case, and by several other courts that have recently struck down school financing in other States, is quite unlike any of the forms of wealth discrimination heretofore reviewed by this Court.

. . . First, in support of their charge that the system discriminates against the "poor," appellees have made no effort to demonstrate that it operates to the peculiar disadvantage of any class fairly definable as indigent, or as composed of persons whose incomes are beneath any designated poverty level. Indeed, there is reason to believe that the poorest families are not necessarily clustered in the poorest property districts. . . .

Second, neither appellees nor the District Court addressed the fact that . . . lack of personal resources has not occasioned an absolute deprivation of the desired benefit. The argument here is not that the children in districts having relatively low assessable property values are receiving no public education; rather, it is that they are receiving a poorer quality education than that available to children in districts having more assessable wealth. Apart from the unsettled and disputed question whether the quality of education may be determined by the amount of money expended for it, a sufficient answer to appellee's argument is that, at least where wealth is involved, the Equal Protection Clause does not require absolute equality or precisely equal advantages. . . .

For these two reasons . . . the disadvantaged class is not susceptible of identification in traditional terms. . . .

. . . [I]t is clear that appellee's suit asks this Court to extend its most exacting scrutiny to review a system that allegedly discriminates against a large, diverse, and amorphous class, unified only by the common factor of residence in districts that happen to have less taxable wealth than other districts. The system of alleged discrimination and the class it defines have none of the traditional indicia of suspectness: the class is not saddled with such disabilities, or subjected to such a history of purposeful unequal treatment, or relegated to such a position of political powerlessness as to command extraordinary protection from the majoritarian political process.

We thus conclude that the Texas system does not operate to the peculiar disadvantage of any suspect class. . . .

Education, of course, is not among the rights afforded explicit protection under our Federal Constitution. Nor do we find any basis for saying it is implicitly so protected. . . .

In sum, to the extent that the Texas system of school financing results in unequal expenditures between children who happen to reside in different districts, we cannot say that such disparities are the product of a system that is so irrational as to be invidiously discriminatory. . . .

Mr. Justice White, with whom Mr. Justice Douglas and Mr. Justice Brennan join, dissenting:

... In my view, the parents and children in Edgewood, and in like districts, suffer from an invidious discrimination violative of the Equal Protection Clause. ...

There is no difficulty in identifying the class that is subject to the alleged discrimination and that is entitled to the benefits of the Equal Protection Clause. I need go no further than the parents and children in the Edgewood district, who are plaintiffs here and who assert that they are entitled to the same choice as Alamo Heights to augment local expenditures for schools but are denied that choice by state law. This group constitutes a class sufficiently definite to invoke the protection of the Constitution. ...

In *San Antonio v. Rodriguez,* the Court did not find that the differences between school districts constituted invidious discrimination. A majority of the justices felt that Texas satisfied constitutional standards under the Equal Protection Clause. On the other hand, four justices in dissenting opinions saw a class (the poor) that was subject to discrimination and that lacked the protection of the Constitution.

X. *BOWERS V. HARDWICK* (1986)

In most of the cases we have considered, plaintiffs have sued on the basis that their rights under the Fourteenth Amendment were violated. However, cases can reach the Supreme Court by several routes, one of which is a *writ of certiorari,* which is directed at an inferior court to bring the record of a case into a superior court for re-examination and review. This was the case in *Bowers v. Hardwick,* in which the constitutionality of a Georgia sodomy statute was challenged. This became a key case in the battle for constitutional rights for gay women and men.

The case of *Bowers v. Hardwick* began on the issue of privacy because the behavior in question took place in Michael Hardwick's home. In deciding the case, however, the justices shifted from the issue of privacy to question whether gays have a fundamental right to engage in consensual sex.

Michael Hardwick's suit was based on the following facts. On August 3, 1982, a police officer went to Hardwick's home to serve Hardwick

a warrant for failure to pay a fine. Hardwick's roommate answered the door, but was not sure if Hardwick was at home. The roommate allowed the officer to enter and approach Hardwick's bedroom. The officer found the bedroom door partly open and observed Hardwick engaged in oral sex with another man. The officer arrested both men, charged them with sodomy, and held them in the local jail for 10 hours.

The Georgia sodomy statute under which the men were charged made "any sexual act involving the sex organs of one person and the mouth or anus of another" a felony punishable by imprisonment for up to 20 years. When the district attorney decided not to submit the case to a grand jury, Hardwick brought suit attacking the constitutionality of the Georgia statute. Later, a divided court of appeals held that the Georgia statute violated Hardwick's fundamental rights. The attorney general of Georgia appealed that judgment to the Supreme Court.

The Court's decision on the case was split. Five justices ruled that the constitutional right of privacy did not apply to Hardwick's case; four argued that it did. While the Georgia statute did not specify that only homosexual sodomy was prohibited, the Court's majority opinion was framed in those terms. (Most legal prohibitions are directed at nonprocreative acts irrespective of the sex of the participants.) The majority opinion also equated consensual sex within the home to criminal conduct within the home, an equation criticized by both gay rights activists and the dissenting justices.

[The majority opinion] emphasized that the home does not confer immunity for criminal conduct, comparing gay sex first to drugs, firearms, and stolen goods and then to adultery, incest, and bigamy. In so doing, the Court evoked images of dissolution, fear, seizure, and instability. ... [and] the stereotypical fear of gay men as predators and child molesters. ... The majority [opinion] advances, mostly by implication, its view of gay sexuality as unrelated to recognized forms of sexual activity or intimate relationships, and as exploitative, predatory, threatening to personal and social stability. [Writing for the dissent]

Justice Blackmun excoriates the majority's choice of analogies and its failure to explain why it did not use nonthreatening analogies such as private, consensual heterosexual activity or even sodomy within marriage for comparison.[20]

While the majority argued that the past criminalization of sodomy argued for its continued criminalization, critics responded that "Whereas the task of the Court was to decide whether the criminalization of sodomy is consistent with the Constitution, the majority treated the fact of past criminalization as determinative. . . . It had no answer to Justice Blackmun's contention 'that by such lights, the Court should have no authority to invalidate miscegenation laws.'"[21]

The Court's decision addressed these key questions:

1. Does Georgia's sodomy law violate the fundamental rights of gays?
2. Does the Constitution confer the fundamental right to engage in homosexual sodomy?
3. Is Georgia's sodomy law selectively being enforced against gays?

Excerpts from the Supreme Court Decision in *Bowers v. Hardwick*[22]

Mr. Justice White delivered the opinion of the Court:

This case does not require a judgment on whether laws against sodomy between consenting adults in general, or between homosexuals in particular, are wise or desirable. . . . The issue presented is whether the Federal Constitution confers a fundamental right upon homosexuals to engage in sodomy and hence invalidates the laws of the many States that still makes such contact illegal and have done so for a very long time.

We first register our disagreement with the Court of Appeals and with respondent that the Court's prior cases have construed the Constitution to confer a right of privacy that extends to homosexual sodomy. . . .

Precedent aside, however, respondent would have us announce, as the Court of Appeals did, a fundamental right to engage in homosexual sodomy. This we are quite unwilling to do. . . .

It is obvious to us that neither of these formulations [*Palko v. Connecticut*, 302 U.S. 319 (1937) and *Moore v. East Cleveland*, 431 U.S. 494 (1977)] would extend a fundamental right to homosexuals to engage in acts of consensual sodomy. Proscriptions against that conduct have ancient roots. . . . Sodomy was a criminal offense at common law and was forbidden by the laws of the original thirteen States when they ratified the Bill of Rights. In 1868, when the Fourteenth Amendment was ratified, all but 5 of the 37 States in the Union had criminal sodomy laws. In fact, until 1961, all 50 States outlawed sodomy, and today 24 States and the District of Columbia continue to provide criminal penalties for sodomy performed in private and between consenting adults. . . . Against this background, to claim that a right to engage in such conduct is "deeply rooted in this Nation's history and tradition" or "implicit in the concept of ordered liberty" is, at best, facetious. . . .

Respondent . . . asserts that the result should be different where the homosexual conduct occurs in the privacy of the home. He relies on *Stanley v. Georgia*, 394 U.S. 557, (1969) . . . where the Court held that the First Amendment prevents conviction for possessing and reading obscene material in the privacy of one's home: "If the First Amendment means anything, it means that a State has no business telling a man, sitting alone in his house, what books he may read or what films he may watch." . . .

Stanley did protect conduct that would not have been protected outside the home, and it partially prevented the enforcement of state obscenity laws; but the decision was firmly grounded in the First Amendment. The right pressed upon us here has no similar support in the text of the Constitution, and it does not qualify for recognition under the prevailing principles for construing the Fourteenth Amendment. Its limits are also difficult to discern. Plainly enough, otherwise illegal conduct is not always immunized whenever it occurs in the home. Victimless crimes, such as the possession and use of illegal drugs, do not escape the law where they are committed at home. *Stanley* itself recognized that its holding offered no protection for the possession in the home of drugs, firearms, or stolen goods. . . . And if respondent's submission is limited to the voluntary sexual conduct between consenting adults, it would be difficult, except by fiat, to limit the claimed right to homosexual conduct while leaving exposed to prosecution adultery, incest, and other sexual crimes even though they are committed in the home. We are unwilling to start down that road. . . .

Justice Blackmun, with whom Justice Brennan, Justice Marshall, and Justice Stevens join, dissenting:

This case is no more about "a fundamental right to engage in homosexual sodomy," as the Court purports to declare, . . . than *Stanley v. Georgia*, 394 U.S. 557 (1969), . . . was about a fundamental right to watch obscene movies. . . . Rather, this case is about "the most comprehensive of rights and the right most valued by civilized men," namely, "the right to be let alone." *Olmstead v. United States*, 277 U.S. 438, (1928) (Brandeis, J., dissenting).

The statute at issue, Ga. Code Ann. section 16-6-2 (1984), denies individuals the right to decide for themselves whether to engage in particular forms of private, consensual sexual activity. The Court concludes that section 16-6-2 is valid essentially because "the laws of . . . many States . . . still make such conduct illegal and have done so for a very long time . . ." (Holmes, J., dissenting). Like Justice Holmes [dissenting in *Lochner v. New York*, 198 U.S. 45 (1905)], I believe that "[i]t is revolting to have no better reason for a rule of law than that it was laid down in the time of Henry IV. It is still more revolting if the grounds upon which it was laid down have vanished long since, and the rule simply persists from blind imitation of the past." Holmes, The Path of Law, 10 *Harvard Law Review* 457, 469 (1897). I believe we must analyze Hardwick's claim in the light of the values that underlie the constitutional right to privacy. If that right means anything, it means that, before Georgia can prosecute its citizens for making choices about the most intimate aspects of their lives, it must do more than assert that the choice they have made is an "'abominable crime not fit to be named among Christians.'"

Like the statute that is challenged in this case, the rationale of the Court's opinion applies equally to the prohibited conduct regardless of whether the parties who engage in it are married or unmarried, or are of the same or different sexes. Sodomy was condemned as an odious and sinful type of behavior during the formative period of the common law. That condemnation was equally damning for heterosexual and homosexual sodomy. Moreover, it provided no special exemption for married couples. The license to cohabit and to produce legitimate offspring simply did not include any permission to engage in sexual conduct that was considered a "crime against nature."

The Court's decision did not uphold Michael Hardwick's contention that his sexual conduct in the privacy of his own home was constitutionally protected. While the decision was seen as a blow to the assertion of gay rights, the majority's narrow one-vote margin also indicated the Court's shifting opinion on this issue.

XI. *REGENTS OF THE UNIVERSITY OF CALIFORNIA V. BAKKE* (1978)

The Supreme Court has reviewed several cases concerning equitable treatment in public education. Key cases include racially separate public schools (*Brown v. Board of Education,* 1954); the practice of English-only instruction for Chinese students in public schools (*Lau v. Nichols,* 1974); and the practice of operating public schools based solely on revenue from local property taxes (*San Antonio School District v. Rodriguez,* 1973).

African Americans not only had to fight for equity in public schools but also had to sue to gain admission to law and medical schools in state universities. See *Sipuel v. Oklahoma,* 1948; *Missouri ex rel Gaines,* 1938; and *Sweatt v. Painter,* 1950.

In 1978, race-based admissions became an issue again when a *white* person sued for admission to the medical school at the University of California at Davis. The case of *The Regents of the University of California v. Bakke,* however, must be seen in light of the policy of affirmative action, which sought to redress historic injustices against racial minorities and other specified groups by providing educational and employment opportunities to members of these groups.

In 1968, the University of California at Davis opened a medical school with a track admission policy for a 100-seat class. In 1974, applicants who identified themselves as economically and/or educationally disadvantaged or a member of a minority group (blacks, Chicanos, Asians, American Indians) were reviewed by a special committee. They could also compete for the remaining 84 seats. However, no disadvantaged white was ever admitted to the school through the special admissions program, although some applied. Bakke, a white male, applied to the medical school in 1973 and 1974 under the general admissions program. He was rejected both times because he did not meet the requisite cutoff score. In both years, special applicants with significantly lower scores than Bakke were admitted. After his second rejection, Bakke sued for admission to the medical school, alleging that the special admissions program excluded him on the basis of his race in violation of the Equal Protection Clause of the Fourteenth Amendment, a provision of the California Constitution, and section 601 of Title VI of the Civil Rights Act of 1964, which provides that no person shall, on the ground of race or color, be excluded from participating in any program receiving federal financial assistance. The California Supreme Court applied a strict-scrutiny standard. It concluded that the special admissions program was not the least intrusive means of achieving the goals of the admittedly compelling state interests of integrating the medical profession and increasing the number of doctors willing to serve minority patients. The California court held that UC Davis's special admissions program violated the Equal Protection Clause of the U.S. Constitution. The Davis School of Medicine was ordered to admit Bakke.

The Court's divided opinion addressed these key questions:

1. Does the University of California Davis School of Medicine admission policy violate the Fourteenth Amendment?
2. Does giving preference to a group of nonwhite applicants constitute discrimination?
3. Does the University of California Davis School of Medicine School use a racial classification that is suspect?

4. Was Bakke denied admission to the University of California Davis School of Medicine on the basis of race?
5. Can race be used as a criterion for admission to a university?

Excerpts from the Supreme Court Decision in *The Regents of the University of California v. Bakke*[23]

Mr. Justice Powell delivered the opinion of the Court:

> The guarantees of the Fourteenth Amendment extend to all persons. Its language is explicit: "No State shall . . . deny to any person within its jurisdiction the equal protection of the laws." . . . The guarantee of equal protection cannot mean one thing when applied to one individual and something else when applied to a person of another color. . . .
>
> . . . the [Fourteenth] Amendment itself was framed in universal terms, without reference to color, ethnic origin, or condition of prior servitude.
>
> Petitioner [University of California, Davis] urges us to adopt for the first time a more restrictive view of the Equal Protection Clause and hold that discrimination against members of the white "majority" cannot be suspect if its purpose can be characterized as "benign."
>
> . . . Moreover, there are serious problems of justice connected with the idea of preference itself. First, it may not always be clear that a so-called preference is in fact benign. . . . Second, preferential programs may only reinforce common stereotypes holding that certain groups are unable to achieve success without special protection based on a factor having no relationship to individual worth. Third, there is a measure of inequity in forcing innocent persons in respondent's position to bear the burdens of redressing grievances not of their making.
>
> . . . When a classification denies an individual opportunities or benefits enjoyed by others solely because of his race or ethnic background, it must be regarded as suspect.
>
> If petitioner's purpose is to assure within its student body some specified percentage of a particular group merely because of its race or ethnic origin, such a preferential purpose must be rejected. . . . Preferring

members of any one group for no reason other than race or ethnic origin is discrimination for its own sake. This the Constitution forbids.

. . . [A] goal asserted by petitioner is the attainment of a diverse student body. This clearly is a constitutionally permissible goal for an institution of higher education. Academic freedom, though not a specifically enumerated constitutional right, long has been viewed as a special concern of the First Amendment. . . .

Ethnic diversity, however, is only one element in a range of factors a university properly may consider in attaining the goal of a heterogeneous student body.

It may be assumed that the reservation of a specified number of seats in each class for individuals from the preferred ethnic groups would contribute to the attainment of considerable ethnic diversity in the student body. But petitioner's argument that this is the only effective means of serving the interest of diversity is seriously flawed. . . . Petitioner's special admissions program, focused solely on ethnic diversity, would hinder rather than further attainment of genuine diversity.

. . . In summary, it is evident that the Davis special admissions program involves the use of an explicit racial classification never before countenanced by this Court. It tells applicants who are not Negro, Asian, or Chicano that they are totally excluded from a specific percentage of the seats in the class.

The fatal flaw in petitioner's preferential program is its disregard of individual rights as guaranteed by the Fourteenth Amendment. Such rights are not absolute.

Mr. Justice Brennan, Mr. Justice White, Mr. Justice Marshall, and Mr. Justice Blackmun, concurring in part and dissenting in part:

We conclude . . . that racial classifications are not *per se* invalid under the Fourteenth Amendment.

Unquestionably we have held that a government practice or statute which restricts "fundamental rights" or which contains "suspect classifications" is to be subjected to "strict scrutiny" and can be justified only if it furthers a compelling government purpose. . . . But no fundamental right is involved here. Nor do whites as a class have any of the "traditional indicia of suspectness; the class is not saddled with such disabilities, or subjected to such a history

of purposeful unequal treatment, or relegated to such a history of purposeful unequal treatment, or relegated to such position of political powerlessness as to command extraordinary protection from the majoritarian political process." . . .

Certainly . . . Davis had a sound basis for believing that the problem of under-representation of minorities was substantial and chronic. . . . Until at least 1973, the practice of medicine in this country was, in fact, if not in law, largely the prerogative of whites. In 1950, for example, while Negroes constituted 10% of the total population, Negro physicians constituted only 2.2% of the total number of physicians. The overwhelming majority of these . . . were educated in two predominantly Negro medical schools, Howard and Meharry. By 1970, the gap between the proportion of Negroes in medicine and their proportion in the population had widened: The number of Negroes employed in medicine remained frozen at 2.2% while the Negro population had increased to 11.1%. The number of Negro admittees to predominantly white medical schools, moreover, had declined in absolute numbers during the years 1955 to 1964.

Moreover, Davis had very good reason to believe that the national pattern of under-representation of minorities in medicine would be perpetuated if it retained a single admissions standard. . . .

Davis clearly could conclude that the serious and persistent under-representation of minorities in medicine depicted by these statistics is the result of handicaps under which minority applicants labor as a consequence of . . . deliberate, purposeful discrimination against minorities in education and in society generally, as well as in the medical profession. . . .

It is not even claimed that Davis' program in any way operates to stigmatize or single out any discrete . . . or even any identifiable, nonminority group. Nor will harm comparable to that imposed upon racial minorities by exclusion or separation on grounds of race be the likely result of the program. . . .

Nor was Bakke in any sense stamped as inferior by the Medical School's rejection of him. Indeed, it is conceded by all that he satisfied those criteria regarded by the school as generally relevant to academic performance better than most of the minority members who were admitted. Moreover, there is absolutely no basis for concluding that Bakke's rejection that was a result of Davis' use of racial preference will affect him throughout his life in the same way as the segregation of the Negro schoolchildren in *Brown I* would have affected them. Unlike discrimination against racial minorities, the use of racial preferences for remedial purposes does not inflict a pervasive injury upon individual whites in the sense that wherever they go or whatever they do there is a significant likelihood that they will be treated as second-class citizens because of their color. . . .

In addition, there is simply no evidence that the Davis program discriminated intentionally or unintentionally against any minority group which it purports to benefit. The program does not establish a quota in the invidious sense of a ceiling on the number of minority applicants to be admitted. . . .

Finally, Davis' special admissions program cannot be said to violate the Constitution. . . .

. . . we would reverse the judgment of the Supreme Court of California holding the Medical School's special admissions program unconstitutional and directing respondent's admission.

Justices Stevens and Stewart, along with Chief Justice Rehnquist, concurred and dissented in part. They found that the university's special admissions program violated Title VI of the Civil Rights Act of 1964, which prohibits discrimination under any program or activity receiving federal funding assistance. This dissent found that Bakke was not admitted to the Davis Medical School because of his race.

Race-based admissions were again considered in *Hopwood v. Texas,* a 1994 case in the Western District of Texas. The suit, brought by four white Texas residents, claimed that the affirmative action admissions program of the University of Texas School of Law violated the Equal Protection Clause of the Fourteenth Amendment and Title VI of the Civil Rights Act of 1964. The district court agreed that the plaintiffs' equal protection rights had been violated, but refused to direct the school to cease making admission decisions based on race. The case was subsequently appealed in the Court of Appeals for the Fifth Circuit, which held that the University of Texas School of Law could not use race as an admissions factor in order to achieve a diverse student body. The holding of the circuit court stands because the Supreme Court refused to hear the case.

This decision in effect overruled Justice Powell's opinion in *Bakke,* which held that universities can take account of an applicant's race in some circumstances. He asserted that the goal of achieving a diverse student body was permissible under the Constitution.

XII. *TENNESSEE V. LANE* (2004)

Historically, disabled people have been thought of as possessed or wicked. Often they were scorned and shut off from society in mental institutions. Today, however, the medical model is the dominant perspective that "those with disabilities have some kind of physical, mental, or emotional defect that not surprisingly limits their performance." Essentially, we don't expect those who are "flawed" to function as well as other people.[24]

Disabled people constantly face discrimination resulting in exclusion from housing, public buildings, and public transportation. This has prevented them from attending school, visiting museums, shopping, or living without assistance.

The 1990 Americans with Disabilities Act forbids discrimination against persons with disabilities in three key areas of public life. Title I covers employment; Title II encompasses public services, programs, and activities; and Title III covers public accommodations. In 2001 Casey Martin sued the PGA Tour,[25] under the public accommodations provisions of Title III to allow him to play golf on the tour while riding a golf cart because he suffers from Klippel-Trenaunay-Weber syndrome, a degenerative circulatory disorder that causes severe pain in his lower leg. Martin won his case when the Court held that the PGA walking rule was not compromised by allowing him to use a cart.

The provisions of Title II, which include access to the services, programs, or activities of a public entity such as a courthouse are questioned in *Tennessee v. Lane.* In this case, residents of the state who are paraplegics sued Tennessee under Title II of the Americans with Disabilities Act (ADA) because they were denied access to a courthouse. Because this case involves a suit by an individual against a state, the Supreme Court has to consider the provisions of the Eleventh Amendment,[26] which provides state immunity against suits by citizens seeking equity and the enforcement clause, Section 5 of the Fourteenth Amendment.[27] After Tennessee was unsuccessful in getting the case dismissed because the plaintiffs sought damages, the case went to the Supreme Court. This issue then became an interpretation of Congress's power to enforce by appropriate legislation (Section 5) the guarantee that "no State shall make or enforce any law which shall abridge the privileges or immunities of citizens of the United States; nor shall any State deprive any person of life, liberty, or property, without due process of law; nor deny to any person within its jurisdiction the equal protection of the laws."

In 1998 George Lane and Beverly Jones, both paraplegics who use wheelchairs, filed suit against the state of Tennessee and a number of counties under Title II of the ADA, which states that no qualified individual with a disability shall, because of the disability be excluded from participation or denied the benefits of the services, programs, or activities of a public entity. Both parties claimed that they were denied access to the state court system because of their disability. Lane alleged that he was forced to appear to answer criminal charges on the second floor of a county courthouse. The courthouse had no elevator. In his first court appearance Lane crawled up two flights to reach the courtroom. When Lane had to return for a second time, he refused to crawl or to be carried to the courtroom. He was arrested and sent to jail for failure to appear for his hearing. Jones, a certified court reporter, claimed that she had not been able to obtain work because she could not gain access to several county courthouses.

The court's decision addressed these key questions:

1. Is Title II a valid exercise of Congress's Section 5 enforcement powers under the Fourteenth Amendment?
2. Does Title II enforce a variety of basic constitutional guarantees such as the right of access to the courts?
3. Does Title II validly enforce these constitutional rights?
4. Is Title II an appropriate response to this history of discrimination and pattern of unequal treatment?

Excerpts from the Supreme Court Decision in *Tennessee v. George Lane et al.*[28]

Mr. Justice Stevens delivered the opinion of the Court:

> The ADA was passed by large majorities in both Houses of Congress after decades of deliberation and investigation into the need for comprehensive legislation to address discrimination against persons with disabilities.
>
> . . . Title II, sections 12131–12134, prohibits any public entity from discrimination against "qualified" persons with disabilities in the provision or operation of public services, programs, or activities. The Act defines the term "public entity" to include state and local governments. . . .
>
> Title II, like Title I, seeks to enforce this prohibition on irrational disability discrimination. But it also seeks to enforce a variety of other basic constitutional guarantees, infringements of which are subject to more searching judicial review. . . . These rights include some, like the right of access to the courts at issue in this case, that are protected by the Due Process Clause of the Fourteenth Amendment. The Due Process Clause [as] applied to the States via the Fourteenth Amendment both guarantee to a criminal defendant such as respondent Lane the "right to be present at all stages of the trial where his absence might frustrate the fairness of the proceedings." . . . The Due Process Clause also requires the States to afford certain civil litigants a "meaningful opportunity to be heard" by removing obstacles to their full participation in judicial proceedings. . . . And, finally, we have recognized that members of the public have a right of access to criminal proceedings secured by the First Amendment.
>
> . . . It is not difficult to perceive the harm that Title II is designed to address. Congress enacted Title II against a backdrop of pervasive unequal treatment in the administration of state services and programs, including systematic deprivations of fundamental rights.

. . . With respect to the particular services at issue in this case, Congress learned that many individuals, in many States across the country, were being excluded from courthouses and court proceedings by reason of their disabilities. A report before Congress showed that some 76% of public services and programs housed in state-owned buildings were inaccessible to and unusable by persons with disabilities. . . .

The conclusion that Congress drew from this body of evidence is set forth in the text of the ADA itself: "Discrimination against individuals with disabilities persists in such critical areas as . . . education, transportation, communication, recreation, institutionalization, health services, voting, and access to public services. . . ." This finding, together with the extensive record of disability discrimination that underlies it, makes clear beyond peradventure that inadequate provision of public services and access to public facilities was an appropriate subject for prophylactic legislation.

. . . Whatever might be said about Title II's other applications, the question presented in this case is not whether Congress can validly subject the States to private suits for money damages for failing to provide reasonable access to hockey rinks, or even to voting booths, but whether Congress had the power under Section 5 to enforce the constitutional right of access to the courts. Because we find that Title II unquestionably is valid Section 5 legislation as it applies to the class of cases implicating the accessibility of judicial services, we need go no further.

. . . Title II's affirmative obligation to accommodate persons with disabilities in the administration of justice cannot be said to be "so out of proportion to a supposed remedial or preventive object that it cannot be understood as responsive to, or designed to prevent, unconstitutional behavior. . . . It is, rather, a reasonable prophylactic measure, reasonably targeted to a legitimate end.

For these reasons, we conclude that Title III, as it applies to the class of cases implicating the fundamental right of access to the courts, constitutes a valid exercise of Congress's Section 5 authority to enforce the guarantees of the Fourteenth Amendment.

XIII. THE MICHIGAN CASES

Gratz v. Bollinger et al. (2003) and *Grutter v. Bollinger et al.* (2003) considered admission standards for the University of Michigan's undergraduate program and its Law School. This marked the first time in the 25 years since the *Bakke* decision that the Supreme Court had considered the legal status of race-conscious admissions. In *Bakke,* Justice Powell held that race could be taken into consideration if it served a compelling government interest. He then held that the goal of achieving a diverse student body was a circumstance where race could be considered. However, the *Bakke* decision generated six separate opinions, but no majority opinion.[29]

The University of Michigan cases question whether Justice Powell's opinion set a precedent for considering diversity a constitutional justification for race-conscious admissions.

Gratz v. Bollinger et al. (2003)

Jennifer Gratz and Patrick Hamacher were both white residents of Michigan who applied for admission to the University of Michigan's College of Literature, Science, and the Arts (LSA). Both were considered qualified for admission. However, both were denied early admission, and upon further review neither was admitted to the university. The university's Undergraduate Admissions Office uses a written guideline system that includes such factors as high school grades, standardized test scores, the quality of the high school, curriculum strength, geography, alumni relationships, leadership, and race. Although the guidelines have changed since 1995, the university consistently considered African Americans, Hispanics, and Native Americans as "underrepresented minorities." The guidelines provided that all applicants from an underrepresented racial or ethnic minority group were automatically given 20 points out of the 100 needed for admission. The university never disputed the claim that practically every qualified applicant from these groups was admitted.

In 1997, Gratz and Hamacher filed a class-action suit alleging violation of their rights under the Fourteenth Amendment and the Civil Rights Act of 1964. The Equal Protection Clause of the Fourteenth Amendment provides that a state cannot act unfairly or arbitrarily toward or discriminate against a person within its jurisdiction because the individual has "the equal protection of the laws."

Title VI of the Civil Rights Act prohibits discrimination on the grounds of race, color, or national origin against anyone participating in a program or activity which receives federal financial assistance.

The Court's decision addressed these key questions:

1. Under strict scrutiny, does the university's use of race in its current admission policy constitute narrowly tailored measures that further compelling government interests?
2. Does the undergraduate admission policy violate the Equal Protection Clause of the Fourteenth Amendment?
3. Does the undergraduate admission policy violate Title VI of the Civil Rights Act of 1964?

Excerpts from the Supreme Court Decision in *Gratz v. Bollinger et al.* (2003)[30]

Chief Justice Rehnquist delivered the opinion of the Court:

> . . . Because the University's use of race in its current freshman admission policy is not narrowly tailored to achieve respondents' asserted interest in diversity, the policy violates the Equal Protection Clause. For the reasons set forth in *Grutter v. Bollinger* . . . the Court has today rejected petitioners' argument that diversity cannot constitute a compelling state interest. However, the Court finds that the University's current policy, which automatically distributes 20 points, or one-fifth of the points needed to guarantee admission, to every single "underrepresented minority" applicant solely because of race, is not narrowly tailored to achieve educational diversity. In *Bakke,* Justice Powell explained his view that it would be permissible for a university to employ an admissions program in which "race or ethnic background may be deemed a 'plus' in a particular applicant's file" . . . he emphasized, however, the importance of considering each particular applicant as an individual, assessing all of the qualities that individual possesses, and in turn, evaluating that individual's ability to contribute to the unique setting of higher education. The admissions program Justice Powell described did not contemplate that any single characteristic automatically

> ensured a specific and identifiable contribution to a university's diversity. . . . The current LSA policy does not provide the individualized consideration Justice Powell contemplated. The only consideration that accompanies the 20-point automatic distribution to all applicants from underrepresented minorities is a factual review to determine whether an individual is a member of one of these minority groups. Moreover, unlike Justice Powell's example, where the race of a "particular black applicant" could be "considered without being decisive" . . . the LSA's 20-point distribution has the effect of making "the factor of race . . . decisive" for virtually every minimally qualified underrepresented minority applicant. The fact that the LSA has created the possibility of an applicant's file being flagged for individualized consideration only emphasizes the flaws of the University's system as a whole when compared to that described by Justice Powell. The record does not reveal precisely how many applications are flagged, but it is undisputed that consideration is the exception and not the rule in the LSA's program. Also, this individualized review is only provided *after* admissions counselors automatically distribute the University's version of a "plus" that makes race a decisive factor for virtually every minimally qualified underrepresented minority applicant. . . . Nothing in Justice Powell's *Bakke* opinion signaled that a university may employ whatever means it desires to achieve diversity without regard to the limits imposed by strict scrutiny. Because the University's use of race in its current freshman admission policy violates the Equal Protection Clause, it also violates Title VI.

Grutter v. Bollinger et al. (2003)

Barbara Grutter, a white Michigan resident, applied to the University of Michigan Law School in 1996. She was originally placed on a waiting list but was ultimately not admitted. She alleged that her application was rejected because the Law School used race as a "predominant" factor, which gave applicants from certain minority groups "a significantly greater chance of admission than students with similar credentials from disfavored racial groups." The Law School asserted that it had a compelling interest in obtaining the educational benefits derived from a diverse student body. Law

School officials contended that the admissions staff was not directed to admit a specific percentage or number of minority students, but rather to consider race among several factors. The goal was to obtain a "critical mass" of underrepresented minority students in order to realize the educational benefits of a diverse student body. The critical mass concept was never stated in terms of a fixed number, or percentage, or even a range of numbers or percentages. Admission officers acknowledged that minority group membership was a strong factor in the acceptance decisions and that applicants from minority groups were given large allowance for admission compared to applicants from non-favored groups. However, it was asserted that race was not considered the predominant factor in the Law School's admission formula.

The Court's decision addressed these key questions:

1. Was race a predominant or a plus factor when reviewing the files of Law School applicants?
2. Did the Law School have a compelling interest in creating a diverse study body?
3. Does seeking a critical mass of minority students equal a quota?
4. Does the Law School admissions policy violate the Fourteenth Amendment and Title VI of the Civil Rights Act of 1964?

Excerpts from the Supreme Court Decision in *Grutter v. Bollinger et al.*[31]

Justice O'Connor delivered the opinion of the Court:

> We last addressed the use of race in public higher education over 25 years ago. In the landmark *Bakke* case, we reviewed a racial set-aside program that reserved 16 out of 100 seats in a medical school class for members of certain minority groups. . . . The decision produced six separate opinions, none of which commanded a majority of the Court. . . . The only holding for the court in *Bakke* was that a "State has a substantial interest that legitimately may be served by a properly devised admissions program involving the competitive consideration of race and ethnic origin."

. . . Public and private universities across the nation have modeled their own admissions programs on Justice Powell's views on permissible race-conscious policies.

. . . Justice Powell approved the university's use of race to further only one interest: "the attainment of a diverse student body" . . . Justice Powell grounded his analysis in the academic freedom that long has been viewed as a special concern of the First Amendment. Justice Powell emphasized that nothing less than the "'nation's future depends upon leaders trained through wide exposure' to the ideas and mores of students as diverse as this Nation of many peoples." . . . Both "tradition and experience lend support to the view that the contribution of diversity is substantial."

Justice Powell was, however, careful to emphasize that in his view race "is only one element in a range of factors a university properly may consider in attaining the goal of a heterogeneous student body." . . . For Justice Powell "[i]t is not an interest in simple ethnic diversity, in which a specified percentage of the student body is in effect guaranteed to be members of selected ethnic groups," that can justify the use of race. . . . Rather, "[t]he diversity that furthers a compelling state interest encompasses a far broader array of qualifications and characteristics of which racial or ethnic origin is but a single though important element."

. . . We have held that all racial classifications imposed by government "must be analyzed by a reviewing court under strict scrutiny." . . . This means that such classifications are constitutional only if they are narrowly tailored to further compelling governmental interests.

. . . The Law School asks us to recognize, in the context of higher education, a compelling state interest in student body diversity.

. . . Today, we hold that the Law School has a compelling interest in attaining a diverse student body.

. . . Our conclusion that the Law School has a compelling interest in a diverse student body is informed by our view that attaining a diverse student body is at the heart of the Law School's proper institutional mission, and that "good faith" on the part of a university is "presumed" absent "a showing to the contrary."

. . . The Law School's concept of critical mass is defined by reference to the educational benefits that diversity is designed to produce.

These benefits are substantial. As the District Court emphasized, the Law School's admissions policy promotes "cross-racial understanding," helps to break down racial stereotypes, and "enables [students] to better understand persons of different races."

. . . The Law School has determined, based on its experience and expertise, that a "critical mass" of underrepresented minorities is necessary to further its compelling interest in securing the educational benefits of a diverse student body.

. . . To be narrowly tailored, a race-conscious admissions program cannot use a quota system—it cannot "insulat[e] each category of applicants with certain desired qualifications from competition with all other applicants" (opinion of Justice Powell). Instead, a university may consider race or ethnicity only as a "'plus' in a particular applicant's file," without "insulat[ing] the individual from comparison with all other candidates for the available seats."

. . . We find that the Law School's admissions program bears the hallmarks of a narrowly tailored plan. As Justice Powell made clear in *Bakke*, truly individualized consideration demands that race be used in a flexible, nonmechanical way.

. . . We are satisfied that the Law School's admissions program . . . does not operate as a quota. Properly understood, a "quota" is a program in which a certain fixed number or proportion of opportunities are "reserved exclusively for certain minority groups."

. . . The Law School's goal of attaining a critical mass of underrepresented minority students does not transform its program into a quota. . . . "[S]ome attention to numbers," without more, does not transform a flexible admissions system into a rigid quota.

. . . The Law School affords this individualized consideration to applicants of all races. There is no policy, either *de jure* or *de facto*, of automatic acceptance or rejection based on any single "soft" variable. Unlike the program at issue in *Gratz v. Bollinger*, the Law School awards no mechanical, predetermined diversity "bonuses" based on race or ethnicity.

. . . What is more, the Law School actually gives substantial weight to diversity factors besides race. The Law School frequently accepts nonminority applicants with grades and test scores lower than underrepresented minority applicants (and other nonminority applicants) who are rejected.

. . . We agree that, in the context of its individualized inquiry into the possible diversity contributions of all applicants, the Law School's race-conscious admissions program does not unduly harm nonminority applicants.

. . . the Equal Protection Clause does not prohibit the Law School's narrowly tailored use of race in admissions decisions to further a compelling interest in obtaining the educational benefits that flow from a diverse student body.

XIV. *RICCI V. DeStefano* (2009)

Racial equity has been an issue in hiring and the promotion of municipal workers such as teachers, police officers, and firefighters since the Civil Rights legislation of 1964. In this case in New Haven, Connecticut, when firefighters sought promotion, questions were raised about racially biased tests and the history of discrimination in the firefighting profession, as well as disparate treatment and impact.

In 2003, the city of New Haven used written and oral examinations to identify which firefighters would be promoted to the rank of lieutenant or captain. Under the "Rule of Three," the City was required to fill vacancies by selecting a candidate from the top three scorers on the list. Application of this rule excluded all black firefighters from promotion because they did not score high enough on the examination. The test results were reviewed by an independent review board because the results created a racial disparity, which could mean that the test was racially biased. The review board split evenly on whether to certify the examination results. The City then decided that no one would be promoted on the basis of the test results. When the city decided not to certify the test results, white and Hispanic firefighters who had passed the exam but were denied promotion, sued the City, alleging that by discarding the test results they had been discriminated against under Title VII of the 1964 Civil Rights Act.

The Court's divided opinion addressed these questions:

1. Can New Haven justify discrimination because it fears a lawsuit?
2. Did the City's action of discarding the test results violate Title VII of the Civil Rights Act?

Excerpts from the Supreme Court Decision in *Ricci v. DeStefano* (2009)[32]

Justice Kennedy delivered the opinion of the Court:

In 2003, 118 New Haven firefighters took examinations to qualify for promotion to the rank of lieutenant or captain. Promotion examinations in New Haven (or City) were infrequent, so the stakes were high. . . .

Certain white and Hispanic firefighters who likely would have been promoted based on their good test performance sued the City . . . the suit alleges that, by discarding the test results, the City . . . discriminated against the plaintiffs based on their race, in violation of . . . Title VII of the Civil Rights Act of 1964. . . .

. . . Title VII of the Civil Rights Act of 1964 . . . as amended, prohibits employment discrimination on the basis of race, color, religion, sex, or national origin. Title VII prohibits both intentional discrimination (known as "disparate treatment") as well as, in some cases, practices that are not intended to discriminate but in fact have a disproportionately adverse effect on minorities (known as "disparate impact").

As enacted in 1964, Title VII's principal nondiscrimination provision held employers liable only for disparate treatment. . . .

Our analysis begins with this premise: The City's actions would violate the disparate-treatment prohibition of Title VII absent some valid defense. All the evidence demonstrates that the City chose not to certify the examination results because of the statistical disparity based on race—i.e., how minority candidates had performed when compared to white candidates. As the District Court put it, the City rejected the test results because "too many whites and not enough minorities would be promoted were the lists to be certified."

The City argues that, even under the strong-basis-in evidence standard, its decision to discard the examination results were permissible under Title VII. . . .

We conclude there is no-strong-basis-in-evidence to establish that the test was deficient. . . .

. . . Fear of litigation alone cannot justify an employer's reliance on race to the detriment of individuals who passed the examinations and qualified for promotions. The City's discarding the test results was impermissible under Title VII. . . .

. . . [T]he City was not entitled to disregard the test based solely on the racial disparity in the results.

Justice Ginsburg, with whom Justice Stevens, Justice Souter, and Justice Breyer join, dissenting:

In assessing claims of race discrimination, [c]ontext matters . . . Congress extended Title VII of the Civil Rights Act of 1964 to cover public employment. At that time, municipal fire departments across the county, including New Haven's pervasively discriminated against minorities . . . . The white firefighters who scored high on New Haven's promotion exams understandably attract this Court's sympathy. But they had no vested right to promotion. Nor have other persons received promotions in preference to them.

. . . The Court's recitation of the facts leaves out important parts of the story. Firefighting is a profession in which the legacy of racial discrimination casts an especially long shadow. In extending Title VII to state and local government employers in 1972, Congress took note of a U.S. Commission on Civil Rights (USCCR) report finding racial discrimination in municipal employment even "more pervasive than in the private sector." . . . According to the report, overt racism was partly to blame but so too was a failure on the part of municipal employers to apply merit-based employment principles. In making hiring and promotion decisions, public employers often "rel[ied] on criteria unrelated to job performance," including nepotism or political patronage. . . . Such flawed selection methods served to entrench preexisting racial hierarchies. The USCCR report singled out police and fire departments for having "[b]arriers to equal employment . . . greater . . . than in any other area of State or local government," with African Americans "hold[ing] almost no position in the officer ranks." . . . (Racial minorities are underrepresented in the fire departments in nearly every community in which they live.")

The city of New Haven (City) was no exception. In the early 1970s, African Americans and Hispanics composed 30 percent of the New Haven's population, but only 3.6 percent of the City's 502 firefighters. The racial disparity in the officer ranks was even more pronounced. . . .

. . . It is against this backdrop of entrenched inequality that the promotion process at issue in this litigation should be assessed. . . .

. . . The (test) results showed significant racial disparities. . . .

These stark disparities, the Court acknowledges, sufficed to state *prima facie* case under Title VII disparate-impact provision. . . . New Haven thus had cause for concern about the prospect of Title VII litigation and liability. . . .

. . . Between January and March 2004, the Civil Service Board (CSB) held five public meetings to consider the proper course. . . .

At its fourth meeting, the CSB solicited the views of three individuals with testing-related expertise. . . . Dr. Christopher Hornick, an industrial/organizational psychology consultant with 25 years' experience with police and firefighter test, described the exam results as having "relatively high adverse impact." . . .

Specifically, Hornick questioned New Haven's union-prompted 60/40 written/oral examination structure, noting the availability of "different types of testing procedures that are much more valid in terms of identifying the best potential supervisors in [the] fire department."

Respondents were no doubt conscious of race during their decision making process, the court acknowledged, but this did not mean they had engaged in racially disparate treatment. The conclusion they had reached and the action thereupon taken were race-neutral in this sense: "[A]ll the test results were discarded. . . . .

. . . Title VII . . . aims to eliminate all forms of employment discrimination, unintentional as well as deliberate. Until today . . . . this Court has never questioned the constitutionality of the disparate-impact component of Title VII. . . .

. . . This Court has repeatedly emphasized that the statute "should not be read to thwart" efforts at voluntary compliance . . . (Title VII permits employers and unions voluntarily to make use of reasonable race-conscious affirmative action") . . .

Applying what I view as the proper standard to the record thus far made, I would hold that New Haven had ample cause to believe its selection process was flawed and not justified by business necessity. Judged by that standard, petitioners have not shown that New Haven's failure to certify the exam results violated Title VII's disparate-treatment provision. . . .

Chief among the City's problems was the very nature of the tests for promotion. In choosing to use written and oral exams with a 60/40 weighting,

the City simply adhered to the union's preference and apparently gave no consideration to whether the weighting was likely to identify the most qualified fire-officer candidates. There is strong reason to think it was not.

Relying heavily on written tests to select fire officers is a questionable practice . . . successful fire officers, the City's description of the position make clear, must have the "[a]bility to lead personnel effectively, maintain discipline, promote harmony, exercise sound judgment, and cooperate with other officials." . . . these qualities are not well measured by written tests. . . .

It is indeed regrettable that the City's noncertification decision would have required all candidates to go through another selection process. But it would have been more regrettable to rely on flawed exams to shut out candidates who may well have the command presence and other qualities needed to excel as fire officers. . . .

NOTES

1. *Privileges and immunities* refer to the ability of one state to discriminate against the citizens of another state. A resident of one state cannot be denied legal protection, access to the courts, or property rights in another state.
2. In *Smith v. Allwright,* 321 U.S. 649 (1944), the Supreme Court held that a 1927 Texas law that authorized political parties to establish criteria for membership in the state Democratic party violated the Fifteenth Amendment. In effect, the criteria excluded nonwhites from the Democratic party. Since only party members could vote in the primary election, the result was a whites-only primary. The Democratic party so dominated politics in the southern states after the Civil War that winning the primary was equivalent to winning the general election.
3. Americans of African descent have been called *blacks*, *Negroes, colored,* or *African Americans,* depending on the historical period.
4. 19 Howard 393 (1857).
5. The Nineteenth Amendment that was ratified on August 18, 1920, stated, "The right of citizens of the United States to vote shall not be denied or abridged by the United States or by any state on account of sex. Congress shall have the power to enforce this article by appropriate legislation."
6. 21 Wallace 162 (1875).
7. Crozier, "Constitutionality of Discrimination Based on Sex," 15 *B.U.L. Review,* 723, 727–28 (1935) as quoted in William Hodes, "Women and the Constitution: Some

Legal History and a New Approach to the Nineteenth Amendment," *Rutgers Law Review,* Vol. 25, 1970, p. 27.

8. Hodes, p. 45.

9. Gunnar Myrdal, *An American Dilemma: The Negro Problem and Modern Democracy.* New York: Harper and Row (2d ed. 1962 [1944]), pp. 1073–74, as quoted in Hodes, p. 29. This same biblical ground has yielded the idea that a woman is an extension of her husband and his status.

10. The states under military rule were Virginia, North Carolina, South Carolina, Georgia, Florida, Tennessee, Alabama, Mississippi, Texas, Louisiana, and Arkansas.

11. The term *colored* was used in Louisiana to describe persons of mixed race who had some African ancestry.

12. 163 U.S. 537 (1896).

13. 118 U.S. 356 (1886).

14. 112 U.S. 94 (1884).

15. Native Americans and slaves posed a problem when taking the census count, which was the basis for apportioning seats in the U.S. House of Representatives. Some states stood to lose representation if some of their slave or Native American population was not counted. Blacks were counted as three-fifths of a white man, and only those Native Americans who were taxed were counted.

16. Restrictive covenants were written in deeds restricting the use of the land. Covenants could prohibit the sale of land to nonwhites or non-Christians.

17. 347 U.S. 483 (1954).

18. 414 U.S. 563 (1974).

19. 411 U.S. 1 (1973).

20. Rhonda Copelon, "A Crime Not Fit to Be Named: Sex, Lies, and the Constitution," p. 182. In David Kairys (ed.), *The Politics of Law,* pp. 177–94, New York: Pantheon 1998.

21. Copelon, p. 184.

22. 478 U.S. 186 (1986).

23. 438 U.S. 265 (1978).

24. Paul C. Higgins, *Making Disability.* Springfield, IL: Charles C. Thomas (1992), pp. 26–27.

25. *PGA Tour, Inc. v. Casey Martin,* 532 U.S. 661.

26. The Eleventh Amendment pertains to suits against the states. The interpretation is that a state cannot be sued by U.S. citizens of that state or another state nor by a foreign country.

27. Section 5 of the Fourteenth Amendment grants Congress the power to enforce the provisions of this amendment by appropriate legislation.

28. 124 S. Ct. 1978 (2004).

29. Four justices supported the University of California's admissions program against all objections on the ground that the government could use race "to remedy disadvantages cast on minorities by past racial prejudice." Four other justices did not interpret *Bakke* on constitutional grounds, but instead struck down the program on statutory grounds. Justice Powell's position was against the set-aside admissions policy, but was also for "reversing the state court's injunction against any use of race whatsoever." The holding in *Bakke* was that a "State has a substantial interest that legitimately may be served by a properly devised admissions program involving the competitive consideration of race and ethnic origin."

30. 539 U.S. 244 (2003).

31. 539 U.S. 982 (2003).

32. 129 S. Ct. 2658.

READING 42

Segregation: The Rising Costs for America

James H. Carr

Nandinee K. Kutty

The grave problem facing us is the problem of economic deprivation, with the syndrome of bad housing and poor education and improper health facilities all surrounding this basic problem.

(The Reverend Dr. Martin Luther King, Jr. in an interview one week before his death in 1968)

The link between access to decent housing and the attainment of economic and social mobility has been known for decades. Access to quality schools, good jobs, healthy and safe environments, supportive social networks, and accumulation of housing wealth are all influenced by the ability to secure housing in neighborhoods of opportunity and choice (Katz, 2004). Denial of access to housing is arguably the single most powerful tool to undermine and marginalize the upward mobility of people. A series of mechanisms directly intended to restrict the housing choice of minority households, beginning in the late 1800s and continuing throughout most of the twentieth century, largely explain the severe wealth disparities in America by race/ethnicity. They also largely explain the seemingly intractable concentrated poverty faced

---

James H. Carr is chief operating officer for the National Community Reinvestment Coalition. Nandinee K. Kutty is an economist and policy consultant.

by a disproportionate share of African American, Latino, and Native American populations. Failure to honestly acknowledge and address this unfortunate, but nevertheless real, past, and its consequences, will increasingly present major economic and social challenges for the nation's future.

Unequal treatment of minorities in the housing markets includes providing them with incomplete or misleading information about available housing units on the market, providing them with inaccurate information about the quality of neighborhoods and local schools, giving them inferior and unnecessarily costly access to mortgage credit, and other unequal costs or terms. These biased practices directly limit housing options for home-seekers, in direct contravention of the law. Moreover, it relegates them, unnecessarily, to severely disadvantaged housing conditions with the attendant problems of poor schools, unsafe streets, limited access to jobs, stifled housing equity accumulation, and concentrated poverty. In the end, housing discrimination artificially limits individuals from achieving their full potential as contributing members of society, stifles human achievement, creates unnecessary social program dependencies, and breeds dysfunctional behavior. It promotes an unproductive and divisive political environment along race, ethnic, and class lines. In short, housing discrimination is counterproductive to the national interest.

As the share of America's minority populations grows relative to the total U.S. population, failure to address lingering and significant roadblocks to economic mobility for minority households presents increasing challenges for the nation as a whole. Issues ranging from the United States' economic status in an increasingly competitive global economy to the solvency of Social Security and Medicare are affected (as the nation's population of financially disadvantaged households grows).

By the middle of this century, today's minorities will constitute half of the U.S. population—and that fast-growing population is disproportionately impoverished, ill-housed, poorly educated, and tenuously linked to labor markets. The first major step toward seriously addressing the substantial

barriers to economic and social mobility for minority households is to eliminate disparate treatment from the housing markets. By taking that single step, hundreds of thousands, if not millions, of households who are ready and prepared to succeed in the competitive marketplace will not be stymied by the continued artificial barrier of illegal discrimination.

[There are] many challenges and obstacles faced by minority households in achieving economic and social mobility. Five key points are discussed:

- America's wealth disparities along race and ethnic lines, as well as the disproportionate concentrated poverty among minority households, are largely the result of decades of public policies intended to economically marginalize minority households.
- The severe levels of concentrated poverty, segregation, and isolation resulting from those policies have created a complex web of socio-economic challenges that defy piecemeal and uncoordinated intervention. The problems are growing. As these problems grow, they increasingly take on grave significance for the nation beyond the sole issue of social justice.
- Housing is the centerpiece of opportunity. Successful housing-based strategies will help overcome barriers to economic mobility, and will thus create positive outcomes that go well beyond just providing affordable shelter.
- The millions of members of minority groups who today find themselves outside the mainstream of opportunities in America are a valuable human resource that is increasingly costly to neglect.
- Successful interventions are not beyond our ability to understand, design, and implement.

THE ROLE OF PUBLIC POLICIES IN THE CREATION OF INEQUALITY

Policies and Programs Impacting Housing Choice and Access to Finance

The hypersegregation and isolation that characterize a majority of African American communities in the United States are a *twentieth century phenomenon*—not the direct extension of slavery. In the late 1800s and early 1900s, African Americans and whites lived in close physical proximity to one another in both the North and the South; middle-class and upper-class African Americans in northern cities often lived as neighbors to whites of similar economic class and professional status. As neighbors and within professional classes, blacks and whites maintained easy interactions with each other.

In fact, only a short period after the Emancipation Proclamation of 1863, African Americans had achieved a measure of success in resettling their lives. They were farming land, acquiring property, establishing trades and businesses, building or buying houses, getting educated, working in jobs

for wages, and raising their families. They were on their way to acquiring economic and political power. They had the right to vote, and they became involved in the political process not only as voters but also as governmental representatives at the local, state, and national levels. It may be surprising to some readers to know that in the 1870s the newly enfranchised voters of South Carolina voted for enough African American representatives to provide African Americans with a majority in the state assembly (Library of Congress, 2002).

African Americans were becoming educated at a rapid rate at the end of the nineteenth century. While only a small proportion of African Americans had been literate at the end of the Civil War (state laws had forbidden literacy for the enslaved), by

FIGURE 1

Black segregation on the rise: northern U.S. cities

Source: Data points are from Douglas S. Massey, "Origins of Economic Disparities: The Historical Role of Housing Segregation," *American Apartheid: Segregation and the Making of the Underclass,* 1993.

Notes: "Indices of black isolation" refers to the percentage of blacks in the ward of the average black citizen. The isolation index measures the extent to which blacks live within neighborhoods that are predominantly black. A value of 100 percent indicates complete ghettoization and means that all blacks live in totally black areas; a value under 50 percent means that blacks are more likely to have whites than blacks as neighbors.

Values have not been estimated where exact figures were not found.

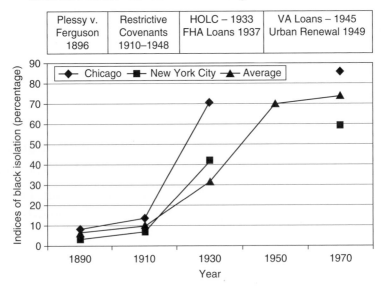

the turn of the twentieth century the majority of all African Americans were literate (Library of Congress, 2002). But this remarkable progress was stalled and tragically reversed with a series of private actions, reinforced and institutionalized by public laws, judicial mandates, and regulatory guidelines.

Programs and practices that systematically harmed minority households and communities included the use of restrictive housing covenants that limited housing location for minorities; a wide range of discriminatory practices by real estate professionals that further marginalized housing choice for African Americans; lack of government redress against violence to minorities who sought to move out of their segregated communities; biased underwriting policies of the Home Owners Loan Corporation (HOLC), the Federal Housing Administration (FHA), and

Veterans Administration (VA) that further limited minority locational choice, as well as undermined the value of properties in minority communities; urban renewal programs that targeted the destruction of minority communities in several U.S. cities; forced relocation of African American families to isolated, unsafe, and poorly constructed high-rise public housing projects; and inferior treatment of minorities in the GI Bill, New Deal programs, and other public housing assistance efforts.

These policies and practices related to housing and other economic areas, as well as the general national climate in which these policies and practices thrived, explain much of the present state of disadvantage faced by millions of American families.

One of the earliest and most important blows to the civil rights of African Americans after the abolishment of slavery came in the form of the

FIGURE 2

Black segregation on the rise: southern U.S. cities
Source: Data points are from Douglas S. Massey, "Origins of Economic Disparities: The Historical Role of Housing Segregation," *American Apartheid: Segregation and the Making of the Underclass,* 1993.
Notes: The index of dissimilarity represented here as "Indices of black–white segregation" gives the percentage of blacks who would have to move to achieve an "even" residential pattern—one where every neighborhood replicates the racial composition of the city.
Values have not been estimated where exact figures were not found.

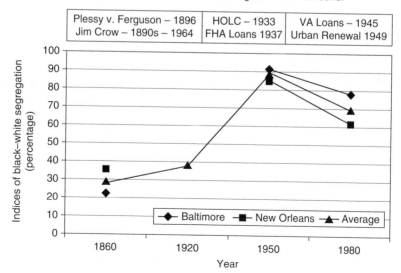

1896 *Plessy v. Ferguson* U.S. Supreme Court decision, which upheld the right of states to require segregation and ruled that segregation did not violate the Thirteenth Amendment of the U.S. Constitution. This decision upheld and established the doctrine of "separate but equal" and viewed the segregation of races as merely a matter of social policy; it asserted that segregation did not imply inequality. In reality, however, segregated facilities such as public schools, parks, swimming pools and other recreation facilities, cafés and restaurants, public facilities, and seating in transportation were systematically and significantly unequal in quality; minority facilities were rarely if ever even close to the same level of quality. The 1896 *Plessy* decision marked a significant turning point after which all levels of government passed further segregation laws and expanded segregation practices.

By 1900, all Deep South states had passed legislation and enforced social behaviors instituting segregation and the subordination of African Americans by whites (Jaynes, 2011). Under these laws, which came to be known as "Jim Crow" laws, African Americans were denied the right to vote through poll taxes, unfair literacy tests, and physical and economic intimidation. Their employment mobility was curtailed by anti-enticement laws that made it a crime for any employer to attempt to hire a worker under contract with another employer. Many agricultural laborers and sharecropper families who had borrowed money from their employer (in order to subsist during the year) were placed in debt peonage for several years. States passed vagrancy laws aimed at restricting the occupational mobility and general free movement of African Americans. One response of some African Americans in the South was to migrate to other parts of the nation (Jaynes, 2011). But the discriminatory practices employed in the South followed African Americans to northern cities, in different guises, and continued to expand and proliferate throughout most of the century.

Douglas Massey (2008) discusses the evolution of the black ghetto in America. Among his other insights, Massey shows that no ethnic or racial group in the history of the United States, other than African Americans, has ever experienced ghettoization, even briefly; while for urban African Americans the ghetto has constituted the typical residential experience for nearly a century. Massey points out that the immigrant ethnic enclaves that have existed in the United States are different from the black ghetto in three important respects. Immigrant enclaves were never homogeneous; they contained a variety of ethnicities, even when they were identified with one particular group. European ethnic groups did not experience the same high degree of isolation from American society as have African Americans living in hyper-segregated communities. And third, most members of other racial, religious, or ethnic groups did not live within the confines of the enclaves named after them. In fact, living in European ethnic enclaves was not the permanent condition for immigrant families; those neighborhoods served as springboards for moving on to a better life. In contrast, African Americans living in black ghettos remained permanently trapped in those surroundings. According to Massey, the American black ghetto has endured now for about a hundred years.

Massey highlights that restrictive covenants were a critical tool in the creation of the ghetto. Restrictive covenants were contractual agreements among property owners to prohibit African Americans from owning or occupying homes in white neighborhoods. After 1910, restrictive covenants were being used widely throughout the United States; indeed, they were found to be very effective in maintaining the color line. Other mechanisms to bring about racial segregation included blockbusting, violence and intimidation, a variety of discriminatory practices by real estate agents, and predatory lending to minorities. African Americans who faced violence to their property and person seldom found any redress from the authorities who chose to look the other way.

The federal government, in the twentieth century, became an instrument of widespread and systematic discrimination in housing through the formal underwriting policies of the HOLC, FHA, and VA. The HOLC, established in 1933 as the first government-sponsored program to introduce long-term, self-amortizing mortgages on a mass scale, institutionalized the practice of redlining. Under its system of rating loan risks, loans for homes located in older central city neighborhoods, with racially or ethnically mixed populations, were rated as too risky; and therefore such loans were seldom approved. Under HOLC criteria, African American neighborhoods were inevitably redlined and not served. The HOLC had not invented these racial standards of evaluating risks; these practices were already widespread in the real estate industry by the 1920s. But the HOLC took the lead in formally institutionalizing them. HOLC practices became models for other lending institutions, both private and public. According to Douglas Massey and Nancy Denton, the authors of the book *American Apartheid,* "It [the HOLC] lent the power, prestige, and support of the federal government to the systematic practice of racial discrimination in housing" (1993, p. 52).

The FHA and VA (established in 1937 and 1944, respectively) followed the HOLC's precedent; they applied similar racially discriminatory standards on a massive scale in housing markets all across the nation. The FHA's 1939 Underwriting Manual stated that "if a neighborhood is to retain stability, it is necessary that properties shall continue to be occupied by the same social and racial classes" (Jackson, 1985, p. 208). The FHA recommended the use of racially restrictive covenants in order to maintain the homogeneity of neighborhoods. The result was that the vast majority of FHA and VA loans were for homes in white middle-class suburbs. The federal transportation policy of this period focused on highway construction on a massive scale. Highways helped the growth of suburban housing markets and accelerated the process of suburbanization. Thus, by the late 1950s many cities fell into a spiral of decline induced by federal housing and transportation policies that encouraged middle-class whites to abandon inner cities for the suburbs. During this period, poor and lower-income African Americans from the South continued to migrate into northern cities, which further induced many middle-class whites to flee these cities (Massey and Denton, 1993).

Seeking a better life, many blacks began to migrate to northern and midwestern cities. As their populations grew, many white households who remained in the cities became concerned for their communities as well as major institutions that could not relocate, such as universities, theaters and other cultural institutions, parks, and other amenities. Viewing blacks as a threat, they appealed to the federal government for help to remove what they viewed to be urban slums that were spoiling the physical and social environment of their cities. The federal government responded by making funds available for local authorities to remove or "redevelop" slums. In many cities, slum removal translated directly into massive destruction of struggling but vibrant lower-income African American communities and the construction of large-scale public housing (Massey and Denton, 1993).

These programs were collectively called urban renewal. Public housing, intended for African Americans in conjunction with urban renewal, was built largely at the most undesirable locations, and frequently at very high densities. Poor and lower-income African Americans were displaced from the more dispersed slums and adjacent black neighborhoods and put into the far more segregated and crowded public housing (Massey and Denton, 1993). There they lived in overcrowded conditions, removed from the rest of society, in unaesthetic concrete spaces. Living conditions were not only physically undesirable but damaging to the human spirit. Residents of public housing projects had few interactions with the rest of society. According to historian Arnold Hirsch, public housing was a federally sponsored "second ghetto" which was "solidly institutionalized and frozen in concrete," where "government took an active hand not merely in reinforcing prevailing patterns of segregation, but in lending them a permanence never seen before" (1983, pp. 252–254).

Collectively, these programs had the impact of denying African Americans access to quality housing in growing and vibrant communities with good access to quality public educational institutions and jobs. This reality greatly undermined the accumulation of black wealth, in the form of housing assets, as well as denying blacks access to broader societal opportunities. Further, within black communities, African Americans were denied equal access to housing finance options available to white families. This further eroded housing wealth within African American communities since home sales were stifled by inadequate access for blacks to mortgage credit. Furthermore, unequal access to finance to renovate and repair the housing stock all but guaranteed its diminished quality.

Contemporary Housing Discrimination and Segregation

Although some progress has been made in purging some of the most blatant and obvious forms of discrimination from the housing markets, significant levels of discrimination continue, much of which builds directly on the infrastructure created by decades of discrimination. This perpetuating nature of discrimination ensures that the legacy of past discriminatory practices will not easily fade as mere relics of the past. In part, this lack of success in purging discrimination from the markets is directly attributable to the fact that enforcement of fair housing and lending laws is woefully underfunded and low on the public policy priority agenda. For example, although the Fair Housing Act was passed in 1968, the U.S. Department of Justice did not prosecute a major case against a mortgage lending institution until the early 1990s—the case against Decatur Federal S&L.

The Fair Housing Amendments Act of 1988 provided enormous enforcement powers to the U.S. Department of Housing and Urban Development (HUD), including the power to the HUD Secretary to initiate fair housing cases even if not connected with a complaint. However, HUD's enforcement powers have for various reasons largely remained underutilized. In 2003 HUD brought only four racial discrimination cases, although it had received more than 2,700 complaints that year. Nearly forty years after the passage of the federal Fair Housing Act, at least 3.7 million fair housing violations still occur each year (National Fair Housing Alliance, 2004). . . .

The Complex Economic and Social Impacts of Segregation

Years of abusive policies and practices of denial of opportunity have led to severe wealth disparities, including significant levels of poverty and concentrated poverty, in both black and Latino communities in cities across the nation. Over 18 percent of poor African Americans and almost 14 percent of poor Latinos live in poverty neighborhoods; in contrast, less than 6 percent of poor whites live in such neighborhoods (Jargowsky, 2003). In fact, it is not only poor African Americans but *most* African Americans who face a significant likelihood of living in poor neighborhoods. Sociologist Lincoln Quillian (2003) has estimated that most African Americans, in contrast with only 10 percent of whites, will live in a poor neighborhood at some point in a decade.

Poor black neighborhoods in U.S. cities underwent a transformation during the late 1970s and the 1980s: the black ghetto increasingly became the jobless ghetto and a place of concentrated poverty (Wilson, 1996). Previously, heavily segregated black neighborhoods contained both workers and jobless people. But in the 1970s and 1980s, structural changes in the economy caused cutbacks in certain types of jobs. Low-skilled and less educated workers who lived in such neighborhoods, and who were precluded by discriminatory housing market practices from relocating to areas of new job growth, were severely impacted by the job cuts. Increasingly, ghettos became dominated by jobless adults and families. High levels of crime, violence, and drug trafficking created extreme social disorder in America's jobless ghettos. Joblessness contributed to a decline in marriage and the growth of out-of-wedlock births (Wilson, 1996).

A complex web of problems began to grow in the segregated, impoverished neighborhoods of America. Hardworking, law-abiding families were not able to find avenues for upward mobility within the desperate conditions of the ghettos. There was a dearth of positive role models in such neighborhoods. Residents here were condemned to the worst poverty of all—a poverty of hope. . . .

HOUSING IS THE CENTERPIECE OF OPPORTUNITY

Housing is the centerpiece of opportunity in America. It is not just shelter, a convenient or pleasant place to live. Housing is much more than that—it determines the opportunity structures on which a family or individual can rely. As is discussed above, housing is the key to asset accumulation for the typical American family. But housing is also the key by which to access quality education, good jobs, convenient transportation, valuable social networks, diverse and well-maintained recreational facilities, and quality physical and mental health centers. Social status and the general well-being of the family or individual are also significantly determined by housing. . . .

Housing and Education

No one understands better the link between housing and schools than housing real estate agents. The quality of schools has for years been, arguably, the single most significant determinant of a quality housing market. The public schools that children in a family will attend are still predominantly decided by the location of housing. Hence, discrimination in housing and residential segregation grievously curtail the access of minority children to good-quality education. . . . Housing opportunities can lead to better schooling opportunities as families move to school districts with better schools. Stable, affordable housing makes long-term uninterrupted attendance in the same school possible for children, thereby enhancing the learning experience for the individual child as well as the entire class. Socioeconomic segregation becomes an important cause of educational inequality in a variety of ways, including its impact on local finances for schools. . . .

Housing and Jobs

Residential segregation contributes to employment inequality across racial and ethnic groups. . . . Housing location has an immediate impact on access to jobs in terms of distance from jobs and commuting costs. In addition, labor-market outcomes are affected by education levels, skills, experience, attitudes, job-related information, referrals, prejudice, and discrimination—all of which are significantly influenced by the neighborhood of residence. For example, residents of neighborhoods that are far from employment centers (such as suburban job centers) may lack information about potential job opportunities. Also, community norms and expectations about education and good jobs tend to be lower in segregated minority neighborhoods; this possibly leads to worse labor market outcomes for the residents of these neighborhoods. . . .

Moreover, some studies indicate that African Americans have worse access to jobs than any other racial or ethnic group. According to economists Steven Raphael and Michael Stoll, despite some improvement in the proximity of African Americans to jobs during the 1990s, African Americans on average remain *more physically isolated from jobs than members of any other racial/ethnic group.* Raphael and Stoll (2002) found that in metropolitan areas with higher levels of segregation, minorities faced larger spatial mismatches between jobs and housing. Employers are known to discriminate against job applicants on the basis of their address; job seekers living in lower-income, minority neighborhoods may be rejected because of where they live (Tilly et al., 2001; Wilson, 1996).

Housing and Health

. . . The link between housing and children's health is best known in the case of lead paint, which has harmful effects on the development of children. Housing features like grab bars can enhance the functionality of disabled or elderly members of the household (Kutty, 2000). Housing location also affects access to good hospitals or other healthcare facilities. Stability of housing tenure reduces stress and stress-related ailments. There is recent evidence that residents in neighborhoods with good walkability features have lower rates of obesity. Housing costs also determine the disposable income left over for the household to spend on health care and healthy foods and behaviors.

Housing and Social Networks

Housing design, neighborhood amenities, and neighborhood composition, in part, determine the social networks formed by members of a family. Some housing developments are designed to promote better interaction with neighbors, with features such as balconies, porches, community spaces, and planned community activities. Social networks can promote emotional well-being and a sense of safety, and can also open up a range of opportunities—economic, educational, and social. . . .

Since housing is the centerpiece of opportunity, housing-related programs can help promote access to economic opportunity. These programs can serve as vehicles for upward economic mobility for families currently living in disadvantaged communities.

SUCCESSFUL INTERVENTIONS ARE ACHIEVABLE

Americans are a feisty people. We are proud of our accomplishments and successes. Our zeal to compliment our achievements sometimes leads us to make inaccurate assumptions regarding the true pillars and foundations of our success. For example, we cherish the view that individual success is a result of our individual investments of time, energy, intelligence, and financial resources. And we often perceive that people who have failed have done so as a result of their own personal limitations. While there is some truth in both of these beliefs, there is also a fair amount of inaccuracy.

Much of our success as a nation is the result of carefully crafted policies that intentionally and directly helped to build the largest and most affluent middle-class society of any nation on earth. As Douglas Massey and others (Katznelson, 2005) point out, programs such as land grants, high-quality public education, a broad range of housing programs, and specially designed financial institutions, and unique legislation in times of particular need, are important pillars of our success. Our shortcoming as a nation was that access to those programs and initiatives was not shared equally among all Americans, and the negative results are clear.

Compensating for decades of denial of opportunity will not be easy. But, it is essential. Equally important, the solutions are not beyond our ability to identify and implement. The first step to redress segregation is to enforce fair housing laws. Failure to enforce the law is both unconscionable and increasingly harmful to society at large. A second step to redressing years of discrimination would be the institution of commonsense consumer financial protections to help financially vulnerable households better engage the financial markets (including home mortgage markets). A final component would be the expansion or creation of programs aimed at repairing the damage to financial markets in lower-income minority communities.

CONCLUSION

. . . [W]e argue that many of the programs or opportunities needed to promote economic mobility for historically disadvantaged groups (racial and ethnic minorities) are the same programs that would benefit most Americans. Good jobs, quality education, decent affordable housing, safe neighborhoods, comprehensive health care, access to mainstream financial services, and a reliable social safety network are keys to upward economic and social mobility. Ensuring these opportunities are available to all residents would empower both traditionally disadvantaged families as well as the broader society as a whole. America has a proud history and heritage of developing and implementing comprehensive public programs and innovative policies to promote upward mobility. Our recommendation is to draw on our past successes and meet the challenges that face us, with sound public policies, as we have done in the past, but this time, for the benefit of all Americans.

DISCUSSION QUESTIONS

1. What is the evidence that "housing is the centerpiece of opportunity in America," as Carr and Kutty claim?
2. Why is housing in America more racially segregated than it was a century ago?

PERSONAL ACCOUNT

Learning My Own Privilege

My social class has afforded me the privilege to go about my daily life and education with relative ease and comfort, despite the fact that as a mixed-race, learning disabled woman I belong to many socially devalued groups. I grew up in a safe yet diverse area where my ethnicity and status as the daughter of an immigrant, on the one hand, and a gay man on the other, had few negative social consequences. My father, an American diplomat, met my mother and got married while stationed in the Philippines. We moved around a lot, which caused a great deal of familial stress. Despite the fact that their marriage was falling apart, my mom and dad provided a very happy home and a good education for both their children. They divorced in the late 1990s; my mother remarried, and while I was in high school, my father came out.

Likely because my father came out later in life, and he and my mother divorced relatively amicably, the legal custody he had over my sister and me was never contested. I also never directly encountered anti-immigrant resentment or the threat of my mother being deported. My parents did such a good job insulating me from the prejudice they encountered, that I did not realize what kind of investments and sacrifices they made until I was in college.

Growing up, I often thought about how my learning disability disadvantaged me. I felt ashamed of being pulled out of my regular class during English. I also resented not being able to take electives because I had to spend that extra time catching up with everyone else in my grade. I remember the summer between third and fourth grade, when I realized that most of my friends were going to the school for "gifted" children. I didn't understand why I couldn't go with them. My father explained that I needed a little bit more help than everyone else, and that I'd be spending a lot more time outside my normal class in the coming years working with "special" teachers. I came to hate the word "special." I wanted to be "special" in the same way the "gifted" kids were—no one cared how great I was at social studies or how fast I could run. I felt like the only thing that made me "special" was the fact I couldn't read well.

I didn't realize how incredibly fortunate I was to be able to attend quality schools that had the resources to detect my disability early and give me the extra attention I desperately needed. The reason I got that kind of help was because my parents could afford to buy a house in a nationally ranked school district. They also had the resources to send me to specialists, as well as the leisure time to help me at home. So, whereas the story of my "overcoming" my disability, eventually taking Advanced Placement classes in high school, and going on to college can be told as a great personal triumph, it can be more fully understood as the most likely outcome for a very upper middle-class girl who was always expected to go to college.

Mireille M. Cecil

REFERENCES

Jackson, Kenneth T. 1985. *Crabgrass Frontier: The Suburbanization of the United States.* Oxford: Oxford University Press.

Jargowsky, Paul A. 2003. *Stunning Progress, Hidden Problems: The Dramatic Decline of Concentrated Poverty in the 1990s.* May. Washington, DC: Brookings Institution.

James, Gerald D. 2011. "Two Evolutions: Black Affluence—Black Poverty." in Henry Louis Gates, Jr., ed., *The Oxford Handbook of African American Citizenship.*

Katz, Bruce. 2004. *Neighborhoods of Choice and Connection: The Evolution of American Neighborhood Policy and What It Means for the United Kingdom.* Washington, DC: Brookings Institution.

Katznelson, Ira. 2005. *When Affirmative Action Was White.* New York: W.W. Norton.

Kutty, Nandinee K. 2000. "Production of Functionality by the Elderly: A Household Production Function Approach," *Applied Economics,* 32, pp. 1269–1280.

Library of Congress. 2002. *The African American Odyssey: A Quest for Full Citizenship.* Library of Congress Exhibition. Available at http://memory.loc.gov/ammem/aaohtml/exhibit/aointro.html (accessed December 16, 2006).

Massey, Douglas S. and Nancy A. Denton. 1993. *American Apartheid: Segregation and the Making of the Underclass.* Cambridge, MA: Harvard University Press.

Massey, Douglas S. 2008. "Origins of Economic Disparities: The Historic Role of Housing Segregation." Chapter 2 in *Segregation: The Rising Costs for America,* edited by James

H. Carr and Nandinee K. Kutty. New York: Routledge, pp. 39–80.

Raphael, Steven and Michael A. Stoll. 2002. *Modest Progress: The Narrowing Spatial Mismatch between Blacks and Jobs in the 1990s.* Washington, DC: Brookings Institution.

Tilly, Chris, Philip Moss, Joleen Kirschenman, and Ivy Kennelly. 2001. "Space as a Signal: How Employers Perceive Neighborhoods in Four Metropolitan Labor Markets." In *Urban Inequality: Evidence from Four Cities,* edited by Alice O'Connor, Chris Tilly, and Lawrence D. Bobo. New York: Russell Sage Foundation.

Wilson, William J. 1996. *When Work Disappears: The World of the New Urban Poor.* New York: Alfred A, Knopf.

READING 43

Land Rich, Dirt Poor: Challenges to Asset Building in Native America

Meizhu Lui

Bárbara J. Robles

Betsy Leondar-Wright

Rose M. Brewer

Rebecca Adamson

"[Tribes] may . . . be denominated domestic dependent nations . . . their relation to the United States resembles that of a ward to his guardian."

—*Chief Justice Marshall, 1831,*
Cherokee Nation v. Georgia

American Indian tribes are the single largest private landholders in the United States today. But their

Meizhu Lui is executive director of United for a Fair Economy. Bárbara Robles is an economist and Senior Community Affairs Research Liaison at the Board of Governors of the Federal Reserve System. Betsy Leondar-Wright is communications director of United for a Fair Economy. Rose M. Brewer is a professor of African American and African Studies at the University of Minnesota. Rebecca Adamson, a Cherokee, is founder and president of First Nations Development Institute and founder of First Peoples Worldwide. United for a Fair Economy is a national non-partisan organization that campaigns against income and wealth inequality.

relationships to this wealth is different than any other group of Americans.

Imagine for a moment that you have inherited a large amount of wealth and property from a rich uncle in Texas. After celebrating your good fortune, you would probably seek to manage and protect this wealth in the best way possible. You may visit with an attorney to set up a trust fund to provide for you and your children. You would receive quarterly statements communicating the particulars of this trust fund—how much wealth it generates in a year, how your money has been invested, how much you are being charged in fees and service costs. More importantly, you would receive regular payments from this trust. If you were dissatisfied with the way your trust fund was being managed, you would have the freedom to hire a new attorney or trust manager, and would seek the most qualified person to manage your valuable assets.

And what about that land in Texas, rich with oil? You would seek to secure the best possible lease for the oil, and would closely monitor the revenues generated from this valuable natural resource. If you felt that you were receiving lower than market rate for your product, you would work to find a new contract that would generate the highest possible return for your goods. If you suspected that your business manager was not finding the best contracts for your oil, you would fire him or her.

These basic principles of asset management are followed by most people who own wealth in America. Yet these basic principles are not available to Native Americans, whose wealth is managed for them by the federal government. The wealth of Native Americans, including the land, natural resources, and income generated from such resources, is "held in trust" for them, meaning that the federal government controls when and how the land is leased, how much money the oil and gas and other resources sell for, and how the money earned is distributed. U.S. courts have ruled that there is a trustee-beneficiary relationship between tribes and the U.S. government, similar to a guardian and a ward, and from this legal opinion emerged the modern paternalistic relationship toward Indian tribes.

Stemming from the doctrine of trust responsibility, the federal government (through the Bureau of Indian Affairs) controls the management of Indian resources "for their best interest." While in writing it may have appeared that the United States government was interested in "protecting" tribal resources, in reality the federal government has mismanaged them, depriving the tribes of untold amounts of revenue.

The Supreme Court has ruled that the treaties entered into with the federal government create a legal relationship between the Indian tribes and the federal government. The government must respect the sovereignty of the tribes and provide "food, services and clothing to the tribes." In exchange for taking Indian lands and restricting tribes to reservation lands set aside for their use, the federal government would be held under the "moral obligations of the highest responsibility and trust" to the tribes. The *Seminole Nation v. United States* decision in 1942 defined the government duty to keep its promises and act in the best interests of the tribes as "the doctrine of trust responsibility."

While under the doctrine of trust responsibility the U.S. government may claim to manage tribal affairs for the best interests of tribes, this doctrine has in fact been applied in a paternalistic fashion over the past two hundred years. In 1977, the American Indian Policy Review Commission reported to the U.S. Senate that "the Bureau of Indian Affairs . . . has used the trust doctrine as a means to develop a paternalistic control over the day-to-day affairs of Indian tribes and individuals."

This doctrine of trust responsibility has affected American Indian tribes in two important ways: First, the trust responsibility promoted federal control of Indian assets, including land and natural resources, throughout U.S. history. Even in the last twenty years, as Native people have found new ways to create wealth, Congress has legislated new methods of exerting control that undermine Native sovereignty and take money out of the Native, wealth pot. Although the original intention of the trust responsibility was to manage tribal resources for the best interests of the tribes, federal appropriation of Native wealth and federal mismanagement has led to lost resources and stolen funds. These facts are the basis for a $137 billion lawsuit against the U.S. Department of the Interior.

Second, the trust responsibility has led to decades of federal policies intended to help Native Americans assimilate into mainstream white society. These policies included: forcing Indians to sell their tribal land to acquire cash; forcing Indians to adopt Western farming techniques; and removing Indian children from their families to attend schools designed to assimilate them into mainstream society. Such policies have been used for nearly two centuries to coerce Native Americans to accept Western models of property ownership, promoting private property ownership instead of collective tribal property ownership, and have attempted to erode the cultural traditions that formed tribal communities and societies. Beyond the physical genocide practiced in the 1700s and 1800s, these policies result in cultural destruction as well.

TRIBAL LAND, TRIBAL POVERTY

There are over 562 federally recognized tribes in the United States, with reservations that range in size from less than 100 acres to the 17 million-acre Navajo reservation. This includes 333 federally recognized tribes in the lower 48 states, and 229 Alaska Native Villages, now legally recognized as tribes.

In the lower 48 states, reservation lands account for over 54 million acres, and if the 42 million acres of Alaska Native lands are added, the aggregate amount would qualify as the fourth largest land base by area in the United States, behind Alaska, Texas, and California. Along with the timber, grazing, and croplands, other natural resources include 4 percent of U.S. oil and gas reserves, 30 percent of the low-sulfur coal reserves, and 40 percent of the privately held uranium deposits.

For most people anywhere in today's economy, such property holdings would equal wealth and money. Not so for the American Indian. Defying the economic tenet that property holdings and wealth are two sides of the same economic coin, today's Native Americans have the highest poverty rate in the nation.[1] Native Americans, as a group, have a 25.7 percent poverty rate, and they suffer from disproportionately low education levels[2] and high levels of chronic diseases. Official unemployment on Indian reservations is close to 22 percent annually, with seasonal employment even higher.[3]

Native Americans have the worst housing of any ethnic group. In 2000, 24 percent of households on Indian reservations were overcrowded, almost double the U.S. average.[4] Nearly 24 percent of homes on reservations lacked complete plumbing, substantially higher than the national rate.[5] Among Native American homeowners, the median home value was $81,000 in 1999, or only two-thirds of the white median.[6]

While net worth data are not available for Native Americans, there is evidence that asset ownership is far lower than for white Americans. Only 18 percent of American Indians had any income from interest, dividends, or rents in 1999,[7] compared with 41 percent of whites.[8] . . .

How did this group of people that was once so rich come to exhibit such signs of poverty? It is through a long history of federal policy that systematically stripped Native Americans of their assets, including land and natural resources such as gas and oil. Tribes are, in effect, "land rich and dirt poor." This overview of federal policy toward Native Americans shows how it has both systematically removed assets from Native American ownership and also reduced Native control of assets that they rightfully own. . . .

NOT A "MINORITY"

While there is no single definition of "Indian," there are some legal definitions that determine who qualifies for federal and tribal programs aimed at Native Americans. Usually, tribes have criteria based on ancestry for determining who is a tribal member. The federal government also uses certain criteria, often based on ancestry and termed "blood quantum." Most tribes require a one-fourth to one-eighth blood quantum, or that one out of four or one out of eight relatives are tribal members, to be a full-blooded tribal member. Unfortunately, many tribal definitions of

tribal members do not match the federal definitions, and this sometimes leads to a confusing situation where an individual may be eligible for a tribal program but not a federal program, or vice versa.[9] The U.S. Census goes with a self-definition approach—anyone who reports that they are Native American on the census is counted as Native American.

It is important to understand that American Indians have a history and a legal status that is different from any other racial group in America. Technically, Indians are not a "minority group," but rather are members of independent, sovereign nations led by sovereign tribal governments. These tribal governments have a unique relationship with the federal government, one that is rooted in American history and federal Indian law. This relationship determines the rights of members of Indian tribes, and determines how the federal government can treat Native Americans given their tribal "citizenship."

As members of a tribe, American Indians are eligible to participate in specific programs sponsored by the U.S. government, including ones designed to take care of the health, educational, and social service needs of tribal members. Individual tribal members may also own land that is held in trust by the federal government. In addition, tribal members can participate in programs related to health, education, and home ownership. These typically are administered by the Bureau of Indian Affairs, which is part of the U.S. Department of the Interior. Historically, the BIA has administered all Indian Health Service programs, all trust funds for tribes, and all land and natural resource leases. More and more tribes are administering programs formerly controlled by the BIA, including health programs, housing programs, and even in a few cases trust funds.

HISTORY OF FEDERAL POLICY TOWARD NATIVE AMERICAN ASSETS

In 1492, the year Columbus accidentally landed in what is now North America, Native populations resided in and controlled the vast land areas of what is now the United States. Different tribes controlled different regions of the continent, and depending on the tribe, were either agrarian populations farming numerous crops, or nomads living off hunting, fishing, and gathering in established territories. The Native population was nearly five million. By 1800, many of these tribes had been forced inland by European settlements, and by 1900 the Native population was less than one million and was residing on less than 4 percent of the original continental United States.[10]

Each tribe in the United States has had a different experience related to treaty making, land theft, and control of tribal resources, but federal policies toward Native Americans on the whole reflect one theme: control of Native assets. Whether it is the relocation of the Cherokee, Chickasaw, and Choctaw tribes in the early 1800s from their rich agricultural land in Georgia and other southern territories, the sale of land on the Osage reservation in Oklahoma to non-Indians to gain access to oil in the early 1900s, or the "termination" of the Klamath tribes in Oregon[11] to sell timber-rich land to a paper company in the 1950s, federal policies toward American Indians have methodically removed wealth from Native populations.

COLONIZATION AND TREATY MAKING (1492–1838)

The first colonists benefited from the knowledge and technology of Native populations in many ways. The pilgrims of Plymouth survived the winter of 1620 with the assistance of the Wampanoag tribe of Massachusetts.[12] Such assistance in the form of food and agricultural help, coupled with a fear of Native populations' often superior military might, contributed to a relationship of respect between the early settlers and Native Americans. As more people from England, France, Spain, and Holland began settling in the eastern colonies, treaties were signed with Indian nations, and for the most part Indian tribes were treated as political equals who were respected for their military strength, advanced agricultural knowledge, and political systems.

As the number of settlers in the "New World" grew, however, conflicts flared between the colonists and the Indian tribes. As the colonists' power increased, they ceased treating Indians as political equals. Conflicts over land led to increased Native resistance, and raids against the European settlements and armed conflicts between settlers and Indians became more frequent.

European colonists in the New World often described the land as barren and empty. This is partly due to their desire to claim ownership of land under the concept of eminent domain, which allowed that if a property was unused it could be claimed by the British Crown.[13] It also stemmed from the settlers' lack of understanding of Native American concepts of property and land use. The Native belief in collective land use, in seasonal agricultural practices in harmony with the environment, and in one's inability to "own" the land often confused the European settlers, who subscribed to individual property rights and strict territorial boundaries. This clash of value systems led to disputes over territorial rights and land use. . . .

Some tribes built strategic alliances with the settlers. As the American colonists began to feud with one another and ultimately with the British Crown, alliances were built with several tribes. The Iroquois Confederacy sided with the British in the French and Indian War, and as a result the English king issued a proclamation to limit colonists' taking of Indian land. The colonists largely ignored this proclamation, however, and when they rebelled against the British Crown in the late 1700s, they preemptively attacked many tribal settlements. Most eastern tribes sided with the British, but the Oneida, Tuscaroras, Mohegans, and Pequots assisted their American neighbors.

After the American Revolutionary War, the tribes that had sided with the British were punished by the new government, while those that had fought on the side of the colonists were rewarded. For example, the Oneida tribe was granted high-quality agricultural land in Wisconsin in exchange for supporting the American colonists. The official position of the new U.S. government after the war was to treat Indian tribes as having status equal to foreign nations, and to respect treaty rights and maintain good relations with them. However, as westward expansion continued, Native Americans increasingly were forced to sign treaties, removed from their land, or relocated to reservations. . . .

Treaties are the most important legal documents in determining the nature of the federal relationship with American Indian tribes. It is from the texts and proceedings of these treaties that the complex legal and political ideas (subsequently called federal Indian law) have emerged, affecting Indians for over two centuries. The Supreme Court has ruled that the treaties entered into with the federal government create a legal relationship between the Indian tribes and the federal government to respect the sovereignty of the tribes and provide "food, services and clothing to the tribes."[14] This was seen as a fair exchange for taking Indian lands and restricting tribes to reservation lands set aside for their use.

The treaties contributed to a loss of tribal wealth because they forced many tribes to relinquish control of traditional territories, including land and natural resources. They also laid the foundation for the modern-day relationship between tribes and the federal government and for the trust funds that the federal government currently manages for Indian nations. These trust funds were first mentioned in a treaty with the Choctaws in the 1820s, in which they ceded lands west of the Mississippi River, and agreed to have funds set aside to support Choctaw schools. Later treaties would establish trusts to manage tribal wealth, administer leases on tribal natural resources, and manage ownership of land.

The "subject of Indian rights can seem complex and terribly confusing. There are thousands of treaties, statutes, executive orders, court decisions, and agency rulings that play integral roles. Indian law is a subject unto itself, having few parallels."[15] As a subcommittee of the U.S. Senate noted in 1977:

> It is almost always a mistake to seek answers to Indian legal issues by making analogies to seemingly similar fields. General notions of civil rights law and public land law, for example, simply fail to resolve many questions

relating to American Indian tribes and individuals. This extraordinary body of law and policy holds its own answers, which are often wholly unexpected to those unfamiliar with it. . . .[16]

RELOCATION AND RESERVATIONS (1828–1887)

When Andrew Jackson was elected president in 1828, federal policy toward American Indians changed dramatically. What had previously been an unofficial policy of increasing control of Indian lands for white settlement became official federal policy. Removal became "the dominant federal Indian policy of the nineteenth century."[17] In the late 1700s and early 1800s, the demand for land had increased even more as new populations arrived and agricultural technology improved. Pressure grew on the federal government to displace many tribes from their rich agricultural land, including the Cherokee, Chickasaw, Choctaw, and Creek. There was also a great deal of interest in newly discovered natural resources in traditional Indian territories. For example, in 1830, the governor of Georgia issued a proclamation that announced that all the lands of the Cherokee, and especially the gold mines, were the property of the state.[18]

The Indian Removal Act of 1830 was drafted to remove eastern tribes to lands west of the Mississippi, thereby opening up former Indian lands in the East for white colonization. Officially, the Native Americans were to be encouraged to move not by force, but by land exchanges. In practice, however, force was often used and the land exchanges were terribly inadequate.

The Cherokee attempted to resist the Indian Removal Act through legal means and brought its case before the United States Supreme Court. In 1832, Chief Justice John Marshall found in favor of the Cherokees in the case of *Worcester v. Georgia,* but President Jackson refused to enforce the court's decision.[19] In the fall and winter of 1838–39, the Cherokee were finally forced westward. Fifteen thousand Cherokee were marched off to "Indian Territory," during what came to be called the Trail of Tears.[20] During the cold, twelve-hundred-mile march, four thousand Cherokee Indians died.[21] The Chickasaw, Choctaw, and Creek tribes were also relocated from their traditional homelands in the Southeast to the newly created Indian Territory in what is now Oklahoma. Of the twenty thousand tribal Choctaw members forcibly relocated from Mississippi, only seven thousand survived.

When Indians, forced westward by the Indian Removal Act, arrived in the so-called Indian Territory, they often discovered the land areas they were compensated with were even smaller than those in the East. Even this meager land in the newly designated Indian Territory was under contest, however. Before all of the primary removals were completed in the East, the secondary removals had begun in the West, "and the land that was supposed to belong to the Indian in perpetuity was in the white man's market."[22] Again Native American value systems and Western concepts of property rights were in conflict. The land, often considered by Indians to be sacred "mother earth," was increasingly being commodified and sold for profit to benefit white settlers.

Ironically, much of the land to which tribes were relocated was later found to contain great natural resource wealth, as had their traditional territories. When this occurred, the federal government often responded by opening up reservations to white ownership, once again removing Indians to other lands or simply appropriating natural resources. . . .

Throughout the second half of the nineteenth century, colonial settlement continued to push westward. The Homestead Act and the Pacific Railway Act, both passed in 1862, brought floods of settlers to the West. The Homestead Act provided that any white male adult eligible for citizenship could claim 160 acres of government-surveyed western land.[23] The result was that by 1900, homesteaders had filed six hundred thousand claims for eighty million acres of land, mostly in the western Plains states of Kansas, Nebraska, Colorado, and Wyoming, displacing the Sioux, Cheyenne, Ute, Pawnee, and many other tribes.[24]

With the Pacific Railway Act, the government gave huge grants of land to the railroad companies for rights-of-way, and the railroad often cut narrow swathes through the middle of Native American lands. The act itself even encouraged this disruption of Indian land, stating, "The United States shall extinguish as rapidly as may be the Indian titles to all lands falling under the operation of this act and required for the said right of way."[25]

Railroad companies also received many additional square miles of land to gather building materials and establish small settlements to support railroad construction, and the lucrative timber and mineral rights to this land.[26] This permanent grant of land and natural resources benefited many white settlers by providing jobs and transportation corridors, but typically extracted land and other wealth from Indian tribes without compensation. . . .

As westward expansion continued, the U.S. Army actively waged battles with tribes to open land for white settlement. In 1845, the U.S. Army clashed with the Sioux in Nebraska, and again in Minnesota in 1862, and also with the Navajo in New Mexico.[27] White settlers often participated in attacks on Native Americans, especially after the U.S. Army went east for the Civil War.[28]

The California Gold Rush, beginning in 1849, was a particularly devastating period in Native American history. Many Indian villages in California were destroyed by order of Congress, and numerous Indians were killed or moved to reservations. In 1853, the California Preemptive Act declared all Indian lands as public domain, open for homesteading.[29] Local tribes were systematically chased off their lands and marched to missions and reservations, and many were enslaved and brutally massacred. In 1851, the California state government provided $1 million for scalping missions. Individuals could get $5 for a severed Indian head in Shasta in 1855, and 25¢ for a scalp in Honey Lake in 1863.[30] All these activities, in addition to the introduction of diseases to the Native populations, reduced the Indian population in California from 310,000 in 1850 to less than 50,000 in 1855.[31] By 1870, there was an estimated population of only 31,000 Californian Indians left. Over

60 percent of the indigenous people died from disease introduced by the hundreds of thousands of so-called 49ers.[32]

ALLOTMENT AND ASSIMILATION (1887–1934)

The loss of Indian land was greatly accelerated in the late 1800s with the passage of the General Allotment Act, also known as the Dawes Act.[33] This piece of legislation, passed by Congress in 1887, was disastrous for tribes and severely reduced their land holdings.

The official purpose of the Dawes Act was to encourage tribal members to adopt a sedentary agricultural lifestyle and to force Indians to assimilate into white society.[34] Other unstated purposes were to break up tribal governments, abolish Indian reservations, promote individual ownership of Indian land instead of traditional collective tribal ownership, and allow white settlers and private business interests increased access to land and other Native natural assets.[35] This was to be accomplished by dividing existing reservations—already diminished by treaties and settlement—into individual Indian allotments of between 80 and 160 acres. Many Indians were given meager farming tools and encouraged to start Western farming practices by Indian Agents dedicated to "civilizing" the Native population. Surplus land not allotted to Indians was typically sold to white farmers and ranchers. This resulted in a massive land transfer from Indians to white settlers over a short period of time. In just one year, 1891, Indian commissioner Thomas Morgan sold off one-seventh of all the Indian lands in the United States to white settlers, over 17.4 million acres.[36]

Native women especially lost property rights under the Dawes Act. The original plan was to distribute land to "heads of families," meaning men, but some tribal leaders objected because women and children had some property rights in their cultures. The plan was changed to a per capita distribution. However, women and children without men in their families were more often challenged in court by white would-be settlers and usually declared incompetent to own land.[37]

The land allotted to American Indians was inferior in terms of quality and quantity, yet there was no provision in the Dawes Act to compensate for low-quality land. Many individual Indian landholders were not successful at agricultural production, partly because of the low quality of the land, and partly because they were being forced to adopt western agricultural practices. By the turn of the century, whether an individual had received good or poor quality land made little difference, as Indian land increasingly fell into the hands of non-Indians through leasing and sales.

Individual Indian allotments were initially to be held in trust for twenty-five years, during which time the state could not tax them nor could they be sold. This was designed to protect individually owned Indian land, as individuals worked to gain economic self-sufficiency through farming. Even this protection, however, was short-lived. The Burke Act, passed in 1890, allowed the Secretary of the Interior to remove allotments from trust before the time set by the Dawes Act to Indian allotees considered competent to manage their own affairs. After allotment lands were taken out of trust, they could be sold and, most importantly, taxed by the state. Many impoverished American Indians sold their allotments or lost them in foreclosures when they were unable to pay the state property taxes. In most instances, this land was quickly sold to local non-Indians usually for below market value amounts. . . .[38]

Instead of the culturally appropriate, tribally owned collective land, the Dawes Act forced private property ownership upon tribal members. The push to individual allotments also resulted in a checkerboard pattern of ownership within the boundaries of many reservations, where Indian allotments were interspersed with non-Indian land plots. This checkerboard pattern of ownership has lead to serious problems on many reservations to this day related to jurisdiction and tribal control of land. Without a unified land base, tribes have had difficulty creating economies of scale or implementing effective economic development strategies.

For the allotments that were not sold or encumbered, the land was partitioned among the heirs upon the original allottee's death, or sold and the money divided. This aspect of the allotment policy, in particular, has been extremely disruptive to Native land ownership patterns. It has resulted in highly fractionated heirships, where dozens or even hundreds of heirs to the original allottee own partial interests in a single 160-acre allotment. Years of government mismanagement of these land trust accounts has led to great confusion over who owns what parcels of land. The parcels of land were supposed to be managed for individuals and their heirs, but these parcels of land have become highly fractionated with each generation. Some original allotments are now owned by over three hundred people, rendering the land useless for homesteading or development. In addition, mismanagement by the federal government has resulted in lost records pertaining to land ownership, so many tribal members have no record of the land they rightfully own. . . .

INDIAN REORGANIZATION: THE INDIAN NEW DEAL (1934–1953)

John Collier, appointed commissioner of Indian Affairs in 1933, held views contrary to most other Indian advocates of the time and believed that all efforts to acculturate and assimilate Indians into white society had failed, and had only served to destroy the inherent strengths of Indian tribal life.[39] Upon assumption of office, Collier acted quickly to try to reform federal Indian policy and guarantee a land base for future generations. As the allotment policy had turned Indians into paupers instead of making them responsible, self-sufficient farmers, and due to strong support for those previous policies, Collier presumed that legislation would be necessary to guarantee the land protections he sought. His extensive plan, known as the Wheeler-Howard Act, was introduced in Congress in 1934, and an amended version was passed in June of that year. This legislation, also known as the Indian Reorganization Act, became the heart of the Indian New Deal.[40] The Indian Reorganization Act prohibited further

allotment of reservation land and extended the trust periods for allotments remaining in trust. Remaining "surplus" land was returned to tribal ownership and held in trust. This policy had a positive impact on many tribes. By 1950, tribes had reacquired four million acres of previously alienated lands.[41]

In its conception, the Indian Reorganization Act, or IRA, was intended to benefit tribes by revitalizing tribal governments, bringing an end to allotment while helping to create new reservation lands, and strengthening relationships between tribal and federal governments. Under the act, tribes would be able to draw up charters for the creation of business corporations, giving tribes a chance for economic expansion and control over corporation affairs independent of the BIA. A revolving credit fund would be established to further aid in economic development while financial aid would assist in providing for college education and technical training. Preference would at last be given to Native Americans for employment in the BIA, allowing tribes greater control over their own affairs. Tribes would be granted the ability to hire attorneys in order to defend their own interests. Moreover, since few tribes were experienced in dealing with modern government affairs, the act provided a model constitution as a guide in restructuring tribal governments. Each tribe had the option of voting on acceptance of a constitution and on the Indian Reorganization Act as a whole.

In practice, however, the IRA quickly made evident a new way of imposing a non-Native system upon tribes. Though the IRA was used to produce much good through the protection of Native lands, its approach also played a part in destroying traditional ways of life and governance, by imposing such foreign concepts as a majority rule government, an adversarial system of justice, a one-person-one-vote concept, and the separation of church and state.[42] Many tribes found themselves willing to reject the promise of federal loans after adoption of the IRA upon learning of a stipulation that they felt continued the influence of the BIA in tribal affairs: for a constitution to be adopted, the Act stated, the document must contain a provision wherein the

Secretary of the Interior must give approval over the final constitution and any amendments. The Secretary was further able to veto new laws, overrule certain council actions, call elections and settle election disputes, oversee economic affairs for the tribe, and approve their choices of legal counsel. The tribes recognized that the Secretary essentially maintained a say over any legislation that might significantly affect the tribe.[43] With these powers, tribes felt that the Secretary would maintain considerable control over tribal affairs. For instance, should a tribe wish to hire an attorney who would help it contest any aspect of the Secretary of Interior's control, the attorney simply would not be approved.

In the end, 181 tribes voted to accept the IRA, while 77 opposed it.[44] Records reveal, however, that votes were frequently mismanaged. The votes of any eligible tribal members who abstained were counted as affirmative ones. This deliberately unorthodox practice took advantage of the traditional right of signifying no by actively boycotting the vote. On the Santa Ysebel Reservation in California for example, forty-three tribal members voted against the IRA, while nine voted in favor. However, sixty-two eligible voters chose to boycott the proceedings; their absences, counted as favorable votes, meant the act was considered passed on the reservation.[45] In other cases, Native voters were ill informed or even subjected to electoral fraud in order to obtain a positive outcome. For instance, the Hopi people were told that the vote was for retention of their land not for reorganization. In addition, many Hopi votes and registration papers were falsified.[46] More controversial still was the Lakota vote, swayed to the affirmative when enough dead persons were registered as having voted changing the outcome of the IRA. . . .[47]

THE TERMINATION PERIOD (1953–1960)

Beginning in the 1940s, war-related industrialization and attempts to terminate the legal recognition of some tribes meant that many Native Americans lost control of more land and natural resources. In 1949, the Hoover Commission issued a report that called for the "complete integration" of Native Americans into mainstream society.[48] In 1953, with direct support from President Dwight D. Eisenhower, Congress passed House Concurrent Resolution No. 108. This resolution, often called "the termination resolution," sought to remove governmental power from tribal governments, discontinue the relationship between the federal government and tribal nations, and discontinue federal benefits and support services that accompanied the trust responsibility. Many of the supporters of the new policy argued that it represented "emancipation" because it would "free" Indians from the oppressive, day-to-day control of the Bureau of Indian Affairs.[49] The resolution stated that

> all of the Indian tribes and the individual members thereof located within the States of California, Florida, New York and Texas, and all of the following named Indian tribes and individual members thereof, should be freed from Federal supervision and control and from all disabilities and limitations specially applicable to Indians.

The policy was implemented by individual congressional acts for each tribe that was slated for termination and was accompanied by a termination plan that transferred tribal land into private ownership and discontinued tribal government powers.

Termination had a devastating effect on tribes. When the federal government terminated a tribe, it once again forced individual private property ownership upon tribal members, often against their will or interest. Individual tribal members, once they became private property owners, were forced to pay taxes to the state. Many Indians either sold their land to whites or were swindled out of it, and many individual Indians lost land that they were not able to pay taxes on. This further contributed to the erosion of the Native land base.[50] By selling Indian land, Congress destroyed the economies of many tribes, reducing them to poverty and dependence on public assistance. In total, approximately 109 tribes and bands were terminated under the policy, and a minimum of 1,362,155 acres and

11,466 individuals were affected. While some of these tribes have since been reinstated, most tribes are still struggling to this day to recover from such a devastating economic blow.

The shameful nature of this period in U.S. history is further reflected in the fact that once again the motivation for tribal termination appeared to be wholly economic, rather than simply misguided social policy. Tribal termination across the nation resulted in the surrender of over twenty million acres of prime timber and farmlands to the United States government. In addition, terminated tribes were cut off from valuable federal services that accompanied the trust responsibility, including health, education, and housing. These terminated tribes have never been compensated for the loss of these services, valued at about $148 million.[51] Because tribal sovereignty is a federal guarantee that insulates tribes from taxation and other economic burdens imposed by the state and local non-Indian governments, the loss of this protection also had high costs. The Native American Rights Fund estimates that these costs may be over $100 million over the period from 1961 to 1986.[52] . . .

CHALLENGES TO HUNTING AND FISHING RIGHTS (1960–1980)

Historically, tribes controlled vast land areas where they actively hunted and fished for food. As tribes increasingly were forced to cede land and accept relocation to reservations, access to these traditional resources became more limited. Competition from corporate interests led to challenges to traditional harvest rights. In addition, the construction of dams, environmental pollution, and other factors seriously diminished the amount available to the tribes. However, since many tribes continued to rely on these natural resources as an important food supply, they have had to work to defend their rights.

In the 1960s, competition from commercial fishing interests and sport hunters and fishermen began to grow. The salmon runs and other fish stock in the Pacific Northwest of the United States were increasingly attractive to corporate interests.

In the 1980s, a legal battle erupted over traditional fishing rights in Wisconsin. A series of court cases was heard by the state and federal courts that ultimately upheld access rights of tribes to their traditional fish harvest. The backlash from corporate interests and sport hunters and fisherman was significant, however, and protest continues to this day.

Indian hunting and fishing rights were the focus of some of the fiercest anti-Indian agitation by sportsmen, who were vocal, active, and even violent in their opposition. Yet the greatest injury from legally allocating a percentage of the catch to Indians was not to sport fishermen, but to the commercial fishing industry. So while the campaign against Indian fishing rights was expressed entirely in terms of sportsmen's interests and environmental protection, the campaign organizers were in fact mostly commercial fisheries. They blamed Indians for smaller fish runs, that were actually caused by normal cyclical patterns and stream pollution from corporations. The response to court protection of tribal fishing rights included fishermen in their boats with guns and the refusal by the state of Washington to enforce the court decision.

WHO BENEFITS FROM TRIBAL NATURAL RESOURCES?

In the lower forty-eight states, tribes hold about 30 percent of the nation's coal resources, 10 percent of the natural gas resources, and 5 percent of the oil resources. According to some estimates, 10 percent of the nation's energy resources lie within the tribal land base.

The electric power industry is a $280 billion per year business in the United States. Coal, natural gas, and some oil are used as the fuels for this industry. If you take the 10 percent of energy resource holdings owned by Indian tribes, then one could assume that the total amount of revenue generated from the tribal energy resources should be around $28 billion per year. Yet in 1999, the annual income to the tribes was less than $1 billion ($900 million).

Until 1962, the Department of the Interior held that it was not legal for Indians to develop their own mineral properties. In practice, Indian mineral owners were simply leaseholders with little say over such matters as air and water pollution and preservation of sacred sites. As the Council of Energy Resource Tribes states:

> It was no longer necessary to move Indians off their land or necessary to send in troops to protect trespass mining; all that was necessary was to induce the Indian landowner to sign a minerals lease, or the government to sign it on behalf of the owner. The location of roads, storage facilities, the use of timber, water, gravel, and the minerals themselves in support of the mining operations become solely the province of the lessee. Until the early 1970s, the only legal role for the Indian mineral owner was that of a passive royalty owner. Under such a scheme, tribes had no opportunity to develop their managerial, technical, or business skills but remained, under the law, wholly dependent upon the integrity of federal institutions for the protection of their interests.

More recently, some tribes have taken a more active role in managing the leases for their natural resources. Only one tribe, the Southern Ute (located in Colorado, New Mexico, and Utah) has complete control of their energy resources. Most tribes have had their energy resources leased to outside corporations, mostly owned by non-Indians. The Bureau of Indian Affairs usually negotiates the leases, often without tribal input, and the corporations pay a percentage in royalties to the tribes. These royalties range from 12 percent to 25 percent of total revenues earned from the resource. While this is changing, the majority of leases for tribally owned natural resources are granted to non-Indian companies. Recently, many lawsuits have emerged that claim the federal government has historically mismanaged these natural resource leases. Litigation in many of these lawsuits is ongoing.

CHALLENGES TO NATIVE WEALTH TODAY

In the 1980s, in an effort to promote economic development on Indian reservations, the Reagan administration encouraged tribes to pursue revenue-generating activities that took advantage of their tribal sovereign jurisdiction. Such activities as cigarette sales and gaming that took advantage of the tribes' unique tax and legal status were promoted. As tribes began to use their governmental status as a vehicle for income-generating activities, however, courts were increasingly called upon to clarify the scope of tribal regulatory and jurisdictional authority. Eyeing profits being generated on Indian reservations, states were eager to impose taxes on tribes.

Taxation

Indians are subject to federal taxation on income, whether it is earned on or off a reservation or tribal lands. However, tribes can operate tribally owned companies that are exempt from federal taxes, even if the company conducts business off the reservation. In addition, most tribes are not subject to state taxation, and therefore tribal businesses can benefit from a significant tax savings. The origin of this legal right is the 1832 opinion by Chief Justice Marshall in *Worcester v. Georgia*, which declares that state laws "can have no force" on an Indian reservation without the consent of Congress.[53] Marshall referred to tribes as "domestic dependent nations" and stated:

> Indian nations had always been considered as distinct, independent political communities, retaining their original natural rights, as the undisputed possessors of the soil.

The U.S. Constitution mentions Indians as distinct and separate identifiable groups twice: once, in the provision for representation in Congress, and the second time in the Fourteenth Amendment, when Indians are exempted from some federal taxation. For the most part, the rights of Indians who live and work on Indian land to avoid state taxation have been upheld including in a 1973 decision.[54] In addition, Indians who buy goods on their reservations, regardless of whether they buy it from an Indian or a non-Indian, do not have to pay state sales tax. This is not true for non-Indians purchasing goods on the reservation. In 1980, the

Supreme Court ruled in *Washington v. Colville* to allow states the authority to tax cigarette sales to non-Indians, effectively stripping tribes of a profit margin for taxing such sales. In *Rice v. Rehner,* in 1983, the Supreme Court ruled that states can regulate the sale of alcohol by requiring tribes to purchase state permits to sell packaged liquors on the reservation. . . .

Gaming

As gaming has become increasingly profitable, states have become more aggressive in their attempts to regulate or tax gaming profits. It all started in 1979, when the Seminole tribe of Florida became the first Indian tribe to operate a high-stakes bingo game.[55] With the advent of more profitable gaming in the early 1980s by the Cazabon Band of Mission Indians and the Morongo Band of Mission Indians, which opened high-stakes poker parlors, tribes began to recognize the income-generating power of gaming operations. More and more tribes began to open casinos or other gaming operations.

Federal Indian law means that Indian reservations are generally exempt from regulation by the states and this, in turn, puts the federal government into a dilemma over the issue of gaming. The issue came to a head in 1987 with *California v. Cazabon Band of Mission Indians.* The Supreme Court found that by allowing any gambling within the bounds of the state, the state could not prohibit gaming on the reservation. In other words, the state could not prohibit gaming on a reservation while it endorsed or participated in similar gaming off the reservation.

As a result of the decision in *Cazabon,* in 1988 Congress enacted the Indian Gaming Regulations Act (IGRA) to provide a statutory basis for the operation of gaming by Indian tribes as a means of promoting tribal economic development, self-sufficiency, and strong tribal governments. IGRA provided a shield from organized crime and other corrupting influences, and it established federal regulatory standards.[56] The Indian Gaming Regulatory Act specified that funds from gaming can only be used for:

- funding tribal government operations or programs;
- providing for the general welfare of the tribe and its members;
- promoting economic development for the tribe;
- donating to charitable organizations;
- helping fund operations of local government agencies. [57]

Many tribes believe that IGRA infringed upon tribal sovereignty because it required tribes to enter into compacts with states before it could offer certain types of gaming, and it restricted the use of gaming funds. While the legislation clearly indicates that states do not have the right to collect taxes on Indian reservations, the state compacts, that tribes must participate in, often require that the tribes pay the state a large portion of their revenues. Rarely does Congress place such restrictions on state or local governments, and privately owned casinos have no such obligations. . . .

LOOKING FORWARD

Native Americans have a history that is different from every other racial group in the United States. While many of the policies that forced tribes to relocate from traditional lands and sell their land and natural resources to whites and non-Natives occurred many years ago, a new set of policies have emerged in the last 20 years that continue to extract newly acquired resources from Indian people.

It is only by understanding the federal policies and actions that led to wealth transfer from Native Americans to white Americans that we can understand why American Indians are "land rich and dirt poor" today. Federal actions, including legislative, judicial, and administrative policies that extracted or mismanaged tribal wealth, have contributed to the current condition of poverty and underdevelopment that many tribes find themselves in today.

Native Americans would be well off if they had gotten the fruits of their assets. It would be simple to make this happen by extending the protections enjoyed by other asset owners to Indians as well.

The United States has a body of law regulating trustees' responsibilities to beneficiaries. The Securities and Exchange Commission (SEC) protects shareholders from conflicts of interest and requires trustees to maximize the benefit to the beneficiary. The Department of the Interior should be held to these same standards, instead of being allowed to cut sweetheart deals . . . at tribes' expense.

To enact these reforms, Native Americans should become legal beneficiaries of their own assets, instead of wards of the government. Indeed, why are Native Americans defined as wards, given that wards are usually children or mentally incompetent adults?

Today tribes have started to build and consolidate their land holdings.

In earlier centuries Native Americans were assumed by white policy makers to be incompetent savages, but now the debate about Native competence should be over. The SEC or another neutral, third-party ombudsman should have the power to audit the Department of the Interior and other trustees managing tribes' assets.

Being land rich should not mean being dirt poor.

DISCUSSION QUESTIONS

1. What forces and events have contributed to the appropriation of Indian assets? What has stemmed the loss of those assets?
2. What are the implications of and consequences that follow from the trust relationship?

NOTES

1. U.S. Census Bureau, 2000 Census Summary File 4, Table QT-P34 "Poverty Status in 1999 of Individuals: 2000."
2. Ibid., QT-P24 "Employment Status by Sex: 2000," QT-P20 "Educational Attainment by Sex: 2000."
3. Taylor and Kalt, 2005, 28.
4. Ibid., 34.
5. Ibid., 36.
6. U.S. Census Bureau, 2000 Census Summary File 4, Table DP-4 "Profile of Selected Housing Characteristics."
7. Many Native people do receive some interest from federally controlled trust accounts such as the Individual Indian Monies accounts.
8. U.S. Census Bureau, 2000 Census Summary File 4, Matrix PCT92 "Interest Dividends, Net Rental Income for 1999 Households."
9. Pevar, 2002, 18–19.
10. Sutton, 1985, passim.
11. In the 1950s, the federal government "terminated" its relationship with several Indian tribes, thus effectively opening up their land for sale to non-Indians and ceasing all federal services to tribes.
12. Weatherford, 1991, 112.
13. Keoke and Porterfield, 2002, 6.
14. Woods, 1994, 1471, 1496–97; Pevar, 1992.
15. Pevar, 1992, xi.
16. American Indian Policy Review Commission, 1977, 99.
17. Pevar, 2002, 7; Deloria and Lytlen, 1984, 242.
18. Fixico, 1998, 88.
19. Axelrod, 1993, 141.
20. A region in the south-central United States, most of which comprises present-day Oklahoma, which in 1834 was set aside by the government specifically for the relocation of Indians from the southeast.
21. Axelrod, 1993, 142.
22. Abel, 1906, 412.
23. U.S. National Archives and Records Administration. *Transcription of Homestead Act (1862)*.
24. U.S. Library of Congress. "The Homestead Act Went Into Effect May 20, 1862."
25. U.S. National Archives and Records Administration. *Transcript of Pacific Railway Act (1862)*.
26. Hartmann, 2002, 83–84, 90.
27. Bartlett, 1974, p. 34
28. Ibid., 33; Amott and Matthaei, 1991, 106.
29. Menchaca, 2002, 257.
30. Project Underground, accessed August 2005.
31. Menchaca, 2002, 257.
32. Project Underground, accessed. August 2005.
33. 24 Stat. 388, as amended, 25 U.S.C. Secs. 331–58.
34. Tyler, 1973, 95.
35. Iverson, 1994, 30.
36. Nabhan, 1989, 61.
37. Amott and Matthaei, 47.
38. McDonnell, 1991, 4.
39. Hurt, 1987, 174.
40. Ibid., 178–79.
41. Parker, 1989, 138.
42. O'Brien, 1989, 294.
43. Ibid., 83.
44. Pevar, 2002, 90.

45. Deloria and Lytle, 1984, 172.
46. Johnson, Troy R., 36.
47. Ibid., 35.
48. Rosenthal, 1996, 253.
49. Canby, 1998, 354–357.
50. Parker, 1989, 53.
51. Don Wharton, Native American Rights Fund, personal correspondence to author, January 2004.
52. Ibid.
53. *Worcester v. Georgia* 31 U.S. 515, 516 (1832); Pevar, 2002, 189–192.
54. *McClanahan v. Arizona Tax Commission* 411 U.S. 164 (1973).
55. Bays, 2002, 85.
56. USC, Title 25, Chapter 29, Section 2702; Mille Lacs Band of Ojibwe.
57. USC, Title 25, Chapter 29, Section 2710 ((b)(2)(b)(i–v).

REFERENCES

Abel, Annie Heloise. 1906. "The History of Events Resulting in the Indian Consolidation West of the Mississippi." *Annual Report of the American Historical Association,* Vol 1, 235–450.

Amott, Teresa, and Julie Matthaei. 1991. *Race, Gender and Work: A Multicultural Economic History of the Women in the United States.* Boston, MA: South End Press.

Axelrod, Alan. 1993. *Chronicle of the Indian Wars: From Colonial Times to Wounded Knee.* New York: Prentice Hall.

Aziz, Nikhil. "Colorblind: White-washing America." *The Public Eye* XVI.2 Summer 2002.

Bartlett, Richard A. 1974. *The New Country: A Social History of the American Frontier 1776–1890.* New York: Oxford University Press.

Bays, Brad A. 2002. "Tribal-State Tobacco Compacts and Motor Fuel Contracts in Oklahoma." In *The Tribes and the States: Geographies of Intergovernmental Interaction,* edited by Brad A. Bays and Erin Hogan Fouberg. New York: Rowman & Littlefield; ch. 9.

Canby, Jr., William C. 1998. *American Indian Law.* St. Paul, MN: West Group.

Deloria, Vine, and Clifford M. Lytle. 1984. *The Nations Within: Past and Future of American Sovereignty.* Austin: University of Texas Press.

Fixico, D.L. 1998. *The Invasion of Indian Country in the Twentieth Century: American Capitalism and Tribal Natural Resources.* Niwot, CO: University Press of Colorado.

Hartmann, Thom. 2002. *Unequal Protection: The Rise of Corporate Dominance and the Theft of Human Rights.* Emmaus, PA: Rodale Books.

Hurt, R.D. 1987. *Indian Agriculture in America: Prehistory to the Present.* Lawrence, KS: University Press of Kansas.

Iverson, P. 1994. *When Indians Became Cowboys.* Norman, OK: University of Oklahoma Press.

Johnson, Troy R., ed. 1999. *Contemporary Native American Political Issues.* Walnut Creek, CA: AltaMira Press, 17–71.

Keoke, E.D., and K.M. Porterfield. 2002. *Encyclopedia of American Indian Contributions to the World: 15,000 Years of Inventions and Innovations.* New York: Facts-on-File.

McDonnell, Janet A., 1991. *The Dispossession of the American Indian: 1887-1934.* Bloomington, IN: Indiana University Press.

Menchaca, Martha. 2002. *Recovering History, Constructing Race: The Indian, Black, and White Roots of Mexican Americans.* Austin, TX: University of Texas Press.

Nabhan, G., 1989. *Enduring Seeds: Native American Agricultural and Wild Plant Conservation.* Tuscon: University of Arizona Press.

O'Brien, Sharon. 1989. *American Indian Tribal Governments.* Norman, OK: University of Oklahoma Press.

Parker, L.S. 1989. *Native American Estate: The Struggle Over Indian and Hawaiian Lands.* Honolulu, HI: University of Hawaii Press.

Pevar, S. 2002. *The Rights of Indians and Tribes.* 3rd ed. Carbondale, IL: Southern Illinois University Press.

Rosenthal, Harvey D. 1996. "Indian Claims Commission." *Native America In the Twentieth Century: An Encyclopedia.* Mary B. Davis, editor. New York: Garland Publishing.

Sutton, Imre, ed. 1985. *Irredeemable America: The Indians Estate and Land Claims.* Tuscon: University of New Mexico Press.

Taylor, Jonathan B., and Joseph P. Kalt. *American Indians on Reservations: A Databook of Socioeconomic Change Between the 1990 and 2000 Censuses.* Cambridge, MA: Harvard Project on American Indian Economic Development, 2005. http://www.ksg.harvard.edu/hpaied/pubs/documents/AmericanIndiansonReservationsADatabookofSocioeconomicChange.pdf (accessed 1/8/05).

U.S. Census Bureau. *2000 Decennial Census,* Summary File 4. Accessed through American Factfinder utility: http://factfinder.census.gov/servlet/BasicFactsServlet

_____. *American Indian- and Alaskan Native-Owned Businesses 1997,* http://www.census.gov/prod/2001pubs/cenbr01-8.pdf

U.S. National Archives and Records Administration. *Transcript of Homestead Act (1862).* http://www.ourdocuments.gov/doc.php?doc=31&page=transcript.

_____. *Transcript of Pacific Railway Act (1862).* http://www.ourdocuments.gov/php?doc=32&page=transcript.

Weatherford, J. 1991. *Native Roots: How the Indians Enriched America.* New York: Fawcett Columbine.

Woods, Mary Christina. "Indian Land and the Promise of Native Sovereignty: The Trust Doctrine Revisited." *Utah Law Review* 4, Fall 1994: 1471, 1496–97.

READING 44

Crossing the Color Line: A Historical Assessment and Personal Narrative of *Loving v. Virginia*

Robert A. Pratt

On many evenings just before sunset, my grandmother and I would sit on our front porch. We lived in the rural black community of Battery, Virginia (approximately forty-five miles east of Richmond) which is located in Essex County. Suddenly, I would hear my grandmother remark: "Well, I see Richard's gone in for the night." I would then turn my head to follow the direction of her gaze, where I would see a white man driving his car down the dirt road leading to a house owned by my great-uncle. It was a two-story wood-frame house, which was one of the biggest in the neighborhood. Most of the rooms were usually rented out to various family-friends, relatives, and occasionally to the families of those who worked at the sawmill—jointly operated by my great-uncle and his older brother, my grandfather.

Raymond and Garnet Hill, along with their two sons, lived there for a time in the early 1960s. Garnet's younger sister, Mildred, was a frequent visitor, especially on weekends. Mildred's three children usually accompanied her on these visits, but her husband never did—at least not during daylight hours. As my grandmother later explained, the white man who occasionally visited my great-uncle's house near nightfall was Richard Loving. The woman whom I knew as Mildred was his wife, and the three children with whom I occasionally played were their children.

If Richard Loving were to spend any time with his family in the state of Virginia, he had

no choice other than to do so under the cover of darkness. He and his part-black, part-Cherokee wife had been banned from the state in 1959 for violating the state's miscegenation laws which prohibited interracial marriage.[1] Although Richard Loving and Mildred Jeter were legally married in Washington, DC, in 1958, Virginia did not recognize the marriage and subsequently banned the couple from their native state.[2] Not until 1967, when the United States Supreme Court declared Virginia's miscegenation statutes unconstitutional in *Loving v. Virginia*,[3] were Richard and Mildred Loving allowed to return to the state of their birth, having spent the first five years of their marriage in exile.[4]

[In 1967], long before the state launched its successful tourism campaign, "Virginia is for Lovers,"[5] the . . . interracial couples[6] who resided there would have been subject to arrest. Had current Supreme Court Justice Clarence Thomas been married to his white wife, Virginia, at the time, he might also have spent some time in jail.[7] Yet, despite the social and historic significance of the Supreme Court's 1967 landmark decision,[8] little has been written on the case, and virtually nothing has been written on the personal lives of this celebrated interracial couple whose very name—Loving—highlights the cruel irony and moral incongruousness of a state law which not that long ago denied two people the right to marry simply because of the color of their skin. Although Richard and Mildred Loving did not set out to make history, their steadfast determination to live as husband and wife has earned them their rightful place in civil rights history and constitutional law. Their courageous decision to challenge racial discrimination remains one of the most compelling personal dramas of our time.

Prohibitions against interracial marriage originated in colonial America, and such restrictions evolved as a natural outgrowth of the colonists' insistence upon rationalizing slavery by equating blackness with inferiority.[9] As A. Leon Higginbotham has written, "from 1662 until approximately 1691, the Virginia legislature passed a series of slave statutes that accomplished what the

---

Robert A. Pratt is a professor of history at the University of Georgia.

courts had failed to do: articulate a clear rationale for the precept of black inferiority and white superiority."[10] If racial inferiority were to be defined in terms of the color of one's skin, then logic would dictate that when blacks began to enter into sexual unions with whites, the offspring of such unions would, over time, appear less black, and hence, less inferior. In that context, interracial unions clearly had the potential to undermine the sanctity of the white race, not to mention the "potentially grave threat to the fledgling institution of slavery."[11]

It is important to note that although sexual intercourse between blacks and whites was deemed to be "abominable," no statute or amendment expressly forbade interracial intercourse.[12] Because the possible birth of a child between white slave-masters and black female slaves was economically profitable for the master, the Virginia legislature was apparently unwilling to pass any law that might interrupt this steady supply of labor.[13] After all, it was cheaper to breed slaves than to import them.[14] As Higginbotham has noted, "interracial sex . . . far from represented a threat to slavery. Rather, it served as its life blood."[15] Nor would such unions undermine the sanctity of the white race so long as lawmakers could be explicit about who was a Negro, and who was not. Legislation in 1785 defined a "mulatto" as any mixed-race Virginian with at least one-fourth African ancestry.[16] This process of racial classification would continue to be modified until the first half of the twentieth century with the intent being to make the definition of a white person increasingly more exclusive.[17]

The Virginia legislature moved to restrict interracial marriage because of its skewed concept of how to preserve the "sanctity" of holy matrimony. As the 1691 statute stipulated, any white person who married a black person would face banishment from the colony for life.[18] The statute provided that "whatsoever English or other white man or woman being free shall intermarry with a negroe, [sic] mulatto, or Indian man or woman bond or free shall within three months after such marriage be banished and removed from this dominion forever."[19] Interestingly, the statute provided for the banishment of the white person but not the black person or the children of the interracial marriage. As property, slaves were far too valuable to be sent into exile. Hence, the intent of the law was not to deprive slave-holders of their property, but to censure publicly those whites who had run afoul of the law.

Virginia's miscegenation laws, which were similar to those of most other states that classified people by race, underwent various changes throughout the eighteenth and nineteenth centuries.[20] But by 1910, some southern states[21] had begun to adopt the "one drop rule"[22] found in Tennessee's law, and a new law in Virginia adjusted the boundaries separating black and white. A 1910 law provided that "every person having one-sixteenth or more of negro blood shall be deemed a colored person."[23] In 1924, the Virginia legislature went a step further by passing the Racial Integrity Act, which defined a white person as having "no trace whatsoever of any blood other than Caucasian" and required all Virginians to register their racial identities with a local registrar as well as with the state registrar of vital statistics.[24] The slightest trace of nonwhite ancestry effectively disqualified a person from marrying someone the state considered to be white. The only exception was the "Pocohontas defense," which in the words of a tract issued by the state registrar of vital statistics, expressed "the desire of all to recognize as an integral and honored part of the white race the descendants of John Rolfe and Pocohontas."[25]

Beginning in the early 1950s, some states began to repeal their miscegenation laws,[26] and the United States Supreme Court's unanimous ruling in *Brown v. Board of Education*,[27] which ended segregation in public education, probably prompted other states to follow suit. Between 1952 and 1967, thirteen states repealed laws that had prohibited interracial marriage,[28] but quite a few other states refused to do so—Virginia foremost among them.[29]

In a case involving a white woman and a Chinese man that came before the Virginia Supreme Court of Appeals in 1955, the court ruled unanimously that its purposes were "to preserve the racial integrity of its citizens," and to prevent "the corruption of blood," "a mongrel breed of citizens," and "the obliteration of racial pride."[30] The court also reasoned that the regulation of marriage was "distinctly one of the rights guaranteed to the States and safeguarded by that bastion of States' rights," namely the Tenth Amendment.[31] Because the United States Supreme Court refused to hear the case on appeal, there was clearly some uncertainty as to where the Justices stood on this issue. Within a few years, however, the Virginia Supreme Court of Appeals would speak yet again on the same issue, this time in a case involving a white man and a black woman—Richard and Mildred Loving.

Richard Perry Loving and Mildred Delores Jeter had known each other practically all of their lives, as their families lived just up the road from each other in the rural community of Central Point, Virginia, located in Caroline County. Central Point had developed an interesting history of black-white sexual relationships over the years, which over time had produced a community in which a considerable number of the blacks were light-skinned.[32] Some of the blacks in the area who were light enough to "pass" as white often did so, and some of those whose complexion was a little darker often claimed to be Native American, even though most of them were known to have black relatives. While there is undoubtedly a Native American presence in Caroline County, not everyone who claimed to be an "Indian" really was, but given the racial climate of the 1950s, some blacks thought it more socially acceptable to emphasize their Native American rather than their African ancestry.[33]

Richard Loving spent most of his time in the company of these light-skinned blacks who accepted him warmly, in part, because his whiteness validated theirs, but also because Richard's parents had lived among these people for most of their lives without asserting any of the prerogatives generally associated with white supremacy. For 23 years, Richard's father had defied the racial mores of southern white society by working for Boyd Byrd, one of the wealthiest black farmers in the community; and apparently, he never had any qualms

about doing so.[34] While the elder Lovings were not oblivious to racial differences, the close-knit nature of their community required a certain degree of interdependence which could sometimes lead to an acceptance of personal relationships in a particular setting that would have been anathema elsewhere. So when white Richard Loving, age seventeen, began courting "colored" Mildred Jeter, age eleven, their budding romance drew little attention from either the white or the black communities.[35]

Mildred (part-black and part-Cherokee) had a pretty light-brown complexion accentuated by her slim figure, which was why practically everyone who knew her called her "Stringbean" or "Bean" for short. Richard (part-English and part-Irish) was a bricklayer by trade, but spent much of his spare time drag racing a car that he co-owned with two black friends, Raymond Green (a mechanic) and Percy Fortune (a local merchant). Despite their natural shyness, both Richard and Mildred were well-liked in the community, and the fact that they attended different churches and different schools did not hinder their courtship. When he was twenty-four and she was eighteen, Richard and Mildred decided to legalize their relationship by getting married.[36]

Mildred did not know that interracial marriage was illegal in Virginia, but Richard did. This explains why, on June 2, 1958, he drove them across the Virginia state line to Washington, DC, to be married. With their union legally validated by the District of Columbia, Mr. and Mrs. Loving returned to Central Point to live with Mildred's parents; however, their marital bliss was short-lived. Five weeks later, on July 11, their quiet life was shattered when they were awakened early in the morning as three law officers "acting on an anonymous tip" opened the unlocked door of their home, walked into their bedroom, and shined a flashlight in their faces.[37] Caroline County Sheriff R. Garnett Brooks demanded to know what the two of them were doing in bed together.[38] Mildred answered, "I'm his wife," while Richard pointed to the District of Columbia marriage certificate that hung on their bedroom wall.[39] "That's no good here,"

Sheriff Brooks replied.[40] He charged the couple with unlawful cohabitation, and then he and his two deputies hauled the Lovings off to a nearby jail in Bowling Green.[41]

At its October term in 1958, a grand jury issued indictments against the couple for violating Virginia's ban on interracial marriages. Specifically, they were charged with violating Virginia's 1924 Racial Integrity Act.[42] The Act stipulated that all marriages between a white person and a colored person shall be absolutely void without any decree of divorce or other legal process,[43] and it prohibited interracial couples from circumventing the law by having their marriages validated elsewhere and later return to Virginia.[44] The Lovings waived their rights to a trial by jury and pled guilty to the charges. On January 6, 1959, Judge Leon M. Bazile, sentenced each of them to 1 year in jail, but he suspended the sentences on the condition that they leave the state of Virginia and not return together or at the same time for a period of 25 years.[45] The Lovings paid their court fees of $36.29 each and moved to Washington, DC, where they would spend their next 5 years in exile.

During their years in the nation's capital, the Lovings lived with Mildred's cousin, Alex Byrd, and his wife Laura at 1151 Neal Street, Northeast. Their first child, Sidney, was born in 1958; Donald was born in 1959; and Peggy, the only girl, was born in 1960. The years in Washington were not happy ones for the couple. Richard struggled to maintain permanent employment while Mildred busied herself tending to the needs of their three children. During this time, they remained oblivious to the civil rights movement that was unfolding in their midst. "I just missed being at home," she told me years later.[46] "I missed being with my family and friends, especially Garnet [her sister]. I wanted my children to grow up in the country, where they could run and play, and where I wouldn't worry about them so much. I never liked much about the city."[47]

Virginia law would not allow Richard and Mildred Loving to live together as husband and wife in the state, nor would they be allowed to raise their mixed-race children (considered illegitimate

under state law) in Virginia.[48] They could visit Virginia, but they could not do so together. They were not even allowed to be in the state at the same time; however, that did not stop them from trying or from succeeding on various occasions. Mildred and the children made frequent visits to Battery, Virginia, the rural black community where her sister and brother-in-law lived. When Mildred would arrive in Battery, some of the neighbors would begin to look at their watches to see how long it would be before Richard's car came cruising through the neighborhood. During those early years, Richard's visits to the "Big House" (the common nickname for my great-uncle's boarding house) occurred almost exclusively after dark; but after a time, he became less cautious. Perhaps, he was confident in the belief that our community would keep his secret, or he was convinced that the local authorities in Essex County (which was adjacent to Caroline County) were not that interested in monitoring his whereabouts. It was on those occasions that I played with the Loving children, especially Sidney who was exactly my age.

The Lovings had not really been that interested in the civil rights movement, nor had they ever given much thought to challenging Virginia's law. But with a major civil rights bill being debated in Congress in 1963,[49] Mildred decided to write to Robert Kennedy, the Attorney General of the United States. The Department of Justice referred the letter to the American Civil Liberties Union. Bernard S. Cohen, a young lawyer doing *pro bono* work for the ACLU in Alexandria, Virginia, agreed to take the case. He would later be joined by another young attorney, Philip J. Hirschkop.[50]

In October 1964, Cohen and Hirschkop filed a class action suit in the U.S. District Court for the Eastern District of Virginia. In January 1965, Judge Bazile presided over a hearing of the Lovings' petition to have his original decision set aside.[51] In a written opinion, he rebutted each of the contentions made by Cohen and Hirschkop that might have resulted in a reconsideration of their clients' guilt. After citing several legal precedents he concluded: "Almighty God created the races white, black, yellow, malay and red, and he placed them on separate continents. And but for the interference with his arrangement, there would be no cause for such marriages. The fact that he separated the races shows that he did not intend for the races to mix."[52] The Lovings' attorneys appealed to the Virginia Supreme Court of Appeals, but their luck was no better there.[53] On March 7, 1966, a unanimous court upheld Judge Bazile's decision.[54] The convictions remained intact. Having exhausted their appeals in Virginia's courts, the Lovings proceeded to the U.S. Supreme Court.

On December 12, 1966, the U.S. Supreme Court agreed to hear the case.[55] The NAACP, the NAACP Legal Defense and Education Fund, the Japanese American Citizens League, and a coalition of Catholic bishops submitted briefs on the couple's behalf.[56] In preparing the brief for their clients, Cohen and Hirschkop reviewed the history of Virginia's miscegenation statutes dating back to the seventeenth century, referring to them as "relics of slavery" and "expressions of modern day racism."[57] In concluding his oral argument on April 10, 1967, Cohen relayed a message to the Justices from Richard Loving: "Tell the Court I love my wife, and it is just unfair that I can't live with her in Virginia."[58]

Two months later on June 12, 1967, Chief Justice Earl Warren delivered the opinion of a unanimous Supreme Court.[59] The Court rejected each of the state's arguments, as well as the legal precedents upon which they rested.[60] The fact that Virginia prohibited only those interracial marriages that involved white persons was evidence that the Racial Integrity Act of 1924 was "designed to maintain White Supremacy."[61] Chief Justice Warren concluded:

> To deny this fundamental freedom [the freedom to marry] on so unsupportable [sic] a basis as the racial classifications embodied in these statutes . . . is surely to deprive all the State's citizens of liberty without due process of law. The Fourteenth Amendment requires that the freedom of choice to marry not be restricted by invidious racial discriminations. Under our Constitution, the freedom to marry, or not marry, a person of another race resides with the individual

and cannot be infringed by the State. . . . These convictions must be reversed.[62]

DISCUSSION QUESTIONS

1. What are the ways in which miscegenation laws contributed to white supremacy?
2. Do you think that the Supreme Court's ruling on *Loving v. Virginia* changed much about American attitudes and practices?

NOTES

1. Appellant's Brief at 2, *Loving v. Virginia,* 388 U.S. 1, No. 395. 1967.
2. *Id.* at 6–7.
3. *Loving v. Virginia,* 388 U.S. 1, 2. 1967.
4. *See* Appellant's Brief at 7–8, *Loving,* No. 395. The Lovings actually returned to Virginia in the fall of 1963 after initiating their legal challenge to the state's miscegenation law. *Id.* On February 11, 1965, a three-judge federal court—consisting of District Court Judge Oren R. Lewis, District Court Judge John D. Butzner, and Circuit Court Judge Albert V. Bryan—entered an interlocutory order which stated:

   > [I]n the event the plaintiffs [Lovings] are taken into custody in the enforcement of the said judgment and sentence, this court, under the provisions of title 28, section 1651, United States Code should grant the plaintiffs [sic] bail in a reasonable amount during the pendency of the State proceedings in the State Courts and in the Supreme Court of the United States, if and when the case should be carried there . . . .

   Id.
5. Adopted in the 1970s to promote tourism, "Virginia is For Lovers" became a popular romantic slogan.
6. *Id.*
7. Civil rights activists and civil libertarians hailed the Supreme Court's ruling in *Loving,* believing that it removed the last barrier to social acceptance and racial equality in the United States. The decision also reinforced the belief that marriage is a personal and private matter which should not be infringed upon by the state, regardless of one's race or gender. In recent years, advocates of same-sex marriage have sought to use *Loving* as a legal precedent, arguing that the Fourteenth Amendment's guarantee of Due Process should prohibit discrimination based on gender just as it does for race. *See, e.g.,* David Orgon Coolidge, *Same-Sex Marriage? Baehr v. Miike and the Meaning of Marriage,* 38 S. Tex. L. Rev. 1, 22–23. 1997.
8. *See, e.g.,* Winthrop D. Jordan, White Over Black: American Attitudes Toward the Negro, 1550–1812 (1968); Edmund S.

Morgan, American Slavery, American Freedom: The Ordeal of Colonial Virginia 293 (1975) (discussing the paradox of slavery and freedom in colonial Virginia).

9. A. Leon Higginbotham, Jr., Shades of Freedom: Racial Politics and Presumptions of the American Legal Process 30. 1996.

10. See id. at 30, 44; A. Leon Higginbotham, Jr. & Barbara K. Kopytoff, *Racial Purity and Interracial Sex in the Law of Colonial and Antebellum Virginia*, 77 Geo. L. J. 1967 (1989).

11. For a historical analysis of Virginia's miscegenation laws, *see generally* Peter Wallenstein, *Race, Marriage, and the Law of Freedom: Alabama and Virginia, 1860s-1960s*, 70 Chi.-Kent L. Rev. 371. 1994.

12. *See* Higginbotham, *supra* note 10, at 44.

13. *Id.*

14. *Id.*

15. The Virginia Legislature changed the definition of "mulatto" in 1785 to those "who shall have one-fourth part or more of negro blood." Act of Oct. 1785, ch. 78, § l, 1785 Va. Acts, *reprinted in* 12 William W. Hening, A Collection of all the Laws of Virginia 184. 1832. Entitled "An Act Declaring what Persons Shall be Deemed Mulattos," it stated:

    [E]very person whose grandfathers or grandmothers any one is, or shall have been a negro, although all his progenitors, except that descending from the negro shall have been white persons, shall be deemed a mulatto; and so every person who shall have one-fourth part or more of negro blood, shall, in like manner, be deemed a mulatto.

    Id.

16. *See* Wallenstein, *supra* note 12, at 408. In 1860, the Code of Virginia specified that "[e]very person who has one-fourth part or more of negro blood shall be deemed a mulatto, and the word 'negro' . . . shall be construed to mean mulatto as well as negro." *See id.* at 395 [citing 30 Va. Code ch. 103, § 9 (1860)]. Following the Civil War, an 1866 act changed the language by dropping the term "mulatto," but left the definitions largely intact. *Id.* at 395. The new act stated that "every person having one-fourth or more of negro blood, shall be deemed a colored person, and every person, not a colored person, having one-fourth or more of Indian blood, shall be deemed an Indian." *Id.*

17. *See* Act of April 1691, No. 16, 1691 Va. Acts, *reprinted in* 3 William W. Hening, A Collection of all the Laws of Virginia 87. 1823.

18. *Id. See generally* Samuel N. Pincus. 1990. The Virginia Supreme Court, Blacks and the Law, 1870–1902.

19. *See* Alfred Avins, *Anti-Miscegenation Laws and the Fourteenth Amendment: The Original Intent*, 52 Va. L. Rev. 1224 (1966); Steven A. Bank, *Anti-Miscegenation Laws and the Dilemma of Symmetry: The Understanding of Equality in the Civil Rights Act of 1875*, 2 U. Chi. L. Sch. Roundtable 303 (1995); Wallenstein, *supra* note 12, at 389–99.

20. Paul Finkelman, *The Crime of Color*, 67 Tul. L. Rev. 2061, 1996. *See also* Wallenstein, *supra* note 12, at 406–07. *See generally* Ian Haney-Lopez, White By Law: The Legal Construction of Race 1996 (discussing the evolving concept of race in America's judicial system).

21. *See* Finkelman, *supra* note 21, at 2110.

22. *See* Wallenstein, *supra* note 12, at 407 n. 180 [citing Act of Mar. 17, 1910, ch. 357 § 49, Va. Acts (amending and reenacting §49 of Va. Code, 1887)].

23. An Act to Preserve Racial Integrity, 1924, ch. 371, §§ 1, 5, Va. Acts.

24. *Loving*, 388 U.S. at 5 n.4. *See also* Walter Wadlington, *The Loving Case: Virginia's Anti-miscegenation Statute in Historical Perspective*, 52 Va. L. Rev. 1189, 1189 n. 1 (1966).

25. *See* Perez v. Sharp, 32 Cal. 2d 711 (1948) (holding that miscegenation laws violated the Equal Protection Clause of the Fourteenth Amendment).

26. Brown v. Board of Education, 347 U.S. 483 (1954).

27. In addition to California (which had acted in 1948), the other states were Arizona, Colorado, Idaho, Indiana, Maryland, Montana, Nebraska, Nevada, North Dakota, Oregon, South Dakota, Utah, and Wyoming. *See Loving*, 388 U.S. at 6 n. 5.

28. When the *Loving* decision was rendered in 1967, sixteen states had laws prohibiting interracial marriages: Alabama, Arkansas, Delaware, Florida, Georgia, Kentucky, Louisiana, Missouri, Mississippi, South Carolina, North Carolina, Oklahoma, Tennessee, Texas, Virginia, and West Virginia. *Id.*

29. Naim v. Naim, 87 S.E.2d 749, 756 (Va. 1955) (preventing white persons in the state from marrying any other ethnicity except "white" and "American Indian"). 1995. *See generally* Edward J. Larson, Sex, Race, and Science: Eugenics in the Deep South. (1995)

30. *Naim*, 87 S.E.2d at 756.

31. Simeon Booker, *The Couple that Rocked Courts*, Ebony, Sept. 1967, at 78.

32. Many light-skinned blacks during this time "crossed over" into the white race when they thought it convenient to do so. For some, it was a form of self-denial; for others, it was their way of playing a "practical joke" on white society. Still others, such as Walter White of the NAACP, used their light complexions to infiltrate white society, enabling them to operate like "secret agents" for the black race. *See generally* James Weldon Johnson, The Autobiography of an Ex-Colored Man (1912); Nella Larsen, Quicksand and Passing 143 (Deborah E. McDowell ed., 1986); Toni Morrison, The Bluest Eye (1970); Wallace Thurman, The Blacker the Berry (1972); Walter White, Rope and Faggot: The Biography of Judge Lynch (1929).

33. Booker, *supra* note 32, at 79.

34. Interview with Mrs. Mildred Loving, in Milford, Va. (Oct. 12, 1994).

35. *Id.*

36. *Id.*

37. *Id.*

38. *Id.*

39. *Id.*

40. *Id.* For a detailed discussion of the Lovings' struggle to secure a legal marriage, *see generally The Crime of Being Married,* Life, Mar. 18, 1966, at 85; Anne Gearan, *Marriage Led Couple to Jail,* Richmond Times-Dispatch, Oct. 11, 1992, at C4.

41. *Loving,* 388 U.S. at 4–5 & nn. 3–4.

42. *Id.* at 5 n. 3.

43. *Id.* at 4.

44. *Id.* at 3.

45. Interview with Mrs. Mildred Loving, *supra* note 35.

46. *Id.*

47. *See, e.g.,* An Act to Preserve Racial Integrity Act, *supra* note 24, §§ 1–7.

48. This civil rights bill would later become the Civil Rights Act of 1964.

49. It is important to note that the ACLU, and not the NAACP, took the lead in *Loving. See generally* Booker, *supra* note 32, at 78 (discussing how the ACLU got involved in the case). In September 1955, NAACP Executive Secretary Roy Wilkins commented that "[m]arriage is a personal matter on which the NAACP takes no position. The only kind of marriage we are for is the happy marriage, the success of which depends on the two individuals involved." *See* Roy Wilkins, Statement on Interracial Marriage, Behind the Scene, Sept. 6, 1955

(located in the NAACP papers with the Manuscript Division of the Library of Congress, filed as II:A:496 in the Publicity, General, 1955 July-Sept. folder). *See also* Chang Moon Sohn, Principle and Expediency in Judicial Review: Miscegenation Cases in the Supreme Court 70–94, 129–47 (1970) (unpublished Ph.D. dissertation, Columbia University) (on file with the Columbia University Library).

50. *Loving,* 388 U.S. at 3.

51. *See id. See also* Wallenstein, *supra* note 12, at 424.

52. *See* Loving v. Commonwealth, 147 S.E.2d 78 (1966).

53. *Id.*

54. *See Supreme Court Agrees to Rule on State Miscegenation Laws,* N.Y. Times, Dec. 13, 1966, at 40. *See also Ban on Interracial Marriages Upheld by Virginia High Court,* N.Y. Times, Mar. 8, 1966, at 26; *Virginia Suit Scores Mixed Marriage Ban,* N.Y. Times, July 30, 1966, at 9.

55. *See* 64 Landmark Briefs and Arguments of the Supreme Court of the United States: Constitutional Law 741, 959 (Philip B. Kurland & Gerhard Casper eds., 1975) [hereinafter Landmark Briefs].

56. Brief for Appellants at 15, Loving v. Virginia, 388 U.S. 1 (1967), *reprinted in* Landmark Briefs, *supra* note 56, at 763.

57. Oral Argument of Philip J. Hirschkop, on behalf of Appellants at 12, Loving v. Virginia, 388 U.S. 1 (1967), *reprinted in* Landmark Briefs, *supra* note 56, at 959, 971.

58. *Loving,* 388 U.S. at 1.

59. *Id.*

60. *Id.* at 11.

61. *Id.* at 12.

62. *Id.* at 6 n.5. *See supra* notes 28 & 29 and accompanying text.

POPULAR CULTURE

READING 45

Framing Class: Media Representations of Wealth and Poverty in America

Diana Kendall

"The Simple Life 2"—the second season of the reality show, on which the celebutante Paris Hilton and her Best Friend Forever, the professional pop-star-daughter

Nicole Richie, are set on a cross-country road trip—*once again takes the heaviest of topics and makes them as weightless as a social X-ray.*[1]

This statement by television critic Choire Sicha in her review of FOX TV's reality-based entertainment show *The Simple Life,* sums up a recurring theme. . . . The media typically take "the heaviest of topics," such as class and social inequality, and trivialize it. Rather than providing a meaningful analysis of inequality and showing realistic portrayals of life in various social classes, the media either play class differences for laughs or sweep the issue of class under the rug so that important distinctions are rendered invisible. By ignoring class or

---

Diana Kendall is a professor of sociology at Baylor University.

trivializing it, the media involve themselves in a social construction of reality that rewards the affluent and penalizes the working class and the poor. In real life, Paris Hilton and Nicole Richie are among the richest young women in the world; however, in the world of *The Simple Life,* they can routinely show up somewhere in the city or the country, pretend they are needy, and rely on the kindness of strangers who have few economic resources. . . .

MEDIA FRAMING AND THE PERFORMANCE OF CLASS IN EVERYDAY LIFE

In a mass-mediated culture such as ours, the media do not simply mirror society; rather, they help to shape it and to create cultural perceptions.[2] The blurring between what is real and what is not real encourages people to emulate the upper classes and shun the working class and the poor. Television shows, magazines, and newspapers sell the idea that the only way to get ahead is to identify with the rich and powerful and to live vicariously through them. From sitcoms to reality shows, the media encourage ordinary people to believe that they may rise to fame and fortune; they too can be the next American Idol. Constantly bombarded by stories about the lifestyles of the rich and famous, viewers feel a sense of intimacy with elites, with whom they have little or no contact in their daily lives.[3] According to the social critic bell hooks, we overidentify with the wealthy, because the media socialize us to believe that people in the upper classes are better than we are. The media also suggest that we need have no allegiance to people in our own class or to those who are less fortunate.[4]

Vicarious living—watching how other individuals live rather than experiencing life for ourselves—through media representations of wealth and success is reflected in many people's reading and viewing habits and in their patterns of consumption. According to hooks, television promotes hedonistic consumerism:

> Largely through marketing and advertising, television promoted the myth of the classless society, offering on one hand images of an American dream fulfilled wherein any and everyone can become rich and on the other suggesting that the lived experience of this lack of class hierarchy was expressed by our *equal right to purchase anything we could afford.*[5]

As hooks suggests, equality does not exist in contemporary society, but media audiences are encouraged to view themselves as having an "equal right" to purchase items that somehow will make them equal to people above them in the social class hierarchy. However, the catch is that we must actually be able to afford these purchases. Manufacturers and the media have dealt with this problem by offering relatively cheap products marketed by wealthy celebrities. Paris Hilton, an heir to the Hilton Hotel fortune, has made millions of dollars by marketing products that give her fans a small "slice" of the good life she enjoys. Middle- and working-class people can purchase jewelry from the Paris Hilton Collection—sterling silver and Swarovski crystal jewelry ranging in price from fifteen to a hundred dollars—and have something that is "like Paris wears." For less than twenty dollars per item, admirers can purchase the Paris Hilton Wall Calendar; a "Paris the Heiress" Paper Doll Book; Hilton's autobiography, *Confessions of an Heiress;* and even her dog's story: *The Tinkerbell Hilton Diaries: My Life Tailing Paris Hilton.* But Hilton is only one of thousands of celebrities who make money by encouraging unnecessary consumerism among people who are inspired by media portrayals of the luxurious and supposedly happy lives of rich celebrities. The title of Hilton's television show, *The Simple Life,* appropriates the image of simple people, such as the working class and poor, who might live happy, meaningful lives, and transfers this image to women whose lives are anything but simple as they flaunt designer clothing and spend collectively millions of dollars on entertainment, travel, and luxuries that can be afforded only by the very wealthy.[6]

How the media frame stories about class *does* make a difference in what we think about other people and how we spend our money. Media frames constitute a mental shortcut (schema) that helps us formulate our thoughts.

The Upper Classes: Affluence and Consumerism for All

Although some media frames show the rich and famous in a negative manner, they still glorify the material possessions and lifestyles of the upper classes. Research has found that people who extensively watch television have exaggerated views of how wealthy most Americans are and what material possessions they own. Studies have also found that extensive television viewing leads to higher rates of spending and to lower savings, presumably because television stimulates consumer desires.[7]

For many years, most media framing of stories about the upper classes has been positive, ranging from *consensus framing* that depicts members of the upper class as being like everyone else, to *admiration framing* that portrays them as generous, caring individuals. The frame most closely associated with rampant consumerism is *emulation framing*, which suggests that people in all classes should reward themselves with a few of the perks of the wealthy, such as buying a piece of Paris's line of jewelry. The writers of television shows such as ABC's *Life of Luxury,* E!'s *It's Good to Be. . .* [a wealthy celebrity, such as Nicole Kidman], and VH1's *The Fabulous Life* rely heavily on admiration and price-tag framing, by which the worth of a person is measured by what he or she owns and how many assistants constantly cater to that person's whims. On programs like FOX's *The O.C.* and *North Shore* and NBC's *Las Vegas,* the people with the most expensive limousines, yachts, and jet aircraft are declared the winners in life. Reality shows like *American Idol, The Billionaire, For Love or Money,* and *The Apprentice* suggest that anyone can move up the class ladder and live like the rich if he or she displays the best looks, greatest talent, or sharpest entrepreneurial skills. It is no wonder that the economist Juliet B. Schor finds that the overriding goal of children age ten to thirteen is to get rich. In response to the statement "I want to make a lot of money when I grow up," 63 percent of the children in Schor's study agreed, whereas only 7 percent disagreed.[8]

Many adults who hope to live the good life simply plunge farther into debt. Many reports show that middle- and working-class American consumers are incurring massive consumer debts as they purchase larger houses, more expensive vehicles, and many other items that are beyond their means. According to one analyst, media portrayals of excessive consumer spending and a bombardment of advertisements by credit-card companies encourage people to load up on debt.[9] With the average U.S. household now spending 13 percent of its after-tax income to *service* debts (not pay off the principal!), people with average incomes who continue to aspire to lives of luxury like those of the upper classes instead may find themselves spending their way into the "poor house" with members of the poverty class.

The Poor and Homeless: "Not Me!"— Negative Role Models in the Media

The sharpest contrasts in media portrayals are between depictions of people in the upper classes and depictions of people at the bottom of the class structure. At best, the poor and homeless are portrayed as deserving of our sympathy on holidays or when disaster strikes. In these situations, those in the bottom classes are depicted as being temporarily down on their luck or as working hard to get out of their current situation but in need of public assistance. At worst, however, the poor are blamed for their own problems; stereotypes of the homeless as bums, alcoholics, and drug addicts, caught in a hopeless downward spiral because of their *individual* pathological behavior, are omnipresent in the media.

For the most part, people at the bottom of the class structure remain out of sight and out of mind for most media audiences. *Thematic framing* depicts the poor and homeless as "faceless" statistics in reports on poverty. *Episodic framing* highlights some problems of the poor but typically does not link their personal situations to such larger societal problems as limited educational opportunities, high rates of unemployment, and jobs that pay depressingly low wages.

The poor do not fare well on television entertainment shows, where writers typically represent them with one-dimensional, bedraggled characters standing on a street corner holding cardboard signs that read "Need money for food." When television writers tackle the issue of homelessness, they often portray the lead characters (who usually are white and relatively affluent) as helpful people, while the poor and homeless are depicted as deviants who might harm themselves or others. Hospital and crime dramas like *E.R., C.S.I.,* and *Law & Order* frequently portray the poor and homeless as "crazy," inebriated in public, or incompetent to provide key information to officials. Television reality shows like *Cops* go so far as to advertise that they provide "footage of debris from the bottom tiers of the urban social order."[10] Statements such as this say a lot about the extent to which television producers, directors, and writers view (or would have us view) the lower classes.

From a sociological perspective, framing of stories about the poor and homeless stands in stark contrast to framing of stories about those in the upper classes, and it suggests that we should distance ourselves from "those people." We are encouraged to view the poor and homeless as the *Other,* the outsider; in the media we find little commonality between our lives and the experiences of people at the bottom of the class hierarchy. As a result, it is easy for us to buy into the dominant ideological construction that views poverty as a problem of individuals, not of the society as a whole, and we may feel justified in our rejection of such people.[11]

The Working Class: Historical Relics and Jokes

As we have seen, the working class and the working poor do not fare much better than the poor and homeless in media representations. The working class is described as "labor," and people in this class are usually nothing more than faces in a crowd on television shows. The media portray people who *produce* goods and services as much less interesting than those who *excessively consume* them, and

this problem can only grow worse as more of the workers who produce the products are thousands of miles away from us, in nations like China, very remote from the typical American consumer.[12]

Contemporary media coverage carries little information about the working class or its problems. Low wages, lack of benefits, and hazardous working conditions are considered boring and uninteresting topics, except on the public broadcasting networks or an occasional television "news show" such as *60 Minutes* or *20/20,* when some major case of worker abuse has recently been revealed. The most popular portrayal of the working class is *caricature framing,* which depicts people in negative ways, such as being dumb, white trash, buffoons, bigots, or slobs. Many television shows featuring working-class characters play on the idea that the clothing, manners, and speech patterns of the working class are not as good as those of the middle or upper classes. For example, working-class characters (such as Roseanne, the animated Homer Simpson, and *The King of Queens'* Doug) may compare themselves to the middle and upper classes by saying that they are not as "fancy as the rich people." Situation comedy writers have perpetuated working-class stereotypes, and now a number of reality shows, such as *The Swan* and *Extreme Makeover,* try to take "ordinary" working-class people and "improve" them through cosmetic surgery, new clothing, and different hairstyles.

Like their upper-class celebrity counterparts, so-called working-class comedians like Jeff Foxworthy have ridiculed the blue-collar lifestyle. They also have marketed products that make fun of the working class. Foxworthy's website, for example, includes figurines ("little statues for *inside* the house"), redneck cookbooks, Games Rednecks Play, and calendars that make fun of the working class generally. Although some people see these items as humorous ("where's yore sense of humor?"), the real message is that people in the lower classes lack good taste, socially acceptable manners, and above all, middle-class values. If you purchase "redneck" merchandise, you too can make fun of the working class and clearly distance yourself from it.

MIDDLE-CLASS FRAMING AND KIDDY-CONSUMERISM

Media framing of stories about the middle class tells us that this economic group is the value center and backbone of the nation. *Middle-class values framing* focuses on the values of this class and suggests that they hold the nation together. Early television writers were aware that their shows needed to appeal to middle-class audiences, who were the targeted consumers for the advertisers' products, and middle-class values of honesty, integrity, and hard work were integral ingredients of early sitcoms. However, some contemporary television writers spoof the middle class and poke fun at values supposedly associated with people in this category. The writers of FOX's *Malcolm in the Middle* and *Arrested Development,* for example, focus on the dysfunctions in a fictional middle-class family, including conflicts between husband and wife, between parents and children, and between members of the family and outsiders.

Why do these shows make fun of the middle class? Because corporations that pay for the advertisements want to capture the attention of males between ages eighteen and thirty-nine, and individuals in this category are believed to enjoy laughing at the uptight customs of conventional middle-class families. In other shows, as well, advertisers realize the influence that their programs have on families. That is why they are happy to spend billions of dollars on product placements (such as a Diet Coke can sitting on a person's desk) in the shows and on ads during commercial breaks. In recent research, Schor examined why very young children buy into the consumerism culture and concluded that extensive media exposure to products was a key reason. According to Schor, "More children [in the United States] than anywhere else believe that their clothes and brands describe who they are and define their social status. American kids display more brand affinity than their counterparts anywhere else in the world; indeed, experts describe then as increasingly 'bonded to brands.'"[13]

Part of this bonding occurs through constant television watching and Internet use, as a steady stream of ads targets children and young people. Schor concludes that we face a greater problem than just excessive consumerism. A child's well-being is undermined by the consumer culture: "High consumer involvement is a significant cause of depression, anxiety, low self-esteem, and psychosomatic complaints."[14] Although no similar studies have been conducted to determine the effects of the media's emphasis on wealth and excessive consumerism among adults, it is likely that today's children will take these values with them into adulthood if our society does not first reach the breaking point with respect to consumer debt.

The issue of class in the United States is portrayed in the media not through a realistic assessment of wealth, poverty, or inequality but instead through its patterns of rampant consumerism. The general message remains, one article stated, "We pledge allegiance to the mall."[15]

DISCUSSION QUESTIONS

1. Does Kendall's discussion of consumerism remind you of any of your own recent purchases?
2. Do you think your view of social class has been influenced by the media as much as Kendall would argue?

NOTES

1. Choire Sicha, "They'll Always Have Paris," *New York Times,* June 13, 2004, AR31 [emphasis added].
2. Tim Delaney and Allene Wilcox. 2002. "Sports and the Role of the Media," in *Values, Society and Evolution,* ed. Harry Birx and Tim Delaney, 199–213. Auburn, N.Y.: Legend.
3. Gloria Watkins. 2000. bell hooks, *Where We Stand: Class Matters* (New York: Routledge, 2000), 73.
4. hooks, *Where We Stand,* 77.
5. hooks, *Where We Stand,* 71 [emphasis added].
6. hooks, *Where We Stand,* 72.
7. Juliet B. Schor. 2004. *Born to Buy: The Commercialized Child and the New Consumer Culture* New York: Scribner.
8. Schor, *Born to Buy.*
9. Joseph Nocera. 1994. *A Piece of the Action: How the Middle Class Joined the Money Class* New York: Simon and Schuster.

10. Karen De Coster and Brad Edmonds, "TV Nation: The Killing of American Brain Cells," Lewrockwell.com, 2004, www.lewrockwell.com/decoster/decoster78.html (accessed July 7, 2004).

11. Judith Butler ["Performative Acts and Gender Constitution: An Essay in Phenomenology and Feminist Theory," in *Performing Feminisms: Feminist Critical Theory and Theatre,* ed. Sue-Ellen Case (Baltimore: Johns Hopkins University Press. 1990), 270] has described gender identity as performative, noted that social reality is not a given but is continually created as an illusion "through language, gesture, and all manner of symbolic social sign." In this sense, class might also be seen as performative, in that people act out their perceived class location not only in terms of their own class-related identity but in regard to how they treat other people, based on their perceived class position.

12. See Thomas Ginsberg, "Union Hopes to Win Over Starbucks Shop Workers," *Austin American-Statesman.* July 2, 2004, D6.

13. Schor, *Born to Buy,* 13.

14. Schor, *Born to Buy,* 167.

15. Louis Uchitelle, "We Pledge Allegiance to the Mall," *New York Times,* December 6, 2004, C12.

READING 46

Loot or Find: Fact or Frame?

Cheryl I. Harris

Devon W. Carbado

EVIDENCE OF THINGS SEEN

What do these images represent? What facts do they convey? We could say that image A depicts a man who, in the aftermath of Katrina, is wading through high waters with food supplies and a big black plastic bag. We might say that image B depicts a man and woman, both wearing backpacks. They, too, are wading through high waters in the aftermath of Katrina, and the woman appears to be carrying food supplies.

Cheryl I. Harris is a professor of law at the University of California, Los Angeles. Devon W. Carbado is a professor of law at the University of California, Los Angeles.

AP Photo/Dave Martin

Chris Graythen/Getty Images

This is not how these images were presented in the press. The captions that appeared with the two photos, both of which ran on Yahoo! news, were quite different. The caption for image A read: "A young man walks through chest-deep flood water after looting a grocery store in New Orleans." The caption for image B read: "Two residents wade through chest-deep waters after finding bread and soda from a local grocery store after Hurricane Katrina came through the area." The caption for image A, then, tells us that a crime has been committed; the caption for image B tells that a fierce, poignant struggle for survival is under way—the subjects have just found food. Image A depicts a young black man; image B shows a white man and woman.

The images and their respective captions almost immediately stirred up significant controversy. People complained that the captions accompanying the images were racially suggestive: black people "loot" and white people "find." *Boston Globe* correspondent Christina Pazzanese wondered, "I am curious how one photographer knew the food was looted by one but not the other. Were interviews conducted as they swam by?"[1]

Not everyone agreed, however, that the images and captions reflected a racial problem. As one commentator put it:

It's difficult to draw any substantiated conclusions from these photos' captions. Although they were both carried by many news outlets, they were taken by two different photographers and came from two different services, the Associated Press (AP) and the Getty Images via Agence France-Presse (AFP). Services make different stylistic standards for how they caption photographs, or the dissimilar wordings may have been due to nothing more than the preferences of different photographers and editors, or the difference might be the coincidental result of a desire to avoid repetitive wording (similar photographs from the same news services variously describe the depicted actions as "looting," "raiding," "taking," "finding," and "making off"). The viewer also isn't privy to the contexts in which the photographs were taken—it's possible that in one case the photographer actually saw his subject exiting an unattended grocery store with an armful of goods, while in the other case the photographer came upon his subjects with supplies in hand and could only make assumptions about how they obtained them.[2]

For the most part, this controversy focused on a question of fact. Did the black person really loot the goods he was carrying? Did the white man and white woman really find the food they were carrying? Indeed, the director of media relations at the Associated Press suggested that, as to image A, "he [the photographer] saw the person go into the shop and take the goods. . . . that's why he wrote 'looting' in the article."[3] In other words, the fact of the matter was that the black man in image A was a looter.

The photographer of image B, Chris Graythen, maintained,

I wrote the caption about the two people who "found" the items. I believed in my opinion, that they did simply find them, and not "looted" them in the definition of the word. The people were swimming in chest deep water, and there were other people in the water, both white and black. I looked for the best picture. There were a million items floating in the water—we were right near a grocery store that had 5+ feet of water in it. It had no doors. The water was moving, and the stuff was floating away. These people were not ducking into a store and busting down windows to get electronics. They picked up bread and Cokes that were floating in the water. They would have floated away anyhow.[4]

To some extent, the credibility of Graythen's explanation is beside the point here. That is, the loot-or-find problem of image A and image B cannot fully be addressed with reference to the individual intent of those who either took the picture or produced the accompanying interpretive text. Indeed, it is entirely plausible that had the photos appeared without any captions, they would have been read the same way.[5] This is because while neither "loot" nor "find" is written on either image, in the context of public disorder, the race of the subjects inscribes those meanings.

THE "COLOR-BLIND" FRAME

Drawing on facts about both Hurricane Katrina and the public's response to it, [we question] whether efforts to change the racial status quo and eliminate inequality should or can rely solely on facts or empiricism. There is a growing sense within the civil rights community that more empirical research is needed to persuade mainstream Americans that racism remains a problem in American society and that the elimination of racial disadvantage is not a do-it-yourself project. The idea seems to be that if only more Americans knew certain "facts" (for example, about the existence of implicit bias) they would be more inclined to support civil rights initiatives (for example, affirmative action). We agree that more empirical research is needed. Facts are important—indeed crucial—since so much of public opinion is grounded in misinformation. We simply do not think that there is a linear progression between raw empiricism and more enlightened public opinion about race and racism. Put another way, we do not believe that facts speak for themselves.

It is precisely the recognition that facts don't speak for themselves that helps to explain why scholars across academic fields and politicians across the political spectrum continue to pay significant attention to the social and cognitive processes that shape how we interpret facts. Of the variety of theories—in sociology, political science, law, anthropology, psychology, and economics—that attempt to explain these processes, most share the idea that we interpret events through frames—interpretational structures that, consciously and unconsciously, shape what we see and how we see it. In the words of one scholar, framing refers to "understanding a story you already know and saying, 'Oh yeah, that one.'"[6] As we process and make sense of an event, we take account of and simultaneously ignore facts that do not fit the frame, and sometimes we supply ones that are missing. Thus, it is sometimes said that "frames trump facts."[7]

The most relevant and dominant frame is color blindness, or the belief that race is *not* a factor in how we make sense of the world. Color blindness is a kind of metaframe that comprises three interwoven racial scripts: (1) because of *Brown v Board of Education* and the civil rights reforms it inaugurated, racism is by and large a thing of the past; (2) when racism does rear its ugly head, it is the product of misguided and irrational behavior on the part of self-declared racial bigots, who are few and far between; and (3) racial consciousness—whether

in the form of affirmative action or Jim Crow–like racism—should be treated with suspicion, if not rejected outright. The gradual ascendancy and eventual racial dominance of color blindness frames the facts of racial inequality (manifested, for example, in disparities in wealth and educational outcomes between blacks and whites) as a function of something other than racism. Because scientists have largely repudiated the notion of biological inferiority, color blindness frames the problem of racial disadvantage in terms of conduct. The problem is not genes but culture, not blood but behavior: were black people to engage in normatively appropriate cultural practices—work hard, attend school, avoid drugs, resist crime—they would transcend their current social status and become part of the truly advantaged. On this view, black disadvantage is both expected and deserved—a kind of natural disaster not produced by racism.

At least initially, Katrina challenged the supremacy of color blindness. The tidal wave of suffering that washed over New Orleans seemed incontrovertible evidence of the salience of race in contemporary U.S. society.[8] The simple fact that the faces of those left to fend for themselves or die were overwhelmingly black raised questions about the explanatory power of color blindness under which race is deemed irrelevant.[9] Racial suffering was everywhere. And black people were dying—prime time live. One had to close one's eyes, or willfully blind oneself, not to see this racial disaster. Everyone, it seemed, except government officials, was riveted. And there was little disagreement that Katrina exposed shameful fissures in America's social fabric; that the precipitating event was an act of God, not the cultural pathology of the victims; and that the government's response, at least in the initial phases, was woefully inadequate. Seasoned mainstream journalists wept and railed, while ordinary Americans flooded relief organizations with money.

The tragedy of Katrina created a rupture in the racial-progress narrative that had all but erased the suffering of poor black people from the political landscape. In contrast to the pre-Katrina picture, black people were perceived to be innocent victims. Black people were perceived to have a legitimate claim on the nation-state. Black people were perceived to be deserving of government help. Katrina—or the *facts* the public observed about its effects—disrupted our tendency to *frame* black disadvantage in terms of cultural deficiency. But how did that happen? And doesn't this disruption undermine our central point about facts and frames?

Not at all. Frames are not static. Epic events like Katrina push up against and can temporarily displace them. All those people. All that suffering. This can't be America. How could we let this happen? That question—how could we let this happen?—reflected a genuine humanitarian concern for fellow human beings. Moreover, the compelling facts about Katrina raised a number of questions about racial inequality previously suppressed under color blindness. Indeed, as the humanitarian crisis peaked with the retreating floodwaters, a debate over the role of race in the disaster quickly emerged. The unrelenting spectacle of black suffering bodies demanded an explanation. Why were those New Orleans residents who remained trapped during Katrina largely black and poor? Was it, as hip-hop artist Kanye West argued, a case of presidential indifference to, or dislike of, poor black people?[10] Or was it, as Ward Connerly asserted, the predictable consequence of a natural disaster that befell a city that just happened to be predominantly black? Was it, as Linda Chavez claimed, the result of a culture of dependency combined with local bureaucratic incompetence? Was race a factor in determining who survived and who did not?[11] Or did class provide a better explanation?[12] Finally, could we ever fully understand Katrina without meaningfully engaging the legacy of slavery?[13] These and other, similar questions were pushed into the foreground by the force of Katrina's devastation.

But the frame of color blindness did not disappear. It manifested itself in the racial divide that emerged with respect to how people answered the foregoing questions. While there is some intraracial diversity of opinion among public figures about the role of race and racism in explaining what happened, there remains a striking racial difference in how the disaster is viewed. According to public opinion polls, whites largely reject the notion that race explains the governmental disregard, while blacks assert that the fact that the victims were black and poor was a significant part of the story.[14] This difference over the difference that race makes reflects competing racial frames. Thus, while the facts of what happened in Katrina's aftermath unsettled the familiar color-blind racial script that poor black people were the authors of their own plight, those facts did not ultimately displace core ideas embedded in the color-blind frame: race is irrelevant and racism largely does not exist. Most whites were able to see black people as victims, but they were unwilling to link their victim status to race or racism. A more acceptable story was that black people in New Orleans suffered only because of bureaucratic inefficiencies in the wake of a natural disaster. Race simply could not be a factor. Katrina then only partially destabilized the frame of color blindness. To the extent that our starting point for thinking about race is that it does not matter, other racial frames or scripts more easily fit within the overarching frame. These frames can both explicitly invoke race and, even more powerfully, implicitly play the race card. After the initial uncertainty, what emerged in the wake of Katrina was the frame of "law and order"—a racial script that permeated the debate over the iconic photographs with which we began our essay, and over the post-Katrina relief efforts. The media were both author and reader of events in ways that both challenged and underwrote this racial frame.

A PICTURE IS WORTH A THOUSAND WORDS

Recall Chris Graythen's response to the racial controversy concerning the images with which we began this [reading]. With regard to image B, Graythen asserted that he "looked for the best picture." More specifically, Graythen searched for an image that would best narrate a particular factual story: that people were wading through water to find food. According to Graythen, both whites and blacks were finding food in the chest-high water. Unlike pre-Katrina New Orleans, this space was racially integrated. Graythen searched this racially integrated body of water for a picture that would most successfully convey the idea of people finding food (as distinct from people "ducking into a store and busting down windows to get electronics"). Graythen's "best picture"—his "Oh yeah, that one"—emerged when he saw the two white people photographed in image B. Their images best fit the caption that Graythen already had in mind, people wading through water to find food. Because people are more likely to associate blacks with looting ("ducking into a store and busting down windows to get electronics") than with finding food, Graythen's selection makes sense. Indeed, one can infer from Graythen's decision to photograph white people that it was easier to frame white people as despondent people finding food than it was to frame black people in that way. To put the point slightly differently, there would be some dissonance between the image of black people in those high waters and a caption describing people finding food. This dissonance is not about facts—whether in fact the black people were finding food; the dissonance is about frames—the racial association between black people and looting, particularly on the heels of a natural disaster or social upheaval.

Two caveats before moving on. First, nothing above is intended to suggest that Graythen's decision to photograph the two white people was racially conscious—that is, intentionally motivated by race. Frames operate both consciously and unconsciously; his selection of whites to photograph (and his "natural selection" against blacks) converged with existing racial frames about criminality and perpetrators, on the one hand, and law-abidingness and victims, on the other. The two photos were perfect mirror images of each other. But only image B could convey a story of survival against adversity; image A was inconsistent with that script. The presence of a black man with a big plastic bag in the context of a natural disaster is already inscribed with meaning. In that sense, the black man in image A did not require a caption to

be framed; nor did the white man and woman in image B. The stereotype of black criminality was activated by image A and the many images like it, which showed the central problem in New Orleans not to be the lack of humanitarian aid, but the lack of law and order.

The second caveat: our analysis should not be read as an argument against empiricism or a claim that facts are irrelevant. We simply mean to say that racial frames shape our perceptions of the facts. This does not mean that we are overdetermined by frames or that we are unable to escape their interpretative strictures. Rather, the point is that dependence on "just the facts" will seldom be enough to dislodge racial frames.[15] Partly this is because racial frames are installed not as the result of empiricism, but in spite of it. Consider color blindness. It is the dominant racial frame for understanding race not because of facts but because of a well-financed political project to entrench and naturalize a color-blind understanding of American race relations.[16] Accordingly, something more than facts is required to undo the racial work color blindness continues to perform; and something more than facts is required to dislodge the normativity of color blindness itself.

FROM RESCUE TO OCCUPATION: SEEING THE INVISIBLE

I'd rather have them here dead than alive. And at least they're not robbing you and you [don't] have to worry about feeding them.[17]

A resident of St. Gabriel when asked for her reactions to the decision to designate the town as a collective morgue

To the extent that our discussion of the problem of racial frames has largely examined representational issues, one might reasonably ask: What are the material consequences of this problem? And how, if at all, did it injure black New Orleanians in the wake of Hurricane Katrina? The answer relates to two interconnected frames: the frame of law and order and the frame of black criminality. Working together, these frames rendered black New Orleanians dangerous, unprotectable, and unrescuable.

In the immediate aftermath of Katrina, the media pointedly criticized the slow pace at which the federal government was responding to the disaster. But the critical stance was short-lived and quickly gave way to a focus on the breakdown of law and order, a frame that activated a familiar stereotype about black criminality. While initially blacks were seen as victims of Hurricane Katrina and a failed governmental response, this victim status proved to be highly unstable. Implicit in the frame that "this can't be America" is the notion that the neglect in the wake of Katrina was a violation of the duty of care owed to all citizens of the nation. This social contract includes blacks as citizens; and indeed the claim by blacks, "We are American"—a statement vigorously asserted by those contained in the convention center[18]—responded to and relied upon that frame.[19]

As time progressed, the social currency of the image of blacks as citizens of the state to whom a duty of care is owed diminished. It rubbed uneasily against the more familiar racial framing of poor black people as lazy, undeserving, and inherently criminal. Concern over the looting of property gradually took precedence over the humanitarian question of when people might be rescued and taken off of the highways and rooftops. Thus, while armed white men were presumed to be defending their property, black men with guns constituted gangs of violent looters who had to be contained. Under this frame, the surrounding towns and parishes that constituted potential refuge for black New Orleans residents who had no means to evacuate before the storm became no-go areas because of concerns about black criminality.

A particularly stark example of this came during the CNN interview on September 8 between Christiane Amanpour and the resident of St. Gabriel quoted above. The sentiment that dead blacks were better than live ones was enforced not only by local authorities who, like the Gretna police, turned people away at gunpoint, but by the National Guard and other local authorities who purportedly denied the Red Cross permission to enter the city shortly after the storm because of concerns about the safety of the rescuers.[20]

These fears were grounded in what ultimately proved to be grossly exaggerated or completely unsubstantiated media accounts of violence and attacks particularly in the Superdome and the convention center.[21] The tone of these reports were hyperbolic, evoking all of the familiar racial subtexts: FOX News, for example, issued a news report the day before the Superdome was evacuated that "there were many reports of robberies, rapes, carjackings, rioters, and murder and that violent gangs are roaming the streets at night, hidden by the cover of darkness." . . . These reports were taken as authoritative by police and other law enforcement officials. Indeed, even the mayor of the city, Ray Nagin, who is black, spoke of "hundreds of armed gang members" killing and raping people inside the Superdome, such that the crowd had descended to an "almost animalistic state."[22]

We are not arguing that there was no violence. There was. But the frames of black criminality and law and order overdetermined how we interpreted both the extent and nature of that violence. For example, consider how the "facts" about rape were interpreted and discussed. . . .

One of the more prominent examples of this official disregard was Charmaine Neville, a member of the family of renowned New Orleans musicians, who was raped by a roving group of men who invaded her community in the Lower Ninth Ward while she and her neighbors struggled unsuccessfully over a series of days to be evacuated and to obtain medical care.[23] Neville's searing account of what happened to her is a clear indictment of the government for its neglect: "What I want people to understand is that if we hadn't been left down there like animals that they were treating us like, all of those things would not have happened." Neville reported that her efforts to tell law enforcement officers and the National Guard of her assault were ignored. Neville's prominence and her fortuitous encounter with a member of the Catholic archdiocese in New Orleans during an interview at a local news station meant that her assault received media attention. Others did not.

Obviously, we are not excusing the conduct of the rapists or blaming that conduct on the government. Our point is simply that the overall governmental response in the aftermath of Katrina, shaped as it was by the racial frame of law and order, created conditions of possibility for rape and increased the likelihood that those rapes would be unaddressed. The sexual assaults against women—the vast majority of them black—became markers of black disorder, chaos, and the "animalistic" nature of New Orleans residents; but black women themselves could not occupy the position of victims worthy of rescue. Their injuries were only abstractions that were marshaled to make the larger point about the descent of New Orleans into a literal and figurative black hole. Black women's rape was invoked but not addressed. . . .

The government focused its attention on violence directed against property and violence directed against the rescuers—reports of which have proven to be false or grossly embellished. While these acts of violence could fit comfortably within the frame of law and order, violence against black women's bodies could not. Images of black criminality could work concomitantly with and help to instantiate the law-and-order frame that relies on black disorder; images of black women as innocent victims could do neither. The frames of law and order and black criminality influenced both the exaggeration (overreporting) and the marginalization (underreporting) of violent crimes in ways that make clear that facts don't speak for themselves. . . .

Only one shooting was confirmed in the Superdome, when a soldier shot himself during a scuffle with an attacker. Though New Orleans police chief Eddie Compass reported that he and his officers had retrieved more than thirty weapons from criminals who had been shooting at the rescuers, he later modified his statement to say that this had happened to another unit, a SWAT team at the convention center. The director of the SWAT team, however, reported that his unit had heard gunshots only one time and that his team had recovered no weapons despite aggressive searches.

In retrospect, it is clear that the media both mischaracterized and exaggerated the security threat to the rescue mission. Certainly the chaos in the wake of Katrina and the breakdown of the communications network helped develop a climate in which rumors could and did flourish. Yet under similarly difficult conditions during other natural disasters and even war, reporters have adhered to basic journalistic standards. That they did not under these conditions could be explained as an isolated case of failure under extremely trying circumstances. That might very well be so. Yet, the important part of this story is not that the media failed to observe the basic rules of journalism; it is that the story they told was one people were all too ready to accept. It was a narrative that made sense within the commonly accepted racial frames of law and order and black criminality.

These frames made it difficult for us to make sense of reported instances of "guys who looked like thugs, with pants hanging down around their asses," engaged in frantic efforts to get people collapsing from heat and exhaustion out of the Superdome and into a nearby makeshift medical facility. These images did not make racial sense. There was no ready-made social frame within which the image of black male rescuers could be placed. Existing outside of standard racial frames, black male rescuers present a socially unintelligible image. That we have trouble *seeing* "guys who look like thugs" as rescuers is not a problem of facts. It is a problem of frames. Indeed, the very use of the term "thug" already frames the fact of what they might be doing in a particular way.

CONCLUSION

. . . Katrina offers profound insights into how race operates in American society, insights into how various facts about our social life are racially interpreted through frames. As a result of racial frames, black people are both visible (as criminals) and invisible (as victims). Racial frames both capture and displace us—discursively and materially. More than shaping whether we see black people as criminal or innocent, perpetrator or victim, these frames shape whether we see black people at all. Indeed, one might reasonably ask: Where have all the black people gone, long time passing? It is not hyperbolic to say that post-Katrina black New Orleanians have become a part of an emerging social category: the disappeared. A critical lesson of Katrina is that civil rights advocacy groups need to think harder about frames, particular when making interventions into natural disasters involving African Americans.

As Michele Landis Dauber reminds us, the template for the American social welfare system has been disaster relief, and the extent to which people are entitled to any form of government resources has always depended upon the claimants' ability to "narrat[e] their deprivation as a disaster—a sudden loss for which the claimant is not responsible."[24] In the case of Katrina, this disaster-relief conception of welfare would seem to promote an immediate national response to aid the hurricane victims. The problem for black people and for other nonwhites, however, as Dauber herself notes, is that racial minorities' claims to victim status have always been fraught "because they are highly likely to be cast as a 'disaster' for the dominant racial group."[25] Implicit in Dauber's analysis is the idea that the move to realign America's racial discourse and policy away from its current distortions must confront the complex problem of racial frames. The existence of racial frames makes it enormously difficult to incorporate "just the facts" into an argument about racism. . . .

What is required is likely to be more in the nature of a social movement than a social survey. Facts will always play a crucial role, but just as the successes of the civil rights movement were born of organized struggle, so too must our efforts to shift racial frames ground themselves in a broader and more organic orientation than raw empiricism. People came to see the facts of de jure segregation differently not because new facts emerged about its harms but because new interpretations of those facts were made possible by social organization on the ground that pushed the courts toward a new consensus. We believe the same is true today.

DISCUSSION QUESTIONS

1. Did the television pictures of Katrina victims challenge the color-blind perspective?
2. Did the media report the facts?

NOTES

1. Cited in Aaron Kinney, "'Looting' or 'Finding'?" *Salon*, September 1, 2005.
2. www.snopes.com/Katrina/photos/looters.asp.
3. Cited in Kinney, "'Looting' or 'Finding'?"
4. Ibid.
5. One study of local television news stories on crime and public opinion illustrates the strong association between criminal behavior and racial identity. Participants were shown an identical news story under three different conditions: one group witnessed a version in which the perpetrator was white; another group saw a version in which the perpetrator was black; and a third group viewed a version in which there was no picture of the perpetrator. Following the screening, the participants in the first, white-perpetrator group were less likely to recall having seen a suspect than subjects in the second, black-perpetrator group. Among those in the third group, who saw no image of the perpetrator, over 60 percent erroneously recalled seeing a perpetrator, and in 70 percent of those cases viewers identified that nonexistent image as black. See Franklin Gilliam Jr. and Shanto Iyengar, "Prime Suspects: The Influence of Local Television News on the Viewing Public," *American Journal of Political Science* 44 (2000):560.
6. Roger Schank, "Tell Me a Story," *Narrative and Intelligence* 71 (1995).
7. A more nuanced formulation suggests, "Like well-accepted theories that guide our interpretation of data, schemas incline us to interpret data consistent with our biases." See Jerry Kang, "Trojan Horses of Races," *Harvard Law Review* 118 (2005):1489, 1515.
8. We do not intend to ignore the tremendous loss suffered in the Gulf region more broadly: we focus on New Orleans because of its unique position in the national imagination, as well as its pre-Katrina racial demographics. Indeed, New Orleans was not just a city that had come to be predominantly black; it was a city that was culturally marked as black. As one noted historian has stated, "The unique culture of south Louisiana derives from black Creole culture." Quoted in "Buffeted by Katrina, City's Complex Black Community Struggles to Regroup," Associated Press, October 4, 2005, www.msnbc.com.
9. Or fend for themselves and be punished for it. A particularly harrowing account of official indifference

and hostility comes from the ordeal of two emergency room workers who had the misfortune of being in New Orleans for a conference when Hurricane Katrina struck. After their hotel in the French Quarter closed, they, along with several hundred others, collected money to hire buses for their evacuation, but the buses were prevented from entering the city. When the workers attempted to flee on foot, they were directed to wait on the interstate for rescue that never came. Neither the police nor the National Guard provided them with food or water. When the group managed to find food for themselves and set up a makeshift camp, they were repeatedly dispersed at gunpoint by the police. When they attempted to walk across the bridge into the neighboring city of Gretna, they were again turned back at gunpoint by Gretna police. See Larry Bradshaw and Lorrie Beth Slonsky, "Trapped in New Orleans," September 6, 2005, www.counterpunch.org/bradshaw09062005.html.

10. On a nationally broadcast telethon to raise money for the victims of Katrina, Kanye West departed from the scripted remarks to say, "I hate the way they portray us in the media. You see a black family: it says they are looting. You see a white family; it says they have been looking for food. And you know, it has been five days, because most of the people are black, and even for me to complain about it, I would be a hypocrite, because I have tried to turn away from the TV because it is too hard to watch. So now I am calling my business manager right now to see what is the biggest amount I can give. And just imagine if I was down there and those are my people down there." Commenting on the slow pace of the government's response, he said, "George Bush doesn't care about black people." NBC immediately cut to another star on the program and censored West's remarks from the West Coast feed of the program. It also issued the following disclaimer: "Kanye West departed from the scripted comments that were prepared for him, and his opinions in no way represent the views of the networks. It would be most unfortunate if the efforts of the artists who participated tonight and the generosity of millions of Americans who are helping those in need are overshadowed by one person's opinion." "Rapper Kanye West Accuses Bush of Racism; NBC Apologizes," *CBC Arts*, September 3, 2005, www.cbc.ca/story/arts/national/2005/09/03/Arts/kanye_west_Katrina20050903.html.

11. This was Howard Dean's view. In an address to the National Baptist Convention he stated, "As survivors are evacuated, order is restored, the water slowly begins to recede, and we sort through the rubble, we must also begin to come to terms with the ugly truth that skin color, age and economics played a deadly role in who survived and who did not." "Excerpts of DNC Chairman Howard Dean's Remarks to the National Baptist Convention of America, Inc.," U.S. Newswire, September 8, 2005, www.usnewswire.com.

12. While some have argued that class was a more salient factor than race in explaining who was affected, we do not think that given the country's history of de jure and de facto racial subordination, race can be so neatly disaggregated from class. Particularly in the context of New Orleans—a city that was predominantly black and predominantly poor—the fact that those left on the overpasses and in the Superdome were black had everything to do with why they were poor. The point is not to reproduce another unhelpful version of the race-versus-class debate but to avoid sublimating the racial dimension of the issues raised by Katrina. Recent survey analysis suggests that race was in fact a crucial factor in explaining who was in harm's way. See "Katrina Hurts Blacks and Poor Victims Most," CNN/*USA Today*/Gallup Poll, October 25, 2005.

13. Both the Reverend Jesse Jackson and Representative Cynthia McKinney drew a link between the events in the Gulf and slavery. In response to a question by Anderson Cooper on CNN about whether race was a determinative factor in the federal government's response to Katrina, Jackson replied, "It is at least a factor. Today I saw 5,000 African Americans on the I–10 causeway desperate, perishing, dehydrated, babies dying. It looked like Africans in the hull of a slave ship. It was so ugly and so obvious. Have we missed this catastrophe because of indifference and ineptitude or is it a combination of both? And certainly I think the issue of race as a factor will not go away from this equation." Jesse Jackson, Remarks on *360 Degrees*, CNN, September 2, 2005. In an address on the floor of the House of Representatives on September 8, 2005, Representative McKinney said, "As I saw the African Americans, mostly African-American families ripped apart, I could only think about slavery, families ripped apart, herded into what looked like concentration camps." Cynthia McKinney, "Text of Remarks Delivered on the Floor of the House on Sept. 8, 2005," reprinted in "A Few Thoughts on the State of Our Nation," September 12, 2005, www.counterpunch.org/mckinney09122005.html.

14. "Huge Racial Divide over Katrina and Its Consequences," Report of the Pew Research Center for People and the Press, September 8, 2005, 2; available at http://people-press.org/reports/display.php3?Report ID=255.

15. As Gary Blasi contends, "If we store social categories in our heads by means of prototypes or exemplars rather than statistics, then our basic cognitive mechanisms not only predispose us toward stereotypes . . . , but also limit the potentially curative effect of information that contradicts the statistical assumptions about base rates that are embedded in our stereotypes." Gary Blasi, "Advocacy Against the Stereotype," *UCLA Law Review* 49 (2002):1241, 1256–57.

PERSONAL ACCOUNT

He Hit Her

I was raised in Charleston, South Carolina, a city where racial and class lines are both evident and defined by street address. I had been taught all my life that black people were different than "us" and were to be feared, particularly in groups.

One summer afternoon when I was 18 or 19, I was sitting in my car at a traffic light at the corner of Cannon and King streets, an area on the edge of the white part of the peninsular city, but progressively being inhabited by more and more blacks. It was hot, had been for weeks, and the sticky heat of South Carolina can be enraging by itself.

As I waited at the light, a young black couple turned the corner on the sidewalk and began to walk towards where I was sitting. The man was yelling and screaming and waving his arms about his head. The woman, a girl really, looked scared and was walking and trying to ignore his tirade. Perhaps it was her seeming indifference that finally did it, perhaps the heat, I don't know. As they drew right up next to my car though, he hit her. He hit her on the side of her head, open palmed, and her head bounced off the brick wall of the house on the corner and she sprawled to the ground, dazed and crying. The man stood over her, shaking his fist and yelling.

I looked around at the other people in cars around me, mostly whites, and at the other people on the sidewalks, mostly blacks, and I realized as everyone gaped that no one was going to do anything, no one was going to help, and neither was I. I don't think it was fear of the man involved that stopped me; rather, I think it was fear generated by what I had been told about the man that stopped me. Physically I was bigger than he was and I knew how to handle myself in a fight: I worked as a bouncer in a nightclub. What I was afraid of was what I had been told about blacks: that *en masse*, they hated whites, and that

given the opportunity they would harm me. I was afraid getting out of the car in that neighborhood would make me the focus of the fight and in a matter of time I would be pummeled by an angry black crowd. Also in my mind were thoughts of things I had heard voiced as a child: "They are different. Violence is a part of life for them. They beat, stab, and shoot each other all the time, and the women are just as bad as the men." So I sat and did nothing. The light changed and I pulled away.

The incident has haunted me over the last almost 15 years. I have often thought about it and felt angry when I did. I believe that as I examined it over time the woman who had been hit, the victim, became less and less prominent, and the black man and myself more prominent. Then I had an epiphany about it.

What bothered me about the incident was not that a man had hit a woman and I had done nothing to intervene, not even to blow my horn, but that a man had hit a woman and I had done nothing to intervene and that this reflected on me as a man. "Men don't hit women, and other men don't let men hit women," was also part of my masculinity training as a boy. There was a whole list of things that "real" men did and things that "real" men didn't do, and somewhere on there was this idea that men didn't let other men hit women. I realized that the incident haunted me not because a man had hit a woman, but because my lack of response was an indictment of *my* masculinity. The horror had become that I was somehow less of a man because of my inaction. Part of the dichotomy that this set up was the notion that the black man had done something to *me*, not to the woman he hit, and it was here that my anger lay. I wonder how this influenced my perception of black men I encountered in the future.

Tim Norton

16. See Lee Cokorinos, *The Assault on Diversity* (Institute for Democracy Studies, 2002), tracing the network of conservative activists and organizations that have waged a well-funded campaign over two decades to change the corpus of civil rights laws, end affirmative action, and reframe the political discourse on race and racism.

17. This should not suggest that she was without any compassion. She went on to say, "[The bodies] have to go somewhere. These are people's families. They have to—they still have to have dignity." It's precisely our

point that one can have compassion and still see black people through racial frames. *Paula Zahn Now*, CNN, September 8, 2005.

18. See Michael Ignatieff, "The Broken Contract," *New York Times,* September 25, 2005 (reporting that a woman held at the convention center asserted, "We are American" during a TV interview, demonstrating both anger and astonishment that she would have to remind Americans of that fact and that the social contract had failed).

19. Note that this frame is simultaneously inclusionary and exclusionary. To the extent that it asserts black citizenship, it seeks to include black people within the nation-state. However, it excludes noncitizens, black as well as others, from the circle of care based on lack of formal American belonging. This is deeply problematic but it reveals the limited space within which blacks could assert legitimate claims on national empathy.

20. See Anna Johnson, "Jackson Lashes Out at Bush over Hurricane Response, Criticizes Media for Katrina Coverage," AP Alert, September 3, 2005 (reporting that the Red Cross asserted that it could not enter New Orleans on orders from the National Guard and local authorities). A principal reason for the delay was that government officials believed that they had to prepare a complicated military operation rather than a relief effort. See "Misinformation Seen Key in Katrina Delays," UPI Top Stories, September 30, 2005.

21. See Brain Thevenot and Gordon Russell, "Reports of Anarchy at the Superdome Overstated," *Seattle Times*, September 26, 2005 (reporting that "the vast majority of reported atrocities committed by evacuees have turned out to be false, or at least unsupported by any evidence, according to key military, law enforcement, medical and civilian officers in a position to know." See also Andrew Gumbel, "After the Storm, US Media Held to Account for Exaggerated Tales of Katrina Chaos," *Los Angeles Times*, September 28, 2005.

22. Thevenot and Russell, "Reports of Anarchy."

23. See Charmaine Neville, "How We Survived the Flood," transcript of interview given to New Orleans media outlets, September 5, 2005, www.counterpunch.org/neville09072005.html.

24. Michele Landis Dauber, "Fate, Responsibility, and 'Natural' Disaster Relief: Narrating the American Welfare State," *Law and Society* 33 (1999):257, 264.

25. Ibid., 307.

READING 47

The Protean N-Word

Randall Kennedy

How should *nigger* be defined? Is it a part of the American cultural inheritance that warrants preservation? Why does *nigger* generate such powerful reactions? Is it a more hurtful racial epithet than insults such as *kike, wop, wetback, mick, chink,* and *gook*? Am I wrongfully offending the sensibilities of readers right now by spelling out *nigger* instead of using a euphemism such as *N-word*? Should blacks be able to use *nigger* in ways forbidden to others? Should the law view *nigger* as a provocation that reduces the culpability of a person who responds to it violently? Under what circumstances, if any, should a person be ousted from his or her job for saying "nigger"? What methods are useful for depriving *nigger* of destructiveness? In the pages that follow, I will pursue these and related questions. I will put a tracer on *nigger,* report on its use, and assess the controversies to which it gives rise. I have invested energy in this endeavor because *nigger* is a key word in the lexicon of race relations and thus an important term in American politics. To be ignorant of its meanings and effects is to make oneself vulnerable to all manner of perils, including the loss of a job, a reputation, a friend, even one's life.[1]

Let's turn first to etymology. *Nigger* is derived from the Latin word for the color black, *niger.*[2] According to the *Random House Historical Dictionary of American Slang,* it did not originate as a slur but took on a derogatory connotation over time. *Nigger* and other words related to it have been spelled in a variety of ways, including niggah, nigguh, niggur, and niggar. When John Rolfe recorded in his journal the first shipment of Africans to Virginia in 1619, he listed them as "negars." A 1689 inventory of an estate in Brooklyn, New York, made mention of an enslaved "niggor" boy. The seminal lexicographer Noah Webster referred to Negroes as "negers." (Currently some people insist upon distinguishing *nigger*—which they see as exclusively an insult—from *nigga,* which they view as a term capable of signaling friendly salutation.)[3] In the 1700s *niger* appeared in what the dictionary describes as "dignified argumentation" such as Samuel Sewall's denunciation of slavery, *The Selling of Joseph.* No one knows precisely when or how *niger* turned derisively into *nigger* and attained a pejorative meaning.[4] We do know, however, that by the end of the first third of the nineteenth century, *nigger* had already become a familiar and influential insult.

Randall Kennedy is a professor of law at Harvard University.

In *A Treatise on the Intellectual Character and Civil* and *Political Condition of the Colored People of the United States: and the Prejudice Exercised Towards Them* (1837), Hosea Easton wrote that *nigger* "is an opprobrious term, employed to impose contempt upon [blacks] as an inferior race. . . . The term in itself would be perfectly harmless were it used only to distinguish one class of society from another; but it is not used with that intent. . . . [I]t flows from the fountain of purpose to injure." Easton averred that often the earliest instruction white adults gave to white children prominently featured the word *nigger*. Adults reprimanded them for being "worse than niggers," for being "ignorant as niggers," for having "no more credit than niggers"; they disciplined them by telling them that unless they behaved they would be carried off by "the old nigger" or made to sit with "niggers" or consigned to the "nigger seat," which was, of course, a place of shame.[5]

Nigger has seeped into practically every aspect of American culture, from literature to political debates, from cartoons to song. Throughout the 1800s and for much of the 1900s as well, writers of popular music generated countless lyrics that lampooned blacks, in songs such as "Philadelphia Riots; or, I Guess It Wasn't de Niggas DisTime," "De Nigga Gal's Dream," "Who's Dat Nigga Dar A-Peepin?," "Run, Nigger, Run," "A Nigger's Reasons," "Nigger Will Be Nigger," "I Am Fighting for the Nigger," "Ten Little Niggers," "Niggas Git on de Boat," "Nigger in a Pit," "Nigger War Bride Blues," "Nigger, Nigger, Never Die," "Li'l Black Nigger," and "He's Just a Nigger." The chorus of this last begins, "He's just a nigger, when you've said dat you've said it all."[6]

Throughout American history, *nigger* has cropped up in children's rhymes, perhaps the best known of which is

Eeny-meeny-miney-mo!
Catch a nigger by the toe!
If he hollers, let him go!
Eeny-meeny-miney-mo!

But there are scores of others as well, including

Nigger, nigger, never die,
Blackface and shiny eye.[7]

And then there is:

Teacher, teacher, don't whip me!
Whip that nigger behind that tree!
He stole honey and I stole money.
Teacher, teacher, wasn't that funny?[8]

Today, on the Internet, whole sites are devoted to nigger jokes. . . .

Nigger has been a familiar part of the vocabularies of whites high and low. It has often been the calling card of so-called white trash—poor, disreputable, uneducated Euro-Americans. Partly to distance themselves from this ilk, some whites of higher standing have aggressively forsworn the use of *nigger*. Such was the case, for example, with senators Strom Thurmond and Richard Russell, both white supremacists who never used the N-word. For many whites in positions of authority, however, referring to blacks as niggers was once a safe indulgence. Reacting to news that Booker T. Washington had dined at the White House, Senator Benjamin Tillman of South Carolina predicted, "The action of President Roosevelt in entertaining that nigger will necessitate our killing a thousand niggers in the South before they will learn their place again." . . .[9]

Nor was *nigger* confined to the language of local figures of limited influence. Supreme Court Justice James Clark McReynolds referred to Howard University as the "nigger university."[10] President Harry S. Truman called Congressman Adam Clayton Powell "that damned nigger preacher."[11] *Nigger* was also in the vocabulary of Senator, Vice President, and President Lyndon Baines Johnson. "I talk everything over with [my wife]," he proclaimed on one occasion early in his political career. Continuing, he quipped, "Of course . . . I have a nigger maid, and I talk my problems over with her, too."[12]

A complete list of prominent whites who have referred at some point or other to blacks demeaningly as niggers would be lengthy indeed. It would include such otherwise disparate figures as Richard Nixon and Flannery O'Connor.[13]

Given whites' use of *nigger*, it should come as no surprise that for many blacks the N-word has constituted a major and menacing presence that has sometimes shifted the course of their lives. . . .

Paul Robeson earned a degree from Columbia Law School but turned his back on a career as an attorney after, among other incidents, a stenographer refused to work for him, declaring, "I never take dictation from a nigger."[14]

Malcolm X remembered that during his childhood, after his family fell apart following the murder of his father, the whites who served as his guardians openly referred to blacks as niggers. And then there was his encounter with a white teacher who, in recommending a career in carpentry rather than the law, urged young Malcolm to be "realistic about being a nigger."[15]

When Jackie Robinson reported to the Brooklyn Dodgers' top minor-league team, the manager earnestly asked the team's owner whether he really thought that niggers were human beings.[16] Robinson, of course, would have to contend with *nigger* throughout his fabled career. During a game played on April 22, 1947, he recalled hearing hatred pour forth from the dugout of the Philadelphia Phillies "as if it had been synchronized by some master conductor."

. . . When Charles McLaurin, an organizer with the Student Nonviolent Coordinating Committee (SNCC), was jailed in Columbia, Mississippi, a patrolman asked him, "Are you a Negro or a nigger?" When McLaurin responded, "Negro," another patrolman hit him in the face. When he gave the same reply to the same question, McLaurin was again beaten. Finally, asked the question a third time, he answered, "I am a nigger." At that point the first patrolman told him to leave town and warned, "If I ever catch you here again I'll kill you."[17]

As a child, the playwright August Wilson stopped going to school for a while after a series of notes were left in his desk by white classmates. The notes read: "Go home nigger."[18]

The Olympic sprinter Tommie Smith remembers an incident from his boyhood in which a white child snatched an ice cream cone out of his hand and snarled, "Niggers don't eat ice cream."[19]

Michael Jordan was suspended from school for hitting a white girl who called him "nigger" during a fight over a seat on a school bus in Wilmington, North Carolina.[20]

Tiger Woods was tied up in kindergarten by older schoolmates who called him "nigger."[21]

Recalling the difficulties she faced in raising her black son in a household with her white female lover, the poet Audre Lorde noted that "for years in the name-calling at school, boys shouted at [her son] not—'your mother's a lesbian'—but rather—'your mother's a nigger.'"[22]

The musician Branford Marsalis has said he cannot remember a time when he was *not* being called "nigger." "If you grew up in the South," he observed, whites "called you nigger from the time you were born." . . . [23]

In 1973, at the very moment he stood poised to break Babe Ruth's record for career home runs, the baseball superstar Hank Aaron encountered *nigger-as-insult* on a massive scale, largely in the form of hateful letters:

Dear Nigger,
Everybody loved Babe Ruth. You will be the most hated man in this country if you break his career home run record.

Dear Black Boy,
Listen Black Boy, we don't want no nigger Babe Ruth.

Dear Mr. Nigger,
I hope you don't break the Babe's record. How can I tell my kids that a nigger did it?

Dear Nigger,
You can hit all dem home runs over dem short fences, but you can't take dat black off yo face.

Dear Nigger,
You black animal, I hope you never live long enough to hit more home runs than the great Babe Ruth. . . .

Dear Nigger Henry,
You are [not] going to break this record established by the great Babe Ruth if you can help it. . . . Whites are far more superior than jungle bunnies. . . . My gun is watching your every black move.[24]

An offshoot of *nigger* is *nigger lover*, a label affixed to nonblacks who become friendly with African Americans or openly side with them in racial controversies. In the Civil War era, Republicans' antislavery politics won them the appellation "black Republicans" or "nigger lovers." . . .

A century later, during the civil rights revolution, whites who joined black civil rights protesters were frequently referred to as nigger lovers. When white and black "freedom riders" rode together on a bus in violation of (unlawful) local Jim Crow custom, a bigoted white driver took delight in delivering them to a furious crowd of racists in Anniston, Alabama. Cheerfully anticipating the beatings to come, the driver yelled to the mob, "Well, boys, here they are. I brought you some niggers and nigger lovers."[25] Speaking to a rally in Baltimore, Maryland, a spokesman for the National States Rights Party declared confidently that most "nigger lovers are sick in the mind" and "should be bound, hung, and killed."[26]

The term *nigger lover* continues to be heard amid the background noise that accompanies racial conflict. Whites who refrain from discriminating against blacks, whites who become intimate with blacks, whites who confront antiblack practices, whites who work on the electoral campaigns of black candidates, whites who nominate blacks for membership in clubs, whites who protect blacks in the course of their official duties, and whites who merely socialize with blacks are all subject to being derided as "nigger lovers."[27]

Over the years, *nigger* has become the best known of the American language's many racial insults, evolving into the paradigmatic slur. It is the epithet that generates epithets. That is why Arabs are called "sand niggers," Irish "the niggers of Europe," and Palestinians "the niggers of the Middle East"; why black bowling balls have been called "nigger eggs," games of craps "nigger golf," watermelons "nigger hams," rolls of one-dollar bills "nigger rolls," bad luck "nigger luck," gossip "nigger news," and heavy boots "nigger stompers."[28]

Observers have made strong claims on behalf of the special status of *nigger* as a racial insult. The journalist Farai Chideya describes it as "the all-American trump card, the nuclear bomb of racial epithets."[29] The writer Andrew Hacker has asserted that among slurs of any sort, *nigger* "stands alone [in] its power to tear at one's insides."[30] Judge Stephen Reinhardt deems *nigger* "the most noxious racial epithet in the contemporary American lexicon."[31] And prosecutor Christopher Darden famously branded *nigger* the "filthiest, dirtiest, nastiest word in the English language."[32]

The claim that *nigger* is the superlative racial epithet—the *most* hurtful, the *most* fearsome, the *most* dangerous, the *most* noxious—necessarily involves comparing oppressions and prioritizing victim status. Some scoff at this enterprise. Objecting to a columnist's assertion that being called a honky was not in the same league as being called a nigger, one reader responded, "We should be in the business of ending racism, not measuring on a politically correct thermometer the degree to which one is more victimized than another"[33] Declining to enter into a discussion comparing the Holocaust with American slavery, a distinguished historian quipped that he refused to become an accountant of atrocity. . . .

We could, of course, avoid making comparisons, Instead of saying that the Holocaust was the *worst* atrocity of the twentieth century, we could say simply that the Holocaust was terrible, Instead of saying that *nigger* has been the *most* socially destructive racial epithet in the American language, we could say merely that, when used derogatorily, *nigger* is a socially destructive epithet. Although such a strategy may have certain diplomatic merits, it deprives audiences of assistance in making qualitative judgments. After all, there is a difference between the massacre that kills fifty and the one that kills five hundred—or five thousand or fifty thousand. By the same token, the stigmatizing power of different racial insults can vary.

A comedy sketch dramatized by Richard Pryor and Chevy Chase on the television show *Saturday Night Live* makes this point vividly. Chase is interviewing Pryor for a job as a janitor and administers a word-association test that goes like this:

"'White,'" says Chase.

"'Black,'" Pryor replies.

"'Bean.'"

"'Pod.'"

"'Negro.'"

"'Whitey,'" Pryor replies lightly.

"'Tarbaby.'"

"What did you say?" Pryor asks, puzzled.

"'Tarbaby,'" Chase repeats, monotone.

"'Ofay,'" Pryor says sharply.

"'Colored.'"

"'Redneck!'"

"'Jungle bunny!'"

"'Peckerwood,'" Pryor yells.

"'Burrhead!'"

"'Cracker.'"

"'Spearchucker!'"

"'White trash!'"

"'Jungle bunny!'"

"'Honky!'"

"'Spade!'"

"'Honky, honky!'"

"'Nigger,'" says Chase smugly [aware that, when pushed, he can always use that trump card].

"'Dead honky!'" Pryor growls [resorting to the threat of violence now that he has been outgunned in the verbal game of racial insult].[34]

It is impossible to declare with confidence that when hurled as an insult, *nigger* necessarily inflicts more distress than other racial epithets. Individuals beset by thugs may well feel equally terrified whether those thugs are screaming "Kill the honky" or "Kill the nigger." In the aggregate, though, *nigger* is and has long been the most socially consequential racial insult. Consider, for example, the striking disparity of incidence that distinguishes *nigger* from other racial epithets appearing in reported court opinions. In reported federal and state cases in the LEXIS-NEXIS data base (as of July 2001), *kike* appears in eighty-four cases, *wetback* in fifty, *gook* in ninety, and *honky* in 286.[35] These cases reveal cruelty, terror, brutality, and heartache. Still, the frequency of these slurs is overwhelmed by that of *nigger,* which appears in 4,219 reported decisions.[36]

Reported court opinions are hardly a perfect mirror of social life in America; they are merely an opaque reflection that poses real difficulties of interpretation. The social meaning of litigation is ambiguous. It may represent an attempt to remedy real injury, or it may mark cynical exploitation of increased intolerance for racism. The very act of bringing a lawsuit may express a sense of empowerment, but declining to bring one may do so as well, signaling that a person or group has means other than cumbersome litigation by which to settle scores or vindicate rights. That there is more litigation in which *nigger* appears could mean that usage of the term is more prevalent than usage of analogous epithets; that its usage is associated with more dramatic injuries; that targets of *nigger* are more aggrieved or more willing and able to sue; or that authorities—police, prosecutors, judges, or juries—are more receptive to this species of complaint. I do not know which of these hypotheses best explains the salience of *nigger* in the jurisprudence of racial epithets. What cannot plausibly be doubted, however, is the fact of *nigger's* baleful preeminence.

Nigger first appears in the reports of the United States Supreme Court in a decision announced in 1871. . . . In the years since, federal and state courts have heard hundreds of cases in which the word *nigger* figured in episodes of racially motivated violence, threats, and arson. Particularly memorable among these was the successful prosecution of Robert Montgomery for violation of federal criminal statutes.[37] In 1988, in Indianapolis, state authorities established a residential treatment center for convicted child molesters in an all-white neighborhood. From the center's opening until mid-1991—a period during which all of the residents of the center were white—neighbors voiced no objections. In June 1991, however, authorities converted the center into a shelter for approximately forty homeless veterans, twenty-five of whom were black. Soon thereafter trouble erupted as a group of whites, including Montgomery, loudly proclaimed their opposition to the encroachment of "niggers" and burned a cross and vandalized a car to express their feelings. An all-white cadre of child molesters was evidently acceptable, but the presence of blacks made a racially integrated group of homeless *veterans* intolerable!

If *nigger* represented only an insulting slur and was associated only with racial animus, this [discussion] would not exist, for the term would be insufficiently interesting to warrant extended study. *Nigger* is fascinating precisely because it has been put to a variety of uses and can radiate a wide array of meanings. Unsurprisingly, blacks have often used *nigger* for different purposes than racist whites. To lampoon slavery, blacks created the story of the slave caught eating one of his master's pigs. "Yes, suh, Massa," the slave quipped, "you got less pig now, but you sho' got more nigger."[38] To poke fun at the grisly phenomenon of lynching, African Americans told of the black man who, upon seeing a white woman pass by, said, "Lawd, will I ever?" A white man responded, "No, nigger, never." The black man replied, "Where there's life, there's hope." And the white man declared, "Where there's a nigger, there's a rope."[39] To dramatize the tragic reality of Jim Crow subjugation, African Americans recounted the tale of the Negro who got off a bus down south. Seeing a white policeman, he politely asked for the time. The policeman hit him twice with a club and said, "Two o'clock, nigger. Why?" "No reason, Cap'n," the black man answered. "I's just glad it ain't twelve."[40] And to satirize "legal" disenfranchisement, African Americans told the joke about the black man who attempted to register to vote. After the man answered a battery of questions that were far more difficult than any posed to whites, an official confronted him with a headline in a Chinese paper and demanded a translation. "Yeah, I know what it means," the black man said. "It means that niggers don't vote in Mississippi again this year."[41]

In the 1960s and 1970s, protest became more direct and more assertive. Drafted to fight a "white man's war" in Vietnam, Muhammad Ali refused to be inducted into the U.S. Army, explaining, "No Vietcong ever called me 'nigger.'"[42] Emphasizing the depth of white racism all across the United States, activists joked, "What is a Negro with a Ph.D.?" Their response? "Dr. Nigger."

In his famous "Letter from a Birmingham Jail," Martin Luther King Jr. continued to agitate, listing in wrenching detail the indignities that prompted his impatience with tardy reform. He cited having to sleep in automobiles because of racial exclusion from motels, having to explain to his children why they could not go to amusement parks open to the white public, and being "harried by day and haunted by night by the fact that you are a Negro, living constantly at tip-toe stance never quite knowing what to expect next." Among King's litany of abuses was the humiliating way in which whites routinely addressed blacks: "Your wife and mother," he observed, "are never given the respected title 'Mrs.,'" and under the etiquette of Jim Crow, "your first name becomes 'nigger' and your middle name becomes 'boy' (however old you are) and your last name becomes 'John.'"[43]

For some observers, the only legitimate use of *nigger* is as a rhetorical boomerang against racists. There are others, however, who approvingly note a wide range of additional usages. According to Professor Clarence Major, when *nigger* is "used by black people among themselves, [it] is a racial term with undertones of warmth and good will—reflecting . . . a tragicomic sensibility that is aware of black history."[44] The writer Claude Brown once admiringly described *nigger* as "perhaps the most soulful word in the world,"[45] and journalist Jarvis DeBerry calls it "beautiful in its multiplicity of functions." "I am not aware," DeBerry writes, "of any other word capable of expressing so many contradictory emotions."[46] Traditionally an insult, *nigger* can also be a compliment, as in "He played like a nigger." Historically a signal of hostility, it can also be a salutation announcing affection, as in "This is my main nigger." A term of belittlement, *nigger* can also be a term of respect, as in "James Brown is a straight-up nigger." A word that can bring forth bitter tears in certain circumstances, *nigger* can prompt joyful laughter in others.[47]

A candid portrayal of the N-word's use among African Americans may be found in Helen Jackson Lee's autobiography, *Nigger in the Window*. It was Lee's cousin who first introduced her to *nigger*'s possibilities. As Lee remembered it, "Cousin Bea had a hundred different ways of saying *nigger;* listening to her, I learned the variety of meanings the word could assume. How it could be opened like an umbrella to cover a dozen different moods, or stretched like a rubber band to wrap up our family with other colored families. . . . *Nigger* was a piece-of-clay word that you could shape . . . to express your feelings." . . .[48]

Before the 1970s, however, *nigger* seldom figured in the routines of professional comedians. It was especially rare in the acts of those who performed for racially mixed audiences. . . .

All that changed with the emergence of Richard Pryor.[49] Through live performances and a string of albums, he brought *nigger* to center stage in stand-up comedy, displaying with consummate artistry its multiple meanings.

Pryor's single best performance may be heard on the aptly titled *That Nigger's Crazy,* winner of the 1974 Grammy Award for best comedy recording. The album explores Pryor's professional fears ("Hope I'm funny . . . because I know niggers ready to kick ass"), blacks' alleged ability to avoid certain sorts of danger ("Niggers never get burned up in buildings. . . . White folks just panic, run to the door, fall all over each other. . . . Niggers get outside, *then* argue"), black parenting styles ("My father was one of them eleven-o'clock niggers"), comparative sociology ("White folks fuck quiet; niggers make noise"), racial anthropology ("White folks . . . don't know how to play the dozens"), and social commentary ("Nothin' can scare a nigger after four hundred years of this shit"). . . .

In the years since the release of *That Nigger's Crazy,* the N-word has become a staple in the routine of many black comedians. Among these, the one who most jarringly deploys it is Chris Rock, whose signature skit begins with the declaration "I love black people, but I hate niggers."[50] He goes on:

> It's like our own personal civil war.
> On the one side, there's black people.
> On the other, you've got niggers.
> The niggers have got to go. Every time black people want to have a good time, niggers mess it up. You

can't do anything without some ignorant-ass niggers fucking it up.

> Can't go to a movie the first week it opens. Why? Because niggers are shooting at the screen. . . .
> You can't have anything in your house. Why? Because the niggers who live next door will break in, take it all, and then come over the next day and go, "We heard you got robbed." . . .

Rap is another genre of entertainment suffused with instances of *nigger.* A cursory survey just of titles yields Dr. Dre's "The Day the Niggas Took Over," A Tribe Called Quest's "Sucka Nigga," Jaz-Z's "Real Nigger," the Geto Boys' "Trigga Happy Nigga," DMX's "My Niggas," and Cypress Hill's "Killa Hill Nigga." In "Gangsta's Paradise," meanwhile, Coolio declares,

> *I'm the kind of nigga*
> *little homies want to be like*
> *on their knees in the night*
> *saying prayers in the streetlights.*[51]

Ice-T says in one of his songs, "I'm a nigger not a colored man or a black or a Negro or an Afro-American."[52] Ice Cube, for his part, dubs himself "the Nigga ya love to hate."[53] And Beanie Sigel promises

> *I'ma ride with my niggas*
> *die with my niggas*
> *get high with my niggas*
> *split pies with my niggas*
> *till my body gets hard*
> *soul touch the sky*
> *till my numbers get called*
> *and God shuts my eyes.*[54]

One of the seminal influences in gangsta rap called itself N.W.A, short for "Niggaz Wit Attitude." One of this group's most popular albums was *Efil4zaggin,* which, read backward, is "Niggaz 4 Life." Tupac Shakur proclaimed that for him, *nigga* stood for "Never Ignorant, Gets Goals Accomplished."[55]

Some people—I call them eradicationists—seek to drive *nigger* out of rap, comedy, and all other categories of entertainment even when (perhaps *especially* when) blacks themselves are the ones using the N-word. They see this usage as bestowing legitimacy on *nigger* and misleading those whites who have little direct interaction with African

Americans. Eradicationists also maintain that blacks' use of *nigger* is symptomatic of racial self-hatred or the internalization of white racism, thus the rhetorical equivalent of black-on-black crime.

There is something to both of these points. The use of *nigger* by black rappers and comedians has given the term a new currency and enhanced cachet such that many young whites yearn to use the term like the blacks whom they see as heroes or trendsetters. It is undoubtedly true, moreover, that in some cases, blacks' use of *nigger* is indicative of an antiblack, self-hating prejudice. I myself first became aware of the term as a child in an all-black setting—my family household in Columbia, South Carolina—in which older relatives routinely attributed to negritude traits they disparaged, including tardiness, dishonesty, rudeness, impoverishment, cowardice, and stupidity. Such racial disparagement *of* blacks *by* blacks was by no means idiosyncratic. It is a widespread feature of African American culture that has given rise to a distinctive corpus of racial abasement typified by admonishments, epigraphs, and doggerel. . . .

This tendency toward racial self-abnegation has been much diminished since the civil rights revolution. But it still retains a grip on the psyches of many black Americans and is searingly evident in a phrase well known in black circles: "Niggers ain't shit."[56]

Self-hatred, however, is an implausible explanation for why many assertive, politically progressive African Americans continue to say "nigger" openly and frequently in conversations with one another. These are African Americans who, in their own minds at least, use *nigger* not in subjection to racial subordination but in defiance of it. Some deploy a long tradition, especially evident in black nationalist rhetoric, of using abusive criticism to spur action that is intended to erase any factual predicate for the condemnation voiced. An example is writing by the Last Poets, a group established in 1968 that merged poetry, music, and politics in forms that anticipated certain types of rap. A famous item in the Last Poets' repertoire was "Niggers Are Scared of Revolution," in which they charged that:

Niggers are scared of revolution but niggers shouldn't be scared of revolution because revolution is nothing but change, and all niggers do is change. Niggers come in from work and change into pimping clothes to hit the streets to make some quick change. Niggers change their hair from black to red to blond and hope like hell their looks will change. Niggers kill other niggers just because one didn't receive the correct change. . . .

Niggers shoot dope into their arms. Niggers shoot guns and rifles on New Year's Eve, a new year that is coming in where white police will do more shooting at them. Where are niggers when the revolution needs some shot? Yeah . . . you know, niggers are somewhere shooting the shit. Niggers are scared of revolution.[57]

Describing their intentions, Umar Bin Hassan writes that the poem constituted a "call to arms" because "niggers are human beings lost in somebody else's system of values and morals."[58]

Many blacks also do with *nigger* what other members of marginalized groups have done with slurs aimed at shaming them. They have thrown the slur right back in their oppressors' faces. They have added a positive meaning to *nigger,* just as women, gays, lesbians, poor whites, and children born out of wedlock have defiantly appropriated and revalued such words as *bitch, cunt, queer, dyke, redneck, cracker,* and *bastard.*[59]

Yet another source of allegiance to *nigger* is a pessimistic view of the African American predicament. Many blacks who use *nigger* in public before racially mixed audiences disdain dressing up their colloquial language. They do not even attempt to put their best foot forward for the purpose of impressing whites or eroding stereotypes because they see such missions as lost causes. They like to use *nigger* because it is a shorthand way of reminding themselves and everyone else precisely where they perceive themselves as standing in American society—the message being, "Always remember you's a nigger." As Bruce A. Jacobs observes, "To proclaim oneself a nigger is to declare to the disapproving mainstream, 'You can't fire me. I quit.' Hence the perennial popularity of the word. Among poor black youth who . . . carry a burning resentment of white society. To growl that one is a nigga is a seductive gesture . . . that can feel bitterly empowering."[60]

Two additional considerations also warrant notice here, both of them having to do with the power of words to simultaneously create and divide communities. Some blacks use *nigger* to set themselves off from Negroes who refuse to use it. To proclaim oneself a nigger is to identify oneself as real, authentic, uncut, unassimilated, and unassimilable—the opposite, in short, of a Negro, someone whose rejection of *nigger* is seen as part of an effort to blend into the white mainstream. Sprinkling one's language with *niggers* is thus a way to "keep it real."[61]

Roping off cultural turf is another aim of some blacks who continue to use *nigger* in spite of its stigmatized status. Certain forms of black cultural expression have become commercially valuable, and black cultural entrepreneurs fear that these forms will be exploited by white performers who will adopt them and, tapping white-skin privilege, obtain compensation far outstripping that paid to black performers. This is, of course, a realistic fear in light of the long history of white entertainers' becoming rich and famous by marketing in white-face cultural innovations authored by their underappreciated black counterparts. A counterstrategy is to seed black cultural expression with gestures that are widely viewed as being off-limits to whites. Saying "nigger" is one such gesture. Even whites who immerse themselves in black hip-hop culture typically refrain from openly and unabashedly saying "nigger" like their black heroes or colleagues, for fear that it might be perceived as a sign of disrespect rather than one of solidarity.

Some [non-black] entertainers have used *nigger* in their acts. John Lennon and Yoko Ono, for example, entitled a song "Woman Is the Nigger of the World,"[62] and Patti Smith wrote "Rock 'n' Roll Nigger."[63] But Lennon, Ono, and Smith performed in overwhelmingly white milieus. Rap, by contrast, is dominated by blacks. A few white rappers have achieved commercial success and won the respect of black artists and audiences. I am thinking here especially of the white rapper Eminem, a superstar

in the hip-hop culture. Eminem has assumed many of the distinctive mannerisms of his black rap colleagues, making himself into a "brother" in many ways—in his music, his diction, his gait, his clothes, his associations. He refuses to say, however, any version of a word that his black hip-hop colleagues employ constantly as a matter of course; the nonchalance with which he tosses around epithets such as *bitch* and *faggot* does not extend to *nigger*. "That word," he insists, "is not even in my vocabulary."[64]

Eminem is certainly following a prudent course, for many people, white and black alike, disapprove of a white person saying "nigger" under virtually any circumstance. "When we call each other 'nigger' it means no harm," Ice Cube remarks. "But if a white person uses it, it's something different, it's a racist word."[65] Professor Michael Eric Dyson likewise asserts that whites must know and stay in their racial place when it comes to saying "nigger." He writes that "most white folk attracted to black culture know better than to cross a line drawn in the sand of racial history. *Nigger* has never been cool when spit from white lips."[66]

The race line that Dyson applauds, however, is a specious divide. There is nothing necessarily wrong with a white person saying "nigger," just as there is nothing necessarily wrong with a black person saying it. What should matter is the context in which the word is spoken—the speaker's aims, effects, alternatives. To condemn whites who use the N-word without regard to context is simply to make a fetish of *nigger*. Harriet Beecher Stowe (*Uncle Tom's Cabin*), Mark Twain (*Huckleberry Finn*), William Dean Howells (*An Imperative Duty*), Edward Sheldon (*The Nigger*), Eugene O'Neill (*All God's Chillun*), Lillian Smith (*Strange Fruit*), Sinclair Lewis (*Kingsblood Royal*), Joyce Carol Oates (*Them*), E. L. Doctorow (*Ragtime*), John Grisham (*A Time to Kill*), and numerous other white writers have unveiled *nigger*-as-insult in order to dramatize and condemn racism's baleful presence.

In 1967, President Lyndon Baines Johnson decided to appoint an African American to the Supreme Court for the first time in American history. First on Johnson's list of candidates was Thurgood Marshall—"Mr. Civil Rights," the hero of *Brown v. Board of Education* and, of course, the man he ended up putting on the Court. But before he announced his selection, Johnson asked an assistant to identify some other possible candidates. The aide mentioned A. Leon Higginbotham, whom Johnson had appointed to the federal trial bench. Reportedly, the president dismissed the suggestion with the comment "The only two people who have ever heard of Judge Higginbotham are you and his momma. When I appoint a nigger to the [Supreme Court], I want everyone to know he's a nigger."[67] Was the use of *nigger* in this context a venting of racial prejudice? Maybe. Johnson had been raised in a thoroughly racist environment, had supported racist policies for a long period, and, as we have seen, casually used *nigger* as part of his private vocabulary before he became president. On this particular occasion, however, it seems likely that he was merely seeking to highlight the racial exclusion against which he was acting, parodying the old regime even as he sought to reform it. If this is an accurate assessment of the situation, I see nothing wrong with what Johnson said, and I applaud what he did.

Can a relationship between a black person and a white one be such that the white person should properly feel authorized, at least within the confines of that relationship, to use the N-word? For me the answer is yes. Carl Van Vechten, for instance, wrote of "niggers" in correspondence with his friend Langston Hughes,[68] and Hughes did not object (though he did once write that *nigger* was a red flag for all Negroes).[69] *Should* Hughes have objected? No. Van Vechten, a key supporter of the Harlem Renaissance, had shown time and again that he abhorred racial prejudice, would do what he could to improve the fortunes of African Americans, and treasured his black friends. It was against this backdrop of achieved trust that Hughes (and other black writers) rightly permitted Van Vechten to use *nigger* as so many African Americans have used it—as an ironic, shorthand spoof on the absurdity of American race relations. . . .[70]

DISCUSSION QUESTIONS

1. Should Kennedy have written on this topic at all? Should his article have been included in this textbook?
2. Kennedy seems to be sketching a contrast between an "eradicationist" and a "social context" position. What are the implications of each position?

NOTES

1. See, e.g., *Ohio v. Howard,* 1995 Ohio App. LEXIS 750 (Ohio Ct. App.) (man killed in altercation sparked by his calling the defendant a nigger); *State v. Higginbotham,* 212 N.W. 2d 881 (Minn. Sup. Ct. 1973) (man killed after calling a woman a nigger lover); "Black Judge Adds 35 Years to Robber's Sentence after Felon Made Racial Slur," *Jet,* October 10, 1994; "School Superintendent in Nevada under Fire for Using Word *Nigger*," *Jet,* August 18, 2000; "White Bishop Steps Down from Charity amid Controversy over Racial Slur," *Jet,* April 21, 1997; "Jaguar Official Suspended after Using Racial Slur," *Jet,* June 13, 1994.
2. On the etymology of *nigger,* see the *Random House Historical Dictionary of American Slang,* ed. J. E. Lighter (1997), 2:657, See also the *Oxford English Dictionary,* eds. J. A. Simpson and E. S. C. Weiner (2d ed., 1989), 10:402–4; Geneva Smitherman, *Black Talk: Words and Phrases from the 'Hood to the Amen Corner* (rev. ed., 2000), 210–13; H. L. Mencken, *The American Language: An Inquiry into the Development of English in the United States,* abridged with annotations and new material by Raven I. McDavid Jr., with the assistance of David W. Maurer (1979), 383–84; Hugh Rawson, *Wicked Words* (1989), 268–70.
3. See Rawson, *Wicked Words,* 268–70; Smitherman, *Black Talk,* 210–13.
4. The linguist Robin Tolmach Lakoff speculates that *nigger* became a slur when users of the term became aware that it was a mispronunciation of *Negro* and decided to continue using the mispronunciation to signal contempt—in much the same way that certain individuals choose to insult others by deliberately mispronouncing their names. Robin Tolmach Lakoff, "The N-Word: Still There, Still Ugly," *Newsday,* September 28, 1995. But see the *Random House Historical Dictionary of Slang,* 2:656, where this theory of mispronunciation is discounted.
5. Hosea Easton, *A Treatise on the Intellectual Character and Civil and Political Condition of the Colored People of the United States; and the Prejudice Exercised Towards Them* (1837), 40–41.

6. See Sam Dennison, *Scandalize My Name: Black Imagery in American Popular Music* (1982).

7. Rawson, *Wicked Words,* 268.

8. Kenneth Porter, "Racism in Children's Rhymes and Sayings, Central Kansas, 1910–1918," *Western Folklore* 24 (1965): 191.

9. Quoted in Stephen Kantrowitz, *Ben Tillman and the Reconstruction of White Supremacy* (2000), 259.

10. William O. Douglas, *The Court Years 1939–1975: The Autobiography of William O. Douglas* (1980), 15.

11. See David G. McCollough, *Truman* (1992), 576.

12. Robert A. Caro, *The Years of Lyndon Johnson: The Means of Ascent* (1990), 70.

13. See, e.g., Anthony Summers with Robbyn Swan, *The Arrogance of Power: The Secret World of Richard Nixon* (2000), 354; Seymour Hersh, *The Price of Power: Kissinger in the Nixon White House* (1983), 110–11; Hilton Als, "This Lonesome Place: Flannery O'Connor on Race and Religion in the Unreconstructed South," *The New Yorker,* Jan. 29, 2001; Ralph C. Wood, "Flannery O'Connor's Racial Morals and Manners," *The Christian Century,* Nov. 16, 1994.

14. Martin B. Duberman, *Paul Robeson* (1988), 55.

15. *The Autobiography of Malcolm X* (1965), 30–37.

16. Arnold Rampersad, *Jackie Robinson: A Biography* (1997), 142.

17. Len Holt, *The Summer That Didn't End: The Story of the Mississippi Civil Rights Project of 1964* (1965: Da Capo Press ed., 1992), 258.

18. William Plummer and Toby Kahn, "Street Talk," *People,* May 13, 1996.

19. Kenny Moore, "The 1968 Olympics: A Courageous Stand," *Sports Illustrated,* August 5, 1991.

20. Marc Appleman, "The Kid!," *Sports Illustrated for Kids,* July 1, 1995.

21. Gary Smith, "The Chosen," *Sports Illustrated,* December 23, 1996.

22. Audre Lorde, *Sister Outsider: Essays and Speeches* (1984), 72.

23. Branford Marsalis, interview, *Playboy,* December 1993.

24. Henry Aaron with Lonnie Wheeler, *I Had a Hammer: The Hank Aaron Story* (1991), 230–48.

25. David Halberstam, *The Children* (1998), 261.

26. *Lynch v. State,* 236 A. 2d 45, 48 (Md. Ct. Spec. App. 1967).

27. See, e.g., *United States v. Pospisil,* 186 F.3d 1023 (8th Cir. 1999); *Clifton v. Mass. Bay Transp. Auth.,* 2000 Mass. Super. LEXIS 22; *Guillory v. Godfrey,* 134 Cal. App. 2d 628 (1955); *United States v. Smith,* 1998 U.S. App. LEXIS 16406 (4th Cir.); *United States v. Hartberger,* 148 F.3d 777 (7th Cir. 1998); *Ohio v. Faye,* 2000 Ohio App. LEXIS 1971; *Norris v. City of Anderson,* 1999 U.S. Dist. LEXIS 22612; *Black Voters v. McDonough,* 421 F.Supp. 165 (D. Mass. 1976); *Solomon v. Liberty County, Fla.,* 951 F.Supp. 1522 (E.D. Fla. 1997); *United States v. Lansdowne Swim Club,* 713 F.Supp. 785 (E.D. Pa. 1989); *People v. MacKenzie,* 34 Cal. App. 4th 1256 (1995); *State v. Palermo,* 765 So. 2d 1139 (2000); *State v. Colella,* 690 A.2d 156 (N.J. Super. Ct. 1997); *Mancha v. Field Museum of Natural History,* 283 N.E. 2d 899 (1972); *City of Minneapolis v. State of Minnesota,* 310 N.W. 2d 485 (1981).

28. *Random House Historical Dictionary of American Slang,* 2:664–65; *DuFlambeau v. Stop Treaty Abuse,* 991 F. 2d 1249 (7th Cir. 1933).

29. Farai Chideya, *The Color of Our Future* (1999), 9.

30. Andrew Hacker, *Two Nations: Black and White, Separate, Hostile, Unequal* (1992), 42.

31. *Monteiro v. Tempe Union High School District,* 158 F.3d 1022 (9th Cir. 1998). Also see *Random House Webster's College Dictionary* (2000), 894: "*Nigger* is now probably the most offensive word in English."

32. Margaret M. Russell, "Representing Race: Beyond 'Sellouts' and 'Race Cards': Black Attorneys and the Straitjacket of Legal Practice," *Michigan Law Review* 95 (1997): 765.

33. Letter to the editor, "End Hatred and Its Code Words," *Des Moines Register,* December 28, 1999.

34. Quoted in Joseph Boskin, *Rebellious Laughter* (1997), 161–62.

35. See, e .g., *Goldberg v. City of Philadelphia,* 1994 U.S. Dist. LEXIS 8969 (D.C.E.D. Pa. 1994) (kike); *Vigil v. City of Las Cruces,* 119 F.3d 871 (10th Cir. 1997) (wetback); *United States v. Piche,* 981 F.2d 706 (4th Cir. 1992) (gook); *Huckaby v. Moore,* 142 F.3d 233 (5th Cir. 1998) (honky).

36. See, e.g., *Gant v. Wallingford Bd. of Educ.,* 69 F.3d 669 (2d Cir. 1995); *United States v. Sowa,* 34 F.3d 447 (7th Cir. 1994); *United States v. Ramey,* 24 F.3d 602 (4th Cir. 1994); *United States v. Juvenile Male J.H.H.,* 22 F.3d 821 (8th Cir. 1994); *United States v. McInnis,* 976 F.2d 1226 (9th Cir. 1992). See also chapter two, ahead, *Nigger* in Court.

37. *United States v. Montgomery,* 23 F.3d 1130 (7th Cir. 1994).

38. Lawrence W. Levine, *Black Culture and Black Consciousness: Afro-American Folk Thought from Slavery to Freedom* (1977), 309.

39. Ibid., 341.

40. Ibid., 344.

41. Ibid., 319.

42. Howard Bingham and Max Wallace, *Muhammed Ali's Greatest Fight: Cassius Clay vs. the United States of America* (2000), 119.

43. *A Testament of Hope: The Essential Writings and Speeches of Martin Luther King, Jr.,* ed. James M. Washington (1986), 293.

44. Clarence Major, *Dictionary of Afro-American Slang* (1970), 84.

45. Claude Brown, "The Language of Soul," *Esquire,* April 1968.

46. Jarvis DeBerry, "Keeping a Hateful Word Inside a Dictionary," *New Orleans Times-Picayune.* June 23, 1998.

47. For an excellent discussion about *nigger*, on which I have drawn, see Smitherman, *Black Talk*, 210–13.

48. Helen Jackson Lee, *Nigger in the Window* (1978), 27.

49. On Richard Pryor, see Richard Pryor with Mike Gold, *Pryor Convictions and Other Life Sentences* (1995); John A. Williams and Dennis A. Williams, *If I Stop I'll Die: The Comedy and Tragedy of Richard Pryor* (1991); Jim Haskins, *Richard Pryor: A Man and His Madness* (1984); Jeff Rovin, *Richard Pryor: Black and Blue* (1983).

50. In print, see Chris Rock, *Rock This!*, 17–19 (1997). In audio, listen to Chris Rock, *Roll with the New* (1997). To view the performance, see the video, Chris Rock, *Bring the Pain* (1996).

51. Coolio, "Gangsta's Paradise," *Gangsta's Paradise* (Tommy Boy, 1995).

52. Ice-T, "Straight up Nigga," *OG: Original Gangster* (Sire Records, 1991).

53. Ice Cube, "The Nigga Ya Love to Hate," in *Amerikkka's Most Wanted* (Priority Records, 1990).

54. Beanie Sigel, "Ride 4. My," *The Truth* (Island Def Jam Music Group, 2000).

55. Listen to 2pac, *2pacalypse Now* (Interscope, 1991).

56. Daryl Cumbers Dance, *Shuckin' and Jivin': Folklore from Contemporary Black Americans* (1978), 77.

57. Abiodun Oyewole and Umar Bin Hassan with Kim Greene, *The Last Poets—On a Mission: Selected Poems and a History of the Last Poets* (1996), 6–63.

58. Ibid., 60.

59. See Michael Thomas Ford, *That's Mr. Faggot to You: Further Trials from My Queer Life* (1999); Michael Warner: *The Trouble with Normal: Sex, Politics and the Ethics of Queer Life* (1999); Eve Ensler, *The Vagina Monologues* (1998); Inga Muscio, *Cunt: A Declaration of Independence* (1998); Elizabeth Wurtzel, *Bitch: In Praise of Difficult Women* (1998); Jim Goad, *The Redneck Manifesto* (1997); *Dyke Life: From Growing Up to Growing Old, a Celebration of the Lesbian Experience* (Karla Jay, ed. 1996); Jonathan Eig, "This Woman Wants You to Call Her Bastard," *Offspring*, June/July 2000 (describing Marley Greiner, founder of Bastard Nation); Kathleen Bishop, "Cracker Day Fun for All" *Flagler—Palm Coast Community Times*, March 29, 2000.

60. Bruce A. Jacobs, *Race Manners: Navigating the Minefield Between Black and White Americans* (1999), 102.

61. See Robin D. G. Kelly, *Race Rebels: Culture, Politics, and the Black Working Class* (1994), 209–14.

62. John Lennon and Yoko Ono, *Same Time in New York City* (Apple Records, 1972)

63. Patti Smith, *Easter* (Arista Records, 1978).

64. Anthony DeCurtis, interview with Eminem, *Rolling Stone*, July 15, 2000.

65. Quoted in Kelly, *Race Rebels,* 209–10.

66. Michael Eric Dyson, "Nigger Gotta Stop," *The Source*, June 1999.

67. Quoted in Robert Dallek, *Flawed Giant: Lyndon Johnson and His Times,* 1961-1973 (1998), 44,

68. See Emily Bernard, ed., *Remember Me to Harlem: The Letters of Langston Hughes and Carl Van Vechten,* 1925–1964 (2001).

69. See Langston Hughes, *The Big Sea* (1940), 268. See also p. 161.

70. Pertinent here is the following story, an anecdote saved from oblivion by the great sociologist Erving Goffman:

> I was once admitted to a group of Negro boys of about my own age with whom I used to fish. When I first began to join them, they would carefully use the word *Negro* in my presence. Gradually, as we went fishing more and more often, they began to joke with each other in front of me and to call each other "nigger.". . . One day when we were swimming, a boy shoved me with mock violence and I said to him, "Don't give me that nigger talk."
>
> He replied, "You bastard," with a big grin.
>
> From that time on, we could all use the word *nigger* but the old categories had totally changed. Never, as long as I live, will I forget the way my stomach felt after I used the word *nigger* without any reservation.
>
> Erving Goffman, *Stigma: Notes on the Management of Spoiled Identity* (1963), 29 (quoting Ray Birdwhistell).

READING 48

Disability and Representation

Rosemarie Garland-Thomson

The way we imagine disability in America is changing. The disability rights movement produced civil rights legislation such as the Americans with Disabilities Act of 1990 that mandates full integration and prohibits discrimination. People with disabilities are leaving the closet and the nursing home and entering workplaces, courtrooms, and public debates. Disabled people are now the largest minority group in the United States, constituting 20 percent of the United States population, according to the National Organization on Disability

Rosemarie Garland-Thomson is a professor of women's studies at Emory University.

(www.nod.org), and increasing dramatically as baby boomers age. According to the National Center for Education Statistics, eleven percent of college undergraduates reported having a sensory, mobility, or other disability ("Note 11").

Disability permeates our national culture and conversation. A Deaf Miss America reigned; Superman became quadriplegic; Barbie came out as a wheelchair user; Gallaudet University students demanded a Deaf president; Casey Martin accessed golf tournaments with a cart; *Shine, Born on the Fourth of July, A Beautiful Mind, Finding Nemo,* and *Million Dollar Baby* earned Oscars; Heather Mills, an amputee fashion model and disability activist, married the Beatle Paul McCartney. The FDR Memorial in Washington, DC, got a new statue of Roosevelt using his wheelchair. The companies Kohler, Pontiac, and Crown Royal recently captured attention by featuring hip young blind people cleverly promoting sinks, cars, and whiskey. All this suggests that disability is becoming a diversity, inclusion, and civil rights issue rather than simply a medical problem, charity case, or personal misfortune.

Humanities scholarship is discovering disability everywhere as well. For example, the blind, mad, lame, crippled, and unusually embodied have fired the imagination and underwritten the metaphors of classic Western literature. From Sophocles to Toni Morrison, disability confers distinction on protagonists and drives narrative. The West's first literary hero, Oedipus—whose name means "swollen foot" or "injured foot"—begins a tradition of garnering literary meaning from disability that continues through Shakespeare's Richard III, Melville's monomaniacal amputee Ahab, and Faulkner's modernist monologuist Benjy Compson. Canonical American literature is rich with disability imagery: Anne Bradstreet, our first poet, imagines her book a deformed child; Nathaniel Hawthorne's revengeful cuckold in *The Scarlet Letter* is disabled; Ralph Waldo Emerson offers the invalid as a contrast to his ideal American individual; Mark Twain uses deafness as humor; the category of illness is fundamental to Walt Whitman's poetic project; Edgar

Allan Poe figures the gothic as disability in stories like "Hop Frog."

To deal in images and narratives—whether they come from literature, art, film, or popular culture—is to focus on issues of representation. I mean here representation in its broadest sense, as a saturating of the material world with meaning. In this sense, disability is a story we tell about bodies. It is a received yet pliable story that changes over time and across place. Representation structures rather than reflects reality. The way we imagine disability through images and narratives determines the shape of the material world, the distribution of resources, our relationships with one another, and our sense of ourselves.

The aim of much disability studies is to reimagine disability, to reveal how the storied quality of disability invents and reinvents the world we share. Disability studies challenges our collective representation of disability, exposing it as an exclusionary and oppressive system rather than the natural and appropriate order of things.

Let me offer two brief examples of how representations can reimagine disability. Recently I heard a National Public Radio music review of the little-known American composer Thomas Greene Wiggins. Listening to the broad outlines of this composer's life, I recognized that Thomas Greene Wiggins was the proper name of the freak-show performer known as "Blind Tom," whom I myself had written about because he was the subject of a nineteenth-century sentimental story by Rebecca Harding Davis. What struck me about this respectful review was that the moniker "Blind Tom" was never used, although his slave status, blindness, and apparent cognitive disability were mentioned. Moreover, in all the research I'd done on this disabled performer, I had never read a reference to him as Thomas Greene Wiggins, let alone as an "American composer." What I realized from this review is that the transformation of knowledge wrought by the civil rights and disability rights movements recast what the nineteenth century imagined as the droll curiosity "Blind Tom" into "an American composer," one whom the *New York*

Times (Riis) called "the most celebrated black concert artist of the 19th century." This is exactly what disability studies does: it recognizes the contributions of a group of people who have historically been dismissed because of deeply rooted cultural bias—in Wiggins's case, both as a black man and as a person with disabilities.

Here is another story about reimagining disability. Both the impressionist artist Claude Monet and the leader of contemporary photographic realism, Chuck Close, developed significant disabilities later in their careers. Monet became almost blind, and Close became paralyzed. Each artist was forced by his disability to change both the way he painted and the content of his art. Monet's aesthetic shift from more representational painting to more intensely impressionistic, literally fuzzier, renderings of his famous gardens and bridges resulted from his diminished sight, while Close's celebrated move away from photographic realism toward an almost cubist rendering of his large-scale portraits resulted from his loss of manual dexterity. In other words, disability enabled what we think of as artistic evolution. Monet and Close did not overcome their disabilities, but, rather, they accommodated their disabilities, and their art changed. They were great artists not in spite of disability but because of disability. This is the story we need to understand.

Reimagining disability in this way accomplishes important cultural work. First, it shows disability as a significant human experience that occurs in every society, every family, and most every life. Second, it helps us accept that fact. Third, it helps integrate disability into our knowledge of human experience and history and to integrate disabled people into our culture.

Disability studies points out that ability and disability are not so much a matter of the capacities and limitations of bodies but more about what we expect from a body at a particular moment and place. Stairs disable people who need to use wheelchairs to get around, but ramps let them go places freely. Reading the print in a phone book or deciphering the patterns on a computer screen is an ability that our moment demands. So if our minds can't make sense of the pattern or our eyes can't register the print, we become disabled. In other words, we are expected to look, act, and move in certain ways so we'll fit into the built and attitudinal environment. If we don't, we become disabled.

Disability studies reminds us that all bodies are shaped by their environments from the moment of conception. We transform constantly in response to our surroundings and register history on our bodies. The changes that occur when body encounters world are what we call disability. The human body varies tremendously in its forms and functions. Our bodies need care; we all need assistance to live. Every life evolves into disability, making it perhaps the essential characteristic of being human.

In spite of or perhaps because of this, the subject of disability both discomforts and compels many people. Even though those of us with disabilities are a visible and vocal constituency, we are also a profoundly economically disenfranchised and excluded group. Thriving alongside the positive images and political empowerment I mentioned earlier are discriminatory attitudes and practices. Our society emphatically denies vulnerability, contingency, and mortality. Modernity pressures us relentlessly toward standardizing bodies, a goal that is now largely accomplishable in the developed world through technological and medical interventions that materially rationalize our bodies under the banner of progress and improvement. We are told that if we buy the right products, cultivate the right habits, pay careful attention, and use the most sophisticated medical technology, we can banish disability from our lives. Strong disincentives such as social stigma and a sense of somehow having failed to "overcome" or "beat" life's inevitable limitations pressure us not to identify ourselves as persons with disabilities. We enact often virulent measures to deny, avoid, and eliminate disability and other forms of human variation we don't value. Despite the popular call for diversity, a deep and seldom-challenged project of creating bodily uniformity marches forward in practices such as genetic engineering, selective abortion, reproductive technology, so-called physician-assisted suicide, surgical normalization, aesthetic-standardization procedures, and ideologies of health and fitness. All these practices are supported by a kind of new eugenics that aims to regularize our bodies. Although we value biodiversity in our environment, we devalue physical and mental variety. In short, we expect medicine to wipe away all disability. As a consequence, when disability enters our lives, often our only available responses are silence, denial, shame, or determined and desperate vows to "fight it." Seldom do we imagine disability as an aspect of all lives that our society, government, and community should accommodate and include.

My work is impelled by the question of how representation can affect social justice. What would happen if our society fully recognized and validated human variation? If we cultivated rather than reduced this rich distinctiveness? How would the public landscape change if the widest possible diversity of human forms, functions, and behaviors were fully accommodated? How would such an understanding alter our collective sense of what is beautiful and proper? What would be the political significance of such inclusion? I argue for applying the vibrant logic of biodiversity to humans. Such a logic reimagines a public sphere that values and makes a tenable space for the kinds of bodies variously considered old, retarded, crippled, blind, deaf, abnormal, ugly, deformed, or excessive.

The theologian and sociologist Nancy Eiesland has argued that, in addition to legislative, economic, and social changes, achieving equality for people with disabilities depends on cultural "resymbolization" (98). Eiesland asserts that the way we imagine disability and disabled people must shift for real social change to occur. Whereas Eiesland's work resymbolizes our conceptions of disability in religious iconography, my current work analyzes representations that resymbolize disability in another cultural arena: that of advertising and fashion photography.

While I can't detail the complexities of my argument, I want to offer some of these visual reimaginings of disability. Until the civil rights understanding of disability opened the door to political action and consumer culture, the only public images of people with disabilities were medical photographs and public charity campaigns. For instance, a 1949 March of Dimes poster shows an appealing little girl stepping out of her wheelchair into the supposed redemption of walking: "Look! I can walk again," the text proclaims, while also charging the viewers with the responsibility of assuring her future ambulation. A paternalistic sentimentality fuses here with the medicalization of disability to elicit money. The ideology of cure and the mandate for normalcy intertwine, crowding out any possible narrative of accommodating rather than eliminating disability.

In contrast, a post-Americans with Disabilities Act image moves disability from the private medical realm into the public arena of consumer culture. [One] conventional, stylized, high-fashion shot features a typical female model: slender, white, blond, clad in a black evening gown—and accompanied by her service dog. The juxtaposition of the elite body of a visually normative fashion model with the mark of disability forces the viewer to reconfigure assumptions about what constitutes the attractive, the desirable, and the livable life. Such images of disabled people as consumer citizens do the cultural work of integrating a previously excluded group into the dominant order. This form of what I call cripsploitation may be inadvertently progressive. As one disabled actor quipped, "The Adonis in a wheelchair is better than the whimpering victim in a corner" (Haller and Ralph 9–10).

To conclude, I offer two images that visually reimagine disability. Both are covers of the *New York Times Magazine*, and both draw from the visual conventions and contexts of commercial fashion photography to do their cultural work. The first is a 1993 image of the fashion model Matushka, boldly exposing her mastectomy-scarred body as a source of pride and as a display of beauty. The text reads, "You Can't Look Away Anymore." This intrepid portrait is a political act that visually deconstructs the normalized body that ableist beauty culture presents to us. Matushka's body presents disability as part of the range of human variation and experience, as the typical rather than the atypical, the beautiful rather than the grotesque.

Ten years later, another image of disability appears on the cover of the *New York Times Magazine*. The arresting portrait of Harriet McBryde Johnson, disability rights activist and lawyer, portrays her as charismatic rather than cute, ironic rather than pathetic. And she certainly is not straining to rise out of her wheelchair into an ableist fantasy of ambulation. The photo answers the rhetorical question sprawled across the cover: "Should I Have Been Killed at Birth?" This is what a life worth living looks like, the picture avows.

The shots of Matushka and Johnson refuse the traditional visual rhetorics that present disability as sentimental, inspirational, curable, shameful, or disposable. Instead these photographs evoke the visual conventions of commercial fashion photography to endow their subjects with authority and grace and to represent disability as a tenable and valued way of being in the world.

Such resymbolization contributes to the project of social justice. Because our prevailing representations constrict disability's complexities, they not only restrict the lives and govern the bodies of people we think of as disabled but also limit the imagination of those who think of themselves as non-disabled. Visual reimaginings such as these begin to fulfill the promise of an egalatarian order.

DISCUSSION QUESTIONS

1. If we value biodiversity in our environment, why don't we value it in human bodies?
2. What are current images that reimagine disability and also do justice to the complexities of being disabled?

REFERENCES

Eiesland, Nancy. *The Disabled God: Toward a Liberatory Theology of Disability*. Nashville: Abingdon, 1994.

Haller, Beth, and Sue Ralph. "Profitability, Diversity, and Disability Images in Advertising in the United States and Great Britain." *Disability Studies Quarterly* 21.2 (2001): 3–22. 25 Feb. 2004 <http://www.dsq-sds.org/_issues_pdf/dsq_2001_Spring.pdf>.

"Note 11: Student Disabilities." *The Condition of Education*. 2003. Natl. Center for Educ. Statistics, US Dept. of Educ. 28 Mar. 2005 <http://www.nces.ed.gov/programs/coe/2003/notes/n11.asp>.

Riis, Thomas L. "The Legacy of a Prodigy Lost in Mystery." *New York Times* 5 Mar. 2000, late ed.: 35.

BRIDGING DIFFERENCES

FRAMEWORK ESSAY

A book such as *The Meaning of Difference* runs the risk of leaving students with the feeling that there is little they can do to challenge the constructions of difference. Having recognized the power of master statuses and the significance of our conceptions of difference in everything from personal identity to world events, it is easy to feel powerless in the face of what appear to be overwhelming social forces.

But we did not write this book because we felt powerless or wanted you to feel that way. For us, the idea of looking at race, sex, social class, sexual orientation, and disability *all together* opened up new possibilities for understanding and creating alliances. When we started to talk about this book fifteen years ago, comparing our teaching experiences in a highly diverse university and our personal experiences of stigma and privilege, we were amazed by the connections we saw. That impression grew as we talked with students and friends who were members of other groups. Over time, we learned that understanding the similarities *across* groups opened up new ways of thinking: experiences could be accumulated toward a big picture, rather than being suffered in relative isolation; people could be different but still have had the same experience; people who never had the experience might still have ways to understand it. We believe the world is more interesting and hopeful with the realization that the experience of being in "the closet" is generally the same irrespective of which status brought you there, or that a variety of race and ethnic groups are subject to racial profiling, or that white women often experience the double consciousness that W. E. B. Du Bois described for blacks. When we realized how readily people could generalize from their own experience of stigma and privilege to what others might experience, we were energized.

That energy led to this book. But what should you do with your energy and insight? Or if you are feeling beaten down and depressed, rather than energized, what can you do about that?

Let us start with the worst-case scenario—that is, the possibility that you feel powerless to bring about social change and hopelessly insignificant in the face of overwhelming social forces. Unfortunately, this is not an uncommon outcome in higher education, nor is it distinctive to this subject matter. The emphasis in higher education is more on "understanding" than "doing." Most university coursework stresses detached, value-neutral reasoning, not passionate advocacy for social change.

> In the natural sciences, it is taken for granted that the aim is to explain an external order of nature. In literature, the text is an object to be interpreted. In politics, government is a phenomenon to be analyzed. Everywhere, it is intimated that the stance of the educated person should be that of the spectator. . . . In the contemporary university, one quickly learns that certain questions are out of order. One does not ask persistently about what ought to be done, for normative questions entail what are called value judgments, and these are said to be beyond the scope of scientific analysis. (Anderson, 1993:34–35, 36)

Paradoxically, however, education is also the source of much social change. We all know this almost instinctively. Educational institutions teach us our rights and our history, sharpen our thinking and decision-making, and open us to others' lived experience. Learning *changes* us, and higher education is explicit in its intention to produce that effect. The university is, after all, "an *educational* institution. As such, it is expected to have an impact on the society of which it is a part. . . . [T]he task of the university is not only to explore, systematically, the nature of the world, but also to scrutinize the practices of everyday life to see if they can be improved" (Anderson, 1993:59).

Recognizing the paradoxical nature of higher education, that it can both empower and disempower, means, in truth, that an element of choice—your choice—is involved in whether you are discouraged or inspired at the end of a course.

There is, however, another reason you might leave this material feeling powerless. This has more to do with the nature of society than with the nature of education, but it again involves paradox and personal choice. Eminent sociologist Peter Berger called this the "Janus-faced" nature of human society. The Roman god Janus, for whom January was named, symbolized beginnings and endings, past and future, change and transition, and was depicted as having two faces looking in opposite directions. Berger used that image to convey that just as individuals are rarely wholly powerful, neither are they wholly powerless. In this analogy, Berger found a visual image for the truth that we are *both* the authors and victims—architects and prisoners—of social life. We *both* make society and are made by it. (And in our own spirit of powerfulness, we have edited out the sexism in Berger's prose below.)

> No social structure, however massive it may appear in the present, existed in this massivity from the dawn of time. Somewhere along the line each one of its salient features was concocted by human beings, whether they were charismatic visionaries, clever crooks, conquering heroes or just individuals in positions of power who hit on what seemed to them a better way of running the show. Since all social systems were created by [humans], it follows that [humans] can also change them.
>
> Every [person] who says "I have no choice" in referring to what his [or her] social role demands of him [or her] is engaged in "bad faith." . . . [People] are responsible for their actions. They are in "bad faith" when they attribute to iron necessity what they themselves are choosing to do. (Berger, 1963:128, 143–44)

While you do not have the power to change everything, you certainly have the power to change some things. Gandhi's paradox, discussed by Allan Johnson in Reading 52, captures this point: "Gandhi once said that nothing we do as individuals matters, but that it's vitally important to do it anyway."

So we urge you to move beyond your sense of being powerless and get on with the work of social change. We offer some suggestions here for that process, much of it drawn from work we have found both inspirational and practical.

We Make the Road by Walking

"We make the road by walking" was Spanish poet Antonio Machado's (1875–1939) adaptation of a proverb: "*se hace camino al andar*," or "you make the way as you go." It is also the title of a published dialogue between two famous educator-activists, Myles Horton and Paulo Freire (Bell, Gaventa, and Peters, 1990).

Myles Horton founded the Highlander Folk School in Tennessee in 1932, when American racial segregation was still firmly in place. A unique school, Highlander offered racially integrated adult education—especially in history, government, and leadership—to the rural poor and working-class residents of the Cumberland Mountain communities. Horton's aim was to "use education as one of the instruments for bringing about a new social order" (Bell et al., 1990: xxiii). While many southern labor union leaders studied at Highlander, the school is probably best known for its contribution to the civil rights movement. Highlander taught the methods of nonviolence and started "Citizenship Schools," which taught southern blacks to read and write, so that they could pass the tests required to vote. (Literacy tests have been used in many countries to keep poor people from voting. In the United States, they were used in southern states to keep African Americans from voting, until passage of the 1965 Voting Rights Act). Probably the most famous Highlander student was Rosa Parks, who attended the school shortly before her refusal to move to the back of the bus sparked the Montgomery, Alabama, bus boycott and the civil rights movement.

The second member of the dialogue, Paulo Freire, was author of the classic, *Pedagogy of the Oppressed*. He was in charge of a Brazilian national literacy program in the 1960s, before the government was overthrown by a military coup. Like American blacks before 1965, Brazil's poor were also denied the right to vote because they were illiterate. After the coup, Freire was forced to flee from Brazil, but he went on to write and develop literacy programs elsewhere. His work was distinguished by its emphasis on teaching literacy through real community issues. His belief that education must operate as a dialogue, rooted in values and committed to transforming the world, made him one of the most influential thinkers of the last century.

Apart from the example that Myles Horton's and Paulo Freire's lives provide for the power of education to produce social change, we turn to them here for some basic lessons about transforming learning into action. First, we hope the phrase "we make the road by walking" helps you remember that *you* are the best person to know which "social interventions" will work for you. There is probably nothing more fundamental to social change than learning who you are; finding and honoring that authentic self; recognizing that it is multifaceted, complex, and *evolving*—and then making sure that the social change methods you use are consistent with that self. If you are going to pursue something as important as social change, it might as well be *you* who is doing it, not your impersonation of someone else.

"We make the road by walking" also conveys that the road has not already been built. Although there are many helpful resources, you will not find a recipe book designed for all the situations you will face, nor would that necessarily be a good idea. One of Horton's experiences with a union strike committee illustrates this point:

> [Members of the committee] were getting desperate. They said: "Well, now you've had more experience than we have. You've got to tell us what to do. You're the expert." I said: "No, let's talk about it a little bit more. In the first place I don't know what to do, and if I did know what to do I wouldn't tell you, because if I had to tell you today then I'd have to tell you tomorrow, and when I'm gone you'd have to get somebody else to tell you." One guy reached in his pocket and pulled out a pistol and says, "Goddamn you, if you don't tell us I'm going to kill you." I was tempted then to become an instant expert, right on the spot! But I knew that if I did that, all would be lost and then all the rest of them would start asking me what to do. So I said: "No. Go ahead and shoot if you want to, but I'm not going to tell you." And the others calmed him down. (Bell et al., 1990:126)

So it is important to recognize that, to some extent, you will need to be your *own* resource, *and* you will never have all the answers you need. Horton described two approaches to this inevitable incompleteness. First, "What I finally decided, after three or four years of reading and studying and trying to figure this thing out, was that *the way to do something was to start doing it and learn from it*" (Bell et al., 1990:40; emphasis added). And second, "*People learn from each other.* You don't need to know the answer" (Bell et al., 1990:55; emphasis added).

President Barack Obama's route to becoming a community organizer in Chicago has some parallels. Without knowing what the job entailed or anyone who made a living that way, he decided that was what he wanted to do when he finished college. Obama goes on to say, "And so, in the months leading up to graduation, I wrote to every civil rights organization I could think of, to any black elected official in the country with a progressive agenda, to neighborhood councils and tenant rights groups" (Obama, 2004:135). No one wrote back. Several months, jobs, and periods of unemployment later, a Jewish community organizer funded by local churches, who was trying to create a coalition of urban blacks and suburban whites to save manufacturing jobs in Chicago, hired him as a trainee. "He needed someone to work with him, he said. Somebody black" (Obama, 2004:141). Things did not go especially well: community members, who had already been at this for several years, were discouraged and ready to quit; the black Chicago political establishment was not supportive; it was difficult to find the issues that could bind and motivate people; and people were skeptical about the involvement of a college student with no apparent religious motivation. Only after many long months did a clear and compelling community issue emerge—the fact that there were no Mayor's Employment and Training (MET) programs in the parts of city where the neediest African Americans lived.

Two weeks of preparation and yet, the night of the meeting, my stomach was tied up in knots. At six forty-five only three people had shown up: a young woman with a baby who was drooling onto her tiny jumper, an older woman who carefully folded a stack of cookies into a napkin that she then stuffed into her purse, and a drunken man who immediately slouched into a light slumber in a back-row seat. As the minutes ticked away, I imagined once again the empty chairs, the official's change of mind at the last minute, the look of disappointment on the leadership's faces—the deathly smell of failure.

Then, at two minutes before seven, people began to trickle in. Will and Mary brought a group from West Pullman; then Shirley's children and grandchildren walked in, filling up an entire row of seats; then other Altgeld residents who owed Angela or Shirley or Mona a favor. There were close to a hundred people in the room by the time Ms. Alvarez [representing MET] showed up—a large imperious, Mexican American woman with two young white men in suits trailing behind her. . . .

The leadership acquitted themselves well that night. Angela laid out the issue for the crowd and explained to Ms. Alvarez what we expected from her. When Ms. Alvarez avoided giving a definite response, Mona jumped in and pushed for a yes-or-no answer. And when Ms. Alvarez finally promised to have a MET intake center in the area within six months, the crowd broke into hearty applause. . . . (Obama, 2004:184-85)

Thus, Obama's experience demonstrates that "we make the road by walking."

Work on Yourself First

Challenging social constructions of difference by working on yourself first may not seem earth shattering, but it is the unavoidable first step on the road. We think there are four main lessons on which to concentrate:

1. Increase your tolerance for making mistakes. In his dialogue with Miles Horton, Paulo Freire remarked, "I am always in the beginning, as you"—and at that point Freire was 66 years old and Horton 82. Realizing how little you know about other people's life experience is a way to prepare for the absolute inevitability that, in trying to build connections across difference, *you will make mistakes.* You must increase your tolerance of your mistakes or risk giving up altogether, and you must try to focus on learning from all these attempts—good, bad, or ugly. As one of our colleagues often tells her students, when you are worried that you'll say the wrong thing, you wind up holding back, not extending yourself—and missing an opportunity for connection. Our advice is to just get used to making mistakes. There is no way around them.

2. Appreciate the statuses you occupy. "Appreciating" your statuses—*stigmatized and privileged*—may sound odd, but it is the foundation that allows you to respond with more clarity to others' experiences of their statuses. By appreciating your own statuses, we mean honoring, valuing, and having some reasonable level of comfort about being white, black, Asian, or Latino; male or female; wealthy, middle class, or poor; disabled or nondisabled; straight or gay. Appreciating your status means not being ashamed of who you are.

> Is there a part of your identity of which you are not proud? Is there a part of who you are that you tend to hide from people? *One of the most profound blows to oppression is claiming legitimate delight in who we are.* . . . Notice where you struggle in claiming pride in who you are. This is the preliminary work that must be done to work against all forms of oppression.
>
> Reclaiming pride in our identities entails knowing our histories, becoming familiar not only with the side of history that causes us shame but also with the side that offers us hope. Ever mindful not to distort historical realities, it is nonetheless possible, even in the midst of the worst acts of oppression, to claim as our ancestors the few people who resisted the oppression. For example, in the present, it is useful for many people of German heritage to remember that there were heroic Germans who resisted Nazi anti-Semitism. . . . [A]long with the unfathomable devastation of the Holocaust, this minority tradition of resistance is also part of the history of the German people. (Brown and Mazza, 1997:5–6; emphasis added)

Ironically, at this juncture in American society, some level of shame seems to adhere to both stigmatized *and* privileged statuses. We don't want to mislead you into thinking that getting over that shame is an easy task, but recognizing the existence of shame and its dysfunction is an important first step. As Brown and Mazza suggest in the previous quote, learning the *full* history of "your people"—good deeds and bad—will help you find heroes, as well as avoid false pride. In Reading 55, Shuddhabrata Sengupta offers a moving vision of the ways that each of us may be oppressor and oppressed.

3. Learn to "sit in the fire." For those in privileged statuses, guilt seems to be the most common reaction to discussions of prejudice and discrimination. For those in stigmatized statuses, anger probably ranks at the top. Those who occupy both privileged and stigmatized statuses are "privileged" to experience both ends of this emotional continuum! Insofar as race, sex, social class, disability, and sexual orientation are *all* on the table, *everyone* will probably have the opportunity for an intense emotional experience. That's a lot of emotion, not to mention that people have varying abilities to talk about—or even experience—those feelings. Either way, bridging differences sometimes means we must be willing to "sit in the fire" (Mindell, 1995) of conflict and intense emotion.

Regarding guilt, our advice is not to succumb to it. It is both immobilizing and distracting. Focusing on how badly *you* feel means that *you* are the subject of attention, not the people whose experience you are trying to understand.

About anger, our advice is more complicated. When it's someone else's anger, listen carefully so that you can understand it. Don't stop listening because you don't like the message or the way it is packaged. Don't take an expression of anger personally unless you are told it actually is about you. Try not to let someone else's anger trigger your own, because that will distract you from listening. Recognize that you can withstand someone's anger.

When you are the one who is angry, try not to let it overwhelm you. Try to distinguish between a setting in which you are under attack and one populated by friends, or potential friends, who are trying to learn about your experience. Try to distinguish people who are malevolent from those who are misguided, or simply awkward in their efforts to help. Try to avoid self-righteousness. Your having been injured doesn't mean that you have not also inflicted injury. Remember that "every person is important, even those who belong to majority groups that have historically oppressed other groups" (Brown and Mazza, 1997:5).

As you experience sitting in the fire, remember that *the benefits of diversity derive from engagement, not passive observation. Contact will inevitably entail periods of disagreement and conflict.* Parker Palmer is a sociologist and nationally renowned expert on higher education. We quote him at length below, because he offers such a clear picture of what both frightens and draws us to engagement across difference.

> We collaborate with the structures of separation because they promise to protect us against one of the deepest fears at the heart of being human—the fear of having a live encounter with alien "otherness," whether the other is a student, a colleague, a subject, or a self-dissenting voice within. *We fear encounters in which the other is free to be itself, to speak its own truth, to tell us what we may not wish to hear. We want those encounters on our own terms, so that we can control their outcomes, so that they will not threaten our view of world and self....*
>
> This fear of the live encounter is actually a sequence of fears that begins in the fear of diversity. As long as we inhabit a university made homogeneous by our refusal to admit otherness, we can maintain the illusion that we possess the truth about ourselves and the world—after all, there is no "other" to challenge us! But as soon as we admit pluralism, we are forced to admit that ours is not the only standpoint, the only experience, the only way, and the truths we have built our lives on begin to feel fragile....
>
> Otherness, taken seriously, always invites transformation, calling us not only to new facts and theories and values but also to new ways of living our lives—and that is the most daunting threat of all. (Palmer, 1998: 36–38; emphasis added)

But what if there appears to be no diversity in the setting in which you find yourself? The odds are that is just how things look. No matter how homogeneous a group may seem, there will be layers of significant difference beneath the appearances. "Taking the time to examine [those less visible differences] can be invaluable, not only for creating a climate that welcomes the differences already present in the group, but also for laying the groundwork for becoming more inclusive of other differences" (Brown and Mazza, 1997:13).

4. Be an ally. Appreciate your allies.   We conclude this list with what we think is the most important of the lessons: Be an ally; find allies; appreciate your allies. There is nothing complicated about the concept of an ally: an ally is simply someone committed to eliminating stigma and the ill-treatment of those in stigmatized statuses. If you remember a time when you were treated unfairly because of a status you occupy and think about what you *wish* someone had done or said on your behalf, you will then understand the critical role an ally can play, and you will have a good sense of what the role calls for. Beyond that, you can learn about being an ally by asking people what would be helpful and by educating yourself about the history and experience of those in stigmatized groups.

Many of the personal accounts in this book are about having or wishing for an ally. Indeed, if "ally" were an entry in the help-wanted section of the newspaper, the opportunities would be described as "unlimited." John Larew's article on legacy admissions (Reading 31) is an example of being an ally. The article—written while he was editor of Harvard's *Crimson Tide*—sparked an extended national discussion on legacy admissions. Larew can take considerable credit for the attention now being paid to the underrepresentation of low-income students in colleges and universities.

While Larew's article grew out of his daily experience and the media access he had as editor of the *Crimson Tide*, other ways of being an ally are available to virtually anyone, anytime—even, for example, at lunch. We single out this meal, because it is generally a public one, in which members of stigmatized categories are likely to find themselves with limited options: eat with other members of the category, eat alone, or hide. So an ally (or potential ally) might extend an invitation to share a sandwich.

Being an ally, however, is not only about what you can do on your own. It is also about joining with others in collective action. The social movements that have historically transformed the status of stigmatized groups in America, such as the women's movement or the civil rights movement, included some people from privileged statuses, just as privileged allies have joined with members of stigmatized groups in innumerable more localized ways: university chapters of Men against Sexism, community groups like Parents and Friends of Lesbians and Gays, elected officials who sponsor antidiscrimination legislation, the 1960s college students who risked their lives to register black voters in the South, the Muslims in Rwanda who helped Tutsis escape from the 1994 genocide. You might consider how you could become an ally who makes a difference.

Still, *getting* allies sometimes requires *asking for help* and even telling people what you specifically want or don't want them to do. People who are disabled do this in a powerful video on YouTube called "A Credo for Support," telling their potential allies:

Do not see my disability as the problem. Recognize that my disability is an attribute.

Do not try to fix me, because I am not broken. Support me. I can make my contribution to the community in my way.

Do not see me as your client. I am your fellow citizen. See me as your neighbor. Remember, none of us can be self-sufficient.

Do not try to change me. You have no right. Help me learn what I want to know.

Do not try to be my friend. I deserve more than that. Get to know me. We may become friends.

Do not help me, even if it does make you feel good. Ask me if I need your help.

Do not admire me. A desire to live a full life does not warrant adoration. Respect me, for respect presumes equality.

Do not tell, correct, and lead. Listen, support, and follow.

Do not work on me. Work with me. (Kunc and Van der Klift, 2007)

While you might wish for allies who could read your mind and step in and out at exactly the right moment, it is unlikely you will find people like that. The people you do find, however, will probably be more easily recruited to become allies with appreciation than with guilt.

> We rarely increase our effectiveness by dwelling on all of the things we still need to get right. This principle is especially important for those of us who are seeking allies. Pointing out only how the people around us have failed usually only increases their discouragement. Remembering the successes can lead to increased confidence and a greater ability to be an effective ally. (Brown and Mazza, 1997:49)

White men who are straight and nondisabled can often be powerful allies. When such a person speaks on behalf of those in stigmatized statuses, he stands a good chance of being heard, if only because he appears not to be acting out of vested interest. His intervention can change the dynamic, provide a role model for others, and give those in stigmatized statuses a break from always being the ones to raise the contentious points. Once, on a panel about gender, we saw one of the men flag issues of sexism that the women panelists would otherwise have had to note. It seemed to us that they appreciated his intervention.

Being an ally is also sometimes called for among one's friends and loved ones, in those more private settings where people feel freer to air and cultivate their prejudices. Like Paul Kivel, who suggests in Reading 54, some ways to respond in these situations, we would also urge you to be an "ally with a heart" in these settings.

> Condemning people, shaming them, and making them feel guilty are all unproductive strategies: They all increase defensiveness rather than creating an opening for change. . . . Condemning people rarely helps them to change their behavior. Instead, think about what you honestly appreciate about the person. Also consider the ways that person has made any progress, even if it's only slight, on the issue that is of concern to you. Practice telling that person the things she is doing right. Appreciation leads to action; condemnation leads to paralysis.
>
> People are often afraid to appreciate someone whose behavior they disapprove of, for fear that the appreciation will keep the oppressive behavior unchallenged. However, only by seeing what is human in the person who acts oppressively can we hope to bring about change. All of us are more receptive to suggestions to change when we know we are liked. (Brown and Mazza, 1997:3)

A Concluding Note

We opened this essay worried that our readers felt powerless and insignificant. We close with the hope that you now understand that challenging the constructions of difference is well within *all* of our capabilities.

KEY CONCEPTS

ally Someone from a privileged status committed to eliminating stigma and the ill-treatment of those in stigmatized statuses. (page 520)

Gandhi's paradox While nothing we do as individuals matters, it is important to take action anyway. (page 515)

Janus-faced nature of society That people create society, but also that society constrains people. (page 515)

REFERENCES

Anderson, Charles W. 1993. *Prescribing the Life of the Mind: An Essay on the Purpose of the University, the Aims of Liberal Education, the Competence of Citizens, and the Cultivation of Practical Reason.* Madison: University of Wisconsin Press.

Bell, Brenda, John Gaventa, and John Peters. 1990. *We Make the Road by Walking: Conversations on Education and Social Change.* Philadephia: Temple University Press.

Berger, Peter L. 1963. *Invitation to Sociology: A Humanistic Perspective.* New York: Anchor Books.

Brown, Cherie R., and George J. Mazza. 1997. *Healing into Action: A Leadership Guide for Creating Diverse Communities.* Washington, DC: National Coalition Building Institute.

Kunc, Norman, and Emma Van der Klift. 2007. A Credo for Support (People 1st Version). People First of San Luis Obispo. http://www.youtube.com/watch?v=wun-HDfZFxXw (accessed May 2007).

Mindell, Arnold. 1995. *Sitting in the Fire: Large Group Transformation Using Conflict and Diversity.* Portland, OR: Lao Tse Press.

Obama, Barack. 2004. *Dreams from My Father: A Story of Race and Inheritance.* New York: Three Rivers Press.

Palmer, Parker J. 1998. *The Courage to Teach: Exploring the Inner Landscape of a Teacher's Life.* San Francisco: Jossey-Bass.

READING 49

Lilly's Big Day

Gail Collins

President Obama [signed] the Lilly Ledbetter Fair Pay Act into law [on January 29, 2009].[1]

"I'm so excited I can hardly stand it," Ledbetter said recently after the bill passed the Senate.

Obama told her story over and over when he campaigned for president: How Ledbetter, now 70, spent years working as a plant supervisor at a tire factory in Alabama. How, when she neared retirement, someone slipped her a pay schedule that showed her male colleagues were making much more money than she was. A jury found her employer, the Goodyear Tire and Rubber Company, to be really, really guilty of pay discrimination. But the Supreme Court, in a 5-to-4 decision led by the Bush appointees, threw out Ledbetter's case, ruling that she should have filed her suit within 180 days of the first time Goodyear paid her less than her peers.

(Let us pause briefly to contemplate the chances of figuring out your co-workers' salaries within the first six months on the job.)

Until the Supreme Court stepped in, courts generally presumed that the 180-day time limit began the last time an employee got a discriminatory pay check, not the first. . . . Ledbetter, who was widowed in December, won't get any restitution of her lost wages; her case can't be retried. She's now part of a long line of working women who went to court and changed a little bit of the world in fights that often brought them minimal personal benefit.

Another was Eulalie Cooper, a flight attendant who sued Delta Air Lines in the mid-'60s when she was fired for being married. Not only did a Louisiana judge uphold the airline industry's bizarre rules requiring stewardesses to be young and single, Cooper was denied unemployment benefits on the grounds that by getting married she left her job "voluntarily."

Gail Collins is a newspaper columnist and writer.

But she began a pattern of litigation that eventually ended the industry's insistence that women needed to look like sex objects in order to properly care for passengers on airplanes. Next time you talk about US Airways Flight 1549's spectacular landing on the Hudson River, remember that the three flight attendants who kept calm in the ditched plane were all women in their 50s and give a nod to people like Eulalie Cooper.

Patricia Lorance, an Illinois factory worker, went to court after her union and employer secretly agreed to new seniority rules that discriminated against the women who had been promoted in the post-Civil Rights Act era of the 1970s. Like Ledbetter, she lost her court fight because of a ridiculous ruling about timing, which had to be fixed by Congress.

Working at a series of lower-paying jobs after the factory closed, and then disabled by physical ailments, Lorance lost track of her case long before it finally wound its way through the Supreme Court. "But to this day, I am rather proud of myself because I was not a dumb person. I believe in just standing up and fighting for your own rights," she said in a phone interview.

Ledbetter's real soul sister is Lorena Weeks of Wadley, Georgia. Weeks, now 80, had worked two jobs to support her orphaned siblings, then struggled with her husband to set enough money aside to assure their children would be able to go to college. A longtime telephone employee, she applied for a higher-paying job overseeing equipment at the central office. Both her union and the management said the job was unsuitable for a woman because it involved pushing 30-pound equipment on a dolly, even though Weeks regularly toted around a 34-pound typewriter at her clerical job.

Weeks v. Southern Bell helped smash employers' old dodge of keeping women out of higher-paying positions by claiming that they required qualifications only men could fulfill. But it was a long, painful fight during which Weeks was terrified that she might lose her job entirely. "I felt like I was so alone, and yet I knew I was doing what God wanted me to do. Going back to the fact my momma had died working so hard. And I knew women worked and needed a place in the world," she said.

It's a good day for the feisty working women who went to court to demand their rights and the frequently underpaid lawyers who championed them. They're strangers to one another; most of them made their stands and then returned to their ordinary lives. But they're a special sorority all the same. And Lilly Ledbetter got to go to the inauguration and dance with the new president.

"Tell her congratulations," said Lorena Weeks.

DISCUSSION QUESTIONS

1. What do you think motivates and sustains people like Ledbetter, Cooper, Lorance, and Weeks?
2. What are the assumptions in Collins's article and can they be supported?

NOTES

1. The Lilly Ledbetter Fair Pay Act of 2009 (S 181) amended or modified title VII of the Civil Rights Act of 1964, the Age Discrimination in Employment Act of 1967, the Americans with Disabilities Act of 1990, and the Rehabilitation Act of 1973 to clarify that a discriminatory compensation decision or other unlawful practice occurs each time compensation is paid.

READING 50

The Other Movement That Rosa Parks Inspired: By Sitting Down, She Made Room for the Disabled

Charles Wilson

On an unseasonably warm September day in 1984, about a dozen men and women rolled their wheelchairs in front of a city bus that was pulling onto State Street in Chicago. Then they sat there and

---

Charles Wilson is a writer who has been published in *The New York Times, The Washington Post*, and *The Economist*.

didn't move. The group had no secret agenda, they simply wanted to make a point. Days before, the Chicago Transit Authority had announced that it was purchasing 363 new public buses—and that none of them would be equipped with wheelchair lifts to serve disabled passengers because the lifts had been deemed too expensive. This ragtag group of wheelchair riders, who were affiliated with a disability rights organization called ADAPT, or Americans Disabled for Accessible Public Transit, decided to protest that decision by obstructing a bus until the police carted them away. Every one of them wore a simple paper name tag, the sort that you would normally see at a meet-and-greet. They all said: "My name is Rosa Parks."

Rosa Parks's act of courage in Montgomery, Ala., in 1955 did more than dismantle the system of racial segregation on public transportation. Her refusal to give up her seat to a white man also created a legacy she never could have foreseen. It was through Parks's example that the disabled community transformed its own often disorganized cause into a unified disability rights movement. "Had it not been for Parks and the bus boycott, there is no question that the disability rights movement would have been light years behind, if it would have ever occurred," says Michael Auberger, a disability rights activist who was one of the first to place his wheelchair in front of a bus in the early 1980s. "Her genius was that she saw the bus as the great integrator. It took you to work, it took you to play, it took you to places that you had never before seen. We began to see the bus the same way, too, and it empowered a group of people who had been just as disenfranchised as African Americans."

The disability rights movement could in no sense have been called a movement when Parks refused to yield her seat. At that time, the unemployment rate for people with disabilities reached over 70 percent, and organizations that rallied for rights for people with disabilities focused on solutions that were specific to a single disorder. "The disability community was fragmented," says Bob Kafka, a quadriplegic who broke his neck in 1973 and who was an early organizer for ADAPT. "The deaf community wanted interpreters. People with mobility issues wanted curb cuts. The blind wanted more sensory communication. Everyone saw themselves as a deaf person, or a blind person, or a mental health person. We were tossed salad, not fondue."

Parks's action offered these separate communities a strategy that unified their various wishes. "Rosa Parks energized us in that she was the perfect symbol for when the meek become militant," says Kafka. "She was someone who was willing to cross the line." And the fight for accessible public transportation was to be the single issue that catalyzed disparate disability groups into a common cause.

By the 1960s, and '70s, many cities had introduced paratransit services that picked up disabled patients. The officials who controlled city budgets, though, typically stipulated that these buses could be used by an individual only a few times a month and that the buses could be used only by appointment. So, in the late '70s and early '80s, some activists began to extend the logic of Parks's silent act of defiance to their own cause: Buses that divided people into separate categories, they said, were inherently unequal. Disabled people shouldn't be limited to using paratransit buses. They deserved to ride the city buses just like everyone else.

"How could you go to school, or go on a date, or volunteer somewhere if the only trips deemed worth funding for you were medical trips?" wrote ADAPT member Stephanie Thomas in her introduction to "To Ride the Public's Buses," a collection of articles about the early bus actions that appeared in *Disability Rag*. "How could you get a job if you could only get 3 rides a week? If you were never on time?"

Parks's method of dissent—sitting still—was well suited to a community in which many people found themselves having to do that very thing all day long. Within two decades of her refusal to give up her seat, disabled people in cities across the country began staging their own "sit-ins" by parking their wheelchairs in front of ill-equipped city buses—or, alternatively, by ditching their wheelchairs and crawling onto the stairs of the bus vestibules.

Some of the sit-ins were individual acts of defiance. In Hartford, Conn., 63-year-old Edith Harris parked her wheelchair in front of 10 separate local buses on a single day after waiting nearly two hours for an accessible bus. Increasingly, though, the sit-ins were organized by ADAPT and involved many wheelchair users at a single location.

These actions began to change both how disabled people were perceived and how they perceived themselves. "Without the history of Parks and Martin Luther King, the only argument that the disability community had was the Jerry Lewis Principle," explains Auberger. "The Poor Pathetic Cripple Principle. But if you take a single disabled person and you show them that they can stop a bus, you've empowered that person. And you've made them feel they had rights."

The sit-ins also began to bring about concrete changes in the policies of urban transportation boards. In 1983, the city of Denver gave up its initial resistance and retrofitted all 250 of its buses with lifts after 45 wheelchair users blocked buses at the downtown intersection of Colfax Avenue and Broadway. Similar moves were made by Washington's Metro board in 1986 and by Chicago's transit authority in 1989. And in 1990, when the landmark Americans With Disabilities Act cleared Congress, the only provisions that went into effect immediately were those that mandated accessible public transportation.

If Rosa Parks left a lasting legacy on the disability rights movement, it is important to recognize that it is a legacy that is largely unfinished. A restored version of the bus that Rosa Parks rode in Montgomery recently went on display at the Henry Ford Museum near Detroit, the city where Parks lived her last decades. . . . Detroit's mayor, Kwame Kilpatrick . . . memorialized Parks by saying that "she stood up by sitting down. I'm only standing here because of her."

Kilpatrick failed to mention a further irony, though: The Justice Department [had] joined a suit against his city. . . . It was initially filed in August 2004, by Richard Bernstein, a blind 31-year-old lawyer from the Detroit suburb of Farmington Hills, on behalf of four disabled inner-city clients. His plaintiffs said that they routinely waited three to four hours in severe cold for a bus with a working lift. Their complaint cited evidence that half of the lifts on the city's bus fleet were routinely broken. The complaint did not ask for compensation. It demanded only that the Motor City comply with the Americans with Disabilities Act. The city recently purchased more accessible buses, but the mayor didn't offer a plan for making sure the buses stayed in good working order. He has publicly disparaged Bernstein on radio as an example of "suburban guys coming into our community trying to raise up the concerns of people when this administration is going to the wall on this issue of disabled riders."

Mayor Kilpatrick is not going to the wall, and neither are many other mayors in this country. A 2002 federal Bureau of Transportation Statistics study found that 6 million Americans with disabilities still have trouble obtaining the transportation they need. Many civic leaders and officials at transit organizations have made arguments about the economic difficulty of installing lifts on buses and maintaining them. But they are seeing only one side of the argument: More people in the disability community would pursue jobs and pay more taxes if they could only trust that they could get to work and back safely.

Public officials who offered elaborate eulogies to Parks's memory . . . should evaluate whether they are truly living up to the power of her ideas. During a visit to Detroit . . . to speak to disabled transit riders for a project I was working on, I met Robert Harvey, who last winter hurled his wheelchair in front of a bus pulling onto Woodward Avenue after four drivers in a row had passed him by. (He was knocked to the curb.) I met Carolyn Reed, who has spina bifida and had lost a job because she could rarely find a bus that would get her to work on time. Her able bodied friends had also recently stopped inviting her to the movies. She guessed why: A few times over the past months, they had found themselves waiting late at night with her for hours to catch a bus with a working lift. "I'd say, 'Go ahead, go ahead, I'll be all right,'" she told me. "And they'd say, 'We're not leaving you out here.'" I also met Willie Cochran, a double amputee who once waited six hours in freezing temperatures for a bus that would take him home from dialysis treatment.

None of this should be happening in America. "Rosa Parks could get on the bus to protest," says Roger McCarville, a veteran in Detroit who once chained himself to a bus. "We still can't get on the bus." A true tribute to Parks would be to ensure that every American can.

DISCUSSION QUESTIONS

1. How did the lack of access to public transportation promote a disability movement?
2. Why are sit-ins an effective form of protest?

READING 51

Influencing Public Policy

Jeanine C. Cogan

. . . Federal and state politics are commonly portrayed as open only to a few select stakeholders, as too complex to maneuver, and/or as too big for an individual to have an impact on. One goal of this [discussion] is to correct these misperceptions with information on and tools for how to successfully influence policy. This [discussion] reflects my experience as a policy advocate at the federal level. However, the basic principles and strategies described here can be applied to other levels of government and policy development. This [discussion] considers three topics: the players in policy development, the lifestyle of policy makers, and how you too can influence policy.

THE PLAYERS IN FEDERAL POLICY DEVELOPMENT

There are at least five central groups or stakeholders involved in influencing the legislative process: constituents, organizations or interest groups, coalitions, members of Congress, and congressional

Jeanine C. Cogan is assistant director of the Other 3Rs Project at the Center for Psychology in Schools and Education at the American Psychological Association.

staffers. The role that each plays in the federal policy-making process is briefly described below.

Constituents

Anyone eligible to vote is a constituent. This probably includes you and many of the people you care about. As such, your primary mechanism for influencing the federal legislative process is through your members of Congress: senators and representatives. According to the American Psychological Association,[1] some members of Congress view their constituents as having the most influence on their voting decisions—more than lobbying groups, their colleagues, and party pressures. Because the people in their districts vote members of Congress into office, members are motivated to attend to constituent concerns. Indeed, constituent service is one of the most important aspects of congressional life.[2]

Constituents articulate their views and concerns to members through visits, letters, e-mail, and/or phone calls. In addition, grassroots activism, such as rallies and protests, is effective in mobilizing constituents within a community and to focus members' attention on specific issues. Constituents may also be members of or become involved in organizations that work to influence policy.

Advocacy Organizations

There are numerous types of organizations and interest groups that advocate for specific policies. They cover a range of issues, including business and industry, science and technology, professional interests, labor, civil rights, public interest, and governmental interests.[3] Organizations often have a person or office responsible for advocating on behalf of their members' interests and concerns. Advocating on behalf of a large number of people across the nation can offer more political weight to a message than simply advocating on behalf of one's own interests as a constituent.[4]

Congressional staff often work closely with advocacy groups.[5] In order to move a bill forward, staffers may work with advocacy groups to identify members in key congressional districts who need to be contacted directly by their local constituents. Such grassroots support for a bill may help it gain active congressional consideration and increase its priority as an issue on the legislative agenda.

... To be able to exert more significant influence, advocacy groups may coordinate efforts and work together through coalitions.

Coalitions

Coalitions typically are composed of clusters of advocacy organizations that share common interests or political positions with the aim of developing strength in numbers in order to influence policy. The coalition is designed to bring diverse organizations together to lobby on national policies, promote grassroots activism, and educate the public.[6] Members of a coalition may establish personal relationships with staff and members of Congress, which can contribute to the success of a bill or other policy initiative. Coalitions vary significantly in their membership, structure, and missions. Their constituencies and agendas may shift and adapt according to the changing policy environment and legislative focus. Membership within a coalition is typically on a group, rather than individual, basis. Coalition activities include regular meetings, federal and local outreach efforts, the sharing of knowledge and resources, and strategizing about how to optimize their influence. Working in coalitions maximizes the likelihood of successfully influencing the legislative process by allowing a large number of people to express their opinion on an issue in a short period of time.

Members of Congress

Certainly, a legislator's colleagues, the other policy makers, are another important influence. Numerous factors contribute to the decisions legislators make.[7] Three primary considerations are key in members' political decisions: (1) to satisfy constituents, (2) to enhance their personal reputations within the political world, and (3) to create good policy. All three can be accomplished when members have the skill to successfully work with and influence one another.[8] Members influence each other through direct one-on-one interaction, legislation, briefings, hearings, speeches, and the press. The well-known "Dear Colleague" letter on Capitol Hill, in which members explain legislation to their colleagues and urge them either to become co-sponsors or to vote along similar lines, is a primary strategy for influencing other members.

Members also influence each other through party affiliation and loyalty. Party politics plays a significant role in members' policy decisions.[9] Party leadership may urge members to vote in a certain way on specific legislation. Partisan politics are most apparent in party "whipping." Whipping occurs when party leadership strongly encourages members to vote in a particular way with the implied assumption that doing so will result in rewards. For voting along party lines, members can be rewarded with positions on more powerful committees, among other things that give them more power and clout with colleagues. This influence with colleagues may translate into a greater likelihood of successfully addressing constituent concerns, thereby improving reelection possibilities.

Congressional Staff

Until the 1950s, the U.S. Congress was a part-time institution that worked for 9 of the 24 months of a congressional session. The congressional workload has doubled in the last 30 years.[10] Currently, members work 18 months per session. The increased workload resulted from a series of decisions that enlarged congressional staff assistance, beginning in 1946 with the Legislative Reorganization Act.[11] For example, in 1967, members of the House of Representatives employed 4,000 people as personal staff. By 1990 that number had doubled. Interestingly, some scholars have argued that the increase of staff has resulted in expanded staff autonomy. With larger staffs, members are able to take on more issues and expand their workload. In turn, members need to rely more on and increasingly delegate independent authority to their staff.

Consequently, staff play a critical role in determining policy. Members rely on staff to track specific issues, write speeches, educate them on a range of topics, advise them on legislation and policy decisions, and write legislation. The autonomy and influence of a staffer depends on a range of factors including their individual personalities, the structure of the office, and the members' style.[12]

THE LIFESTYLE OF A POLICY MAKER

"To best understand the way in which federal policy is formulated, it helps to think of Capitol Hill as a community, or culture, with its own inhabitants, rules, norms, and social processes."[13] Only by understanding the culture of politicians can scientists, lobbyists, activists, or anyone else hope to influence the federal process and shape public policy.[14] Four central characteristics of congressional offices are the rapid pace, the large workload, the valuing of direct experience over other data, and the need to compromise.

Political life is typically a lifestyle of unanticipated, urgent deadlines. Given these tight timelines, it is not uncommon for staffers to become "experts" on a specific topic in a few days or mere hours. Therefore, as they are searching for facts on a topic, staffers must rely on easily accessible, digestible resources—typically the Internet or talking points provided by advocates. The outcome of such quick research is often a blend of substantive and political information. Also, with the expanded congressional workload, staffers are typically stretched so thin that reading one-page summaries is all they have time to do. Extensive reports are often useless unless there is a one- or two-page summary (called talking points or briefing memo).[15] Boxes 1 and 2 explain how to prepare such documents.

Although some policy makers appreciate the importance and usefulness of considering scientific data in their decision-making process, they tend to place greater value on precedent and anecdotal evidence. It is not unusual for legislation to remain stagnant until an event occurs to galvanize members of Congress. For example, in 1998 the Hate Crimes

BOX 1

Write an Effective Briefing Sheet or Talking Points

1. *First identify the goal and state it clearly.* Why are you lobbying the member? What is the reason for meeting with the staffer?
2. *Summarize the research and main arguments using bullet points.*
3. *Stay focused on one topic.* If you wish to discuss more than one topic, prepare separate briefing memos (one per topic).
4. *Be concise.* Keep briefing memos to one page, if possible. If the message cannot be conveyed in a page or two, you will likely lose the opportunity to influence the staff.
5. *Make the briefing memo easy to read and visually appealing.*

Prevention Act received attention, with hearings in both the House and Senate, only after an African American man was brutally murdered in Jasper, Texas. Similarly, critical gun control legislation that had been introduced each session of Congress for a number of years was not seriously considered until after the Columbine High School shooting in Littleton, Colorado, in 1999. The palpable role of real-life stories in members' policy decisions may in part reflect that they are primarily motivated to address the needs of their constituents and do so after hearing of their concerns and hardships. Additionally, research on persuasion shows that, depending on the audience, appealing to one's emotions, especially with fear-arousing messages, can be a powerful method of communication.[16] This lesson has not gone unnoticed by policy makers.

Given the nature of our two-party system of government, members must work with individuals who may have very different opinions and perspectives on an issue. As a consequence, to move a policy initiative forward one must have enough support, which often requires negotiation and compromise. This tendency to compromise may collide with the desires and expectations of constituents and advocacy groups.

BOX 2

An Effective Briefing Memo

GOAL: WE URGE YOUR BOSS TO SUPPORT THE HATE CRIMES PREVENTION ACT (HCPA)

WHY WE NEED THE HCPA

- According to community surveys, violence against individuals on the basis of their real or perceived race, ethnicity, religion, sexual orientation, gender, disability, and other social groupings is a fact of life in the United States.
- A civil rights statute, Section 245 of Title 18 U.S.C., gives federal prosecutors the authority to investigate allegations of hate violence based on race, religion, and national origin. This avenue for federal involvement is necessary in order to address cases where state and local authorities fail to properly respond to victims' allegations. Currently such federal investigations are minimal, with typically less than 10 prosecutions annually.
- This statute is critical for responding to the problem of hate violence, yet it does not include a broad definition of hate crimes in line with more recent legislation. In 1994 Congress passed the Hate Crimes Sentencing Enhancement Act as part of the Violent Crime Control and Law Enforcement Act of 1994. In this law, hate crimes were defined broadly as a crime committed against the person:

  > "because of the actual or perceived race, color, religion, national origin, ethnicity, gender, disability, or sexual orientation of that person."

PURPOSE OF THE HCPA

- The main purpose of the HCPA is to bring Section 245 of Title 18 U.S.C. in line with this recent hate crimes definition so that federal officials can investigate and prosecute crimes motivated by hate based on the victim's real or perceived gender, disability, or sexual orientation.
- The Department of Justice (DOJ) receives inquiries from families of gay victims asking for their involvement when local authorities have failed to respond. Unfortunately, the DOJ does not have the authority to investigate such cases. The DOJ considers this bill an important measure in assisting them to properly respond to victims' concerns.

I wrote this example of a briefing memo specifically for the purposes of this [discussion]. The material is based on my advocacy work in the Public Policy Office at the American Psychological Association.

Understanding the unique culture of policy makers allows you to be more effective in influencing federal policy. Given the rapid pace and heavy workload you can increase your effectiveness in working with congressional offices by interacting with staff in a way that shows respect for staffers' time and efforts. Additionally, when working with staff it is useful to offer both data and personal stories of affected individuals. Finally, you may be more successful working with staff if you have an understanding of the limitations of members of Congress due to the institutional tendency toward compromise.

INFLUENCING PUBLIC POLICY

There are two basic avenues by which you can shape policy. In some cases, you will want to influence legislators on issues that are already on the public agenda. In others, you will want to create legislative support for an unknown or invisible issue.

Influencing Legislators on Existing Issues

As you already know, voting constituents are greatly valued in legislative offices. A constituent communicating concerns to members of Congress can play an influential role in the legislative process. The most common way in which individuals can influence policy is to register opinions on already existing bills. Interested constituents can communicate with members of Congress or work in coalitions to promote or prevent the passage of particular legislation.

Contacting Members of Congress The first step in effective communication with Congress is to determine the best person to contact. Usually, contacting your own legislator—the person who represents your congressional district—is most effective. As your elected official, this is the person who represents you and therefore must be sensitive to your views and concerns. Occasionally, however, in order to achieve a certain goal it will be more appropriate to contact other members of Congress. For example, if a member is recognized as a leader

BOX 3

Contact Your Legislators

FEDERAL LEVEL
When writing a letter to your member of Congress use the following congressional addresses:

(Your Congressperson) The Honorable First, Last Name
U.S. House of Representatives
Washington, DC 20515

(Your Senator) The Honorable First, Last Name
U.S. Senate
Washington, DC 20510

When calling your member of Congress, use the U.S. Capitol Switchboard at 202-224-3121. Constituents should ask for their representative and/or senator.

STATE AND LOCAL LEVEL
Use GovSpot at *www.govspot.com* to identify and contact your state and local leaders. GovSpot.com is a nonpartisan government information portal designed to simplify the search for relevant government information online. This resource offers a collection of top government and civic resources such as government websites and documents, facts and figures, news, political information, and how to locate state and local policy makers.

on an issue in which you have expertise or interest, then contacting that member is appropriate, even if he or she does not represent your congressional district or state.

Constituents can contact members of Congress through phone calls, letter writing, e-mail, or a visit (see Boxes 3 and 4). The purpose of the communication often determines which mode of communication to use. For example, is the communication meant to register an opinion or to educate members of Congress on a particular issue? Is it designed to establish a relationship with the congressional office? Is an immediate response and action needed?

If a bill is currently being debated, it is controversial, and/or there are other time pressures, you

BOX 4

Organize Visits with Elected Officials

One of the best avenues to equality for LGB Americans is through establishing a personal relationship with your elected officials. Like any relationship, these relationships require cultivation over time and will involve developing ties to the elected official as well as members of their staff. A personal visit can be key to this kind of interaction. For state and local officials, this may not be difficult. If a visit to Washington D.C., is difficult, you can arrange to visit your members of Congress when they return to their district office.

When you schedule such a visit, it may be helpful to organize a small group of like-minded voters. Taking a delegation of interested persons with you will enhance your visit. If this is not possible, bring at least one other person with you for support.

Your meeting will be most effective by doing the following:

- Identify the "visit team" (no more than six individuals) from your state or district who are interested in LGB issues.
- If you are from a big state and you are meeting with your senator, you may want to include individuals from several points around the state. The same is true for congressional districts and for state and local officials.
- The official's political party doesn't really matter. However, it helps if you can get someone on your team who is politically well connected or has a good sense of the local political dynamic.
- Make sure members of your team are comfortable with the process. If they are truly uncomfortable, they may detract from the overall impression you want to leave with your elected official.
- Arrange the date, time, and place for a premeeting of the visit team. Use this meeting (or at least a conference call) to make sure everyone is on board. You do not want questions or disagreements within your group during the visit.
- Arrange the date, time, and place for a meeting by contacting the state, district, or local office of the elected official you wish to meet.
- Coordinate the participants in the meeting to make sure that the visit team "sings with one voice" in making points with the elected official.
- Use the material in *Everyday Activism* to arm the team with the facts. In addition, do some research on the local situation so that you can personalize your arguments.
- Visit-team leaders should be prepared to guide and direct the meeting. After assembling at the office, team members should introduce themselves and identify the organization or institution with which they are affiliated.
- The visit-team leader should then lay out the problem and briefly outline the impact of the issue on the official's constituency.
- An open discussion should follow, with each team member providing his or her input while maintaining as much of a conversational tone as possible.
- Above all **listen.** Try to ascertain where your official is coming from. Employ active listening techniques to show her or him that you understand the concerns being raised. Try to answer objections and concerns as appropriate but don't get into a fight. Be firm and assertive but **not** combative.
- Be sure that the elected official is asked at some point to take a certain action, to support a policy initiative, or vote in a particular way on current legislation. For example:

  "Will you please assist our efforts to overturn the ban on lesbian and gay men in the military? Specifically, we would like for you to sponsor legislation to repeal the ban."
  "Will you support efforts to end workplace discrimination against lesbian and gay men? Specifically, we would like for you to co-sponsor ENDA."

- If the official expresses uncertainty about the facts, offer to provide further information to document the facts. . . .
- After the visit, send a follow-up letter thanking the official for his or her time and consideration. Include the information you offered to provide (e.g., a copy of the relevant policy brief) with your letter.

Adapted from unpublished materials originally drafted by William Baily, American Psychological Association.

may be more successful communicating with members by phone. Members of Congress may inquire from staff what their constituents are expressing and consider this when making policy decisions. Constituents interested in calling members should call the U.S. Capitol Switchboard at 202-224-3121 and ask for their representative and/or senator.

If you are interested in receiving a response to an inquiry or educating members of Congress, then writing a letter or setting up a visit is preferable. (For help organizing and conducting visits to congressional offices, refer to Box 4.) The most effective letters are those that are concise and focused on one issue. (An example of a sample letter is shown in Box 5.) To write an effective letter, you should follow these three steps:

1. *State the purpose.* The first paragraph should include who you are and why you are writing this particular member of Congress. For example, "I am writing you as a constituent in your district." This is followed by the purpose of the letter. Bill names and/or numbers should be used if possible and applicable; for example, "I am writing to urge you to vote for the Hate Crimes Prevention Act."

2. *State the evidence/argument.* The purpose is followed by a rationale for the requested action. For example, "Given that so many states currently do not have laws that allow crimes to be investigated as hate crimes, the passage of this bill is necessary." Personal experiences that support the stated position can be concisely summarized as well. If you would like to make a research-based argument, then a short summary of the research or the presentation of some data can be effective.

3. *Ask for a response.* To optimize the impact of a correspondence, you should conclude by specifically asking members to reply. Responding to constituent mail is a vital role of congressional offices. The last paragraph should reiterate your concern and request a response.[17]

Effective Advocacy When interacting with policy makers, advocates may err by being overly critical without offering specific suggestions or

---

BOX 5

An Effective Constituent Letter

The Honorable John Doe
U.S. House of Representatives
Washington, DC 20515

Dear Representative John Doe:

I am a constituent and am writing to ask you to oppose the proposed amendment by Congressman Todd Tiahrt (R-Kan.) to the D.C. appropriations bill that would prevent unmarried couples from adopting children in Washington, D.C. This current bill is ill-conceived and based on a number of inaccurate beliefs about lesbians and gay men as parents.

As a lesbian mother, I live in constant fear of losing custody of my child even though I am a nurturing, committed parent. I participate actively in the school board and related activities. My ability to be a caring and effective parent has nothing to do with my sexual orientation. This current amendment further threatens my daily existence as a parent.

According to the American Psychological Association, research shows that lesbians and gay men are fit parents. Contrary to the belief that gay parents may have a negative influence on their children, when compared with children of heterosexual parents, children of gay men or lesbians show no marked difference in their intelligence, psychological adjustment, social adjustment, popularity with friends, development of sex role identity, or development of sexual orientation. Overall, the belief that children of gay and lesbian parents suffer deficits in personal development has no empirical foundation.

In sum, the characterization of homosexual parents as being a threat to children is inaccurate, therefore calling into question policy decisions based on this belief. I urge you to oppose this amendment. I look forward to hearing your perspective.

Respectfully,
Jane Smith

I wrote this as an example of a good constituent letter. The Tiahrt amendment was introduced to the D.C. appropriations bill in 1997. Although it was eliminated, a similar amendment had been introduced every year since.

alternatives. Making this mistake will limit your effectiveness. Most legislators and their staff want to write the best bills possible and implement effective policies. For this reason, you should view the staffer as a friend, not a foe. Many staffers will be open to your expertise and ideas (though they may not always implement them). Therefore, when possible, it is useful to offer particular strategies for implementing the goals or ideas you want to promote.

For example, if you support the overall purpose of a bill but think it has flaws, prepare talking points that outline the concerns and offer alternatives. When I served as a legislative assistant for Congresswoman DeGette, I wrote a bill that health consumers supported but health providers opposed. After introducing the bill, many provider groups were critical and some raised legitimate concerns. The groups who were most effective were those that offered alternative language for the bill. Even if they agree with your perspective, legislative staffers may not have the time or expertise to find a solution for your concern. However, you can play a unique role in the legislative process by offering specific solutions and assistance to the congressional staff.

Creating Congressional Support for an Unknown Issue

In addition to influencing important policy decisions about existing legislation and visible issues, you can also help set the legislative agenda. For example, hate crimes legislation grew out of a national coordinated movement that promoted this issue as an important policy priority. Individuals and organizations met with members of Congress urging them to recognize and address this growing problem.

Finding Members to Support and Promote an Issue
Members of Congress become known for their leadership in particular areas. You should research which member is likely to support and promote your issue. Given the continuing hostile environment toward LGBs, most members, even leaders on LGB-positive policies, will not showcase

their work on LGB rights. So while information about members' policy priorities and accomplishments is available on their websites, you may have to look beyond their bios or issues of interest. For example, Rep. Christopher Shays (R-Conn.) has been a leading advocate for [the Employment Nondiscrimination Act]. However, his endless support for LGB protections against workplace discrimination is not obvious from his website under the heading "issues." Instead, you have to look under "press releases." Keep this in mind as you explore members' homepages and other information. The Internet address for members' homepages for the House of Representatives is www.house.gov. For the Senate, it is www.senate.gov. Members' biographies are also available by accessing the website on biographical directories of members of Congress at bioguide.congress.gov. An excellent book, titled *Politics in America,* provides descriptions of the members of Congress and is published each year by the *Congressional Quarterly.*

Another useful avenue for learning the legislative priorities of members is to see what bills they introduced or co-sponsored through accessing the Thomas website at thomas.loc.gov. This site provides information about the bills members have introduced and/or co-sponsored, as well as the text of legislation, congressional records, committee information, and bill status and summaries.

Establishing Relationships with Congressional Staff

As you have learned already, congressional staff are critical in policy development and their influence can be substantial. Staffers serve as gatekeepers to members of Congress by deciding who receives entrée into the office. If staff advise the member of Congress to meet with a particular advocacy group, the member is likely to do so. Given this influence, advocates interested in making contact with their representatives should establish rapport with the legislative staff. To this end, you can seek an appointment by calling the legislative assistant currently working on the issue of interest. In order to increase the chances of success, you should offer an explanation for choosing this particular member and state the purpose of the proposed meeting. For example, "I am calling you because your boss is a leader on employment issues. I know she led the fight to save small businesses last year. I would like to schedule an appointment with you to discuss another important employment issue: the need for legislation to prevent work-related discrimination based on sexual orientation."

Educating Staff   The primary goal of working with congressional members is to increase their knowledge and understanding of a particular topic that can lead to congressional interest and action. Because advocates tend to hold detailed knowledge on a specific topic while staffers have a little information about many topics, staffers typically welcome information. Due to the workload constraints, you should present concise summaries and clearly outlined points and goals. To facilitate this process, prepare handouts for congressional staff with talking points or briefing memos that summarize the topic. . . . As you have already seen, Box 1 provides guidelines for writing an effective policy brief and Box 2 contains an example.

Addressing Inaccurate Perceptions and Reaching a Broader Audience   Given that there is so much misinformation about the lives of LGBs, one of the most important roles you can play is to correct myths and stereotypes. This is where research is particularly helpful. The American Psychological Association (APA) has created many documents based on solid social science evidence. Summaries of research that clarify the truth about LGBs' lives and experiences are readily available by accessing the American Psychological Association Lesbian, Gay, and Bisexual Concerns Office website at www.apa.org/ pi/lgbc/publications/pubsreports.html.

In addition to educating the major players in the policy process, you may need to reach broader audiences with your efforts to raise awareness and correct misinformation. Writing letters to the editor of local, regional, and national publications is one way to do this. Most policy makers pay close attention to the

---

BOX 6

Write a Letter to the Editor

- Make one point (or at most two) in your letter or fax. State the point clearly, ideally in the first sentence.
- Make your letter timely. If you are not addressing a specific article, editorial, or letter that recently appeared in the paper you are writing to, then tie your issue to a recent event.
- Familiarize yourself with the coverage and editorial position of the paper to which you are writing. Refute or support specific statements, address relevant facts that are ignored, but avoid blanket attacks on the media in general or the newspaper in particular.
- Check the letter specifications of the newspaper to which you are writing. Length and format requirements vary from paper to paper. (Generally, roughly two short paragraphs are ideal.) You also must include your name, signature, address, and phone number.
- Look at the letters that appear in your paper. Are the letters printed usually of a certain type?
- Support your facts. If the topic you address is controversial, consider sending documentation along with your letter. But don't overload the editors with too much information.
- Keep your letter brief. Type it.
- Find others to write letters when possible. This will show that other individuals in the community are concerned about the issue. If your letter doesn't get published, perhaps someone else's on the same topic will.
- Monitor the paper for your letter. If your letter has not appeared within a week or two, follow up with a call to the editorial department of the newspaper.
- Write to different sections of the paper when appropriate. Sometimes the issue you want to address is relevant to the lifestyle, book review, or other section of the paper.

Text adapted from Fairness and Accuracy in Reporting (FAIR) at www.fair.org.

---

media in their districts, so such letters can also have an impact on policy making. In addition, many newspapers welcome well-written op-ed columns on issues of concern to their readers. The guidance provided in Boxes 6 and 7 may help you get your ideas into print.

BOX 7

Write an Op-Ed

An op-ed gets its name because of its placement opposite the editorial page. It is longer than a letter to the editor—usually 500–800 words. Also often referred to as an opinion editorial, these are more difficult to get printed than a letter to the editor but can be very effective.

Getting It in Print

- *Pick the right author.* Many papers will only print an op-ed from a representative of an organization or from a noted authority. A meeting with the editor can also help to establish the author as credible. Using a local spokesperson increases the local perspective or interest, especially on issues with national significance.

- *Pitch the article ahead of time.* Ideally, pitch your idea to the editor about 2 weeks before you want it to run. If you are responding to an op-ed that has just been published, contact the op-ed page editor right away to ask about a response. Even if they don't ask, offer to send a draft for their consideration.

- *Follow the guidelines.* Call your paper to find out the preferred length for an op-ed, deadlines, and any other requirements. Unless guidelines say otherwise, submit the piece typed and double-spaced on white paper with 1-inch margins. Ideally, the first page should be on your letterhead. Have a header at the top of each additional page with your name, the date, and the page number. Fax, mail, e-mail, or hand deliver the piece to the op-ed page editor.

- *Have a specific point of view and something fresh to offer.* Try to be ahead of the curve in public discussion of an issue. Let friends and peers review the piece and offer comments.

- *Follow up.* Follow the mailing with a phone call to the op-ed page editor. Be polite and respectful of his or her schedule, but try to emphasize again, as feels appropriate, why the paper should run the piece. Remember—there is a lot of competition for space on the op-ed page. If you are not successful on your first try, don't give up.

Text adapted from PFLAG at www.pflag.org.

CONCLUSION

Every day, thousands of people are actively lobbying members of Congress in an effort to influence policy. In order to defend against anti-LGB policies and to advocate for policies that are proactive in improving the lives of lesbian, gay, and bisexual people, we must remain active participants in the legislative process. From writing letters to establishing more enduring relationships with congressional staffers, we all can and do influence policy.

To some this process may seem cumbersome and complicated. However, please remember that help is always available. If you have questions about the federal government, trained staff at the Federal Consumer Information Center will answer your questions about federal programs, benefits, or services. You can call their toll-free hotline at 800-688-9889 (TTY 800-326-2996) between 9 A.M. and 8 P.M. Eastern time or use their website (www.info.gov).

Although this [discussion] has focused on advocacy at the federal level, the same basic principles and processes can be applied at any level. Whether you want to push for LGB-affirming legislation on Capitol Hill, in your state legislature, or with local elected officials, you will be most effective when you educate yourself and share that knowledge with those you wish to influence. Developing relationship networks can be an effective strategy for educating officials and members of their staffs regardless of the level of government. Well-crafted letters to the editor and op-ed columns can raise awareness of the issues locally, regionally, and nationally. . . . Use the lessons you have learned from this discussion and make a difference.

DISCUSSION QUESTIONS

1. Does Cogan's description of "Capitol Hill culture" fit with your assumptions about how government works? What surprised you in her description? What didn't?

2. Does the information in Cogan's article make you feel any more comfortable about pursuing "everyday activism" on issues important to you? Why or why not?

NOTES

1. American Psychological Association. 1995. *Advancing psychology in the public interest: A psychologist's guide to participation in federal policy making*. Washington, DC: Author.

2. Wells, W. G. 1996. *Working with Congress: A practical guide for scientists and engineers*. Washington, DC: American Association for the Advancement of Science.

3. Lorion, R. P., & Iscoe, I. 1996. Reshaping our views of our field. In R. P. Lorion, I. Iscoe, P. H. DeLeon, & G. R. VandenBos (Eds.), *Psychology and public policy* (pp. 1–19). Washington, DC: American Psychological Association. Truman, D. B. 1987. The nature and functions of interest groups: The governmental process. In P. Woll (Ed.), *American government: Readings and cases* (pp. 255–262). Boston: Little, Brown.

4. Ceaser, J. W., Bessette, J. M., O'Toole, L. J., & Thurow, G. 1995. *American government: Origins, institutions, and public policy* (4th ed.). Dubuque, IA: Kendall/Hunt.

5. Nickels, I. B. 1994. *Guiding a bill through the legislative process* (Congressional Research Service Report for Congress, 94-322 GOV). Washington, DC: Library of Congress.

6. Key, V. O. 1987. The nature and functions of interest groups: Pressure groups. In P. Woll (Ed.), *American government: Readings and cases* (pp. 266–273). Boston: Little, Brown.

7. American Psychological Association, 1995 (see note 1). Wells, 1996 (see note 2).

8. Drew, E. 1987. A day in the life of a United States Senator. In P. Woll (Ed.), *American government: Readings and cases* (pp. 487–497). Boston: Little, Brown. Vincent, T. A. 1990. A view from the Hill: The human element in policy making on Capitol Hill. American Psychologist, 45(1), 61–64.

9. American Psychological Association, 1995.

10. Wells, 1996.

11. Rundquist, P. S., Schneider, J., & Pauls, F. H. 1992. *Congressional staff: An analysis of their roles, functions, and impacts* (Congressional Research Service Report for Congress, 92-90S). Washington, DC: Library of Congress.

12. Redman, E. 1987. Congressional staff: The surrogates of power. In P. Woll (Ed.), *American government: Readings and cases* (pp. 452–461). Boston: Little, Brown. Rundquist, Scheider, & Pauls, 1992.

13. Vincent, T. A., 1990, p. 61 (see note 8).

14. Bevan, W. 1996. On getting in bed with a lion. In R. P. Lorion, I. Iscoe, P. H. DeLeon, & G. R. VandenBos (Eds.), *Psychology and public policy* (pp. 145–163). Washington, DC: American Psychological Association. Nissim-Sabat, D. (1997). Psychologists, Congress, and public policy.

Professional Psychology: Research and Practice, 28(3). 275–280. Wells, 1996 (see note 2).

15. This is the rationale for including briefing memos throughout this [discussion].

16. For example, Wilson, D. K., Purdon, S. E., & Wallston, A. 1988. Compliance to health recommendations: A theoretical overview of message framing. *Health Education Research, 3*, 161–171.

17. American Psychological Association, 1995 (see note 1). For more information on how to write an effective letter, the reader is referred to the information brochure written by the APA titled: Calkins, B. J. 1995. *Psychology in the public interest: A psychologist's guide to participation in federal policy making*. Washington, DC: APA. Available at www.apa.org/ppo/grassroots/sadguide.html.

READING 52

What Can We Do? Becoming Part of the Solution

Allan G. Johnson

The challenge we face is to change patterns of exclusion, rejection, privilege, harassment, discrimination, and violence that are everywhere in this society and have existed for hundreds (or, in the case of gender, thousands) of years. We have to begin by thinking about the trouble and the challenge in new and more productive ways. . . .

Large numbers of people have sat on the sidelines and seen themselves as neither part of the problem nor the solution. Beyond this shared trait, however, they are far from homogeneous. Everyone is aware of the whites, heterosexuals, and men who intentionally act out in oppressive ways. But there is less attention to the millions of people who know inequities exist and want to be part of the solution. Their silence and invisibility allow the trouble to continue. Removing what silences them and stands in their way can tap an enormous potential of energy for change. . . .

Allan G. Johnson is a sociologist, writer, and public speaker who has worked on issues of privilege, oppression, and social unequality.

MYTH 1: "IT'S ALWAYS BEEN THIS WAY, AND IT ALWAYS WILL"

If you don't make a point of studying history, it's easy to slide into the belief that things have always been the way we've known them to be. But if you look back a bit further, you find racial oppression has been a feature of human life for only a matter of centuries, and there is abundant evidence that male dominance has been around for only seven thousand years or so, which isn't very long when you consider that human beings have been on the earth for hundreds of thousands of years.[1] So when it comes to human social life, the smart money should be on the idea that *nothing* has always been this way or any other.

This idea should suggest that nothing *will* always be this way or any other, contrary to the notion that privilege and oppression are here to stay. If the only thing we can count on is change, then it's hard to see why we should believe for a minute that *any* kind of social system is permanent. Reality is always in motion. Things may appear to stand still, but that's only because humans have a short attention span, dictated perhaps by the shortness of our lives. If we take the long view—the *really* long view—we can see that everything is in process all the time.

Some would argue that everything *is* process, the space between one point and another, the movement from one thing toward another. What we may see as permanent end points—world capitalism, Western civilization, advanced technology, and so on—are actually temporary states on the way to other temporary states. Even ecologists, who used to talk about ecological balance, now speak of ecosystems as inherently unstable. Instead of always returning to some steady state after a period of disruption, ecosystems are, by nature, a continuing process of change from one arrangement to another. They never go back to just where they were.

Social systems are also fluid. A society isn't some hulking *thing* that sits there forever as it is. Because a system happens only as people participate in it, it can't help being a dynamic process of creation and re-creation from one moment to the next.

In something as simple as a man following the path of least resistance toward controlling conversations (and a woman letting him do it), the reality of male privilege in that moment comes into being. This is how we *do* male privilege, bit by bit, moment by moment. This is also how individuals can contribute to change: by choosing paths of *greater* resistance, as when men don't take control and women refuse their own subordination.

Since people can always choose paths of greater resistance or create new ones entirely, systems can only be as stable as the flow of human choice and creativity, which certainly isn't a recipe for permanence. In the short run, systems of privilege may look unchangeable. But the relentless process of social life never produces the exact same result twice in a row, because it's impossible for everyone to participate in any system in an unvarying and uniform way. Added to this are the dynamic interactions that go on among systems—between capitalism and the state, for example, or between families and the economy—that also produce powerful and unavoidable tensions, contradictions, and other currents of change. Ultimately, systems can't help changing.

Oppressive systems often *seem* stable because they limit people's lives and imaginations so much that they can't see beyond them. But this masks a fundamental long-term instability caused by the dynamics of oppression itself. Any system organized around one group's efforts to control and exploit another is a losing proposition, because it contradicts the essentially uncontrollable nature of reality and does violence to basic human needs and values. For example, as the last two centuries of feminist thought and action have begun to challenge the violence and break down the denial, patriarchy has become increasingly vulnerable. This is one reason male resistance, backlash, and defensiveness are now so intense. Many men complain about their lot, especially their inability to realize ideals of control in relation to their own lives,[2] women, and other men. Fear of and resentment toward women are pervasive, from worrying about being accused of sexual harassment to railing against affirmative action.

No social system lasts forever, but this is especially true of oppressive systems of privilege. We can't know what will replace them, but we can be confident that they will go, that they *are* going at every moment. It's only a matter of how quickly, by what means, and toward what alternatives, and whether each of us will do our part to make it happen sooner rather than later and with less rather than more human suffering in the process.

MYTH 2: GANDHI'S PARADOX AND THE MYTH OF NO EFFECT

Whether we help change oppressive systems depends on how we handle the belief that nothing we do can make a difference, that the system is too big and powerful for us to affect it. The complaint is valid if we look at society as a whole: it's true that we aren't going to change it in our lifetime. But if changing the entire system through our own efforts is the standard against which we measure the ability to do something, then we've set ourselves up to feel powerless. It's not unreasonable to want to make a difference, but if we have to *see* the final result of what we do, then we can't be part of change that's too gradual and long term to allow that. We also can't be part of change that's so complex that we can't sort out our contribution from countless others that combine in ways we can never grasp. The problem of privilege and oppression requires complex and long-term change coupled with short-term work to soften some of its worst consequences. This means that if we're going to be part of the solution, we have to let go of the idea that change doesn't happen unless we're around to see it happen.

To shake off the paralyzing myth that we cannot, individually, be effective, we have to alter how we see ourselves in relation to a long-term, complex process of change. This begins by altering how we relate to time. Many changes can come about quickly enough for us to see them happen. When I was in college, for example, there was little talk about gender inequality as a social problem, whereas now there are more than five hundred women's studies

programs in the United States. But a goal like ending oppression takes more than this and far more time than our short lives can encompass. If we're going to see ourselves as part of that kind of change, we can't use the human life span as a significant standard against which to measure progress.

To see our choices in relation to long-term change, we have to develop what might be called "time constancy," analogous to what psychologists call "object constancy." If you hold a cookie in front of very young children and then put it behind your back while they watch, they can't find the cookie because they apparently can't hold on to the image of it and where it went. They lack object constancy. In other words, if they can't see it, it might as well not even exist. After a while, children develop the mental ability to know that objects or people exist even when they're out of sight. In thinking about change and our relation to it, we need to develop a similar ability in relation to time that enables us to carry within us the knowledge, the faith, that significant change happens even though we aren't around to see it.

Along with time constancy, we need to clarify for ourselves how our choices matter and how they don't. Gandhi once said nothing we do as individuals matters, but that it's vitally important to do it anyway. This touches on a powerful paradox in the relationship between society and individuals. Imagine, for example, that social systems are trees and we are the leaves. No individual leaf on the tree matters; whether it lives or dies has no effect on much of anything. But collectively, the leaves are essential to the whole tree because they photosynthesize the sugar that feeds it. Without leaves, the tree dies.

So leaves matter and they don't, just as we matter and we don't. What each of us does may not seem like much, because in important ways, it *isn't* much. But when many people do this work together, they can form a critical mass that is anything but insignificant, especially in the long run. If we're going to be part of a larger change process, we have to learn to live with this sometimes uncomfortable paradox.

A related paradox is that we have to be willing to travel without knowing where we're going. We need faith to do what seems right without necessarily being sure of the effect that will have. We have to think like pioneers who may know the direction they want to move in or what they would like to find, without knowing where they will wind up. Because they are going where they've never been before, they can't know whether they will ever arrive at anything they might consider a destination, much less the kind of place they had in mind when they first set out. If pioneers had to know their destination from the beginning, they would never go anywhere or discover anything.

In similar ways, to seek out alternatives to systems of privilege it has to be enough to move away from social life organized around privilege and oppression and to move toward the certainty that alternatives are possible, even though we may not have a clear idea of what those are or ever experience them ourselves. It has to be enough to question how we see ourselves as people of a certain race, gender, class, and sexual orientation, for example, or examine how we see capitalism and the scarcity and competition it produces in relation to our personal striving to better our own lives, or how oppression works and how we participate in it. Then we can open ourselves to experience what happens next.

When we dare ask core questions about who we are and how the world works, things happen that we can't foresee; they don't happen unless we *move,* if only in our minds. As pioneers, we discover what's possible only by first putting ourselves in motion, because we have to move in order to change our position—and hence put perspective—on where we are, where we've been, and where we might go. This is how alternatives begin to appear.

The myth of no effect obscures the role we can play in the long-term transformation of society. But the myth also blinds us to our own power in relation to other people. We may cling to the belief that there is nothing we can do precisely because we subconsciously know how much power we *do* have and are afraid to use it because people may not like it. If we deny our power to affect people, then we don't have to worry about taking responsibility for how we use it or, more significant, how we don't.

This reluctance to acknowledge and use power comes up in the simplest everyday situations, as when a group of friends starts laughing at a racist, sexist, or homophobic joke and we have to decide whether to go along. It's just a moment among countless such moments that constitute the fabric of all kinds of oppressive systems. But it's a crucial moment, because the group's seamless response to the joke affirms the normalcy and unproblematic nature of it in a system of privilege. It takes only one person to tear the fabric of collusion and apparent consensus. On some level, we each know we have this potential, and this knowledge can empower us or scare us into silence. We can change the course of the moment with something as simple as visibly not joining in the laughter, or saying "I don't think that's funny." We know how uncomfortable this can make the group feel and how they may ward off their discomfort by dismissing, excluding, or even attacking us as bearers of bad news. Our silence, then, isn't because nothing we do will matter, our silence is our not *daring* to matter.

Our power to affect other people isn't simply the power to make them feel uncomfortable. Systems shape the choices people make primarily by providing paths of least resistance. Whenever we openly choose a different path, however, we make it possible for others to see both the path of least resistance they're following and the possibility of choosing something else.

If we choose different paths, we usually won't know if we're affecting other people, but it's safe to assume that we are. When people know that alternatives exist and witness other people choosing them, things become possible that weren't before. When we openly pass up a path of least resistance, we increase resistance for other people around that path, because now they must reconcile their choice with what they've seen us do, something they didn't have to deal with before. There's no way to predict how this will play out in the long run, but there's certainly no good reason to think it won't make a difference.

The simple fact is that we affect one another all the time without knowing it. When my family moved to our house in the woods of northwestern Connecticut, one of my first pleasures was blazing walking trails through the woods. Some time later I noticed deer scat and hoofprints along the trails, and it pleased me to think they had adopted the trail I'd laid down. But then I wondered if perhaps I had followed a trail laid down by others when I cleared "my" trail. I realized that there is no way to know that anything begins or ends with me and the choices I make. It's more likely that the paths others have chosen influence the paths I choose.

This suggests that the simplest way to help others make different choices is to make them myself, and to do it openly. As I shift the patterns of my own participation in systems of privilege, I make it easier for others to do so as well, and harder for them not to. Simply by setting an example—rather than trying to change them—I create the possibility of their participating in change in their own time and in their own way. In this way I can widen the circle of change without provoking the kind of defensiveness that perpetuates paths of least resistance and the oppressive systems they serve.

It's important to see that in doing this kind of work, we don't have to go after people to change their minds. In fact, changing people's minds may play a relatively small part in changing societies. We won't succeed in turning diehard misogynists into practicing feminists, for example, or racists into civil rights activists. At most, we can shift the odds in favor of new paths that contradict the core values that systems of privilege depend on. We can introduce so many exceptions to the paths that support privilege that the children or grandchildren of diehard racists and misogynists will start to change their perception of which paths offer the least resistance. Research on men's changing attitudes toward the male provider role, for example, shows that most of the shift occurs *between* generations, not within them.[3] This suggests that rather than trying to change people, the most important thing we can do is contribute to the slow evolution of entire cultures so that forms and values which support privilege begin to lose their "obvious" legitimacy and normalcy and new forms emerge to challenge their privileged place in social life.

In science, this is how one paradigm replaces another.[4] For hundreds of years, for example, Europeans believed that the stars, planets, and sun revolved around Earth. But scientists such as Copernicus and Galileo found that too many of their astronomical observations were anomalies that didn't fit the prevailing paradigm: if the sun and planets revolved around the Earth, then they wouldn't move as they did. As such observations accumulated, they made it increasingly difficult to hang on to an Earth-centered paradigm. Eventually the anomalies became so numerous that Copernicus offered a new paradigm, which he declined to publish for fear of persecution as a heretic, a fate that eventually befell Galileo when he took up the cause a century later. Eventually, however, the evidence was so overwhelming that a new paradigm replaced the old one.

In similar ways, we can see how systems of privilege are based on paradigms that shape how we think about difference and how we organize social life in relation to it. We can openly challenge those paradigms with evidence that they don't work and produce unacceptable consequences for everyone. We can help weaken them by openly choosing alternative paths in our everyday lives and thereby provide living anomalies that don't fit the prevailing paradigm. By our example, we can contradict basic assumptions and their legitimacy over and over again. We can add our choices and our lives to tip the scales toward new paradigms that don't revolve around privilege and oppression. We can't tip the scales overnight or by ourselves, and in that sense we don't amount to much. But on the other side of Gandhi's paradox, it is crucial where we choose to place what poet Bonaro Overstreet called "the stubborn ounces of my weight":

STUBBORN OUNCES

(To One Who Doubts the Worth of Doing Anything If You Can't Do Everything)

You say the little efforts that I make
will do no good; they will never prevail

PERSONAL ACCOUNT

Parents' Underestimated Love

"Coming out of the closet" to my parents has been the most liberating thing that I have done in my life because having my homosexuality discovered by my parents was my biggest fear. Although I didn't grow up in a particularly homophobic environment, innately I knew that homosexuality was different and wasn't accepted because of rigid social norms and religious doctrines. I lived in anguish of being exposed and of the consequences that would come with being the queer one.

Keeping the secret from my traditional Salvadoran parents created a wedge that made it difficult for me to bond with my parents and have them participate fully in my life. I became a recluse and avoided much parental interaction to avoid questions about girlfriends. During my teenage years, girlfriends were expected from a "good and healthy" boy such as myself. I felt that my lack of interest in girls would have led to probes from my parents, and plus, I wasn't the typical macho boy who was into sports, cars, etc. . . . I was the "sensitive type." To avoid any suspicion, I limited my interaction with my parents. I felt that if I opened up to them, my sexuality would be questioned and questions like "Are you gay?" would follow. Being an academic overachiever in high school made things easier for me. Whenever the question was asked of why I didn't have a girlfriend, I had the perfect excuse, "I'm too busy with school to focus on girls . . . do you want a *Playboy* or an honor student?"

During my sophomore year in college I took a bold step and moved out of my parents' house. My move facilitated my "coming out" to my parents because the possibility of being kicked out of the house when I told them I was gay wouldn't loom over me. I didn't know if my parents would kick me out, but I couldn't run the risk of finding out. One year after moving out, I "came out." Ironically it didn't come as a surprise to my parents, and frankly it wasn't a big deal! After years of living in fear of rejection and shame, my parents accepted and reaffirmed their love and support. I underestimated the power of my parents' love.

Octavio N. Espinal

to tip the hovering scale
where Justice hangs in balance.
       I don't think
I ever thought they would.
But I am prejudiced beyond debate
In favor of my right to choose which side
shall feel the stubborn ounces of my weight.[5]

It is in such small and humble choices that oppression and the movement toward something better actually happen.

DISCUSSION QUESTIONS

1. In a sense, Allan Johnson's discussion highlights the paradoxes inherent in the efforts to create social change. What are those paradoxes, and how does Johnson resolve them?

2. What would Johnson's advice be to someone who wants to make a difference in society? Can it be summarized in a sentence or two?

NOTES

1. See Elizabeth Fisher, *Woman's Creation: Sexual Evolution and the Shaping of Society* (New York: McGraw-Hill, 1979); Gerda Lerner, *The Creation of Patriarchy* (New York: Oxford University Press, 1986).
2. This is what Warren Farrell means when he describes male power as mythical. In this case, he's right. See *The Myth of Male Power* (New York: Berkley Books, 1993).
3. J. R. Wilkie, "Changes in U.S. Men's Attitudes towards the Family Provider Role, 1972–1989," *Gender and Society* 7, no. 2 (1993): 261–79.
4. The classic statement of how this happens is by Thomas S. Kuhn, *The Structure of Scientific Revolutions* (Chicago: University of Chicago Press, 1970).
5. Bonaro W. Overstreet, *Hands Laid Upon the Wind* (New York: Norton, 1955), p. 15.

READING 53

In Defense of Rich Kids

William Upski Wimsatt

My family never talked much about money, except to say that we were "middle-class . . . well maybe upper-middle-class." A few years ago, it became clear that both my parents and my grandmother had a lot more money than I realized. As an only child, I stood to inherit a nice chunk of it. I didn't know how much and I didn't know when. They did not want me to become spoiled or think I didn't have to work.

A lot of people will use this information to write me off. Oh, he's a rich kid. No wonder he could publish a book, probably with his parents' money. And why's he going around bragging about it? What is he, stupid? Some of us have to work for a living, etc.

You can hate me if you want to. I am the beneficiary of a very unfair system. The system gives me tons of free money for doing nothing, yet it forces you to work two and three jobs just to get out of debt.

On top of that, I have the nerve to sit up here and talk about it and—for some it will seem—to rub it in. Most rich people are considerate enough to shut their mouths and pretend they're struggling too. To get on TV talking about, "I got this on sale."

I didn't really have anyone to talk about it with. I knew a lot of the kids I had gone to school with were in a similar situation but we never discussed our family money, except in really strange ways like how broke we were and how those other rich people were so spoiled/lucky. Our judgments of them betrayed our own underlying shame.

And let's talk right now about motives. As soon as you bring up philanthropy, people want to talk about motives. "Is he doing this for the right reasons or is he just doing this to make himself feel good?" Well, let me tell you, I am definitely doing this to make myself feel good and—call me crazy—I believe doing what you feel good about is one of the right reasons.

Yes, I have the luxury to give my money away because I know I'm going to inherit more later in life. But don't come to me with this bullshit, "Oh, it's easy for you to give away your money because you're gonna inherit more later." If it's so easy, how come more rich people aren't doing it? How come Americans only give 2% to charity across the board, whether they are rich, poor, or middle-class? I usually give away 20–30% of my income every year. But I just got my first steady job, so this year, if you throw in the book, I'll probably be giving away more like 50%.

Hell no, I'm not some kind of saint who has taken a vow of poverty and is now sitting in judgment of you or anyone else's money decisions. But be aware, it's easy to criticize my actions when you don't have much money. If you were in my situation, who's to say you'd be any different from 99% of other rich people who keep it all for themselves. Or if they do give it away, it's to big colleges, big arts, big religion, or big service, supporting bureaucratic institutions that maintain systemic problems by treating symptoms and obscuring root causes.

Which brings me to the next very selfish reason for my philanthropy. I have a political agenda and my philanthropic "generosity" plus my sense of strategy gives me more philanthropic power to change the world than people with 50 times my income.

The deeper reason why I give away my money is because I love the world. Because I'm grateful to be alive at all. Because I'm scared about where we're headed. Because we owe it to our great-grandchildren. Because we owe it to the millions of years of evolution it took to get us here. And to everyone before us who fought to change history and make things as good as they are now. Because I know how to change history and I know it takes money. Because I get more joy out of making

---

William Upski Wimsatt is a social entrepreneur, political activist, and author of *Bomb the Suburbs* and *No More Prisons*. He has also written for the *Chicago Tribune* and *Vibe*.

things better for everyone than I get out of making things materially better for myself. Because I know how to make and spend money on myself. It's boring. There's no challenge in it. And no love in it. I love helping good things happen, and supporting people I believe in. Especially people and organizations that have NO money put into them by traditional foundations and charities. I'm not talking about your everyday charities like diabetes or your college(s) that already have multi-million dollar budgets set up to fight for them.

They're new.

They don't exist yet.

They're like diabetes in 1921, the year before they extracted insulin.

They're like your college the year before it was founded.

Don't get me wrong. My father has juvenile diabetes. And I love my college too. But the money supporting the Juvenile Diabetes Foundation, and my college is already so big, their fundraising operations so effective, that giving my money to them is a drop in the bucket.

For the organizing efforts I want to support, every dollar is like a seed, helping not only to create a new kind of organization, but an organization that will be copied and that decades from now will establish new fields of work. It is the most strategic way possible to change the course of history, and the most unpopular because it's so high-risk. . . .

THE MOST EFFECTIVE THING YOU EVER DO

. . . What if we could double the number of cool rich people who are funding social change from say five hundred to a thousand? Then we could double the number of organizers on the street, lawyers in the court rooms, lobbyists in Congress. Double the number of investigative reporters. There are so many people who want to do progressive work who can't because there aren't enough activist jobs. People come out of law school to become environmental lawyers and they end up having to defend corporations because they have to pay off their student loans. Environmental groups can't afford to hire them. The same goes for radical artists and journalists, forced to get jobs in advertising and public relations.

Five hundred more cool rich people could change all that.

Five hundred cool rich people could change the political landscape of this country.

Now don't get me wrong. I'm not saying philanthropy will solve all our problems, especially not the way 99% of it is done now. I'm not saying cool rich people are any more important or worthy than any other people. Poor people are made to feel like they aren't worth anything and that's wrong. I don't want to feed into that by focusing on rich people for a while. We need billions of people from billions of backgrounds trying billions of strategies to save this planet. It's just that every serious effort to change things takes people with money who understand how to support a movement. All these naive college or punk or hip-hop revolutionaries talking about, "Fuck that. I don't know any rich people and if I do they're assholes and anyway, I don't need their money." I only have one thing to say. Wait until your community center gets shut down. Wait until your broke grassroots genius friends start burning out because they have to do menial shit all day because they don't have the time or capital to make their dreams come true.

Consider these statistics. There are about five million millionaire households in the U.S. That's approximately one out of every 50 people. So, if you are a social person (not a hermit) and you are not currently serving a life sentence in prison, then chances are you will have the opportunity at some point in your life to get to know a number of people who are, at the very least, millionaires. Most of the time you will not know they are millionaires. Half of the time, millionaires don't even realize they are millionaires. My parents didn't realize they were. People usually have their assets tied up in many different forms such as houses, trusts, mutual funds, stocks, bonds and retirement accounts.

Less than 1% of all charitable giving ends up in the hands of people who are working to change the system. As Teresa Odendahl has pointed out in her ironically titled book *Charity Begins at Home,* contrary to popular belief, most charity money does not go to help poor children help themselves. The vast majority of money goes to big churches, big colleges, big hospitals, big arts and social service organizations which either directly cater to privileged people, or which treat the symptoms of social ills without ever addressing the root causes. . . .

Over the next 50 years, the upper-classes of my generation stand to inherit or earn the greatest personal fortune in history, while the lower classes both here and internationally will continue slipping deeper into poverty and debt.

That's where the Cool Rich Kids Movement comes in. Actually there isn't much of a "Cool Rich Kids Movement." That's just what I call the loose-knit network of maybe 100 of us young people with wealth who are in conversation with each other, and who support each other in taking small but significant actions. We are asking our parents to teach us about money. We are helping our families make responsible decisions about investments. Some of us are getting on the boards of family foundations or helping our families to start them. We introduce each other to amazing grassroots people to break the isolation of wealth. We are just in the process of getting organized. We had our first conference last spring, sponsored by the Third Wave Foundation in New York. More are planned.

My goal is to get more young people with wealth in on the conversation. With five million millionaires in the U.S., even if we only spoke to the coolest 1% of all millionaire kids, that's still 50,000 people!

One half of the money I give away every year goes directly to grassroots youth activist organizations that I have a relationship with. (No, I don't make them kiss up to me. I just give it to them, thank them for their hard work and if they feel funny about it, I remind them that the only reason I have the money in the first place is because I've been so privileged and so many people have helped me. So it wasn't really "my" money

to begin with. Oftentimes I have to *insist* that people take my money. We've all had so many bad experiences.)

The other half of my money I donate to organizing people with wealth.

That may seem strange at first.

Why give money to people who already have wealth?

From all my experience with grassroots organizations, I believe that organizing people with wealth is the most powerful work I do. And paradoxically, it is some of the hardest work to fundraise for because everybody including rich people thinks, "Why give rich people more money?" And that's why only a few dozen people in America have the job of helping rich people figure out how to come to terms with and do cool things with their money.

I think we need more of those people in the world.

So recently, I've changed my focus in a big way.

I joined the board of More Than Money. I am helping to start the Active Element Foundation, which is the first foundation that will specifically work with young donors on funding grassroots youth activism. And I'm also helping to start the Self-Education Foundation, which will tap successful people who either didn't like school or who dropped out to fund self-education resource centers which will support poor kids to take learning into their own hands. I am helping to organize a series of conferences around the country for young people with wealth, put on by The Third Wave Foundation and the Comfort Zone. . . .

I believe the most effective thing I do for the world every year is to buy gift subscriptions of *More Than Money Journal* for my privileged friends and to keep a ready supply of *Money Talks. So Can We.* for every cool young person I meet who has money. This is the most effective action I do. Any other possible action I could do, one cool rich person could hire ten more people to take my place.

But there's very little room in our culture to talk about having money and funding renegade work. Most rich people be like, "See you later." And most grassroots people be like, "It's easy for you because

PERSONAL ACCOUNT

Where Are You From?

As a freshman at a predominantly white private college, I was confronted with a number of unusual situations. I was extremely young for a college freshman (I was sixteen), I was African American, and I was placed in upper-division courses, because of my academic background. So being accepted and fitting in were crucial to me.

I was enrolled in a course, political thought, with approximately thirty other students, mostly juniors and seniors who had taken courses with this professor before. I was the only African American in the class. During introductions for the first class, he never got around to letting me speak, even though he went alphabetically on the list (my last name begins with a "C"). Later, I began to be aware of his exclusion of me from class discussion.

By the third class, I guess he felt there was no longer any way he could avoid speaking to me. He asked me a few questions about myself—where I was from, what high school had I attended, and what was my major. His questions began to seem like a personal attack, and then finally he asked, "Why are you here?" "Where are you from?" I was quite taken aback by his line of questioning, when one of the upperclassmen (a white man) responded for me. "She's a freshman, Dr. B. Any more questions?" That guy became one of my closest friends. We have maintained contact ever since college. His response to Dr. B. totally changed the professor's way of treating me.

C.C.

you're rich." There's resentment either way. People who aren't rich can play a huge role supporting us. So many of my friends who aren't wealthy act like, "Ha ha ha, going to your rich kids conference." That's not going to make me want to talk to you. If you are truly down to change the world, don't try to score points by alienating your rich friends with snide remarks. If you take the time to truly understand us and support us as people, more than likely, we will do the same for you. Rich people don't choose to be born rich any more than poor people choose to be born poor. The sickness of our society damages us each in different and complicated ways, and we sometimes forget that rich people get damaged too. Not just in a mocking way, like, "Oh, they're so spoiled." But in a real way. One of the most common ways privileged people get damaged is that we are taught not to talk about money. We put a wall around ourselves, and then it is hard for us to be honest with people who aren't rich. This makes us cold and creates a vicious cycle of not trusting and not sharing ourselves or our money.

There are only a few of us out here doing this work, which is why I have been thrust into the spotlight. It's a little ridiculous actually that I am speaking for rich kids when I haven't even inherited my money yet. But there was a deafening silence and someone needed to come out here and give us a bold public voice. Do you have any cool rich friends who may be looking for people in similar situations to talk to?

Hint: You do.

Please please please pass this along to them.

It just might be the most effective thing you ever do.

DISCUSSION QUESTIONS

1. Would you rather have money or a large number of supporters if you were seeking to create social change?

2. How much money would you want to have before you considered giving away some of it to create social change?

READING 54

Uprooting Racism: How White People Can Work for Racial Justice

Paul Kivel

"THANK YOU FOR BEING ANGRY"

A person of color who is angry about discrimination or harassment is doing us a service. That person is pointing out something wrong, something that contradicts the ideals of equality set forth in our Declaration of Independence and Bill of Rights. That person is bringing our attention to a problem that needs solving, a wrong that needs righting. We could convey our appreciation by saying, "Thank you, your anger has helped me see what's not right here." What keeps us from responding in this way?

Anger is a scary emotion in our society. In mainstream white culture we are taught to be polite, never to raise our voices, to be reasonable and to keep calm. People who are demonstrative of their feelings are discounted and ridiculed. We are told by parents just to obey "because I said so." We are told by bosses, religious leaders and professional authorities not to challenge what they say, "or else" (or else you'll be fired, go to hell, be treated as "crazy"). When we do get angry we learn to stuff it, mutter under our breath and go away. We are taught to turn our anger inward in self-destructive behaviors. If we are men we are taught to take out our frustrations on someone weaker and smaller than we are.

When we have seen someone expressing anger, it has often been a person with power who was abusing us or someone else physically, verbally or emotionally. We were hurt, scared or possibly confused. Most of us can remember a time from our youth when a parent, teacher, coach, boss or other adult was yelling at us abusively. It made us afraid when those around us became angry. It made us afraid of our own anger.

A similar response is triggered when a person of color gets angry at us about racism. We become scared, guilty, embarrassed, confused and we fear everything is falling apart and we might get hurt. If the angry person would just calm down, or go away, we could get back to the big, happy family feeling.

Relationships between people of color and whites often begin as friendly and polite. We may be pleased that we know and like a person from another cultural group. We may be pleased that they like us. We are encouraged because despite our fears, it seems that it may be possible for people from different cultures to get along together. The friendships may confirm our feelings that we are different from other white people.

But then the person of color gets angry. Perhaps they are angry about something we do or say. Perhaps they are angry about a comment or action by someone else, or about racism in general. We may back off in response, fearing that the relationship is falling apart. We aren't liked anymore. We've been found out to be racist. For a person of color, this may be a time of hope that the relationship can become more intimate and honest. The anger may be an attempt to test the depths and possibilities of the friendship. They may be open about their feelings, to see how safe we are, hoping that we will not desert them. Or the anger may be a more assertive attempt to break through our complacency to address some core assumptions, beliefs or actions.

Many white people have been taught to see anger and conflict as a sign of failure. They may instead be signs that we're becoming more honest, dealing with the real differences and problems in our lives. If it is not safe enough to argue, disagree, express anger and struggle with each other what kind of relationship can it be?

Paul Kivel is a social justice educator, activist, writer, trainer, and speaker on men's issues.

We could say, "Thank you for pointing out the racism because I want to know whenever it is occurring." Or, "I appreciate your honesty. Let's see what we can do about this situation." More likely we get scared and disappear, or become defensive and counterattack. In any case, we don't focus on the root of the problem, and the racism goes unattended.

When people of color are angry about racism it is legitimate anger. It is not their oversensitivity, but our lack of sensitivity, that causes this communication gap. They are vulnerable to the abuse of racism every day. They are experts on it. White society, and most of us individually, rarely notice racism.

It is the anger and actions of people of color that call our attention to the injustice of racism. Sometimes that anger is from an individual person of color who is talking to us. At other times it is the rage of an entire community protesting, bringing legal action or burning down buildings. Such anger and action is almost always a last resort, a desperate attempt to get our attention when all else fails.

It is tremendously draining, costly and personally devastating for people of color to have to rage about racism. They often end up losing their friends, their livelihoods, even their lives. Rather than attacking them for their anger, we need to ask ourselves how many layers of complacency, ignorance, collusion, privilege and misinformation have we put into place for it to take so much outrage to get our attention?

The 1965 riots in Watts, as never before, brought our attention to the ravages of racism on the African-American population living there. In 1968 a national report by the Kerner Commission warned us of the dangers of not addressing racial problems. Yet in 1992, when there were new uprisings in Los Angeles, we focused again on the anger of African Americans, on containing that anger, protecting property and controlling the community, rather than on solving the problems that cause poverty, unemployment, crime and high drop-out rates. As soon as the anger was contained, we turned our attention elsewhere and left the underlying problems unaddressed.

The only way to break this cycle of rage is for us to seriously address the sources of the anger, the causes of the problems. And in order to do that, we need to talk about racism directly with each other.

BEING A STRONG WHITE ALLY

What kind of active support does a strong white ally provide? People of color that I have talked with over the years have been remarkably consistent in describing the kinds of support they need from white allies. The following list is compiled from their statements at workshops I have facilitated. The focus here is on personal qualities and interpersonal relationships. More active interventions are discussed in the next part of [this discussion].

What people of color want from white allies:

"Respect"
"Find out about us"
"Don't take over"
"Provide information"
"Resources"
"Money"
"Take risks"
"Don't take it personally"
"Understanding"
"Teach your children about racism"
"Speak up"
"Don't be scared by my anger"
"Support"
"Listen"
"Don't make assumptions"
"Stand by my side"
"Don't assume you know what's best for me"
"Your body on the line"
"Make mistakes"
"Honesty"
"Talk to other white people"
"Interrupt jokes and comments"
"Don't ask me to speak for my people"

BASIC TACTICS

Every situation is different and calls for critical thinking about how to make a difference. Taking the statements above into account, I have compiled some general guidelines.

1. *Assume racism is everywhere, every day.* Just as economics influences everything we do, just as our gender and gender politics influence everything we do, assume that racism is affecting whatever is going on. We assume this because it's true, and because one of the privileges of being white is not having to see or deal with racism all the time. We have to learn to see the effect that racism has. Notice who speaks, what is said, how things are done and described. Notice who isn't present. Notice code words for race, and the implications of the policies, patterns and comments that are being expressed. You already notice the skin color of everyone you meet and interact with—now notice what difference it makes.

2. *Notice who is the center of attention and who is the center of power.* Racism works by directing violence and blame toward people of color and consolidating power and privilege for white people.

3. *Notice how racism is denied, minimized and justified.*

4. *Understand and learn from the history of whiteness and racism.* Notice how racism has changed over time and how it has subverted or resisted challenges. Study the tactics that have worked effectively against it.

5. *Understand the connections between racism, economic issues, sexism and other forms of injustice.*

6. *Take a stand against injustice.* Take risks. It is scary, difficult, risky and may bring up many feelings, but ultimately it is the only healthy and moral human thing to do. Intervene in situations where racism is being passed on.

7. *Be strategic.* Decide what is important to challenge and what's not. Think about strategy in particular situations. Attack the source of power.

8. *Don't confuse a battle with the war.* Behind particular incidents and interactions are larger patterns. Racism is flexible and adaptable. There will be gains and losses in the struggle for justice and equality.

9. *Don't call names or be personally abusive.* Since power is often defined as power over others— the ability to abuse or control people—it is easy to become abusive ourselves. However, we usually end up abusing people who have less power than we do because it is less dangerous. Attacking people doesn't address the systemic nature of racism and inequality.

10. *Support the leadership of people of color.* Do this consistently, but not uncritically.

11. *Don't do it alone.* You will not end racism by yourself. We can do it if we work together. Build support, establish networks, work with already established groups.

12. *Talk with your children and other young people about racism.*

IT'S NOT JUST A JOKE

"Let me tell you about the Chinaman who . . . " What do you do when someone starts to tell a joke which you think is likely to be a racial put-down? What do you do if the racial nature of the joke is only apparent at the punchline? How do you respond to a comment which contains a racial stereotype?

Interrupting racist comments can be scary because we risk turning the attack or anger toward us. We are sometimes accused of dampening the mood, being too serious or too sensitive. We may be ridiculed for being friends of the _____. People may think we're arrogant or trying to be politically correct. They may try to get back at us for embarrassing them. If you're in an environment where any of this could happen, then you know that it is not only not safe for you, it's even more unsafe for people of color.

People tell jokes and make comments sometimes out of ignorance, but usually knowing at some level that the comment puts down someone else and creates a collusion between the speaker and the listener. The joketeller is claiming that we're normal, intelligent and sane, and others are not. The effect is to exclude someone or some group of people from the group, to make it a little (or a lot) more unsafe for them to be there. Furthermore, by objectifying someone, it makes it that much easier for the next person to tell a joke, make a comment or take stronger action against any member of the objectified group.

The reverse is also true. Interrupting such behavior makes it less safe to harass or discriminate, and more safe for the intended targets of the abuse. Doing nothing is tacit approval and collusion with the abuse. There is no neutral stance. If someone is being attacked, even by a joke or teasing, there are no innocent bystanders.

As a white person you can play a powerful role in such a situation. When a person of color protests against being put down in an atmosphere where they are already disrespected, they are often discounted as well. You, as a white person interrupting verbal abuse, may be listened to and heeded because it breaks the collusion from other white people that was expected by the abuser. If a person of color speaks up first then you can support them by stating why you think it is right to challenge the comments. In either case, your intervention as a white person challenging racist comments is important and often effective.

What can you actually say in the presence of derogatory comments? There are no right or wrong answers. The more you do it the better you get. Even if it doesn't come off as you intended, you will influence others to be more sensitive and you will model the courage and integrity to interrupt verbal abuse. Following are suggestions for where to start.

If you can tell at the beginning that a joke is likely to be offensive or involves stereotypes and putdowns, you can say something like, "I don't want to hear a joke or story that reinforces stereotypes or puts down a group of people." Or, "Please stop right there. It sounds like your story is going to make fun of a group of people and I don't want to hear about it." Or, "I don't like humor that makes it unsafe for

people here." Or, "I don't want to hear a joke that asks us to laugh at someone else's expense." There are many ways to say something appropriate without attacking or being offensive yourself.

Using "I" statements should be an important part of your strategy. Rather than attacking someone, it is stronger to state how you feel, what you want. Other people may still become defensive, but there is more opportunity for them to hear what you have to say if you word it as an "I" statement.

Often you don't know the story is offensive until the punchline. Or you just are not sure what you're hearing, but it makes you uncomfortable. It is appropriate to say afterwards that the joke was inappropriate because . . . , or the story was offensive because . . . , or it made you feel uncomfortable because . . . Trust your feelings about it!

In any of these interactions you may need to explain further why stories based on stereotypes reinforce abuse, and why jokes and comments that put people down are offensive. Rather than calling someone racist, or writing someone off, interrupting abuse is a way to do public education. It is a way to put what you know about racial stereotypes and abuse into action to stop them.

Often a person telling a racial joke is defensive about being called on the racism and may argue or defend themselves. You don't have to prove anything, although a good discussion of the issues is a great way to do more education. It's now up to the other person to think about your comments and to decide what to do. Everyone nearby will have heard you make a clear, direct statement challenging verbal abuse. Calling people's attention to something they assumed was innocent makes them more sensitive in the future and encourages them to stop and think about what they say about others.

Some of the other kinds of reactions you can expect are:

"It's only a joke." "It may 'only' be a joke but it is at someone's expense. It creates an environment that is less safe for the person or group being joked about. Abuse is not a joke."

"I didn't mean any harm." "I'm sure you didn't. But you should understand the harm that results even if you didn't mean it, and change what you say."

"Is this some kind of thought patrol?" "No, people can think whatever they want to. But we are responsible for what we say in public. A verbal attack is like any other kind of attack, it hurts the person attacked. Unless you intentionally want to hurt someone, you should not tell jokes or stories like this."

"This joke was told to me by a member of that group." "It really makes no difference who tells it. If it is offensive then it shouldn't be told. It is sad but true that some of us put down our own racial or ethnic group. That doesn't make it okay or less hurtful."

Sometimes the speaker will try to isolate you by saying that everyone else likes the story, everyone else laughed at the joke. At that point you might want to turn to the others and ask them if they like hearing jokes that are derogatory, do they like stories that attack people?

Sometimes the joke or derogatory comment will be made by a member of the racial group the comment is about. They may believe negative stereotypes about their racial group, they may want to separate themselves from others like themselves, or they may have accepted the racial norms of white peers in order to be accepted. In this situation it is more appropriate, and probably more effective, to talk to that person separately and express your concerns about how comments reinforce stereotypes and make the environment unsafe.

Speaking out makes a difference. Even a defensive speaker will think about what you said and probably speak more carefully in the future. I have found that when I respond to jokes or comments, other people come up to me afterwards and say they are glad I said something because the comments bothered them too but they didn't know what to say. Many of us stand around, uneasy but hesitant to intervene. By speaking out we model effective intervention and encourage other people to do the same. We set a tone for being active rather than passive, challenging racism rather than colluding with it.

The response to your intervention also lets you know whether the abusive comments are intentional or unintentional, malicious or not. It will give you information about whether the speaker is willing to take responsibility for the effects words have on others. We all have a lot to learn about how racism hurts people. We need to move on from our mistakes, wiser from the process. No one should be trashed.

If the speaker persists in making racially abusive jokes or comments, then further challenge will only result in arguments and fights. People around them need to take the steps necessary to protect themselves from abuse. You may need to think of other tactics to create a safe and respectful environment, including talking with peers to develop a plan for dealing with this person, or talking with a supervisor.

If you are in a climate where people are being put down, teased or made the butt of jokes based on their race, gender, sexual orientation, age or any other factor, you should investigate whether other forms of abuse such as sexual harassment or racial discrimination are occurring as well. Jokes and verbal abuse are obviously not the most important forms that racism takes. However, we all have the right to live, work and socialize in environments free from verbal and emotional harassment. In order to create contexts where white people and people of color can work together to challenge more fundamental forms of racism, we need to be able to talk to each other about the ways that we talk to each other.

DISCUSSION QUESTIONS

1. When is anger about racism appropriate?
2. What are some of the contradictions between the American ideals of equality and reality?

READING 55

I/Me/Mine—Intersectional Identities as Negotiated Minefields

Shuddhabrata Sengupta

Identities can occasionally be weapons of mass destruction (lite). They can be invading armies and besieged cities. They can be maps waiting to be redrawn. Or a people, anticipating measures of "freedom" and "occupation" to come their way from an armored vehicle, or a cluster bomb, or depleted uranium.

To speak of identities in times of war and in the aftermath of war is to be compelled to recognize how certain methods of identification—the ascription of citizenship to a subject of a nation-state, for instance—also automatically confers on the being so described partisanship vis-à-vis one or the other forces engaged in the battle. The same could be said of religious or ethnic identity, or color, and in some cases of gender, and the battlefields that lie on the terrain within and between these categories. Let me sketch a few scenarios for you, to make all my dilemmas when talking about identities explicit.

Are you the internationally recognized and feted artist or academic woman of color who considers herself to be more oppressed than the working-class Caucasian woman in prison—let's say a blonde Bosnian Muslim immigrant sex worker who happens to have charges of manslaughter against her for killing her abusive Jamaican pimp? Here, the index of oppression is melanin, not life.

Are you a Caucasian, which translates as "black" in Russia?

Or are you the African American man in prison who considers himself to be less oppressed, because he is a man, than the African American woman on the street, whom he is happy to call a "ho"?

Shuddhabrata Sengupta is a media practitioner, filmmaker, and writer with the Raqs Media Collective and one of the initiators of the Sarai Media Lab. His work involves textual explorations of aesthetics, surveillance, and cyberculture.

Are you the African American GI in Iraq, sucked into a war by the poverty draft at home and face to face with the anger of a subject population that considers you to be the brutal enforcer of an occupying army that possesses the greatest number of weapons of mass destruction on earth? In combat fatigues, and under camouflage striping, white shades into dark, and dark can pale to white.

Are you the white working-class woman, perhaps a single mother, who is herself a victim of insidious sexism within the military and within working-class subcultures, who nevertheless becomes a willing enforcer of the apparatus of humiliation in the Abu Ghraib prison?

Are you the South Asian illegal alien in New York who washes dishes in a restaurant, is hoping to be a taxi driver, and really wishes he could be a Chinese grocer on the make?

Are you the recently arrived, already battered, non-English-speaking Indian or Pakistani "passport bride" caught between her aggressive husband, notions of community honor, shame, and the (amended) marriage fraud provisions of the 1952 Immigration and Naturalization Act of the United States?

Are you the Palestinian teenager throwing rocks at an Israeli military bulldozer who wishes he were a black rap artist from the Bronx with a Jewish record producer?

Are you the Iraqi woman, relieved that Saddam Hussein is no more, angry about U.S. bombs landing in her neighborhood, worried about the calls for the veil that emanate from Shiite clerics asserting their long oppressed identities by demanding a Shiite Islamic state in Iraq, and equally worried about having been "liberated" from a dictator only to be delivered as a subject to a convicted fraudster,[1] all in the name of her freedom, her honor, and her dignity as an Iraqi?

Are you the rich Indian racist who thinks that white women were made white in order for him to harass them on the streets of New Delhi? Are you the British exchange student of Nigerian origin in an Indian city who can't find a room to rent because of her color and who listens patiently to stories about how Indians suffer racism in the city where she grew up?

Are you one of the 15 million Bangladeshi illegal immigrants whom the Indian government now plans to identify and deport? Have you given thought to how you might change your accent, or your name, or adjust a few facts in your biography, and tell your children a few stories so that they don't let slip that you walked across the border when the police, accompanied by ethnographers, come knocking on your shack in New Delhi for an interview? Can you exchange one biography of oppression for another that might be more suitable for survival under the present circumstances?

Are you the anti-Semitic black Muslim descendent of slaves? Are you the racist Jewish granddaughter of concentration camp survivors? Are you the white supremacist descendent of refugees from the potato famine in Ireland? Are you the Hindu fundamentalist who has fantasies of raping Muslim women and who will defend the honor of his sister with an automatic weapon? Are you the Kashmiri Muslim woman suicide bomber with a sharp memory of being raped by an Indian army major when you were a teenager?

Is what you call your identity a weapon, a shield, a fortress, a battering ram, an unexploded land mine? The trouble with the deployment of identities as means of offense or defense is that, given a change in the equations of violence in any instance, which may have to do with anything from local politics to broader geopolitical crosscurrents, the victim very quickly becomes the oppressor. And so the idealist builder of Zion becomes a tyrant. Yesterday's Kurdish peshmarga (guerrilla fighter), forgotten by the world, becomes today's policeman for an occupying power because of the way the cartographic dice happen to be loaded at present. The players in the game may change; the Kurd may well go back up the mountain, fleeing like he had to the last time Saddam Hussein gassed him with helicopters that were bought with the help of today's "liberators."

The history of the twentieth century bears witness to the fact that the project of national liberation has inevitably turned the dream of freedom into the nightmare of refugee and prison camps and exile. The victims have changed; the rules haven't. And the assertion of the identity of an oppressed people becomes the excuse for silencing any question about the networks of power and privilege within the community.

As someone carrying an Indian passport, I am only too keenly aware that the rhetoric of nationalism and anticolonialism, a constituent of the chimera of what an Indian identity is seen to be, is the currency that enables the Indian state to act exactly as brutally as any colonial or imperial power within the borders of the republic. I do not doubt that colonialism was brutal, but I see colonialism as the instance by which a network of oppression stretched across the world. The white convict in Australia, the East Indian indentured worker in Trinidad, the pauperized peasant in Bihar, and the dispossessed African pastoralist were as much at the receiving end of violence as local landed elites—native princes, rubber plantation owners, administrators, and policemen of all colors—were perpetuators of that violence. I long to be able to recover what I call the history and buried memory of the detritus of empire that enables me to see the flow and network of power in structures and institutions that, though they may on occasion take on the patina of race and color, were just as able to discard it when it suited their purpose. Sometimes they could do both at once, as in the upper-class railway carriages in India during British rule, which were always desegregated so that the Indian prince, no matter how dark, could drink gin and tonic with the English colonist, and the second- and third-class carriages, which were often segregated so that the Irish subaltern could always be kept at arm's length from the Indian sepoy, cootie, or pilgrim.

Once you position or foreground a particular circumstance of victimhood, it enables a scotoma, an inability to see oneself as anything other than a victim, and this, if anything, propels and unleashes the greatest violence. And so it is that the United States can disperse depleted uranium in faraway lands because Americans have been persuaded that 9/11, a tragedy for the whole world like any tragedy (be it the violence in Kashmir, or Afghanistan, or Palestine, or Rwanda, or Vietnam), comes to be seen as the special, particular tragedy of the American people and thereby the launching pad for the exclusive claim to the righteous use of force on their behalf by the U.S. government.

It is only when we examine identities as fields of intersection and therefore always of contestation that we can imagine possibilities other than the binaries of "Are you with the besieged dictator or are you with the invading army?" It is possible to be neither. Or in the case of another example, "Are you critical of patriarchy within the African American community and of racism in the United States?" or "Can you be critical of patriarchy in the minority Muslim community in India and be critical at the same time of the anti-Muslim prejudices of Hindu fundamentalists?" It is possible to be both. And can you break your silences about being neither, in the first instance, and about being both in the latter two instances? Or will you choose to voice one opposition and be silent about another because of fears of betrayal, of letting who you are in one sense be held against who you are in another? Being neither in the first instance and being both in the second are concomitant to our admitting to our identities as force fields of different kinds of motivations, of different and sometimes conflicting intersections, of varied yet interlinked trajectories and histories of power and powerlessness.

Kimberle Williams Crenshaw puts this quite succinctly in her essay "Mapping the Margins: Inter-sectionality, Identity Politics, and Violence against Women of Color" (1991) when she says, and I quote:

> Among the most troubling political consequences of the failure of antiracist and feminist discourses to address the intersections of racism and patriarchy is the fact that, to the extent they forward the interest of people of color and "women," respectively, one analysis often implicitly denies the validity of the other. The failure of feminism to interrogate race means that the resistance strategies of feminism will often replicate and reinforce the subordination of people of color, and the failure of antiracism to interrogate patriarchy means that antiracism will frequently reproduce the subordination of women. These mutual elisions present a particularly difficult political dilemma for women of color. Adopting either analysis constitutes a denial of a fundamental dimension of our subordination and works to preclude the development of a political discourse that more fully empowers women of color.

A call center worker in a suburb of Delhi, the city where I live, performs a Californian accent as she pursues a loan defaulter in a poor Los Angeles neighborhood on the telephone. She threatens and cajoles him. She scares him, gets underneath his skin, because she is scared that he won't agree to pay and that this will translate as a cut in her salary. Latitudes away from him, she has a window open on her computer telling her about the weather in his backyard, his credit history, his employment record, his prison record. Her skin is darker than his, but her voice is trained to be whiter on the phone. Her night is his day. She is a remote agent with a talent for impersonation in the information-technology-enabled industry in India. She never gets paid extra for the long hours she puts in. He was laid off a few months ago and hasn't been able to sort himself out, which is why she is calling him on behalf of the company she works for. He lives in a third-world neighborhood in a first-world city; she works in a free trade zone in a third-world country. The army of the government that rules him is busy with shock and awe; the army of the government that rules her is always prepared to go to war on her behalf. She wants a green card; he wants credit. They both want out. Neither knows the other as anything other than as case and agent. The conversation between them is a denial of their realities and an assertion of many identities, each with their truths, all at once.

Identities are minefields, and the mines have been lain by armies that have forgotten the map. The arsenal is familiar; it's just that we don't know which mine (as in "weapon" and as in "first-person possessive singular personal pronoun") will claim which part of me. I negotiate them at my peril, never very sure about what I am stepping on and which aspect of my beings will blow up in my face. . . .

An understanding of the networked nature of the contemporary world and of the history of this world will help us understand that there are crosscutting histories of oppression and violence, that no one is innocent, and that all of us are implicated somewhere in our histories or in the histories of our ancestors as victims and as aggressors. If you take, for instance, the Middle East, it is easy to blame the current mess on the shortsighted policies of European colonialism. While the latter dynamic is to a large extent totally true, European colonialism in the Middle East has a comparatively recent history. We forget, for instance, that it was immediately preceded by the no less lethal achievement of the Islamic Ottoman Empire, which, right up to the closing of the first decade of the twentieth century, underlay by its many vexations the further complexities that the enterprise of competing European colonialisms was due to unleash. A vulgar Eurocentric view of history would not even recognize the Ottoman project or the Islamicate achievement as worthy of consideration and would mistakenly consider itself (Europe) to be the harbinger of "civilization and urbanity" in the Arab and Islamic world. But a counter-Eurocentric or even a specifically Turkic Islamist project, one that seeks to invert Eurocentrism, would no doubt either neglect to mention that a non-European power had a pretty lethal record of colonialism, even in fairly recent times, or romanticize the Ottoman achievement in terms of its tolerance, its catholicity, and so on—all of which, of course, have some basis in truth.

The understanding of the dynamics of power versus powerlessness, however, lies in taking account of both the interweaving of the histories of the Ottoman and European enterprises and their many internal contradictions. Consequently, looking for this interwovenness as well as acknowledging the gaps—those spaces of incommensurability that make it difficult to speak in binaries of Ottoman versus European, or black versus white—is a project of vastly different epistemological challenges to the projects that dominate the current scene and tend to oversimplify these histories. Just as parallel lines meet and intersect when one moves from Euclidean two-dimensional geometry to non-Euclidean three-dimensional geometry, so too an entirely different vision of the same realities becomes contingent on how one chooses to see. . . .

DISCUSSION QUESTIONS

1. How are identities fields of intersection?
2. What impact did British colonialism have on Indian identity?

NOTE

1. Convicted fraudster here refers to Ahmed Husain Chalabi. Chalabi, an Iraqi politician, belongs to the Shia community and is associated with the Iraqi National Congress (INC). One of the key figures to emerge in the political scenario of post-Saddam Hussein Iraq, Chalabi was a favorite of his Pentagon backers and occupied a prominent position in the new Iraqi regime. He fell from grace in August 2004 when corruption charges against him resurfaced but was reinducted into the interim Iraqi authority as a deputy prime minister in April 2005. In 1992 he was sentenced in absentia by a Jordanian court to twenty-two years in prison with hard labor for bank fraud after the 1990 collapse of Petra Bank, which he had founded in 1977. Although he has always maintained that the case was a plot to frame him by Baghdad, the issue was revisited later when the State Department raised questions about the INC's accounting practices.

REFERENCES

Crenshaw, Kimberle Williams. 1991. "Mapping the Margins: Intersectionality, Identity Politics, and Violence against Women of Color." http://www.hsph.harvard.edu/Organizations/healthnet/WoC/feminisms/crenshaw.html.

CREDITS

Timothy Beneke, "Proving Manhood" from *Proving Manhood: Reflections on Men and Sexism*, pp. 35–48. Copyright © 1997. Reprinted with the permission of the author.

Po Bronson and Ashley Merryman, "See Baby Discriminate" from *Newsweek* (September 14, 2009). Copyright © 2009 by Newsweek, Inc. All rights reserved. Used by permission and protected by the Copyright Laws of the United States. The printing, copying, redistribution, or retransmission of the Material without express written permission is prohibited.

James H. Carr and Nandinee K. Kutty, from "The New Imperative for Equality" in *Segregation: The Rising Costs for America*, edited by James H. Carr and Nandinee K. Kutty. Copyright © 2008 by Routledge. Reprinted with the permission of Routledge/Taylor & Francis Books, Inc.

Jeanine Cogan, "Influencing Public Policy" from *Everyday Activism: A Handbook for Lesbian, Gay, and Bisexual People and Their Allies*, edited by Michael R. Stevenson and Jeanine C. Cogan. Copyright © 2003 by Routledge. Reprinted with the permission of Routledge/Taylor & Francis Books, Inc.

Gail Collins, "Lilly's Big Day" from *The New York Times* (January 29, 2009). Copyright © 2009 by The New York Times Company. All rights reserved. Used by permission and protected by the Copyright Laws of the United States. The printing, copying, redistribution, or retransmission of the Material without express written permission is prohibited.

Patricia Hill Collins, "It's All in the Family: Intersection of Gender, Race, and Nation" from *Hypatia, Journal of Feminist Philosophy* 13(3) (Summer 1998): 62–82. Copyright © 1998 by Hypatia, Inc. Reprinted by permission of John Wiley & Sons, Inc.

F. James Davis, "Who is Black? One Nation's Definition" (originally titled "The Nation's Rule") from *Who is Black? One Nation's Definition*. Copyright © 1991 by The Pennsylvania State University. Reprinted with the permission of The Pennsylvania State University Press.

Alice Dreger, "Where's the Rulebook for Sex Verification?" from *The New York Times* (August 22, 2009). Copyright ©

2009 by The New York Times Company. All rights reserved. Used by permission and protected by the Copyright Laws of the United States. The printing, copying, redistribution, or retransmission of the Material without express written permission is prohibited.

The Economist, "More or less equal?" from *The Economist* 390 (April 4, 2009). Copyright © 2009 by The Economist. Reprinted by permission.

Paula England, excerpts from "The Gendered Revolution: Stalled and Uneven" from *Gender & Society* 24, no 2 (April 2010). Copyright © 2010 by Sociologists for Women in Society. Reprinted by permission of Sage Publications, Ltd.

Yen Le Espiritu, "Asian American Panethnicity: Contemporary National and Transnational Possibilities" from *Not Just Black and White: Historical and Contemporary Perspectives on Immigration, Race, and Ethnicity in the United States*, edited by Nancy Foner and George M. Frederickson. Copyright © 2004 by Russell Sage Foundation. Reprinted with the permission of Russell Sage Foundation, 112 East 64th Street, New York, NY 10021.

Ruth Frankenberg, "Whiteness as an 'Unmarked' Cultural Category" from *White Women, Race Matters*. Copyright © 1993 by the Regents of the University of Minnesota. Reprinted with the permission of the author and the University of Minnesota Press.

Sally French, "'Can You See the Rainbow?' The Roots of Denial" from John Swain, Vic Finkelstein, Sally French, and Mike Oliver (eds.), *Disabling Barriers—Enabling Environments*. Copyright © 1993 by The Open University. Reprinted by permission of Sage Publications, Ltd.

Reproduced by permission of SAGE Publications, London, Los Angeles, New Delhi, and Singapore.

Rosemarie Garland-Thomson, "Disability and Representation" from the Conference on Disability Studies and the University (Emory University, March 5–7, 2004) in *PMLA* 120.2 (2005): 522–527. Copyright © 2005. Reprinted by permission of The Modern Language Association of America.

Eva Marie Garroutte, excerpt from *Real Indians: Identity and the Survival of Native America*. Copyright © 2003 by The

Malcolm Gladwell, excerpt from Chapter Three, common no "from" *Blink: The Power of Thinking Without Thinking.* Copyright © 2005 by Malcolm Gladwell. Reprinted by permission of Little Brown and Company.

Laura Hamilton and Elizabeth A. Armstrong, excerpts from "Gendered Sexuality in Young Adulthood: Double Binds and Flawed Options" from *Gender & Society* 23, no. 5 (2009). Copyright © 2009 by Sociologists for Women in Society. Reprinted by permission of Little Brown and Company.

Cheryl Harris and Devon Carbado, "Loot or Find: Fact or Frame?" from *After the Storm: Black Intellectuals Explore the Meaning of Hurricane Katrina*, edited by David Dante Troutt. Copyright © 2006. Reprinted with the permission of the authors.

John Hockenberry, "Public Transit" (excerpts from Public Transportation) from *Moving Violations.* Copyright © 1995 by John Hockenberry. Reprinted with the permission of Hyperion. All rights reserved.

Allan Johnson, "What Can We Do?: Becoming Part of the Solution" from *Privilege, Power, and Difference.* Copyright © 2001. Reprinted with the permission of The McGraw-Hill Companies, Inc.

Diana Kendall, "Framing Class: Media Representations of Wealth and Poverty in America" from *Framing Class: Media Representations of Wealth and Poverty in America.* Copyright © 2005 by Rowman & Littlefield Publishing Group. Reprinted with permission.

Randall Kennedy, "The Protean N-Word" from *Nigger: The Strange Career of a Troublesome Word.* Copyright © 2002 by Randall Kennedy. Used by permission of Pantheon Books, a division of Random House, Inc.

Michael S. Kimmel, excerpt from *The Gendered Society, Second Edition.* Copyright © 2000, 2004 by Michael S. Kimmel. Reprinted with the permission of Oxford University Press, Ltd.

Paul Kivel, excerpt from *Uprooting Racism: How White People Can Work for Racial Justice.* Copyright © 1996 by Paul Kivel. Reprinted with the permission of New Society Publishers.

Roger N. Lancaster, excerpts from "The Biology of the Homosexual" from *The Trouble With Nature: Sex in Science and Popular Culture.* Copyright © 2003 by the Regents of the University of California. Reprinted by permission of the University of California Press.

Harlan Lane, excerpts from "Ethnicity, Ethics, and the Deaf-World" from *Journal of Deaf Studies and Deaf Education* 10.3 (Summer 2005). Copyright © 2005. Reprinted with the permission of Oxford University Press, Ltd.

Annette Lareau and Elliot B. Weininger, excerpts from "Class and the Transition to Adulthood" from *Social Class: How Does it Work?*, edited by Annette Lareau and Dalton Conley. Copyright © 2008 by the Russell Sage Foundation. Reprinted with the permission of Russell Sage Foundation, 112 East 64th Street, New York, NY 10021.

John Larew, "Why Are Droves of Unqualified, Unprepared Kids Getting into Our Colleges? Because Their Dads Are Alumni" from *The Washington Monthly* (June 1991). Copyright © 1991 The Washington Monthly Company. Reprinted with the permission of *The Washington Monthly*, 1611 Connecticut Avenue, N.W., Washington, DC 20009.

Jennifer Lee and Frank D. Bean, "America's Changing Color Lines: Immigration, Race/Ethnicity, and Multiracial Identification" from *Annual Review of Sociology* 39 (Annual 2004). Reprinted with the permission of Annual Review of Sociology and Frank D. Bean.

Meizhu Lui, Barbara J. Robles, Betsy Leondar-Wright, Rose M. Brewer, and Rebecca Adamson, excerpts from "Land Rich, Dirt Poor: Challenges to Asset Building in Native America" from *The Color of Wealth: The Story Behind the U.S. Racial Wealth Divide.* Copyright © 2006 by United for a Fair Economy. Reprinted by permission of The New Press, www.thenewpress.com.

Jelita McLeod, "Everybody's Ethnic Enigma" from *The Washington Post* (July 7, 2003). Copyright © 2003 by Jelita McLeod. Reprinted with the permission of the author.

Stephen J. McNamee and Robert K. Miller, Jr., excerpt from "The Silver Spoon: Inheritance and the Staggered Start" from *The Meritocracy Myth,* Second Edition. Copyright © 2009. Reprinted with the permission of Rowman & Littlefield Publishing Group. This piece contains excerpts from Lawrence Mishel, Jared Bernstein, and Sylvia Allegretto, *The State of Working America: 2006/2007.* Copyright © 2007 by Cornell University. Used by permission of the publisher, Cornell University Press.

Liza Mundy, "A World of Their Own" from *The Washington Post* (March 31, 2002). Copyright © 2002 by The Washington Post. All rights reserved. Used by permission and protected by the Copyright Laws of the United States. The printing, copying, redistribution, or retransmission of the Material without express written permission is prohibited.

Michael Oliver, excerpts from "Disability Definitions: The Politics of Meaning" and "The Cultural Production of Impairment and Disability" from *The Politics of Disablement: A Sociological Approach.* Copyright © 1990 by Michael Oliver. Reprinted with the permission of Palgrave Macmillan.

Beth Fay Omansky, "Not Blind Enough: Living in the Borderland Called Legal Blindness." Reprinted with permission.

Sarah Faragalla, "Hair"

Ruth C. Feldsberg, "What's in a Name?"

Niah Grimes, "A Loaded Vacation"

Francisco Hernandez, "Just Something You Did as a Man"

Eric Jackson, "My Strategies"

Anthony McNeill, "Just Like My Mama Said"

Julia Morgenstern, "The Price of Nonconformity"

Isabelle Nguyen, "Let Me Work for It!"

Tim Norton, "He Hit Her"

Rose B. Pascarell, "That Moment of Visibility"

Sherri H. Pereira, "I Thought My Race Was Invisible"

Heather L. Shaw, "Invisibly Disabled"

Hoorie I. Siddique, "I Am a Pakistani Woman"

Photo Credits:

page 1, John A. Rizzo/Getty Images

page 193, © Bob Daemmrich/The Image Works

page 331, Hisham F. Ibrahim/Getty Images

page 353, (top) Royalty-Free/CORBIS, (bottom) RubberBall Productions

page 453, (top) AP Photo/Dave Martin, (bottom) Chris Graythen/Getty Images

page 479, David Young-Wolff/PhotoEdit

INDEX

A page number followed by *b* indicates a box; one followed by *fig* indicates an illustrated figure; one followed by *n* indicates a note; one followed by *t* indicates a table.

Aaron, Henry, 465
Abberley, P., 170, 185
ableism/disableism, **5**
Aboufadel, K., 339
Accordian Crimes (Proulx), 224
achieved identities, 223
ACLU, *Loving* case and, 448*n*
Active Element Foundation, 510
ACT UP, 272
Adams, G.R., 34
Adams, P.L., 226
Adamson, Rebecca, 428
ADAPT (Americans Disabled for Accessible Public Transit), 490–491
admiration framing, 450
adulthood, social class and transition to, 292–301
advocacy, effectiveness of, 498–499
advocacy organizations, 493
affirmative action, 378*n*
    Gratz v. Bollinger et al. on, 412–413
    privilege of "legacy" admission versus, 305–310
African Americans
    as aggregate classification, 16–17
    ascribed identity of, 223
    assumption of criminality of, 196–198
    census enumeration of, 61–62
    characterization of women, 36*n*
    defining black identity, 56–63
    "double consciousness" experience, 94*n*, **208**, 333
    health issues and inequalities, 302, 303–304
    one-drop rule, 62–63
    personal accounts on being, 66, 356, 511

post-Civil War status, 51
racial identity/self-esteem and, 216–217
racializing "the fag," 283–285
residential segregation and, 335–336
Social Security and, 250
stereotypes of, 336–337
stigmatized status of, 213
African Diaspora, 51, 54
African societies, social/ethnic identities of, 47
Afrocentrism, 51–52
Agassi, Andre, 107
Agassiz, Louis, 344, 347
aggregated categories, **14**–17
Ahab, 475
Ahearn, F.L., 222
Ahmad, Muneer I., 113*n*
Aid to Families with Dependent Children and Temporary Assistance to Needy Families, 38*n*
Alba, R.D., 95–97, 216
Alexander the Great, 46–47
Al-Fayed, Dodi, 108
Alger, Horatio, 371
Al-Hajebi, Sumaya, 111
Ali, Lorraine, 112*n*
Ali, Muhammad, 254, 255, 468
Alien Land Law, 15*n*
Allegretto, Sylvia, 138–140
Allen, K.R., 164
Allen, T.E., 186
Allen, Theodore, 50, 54
Allison, P., 381
Allport, G., 35
ally/allies, **486**–487
    being a strong ally, 513
Almagauer, T., 278

Alsadir, Nuar, 226
alternative family structures, 222
Alvarez, Sandy, 90
Amanpour, Christiane, 458
Amaro, H., 158
Amendment XI (1794), 418
Amendment XIII (1865), 390
Amendment XIV (1868), 390–391, 408, 412
Amendment XIX (1920), 417*n*
Amendment XV (1870), 391
American Anthropological Association (AAA), 24
American Apartheid (Massey and Denton), 423
American Breeders Association, 187
American identity, privileges of, 249–250
American Indians. *See* Native Americans
Americanization (Talbot), 94*n*
American Journal of Public Health, 303
American Psychological Association (APA), 500
American Sign Language (ASL), 171, 173
American Sociological Association (ASA), 24
Americans with Disabilities Act (1990), 16, 410, 474, 491
Amnesty International, 39
Andersen, M.L., 246
Anderson, C.W., 480, 481
Andre, J., 336
androcentrism, **18**
Androgen Insensitivity Syndrome, 123
anger, 485
Angier, Natalie, 156*n*, 157*n*
Anka, Paul, 107

anti-enticement laws, 422
Anti-intellectualism in American Life (Hofstadter), 371
Antiterrorism and Effective Death Penalty Act, 200
Anwar, Gabrielle, 107
A Part, Yet Apart (Shankar), 79
Apostle, R., 341
Arab Americans. *See* Middle Eastern Americans/immigrants
Archer, B., 26
Armstrong, Elizabeth A., 4, 259, 262, 382
Arnett, J.J., 224, 232
Arocha, J., 237
Arrow, K., 29
arts, of an ethnic group, 179
Asayesh, Gelareh, 109
ascribed identitites, 223
Ashe, Arthur, 210–211
Asian American Panethnicity: Bridging Institutions and Identities (Espiritu), 75
Asian Americans. *See also* pan-Asianism; panethnicity
    class diversification, 78
    ethnic diversification, 77–79
    generational diversification, 78
    Harvard admissions and, 309
    increasing population of, 95
    intermarriage among, 83
    model-minority myth of, 337, 370–377
    personal account on being, 88, 377
    politics of, 77
    post-1965 immigration and, 75
    stereotypes of, 336
Asian Americans United, 83
Asian Immigrant Women Advocates, 84
Asian Pacific Americans, 78
Atencia, D.P., 200
Athens, Greece, 47
Athey, J.L., 222
Atkinson, D.R., 215
Auberger, Michael, 490, 491
aversive racism, **340**
Ayatollah Khomeini, 107
Azores, T., 81

Bacon's Rebellion, 50
Bahan, B., 177, 179, 186, 187
Bahr, H.M., 58

Bailey, B.H., 229
Bailey, J.M., 159, 161
Bailey, Michael J., 147–150, 156*n*, 378
Baker, J.B., 279
Bakke, Alan, 307, 408–410
Bakke, University of California Board of Regents v. (1978), 307, 407–410, 418*n*
Baldwin, James, 62
Baldwin, J.D., 164
Baldwin, J.I., 164
Balkany, T., 186
Banaji, Mahzarin, 351, 354
Bane, M.J., 38
Bankston, C.L., III, 99
Barnes, C., 5
Barnes, J., 83, 85*n*
Barnett, Doug, 149
Baron, R.A., 36
Barrett, D., 170
Barrett, Todd, 156*n*
Barringer, Herbert, 373
Bart, P., 160
Barth, F., 178, 180
Bartky, Sandra, 215
Bartky, S.L., 287
base roll, 69
Basow, Susan, 32, 36*n*
Bates, N.A., 238
"battle of the sexes," 260
Baumeister, Roy F., 159–162
Baynton, B., 182–184
Bazile, Leon M., 445, 446
Bean, Frank D., 21, 94, 95, 97, 98, 100, 101, 336
Beckham, David, 135
Begley, S., 23
behavior norms, in ethnic group, 178
Belanger, M., 225, 227
Bell, Alexander Graham, 187
Bell, A.P., 161
Bell, B., 481–483
Bell, Buck v. (1927), 346
Bell, Catherine, 107
Bell, D., 239
The Bell Curve (Herrnstein and Murray), 53
Bellow, Saul, 254
Bem, S.L., 288
Beneke, Timothy, 212, 254
Bennett, C., 97
Bennett, C.E., 83, 85*n*, 98

Berger, P.L., 35, 481
Bergmann, B., 379
Berlant, L., 18
Bernstein, Jared, 138–140
Bernstein, Richard, 491
Berry, B., 58, 60
Berry, Lorraine, 222, 224, 230
Berscheid, E., 163
Best, 284
Bhutto, Benazir, 367
Bianchi, S., 380
bias, preparation for, 361–362
bicultural competence, 221
BiDil, 24–25
Bigler, Rebecca, 358, 360, 361
bilingual competence, 221
bilingual education, 401–402
Binet, Alfred, 345
bin Laden, Osama, 107
Binnie, C., 177
birth control, 378
bisexuality, 25, 288
Black Codes, 369, 370*n*
"A Black Feminist Statement" (Combahee River Collective), 252*n*
Blackmun, Harris, 307
Blackmun, Harry A., 406, 407, 409
Blacks. *See* African Americans
Blasi, Gary, 461*n*
Blauner, R., 21, 77
Blinde, E.M., 163
blindness
    borderline, 323–329
    experience with being legally blind, 323–329
    job discrimination and, 322–323
    personal accounts of being blind, 317–320
Blind Tom, 475
blood quantum, 66–72, 430
"blood ties," 248–249
Bloom, D.E., 229
blue-collar jobs, women in, 383–385, 386*n*
Blumstein, P., 160, 162, 289
Boardman, J., 47, 55*n*
Board of Education, Brown v. (1954), 396, 400–401, 407, 443, 455
Boas, Franz, 347
Bobo, L., 95
Bobo, L.D., 340, 341
Bodziock, J., 348
Bogle, K.A., 259, 260

Bohan, J.S., 161
Bohannan, P., 56*n*
Bok, Derek, 305, 309
Bollinger et al, Gratz v. (2003), 412–413
Bollinger et al, Grutter v. (2003), 413–415
Bonacich, Edna, 80
Bonastia, C., 335
Bonilla-Silva, E., 21
borderline blindness, 323–329
Boswell, A. Ayres, 262
Bowen, Patricia, 92
Bowers v. Hardwick (1986), 405–407
Bowles, S., 29
Bowman, Joy, 362
Boy Scout Manual (1914), 255
Bracken, K., 238
Bradley, K., 379, 384, 385
Bradley, S.U., 159
Bradstreet, Anne, 475
"brain-drain," 374
Brandeis, Louis, 407
Brandon, P., 231
Brantlinger, P., 332
Brehony, Kathy, 290
Brennan, William J., Jr., 404, 407, 409
Brewer, Rose M., 428
Breyer, Stephen, 416
briefing memo, 495*b*
briefing sheet, 495*b*
Brodkin, K., 96
The Broken Cord (Dorris), 72
Bronson, Po, 214, 340, 356
Brooke, James, 122
Brooks, R. Garnett, 444
Brown, Claude, 468
Brown, C.R., 484–487
Brown, Henry B., 394
Brown, James, 468
Brown v. Board of Education (1954), 396, 400–401, 407, 443, 455
Buckley, Chris, 306
Buckley, G.L., 57
Buckley, William F., Jr., 306
Buck v . Bell (1927), 346
Budrys, Grace, 144
Bullard, D., 179
Bullough, B., 158
Bullough, V.L., 158
Burawoy, M., 80
Burke Act, 434
Burn, S.M., 277
Burstein, P., 378, 386*n*

Busch, Andrea M., 122
Bush, George H.W., 371
Butler, J., 285
Butler, Judith, 453*n*
Byne, W., 159
Byrd, Alex, 445
Byrd, Boyd, 444
Byrd, Laura, 445
Byrne, D., 36

Cable, Daniel M., 355*n*
Cainkar, Louise, 112*n*
California Gold Rush, 433
California v. Cazabon Band of Mission Indians (1987), 439
Callender, Heather, 330
Campanelli, P.C., 238
Campbell, J.C., 260
Campomanes, Oscar, 85*n*
Canny, N.P., 50
Canterbery, E. Ray, 141
Cantril, Hadley, 2
capitalist social class, 131
Carbado, Devon W., 453
Carr, James, 335, 418
Carter, T., 201
Carthage, 47
Cartwright, Samuel, 369
Cary, L., 194
Cass, V.C., 288
Cassidy, R.C., 95
Castro, A., 48
categorical definitions, 287
Catholic ethnics, 216*n*
Cayton, H.R., 95
Cazabon Band of Mission Indians, California v. (1987), 439
CDIB, 67
Cecil, Mireille M., 427
CEOs, 139, 354–355
Chadwick, B.A., 58
Chan, Jackie, 368
Chan, S., 82
Charity Begins at Home (Odendahl), 510
Charles, Kerwin, 140, 141
Charles, M., 379, 383–385
Charles, Prince of Wales, 108
Charles, Suzette, 57
Charlton, J., 37
Charo, R. Alta, 173
Chase, Cheryl, 125–128

Chase, Chevy, 466
Chavez, Linda, 456
Chenault, Kenneth, 355
Cheney, Richard, 131
Cheng, L., 81
Cheng, Lucie, 80
Cher, 107
Cherny, S.S., 157*n*
Chicago Transit Authority, 490
Chideya, Farai, 466
Child, I.L., 227
children
    of college alumni, 305–310
    communication with, about race, 361
    consumer culture and, 450, 452
    deaf child born of lesbian mothers, 171–177
    exposure to other races and cultures, 359
    health issues of white vs. African American, 302–303
    of immigrants, 222–229
    in-group preferences of, 358
    inherited wealth and quality of life, 142
    multiracial, 83
    racial attitudes of, 356–363
    surnames of, 382
Chin, Frank, 375
Chinese Americans, 77, 374, 375
Chinese Exclusion Act (1882), 342, 396
Cho, Margaret, 244
Cho, Sumi, 375
Christiansen, J.D., 187
citizenship
    Elk v. Wilkins on Native Americans and, 397–400
    Minor v. Happersett defining, 391–393
    Plessy v. Ferguson on equal protection of, 393–396
    privilege of national identity and, 249–250
    Yick Wo v. Hopkins on immigrants and, 396–397
Citizenship Schools, 482
City of Boston, Roberts v. (1849), 396
Civil Rights Act of 1964, 412
civil rights movement
    disabled movement and, 490–492
    Highlander Folk School and, 482
Civil Rights Project, 360

Civil War Amendments
 Amendment XIII (1865), 390
 Amendment XIV (1868), 390–391
 Amendment XV (1870), 391
Clark, K., 95
Clarke, Edward, 343, 344
class. *See* social class
class privilege, 202–203
Clausen, Jens, 155, 157*n*
Clinton, Bill, 38
Clinton, Hillary, 367
Close, Chuck, 476
coalitions, 493
cocaine use, 198–199
cochlear implant surgery, 186–187
Cochran, Willie, 492
Cockerham, William, 144, 145
code-switch, 221
coethnic identities, 229–230
Coffman, T.L., 339
Cogan, Jeanine, C., 492
Cohen, Bernard, 446
Cohen, Felix S., 73*n*
Cohen, M.N., 24, 346
Cohen, Richard, 366
Cohn, D., 12
Cole, S., 170
Coleman, E., 288
Coleman, J., 228
college. *See* higher education
Collier, Jane, 252*n*
Collier, John, 435
Collins, Chuck, 141
Collins, Gail, 489
Collins, Patricia Hill, 4, 94*n*, 212, 245
color blindness, 454–456
Columbus, Christopher, 430
communication
 about race, 361
 natural-law language used during,
  333–335
community feeling, in ethnic group,
 178
Compass, Eddie, 459
Compson, Benjy, 475
compulsive masculinity
 creativity and, 258*n*
 description and categories of, 254
 sexism and, 257
 in the United States, 254–257
Congenital Adrenal Hyperplasia, 123
Congress
 contacting members of, 496*b*,
  497–498

creating support for an unknown
 issue, 499
congressional staff, 494
 educating, 500
 establishing relationships with,
  499–500
Conley, T.D., 158, 159
Connah, G., 47
Connecticut, Palko v. (1937), 406
Connell, R.W., 119, 122, 280
Connerly, Ward, 367, 456
Conrad, E., 51
Conrad, P., 181, 184, 186, 344
consensus framing, 450
constituent letter, 498*b*
constituents, 493
constructionist orientation, 2–7
consumer debt, 450
consumerism, 449
Coolio, 469
"cool pose," 284
Cool Rich Kids Movement, 510
Coontz, Stephanie, 250, 252*n*
Cooper, Anderson, 461*n*
Cooper, Eulalie, 489
Copeland, Peter, 156*n*, 157*n*
Copenhaver-Johnson, Jeane, 362
Copernicus, 506
Corbett, K., 281
Cordero-Guzmán, H., 238
core identity, 269
Cotter, D.A., 378, 380, 381, 383, 384,
 386
covering of disfavored identities,
 108–110
crack cocaine, 198–199
Crenshaw, Kimberle Williams,
 248, 519
crime
 assumption of white non-
  criminality, 198
 intraracial nature of, 196*n*
Cross, W.E., Jr., 214
cross-race collaboration, in Obama
 election, 364
cross-race relationships, 360–361
Crouch, B., 179
cultural homogenization, 93
cultural identity
 achieved and ascribed identities, 223
 ethos of reception, 225
 performing identity, 224–225
 social disparagement and academic
  outcomes, 227–229

social mirror, 225–227
 stage vs. context, 222–223
 sustained contact and, 223–224
culture, as learned behavior, 53
culture-specific knowledge, in ethnic
 group, 179
Curtin, P., 56*n*
customs, of ethnic group, 179

DaCosta, K., 98
Dalmage, H.M., 99
Daneshi, A., 186
Daniels, R., 76
Darden, Christopher, 466
Dartmouth Review, 309
Dartmouth University, 305
Darwin, Charles, 342, 343
Dauber, Michele Landis, 460
David, Worth, 305
Davidson, B., 47
Davis, Angela, 84, 252*n*
Davis, A.Y., 252
Davis, D.B., 49
Davis, D.S., 182
Davis, F. James, 21, 33, 56, 99, 100, 205
Davis, John, 62
Davis, K., 97
Davis, Katherine, 162
Davis, Lennard, 183
Davis, Rebecca Harding, 475
Dawes Act of 1887, 69, 434
Dawood, K., 161
deafness
 cochlear implant surgery, 186–187
 deaf child born of lesbian mothers,
  171–177
 deaf eugenics today, 188
 Deaf-World/hearing world
  boundaries, 181*t*
 ethnicity, ethics and, 177–189
Deaf-World, 21
 as disability group, 181–184
 oppression of, 182–183
 reasons to reject disability label,
  184–189
 risk for the deaf child, 185–187
 shared struggle for rights, 183–184
 survival risk for, 187–188
Dean, Howard, 461*n*
Deaux, K., 163
de Bango, G., 238
DeBerry, Jarvis, 468
debt, consumer, 450

Defense of Marriage Act, 275
Degler, C.H., 341, 343–347
de jure segregation, 33
De la Fuente, A., 237
de la Garza, R.O., 15
DeLamater, J., 164
DeLap, Jan, 172
Delgado, Richard, 105, 112*n*
Delshad, Jimmy, 110
DeMaio, T.J., 238
D'Emilio, John, 324
Demo, D.H., 164
Dennis, J., 19
Denton, N., 95, 228, 238
Denton, Nancy, 423
deportation, 200–201
The Descent of Man (Darwin), 342
desegregation, 360
    of male-oriented jobs, 383–384, 386
Deshen, S., 185
DeStefano, Ricci v. (2009), 415–417
Devine, P.G., 339
DeVos, George, 223, 224, 227, 228, 230
Dew-Becker, Ian, 134, 135
Diamant, A.L., 160
Diamond, L.M., 161, 164
Diana, Princess of Wales, 108
dichotomania, 19*n*
dichotomizing, **19**–21
    class, 28–29
    disability, 30–31
    race, 19–21
    sex, 30
    sexual orientation, 25–28
Dickens, Charles, 117
difference
    challenging social constructions of,
        484–487
    conceptions of, 2
    meaning and ideology of, 332–348
differential socialization, 115
differential undercount, **11**
di Leonardo, Micaela, 156*n*
disability
    definition of, **5**
    dichotomization and, 30–31
    in humanities scholarship, 475
    importance of definitions related to,
        167–168
    in national culture, 475
    personal account of, 171
    politics of meaning, 168–169
    reaction to relatively invisible
        disabilities, 207

representation of, 474–478
resymbolization of, 477–478
social and medical models of, 6
stigmatized status of, 213
structured account of impairment,
    169–170
studies, 475–476
survey of disabled adults, 168*t*, 169*t*
disability rights movement, 16, 474
    inspired by Rosa Parks, 490–492
disabled people
    on blindness, 317–320
    deafness, 171–177
    public transit, 310–317
    Tennessee v. Lane on discrimination
        against, 410–412
disaggregate, **15**
discredited and discreditable, **205**–210
discrimination
    audit studies and benefits of, 211
    blindness and job, 322–323
    against immigrants, 225
    income levels and, 381
    institutionalized, 239
    LGB protections against workplace,
        499
    natural-law language and, 334
    preparation-for-bias, 361–362
    racial attitudes of children and,
        356–363
    relationship to prejudice and
        stereotypes, 339–341
    reverse discrimination, 211–212
    segregation, 335
    against stigmatized people, 215–216
    white denial of, 368
Diverse Environment Theory, 359–360
Dixon, T.L., 198
DMX, 469
Doctorow, E.L., 471
Dominguez, V.R., 240*n*
Dorris, Michael, 72
double consciousness, 94*n*, **208,** 333
Douglas, William O., 402, 404
Douglass, Frederick, 59, 348
Dovidio, J.F., 34, 340
Downey, J.I., 161
Downie, A.B., 182
Doyal, L., 170
Dr. Dre, 469
Drake, S.C., 95
Dred Scott v. Sanford (1857), 334,
    389–390
Dreger, Alice, 30, 123, 186

Dreifus, C., 25
drugs, perceptions of white vs. black
    use of, 198–199
D'Souza, Dinesh, 306
Du Bois, W.E.B., 94*n*, 95, 208, 226,
    228, 232, 239, 333, 347, 480
Dubos, Rene, 31
Duchesneau, Sharon, 171–173
Dunn, J.L., 260
Dupas, Ralph, 60
Durlauf, S., 29
Duster, Troy, 25
Dyson, Michael Eric, 471

East Cleveland, Moore v. (1977), 406
Easton, Hosea, 464
Edelin, Ramona H., 8
Edin, K., 386*n*
Edmonston, B., 95, 98, 229
education. *See also* higher education
    Bakke decision on equitable, 307,
        407–410, 418*n*
    bilingual, 401–402
    Brown v. Board of Education on
        equal access to, 400–401
    of children of immigrants, 227–229
    high school drop-outs, 295
    housing and, 425
    Lau v. Nichols on discrimination in,
        401–403
    peer pressure to reject school,
        231–232
    *San Antonio School District v.
        Rodriguez* on funding, 403–405
    school diversity and cross-race
        relationships, 360–361
    social class and parental
        involvement in, 295–297
    social Darwinism opposing female
        access to, 343–344
    transition to adulthood and,
        292–301
effeminacy, 280
Eichen, E., 186
Eiesland, Nancy, 477
Eisenhart, M.A., 265
Eisenhower, Dwight D., 436
elected officials, organizing visits with,
    497*b*
Eleventh Amendment (1794), 418,
    418*n*
Elk, John, 398, 400
Elkins, James, 324

Elk v. Wilkins (1884), 334, 397–400
Elliot, D., 168
Elliott, A.J., 339
Ellis, A., 159
Ellis, Havelock, 158
Ellison, Tara S., 276
Emerson, John, 389
Emerson, Ralph Waldo, 475
Eminem, 280, 471
employment
  housing and, 425
  increased employment of women,
    379–381
  Ricci v. DeStefano on hiring of
    municipal workers, 415–417
  sex segregation of U.S. occupations,
    383–385, 383*f*
  women moving into "male jobs,"
    381–382, 384
emulation framing, 450
Engels, Friedrich, 332
England, P., 259, 380–382, 385
England, Paula, 378
Engle, Karen, 106, 112*n*
entitlement, **203**–204
Entman, R.M., 198
episodic framing, 450
Epstein, Cynthia Fuchs, 119, 122
Equal Employment Opportunity
  Commission, 386*n*
Equal Protection Clause, of
  Fourteenth Amendment, 408, 412
eradicationists, 469–470
Erickson, Ken, 260
Erikson, Erik, 222, 229
Ernest Martin Hopkins Institute, 309
Erting, C., 179–181
Eschbach, K., 98–100
Eshbaugh, E.M., 260
Espenshade, T., 225, 227
Espinal, Octavio N., 507
Espiritu, Yen Le, 15*n*, 16, 75, 77, 79,
  83, 84, 85*n*
essential identity, **27**
essentialist orientation, 2–7
ethnic affiliation, demonstration of,
  224–225
ethnic boundaries, 181
ethnic communities, 224
ethnic disidentification, 76
ethnic groups
  defined, **21**
  internal properties of, 178–181,
    178*t*

ethnic identity
  envy of, 216
  historical constructions of, 46–49
ethnicity
  classification mentality, 242,
    244–245
  deafness as, 178–181
  historical constructions of identity,
    46–49
  personal account on identifying
    with, 243–244
  and race defined, 21–31
ethos of reception
  academic achievement and, 227
  immigrant adaptation and,
    225, 227
Ettinger, M., 204
eugenics movement, 187–188,
  251–252, 345–346
Eurocentric, **18**
evolutionary change, 342–343
Ewing, Patricia, 124
executives, 354–355

Faderman, L., 4, 162
Fadiman, A., 224
"fag," adolescent use of term, 278–283
"fag discourse," 281
Fair Housing Act, 424
Fair Housing Amendments Act of
  1988, 424
Falicov, C.J., 230
families
  "blood ties" presumptions of,
    248–249
  economic and wealth issues of,
    250–251
  gender roles in, 120
  hierarchy within unity context of,
    246–248
  intersectionality paradigm and, 246
  meaning of home and, 248
  privilege of single-race, 201
  rights, obligations, and rules of,
    249–250
  traditional family ideal, 245–246
family values, 245, 246–247, 252
Faragalla, Sarah, 235
Farkas, G., 385
Farley, R., 95, 98
Faulkner, William, 475
Fausto-Sterling, Anne, 125, 156*n*
Feagin, Joe R., 145

Federal Housing Administration
  (FHA), 421, 423
federal identification policies
  aggregating and disaggregating,
    14–19
  creating categories of people,
    10–14
federal policy development, 492–494
  advocacy organizations and, 493
  coalitions and, 493
  congressional staff, 494
  constituents and, 493
  members of Congress and, 493–494
  policy maker lifestyle, 494–496
  writing an effective briefing memo,
    495*b*
  writing an effective briefing sheet/
    talking points, 495*b*
Fehr, B., 287
Feldman, S.S., 226
Feliciano, C., 336
femininity
  changing meanings of, over course
    of life, 115
  "emphasized," 119
  men and stigma of traits of,
    33–34, 36
  plural definitions of, 118–119
feminism
  family and gender oppression, 252*n*
  gender revolution, 378–386
  gender visibility for men/women,
    116–117
  labor and, 84
Ferguson, Plessy v. (1896), 19, 59, 334,
  393–396, 422
Fernandez, M., 97
Ferree, M.M., 386*n*
Fifteenth Amendment (1870), 391
Filipino Americans, 77, 80–81, 374
film, homosexual portrayal in, 271
Fine, H., 184
Fine, P., 184
Finkelstein, V., 182, 184
Firestein, B.A., 159
First Americans in the Arts (FAITA),
  68
Fiscella, Kevin, 303
Fishbein, H.D., 279
Fishman, J., 179
Fishman, Joshua, 180
Fitzsimmons, William, 305, 308, 309
Fix, M., 229
Flagg, B.J., 20

Flutie, Doug, 107
Fogarty, A.C.K., 259, 382
Folbre, N., 381
Foner, N., 96
Fong, R., 101
Foote, Donna, 156*n*
Forbes, Jack, 70
forced sterilization. *See* eugenics
     movement
Fordham, S., 230
Fortune, Percy, 444
Foucault, Michel, 126, 182, 276*n*
Fourteenth Amendment (1868),
     390–391
Fox, R., 158, 159
Foxworthy, Jeff, 451
Frank, 145
Frankenberg, Ruth, 18, 88, 214, 253*n*
Franks, Peter, 303
Fraser, G.R., 188
Fraser, N., 213
Frazier, E. Franklin, 347
Frazier, Joe, 254, 255
Freire, P., 227
Freire, Paulo, 481, 482, 484
French, M., 182
French, Marilyn, 341
French, Sally, 317, 324, 328
Freud, S., 281
Frey, Bruno S., 145
Friedman, R.C., 161
Frye, Marilyn, 332
Fu, V., 97
Fulker, D.W., 157*n*

Gabriela (women's organization), 84
Gaertner, Samuel, 340
Gaertner, S.L., 34
Gagnon, J.H., 160
Galbraith, John Kenneth, 142
Gale, William G., 143
Galileo, 506
Gallup, Inc., 202
gaming, 439
Gandhi, Mohandas K., 481, 504
Gandhi's paradox, **481,** 504–507
gangs
     as alternative family structure, 222
     negative social mirroring and, 226
Gans, H., 227
Gans, H.J., 95, 96
Garcia-Beaulieu, C., 380
Gardner, H., 221

Garland-Thomson, Rosemarie, 474
Garnets, L.D., 288
Garnets, Linda D., 26, 157
Garroutte, Eva Marie, 66
Gastman, B.R., 186
Gates, Henry Louis, 232
Gatewood, James V., 77–78, 81
Gaventa, J., 481
"gay," adolescent use of term, 279
gay and lesbian, as aggregate
     classification, 17
"gay brain" research, 147–148
"gay gene" study, 147, 150–156
gay men
     accusations of "flaunting" sexuality,
          202
     gendered homophobia, 278–281
     personal account of, 507
     sexual identity transformation of,
          269–276
gay movement, 272–273
"gay twins" survey, 147, 148–150
Gebhard, P.H., 289
Geers, A.E., 187
Gelareh, Asayesh, 113*n*
Gelb, S.A., 182
Gelman, David, 156*n*
gender
     behavior characteristics, 121*f*
     "deceptive distinctions" of, 119–120
     defined, **30**
     differences, meaning of mean
          differences of, 120–121
     egalitarianism, 379, 384
     essentialism, 379, 383–385
     family and oppression, 252*n*
     inequality, 114
     "interplanetary" theory of
          differences in, 113–114, 121
     intersexuality and, 124–129
     personal account of, 122
     privilege of, 250
     universal inequality related to, 114
     visibility, 116–117
gendered homophobia, 278–281
gendered sexuality in young adults
     study
     appeal of hookups and sexual
          double bind, 265–266
     contradictions between class/
          gender, 263–267
     gender beliefs, 261–263
     less privileged women and, 266
     method, 260–261

the relationship imperative,
     262–263
"slut" stigma, 261–262
gendered society, nature and nurture
     positions on, 114–115
gender identity, 453*n*
Gender Identity Disorder, 127, 280
gender revolution, 378–386
     devaluation of traditional female
          jobs/activities, 379–383
genealogical identity, 46
General Allotment Act of 1887, 69,
     434
genetic research, into homosexuality,
     147, 150–156
George, Jeff, 107
Georgia, Stanley v. (1969), 406, 407
Georgia, Worcester v. (1832), 432, 438
The German Ideology (Marx and
     Engels), 332
Gerson, Kathleen, 120, 123
Gerstle, G., 96, 97
ghettoization, 422, 424
Gibson, M.A., 231, 232
Gilbert, G.M., 339
Gilbertson, G., 97
Gilman, S., 38
Gingrich, Newt, 371
Gini coefficient, 134
Ginsburg, Ruth Bader, 416
Giordano, P.C., 259
Gitlin, T., 95
Giuliani, Rudy, 366
Gladwell, Malcolm, 156*n*, 340, 351
Glass, R.M., 186
"glass ceiling," 386*n*
GLBTQ acronym, 9
Glebocki, Louise, 90, 92
Glenn, N., 259, 260
global identity, 232
globalization, social inequalities and,
     134–135
Glunt, E.K., 207
Goddard, H.H., 345
Godolphin, F.R.B., 47, 55*n*
Goetz, Bernard, 311
Goffman, Erving, 34, 37, 108, 112*n*,
     119, 205, 207, 275*n*, 328, 474*n*
Goldberg, D.T., 247
Golden, C., 163
Goldin, C., 382
Gomez, C., 100
Gonsiorek, J., 158
Gonsoulin, T.P., 182, 184

Goodyear Tire and Rubber Company, 489
Gordon, Beth, 326
Gordon, L., 250
Gordon, M., 97
Gordon, M.M., 227
Gordon, Robert, 134, 135
Gornick, J.C., 381
Gould, S.J., 249, 334, 342, 344–346
Goyette, K., 98, 99
Gracia, J.J.E., 15
Graham, R., 55
Gramsci, Antonio, 333
Grant, Madison, 62
Gratz, Jennifer, 412
Gratz v. Bollinger et al (2003), 412–413
Graubard, Stephen, 371
Gray, Horace, 398
Gray, John, 122
Graythen, B. Chris, 454, 456
Great Migration (1920s), 347. *See also* immigration
Green, Raymond, 444
Greenwald, Anthony G., 351, 352
Greico, E.M., 95
Grello, C.M., 260
Greve, Michael, S., 375
Grimes, Niah, 66
Grisham, John, 471
Grusky, D.B., 383
Grutter, Barbara, 413
Grutter v. Bollinger et al (2003), 413–415
Guillory, Jean Gregoire, 60
guilt, 484–485
Gusfield, J., 181, 182, 184
Gute, G., 260
Guyll, M., 339
Gwaltney, J.L., 56

Hacker, Andrew, 466
Hagan, J., 238
Hagopian, Elaine C., 112*n*
Haines, D.W., 22, 338
hair, 235
Hall, People v. (1854), 19
Hall, Stuart, 246
Haller, Beth, 477
Haller, M.H., 251
halo effect, 135
Hamacher, Patrick, 412
Hamer, Dean, 26, 147, 150–153, 155, 156*n*, 157*n*

Hamilton, Laura, 259, 262, 382
Hammersmith, S.K., 161
Handlon, Melanie, 298, 301*n*
Haney Lopez, I.F., 100
Hapa Issues Forum (HIF), 83
Happersett, Minor v. (1875), 334, 391–393
Haraway, D., 253*n*
Hardwick, Bowers v. (1986), 405–407
Hardwick, Michael, 405, 407
Hardy, Thomas, 117
Hare, N., 208
Harlan, John M., 394, 395, 399
Harlem Renaissance (1920s), 347
Harper, M.S., 260
Harris, A., 168
Harris, Cheryl I., 453
Harris, D., 201
Harris, D.R., 99, 100
Harris, Edith, 491
Harris, M., 58
Harris-Britt, April, 361, 362
Harrison, R., 97
Harvard Crimson, 305
Harvard Immigration Project, 226
Harvard Longitudinal Immigrant Student Adaptation study, 228
Harvard University admissions, 305–310
Harvey, Robert, 492
Hassan, Umar Bin, 470
Hastie, William, 400
Hate Crimes Prevention Act, 494–495
Havens, John J., 141
Hawthorne, Nathaniel, 475
Hayano, D., 76
Hayek, Selma, 107
Hayes, A., 259
Hayton, Lennie, 58
Hazen, S.H., 214–217
health/health inequalities, 136
    comparing U.S. to international, 302
    consequences of, 301–302
    diseases of affluence, 303
    housing and, 425
    individual behaviors and, 144–145
    link between income and, 303
    link between social status and, 303–304
    nonmedical consequences of, 302–303
    occupational hazards to, 144
health insurance, 302

health professionals
    increasing numbers of women as, 381
    from Philippines, 81, 374
Hee, Suzanne, 78
hegemonic (or ruling) ideology, 333, **333**
height-salary study, 355
Heisey, William, 155, 157*n*
Helms, J.E., 215
Henshel, R.L., 3
Herbert, S., 231
Herek, G.M., 18, 158, 163, 202, 207
Hermsen, J.M., 378–381, 383, 384, 386
Herodotus, 47, 49, 55*n*
Herrera, E., 238
heteronormativity, **18**
heterosexism, 18
heterosexuality
    among women, 287
    dominance of, 270–271
    presumption of, 206
    privilege, 201–202
heterosexual questionnaire, 166
Heyl, Sherman, 26
hierarchies
    challenging the family, 252
    families, unity and, 246–248
    natural-law language and, 335–336
    privileges of national identity and gender, 250
Higginbotham, A. Leon, 442, 472
Higgins, P.C., 6
Higham, J., 227
high blood pressure, 303–304
higher education
    Grutter v. Bollinger et al on diversity of student body, 413–415
    legacy admissions to, 305–310
    needs-blind admissions, 308
    paradoxical nature of, 481
    personal account of black experience with, 511
    privilege and, 203
    race-based admissions to (*See* *Hopwood v. Texas* (1994); *Regents of the University of California v. Bakke* (1978))
    self-development imperative, 264
    women graduates of, 378
    women in "male" areas of study, 381–382
Highlander Folk School, 481–482
high school drop-outs, 295

Hill, Garnet, 442
Hill, L., 286
Hill, Raymond, 442
Hillary, Edmund, 317
Hilton, Paris, 448, 449
Hirsch, Arnold, 423
Hirschkop, Philip J., 445, 446
Hirschman, C., 98
Hirsh, C.E., 378, 382
Hispanics. *See* Latinos/Hispanics
history, of ethnic group, 179
Hitti, P., 48
Hockenberry, John, 6, 196, 310
Hoffman, E., 224
Hoffman, Marjorie, 92
Hoffmeister, 179
Hofstadter, Richard, 371
Holima, Mahmoud Abu, 313, 314
Holland, D.C., 265
Hollinger, D.A., 95
Holmes, Oliver Wendell, Jr., 346, 407
home, 248
*Home Girls: A Black Feminist
    Anthology* (Smith), 253*n*
homeless, media portrayal of,
    450–451
Home Owners Loan Corporation
    (HOLC), 421, 422–423
Homestead Act, 433
homicide, 303
homophobia, 18, 269–270
    adolescent males and, 277–285
    gendered, 278–281
    teen's personal experience of,
        281–283
homosexuality. *See also* gay men;
    lesbians
    biology of, 147–156
    Bowers v. Hardwick on sodomy and,
        405–407
    coming out, 288
    essentialist and constructionist
        perspectives of, 4–5
    German criminal codes penalizing,
        344
    personal account of, 507
    racializing, 283–285
    transformation of gay and lesbian
        life, 269–276
hooks, bell, 208, 449
hookups, 259–260, 265–266
Hopkins, Yick Wo v. (1886), 396–397
Hopwood v. Texas (1994), 410
Horgan, John, 157*n*

Horne, Lena, 57–58
Horsman, R., 50
Horton, Myles, 481, 482, 484
Hossfeld, K., 84
House Concurrent Resolution, 436
housing
    discrimination, 335, 418–426
    education and, 425
    health and, 425
    jobs and, 425
    social networks and, 426
Housing and Urban Development
    (HUD), 424
Houston, Charles, 400
Howells, William Dean, 471
Hu, Arthur, 309
Hu, Nan, 156*n*
Hu, Stella, 156*n*, 157*n*, 159
Hubbard, Ruth, 149, 156*n*, 157*n*
Hu-DeHart, Evelyn, 15, 81
Hughes, D., 188
Hughes, Langston, 92, 472
Hull, John, 324, 326–328
Hummer, R.A., 262
Humphrey, Dot, 91
Humphries, Tom, 177, 184
Hune, Shirley, 85*n*
Hunt, J., 5
Huntington, Samuel P., 112*n*
Hurricane Katrina
    "color-blind" frame applied to
        images of, 454–456
    photographic images following,
        453–454
    reality versus perceptions of,
        457–459
    responding to racial controversy
        over images of, 456–457
Hurst, Erik, 140, 141
Hurtado, Aida, 94*n*
Huygen, P.L., 186
Hyde, J.S., 163, 164, 287
hypersegregation, 419, 422
hypodescent, 58, 238, 240*n*

Ice Cube, 469, 471
Ice-T, 469
Ichioka, Y., 76
identity. *See also* cultural identity;
    sexual identity
    adolescents and, 223
    core identity, 269
    covering of disfavored, 108–110

evolution of, 65
    globalization and, 221
    historical constructions of, 46–49
    immigrants and (*See* identity
        pathways)
    invisible identities, 276
    lack of "racial designations" in early
        history, 48–49
    modern conception of human
        differences and, 49–51
    negotiating minefield of I/me/mine,
        517–520
    the non-problem of "mixed-race"
        people and, 52–53
identity development, by stigmatized
    people, 214–217
identity pathways
    coethnic identities, 229–230
    ethnic flight, 230
    gendered differences, 231–232
    transcultural identities, 230–231
ideologies
    description of, 332–333, 348
    hegemonic (or ruling), 333
    natural-law language describing,
        333–335
    social institutions and support of,
        341–348
    stereotypes used to convey, 336–341
    supported by science, 341–347
ideology, **332–333**
Ignatiev, Noel, 96, 113*n*, 239
I Grew Up Thinking I Was White
    (Asayesh), 109
"I Have a Dream" speech (King), 369
Illegal Immigration Reform and
    Immigrant Responsibility Act,
    200
Illiberal Education (D'Souza), 306
illness model of sexual orientation,
    158
immigrants
    coethnic identities, 229–230
    deportation of and federal
        immigration laws, 200–201
    ethnic disidentification and, 76
    ethnic flight, 230
    Filipinos' experience as, 80–81
    gendered differences, 231–232
    housing of, 422
    increasing numbers of, 221
    from India, 374
    nineteenth-century Asian, 76
    personal account of, 145, 235

immigrants (*Continued*)
    race, color, and adaptation of, 228
    second generation, 222
    stress of, 221–222
    top Asian countries sending, 78
    transcultural identities, 230–231
    Vietnamese experience as, 81–82
immigration
    "America-centric" nature of studies
      of, 76
    "brain-drain" and, 374
    globalization and, 221
    increasing multiracial identification
      due to, 94–96
    model-minority stereotypes and,
      337–339
    quota system, 338–339
Immigration Act (1924), 76
Immigration Act (1965), 80, 81
Immigration Restriction Act, 346
impairment, 5. *See also* disability
    social class and causes of, 170
Implicit Association Test (IAT),
    351–355
implicit bias, 455
"The Importance of Collecting Data
    and Doing Social Scientific
    Research on Race" (ASA), 24
income levels
    in "female" occupations, 381
    height-salary study, 355
    intergenerational mobility and,
      140–142, 141*t*
    link between health and, 303
    share of, and total net worth, 139*t*
Indian Americans (immigrants from
    India), 374
Indian Gaming Regulations Act
    (IGRA), 439
Indian New Deal, 435
Indian Removal Act (1830), 342,
    432–433
Indian Reorganization Act (1934), 435
individual merit, 29
inequality. *See also* health/health
    inequalities
    medical consequences of, 301–304
    role of public policies in creation
      of, 419–424
    in social class, 133–136
inheritance of wealth, 142–146
intelligence testing, 345
interethnic marriage, 83
intergenerational mobility, 140–142

intermarriage
    among Asian Americans, 83
    with conquered peoples, 46–47
    of deaf people, 187
    increasing multiracial identification
      due to, 95
    as political or economic strategy, 47
    in the United States, 97–98
interracial friendship, 357
interracial marriage
    Loving v. Virginia and legalization
      of, 442–446
    personal account of, 101
    rejection of state laws banning, 336
intersectionality
    contradictions between class and
      gender, 263–267
    definition of, 4
    equality and hierarchy context of,
      246–248
    of multiple statuses, 212–213
    negotiating minefield of I/me/mine,
      517–520
    scholarly analysis of, 245–246
    sexuality and Black women, 253*n*
intersex genital mutilation (IGM),
    126
Intersex Society of North America,
    125
intersexuality
    Cheryl Chase's experience with,
      125–127, 129
    clinical description of, 125–126
    identity politics and, 128–129
inversion model of sexual orientation,
    158–159
"involuntary minorities," 228
IQ (intelligence quotient) testing,
    345, 346
Iranians, 110
Isaacs, Julia, 140
Ivy League admissions, 305
Iwasaki, Naomi, 75
Iyer, P., 221

Jackson, Andrew, 432
Jackson, Eric, 244
Jackson, Jesse, 461*n*
Jackson, Kenneth T., 423
Jackson, R.M., 382
Jacobs, Bruce A., 470
Jacobs, D., 39
Jacobsen, M.F., 96

Jacobson, M., 239
Jacoby, T., 95, 97
Jaffee, S.R., 163, 287
Jalbert, Y., 186
James, Henry, 117
Jane Doe v. State of Louisiana (1983),
    60–61
Janus-faced nature of society, **481**
Japanese American Citizens League,
    378*n*
Japanese Americans, 375
    personal account on, 88
    U.S. census and, 77, 85*n*
Jargowsky, Paul A., 424
Jaynes, 422
Jay-Z, 469
Jenkins, A., 14
Jerry Lewis Principle, 491
"Jewishness," 110
Jewish women, 36*n*
"Jim Crow" laws and racism, 205,
    422, 455
job discrimination, 322–323
jobs. *See* employment
Jobs, Steve, 107
John, Elton, 280
Johnson, Allan, G., 481, 502
Johnson, Angela, 362, 363
Johnson, Harriet McBride, 478
Johnson, L.D., 199
Johnson, Lyndon Baines, 464,
    471, 472
Johnson, R.E., 179–181
Johnson, T.P., 99
Jones, Beverly, 411
Jones, J.M., 38
Jordan, I. King, 184
Jordan, Michael, 465
Judge, Timothy, 355
judicial interpretation. *See* specific
    legal case
Julien, I., 278

Kafka, Bob, 490, 491
Kahlenberg, R.D., 29
Kalmijn, M., 97, 98
Kamin, Leon J., 154, 157*n*
Kang, L.H.Y., 80, 84
Kanter, Rosabeth Moss,
    120, 123, 209
Karabel, Jerome, 306
Karen, David, 306
Karlins, M., 339

Kasem, Casy, 107
Katz, Bruce, 418
Katz, J., 27
Katz, J.N., 162
Katz, M., 37
Katz, M.B., 339
Katz, Phyllis, 359, 361
Katznelson, Ira, 426
Kazen, Freida, 91
Keats, B.J.B., 156n
Keck, David, 155, 157n
Kefalas, M., 386n
Kehily, M.J., 281
Kelley, R.D.G., 284
Kelsall, D.C., 186
Kendall, Diana, 448
Kennedy, Anthony M., 416
Kennedy, D., 186
Kennedy, Florynce, 208
Kennedy, Randall, 463
Kennedy, Robert, 445
Kerbo, Harold R., 140
Kessler, S.J., 30
Kia, Mansour, 113n
Kidman, Nicole, 450
Kilbourne, B.S., 381
Killebrew, Paul, 308
Kilpatrick, Kwame, 491, 492
Kim, C.J., 239
Kim, Claire, 375
Kimmel, D.C., 158, 288
Kimmel, Michael, 113, 122, 195, 255, 277, 341
King, D.L., 278
King, Martin Luther, Jr., 369, 418, 491
King, R.C., 85n
King, Rodney, 248
Kinsey, A.C., 289
Kinsey, Alfred, 26, 156n
kinship, in ethnic group, 179–180
kinship connections, 46
Kissam, E., 238
Kite, M.E., 163
Kitzinger, C., 160
Kivel, Paul, 487, 512
Kiviat, B., 8
Klinkenberg, D., 290
Kluegel, J., 341
Knight, Davis, 60
Knipfel, Jim, 326
Knoeber, Alfred, 347
Kocieniewski, D., 200
Kohn, Alfie, 123
Koppes, Clayton R., 112n

Korean Americans, 374
Korean War, 82
Korgen, K.O., 99, 100
Krafft-Ebing, R., 158
Kruglak, L., 157n
Kudlick, Catherine J., 326
Kunc, Norman, 487
Kuperberg, A., 379
Kurashige, S., 83, 84
Kutty, Nandinee, 335, 418, 425
Kuusisto, Stephen, 325, 326
Kwan, Michelle, 20

labor unions, 131
Laciner, Sadat, 104
Ladd, Paddy, 184
Lakoff, Robin Tolmach, 472
Lancaster, Roger, 4, 26, 147, 341
Lane, George, 411
Lane, Harlan, 21, 177–179, 182, 185–187
Lane, Tennessee v. (2004), 196
language
  of ethnic group, 179
  natural-law, **333**–335
Lapinsky, Tara, 20
Lareau, Annette, 142, 203, 292
Larew, John, 202, 305, 310n, 486
Last Poets, 470
Latinos/Hispanics
  celebration of African roots, 240
  characteristics of women, 36n
  housing and, 424
  increasing intermarriage among, 95
  increasing population of, 95
  racial associations, 240n
  racial profiling and, 199, 201
  stigmatized status of, 213
  U.S. race structure and, 235–240
  use of terms, 239, 240n
Laumann, E.O., 160, 290
Lau v. Nichols (1974), 401–403, 407
lawful permanent resident, **200**
"law of the excluded middle," 119
Le, C.H., 337
Lea, Homer, 255
learning disabilities, 6, 330, 427
Ledbetter, Lilly, 489, 490
Lee, Helen Jackson, 468
Lee, Jennifer, 21, 94, 95, 97, 100, 101, 336

Lee, S., 232
Lee, S.M., 97
legacy admissions, 305–310
legal blindness, 323–329
legal cases. *See* specific case
Legislative Reorganization Act, 494
legislators
  contacting, 496b, 497–498
  influencing, 496, 498–499
  organizing visits with elected officials, 497b
Le Grand, J., 170
Lehne, G., 277
Leigh, L.W., 187
Lennon, John, 471
Leondar-Wright, Betsy, 428
Lesbian Mental Health Survey, 288
lesbians
  accusations of "flaunting" sexuality, 202
  child born of deaf mothers, 171–177
  childhood influences on, 161–162
  conceptual issues of, 286–291
  personal account of, 276
  sexual identity transformation of, 269–276
  sociocultural influences on, 162–163
  stereotypes of, 36n
  within-person variation or change over time, 160–161
Lesbian Wellness Survey, 289
Lester, J., 201
"Letter from a Birmingham Jail" (King), 468
letter to the editor, 500b
Levanon, A., 381
LeVay, Simon, 147, 148, 152, 156n
Lever, J., 160
Levesque, J., 179
Levin, J., 35
Levine, H.G., 198
Levitt, P., 224
Lewis, Sinclair, 471
Lewontin, Richard C., 154, 157n
LGB rights, 499
LGBTQ acronym, 9
Li, Joshua, 309
Li, L., 157n
Li, Su, 378, 381
Liddy, G. Gordon, 255
Lieberman, L., 24
Lieberson, S., 96, 97

life expectancy, 136, 302. *See also*
   health/health inequalities
   differences in, between African
      Americans and whites, 303–304
   socioeconomic status and, 144–146
Liggio, L.P., 50
Lilly Ledbetter Fair Pay Act, 489
Lim, L.Y.C., 84
Lincoln, Robert, 57
Ling, S.H., 76
Linton, Simi, 326, 327
Linz, D., 198
literature, homosexual representation
   in, 280
Liu, J., 81
Liu, Lucy, 368
Liu, William, 77
Lochner v. New York (1905), 407
Loewen, J., 96, 101, 239
Lombardo, P., 345, 346
Longmore, M.A., 259
looping, **205**
Lopez, D., 16
Lopez, Jennifer, 368
López, N., 229, 231
Lorance, Patricia, 489
Lorde, Audre, 252*n*, 465
Lott, J., 77
Louie, J., 222, 225
Louima, Abner, 340
Loulan, J., 289, 290
Loving, Mildred, 442, 444
Loving, Richard, 442, 444
Loving v. Virginia (1967), 336,
   442–446
Lowe, L., 76, 77, 80, 84
Lowry Sullivan, C.B., 159
Ludwig, J., 336
Lugones, M., 237
Lui, Meizhu, 428
Lun, J., 339
Lyman, P., 281

Machado, Antonio, 481
Maden, S., 339
Madonna, 135
Maestes, M., 224, 225
Magnuson, Victoria, 156*n*
Mahan, Alfred T., 104, 112*n*
Mailer, Norman, 254, 255
Maira, S., 226
Major, Clarence, 468
Major Crimes Act of 1885, 73*n*

Majors, Richard, 284
Malcolm X, 465
Males, M., 39
Maloof family, 107
Mangum, C.S., Jr., 60
Manning, W.D., 259
Marcia, J., 223
Mare, R.D., 380
marked and unmarked statuses, **204**
Markowicz, H., 181
Marks, J., 52, 241*n*
Marks, Jonathan, 153, 157*n*
Marmot, Michael, 303, 304
Marquardt, E., 260
Marsalis, Branford, 465
Marshall, G., 2, 24
Marshall, John, 432, 438
Marshall, Thurgood, 54, 400, 407, 409,
   428, 472
Martin, C., 289
Martin, Casey, 410, 475
Martin, E., 238
Martin, J., 168, 169
Martin, P.Y., 262
Marx, Karl, 332
masculinity
   changing meanings of, over course
      of life, 115
   compulsive, 254–257
   current debate on, 117–118
   forces constructing, 258*n*
   personal accounts on sense of, 258
   plural definitions of, 118–119
Massey, Douglas S., 29, 95, 228, 238,
   420–423, 426
master statuses
   appreciating your own, 484
   definition of, **2**
   essentialist versus constructionist
      perspectives of, 2–7
   examples of stigmatized, 35–37
   intersection experience of, 213
   multiple occupations of, 212
   Muslim, personal account of
      being, 111
   stereotypes about people in
      stigmatized, 37–39
Materazzi, Marco, 108
matrix of domination, 253*n*
Matsuda, Mari, 375
Matthews, Stanley, 397
Matushka, 477, 478
Matute-Bianchi, M.E., 224, 228
Maugh, Thomas, H., II, 156*n*

May, D., 188
Mayberry, R., 186
Mazumdar, Sucheta, 85*n*
Mazza, G.J., 484–487
McCain, John, 363, 366
McCann, E., 170
McCartney, Paul, 475
McCarville, Roger, 492
McClintock, Anne, 246, 253*n*
McClintock, E.A., 382
McCullough, Candace, 172, 173
McCullough, Gauvin Hughes, 172
McCune, P., 213
McDevitt, J., 35
McGuigan, K., 160
McGuire, T.R., 159
McGurn, William, 371
McIntosh, Peggy, 195, 196
McKenna, W., 30
McKenney, N.R., 98
McKinney, Cynthia, 461*n*
McKinney, K., 164
McKinney, Mary D., 145
McLanahan, S., 382
McLaurin, Charles, 465
McLeod, Jelita, 3, 242
McManus, B., 259
McNamee, Stephen J., 29, 136, 332
McNeill, Anthony, 356
McQuillan, J., 386*n*
McReynolds, James Clark, 464
meaning of difference, 332–348
media
   framing social class by, 448–452
   Hurricane Katrina coverage by the,
      453–460
   negative images of the poor and
      homeless by, 450–451
   upper-class consumerism portrayed
      in, 450
Melton, G.B., 158
Meltzer, H., 168
Melville, Herman, 475
*Memoir Upon the Formation of a Deaf
   Variety of the Human Race* (Bell),
   187
men
   compulsive masculinity and,
      254–257
   health inequalities and, 302
   unconcious male associations,
      351–352
"mental defectives," 345
Mercer, G., 5

Mercer, K., 278
merit-based reward, 332–333
Merryman, Ashley, 214, 340, 356
Merton, R.K., 97
Messner, M.A., 195, 277
mestizaje, 237
Michael, R.T., 27, 160
Michaels, S., 160
Michalko, Rod, 326–329
middle class
  media portrayal of, 452
  parental involvement in children's
    education, 297
  society role of, 131–132
middle-class values framing, 452
Middle Eastern Americans/
    immigrants
  covering and its implications,
    108–110
  as "enemy race," 105–106
  mistaken for blacks, 56n
  negotiation of identity by, 104–111
  racial profiling of, 200
  selective radicalization and
    covering, 106–111
Middle East/Middle Eastern
    category, 16
Mihesuah, Devon, 70
Miles, I., 170
Milkie, M.A., 380
Miller, A., 382
Miller, Lucius Hopkins, 112n
Miller, Robert, 29, 332
Miller, Robert K., Jr., 136
Mills, Heather, 475
Mills, J., 9n
Mills, M., 185
Mincey, R.B., 29
Mindell, A., 485
Mindess, A., 178
Minh-ha, Trinh T., 93
Minor, Virginia, 392
minorities
  children and racial identity, 361
  disabled people as largest group
    of, 474
  in executive positions, 355
  housing segregation and, 418–427
  "politics of minority groups," 168
Minor v. Happersett (1875), 334,
    391–393
Minstrel show stereotypes, 347–348
miscegenation, 59, 62, 63, 442, 443
Mishel, Lawrence, 135, 138–140

Misir, D.N., 82
Missouri ex rel Gaines (1938), 407
Mitchell, George, 107
Mitchell, S.H., 187
Mitchell-Kernan, C., 97
"mixed-race" people, 52–53
model-minority myth, 337–339,
    370–377
Mohawk, J., 17
Monbeck, Michael, 324, 325, 329
Monet, Claude, 476
Montgomery, Robert, 467
Moody, James, 360
Moore v. East Cleveland (1977), 406
Morales, Ed, 230
Moran, R.F., 97, 98
Morgan, Edmund S., 49, 51, 56n
Morgan, S.P., 97
Morgan, Stephen, 299
Morgan, Thomas, 434
Morganstern, Julie, 101
Morner, M., 55
Morning, A., 98
Morris, Jessica, 288
Morris, M., 29, 386n
Morrison, T., 239
Morrison, Toni, 20, 475
Morsy, S., 56n
mortality statistics, 302. *See also*
    health/health inequalities
Morton, G., 215
Morton, Samuel, 344
Muhammad Ali, 254–255
"mulatto" designation, 443, 447n
  in early census reports, 61
  original use of, 59
multiplicity of sex, 127
multiracial
  children, 83
  identification patterns, 99–101
  population, of the U.S., 98–101
Mundy, Liza, 171
Murray, Nancy, 112n
Myrdal, G., 58, 95
myth of no effect, 504–507

NAACP, 448n
Nabrit, James, 400
Nader, Ralph, 107
Nagel, J., 179
Nagin, Ray, 458
Najimi, Kathy, 107
Nakamoto, J.M., 238

naming/names
  asserting, 7–10
  constructing difference through, 7
  creating categories of people
    through, 10–14
Nash, G., 49
National Center for Health Statistics,
    144
National Health and Social Life Survey
    (NHSLS), 27n
National Institute on Deafness
    and Other Communication
    Disorders, 188
national origins quota laws, 62
National Security Entry-Exit
    Registration System, 200
Native Americans
  as aggregate classification, 16–17
  allotment and assimilation,
    434–435
  appropriation of territories, 342
  biological definition contexts/
    consequences for, 70–72
  "blood quantum" for tribal
    membership, 66–72
  challenges to asset building by,
    428–440
  challenges to hunting/fishing rights,
    437
  characterization of women, 36n
  colonization and treaties with,
    431–432
  federal policy toward assets of,
    430–431
  gaming, 439
  Indian Reorganization Act and,
    435–436
  mention of "Indians" in U.S.
    Constitution, 67, 73n
  racial identity and, 51
  relocation and reservations,
    432–434
  resources and programs for, 67, 73n
  taxation of, 438
  termination period, 436–437
  tribal natural resources, 437–438
  tribal poverty, 429–430
Nativism, 51
Naturalization Law of 1790, 398
natural-law language, **333**–335
natural selection, 343
"nature-nurture" conflict, 341–342
Nayak, A., 281
"need for income" effect, 380

"negro." *See also* African Americans
  as social and legal definition, 63
  as U.S. census racial category, 10, 12, 19
  use of term, 8, 58
Nelson, Mecca, 309
Neuburger, H., 186
Never Say Never (Hill), 286
Neville, Charmaine, 458
New Orleans. *See* Hurricane Katrina
Newport, E., 186
New York, Lochner v. (1905), 407
Nguyen, Isabelle, 377
Nguyen, V.T., 82
Nicholas, J.G., 187
Nichols, Lau v. (1974), 401–403, 407
Nigger in the Window (Lee), 468–469
"nigger lover" label, 466
"nigger," use of term, 463–472
  in American culture, 464, 469, 471
  by blacks, 468–471
  in court opinions, 467
  etymology of, 463, 472*n*
  menacing connotation of, to blacks, 464–465
  as paradigmatic slur, 466–467
Nineteenth Amendment (1920), 417, 417*n*
Nixon, Richard, 464
Nobles, M., 100
"no-race" theory, 24
norms for behavior, in ethnic group, 178
North America colonization and structured inequality, 49–51
Norton, Tim, 462
Nosari, Joe, 141
Nosek, Brian, 351
Notre Dame University, 307
Nsamenang, B., 232
Nsiah-Jefferson, L., 252
NurtureShock (Bronson and Merryman), 358
N.W.A., 469

Oates, Joyce Carol, 471
Obama, Barack, 21, 340, 358, 363–369, 483, 489
O'Barr, Jean F., 123
O'Barr, William, 120, 123
Occupation, identity and, 46
occupational health hazards, 144
O'Connor, Flannery, 464

O'Connor, Sandra Day, 414
OCR (U.S. Department of Education's Office for Civil Rights), 305, 307, 308
octoroon, 59
Odendahl, Teresa, 510
Oetjen, H., 288
Ogbu, John U., 227, 228, 230, 231
Okizaki, C.L., 21
Oklahoma, Sipuel v. (1948), 407
Oklahoma, Skinner v. (1942), 346
O'Leary, Hazel, 54
Oliver, M.B., 164, 198
Oliver, Michael, 5, 6, 10, 167
Olmstead v. United States (1928), 407
Olsen, L., 232
Omansky, Beth, 5, 10, 207, 323
Omansky Gordon, Beth, 329
Omatsu, G., 77
Omi, Michael, 16, 17, 19, 23, 75, 105, 112*n*, 252, 333
one-drop rule, 62–63, 240*n*, 443
O'Neill, Eugene, 471
Ong, Aihwa, 79
Ong, Paul, 76, 78, 79, 81
Online College Social Life Survey (OCSLS), 259
Ono, Yoko, 471
OPCS (Office of Population Censuses and Surveys), 168
op-ed pieces, writing, 501*b*
"opportunity cost" factor, 380
oppression, 332, 503
Orfield, G., 228
The Origin of the Species (Darwin), 342–343
Ortiz, V., 238
Ortner, S.B., 28
"Other," 485
  constructed as profoundly different, 31–33
  defined, **31**
  sanctioning those who associate with the, 33–34
Ottley, Roi, 57
outrage constraint, 135
Overstreet, Bonaro, 506
Owen, 260

P. Diddy, 368
Pacific Railway Act, 433
Padden, C., 177, 181, 187
Paez, M.M., 227

Pager, D., 211, 335
Pagnini, D.L., 97
Painter, Kim, 156*n*
Painter, Sweatt v. (1950), 407
Palko v. Connecticut (1937), 406
Palmer, Parker, 485
pan-Asianism. *See also* Asian Americans
  emergence of, 76–77
  national/transnational possibilities, 82–84
  transnational approach to, 79–82
  transnational possibilities of, 75–76
panethnicity
  Asian American implications for, 78–79
  definition of, **16**
  emergence of pan-Asianism and, 76–77
panethnic terms, **16**
Pang, Gin Yong, 83
Parham, T., 223
Parks, Rosa, 482, 490–492
Pascarell, Rose B., 300
Pascoe, C.J., 33–34, 212, 277
Passel, J., 229
passing, **205**–208
  immigrants and, 223
  inadvertent, 206–207
  as sighted, 327–329
"passing as white" phenomenon, 62–63, 205
The Passing of the Great Race (Grant), 62
pastoralism, 91
Patel, Sunita, 112*n*, 113*n*
paternalism, 37
Pattatucci, Angela, 156*n*, 157*n*, 164
Patterson, Chris, 89–90
Patterson, C.J., 157*n*, 158, 161
Patterson, O., 95
Paul, E.L., 259
Paul of Tarsus, 47
Pazzanese, Christina, 454
Pearlman, S.F., 160
Pedagogy of the Oppressed, 482
pedigree studies, 150–151
People v. Hall (1854), 19
Peplau, Letitia Anne, 26, 157–159
Percheski, C., 379
Pereira, Sherri H., 88
Perlmann, J., 96, 98
"perpetual foreigner syndrome," 223
Perrucci, R., 28

Peters, J., 481
Petersen, W., 180
Petras, J., 80
Pettito, L., 186
Pfuhl, E.H., 3
Phelps, Michele, 124
philanthropy, 508–511
Philippines
  colonized immigrants from, 80–81
  health professional infrastructure
    in, 81
Phillips, Margaret, 90
Phipps, Susie Guillory, 60–61
Phoenix, A., 99
photographic images
  "color-blind" frame applied to,
    454–456
  Hurricane Katrina and power of,
    453–454
  responding to racial controversy
    over, 456–457
physicalist perspective, 18
Pierce, C., 333, 334
Piketty, Thomas, 134
Pillard, Richard, 147–150, 156*n*,
  159, 182
"place," 248
plasticity hypothesis, 160–161
Plessy, Homer A., 59, 394
Plessy v. Ferguson (1896), 19, 59, 334,
  393–396, 422
Plummer, D.C., 277, 278
"Pocohontas defense," 443
Poe, Edgar Allan, 475
police-on-police shootings, 197–198
"politics of minority groups," 168
Pomeroy, W., 289
popular culture, and media framing of
  social class, 448–452
Portes, A., 80, 81, 99, 224, 228, 231
Portes, Alejandro, 229
poverty
  attributing individual merit to, 29
  inequality and, 303
  media portrayal of, 450–451
  Native Americans and, 429–430
Powell, Adam Clayton, 464
Powell, Adam Clayton, Jr., 57
Powell, Colin, 368
Powell, Lewis F., Jr., 403, 408, 410
power relationships, social class in
  context of, 130–133
Pratt, Robert, 336, 442
Preferential Policies (Sowell), 306

prejudice, relationship to stereotypes
  and discrimination, 339–341
Preston, D.J., 59
Price, Joyce Howard, 112*n*
Prinz, P., 187
privilege. *See also* gendered sexuality
  in young adults study
  of class, 202–203
  in defense of rich kids with,
    508–511
  double binds experience, 264–267
  effects of stigma on, 212
  emotional experience of, 484
  entitlement belief and, 203–204
  examples of, **195**–204
  experience of, 195
  guilt over, 215–216
  of heterosexuals, 201–202
  hierarchies of national identity,
    gender, and, 250
  higher education and, 203
  inherited wealth and, 136–146
  of legacy admissions, 305–310
  stigmatized versus privileged
    experience with, 211–217
privileges and immunities, 388, 417*n*
Proctor, R.N., 251
Proulx, E.A., 224
Pryor, D.W., 160
Pryor, Richard, 466, 469
psychological disparagement, 227
public housing, 423
public policy
  addressing inaccurate perceptions/
    reaching a broader audience, 500
  federal policy development,
    492–494
  influencing, 496–500
  policy maker lifestyle, 494–496
public policy influence
  lifestyle of policy maker with,
    494–496
  players in federal policy
    development, 492–494
public transit challenges, 310–317
"Pygmalion in the Classroom"
  study, 226

Qian, Z., 98
Qin-Hilliard, D.B., 221, 229, 231
Quadagno, Jill, 250, 251
quadroon, 59
Quayle, Dan, 245

Queer Nation, 272
Quillian, Lincoln, 424

race
  association of racial identity and
    criminal behavior, 460*n*
  biological distinctiveness of
    categories of, 23–25
  biophysical traits and, 48, 51, 54
  definition as family, 249
  dichotomizing, 19–21
  and ethnicity defined, 21–31
  folk concepts of, 241*n*
  foundations of race ideology, 49–51
  as identity, 51–52 (*See also* racial
    identity)
  Latinos and U.S. structure of,
    235–240
  social geography of, 84
  as social status, 53
"Race and Ethnic Standards for Federal
  Statistics and Administrative
  Reporting" (OMB), 12
Race IAT, 352–354
race relations, impact of Great
  Migration on, 347
racial consciousness, 455
racial identity
  changing boundaries of ethnicity
    and, 94–101
  historical constructions of, 46–49
  transcending restrictions of, 53–55
Racial Integrity Act, 443, 445
racialization process, 239–240
racial justice
  basic tactics for promoting, 514
  being angry over racism for,
    512–513
  being a strong white ally for, 513
racial mixture, 237, 238
racial profiling, **199**–201
racial triangulation, 375
racism
  aversive, **340**
  basic tactics for fighting, 514
  being angry over, 512–513
  election of Barack Obama and,
    363–369
  how white people can fight, 512–516
  institutionalized, 250
  it's not just a joke, 514–516
  War on Poverty undermined by, 250
  white denial of, 366–369

Rahal, Bobby, 107
Ralph, Sue, 477
Ramsey, C., 187
Raphael, Steven, 425
rap music, 469, 471
Rarus, Nancy, 173
Raspberry, William, 371
Rawlings, B.W., 186
Raymond, J., 251, 252
Reagan, Ronald, 371
Reardon, W., 180
Redding, R.E., 158
redlining, 423
Reed, Carolyn, 492
Reed, T.E., 52
Reefhuis, J., 186
refugees. *See also* immigrants
    model minority stereotypes, 337–338
    motivations of, 221
    Vietnamese, 81–82
Regan, P.C., 163
*Regents of the University of California
    v. Bakke* (1978), 307, 407–410,
    418*n*
Rehnquist, William H., 410, 413
Reinarman, C., 198
Reinhardt, Stephen, 466
Reisenberg, D., 186
relational double bind, 264–265
relationship hierarchies, 246–247
relationship imperative, 262–263
religion, identity and, 48
Remington, F., 186
rereading, **205**
residential segregation, 335–336
restrictive covenants, 400, 418*n*,
    421–423
resymbolization, 477–478
Reuss, Alejandro, 301
reverse discrimination, 211–212
Ricci v. DeStefano (2009), 415–417
Rice, G. William, 68
Rich, Frank, 366
Richard III, 475
Richards, R., 200
Richardson, L., 36
Richie, Nicole, 448, 449
rich kids, 508–511
Ridgeway, C.L., 379, 384, 385
Riggs, M., 278, 348
Riis, Thomas L., 476
Risch, Neil, 156*n*
Risman, Barbara, 120, 122, 123, 386*n*
Risman, B.J., 268, 385

Rist, Darryl, 5
Rivera, E., 240
Roberts, Suzie, 89
Roberts v. City of Boston (1849), 396
Robeson, Paul, 465
Robinson, Jackie, 361, 465
Robinson, J.P., 380
Robles, Bárbara J., 428
Rochlin, Martin, 26, 166
Rock, Chris, 469
Rodriguez, C., 237–240
Rodriguez, C.E., 95, 235
Rodriguez, N., 238
Rodriguez, Richard, 371
*Rodriguez, San Antonio School District
    v.* (1973), 403–405, 407
Roediger, D., 20
Roediger, D.R., 96
Rojeck, A., 198
Rolfe, John, 443, 463
Romero, M., 238
Romero, Victor, 106, 112*n*
Roosens, Eugeen, 68
Roosevelt, Franklin Delano, 475
Roosevelt, Theodore, 464
Root, M.P.P., 99
Rosales, Melodye, 362
Rosch, E., 287
Rose, Peter, 371
Rose, S., 290
Rose, Steven, 154, 157*n*
Rosenblum, K.E., 327
Rosenbluth, S., 160
Rosenfeld, Jeffrey P., 136
Rosenfeld, M.J., 97
Rosenhan, D.L., 205
Rosenthal, D.A., 226
Ross, M., 380
Rothblum, Esther D., 26, 286, 288–290
Royster, Diedre A., 211, 212
Rubin, Gayle, 121, 123
Rubio, P.F., 25
Rule of Three, 415
Rumbaut, R.G., 81, 99, 224, 228, 231
Russell, Bill, 337
Russell, M., 18
Russell, Richard, 464
Rust, P.C., 158, 160, 162, 163, 288
Rustin, Bayard, 324
Ruth, George Herman, "Babe," 465

Sacks, K., 84
Saenz, R., 98, 99

Saez, Emmanuel, 134
Saito, L., 84
Salazar, Ruben, 9
Salgado de Snyder, N., 99
Salient, 309
Saltus, R., 185
same-sex relationships. *See also* gay
    men; homosexuality; lesbians
    ideas of, shaped by science, 344
    public affection and, 202
*San Antonio School District v.
    Rodriguez* (1973), 403–405, 407
Sanford, Dred Scott v. (1857), 334,
    389–390
Sanford, John, 389
Sanjek, R., 95
Santiago, R., 240
Sapir, Edward, 347
Sarroub, L.K., 232
Sassen, Saskia, 80
Sassler, S., 382
Savin-Williams, R.C., 162–164
Sayers, J., 343, 344
Schein, J.D., 178, 185
Scheper-Hughes, N., 84
Schervish, Paul G., 141
Schickel, R., 57
Schmidt, P., 8
Schneider, David M., 156*n*, 180
Schneider, J., 6, 181, 184, 186
Schneider, J.W., 344
Schnittker, 145
Scholz, John Karl, 143
Schor, Juliet B., 450
Schram, S., 38
Schuman, H., 341
Schur, E., 35, 39, 205
Schuster, M.A., 160
Schwartz, P., 160, 162, 289
Schwartz, T.P., 138
Schwarz, J.E., 29
science
    American slavery defense
        using, 344
    ideologies supported by, 341–347
    "nature-nurture" conflict of,
        341–342
    same-sex relationship ideas shaped
        by, 344
    social Darwinism, **343**–344
Scott, Dred, 389, 390, 398, 400
Scott, J., 2
Sczesny, S., 36
second generation, 222

Sedat, Laciner, 112*n*
Sedey, A.L., 187
Sedgwick, E.K., 206
Sedgwick, Eve, 280
segregation, 335
  blacks in northern U.S. cities, 420*f*, 423
  blacks in southern U.S. cities, 421*f*
  contemporary housing discrimination and, 424
  economic and social impacts of, 424
  housing access and, 418–426
  role of public policies in, 419–424
  successful inteventions in, 426
Seidman, Steven, 206, 269
selective radicalization, 107–108
self-development imperative, 264–267
Semenya, Caster, 30, 123, 124
Sengupta, Shuddhabrata, 213, 517
"separate-but-equal" case *(Plessy v. Ferguson)*, 19, 59, 334, 393–396, 422
September 11, 2001 terrorist attacks, 200
Sewall, Samuel, 463
sex
  biology of, 123
  defined, **30**
  dichotomizing, 30
  multiplicity of, 127
Sex in Education (Clarke), 343
sexism, compulsive masculinity and, 257
sexual activity
  conceptual issues in female, 289–290
  hookups, 259–260
sexual citizenship politics, 271–273
sexual fluidity, 159–161
sexual identity, 4*n*
  transformation of gay and lesbian, 269–276
sexuality, gender differences in, 164
sexual orientation, 4*n. See also* sexual identity
  biology of the homosexual, 147–156
  bisexuality, 288
  childhood influences on women's, 161–162
  continuous definition of, 288
  dichotomizing, 25–28

dichotomous definitions of, 287–288
essentialist perspective of, 4
heterosexual questionnaire, 166–167
illness model of, 158
inversion model of, 158–159
multidimensional concept of, 288
parallels beween classifications of race and, 27–28
research on, 288–289
sociocultural influences on women's, 162–163
transformation of, 269–276
understanding women's sexuality and, 157–164
women and conceptual issues of, 286–291
sexual plasticity hypothesis, 160–161
sexual preference, constructionist perspective of, 4
sexual prejudice, 162–163
sex verification, 123–124
Shafer, E.F., 259
Shafer, E.M., 381, 382
Shah, B., 84
Shakespeare, William, 475
Shakira, 107
Shakur, Tupac, 469
Shalhoub, Tony, 107
Shankar, Rajiv, 79
Shapiro, J.P., 189
Shaw, Heather L., 171
Shaw, Risa, 172
Shays, Christopher, 499
Sheldon, Edward, 471
Shepard, Matthew, 117
Sheperd, H., 211, 335
Shim, M., 382
Shinagawa, Larry Hajime, 83
Shipman, P., 342, 343
Shirley, O., 169
Shobat, E., 236
Shorris, E., 9
Sicha, Choire, 448
Siddique, Hoorie, I., 145
Sieber, Sam D., 140
Sigel, Beanie, 469
Silverman, R.A., 3
Silverstone, Alicia, 109
Sim, J., 99, 100
Simmons, Russell, 368
Simon, Scott J., 112*n*
The Simple Life (TV show), 448–449

Sinclair, S., 339
Sipuel v. Oklahoma (1948), 407
Sister Outsider (Lorde), 253*n*
skin color
  children's perception of, 358–359
  lack of "racial designations" in early history, 48–49
  Latinos and, 235
Skinner v. Oklahoma (1942), 346
Skrentny, J., 12
Skrentny, J.D., 96, 338
Slack, J.D., 246
slaves/slavery
  in ancient Europe, 48–49
  ban on interracial unions and, 442–443
  early constructs of, 48
  interracial sex and, 443
  minstrel show characters depicting, 348
  science used as defense of, 344
"slut" stigma, 261–262, 267
Smedley, Audrey, 22–23, 46, 48, 49
Smelser, N.J., 95
Smith, Arthur D., 178–180
Smith, Barbara, 253*n*
Smith, Chad, 70
Smith, D., 333
Smith, E., 341
Smith, G.W., 277
Smith, James P., 95, 98, 144
Smith, Lillian, 471
Smith, Patti, 471
Smith, R., 232
Smith, Raymond T., 156*n*
Smith, S., 180
Smith, T., 178
Smith, Tommie, 465
Smith, T.W., 8, 196
Smith v. Allwright (1944), 417*n*
Snowden, Frank, 48
social change
  becoming part of the solution, 502–507
  commitment of the privileged to, 215–216
  education as source of, 480–481
  Gandhi's paradox on, 481, 504–507
  influencing public policy for, 492–501
  philanthropy for, 508–511
  whites working for racial justice, 512–516

social class. *See also* middle class; working class
  causes of impairment and, 170
  dichotomizing, 28–29
  educational involvement of parents and, 295–297
  gendered sexuality in young adults, 259–268
  halo effect, 135
  inequalities in, 133–136
  inheritance and, 136–146
  meaning and implications of, 130–133
  media representation and framing of, 448–452
  norm and the exception in, 134–135
  transition to adulthood and, 292–301
social Darwinism, **343**–344
social dislocation, 324
social exclusion, of immigrants, 225
social geography of race, 84
social institution, **341**
social isolation, 303
social mirror, 225–227
social networks, housing and, 426
social organization, family as fundamental principle of, 246
social position, identity and, 48
social processes, and creation of differences, 3
Social Security, 250
social status
  experiencing, 194–195
  link between health and, 303–304
  marked vs. unmarked, 203–204
  transformation of gay and lesbian, 269–276
social structure, of ethnic group, 178
society
  changing negative patterns of, 502–507
  the gendered, 113–122
  women's sexuality and environment of, 160
Society and the Healthy Homosexual (Weinberg), 18
sociocultural influences on sexual orientation
  identity, 162
  institutions, 162
  sexual prejudice, 162–163
Sollors, W., 180
Sommer, D., 221

Sophocles, 475
Soss, J., 38
The Souls of Black Folk (Du Bois), 208
"Southern Manifesto," 369
Sowell, Thomas, 306
Spade, Joan Z., 262
Spalding, L.R., 158
Spanglish, 230
Spencer, Herbert, 343
Spencer, J.M., 99
Spickard, P.R., 96, 99, 101
Spivak, G., 216
Sprecher, S., 164
Squires-Wheeler, E., 156*n*
Stabile, Carol, 198
Stacey, J., 252*n*
Stam, R., 236
Standish, Helen, 90, 91
Stanley v. Georgia (1969), 406, 407
Starkey, Marion, 74*n*
"Statement on Race" (AAA), 24
State of Louisiana, Jane Doe v. (1983), 60–61
status. *See also* master statuses
  appreciating your statuses, 484
  definition of, **2**
Stauss, J.H., 58
Steele, Claude, 228
Steele, Richard, 308
Stefancic, Jean, 112*n*
Stein, Edward, 151, 156*n*
Steinberg, R.J., 381
Steinberg, S., 338
Stephan, C.W., 99, 100
Stephan, W.G., 99, 100
Stepick, A., 229
Stepp, 260
stereotypes
  about African Americans, 336–337
  about Asian Americans, 336
  about stigmatized master statuses, 37–39
  definition of, **336**
  identity threats and, 228
  ideology conveyed through, 336–341
  interpretation of behavior based on, 209
  minstrel shows, 347–348
  model minority, 337–339, 370–377
  relationship to prejudice and discrimination, 339–341
sterilization. *See* eugenics movement
Stevens, G., 95, 97, 98, 100

Stevens, J., 201
Stevens, John P., 407, 410, 411
Stewart, Potter, 410
stigma
  complexities in experience of privilege and, 211–217
  definition of, **34**
  the discredited and visibility, 208–210
  examples of stigmatized master statuses, 35–37
  expectations of those sharing one's, 210–211
  "passing" phenomenon to escape, 62–63, 205–208
stigmatized people
  allies of, 486–487
  codes of conduct for categories of, 211
  connections between, 480
  disabled, 476–477
  emotional experience of, 484
  homosexuals, 271–273
  identity development by, 214–217
  overt displays of stigmatized status by, 210
  stereotypes about master statuses of, 37–39
  treatment of violence against, 39
  visibility problems of, 208–210
Stimpson, Catherine, 116, 122
Stoll, Michael, 425
Stone, D., 167
Stone, P., 379
Stonequist, E.V., 221, 231
Stowe, Harriet Beecher, 471
strength, overlapping normal curves of, 32*f*
Strobel, L.M., 82
Strong, M., 187
structural exclusion, 225
"Stubborn Ounces," 506–507
Stull, Donald, 260
Sturm, Circe, 74*n*
Stutzer, Alois, 145
Suárez-Orozco, Carola, 221–223, 225–227, 229, 232
Suárez-Orozco, M., 222–229, 231, 232
Sununu, John, 107
Suplee, Curt, 156*n*
"survival of the fittest," 343
Susser, M., 169, 170
Sussman, Juniper, 172
Svirsky, M., 186

Sweatt v. Painter (1950), 407
Sweeney, B.N., 262
symbolic violence, 227

Takagi, D.Y., 38
Takaki, R.M., 19, 76, 226, 239, 338
Talan, Jamie, 156*n*
Talbot, Mary, 156*n*
talking points, 495*b*
tallness, 354–355
Taney, Roger B., 390
Tannen, Deborah, 119, 122
Tatum, B., 225
Taub, D.E., 163
Tavris, Carol, 119, 122
Taylor, Charles, 225
Taylor, D., 169
Tehranian, John, 16, 104, 200, 206
Tennessee v. Lane (2004), 196, 410–412
Teoh, S.-W., 186
Terman, Lewis M., 345
termination resolution, 436
terrorist attacks of September 11,
    2001, 200
Texas, Hopwood v. (1994), 410
That Nigger's Crazy (Pryor), 469
thematic framing, 450
Thernstrom, Abigail, 367
Third World countries, and
    impairments, 169–170
Thirteenth Amendment (1865), 390
Thomas, C., 215
Thomas, Cathy, 89, 91, 92
Thomas, Clarence, 442
Thomas, Danny, 107
Thomas, P., 240
Thomas, S., 215
Thomas, Stephanie, 491
Thomas, Virginia, 442
Thomas, W.I., 167
Thompson, E.C., 25
Thornton, R., 72*n*–73*n*
Thurmond, Strom, 464
Thurow, Lester, 139
Tienda, M., 238
Tillman, Benjamin, 464
Tilly, Chris, 425
Tipton, Sean, 174
Tischler, H.L., 58
Title VI of the Civil Rights Act of
    1964, 408, 410
Title VII of the Civil Rights Act of
    1964, 415

Titone, R., 221
Tizard, B., 99
Tocqueville, Alexis de, 113
Todorova, T., 222
Tokarczyk, M.M., 203
"To Ride the Public's Buses"
    (Thomas), 491
Torres, A., 239
"traceable amount rule," 58
trade unionism, decline in, 134
Trail of Tears, 432–433
transcultural identitites, 230–231
transgender, **40**
transgendered people, **30**
Traverso, Clare, 91
Travis, T.-M.C., 327
*Treatise on the Intellectual Character
    and Civil and Political Condition
    of the Colored People of the United
    States* (Easton), 464
Treaty of Guadalupe Hidalgo (1848),
    19, 342
Trillin, C., 60
Trudeau, Gary, 370
Truman, Harry S., 464
Trumka, Richard, 364
Tsuda, T., 225
Tucker, M.B., 97
Turnbull, C.M., 182
Twain, Mark, 471, 475
Twain, Shania, 67–68
Tye-Murray, N., 186
Tynes, Brendesha, 361

Umiker-Sebeok, J., 287
unconscious attitudes, 351–355
Unequal Childhoods (Lareau), 296, 300
Union of the Physically Impaired
    Against Segregation (UPIAS), 5
United Nations Convention on
    the Rights of Persons with
    Disabilities, 5–6
United States. *See also* Native
    Americans
    colonization of, 431–432
    compulsive masculinity in,
        254–257
    family planning issues in, 251–252
    gays' changing social status role in
        multicultural, 273–275
    health inequalities in, 301–304
    immigration quota policy, 338–339
    imperialism, 80

increasing multiracial identification
    in, 94–101
intermarriage in, 97–98
as multicultural nation, 273–275
multiracial population of, 98–101
national identity privilege in,
    249–250
United States, Olmstead v. (1928), 407
"universal" humans, 55
University of California at Berkeley,
    307
*University of California Board of
    Regents v. Bakke* (1978), 307
University of Michigan cases,
    412–415
University of Pennsylvania, 305
University of Texas Children's
    Research Lab, 356, 357
University of Virginia, 307
unmarked social status, 203–204
Unz, Ron, 371
urban renewal, 423
U.S. Census Bureau
    Arab/Middle Eastern category, 12
    Asian and Other Asian categories,
        15*n*
    Asian population, 85*n*
    definition of blacks and
        enumeration of, 61–62
    evolution of race and ethnicity
        classifications, 65
    Hispanic origin categories, 14*n*
    Hispanic responses to, 238, 240*n*
    Native Americans, slaves, and state
        representation, 418*n*
    Pacific Islander and Other Pacific
        Islander categories, 15*n*
    race and ethnicity questions,
        10–11, 238
    undercounting, 12
U.S. Immigration and Naturalization
    Service, 94–95

Valenstein, E., 186
Valenzuela, A., 232
values, of ethnic group, 178
Van Cleve, J., 179
Van der Klift, Emma, 487
Vanneman, R., 378–381, 383, 384, 386
Vechten, Carl Van, 472
Veniegas, R.C., 158, 159
Vermont Youth Behavior Risk Survey
    (1999), 289

Veterans Administration (VA), 421, 423
vicarious living, 449
Vietnamese Americans, 373, 377
Vietnamese immigrants, 81–82
Vietnam War, 81–82
Vigil, J.D., 222, 229
Vines, Gail, 156*n*
violence
   hierarchy context of, 247–248
   homicide, 303
   personal account of, 462
   against stigmatized people, 39
   symbolic, 227
Virginia, Loving v. (1967), 336, 442–446
visibility, discredited and problem of, 208–210
Vittrup, Birgitte, 356, 357
Viviani, N., 82
Volgy, T.J., 29
Volpp, L., 200

Waite, Morrison R., 392
Wald, Elijah, 149, 156*n*, 157*n*
Waldinger, R., 95, 96
Walker, C.J., 367
Wallenstein, Peter, 113*n*
Walmsley, R., 199
Walters, G., 339
Walton, Sam, 141
Warner, Michael, 18, 19
War on Poverty, 250
Warren, Earl, 400, 446
Washington, Booker T., 59, 464
Washington, Denzel, 368
Waters, M., 224, 228, 229, 231, 232
Waters, M.C., 95–98
Watson, W., 169, 170
Wayne, John, 109
wealth
   attributing individual merit to, 29
   cumulative advantages of inheritance of, 142–146
   in defense of, 508–511
   disparities, 133–136
   housing segregation and disparities in, 418, 419
   inequality of income and, 28–29, 138–140
   inheritance of, 136–146, 250–251
Webster, Noah, 463
Weeks, Lorena, 489, 490

Weeks v. Southern Bell, 489–490
Weinberg, George, 18
Weinberg, M.S., 160, 161, 163
Weininger, Elliot, 203, 292
Weinrich, J.D., 161, 163
Weiss, Ira, 176
Welsh, D.P., 260
Wermuth, Laurie, 144
Werth, B., 182
West, C., 384
West, Kanye, 456, 461*n*
Western, B., 199, 386*n*
Wharton, Edith, 117
Wheeler-Howard Act, 435
Whisman, V., 160
White, Byron R., 404, 406, 409
White, Jane, 58
White, Walter, 58
White, Wendy S., 298
Whitehall I, 304
whites/whiteness, 253*n*
   assumption of non-criminality with, 198
   being a strong ally, 513
   Catholic ethnics, 216*n*
   "culturelessness" of, 88
   denial of racism, 366–369
   stereotypes held by, 339–341
   as "unmarked" cultural category, 88–94
Whitman, Walt, 475
Whitten, N.E., Jr., 239
WHO (World Health Organization), 168
Wickenden, James, 308
Wiefek, N., 28
Wiggins, Thomas Greene, 475
Wilchins, Riki, 30, 124, 280, 341
Wilde, Oscar, 342, 344
Wilkins, Charles, 398
Wilkins, Elk v. (1884), 334, 397–400
Wilkins, Roy, 448*n*
Wilkinson, R.G., 303
Wilkinson, S., 160
Willenbacher, Barbara, 138
Williams, B.F., 248
Williams, Christine, 258*n*
Williams, C.J., 160
Williams, K., 98
Williams, Patricia, J., 197
Williams, Raymond, 91
Williams, Serena, 368
Williams, Vanessa, 57
Williams, Venus, 368

Williamson, J., 58
Williamson, J.B., 29
Williamson, Thad, 303
Wilson, August, 465
Wilson, Charles, 6, 490
Wilson, Pete, 371
Wilson, Terry, 72
Wilson, W.J., 95, 424, 425
Wimsatt, William, Upski, 508
Winant, H., 17, 19, 23, 75, 252, 333, 336
Winant, Howard, 105, 112*n*
Winfrey, Oprah, 368
Winicott, D.W., 225
Winzer, M.A., 179
Wise, Tim, 38, 340, 363
Wittig, Monique, 124
Wo, Yick, 396
Wolfe, Tom, 255
Wolff, Edward N., 136, 139
women. *See also* gender revolution
   African American feminists, 252*n*
   characterization of women by race, 36*n*
   childhood influences on sexual orientation of, 161–162
   conceptual issues in sexual desire, 290–291
   conceptual issues of sexual orientation of, 286–291
   on "culturelessness" of white identity, 88–93
   devaluation of traditional female activities/jobs, 379–383
   "double conscious" experience, 333
   double standard of aging, 382
   in executive positions, 355
   fluidity of sexuality of, 159–161
   health inequalities and, 302
   heterosexuality among, 287
   hookups and, 259–260
   increased employment of, 379–381, 380*f*
   with less education, employment rates of, 380, 386*n*
   in "masculine" workforce, 258*n*
   in migratory and international workforce, 84
   Native American, 434
   relationships and sexuality/sexual orientation of, 163–164
   rights of, to upward mobility/ gender essentialism, 383–385
   rights of working women, 489–490

social class and sex in relationships,
  260–268
social Darwinism opposing equal
  education for, 343–344
Social Security and, 250
sociocultural influences on sexual
  orientation of, 162–163
surnames of, after marriage, 382
unconcious female associations,
  351–352
understanding sexuality/sexual
  orientation of, 157–164
violence against, personal account
  of, 462
Women, Race, and Class (Davis),
  252*n*
women's movement, 274
Wong, Paul, 77
Woo, Deborah, 374
Wood, J., 277

Wood, P., 168
Woods, Tiger, 368, 465
Woodward, Grace Steele, 74*n*
Woodward, J., 181
Woolf, Virginia, 118, 122
Worcester v. Georgia (1832),
  432, 438
working class
  characterization of women of, 36*n*
  media portrayal of, 451
  overview and description of,
    130–133
  personal account of, 300
  students, 203
Wright, Luther, Jr., 113*n*
Wu, Frank, H., 223, 336, 370
Wysong, E., 28

Xie, Y., 98, 99

Yale University, 305
Yick Wo v. Hopkins (1886), 396–397
Yoshino, Kenji, 108, 110, 112*n*, 113*n*
You Just Don't Understand (Tannen),
  119
Young, R.J.C., 249
Yun, J.T., 228

Zack, N., 99
Zamichow, Nora, 156*n*
Zéphir, F., 229
Zhou, Min, 77–78, 81, 82, 99, 228
Zicklin, Gilbert, 149, 150, 156*n*
Zidane, Zenadine, 108
Zimmerman, D.H., 384
Zola, Irving K., 31, 184
Zolberg, A., 80
Zucker, K.J., 159, 161
Zweig, Michael, 28, 130, 133